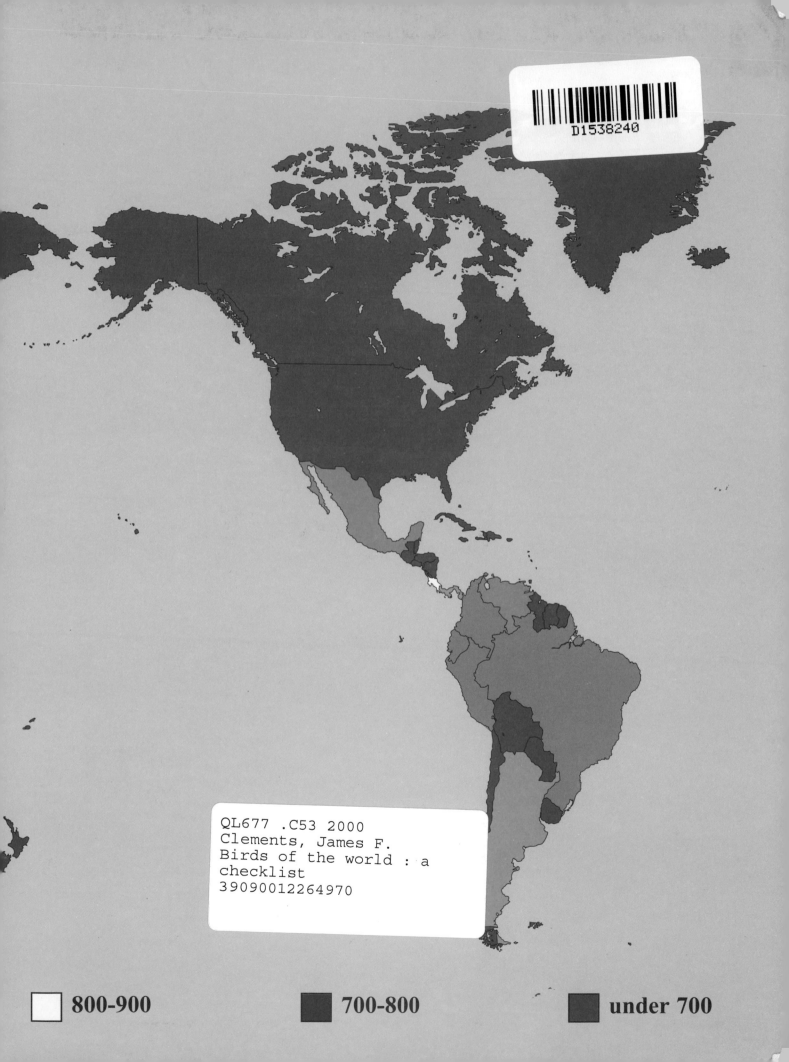

800-900   700-800   under 700

BIRDS OF THE WORLD:

A CHECKLIST

James F. Clements

Ibis Publishing Company

BIRDS OF THE WORLD:
A CHECKLIST

Fifth Edition

© Copyright James F. Clements 2000

IBIS PUBLISHING COMPANY
3420 Freda's Hill Road
Vista, CA 92084-7466

Visit our website: www.ibispub.com

ISBN Number 0-934797-16-1

Library of Congress Catalog Card Number 99-97638

Dust jacket photograph of Hawaiian Goose (*Branta sandvicensis*) by Frank S. Todd
Dust jacket design and end sheet maps by John Bass
Printed in Verona, Italy by Artegrafica

In fond memory of Arnold Small

**Ornithologist, scholar, friend
and my birding companion
for fifty years on every continent
on planet earth**

Que en paz descanse

Contents

Since the first edition of *Birds of the World: A Checklist* appeared in 1974, I have received numerous suggestions from members of the ornithological community for improving future editions. Most of these suggestions were incorporated and acknowledged in the second, third and fourth editions.

I am deeply indebted to the late Burt Monroe and Charles Sibley, both of whom were always ready to assist me with even the most trivial taxonomic problem.

Tom Schulenberg has been a tremendous aid in helping to sort out the almost impossible *Scytalopus* genus of tapaculos. Mort and Phyllis Isler reviewed the Thamnophilidae and Formicariidae and contributed valuable and up-to-date information regarding the taxonomy and ranges of these two controversial families.

Josep del Hoyo and Andy Elliot, editors of the *Handbook of the Birds of the World*, kindly furnished me with the higher taxonomy for the proposed twelve-volume series.

I remain in debt to Dr. Robert S. Ridgely, who reviewed the entire draft of the South American avifauna for the fourth edition, and whose assistance with ranges worldwide was extremely helpful with this fifth edition.

Others who have made suggestions or contributions to this edition include Keith Axelson, Dr. Luis Baptista, Dr. Bruce Beehler, Dr. Les Christidis, Dr. Robert Eisberg, Bill Everett, Shawneen Finnegan, Dr. John P. O'Neill, Nigel Redman, Noam Shany, Dr. Arnold Small, Frank Todd, Phil Unitt and Dr. Hartmut Walter.

There is no way I can thank Donna O'Daniel enough for the outstanding job she did on editing the entire manuscript. Each time one of the sections would reach me from Donna's remote outpost on Johnston Atoll, I would gaze in awe on the corrections and comments that she made. Even in this age of computer spell-checking programs, Donna proved that there is no substitute for a critical eye.

Last, but not least, my wife Karen was a constant inspiration during the five years I have been working on this edition. Several times she had to shut the door to my office when I was trying to wade through some difficult section, but neither her encouragement nor her patience ever waned.

Despite all the help I received from scientists, taxonomists and fellow birders from around the world, this book is of necessity the product of my own research. Some errors in a work of this magnitude are almost inevitable. Any errors, omissions or commissions are solely my responsibility. Hopefully, none of these will affect the usefulness of this checklist.

James F. Clements
January 2000

Before the first edition of Clements' *Birds of the World: A Checklist* appeared in 1972, birders, field ornithologists, museum curators, aviculturalists, conservationists, interested scientists, and laymen who wanted an overview of the world's birds had little published information to guide them. Indeed, the standard reference of the time was the multi-volume J. L. Peters *Checklist of the Birds of the World*. This mammoth, highly detailed work saw its first volume published in 1931, and even before the last volume was completed (in 1986), the first was so obsolete that it had to be revised in 1979. Unfortunately, as so often has been the case with such colossal undertakings, the sheer magnitude of the task made the production span decades. Peters *Checklist* is, in many ways, now only a historical document. The cost of Peters' *Checklist* was also prohibitive, requiring most of us to have to visit our nearest major museum to get a glimpse of it—even most university libraries did not carry the series.

At the time of the publication of Clements' first edition, there were no authoritative field guides for many areas outside of Europe and North America. Clements' first *Checklist* became instant required reading, and was soon followed by several attempts by others to synopsize a world summary of bird systematics and distribution. With its concise and useful presentation, however, it was Clements' work that became the standard reference. The 1980s, however, saw an unprecedented proliferation of research and knowledge on bird taxonomy and distribution. In an admirable effort to remain current, Clements followed suit and produced subsequent editions to reflect the significant changes and advances in ornithological knowledge, with each of his editions improving and refining the information presented.

The 1990s have introduced a new factor into the picture, with the widespread application of DNA and other molecular analytical approaches being applied to bird taxonomy. This has brought about radical changes within the world of birds at nearly every level of systematics from species concepts through higher order relationships. Whether one agrees with the conclusions of various researchers or not,

what is clear is that we have entered what is likely the second most dynamic phase in the history of the study of birds—the first being the discovery and description of most of the world's species and subspecies as we have known them to this point. What lies ahead—the second phase—is certainly a very long period of reorganization and shuffling, differing opinions, and ultimately, something hopefully approaching real understanding and consensus. I expect this process will take generations, especially considering the work to be done at the subspecies level.

This is how science progresses but it is not particularly great news, for example, to birders who want to keep track of their observations or curators who have to keep thousands of avian specimens properly cataloged, sorted and organized. Since future taxonomic work will be accomplished in many discrete steps, so will the bigger picture change. Therein lies the challenge.

In the last decade, there have been several attempts to either put forth new checklist "paradigms" or get in under the wire—that is—to publish checklists of the world's birds that closely resemble the sequence and species concepts to which we have become accustomed. Each of these efforts have their particular merits, but all have the inevitable fate of becoming at least partially obsolete almost the moment they are published. In this uncertain environment a new mode of keeping current is required, and it is this volume that, once again, will begin to set such a new standard. This is indeed no simple task given the variance of opinion and mass of detailed information, but Clements has an excellent foundation from which to start based on his previous editions.

One could, and some have, prepared world bird checklists after only reviewing the ornithological literature and cobbling together information from hundreds of different sources. In the end, arbitrary choices are usually made regarding what authorities to follow and include. This approach includes no "ground truthing" of the information put forth. A unique and valuable facet of this edition is that it also benefits from the vast field experience that Jim Clements has acquired over the last nearly

50 years, visiting virtually every remote corner of the globe in search of rare and uncommon species. It is only through this kind of in-depth field work and first-hand knowledge that what has been written can be verified.

If one word can be described to describe this edition, it would be "useful." Clements has labored to present a vast amount of information in as organized and concise a manner as possible. The English and scientific name indices alone are a major stride forward in sorting out a veritable ornithological Tower of Babel. It is also a major benefit that Clements does not use this *Checklist* as a platform to promote a personal major taxonomic agenda. In virtually every case, he follows (for North America) the American Ornithologists' Union, or, for the species that occur outside the AOU area, the most widely currently accepted nomenclature. Where he varies, he states his reasons and sources.

The inclusion of subspecies in this edition is also a major advancement. It will aid not only species identification but heighten awareness of the variation within species and the known limits of species and subspecies distribution. Again, every other previously published overview of subspecies is essentially obsolete.

Perhaps exceeding the value of the powerful indexing features of this edition is the more detailed information on distribution than can be found in virtually any other recently published world checklist. Clements also recognized that the world is large and distributions sometimes small, so he has spared us all an enormous amount of work by providing an extensive gazetteer. I am hard pressed to conceive what other features could have improved this printed edition, which perhaps leads to what will likely be the ultimate functionality of this work. Clements plans to provide periodic updates to this work via the Internet—perhaps the only way to really avoid obsolescence. In an increasingly complex and dynamic scientific setting, Clements has provided the ideal solution...one that will likely accompany the most tattered book on our shelves.

Lastly, I hope that all users of this reference work will be constantly mindful that, by some estimates, fifteen percent or more of the world's species of birds are threatened or endangered. Basic knowledge such as is presented herein is fundamental to understanding the gravity and extent of this situation. Armed at first with knowledge, we can hopefully take the appropriate steps to avoid the unimaginable tragedy that future generations might not have the pleasure and privilege of seeing and enjoying many of our world's avian gems. Let us hope the list increases in numbers.

William T. Everett, President
Endangered Species Recovery Council

Almost twenty-five years have passed since the first edition of *Birds of the World: A Checklist* was published. During the intervening years, four editions of the checklist have appeared, and the number of species described has grown from 8600 to over 9700. There have been monumental strides in taxonomic treatment, especially in the last decade since the publication of the fourth edition—much of which has led to a great deal of confusion in the birding world.

I could write an entire book just dealing with the current taxonomic problems facing the ornithological community. Almost every issue of the *Auk, Wilson Bulletin, Ibis, Condor, Bulletin of the B.B.C.* or any of the other prominent ornithological journals contains an article about recent changes in taxonomy.

This fifth edition follows the higher taxonomic sequence outlined in the *Handbook of the Birds of the World* series published by Lynx Edicions. Five of these comprehensive volumes have been published to date, and the editors have graciously sent me the taxonomic sequence of families for the entire series. I have chosen to follow their sequence of higher taxa since less than half of the families of birds occur in the region covered by the AOU. Aside from this change, I still follow the AOU for almost all species names. In some cases where there is a conflict in the AOU area with a long-standing name in the Palearctic region, I have chosen to use the accepted name in use by the British Ornithologists' Union. Thus readers will understand my choice of using White-throated Robin for the Eurasian *Irania gutturalis*, and White-throated Thrush for *Turdus assimilis*. The late Burt Monroe (formerly president of the AOU Checklist Committee) was keenly aware of these potential conflicts on the international scene, and I have followed many of his suggestions where these conflicts presented themselves.

This fifth edition of the checklist reflects the many changes that have occurred since publication of the fourth edition in 1991. I have historically been heavily in favor of the Biological Species Concept, and the current edition of the checklist, in addition to the previous four editions, continues this view. Despite the fact that I worked in close collaboration with the late Burt Monroe Jr. in the preparation of the fourth edition of the checklist, many of the Sibley-Monroe species were not accepted by the AOU checklist committee. In all cases where I have added new species, appropriate citations are noted. In certain cases I have included allopatric species that have appeared in major ornithological journals. I do not go as far as the late Charles Sibley, however, in considering a vast array of insular forms valid species.

The most important addition to previous editions of the checklist is the inclusion of subspecies. There is possibly even more controversy in the ornithological community regarding subspecies than species, but with the major changes taking place in species-level taxonomy, I felt the addition of subspecies at this time to be of paramount importance. The basic reference for subspecies classification was the monumental 15-volume Peters *Check-list of Birds of the World*. Since some of this series is over 50 years old, the changes in the number of species (and subspecies) during the intervening half century have been monumental. This has been updated by the first five volumes of the *Handbook of the Birds of the World* series, and by the 9-volume *Birds of the Western Palearctic*.

A major addition to the fifth edition is the addition of a complete English-name index, which should make it fairly easy for even the layman to find the majority of birds with little or no trouble. One of the major problems facing users of this volume is the constant changing of English names by authors of the prolific number of field guides and family monographs that have been published in recent years. In addition, such splits as the Long-tailed Hermit into the Eastern Long-tailed and Western Long-tailed do not make it any easier to find some species.

Because of the confusing use of various English names for certain species, it is often much simpler to use the scientific name to look up a particular bird. Thus if you searching for the American Robin (*Turdus migratorius*), the quickest way is to look up *migratorius* in the scientific index (where you only have to deal with the extant thrush and the extinct Passenger Pigeon). You could look up *Turdus* in the scientific index, which would necessitate looking through 65 entries in the *Turdus* genus. Similarly, looking up Robin in the English-name index would require a search of the 91 Robins listed.

Despite the fact that some English names that have been in the literature for years could undoubtedly be improved upon, I have chosen in most cases to maintain my conservative posture and not change any long-standing names. With several exceptions I follow the American Ornithologists' Union nomenclature, even where I disagree with their choice of names.

Because of the inclusion of subspecies in this edition, I have tried to describe the ranges of each form so that the reader in most cases can determine the correct race in a given area. With the exception of disjunct populations this becomes a difficult decision in many instances, since the ranges of most subspecies have areas of overlap. Ranges generally are given from northwest to southeast. Ranges separated by a semicolon indicate disjunct or isolated populations.

In addition to incorporating the numerous taxonomic changes that have occurred in the past ten years, I have added a gazetteer of some 2000 place names that are mentioned in the text. This will enable readers to instantly locate a remote island or topographic feature by using their geographic coordinates. This was suggested to me years ago by Jim Tucker, former executive director of the American Birding Association, whose occasional greeting to me was, "Where in the world are the Daito Islands, the Bolavens Plateau," or some equally obscure location that he was unable (or unwilling) to locate in the standard atlases of the day.

Another addition to the fifth edition is a numerical listing of the distribution of bird species by country—one by total species and another by total endemics. The front and back end sheets replace the zoogeographic map of the previous editions, and give a graphic presentation of worldwide bird distribution. Wherever possible I

have given ranges in geographic descriptions as well as (or rather than) political units, since birds do not generally heed political borders. Mountain ranges, deserts, oceans and major rivers serve as more effective boundaries for most birds than arbitrary country borders.

An excellent companion to this volume is a Windows software program that contains the common name of every family and species, the scientific name of every order, family, genus and species, and the range of each species. When sightings are recorded, the software automatically updates both annual and life lists. It also produces such lists for all faunal zones, ABA reporting areas, all countries, major island groups, U.S. states and Canadian provinces. It can also produce checklists of the birds of any of these world regions, labeling endemics and species previously seen in the region, outside it, or both. Also available is a lexicon file used to add the scientific names to spelling checkers of most Windows or Macintosh word processors. Further information can be obtained from Santa Barbara Software Products, Inc., 1400 Dover Road, Santa Barbara, CA 93103, USA. Telephone/fax: (805) 963-4886 or e-mail: sbsp@aol.com Website: http://members.aol.com/sbsp

This checklist is the official world checklist of the American Birding Association, and future changes will be posted on the internet on the Ibis Publishing Co. website (www.ibispub.com). The author enthusiastically welcomes any items of potential interest to readers. These should be sent to the publisher at 3420 Freda's Hill Road, Vista, CA 92084-7466, USA, by fax to (760) 598-0066 or by e-mail to ibispub@msn.com

adjacent	adj.	Netherlands Antilles	Neth. Ant.
Afghanistan	Afghan.	New Hampshire	N Hamp.
Amazonian	Amaz.	New Mexico	N Mex.
America	Am.	New South Wales	NSW
Archipelago	Arch.	New York	NY
Arizona	Ariz.	New Zealand	NZ
Atlantic Ocean	Atl. Oc.	North	N; n
British	Br.	North America	N Am
British Columbia	Br. Col.	North Carolina	N Car.
California	Calif.	N. Dakota	N Dak.
Cape Province	C. Prov.	Northeast	NE; ne
Central	C; c, cent.	Northwest	NW; nw
Central African Republic	Cent. African Rep.	Northwest Territory	NWT
cerca	ca	New York	NY
Colorado	Colo.	Pacific Ocean	Pac. Oc.
Connecticut	Conn.	Papua New Guinea	Papua NG
County	Co.	Peninsula	Pen.
District	Dist.	Queensland	Queens.
Dominican Republic	Dom. Rep.	Republic	Rep.
East	E; e	River	R.
El Salvador	El Sal.	Siberia	Sib.
Extinct	†	South	S; s
Federal	Fed.	South America	S Am.
French	Fr.	South Carolina	S Car.
Greater	Gr.	Southeast	SE; se
Indian Ocean	Ind. Oc.	Southwest	SW; sw
Introduced	Introd.	Strait	Str.
Isla	I.	Subtropical	Subtrop.
Island	I.	Synonymous	Syn.; syn.
Islands	Is., is.	Tasmania	Tas.
Lake	L.	Tierra del Fuego	T. D. Fuego
Madagascar	Madag.	Tropical	Trop.; trop.
Massachusetts	Mass.	United Kingdom	UK
Mediterranean	Medit.	United States	US
Montana	Mont.	Washington	Wash.
Mountain	Mt.	West	W, w
Mountains	Mts.; mts.	Wyoming	Wyo.

PART I: Non-Passerines

	Order	Family	Species	Page
Ostrich	Struthioniformes	Struthionidae	1	1
Rheas	Struthioniformes	Rheidae	2	1
Cassowaries	Struthioniformes	Casuariidae	3	1
Emu	Struthioniformes	Dromaiidae	1	1
Kiwis	Struthioniformes	Apterygidae	3	1
Tinamous	Tinamiformes	Tinamidae	47	2-5
Penguins	Sphenisciformes	Spheniscidae	17	5-6
Loons	Gaviiformes	Gaviidae	5	6
Grebes	Podicipediformes	Podicipedidae	19	7-8
Albatrosses	Procellariiformes	Diomedeidae	14	8-9
Shearwaters and Petrels	Procellariiformes	Procellariidae	72	9-12
Storm-Petrels	Procellariiformes	Hydrobatidae	20	12-13
Diving-Petrels	Procellariiformes	Pelecanoididae	4	14
Tropicbirds	Pelecaniformes	Phaethontidae	3	14
Pelicans	Pelecaniformes	Pelecanidae	8	14-15
Boobies and Gannets	Pelecaniformes	Sulidae	9	15
Cormorants	Pelecaniformes	Phalacrocoracidae	39	15-17
Anhinga and Darters	Pelecaniformes	Anhingidae	2	17
Frigatebirds	Pelecaniformes	Fregatidae	5	18
Herons, Egrets and Bitterns	Ciconiiformes	Ardeidae	63	18-22
Hamerkop	Ciconiiformes	Scopidae	1	22
Storks	Ciconiiformes	Ciconiidae	19	22-23
Shoebill	Ciconiiformes	Balaenicipitidae	1	23
Ibises and Spoonbills	Ciconiiformes	Threskiornithidae	33	23-25
Flamingos	Phoenicopteriformes	Phoenicopteridae	5	25
Screamers	Anseriformes	Anhimidae	3	25
Ducks, Geese and Swans	Anseriformes	Anatidae	157	25-33
New World Vultures	Falconiformes	Cathartidae	7	33
Osprey	Falconiformes	Pandionidae	1	34
Hawks, Eagles and Kites	Falconiformes	Accipitridae	236	34-48
Secretary-bird	Falconiformes	Sagittariidae	1	49
Falcons and Caracaras	Falconiformes	Falconidae	62	49-53
Megapodes	Galliformes	Megapodiidae	21	53-54
Guans, Chachalacas and Allies	Galliformes	Cracidae	50	54-57
Turkeys	Galliformes	Meleagridae	2	57
Grouse	Galliformes	Tetraonidae	17	57-60
New World Quail	Galliformes	Odontophoridae	31	60-63
Pheasants and Partridges	Galliformes	Phasianidae	155	63-73
Guineafowl	Galliformes	Numididae	6	74
Hoatzin	Opisthocomiformes	Opisthocomidae	1	75
Mesites	Gruiformes	Mesitornithidae	3	75
Buttonquail	Gruiformes	Turnicidae	16	75-76
Cranes	Gruiformes	Gruidae	15	76-77
Limpkin	Gruiformes	Aramidae	1	77
Trumpeters	Gruiformes	Psophiidae	3	77-78
Rails, Gallinules and Coots	Gruiformes	Rallidae	134	78-86
Sungrebe and Finfoots	Gruiformes	Heliornithidae	3	86
Kagu	Gruiformes	Rhynochetidae	1	87
Sunbittern	Gruiformes	Eurypygidae	1	87
Seriemas	Gruiformes	Cariamidae	2	87
Bustards	Gruiformes	Otididae	25	87-88
Jacanas	Charadriiformes	Jacanidae	8	88-89
Painted-Snipe	Charadriiformes	Rostratulidae	2	89

Crab Plover	Charadriiformes	Dromadidae	1	89
Oystercatchers	Charadriiformes	Haematopodidae	11	89-90
Ibisbill	Charadriiformes	Ibidorhynchidae	1	90
Avocets and Stilts	Charadriiformes	Recurvirostridae	10	90
Thick-knees	Charadriiformes	Burhinidae	9	91
Pratincoles and Coursers	Charadriiformes	Glareolidae	17	91-92
Plovers and Lapwings	Charadriiformes	Charadriidae	66	92-96
Magellanic Plover	Charadriiformes	Pluvianellidae	1	96
Sandpipers and Allies	Charadriiformes	Scolopacidae	87	96-99
Plains-wanderer	Charadriiformes	Pedionomidae	1	100
Seedsnipes	Charadriiformes	Thinocoridae	4	100
Sheathbills	Charadriiformes	Chionidae	2	101
Skuas and Jaegers	Charadriiformes	Stercoraiidae	7	101
Gulls	Charadriiformes	Laridae	51	101-104
Terns	Charadriiformes	Sternidae	44	104-107
Skimmers	Charadriiformes	Rynchopidae	3	107
Auks, Murres and Puffins	Charadriiformes	Alcidae	23	107-109
Sandgrouse	Pterocliformes	Pteroclidae	16	109-110
Pigeons and Doves	Columbiformes	Columbidae	308	110-130
Cockatoos and Allies	Psittaciformes	Cacatuidae	21	131-132
Parrots, Macaws and Allies	Psittaciformes	Psittacidae	331	132-152
Turacos	Cuculiformes	Musophagidae	23	152-153
Cuckoos	Cuculiformes	Cuculidae	138	153-162
Barn-Owls	Strigiformes	Tytonidae	16	162-163
Typical Owls	Strigiformes	Strigidae	188	163-178
Oilbird	Caprimulgiformes	Steatornithidae	1	178
Owlet-Nightjars	Caprimulgiformes	Aegothelidae	9	178
Frogmouths	Caprimulgiformes	Podargidae	12	178-179
Potoos	Caprimulgiformes	Nyctibiidae	7	179-180
Nightjars and Allies	Caprimulgiformes	Caprimulgidae	89	180-186
Swifts	Apodiformes	Apodidae	98	186-193
Treeswifts	Apodiformes	Hemiprocnidae	4	193-194
Hummingbirds	Apodiformes	Trochilidae	335	194-214
Mousebirds	Coliiformes	Coliidae	6	214
Trogons	Trogoniformes	Trogonidae	39	214-218
Kingfishers	Coraciiformes	Alcedinidae	93	218-226
Todies	Coraciiformes	Todidae	5	226-227
Motmots	Coraciiformes	Momotidae	10	227-228
Bee-eaters	Coraciiformes	Meropidae	26	228-229
Typical Rollers	Coraciiformes	Coraciidae	12	230
Ground-Rollers	Coraciiformes	Brachypteraciidae	5	231
Cuckoo-Roller	Coraciiformes	Leptosomidae	1	231
Hoopoes	Upupiformes	Upupidae	2	231
Woodhoopoes	Upupiformes	Phoeniculidae	8	231-232
Hornbills	Coraciiformes	Bucerotidae	57	232-235
Jacamars	Piciformes	Galbulidae	18	235-236
Puffbirds	Piciformes	Bucconidae	33	236-238
Barbets	Piciformes	Capitonidae	83	238-245
Toucans	Piciformes	Ramphastidae	41	245-247
Honeyguides	Piciformes	Indicatoridae	17	247-248
Woodpeckers and Allies	Piciformes	Picidae	217	248-266

Part II: Passerines

	Order	Family	Species	Page
Broadbills	Passeriformes	Eurylaimidae	15	269-270
Asities	Passeriformes	Philepittidea	4	270
Ovenbirds	Passeriformes	Furnariidae	240	270-286
Woodcreepers	Passeriformes	Dendrocolaptidae	51	286-293
Typical Antbirds	Passeriformes	Thamnophilidae	207	293-307
Antthrushes and Antpittas	Passeriformes	Formicariidae	62	307-312
Gnateaters	Passeriformes	Conopophagidae	8	312
Tapaculos	Passeriformes	Rhinocryptidae	56	312-315
Plantcutters	Passeriformes	Phytotomidae	3	315
Cotingas	Passeriformes	Cotingidae	68	315-318
Manakins	Passeriformes	Pipridae	52	318-322
Tyrant Flycatchers	Passeriformes	Tyrannidae	425	322-352
Sharpbill	Passeriformes	Oxyruncidae	1	352
Pittas	Passeriformes	Pittidae	32	353-355
Scrub-birds	Passeriformes	Atrichornithidae	2	355
Lyrebirds	Passeriformes	Menuridae	2	355
New Zealand Wrens	Passeriformes	Acanthisittidae	3	355-356
Larks	Passeriformes	Alaudidae	91	356-365
Swallows	Passeriformes	Hirundinidae	90	365-371
Wagtails and Pipits	Passeriformes	Motacillidae	62	371-376
Cuckoo-shrikes	Passeriformes	Campephagidae	82	376-384
Bulbuls	Passeriformes	Pycnonotidae	130	384-394
Kinglets	Passeriformes	Regulidae	6	394
Leafbirds	Passeriformes	Chloropseidae	8	394-395
Ioras	Passeriformes	Aegithinidae	4	395-396
Silky-flycatchers	Passeriformes	Ptilogonatidae	4	396
Waxwings	Passeriformes	Bombycillidae	3	396
Hypocolius	Passeriformes	Hypocoliidae	1	396
Palmchat	Passeriformes	Dulidae	1	396
Dippers	Passeriformes	Cinclidae	5	397
Wrens	Passeriformes	Troglodytidae	79	397-406
Mockingbirds and Thrashers	Passeriformes	Mimidae	35	406-409
Accentors	Passeriformes	Prunellidae	13	409-410
Thrushes and Allies	Passeriformes	Turdidae	175	410-424
Cisticolas and Allies	Passeriformes	Cisticolidae	111	424-434
Old World Warblers	Passeriformes	Sylviidae	279	435-454
Gnatcatchers	Passeriformes	Polioptilidae	15	454-456
Old World Flycatchers	Passeriformes	Muscicapidae	270	456-476
Wattle-eyes	Passeriformes	Platysteiridae	31	476-477
Fantails	Passeriformes	Rhipiduridae	43	478-481
Monarch Flycatchers	Passeriformes	Monarchidae	98	481-489
Australasian Robins	Passeriformes	Petroicidae	44	489-492
Whistlers and Allies	Passeriformes	Pachycephalidae	57	492-498
Rockfowl	Passeriformes	Picathartidae	2	498
Babblers	Passeriformes	Timaliidae	265	498-521
Pseudo-babblers	Passeriformes	Pomatostomidae	5	521
Parrotbills	Passeriformes	Paradoxornithidae	20	521-523
Logrunner and Chowchilla	Passeriformes	Orthonychidae	2	523
Whipbirds and Quail-thrushes	Passeriformes	Cinclosomatidae	15	523-524
Long-tailed Tits	Passeriformes	Aegithalidae	8	524-525
Fairywrens	Passeriformes	Maluridae	25	525-527
Thornbills and Allies	Passeriformes	Acanthizidae	65	527-532
Australian Chats	Passeriformes	Epthianuridae	5	532

Part I

Non-Passerines

ORDER: STRUTHIONIFORMES
FAMILY: STRUTHIONIDAE (Ostrich—1)

☐ **Ostrich** *Struthio camelus*

____	*S. c. camelus*	Sahel of North Africa and the Sudan
____	*S. c. syriacus†*	Formerly Syrian and Arabian deserts. Extinct ca 1966
____	*S. c. molybdophanes*	S Ethiopia to Somalia and adjacent ne Kenya
____	*S. c. massaicus*	S Kenya and e Tanzania
____	*S. c. australis*	Southern Africa

ORDER: RHEIFORMES
FAMILY: RHEIDAE (Rheas—2)

☐ **Greater Rhea** *Rhea americana*

____	*R. a. americana*	Campos of n and e Brazil
____	*R. a. intermedia*	Extreme se Brazil (Rio Grande do Sul) and Uruguay
____	*R.. a. nobilis*	E Paraguay (east of the Río Paraguay)
____	*R.. a. araneipes*	*Chaco* of Paraguay to Bolivia and Brazilian Mato Grosso
____	*R. a. albescens*	Plains of Argentina south to Río Negro

☐ **Lesser Rhea** *Rhea pennata*

____	*R. p. garleppi*	Desert *puna* of se Peru, sw Bolivia and nw Argentina
____	*R. p. tarapacensis*	*Puna* of n Chile (Arica to Atacama)
____	*R. p. pennata*	Patagonian steppes of s Argentina and Magellanic Chile

ORDER: CASUARIIFORMES
FAMILY: CASUARIIDAE (Cassowaries—3)

☐ **Southern Cassowary** *Casuarius casuarius*

Humid forests of ne Australia, New Guinea and Aru Islands

☐ **Dwarf Cassowary** *Casuarius bennetti*

New Guinea, Yapen I. and New Britain

☐ **Northern Cassowary** *Casuarius unappendiculatus*

Lowlands of New Guinea, Yapen I. and w Papuan islands

ORDER: CASUARIIFORMES
FAMILY: DROMAIIDAE (Emu—1)

☐ **Emu** *Dromaius novaehollandiae*

____	*D. n. novaehollandiae*	Australia
____	*D. n. diemenensis†*	Formerly Tasmania. Extinct ca 1865

ORDER: DINORNITHIFORMES
FAMILY: APTERYGIDAE (Kiwis—3)

☐ **Brown Kiwi** *Apteryx australis*

____	*A. a. mantelli*	North I. (New Zealand)
____	*A. a. australis*	South I. (New Zealand)
____	*A. a. lawryi*	Stewart I. (New Zealand)

☐ **Little Spotted Kiwi** *Apteryx owenii*

Kapiti I., South I. and formerly North I. (New Zealand)

☐ **Great Spotted Kiwi** *Apteryx haastii*

Forests of South I. (New Zealand)

ORDER: TINAMIFORMES
FAMILY: TINAMIDAE (Tinamous—47)

☐ **Gray Tinamou** *Tinamus tao*

____	*T. t. larensis*	Montane forests of central Colombia and nw Venezuela
____	*T. t. kleei*	S-c Colombia to e Ecuador, e Peru, e Bolivia and w Brazil
____	*T. t. septentrionalis*	NE Venezuela and (?) nw Guyana
____	*T. t. tao*	N-central Brazil to borders of e Peru and Bolivia

☐ **Solitary Tinamou** *Tinamus solitarius*

____	*T. s. pernambucensis*	E-central Brazil (Pernambuco and Alagoas)
____	*T. s. solitarius*	SE Paraguay to e Brazil and extreme ne Argentina (Misiones)

☐ **Black Tinamou** *Tinamus osgoodi*

____	*T. o. hershkovitzi*	Andes of s-central Colombia
____	*T. o. osgoodi*	Andes of se Peru

☐ **Great Tinamou** *Tinamus major*

____	*T. m. robustus*	Lowlands of se Mexico to Guatemala and n Nicaragua
____	*T. m. percautus*	SE Mexico (Yucatán Pen.) to Petén of Guatemala and Belize
____	*T. m. fuscipennis*	N Nicaragua to Costa Rica and w Panama
____	*T. m. castaneiceps*	SW Costa Rica and w Panama
____	*T. m. brunneiventris*	S-central Panama
____	*T. m. saturatus*	Pacific slope of e Panama and nw Colombia
____	*T. m. latifrons*	SW Colombia and w Ecuador
____	*T. m. zuliensis*	Tropical ne Colombia and w Venezuela
____	*T. m. peruvianus*	SE Colombia east of the Andes to Bolivia and extreme w Brazil
____	*T. m. serratus*	Extreme s Venezuela and adjacent nw Brazil
____	*T. m. major*	E Venezuela to the Guianas and ne Brazil
____	*T. m. olivascens*	Amazonian Brazil

☐ **White-throated Tinamou** *Tinamus guttatus*

SE Colombia and s Venezuela to n Bolivia and Amaz. Brazil

☐ **Highland Tinamou** *Nothocercus bonapartei*

____	*N. b. frantzii*	Highlands of Costa Rica and w Panama
____	*N. b. intercedens*	W Andes of Colombia
____	*N. b. discrepans*	Base of Eastern Andes of Colombia (Tolima and Meta)
____	*N. b. bonapartei*	Central and E Andes of Colombia and w Venezuela
____	*N. b. plumbeiceps*	Andes of e Ecuador to extreme n Peru

☐ **Tawny-breasted Tinamou** *Nothocercus julius*

Andes of central Colombia and extreme w Venezuela; s-c Peru

☐ **Hooded Tinamou** *Nothocercus nigrocapillus*

____	*N. n. cadwaladeri*	Andes of nw Peru
____	*N. n. nigrocapillus*	Andes of central Peru to Bolivia

☐ **Berlepsch's Tinamou** *Crypturellus berlepschi*

Tropical forests of nw Colombia to nw Ecuador

☐ **Cinereous Tinamou** *Crypturellus cinereus*

SE Colombia to Guianas, s Venezuela, n Bolivia and ne Brazil

☐ **Red-legged Tinamou** *Crypturellus erythropus*

____	*C. e. columbianus*	Tropical north-central Colombia
____	*C. e. saltuarius*	NE Colombia (Sierra de Ocaña)
____	*C. e. idoneus*	NE Colombia and adjacent nw Venezuela
____	*C. e. cursitans*	N Colombia east of the Andes and nw Venezuela
____	*C. e. spencei*	N Venezuela
____	*C. e. margaritae*	Margarita I. (off Venezuela)
____	*C. e. erythropus*	E Venezuela to Guyana, Suriname and ne Brazil

☐ **Little Tinamou** *Crypturellus soui*

____	*C. s. meserythrus*	Tropical s Mexico to Belize, Honduras and se Nicaragua
____	*C. s. modestus*	Costa Rica and w Panama
____	*C. s. capnodes*	Humid lowlands of nw Panama
____	*C. s. poliocephalus*	Pacific slope of Panama (Veraguas to Canal Zone)
____	*C. s. panamensis*	Pacific and Caribbean slopes of Panama
____	*C. s. harterti*	Pacific slope of Colombia and Ecuador
____	*C. s. caucae*	Magdalena Valley of n-central Colombia
____	*C. s. mustelinus*	NE Colombia and extreme nw Venezuela
____	*C. s. soui*	E Colombia to the Guianas and ne Brazil
____	*C. s. caquetae*	SE Colombia (Meta to Caquetá)
____	*C. s. andrei*	Coastal n Venezuela (Falcón to Monagas); Trinidad
____	*C. s. nigriceps*	Tropical e Ecuador and ne Peru
____	*C. s. inconspicuus*	Central and e Peru and n Bolivia
____	*C. s. albigularis*	N and e Brazil

☐ **Tepui Tinamou** *Crypturellus ptaritepui*

Tepuis of s Venezuela (Ptari-tepui and Sororopán-tepui)

☐ **Brown Tinamou** *Crypturellus obsoletus*

____	*C. o. castaneus*	Tropical e Colombia to e Ecuador and n Peru
____	*C. o. ochraceiventris*	Subtropical central Peru (Huánuco to Cuzco)
____	*C. o. traylori*	Subtropical se Peru (Marcapata Valley of Cuzco)
____	*C. o. punensis*	Extreme se Peru and *yungas* of n Bolivia
____	*C. o. cerviniventris*	N Venezuela
____	*C. o. knoxi*	Subtropical nw Venezuela
____	*C. o. griseiventris*	N-central Brazil (Santarém region along Rio Tapajós)
____	*C. o. hypochracea*	SW Brazil (upper Río Madeira in Rondônia)
____	*C. o. obsoletus*	E Paraguay to se Brazil and extreme ne Argentina (Misiones)

☐ **Undulated Tinamou** *Crypturellus undulatus*

	C. u. manapiare	S Venezuela (upper Río Ventuari in Amazonas)
____	*C. u. simplex*	SW Guyana and immediately adjacent Brazil
____	*C. u. yapura*	SE Colombia to e Ecuador, e Peru and nw Brazil
____	*C. u. vermiculatus*	E Brazil (s Maranhão to Mato Grosso)
____	*C. u. adspersus*	Brazil south of the Amazon (Rio Madeira to Rio Tapajós)
____	*C. u. undulatus*	SE Peru to n Argentina

☐ **Pale-browed Tinamou** *Crypturellus transfasciatus*

Tropical forests of w Ecuador to nw Peru

☐ **Brazilian Tinamou** *Crypturellus strigulosus*

Tropical s Amazonian Brazil, adjacent e Peru and nw Bolivia

☐ **Gray-legged Tinamou** *Crypturellus duidae*

Tropical forests of e-central Colombia to s Venezuela

☐ **Yellow-legged Tinamou** *Crypturellus noctivagus*

____	*C. n. zabele*	Lowlands of ne Brazil (Piauí to Bahia and Minas Gerais)
____	*C. n. noctivagus*	Coastal se Brazil (Minas Gerais to Rio Grande do Sul)

☐ **Black-capped Tinamou** *Crypturellus atrocapillus*

____	*C. a. atrocapillus*	Lowlands of se Peru
____	*C. a. garleppi*	Lowlands of n Bolivia

☐ **Slaty-breasted Tinamou** *Crypturellus boucardi*

____	*C. b. boucardi*	Gulf-Caribbean lowlands of se Mexico to nw Honduras
____	*C. b. costaricensis*	Caribbean slope of Honduras to n Costa Rica

☐ **Choco Tinamou** *Crypturellus kerriae*

Humid foothills of extreme se Panama and nw Colombia

☐ **Variegated Tinamou** *Crypturellus variegatus*

Colombia to Venezuela, the Guianas, n Bolivia and Amaz. Brazil

☐ **Thicket Tinamou** *Crypturellus cinnamomeus*

____	*C. c. occidentalis*	Coastal w Mexico (Sinaloa to Guerrero)
____	*C. c. soconuscensis*	Pacific slope of s Mexico (Oaxaca and Chiapas)
____	*C. c. mexicanus*	Atlantic coast of Mexico (Tamaulipas to Puebla)
____	*C. c. sallaei*	S Mexico (Puebla to s Veracruz, Oaxaca and Chiapas)
____	*C. c. goldmani*	SE Mexico (Yucatán Peninsula) to n Guatemala and n Belize
____	*C. c. vicinior*	Highlands of s Mexico (Chiapas) to Guatemala and c Honduras
____	*C. c. cinnamomeus*	Coastal se Mexico (Chiapas) to El Salvador and Honduras
____	*C. c. delattrii*	Pacific lowlands of Nicaragua
____	*C. c. praepes*	Lowlands of nw Costa Rica

☐ **Rusty Tinamou** *Crypturellus brevirostris*

French Guiana and extreme ne Brazil; e Peru and nw Brazil

☐ **Bartlett's Tinamou** *Crypturellus bartletti*

Tropical w Amazonian Brazil, e Peru and n Bolivia

☐ **Small-billed Tinamou** *Crypturellus parvirostris*

Patchily distributed Amazon basin south to ne Argentina

☐ **Barred Tinamou** *Crypturellus casiquiare*

Extreme e Colombia and adjacent s Venezuela

☐ **Tataupa Tinamou** *Crypturellus tataupa*

____	*C. t. inops*	Marañón Valley of nw Peru
____	*C. t. peruviana*	W-central Peru (Chanchamayo Valley of Junín)
____	*C. t. lepidotus*	NE Brazil (Maranhão, Ceará, Piauí, Pernambuco and Bahia)
____	*C. t. tataupa*	E Bolivia to Paraguay, s Brazil and n Argentina

☐ **Red-winged Tinamou** *Rhynchotus rufescens*

____	*R. r. catingae*	Central and ne Brazil
____	*R. r. rufescens*	SE Peru to Bolivia, e Paraguay, se Brazil and ne Argentina
____	*R. r. maculicollis*	Andes of nw Bolivia to nw Argentina
____	*R. r. pallescens*	N Argentina (e Formosa to Río Negro)

☐ **Ornate Tinamou** *Nothoprocta ornata*

____	*N. o. branickii*	*Puna* of central Peru (Ancash to Apurímac)
____	*N. o. ornata*	Andes of se Peru to Bolivia and extreme n Chile
____	*N. o. rostrata*	Andes of nw Argentina (Jujuy and La Rioja)

☐ **Chilean Tinamou** *Nothoprocta perdicaria*

____	*N. p. perdicaria*	Semiarid grasslands of n-central Chile (Atacama to Ñuble)
____	*N. p. sanborni*	S-central Chile (Maule to Llanquihue) and adjacent Argentina

☐ **Brushland Tinamou** *Nothoprocta cinerascens*

____	*N. c. cinerascens*	SE Bolivia to nw Paraguay and central Argentina
____	*N. c. parvimaculata*	Arid nw Argentina (e La Rioja)

☐ **Andean Tinamou** *Nothoprocta pentlandii*

____	*N. p. ambigua*	Andes of s Ecuador and nw Peru
____	*N. p. oustaleti*	W slope of Andes of central and s Peru
____	*N. p. niethammeri*	Coastal central Peru
____	*N. p. fulvescens*	Andes of se Peru
____	*N. p. pentlandii*	Andes of w Bolivia to nw Argentina and extreme n Chile
____	*N. p. doeringi*	Mountains of central Argentina (San Luis and Córdoba)
____	*N. p. mendozae*	Mountains of w-central Argentina (n Neuquén and Mendoza)

☐ **Curve-billed Tinamou** *Nothoprocta curvirostris*

____	*N. c. curvirostris*	Andes of central Ecuador to n Peru (Cordillera del Condor)
____	*N. c. peruviana*	Andes of n and central Peru (south to Huánuco)

☐ **Taczanowski's Tinamou** *Nothoprocta taczanowskii*

Andes of s-central Peru (Junín to Puno)

4

☐ **Kalinowski's Tinamou** *Nothoprocta kalinowskii*

Known from two specimens ca 1900 from Andes of Peru

☐ **White-bellied Nothura** *Nothura boraquira*

NE Brazil to e Bolivia and ne Paraguay

☐ **Lesser Nothura** *Nothura minor*

Semiarid grasslands and scrub of interior se Brazil

☐ **Darwin's Nothura** *Nothura darwinii*

____ *N. d. peruviana*	Highlands of s Peru (Urubamba Valley of Cuzco)
____ *N. d. agassizii*	Altiplano of extreme se Peru and w Bolivia
____ *N. d. boliviana*	Highlands of w Bolivia (Cochabamba to Tarija)
____ *N. d. salvadorii*	Semiarid subtropical w Argentina
____ *N. d. darwinii*	Patagonian steppes of s-central Argentina

☐ **Spotted Nothura** *Nothura maculosa*

____ *N. m. cearensis*	NE Brazil (s Ceará)
____ *N. m. major*	Interior e-c Brazil (Minas Gerais, Goiás and adjacent Bahia)
____ *N. m. paludivaga*	Central Paraguay and n-central Argentina
____ *N. m. maculosa*	SE Brazil to e Paraguay, Uruguay and ne Argentina
____ *N. m. pallida*	Moist *chaco* grasslands of nw Argentina
____ *N. m. annectens*	Moist grasslands of e Argentina
____ *N. m. submontana*	Andean foothills of sw Argentina (Neuquén to Chubut)
____ *N. m. nigroguttata*	Plains of s-central Argentina (Río Negro to se Neuquén)

☐ **Chaco Nothura** *Nothura chacoensis*

Chaco of nw Paraguay and n-central Argentina

☐ **Dwarf Tinamou** *Taoniscus nanus*

Interior se Brazil and ne Argentina (Misiones)

☐ **Elegant Crested Tinamou** *Eudromia elegans*

____ *E. e. intermedia*	Andes of nw Argentina (Salta to Catamarca)
____ *E. e. magnistriata*	Andes of nw Argentina (Tucumán and n Córdoba)
____ *E. e. riojana*	Andes of nw Argentina (La Rioja and San Juan)
____ *E. e. albida*	Dry savanna of w Argentina (San Juan)
____ *E. a. wetmorei*	Andean foothills in w Argentina (n-central Mendoza)
____ *E. e. devia*	SW Argentina at base of Andes (Neuquén)
____ *E. e. numida*	Dry grasslands of central Argentina
____ *E. e. multiguttata*	Dry grasslands of e-central Argentina
____ *E. e. elegans*	Central Argentina (Río Negro and Neuquén)
____ *E. e. patagonica*	S Argentina (Neuquén to Santa Cruz) and adjacent s Chile

☐ **Quebracho Crested Tinamou** *Eudromia formosa*

____ *E. f. mira*	Arid *chaco* of Paraguay and (?) possibly adjacent n Argentina
____ *E. f. formosa*	Arid *quebracho* woodlands of n-central Argentina

☐ **Puna Tinamou** *Tinamotis pentlandii*

Andes of Peru to n Bolivia, Chile and nw Argentina

☐ **Patagonian Tinamou** *Tinamotis ingoufi*

Savanna of sw Argentina and s Chile

ORDER: SPHENISCIFORMES
FAMILY: SPHENISCIDAE (Penguins—17)

☐ **King Penguin** *Aptenodytes patagonicus*

____ *A. p. patagonicus*	Staten I., South Georgia I. and Falkland Islands
____ *A. p. halli*	Macquarie, Kerguelen, Crozet and Marion islands

☐ **Emperor Penguin** *Aptenodytes forsteri*

Antarctic continent and seas to edge of ice pack

☐ **Gentoo Penguin** *Pygoscelis papua*

_____ *P. p. papua*

_____ *P. p. ellsworthi*

Subantarctic regions south to ca 60°S

Antarctic Peninsula to South Sandwich Islands

☐ **Adelie Penguin** *Pygoscelis adeliae*

Circumpolar Antarctic seas to edge of ice pack

☐ **Chinstrap Penguin** *Pygoscelis antarctica*

Circumpolar Antarctic seas and adjacent islands

☐ **Fiordland Penguin** *Eudyptes pachyrhynchus*

South I. (New Zealand) and adjacent subantarctic islands

☐ **Snares Penguin** *Eudyptes robustus*

Snares I. and adjacent waters off New Zealand

☐ **Erect-crested Penguin** *Eudyptes sclateri*

Subantarctic New Zealand and Australian waters

☐ **Rockhopper Penguin** *Eudyptes chrysocome*

_____ *E. c. chrysocome*

_____ *E. c. filholi*

_____ *E. c. moseleyi*

Cape Horn Archipelago and Falkland Islands

Kerguelen Islands and subantarctic New Zealand islands

Tristan da Cunha, Gough, St. Paul and Amsterdam islands

☐ **Royal Penguin** *Eudyptes schlegeli*

Macquarie I. and adjacent islets

☐ **Macaroni Penguin** *Eudyptes chrysolophus*

Subantarctic islands in s Atlantic Ocean and s Indian Ocean

☐ **Yellow-eyed Penguin** *Megadyptes antipodes*

Auckland I., Stewart I., Campbell I. and South I. (New Zealand)

☐ **Little Penguin** *Eudyptula minor*

_____ *E. m. novaehollandiae*

_____ *E. m. iredalei*

_____ *E. m. variabilis*

_____ *E. m. albosignata*

_____ *E. m. minor*

_____ *E. m. chathamensis*

South Australia and Tasmania

Northern North I. (New Zealand)

Southern North I. and Cook Strait (New Zealand)

Eastern South I. (New Zealand)

Western and southern South I. and Stewart I. (New Zealand)

Chatham Islands

☐ **Jackass Penguin** *Spheniscus demersus*

Coasts and islands off Namibia, South Africa and adj. waters

☐ **Humboldt Penguin** *Spheniscus humboldti*

Humboldt Current region of coastal n Peru to s Chile

☐ **Magellanic Penguin** *Spheniscus magellanicus*

Patagonian coasts, Staten, Falkland and Juan Fernández islands

☐ **Galapagos Penguin** *Spheniscus mendiculus*

Galapagos Islands (Fernandina and Isabela)

ORDER: GAVIIFORMES
FAMILY: GAVIIDAE (Loons—5)

☐ **Red-throated Loon** *Gavia stellata*

N Eurasia and n N Am.; winters to Caspian and Mediterranean

☐ **Arctic Loon** *Gavia arctica*

Arctic Eurasia and w Alaska; winters to s Palearctic region

☐ **Pacific Loon** *Gavia pacifica*

Coastal e Siberia and n N America; winters to Japan, s Baja

☐ **Common Loon** *Gavia immer*

W Palearctic and N America; winters to s US and s Palearctic

☐ **Yellow-billed Loon** *Gavia adamsii*

N Eurasia and n North America; winters to n Baja California

ORDER: PODICIPEDIFORMES
FAMILY: PODICIPEDIDAE (Grebes—19)

☐ **Little Grebe** *Tachybaptus ruficollis*

___	*T. r. ruficollis*	Europe east to Ural Mountains and nw Africa
___	*T. r. iraquensis*	Iraq and sw Iran
___	*T. r. capensis*	Caucasus to Myanmar and Sri Lanka; Africa s of the Sahara
___	*T. r. poggei*	SE to ne Asia, Hainan, Taiwan, Japan and s Kuril Islands
___	*T. r. philippensis*	N Philippine Islands
___	*T. r. cotabato*	Mindanao (s Philippines)
___	*T. r. tricolor*	Sulawesi to New Guinea and Lesser Sundas
___	*T. r. vulcanorum*	Java to Timor
___	*T. r. collaris*	NE New Guinea to Bougainville (Solomon Islands)

☐ **Australasian Grebe** *Tachybaptus novaehollandiae*

___	*T. n. novaehollandiae*	S New Guinea to Australia, Tasmania and New Zealand
___	*T. n. leucosternos*	Vanuatu and New Caledonia
___	*T. n. renellianus*	Rennell (Solomon Islands)
___	*T. n. javanicus*	Java
___	*T. n. timorensis*	Timor (e Lesser Sundas)
___	*T. n. fumosus*	Sangihi I. and Talaud Islands (off ne Sulawesi)
___	*T. n. incola*	N New Guinea

☐ **Madagascar Grebe** *Tachybaptus pelzelnii*

Madagascar

☐ **Least Grebe** *Tachybaptus dominicus*

___	*T. d. brachypterus*	S Texas to w-central Mexico and Panama
___	*T. d. bangsi*	W Mexico (southern half of Baja California and s Sonora)
___	*T. d. dominicus*	Cozumel I., Bahamas, Greater Antilles and Virgin Islands
___	*T. d. speciosus*	Tropical n South America to s Brazil and n Argentina

☐ **Pied-billed Grebe** *Podilymbus podiceps*

___	*P. p. podiceps*	Alaska to Panama and Cuba
___	*P. p. antillarum*	Greater and Lesser Antilles
___	*P. p. antarcticus*	Northern South America to s Argentina

☐ **White-tufted Grebe** *Rollandia rolland*

___	*R. r. morrisoni*	Andes of central Peru (Lake Junín)
___	*R. r. chilensis*	S Peru and s Brazil to Tierra del Fuego and Cape Horn Arch.
___	*R. r. rolland*	Falkland Islands

☐ **Short-winged Grebe** *Rollandia microptera*

Andes of s Peru and w Bolivia (Lake Titicaca basin)

☐ **Hoary-headed Grebe** *Poliocephalus poliocephalus*

Australia, Tasmania and South I. (New Zealand)

☐ **New Zealand Grebe** *Poliocephalus rufopectus*

North I. (New Zealand)

☐ **Great Grebe** *Podiceps major*

___	*P. m. major*	S Brazil to s Argentina and central Chile; coastal Peru
___	*P. m. navasi*	S Argentina and s Chile

☐ **Red-necked Grebe** *Podiceps grisegena*

___	*P. g. grisegena*	Locally in Eurasia
___	*P. g. holboellii*	North America and ne Asia

☐ **Great Crested Grebe** *Podiceps cristatus*

___	*P. c. cristatus*	Palearctic region
___	*P. c. infuscatus*	Afrotropical region
___	*P. c. australis*	Australia, Tasmania and South I. (New Zealand)

☐ **Horned Grebe** *Podiceps auritus*

____ *P. a. auritus* — Locally in Palearctic region
____ *P. a. cornutus* — Locally in North America

☐ **Eared Grebe** *Podiceps nigricollis*

____ *P. n. nigricollis* — Locally in Eurasia
____ *P. n. gurneyi* — Africa south of the Sahara
____ *P. n. californicus* — Canada to Mexico; winters to Guatemala

☐ **Silvery Grebe** *Podiceps occipitalis*

____ *P. o. juninensis* — Locally in Andes of Colombia to n Chile and Argentina
____ *P. o. occipitalis* — Andes of c Argentina to Tierra del Fuego and Falkland Islands

☐ **Junin Grebe** *Podiceps taczanowskii*

Andes of central Peru (Lake Junín)

☐ **Hooded Grebe** *Podiceps gallardoi*

SW Argentina (w Santa Cruz); winter range unknown

☐ **Western Grebe** *Aechmophorus occidentalis*

____ *A. o. occidentalis* — W North America (se Alaska to n Mexico and Baja Calif.)
____ *A. o. ephemeralis* — Western Mexico

☐ **Clark's Grebe** *Aechmophorus clarkii*

____ *A. c. clarkii* — W North America (se Alaska to n Mexico)
____ *A. c. transitionalis* — Coastal w Mexico (Nayarit) and Mexican plateau

ORDER: PROCELLARIIFORMES
FAMILY: DIOMEDEIDAE (Albatrosses—14)

☐ **Wandering Albatross** *Diomedea exulans*

____ *D. e. exulans* — Southern oceans in South Georgia area
____ *D. e. dabbenena* — Tristan da Cunha and Gough islands
____ *D. e. antipodensis* — Antipodes Islands
____ *D. e. gibsoni* — Marion and Crozet islands

☐ **Royal Albatross** *Diomedea epomophora*

____ *D. e. sanfordi* — Chatham Islands and New Zealand; ranges circumpolar s oceans
____ *D. e. epomophora* — Campbell and Auckland islands; ranges circumpolar s oceans

☐ **Amsterdam Island Albatross** *Diomedea amsterdamensis*

Breeds Amsterdam I. (French subantarctic islands)

☐ **Short-tailed Albatross** *Phoebastria albatrus*

Breeds Torishima (Izu Islands); ranges at sea through n Pacific

☐ **Waved Albatross** *Phoebastria irrorata*

Breeds Hood (Galapagos Is.) and Isla La Plata off Ecuador

☐ **Laysan Albatross** *Phoebastria immutabilis*

Breeds w Hawaiian and Revillagigedo islands; ranges n Pacific

☐ **Black-footed Albatross** *Phoebastria nigripes*

W Hawaiian, Izu, Bonin and s Ryukyu islands

☐ **Gray-headed Albatross** *Thalassarche chrysostoma*

Circumpolar high s latitudes; ranges s oceans north to 35°S

☐ **Black-browed Albatross** *Thalassarche melanophris*

____ *T. m. impavida* — Campbell Islands and adjacent islands off New Zealand
____ *T. m. melanophris* — Cape Horn Archipelago to Antipodes Islands

☐ **Buller's Albatross** *Thalassarche bulleri*

____ *T. b. bulleri* — Solander and Snares islands; disperses to Australasian seas
____ *T. b. platei* — Three Kings and Chatham islands; ranges to s South America

☐ **Shy Albatross** *Thalassarche cauta*

____ *T. c. cauta*	Auckland Islands
____ *T. c. eremita*	Chatham Islands
____ *T. c. salvini*	Crozet, Snares and Bounty islands

☐ **Yellow-nosed Albatross** *Thalassarche chlororhynchos*

____ *T. c. chlororhynchos*	Tristan da Cunha and Gough islands.; ranges southern oceans
____ *T. c. bassi*	Breeds on s Indian Ocean islands; ranges southern oceans

☐ **Sooty Albatross** *Phoebetria fusca*

S Atlantic Ocean and Indian Ocean north to about 30°S

☐ **Light-mantled Albatross** *Phoebetria palpebrata*

Circumpolar subantarctic islands; ranges north to 35°S

ORDER: PROCELLARIIFORMES
FAMILY: PROCELLARIIDAE (Shearwaters and Petrels—72)

☐ **Antarctic Giant Petrel** *Macronectes giganteus*

Circumpolar southern oceans south to the pack ice

☐ **Hall's Giant Petrel** *Macronectes halli*

Southern oceans, generally north of Antarctic convergence

☐ **Northern Fulmar** *Fulmarus glacialis*

____ *F. g. glacialis*	Breeds high Arctic regions of North Atlantic; ranges widely
____ *F. g. auduboni*	Breeds low Arctic and boreal North Atlantic; ranges widely
____ *F. g. rodgersii*	Breeds coasts of e Siberia and Alaskan peninsula; ranges widely

☐ **Southern Fulmar** *Fulmarus glacialoides*

Antarctic circumpolar; ranges widely southern oceans

☐ **Antarctic Petrel** *Thalassoica antarctica*

Breeds Antarctic islands and coasts; ranges southern oceans

☐ **Cape Petrel** *Daption capense*

____ *D. c. capense*	Breeds circumpolar subantarctic islands; ranges southern oceans
____ *D. c. australe*	Breeds New Zealand subantarctic islands; ranges southern oceans

☐ **Snow Petrel** *Pagodroma nivea*

____ *P. n. nivea*	South Georgia and adj. islands, Scotia Arc and Antarctic Pen.
____ *P. n. confusa*	South Sandwich Islands and Géologie Archipelago

☐ **Great-winged Petrel** *Pterodroma macroptera*

____ *P. m. macroptera*	Breeds and ranges islands and seas in southern oceans
____ *P. m. gouldi*	Breeds on islands off North I. (New Zealand)

☐ **Mascarene Petrel** *Pterodroma aterrima*

Réunion (Mascarene Islands); ranges adjacent Indian Ocean

☐ **Tahiti Petrel** *Pterodroma rostrata*

____ *P. r. rostrata*	Breeds Marquesas and Society islands; confined to trop. Pacific
____ *P. r. becki*	Known from two 1928 specimens from Rendova (Solomon Is.)
____ *P. r. trouessarti*	Breeds New Caledonia; ranges s Pacific Ocean

☐ **White-headed Petrel** *Pterodroma lessonii*

Islands in s Indian Ocean and s Pacific Ocean

☐ **Black-capped Petrel** *Pterodroma hasitata*

____ *P. h. hasitata*	Cuba, Hispaniola, Guadeloupe and Dominica ; ranges w Atlantic
____ *P. h. caribbaea†*	Formerly Jamaica. Extinct ca 1936

☐ **Bermuda Petrel** *Pterodroma cahow*

Breeds Nonsuch I. (Bermuda); disperses to Gulf Stream

☐ **Atlantic Petrel** *Pterodroma incerta*

Tristan da Cunha and Gough islands; ranges s Atlantic Ocean

☐ **Phoenix Petrel** *Pterodroma alba*

Breeds French Polynesia to Kermadec I.; ranges s Pacific waters

☐ **Mottled Petrel** *Pterodroma inexpectata*

Breeds Stewart I., Snares Islands and sw South I. (New Zealand)

☐ **Providence Petrel** *Pterodroma solandri*

Breeds Lord Howe I. and Philip I.; ranges to nw Pacific

☐ **Kerguelen Petrel** *Pterodroma brevirostris*

Tristan da Cunha, Gough, Prince Edward, Crozet and Kergulen is.

☐ **Murphy's Petrel** *Pterodroma ultima*

Tuamotu Archipelago, Austral Islands and Pitcairn I.

☐ **Kermadec Petrel** *Pterodroma neglecta*
____ *P. n. neglecta*
____ *P. n. juana*

Breeds South Pacific islands from New Zealand to Easter I.
Juan Fernández, San Ambrosio and San Félix islands (off Chile)

☐ **Magenta Petrel** *Pterodroma magentae*

Chatham Islands (population ±50 birds in 1992)

☐ **Herald Petrel** *Pterodroma arminjoniana*
____ *P. a. arminjoniana*
____ *P. a. heraldica*

Breeds Trindade I. and Martín Vaz I. (s Atlantic Ocean)
Breeds Raine I., Tonga and French Polynesia to Easter I.

☐ **Soft-plumaged Petrel** *Pterodroma mollis*
____ *P. m. mollis*
____ *P. m. dubia*

Gough, Tristan da Cunha and Antipodes islands
Marion, Crozet, Kerguelen and Amsterdam islands

☐ **Cape Verde Petrel** *Pterodroma feae*

Cape Verde and Desertas islands; ranges e Atlantic Ocean

☐ **Madeira Petrel** *Pterodroma madeira*

Highlands of Madeira I.; ranges e Atlantic Ocean

☐ **Barau's Petrel** *Pterodroma baraui*

Breeds Réunion I. and Rodrigues I.; pelagic range unknown

☐ **Dark-rumped Petrel** *Pterodroma phaeopygia*
____ *P. p. phaeopygia*
____ *P. p. sandwichensis*

Galapagos Islands; ranges w Mexico to n Peru
Hawaiian Islands; ranges south to Polynesia

☐ **Juan Fernandez Petrel** *Pterodroma externa*

Alejandro Selkirk I. (Juan Fernández Islands off Chile)

☐ **White-necked Petrel** *Pterodroma cervicalis*

Breeds Kermadec Islands; ranges s Pacific Ocean

☐ **Cook's Petrel** *Pterodroma cookii*

Breeds islands off New Zealand; ranges to e and n Pacific

☐ **Defilippe's Petrel** *Pterodroma defilippiana*

Juan Fernández, San Ambrosio and San Félix islands (off Chile)

☐ **Gould's Petrel** *Pterodroma leucoptera*
____ *P. l. leucoptera*
____ *P. l. caledonica*
____ *P. l. brevipes*

Breeds Cabbage Tree Is. (off e Australia); ranges s Pacific Ocean
New Caledonia
Fiji and Cook Islands

☐ **Bonin Petrel** *Pterodroma hypoleuca*

Volcano, Bonin and w Hawaiian islands; ranges to Polynesia

☐ **Black-winged Petrel** *Pterodroma nigripennis*

Breeds sw Pacific; ranges s-central Pacific Ocean

☐ **Chatham Petrel** *Pterodroma axillaris*

Rangitira I. (Chatham Islands) and adjacent seas

☐ **Stejneger's Petrel** *Pterodroma longirostris*

Alejandro Selkirk I. (off Chile); ranges e and n Pacific

☐ **Pycroft's Petrel** *Pterodroma pycrofti*

Breeds small islands off New Zealand coast; ranges to n Pacific

☐ **Fiji Petrel** *Pterodroma macgillivrayi*

Breeds Gau I. (Fiji). Status uncertain

☐ **Blue Petrel** *Halobaena caerulea*

Islands in subantarctic southern oceans and islands off Cape Horn

☐ **Broad-billed Prion** *Pachyptila vittata*

Breeds islands off New Zealand and Tristan da Cunha group

☐ **Salvin's Prion** *Pachyptila salvini*
____ *P. s. salvini*
____ *P. s. macgillivrayi*

Prince Edward and Crozet islands
Amsterdam and St. Paul islands

☐ **Antarctic Prion** *Pachyptila desolata*
____ *P. d. desolata*
____ *P. d. alter*
____ *P. d. banksi*

Crozet, Kerguelen and Macquarie islands
Auckland and Heard islands
Scotia Arc, South Georgia, South Sandwich and Scott islands

☐ **Slender-billed Prion** *Pachyptila belcheri*

Crozet, Kerguelen and Falkland islands; Noir I. (off s Chile)

☐ **Fulmar Prion** *Pachyptila crassirostris*
____ *P. c. eatoni*
____ *P. c. crassirostris*

Breeds Heard and Auckland islands (New Zealand)
Snares, Bounty and Chatham islands (New Zealand)

☐ **Fairy Prion** *Pachyptila turtur*

Breeds scattered subtropical and subantarctic islands

☐ **Bulwer's Petrel** *Bulweria bulwerii*

Azores to Cape Verde, Johnston and nw Hawaiian islands

☐ **Jouanin's Petrel** *Bulweria fallax*

NW Indian Ocean and s Arabian Sea; breeding grounds unknown

☐ **Gray Petrel** *Procellaria cinerea*

Breeds and ranges circumpolar subantarctic seas

☐ **White-chinned Petrel** *Procellaria aequinoctialis*
____ *P. a. aequinoctialis*
____ *P. a. conspicillata*

Circumpolar subantarctic islands
Inaccessible I. (Tristan da Cunha)

☐ **Parkinson's Petrel** *Procellaria parkinsoni*

Little and Great Barrier is. (New Zealand); ranges to S America

☐ **Westland Petrel** *Procellaria westlandica*

Breeds South I. (New Zealand); disperses to Australia

☐ **Streaked Shearwater** *Calonectris leucomelas*

Breeds coastal islands off Japan and China; ranges to s Pacific

☐ **Cory's Shearwater** *Calonectris diomedea*
____ *C. d. diomedea*
____ *C. d. borealis*
____ *C. d. edwardsii*

Breeds Mediterranean islands
Breeds Azores, Madeira, Canary and Berlenga islands
Breeds Cape Verde Islands

☐ **Pink-footed Shearwater** *Puffinus creatopus*

Mocha and Juan Fernández islands off Chile; ranges to n Pacific

☐ **Flesh-footed Shearwater** *Puffinus carneipes*

Transequatorial migrant from sw to n Pacific Ocean

☐ **Greater Shearwater** *Puffinus gravis*

Islands in s Atlantic Ocean; ranges n Atlantic to Arctic Circle

☐ **Wedge-tailed Shearwater** *Puffinus pacificus*

Widespread tropical Pacific and Indian oceans

☐ **Buller's Shearwater** *Puffinus bulleri*

Breeds islands off New Zealand; wide transpacific dispersal

☐ **Sooty Shearwater** *Puffinus griseus*

Transequatorial migrant from s S Am. and Australia to n Pacific

☐ **Short-tailed Shearwater** *Puffinus tenuirostris*

Australia and s Tasmania; transequatorial migrant to n Pacific

☐ **Christmas Shearwater** *Puffinus nativitatis*

Widespread throughout tropical central Pacific Ocean

☐ **Manx Shearwater** *Puffinus puffinus*

Breeds n Atlantic; ranges to Argentina and s African waters

☐ **Mediterranean Shearwater** *Puffinus yelkouan*
____ *P. y. mauritanicus*
____ *P. y. yelkouan*

Breeds Balearic Islands; ranges to coastal n Europe
Breeds central and e Mediterranean islands

☐ **Hutton's Shearwater** *Puffinus huttoni*

Breeds ne South I. (New Zealand); ranges to Australia

☐ **Black-vented Shearwater** *Puffinus opisthomelas*

Islands off w coast of Baja Calif.; disperses adj. Mexican waters

☐ **Townsend's Shearwater** *Puffinus auricularis*
____ *P. a. newelli*
____ *P. a. auricularis*

Breeds Kauai (Hawaiian Islands); dispersal unknown
Breeds Revillagigedo Islands (off w Mexico); disperses to 8°N

☐ **Fluttering Shearwater** *Puffinus gavia*

Breeds is. off New Zealand; ranges to Tasman Sea and Vanuatu

☐ **Little Shearwater** *Puffinus assimilis*
____ *P. a. baroli*
____ *P. a. boydi*
____ *P. a. tunneyi*
____ *P. a. assimilis*
____ *P. a. kermadecensis*
____ *P. a. haurakiensis*
____ *P. a. elegans*
____ *P. a. myrtae*

Azores, Desertas, Salvage and Canary islands
Cape Verde Islands
Islands off sw Australia (Abrolhos Islands to Récherche Arch.)
Norfolk and Lord Howe islands
Kermadec Islands
Islets off ne coast of North I. (New Zealand)
Tristan da Cunha, Gough, Chatham and Antipodes islands
Rapa I. (Austral Islands)

☐ **Audubon's Shearwater** *Puffinus lherminieri*
____ *P. l. lherminieri*
____ *P. l. loyemilleri*
____ *P. l. subalaris*
____ *P. l. dichrous*
____ *P. l. gunax*
____ *P. l. bannermani*
____ *P. l. bailloni*
____ *P. l. nicolae*
____ *P. l. temptator*

Breeds Bahamas and West Indies; formerly Bermuda
Islets in sw Caribbean
Breeds Galapagos Islands
Islands throughout central Pacific (Samoa to Marquesas Islands)
Breeds Banks Group (Vanuatu)
Breeds Bonin and Volcano islands (off Japan)
Mascarene Islands
NW Indian Ocean (Aldabra to Seychelles and Maldives)
Mohéli I. (Comoro Islands)

☐ **Persian Shearwater** *Puffinus persicus*

Breeds and ranges Arabian Sea and adjacent waters

☐ **Heinroth's Shearwater** *Puffinus heinrothi*

New Britain and Solomon Islands

☐ **Mascarene Shearwater** *Puffinus atrodorsalis*

Southwestern Indian Ocean

ORDER: PROCELLARIIFORMES
FAMILY: HYDROBATIDAE (Storm-Petrels—20)

☐ **Gray-backed Storm-Petrel** *Garrodia nereis*

Circumpolar subantarctic waters, north to about 35°S

☐ **Wilson's Storm-Petrel** *Oceanites oceanicus*
____ *O. o. oceanicus*
____ *O. o. exasperatus*

Subantarctic islands from Cape Horn to Kerguelen Islands
South Shetland Is., South Sandwich Is. and adj. Antarctic coast

☐ **White-vented Storm-Petrel** *Oceanites gracilis*
____ *O. g. galapagoensis*
____ *O. g. gracilis*

Galapagos Islands (breeding grounds unknown)
Coast of Ecuador to Chile (breeding grounds unknown)

☐ **White-faced Storm-Petrel** *Pelagodroma marina*

____ *P. m. hypoleuca*	Salvage I. (North Atlantic Ocean)
____ *P. m. eadesi*	Cape Verde Islands
____ *P. m. marina*	Tristan da Cunha and Gough islands
____ *P. m. dulciae*	Breeds islands off w and s Australia
____ *P. m. maoriana*	Stewart, Auckland, Chatham and islands off New Zealand
____ *P. m. albiclunis*	Kermadec Islands

☐ **Black-bellied Storm-Petrel** *Fregetta tropica*

____ *F. t. tropica*	Subantarctic circumpolar islands; ranges north to tropics
____ *F. t. melanoleuca*	Tristan da Cunha and Gough islands

☐ **White-bellied Storm-Petrel** *Fregetta grallaria*

____ *F. g. leucogaster*	Tristan da Cunha, Gough, Amsterdam and St. Paul islands
____ *F. g. grallaria*	Lord Howe and Kermadec islands
____ *F. g. segethi*	Juan Fernández Islands (off Chile)
____ *F. g. titan*	Rapa I. (Austral Islands)

☐ **Polynesian Storm-Petrel** *Nesofregetta fuliginosa*

Tropical central and w Pacific Ocean

☐ **European Storm-Petrel** *Hydrobates pelagicus*

E Atlantic and Mediterranean; ranges to Indian Ocean

☐ **Least Storm-Petrel** *Oceanodroma microsoma*

Breeds islands off Baja Calif.; ranges south to extreme n Peru

☐ **Wedge-rumped Storm-Petrel** *Oceanodroma tethys*

____ *O. t. tethys*	Galapagos Islands (Pitt, Tower and Redonda)
____ *O. t. kelsalli*	Islas Pescadores and San Gallán (off coast of Peru)

☐ **Band-rumped Storm-Petrel** *Oceanodroma castro*

Breeds and ranges tropical Atlantic and Pacific Oceans

☐ **Leach's Storm-Petrel** *Oceanodroma leucorhoa*

____ *O. l. leucorhoa*	N Atlantic; Japan to Aleutians and islands off n Mexico
____ *O. l. willeti*	Coronados Islands (off w Mexico)
____ *O. l. chapmani*	San Benito Islands (off w Mexico)
____ *O. l. socorroensis*	Summer breeder on Guadalupe I. (off w Mexico)
____ *O. l. cheimomnestes*	Winter breeder on Guadalupe I. (off w Mexico)

☐ **Swinhoe's Storm-Petrel** *Oceanodroma monorhis*

Breeds islands off Japan; disperses to n Indian Ocean

☐ **Tristram's Storm-Petrel** *Oceanodroma tristrami*

Breeds and ranges Hawaii, Izu and Volcano islands

☐ **Markham's Storm-Petrel** *Oceanodroma markhami*

Breeds Paracas Peninsula (Peru); ranges to s Mexico and Chile

☐ **Matsudaira's Storm-Petrel** *Oceanodroma matsudairae*

Breeds Volcano Islands (Japan); disperses to Indian Ocean

☐ **Black Storm-Petrel** *Oceanodroma melania*

Breeds islands off California and Baja; ranges to Peru

☐ **Ashy Storm-Petrel** *Oceanodroma homochroa*

Breeds islands off California; ranges to s Baja California

☐ **Ringed Storm-Petrel** *Oceanodroma hornbyi*

Ranges coastal Ecuador to central Chile

☐ **Fork-tailed Storm-Petrel** *Oceanodroma furcata*

____ *O. f. furcata*	N Kuril, Komandorskiye and Aleutian islands
____ *O. f. plumbea*	Islands off s Alaska to n California

ORDER: PROCELLARIIFORMES
FAMILY: PELECANOIDIDAE (Diving-Petrels—4)

☐ **Peruvian Diving-Petrel** *Pelecanoides garnotii*

Arid coasts of Peru and n Chile

☐ **Magellanic Diving-Petrel** *Pelecanoides magellani*

Islands and fiords of s Chile and s Argentina

☐ **South Georgia Diving-Petrel** *Pelecanoides georgicus*

Subantarctic circumpolar regions

☐ **Common Diving-Petrel** *Pelecanoides urinatrix*
____ *P. u. berard* — Falkland Islands
____ *P. u. dacunhae* — Tristan da Cunha and Gough islands
____ *P. u. exsul* — South Georgia I. east to Antipodes Islands
____ *P. u. urinatrix* — Tasmania, New Zealand and islands in Bass Strait
____ *P. u. chathamensis* — Chatham and Snares islands (off New Zealand)
____ *P. u. copperingeri* — Southern Chile

ORDER: PELECANIFORMES
FAMILY: PHAETHONTIDAE (Tropicbirds—3)

☐ **Red-billed Tropicbird** *Phaethon aethereus*
____ *P. a. mesonauta* — Subtropical and tropical e Pacific, Caribbean and e Atlantic
____ *P. a. aethereus* — Fernando de Noronha, Ascension and St. Helena is. (s Atlantic)
____ *P. a. indicus* — Red Sea, Persian Gulf and Gulf of Aden

☐ **Red-tailed Tropicbird** *Phaethon rubricauda*
____ *P. r. melanorhynchos* — Breeds and disperses widely in tropical Pacific Ocean
____ *P. r. roseotincta* — Breeds sw Pacific islands
____ *P. r. rubricauda* — Breeds islands in w Indian Ocean
____ *P. r. westralis* — Islands in e Indian Ocean and Easter I.

☐ **White-tailed Tropicbird** *Phaethon lepturus*
____ *P. l. lepturus* — Islands in Indian Ocean
____ *P. l. fulvus* — Christmas I. (Indian Ocean)
____ *P. l. europae* — Europa I. (s Mozambique Channel)
____ *P. l. dorothea* — Islands in tropical w Pacific (Hawaii to New Caledonia)
____ *P. l. catesbyi* — Breeds islands in tropical Atlantic Ocean
____ *P. l. ascensionis* — Fernando de Noronha and Ascension islands

ORDER: PELECANIFORMES
FAMILY: PELECANIDAE (Pelicans—8)

☐ **Great White Pelican** *Pelecanus onocrotalus*

Locally in s-central Eurasia, s Asia and Africa

☐ **Pink-backed Pelican** *Pelecanus rufescens*

Locally in Africa south of the Sahara and Madagascar

☐ **Spot-billed Pelican** *Pelecanus philippensis*

Lowlands of India to SE Asia and Philippines

☐ **Dalmatian Pelican** *Pelecanus crispus*

Breeds s Eurasia; winters to India

☐ **Australian Pelican** *Pelecanus conspicillatus*

Australia and Tasmania; winters to New Guinea region

☐ **American White Pelican** *Pelecanus erythrorhynchos*

S Canada to s US; winters to Costa Rica

☐ **Peruvian Pelican** *Pelecanus thagus*

Pacific coast of s Ecuador to s Chile

☐ **Brown Pelican** *Pelecanus occidentalis*

____ *P. o. occidentalis*	West Indies and Caribbean to islands off Venezuela
____ *P. o. carolinensis*	Locally on Atlantic coast of tropical America
____ *P. o. californicus*	Anacapa I. and islands off Baja and in Gulf of California
____ *P. o. murphyi*	Pacific coast of nw South America from Colombia to Peru
____ *P. o. urinator*	Galapagos Islands

ORDER: PELECANIFORMES
FAMILY: SULIDAE (Gannets and Boobies—9)

☐ **Northern Gannet** *Morus bassanus*

Breeds n Atlantic coasts; ranges to coastal nw Africa

☐ **Cape Gannet** *Morus capensis*

Islands off s Africa; disperses to coastal Mozambique

☐ **Australian Gannet** *Morus serrator*

Islands and coasts of Australia, Tasmania and New Zealand

☐ **Abbott's Booby** *Sula abbotti*

Christmas I. (e Indian Ocean)

☐ **Blue-footed Booby** *Sula nebouxii*

____ *S. n. nebouxii*	Pacific coast of Mexico to Peru
____ *S. n. excisa*	Galapagos Islands

☐ **Peruvian Booby** *Sula variegata*

Coastal sw Colombia to s Chile

☐ **Masked Booby** *Sula dactylatra*

____ *S. d. personata*	Islands in central and w Pacific to islands off w Australia
____ *S. d. fullagari*	Islands in n Tasman Sea
____ *S. d. granti*	Breeds islands off w Mexico to Chile
____ *S. d. dactylatra*	Breeds islands in Caribbean and sw Atlantic Ocean
____ *S. d. melanops*	Breeds islands in w Indian Ocean

☐ **Red-footed Booby** *Sula sula*

____ *S. s. sula*	Breeds islands in Caribbean and off Brazil
____ *S. s. rubripes*	Breeds islands in tropical Pacific and Indian oceans
____ *S. s. websteri*	Islands off w Mexico, Central America and Galapagos Islands

☐ **Brown Booby** *Sula leucogaster*

____ *S. l. brewsteri*	Islands in Gulf of California and off w Mexico
____ *S. l. etesiaca*	Islands off Central America and Colombia
____ *S. l. leucogaster*	Islands in Gulf of Mexico, Caribbean and tropical Atlantic
____ *S. l. plotus*	Islands in Red Sea, tropical Indian Ocean and s China Sea

ORDER: PELECANIFORMES
FAMILY: PHALACROCORACIDAE (Cormorants—39)

☐ **Little Black Cormorant** *Phalacrocorax sulcirostris*

Australasian region and Malay Archipelago

☐ **Double-crested Cormorant** *Phalacrocorax auritus*

____ *P. a. cincinatus*	Aleutian Islands across Gulf of Alaska to Yakutat Peninsula
____ *P. a. albociliatus*	SW British Columbia to Gulf of California
____ *P. a. auritus*	Gulf of St. Lawrence to Cape Cod and locally west to Utah
P. a. floridanus	Coastal North Carolina to Florida, Bahamas and Cuba

☐ **Indian Cormorant** *Phalacrocorax fuscicollis*

Lowlands of India and SE Asia

☐ **Neotropic Cormorant** *Phalacrocorax brasilianus*
___ *P. b. mexicanus* — Extreme s US to Nicaragua, Bahamas, Cuba and Isle of Pines
___ *P. b. brasilianus* — Costa Rica s through South America to Tierra del Fuego

☐ **Great Cormorant** *Phalacrocorax carbo*
___ *P. c. carbo* — N Europe and n N America; winters to Gulf coast, nw Africa
___ *P. c. sinensis* — N-central Europe to s China; winters to SE Asia and Indonesia
___ *P. c. hanedae* — Honshu I. (Japan)
___ *P. c. maroccanus* — Coastal nw Africa (Morocco to Mauritania)
___ *P. c. lucidus* — Africa south of the Sahara and Cape Verde Islands
___ *P. c. novaehollandiae* — Australia, Tasmania, New Zealand and Chatham Islands

☐ **Cape Cormorant** *Phalacrocorax capensis* — Coastal sw Namibia and s South Africa

☐ **Socotra Cormorant** *Phalacrocorax nigrogularis* — Seacoasts and islands in Persian Gulf

☐ **Bank Cormorant** *Phalacrocorax neglectus* — Coastal sw Africa (Namibia to sw Cape Province)

☐ **Japanese Cormorant** *Phalacrocorax capillatus* — Rocky seacoasts and islands of ne Asia

☐ **Brandt's Cormorant** *Phalacrocorax penicillatus* — Coastal s Alaska to Baja California

☐ **European Shag** *Phalacrocorax aristotelis*
___ *P. a. aristotelis* — Iceland and n Scandinavia south to Iberian Peninsula
___ *P. a. desmarestii* — Mediterranean coasts and islands
___ *P. a. riggenbachi* — W coast of Morocco (Casablanca to Puerto Cansado)

☐ **Pelagic Cormorant** *Phalacrocorax pelagicus*
___ *P. p. pelagicus* — Coastal ne Asia, Bering Sea and Arctic Ocean islands
___ *P. p. resplendens* — Coastal sw British Columbia to s Baja California

☐ **Red-faced Cormorant** *Phalacrocorax urile* — Islands off n Japan to coastal s Alaska

☐ **Rock Shag** *Phalacrocorax magellanicus* — Coasts of Chile, Argentina and Falkland Islands

☐ **Guanay Cormorant** *Phalacrocorax bougainvillii* — Seacoasts and islands off Peru and Chile

☐ **Pied Cormorant** *Phalacrocorax varius*
___ *P. v. hypoleucos* — Coastal and interior Australia; rare vagrant to Tasmania
___ *P. v. varius* — Coastal New Zealand and Stewart I.

☐ **Black-faced Cormorant** *Phalacrocorax fuscescens* — Coastal s Australia, Tasmania and islands in Bass Strait

☐ **Rough-faced Shag** *Phalacrocorax carunculatus* — Islands in Cook Strait (New Zealand)

☐ **Bronze Shag** *Phalacrocorax chalconotus* — Coasts of Otago, Stewart and South islands (New Zealand)

☐ **Chatham Islands Shag** *Phalacrocorax onslowi* — Chatham Islands

☐ **Auckland Islands Shag** *Phalacrocorax colensoi* — Auckland Islands

☐ **Campbell Islands Shag** *Phalacrocorax campbelli* — Campbell Islands

☐ **Bounty Islands Shag** *Phalacrocorax ranfurlyi* — Bounty Islands (New Zealand); vagrant to Antipodes Islands

☐ **Antarctic Shag** *Phalacrocorax bransfieldensis* — South Shetland Islands and Antarctic Peninsula

☐ **South Georgia Shag** *Phalacrocorax georgianus* — South Georgia, South Sandwich and South Orkney islands

☐ **Imperial Shag** *Phalacrocorax atriceps*
___ *P. a. atriceps* — Islands and coasts of s Argentina and Chile
___ *P. a. albiventer* — Falkland Islands

☐ **Heard Island Shag** *Phalacrocorax nivalis* — Heard I. (s Indian Ocean)

☐ **Crozet Shag** *Phalacrocorax melanogenis* — Prince Edward, Marion and Crozet islands

☐ **Kerguelen Shag** *Phalacrocorax verrucosus* — Kerguelen I. (s Indian Ocean)

☐ **Macquarie Shag** *Phalacrocorax purpurascens* — Macquarie I. and adjacent Bishop and Clerk Rocks

☐ **Red-legged Cormorant** *Phalacrocorax gaimardi* — Coastal Peru and Chile; isolated population in s Argentina

☐ **Spotted Shag** *Phalacrocorax punctatus*
___ *P. p. punctatus* — North I. and South I. (New Zealand)
___ *P. p. oliveri* — Stewart I. and adjacent w coast of South I. (New Zealand)

☐ **Pitt Island Shag** *Phalacrocorax featherstoni* — Chatham Islands (New Zealand)

☐ **Little Pied Cormorant** *Phalacrocorax melanoleucos*
___ *P. m. melanoleucos* — Lesser Sundas to Solomon Islands, Australia and Tasmania
___ *P. m. brevicauda* — Rennel I. (Solomon Islands)
___ *P. m. brevirostris* — New Zealand, Stewart and Campbell islands

☐ **Long-tailed Cormorant** *Phalacrocorax africanus*
___ *P. a. africanus* — Africa south of the Sahara
___ *P. a. pictilis* — Madagascar

☐ **Crowned Cormorant** *Phalacrocorax coronatus* — Coastal sw Africa (Angola to South Africa)

☐ **Little Cormorant** *Phalacrocorax niger* — Lowlands of India to SE Asia and n Java

☐ **Pygmy Cormorant** *Phalacrocorax pygmaeus* — Inland lakes and rivers of se Europe to central Asia

☐ **Flightless Cormorant** *Phalacrocorax harrisi* — Galapagos Islands (coasts of Fernandina and Isabela)

ORDER: PELECANIFORMES
FAMILY: ANHINGIDAE (Anhingas—2)

☐ **Anhinga** *Anhinga anhinga*
___ *A. a. leucogaster* — SE US to Panama, Cuba and Isle of Pines
___ *A. a. anhinga* — Trinidad, Tobago and n South America to n Argentina

☐ **Darter** *Anhinga melanogaster*
___ *A. m. rufa* — Africa south of the Sahara and Middle East
___ *A. m. vulsini* — Madagascar
___ *A. m. melanogaster* — India to SE Asia, Malay Archipelago and Philippine Islands
___ *A. m. novaehollandiae* — Australia to Lesser Sundas, Moluccas and New Guinea

ORDER: PELECANIFORMES
FAMILY: FREGATIDAE (Frigatebirds—5)

☐ **Ascension Island Frigatebird** *Fregata aquila*

Breeds Ascension I.; ranges to w African coast

☐ **Christmas Island Frigatebird** *Fregata andrewsi*

Christmas I.; ranges to s China Sea and Australia

☐ **Magnificent Frigatebird** *Fregata magnificens*

Tropical w Atlantic and e Pacific oceans

☐ **Great Frigatebird** *Fregata minor*

____	*F. m. palmerstoni*	Breeds islands in w and central Pacific
____	*F. m. ridgwayi*	Breeds e Pacific on Revillagigedo, Cocos and Galapagos islands
____	*F. m. nicolli*	Breeds Trindade I. and Martín Vaz I.; ranges to Brazil
____	*F. m. aldabrensis*	Breeds w Indian Ocean on Aldabra and adjacent islands
____	*F. m. minor*	Cocos and Christmas is. (Indian Ocean); Paracel Is. (S China Sea)

☐ **Lesser Frigatebird** *Fregata ariel*

____	*F. a. ariel*	Islands in Indian and Pacific oceans
____	*F. a. trinitatis*	Trindade I. and Martín Vaz I.; wanders to coastal Brazil
____	*F. a. iredalei*	Mascarene Islands; disperses to coasts of India and Somalia

ORDER: CICONIIFORMES
FAMILY: ARDEIDAE (Herons, Egrets and Bitterns—63)

☐ **Whistling Heron** *Syrigma sibilatrix*

____	*S. s. fostersmithi*	E Colombia and Venezuela
____	*S. s. sibilatrix*	Wet grasslands of Bolivia to se Brazil and ne Argentina

☐ **Capped Heron** *Pilherodius pileatus*

Lowlands of e Panama to the Guianas, Brazil and n Paraguay

☐ **Gray Heron** *Ardea cinerea*

____	*A. c. cinerea*	Eurasia to Manchuria, India, Africa and Comoro Islands
____	*A. c. jouyi*	Japan, China, Indochina, Malaya, Sumatra and Java
____	*A. c. firasa*	Madagascar
____	*A. c. monicae*	Islands off Banc d'Arguin (Mauritania)

☐ **Great Blue Heron** *Ardea herodias*

____	*A. h. fannini*	SE Alaska to coastal Washington
____	*A. h. herodias*	S Canada to s Baja California and Central America
____	*A. h. wardi*	S-central US to Gulf Coast and Florida
____	*A. h. occidentalis*	S Florida through West Indies to islands off Venezuela
____	*A. h. cognata*	Galapagos Islands

☐ **Cocoi Heron** *Ardea cocoi*

Widespread South America (excluding the Andes)

☐ **Pacific Heron** *Ardea pacifica*

Lakes, ponds and marshes of Australia and Tasmania

☐ **Black-headed Heron** *Ardea melanocephala*

Grasslands and savanna of Africa south of the Sahara

☐ **Humblot's Heron** *Ardea humbloti*

Aquatic lowlands of Madagascar and Comoro Islands

☐ **White-bellied Heron** *Ardea insignis*

Himalayan foothills (Nepal to ne India and Myanmar)

☐ **Great-billed Heron** *Ardea sumatrana*

____	*A. s. sumatrana*	Coasts of SE Asia, Indonesia, Philippines and New Guinea
____	*A. s. mathewsae*	Coasts of tropical n Australia

☐ **Goliath Heron** *Ardea goliath*

Locally in Africa, Iraq and Iran; casual to India and Sri Lanka

☐ **Purple Heron** *Ardea purpurea*
_____ *A. p. purpurea (bournei)* — SW Palearctic to Iran, Africa s of the Sahara and Cape Verde Is.
_____ *A. p. madagascariensis* — Madagascar
_____ *A. p. manilensis* — Southern and e Asia, Indonesia and Philippine Islands

☐ **Great Egret** *Ardea alba*
_____ *A. a. egretta* — S Canada to Tierra del Fuego and West Indies
_____ *A. a. alba* — Central Europe to central Asia (south to Iran)
_____ *A. a. melanorhyncha* — Africa south of the Sahara and Madagascar
_____ *A. a. modesta* — Southern and e Asia to Indonesia, Australia and New Zealand

☐ **Reddish Egret** *Egretta rufescens*
_____ *E. r. rufescens* — S US, Bahamas and West Indies; winters to nw South America
_____ *E. r. dickeyi* — S Baja California; winters to Guatemala and El Salvador

☐ **Pied Heron** *Egretta picata*

Locally from New Guinea to Indonesia and n Australia

☐ **Slaty Egret** *Egretta vinaceigula*

Swamps and reedbeds of s-central Africa

☐ **Black Heron** *Egretta ardesiaca*

Locally in Africa south of the Sahara and Madagascar

☐ **Tricolored Heron** *Egretta tricolor*
_____ *E. t. ruficollis (occidentalis)* — Tropical s US to Colombia, nw Venezuela and West Indies
_____ *E. t. tricolor* — NE Venezuela and the Guianas to s Peru and ne Brazil; Trinidad

☐ **Intermediate Egret** *Egretta intermedia*
_____ *E. i. intermedia* — Japan to s India and Greater Sundas
_____ *E. i. plumifera* — New Guinea, eastern Indonesia and Australia
_____ *E. i. brachyrhyncha* — Africa south of the Sahara

☐ **White-faced Heron** *Egretta novaehollandiae*
_____ *E. n. novaehollandiae* — Indonesia and Australasian region
_____ *E. n. parryi* — NW Australia

☐ **Little Blue Heron** *Egretta caerulea*

US to s Brazil, Uruguay and West Indies

☐ **Snowy Egret** *Egretta thula*
_____ *E. t. thula* — Western US to Baja California and coastal nw Mexico
_____ *E. t. brewsteri* — Locally from US to central Argentina and West Indies

☐ **Little Egret** *Egretta garzetta*
_____ *E. g. garzetta* — Widespread Eurasia and Africa
_____ *E. g. nigripes* — Java and Philippines to New Guinea
_____ *E. g. immaculata* — N and e Australia; occasional New Zealand
_____ *E. g. gularis* — Coastal w Africa to Gulf of Guinea islands and Gabon
_____ *E. g. schistacea* — Coastal e Africa to Red Sea, Persian Gulf and se India
_____ *E. g. dimorpha* — SE Kenya to Tanzania, Madagascar, Aldabra and Comoro islands

☐ **Chinese Egret** *Egretta eulophotes*

E Asia; winters to SE Asia, Philippines and Indonesia

☐ **Pacific Reef-Heron** *Egretta sacra*
_____ *E. s. sacra* — Coastal SE Asia, Malay Archipelago, Oceania and Australasia
_____ *E. s. albolineata* — New Caledonia and Loyalty Islands

☐ **Squacco Heron** *Ardeola ralloides*

Locally in s Palearctic region, Africa and Madagascar

☐ **Indian Pond-Heron** *Ardeola grayii*

Persian Gulf to India, Myanmar, Andaman and Nicobar islands

☐ **Chinese Pond-Heron** *Ardeola bacchus*

Lowlands of s Asia; winters to Greater Sundas

☐ **Javan Pond-Heron** *Ardeola speciosa*
____ *A. s. continentalis*   Central Thailand to s Indochina
____ *A. s. speciosa*   West and central Indonesian Archipelago

☐ **Madagascar Pond-Heron** *Ardeola idae*

Madagascar and Aldabra; post-breeding dispersal to c Africa

☐ **Rufous-bellied Heron** *Ardeola rufiventris*

Locally in e and se Africa

☐ **Cattle Egret** *Bubulcus ibis*
____ *B. i. ibis*   W Palearctic, Africa, North and South America
____ *B. i. coromandus*   S Japan to Philippines, Moluccas and Indian subcontinent
____ *B. i. seychellarum*   Seychelles

☐ **Striated Heron** *Butorides striatus*
____ *B. s. anthonyi*   Western US and n Baja California
____ *B. s. frazari*   S Baja California
____ *B. s. bahamensis*   Bahamas
____ *B. s. striatus*   E Panama and all South America to n Argentina and Chile
____ *B. s. atricapillus*   Africa south of the Sahara and islands in Gulf of Guinea
____ *B. s. rutenbergi*   Madagascar
____ *B. s. brevipes*   Red Sea environs and n Somalia
____ *B. s. crawfordi*   Aldabra and Amirante islands
____ *B. s. rhizophorae*   Comoro Islands
____ *B. s. degens*   Seychelles
____ *B. s. albolimbatus*   Diego Garcia, Chagos and Maldive islands
____ *B. s. chloriceps*   Indian subcontinent, Sri Lanka and Laccadive Islands
____ *B. s. javanicus*   Myanmar and Thailand to Greater Sundas and Mascarene Islands
____ *B. s. amurensis*   Manchuria to ne China, Japan, Ryukyu and Bonin islands
____ *B. s. actophilus*   E China to n Vietnam and n Myanmar
____ *B. s. spodiogaster*   Andaman Islands, Nicobar Islands and islands off w Sumatra
____ *B. s. carcinophilus*   Taiwan, Philippines and Sulawesi
____ *B. s. steini*   Lesser Sundas
____ *B. s. moluccarum*   Moluccas
____ *B. s. papuensis*   Aru Islands and nw New Guinea
____ *B. s. idenburgi*   N-central New Guinea
____ *B. s. rogersi*   NW Western Australia
____ *B. s. cinereus*   NE Western Australia
____ *B. s. stagnatilis*   N-central Australia
____ *B. s. littleri*   South-central New Guinea and ne Queensland
____ *B. s. macrorhynchus*   E Queensland, New Caledonia and Loyalty Islands
____ *B. s. solomonensis*   Melanesia (New Hanover to w Fiji)
____ *B. s. patruelis*   Tahiti (Society Islands)

☐ **Green Heron** *Butorides virescens*

North America, Central America and West Indies

☐ **Galapagos Heron** *Butorides sundevalli*

Coasts and mangroves of Galapagos Islands

☐ **Agami Heron** *Agamia agami*

Tropical s Mexico to n Bolivia and w Amazonian Brazil

☐ **Black-crowned Night-Heron** *Nycticorax nycticorax*
____ *N. n. nycticorax*   Eurasia south to Indonesia, Africa and Madagascar
____ *N. n. hoactli*   S Canada to n Argentina and Chile
____ *N. n. obscurus*   N Chile and n-central Argentina to Tierra del Fuego
____ *N. n. falklandicus*   Falkland Islands

☐ **Rufous Night-Heron** *Nycticorax caledonicus*

____	*N. c. manillensis*	Philippines, e Borneo and Sulawesi
____	*N. c. hilli*	Australia, Indonesia and New Guinea
____	*N. c. mandibularis*	Bismarck Archipelago to Solomon Islands
____	*N. c. pelewensis*	Palau and Caroline islands
____	*N. c. caledonicus*	New Caledonia

☐ **Yellow-crowned Night-Heron** *Nyctanassa violacea*

____	*N. v. violacea*	Central and e US to e Mexico and Honduras
____	*N. v. bancrofti*	Baja California and w Mexico to El Salvador and West Indies
____	*N. v. gravirostris*	Socorro I. (Revillagigedo Islands off w Mexico)
____	*N. v. calignis*	Panama to Peru
____	*N. v. pauper*	Galapagos Islands
____	*N. v. cayennensis*	Colombia to e Brazil

☐ **White-backed Night-Heron** *Gorsachius leuconotus*

Locally in Africa south of the Sahara

☐ **White-eared Night-Heron** *Gorsachius magnificus*

Highlands of Hainan; ranges to adjacent se China

☐ **Japanese Night-Heron** *Gorsachius goisagi*

S Japan; winters se China to Ryukyu Islands and Indonesia

☐ **Malayan Night-Heron** *Gorsachius melanolophus*

Humid forests of s Asia and Malay Archipelago

☐ **Boat-billed Heron** *Cochlearius cochlearius*

____	*C. c. zeledoni*	W-central Mexico
____	*C. c. phillipsi*	Tropical e Mexico and Belize
____	*C. c. ridgwayi*	Tropical s Mexico to w Honduras and El Salvador
____	*C. c. panamensis*	Costa Rica and Panama
____	*C. c. cochlearius*	E Panama to the Guianas, Amazon basin and ne Argentina

☐ **Bare-throated Tiger-Heron** *Tigrisoma mexicanum*

Wet lowlands of Mexico to nw Colombia

☐ **Fasciated Tiger-Heron** *Tigrisoma fasciatum*

____	*T. f. salmoni*	Costa Rica to Venezuela and n Bolivia
____	*T. f. fasciatum*	SE Brazil to ne Argentina
____	*T. f. pallescens*	NW Argentina

☐ **Rufescent Tiger-Heron** *Tigrisoma lineatum*

____	*T. l. lineatum*	SE Mexico to Amazonian Brazil and n Argentina
____	*T. l. marmoratum*	Central Bolivia to e Brazil and ne Argentina

☐ **Forest Bittern** *Zonerodius heliosylus*

Lowlands of New Guinea, Salawati I. and Aru Islands

☐ **White-crested Bittern** *Tigriornis leucolophus*

Sierra Leone to Cameroon, Gabon, Zaire and Cent. African Rep.

☐ **Zigzag Heron** *Zebrilus undulatus*

Locally in ponds and streams of Amazon basin

☐ **Stripe-backed Bittern** *Ixobrychus involucris*

Colombia to the Guianas, s Venezuela, c Argentina and c Chile

☐ **Least Bittern** *Ixobrychus exilis*

____	*I. e. exilis*	S Canada to Central America and West Indies
____	*I. e. pullus*	NW Mexico
____	*I. e. erythromelas*	E Panama to the Guianas, se Brazil and Paraguay
____	*I. e. bogotensis*	Central Colombia (declining due to habitat destruction)
____	*I. e. peruvianus*	W-central Peru

☐ **Yellow Bittern** *Ixobrychus sinensis*

S Asia, Malay Archipelago, New Guinea region and s Oceania

21

☐ **Black-backed Bittern** *Ixobrychus novaezelandiae*
____   *I. n. dubius*   SW and e Australia and New Guinea
____   *I. n. novaezelandiae†*   Formerly South I. (New Zealand). Probably extinct

☐ **Little Bittern** *Ixobrychus minutus*
____   *I. m. minutus*   Central and s Europe to Siberia; North Africa
____   *I. m. payesii*   Africa south of the Sahara
____   *I. m. podiceps*   Madagascar

☐ **Schrenck's Bittern** *Ixobrychus eurhythmus*
      E Asia; winters to SE Asia, Philippines and Greater Sundas

☐ **Cinnamon Bittern** *Ixobrychus cinnamomeus*
      India to SE Asia, Philippines and Indonesia

☐ **Dwarf Bittern** *Ixobrychus sturmii*
      Africa south of the Sahara

☐ **Black Bittern** *Ixobrychus flavicollis*
____   *I. f. flavicollis*   India and SE Asia to Indonesia and Philippines
____   *I. f. australis*   Moluccas, New Guinea and Bismarck Arch. to n Australia
____   *I. f. woodfordi*   Solomon Islands

☐ **Pinnated Bittern** *Botaurus pinnatus*
____   *B. p. caribaeus*   Lowlands of e Mexico
____   *B. p. pinnatus*   SE Nicaragua to Ecuador, the Guianas, n Argentina and Brazil

☐ **American Bittern** *Botaurus lentiginosus*
      Alaska to Mexico; winters to Panama and West Indies

☐ **Great Bittern** *Botaurus stellaris*
____   *B. s. stellaris*   Palearctic and n Afrotropical region; winters to Philippines
____   *B. s. capensis*   Southern Africa

☐ **Australasian Bittern** *Botaurus poiciloptilus*
      S Australia, Tasmania, New Zealand and New Caledonia

ORDER: CICONIIFORMES
FAMILY: SCOPIDAE (Hamerkop—1)

☐ **Hamerkop** *Scopus umbretta*
____   *S. u. umbretta*   Tropical Africa, Madagascar and sw Arabia
____   *S. u. minor*   Coastal w Africa (Sierra Leone to e Nigeria)

ORDER: CICONIIFORMES
FAMILY: CICONIIDAE (Storks—19)

☐ **Wood Stork** *Mycteria americana*
      S US to n Argentina, Brazil, Cuba and Hispaniola

☐ **Milky Stork** *Mycteria cinerea*
      Lowlands of Malaya, Indochina, Greater Sundas and Sulawesi

☐ **Yellow-billed Stork** *Mycteria ibis*
      Africa south of the Sahara and Madagascar

☐ **Painted Stork** *Mycteria leucocephala*
      Lowlands of Indian subcontinent to s China and SE Asia

☐ **Asian Openbill** *Anastomus oscitans*
      Lowlands of Indian subcontinent to SE Asia

☐ **African Openbill** *Anastomus lamelligerus*
____   *A. l. lamelligerus*   Africa south of the Sahara
____   *A. l. madagascariensis*   Madagascar

☐ **Black Stork** *Ciconia nigra*

Central and s Eurasia; s Africa; winters to c Africa and India

☐ **Abdim's Stork** *Ciconia abdimii*

Sub-Saharan Africa and sw Arabia

☐ **Woolly-necked Stork** *Ciconia episcopus*
____ *C. e. microscelis*
____ *C. e. episcopus*
____ *C. e. neglecta*

Tropical Africa
India to Indochina, n Malay Peninsula and Philippines
Java and Wallacea

☐ **Storm's Stork** *Ciconia stormi*

Lowlands of Borneo, e Sumatra and Malay Peninsula

☐ **Maguari Stork** *Ciconia maguari*

Tropical plains and marshes of South America east of the Andes

☐ **White Stork** *Ciconia ciconia*
____ *C. c. ciconia*
____ *C. c. asiatica*

W Palearctic and w Asia: winters to tropical and South Africa
Turkestan; winters to Iran and India

☐ **Oriental Stork** *Ciconia boyciana*

Siberia, Manchuria and Korea; winters to s China and n India

☐ **Black-necked Stork** *Ephippiorhynchus asiaticus*
____ *E. a. asiaticus*
____ *E. a. australis*

Indian subcontinent and SE Asia
Australia and s New Guinea

☐ **Saddle-billed Stork** *Ephippiorhynchus senegalensis*

Locally in Africa south of the Sahara

☐ **Jabiru** *Jabiru mycteria*

Tropical s Mexico through South America to ne Argentina

☐ **Lesser Adjutant** *Leptoptilos javanicus*

India and Sri Lanka to s China, Indochina and Indonesia

☐ **Marabou Stork** *Leptoptilos crumeniferus*

Tropical Africa south of the Sahara

☐ **Greater Adjutant** *Leptoptilos dubius*

NE India (population ±300 birds 1992)

ORDER: CICONIIFORMES
FAMILY: BALAENICIPIDIDAE (Shoebill—1)

☐ **Shoebill** *Balaeniceps rex*

Dense swamps of central Africa

ORDER: CICONIIFORMES
FAMILY: THRESKIORNITHIDAE (Ibis and Spoonbills—33)

☐ **Sacred Ibis** *Threskiornis aethiopicus*
____ *T. a. aethiopicus*
____ *T. a. bernieri*
____ *T. a. abbotti*

Africa south of the Sahara and se Iraq; formerly Egypt
Madagascar
Aldabra I.

☐ **Black-headed Ibis** *Threskiornis melanocephalus*

India to SE Asia; winters to e China, Sumatra and Philippines

☐ **Australian Ibis** *Threskiornis molucca*
____ *T. m. molucca*
____ *T. m. pygmaeus*

Australia to s New Guinea, s Moluccas and e Lesser Sundas
Solomon Islands (Rennell and Bellona)

☐ **Straw-necked Ibis** *Threskiornis spinicollis*

Australia; ranges to n Tasmania and s New Guinea

☐ **Red-naped Ibis** *Pseudibis papillosa*

Semiarid lowlands of India and Pakistan

☐ **White-shouldered Ibis** *Pseudibis davisoni*

SW China to Myanmar, peninsular Thailand and Indochina

☐ **Giant Ibis** *Pseudibis gigantea*

Lowlands of Thailand, Cambodia, Laos and s Vietnam

☐ **Waldrapp** *Geronticus eremita*

Patchily distributed mountains of Morocco and Red Sea area

☐ **Bald Ibis** *Geronticus calvus*

Mountains of inland regions of South Africa

☐ **Crested Ibis** *Nipponia nippon*

China (±50 birds in Shaanxi Province in 1998)

☐ **Olive Ibis** *Bostrychia olivacea*
  ____ *B. o. olivacea*   Lowland forests of Sierra Leone and Liberia
  ____ *B. o. cupreipennis*   Lowland forests of Cameroon, Gabon, Congo and Zaire
  ____ *B. o. rothschildi†*   Formerly Príncipe I. (Gulf of Guinea). Extinct ca 1901
  ____ *B. o. bocagei*   São Tomé I. (Gulf of Guinea)
  ____ *B. o. akleyorum*   Montane forests of Kenya and Tanzania

☐ **Spot-breasted Ibis** *Bostrychia rara*

Liberia to Cameroon, Gabon, Zaire and extreme ne Angola

☐ **Hadada Ibis** *Bostrychia hagedash*
  ____ *B. h. brevirostris*   Senegal to Kenya and south to Zambezi Valley
  ____ *B. h. nilotica*   Sudan and Ethiopia to Uganda and nw Tanzania
  ____ *B. h. hagedash*   Southern Africa (south of the Zambezi Valley)

☐ **Wattled Ibis** *Bostrychia carunculata*

Highlands of Ethiopia

☐ **Plumbeous Ibis** *Theristicus caerulescens*

Lowlands of s Brazil to Bolivia, Paraguay and ne Argentina

☐ **Buff-necked Ibis** *Theristicus caudatus*
  ____ *T. c. caudatus*   E Colombia to Venezuela, Guianas and sw Brazil (Mato Grosso)
  ____ *T. c. hyperorius*   E Bolivia to se Brazil, Paraguay, Uruguay and n Argentina

☐ **Andean Ibis** *Theristicus branickii*

Andes of Ecuador to extreme n Chile

☐ **Black-faced Ibis** *Theristicus melanopis*

Coastal Peru, n Chile and Argentina south to Tierra del Fuego

☐ **Sharp-tailed Ibis** *Cercibis oxycerca*

Llanos of e Colombia to the Guianas and w Amazonian Brazil

☐ **Green Ibis** *Mesembrinibis cayennensis*

Lowlands of Costa Rica to ne Argentina and Brazil

☐ **Bare-faced Ibis** *Phimosus infuscatus*
  ____ *P. i. berlepschi*   E Colombia to the Guianas, Suriname and adjacent nw Brazil
  ____ *P. i. nudifrons*   Brazil south of the Amazon
  ____ *P. i. infuscatus*   E Bolivia to Paraguay, ne Argentina and Uruguay

☐ **White Ibis** *Eudocimus albus*

Southern US to se Brazil, Bahamas and Greater Antilles

☐ **Scarlet Ibis** *Eudocimus ruber*

Coastal Colombia to the Guianas and ne Brazil; Trinidad

☐ **Glossy Ibis** *Plegadis falcinellus*

Locally in e N America, n S America, Eurasia and Africa

☐ **White-faced Ibis** *Plegadis chihi*

Great Basin of w US to sw Brazil and central Argentina

☐ **Puna Ibis** *Plegadis ridgwayi*

High Andes of central Peru to nw Argentina and n Chile

☐ **Madagascar Ibis** *Lophotibis cristata*
    ____ *L. c. cristata* — Forests of e Madagascar
    ____ *L. c. urschi* — Forests of w Madagascar

☐ **Eurasian Spoonbill** *Platalea leucorodia*
    ____ *P. l. leucorodia* — S Palearctic to India; winters to central Africa and se China
    ____ *P. l. balsaci* — Banc d'Arguin (off coast of Mauritania)
    ____ *P. l. archeri* — Coasts of Red Sea and Somalia

☐ **Royal Spoonbill** *Platalea regia* — Australia, New Zealand, Indonesia, New Guinea and Solomon Is.

☐ **African Spoonbill** *Platalea alba* — Africa south of the Sahara and Madagascar

☐ **Black-faced Spoonbill** *Platalea minor* — Breeds ne China and Korea; winters to SE Asia

☐ **Yellow-billed Spoonbill** *Platalea flavipes* — Australia; vagrant to Tasmania and New Zealand

☐ **Roseate Spoonbill** *Ajaia ajaja* — S US to n Argentina, Brazil and West Indies

ORDER: PHOENICOPTERIFORMES
FAMILY: PHOENICOPTERIDAE (Flamingos—5)

☐ **Greater Flamingo** *Phoenicopterus ruber*
    ____ *P. r. ruber* — Locally from Caribbean to ne Brazil; Galapagos Islands
    ____ *P. r. roseus* — S Europe and Mediterranean basin to Indian subcontinent

☐ **Chilean Flamingo** *Phoenicopterus chilensis* — Andes of s South America; pampas of s Brazil to s Argentina

☐ **Lesser Flamingo** *Phoenicopterus minor* — Locally from Africa and Madagascar to nw India

☐ **Andean Flamingo** *Phoenicopterus andinus* — High Andes of s Peru to nw Argentina and n Chile

☐ **Puna Flamingo** *Phoenicopterus jamesi* — High Andes of s Peru to nw Argentina and n Chile

ORDER: ANSERIFORMES
FAMILY: ANHIMIDAE (Screamers—3)

☐ **Horned Screamer** *Anhima cornuta* — Lowlands of Venezuela to n Bolivia and Amazonian Brazil

☐ **Northern Screamer** *Chauna chavaria* — N Colombia and nw Venezuela

☐ **Southern Screamer** *Chauna torquata* — Wet lowlands of se Peru to n Argentina and s Brazil

ORDER: ANSERIFORMES
FAMILY: ANATIDAE (Ducks, Geese and Swans—157)

☐ **Magpie Goose** *Anseranas semipalmata* — Coastal n Australia and Trans-Fly savanna of s New Guinea

☐ **Spotted Whistling-Duck** *Dendrocygna guttata* — Sulawesi to New Guinea, Bismarck Arch. and s Philippines

☐ **Plumed Whistling-Duck** *Dendrocygna eytoni* — Lowlands of n and e Australia

☐ **Fulvous Whistling-Duck** *Dendrocygna bicolor*

S US to Argentina; e Africa, Madagascar and s Asia

☐ **Wandering Whistling-Duck** *Dendrocygna arcuata*
____ *D. a. arcuata*
____ *D. a. australis*
____ *D. a. pygmaea*

Philippines to Indonesia
Tropical s New Guinea and n Australia
New Britain I. (Bismarck Archipelago)

☐ **Lesser Whistling-Duck** *Dendrocygna javanica*

Indian subcontinent to SE Asia and Greater Sundas

☐ **White-faced Whistling-Duck** *Dendrocygna viduata*

Costa Rica to Brazil; Africa, Madagascar and Comoro Islands

☐ **West Indian Whistling-Duck** *Dendrocygna arborea*

Bahamas, Greater Antilles and n Lesser Antilles

☐ **Black-bellied Whistling-Duck** *Dendrocygna autumnalis*

Extreme s Texas to n Argentina (mainly east of Andes)

☐ **White-backed Duck** *Thalassornis leuconotus*
____ *T. l. leuconotus*
____ *T. l. insularis*

Locally in Africa south of the Sahara
Locally in aquatic lowlands of Madagascar

☐ **Mute Swan** *Cygnus olor*

Palearctic region; winters to India and se China

☐ **Black Swan** *Cygnus atratus*

Australia and Tasmania; introduced New Zealand

☐ **Black-necked Swan** *Cygnus melanocorypha*

S Brazil to Tierra del Fuego and Falkland Islands

☐ **Trumpeter Swan** *Cygnus buccinator*

Western North America

☐ **Whooper Swan** *Cygnus cygnus*

Palearctic; winters to India and se China

☐ **Tundra Swan** *Cygnus columbianus*
____ *C. c. bewickii*
____ *C. c. columbianus*

Kola Peninsula to arctic n Siberia; winters w Europe to s Asia
Tundra of arctic North America; winters to w and coastal e US

☐ **Coscoroba Swan** *Coscoroba coscoroba*

S Brazil to Paraguay, Uruguay, Tierra del Fuego and Falkland Is.

☐ **Swan Goose** *Anser cygnoides*

N-central Asia (s-central Siberia to n China)

☐ **Bean Goose** *Anser fabalis*
____ *A. f. fabalis*
____ *A. f. johanseni*
____ *A. f. middendorffii*
____ *A. f. rossicus*
____ *A. f. serrirostris*

Taiga of Scandinavia to Ural Mountains
Taiga and wooded tundra of Ural Mountains to Lake Baikal
Taiga of e Siberia (east of Lake Baikal)
Tundra of n Russia and nw Siberia
Tundra of ne Siberia

☐ **Pink-footed Goose** *Anser brachyrhynchus*

Breeds Greenland, Iceland and Spitzbergen; winters nw Europe

☐ **Greater White-fronted Goose** *Anser albifrons*
____ *A. a. albifrons*
____ *A. a. frontalis*
____ *A. a. flavirostris*
____ *A. a. gambelli*
____ *A. a. elgasi*

N Russia and Siberia; winters to Mediterranean and n India
E Siberia to n Canada; winters w US, n Mexico and China
Breeds w coast of Greenland; winters mainly in Ireland
Taiga of nw Canada and w Alaska; winters Gulf Coast
Taiga south of Alaskan tundra; winters Sacramento Valley

☐ **Lesser White-fronted Goose** *Anser erythropus*

Arctic Eurasia; winters to s Europe, India and China

☐ **Greylag Goose** *Anser anser*
____ *A. a. anser*
____ *A. a. rubrirostris*

Breeds nw Eurasia; winters to North Africa, Turkey and Iran
NE Eurasia; winters to Asia Minor, India and n Indochina

☐ **Bar-headed Goose** *Anser indicus*

Alpine lakes in central Asia; winters to India and Myanmar

☐ **Snow Goose** *Chen caerulescens*
_____ *C. c. caerulescens*
_____ *C. c. atlanticus*

Siberia and Alaska; winters to California and Gulf Coast
NW Greenland and islands in Baffin Bay; winters to ne Mexico

☐ **Ross' Goose** *Chen rossii*

Tundra of Arctic Canada; winters to s US

☐ **Emperor Goose** *Chen canagica*

NE Siberia to w Alaska; winters s Alaska to n California

☐ **Hawaiian Goose** *Branta sandvicensis*

Upland lava flows of Hawaii; introduced to Maui

☐ **Canada Goose** *Branta canadensis*
_____ *B. c. leucopareia*
_____ *B. c. minima*
_____ *B. c. taverneri*
_____ *B. c. occidentalis*
_____ *B. c. fulva*
_____ *B. c. parvipes*
_____ *B. c. moffitti*
_____ *B. c. maxima*
_____ *B. c. hutchinsii*
_____ *B. c. interior*
_____ *B. c. canadensis*

Buldir I. (w Alaska). Formerly Kuril Is. and Aleutian Is.
Coastal w Alaska to Mackenzie delta; winters to s California
Central Alaska to Mackenzie River delta; winters to Mexico
SW Alaska (Prince William Sound to Copper River Delta)
Coastal s Alaska to British Columbia; occasional n California
Central Alaska to Canadian prairie provinces; winters s US
N Great Plains and s Canada; disperses southward in winter
Formerly Great Plains; now only on wildlife reserves
Breeds n-c Canada and Greenland; winters Texas and Mexico
Breeds ne Canada; winters to Florida and Louisiana
Breeds Labrador and Newfoundland; winters to Florida

☐ **Barnacle Goose** *Branta leucopsis*

Greenland to Novaya Zemlya; winters to n Mediterranean

☐ **Brant** *Branta bernicla*
_____ *B. b. bernicla*
_____ *B. b. orientalis*
_____ *B. b. hrota*
_____ *B. b. nigricans*

N-central Siberia; winters coastal England and nw Europe
NE Siberia
E Arctic Canada, Greenland and Spitzbergen; winters e N Am.
Extreme ne Siberia to n Canada; winters to n Mexico and China

☐ **Red-breasted Goose** *Branta ruficollis*

Siberian tundra; winters Black, Caspian and Aral seas

☐ **Cape Barren Goose** *Cereopsis novaehollandiae*

Islands in Bass Strait, adjacent Australia and Tasmania

☐ **Freckled Duck** *Stictonetta naevosa*

Locally in se and extreme sw Australia

☐ **Blue-winged Goose** *Cyanochen cyanopterus*

Highlands of Ethiopia

☐ **Andean Goose** *Chloephaga melanoptera*

Andes of s Peru to nw Argentina and central Chile

☐ **Upland Goose** *Chloephaga picta*
_____ *C. p. picta*
_____ *C. p. leucoptera*

Mountains of central Argentina and Chile to Tierra del Fuego
Falkland Islands

☐ **Kelp Goose** *Chloephaga hybrida*
_____ *C. h. hybrida*
_____ *C. h. malvinarum*

Coastal s Argentina and Chile to Tierra del Fuego
Falkland Islands

☐ **Ashy-headed Goose** *Chloephaga poliocephala*

S Argentina and s Chile to Tierra del Fuego

☐ **Ruddy-headed Goose** *Chloephaga rubidiceps*

Tierra del Fuego and Falkland Islands

☐ **Orinoco Goose** *Neochen jubata*

Orinoco and Amazon River basins to nw Argentina

☐ **Egyptian Goose** *Alopochen aegyptiacus*

Africa south of the Sahara and Nile Valley

☐ **Ruddy Shelduck** *Tadorna ferruginea*

S Mediterranean basin to e Asia

☐ **South African Shelduck** *Tadorna cana*

Karoo of s Africa

☐ **Australian Shelduck** *Tadorna tadornoides*

Patchily distributed sw and se Australia and Tasmania

☐ **Paradise Shelduck** *Tadorna variegata*

North, South and Stewart islands (New Zealand)

☐ **Common Shelduck** *Tadorna tadorna*

Palearctic region; winters to Near East, India and Myanmar

☐ **Radjah Shelduck** *Tadorna radjah*
____ *T. r. radjah*
____ *T. r. rufitergum*

Moluccas to New Guinea and adjacent islands
Coastal n and e tropical Australia

☐ **Flightless Steamerduck** *Tachyeres pteneres*

S South America (Tierra del Fuego and Cape Horn Archipelago)

☐ **White-headed Steamerduck** *Tachyeres leucocephalus*

S Argentina (s coast of Chubut Province)

☐ **Falkland Steamerduck** *Tachyeres brachypterus*

Falkland Islands

☐ **Flying Steamerduck** *Tachyeres patachonicus*

Coastal s Chile, Argentina and Falkland Islands

☐ **Spur-winged Goose** *Plectropterus gambensis*
____ *P. g. gambensis*
____ *P. g. niger*

Gambia to Ethiopia and south to the Zambesi River
Namibia and Zimbabwe to Cape Province

☐ **Muscovy Duck** *Cairina moschata*

Lowlands of s Mexico to ne Argentina and Brazil

☐ **White-winged Duck** *Cairina scutulata*

India to SE Asia, Sumatra and Java

☐ **Comb Duck** *Sarkidiornis melanotos*
____ *S. m. melanotos*
____ *S. m. sylvicola*

Tropical Africa and Madagascar; India to s China
Tropical South America (east of the Andes) to n Argentina

☐ **Hartlaub's Duck** *Pteronetta hartlaubii*

Locally in forest streams of equatorial w Africa

☐ **Green Pygmy-goose** *Nettapus pulchellus*

Sulawesi to Moluccas, New Guinea and tropical n Australia

☐ **Cotton Pygmy-goose** *Nettapus coromandelianus*
____ *N. c. coromandelianus*
____ *N. c. albipennis*

Lowlands of India, s Asia, Indonesia and New Guinea
Lowlands of coastal ne Australia (south to Townsville)

☐ **African Pygmy-goose** *Nettapus auritus*

Africa south of the Sahara (except sw Africa) and Madagascar

☐ **Ringed Teal** *Callonetta leucophrys*

S Brazil to Bolivia, Paraguay, Uruguay and ne Argentina

☐ **Wood Duck** *Aix sponsa*

Inland waters of Canada to n Mexico, Cuba and Bahamas

☐ **Mandarin Duck** *Aix galericulata*

Wooded ponds, swamps and streams of ne Asia

☐ **Maned Duck** *Chenonetta jubata*

E and sw Australia and Tasmania

☐ **Brazilian Teal** *Amazonetta brasiliensis*
____ *A. b. brasiliensis*
____ *A. b. ipecutiri*

Colombia and Venezuela south to Brazil
S Brazil to e Bolivia, Uruguay and Argentina

☐ **Blue Duck** *Hymenolaimus malacorhynchos*
____ *H. m. malacorhynchos*
____ *H. m. hymenolaimus*

Mountain streams of w South I. (New Zealand)
Mountain streams of central North I. (New Zealand)

☐ **Torrent Duck** *Merganetta armata*
____ *M. a. colombiana*
____ *M. a. leucogenis*
____ *M. a. turneri*
____ *M. a. garleppi*
____ *M. a. berlepschi*
____ *M. a. armata*

Andes of Colombia, adjacent nw Venezuela and Ecuador
Andes of central and s Ecuador and Peru
Andes of s Peru (Cuzco and Arequipa)
Andes of Bolivia
Andes of nw Argentina and n Chile
Andes of Chile and adjacent Argentina south to Tierra del Fuego

☐ **Salvadori's Teal** *Salvadorina waigiuensis*

Mountain streams of New Guinea

☐ **African Black Duck** *Anas sparsa*
____ *A. s. leucostigma*
____ *A. s. sparsa*

W equatorial Africa; Ethiopia and Sudan to Zimbabwe
Southern Africa (south of Zimbabwe)

☐ **Eurasian Wigeon** *Anas penelope*

N and central Eurasia; winters to Africa and s Asia

☐ **American Wigeon** *Anas americana*

Alaska to s US; winters to nw South America

☐ **Chiloe Wigeon** *Anas sibilatrix*

S South America and Falkland Islands; winters to se Brazil

☐ **Falcated Duck** *Anas falcata*

E Siberia and Mongolia to n Japan; winters to India

☐ **Gadwall** *Anas strepera*
____ *A. s. strepera*
____ *A. s. couesi†*

Widespread Palearctic and Nearctic regions
Formerly Fanning Islands (central Pacific). Extinct ca 1874

☐ **Baikal Teal** *Anas formosa*

E Siberia to Kamchatka; winters to India, Myanmar and Japan

☐ **Green-winged Teal** *Anas crecca*
____ *A. c. crecca*
____ *A. c. nimia*
____ *A. c. carolinensis*

Nearctic region; winters to Africa, India and SE Asia
Aleutian Islands
Breeds North America; winters to Mexico and West Indies

☐ **Speckled Teal** *Anas flavirostris*
____ *A. f. altipetens*
____ *A. f. andium*
____ *A. f. oxyptera*
____ *A. f. flavirostris*

Andes of Colombia to nw Venezuela
Andes of Colombia and n Ecuador
Andes of central Peru to n Chile and Argentina
N Argentina to Tierra del Fuego, South Georgia and Falkland Is.

☐ **Cape Teal** *Anas capensis*

Locally from Sudan and Ethiopia to Namibia and South Africa

☐ **Bernier's Teal** *Anas bernieri*

Lowlands of w Madagascar (population ±20 birds 1993)

☐ **Sunda Teal** *Anas gibberifrons*
____ *A. g. gibberifrons*
____ *A. g. remissa†*

Java and Sulawesi to e Lesser Sundas (Timor and Wetar)
Formerly Rennell (Solomon Islands). Extinct ca 1959

☐ **Andaman Teal** *Anas albogularis*

Andaman Islands and Great Coco I.

☐ **Gray Teal** *Anas gracilis*

Australia and Tasmania to New Guinea and New Caledonia

☐ **Chestnut Teal** *Anas castanea*

Swamps and marshes of sw and se Australia and Tasmania

☐ **Auckland Islands Teal** *Anas aucklandica*

Islets off Auckland Islands

☐ **Campbell Islands Teal** *Anas nesiotis*

Rediscovered 1975 on Campbell Islands after considered extinct

☐ **Brown Teal** *Anas chlorotis*

New Zealand and offshore islands

☐ **Mallard** *Anas platyrhynchos* | Holarctic; winters to Mexico, North Africa, India and Borneo
____ *A. p. platyrhynchos* | Holarctic; winters to Mexico, North Africa, India and Borneo
____ *A. p. conboschas* | Coastal sw Greenland
____ *A. p. maculosa* | Atlantic s US to Mexico
____ *A. p. oustaletti†* | Formerly Marianas Archipelago. Extinct ca 1974
____ *A. p. diazi* | S Texas, New Mexico and Arizona south to central Mexico

☐ **Laysan Duck** *Anas laysanensis*

Laysan I. (nw Hawaiian Islands)

☐ **Hawaiian Duck** *Anas wyvilliana*

Hawaiian Islands (Kauai and Oahu)

☐ **Mottled Duck** *Anas fulvigula*

Florida and coastal s Texas to se Mexico

☐ **American Black Duck** *Anas rubripes*

NE North America; winters to Bahamas and Gulf Coast

☐ **Yellow-billed Duck** *Anas undulata*
____ *A. u. undulata* | Locally from Kenya and Uganda to Angola and South Africa
____ *A. u. rueppelli* | Ethiopia (upper Blue Nile region) to n Kenya and s Sudan

☐ **Meller's Duck** *Anas melleri*

High plateau and e Madagascar

☐ **Spot-billed Duck** *Anas poecilorhyncha*
____ *A. p. poecilorhyncha* | Indian subcontinent and Sri Lanka
____ *A. p. haringtoni* | Myanmar and Assam to extreme s China and Laos
____ *A. p. zonorhyncha* | Breeds ne Asia; winters to s China, Taiwan and Philippines

☐ **Pacific Black Duck** *Anas superciliosa*
____ *A. s. superciliosa* | New Zealand, Auckland, Campbell and Macquarie islands
____ *A. s. pelewensis* | New Guinea to Solomon Islands and French Polynesia
____ *A. s. rogersi* | Widespread throughout Australasia and Indonesia

☐ **Philippine Duck** *Anas luzonica*

Philippine Islands

☐ **Spectacled Duck** *Anas specularis*

Mainly forested regions of s Argentina and Chile

☐ **Crested Duck** *Anas specularioides*
____ *A. s. alticola* | Andes of Peru and Bolivia to nw Argentina and Chile
____ *A. s. specularioides* | Central Chile and Argentina to Tierra del Fuego and Falkland Is.

☐ **Northern Pintail** *Anas acuta*

Palearctic and N America; winters to s Eurasia and n S America

☐ **Eaton's Pintail** *Anas eatoni*
____ *A. e. eatoni* | Kerguelen Islands
____ *A. e. drygalskii* | Crozet I.

☐ **Yellow-billed Pintail** *Anas georgica*
____ *A. g. spinicauda* | Highlands of s Colombia to Tierra del Fuego and Falkland Islands
____ *A. g. georgica* | South Georgia I.
____ *A. g. nicefori†* | Formerly Andes of Colombia. Extinct ca 1952

☐ **White-cheeked Pintail** *Anas bahamensis*
____ *A. b. bahamensis* | Locally in West Indies and n South America
____ *A. b. rubrirostris* | S Brazil and Bolivia to Argentina and Chile
____ *A. b. galapagensis* | Galapagos Islands

☐ **Red-billed Duck** *Anas erythrorhyncha*

Locally in e and s Africa and Madagascar

☐ **Puna Teal** *Anas puna*

Andes of Peru to nw Argentina and n Chile

☐ **Silver Teal** *Anas versicolor*
____ *A. v. versicolor* — S Bolivia, Paraguay and s Brazil to Tierra del Fuego
____ *A. v. fretensis* — S Chile, s Argentina and Falkland Islands

☐ **Hottentot Teal** *Anas hottentota* — Locally in Africa south of the Sahara and Madagascar

☐ **Garganey** *Anas querquedula* — Palearctic; winters to s Africa and Australasian region

☐ **Blue-winged Teal** *Anas discors* — North America; winters s US to central Argentina

☐ **Cinnamon Teal** *Anas cyanoptera*
____ *A. c. septentrionalium* — British Columbia to nw Mexico; winters to nw South America
____ *A. c. tropica* — Cauca and Magdalena valleys of Colombia
____ *A. c. borreroi* — E Andes of Colombia
____ *A. c. orinomus* — Altiplano of Peru and Bolivia to n Chile
____ *A. c. cyanoptera* — S Peru and s Brazil to Tierra del Fuego and Falkland Islands

☐ **Red Shoveler** *Anas platalea* — S Peru and s Brazil to Tierra del Fuego and Falkland Islands

☐ **Cape Shoveler** *Anas smithii* — Locally in southern Africa

☐ **Australian Shoveler** *Anas rhynchotis*
____ *A. r. rhynchotis* — Discontinuously distributed sw and se Australia and Tasmania
____ *A. r. variegata* — New Zealand

☐ **Northern Shoveler** *Anas clypeata* — Holarctic; winters to Africa, n South America and Malay Arch.

☐ **Pink-eared Duck** *Malacorhynchus membranaceus* — Nomadic throughout Australia

☐ **Marbled Teal** *Marmaronetta angustirostris* — Canary Islands and Mediterranean basin to extreme sw China

☐ **Red-crested Pochard** *Netta rufina* — Locally from Mediterranean basin to central Asia

☐ **Rosy-billed Pochard** *Netta peposaca* — Lowlands of se Brazil to s Argentina and Chile

☐ **Southern Pochard** *Netta erythrophthalma*
____ *N. e. erythrophthalma* — Northern half of South America
____ *N. e. brunnea* — Patchily distributed Sudan and Ethiopia to South Africa

☐ **Common Pochard** *Aythya ferina* — Palearctic; winters to tropical Africa, India and SE Asia

☐ **Canvasback** *Aythya valisineria* — Breeds North America; winters to s Mexico

☐ **Redhead** *Aythya americana* — Alaska to s US; winters to Guatemala and Greater Antilles

☐ **Ring-necked Duck** *Aythya collaris* — Breeds Alaska to s US; winters to Panama and s Lesser Antilles

☐ **Ferruginous Pochard** *Aythya nyroca* — Discontinuous Palearctic; winters to India, SE Asia and e China

☐ **Madagascar Pochard** *Aythya innotata* — Lake Alaotra (Madagascar). On verge of extinction

☐ **Baer's Pochard** *Aythya baeri* — NE Eurasia; winters to India, SE Asia and se China

☐ **White-eyed Duck** *Aythya australis* — Australian region and sw Oceania

☐ **Tufted Duck** *Aythya fuligula* — N Palearctic region; winters to n Africa and s Asia

☐ **New Zealand Scaup** *Aythya novaeseelandiae* — New Zealand

☐ **Greater Scaup** *Aythya marila*
_____ *A. m. marila* — N Eurasia; winters to Mediterranean region and India
_____ *A. m. mariloides* — N Asia and n North America; winters to s US and China

☐ **Lesser Scaup** *Aythya affinis*

Alaska to s US; winters n South America and Hawaiian Islands

☐ **Common Eider** *Somateria mollissima*
_____ *S. m. mollissima* — Coast of nw Eurasia; winters to coastal s France
_____ *S. m. faeroeensis* — Faeroe Islands
_____ *S. m. v-nigra* — Arctic coasts of ne Siberia to Alaska and s British Columbia
_____ *S. m. borealis* — Arctic coast of e Canada and Greenland; winters to Long Island
_____ *S. m. sedentaria* — Coasts and islands of Hudson Bay to James Bay
_____ *S. m. dresseri* — Coastal Labrador to Maine; winters to Long Island

☐ **King Eider** *Somateria spectabilis*

Arctic Eurasia and n North America

☐ **Spectacled Eider** *Somateria fischeri*

Coastal n Siberia east to n Alaska

☐ **Steller's Eider** *Polysticta stelleri*

Arctic Siberia (Taymyr Peninsula) east to n Alaska

☐ **Harlequin Duck** *Histrionicus histrionicus*
_____ *H. h. histrionicus* — Greenland, Baffin I. and n Labrador; winters to Long Island
_____ *H. h. pacificus* — N and e Palearctic and Bering Sea islands to central California

☐ **Oldsquaw** *Clangula hyemalis*

Coasts of Holarctic region

☐ **Black Scoter** *Melanitta nigra*
_____ *M. n. nigra* — N Eurasia; winters w Europe to Mediterranean and Caspian Sea
_____ *M. n. americana* — Breeds n Siberia to Alaska; winters to n US

☐ **Surf Scoter** *Melanitta perspicillata*

Northern North America; winters to Baja California and s US

☐ **White-winged Scoter** *Melanitta fusca*
_____ *M. f. fusca* — N Eurasia; winters Norway to Spain and Caspian Sea
_____ *M. f. stejnegeri* — Breeds ne Asia; winters coastal e Asia to Japan and China
_____ *M. f. deglandi* — Northern North America; winters to coastal s US
_____ *M. f. dixoni* — Breeds nw Alaska; winters Aleutians and Alaska Pen. to Baja

☐ **Common Goldeneye** *Bucephala clangula*
_____ *B. c. clangula* — N Eurasia; winters to Mediterranean, Persian Gulf and s China
_____ *B. c. americana* — Breeds n North America; winters to California and Florida

☐ **Barrow's Goldeneye** *Bucephala islandica*

Disjunct populations in w Palearctic and n North America

☐ **Bufflehead** *Bucephala albeola*

Breeds n North America; winters to Mexico and Greater Antilles

☐ **Smew** *Mergellus albellus*

N Eurasia; winters to North Africa, India and e China

☐ **Hooded Merganser** *Lophodytes cucullatus*

Breeds n North America; winters to Mexico and West Indies

☐ **Brazilian Merganser** *Mergus octosetaceus*

S-central South America (Paraguai-Paraná drainage system)

☐ **Red-breasted Merganser** *Mergus serrator*

N Palearctic and n N America; winters s Palearctic and Mexico

☐ **Common Merganser** *Mergus merganser*
_____ *M. m. merganser* — Palearctic region; winters Mediterranean to n India and China
_____ *M. m. orientalis* — Afghanistan to Tibet and s China; winters to India and sw China
_____ *M. m. americanus* — Widespread North America

☐ **Scaly-sided Merganser** *Mergus squamatus*

Manchuria and extreme se Siberia; winters to s China

☐ **Black-headed Duck** *Heteronetta atricapilla*

Lowlands of s South America

☐ **Masked Duck** *Nomonyx dominica*

S Texas to n Argentina and Brazil; West Indies

☐ **Ruddy Duck** *Oxyura jamaicensis*
_____ *O. j. jamaicensis* — Interior nw N America (sw Canada to Mexico); West Indies
_____ *O. j. andina* — Lakes and marshes of Central and E Andes of Colombia

☐ **Andean Duck** *Oxyura ferruginea*

Locally from Andes of s Colombia to s Argentina and s Chile

☐ **White-headed Duck** *Oxyura leucocephala*

Patchily distributed Mediterranean basin to central Asia

☐ **Maccoa Duck** *Oxyura maccoa*

Locally in highlands of e and s Africa

☐ **Lake Duck** *Oxyura vittata*

S Argentina and Chile; winters north to s Brazil and Paraguay

☐ **Blue-billed Duck** *Oxyura australis*

Patchily distributed Australia and Tasmania

☐ **Musk Duck** *Biziura lobata*

Lakes and swamps of s and w Australia and Tasmania

ORDER: FALCONIFORMES
FAMILY: CATHARTIDAE (New World Vultures—7)

☐ **Black Vulture** *Coragyps atratus*
_____ *C. a. atratus* — Extreme s US and n Mexico
_____ *C. a. brasiliensis* — Central America to n and e South America
_____ *C. a. foetens* — Western South America

☐ **Turkey Vulture** *Cathartes aura*
_____ *C. a. aura* — W North America south to Costa Rica; Greater Antilles
_____ *C. a. septentrionalis* — E North America
_____ *C. a. ruficollis* — Central America and lowlands of South America; Trinidad
_____ *C. a. jota* — Pacific coast of Ecuador to Tierra del Fuego and Falkland Islands

☐ **Lesser Yellow-headed Vulture** *Cathartes burrovianus*
_____ *C. b. burrovianus* — S Mexico to central Colombia and nw Venezuela
_____ *C. b. urubitinga* — S America to Argentina and Brazil (east of the Andes)

☐ **Greater Yellow-headed Vulture** *Cathartes melambrotus*

Guianas and s Venezuela to n Bolivia and n Brazil

☐ **California Condor** *Gymnogyps californianus*

Formerly s California. ±132 birds extant in 1998

☐ **Andean Condor** *Vultur gryphus*

Andes and coasts of Colombia to Tierra del Fuego

☐ **King Vulture** *Sarcoramphus papa*

S Mexico to n Argentina and Brazil

ORDER: FALCONIFORMES
FAMILY: PANDIOIDAE (Osprey—1)

☐ **Osprey** *Pandion haliaetus*

____ *P. h. haliaetus*	Palearctic; winters to South Africa, India and Philippines
____ *P. h. carolinensis*	Canada to s US; winters to Peru and Brazil
____ *P. h. ridgwayi*	Caribbean (including Bahamas, Cuba and Belize)
____ *P. h. cristatus*	Australia to New Caledonia, New Guinea, Java and Sulawesi

ORDER: FALCONIFORMES
FAMILY: ACCIPITRIDAE (Hawks, Eagles and Kites—234)

☐ **African Cuckoo-Hawk** *Aviceda cuculoides*

____ *A. c. cuculoides*	Senegal to sw Ethiopia and n Zaire
____ *A. c. batesi*	Sierra Leone to Uganda and n Angola
____ *A. c. verreauxii*	Kenya to Namibia and South Africa

☐ **Madagascar Cuckoo-Hawk** *Aviceda madagascariensis*

	Woodlands and scrub of Madagascar

☐ **Jerdon's Baza** *Aviceda jerdoni*

____ *A. j. ceylonensis*	SW India and Sri Lanka
____ *A. j. jerdoni*	NE India to Myanmar, s China and n Malay Peninsula
____ *A. j. borneensis*	Borneo
____ *A. j. magnirostris*	Philippine Islands
____ *A. j. celebensis*	Sulawesi, Banggai and Sula islands

☐ **Pacific Baza** *Aviceda subcristata*

____ *A. s. timorlaoensis*	Lesser Sundas and islands off Sulawesi
____ *A. s. pallida*	Seram Laut (Manawoka and Gorong) and Kai Islands
____ *A. s. reinwardtii*	S Moluccas (Boano, Seram, Ambon and Haruku)
____ *A. s. stresemanni*	Buru (central Moluccas)
____ *A. s. rufa*	Moluccas (Morotai, Halmahera, Ternate, Tidore, Bacan and Obi)
____ *A. s. waigeuensis*	Waigeo I. (off n New Guinea)
____ *A. s. obscura*	Biak I. (off n New Guinea)
____ *A. s. stenozoma*	Aru Islands and w New Guinea
____ *A. s. megala*	Eastern New Guinea
____ *A. s. coultasi*	Admiralty Islands
____ *A. s. bismarckii*	Bismarck Archipelago
____ *A. s. gurneyi*	Solomon Islands
____ *A. s. subcristata*	N and ne Australia

☐ **Black Baza** *Aviceda leuphotes*

____ *A. l. wolfei*	W-central China (Sichuan)
____ *A. l. syama*	NE India to s China; winters to SE Asia and Sumatra
____ *A. l. leuphotes*	SW India to s Myanmar and w Thailand
____ *A. l. andamanica*	Andaman Islands

☐ **Gray-headed Kite** *Leptodon cayanensis*

____ *L. c. cayanensis*	SE Mexico to w Ecuador, the Guianas and Amazonia; Trinidad
____ *L. c. monachus*	Central Brazil to e Bolivia, n Argentina and Paraguay

☐ **White-collared Kite** *Leptodon forbesi*

	NE Brazil (Pernambuco and Alagoas)

☐ **Hook-billed Kite** *Chondrohierax uncinatus*

____ *C. u. uncinatus*	S US and w Mexico to Brazil and n Argentina
____ *C. u. wilsonii*	E Cuba
____ *C. u. mirus*	Grenada (Lesser Antilles)

☐ **Long-tailed Honey-buzzard** *Henicopernis longicauda*

New Guinea, Aru, Yapen and w Papuan islands

☐ **Black Honey-buzzard** *Henicopernis infuscatus*

New Britain (Bismarck Archipelago)

☐ **European Honey-buzzard** *Pernis apivorus*

W Palearctic; winters s Europe and Iran to s Africa

☐ **Barred Honey-buzzard** *Pernis celebensis*
____ *P. c. celebensis*   Sulawesi, Muna, Butung and Peleng islands
____ *P. c. steerei*   Philippine Islands (except Palawan)

☐ **Oriental Honey-buzzard** *Pernis ptilorhynchus*
____ *P. p. orientalis*   S Siberia to Manchuria and Japan; winters to Greater Sundas
____ *P. p. ruficollis*   India and Sri Lanka to Myanmar and extreme sw China
____ *P. p. philippensis*   N and e Philippine Islands
____ *P. p. palawanensis*   S Philippines (Palawan and Calauit)
____ *P. p. torquatus*   Malay Peninsula, Sumatra and Borneo
____ *P. p. ptilorhynchus*   Java

☐ **Square-tailed Kite** *Lophoictinia isura*

Locally in scrub and open country of Australia

☐ **Black-breasted Kite** *Hamirostra melanosternon*

N and interior plains and scrub of Australia

☐ **Swallow-tailed Kite** *Elanoides forficatus*
____ *E. f. forficatus*   Lowlands of coastal se US to n Mexico
____ *E. f. yetapa*   S Mexico (except Yucatán Peninsula) to Brazil and ne Argentina

☐ **Bat Hawk** *Macheiramphus alcinus*
____ *M. a. alcinus*   S Myanmar to Malay Peninsula, Sumatra, Borneo and Sulawesi
____ *M. a. papuanus*   E New Guinea
____ *M. a. anderssoni*   Africa south of the Sahara and Madagascar

☐ **Pearl Kite** *Gampsonyx swainsonii*
____ *G. s. leonae*   Nicaragua; n South America south to the Amazon
____ *G. s. swainsonii*   Brazil south of the Amazon to e Peru, Bolivia and ne Argentina
____ *G. s. magnus*   Coastal w Colombia to Ecuador and n Peru

☐ **Black-shouldered Kite** *Elanus caeruleus*
____ *E. c. caeruleus*   SW Iberian Peninsula, Africa and sw Arabia
____ *E. c. vociferus*   Pakistan to e China, Indochina and Malay Peninsula
____ *E. c. hypoleucos*   Greater and Lesser Sundas, Sulawesi and Philippines
____ *E. c. wahgiensis*   New Guinea

☐ **Australian Kite** *Elanus axillaris*

Savanna and dry forests throughout Australia

☐ **White-tailed Kite** *Elanus leucurus*
____ *E. l. majusculus*   W and s US to w Panama
____ *E. l. leucurus*   E Panama to Brazil, central Argentina and central Chile

☐ **Letter-winged Kite** *Elanus scriptus*

Dry open country of interior of Australia

☐ **Scissor-tailed Kite** *Chelictinia riocourii*

Savanna of sub-Saharan Africa

☐ **Snail Kite** *Rostrhamus sociabilis*
____ *R. s. plumbeus*   Freshwater marshes of Florida, Cuba and Isle of Pines
____ *R. s. major*   E Mexico and Petén of n Guatemala
____ *R. s. sociabilis*   Honduras and Nicaragua to Brazil and ne Argentina

☐ **Slender-billed Kite** *Rostrhamus hamatus*

E Panama to the Guianas, n Bolivia and Amazonian Brazil

☐ **Double-toothed Kite** *Harpagus bidentatus*
_____ *H. b. fasciatus* | SE Mexico to w Colombia and w Ecuador
_____ *H. b. bidentatus* | E Colombia and Ecuador through Amazonia to se Brazil

☐ **Rufous-thighed Kite** *Harpagus diodon*

Lowlands of the Guianas to n Argentina and all of Brazil

☐ **Mississippi Kite** *Ictinia mississippiensis*

S US (Arizona to Florida); winters in South America

☐ **Plumbeous Kite** *Ictinia plumbea*

E Mexico to ne Argentina and all of Brazil

☐ **Red Kite** *Milvus milvus*
_____ *M. m. milvus* | Locally in western Palearctic region
_____ *M. m. fasciicauda* | Cape Verde Islands

☐ **Black Kite** *Milvus migrans*
_____ *M. m. migrans* | NW Africa and Europe to s-central Asia; winters to s Africa
_____ *M. m. lineatus* | Siberia to n India, China and Ryukyu Is.; winters to Iraq, SE Asia
_____ *M. m. formosanus* | Taiwan and Hainan (s China)
_____ *M. m. govinda* | Indian subcontinent to Indochina and Malay Peninsula
_____ *M. m. affinis* | Sulawesi to Moluccas, New Guinea, Solomons and Australia
_____ *M. m. aegyptius* | Egypt, sw Arabia and coastal ne Africa
_____ *M. m. parasitus* | Africa s of the Sahara, Madagascar, Cape Verde and Comoro is.

☐ **Whistling Kite** *Haliastur sphenurus*

Australia, New Guinea and New Caledonia

☐ **Brahminy Kite** *Haliastur indus*
_____ *H. i. indus* | Indian subcontinent and SE Asia to s China
_____ *H. i. intermedius* | Malay Peninsula, Indonesian Archipelago and Philippine Islands
_____ *H. i. girrenera* | Moluccas, New Guinea, Bismarck Archipelago and Australia
_____ *H. i. flavirostris* | Solomon Islands

☐ **White-bellied Sea-Eagle** *Haliaeetus leucogaster*

Coasts and islands of s Asia, Malay Archipelago and Australasia

☐ **Solomon Sea-Eagle** *Haliaeetus sanfordi*

Solomon Islands

☐ **African Fish-Eagle** *Haliaeetus vocifer*

Africa south of the Sahara

☐ **Madagascar Fish-Eagle** *Haliaeetus vociferoides*

Locally along coasts, lakes and rivers of nw Madagascar

☐ **Pallas' Fish-Eagle** *Haliaeetus leucoryphus*

Central Asia to India, Myanmar and s-central China (Sichuan)

☐ **White-tailed Eagle** *Haliaeetus albicilla*

Locally in Palearctic, sw Greenland, w Iceland and w Alaska

☐ **Bald Eagle** *Haliaeetus leucocephalus*
_____ *H. l. washingtoniensis* | Locally in Aleutian Islands, Alaska, Canada and n US
_____ *H. l. leucocephalus* | Locally from southern US to nw Mexico

☐ **Steller's Sea-Eagle** *Haliaeetus pelagicus*

Coastal e Siberia; winters to China, Korea, Japan and Ryukyu Is.

☐ **Lesser Fish-Eagle** *Ichthyophaga humilis*
_____ *I. h. plumbea* | Kashmir to SE Asia and Hainan (s China)
_____ *I. h. humilis* | Malaya to Borneo, Sumatra, Sulawesi, Banggai and Sula islands

☐ **Gray-headed Fish-Eagle** *Ichthyophaga ichthyaetus*

Lowlands of India to SE Asia, Borneo, Java and Philippines

☐ **Palm-nut Vulture** *Gypohierax angolensis*

Oil-palm forests and savanna of tropical Africa

☐ **Hooded Vulture** *Necrosyrtes monachus*

Savanna of Africa south of the Sahara

☐ **Lammergeier** *Gypaetus barbatus*
____ *G. b. barbatus* — Mountains of s Europe and nw Africa to central and ne China
____ *G. b. meridionalis* — Locally in e and s Africa and sw Arabia

☐ **Egyptian Vulture** *Neophron percnopterus*
____ *N. p. percnopterus* — Africa, s Europe to nw India; Canary Is. and Cape Verde Is.
____ *N. p. ginginianus* — Nepal and India (except northwest)

☐ **White-backed Vulture** *Gyps africanus* — Open plains and savanna of Africa south of the Sahara

☐ **White-rumped Vulture** *Gyps bengalensis* — Lowlands of Iran to India, sw China and SE Asia

☐ **Long-billed Vulture** *Gyps indicus*
____ *G. i. tenuirostris* — Kashmir through lower Himalayas to SE Asia
____ *G. i. indicus* — Pakistan and India (south of the Ganges River)

☐ **Rueppell's Griffon** *Gyps rueppellii*
____ *G. r. rueppellii* — SW Mauritania to e Sudan, Uganda, Kenya and Tanzania
____ *G. r. erlangeri* — Ethiopia, Eritrea and nw Somalia; s Arabia?

☐ **Himalayan Griffon** *Gyps himalayensis* — Himalayas from nw India to Tibet and w-central China

☐ **Eurasian Griffon** *Gyps fulvus*
____ *G. f. fulvus* — NW Africa and Iberian Peninsula to Middle East
____ *G. f. fulvescens* — Afghanistan, Pakistan and n India to Assam

☐ **Cape Griffon** *Gyps coprotheres* — Open plains and mountains of southern Africa

☐ **Cinereous Vulture** *Aegypius monachus* — Mediterranean basin environs to e Asia

☐ **Lappet-faced Vulture** *Torgos tracheliotus*
____ *T. t. tracheliotus* — SW Morocco and Africa south of the Sahara
____ *T. t. nubicus* — Egypt and n Sudan
____ *T. t. negevensis* — S Israel and Arabian Peninsula

☐ **White-headed Vulture** *Trigonoceps occipitalis* — Thornscrub and deserts of Africa south of the Sahara

☐ **Red-headed Vulture** *Sarcogyps calvus* — India and SE Asia

☐ **Short-toed Eagle** *Circaetus gallicus* — W Palearctic to c Asia, Indian subcontinent and Lesser Sundas

☐ **Beaudouin's Snake-Eagle** *Circaetus beaudouini* — Senegal and Mauritania to s Sudan, n Uganda and nw Kenya

☐ **Black-breasted Snake-Eagle** *Circaetus pectoralis* — E Sudan and Ethiopia to South Africa

☐ **Brown Snake-Eagle** *Circaetus cinereus* — Senegambia to n Ethiopia and south to South Africa

☐ **Fasciated Snake-Eagle** *Circaetus fasciolatus* — Mainly coastal districts of s Somalia to e South Africa

☐ **Banded Snake-Eagle** *Circaetus cinerascens* — Savanna and thornscrub of Africa south of the Sahara

☐ **Bateleur** *Terathopius ecaudatus* — Savanna and thornscrub of Africa south of the Sahara

☐ **Nicobar Serpent-Eagle** *Spilornis klossi* — Great Nicobar I. (Nicobar Islands)

☐ **Sulawesi Serpent-Eagle** *Spilornis rufipectus*
____ *S. r. rufipectus* — Sulawesi and adjacent islands
____ *S. r. sulaensis* — Banggai and Sula islands (off e Sulawesi)

☐ **Mountain Serpent-Eagle** *Spilornis kinabaluensis*

Mountains of n Borneo

☐ **Crested Serpent-Eagle** *Spilornis cheela*

____ *S. c. cheela*	N India and Nepal
____ *S. c. melanotis*	Indo-Gangetic plain
____ *S. c. spilogaster*	Sri Lanka
____ *S. c. burmanicus*	Myanmar to sw China, Thailand and Indochina
____ *S. c. davisoni*	Andaman Islands
____ *S. c. minimus*	Nicobar Islands
____ *S. c. ricketti*	Southern China and n Vietnam
____ *S. c. perplexus*	S Ryukyu Islands
____ *S. c. hoya*	Taiwan
____ *S. c. rutherfordi*	Hainan (s China)
____ *S. c. palawanensis*	Palawan (sw Philippines)
____ *S. c. pallidus*	Lowlands of n Borneo
____ *S. c. richmondi*	S Borneo
____ *S. c. natunensis*	Natunas and Belitung islands (off Borneo)
____ *S. c. malayensis*	Malay Peninsula, n Sumatra and Anambas Islands
____ *S. c. batu*	S Sumatra and Batu Islands
____ *S. c. abbotti*	Simeulue I. (off w Sumatra)
____ *S. c. asturinus*	Nias I. (off w Sumatra)
____ *S. c. sipora*	Mentawai Archepelago (off w Sumatra)
____ *S. c. bido*	Java and Bali
____ *S. c. baweanus*	Bawean I. (off n Java)

☐ **Philippine Serpent-Eagle** *Spilornis holospilus*

Forests of larger Philippine Islands (except Palawan)

☐ **Andaman Serpent-Eagle** *Spilornis elgini*

Forests of Andaman Islands

☐ **Congo Serpent-Eagle** *Dryotriorchis spectabilis*

____ *D. s. spectabilis*	Sierra Leone to Nigeria and nw Cameroon
____ *D. s. batesi*	S Cameroon to Uganda, Gabon and n Angola

☐ **Madagascar Serpent-Eagle** *Eutriorchis astur*

Rainforests of ne Madagascar (on verge of extinction)

☐ **Western Marsh-Harrier** *Circus aeruginosus*

____ *C. a. aeruginosus*	W and central Palearctic; winters to SE Asia and Greater Sundas
____ *C. a. harterti*	Morocco to Tunisia

☐ **African Marsh-Harrier** *Circus ranivorus*

Marshes and grasslands of e and s Africa

☐ **Eastern Marsh-Harrier** *Circus spilonotus*

____ *C. s. spilonotus*	E Asia; winters to SE Asia, Philippines and Indonesia
____ *C. s. spilothorax*	Central and e New Guinea

☐ **Swamp Harrier** *Circus approximans*

Australasian region and sw Oceania

☐ **Reunion Harrier** *Circus maillardi*

____ *C. m. maillardi*	Réunion (w Indian Ocean)
____ *C. m. macrosceles*	Madagascar and Comoro Islands

☐ **Long-winged Harrier** *Circus buffoni*

Grasslands of tropical South America, Trinidad and Tobago

☐ **Spotted Harrier** *Circus assimilis*

Sulawesi, Sula Islands, e Lesser Sundas and Australia

☐ **Black Harrier** *Circus maurus*

Arid grasslands of s Namibia, sw Botswana and South Africa

☐ **Cinereous Harrier** *Circus cinereus*

Andes of Colombia to Tierra del Fuego and Falkland Islands

☐ **Northern Harrier** *Circus cyaneus*
____ *C. c. cyaneus* — Widespread Eurasia
____ *C. c. hudsonius* — Widespread North America; winters to n South America

☐ **Pallid Harrier** *Circus macrourus* — Central Eurasia; winters to s Africa, India and Myanmar

☐ **Pied Harrier** *Circus melanoleucos* — E Asia; winters to s Asia, Philippines and Greater Sundas

☐ **Montagu's Harrier** *Circus pygargus* — N Palearctic; winters to s Africa, Iran and India

☐ **African Harrier-Hawk** *Polyboroides typus*
____ *P. t. pectoralis* — Senegambia to w Sudan, Niger and Zaire
____ *P. t. typus* — E Sudan to Eritrea, Angola and South Africa

☐ **Madagascar Harrier-Hawk** *Polyboroides radiatus* — Woodlands and savanna of Madagascar

☐ **Lizard Buzzard** *Kaupifalco monogrammicus*
____ *K. m. monogrammicus* — Senegambia to Ethiopia, Uganda and Kenya
____ *K. m. meridionalis* — S Kenya to Angola, n Namibia and n South Africa

☐ **Dark Chanting-Goshawk** *Melierax metabates*
____ *M. m. theresae* — SW Morocco
____ *M. m. neumanni* — Mali east to n Sudan
____ *M. m. ignoscens* — SW Arabian Peninsula
____ *M. m. metabates* — Senegambia to Ethiopia and south to Zaire and n Tanzania
____ *M. m. mechowi* — Angola to s Tanzania and s to n Namibia and ne South Africa

☐ **Eastern Chanting-Goshawk** *Melierax poliopterus* — SE Ethiopia and Somalia to e Uganda and n Tanzania

☐ **Pale Chanting-Goshawk** *Melierax canorus*
____ *M. c. argentior* — S Angola to Zimbabwe and ne South Africa
____ *M. c. canorus* — Southern South Africa

☐ **Gabar Goshawk** *Micronisus gabar*
____ *M. g. niger* — Senegambia to Sudan, n Ethiopia and sw Arabia
____ *M. g. aequatorius* — Highlands of Ethiopia to Zaire, Zambia and n Mozambique
____ *M. g. gabar* — S Angola to Zambia, Mozambique and South Africa

☐ **Gray-bellied Goshawk** *Accipiter poliogaster* — Locally in humid forests of South America east of the Andes

☐ **Crested Goshawk** *Accipiter trivirgatus*
____ *A. t. indicus* — India and Nepal to s China, Indochina and Malay Peninsula
____ *A. t. peninsulae* — SW India
____ *A. t. layardi* — Sri Lanka
____ *A. t. formosae* — Taiwan
____ *A. t. trivirgatus* — Sumatra
____ *A. t. niasensis* — Nias I. (off w Sumatra)
____ *A. t. javanicus* — Java (vagrant to Bali)
____ *A. t. microstictus* — Borneo
____ *A. t. palawanus* — SW Philippines (Palawan and Calamianes)
____ *A. t. extimus* — SE Philippine Islands
____ *A. t. castroi* — Polillo (off Luzon in n Philippines)

☐ **Red-chested Goshawk** *Accipiter toussenelii*
____ *A. t. macroscelides* — Rainforests of Senegambia to w Cameroon
____ *A. t. toussenelii* — Lower Zaire River basin (s Cameroon to Gabon)
____ *A. t. canescens* — Upper Zaire River basin
____ *A. t. lopezi* — Bioko (Gulf of Guinea)

☐ **Sulawesi Goshawk** *Accipiter griseiceps*

Sulawesi, Muna, Butung and Togian islands

☐ **African Goshawk** *Accipiter tachiro*
_____ *A. t. unduliventer* — Highlands of Ethiopia
_____ *A. t. croizati* — SW Ethiopia
_____ *A. t. sparsimfasciatus* — Somalia to n Zaire, Angola, Zambia and Mozambique
_____ *A. t. pembaensis* — Pemba I. (off Tanzania)
_____ *A. t. tachiro* — S Angola to Mozambique and South Africa

☐ **Chestnut-flanked Sparrowhawk** *Accipiter castanilius*

Dense forests of Nigeria to Zaire River basin

☐ **Shikra** *Accipiter badius*
_____ *A. b. cenchroides* — Azerbaijan to Kazakstan, Iran and nw India
_____ *A. b. dussumieri* — Central India and Bangladesh
_____ *A. b. badius* — SW India and Sri Lanka
_____ *A. b. poliopsis* — N India to s China, Thailand and Vietnam
_____ *A. b. sphenurus* — Senegambia to sw Arabia, n Zaire and n Tanzania
_____ *A. b. polyzonoides* — S Zaire and s Tanzania to n South Africa

☐ **Nicobar Sparrowhawk** *Accipiter butleri*
_____ *A. b. butleri* — Car Nicobar (north Nicobar Islands)
_____ *A. b. obsoletus* — Central Nicobar Islands (Katchall and Camorta)

☐ **Levant Sparrowhawk** *Accipiter brevipes*

Balkans to Russia; winters to ne Africa and Arabian Peninsula

☐ **Chinese Goshawk** *Accipiter soloensis*

China and Korea; winters to SE Asia, Philippines and Indonesia

☐ **Frances' Goshawk** *Accipiter francesii*
_____ *A. f. francesii* — Madagascar
_____ *A. f. griveaudi* — Grand Comoro I. (Comoro Islands)
_____ *A. f. pusillus* — Anjouan (Comoro Islands)
_____ *A. f. brutus* — Mayotte (Comoro Islands)

☐ **Spot-tailed Goshawk** *Accipiter trinotatus*

Sulawesi, Talisei, Muna and Butung islands

☐ **Variable Goshawk** *Accipiter hiogaster*
_____ *A. h. sylvestris* — Lesser Sundas
_____ *A. n. polionotus* — Banda and Tanimbar islands (e Indonesian Archipelago)
_____ *A. h. albiventris* — Tayandu and Kai islands (e Indonesian Archipelago)
_____ *A. h. obiensis* — Obi I. (central Moluccas)
_____ *A. h. griseogularis* — N Moluccas (Halmahera, Ternate, Tidore and Bacan)
_____ *A. h. mortyi* — Morotai I. (n Moluccas)
_____ *A. h. hiogaster* — South Moluccas
_____ *A. h. pallidiceps* — Buru I. (s Moluccas)
_____ *A. h. leucosomus* — New Guinea
_____ *A. h. pallidimas* — D'Entrecasteaux Archipelago
_____ *A. h. manusi* — Admiralty Islands
_____ *A. h. bougainvillei* — Bougainville (n Solomon Islands)
_____ *A. h. rufoschistaceus* — Solomon Islands (Choiseul, Santa Isabel and Florida Group)
_____ *A. h. rubianae* — Central Solomon Islands
_____ *A. h. pulchellus* — Guadalcanal (sw Solomon Islands)
_____ *A. h. malaitae* — Malaita (se Solomon Islands)
_____ *A. h. misulae* — Louisiade Archipelago
_____ *A. h. misoriensis* — Biak I. (New Guinea)
_____ *A. h. dampieri* — New Britain (Bismarck Archipelago)
_____ *A. h. lavongai* — Bismarck Archipelago (New Hanover and New Ireland)
_____ *A. h. lihirensis* — Bismarck Archipelago (Lihir and Tanga)
_____ *A. h. matthiae* — St. Matthias I. (Bismarck Archipelago)

☐ **Gray Goshawk** *Accipiter novaehollandiae*

N and e Australia and Tasmania

☐ **Brown Goshawk** *Accipiter fasciatus*
- ____ *A. f. natalis* — Christmas I. (Indian Ocean)
- ____ *A. f. tjendanae* — Sumba (Lesser Sundas)
- ____ *A. f. wallacii* — Lombok, Sumbawa, Flores and adjacent Lesser Sundas
- ____ *A. f. stresemanni* — Tanahjampea, Kalao, Bonerate, Kalaotoa, Madu and Tukanbesi is.
- ____ *A. f. hellmayri* — Lesser Sundas (Timor, Alor, Semau and Roti)
- ____ *A. f. savu* — Sawu (Lesser Sundas)
- ____ *A. f. polycryptus* — E New Guinea
- ____ *A. f. dogwa* — S New Guinea
- ____ *A. f. didimus (buruensis)* — Buru (s Moluccas) and n Australia
- ____ *A. f. fasciatus* — Australia, Tasmania, Solomon Is. (Rennell, Bellona) and Timor
- ____ *A. f. vigilax* — New Caledonia, Loyalty Islands and Vanuatu

☐ **Black-mantled Goshawk** *Accipiter melanochlamys*
- ____ *A. m. melanochlamys* — W New Guinea (Vogelkop Mountains)
- ____ *A. m. schistacinus* — Montane forests of central and e New Guinea

☐ **Pied Goshawk** *Accipiter albogularis*
- ____ *A. a. eichhorni* — Feni I. (Bismarck Archipelago)
- ____ *A. a. woodfordi* — Solomon Islands
- ____ *A. a. albogularis* — Solomon Islands (San Cristóbal and Santa Anna)
- ____ *A. a. gilvus* — Central Solomon Islands
- ____ *A. a. sharpei* — Lowlands of Santa Cruz Group (Solomon Islands)

☐ **New Caledonia Goshawk** *Accipiter haplochrous*

New Caledonia

☐ **Fiji Goshawk** *Accipiter rufitorques*

Fiji Islands

☐ **Moluccan Goshawk** *Accipiter henicogrammus*

N Moluccas (Bacan, Halmahera, Ternate and Morotai)

☐ **Slaty-mantled Goshawk** *Accipiter luteoschistaceus*

Mountains of New Britain (Bismarck Archipelago)

☐ **Imitator Sparrowhawk** *Accipiter imitator*

Solomon Islands (Bougainville, Choiseul and Santa Isabel)

☐ **Gray-headed Goshawk** *Accipiter poliocephalus*

New Guinea, Aru Is., D'Entrecasteaux Arch. and Louisiade Arch.

☐ **New Britain Goshawk** *Accipiter princeps*

Highlands of New Britain (Bismarck Archipelago)

☐ **Tiny Hawk** *Accipiter superciliosus*
- ____ *A. s. fontanieri* — Nicaragua to w Colombia and Ecuador
- ____ *A. s. superciliosus* — S America east of the Andes to extreme ne Argentina and Brazil

☐ **Semicollared Hawk** *Accipiter collaris*

Mountains of Colombia to sw Venezuela, Ecuador and s Peru

☐ **Red-thighed Sparrowhawk** *Accipiter erythropus*
- ____ *A. e. erythropus* — Senegambia to Nigeria
- ____ *A. e. zenkeri* — Cameroon to w Uganda, central Zaire, Gabon and n Angola

Lowland forests and savanna of w and central Africa

☐ **Little Sparrowhawk** *Accipiter minullus*

Forests and thornscrub of e and s Africa

☐ **Japanese Sparrowhawk** *Accipiter gularis*
- ____ *A. g. sibiricus* — Mongolia to e China and Taiwan; winters to India and Indonesia
- ____ *A. g. gularis* — Sakhalin, Kuril Is. and Japan; winters to Philippines and Indonesia
- ____ *A. g. iwasakii* — S Ryukyu Islands (Iriomote and Ishigaki)

☐ **Small Sparrowhawk** *Accipiter nanus*

Montane forests of Sulawesi

☐ **Besra** *Accipiter virgatus*

____	*A. v. affinis*	N India and Nepal to central China and Indochina
____	*A. v. fuscipectus*	Mountains of Taiwan
____	*A. v. besra*	S India and Sri Lanka
____	*A. v. abdulali*	Andaman and Nicobar islands
____	*A. v. nisoides*	Myanmar, Thailand and n Malay Peninsula
____	*A. v. confusus*	Philippines (Luzon, Mindoro, Negros and Catanduanes)
____	*A. v. quagga*	Philippines (Cebu, Bohol, Leyte, Samar, Siquijor and Mindanao)
____	*A. v. rufotibialis*	N Borneo
____	*A. v. vanbemmeli*	Sumatra
____	*A. v. virgatus*	Java and Bali
____	*A. v. quinquefasciatus*	Flores (Lesser Sundas)

☐ **Rufous-necked Sparrowhawk** *Accipiter erythrauchen*

____	*A. e. erythrauchen*	N Moluccas (Morotai, Halmahera, Bacan and Obi)
____	*A. e. ceramensis*	S Moluccas (Buru, Ambon and Seram)

☐ **Collared Sparrowhawk** *Accipiter cirrocephalus*

____	*A. c. papuanus*	New Guinea, w Papuan islands and Aru Islands
____	*A. c. rosselianus*	Rossell (Louisiade Archipelago)
____	*A. c. cirrocephalus*	Australia and Tasmania

☐ **New Britain Sparrowhawk** *Accipiter brachyurus*

New Britain (Bismarck Archipelago)

☐ **Vinous-breasted Sparrowhawk** *Accipiter rhodogaster*

____	*A. r. rhodogaster*	Sulawesi
____	*A. r. butonensis*	Muna and Butung islands (off Sulawesi)
____	*A. r. sulaensis*	Banggai and Sula islands (off Sulawesi)

☐ **Madagascar Sparrowhawk** *Accipiter madagascariensis*

Scrub and savanna of Madagascar

☐ **Ovampo Sparrowhawk** *Accipiter ovampensis*

Locally in savanna and thornscrub of Africa south of the Sahara

☐ **Eurasian Sparrowhawk** *Accipiter nisus*

____	*A. n. granti*	Madeira and Canary Islands
____	*A. n. nisus*	Europe to Asia Minor and Siberia; winters to Africa
____	*A. n. wolterstorffi*	Corsica and Sardinia
____	*A. n. punicus*	NW Africa (Morocco to Tunisia)
____	*A. n. nisosimilis*	Central and e Asia; winters to India, Sri Lanka and Indochina
____	*A. n. melaschistos*	Himalayas and mountains of central Asia

☐ **Rufous-chested Sparrowhawk** *Accipiter rufiventris*

____	*A. r. perspicillaris*	Highland forests of Ethiopia
____	*A. r. rufiventris*	Montane forests of Kenya and e Zaire to South Africa

☐ **Sharp-shinned Hawk** *Accipiter striatus*

____	*A. s. perobscurus*	Queen Charlotte Is. and (?) adjacent coastal British Columbia
____	*A. s. velox*	Alaska and Canada to s US; winters to Panama
____	*A. s. suttoni*	Locally from extreme s New Mexico to se Mexico (Veracruz)
____	*A. s. madrensis*	W Mexico (Guerrero and w Oaxaca)
____	*A. s. chionogaster*	Oak-pine highlands of s Mexico (Chiapas) to Nicaragua
____	*A. s. fringilloides*	Cuba
____	*A. s. striatus*	Hispaniola
____	*A. s. venator*	Puerto Rico

☐ **Plain-breasted Hawk** *Accipiter ventralis*

Andes of Colombia and w Venezuela to w Bolivia

☐ **Rufous-thighed Hawk** *Accipiter erythronemius*

Bolivia and Paraguay to n Argentina and s Brazil

☐ **Cooper's Hawk** *Accipiter cooperii*

Woodlands of s Canada and US; winters to Central America

☐ **Gundlach's Hawk** *Accipiter gundlachi*
    ____ *A. g. gundlachi*
    ____ *A. g. wileyi*

Lowland forests of w and central Cuba
Lowland forests of e Cuba

☐ **Bicolored Hawk** *Accipiter bicolor*
    ____ *A. b. fidens*
    ____ *A. b. bicolor*
    ____ *A. b. pileatus*
    ____ *A. b. guttifer*

Lowlands of s Mexico (Oaxaca, Veracruz and Yucatán Peninsula)
SE Mexico (Yucatán Pen.) to the Guianas, Brazil and nw Peru
Brazil south of the Amazon to ne Argentina
Bolivia to Paraguay, sw Brazil (Mato Grosso) and n Argentina

☐ **Chilean Hawk** *Accipiter chilensis*

Andes of central Chile and Argentina to Tierra del Fuego

☐ **Black Goshawk** *Accipiter melanoleucus*
    ____ *A. m. temminckii*
    ____ *A. m. melanoleucus*

Senegambia to Gabon, Congo and Central African Republic
E Sudan and nw Ethiopia; Kenya to Angola and South Africa

☐ **Henst's Goshawk** *Accipiter henstii*

Forests and savanna of Madagascar

☐ **Northern Goshawk** *Accipiter gentilis*
    ____ *A. g. gentilis*
    ____ *A. g. arrigonii*
    ____ *A. g. buteoides*
    ____ *A. g. albidus*
    ____ *A. g. schvedowi*
    ____ *A. g. fujiyamae*
    ____ *A. g. atricapillus*
    ____ *A. g. laingi*

Europe and extreme nw Africa
Corsica and Sardinia
N Eurasia (Sweden to Lena River); winters to central Asia
NE Siberia to Kamchatka Peninsula
NE Asia to central China; winters to n Indochina
Japan
North America south to s US and w Mexico
SW Canada (Queen Charlotte Islands and Vancouver I.)

☐ **Meyer's Goshawk** *Accipiter meyerianus*

Moluccas to New Guinea, New Britain and Solomon Islands

☐ **Chestnut-shouldered Goshawk** *Erythrotriorchis buergersi*

Montane forests of n and e New Guinea

☐ **Red Goshawk** *Erythrotriorchis radiatus*

Dry woodlands of n and e Australia

☐ **Doria's Goshawk** *Megatriorchis doriae*

New Guinea and Batanta I.

☐ **Long-tailed Hawk** *Urotriorchis macrourus*

Rainforests of Liberia to w Uganda and s Zaire

☐ **Grasshopper Buzzard** *Butastur rufipennis*

Savanna and grasslands of sub-Saharan Africa

☐ **White-eyed Buzzard** *Butastur teesa*

Woodlands and plains of se Iran to India, s Tibet and Myanmar

☐ **Rufous-winged Buzzard** *Butastur liventer*

Savanna and woodlands of SE Asia, Java and Sulawesi

☐ **Gray-faced Buzzard** *Butastur indicus*

NE Asia; winters SE Asia to Philippines and Indonesia

☐ **Crane Hawk** *Geranospiza caerulescens*
    ____ *G. c. livens*
    ____ *G. c. nigra*
    ____ *G. c. balzarensis*
    ____ *G. c. caerulescens*
    ____ *G. c. gracilis*
    ____ *G. c. flexipes*

NW Mexico
Northern Mexico to central Panama
E Panama to w Colombia, Ecuador and extreme nw Peru
Guianas and Amazonian Brazil to e Colombia and Peru
NE Brazil (Maranhão, Ceará and Piauí to Bahia)
S Brazil to *chaco* of Paraguay, Bolivia and n Argentina

☐ **Plumbeous Hawk** *Leucopternis plumbea*

E Panama to w Colombia, Ecuador and extreme nw Peru

☐ **Slate-colored Hawk** *Leucopternis schistacea*

Tropical s Venezuela to e Bolivia and Amazonian Brazil

☐ **Barred Hawk** *Leucopternis princeps*

Montane forests of Costa Rica to Colombia and n Ecuador

☐ **Black-faced Hawk** *Leucopternis melanops*

SE Colombia to s Venezuela, ne Ecuador and n Amaz. Brazil

☐ **White-browed Hawk** *Leucopternis kuhli*

Rainforests of e Peru, n Bolivia and s Amazonian Brazil

☐ **White-necked Hawk** *Leucopternis lacernulata*

Lowland forests of coastal se Brazil

☐ **Semiplumbeous Hawk** *Leucopternis semiplumbea*

Humid forests of Honduras to w Colombia and nw Ecuador

☐ **White Hawk** *Leucopternis albicollis*
     ____ *L. a. ghiesbreghti*   Tropical forests of s Mexico to Guatemala and Belize
     ____ *L. a. costaricensis*   Honduras to Panama and w Colombia
     ____ *L. a. williaminae*   NW Colombia to extreme nw Venezuela
     ____ *L. a. albicollis*   Humid forests of the Guianas and Amazonian basin; Trinidad

☐ **Gray-backed Hawk** *Leucopternis occidentalis*

Montane forests of w Ecuador and adjacent nw Peru

☐ **Mantled Hawk** *Leucopternis polionota*

Tropical forests of e Brazil to e Uruguay and e Paraguay

☐ **Rufous Crab-Hawk** *Buteogallus aequinoctialis*

NE Venezuela (Orinoco delta) to e Brazil (Paraná)

☐ **Common Black-Hawk** *Buteogallus anthracinus*
     ____ *B. a. anthracinus*   SW US to n South America, St. Vincent and Trinidad
     ____ *B. a. gundlachii*   Cuba and Isle of Pines
     ____ *B. a. utilensis*   Cancún, Cozumel I. and islands in Gulf of Honduras

☐ **Mangrove Black-Hawk** *Buteogallus subtilis*
     ____ *B. s. rhizophorae*   Pacific coast of El Salvador and Honduras
     ____ *B. s. bangsi*   Pacific coast of Costa Rica and Panama; Pearl Islands
     ____ *B. s. subtilis*   Pacific coast of Colombia, Ecuador and extreme n Peru

☐ **Great Black-Hawk** *Buteogallus urubitinga*
     ____ *B. u. ridgwayi*   Lowlands of n Mexico to w Panama
     ____ *B. u. urubitinga*   E Panama through South America to n Argentina

☐ **Savanna Hawk** *Buteogallus meridionalis*

Savanna and marshes of w Panama to Brazil and n Argentina

☐ **Harris' Hawk** *Parabuteo unicinctus*
     ____ *P. u. harrisi*   Arid sw US to Pacific slope of Colombia, Ecuador and Peru
     ____ *P. u. unicinctus*   E Colombia and Venezuela to Brazil, s Argentina and s Chile

☐ **Black-collared Hawk** *Busarellus nigricollis*
     ____ *B. n. nigricollis*   Lowlands of central Mexico to Amazonian Brazil and e Bolivia
     ____ *B. n. leucocephalus*   Paraguay, Uruguay and n Argentina

☐ **Black-chested Buzzard-Eagle** *Geranoaetus melanoleucus*
     ____ *G. m. australis*   Andes of w Venezuela to Tierra del Fuego
     ____ *G. m. melanoleucus*   SE Brazil to Paraguay, Uruguay and ne Argentina

☐ **Solitary Eagle** *Harpyhaliaetus solitarius*
     ____ *H. s. sheffleri*   Locally in montane forests of s Mexico to Panama
     ____ *H. s. solitarius*   Locally in montane forests of Venezuela to nw Argentina

☐ **Crowned Eagle** *Harpyhaliaetus coronatus*

Savanna of s Brazil, Paraguay and Bolivia to n Argentina

☐ **Gray Hawk** *Asturina nitida*
____	*A. n. plagiata*	Lowlands of sw US to nw Costa Rica
____	*A. n. costaricensis*	SW Costa Rica to n Colombia and w Ecuador
____	*A. n. nitida*	E Colombia and Ecuador to the Guianas and Amazonian Brazil
____	*A. n. pallida*	S-central Brazil to e Bolivia, Paraguay and n Argentina

☐ **Roadside Hawk** *Buteo magnirostris*
____	*B. m. griseocauda*	Mexico to nw Costa Rica and w Panama
____	*B. m. conspectus*	SE Mexico (Tabasco and Yucatán Peninsula) to n Belize
____	*B. m. gracilis*	Cozumel and Holbox islands (off Yucatán Peninsula)
____	*B. m. sinushonduri*	Bonacca and Roatán islands (Honduras)
____	*B. m. petulans*	SW Costa Rica and w Panama and adjacent islands
____	*B. m. alius*	Pearl Islands (San José and San Miguel) in Gulf of Panama
____	*B. m. magnirostris*	Colombia and w Ecuador to the Guianas and Amazonian Brazil
____	*B. m. occiduus*	W Amazonian Brazil, e Peru and n Bolivia
____	*B. m. saturatus*	SW Brazil to Paraguay, Bolivia and w Argentina
____	*B. m. nattereri*	NE Brazil (south to Bahia)
____	*B. m. magniplumis*	S Brazil to ne Argentina (Misiones) and adjacent Paraguay
____	*B. m. pucherani*	Uruguay and ne Argentina (south to Buenos Aires Province)

☐ **Red-shouldered Hawk** *Buteo lineatus*
____	*B. l. elegans*	S Oregon to n Baja California
____	*B. l. lineatus*	E North America (s Canada to central US)
____	*B. l. texanus*	S Texas to se Mexico (Veracruz)
____	*B. l. alleni*	S-central Texas to South Carolina and n Florida
____	*B. l. extimus*	Florida and Florida Keys

☐ **Ridgway's Hawk** *Buteo ridgwayi*

Lowlands of Hispaniola and satellite islands

☐ **Broad-winged Hawk** *Buteo platypterus*
____	*B. p. platypterus*	Central and s Canada to s US; winters to Brazil and Bolivia
____	*B. p. cubanensis*	Cuba
____	*B. p. brunnescens*	Puerto Rico
____	*B. p. insulicola*	Antigua (Lesser Antilles)
____	*B. p. rivierei*	Lesser Antilles (Dominica, Martinique and St. Lucia)
____	*B. p. antillarum*	Lesser Antilles (St. Vincent and Grenada) to Tobago

☐ **White-rumped Hawk** *Buteo leucorrhous*

Forests of Venezuela to n Argentina and s Brazil

☐ **Short-tailed Hawk** *Buteo brachyurus*
____	*B. b. fuliginosus*	S Florida; e Mexico to Panama
____	*B. b. brachyurus*	N South America to Brazil, Bolivia, Paraguay and n Argentina

☐ **White-throated Hawk** *Buteo albigula*

Andes of Venezuela to nw Argentina and Chile

☐ **Swainson's Hawk** *Buteo swainsoni*

W N America; winters to n Argentina, s Brazil and Paraguay

☐ **White-tailed Hawk** *Buteo albicaudatus*
____	*B. a. hypospodius*	S Texas and nw Mexico to n Colombia and nw Venezuela
____	*B. a. colonus*	Netherlands Antilles, n South America and Amazon basin
____	*B. a. albicaudatus*	SE Peru to Bolivia, Paraguay, se Brazil, Uruguay, n Argentina

☐ **Galapagos Hawk** *Buteo galapagoensis*

Galapagos Islands

☐ **Variable Hawk** *Buteo polyosoma*
____	*B. p. polyosoma*	Andes of sw Colombia to Tierra del Fuego and Falkland Islands
____	*B. p. poecilochrous*	High Andes of Ecuador to nw Argentina
____	*B. p. exsul*	Juan Fernández Islands (off Chile)

☐ **Zone-tailed Hawk** *Buteo albonotatus*

Arid sw US to n Bolivia, Paraguay and Brazil

☐ **Hawaiian Hawk** *Buteo solitarius*

Forests of Hawaii (Hawaiian Islands)

☐ **Red-tailed Hawk** *Buteo jamaicensis*

____	*B. j. alascensis*	SE Alaska and coastal British Columbia
____	*B. j. harlani*	Interior Alaska to sw Yukon and n British Columbia
____	*B. j. calurus*	W North America (west of the Great Plains)
____	*B. j. borealis*	North America (east of the Great Plains)
____	*B. j. kriderii*	Plains of s-central Canada to n-central US
____	*B. j. fuertesi*	Texas to n Mexico
____	*B. j. hadropus*	Highlands of central Mexico
____	*B. j. kemsiesi*	S Mexico (Chiapas) to n Nicaragua
____	*B. j. costaricensis*	Costa Rica
____	*B. j. fumosus*	Tres Marías Islands (off w Mexico)
____	*B. j. socorroensis*	Socorro I. (Revillagigedo Islands off w Mexico)
____	*B. j. umbrinus*	Florida
____	*B. j. solitudinis*	Bahamas and Cuba
____	*B. j. jamaicensis*	Jamaica, Hispaniola, Puerto Rico and n Lesser Antilles

☐ **Rufous-tailed Hawk** *Buteo ventralis*

Patagonian forests of s Chile and Argentina

☐ **Eurasian Buzzard** *Buteo buteo*

____	*B. b. buteo*	W Palearctic region and Madeira; winters to w Africa
____	*B. b. arrigonii*	Corsica and Sardinia
____	*B. b. rothschildi*	Azores
____	*B. b. insularum*	Canary Islands
____	*B. b. bannermani*	Cape Verde Islands
____	*B. b. vulpinus*	N Palearctic; winters to s Asia and Africa south of the Sahara
____	*B. b. menetriesi*	S Crimea and Caucasus to n Iran
____	*B. b. japonicus*	Central Asia to Japan and Tibet; winters India to Japan
____	*B. b. refectus*	Himalayas and w China
____	*B. b. toyoshimai*	Izu Islands and Bonin Islands
____	*B. b. oshiroi*	Daito Islands

☐ **Mountain Buzzard** *Buteo oreophilus*

____	*B. o. oreophilus*	Highlands of Ethiopia to Tanzania and Malawi
____	*B. o. trizonatus*	Locally in montane forests of e and s Africa

☐ **Madagascar Buzzard** *Buteo brachypterus*

Woodlands and savanna of Madagascar

☐ **Long-legged Buzzard** *Buteo rufinus*

____	*B. r. rufinus*	SE Europe to Mongolia and India; winters to Africa
____	*B. r. cirtensis*	Mauritania to Egypt and Arabian Peninsula

☐ **Upland Buzzard** *Buteo hemilasius*

Open steppes and montane slopes of e Asia

☐ **Ferruginous Hawk** *Buteo regalis*

Prairies and plains of s Canada to n Mexico

☐ **Rough-legged Hawk** *Buteo lagopus*

____	*B. l. lagopus*	Tundra and grasslands of n Eurasia; winters central Eurasia
____	*B. l. menzbieri*	NE Asia; winters to central Asia, n China and Japan
____	*B. l. kamtschatkensis*	Kamchatka Peninsula; winters in e-central Asia
____	*B. l. sanctijohannis*	Alaska and n Canada; winters to s US

☐ **Red-necked Buzzard** *Buteo auguralis*

Sub-Saharan and w-central Africa; disperses to Sahel

☐ **Augur Buzzard** *Buteo augur*

Highlands of Ethiopia to Zimbabwe, Angola and Namibia

☐ **Archer's Buzzard** *Buteo archeri*

Highlands of n Somalia

☐ **Jackal Buzzard** *Buteo rufofuscus*

Savanna of s Africa

☐ **Crested Eagle** *Morphnus guianensis*

Forests of e Guatemala to ne Argentina and s Brazil

☐ **Harpy Eagle** *Harpia harpyja*

Forests of Central America to ne Argentina and s Brazil

☐ **New Guinea Eagle** *Harpyopsis novaeguineae*

Forests of New Guinea

☐ **Great Philippine Eagle** *Pithecophaga jefferyi*

Philippines (Luzon, Leyte, Samar and Mindanao)

☐ **Black Eagle** *Ictinaetus malayensis*
____ *I. m. perniger*
____ *I. m. malayensis*

N India and Nepal; s India and Sri Lanka
Myanmar to s China, SE Asia and Indonesia

☐ **Lesser Spotted Eagle** *Aquila pomarina*
____ *A. p. pomarina*
____ *A. p. hastata*

Locally in e Europe to Caspian lowlands; winters to s Africa
India, Bangladesh and n Myanmar

☐ **Greater Spotted Eagle** *Aquila clanga*

C Eurasia and s Asia; winters to Africa, China and Indochina

☐ **Tawny Eagle** *Aquila rapax*
____ *A. r. belisarius*
____ *A. r. rapax*
____ *A. r. vindhiana*

Morocco and Algeria; s Arabia and w Africa to n Kenya
S Kenya and Zaire to Angola, Namibia and South Africa
Locally in Pakistan, India and s Nepal

☐ **Steppe Eagle** *Aquila nipalensis*
____ *A. n. orientalis*
____ *A. n. nipalensis*

Central Eurasia; winters to Middle East, Arabia and s Africa
Altai Mts. to Tibet and Manchuria; winters India to se China

☐ **Spanish Eagle** *Aquila adalberti*

Locally in Iberian Peninsula; formerly Morocco

☐ **Imperial Eagle** *Aquila heliaca*

C Europe to Mongolia; winters to Africa, n India and China

☐ **Wahlberg's Eagle** *Aquila wahlbergi*

Savanna of Africa south of the Sahara

☐ **Gurney's Eagle** *Aquila gurneyi*

Moluccas to New Guinea, w Papuan islands and Aru Islands

☐ **Golden Eagle** *Aquila chrysaetos*
____ *A. c. homeyeri*
____ *A. c. chrysaetos*
____ *A. c. daphanea*
____ *A. c. japonica*
____ *A. c. kamtschatica*
____ *A. c. canadensis*

Iberian Peninsula; nw Africa to Arabia and Iran
Western Palearctic region to Siberia and Altai Mountains
Turkestan to Manchuria, Pakistan, Himalayas and sw China
Korea and Japan
Siberia and Altai Mountains to Kamchatka Peninsula
Alaska to w-central Mexico and coastal ne US

☐ **Wedge-tailed Eagle** *Aquila audax*
____ *A. a. audax*
____ *A. a. fleayi*

Savanna of Australia and Trans-Fly of s New Guinea
Tasmania

☐ **Verreaux's Eagle** *Aquila verreauxii*

Locally in Africa south of the Sahara and s Arabian Peninsula

☐ **Bonelli's Eagle** *Hieraaetus fasciatus*
____ *H. f. fasciatus*
____ *H. f. renschi*

Mediterranean basin to India, s China and Indochina
Lesser Sundas

☐ **African Hawk-Eagle** *Hieraaetus spilogaster*

Woodlands and savanna of Africa south of the Sahara

☐ **Booted Eagle** *Hieraaetus pennatus*

S Palearctic and Africa s of the Sahara; winters to SE Asia, India

☐ **Little Eagle** *Hieraaetus morphnoides*
_____ *H. m. weiskei*
_____ *H. m. morphnoides*

New Guinea; vagrant to Moluccas (Halmahera and Seram)
Moist woodlands of Australia

☐ **Ayres' Hawk-Eagle** *Hieraaetus ayresii*

Woodlands and savanna of Africa south of the Sahara

☐ **Rufous-bellied Eagle** *Hieraaetus kienerii*
_____ *H. k. kienerii*
_____ *H. k. formosus*

NE India and Nepal; sw India (Western Ghats) and Sri Lanka
Myanmar to Indochina, Malay Pen., Indonesia and Philippines

☐ **Martial Eagle** *Polemaetus bellicosus*

Savanna and thornbush of Africa south of the Sahara

☐ **Black-and-white Hawk-Eagle** *Spizastur melanoleucus*

Forests of s Mexico to n Argentina and Brazil

☐ **Long-crested Eagle** *Lophaetus occipitalis*

Savanna of Africa south of the Sahara

☐ **Cassin's Hawk-Eagle** *Spizaetus africanus*

Humid forests of w and central Africa

☐ **Changeable Hawk-Eagle** *Spizaetus cirrhatus*
_____ *S. c. limnaeetus*
_____ *S. c. cirrhatus*
_____ *S. c. ceylanensis*
_____ *S. c. andamanensis*
_____ *S. c. vanheurni*
_____ *S. c. floris*

N India to Indochina, Malaya, Greater Sundas and Philippines
Peninsular India
Sri Lanka
Andaman Islands
Simeulue I. (off w Sumatra)
Lesser Sundas (Sumbawa, Komodo, Flores and Paloe)

☐ **Mountain Hawk-Eagle** *Spizaetus nipalensis*
_____ *S. n. orientalis*
_____ *S. n. nipalensis*
_____ *S. n. kelaarti*

Japan
India to e China, Taiwan, Indochina and Malay Peninsula
SW India (Western Ghats) and Sri Lanka

☐ **Blyth's Hawk-Eagle** *Spizaetus alboniger*

Forests of s Myanmar to Malay Peninsula, Sumatra and Borneo

☐ **Javan Hawk-Eagle** *Spizaetus bartelsi*

Wooded hills of w Java

☐ **Sulawesi Hawk-Eagle** *Spizaetus lanceolatus*

Forests of Sulawesi, Banggai and Sula islands

☐ **Philippine Hawk-Eagle** *Spizaetus philippensis*

Philippine Islands

☐ **Wallace's Hawk-Eagle** *Spizaetus nanus*
_____ *S. n. nanus*
_____ *S. n. stresemanni*

S Myanmar and Thailand to Malay Pen., Sumatra and Borneo
Nias I. (off w Sumatra)

☐ **Black Hawk-Eagle** *Spizaetus tyrannus*
_____ *S. t. serus*
_____ *S. t. tyrannus*

Forests of s Mexico to ne Argentina and Brazil; Trinidad
E and s Brazil to extreme ne Argentina (Misiones)

☐ **Ornate Hawk-Eagle** *Spizaetus ornatus*
_____ *S. o. vicarius*
_____ *S. o. ornatus*

Humid forests of s Mexico to w Colombia and w Ecuador
Humid tropical n South America to n Argentina and Brazil

☐ **Crowned Hawk-Eagle** *Stephanoaetus coronatus*

Forests of Africa south of the Sahara

☐ **Black-and-chestnut Eagle** *Oroaetus isidori*

Coastal mountains of Venezuela to Andes of nw Argentina

ORDER: FALCONIFORMES
FAMILY: SAGITTARIIDAE (Secretary-bird—1)

☐ **Secretary-bird** *Sagittarius serpentarius*

	Savanna and grasslands of Africa south of the Sahara

ORDER: FALCONIFORMES
FAMILY: FALCONIDAE (Falcons and Caracaras—62)

☐ **Black Caracara** *Daptrius ater*

Guianas and s Venezuela to n Bolivia and Amazonian Brazil

☐ **Red-throated Caracara** *Daptrius americanus*

Extreme s Mexico to n Bolivia and s Brazil

☐ **Carunculated Caracara** *Phalcoboenus carunculatus*

Páramo of sw Colombia and Ecuador

☐ **Mountain Caracara** *Phalcoboenus megalopterus*

Páramo of n Peru to nw Argentina and central Chile

☐ **White-throated Caracara** *Phalcoboenus albogularis*

Andes of s Argentina and s Chile to Tierra del Fuego

☐ **Striated Caracara** *Phalcoboenus australis*

Tierra del Fuego, Staten I., Navarino I. and Falkland Islands

☐ **Crested Caracara** *Caracara plancus*
- ____ *C. p. pallidus* — Tres Marías Islands (off w Mexico)
- ____ *C. p. audubonii* — S US to w Panama, Cuba and Isle of Pines
- ____ *C. p. cheriway* — E Panama and n S Am. to n Peru, Brazil, Aruba and Trinidad
- ____ *C. p. plancus* — Amazon basin to Peru, Tierra del Fuego and Falkland Islands

☐ **Yellow-headed Caracara** *Milvago chimachima*
- ____ *M. c. cordatus* — Savanna of sw Costa Rica to Brazil n of the Amazon; Trinidad
- ____ *M. c. chimachima* — Brazil s of the Amazon to e Bolivia, Paraguay and n Argentina

☐ **Chimango Caracara** *Milvago chimango*
- ____ *M. c. chimango* — Forests of s Brazil and Paraguay to c Argentina and c Chile
- ____ *M. c. temucoensis* — S Chile and s Argentina to Tierra del Fuego and Cape Horn Arch.

☐ **Laughing Falcon** *Herpetotheres cachinnans*
- ____ *H. c. chapmani* — Lowlands of n Mexico to Honduras
- ____ *H. c. cachinnans* — Nicaragua to Colombia, Peru and central Brazil
- ____ *H. c. queribundus* — E Bolivia and Brazil to Paraguay and n Argentina

☐ **Barred Forest-Falcon** *Micrastur ruficollis*
- ____ *M. r. guerilla* — Humid forests of s Mexico to Nicaragua
- ____ *M. r. interstes* — Costa Rica and Panama to w Colombia and w Ecuador
- ____ *M. r. zonothorax* — E Andean foothills of Colombia and Venezuela to Bolivia
- ____ *M. r. concentricus* — S Venezuela to the Guianas and Amazonian Brazil
- ____ *M. r. ruficollis* — S Brazil to Paraguay and n Argentina
- ____ *M. r. olrogi* — Subtropical forests of nw Argentina

☐ **Plumbeous Forest-Falcon** *Micrastur plumbeus*

Humid forests of sw Colombia and nw Ecuador

☐ **Lined Forest-Falcon** *Micrastur gilvicollis*

Guianas and s Venezuela to Bolivia and Amazonian Brazil

☐ **Slaty-backed Forest-Falcon** *Micrastur mirandollei*

Humid Costa Rica to Bolivia and Amazonian Brazil

☐ **Collared Forest-Falcon** *Micrastur semitorquatus*
- ____ *M. s. naso* — N-central Mexico to Ecuador
- ____ *M. s. semitorquatus* — Rainforests of n South America to Brazil and n Argentina

☐ **Buckley's Forest-Falcon** *Micrastur buckleyi*

Humid Amazon forests of e Ecuador and e Peru

☐ **Spot-winged Falconet** *Spiziapteryx circumcinctus*

Chaco of n Argentina, w Paraguay and e Bolivia

☐ **Pygmy Falcon** *Polihierax semitorquatus*

Discontinuously distributed acacia thornscrub of ne and s Africa

☐ **White-rumped Falcon** *Polihierax insignis*
____ *P. i. insignis* — Myanmar (valley of Irrawaddy River)
____ *P. i. cinereiceps* — S Myanmar and Thailand
____ *P. i. harmandi* — S Indochina

☐ **Collared Falconet** *Microhierax caerulescens*
____ *M. c. caerulescens* — Himalayas of India and Nepal to Assam
____ *M. c. burmanicus* — Myanmar to s Indochina

☐ **Black-thighed Falconet** *Microhierax fringillarius*

Forests of Myanmar to Malay Peninsula and Greater Sundas

☐ **White-fronted Falconet** *Microhierax latifrons*

Forests of n Borneo

☐ **Philippine Falconet** *Microhierax erythrogenys*
____ *M. e. erythrogenys* — N Philippines (Luzon, Mindoro, Negros and Bohol)
____ *M. e. meridionalis* — S Philippines (Samar, Leyte and Cebu to Mindanao)

☐ **Pied Falconet** *Microhierax melanoleucus*

Forests of ne India to s China and n Indochina

☐ **Lesser Kestrel** *Falco naumanni*

Mediterranean basin to e China; winters to s Asia and s Africa

☐ **Eurasian Kestrel** *Falco tinnunculus*
____ *F. t. tinnunculus* — N Africa, Europe and Middle East to Siberia
____ *F. t. interstinctus* — Tibet to China and Japan; winters to India, Malaya, Philippines
____ *F. t. objurgatus* — S India (Western and Eastern Ghats) and Sri Lanka
____ *F. t. canariensis* — Madeira and w Canary Islands
____ *F. t. dacotiae* — E Canary Islands
____ *F. t. neglectus* — N Cape Verde Islands
____ *F. t. alexandri* — SE Cape Verde Islands
____ *F. t. rupicolaeformis* — NE Africa and Arabia
____ *F. t. archerii* — Somalia, coastal Kenya and Socotra
____ *F. t. rufescens* — West Africa to Ethiopia, Tanzania and n Angola
____ *F. t. rupicolus* — N Angola to s Zaire, s Tanzania and South Africa

☐ **Madagascar Kestrel** *Falco newtoni*

Madagascar and Aldabra

☐ **Mauritius Kestrel** *Falco punctatus*

Dense forests of sw Mauritius (w Indian Ocean)

☐ **Seychelles Kestrel** *Falco araea*

Locally in Seychelles

☐ **Spotted Kestrel** *Falco moluccensis*
____ *F. m. moluccensis* — N and s Moluccas
____ *F. m. microbalia* — Java to Lesser Sundas, Sulawesi and Tanimbar Islands

☐ **Australian Kestrel** *Falco cenchroides*
____ *F. c. cenchroides* — Australian region; winters to Java, Lesser Sundas and Moluccas
____ *F. c. baru* — Montane forests of w-central New Guinea

☐ **Greater Kestrel** *Falco rupicoloides*
____ *F. r. fieldi* — Ethiopia and Somalia
____ *F. r. arthuri* — Kenya and ne Tanzania
____ *F. r. rupicoloides* — Acacia steppes of southern Africa

☐ **American Kestrel** *Falco sparverius*
    ____ *F. s. sparverius* — North America (Alaska to Newfoundland, south to w Mexico)
    ____ *F. s. paulus* — Coastal s US to Florida
    ____ *F. s. peninsularis* — W Mexico (s Baja California, Sonora and Sinaloa)
    ____ *F. s. tropicalis* — S Mexico to n Honduras
    ____ *F. s. nicaraguensis* — Savanna of Honduras and Nicaragua
    ____ *F. s. sparverioides* — Bahamas, Cuba and Isle of Pines
    ____ *F. s. dominicensis* — Hispaniola
    ____ *F. s. caribaearum* — West Indies (Puerto Rico to Grenada)
    ____ *F. s. brevipennis* — Netherlands Antilles (Aruba, Curaçao and Bonaire)
    ____ *F. s. ochraceus* — Mountains of e Colombia and nw Venezuela
    ____ *F. s. caucae* — Mountains of w Colombia
    ____ *F. s. isabellinus* — Venezuela to n Brazil
    ____ *F. s. aequatorialis* — Subtropical n Ecuador
    ____ *F. s. peruvianus* — Subtropical sw Ecuador, Peru and n Chile
    ____ *F. s. fernandensis* — Robinson Crusoe I. (Juan Fernández Islands off Chile)
    ____ *F. s. cinnamonimus* — SE Peru, Chile and Argentina to Tierra del Fuego
    ____ *F. s. cearae* — Tablelands of ne Brazil to e Bolivia

☐ **Fox Kestrel** *Falco alopex* — Rocky hills and gorges of sub-Saharan Africa

☐ **Gray Kestrel** *Falco ardosiaceus* — Savanna and woodlands of Africa south of the Sahara

☐ **Dickinson's Kestrel** *Falco dickinsoni* — Palms and savanna of e-central and ne South Africa

☐ **Banded Kestrel** *Falco zoniventris* — Humid lowlands and subdesert of Madagascar

☐ **Red-necked Falcon** *Falco chicquera*
    ____ *F. c. chicquera* — Iran to India, Nepal and Bangladesh
    ____ *F. c. ruficollis (horsbrughi)* — Africa south of the Sahara

☐ **Red-footed Falcon** *Falco vespertinus* — Central Eurasia; winters in Africa south of the Sahara

☐ **Amur Falcon** *Falco amurensis* — Steppes of ne Asia; winters from Malawi to South Africa

☐ **Eleonora's Falcon** *Falco eleonorae* — Mediterranean islands and coasts; winters to Madagascar

☐ **Sooty Falcon** *Falco concolor* — Rocky areas of ne Africa; winters to s Africa and Madagascar

☐ **Aplomado Falcon** *Falco femoralis*
    ____ *F. f. septentrionalis* — Savanna and woodlands of n Mexico and Guatemala
    ____ *F. f. femoralis* — Nicaragua and Belize through S America to Tierra del Fuego
    ____ *F. f. pichinchae* — Temperate Colombia to n Chile and nw Argentina

☐ **Merlin** *Falco columbarius*
    ____ *F. c. subaesalon* — Iceland
    ____ *F. c. aesalon* — N Eurasia (Faeroes to central Siberia); winters to N Africa
    ____ *F. c. insignis* — Siberia (Yenisey River to Kolyma River)
    ____ *F. c. pacificus* — NE Asia and Sakhalin
    ____ *F. c. pallidus* — Steppes of Asia (Aral Sea to Altai Mountains)
    ____ *F. c. lymani* — Mountains of central Asia
    ____ *F. c. suckleyi* — Alaska and British Columbia to n Washington
    ____ *F. c. columbarius* — North America (except for Pacific coast and Great Plains)
    ____ *F. c. richardsoni* — Great Plains of North America (central Alberta to Wyoming)

☐ **Bat Falcon** *Falco rufigularis*
    ____ *F. r. petoensis* — Humid lowlands of n Mexico to s Ecuador (west of the Andes)
    ____ *F. r. rufigularis* — Lowlands of n S America to s Brazil and n Argentina; Trinidad
    ____ *F. r. ophryophanes* — Tableland of Brazil, adjacent Bolivia, Paraguay and Argentina

☐ **Orange-breasted Falcon** *Falco deiroleucus*

Locally from s Mexico to n Argentina and Brazil

☐ **Eurasian Hobby** *Falco subbuteo*
____ *F. s. subbuteo*
____ *F. s. streichi*

Palearctic; winters to s Africa, s Eurasia and Greater Sundas
S and e China to Myanmar and n Indochina

☐ **African Hobby** *Falco cuvierii*

Savanna of Africa south of the Sahara

☐ **Oriental Hobby** *Falco severus*

S Asia, Malay Arch. and New Guinea region; winters to s India

☐ **Australian Hobby** *Falco longipennis*
____ *F. l. hanieli*
____ *F. l. longipennis*

Lesser Sundas (Lombok to Timor)
Australia and Tasmania; winters to New Guinea and Moluccas

☐ **New Zealand Falcon** *Falco novaeseelandiae*

Locally in New Zealand, Stewart I. and Auckland Islands

☐ **Brown Falcon** *Falco berigora*
____ *F. b. novaeguineae*
____ *F. b. berigora*
____ *F. b. occidentalis*

E and central New Guinea and coastal n Australia
Australia (except west and south) and Tasmania
SW and w-central Australia

☐ **Gray Falcon** *Falco hypoleucos*

Arid interior and coastal Australia

☐ **Black Falcon** *Falco subniger*

Woodlands and grasslands of Australia

☐ **Lanner Falcon** *Falco biarmicus*
____ *F. b. feldeggii*
____ *F. b. erlangeri*
____ *F. b. tanypterus*
____ *F. b. abyssinicus*
____ *F. b. biarmicus*

Sicily and s Italy to Armenia, Azerbaijan and Lebanon
Mauritania to Morocco and Tunisia
Egypt and Sudan to Arabia, Israel and Iraq
Senegal and Ghana to Ethiopia, Somalia, Uganda and n Zaire
Angola to s Zaire, Kenya and South Africa

☐ **Laggar Falcon** *Falco jugger*

SE Iran to India and Myanmar

☐ **Saker Falcon** *Falco cherrug*
____ *F. c. cherrug*
____ *F. c. milvipes*

S-cent. Eurasia to Altai Mts.; winters to ne Africa and nw India
NE Asia; winters to Iran, nw India, Tibet and central China

☐ **Gyrfalcon** *Falco rusticolus*

Mountains and tundra of n Palearctic region and n North America

☐ **Prairie Falcon** *Falco mexicanus*

Arid North America (British Columbia to n Mexico)

☐ **Barbary Falcon** *Falco pelegrinoides*

Canary Islands; locally from n Africa (Morocco) to w Iran

☐ **Taita Falcon** *Falco fasciinucha*

Locally in highlands of sw Ethiopia to sw Mozambique

☐ **Peregrine Falcon** *Falco peregrinus*
____ *F. p. tundrius*
____ *F. p. anatum*
____ *F. p. pealei*
____ *F. p. cassini*
____ *F. p. japonensis*
____ *F. p. furuitii*
____ *F. p. calidus*
____ *F. p. peregrinus*
____ *F. p. brookei*
____ *F. p. babylonicus*
____ *F. p. madens*

Arctic tundra of North America (Alaska to Greenland)
North America (south of tundra) to n Mexico
Coastal w North America (Aleutian Islands to Washington)
W South America (Ecuador to Tierra del Fuego and Falkland Is.)
NE Siberia to Kamchatka Peninsula and Japan
Volcano Islands and Bonin Islands
Tundra of Eurasia (Lapland to ne Siberia)
N Eurasia (south of the tundra)
Mediterranean basin east to the Caucasus Mountains
E Iran to Mongolia
Cape Verde Islands

____	*F. p. minor*	Morocco, Mauritania and Africa south of the Sahara
____	*F. p. radama*	Madagascar and Comoro Islands
____	*F. p. peregrinator*	Pakistan, India and Sri Lanka to se China
____	*F. p. ernesti*	Philippines to New Guinea, Bismarck Arch. and Indonesia
____	*F. p. nesiotes*	Vanuatu and New Caledonia
____	*F. p. macropus*	Australia (expect for sw part)
____	*F. p. submelanogenys*	SW Australia

ORDER: GALLIFORMES
FAMILY: MEGAPODIIDAE (Megapodes—21)

☐ **Australian Brush-turkey** *Alectura lathami*

____	*A. l. purpureicollis*	NE Australia (n Queensland)
____	*A. l. lathami*	E Australia (central and s Queensland to New South Wales)

☐ **Wattled Brush-turkey** *Aepypodius arfakianus*

____	*A. a. arfakianus*	High mountains of New Guinea and Yapen I.
____	*A. a. misoliensis*	Mountains of Misool I. (off nw New Guinea)

☐ **Bruijn's Brush-turkey** *Aepypodius bruijnii*

Waigeo I. (off New Guinea)

☐ **Red-billed Brush-turkey** *Talegalla cuvieri*

Lowlands of nw New Guinea, Misool and Salawati islands

☐ **Black-billed Brush-turkey** *Talegalla fuscirostris*

____	*T. f. occidentis*	Lowlands of sw New Guinea and Aru Islands
____	*T. f. fuscirostris*	Lowlands of se New Guinea

☐ **Brown-collared Brush-turkey** *Talegalla jobiensis*

____	*T. j. jobiensis*	Lowland forests of n-central New Guinea and Yapen I.
____	*T. j. longicauda*	Lowland forests of e New Guinea

☐ **Malleefowl** *Leipoa ocellata*

Scrub and heath of sw and s Australia

☐ **Maleo** *Macrocephalon maleo*

Sulawesi, Bangka, Lembeh and Butung islands

☐ **Moluccan Scrubfowl** *Megapodius wallacei*

Moluccas and Misool I.

☐ **Niaufoou Scrubfowl** *Megapodius pritchardii*

Forests of Niuafo'ou I. (n Tonga)

☐ **Micronesian Scrubfowl** *Megapodius laperouse*

____	*M. l. laperouse*	Locally in n Mariana Islands
____	*M. l. senex*	Locally on Palau Is. (w Caroline Islands)

☐ **Nicobar Scrubfowl** *Megapodius nicobariensis*

____	*M. n. nicobariensis*	Lowlands of central and n Nicobar Islands
____	*M. n. abbotti*	Lowlands of Great Nicobar I. and Little Nicobar I.

☐ **Tabon Scrubfowl** *Megapodius cumingii*

____	*M. c. pusillus*	N and e Philippine Islands
____	*M. c. cumingii*	N Borneo, Palawan and Sulu Archipelago
____	*M. c. gilberti*	Sulawesi, Talisei, Tendila, Lembeh and Togian islands
____	*M. c. talautensis*	Talaud Islands (n Moluccas)
____	*M. c. sanghirensis*	Sangihe, Siau, Tahulandang and Ruang islands (off Sulawesi)

☐ **Sula Scrubfowl** *Megapodius bernsteinii*

Lowlands of Banggai and Sula islands (off Sulawesi)

☐ **Tanimbar Scrubfowl** *Megapodius tenimberensis*

Tanimbar I. (Banda Sea)

☐ **Dusky Scrubfowl** *Megapodius freycinet*
____ *M. f. freycinet* — N Moluccas and west Papuan islands (off New Guinea)
____ *M. f. geelvinkianus* — Islands in Geelvink Bay (n New Guinea)

☐ **Forsten's Scrubfowl** *Megapodius forstenii*

Moluccas (Ambon, Seram, Haruku, Gorang and Buru)

☐ **Melanesian Scrubfowl** *Megapodius eremita*

Admiralty Is., New Britain, New Ireland and Solomon Is.

☐ **Vanuatu Scrubfowl** *Megapodius layardi*

Forests of Vanuatu and Banks Group

☐ **New Guinea Scrubfowl** *Megapodius affinis*

N New Guinea and adjacent islands

☐ **Orange-footed Scrubfowl** *Megapodius reinwardt*
____ *M. r. buruensis* — Buru I. (s Moluccas)
____ *M. r. forstenii* — S Moluccas (Seram, Ambon and adjacent islands)
____ *M. r. reinwardt* — Lesser Sundas, se Moluccas, Aru and adjacent islands
____ *M. r. macgillivrayi* — D'Entrecasteaux and Louisiade archipelagos
____ *M. r. tumulus* — N Australia
____ *M. r. yorki* — NE Australia (Cape York Peninsula and adjacent islands)
____ *M. r. castanonotus* — E Queensland (Cooktown to Yeppoon and offshore islands)

ORDER: GALLIFORMES
FAMILY: CRACIDAE (Guans, Chachalacas and Curassows—50)

☐ **Plain Chachalaca** *Ortalis vetula*
____ *O. v. mccallii* — Extreme s Texas to ne Mexico (n Veracuz)
____ *O. v. vetula* — SE Mexico (s Veracruz) to nw Costa Rica
____ *O. v. pallidiventris* — SE Mexico (n Yucatán Peninsula)
____ *O. v. deschauenseei* — Utila I. (off n Honduras)

☐ **Gray-headed Chachalaca** *Ortalis cinereiceps*

Tropical e Honduras to nw Colombia

☐ **Chestnut-winged Chachalaca** *Ortalis garrula*

Woodlands and scrub of n Colombia

☐ **Rufous-vented Chachalaca** *Ortalis ruficauda*
____ *O. r. ruficrissa* — Tropical n Colombia and nw Venezuela
____ *O. r. ruficauda* — NE Colombia to n Venezuela, Tobago and Isla Margarita

☐ **Rufous-headed Chachalaca** *Ortalis erythroptera*

W Ecuador and extreme nw Peru

☐ **Rufous-bellied Chachalaca** *Ortalis wagleri*

Semiarid nw Mexico (Sonora to Jalisco)

☐ **West Mexican Chachalaca** *Ortalis poliocephala*

Semiarid w Mexico (c Jalisco and Michoacán to Chiapas)

☐ **Chaco Chachalaca** *Ortalis canicollis*
____ *O. c. canicollis* — *Chaco* of e Bolivia to w Paraguay and n Argentina
____ *O. c. pantanalensis* — W Brazil (sw Mato Grosso)

☐ **White-bellied Chachalaca** *Ortalis leucogastra*

Pacific slope of s Mexico (Chiapas) to nw Costa Rica

☐ **Little Chachalaca** *Ortalis motmot*
____ *O. m. motmot* — Guianas to s Venezuela and n Amazonian Brazil
____ *O. m. ruficeps* — N-central Brazil (south of the Amazon)

☐ **Speckled Chachalaca** *Ortalis guttata*
_____ *O. g. columbiana* — N and central Colombia
_____ *O. g. guttata* — E Colombia to Ecuador, Peru, Bolivia and adjacent w Brazil
_____ *O. g. subaffinis* — E and ne Bolivia and adjacent Brazil
_____ *O. g. araucuan* — E Brazil
_____ *O. g. squamata* — SE Brazil

☐ **Buff-browed Chachalaca** *Ortalis superciliaris*

NE Brazil south of the Amazon (Pará to Piauí and n Goiás)

☐ **Band-tailed Guan** *Penelope argyrotis*
_____ *P. a. albicauda* — Sierra de Perijá (Colombia/ Venezuela border)
_____ *P. a. colombiana* — Santa Marta Mountains (ne Colombia)
_____ *P. a. argyrotis* — Montane forests of n Colombia and n Venezuela

☐ **Bearded Guan** *Penelope barbata*

Locally in Western Andes of sw Ecuador and nw Peru

☐ **Baudo Guan** *Penelope ortoni*

W slope of Andes of Colombia and Ecuador

☐ **Andean Guan** *Penelope montagnii*
_____ *P. m. montagnii* — N and central Colombia and nw Venezuela
_____ *P. m. atrogularis* — W slope of Andes of s Colombia and Ecuador
_____ *P. m. brooki* — E slope of Andes of s Colombia and Ecuador
_____ *P. m. plumosa* — E slope of Andes of Peru
_____ *P. m. sclateri* — *Yungas* of Bolivia

☐ **Marail Guan** *Penelope marail*
_____ *P. m. marail* — Tropical Guianas and e Venezuela (south of the Orinoco)
_____ *P. m. jacupeba* — SE Venezuela and n Amazonian Brazil

☐ **Rusty-margined Guan** *Penelope superciliaris*
_____ *P. s. superciliaris* — Amazonian Brazil
_____ *P. s. jacupemba* — Central and s Brazil to e Bolivia
_____ *P. s. major* — Extreme s Brazil to e Paraguay and ne Argentina

☐ **Red-faced Guan** *Penelope dabbenei*

Humid Andes of se Bolivia to extreme nw Argentina

☐ **Crested Guan** *Penelope purpurascens*
_____ *P. p. purpurascens* — Humid forests of Mexico to Honduras and Nicaragua
_____ *P. p. aequatorialis* — S Honduras and Nicaragua to nw Colombia and se Ecuador
_____ *P. p. brunnescens* — N Colombia to e Venezuela

☐ **Cauca Guan** *Penelope perspicax*

Subtropical W and C Andes of Colombia (possibly extinct)

☐ **White-winged Guan** *Penelope albipennis*

Dry forests of nw Peru (Tumbes, Piura and Lambayeque)

☐ **Spix's Guan** *Penelope jacquacu*
_____ *P. j. granti* — S Venezuela to the Guianas and n Amazonian Brazil
_____ *P. j. orienticola* — SE Venezuela and nw Brazil north of the Amazon
_____ *P. j. jacquacu* — E Colombia to Bolivia and adjacent w Amazonian Brazil
_____ *P. j. speciosa* — E Bolivia

☐ **Dusky-legged Guan** *Penelope obscura*
_____ *P. o. bronzina* — E Brazil (Espíritu Santo to Santa Catarina)
_____ *P. o. obscura* — Extreme se Brazil to se Paraguay, Uruguay and ne Argentina
_____ *P. o. bridgesi* — E slope of Andes of Bolivia to nw Argentina

☐ **White-crested Guan** *Penelope pileata*

Amazonian Brazil (lower Rio Madeira to Rio Tapajós)

☐ **Chestnut-bellied Guan** *Penelope ochrogaster*

Lowlands of e Brazil (west to Mato Grosso)

☐ **White-browed Guan** *Penelope jacucaca*

Interior ne Brazil (Ceará and Paraíba to Bahia)

☐ **Blue-throated Piping-Guan** *Pipile cumanensis*
____ *P. c. cumanensis* E Colombia to Venezuela, the Guianas, w Brazil and Peru
____ *P. c. grayi* SW Brazil to Bolivia, ne Paraguay and se Peru

☐ **Trinidad Piping-Guan** *Pipile pipile*

Forests of Trinidad (seriously endangered)

☐ **Red-throated Piping-Guan** *Pipile cujubi*
____ *P. c. cujubi* Forests of w Amazonian Brazil (Rio Madeira to n Pará)
____ *P. c. nattereri* W Amazonian Brazil to extreme ne Bolivia

☐ **Black-fronted Piping-Guan** *Pipile jacutinga*

E Brazil (Bahia) to se Paraguay and ne Argentina

☐ **Wattled Guan** *Aburria aburri*

Montane forests of w Venezuela to n Peru

☐ **Black Guan** *Chamaepetes unicolor*

Montane forests of Costa Rica and w Panama

☐ **Sickle-winged Guan** *Chamaepetes goudotii*
____ *C. g. goudotii* Andes of n Colombia
____ *C. g. sanctaemarthae* Santa Marta Mountains (ne Colombia)
____ *C. g. fagani* W slope of Andes of sw Colombia and Ecuador
____ *C. g. tschudii* E slope of Andes of s Colombia, Ecuador and n Peru
____ *C. g. rufiventris* E slope of Andes of central Peru
____ *C. g. ssp.* Undescribed race from mountains of Bolivia (La Paz)

☐ **Highland Guan** *Penelopina nigra*

Humid montane forests of s Mexico to Nicaragua

☐ **Horned Guan** *Oreophasis derbianus*

Humid forests of s Mexico (Chiapas) and Guatemala

☐ **Nocturnal Curassow** *Nothocrax urumutum*

Humid s Venezuela to ne Peru and w Amazonian Brazil

☐ **Crestless Curassow** *Mitu tomentosa*

Guyana to s Venezuela, e Colombia and adjacent nw Brazil

☐ **Salvin's Curassow** *Mitu salvini*

Humid lowlands of s Colombia to e Ecuador and ne Peru

☐ **Razor-billed Curassow** *Mitu tuberosa*

Tropical se Colombia to n Bolivia and Amazonian Brazil

☐ **Alagoas Curassow** *Mitu mitu*

Coastal e Brazil (Alagoas); possibly extinct in wild

☐ **Helmeted Curassow** *Pauxi pauxi*
____ *P. p. pauxi* Montane forests of Venezuela and adjacent ne Colombia
____ *P. p. gilliardi* Sierra de Perijá (Colombia/Venezuela border)

☐ **Horned Curassow** *Pauxi unicornis*
____ *P. u. koepckeae* Andes of se Peru (Cerros del Sira)
____ *P. u. unicornis* E slope of Andes of central Bolivia

☐ **Great Curassow** *Crax rubra*
____ *C. r. rubra* Humid forests of e Mexico to w Ecuador
____ *C. r. griscomi* Cozumel I. (off Yucatán coast of Mexico). Possibly extirpated

☐ **Blue-knobbed Curassow** *Crax alberti*

Humid forests of n Colombia

☐ **Yellow-knobbed Curassow** *Crax daubentoni*

Llanos of ne Colombia and adjacent n Venezuela

☐ **Black Curassow** *Crax alector*
    ____ *C. a. erythrognatha*   E Colombia and Venezuela (south of the Orinoco River)
    ____ *C. a. alector*   Extreme e Venezuela to Guianas and Brazil (n of the Amazon)

☐ **Bare-faced Curassow** *Crax fasciolata*
    ____ *C. f. pinima*   NE Brazil
    ____ *C. f. fasciolata*   Lowlands of Brazil to Paraguay and ne Argentina
    ____ *C. f. grayi*   E Bolivia

☐ **Wattled Curassow** *Crax globulosa*
    Humid se Colombia to n Bolivia and w Amazonian Brazil

☐ **Red-billed Curassow** *Crax blumenbachii*
    Lowland forests of se Brazil (on verge of extinction)

ORDER: GALLIFORMES
FAMILY: MELEAGRIDIDAE (Turkeys—2

☐ **Wild Turkey** *Meleagris gallopavo*
    ____ *M. g. silvestris*   Central and e US
    ____ *M. g. osceola*   Locally in Florida
    ____ *M. g. intermedia*   N Texas to e-central Mexico
    ____ *M. g. merriami*   Western US
    ____ *M. g. mexicana*   Mountains west of central plateau of Mexico
    ____ *M. g. gallopavo*   S Mexico (Jalisco to Veracruz and south to Guerrero)

☐ **Ocellated Turkey** *Meleagris ocellata*
    SE Mexico (Yucatán Pen.) to n Guatemala (Petén) and Belize

ORDER: GALLIFORMES
FAMILY: TETRAONIDAE (Grouse, Ptarmigans and Prairie-chickens—17)

☐ **Spruce Grouse** *Falcipennis canadensis*
    ____ *F. c. osgoodi*   Alaska and Yukon to Great Slave Lake and Lake Athabasca
    ____ *F. c. atratus*   S Alaska (Bristol Bay) to Prince William Sound and Kodiak I.
    ____ *F. c. franklinii*   Coniferous forests of extreme se Alaska to nw US
    ____ *F. c. canadensis*   Coniferous forests of Canada (central Alberta to Labrador)
    ____ *F. c. canace*   SE Canada and adjacent US (Minnesota to Maine)
    ____ *F. c. torridus*   Nova Scotia

☐ **Blue Grouse** *Dendragapus obscurus*
    ____ *D. o. sitkensis*   SE Alaska to Queen Charlotte Islands
    ____ *D. o. fuliginosus*   Yukon/Alaska border to nw California; Vancouver I.
    ____ *D. o. richardsoni*   Alaska and s Yukon to Idaho, w Montana and nw Wyoming
    ____ *D. o. pallidus*   S-central British Columbia to e Washington and ne Oregon
    ____ *D. o. sierrae*   Cascades from Washington to California and Nevada
    ____ *D. o. howardi*   S California (s Sierra Nevada and Tehachapi Mountains)
    ____ *D. o. oreinus*   Mountains of ne Nevada and adjacent Utah
    ____ *D. o. obscurus*   Mts. of Wyoming to Colorado, Arizona and New Mexico

☐ **Siberian Grouse** *Dendragapus falcipennis*
    Coniferous forests of ne Asia

☐ **White-tailed Ptarmigan** *Lagopus leucurus*
    ____ *L. l. peninsularis*   Mountains of s-central Alaska to Glacier Bay and White Pass
    ____ *L. l. leucurus*   N Yukon, w Br. Columbia and w Alberta to n border of US
    ____ *L. l. saxatilis*   Higher peaks of Vancouver I.
    ____ *L. l. rainierensis*   Alpine summits of Cascades of Washington
    ____ *L. l. altipetens*   Rocky Mountains (Montana to New Mexico)

☐ **Willow Ptarmigan** *Lagopus lagopus*

____	*L. l. scoticus*	British Isles
____	*L. l. variegatus*	Coastal Norway (islands off Trondheim Fjord)
____	*L. l. lagopus*	Scandinavia and n Russia
____	*L. l. rossicus*	Baltic countries to central Russia
____	*L. l. birulai*	New Siberian Islands
____	*L. l. koreni*	Siberia to Kamchatka Peninsula
____	*L. l. kamtschatkensis*	Kamchatka Peninsula and Kuril Islands
____	*L. l. maior*	Steppes of sw Siberia and n Kazakstan
____	*L. l. brevirostris*	Altai Mountains and Sayan Mountains
____	*L. l. kozlowae*	W Mongolia (Tanmu-Ola, Khangai and Kentei Mountains)
____	*L. l. sserebrowsky*	E Siberia (Lake Baikal to Sea of Okhotsk and Sikhote Alin Mts.)
____	*L. l. okadai*	Sakhalin I.
____	*L. l. muriei*	E Aleutian Islands and Kodiak I.
____	*L. l. alexandrae*	Alaskan Peninsula to nw British Columbia
____	*L. l. alascensis*	Alaska
____	*L. l. leucopterus*	Arctic islands of n Canada and adjacent mainland to s Baffin I.
____	*L. l. albus*	Tundra of n Yukon and c Br. Columbia to Gulf of St. Lawrence
____	*L. l. ungavus*	N Quebec and n Labrador
____	*L. l. alleni*	Newfoundland

☐ **Rock Ptarmigan** *Lagopus mutus*

____	*L. m. hyperboreus*	Svalbard, Franz Josef Land and Bear I.
____	*L. m. mutus*	Norway, n Sweden, n Finland and Kola Peninsula
____	*L. m. millaisi*	Scotland
____	*L. m. pyrenaicus*	Pyrénées
____	*L. m. helveticus*	Alps (Savoie to central Austria)
____	*L. m. komensis*	N Ural Mountains
____	*L. m. pleskei*	N Siberia (Taymyr Peninsula to Chukotsk Peninsula)
____	*L. m. macrorhynchus*	Tarbagatay Mountains (Russia)
____	*L. m. ssp.*	Undescribed race from Pamir Alaï Mts. (Tajikistan)
____	*L. m. nadezdae*	Mountains of s Siberia and Mongolia
____	*L. m. transbaicalicus*	SE Siberia (Lake Baikal to Sea of Okhotsk)
____	*L. m. kraschennikovi*	Kamchatka Peninsula
____	*L. m. ridgwayi*	Komandorskiye Islands
____	*L. m. kurilensis*	Kuril Islands
____	*L. m. japonicus*	Honshu I. (Japan)
____	*L. m. evermanni*	Attu I. (Aleutian Islands)
____	*L. m. townsendi*	Aleutian Islands (Kiska and Little Kiska)
____	*L. m. gabrielsoni*	Aleutian Islands (Amchitka, Little Sitkin and Rats)
____	*L. m. sanfordi*	Aleutian Islands (Tanaga and Kanaga)
____	*L. m. chamberlaini*	Adak I. (Aleutian Islands)
____	*L. m. atkhensis*	Atka I. (Aleutian Islands)
____	*L. m. yunaskensis*	Yunaska I. (Aleutian Islands)
____	*L. m. nelsoni*	Aleutian Islands (Unimak, Unalaska and Amaknak)
____	*L. m. dixoni*	Coasts and mountains of Glacier Bay to nw British Columbia
____	*L. m. kelloggae*	Alaska and n Yukon
____	*L. m. rupestris*	Tundra of n North America
____	*L. m. saturatus*	NW Greenland
____	*L. m. captus*	E Greenland
____	*L. m. reinhardti*	SW Greenland
____	*L. m. welchi*	Newfoundland
____	*L. m. islandorum*	Iceland

☐ **Black-billed Capercaillie** *Tetrao parvirostris*

____	*T. p. parvirostris*	E Siberia to n Manchuria, Ussuriland and Sakhalin I.
____	*T. p. kamschaticus*	Kamchatka Peninsula
____	*T. p. stegmanni*	Lake Baikal region, Sayan Mountains and n Mongolia

☐ **Eurasian Capercaillie** *Tetrao urogallus*

_____	*T. u. cantabricus*	Cantabrian Mountains (nw Spain)
_____	*T. u. aquitanicus*	Pyrénées
_____	*T. u. major*	Germany to sw Baltic countries and Balkan Peninsula
_____	*T. u. rudolfi*	Carpathian Mountains and Rhodope Mountains
_____	*T. u. urogallus*	Scandinavia
_____	*T. u. lonnbergi*	Kola Peninsula
_____	*T. u. karelicus*	Finland and n Russian (Karelia)
_____	*T. u. pleskei*	Belarus, n Ukraine and European Russia
_____	*T. u. obsoletus*	N Russia and n Siberia to upper Lena River
_____	*T. u. volgensis*	Central and se Russia
_____	*T. u. uralensis*	S Ural Mountains and sw Siberia
_____	*T. u. taczanowskii*	Central Siberia to Altai Mountains and nw Mongolia

☐ **Black Grouse** *Tetrao tetrix*

_____	*T. t. britannicus*	N England, Scotland and Inner Hebrides
_____	*T. t. tetrix*	Scandinavia to France and n Italy east to Siberia
_____	*T. t. viridanus*	SE Russia to Siberian steppes
_____	*T. t. tschusii*	S Siberia south to nw Altai and Sayan mountains
_____	*T. t. baikalensis*	SE Siberia to n Mongolia and nw Manchuria
_____	*T. t. mongolicus*	Russian Altai to Chinese Turkestan
_____	*T. t. ussuriensis*	SE Siberia (Lake Baikal) to nw Korea and n Mongolia

☐ **Caucasian Grouse** *Tetrao mlokosiewiczi*

	Caucasus Mountains to ne Turkey and nw Iran

☐ **Hazel Grouse** *Bonasa bonasia*

_____	*B. b. styriaca*	Jura Mountains, Alps, Hungary, Slovakia and s Poland
_____	*B. b. rhenana*	NE France, Luxembourg, Belgium and West Germany
_____	*B. b. rupestris*	S Germany, Bohemia and Sudety Mountains
_____	*B. b. schiebeli*	Balkan Peninsula
_____	*B. b. volgensis*	Poland and Ukraine to central European Russia
_____	*B. b. bonasia*	S Scandinavia, Finland and n European Russia to Ural Mts.
_____	*B. b. griseonota*	N Sweden
_____	*B. b. sibirica*	Siberia to Altai Mountains, Sayan Mountains and n Mongolia
_____	*B. b. kolymensis*	Extreme e Siberia to Sea of Okhotsk
_____	*B. b. amurensis*	S Amurland and Little Khingan Mountains to n Korea
_____	*B. b. yamashinai*	Sakhalin (Russia)
_____	*B. b. vicinitas*	Hokkaido (n Japan)

☐ **Severtzov's Grouse** *Bonasa sewerzowi*

	Mts. of w China (Gansu to e Tibet, nw Yunnan and n Sichuan)

☐ **Ruffed Grouse** *Bonasa umbellus*

_____	*B. u. yukonensis*	W Alaska and Yukon to s Mackenzie and nw Saskatchewan
_____	*B. u. umbelloides*	SE Alaska to British Columbia and east to Quebec
_____	*B. u. labradorensis*	Labrador
_____	*B. u. sabini*	Coastal sw British Columbia to nw California
_____	*B. u. brunnescens*	Vancouver I. and adjacent mainland
_____	*B. u. castanea*	Olympic Peninsula (nw Washington)
_____	*B. u. affinis*	Inland British Columbia to Washington and central Oregon
_____	*B. u. phaia*	SE Br. Columbia and e Washington to Rocky Mts. of s Idaho
_____	*B. u. incana*	SE Idaho, Wyoming, N Dakota to Colorado and w S Dakota
_____	*B. u. mediana*	Minnesota and s Wisconsin
_____	*B. u. togata*	S Ontario and s Quebec to n Wisconsin, c Michigan and c NY
_____	*B. u. thayeri*	Nova Scotia
_____	*B. u. umbellus*	NY and Massachusetts to e Pennsylvania and New Jersey
_____	*B. u. monticola*	S Michigan, Ohio and Pennsylvania to n Georgia

☐ **Sage Grouse** *Centrocercus urophasianus*

Prairies and sage grasslands of w Canada to sw US

☐ **Sharp-tailed Grouse** *Tympanuchus phasianellus*

_____ *T. p. caurus*	N Alaska to s Yukon, n British Columbia and n Alberta
_____ *T. p. kennicotti*	Mackenzie River to Great Slave Lake
_____ *T. p. phasianellus*	N Manitoba to n Ontario and w-central Quebec
_____ *T. p. campestris*	S Manitoba to n Michigan, Minnesota and Wisconsin
_____ *T. p. jamesi*	N-c Alberta and Saskatchewan to Colorado and Nebraska
_____ *T. p. columbianus*	N-c British Columbia to e Oregon, n Utah and w Colorado

☐ **Greater Prairie-Chicken** *Tympanuchus cupido*

_____ *T. c. cupido†*	Formerly ne US; extirpated ca 1932
_____ *T. c. pinnatus*	S-central Canada to ne Texas
_____ *T. c. attwateri*	Coastal se Texas

☐ **Lesser Prairie-Chicken** *Tympanuchus pallidicinctus*

Arid grasslands of s-central US

ORDER: GALLIFORMES
FAMILY: ODONTOPHORIDAE (New World Quail—31)

☐ **Bearded Wood-Partridge** *Dendrortyx barbatus*

Humid montane forests of ne Mexico

☐ **Long-tailed Wood-Partridge** *Dendrortyx macroura*

_____ *D. m. macroura*	S Mexico (valley of México and Veracruz)
_____ *D. m. diversus*	SW Mexico (montane oak-pine forests of nw Jalisco)
_____ *D. m. griseipectus*	W slope of mts. of Distrito Federal, México and Morelos
_____ *D. m. striatus*	SW Mexico (s Jalisco to Michoacán and Guerrero)
_____ *D. m. inesperatus*	S Mexico (Chilpancingo area of Guerrero)
_____ *D. m. oaxacae*	S Mexico (montane oak-pine forests w Oaxaca)

☐ **Buffy-crowned Wood-Partridge** *Dendrortyx leucophrys*

_____ *D. l. leucophrys*	Mountains of s Mexico (Chiapas) to Nicaragua
_____ *D. l. hypospodius*	Mountains of n Costa Rica

☐ **Mountain Quail** *Oreortyx pictus*

_____ *O. p. pictus*	Cascades of Washington to coastal mountains of c California
_____ *O. p. plumiferus*	S Washington to w Nevada and central California
_____ *O. p. russelli*	S California (Little San Bernardino Mountains)
_____ *O. p. palmeri*	S Washington to c California (nw San Luis Obispo County)
_____ *O. p. eremophila*	Sierra Nevada of s California to n Baja, extreme sw Nevada
_____ *O. p. confinis*	Mts. of n Baja California (Sierra Juárez and San Pedro Mártir)

☐ **Scaled Quail** *Callipepla squamata*

_____ *C. s. hargravi*	SE Colorado to Oklahoma, sw Kansas and nw Texas
_____ *C. s. pallida*	S Arizona to w Texas, n Sonora and Chihuahua
_____ *C. s. squamata*	N Mexico (n Sonora and Tamaulipas s to valley of México)
_____ *C. s. castanogastris*	S Texas to n Mexico (Tamaulipas, Nuevo León, e Coahuila)

☐ **Elegant Quail** *Callipepla douglasii*

_____ *C. d. bensoni*	Arid nw Mexico (Sonora)
_____ *C. d. languens*	Arid nw Mexico (w Chihuahua)
_____ *C. d. douglasii*	W Mexico (extreme s Sonora to Sinaloa and nw Durango)
_____ *C. d. impedita*	Arid w Mexico (Nayarit)
_____ *C. d. teres*	Arid w Mexico (nw Jalisco)

☐ **California Quail** *Callipepla californica*

____	*C. c. californica*	N Oregon and w Nevada to s California and Coronados Islands
____	*C. c. orecta*	SE Oregon (Warner Valley) and extreme n California
____	*C. c. brunnescens*	Extreme n coastal California to s Santa Cruz County
____	*C. c. catalinensis*	Santa Catalina I. (off s California)
____	*C. c. canfieldae*	Owens Valley of e-central California
____	*C. c. plumbea*	San Diego County south through nw Baja California
____	*C. c. decoloratus*	Baja California between latitude 25°N and 30°N
____	*C. c. achrustera*	S Baja California

☐ **Gambel's Quail** *Callipepla gambelii*

____	*C. g. gambelii*	Utah and Nevada to Colorado, Mohave deserts and ne Baja
____	*C. g. sana*	Arid scrub of w Colorado
____	*C. g. ignoscens*	S New Mexico and extreme w Texas
____	*C. g. pembertoni*	Isla Tiburón (Gulf of California)
____	*C. g. fulvipectus*	SE Arizona and sw New Mexico to nw Mexico (s Sonora)
____	*C. g. stephensi*	W Mexico (s Sonora adjacent to Sinaloa border)
____	*C. g. friedmanni*	W Mexico (coastal Sonora from Río Fuerte to Río Culiacán)

☐ **Banded Quail** *Philortyx fasciatus*

Arid w Mexico (sw Jalisco to se Guerrero, Morelos and Puebla)

☐ **Northern Bobwhite** *Colinus virginianus*

____	*C. v. marilandicus*	NE US (se Maine to Pennsylvania and central Virginia)
____	*C. v. virginianus*	Atlantic coast (Virginia to n Florida and se Alabama)
____	*C. v. floridanus*	Peninsular Florida
____	*C. v. cubanensis*	Cuba and Isle of Pines
____	*C. v. mexicanus*	E US west of Atlantic seaboard to Great Plains
____	*C. v. taylori*	S Dakota to n Texas, w Missouri and nw Arkansas
____	*C. v. texanus*	SW Texas to n Mexico (Coahuila, Nuevo León, Tamaulipas)
____	*C. v. ridgwayi*	NW Mexico (n-central Sonora); extirpated in Arizona
____	*C. v. maculatus*	E Mexico (c Tamaulipas to n Veracruz and se San Luis Potosí)
____	*C. v. aridus*	E Mexico (c and w-central Tamaulipas to se San Luis Potosí)
____	*C. v. graysoni*	W-c Mexico (s Nayarit to Morelos, s Hidalgo, San Luis Potosí)
____	*C. v. nigripectus*	E Mexico (Puebla, Morelos and México)
____	*C. v. pectoralis*	SE Mexico (e slopes of mountains of central Veracruz)
____	*C. v. godmani*	Lowlands of se Mexico (Veracruz)
____	*C. v. minor*	SE Mexico (ne Chiapas and adjacent Tabasco)
____	*C. v. atriceps*	S Mexico (interior of w Oaxaca)
____	*C. v. thayeri*	S Mexico (ne Oaxaca)
____	*C. v. harrisoni*	S Mexico (sw Oaxaca)
____	*C. v. coyolcos*	Pacific coast of s Mexico (Oaxaca and Chiapas)
____	*C. v. salvini*	S Mexico (coastal southern Chiapas)
____	*C. v. insignis (nelsoni)*	S Mexico (s Chiapas) and adjacent Guatemala

☐ **Black-throated Bobwhite** *Colinus nigrogularis*

____	*C. n. persiccus*	SE Mexico (Progresso area of Yucatán Peninsula)
____	*C. n. caboti*	SE Mexico (n Campeche, Yucatán and n Quintana Roo)
____	*C. n. nigrogularis*	Belize and adjacent n Guatemala
____	*C. n. segoviensis*	E Honduras and ne Nicaragua

☐ **Crested Bobwhite** *Colinus cristatus*

____	*C. c. incanus*	S Guatemala
____	*C. c. hypoleucus*	W El Salvador and adjacent Guatemala
____	*C. c. leucopogon*	SE El Salvador and w Honduras
____	*C. c. leylandi*	NW Honduras
____	*C. c. sclateri*	Central Honduras to nw Nicaragua
____	*C. c. dickeyi*	NW and central Costa Rica
____	*C. c. mariae*	Savanna of e Panama (Chiriquí)

____	*Colinus cristatus panamensis*	Lowlands of Pacific slope of Panama
____	*C. c. decoratus*	Caribbean coast of Colombia
____	*C. c. cristatus*	NE Colombia and nw Venezuela
____	*C. c. continentis*	Coastal nw Venezuela, Aruba and Curaçao
____	*C. c. littoralis*	N base of Santa Marta Mountains (ne Colombia)
____	*C. c. badius*	Cauca Valley to Pacific slope of Western Andes of Colombia
____	*C. c. leucotis*	N Colombia (Magdalena and Sinú valleys)
____	*C. c. bogotensis*	E Andes of Colombia (Boyacá and Cundinamarca)
____	*C. c. parvicristatus*	E slope of e Andes of Colombia and adjacent Venezuela
____	*C. c. horvathi*	Andes of nw Venezuela (Mérida)
____	*C. c. barnesi*	W-central Venezuela (Portuguesa and Barinas)
____	*C. c. mocquerysi*	NE Venezuela (Sucre, n Monagas and n Anzoátegui)
____	*C. c. sonnini*	Coastal n Venezuela to the Guianas and extreme n Brazil

☐ **Marbled Wood-Quail** *Odontophorus gujanensis*

____	*O. g. castigatus*	SW Costa Rica and (?) w Panama
____	*O. g. marmoratus*	E Panama to n Colombia and nw Venezuela
____	*O. g. gujanensis*	SE Venezuela to the Guianas, Brazil and extreme ne Paraguay
____	*O. g. medius*	S Venezuela to nw Brazil
____	*O. g. buckleyi*	Base of Eastern Andes of Colombia to e Ecuador and n Peru
____	*O. g. rufogularis*	NE Peru (upper Río Javarí)
____	*O. g. pachyrhynchus*	E-central Peru (Junín and Ayacucho)
____	*O. g. simonsi*	Tropical e Bolivia

☐ **Spot-winged Wood-Quail** *Odontophorus capueira*

____	*O. c. plumbeicollis*	Tropical ne Brazil (Ceará and Alagoas)
____	*O. c. capueira*	Tropical e Brazil to e Paraguay and ne Argentina

☐ **Black-eared Wood-Quail** *Odontophorus melanotis*

____	*O. m. verecundus*	Humid Caribbean lowlands of Honduras
____	*O. m. melanotis*	SE Honduras to Nicaragua, Costa Rica and Panama

☐ **Rufous-fronted Wood-Quail** *Odontophorus erythrops*

____	*O. e. parambae*	Tropical Colombia and w Ecuador
____	*O. e. erythrops*	Tropical sw Ecuador

☐ **Black-fronted Wood-Quail** *Odontophorus atrifrons*

____	*O. a. atrifrons*	Santa Marta Mountains (ne Colombia)
____	*O. a. variegatus*	E Andes of ne Colombia
____	*O. a. navai*	Sierra de Perijá (Colombia/Venezuela border)

☐ **Chestnut Wood-Quail** *Odontophorus hyperythrus*

Western and Central Andes of Colombia

☐ **Dark-backed Wood-Quail** *Odontophorus melanonotus*

Montane forests of nw Ecuador and adjacent sw Colombia

☐ **Rufous-breasted Wood-Quail** *Odontophorus speciosus*

____	*O. s. soederstroemii*	Tropical forests of e Ecuador
____	*O. s. speciosus*	Tropical e-central Peru
____	*O. s. loricatus*	Tropical se Peru and e Bolivia

☐ **Tacarcuna Wood-Quail** *Odontophorus dialeucos*

Extreme e Panama and adjacent nw Colombia (Chocó)

☐ **Gorgeted Wood-Quail** *Odontophorus strophium*

Temp. E Andes of Colombia (Santander and Cundinamarca)

☐ **Venezuelan Wood-Quail** *Odontophorus columbianus*

W Venezuela (sw Táchira) and coastal cordillera e to Miranda

☐ **Black-breasted Wood-Quail** *Odontophorus leucolaemus*

Tropical and subtropical forests of Costa Rica and w Panama

☐ **Stripe-faced Wood-Quail** *Odontophorus balliviani*

Andes of se Peru and n Bolivia

☐ **Starred Wood-Quail** *Odontophorus stellatus*

Tropical forests of w Amazon basin

☐ **Spotted Wood-Quail** *Odontophorus guttatus*

Forests of se Mexico to extreme w Panama

☐ **Singing Quail** *Dactylortyx thoracicus*

____	*D. t. pettingilli*	E Mexico (sw Tamaulipas and se San Luis Potosí)
____	*D. t. thoracicus*	E Mexico (ne Puebla and central Veracruz)
____	*D. t. devius*	W Mexico (Jalisco)
____	*D. t. molodus*	W Mexico (central Guerrero)
____	*D. t. ginetensis*	S Mexico (Chiapas/Oaxaca border region)
____	*D. t. edwardsi*	S Mexico (mountains of Chiapas adjacent to Oaxaca border)
____	*D. t. chiapensis*	S Mexico (central Chiapas)
____	*D. t. moorei*	S Mexico (mountains of central Chiapas)
____	*D. t. dolichonyx*	S Mexico (Sierra Madre del Sur of Chiapas)
____	*D. t. sharpei*	Campeche, Yucatán and Quintana Roo to Petén of Guatemala
____	*D. t. paynteri*	S Mexico (s-central Quintana Roo)
____	*D. t. calophonus*	Pacific Cordillera of Guatemala
____	*D. t. salvadoranus*	El Salvador (Volcán de San Miguel)
____	*D. t. taylori*	El Salvador (Mt. Cacaguatique region)
____	*D. t. fuscus*	Honduras (Tugucigalpa region)
____	*D. t. rufescens*	Honduras (San Juancito Mountains)
____	*D. t. conoveri*	Honduras (Department of Olancho)

☐ **Montezuma Quail** *Cyrtonyx montezumae*

____	*C. m. mearnsi*	W Texas to central Arizona and n Mexico (n Coahuila)
____	*C. m. montezumae*	E Mexico (Tamaulipas to Hidalgo, Puebla and Oaxaca)
____	*C. m. merriami*	SE Mexico (Mt. Orizaba area of Veracruz)
____	*C. m. sallei*	S Mexico (s Michoacán to Guerrero and w Oaxaca)
____	*C. m. rowleyi*	S Mexico (Sierra de Miahuatlán of Guerrero and Oaxaca)

☐ **Ocellated Quail** *Cyrtonyx ocellatus*

Oak-pine forests of s Mexico to n Nicaragua

☐ **Tawny-faced Quail** *Rhynchortyx cinctus*

____	*R. c. pudiobundus*	Caribbean lowlands of ne Honduras and e Nicaragua
____	*R. c. cinctus*	Caribbean coast of Costa Rica and Panama
____	*R. c. australis*	Pacific coast of Colombia and nw Ecuador

ORDER: GALLIFORMES
FAMILY: PHASIANIDAE (Pheasants and Partridges—155)

☐ **Snow Partridge** *Lerwa lerwa*

Himalayas of e Afghanistan to s Tibet and sw China

☐ **Verreaux's Partridge** *Tetraophasis obscurus*

Alpine mountain slopes of ne Tibet

☐ **Szecheny's Partridge** *Tetraophasis szechenyii*

Mountains of e Tibet, sw China and extreme ne India

☐ **Caucasian Snowcock** *Tetraogallus caucasicus*

Rocky heights of Caucasus Mountains

☐ **Caspian Snowcock** *Tetraogallus caspius*

____	*T. c. caspius*	Mountains of e Turkey, s Russia and w Iran
____	*T. c. semenowtianschanskii*	Zagros Mountains (sw Iran)

☐ **Altai Snowcock** *Tetraogallus altaicus*

Mountains of sw Siberia and w Mongolia

☐ **Tibetan Snowcock** *Tetraogallus tibetanus*
____ *T. t. tibetanus*	Pamir Mountains to w Tibet and Ladakh
____ *T. t. przewalskii*	NE India to w-central China and nw Sichuan
____ *T. t. aquilonifer*	W Nepal to Bhutan
____ *T. t. henrici*	E Tibet to nw Sichuan

☐ **Himalayan Snowcock** *Tetraogallus himalayensis*
____ *T. h. sewerzowi*	Tien Shan Mountains to nw China (e Xinjiang)
____ *T. h. incognitus*	Mountains of s Tajikistan and n Afghanistan
____ *T. h. himalayensis*	E Afghanistan to nw India and Nepal
____ *T. h. grombczewskii*	W China (Kunlun Mountains) to n Tibet and s Xinjiang
____ *T. h. koslowi*	W China (Nam Shan and Ching Hai Ku Mountains)

☐ **Rock Partridge** *Alectoris graeca*
____ *A. g. saxatilis*	Alps (France to Austria and w Yugoslavia) and Appennines
____ *A. g. graeca*	SE Yugoslavia to Greece and Bulgaria
____ *A. g. whitakeri*	Sicily

☐ **Chukar** *Alectoris chukar*
____ *A. c. cypriotes*	SE Bulgaria to s Syria, Crete, Rhodes, and Cyprus
____ *A. c. sinaica*	N Syrian Desert south to Sinai Peninsula
____ *A. c. kurdestanica*	Caucasus Mountains to Iran
____ *A. c. werae*	E Iraq and sw Iran
____ *A. c. koroviakovi*	E Iran to Pakistan
____ *A. c. subpallida*	Tajikistan (Kyzl Kum and Kara Kum mountains)
____ *A. c. falki*	N-central Afghanistan to Pamirs and w China (w Xinjiang)
____ *A. c. dzungarica*	NW Mongolia to Russian Altai and e Tibet
____ *A. c. pallescens*	NE Afghanistan to Ladakh and w Tibet
____ *A. c. pallida*	NW China (Tarim basin of w Xinjiang)
____ *A. c. fallax*	NW China (e and s Tien Shan Mountains of Xinjiang)
____ *A. c. chukar*	E Afghanistan to e Nepal
____ *A. c. pubescens*	Inner Mongolia to nw Sichuan and e Qinghai
____ *A. c. potanini*	W Mongolia

☐ **Philby's Partridge** *Alectoris philbyi*
	Rocky deserts of sw Saudi Arabia and n Yemen

☐ **Przevalski's Partridge** *Alectoris magna*
	Desolate regions of n-central China (Qinghai and Gansu)

☐ **Barbary Partridge** *Alectoris barbara*
____ *A. b. koenigi*	NW Morocco; introduced to Canary Islands and s Spain
____ *A. b. barbara*	N Morocco and n Algeria; Sardinia (introduced?)
____ *A. b. spatzi*	S Morocco to central Algeria and s Tunisia
____ *A. b. barbata*	Libya and nw Egypt

☐ **Red-legged Partridge** *Alectoris rufa*
____ *A. r. rufa*	France, nw Italy, Elba and Corsica
____ *A. r. hispanica*	N and w Iberian Peninsula
____ *A. r. intercedens*	E and s Iberian Peninsula and Balearic Islands

☐ **Arabian Partridge** *Alectoris melanocephala*
	Arid regions of s Arabian Peninsula

☐ **See-see Partridge** *Ammoperdix griseogularis*
	Arid se Turkey and Middle East to sw Russia and Pakistan

☐ **Sand Partridge** *Ammoperdix heyi*
____ *A. h. heyi*	Jordan Valley to Sinai Peninsula and w Saudi Arabia
____ *A. h. nicolli*	N Egypt east of the Nile
____ *A. h. cholmleyi*	Central Egypt east of the Nile to n Sudan
____ *A. h. intermedia*	S Arabian Peninsula

☐ **Black Francolin** *Francolinus francolinus*
- ____ *F. f. francolinus* — Cyprus and Asia Minor to Iraq and Iran
- ____ *F. f. arabistanicus* — S Iraq and w Iran
- ____ *F. f. bogdanovi* — S Iran and Afghanistan to s Pakistan
- ____ *F. f. henrici* — S Pakistan to w India
- ____ *F. f. asiae* — N India
- ____ *F. f. melanonotus* — E India to Sikkim and Bangladesh

☐ **Painted Francolin** *Francolinus pictus*
- ____ *F. p. pallidus* — N-central India
- ____ *F. p. pictus* — Central and s India
- ____ *F. p. watsoni* — Sri Lanka

☐ **Chinese Francolin** *Francolinus pintadeanus*
- ____ *F. p. phayrei* — Dry scrub of ne India to Myanmar and Indochina
- ____ *F. p. pintadeanus* — SE China and Hainan

☐ **Gray Francolin** *Francolinus pondicerianus*
- ____ *F. p. mecranensis* — Arid se Iran and s Pakistan
- ____ *F. p. interpositus* — NW India and Pakistan
- ____ *F. p. pondicerianus* — S India and Sri Lanka

☐ **Swamp Francolin** *Francolinus gularis*

Terai of n India to s Nepal and Bangladesh

☐ **Coqui Francolin** *Francolinus coqui*
- ____ *F. c. spinetorum* — Mali to Nigeria and Angola
- ____ *F. c. maharao* — Ethiopia to s Uganda, Kenya and n Tanzania
- ____ *F. c. hubbardi* — W and s Kenya to central Tanzania
- ____ *F. c. coqui* — Kenya to Zaire, Botswana, Natal and n Namibia

☐ **White-throated Francolin** *Francolinus albogularis*
- ____ *F. a. albogularis* — Senegambia to Ivory Coast
- ____ *F. a. buckleyi* — E Ivory Coast to Cameroon
- ____ *F. a. dewittei* — SE Zaire to e Angola and nw Zambia

☐ **Schlegel's Francolin** *Francolinus schlegelii*

Savanna of Cameroon and s Chad to sw Sudan

☐ **Forest Francolin** *Francolinus lathami*
- ____ *F. l. lathami* — Sierra Leone to Gabon, nw Zaire and Angola
- ____ *F. l. schubotzi* — W Zaire to extreme sw Sudan, w Uganda and nw Tanzania

☐ **Crested Francolin** *Francolinus sephaena*
- ____ *F. s. grantii* — Ethiopia to s Sudan, Uganda and n-central Tanzania
- ____ *F. s. spilogaster* — E Ethiopia to Somalia and ne Kenya
- ____ *F. s. rovuma* — Coastal Kenya and Tanzania to n Mozambique
- ____ *F. s. sephaena* — E Zimbabwe to se Botswana and ne South Africa
- ____ *F. s. zambesiae* — W-central Mozambique to nw Namibia and s Angola

☐ **Ring-necked Francolin** *Francolinus streptophorus*

Southwest Cameroon; w Uganda to w Kenya and nw Tanzania

☐ **Finsch's Francolin** *Francolinus finschi*

Brachystegia belt of nw Angola, Gabon and sw Zaire

☐ **Red-winged Francolin** *Francolinus levaillantii*
- ____ *F. l. kikuyuensis* — Angola to e Zaire, w-central Kenya and Zambia
- ____ *F. l. levaillantii* — Malawi and ne Zambia to e South Africa

☐ **Gray-winged Francolin** *Francolinus africanus*

Grasslands of Lesotho and w-central South Africa

☐ **Moorland Francolin** *Francolinus psilolaemus*
_____ *F. p. psilolaemus* — Montane moorlands of central and s Ethiopia
_____ *F. p. elgonensis* — Montane moorlands of e Uganda to central Kenya

☐ **Shelley's Francolin** *Francolinus shelleyi*
_____ *F. s. shelleyi* — S Uganda and sw Kenya to ne South Africa
_____ *F. s. whytei* — SE Zaire to n Zambia and n Malawi

☐ **Orange River Francolin** *Francolinus levaillantoides*
_____ *F. l. gutturalis* — N Ethiopia
_____ *F. l. lorti* — Uganda to Sudan, s Ethiopia and Somalia
_____ *F. l. jugularis* — Kalahari Desert of n Namibia to sw Angola
_____ *F. l. levaillantoides* — S Botswana to e Namibia, Lesotho and n South Africa

☐ **Scaly Francolin** *Francolinus squamatus* — Equatorial Africa from s-c Nigeria to s Ethiopia and Malawi

☐ **Ahanta Francolin** *Francolinus ahantensis* — Discontinuous in lowlands of Senegambia to sw Nigeria

☐ **Gray-striped Francolin** *Francolinus griseostriatus* — Locally in escarpment of w Angola. Last recorded 1954

☐ **Nahan's Francolin** *Francolinus nahani* — Humid forests of w Uganda and ne Zaire

☐ **Hartlaub's Francolin** *Francolinus hartlaubi* — Rocky hill country of sw Angola to central Namibia

☐ **Double-spurred Francolin** *Francolinus bicalcaratus*
_____ *F. b. ayesha* — W Morocco (Rabat to Essaouira)
_____ *F. b. bicalcaratus* — Senegambia to Central African Republic

☐ **Heuglin's Francolin** *Francolinus icterorhynchus* — Central African Republic to s Sudan, n Zaire and w Uganda

☐ **Clapperton's Francolin** *Francolinus clappertoni* — Sub-Saharan Africa (Mali to Sudan and Ethiopia)

☐ **Harwood's Francolin** *Francolinus harwoodi* — Highlands of central Ethiopia

☐ **Red-billed Francolin** *Francolinus adspersus* — S Angola to Namibia, Botswana, sw Zambia and w Zimbabwe

☐ **Cape Francolin** *Francolinus capensis* — South Africa (riverine scrub of s and w Cape Province)

☐ **Natal Francolin** *Francolinus natalensis* — Zambia and Mozambique to Cape Province

☐ **Hildebrandt's Francolin** *Francolinus hildebrandti* — Kenya to Tanzania, se Zaire, ne Zambia and s Malawi

☐ **Yellow-necked Francolin** *Francolinus leucoscepus* — SE Sudan to Ethiopia, Somalia, Kenya and n Tanzania

☐ **Gray-breasted Francolin** *Francolinus rufopictus* — NW Tanzania (Lake Victoria to Serengeti and s to Wembere)

☐ **Red-necked Francolin** *Francolinus afer*
_____ *F. a. cranchii* — W Congo to e Uganda and w Kenya, south to ne Zambia
_____ *F. a. harterti* — N shore of Lake Tanganyika (Burundi, ne Tanzania, e Zaire)
_____ *F. a. leucoparaeus* — Coastal Kenya (Tana River to Tanzania border)
_____ *F. a. afer* — W Angola and extreme nw Namibia
_____ *F. a. melanogaster* — Mozambique n of Zambezi R. to e Tanzania and e Zambia
_____ *F. a. swynnertoni* — Interior Mozambique s of Zambezi River to se Zimbabwe
_____ *F. a. castaneiventer* — South Africa (s and e Cape Province)

☐ **Swainson's Francolin** *Francolinus swainsonii*
_____ *F. s. swainsonii* — SE Angola to n Namibia, s Botswana and ne South Africa
_____ *F. s. lundazi* — N and w Zimbabwe to s Mozambique

☐ **Jackson's Francolin** *Francolinus jacksoni*

Montane forests of w and central Kenya

☐ **Handsome Francolin** *Francolinus nobilis*

Montane forests of sw Uganda, e Zaire and Rwanda

☐ **Cameroon Francolin** *Francolinus camerunensis*

Montane forests of Cameroon Mountain

☐ **Swierstra's Francolin** *Francolinus swierstrai*

Montane forests of w Angola (Cuanza Sul to Huila)

☐ **Chestnut-naped Francolin** *Francolinus castaneicollis*
____ *F. c. castaneicollis* — Mountains of ne Ethiopia and Somalia to Kenya border
____ *F. c. atrifrons* — S Ethiopia and extreme n Kenya

☐ **Erckel's Francolin** *Francolinus erckelii*

Eritrea to n Ethiopia and e Sudan (Red Sea Province)

☐ **Djibouti Francolin** *Francolinus ochropectus*

Montane forests of Forêt du Day (Djibouti)

☐ **Gray Partridge** *Perdix perdix*
____ *P. p. perdix (italica)* — British Isles and s Scandinavia to Alps, Italy and Balkans
____ *P. p. sphangnetorum* — Moors of n Holland and nw Germany
____ *P. p. armoricana* — Locally in France
____ *P. p. hispaniensis* — Central Pyrénées (ne Portugal and n Spain)
____ *P. p. lucida* — Finland east to Ural Mts. and s to Black Sea and n Caucasus
____ *P. p. robusta* — Ural Mountains to sw Siberia and nw China
____ *P. p. canescens* — Turkey east to the Caucasus, Transcaucasia and nw Iran

☐ **Daurian Partridge** *Perdix dauurica*
____ *P. d. dauurica* — Steppes of Mongolia and n China (Xinjiang)
____ *P. d. suschkini* — Steppes of Manchuria to w China (Gansu and Qinghai)

☐ **Tibetan Partridge** *Perdix hodgsoniae*
____ *P. h. sifanica* — E Tibet to w-central China
____ *P. h. caraganae* — E Kashmir to extreme e Tibet
____ *P. h. hodgsoniae* — Himalayas (w Nepal to Assam and e Tibet)

☐ **Long-billed Partridge** *Rhizothera longirostris*
____ *R. l. longirostris* — Myanmar, Malay Pen. and s Thailand to Sumatra and Borneo
____ *R. l. dulitensis* — N Borneo (Buto Song Mountains and Sarawak)

☐ **Madagascar Partridge** *Margaroperdix madagascarensis*

Madagascar; introduced Réunion

☐ **Black Partridge** *Melanoperdix nigra*
____ *M. n. nigra* — Lowland forests of Malay Peninsula and Sumatra
____ *M. n. borneensis* — Lowland forests of Borneo

☐ **Japanese Quail** *Coturnix japonica*

E Palearctic; winters to SE Asia and e China

☐ **Common Quail** *Coturnix coturnix*
____ *C. c. coturnix* — W Eurasia and nw Africa
____ *C. c. confisa* — Canary Islands, Madeira and Azores
____ *C. c. inopinata* — Cape Verde Islands
____ *C. c. erlangeri* — Highlands of Ethiopia
____ *C. c. africana* — Kenya and Uganda to S Africa, Madagascar and Comoro Is.

☐ **Harlequin Quail** *Coturnix delegorguei*
____ *C. d. delegorguei* — Grasslands of Africa south of the Sahara and Madagascar
____ *C. d. histrionica* — São Tomé (Gulf of Guinea)
____ *C. d. arabica* — Known from some old specimens from sw Arabia

☐ **Rain Quail** *Coturnix coromandelica*

Pakistan to Myanmar and w Thailand

☐ **Stubble Quail** *Coturnix pectoralis*

Grasslands of Australia and Tasmania

☐ **Brown Quail** *Coturnix ypsilophora*

____ *C. y. raaltenii*	Lesser Sundas (Flores, Timor and adjacent islands)
____ *C. y. pallidior*	Lesser Sundas (Sumba and Sawu)
____ *C. y. saturatior*	Lowlands of n New Guinea
____ *C. y. lamonti*	Mid-montane central highlands of New Guinea
____ *C. y. dogwa*	Lowlands of s New Guinea
____ *C. y. plumbeus*	Lowlands of e New Guinea
____ *C. y. monticola*	Alpine grasslands of se New Guinea
____ *C. y. mafulu*	S slopes of mountains of se New Guinea
____ *C. y. australis*	Moist areas of Australia
____ *C. y. ypsilophora*	Tasmania

☐ **Blue-breasted Quail** *Coturnix chinensis*

____ *C. c. chinensis*	India to Sri Lanka, Malaya, Indochina, se China and Taiwan
____ *C. c. trinkutensis*	Andaman Islands and Nicobar Islands
____ *C. c. palmeri*	Sumatra and Java
____ *C. c. lineata*	Philippines, Borneo, Sulawesi and Sula Islands
____ *C. c. lineatula*	Lesser Sundas (Lombok to Sumba, Flores and Timor)
____ *C. c. novaeguineae*	Montane forests of New Guinea
____ *C. c. papuensis*	SE New Guinea
____ *C. c. lepida*	Bismarck Archipelago
____ *C. c. colletti*	N Australia (Northern Territory)
____ *C. c. victoriae*	E Australia (Queensland to Victoria)

☐ **Blue Quail** *Coturnix adansonii*

Wet grasslands of Africa south of the Sahara

☐ **Snow Mountain Quail** *Anurophasis monorthonyx*

W New Guinea (alpine grasslands of Snow Mountains)

☐ **Jungle Bush-Quail** *Perdicula asiatica*

____ *P. a. punjabi*	NW India (Kashmir to Uttar Pradesh)
____ *P. a. vidali*	W India
____ *P. a. asiatica*	Central and ne India (Gujarat to Bihar)
____ *P. a. ceylonensis*	Sri Lanka

☐ **Rock Bush-Quail** *Perdicula argoondah*

____ *P. a. meinertzhageni*	NW India (south to Rann of Kutch and Madhya Pradesh)
____ *P. a. argoondah*	Peninsular India south to Madras
____ *P. a. salimali*	S India (stony lateritic soils of e-central Mysore)

☐ **Painted Bush-Quail** *Perdicula erythrorhyncha*

____ *P. e. erythrorhyncha*	W India (Western Ghats)
____ *P. e. blewitti*	Central and eastern India

☐ **Manipur Bush-Quail** *Perdicula manipurensis*

____ *P. m. manipurensis*	Manipur and Assam hills (south of the Brahmaputra River)
____ *P. m. inglisi*	W Bengal and Assam (north of the Brahmaputra River)

☐ **Udzungwa Partridge** *Xenoperdix udzungwensis*

S Tanzania (Udzungwa Mountains)

☐ **Hill Partridge** *Arborophila torqueola*

____ *A. t. millardi*	W Himalayas (Himanchal Pradesh to w Nepal)
____ *A. t. torqueola*	E Himalayas (Nepal to Tibet and n Myanmar)
____ *A. t. batemani*	N Myanmar to sw China (w Yunnan and sw Sichuan)
____ *A. t. griseata*	NW Vietnam

☐ **Sichuan Partridge** *Arborophila rufipectus*

SW China (hills of s-central Sichuan)

☐ **Chestnut-breasted Partridge** *Arborophila mandellii*

Coniferous foothill forests of Sikkim to se Tibet

☐ **White-necklaced Partridge** *Arborophila gingica*

Montane forests of se China

☐ **Rufous-throated Partridge** *Arborophila rufogularis*

____ *A. r. rufogularis* — N India (Uttar Pradesh to Assam) and Nepal
____ *A. r. intermedia* — NE India to Myanmar and extreme nw Yunnan
____ *A. r. tickelli* — E Myanmar to Thailand and sw Laos
____ *A. r. euroa* — S China (se Yunnan) to n Laos
____ *A. r. guttata* — Central Vietnam and n Laos
____ *A. r. vietnamensis* — S Vietnam (Langbian Plateau region)

☐ **White-cheeked Partridge** *Arborophila atrogularis*

Humid forests of ne India to Myanmar and sw China (Yunnan)

☐ **Taiwan Partridge** *Arborophila crudigularis*

Montane forests of Taiwan

☐ **Hainan Partridge** *Arborophila ardens*

Montane forests of Hainan I. (s China)

☐ **Chestnut-bellied Partridge** *Arborophila javanica*

____ *A. j. javanica* — Mountains of w Java
____ *A. j. bartelsi* — Mountains of w-central Java
____ *A. j. lawuana* — Mountains of e-central Java

☐ **Gray-breasted Partridge** *Arborophila orientalis*

____ *A. o. campbelli* — Mountains of Malay Peninsula
____ *A. o. rolli* — NW Sumatra (Batak highlands)
____ *A. o. sumatrana* — Mountains of central Sumatra
____ *A. o. orientalis* — Mountains of e Java

☐ **Bar-backed Partridge** *Arborophila brunneopectus*

____ *A. b. brunneopectus* — SW China (sw Yunnan) to e Myanmar, n Laos and w Thailand
____ *A. b. henrici* — N and central Vietnam
____ *A. b. albigula* — S-central Vietnam

☐ **Orange-necked Partridge** *Arborophila davidi*

Single 1927 specimen from s Vietnam; rediscovered 1988

☐ **Chestnut-headed Partridge** *Arborophila cambodiana*

____ *A. c. diversa* — Tropical forests of se Thailand
____ *A. c. cambodiana* — Tropical forests of sw Cambodia

☐ **Red-breasted Partridge** *Arborophila hyperythra*

____ *A. h. hyperythra* — Montane forests of n-central Borneo
____ *A. h. erythrophrys* — Mt. Kinabalu (n Borneo)

☐ **Red-billed Partridge** *Arborophila rubrirostris*

Montane forests of Sumatra

☐ **Scaly-breasted Partridge** *Arborophila chloropus*

____ *A. c. chloropus* — Extreme sw China (Yunnan) to Myanmar and w Thailand
____ *A. c. peninsularis* — SW Thailand
____ *A. c. tonkinensis* — N Vietnam
____ *A. c. olivacea* — Laos and Cambodia
____ *A. c. cognacqi* — S Vietnam

☐ **Vietnam Partridge** *Arborophila merlini*

____ *A. m. merlini* — Interior of central Vietnam
____ *A. m. vivida* — Coastal hills of central Vietnam

☐ **Chestnut-necklaced Partridge** *Arborophila charltonii*
_____ *A. c. charltonii*   S Thailand to s Myanmar and Malay Peninsula
_____ *A. c. atjenensis*   N Sumatra (Aceh Province)
_____ *A. c. graydoni*   N Borneo (Sabah)

☐ **Ferruginous Partridge** *Caloperdix oculea*
_____ *C. o. oculea*   SE Myanmar and sw Thailand to Malay Peninsula
_____ *C. o. ocellata*   Sumatra
_____ *C. o. borneensis*   Borneo

☐ **Crimson-headed Partridge** *Haematortyx sanguiniceps*

Montane forests of n Borneo

☐ **Crested Partridge** *Rollulus rouloul*

Malay Pen., Sumatra, Borneo, Banka and Belitung islands

☐ **Stone Partridge** *Ptilopachus petrosus*
_____ *P. p. petrosus*   Senegambia to s Sudan, n Uganda and n Kenya
_____ *P. p. major*   Rocky areas of nw Ethiopia

☐ **Mountain Bamboo-Partridge** *Bambusicola fytchii*
_____ *B. f. hopkinsoni*   NE India to Bangladesh and n Myanmar
_____ *B. f. fytchii*   SW China (Sichuan and Yunnan) to Myanmar and n Vietnam

☐ **Chinese Bamboo-Partridge** *Bambusicola thoracica*
_____ *B. t. thoracica*   Arid bush of s and central China
_____ *B. t. sonorivox*   Taiwan

☐ **Red Spurfowl** *Galloperdix spadicea*
_____ *G. s. caurina*   W India (Arvalli Hills of s Rajasthan)
_____ *G. s. spadicea*   N India (Uttar Pradesh) and *terai* of w Nepal to s India
_____ *G. s. stewarti*   S India (Kerala coast)

☐ **Painted Spurfowl** *Galloperdix lunulata*

Semiarid steppes of peninsular India

☐ **Ceylon Spurfowl** *Galloperdix bicalcarata*

Humid forests of s Sri Lanka

☐ **Blood Pheasant** *Ithaginis cruentus*
_____ *I. c. cruentus*   N Nepal to nw Bhutan
_____ *L. c. affinis*   Sikkim
_____ *I. c. tibetanus*   E Bhutan and s Tibet
_____ *I. c. kuseri*   NE India (upper Assam) and se Tibet
_____ *I. c. geoffroyi*   W China (w Sichuan) and se Tibet
_____ *I. c. marionae*   Mountains of sw China (nw Yunnan) and ne Myanmar
_____ *I. c. rocki*   SW China (Mekong Valley of nw Yunnan)
_____ *I. c. holoptilus*   SW China (Likiang District of Yunnan)
_____ *I. c. clarkei*   SW China (Likiang Mountains of nw Yunnan)
_____ *I. c. michaelis*   N-central China (Nan Shan Mountains of nw Gansu)
_____ *I. c. beicki*   N-central China (ne Qinghai and adjacent Gansu)
_____ *I. c. berezowskii*   Mountains of central China (s Gansu and n Sichuan)
_____ *I. c. annae*   Mountains of sw China (nw Sichuan)
_____ *I. c. sinensis*   C China (Tsinling Mountains of s Shensi and sw Hunan)

☐ **Western Tragopan** *Tragopan melanocephalus*

Himalayas of n Pakistan to nw India and adjacent sw Tibet

☐ **Satyr Tragopan** *Tragopan satyra*

Oak-rhododendron forests of n India to Nepal and se Tibet

☐ **Blyth's Tragopan** *Tragopan blythii*
_____ *T. b. blythii*   Himalayas of ne India to sw China and adjacent Myanmar
_____ *T. b. molesworthi*   Known from 3 specimens from e Bhutan

☐ Temminck's Tragopan *Tragopan temminckii*

Mts. of ne India to central China, n Myanmar and nw Tonkin

☐ Cabot's Tragopan *Tragopan caboti*

____ *T. c. caboti* Foothill forests of se China
____ *T. c. guangxiensis* SE China (ne Guangxi Zhuangu Autonomous Region)

☐   *Pucrasia macrolopha*

____ *P. m. castanea* Mountains of e Afghanistan and adjacent Pakistan
____ *P. m. biddulphi* Himalayas of Kashmir
____ *P. m. bethelae* NW India (Kulu Valley)
____ *P. m. macrolopha* W Himalayas (Kashmir to Kumaon)
____ *P. m. nipalensis* Mountains of w Nepal
____ *P. m. meyeri* Mountains of s-central China (w Sichuan to nw Yunnan)
____ *P. m. ruficollis* Mountains of central China (s Gansu, Shaanxi and w Sichuan)
____ *P. m. xanthospila* N Shaanxi to Inner Mongolia, w Liaoning and sw Manchuria
____ *P. m. joretiana* Mountains of e-central China (sw Anhui)
____ *P. m. darwini* Mountains of c China (Hubei and se Sichuan to Fujian)

☐ Himalayan Monal *Lophophorus impejanus*

Himalayas of Afghanistan to s Tibet, sw China and ne Myanmar

☐ Sclater's Monal *Lophophorus sclateri*

Himalayas of ne India to sw China

☐ Chinese Monal *Lophophorus lhuysii*

Mountains of sw China (s Gansu, nw Sichuan and Yunnan)

☐ Red Junglefowl *Gallus gallus*

____ *G. g. murghi* N India and adjacent Nepal and Bangladesh
____ *G. g. spadiceus* Myanmar to sw Yunnan, Malay Peninsula and n Sumatra
____ *G. g. jabouillei* N Vietnam to s China (se Yunnan, Guangxi and Hainan I.)
____ *G. g. gallus* N Indochina to e Thailand
____ *G. g. bankiva* S Sumatra, Java and Bali

☐ Gray Junglefowl *Gallus sonneratii*

Peninsular India

☐ Ceylon Junglefowl *Gallus lafayetii*

Sri Lanka

☐ Green Junglefowl *Gallus varius*

Java, Bali, Lombok, Sumbawa, Flores and Alor islands

☐ Kalij Pheasant *Lophura leucomelanos*

____ *L. l. hamiltoni* Western Himalayas (Indus River to w Nepal)
____ *L. l. leucomelanos* Subtropical pine, *sal*, and moist temperate forests of Nepal
____ *L. l. melanota* Sikkim and w Bhutan
____ *L. l. moffitti* Range unknown; possibly central Bhutan
____ *L. l. lathami* E Bhutan and n India to Myanmar
____ *L. l. williamsi* W Myanmar (east to Irrawaddy River)
____ *L. l. oatesi* S Myanmar (Arakan Yoma Mountains)
____ *L. l. lineata* S Myanmar (east of Irrawaddy River) to nw Thailand
____ *L. l. crawfurdi* SE Myanmar (Tenasserim) and peninsular Thailand

☐ Imperial Pheasant *Lophura imperialis*

Limestone mountains of central Vietnam

☐ Edwards' Pheasant *Lophura edwardsi*

Lowlands of central Vietnam (on verge of extinction in wild)

☐   *Lophura hatinhensis*

Lowlands of n-central Vietnam

☐ Swinhoe's Pheasant *Lophura swinhoii*

Montane forests of central Taiwan

☐ Salvadori's Pheasant *Lophura inornata*

____ *L. i. inornata* Montane forests of s Sumatra
____ *L. i. hoogerwerfi* NW Sumatra (known from two female specimens ca 1939)

☐ **Silver Pheasant** *Lophura nycthemera*

____	*L. n. occidentalis*	S-central China (nw Yunnan) and ne Myanmar
____	*L. n. rufipes*	Highlands of n Myanmar (Northern Shan States)
____	*L. n. ripponi*	Highlands of n Myanmar (Southern Shan States)
____	*L. n. jonesi*	Myanmar to sw China (sw Yunnan) and central Thailand
____	*L. n. omeiensis*	S-central China (s Sichuan)
____	*L. n. rongjiangensis*	S-central China (se Guizhou)
____	*L. n. beaulieui*	S-central China (se Yunnan) to n Laos and n Vietnam
____	*L. n. nycthemera*	S China (Guangdong and Guangxi) to n Vietnam
____	*L. n. whiteheadi*	Hainan (s China)
____	*L. n. fokiensis*	SE China (nw Fujian and (?) Zhejiang
____	*L. n. berliozi*	Central Vietnam (w slope of Annamitic Mountains)
____	*L. n. beli*	Central Vietnam (e slope of Annamitic Mountains)
____	*L. n. engelbachi*	S Laos (Bolavens Plateau)
____	*L. n. lewisi*	Mountains of sw Cambodia and se Thailand
____	*L. n. annamensis*	Montane forests of s Vietnam

☐ **Crestless Fireback** *Lophura erythrophthalma*

____	*L. e. erythrophthalma*	Lowland forests of Malay Peninsula and Sumatra
____	*L. e. pyronota*	Lowland forests of n Borneo

☐ **Crested Fireback** *Lophura ignita*

____	*L. i. rufa*	Malay Peninsula and Sumatra (except for range of *macartneyi*)
____	*L. i. macartneyi*	SE Sumatra
____	*L. i. ignita*	Kalimantan (Borneo) and Banka I. (off se Sumatra)
____	*L. i. nobilis*	N Borneo (Sarawak and Sabah)

☐ **Siamese Fireback** *Lophura diardi*

Lowlands of e Myanmar, Thailand and Indochina

☐ **Bulwer's Pheasant** *Lophura bulweri*

Submontane forests of interior Borneo

☐ **White Eared-Pheasant** *Crossoptilon crossoptilon*

____	*C. c. harmani*	Rhododendron forests of s Tibet and adjacent ne India
____	*C. c. drouynii*	Montane forests of e Tibet
____	*C. c. dolani*	W-central China (s Qinghai)
____	*C. c. crossoptilon*	SW China (w Sichuan) to se Tibet and extreme ne India
____	*C. c. lichiangense*	S-central China (nw Yunnan)

☐ **Brown Eared-Pheasant** *Crossoptilon mantchuricum*

Montane forests of ne China (Liaoning and Shanxi)

☐ **Blue Eared-Pheasant** *Crossoptilon auritum*

Montane forests of n-central China

☐ **Cheer Pheasant** *Catreus wallichi*

Montane forests of e Afghanistan to central Nepal

☐ **Elliot's Pheasant** *Syrmaticus ellioti*

Montane bamboo forests of se China

☐ **Hume's Pheasant** *Syrmaticus humiae*

____	*S. h. humiae*	Montane forests of extreme ne India and n Myanmar
____	*S. h. burmanicus*	SW China (sw Yunnan) to Myanmar and nw Thailand

☐ **Mikado Pheasant** *Syrmaticus mikado*

Montane forests of central Taiwan

☐ **Copper Pheasant** *Syrmaticus soemmerringii*

____	*S. s. scintillans*	Japan (coniferous forests of n and central Honshu)
____	*S. s. intermedius*	Japan (coniferous forests of sw Honshu and Shikoku)
____	*S. s. subrufus*	Japan (coniferous forests of s Honshu and sw Shikoku)
____	*S. s. soemmerringii*	Japan (coniferous forests of n and central Kyushu)
____	*S. s. ijimae*	Japan (coniferous forests of se Kyushu)

☐ **Reeves' Pheasant** *Syrmaticus reevesii*

Low altitude deciduous forests of n-central China

☐ **Ring-necked Pheasant** *Phasianus colchicus*

____	*P. c. septentrionalis*	N Caucasus
____	*P. c. colchicus*	E Georgia to ne Azerbaijan, s Armenia and nw Iran
____	*P. c. talischensis*	SE Transcaucasia
____	*P. c. persicus*	SW Transcaspia
____	*P. c. bergii*	Islands in Aral Sea
____	*P. c. turcestanicus*	Kazakstan (Valley of River Syrdar'ya)
____	*P. c. mongolicus*	NE Russian Turkestan
____	*P. c. principalis*	S Russian Turkestan and n Afghanistan
____	*P. c. chrysomelas*	Turkestan (upper River Amudar'ya)
____	*P. c. zerafschanicus*	S Uzbekistan (Bukhara and Zerafshan Valley)
____	*P. c. zarudnyi*	Turkestan (valleys of central Amudar'ya)
____	*P. c. bianchii*	Turkestan (Amudar'ya delta)
____	*P. c. shawii*	Chinese Turkestan
____	*P. c. tarimensis*	E-central Chinese Turkestan
____	*P. c. hagenbecki*	NW Mongolia
____	*P. c. edzinensis*	S-central Mongolia
____	*P. c. satschuensis*	N-central China (extreme w Gansu)
____	*P. c. vlangallii*	N-central China (n Qinghai)
____	*P. c. alashanicus*	N-central China (foothills of Alaschan Mountains)
____	*P. c. sohokhotensis*	N-central China (Sohokhoto Oasis and Qilian Shan)
____	*P. c. pallasi*	SE Siberia and ne China
____	*P. c. karpowi*	NE China (s Manchuria and n Liaoning) to Korea
____	*P. c. kiangsuensis*	NE China (n Shanxi and Shaanxi) to se Mongolia
____	*P. c. strauchi*	Central China (s Shaanxi and s Gansu)
____	*P. c. suehschanensis*	W-central China (nw Sichuan)
____	*P. c. elegans*	W-central China (w Sichuan)
____	*P. c. decollatus*	Central China (Sichuan to Liaoning, ne Yunnan and Guizhou)
____	*P. c. torquatus*	E China (Shandong) to Vietnam border
____	*P. c. rothschildi*	SW China (e Yunnan) and n Vietnam
____	*P. c. takatsukasae*	S China and n Vietnam
____	*P. c. formosanus*	Taiwan

☐ **Green Pheasant** *Phasianus versicolor*

____	*P. v. versicolor*	Japan (sw Honshu and Kyushu)
____	*P. v. tanensis*	Japan (central Honshu) and Izu Islands
____	*P. v. robustipes*	Japan (nw Honshu and Sado I.)

☐ **Golden Pheasant** *Chrysolophus pictus*

Mountain slopes of central and s China

☐ **Lady Amherst's Pheasant** *Chrysolophus amherstiae*

Mountains of se Tibet and sw China to n Myanmar

☐ **Bronze-tailed Peacock-Pheasant** *Polyplectron chalcurum*

____	*P. c. scutulatum*	Mountains of n Sumatra
____	*P. c. chalcurum*	Mountains of s Sumatra

☐ **Mountain Peacock-Pheasant** *Polyplectron inopinatum*

Montane forests of Malay Peninsula

☐ **Germain's Peacock-Pheasant** *Polyplectron germaini*

Humid forests of s Vietnam

☐ **Gray Peacock-Pheasant** *Polyplectron bicalcaratum*

____	*P. b. bakeri*	Humid forests of ne India and Bhutan
____	*P. b. bailyi*	Patchily distributed w Assam and adjacent e Himalayas
____	*P. b. bicalcaratum*	NE Assam and Myanmar to sw Thailand and central Laos
____	*P. b. ghigii*	Central and n Vietnam to e Tonkin and central Laos
____	*P. b. katsumatae*	Hainan (s China)

☐ **Malayan Peacock-Pheasant** *Polyplectron malacense*

S Myanmar to s Thailand and Malay Peninsula

☐ **Bornean Peacock-Pheasant** *Polyplectron schleiermacheri*

Lowland primary forests of Borneo

☐ **Palawan Peacock-Pheasant** *Polyplectron emphanum*

Humid forests of Palawan (sw Philippines)

☐ **Crested Argus** *Rheinardia ocellata*
    ____ *R. o. ocellata* — Mountains of central Vietnam and e Laos
    ____ *R. o. nigrescens* — Mts. of central Malay Peninsula (Taman Nagara Nat. Park)

☐ **Great Argus** *Argusianus argus*
    ____ *A. a. argus* — Malay Peninsula and Sumatra
    ____ *A. a. grayi* — Borneo

☐ **Indian Peafowl** *Pavo cristatus*

Forests and scrub of e Pakistan, India and Sri Lanka

☐ **Green Peafowl** *Pavo muticus*
    ____ *P. m. spificer* — NE India and se Bangladesh to nw Myanmar
    ____ *P. m. imperator* — Myanmar to Thailand, s China and Indochina
    ____ *P. m. muticus* — Locally in Java; formerly Malay Peninsula

☐ **Congo Peacock** *Afropavo congensis*

Locally in humid forests of central Zaire

ORDER: GALLIFORMES
FAMILY: NUMIDIDAE (Guineafowl—6)

☐ **White-breasted Guineafowl** *Agelastes meleagrides*

SE Sierra Leone to Ivory Coast and w Ghana

☐ **Black Guineafowl** *Agelastes niger*

SE Nigeria to n Angola and extreme ne Zaire

☐ **Helmeted Guineafowl** *Numida meleagris*
    ____ *N. m. sabyi* — NW Morocco
    ____ *N. m. galeata* — W Africa to s Chad, central Zaire and n Angola
    ____ *N. m. meleagris* — E Chad to Ethiopia, n Zaire, Uganda and n Kenya
    ____ *N. m. somaliensis* — NE Ethiopia and Somalia
    ____ *N. m. reichenowi* — Kenya and central Tanzania
    ____ *N. m. mitrata* — Tanzania to e Mozambique, Zambia and n Botswana
    ____ *N. m. marungensis* — S Congo basin to w Angola and Zambia
    ____ *N. m. damarensis* — S Angola to Botswana and Namibia
    ____ *N. m. coronata* — E South Africa

☐ **Plumed Guineafowl** *Guttera plumifera*
    ____ *G. p. plumifera* — S Cameroon to Congo basin, n Gabon and n Angola
    ____ *G. p. schubotzi* — N Zaire to Rift Valley and forests west of Lake Tanganyika

☐ **Crested Guineafowl** *Guttera pucherani*
    ____ *G. p. verreauxi* — Guinea-Bissau to w Kenya, Angola and Zambia
    ____ *G. p. sclateri* — NW Cameroon
    ____ *G. p. pucherani* — Somalia to Tanzania, Zanzibar and Tumbatu I.
    ____ *G. p. barbata* — SE Tanzania to e Mozambique and Malawi
    ____ *G. p. edouardi* — E Zambia to Mozambique and ne South Africa

☐ **Vulturine Guineafowl** *Acryllium vulturinum*

Arid acacia scrub of s Ethiopia and Somalia to ne Tanzania

ORDER: OPISTHOCOMIFORMES
FAMILY: OPISTHOCOMIDAE (Hoatzin—1)

☐ **Hoatzin** *Opisthocomus hoazin*

Amazon and Orinoco basin lowlands and the Guianas

FAMILY: MESITORNITHIDAE (Mesites—3)

☐ **White-breasted Mesite** *Mesitornis variegata*

Deciduous dry forests of w Madagascar

☐ **Brown Mesite** *Mesitornis unicolor*

Rainforests of e Madagascar

☐ **Subdesert Mesite** *Monias benschi*

Coastal subdeserts of sw Madagascar

ORDER: GRUIFORMES
FAMILY: TURNICIDAE (Buttonquail—16)

☐ **Small Buttonquail** *Turnix sylvatica*

___ *T. s. sylvatica*	S Iberian Peninsula, n Morocco, Algeria and Tunisia
___ *T. s. lepurana (alleni)*	Africa south of the Sahara and extreme s Arabian Peninsula
___ *T. s. dussumier*	Extreme e Iran to India and Myanmar
___ *T. s. davidi (mikado)*	Peninsular Thailand to s China, n Indochina and Taiwan
___ *T. s. whiteheadi*	Luzon (n Philippines)
___ *T. s. nigrorum*	Negros (Philippines)
___ *T. s. celestinoi*	S Philippines (Bohol and Mindanao)
___ *T. s. suluensis*	Sulu Archipelago
___ *T. s. bartelsorum*	Java and Bali

☐ **Red-backed Buttonquail** *Turnix maculosa*

___ *T. m. beccarii*	Sulawesi, Muna and Tomia I. (Tukangbesi Islands)
___ *T. m. kinneari*	Peleng I. (Banggai Islands off e Sulawesi)
___ *T. m. obiensis*	Obi I., Kai Kecil I. (Kai Islands) and Babar I.
___ *T. m. sumbana*	Sumba I. (Lesser Sundas)
___ *T. m. floresiana*	Lesser Sundas (Sumbawa, Komodo, Padar, Flores and Alor)
___ *T. m. maculosa*	Lesser Sundas (Roti, Semau, Timor, Wetar, Moa and Kisar)
___ *T. m. savuensis*	Sawu I. (Lesser Sundas)
___ *T. m. saturata*	Bismarck Archipelago (New Britain and Duke of York)
___ *T. m. furva*	Huon Peninsula (ne New Guinea)
___ *T. m. giluwensis*	E-central New Guinea
___ *T. m. horsbrughi*	S New Guinea
___ *T. m. mayri*	Louisiade Archipelago
___ *T. m. salamonis*	Guadalcanal (Solomon Islands)
___ *T. m. melanota (yorki, pseutes)*	N and e Australia

☐ **Hottentot Buttonquail** *Turnix hottentotta*

___ *T. h. nana*	Ghana to Kenya, Uganda and se Cape Province
___ *T. h. hottentotta*	Mts. of South Africa (sw Cape Province to Port Elizabeth)

☐ **Yellow-legged Buttonquail** *Turnix tanki*

___ *T. t. tanki*	Indian subcontinent, Andaman and Nicobar Islands
___ *T. t. blanfordii*	Manchuria to Myanmar, s China and Indochina

☐ **Spotted Buttonquail** *Turnix ocellata*

___ *T. o. benguetensis*	Mountains of n Luzon (n Philippines)
___ *T. o. ocellata*	S and central Luzon (n Philippines)

☐ **Barred Buttonquail** *Turnix suscitator*

_____ *T. s. taigoor*	India
_____ *T. s. leggei*	Sri Lanka
_____ *T. s. plumbipes*	Nepal, Sikkim and Bangladesh to n Myanmar
_____ *T. s. bengalensis*	NE India (lower w Bengal)
_____ *T. s. okinavensis*	S Kyushu and Makenoshima I. south to Ryukyu Islands
_____ *T. s. rostrata*	Taiwan
_____ *T. s. blakistoni*	Myanmar to s China, n Indochina and Hainan
_____ *T. s. pallescens*	S-central Myanmar
_____ *T. s. thai*	Central Thailand
_____ *T. s. interrumpens*	Peninsular Myanmar and Thailand
_____ *T. s. atrogularis*	Peninsular Malaysia
_____ *T. s. suscitator (machetes, kuiperi)*	Sumatra, Belitung I. and Bangka I. to Java and Bali
_____ *T. s. baweanus*	Bawean I. (off Java)
_____ *T. s. fasciata*	N Philippines (Luzon to Mindoro, Sibuyan and Masbate)
_____ *T. s. haynaldi*	SW Philippines (Palawan and Calamian Islands)
_____ *T. s. nigrescens*	Philippines (Negros, Cebu and Panay)
_____ *T. s. rufilata*	Sulawesi
_____ *T. s. powelli*	Lesser Sundas

☐ **Madagascar Buttonquail** *Turnix nigricollis*

Madagascar; introduced (?) Mauritius, Réunion and Glorieuses

☐ **Black-breasted Buttonquail** *Turnix melanogaster*

Coastal e Australia (se Queensland and n New South Wales)

☐ **Chestnut-backed Buttonquail** *Turnix castanota*

Locally in coastal n Australia and offshore islands

☐ **Buff-breasted Buttonquail** *Turnix olivii*

N Australia (Cape York Peninsula of n Queensland)

☐ **Painted Buttonquail** *Turnix varia*

_____ *T. v. novaecaledoniae*	New Caledonia
_____ *T. v. scintillans*	Houtman Abrolhos Islands (off sw Australia)
_____ *T. v. varia*	SW, e and se Australia and Tasmania

☐ **Luzon Buttonquail** *Turnix worcesteri*

Known from four specimens from Luzon (n Philippines)

☐ **Sumba Buttonquail** *Turnix everetti*

Sumba I. (Lesser Sundas)

☐ **Red-chested Buttonquail** *Turnix pyrrhothorax*

Savanna and scrub of n and e Australia

☐ **Little Buttonquail** *Turnix velox*

Grasslands and woodlands throughout Australia

☐ **Quail-plover** *Ortyxelos meiffrenii*

Discontinuously distributed sahel of sub-Saharan Africa

ORDER: GRUIFORMES
FAMILY: GRUIDAE (Cranes—15)

☐ **Gray Crowned-Crane** *Balearica regulorum*

_____ *B. r. gibbericeps*	Uganda and Kenya to n Zimbabwe and n Mozambique
_____ *B. r. regulorum*	S Angola and n Namibia to Zimbabwe and e South Africa

☐ **Black Crowned-Crane** *Balearica pavonina*

_____ *B. p. pavonina*	Sub-Saharan Africa (Senegambia to Lake Chad)
_____ *B. p. ceciliae*	Sub-Saharan Africa (Chad to Ethiopia and Kenya)

☐ **Demoiselle Crane** *Anthropoides virgo*

Palearctic; winters in ne Africa and s Asia

☐ **Blue Crane** *Grus paradisea*

Locally in n Namibia, s Zimbabwe and South Africa

☐ **Wattled Crane** *Bugeranus carunculatus*

Patchily distributed ne and s Africa

☐ **Siberian Crane** *Grus leucogeranus*

Breeds Arctic Siberia; winters to n India and China

☐ **Sandhill Crane** *Grus canadensis*

_____	*G. c. canadensis*	Arctic N America and e Siberia; winters sw US and n Mexico
_____	*G. c. rowani*	British Columbia to n Ontario; winters to n Mexico
_____	*G. c. tabida*	Mid-continental North America; winters s US and n Mexico
_____	*G. c. pulla*	Gulf Coast of s US
_____	*G. c. pratensis*	Georgia and Florida
_____	*G. c. nesiotes*	Cuba and Isle of Pines

☐ **Sarus Crane** *Grus antigone*

_____	*G. a. antigone*	N India to Nepal and (?) formerly Bangladesh
_____	*G. a. sharpii*	Cambodia and s Laos; winters in Vietnam
_____	*G. a. gilliae*	Spottily distributed coastal n Australia (mainly Queensland)

☐ **Brolga** *Grus rubicunda*

N and e Australia and Trans-Fly lowlands of s New Guinea

☐ **White-naped Crane** *Grus vipio*

Siberia and Manchuria; winters to s China, Korea and Japan

☐ **Common Crane** *Grus grus*

Breeds n Eurasia; winters to n Africa, s India and SE Asia

☐ **Hooded Crane** *Grus monacha*

Siberia and nw Manchuria; winters to e China, Korea, and Japan

☐ **Whooping Crane** *Grus americana*

Breeds n Canada; winters coastal se Texas

☐ **Black-necked Crane** *Grus nigricollis*

Breeds Tibetan plateau; winters to ne India and s China

☐ **Red-crowned Crane** *Grus japonensis*

Siberia, Hokkaido and Mongolia; winters e China and Korea

ORDER: GRUIFORMES
FAMILY: ARAMIDAE (Limpkin—1)

☐ **Limpkin** *Aramus guarauna*

_____	*A. g. pictus*	Florida, Cuba and Jamaica
_____	*A. g. elucus*	Hispaniola and Puerto Rico
_____	*A. g. dolosus*	SE Mexico to Panama
_____	*A. g. guarauna*	S America (except for arid w coast, Andes and extreme south)

ORDER: GRUIFORMES
FAMILY: PSOPHIIDAE (Trumpeters—3)

☐ **Gray-winged Trumpeter** *Psophia crepitans*

_____	*P. c. napensis*	SE Colombia to ne Peru and extreme nw Brazil
_____	*P. c. crepitans*	SE Colombia to Venezuela, the Guianas and n Brazil

☐ **Dark-winged Trumpeter** *Psophia viridis*

_____	*P. v. viridis*	Brazil s of the Amazon between Rio Madeira and Rio Tapajós
_____	*P. v. dextralis*	E Brazil s of Amazon between Rio Tapajós and Rio Tocantins
_____	*P. v. obscura*	NE Brazil south of the Amazon (ne Pará east of Rio Tocantins)

☐ **Pale-winged Trumpeter** *Psophia leucoptera*

_____ *P. l. ochroptera*	NW Brazil (north of the Amazon and west of Rio Negro)
_____ *P. l. leucoptera*	E Peru to central Brazil and ne Bolivia

ORDER: GRUIFORMES
FAMILY: RALLIDAE (Rails, Gallinules and Coots—134)

☐ **White-spotted Flufftail** *Sarothrura pulchra*

_____ *S. p. pulchra*	S Senegal to n Cameroon
_____ *S. p. zenkeri*	Extreme se Nigeria, coastal Cameroon and n Gabon
_____ *S. p. batesi*	S Cameroon
_____ *S. p. centralis*	Congo to s Sudan, w Kenya, nw Tanzania and n Angola

☐ **Buff-spotted Flufftail** *Sarothrura elegans*

_____ *S. e. reichenovi*	W Africa to Uganda and Angola
_____ *S. e. elegans*	Ethiopia to Somalia, e Kenya and south to South Africa

☐ **Red-chested Flufftail** *Sarothrura rufa*

_____ *S. r. bonapartii*	Sierra Leone to Gabon and Congo
_____ *S. r. elizabethae*	C African Rep. to ne Zaire, Ethiopia, Uganda and w Kenya
_____ *S. r. rufa*	Central Kenya to s Zaire, Angola and South Africa

☐ **Chestnut-headed Flufftail** *Sarothrura lugens*

_____ *S. l. lugens*	Swamps of Cameroon to Zaire and w Tanzania
_____ *S. l. lynesi*	Angola to Zambia and Zimbabwe

☐ **Streaky-breasted Flufftail** *Sarothrura boehmi*

Locally in wet grasslands of central Africa

☐ **Striped Flufftail** *Sarothrura affinis*

_____ *S. a. antonii*	Montane grasslands of extreme s Sudan to e Zimbabwe
_____ *S. a. affinis*	Montane grasslands of South Africa

☐ **Madagascar Flufftail** *Sarothrura insularis*

Humid forests of e and nw Madagascar

☐ **White-winged Flufftail** *Sarothrura ayresi*

Highlands of Ethiopia and e South Africa

☐ **Slender-billed Flufftail** *Sarothrura watersi*

Highlands of e Madagascar

☐ **Nkulengu Rail** *Himantornis haematopus*

Humid forests of Sierra Leone to ne Zaire and Gabon

☐ **Gray-throated Rail** *Canirallus oculeus*

Rainforests of Sierra Leone to w Uganda and e Zaire

☐ **Madagascar Wood-Rail** *Canirallus kioloides*

_____ *C. k. kioloides*	Humid rainforests of eastern and high plateau of Madagascar
_____ *C. k. berliozi*	Locally in nw Madagascar (Sambirano district)

☐ **Swinhoe's Rail** *Coturnicops exquisitus*

Siberia and n Manchuria; winters to s China and Ryukyu Is.

☐ **Yellow Rail** *Coturnicops noveboracensis*

_____ *C. n. noveboracensis*	Disjunct in marshes of Canada and n US; winters to s US
_____ *C. n. goldmani*	Locally in marshes central Mexico (Río Lerma environs)

☐ **Speckled Rail** *Coturnicops notatus*

Locally in lowlands of South America east of the Andes

☐ **Ocellated Crake** *Micropygia schomburgkii*

_____ *M. s. schomburgkii*	Locally in Guyana and French Guiana
_____ *M. s. chapmani*	E Brazil (Bahia) to Mato Grosso and n Bolivia

☐ **Chestnut Forest-Rail** *Rallina rubra*

____ *R. r. rubra*	Arfak Mountains (w New Guinea)
____ *R. r. klossi*	New Guinea (Weyland Mts. to Jayawijaya Mts.)
____ *R. r. telefolminensis*	E New Guinea (Victor Emanuel and Hindenberg mountains)

☐ **White-striped Forest-Rail** *Rallina leucospila*

Montane forests of w New Guinea (Vogelkop Peninsula)

☐ **Forbes' Rail** *Rallina forbesi*

____ *R. f. steini*	New Guinea (Weyland Mts. to Bismarck Mts.)
____ *R. f. parva*	NE New Guinea (Mt. Mengam in Adelbert Range)
____ *R. f. dryas*	SE New Guinea (Huon Peninsula)
____ *R. f. forbesi*	SE New Guinea (Herzog Mts. to Owen Stanley Mts.)

☐ **Mayr's Rail** *Rallina mayri*

____ *R. m. mayri*	W New Guinea (Cyclops Mountains)
____ *R. m. carmichaeli*	NW Papua New Guinea (Torricelli and Bewani mountains)

☐ **Red-necked Crake** *Rallina tricolor*

New Guinea to Bismarck Arch., Lesser Sundas and ne Australia

☐ **Andaman Crake** *Rallina canningi*

Andaman Islands

☐ **Red-legged Crake** *Rallina fasciata*

Lowlands of SE Asia, Malay Archipelago and Philippines

☐ **Slaty-legged Crake** *Rallina eurizonoides*

____ *R. e. amauroptera*	Pakistan and India to Assam; winters to Sri Lanka
____ *R. e. telmatophila*	Myanmar to n Thailand, Sumatra and Java
____ *R. e. sepiaria*	Ryukyu Islands
____ *R. e. formosana*	Taiwan and Lan-yü I.
____ *R. e. eurizonoides*	Philippines; vagrant to Palau Islands (w Micronesia)
____ *R. e. alvarezi*	Batan Islands (n Philippines)
____ *R. e. minahasa*	Sulawesi and Sula Islands

☐ **Chestnut-headed Crake** *Anurolimnas castaneiceps*

____ *A. c. coccineipes*	Tropical forests of sw Colombia and ne Ecuador
____ *A. c. castaneiceps*	E Ecuador to e Peru and extreme nw Bolivia (Pando)

☐ **Russet-crowned Crake** *Anurolimnas viridis*

____ *A. v. brunnescens*	E Colombia (middle Magdalena Valley)
____ *A. v. viridis*	S Venezuela to Guianas, Amaz. Brazil, e Peru and n Bolivia

☐ **Black-banded Crake** *Anurolimnas fasciatus*

Marshes of se Colombia to e Peru and w Amazonian Brazil

☐ **Rufous-sided Crake** *Laterallus melanophaius*

____ *L. m. oenops*	Tropical se Colombia to e Peru and extreme w Brazil
____ *L. m. melanophaius*	S Venezuela to the Guianas, Brazil, Bolivia and n Argentina

☐ **Rusty-flanked Crake** *Laterallus levraudi*

Locally in wetlands of n Venezuela (north of the Orinoco)

☐ **Ruddy Crake** *Laterallus ruber*

Lowlands of s Mexico to nw Costa Rica (n Guanacaste)

☐ **White-throated Crake** *Laterallus albigularis*

____ *L. a. cinereiceps*	SE Honduras and Caribbean slope of Nicaragua to nw Panama
____ *L. a. albigularis*	Pacific lowlands of Costa Rica to w Colombia and w Ecuador
____ *L. a. cerdaleus*	E Colombia (Córdoba to Santa Marta)

☐ **Gray-breasted Crake** *Laterallus exilis*

Guatemala and Belize to n Bolivia, Amazonian and e Brazil

☐ **Junin Rail** *Laterallus tuerosi*

Andes of central Peru (Lake Junín)

☐ **Black Rail** *Laterallus jamaicensis*

_____ *L. j. coturniculus*   Coastal central California south to n Baja California
_____ *L. j. jamaicensis*   E US to Belize and Cuba; winters to C America and W Indies
_____ *L. j. murivagans*   Arid littoral of Peru
_____ *L. j. salinasi*   Central Chile (Atacama to Malleco) and extreme w Argentina

☐ **Galapagos Rail** *Laterallus spilonotus*

Galapagos Islands

☐ **Red-and-white Crake** *Laterallus leucopyrrhus*

Marshes of se Brazil to Uruguay, Paraguay and n Argentina

☐ **Rufous-faced Crake** *Laterallus xenopterus*

Marshes of se Paraguay, Bolivia (Beni) and adjacent se Brazil

☐ **Woodford's Rail** *Nesoclopeus woodfordi*

_____ *N. w. tertius*   Bougainville (Solomon Islands)
_____ *N. w. immaculatus*   Locally on Santa Isabel (Solomon Islands)
_____ *N. w. woodfordi*   Guadalcanal (Solomon Islands)

☐ **Bar-winged Rail** *Nesoclopeus poecilopterus*

Fiji Islands (Viti Levu and Ovalau); extirpated on Taveuni

☐ **Weka** *Gallirallus australis*

_____ *G. a. greyi*   North I. (New Zealand)
_____ *G. a. australis*   Western region of South I. (New Zealand)
_____ *G. a. hectori*   Formerly South I. (New Zealand); introduced Chatham Islands
_____ *G. a. scotti*   Stewart, Solander and Codfish islands (off New Zealand)

☐ **New Caledonian Rail** *Gallirallus lafresnayanus*

Forests of New Caledonia (possibly extinct)

☐ **Lord Howe Rail** *Gallirallus sylvestris*

Highlands of Lord Howe I. (on verge of extinction)

☐ **Okinawa Rail** *Gallirallus okinawae*

Swamps of n Okinawa (s Ryukyu Islands)

☐ **Buff-banded Rail** *Gallirallus philippensis*

_____ *G. p. andrewsi*   Cocos Islands (Bay of Bengal)
_____ *G. p. philippensis*   Philippine Islands
_____ *G. p. pelewensis*   Palau Islands (w Caroline Islands)
_____ *G. p. xerophilus*   Gunungapi I. (Banda Sea)
_____ *G. p. wilkinsoni*   Flores (e Lesser Sundas)
_____ *G. p. lacustris*   N New Guinea
_____ *G. p. reductus (wahgiensis)*   Central highlands, coastal ne New Guinea and Long I.
_____ *G. p. anachoretae*   Anchorite Is. (Admiralty Islands)
_____ *G. p. admiralitatis*   Admiralty Islands
_____ *G. p. praedo*   Skoki I. (Admiralty Islands)
_____ *G. p. lesouefi*   Bismarck Arch. (New Hanover, New Ireland, Tabar and Tanga)
_____ *G. p. meyeri*   Bismarck Archipelago (Witu Islands and New Britain)
_____ *G. p. christophori*   Solomon Islands
_____ *G. p. mellori (randi, norfolkensis, australis)*   S New Guinea, Australia and Norfolk I.
_____ *G. p. assimilis*   New Zealand
_____ *G. p. tounelierie (yorki)*   Coral Sea islets (se New Guinea to n New Caledonia)
_____ *G. p. swindellsi*   New Caledonia and Loyalty Islands
_____ *G. p. sethsmithi*   Fiji Islands and Vanuatu
_____ *G. p. ecaudatus*   Tonga Islands
_____ *G. p. goodsoni*   Samoa Islands and Niue I.
_____ *G. p. macquariensis†*   Macquarie I. Extinct

☐ **New Britain Rail** *Gallirallus insignis*

Forests of New Britain (Bismarck Archipelago)

☐ **Guam Rail** *Gallirallus owstoni*

Forests of Guam (s Mariana Islands). On verge of extinction

☐ **Barred Rail** *Gallirallus torquatus*
____	*G. t. torquatus*	Philippine Islands
____	*G. t. celebensis*	Sulawesi, Muna and adjacent islands
____	*G. t. sulcirostris*	Peleng I. (Banggai Is.) and Sula Is. (Taliabu, Mangole, Sanana)
____	*G. t. kuehni*	Tukangbesi Islands (Binongka and Kaledupa)
____	*G. t. limarius*	Salawati I. and nw New Guinea

☐ **Roviana Rail** *Gallirallus rovianae*

New Georgia Group (Solomon Islands)

☐ **Slaty-breasted Rail** *Gallirallus striatus*
____	*G. s. albiventer*	India and Sri Lanka to s China (Yunnan) and Thailand
____	*G. s. obscurior*	Andaman and Nicobar islands
____	*G. s. jouyi*	Coastal s China and Hainan I.
____	*G. s. taiwanus*	Taiwan
____	*G. s. gularis*	Malaysia to Indochina, Sumatra, Java and s Borneo
____	*G. s. striatus*	Philippines, Sulu Archipelago, n Borneo and Sulawesi
____	*G. s. paratermus*	Samar I. (Philippines)

☐ **Clapper Rail** *Rallus longirostris*
____	*R. l. obsoletus*	N California (Humboldt Bay to Monterey Bay)
____	*R. l. levipes*	S Calif. (Santa Barbara) to Baja Calif. (Scammons Lagoon)
____	*R. l. yumanensis*	Salton Sea and Colorado River basin to w Mexico (Nayarit)
____	*R. l. beldingi*	S Baja California (Magdalena Bay to Espírito Santo I.)
____	*R. l. crepitans*	Atlantic coast (Connecticut to ne North Carolina)
____	*R. l. waynei*	Coastal Atlantic salt marshes (se North Carolina to e Florida)
____	*R. l. saturatus*	Gulf Coast (sw Alabama to Texas and Tamaulipas)
____	*R. l. scotti*	Coastal Florida (Pensacola to Cape Sable and Jupiter)
____	*R. l. insularum*	Mangrove swamps of Florida Keys
____	*R. l. coryi*	Mangrove swamps of Bahamas
____	*R. l. pallidus*	Mangroves of se Mexico (coastal n Yucatán Peninsula)
____	*R. l. grossi*	SE Mexico (islands on Chinchorro Bank off Quintana Roo)
____	*R. l. belizensis*	Belize (Ycacos Lagoon)
____	*R. l. leucophaeus*	Isle of Pines
____	*R. l. caribaeus*	Cuba, Hispaniola and Puerto Rico to Antigua and n Antilles
____	*R. l. cypereti*	Coastal sw Colombia to Ecuador and nw Peru (Tumbes)
____	*R. l. phelpsi*	Extreme ne coastal Colombia and extreme nw Venezuela
____	*R. l. margaritae*	Margarita I. (Venezuela)
____	*R. l. pelodramus*	Trinidad
____	*R. l. longirostris*	Coasts of Guyana, Suriname and French Guiana
____	*R. l. crassirostris*	Coastal e Brazil (Amazon estuary to Santa Catarina)

☐ **King Rail** *Rallus elegans*
____	*R. e. elegans*	E Canada and ne US; winters to e Mexico
____	*R. e. tenuirostris*	Central Mexico
____	*R. e. ramsdeni*	Cuba and Isle of Pines

☐ **Plain-flanked Rail** *Rallus wetmorei*

Coastal swamps of nw Venezuela (status unknown)

☐ **Virginia Rail** *Rallus limicola*
____	*R. l. limicola*	S Canada and US; winters to Baja and Guatemala
____	*R. l. friedmanni*	SE Mexico (Puebla, México, Veracruz and Chiapas)
____	*R. l. aequatorialis*	Locally in mountains of sw Colombia, Ecuador and Peru

☐ **Bogota Rail** *Rallus semiplumbeus*
____	*R. s. semiplumbeus*	E Andes of Colombia (Boyacá and Cundinamarca)
____	*R. s. peruvianus*	One 1886 record from an unknown location in Peru

☐ **Austral Rail** *Rallus antarcticus*

Marshes of central Chile and Argentina to Tierra del Fuego

☐ **Water Rail** *Rallus aquaticus*

____	*R. a. hibernans*	Iceland
____	*R. a. aquaticus*	W Palearctic
____	*R. a. korejewi*	Iran to nw China; winters to India and s China
____	*R. a. indicus*	E Siberia to Japan; winters to SE Asia and Borneo

☐ **African Rail** *Rallus caerulescens*

Swamps and reedbeds of e and s Africa

☐ **Madagascar Rail** *Rallus madagascariensis*

Humid forests of e Madagascar

☐ **Luzon Rail** *Rallus mirificus*

Wetlands of Luzon (n Philippines). Status unknown

☐ **Lewin's Rail** *Rallus pectoralis*

____	*R. p. exsul*	Known from 4 specimens from w Flores (Lesser Sundas)
____	*R. p. mayri*	W New Guinea (Arfak and Weyland mountains)
____	*R. p. captus*	Central Highlands of New Guinea
____	*R. p. insulsus*	E New Guinea (Herzog Mountains)
____	*R. p. alberti*	Mountains of s-central Papua New Guinea
____	*R. p. clelandi†*	SW Australia. Extinct
____	*R. p. pectoralis*	S Queensland to Victoria and South Australia
____	*R. p. brachipus*	Tasmania

☐ **Auckland Islands Rail** *Lewinia muelleri*

Auckland Islands (Adams and Disappointment)

☐ **White-throated Rail** *Dryolimnas cuvieri*

____	*D. c. cuvieri*	Lowlands of Madagascar; formerly Mauritius
____	*D. c. abbotti†*	Formerly Assumption I. Extinct
____	*D. c. aldabranus*	Aldabra I.

☐ **African Crake** *Crecopsis egregia*

Africa south of the Sahara

☐ **Corn Crake** *Crex crex*

Palearctic; winters Mediterranean to Africa and Madagascar

☐ **Rouget's Rail** *Rougetius rougetii*

Highlands of Eritrea and Ethiopia

☐ **Platen's Rail** *Aramidopsis plateni*

Sulawesi

☐ **Inaccessible Island Rail** *Atlantisia rogersi*

Inaccessible I. (Tristan da Cunha)

☐ **Little Wood-Rail** *Aramides mangle*

Coastal e Brazil (Maranhão to Rio de Janeiro)

☐ **Rufous-necked Wood-Rail** *Aramides axillaris*

Coastal nw Mexico to w Ecuador, Suriname and Trinidad

☐ **Gray-necked Wood-Rail** *Aramides cajanea*

____	*A. c. mexicanus*	S Mexico (Tamaulipas to Chiapas)
____	*A. c. albiventris*	Yucatán Peninsula, Cozumel I., Belize and adj. n Guatemala
____	*A. c. vanrossemi*	S Mexico (Oaxaca) to sw Guatemala and w El Salvador
____	*A. c. pacificus*	Caribbean slope of Honduras and Nicaragua
____	*A. c. plumbeicollis*	Caribbean lowlands of ne Costa Rica
____	*A. c. latens*	San Miguel Islands and Pearl Islands (Panama)
____	*A. c. morrisoni*	Pearl Islands (San José and Pedro González)
____	*A. c. cajanea*	Costa Rica to n Argentina, Uruguay, Brazil and the Guianas

☐ **Brown Wood-Rail** *Aramides wolfi*

W Colombia to sw Ecuador and extreme n Peru

☐ **Giant Wood-Rail** *Aramides ypecaha*

Marshes of se Brazil to Paraguay, Uruguay and ne Argentina

☐ **Slaty-breasted Wood-Rail** *Aramides saracura*

Forests of se Brazil to Paraguay and ne Argentina (Misiones)

☐ **Red-winged Wood-Rail** *Aramides calopterus*

E Ecuador to ne Peru (Loreto) and w Amazonian Brazil

☐ **Uniform Crake** *Amaurolimnas concolor*
____ *A. c. concolor†*
____ *A. c. guatemalensis*
____ *A. c. castaneus*

Formerly Jamaica. Extinct
S Mexico to Ecuador
Venezuela to the Guianas, Brazil, e Peru and Bolivia

☐ **Bare-faced Rail** *Gymnocrex rosenbergii*

Sulawesi and Peleng I.

☐ **Bare-eyed Rail** *Gymnocrex plumbeiventris*
____ *G. p. plumbeiventris*
____ *G. p. hoeveni*

N Moluccas, New Guinea, Misool, Karkar and New Ireland
Aru Islands and Trans-Fly lowlands of s New Guinea

☐ **Brown Crake** *Amaurornis akool*
____ *A. a. akool*
____ *A. a. coccineipes*

India to Bangladesh and w Myanmar
SE China to ne Vietnam

☐ **Isabelline Bush-hen** *Amaurornis isabellinus*

Lowlands of Sulawesi

☐ **Plain Bush-hen** *Amaurornis olivaceus*

Philippine Islands (except Palawan)

☐ **White-breasted Waterhen** *Amaurornis phoenicurus*
____ *A. p. phoenicurus*
____ *A. p. insularis*
____ *A. p. midnicobaricus*
____ *A. p. leucomelanus*

S Asia, Malay Archipelago and Philippine Islands
Andaman and Nicobar islands
Central Nicobar Islands
Sulawesi, w Moluccas and Lesser Sundas

☐ **Talaud Bush-hen** *Amaurornis magnirostris*

Talaud Islands (n Moluccas)

☐ **Rufous-tailed Bush-hen** *Amaurornis moluccanus*
____ *A. m. moluccanus*
____ *A. m. nigrifrons*
____ *A. m. ultimus*
____ *A. m. ruficrissus*

Sangihe I., Moluccas, Misool I., w and n New Guinea
Bismarck Archipelago and Solomon Islands
E Solomon Islands
S and e New Guinea; n and e Australia

☐ **Black Crake** *Amaurornis flavirostris*

Africa south of the Sahara

☐ **Sakalava Rail** *Amaurornis olivieri*

Sakalava region of nw Madagascar (status unknown)

☐ **Black-tailed Crake** *Amaurornis bicolor*

NE India and Myanmar to sw China and n SE Asia

☐ **Little Crake** *Porzana parva*

S Palearctic region; winters Mediterranean to Africa and India

☐ **Baillon's Crake** *Porzana pusilla*
____ *P. p. intermedia (obscura)*
____ *P. p. pusilla*
____ *P. p. mira*
____ *P. p. mayri*
____ *P. p. palustris*
____ *P. p. affinis*

Europe to Asia Minor, e and s Africa and Madagascar
Central and e Asia; winters to India, Malaya and Philippines
Known from a 1912 specimen from Borneo
Known from 4 specimens from New Guinea
E New Guinea, Australia and Tasmania
New Zealand and Chatham Islands

☐ **Spotted Crake** *Porzana porzana*

Palearctic; winters Mediterranean to s Africa and SE Asia

☐ **Australian Crake** *Porzana fluminea*

Moist areas of Australia and Tasmania

☐ **Sora** *Porzana carolina*

S Alaska to n Baja and s US; winters to W Indies and n S Am.

☐ **Dot-winged Crake** *Porzana spiloptera*

S Uruguay and n Argentina (status unknown)

☐ **Ash-throated Crake** *Porzana albicollis*
_____ *P. a. olivacea*   N Colombia to Venezuela, the Guianas and Suriname; Trinidad
_____ *P. a. albicollis*   E Brazil to Paraguay, e Bolivia and extreme n Argentina

☐ **Ruddy-breasted Crake** *Porzana fusca*
_____ *P. f. fusca*   Pakistan and India to Malaysia, Indonesia and Philippines
_____ *P. f. zeylonica*   W peninsular India and Sri Lanka
_____ *P. f. erythrothorax*   Japan, e China, Manchuria, Indochina and Taiwan
_____ *P. f. phaeopyga*   Ryukyu Islands

☐ **Band-bellied Crake** *Porzana paykullii*
     NE Asia; winters in SE Asia and Greater Sundas

☐ **Spotless Crake** *Porzana tabuensis*
_____ *P. t. tabuensis*   Philippines, Australasian region and Oceania
_____ *P. t. edwardi*   Central highlands of Papua New Guinea
_____ *P. t. richardsoni*   W New Guinea (Jayawijaya Mountains)
_____ *P. t. plumbea*   S Australia, Tasmania, New Zealand and Chatham Islands

☐ **Henderson Island Crake** *Porzana atra*
     Henderson I. (Tuamotu Archipelago)

☐ **Yellow-breasted Crake** *Porzana flaviventer*
_____ *P. f. gossii*   Cuba and Jamaica
_____ *P. f. hendersoni*   Hispaniola and Puerto Rico
_____ *P. f. woodi*   S Mexico to nw Costa Rica
_____ *P. f. flaviventer*   Panama to the Guianas, e Brazil, Paraguay and n Argentina
_____ *P. f. bangsi*   Tropical n Colombia

☐ **White-browed Crake** *Porzana cinerea*
     SE Asia, Malay Archipelago, Australasia and sw Oceania

☐ **Striped Crake** *Aenigmatolimnas marginalis*
     Locally in Africa south of the Sahara

☐ **Zapata Rail** *Cyanolimnas cerverai*
     SW Cuba (Zapata Swamp)

☐ **Colombian Crake** *Neocrex colombianus*
_____ *N. c. ripleyi*   Caribbean lowlands of Panama and adjacent nw Colombia
_____ *N. c. colombianus*   Santa Marta Mountains (ne Colombia) to coastal nw Ecuador

☐ **Paint-billed Crake** *Neocrex erythrops*
_____ *N. e. olivascens*   W Panama to Venezuela, the Guianas, nw Argentina and Brazil
_____ *N. e. erythrops*   Galapagos Islands; coastal Peru (Lima to Lambayeque)

☐ **Spotted Rail** *Pardirallus maculatus*
_____ *P. m. insolitus*   Locally from s Mexico to Costa Rica
_____ *P. m. maculatus*   Cuba, Trinidad and Tobago; Venezuela to Argentina and Peru

☐ **Blackish Rail** *Pardirallus nigricans*
_____ *P. n. caucae*   Cauca Valley of Colombia (status unknown)
_____ *P. n. nigricans*   E Ecuador to e Peru, e Brazil, Paraguay and ne Argentina

☐ **Plumbeous Rail** *Pardirallus sanguinolentus*
_____ *P. s. simonsi*   Arid littoral of Peru to n Chile
_____ *P. s. tschudii*   Temperate Peru (upper Río Marañón) to Lake Titicaca
_____ *P. s. zelebori*   SE Brazil
_____ *P. s. sanguinolentus*   Extreme se Brazil to Uruguay, Paraguay and n Argentina
_____ *P. s. landbecki*   Central Chile (Atacama to Llanquihue) and adjacent Argentina
_____ *P. s. luridus*   Tierra del Fuego and Cape Horn Archipelago

☐ **Invisible Rail** *Habroptila wallacii*
     Halmahera (n Moluccas)

☐ **Chestnut Rail** *Eulabeornis castaneoventris*
_____ *E. c. sharpei* — Aru Islands
_____ *E. c. castaneoventris* — Coastal n Australia (n Western Australia to nw Queensland)

☐ **New Guinea Flightless Rail** *Megacrex inepta*
_____ *M. i. pallida* — Coastal n New Guinea (Idenburg River to Sepik River)
_____ *M. i. inepta* — Trans-Fly lowlands of se New Guinea

☐ **Watercock** *Gallicrex cinerea* — Lowlands of s and e Asia and Malay Archipelago

☐ **Purple Swamphen** *Porphyrio porphyrio*
_____ *P. p. porphyrio* — Iberian Peninsula and nw Africa
_____ *P. p. madagascariensis* — Egypt, Africa south of the Sahara and Madagascar
_____ *P. p. caspius* — Caspian Sea to nw Iran and Turkey
_____ *P. p. seistanicus* — Iraq and s Iran to Afghanistan, Pakistan and nw India
_____ *P. p. poliocephalus* — India to Sri Lanka, s China, n Thailand, Andamans, Nicobars
_____ *P. p. viridis* — S Myanmar to s Thailand, s China, Malay Pen. and Indochina
_____ *P. p. indicus* — Sumatra, Java, Bali, Borneo and Sulawesi
_____ *P. p. pulverulentus* — Karekelong I. (Talaud Islands) and Philippine Islands
_____ *P. p. pelewensis* — Palau Islands (Koror and Anguar)
_____ *P. p. melanopterus* — Moluccas and Lesser Sundas to Aru Islands and New Guinea
_____ *P. p. bellus* — Extreme sw Australia
_____ *P. p. melanotus (chathamensis)* — Australia, Tasmania, New Zealand, Kermadec and Chatham is.
_____ *P. p. samoensis* — Admiralty Is. to Samoa, New Caledonia, Solomon Is. and Fiji

☐ **Takahe** *Porphyrio mantelli*
_____ *P. m. mantelli†* — Formerly North I. (New Zealand). Extinct ca 1894
_____ *P. m. hochstetteri* — Mountains of s South I. (New Zealand). On verge of extinction

☐ **Allen's Gallinule** *Porphyrio alleni* — Africa south of the Sahara, Madagascar and Comoro Islands

☐ **Purple Gallinule** *Porphyrula martinica* — Locally from s US to n Argentina and West Indies

☐ **Azure Gallinule** *Porphyrula flavirostris* — E Colombia to s Venezuela, the Guianas, n Argentina and Brazil

☐ **San Cristobal Moorhen** *Gallinula silvestris* — Known from a 1929 specimen from San Cristóbal (Solomon Is.)

☐ **Tristan Moorhen** *Gallinula nesiotis*
_____ *G. n. nesiotis†* — Formerly Tristan da Cunha. Extinct
_____ *G. n. comeri* — Gough I. (South Atlantic Ocean)

☐ **Common Moorhen** *Gallinula chloropus*
_____ *G. c. chloropus (correina, indica)* — Palearctic; winters to Arabia and s China
_____ *C. c. meridionalis* — Africa south of the Sahara and St. Helena I.
_____ *G. c. pyrrhorrhoa* — Madagascar, Réunion, Mauritius and Comoro Islands
_____ *G. c. orientalis* — Seychelles, Andamans, Malay Pen., Indonesia and Philippines
_____ *G. c. guami* — N Marianas (Guam, Saipan, Tinian and Pagan)
_____ *G. c. sandvicensis* — Hawaiian Islands
_____ *G. c. cachinnans* — SE Canada to w Panama, Bermuda and Galapagos Islands
_____ *G. c. cerceris* — Greater and Lesser Antilles
_____ *G. c. barbadensis* — Barbados
_____ *G. c. pauxilla* — E Panama to n and w Colombia, arid w Ecuador and nw Peru
_____ *G. c. garmani* — Andes of Peru to Chile, Bolivia and nw Argentina
_____ *G. c. galeata* — Guianas to n Argentina, Uruguay and Brazil; Trinidad

☐ **Dusky Moorhen** *Gallinula tenebrosa*
_____ *G. t. frontata* — SE Borneo to Sulawesi, Moluccas, L Sundas, se New Guinea
_____ *G. t. neumanni* — N New Guinea
_____ *G. t. tenebrosa* — Locally in Australia

☐ **Lesser Moorhen** *Gallinula angulata*

Aquatic habitats of Africa south of the Sahara

☐ **Spot-flanked Gallinule** *Gallinula melanops*
____ *G. m. bogotensis*
____ *G. m. melanops*
____ *G. m. crassirostris*

Temperate Eastern Andes of Colombia
E Brazil to Uruguay, Paraguay, e Bolivia and Peru
Argentina and Chile (except extreme south)

☐ **Black-tailed Native-hen** *Gallinula ventralis*

Aquatic habitats of Australia

☐ **Tasmanian Native-hen** *Gallinula mortierii*

Tasmania

☐ **Red-knobbed Coot** *Fulica cristata*

S Spain and Morocco; e and s Africa and Madagascar

☐ **Eurasian Coot** *Fulica atra*
____ *F. a. atra*
____ *F. a. lugubris*
____ *F. a. novaeguinea*
____ *F. a. australis*

Palearctic; winters to Africa, Indonesia and Philippines
Mountains of Java and nw New Guinea
Mountains of central New Guinea
Australia, New Zealand and Buru I.; winters to Tasmania

☐ **Hawaiian Coot** *Fulica alai*

Main Hawaiian Islands (except Lanai)

☐ **American Coot** *Fulica americana*
____ *F. a. americana*
____ *F. a. columbiana*

Alaska to nw Costa Rica, Cuba, Jamaica and Grand Cayman I.
Andes of Colombia to n Ecuador

☐ **Caribbean Coot** *Fulica caribaea*

S Bahamas to Greater and Lesser Antilles and extreme n S Am.

☐ **White-winged Coot** *Fulica leucoptera*

Extreme se Brazil to e Bolivia and south to Tierra del Fuego

☐ **Slate-colored Coot** *Fulica ardesiaca*

Andes of Ecuador to nw Argentina and n Chile

☐ **Red-gartered Coot** *Fulica armillata*

Paraguay to Uruguay, se Brazil and Tierra del Fuego

☐ **Red-fronted Coot** *Fulica rufifrons*

Paraguay to Uruguay, se Brazil, s Peru and Tierra del Fuego

☐ **Giant Coot** *Fulica gigantea*

Andes of s Peru to n Chile and nw Argentina

☐ **Horned Coot** *Fulica cornuta*

High Andean lakes of sw Bolivia to n Chile and nw Argentina

ORDER: GRUIFORMES
FAMILY: HELIORNITHIDAE (Finfoots—3)

☐ **African Finfoot** *Podica senegalensis*
____ *P. s. senegalensis*
____ *P. s. somereni*
____ *P. s. camerunensis*
____ *P. s. petersii*

Senegal to e Zaire, Uganda, nw Tanzania and Ethiopia
Kenya and ne Tanzania
S Cameroon to Gabon, Congo and n Zaire
Angola to se Zaire, Zambia, Mozambique and e South Africa

☐ **Masked Finfoot** *Heliopais personata*

Bangladesh and ne India to Indochina; winters to Sumatra

☐ **Sungrebe** *Heliornis fulica*

Tropical lowlands of s Mexico to ne Argentina and Brazil

ORDER: GRUIFORMES
FAMILY: RHYNOCHETIDAE (Kagu—1)

☐ **Kagu** *Rhynochetos jubatus*

New Caledonia

ORDER: GRUIFORMES
FAMILY: EURYPYGIDAE (Sunbittern—1)

☐ **Sunbittern** *Eurypyga helias*

___ *E. h. major*	Extreme s Mexico and Guatemala to w Ecuador
___ *E. h. meridionalis*	S-central Peru (Junín and Cuzco)
___ *E. h. helias*	Colombia to Venezuela, Guianas, Amaz. Brazil and e Bolivia

ORDER: GRUIFORMES
FAMILY: CARIAMIDAE (Seriemas—2)

☐ **Red-legged Seriema** *Cariama cristata*

C and e Brazil to Bolivia, Paraguay and central Argentina

☐ **Black-legged Seriema** *Chunga burmeisteri*

Chaco of Paraguay and adjacent Bolivia to central Argentina

ORDER: GRUIFORMES
FAMILY: OTIDIDAE (Bustards—25)

☐ **Great Bustard** *Otis tarda*

___ *O. t. tarda*	S Palearctic
___ *O. t. dybowskii*	SE Russia to Mongolia and ne China

☐ **Arabian Bustard** *Ardeotis arabs*

___ *A. a. lynesi*	W Morocco (probably extinct)
___ *A. a. stieberi*	SW Mauritania and Senegambia to ne Sudan
___ *A. a .butleri*	S Sudan; single record for nw Kenya
___ *A. a. arabs*	Ethiopia to nw Somalia, sw Saudi Arabia and w Yemen

☐ **Kori Bustard** *Ardeotis kori*

___ *A. k. struthiunculus*	Ethiopia to nw Somalia, se Sudan, ne Uganda and n Tanzania
___ *A. k. kori*	S Angola to Namibia, Botswana, s Zimbabwe and Mozambique

☐ **Indian Bustard** *Ardeotis nigriceps*

Semiarid grasslands of nw and central India

☐ **Australian Bustard** *Ardeotis australis*

Lowlands of Australia and Trans-Fly of s New Guinea

☐ **Houbara Bustard** *Chlamydotis undulata*

___ *C. u. fuertaventurae*	E Canary Islands (Fuerteventura and Lanzarote)
___ *C. u. undulata*	North Africa (Morocco to western Nile Valley)
___ *C. u. macqueenii*	Nile Valley of Egypt to Arabian Peninsula and Pakistan

☐ **Ludwig's Bustard** *Neotis ludwigii*

Extreme sw Angola to Namibia, sw Botswana and South Africa

☐ **Stanley Bustard** *Neotis denhami*

___ *N. d. denhami*	SW Mauritania and Senegambia to n Uganda and Ethiopia
___ *N. d. jacksoni*	Kenya and w Tanzania to Botswana, Zimbabwe and s Angola
___ *N. d. stanleyi*	Swaziland and South Africa

□ **Heuglin's Bustard** *Neotis heuglinii*

Savanna of Eritrea to s Ethiopia, n Somalia and n Kenya

□ **Nubian Bustard** *Neotis nuba*

Sahel from w Mauritania to e Sudan

□ **White-bellied Bustard** *Eupodotis senegalensis*

____ *E. s. senegalensis*	SW Mauritania to Guinea, Central African Rep. and s Sudan
____ *E. s. canicollis*	Ethiopia to Kenya and ne Tanzania
____ *E. s. erlangeri*	S Kenya and w Tanzania
____ *E. s. mackenziei*	E Gabon to s Zaire, e Angola and w Zambia
____ *E. s. barrowii*	Botswana to Transvaal, Swaziland and e Cape Province

□ **Blue Bustard** *Eupodotis caerulescens*

Acacia and grasslands of South Africa

□ **Karoo Bustard** *Eupodotis vigorsii*

____ *E. v. namaqua*	Arid s Namibia and nw Cape Province
____ *E. v. vigorsii*	Orange Free State to s Cape Province

□ **Rueppell's Bustard** *Eupodotis rueppellii*

____ *E. r. rueppellii*	Arid coastal sw Angola (Benguela) to nw Namibia
____ *E. r. fitzsimonsi*	S Namibia (Maltahöhe to Windhoek)

□ **Little Brown Bustard** *Eupodotis humilis*

Acacia and thornbush of e Ethiopia and n Somalia

□ **Savile's Bustard** *Eupodotis savilei*

SW Mauritania and Senegal to Nigeria, Chad and s Sudan

□ **Buff-crested Bustard** *Eupodotis gindiana*

SE Sudan to s Ethiopia, Somalia, Kenya and n Tanzania

□ **Red-crested Bustard** *Eupodotis ruficrista*

S Angola to ne Namibia, Botswana, s Zambia and n S Africa

□ **Black Bustard** *Eupodotis afra*

Grasslands of sw Africa (Cape Province)

□ **White-quilled Bustard** *Eupodotis afraoides*

____ *E. a. etoschae*	NW Namibia and n Botswana
____ *E. a. damarensis*	Namibia and central Botswana
____ *E. a. afraoides*	SE Botswana to ne South Africa and Lesotho

□ **Black-bellied Bustard** *Lissotis melanogaster*

____ *E. m. melanogaster*	Senegal to Ethiopia, s Angola and Mozambique
____ *E. m. notophila*	SE Africa s of the Zambezi to w Zimbabwe and South Africa

□ **Hartlaub's Bustard** *Lissotis hartlaubii*

E Sudan to Ethiopia, Somalia, ne Uganda and n Tanzania

□ **Bengal Florican** *Houbaropsis bengalensis*

____ *E. b. bengalensis*	Grasslands of e and n India and *terai* of Nepal
____ *E. b. blandini*	Cambodia to Cochinchina and sw Vietnam

□ **Lesser Florican** *Sypheotides indica*

Locally in grasslands of Indian subcontinent

□ **Little Bustard** *Tetrax tetrax*

S Palearctic region

ORDER: CHARADRIIFORMES
FAMILY: JACANIDAE (Jacanas—8)

□ **Lesser Jacana** *Microparra capensis*

Lakes, ponds and marshes of Africa south of the Sahara

☐ **African Jacana** *Actophilornis africanus*

Lakes, ponds and marshes of Africa south of the Sahara

☐ **Madagascar Jacana** *Actophilornis albinucha*

Lakes, ponds and marshes of Madagascar

☐ **Comb-crested Jacana** *Irediparra gallinacea*

_____ *I. g. gallinacea* — S Borneo, Sulawesi, Mindanao, Moluccas and Lesser Sundas
_____ *I. g. novaeguinae* — N and central New Guinea, Misool I. and Aru Islands
_____ *I. g. novaehollandiae* — S New Guinea, D'Entrecasteaux Arch. and n and e Australia

☐ **Pheasant-tailed Jacana** *Hydrophasianus chirurgus*

Swamps and marshes of India, SE Asia and Philippine Islands

☐ **Bronze-winged Jacana** *Metopidius indicus*

Lowlands of India to sw China, SE Asia, Sumatra and Java

☐ **Northern Jacana** *Jacana spinosa*

_____ *J. s. gymnostoma* — N Mexico to Chiapas, Yucatán Peninsula and Cozumel I.
_____ *J. s. spinosa* — Belize and Guatemala to w Panama
_____ *J. s. violacea* — Cuba, Isle of Pines, Jamaica and Hispaniola

☐ **Wattled Jacana** *Jacana jacana*

_____ *J. j. hypomelaena* — W-central Panama to n Colombia
_____ *J. j. melanopygia* — W Colombia to w Venezuela
_____ *J. j. jacana* — SE Colombia to the Guianas, Brazil, Uruguay and n Argentina
_____ *J. j. intermedia* — N and central Venezuela
_____ *J. j. scapularis* — Lowlands of w Ecuador and nw Peru
_____ *J. j. peruviana* — NE Peru (lower Río Ucayalí) and adjacent nw Brazil

ORDER: CHARADRIIFORMES
FAMILY: ROSTRATULIDAE (Painted-snipes—2)

☐ **Greater Painted-snipe** *Rostratula benghalensis*

_____ *R. b. benghalensis* — Locally in Africa, Madagascar and Oriental region
_____ *R. b. australis* — Australia

☐ **American Painted-snipe** *Rostratula semicollaris*

Lowlands of se Brazil to Paraguay, cent. Argentina and Chile

ORDER: CHARADRIIFORMES
FAMILY: DROMADIDAE (Crab Plover—1)

☐ **Crab Plover** *Dromas ardeola*

Coastal n Indian Ocean; ranges to Madagascar and Andaman Is.

ORDER: CHARADRIIFORMES
FAMILY: HAEMATOPODIDAE (Oystercatchers—11)

☐ **Magellanic Oystercatcher** *Haematopus leucopodus*

S-c Chile and Argentina to Cape Horn Arch. and Falkland Is.

☐ **Blackish Oystercatcher** *Haematopus ater*

N Peru to Tierra del Fuego and Falkland Is.; winters to Uruguay

☐ **Black Oystercatcher** *Haematopus bachmani*

W Aleutians to central Baja Calif. and Los Coronados Islands

☐ **American Oystercatcher** *Haematopus palliatus*

_____ *H. p. palliatus* — Seacoasts and islands of US to s S America and West Indies
_____ *H. p. galapagensis* — Galapagos Islands

☐ **African Oystercatcher** *Haematopus moquini*

Coasts of s Africa (n Namibia to e Cape Province)

☐ **Eurasian Oystercatcher** *Haematopus ostralegus*

_____ *H. o. ostralegus*   Iceland and Scandinavia to s Europe; winters to Africa
_____ *H. o. longipes*   Russia to Siberia and south to Caspian Sea and Aral Sea
_____ *H. o. osculans*   Kamchatka Peninsula and North Korea; winters e China

☐ **Pied Oystercatcher** *Haematopus longirostris*

Australia, Tasmania, Aru and Kai islands; coastal s New Guinea

☐ **South Island Oystercatcher** *Haematopus finschi*

Highlands of South I. (New Zealand); winters to North I.

☐ **Chatham Oystercatcher** *Haematopus chathamensis*

Chatham Islands (Chatham, Mangere, Rangatira and Pitt)

☐ **Variable Oystercatcher** *Haematopus unicolor*

Coasts and islands of New Zealand

☐ **Sooty Oystercatcher** *Haematopus fuliginosus*

_____ *H. f. opthalmicus*   Coasts and islands of n Australia (Shark Bay to Lady Elliot)
_____ *H. f. fuliginosus*   Coasts and islands of W Australia (n to Brisbane); Tasmania

ORDER: CHARADRIIFORMES
FAMILY: IBIDORHYNCHIDAE (Ibisbill—1)

☐ **Ibisbill** *Ibidorhyncha struthersii*

Rocky mountain streams and rivers of central Asia

ORDER: CHARADRIIFORMES
FAMILY: RECURVIROSTRIDAE (Avocets and Stilts—10)

☐ **Black-winged Stilt** *Himantopus himantopus*

Mediterranean and sub-Saharan Africa to SE Asia and Taiwan

☐ **White-headed Stilt** *Himantopus leucocephalus*

Indonesia to Australia and New Zealand; winters to Philippines

☐ **Black Stilt** *Himantopus novaezelandiae*

MacKenzie Basin (South I., New Zealand); winters to North I.

☐ **Black-necked Stilt** *Himantopus mexicanus*

_____ *H. m. mexicanus*   W and s US to e Ecuador, sw Peru and ne Brazil; West Indies
_____ *H. m. knudseni*   Hawaiian Islands

☐ **White-backed Stilt** *Himantopus melanurus*

N Chile and e-central Peru to se Brazil and c Argentina

☐ **Banded Stilt** *Cladorhynchus leucocephalus*

Inland salt lakes of w and s Australia

☐ **Pied Avocet** *Recurvirostra avosetta*

N Africa and Eurasia; winters to South Africa and s Asia

☐ **American Avocet** *Recurvirostra americana*

S Canada to n Mexico; winters s US to Costa Rica and Cuba

☐ **Red-necked Avocet** *Recurvirostra novaehollandiae*

Locally in Australia; vagrant to Tasmania and New Zealand

☐ **Andean Avocet** *Recurvirostra andina*

Andes of s Peru to nw Argentina and n Chile

ORDER: CHARADRIIFORMES
FAMILY: BURHINIDAE (Thick-knees—9)

☐ **Water Thick-knee** *Burhinus vermiculatus*

____	*B. v. buettikoferi*	Liberia to Nigeria and Gabon; vagrant to Senegambia
____	*B. v. vermiculatus*	Zaire to Somalia and South Africa

☐ **Eurasian Thick-knee** *Burhinus oedicnemus*

____	*B. o. distinctus*	W Canary Islands
____	*B. o. insularum*	E Canary Islands
____	*B. o. saharae*	N Africa, Mediterranean is., Greece, Turkey to Iraq and Iran
____	*B. o. oedicnemus*	S Britain and Iberian Peninsula to n Balkans and Caucasus
____	*B. o. harterti*	Volga River to Turkestan, Pakistan and extreme nw India
____	*B. o. indicus*	India and Sri Lanka to Indochina; winters to Africa and Arabia

☐ **Senegal Thick-knee** *Burhinus senegalensis*

Sandy lake and river banks of sub-Saharan Africa

☐ **Spotted Thick-knee** *Burhinus capensis*

____	*B. c. maculosus*	Senegal to Somalia, Uganda and Kenya
____	*B. c. dodsoni*	Coastal Somalia and Saudi Arabia
____	*B. c. capensis*	Kenya to South Africa and west from Zambia to Angola
____	*B. c. damarensis*	Namibia to Botswana and Cape Province

☐ **Double-striped Thick-knee** *Burhinus bistriatus*

____	*B. b. bistriatus*	Arid s Mexico to nw Costa Rica
____	*B. b. dominicensis*	Hispaniola
____	*B. b. pediacus*	Savanna and pastures of n Colombia
____	*B. b. vocifer*	Venezuela to Guyana and extreme n Brazil

☐ **Peruvian Thick-knee** *Burhinus superciliaris*

Arid littoral of sw Ecuador to s Peru; one record from n Chile

☐ **Bush Thick-knee** *Burhinus grallarius*

Australia; winters to Tasmania and s New Guinea

☐ **Great Thick-knee** *Burhinus recurvirostris*

SE Iran to Indian subcontinent, Indochina and Hainan I.

☐ **Beach Thick-knee** *Burhinus magnirostris*

Andaman Is. and Malay Pen. to Philippines and Australasia

ORDER: CHARADRIIFORMES
FAMILY: GLAREOLIDAE (Pratincoles and Coursers—17)

☐ **Egyptian Plover** *Pluvianus aegyptius*

Sub-Saharan Africa south to n Zaire and extreme n Angola

☐ **Cream-colored Courser** *Cursorius cursor*

____	*C. c. bogolubovi*	SE Turkey to Iran, Afghanistan, s Pakistan and nw India
____	*C. c. cursor*	Canary Islands, North Africa, Arabian Pen. and Socotra I.
____	*C. c. exsul*	Cape Verde Islands
____	*C. c. somalensis*	Eritrea to Ethiopia and Somalia
____	*C. c. littoralis*	Extreme se Sudan to n Kenya and s Somalia

☐ **Burchell's Courser** *Cursorius rufus*

Semi-deserts of sw Angola to Namibia, Botswana and S Africa

☐ **Temminck's Courser** *Cursorius temminckii*

Savanna of sub-Saharan Africa to n South Africa

☐ **Indian Courser** *Cursorius coromandelicus*

Patchily distributed Pakistan to India and Sri Lanka

☐ **Double-banded Courser** *Smutsornis africanus*

____	*S. a. raffertyi*	Eritrea to Ethiopia and Djibouti
____	*S. a. hartingi*	SE Ethiopia (Ogaden Depression) and Somalia
____	*S. a. gracilis*	Kenya and Tanzania
____	*S. a. bisignatus*	SW Angola
____	*S. a. traylori*	Namibia (Etosha region) to Botswana (Makgadikgadi area)
____	*S. a. sharpei*	Central Namibia
____	*S. a. africanus*	Central Kalahari and s Namibia to n Cape Province
____	*S. a. granti*	W Cape Province and Karoo of South Africa

☐ **Three-banded Courser** *Rhinoptilus cinctus*

____	*R. c. cinctus*	SE Sudan to e Ethiopia, Somalia and n Kenya
____	*R. c. emini*	S Kenya to Tanzania and n Zambia
____	*R. c. seebohmi*	S Angola and n Namibia to Zimbabwe and n South Africa

☐ **Bronze-winged Courser** *Rhinoptilus chalcopterus*

Open woodlands of Africa south of the Sahara

☐ **Jerdon's Courser** *Rhinoptilus bitorquatus*

SE India (Andhra Pradesh). On verge of extinction

☐ **Australian Pratincole** *Stiltia isabella*

Australia; winters to s New Guinea and Greater Sundas

☐ **Collared Pratincole** *Glareola pratincola*

____	*G. p. pratincola*	S Europe to Pakistan; winters sub-Saharan Africa n of 5°N
____	*G. p. erlangeri*	Coastal plains of s Somalia and n Kenya
____	*G. p. fuelleborni*	Senegal to s Kenya, Zaire, Namibia and e South Africa

☐ **Oriental Pratincole** *Glareola maldivarum*

E Asia; winters India to SE Asia, Philippines and Australasia

☐ **Black-winged Pratincole** *Glareola nordmanni*

Romania to sw Russia and n Kazakstan; winters to S Africa

☐ **Madagascar Pratincole** *Glareola ocularis*

Madagascar; winters coastal Somalia to n Mozambique

☐ **Rock Pratincole** *Glareola nuchalis*

____	*G. n. liberiae*	Sierra Leone to w Cameroon
____	*G. n. nuchalis*	Chad to Ethiopia and s to Zambia, Namibia and Mozambique

☐ **Gray Pratincole** *Glareola cinerea*

Rivers of Mali to Cameroon, w Zaire and nw Angola

☐ **Small Pratincole** *Glareola lactea*

E Afghanistan and Pakistan to India and Indochina

ORDER: CHARADRIIFORMES
FAMILY: CHARADRIIDAE (Plovers and Lapwings—66)

☐ **Northern Lapwing** *Vanellus vanellus*

Palearctic; winters to n Africa, India, Myanmar and s China

☐ **Long-toed Lapwing** *Vanellus crassirostris*

____	*V. c. crassirostris*	S Sudan to e Zaire, n Malawi and w Angola
____	*V. c. leucopterus*	Tanzania to Zaire, Angola, n Botswana and ne South Africa

☐ **Blacksmith Plover** *Vanellus armatus*

Lakes and marshes of eastern and southern Africa

☐ **Spur-winged Plover** *Vanellus spinosus*

Senegambia to Red Sea, ne Tanzania and e Mediterranean

☐ **River Lapwing** *Vanellus duvaucelii*

Rivers of India and Nepal to sw China and Indochina

☐ **Yellow-wattled Lapwing** *Vanellus malabaricus*

Lowlands of s Pakistan, India, Bangladesh and Sri Lanka

☐ **Black-headed Lapwing** *Vanellus tectus*
_____ *V. t. tectus* — Senegambia to Ethiopia, Kenya and Uganda
_____ *V. t. latifrons* — S Somalia to e Kenya

☐ **White-headed Lapwing** *Vanellus albiceps* — Sandy riverbanks of Africa south of the Sahara

☐ **Senegal Lapwing** *Vanellus lugubris* — Savanna of Africa south of the Sahara

☐ **Black-winged Lapwing** *Vanellus melanopterus*
_____ *V. m. melanopterus* — Extreme s Sudan to Ethiopia; sw Kenya to central Tanzania
_____ *V. m. minor* — E Cape Province to ne Transvaal; winters to s Mozambique

☐ **Crowned Lapwing** *Vanellus coronatus*
_____ *V. c. coronatus* — Arid brush and deserts of Ethiopia to South Africa
_____ *V. c. demissus* — Arid brush and deserts of Somalia

☐ **Wattled Lapwing** *Vanellus senegallus*
_____ *V. s. senegallus* — Senegambia to s Sudan, ne Zaire and n Uganda
_____ *V. s. major* — Eritrea and Ethiopia
_____ *V. s. lateralis* — S Congo and Angola to Mozambique and ne South Africa

☐ **Spot-breasted Lapwing** *Vanellus melanocephalus* — Montane grasslands of Ethiopia

☐ **Brown-chested Lapwing** *Vanellus superciliosus* — Ghana to Cameroon and Zaire; winters in e Africa

☐ **Gray-headed Lapwing** *Vanellus cinereus* — Breeds ne China and Japan; winters to India and SE Asia

☐ **Red-wattled Lapwing** *Vanellus indicus*
_____ *V. i. aigneri* — SE Turkey to Pakistan
_____ *V. i. indicus* — E Pakistan, India, Nepal and Bangladesh
_____ *V. i. lankae* — Sri Lanka
_____ *V. i. atronuchalis* — NE India and Myanmar to n Malaysia and Indochina

☐ **Sunda Lapwing** *Vanellus macropterus* — Formerly Sumatra and Java. Last recorded ca 1920

☐ **Banded Lapwing** *Vanellus tricolor* — Southern Australia and Tasmania

☐ **Masked Lapwing** *Vanellus miles*
_____ *V. m. miles* — S Moluccas and e Lesser Sundas to New Guinea and n Australia
_____ *V. m. novaehollandiae* — E and se Australia, Tasmania and New Zealand

☐ **Sociable Lapwing** *Vanellus gregarius* — S-central Russia and Kazakstan; winters ne Africa to India

☐ **White-tailed Lapwing** *Vanellus leucurus* — SE Turkey to Afghanistan; winters ne Africa to India

☐ **Pied Lapwing** *Vanellus cayanus* — S America east of the Andes to se Brazil and ne Argentina

☐ **Southern Lapwing** *Vanellus chilensis*
_____ *V. c. cayennensis* — N South America north of the Amazon
_____ *V. c. lampronotus* — Amazonia s of the Amazon to s Brazil, n Chile and n Argentina
_____ *V. c. chilensis* — Argentina (Comodoro Rivadavia) to Chile (Chiloé I.)
_____ *V. c. fretensis* — S Argentina and s Chile

☐ **Andean Lapwing** *Vanellus resplendens* — Andes of sw Colombia to nw Argentina and n Chile

☐ **Red-kneed Dotterel** *Erythrogonys cinctus* — Interior of Australia; several records from s New Guinea

☐ **Pacific Golden-Plover** *Pluvialis fulva* — Siberia and w Alaska; winters to Africa, s Asia and Australasia

93

☐ **American Golden-Plover** *Pluvialis dominica*

Breeds Arctic North America; winters s South America

☐ **Eurasian Golden-Plover** *Pluvialis apricaria*
_____ *P. a. albifrons*
_____ *P. a. apricaria*

E-central Greenland, Iceland and Faeroes to Taymyr Peninsula
Br. Isles to Baltic Pen.; winters Mediterranean and Persian Gulf

☐ **Black-bellied Plover** *Pluvialis squatarola*

Holarctic; almost cosmopolitan post-breeding dispersal

☐ **Red-breasted Dotterel** *Charadrius obscurus*
_____ *C. o. aquilonius*
_____ *C. o. obscurus*

North I. (New Zealand)
Stewart I. (New Zealand)

☐ **Common Ringed Plover** *Charadrius hiaticula*
_____ *C. h. hiaticula*
_____ *C. h. tundrae*

NE Canada and Greenland to Scandinavia; winters to Africa
Russia and Siberia; winters Caspian Sea, sw Asia to S Africa

☐ **Semipalmated Plover** *Charadrius semipalmatus*

Breeds n N America; winters to s S America and Hawaiian Is.

☐ **Long-billed Plover** *Charadrius placidus*

Breeds e Asia; winters to India and Indochina

☐ **Little Ringed Plover** *Charadrius dubius*
_____ *C. d. curonicus*
_____ *C. d. jerdoni*
_____ *C. d. dubius*

Palearctic; winters to Africa, Arabia, e China and Indonesia
India and SE Asia
Philippines to New Guinea and Bismarck Archipelago

☐ **Wilson's Plover** *Charadrius wilsonia*
_____ *C. w. wilsonia*
_____ *C. w. beldingi*
_____ *C. w. cinnamominus*

Coastal e US to Belize and West Indies; winters to e Brazil
Pacific coast of Baja California to s Peru
Colombia to French Guiana; Netherlands Antilles

☐ **Killdeer** *Charadrius vociferus*
_____ *C. v. vociferus*
_____ *C. v. ternominatus*
_____ *C. v. peruvianus*

Canada, US and Mexico; winters to nw South America
Greater Antilles
Peru and nw Chile

☐ **Piping Plover** *Charadrius melodus*

E Canada and US; winters se US, Bahamas and Gr. Antilles

☐ **Madagascar Plover** *Charadrius thoracicus*

Coastal sw Madagascar

☐ **Kittlitz's Plover** *Charadrius pecuarius*

Africa south of the Sahara, ne Egypt and Madagascar

☐ **St. Helena Plover** *Charadrius sanctaehelenae*

St. Helena I. (s Atlantic Ocean)

☐ **Three-banded Plover** *Charadrius tricollaris*
_____ *C. t. tricollaris*
_____ *C. t. bifrontatus*

Ethiopia to Tanzania, Gabon, Chad and South Africa
Madagascar

☐ **Forbes' Plover** *Charadrius forbesi*

Grasslands and rocky hillsides of west and central Africa

☐ **White-fronted Plover** *Charadrius marginatus*
_____ *C. m. mechowi*
_____ *C. m. marginatus*
_____ *C. m. arenaceus*
_____ *C. m. tenellus*

Africa s of Sahara to n Angola, Botswana and Mozambique
S Angola to sw Cape Province
S Mozambique to s Cape Province
Madagascar

☐ **Chestnut-banded Plover** *Charadrius pallidus*
_____ *C. p. venustus*
_____ *C. p. pallidus*

Rift Valley soda lakes on Kenya/Tanzania border
Locally in southern Africa

☐ **Snowy Plover** *Charadrius alexandrinus*
  ____ *C. a. alexandrinus*
  ____ *C. a. dealbatus*
  ____ *C. a. seebohmi*
  ____ *C. a. nivosus*
  ____ *C. a. occidentalis*

W Palearctic to ne China; winters to Africa, s Asia, Indonesia
S Japan, Ryukyu Is. and e China; winters to Philippines, Borneo
SE India and Sri Lanka
US to Mexico and West Indies; winters to Panama
Coastal Peru to s-central Chile

☐ **Javan Plover** *Charadrius javanicus*

Coastal lowlands of Java, Bali and Kangean Islands

☐ **Red-capped Plover** *Charadrius ruficapillus*

Australia and Tasmania

☐ **Malaysian Plover** *Charadrius peronii*

Sandy coasts of SE Asia to Philippines and Indonesia

☐ **Collared Plover** *Charadrius collaris*

Mexico to n Argentina and central Chile

☐ **Puna Plover** *Charadrius alticola*

Andes of Peru to nw Argentina and n Chile

☐ **Two-banded Plover** *Charadrius falklandicus*

S Chile, Argentina and Falkland Islands; winters to s Brazil

☐ **Double-banded Plover** *Charadrius bicinctus*
  ____ *C. b. bicinctus*
  ____ *C. b. exilis*

New Zealand and Chatham Islands; winters to Australasia
Auckland Islands

☐ **Mongolian Plover** *Charadrius mongolus*
  ____ *C. m. pamirensis*
  ____ *C. m. atrifrons*
  ____ *C. m. schaeferi*
  ____ *C. m. mongolus*
  ____ *C. m. stegmanni*

Pamirs to w China (w Xinjiang); winters to Africa and w India
Himalayas and s Tibet: winters from India to Sumatra
E Tibet to s Mongolia; winters Thailand to Greater Sundas
E Siberia and Russian Far East; winters Taiwan to Australia
Kamchatka to Chukotsk Peninsula; winters to Australia

☐ **Greater Sandplover** *Charadrius leschenaultii*
  ____ *C. l. columbinus*
  ____ *C. l. crassirostris*
  ____ *C. l. leschenaultii*

Turkey to s Afghanistan; winters se Mediterranean and Red Sea
Transcaspia to se Kazakstan; winters to South Africa
W China to s Mongolia and s Siberia; winters Australasia

☐ **Caspian Plover** *Charadrius asiaticus*

Caspian Sea to extreme w China; winters in e and s Africa

☐ **Oriental Plover** *Charadrius veredus*

Siberia to Manchuria and Mongolia; winters to Australasia

☐ **Eurasian Dotterel** *Charadrius morinellus*

W Alaska and n Palearctic; winters North Africa to w Iran

☐ **Rufous-chested Dotterel** *Charadrius modestus*

Tierra del Fuego and Falkland Islands; winters to se Brazil

☐ **Mountain Plover** *Charadrius montanus*

Great Plains of w Canada to sw US; winters to n Mexico

☐ **Hooded Plover** *Thinornis cucullatus*

Coastal s Australia, Tasmania and islands in Bass Strait

☐ **Shore Plover** *Thinornis novaeseelandiae*

Rangitara I. (Chatham Islands off New Zealand)

☐ **Black-fronted Dotterel** *Elseyornis melanops*

Australia, Tasmania and New Zealand

☐ **Inland Dotterel** *Peltohyas australis*

Arid interior of Australia

☐ **Wrybill** *Anarhynchus frontalis*

Breeds n South I. (New Zealand); winters North I.

☐ **Diademed Sandpiper-Plover** *Phegornis mitchellii*

High elevation bogs of s Peru to w Argentina and Chile

☐ **Tawny-throated Dotterel** *Oreopholus ruficollis*
_____ *O. r. pallidus* — Arid littoral of sw Ecuador and n Peru
_____ *O. r. ruficollis* — Coastal central Peru to Tierra del Fuego; winters to se Brazil

ORDER: CHARADRIIFORMES
FAMILY: PLUVIANELLIDAE (Magellanic Plover—1)

☐ **Magellanic Plover** *Pluvianellus socialis*
Lagoons and ponds of extreme s Argentina and Chile

ORDER: CHARADRIIFORMES
FAMILY: SCOLOPACIDAE (Sandpipers—87)

☐ **Eurasian Woodcock** *Scolopax rusticola*
Locally in moist woodlands and bogs of Eurasia

☐ **Amami Woodcock** *Scolopax mira*
Amami-O-Shima, Tokuno-Shima, Okinawa, Tokashiki-Shima

☐ **Dusky Woodcock** *Scolopax saturata*
_____ *S. s. saturata* — Mountains of Sumatra and w Java
_____ *S. s. rosenbergii* — Mountains of New Guinea

☐ **Sulawesi Woodcock** *Scolopax celebensis*
Montane forests of Sulawesi

☐ **Moluccan Woodcock** *Scolopax rochussenii*
Known from 8 specimens from n Moluccas (Obi and Bacan)

☐ **American Woodcock** *Scolopax minor*
Breeds e Canada and US; winters to Gulf Coast

☐ **Chatham Islands Snipe** *Coenocorypha pusilla*
Chatham Islands (Rangitara, Mangere and Star Keys)

☐ **Subantarctic Snipe** *Coenocorypha aucklandica*
_____ *C. a. iredalei* — Islands off Stewart I. (New Zealand)
_____ *C. a. huegeli* — Snares Islands (Northeast, Broughton and Alert Stack)
_____ *C. a. aucklandica* — Auckland Islands
_____ *C. a. meinertzhagenae* — Antipodes Islands
_____ *C. a. ssp.* — Undescribed form from Campbell Islands

☐ **Jack Snipe** *Lymnocryptes minimus*
Scandinavia to Siberia; winters tropical Africa and SE Asia

☐ **Solitary Snipe** *Gallinago solitaria*
_____ *G. s. solitaria* — High mts. of central Asia; winters to Pakistan and n India
_____ *G. s. japonica* — Sakhalin and ne China; winters Korea, Japan and e China

☐ **Latham's Snipe** *Gallinago hardwickii*
Sakhalin and Japan; winters Australia, Tasmania, New Guinea

☐ **Wood Snipe** *Gallinago nemoricola*
Breeds Himalayas and Tibet; winters in India and SE Asia

☐ **Pintail Snipe** *Gallinago stenura*
Siberia; winters India to SE Asia, Indonesia and Philippines

☐ **Swinhoe's Snipe** *Gallinago megala*
Siberia; winters India to SE Asia, Philippines and n Australia

☐ **African Snipe** *Gallinago nigripennis*
_____ *G. n. aequatorialis* — Ethiopia to e Zaire, Tanzania, Malawi and Mozambique
_____ *G. n. angolensis* — Angola and Namibia to Zambia and w Zimbabwe
_____ *G. n. nigripennis* — S Mozambique and South Africa

☐ **Madagascar Snipe** *Gallinago macrodactyla*
Marshes of e and central massif of Madagascar

☐ **Great Snipe** *Gallinago media*

Breeds n Palearctic region; winters in sub-Saharan Africa

☐ **Common Snipe** *Gallinago gallinago*
_____ *G. g. faeroeensis*
_____ *G. g. gallinago*
_____ *G. g. delicata*

Iceland, Faeroe, Orkney and Sheltand is.; winters in British Is.
N Palearctic and Aleutians; winters to Africa, India, Indonesia
Aleutian Is. and Alaska to s US; winters to n South America

☐ **South American Snipe** *Gallinago paraguaiae*
_____ *G. p. paraguaiae*
_____ *G. p. magellanica*

E Colombia to the Guianas, Brazil, n Argentina and Trinidad
C Chile and Argentina to Tierra del Fuego and Falkland Islands

☐ **Puna Snipe** *Gallinago andina*

Andes of n Peru to nw Argentina and n Chile

☐ **Noble Snipe** *Gallinago nobilis*

Andes of Colombia to sw Venezuela, Ecuador and n Peru

☐ **Giant Snipe** *Gallinago undulata*
_____ *G. u. undulata*
_____ *G. u. gigantea*

Colombia to Venezuela, the Guianas and adjacent n Brazil
E Bolivia to Paraguay, se Brazil and ne Argentina

☐ **Fuegian Snipe** *Gallinago stricklandii*

Andes of s Argentina and s Chile to Tierra del Fuego

☐ **Andean Snipe** *Gallinago jamesoni*

Andes of Colombia to w Venezuela and e Bolivia

☐ **Imperial Snipe** *Gallinago imperialis*

Locally in Andes of Colombia to e Peru

☐ **Short-billed Dowitcher** *Limnodromus griseus*
_____ *L. g. caurinus*
_____ *L. g. hendersoni*
_____ *L. g. griseus*

S Alaska and s Yukon; winters coastal w US to s Peru
Plains of central Canada; winters se US to Panama
Quebec and Labrador; winters coastal e US to Brazil

☐ **Long-billed Dowitcher** *Limnodromus scolopaceus*

Breeds Siberia and Alaska; winters s US to Panama

☐ **Asian Dowitcher** *Limnodromus semipalmatus*

Siberia and Manchuria; winters to s Asia and n Australia

☐ **Black-tailed Godwit** *Limosa limosa*
_____ *L. l. islandica*
_____ *L. l. limosa*
_____ *L. l. melanuroides*

Iceland, Faeroe Is. and Shetland Is.; winters to sw Europe
W Palearctic; winters to sub-Saharan Africa and India
E Palearctic; winters to SE Asia, Philippines and Australia

☐ **Hudsonian Godwit** *Limosa haemastica*

Canadian Arctic; winters Atlantic coast of s South America

☐ **Bar-tailed Godwit** *Limosa lapponica*
_____ *L. l. lapponica*
_____ *L. l. menzbieri*
_____ *L. l. baueri*

Lapland to Taymyr Peninsula; winters to Africa and India
N Siberia; winters SE Asia to n Australia
NE Siberia to w Alaska; winters China to New Zealand

☐ **Marbled Godwit** *Limosa fedoa*
_____ *L. f. beringiae*
_____ *L. f. fedoa*

Alaskan Peninsula; winters coastal Washington to California
Great Plains of North America; winters to Argentina and Chile

☐ **Eskimo Curlew** *Numenius borealis*

Canadian Arctic; winters to s South America (possibly extinct)

☐ **Little Curlew** *Numenius minutus*

Siberia; winters to Philippines, Indonesia and Australia

☐ **Whimbrel** *Numenius phaeopus*
_____ *N. p. phaeopus*
_____ *N. p. alboaxillaris*
_____ *N. p. variegatus*
_____ *N. p. hudsonicus*

NW Palearctic; winters to Africa and India
Steppes n of Caspian Sea; winters coastal w Indian Ocean
Siberia; winters to India, Philippines, Indonesia and Australia
Alaska to n Canada; winters to s South America

☐ **Bristle-thighed Curlew** *Numenius tahitiensis*

Breeds w Alaska; winters Hawaii and Micronesia to Polynesia

☐ **Slender-billed Curlew** *Numenius tenuirostris*

Breeds sw Siberia and n Kazakstan; winters nw Africa

☐ **Eurasian Curlew** *Numenius arquata*
____ *N. a. arquata*
____ *N. a. orientalis*

British Isles to Ural Mts.; winters to nw Africa and India
E Russia, Manchuria; winters to Africa, SE Asia and Indonesia

☐ **Long-billed Curlew** *Numenius americanus*
____ *N. a. parvus*
____ *N. a. americanus*

SW Canada to California; winters to Mexico
W US; winters to Central America

☐ **Far Eastern Curlew** *Numenius madagascariensis*

Breeds ne Asia; winters to Philippines, Indonesia and Australia

☐ **Upland Sandpiper** *Bartramia longicauda*

Breeds Alaska to s US; winters in South America

☐ **Spotted Redshank** *Tringa erythropus*

Breeds n Eurasia; winters Mediterranean region to SE Asia

☐ **Common Redshank** *Tringa totanus*
____ *T. t. robusta*
____ *T. t. totanus*
____ *T. t. ussuriensis*
____ *T. t. terrignotae*
____ *T. t. craggi*
____ *T. t. eurhinus*

Iceland, Faeroes and Scotland; winters Br. Isles and w Europe
Scandinavia to Iberia; winters to Africa, India and Indonesia
Siberia and Mongolia to e Russia; winters to Africa and India
S Manchuria; winters in SE Asia
NW China (nw Xinjiang); winter grounds unknown
Pamir Mountains to n India and Tibet; winters in India

☐ **Marsh Sandpiper** *Tringa stagnatilis*

Palearctic; winters to s Africa, s Asia and Australasia

☐ **Common Greenshank** *Tringa nebularia*
____ *T. n. nebularia*
____ *T. n. glottoides*

Palearctic; winters to s Africa, s Asia, Philippines and Australia
Siberia to Kamchatka Peninsula; winters to Australasia

☐ **Nordmann's Greenshank** *Tringa guttifer*

E Siberia; winters SE Asia to Philippines and Indonesia

☐ **Greater Yellowlegs** *Tringa melanoleuca*

Alaska and Canada; winters to s South America

☐ **Lesser Yellowlegs** *Tringa flavipes*

Alaska and Canada; winters to Tierra del Fuego and Galapagos

☐ **Green Sandpiper** *Tringa ochropus*

N Eurasia; winters to s Africa, s Asia, Philippines and Australia

☐ **Solitary Sandpiper** *Tringa solitaria*
____ *T. s. cinnamomea*
____ *T. s. solitaria*

Alaska and w Canada; winters n South America to Argentina
E British Columbia to Labrador; winters Cent. and S America

☐ **Wood Sandpiper** *Tringa glareola*

Breeds n Eurasia; winters to s Africa, s Asia and Australia

☐ **Terek Sandpiper** *Xenus cinereus*

Breeds n Eurasia; winters to s Africa, s Asia and Philippines

☐ **Common Sandpiper** *Actitis hypoleucos*

Palearctic; winters to s Africa, c Asia, Philippines and Australia

☐ **Spotted Sandpiper** *Actitis macularia*

Breeds North America; winters to s South America

☐ **Gray-tailed Tattler** *Heterosceles brevipes*

Mountains of Siberia; winters to SE Asia and Australasia

☐ **Wandering Tattler** *Heterosceles incanus*

Siberia and Alaska; winters to n S Am., Hawaii and sw Oceania

☐ **Willet** *Catoptrophorus semipalmatus*
____ *C. s. inornatus*
____ *C. s. semipalmatus*

Central Canada to Nebraska and Colorado; winters to n Chile
SE Canada to Gulf Coast and West Indies; winters to s Brazil

☐ **Tuamotu Sandpiper** *Prosobonia cancellata*

Isolated islands in Tuamotu Archipelago (French Polynesia)

☐ **Ruddy Turnstone** *Arenaria interpres*
____ *A. i. interpres*
____ *A. i. morinella*

Alaska, n N Am. and n Eurasia, winters to Africa, Australasia
NE Alaska and Arctic Canada; winters se US to s S America

☐ **Black Turnstone** *Arenaria melanocephala*

Breeds coastal Alaska; winters se Alaska to nw Mexico

☐ **Surfbird** *Aphriza virgata*

Breeds Alaska and Yukon; winters to Straits of Magellan

☐ **Great Knot** *Calidris tenuirostris*

NE Siberia; winters to India, SE Asia, Philippines and Australia

☐ **Red Knot** *Calidris canutus*
____ *C. c. canutus*
____ *C. c. rogersi*
____ *C. c. roselaari*
____ *C. c. rufa*
____ *C. c. islandica*

Siberia; winters to South Africa and Australasia
Chukotsk Peninsula (Russia); winters Australasia
Wrangel I. (Russia) and nw Alaska; winters to n Venezuela
Canadian low Arctic; winters to s South America
Canadian high Arctic and n Greenland; winters in w Europe

☐ **Sanderling** *Calidris alba*

Breeds Holarctic; worldwide coastal post-breeding dispersal

☐ **Semipalmated Sandpiper** *Calidris pusilla*

Breeds Arctic North America; winters to s South America

☐ **Western Sandpiper** *Calidris mauri*

Breeds Siberia and Alaska; winters to n South America

☐ **Red-necked Stint** *Calidris ruficollis*

Breeds Siberia and Alaska; disperses to s Asia and Australasia

☐ **Little Stint** *Calidris minuta*

N Palearctic; winters to Africa and Indian subcontinent

☐ **Temminck's Stint** *Calidris temminckii*

N Palearctic; winters to Africa, Indonesia and Philippines

☐ **Long-toed Stint** *Calidris subminuta*

NE Palearctic; winters SE Asia to Philippines and Australia

☐ **Least Sandpiper** *Calidris minutilla*

Breeds n N America; winters to s S America and Hawaiian Is.

☐ **White-rumped Sandpiper** *Calidris fuscicollis*

Breeds Arctic North America; winters to Tierra del Fuego

☐ **Baird's Sandpiper** *Calidris bairdii*

Siberia, n Alaska to Greenland; winters in Andes to s S America

☐ **Pectoral Sandpiper** *Calidris melanotos*

Arctic N America and Siberia; winters to s S America, Australia

☐ **Sharp-tailed Sandpiper** *Calidris acuminata*

Breeds ne Siberia; winters in Australasia and Polynesia

☐ **Curlew Sandpiper** *Calidris ferruginea*

Arctic Siberia; winters to s Africa, SE Asia and Australasia

☐ **Dunlin** *Calidris alpina*
____ *C. a. arctica*
____ *C. a. schinzii*
____ *C. a. alpina*
____ *C. a. sakhalina*
____ *C. a. actites*
____ *C. a. kistchinskii*
____ *C. a. arcticola*
____ *C. a. pacifica*
____ *C. a. hudsonia*

NE Greenland; winters mainly nw Africa
Greenland and Iceland to s Scandinavia; winters to nw Africa
Scandinavia to e Russia; winters to Mediterranean and India
Russia to Chukotsk Pen.; winters China, Japan and Taiwan
N Sakhalin; wintering grounds unknown
Sea of Okhotsk to Kuril Islands; wintering grounds unknown
NW Alaska and nw Canada; winters e China, Korea and Japan
SW Alaska; winters in w US and w Mexico
Central Canada; winters se US and e Mexico

☐ **Purple Sandpiper** *Calidris maritima*

Holarctic tundra; winters coastal e US and nw Europe

☐ **Rock Sandpiper** *Calidris ptilocnemis*

_____	*C. p. quarta*	Kuril Islands, s Kamchatka Pen. and Komandorskiye Islands
_____	*C. p. tschuktschorum*	Chukotsk Pen. to w Alaska; winters nw N Am. and e Japan
_____	*C. p. ptilocnemis*	Pribilof, St. Matthew and Hall islands; winters Alaska Pen.
_____	*C. p. couesi*	Aleutian Islands and Alaska Peninsula

☐ **Stilt Sandpiper** *Calidris himantopus*

Breeds n North America; winters sw US to s South America

☐ **Spoonbill Sandpiper** *Eurynorhynchus pygmeus*

Breeds ne Siberia; winters in SE Asia

☐ **Broad-billed Sandpiper** *Limicola falcinellus*

_____	*L. f. falcinellus*	Scandinavia and nw Russia; winters to s Africa and India
_____	*L. f. sibirica*	N Russia; winters to India, SE Asia, Philippines and Australia

☐ **Buff-breasted Sandpiper** *Tryngites subruficollis*

Breeds Arctic North America; winters in s South America

☐ **Ruff and Reeve** *Philomachus pugnax*

Breeds n Palearctic; winters to s Africa, s Asia and Australia

☐ **Wilson's Phalarope** *Phalaropus tricolor*

Breeds Canada and US; winters in w and s South America

☐ **Red-necked Phalarope** *Phalaropus lobatus*

Holarctic circumpolar; winters at sea in southern hemisphere

☐ **Red Phalarope** *Phalaropus fulicaria*

Holarctic circumpolar; winters at sea in southern hemisphere

ORDER: CHARADRIIFORMES
FAMILY: PEDIONOMIDAE (Plains-wanderer—1)

☐ **Plains-wanderer** *Pedionomus torquatus*

Locally in sparse grasslands of inland se Australia

ORDER: CHARADRIIFORMES
FAMILY: THINOCORIDAE (Seedsnipes—4)

☐ **Rufous-bellied Seedsnipe** *Attagis gayi*

_____	*A. g. latreillii*	Andes of n Ecuador
_____	*A. g. simonsi*	Andes of Peru to n Chile and extreme nw Argentina
_____	*A. g. gayi*	Andes of Chile and Argentina to Tierra del Fuego

☐ **White-bellied Seedsnipe** *Attagis malouinus*

S Argentina, s Chile, Cape Horn Archipelago and Staten I.

☐ **Gray-breasted Seedsnipe** *Thinocorus orbignyianus*

_____	*T. o. ingae*	Andes of n Peru to n Chile and nw Argentina
_____	*T. o. orbignyianus*	Andes of n-central Chile and Argentina to Tierra del Fuego

☐ **Least Seedsnipe** *Thinocorus rumicivorus*

_____	*T. r. pallidus*	Arid littoral of sw Ecuador and extreme nw Peru
_____	*T. r. cuneicauda*	Arid littoral of Peru
_____	*T. r. bolivianus*	Altiplano of s Peru to n Chile and extreme nw Argentina
_____	*T. r. rumicivorus*	Patagonia to Tierra del Fuego; winters to c Argentina and Chile

ORDER: CHARADRIIFORMES
FAMILY: CHIONIDIDAE (Sheathbills—2)

☐ **Snowy Sheathbill** *Chionis alba*

S Argentina, s Chile, Antarctic Peninsula and Falkland Islands

☐ **Black-faced Sheathbill** *Chionis minor*

____	*C. m. marionensis*	Marion and Prince Edward islands
____	*C. m. crozettensis*	Crozet Islands
____	*C. m .minor*	Kerguelen Islands
____	*C. m. nasicornis*	Heard and McDonald islands

ORDER: CHARADRIIFORMES
FAMILY: STERCORARIIDAE (Jaegers and Skuas—7)

☐ **Chilean Skua** *Catharacta chilensis*

Coasts of s Chile and s Argentina; ranges north to tropics

☐ **South Polar Skua** *Catharacta maccormicki*

Antarctica; ranges to n Atlantic, n Pacific and Indian oceans

☐ **Brown Skua** *Catharacta antarctica*

____	*C. a. antarctica*	Falkland Is. and se Argentina; winters off se South America
____	*C. a. hamiltoni*	Tristan da Cunha and Gough I.
____	*C. a. lonnbergi*	Antarctic Pen. and circumpolar subantarctic s ocean islands

☐ **Great Skua** *Catharacta skua*

Arctic nw Eurasia; ranges to Mediterranean and n S America

☐ **Pomarine Jaeger** *Stercorarius pomarinus*

Circumpolar Arctic tundra; winters at sea in southern oceans

☐ **Parasitic Jaeger** *Stercorarius parasiticus*

Circumpolar Arctic tundra; winters at sea in southern oceans

☐ **Long-tailed Jaeger** *Stercorarius longicaudus*

____	*S. l. longicaudus*	N Scandinavia and Russia; winters to s S America and S Africa
____	*S. l. pallescens*	Arctic N Am and Siberia; winters to s S America and S Africa

ORDER: CHARADRIIFORMES
FAMILY: LARIDAE (Gulls —51)

☐ **Dolphin Gull** *Larus scoresbii*

Coasts of s Chile, Argentina and Falkland Islands

☐ **Pacific Gull** *Larus pacificus*

____	*L. p. georgii*	Coastal Western Australia to South Australia and Kangaroo I.
____	*L. p. pacificus*	SE Australia (Victoria) and Tasmania; casual to Queensland

☐ **Band-tailed Gull** *Larus belcheri*

Humboldt Current of Peru and Chile; disperses to Ecuador

☐ **Olrog's Gull** *Larus atlanticus*

Atlantic coast of ne Argentina; winters north to Uruguay

☐ **Black-tailed Gull** *Larus crassirostris*

Coastal Siberia, Kuril Islands, Korea, China and Japan

☐ **Gray Gull** *Larus modestus*

Inland nitrate deserts of Peru and Chile; ranges to Ecuador

☐ **Heermann's Gull** *Larus heermanni*

Coastal w Mexico; winters British Columbia to Guatemala

☐ **White-eyed Gull** *Larus leucophthalmus*

Red Sea and Gulf of Aqaba to Gulf of Aden

☐ **Sooty Gull** *Larus hemprichii*

Red Sea and Persian Gulf area to s Pakistan and n Kenya

☐ Mew Gull *Larus canus*
- _____ *L. c. canus* — Iceland and British Isles to White Sea; winters to N Africa
- _____ *L. c. heinei* — W Russia to Siberia; winters to Black Sea and Caspian Sea
- _____ *L. c. kamtschatschensis* — NE Siberia; winters SE Asia
- _____ *L. c. brachyrhynchus* — Alaska to Br. Columbia and Saskatchewan; winters to California

☐ Audouin's Gull *Larus audouinii*

Mediterranean basin; winters to Senegambia

☐ Ring-billed Gull *Larus delawarensis*

N America; winters to s Mexico, Bahamas and Gr. Antilles

☐ Kelp Gull *Larus dominicanus*

Circumpolar southern hemisphere coasts

☐ California Gull *Larus californicus*
- _____ *L. c. albertaensis* — S Mackenzie, Alberta and w Manitoba to South Dakota
- _____ *L. c. californicus* — E Washington to Wyoming and Calif.; winters to s Mexico

☐ Great Black-backed Gull *Larus marinus*

Palearctic and ne N Am.; winters to W Indies and Iberian Pen.

☐ Glaucous-winged Gull *Larus glaucescens*

Bering Sea to nw Oregon; winters to Japan and nw Mexico

☐ Western Gull *Larus occidentalis*
- _____ *L. o. occidentalis* — Pacific coast of British Columbia to central California
- _____ *L. o. wymani* — Central California (Monterey Bay) to s Baja California

☐ Yellow-footed Gull *Larus livens*

Islands in Gulf of California; ranges north to Salton Sea

☐ Glaucous Gull *Larus hyperboreus*
- _____ *L. h. hyperboreus* — Jan Mayen and Spitsbergen east to Taymyr Peninsula
- _____ *L. h. pallidissimus* — Taymyr Peninsula east to Bering Sea and Pribilof Islands
- _____ *L. h. barrovianus* — Alaska to w Canada (nw Mackenzie)
- _____ *L. h. leuceretes* — E Mackenzie and n Canadian Arch. to Greenland and Iceland

☐ Iceland Gull *Larus glaucoides*
- _____ *L. g. kumlieni* — NE Canada (Baffin I. and nw Ungava); winters to n US
- _____ *L. g. glaucoides* — S and w Greenland; winters to n Europe

☐ Thayer's Gull *Larus thayeri*

Hudson Bay to w Greenland; winters British Columbia to Baja

☐ Herring Gull *Larus argentatus*
- _____ *L. a. smithsonianus* — North America; winters to Central America
- _____ *L. a. argenteus* — Iceland, Faeroes, Br. Isles and w France; winters to n Iberia
- _____ *L. a. argentatus* — Scandinavia to Kola Peninsula; winters n and w Europe
- _____ *L. a. vegae* — NE Siberia; winters south to China

☐ Yellow-legged Gull *Larus cachinnans*
- _____ *L. c. atlantis* — Azores to Madeira and Canary Islands
- _____ *L. c. michahellis* — W and s Europe and nw Africa east through Mediterranean
- _____ *L. c. cachinnans* — Transcaucasus to Kazakstan; winters to s Asia and ne Africa
- _____ *L. c. barabensis* — Steppes of central Asia; winters mainly in sw Asia
- _____ *L. c. mongolicus* — SE Altai and Lake Baikal to Mongolia; winters s Asia

☐ Armenian Gull *Larus armenicus*

Lakes of Caucasus to e Turkey and Iran; winters to Red Sea

☐ Lesser Black-backed Gull *Larus fuscus*
- _____ *L. f. graellsii* — Iceland, Faeroes, Br. Isles, France, Iberia; winters to w Africa
- _____ *L. f. fuscus* — Scandinavia to White Sea; winters to Africa and sw Asia
- _____ *L. f. intermedius* — NW Europe and ne Spain; winters to w Africa
- _____ *L. f. heuglini* — N Siberia; winters to Middle East, South Africa and nw India

☐ **Great Black-headed Gull** *Larus ichthyaetus*

S-central Asia; winters Mediterranean to SE Asia

☐ **Slaty-backed Gull** *Larus schistisagus*

Breeds ne Siberia to Japan; winters south to Taiwan

☐ **Brown-headed Gull** *Larus brunnicephalus*

Mts. of s-central Asia; winters to Arabia, India and SE Asia

☐ **Gray-headed Gull** *Larus cirrocephalus*
____ *L. c. cirrocephalus*
____ *L. c. poiocephalus*

Ecuador and Peru; coastal central Brazil to Argentina
Coasts and rivers of sub-Saharan Africa and Madagascar

☐ **Hartlaub's Gull** *Larus hartlaubii*

Coastal sw Namibia to sw South Africa

☐ **Silver Gull** *Larus novaehollandiae*
____ *L. n. forsteri*
____ *L. n. novaehollandiae*

N Australia, New Caledonia and Loyalty Islands
S Australia and Tasmania

☐ **Red-billed Gull** *Larus scopulinus*

New Zealand, Chatham, Auckland and adjacent islands

☐ **Black-billed Gull** *Larus bulleri*

South I. (New Zealand); winters to North I.

☐ **Brown-hooded Gull** *Larus maculipennis*

Lakes, rivers and coasts of s South America and Falkland Is.

☐ **Black-headed Gull** *Larus ridibundus*

N Palearctic; winters to Africa, s Asia and e North America

☐ **Slender-billed Gull** *Larus genei*

Mediterranean basin to nw India; winters to ne Africa

☐ **Bonaparte's Gull** *Larus philadelphia*

N North America; winters to Mexico and Greater Antilles

☐ **Saunders' Gull** *Larus saundersi*

Coastal e China; winters South Korea and s Japan to n Vietnam

☐ **Andean Gull** *Larus serranus*

Andean lakes of Ecuador to n Argentina and central Chile

☐ **Mediterranean Gull** *Larus melanocephalus*

North Sea to Mediterranean and Black Sea; winters to n Africa

☐ **Relict Gull** *Larus relictus*

Kazakstan to Mongolia; winters to eastern China Sea

☐ **Lava Gull** *Larus fuliginosus*

Galapagos Islands

☐ **Laughing Gull** *Larus atricilla*
____ *L. a. megalopterus*
____ *L. a. atricilla*

SE California to w Mexico; Maine to C Am.; winters to Peru
West Indies to Trinidad; winters to n Brazil

☐ **Franklin's Gull** *Larus pipixcan*

W-central N America; winters Pacific coasts of S America

☐ **Little Gull** *Larus minutus*

N Eurasia and ne North America

☐ **Ivory Gull** *Pagophila eburnea*

Arctic circumpolar (mainly associated with ice pack)

☐ **Ross' Gull** *Rhodostethia rosea*

Locally in Siberia and Arctic North America

☐ **Sabine's Gull** *Xema sabini*
____ *X. s. palaearctica*
____ *X. s. tschuktschorum*
____ *X. s. woznesenskii*
____ *X. s. sabini*

Spitsbergen east to Taymyr Peninsula and Lena Delta
Chukotsk Peninsula (Russia)
NE Siberia to Alaska
N Canada to Greenland; winters sw Africa and nw S America

☐ **Swallow-tailed Gull** *Creagrus furcatus*

Galapagos Islands; winters coastal Colombia to Chile

☐ **Red-legged Kittiwake** *Rissa brevirostris*

Komandorskiye, Aleutian and Pribilof islands; winters n Pacific

☐ **Black-legged Kittiwake** *Rissa tridactyla*

_____ *R. t. tridactyla* — Circumpolar n Atlantic; winters to Saragossa Sea and w Africa
_____ *R. t. pollicaris* — Circumpolar n Pacific; winters to e China Sea and nw Mexico

ORDER: CHARADRIIFORMES
FAMILY: STERNIDAE (Terns—44)

☐ **Gull-billed Tern** *Sterna nilotica*

_____ *S. n. nilotica* — Palearctic; winters tropical Africa and Persian Gulf to India
_____ *S. n. addenda* — Transbaikalia to Manchuria and e China; winters SE Asia
_____ *S. n. macrotarsa* — Australia
_____ *S. n. arenea* — E US to Gr. Antilles and Yucatán; winters to Brazil and Peru
_____ *S. n. vanrossemi* — California to n Baja and nw Mexico; winters to Ecuador
_____ *S. n. groenvoldi* — Coasts and rivers of French Guiana to ne Argentina

☐ **Caspian Tern** *Sterna caspia*

Cosmopolitan—wide distribution worldwide

☐ **Elegant Tern** *Sterna elegans*

S California to w Mexico (Nayarit); winters Guatemala to Chile

☐ **Lesser Crested Tern** *Sterna bengalensis*

_____ *S. b. emigrata* — Libya; winters off w African coast
_____ *S. b. bengalensis* — Red Sea, Pakistan, Laccadives and Maldives; winters S Africa
_____ *S. b. torresii* — Persian Gulf; Sulawesi to New Guinea and n Australia

☐ **Sandwich Tern** *Sterna sandvicensis*

_____ *S. s. sandvicensis* — Europe to Caspian Sea; winters to S Africa, India, Sri Lanka
_____ *S. s. acuflavidus* — E N America to s Caribbean; winters to s Peru and Uruguay
_____ *S. s. eurygnatha* — Islands off Venezuela, the Guianas, e Brazil and n Argentina

☐ **Chinese Crested Tern** *Sterna bernsteini*

Coastal e China; winters to Thailand, Borneo and Moluccas

☐ **Royal Tern** *Sterna maxima*

_____ *S. m. albididorsalis* — Coastal Mauritania to Guinea; winters to Namibia
_____ *S. m. maxima* — Coastal US to W Indies, Guianas, Brazil; winters to Argentina

☐ **Great Crested Tern** *Sterna bergii*

_____ *S. b. bergii* — Namibia to South Africa; disperses to Mozambique
_____ *S. b. enigma* — Islands off Mozambique, Zambezi River delta and Madagascar
_____ *S. b. thalassina* — Tanzania, Seychelles, Aldabra and Rodriques I.
_____ *S. b. velox* — Red Sea and nw Somalia to Maldives, Myanmar and Sri Lanka
_____ *S. b. cristata* — Malaysia to Philippines and Ryukyus; e Australia to Society Is.
_____ *S. b. gwendolenae* — W and nw Australia

☐ **River Tern** *Sterna aurantia*

Pakistan to s India, Sri Lanka, Nepal and sw China

☐ **Roseate Tern** *Sterna dougallii*

_____ *S. d. dougallii* — Coastal e N America to W Indies; Azores, Europe and Africa
_____ *S. d. arideensis* — Seychelles to Madagascar and Rodrigues I.
_____ *S. d. korustes* — Sri Lanka, Andaman Islands and Mergui Archipelago
_____ *S. d. bangsi* — Arabian Sea; e China to New Guinea, Solomons and Ryukyus
_____ *S. d. gracilis* — Moluccas and Australia

☐ **Black-naped Tern** *Sterna sumatrana*

_____ *S. s. sumatrana* — Andaman and Nicobar is. to Japan, Malaysia and Australasia
_____ *S. s. mathewsi* — Aldabra, Amirante, Chagos and Maldive islands

☐ **White-fronted Tern** *Sterna striata*

____ *S. s. incerta* — Flinders I. and Cape Barren I. (off Tasmania)
____ *S. s. striata* — North, South and Stewart islands (New Zealand)
____ *S. s. aucklandorna* — Chatham Islands, Auckland Islands and (?) Snares Islands

☐ **South American Tern** *Sterna hirundinacea*

Coasts and islands of s South America and Falkland Islands

☐ **Common Tern** *Sterna hirundo*

____ *S. h. hirundo* — N Am., S Am., Atlantic islands, Europe and w Africa to China
____ *S. h. minussensis* — C Asia to n Mongolia and s Tibet; winters Indian Ocean
____ *S. h. tibetana* — W Mongolia to Kashmir and Tibet; winters e Indian Ocean
____ *S. h. longipennis* — NE Siberia to ne China; winters SE Asia to Australia

☐ **Arctic Tern** *Sterna paradisaea*

Arctic circumpolar; winters sub-Antarctic and Antarctic seas

☐ **Antarctic Tern** *Sterna vittata*

____ *S. v. tristanensis* — Tristan da Cunha, Gough I.; Amsterdam I. and (?) St. Paul I.
____ *S. v. georgiae* — South Georgia I.; possibly S Orkney and S Sandwich islands
____ *S. v. gaini* — South Shetland Islands
____ *S. v. vittata* — Prince Edward, Marion, Crozet and Kerguelen islands
____ *S. v. bethunei* — Stewart, Snares, Auckland, Bounty, Antipodes, Campbell is.
____ *S. v. macquariensis* — Macquarie I.

☐ **Kerguelen Tern** *Sterna virgata*

Marion, Crozet, and Kerguelen islands

☐ **Forster's Tern** *Sterna forsteri*

N America; winters s US to Costa Rica and Greater Antilles

☐ **Snowy-crowned Tern** *Sterna trudeaui*

Lagoons and marshes of se Brazil and Uruguay to Patagonia

☐ **Little Tern** *Sterna albifrons*

____ *S. a. albifrons* — Europe to w Asia and w Indian Ocean; winters Africa to India
____ *S. a. guineae* — Ghana to Gabon
____ *S. a. innominata* — Islands in Persian Gulf
____ *S. a. pusilla* — NE India, Sri Lanka, Myanmar and islands off Sumatra and Java
____ *S. a. sinensis* — SE Russia to Japan, SE Asia, Philippines and New Guinea
____ *S. a. placens* — E Australia and e Tasmania

☐ **Saunders' Tern** *Sterna saundersi*

Red Sea to India and Sri Lanka; winters to Malay Peninsula

☐ **Least Tern** *Sterna antillarum*

____ *S. a. browni* — S California to Baja and w Mexico; winters to Central America
____ *S. a. athalassos* — N Great Plains to Louisiana and Texas; winters to n Brazil
____ *S. a. antillarum* — E US to Honduras, Caribbean and Guianas; winters to n Brazil

☐ **Yellow-billed Tern** *Sterna superciliaris*

Rivers and lakes of South America east of the Andes

☐ **Peruvian Tern** *Sterna lorata*

Arid Humboldt Current coasts of Ecuador to n Chile

☐ **Fairy Tern** *Sterna nereis*

____ *S. n. horni* — Western Australia
____ *S. n. nereis* — South Australia, Victoria and Tasmania
____ *S. n. exsul* — New Caledonia
____ *S. n. davisae* — N North I. (New Zealand)

☐ **Damara Tern** *Sterna balaenarum*

Coastal Namibia to Cape Province; winters to n Angola

☐ **White-cheeked Tern** *Sterna repressa*

Islands and coasts of Red Sea and Persian Gulf to India

☐ **Black-bellied Tern** *Sterna acuticauda*

Pakistan, Nepal and India to sw China, Myanmar and SE Asia

☐ **Aleutian Tern** *Sterna aleutica*

Alaska and Siberia; winters to Philippines and Hong Kong

☐ **Gray-backed Tern** *Sterna lunata*

Islands in tropical Pacific Ocean

☐ **Black-fronted Tern** *Sterna albostriata*

South I.; disperses to Stewart I. and North I. (New Zealand)

☐ **Bridled Tern** *Sterna anaethetus*

_____ *S. a. melanoptera*	Coastal w Africa
_____ *S. a. fuligula*	Red Sea and East Africa to India
_____ *S. a. antarctica*	Madagascar, Aldabra, Seychelles, Mascarene and Andaman is.
_____ *S. a. anaethetus*	Ryukyu Is., Taiwan, Philippines, Indonesia and Australia
_____ *S. a. nelsoni*	W coast of Mexico and Central America
_____ *S. a. recognita*	West Indies, Belize and islands off Venezuela

☐ **Sooty Tern** *Sterna fuscata*

_____ *S. f. fuscata*	Gulf of Mexico, e Mexico and W Indies; Gulf of Guinea islands
_____ *S. f. nubilosa*	S Red Sea and Indian Ocean to Ryukyu Is. and Philippines
_____ *S. f. infuscata*	Central Indonesia
_____ *S. f. serrata*	New Guinea, Australia and New Caledonia
_____ *S. f. kermadeci*	Kermadec Islands
_____ *S. f. oahuensis*	Bonin Islands to Hawaii and South Pacific islands
_____ *S. f. crissalis*	Islands off w Mexico and Central America to Galapagos Is.
_____ *S. f. luctuosa*	Juan Fernández Islands (off Chile)

☐ **Whiskered Tern** *Chlidonias hybridus*

_____ *C. h. hybridus*	SW Europe to Kazakstan; winters Africa and sw Asia
_____ *C. h. swinhoei*	Transbaikalia to e China and Taiwan
_____ *C. h. indicus*	E Iran and Pakistan to n India
_____ *C. h. javanicus*	NE India and Sri Lanka; winters Malaysia and Indonesia
_____ *C. h. sclateri*	Kenya to South Africa and Madagascar
_____ *C. h. fluviatilis*	Australia; disperses to New Guinea and Moluccas

☐ **White-winged Tern** *Chlidonias leucopterus*

Palearctic; winters to Africa, s Asia and Australasia

☐ **Black Tern** *Chlidonias niger*

_____ *C. n. niger*	W Palearctic; winters in Africa
_____ *C. n. surinamensis*	N North America; winters Central America and n S America

☐ **Large-billed Tern** *Phaetusa simplex*

_____ *P. s. simplex*	E Colombia to e Brazil and Amazonia; Trinidad; w Ecuador
_____ *P. s. chloropoda*	Basins of Río Paraguay and Río Paraná to n Argentina

☐ **Lesser Noddy** *Anous tenuirostris*

_____ *A. t. tenuirostris*	Seychelles, Mascarene and Maldive islands
_____ *A. t. melanops*	Houtman Abrolhos Islands (w Australia); formerly Indonesia

☐ **Black Noddy** *Anous minutus*

_____ *A. m. worcesteri*	Cavilli I. and Tubbataha Reef (Sulu Sea)
_____ *A. m. minutus*	NE Australia and New Guinea to Tuamotu Archipelago
_____ *A. m. marcusi*	Marcus I. and Wake I. through Micronesia to Caroline Islands
_____ *A. m. melanogenys*	Hawaiian Islands
_____ *A. m. diamesus*	Clipperton I. (off w Mexico) and Cocos I. (off Costa Rica)
_____ *A. m. americanus*	Islands off Central America and Venezuela; Lesser Antilles
_____ *A. m. atlanticus*	St. Helena and adjacent s Atlantic islands to Gulf of Guinea

☐ **Brown Noddy** *Anous stolidus*

____	*A. s. plumbeigularis*	S Red Sea and Gulf of Aden
____	*A. s. pileatus*	Seychelles and Madagascar to Australia, Polynesia and Hawaii
____	*A. s. galapagensis*	Galapagos Islands
____	*A. s. ridgwayi*	W Mexico (Revillagigedo Islands) to Costa Rica (Cocos I.)
____	*A. s. stolidus*	Caribbean and s Atlantic islands; Gulf of Guinea to Cameroon

☐ **Blue Noddy** *Procelsterna cerulea*

____	*P. c. saxatilis*	Marcus I. and n Marshall Islands to nw Hawaiian Islands
____	*P. c. nebouxi*	Ellice I. to Phoenix Islands, Fiji and Western Samoa
____	*P. c. cerulea*	Christmas I. (Line Islands) and Marquesas Islands
____	*P. c. teretirostris*	Tuamotu Archipelago, Cook, Austral and Society islands
____	*P. c. murphyi*	Gambier Islands

Gray Noddy *Procelsterna albivitta*

____	*P. a. albivitta*	Lord Howe I., Norfolk I., Kermadec Islands and Tonga
____	*P. a. skottsbergii*	Henderson I., Easter I. and Sala y Gómez I. (Chile)
____	*P. a. imitatrix*	Desaventurados Is. off Chile (San Ambrosio and San Félix)

☐ **White Tern** *Gygis alba*

____	*G. a. alba*	Caroline Is. to Hawaii, Clipperton, Cocos and s Atlantic islands
____	*G. a. candida*	Seychelles and Mascarene islands to s-central Pacific
____	*G. a. leucopes*	Henderson I. and Pitcairn I.
____	*G. a. microrhyncha*	Marquesas, Phoenix and Line islands

☐ **Inca Tern** *Larosterna inca*

Islands off Peru and Chile; ranges rarely n to Ecuador

ORDER: CHARADRIIFORMES
FAMILY: RYNCHOPIDAE (Skimmers—3)

☐ **Black Skimmer** *Rynchops niger*

____	*R. n. niger*	Coastal US and Mexico; winters to Panama
____	*R. n. cinerascens*	Coasts and rivers of n S America to Bolivia and nw Argentina
____	*R. n. intercedens*	E Brazil to Paraguay, Uruguay and ne Argentina

☐ **African Skimmer** *Rynchops flavirostris*

Major rivers, lakes and coasts of Africa south of the Sahara

☐ **Indian Skimmer** *Rynchops albicollis*

Rivers and lakes of Indian subcontinent and Mekong Delta

ORDER: CHARADRIIFORMES
FAMILY: ALCIDAE (Auks, Murres and Puffins—23)

☐ **Dovekie** *Alle alle*

____	*A. a. alle*	Baffin I., Greenland and Iceland to Novaya Zemlya
____	*A. a. polaris*	Frans Josef Land to St. Lawrence I.; winters to Maine

☐ **Common Murre** *Uria aalge*

____	*U. a. aalge*	E N America, Greenland and Iceland to Norway and Baltic Sea
____	*U. a. albionis*	British Isles to w Iberian Peninsula; Helgoland
____	*U. a. hyperborea*	Svalbard and n Norway to Murmansk and Novaya Zemlya
____	*U. a. inornata*	Korea, Japan and Kamchatka to Bering Sea and Br. Columbia
____	*U. a. californica*	N Washington to s California

☐ **Thick-billed Murre** *Uria lomvia*

____   *U. l. lomvia*   Gulf of St. Lawrence to Greenland and Novaya Zemlya

____   *U. l. eleonorae*   E Taymyr Peninsula to New Siberian Islands (Russia)

____   *U. l. heckeri*   Wrangel I., Herald I. and n Chukotsk Peninsula

____   *U. l. arra*   N Japan and Aleutian Islands to se Alaska

☐ **Razorbill** *Alca torda*

____   *A. t. torda*   NE North America; Scandinavia to Murmansk and White Sea

____   *A. t. islandica*   Iceland and Br. Isles to France; winters to Mediterranean

☐ **Black Guillemot** *Cepphus grylle*

____   *C. g. mandtii*   Arctic e North America and Arctic n Palearctic

____   *C. g. arcticus*   Subarctic e N America and s Greenland to Br. Isles, Scandinavia

____   *C. g. islandicus*   Iceland

____   *C. g. faeroeensis*   Faeroe Islands

____   *C. g. grylle*   Baltic Sea

☐ **Pigeon Guillemot** *Cepphus columba*

____   *C. c. columba*   NE Siberia to Bering Sea and w Alaska

____   *C. c. snowi*   Kuril Islands

____   *C. c. kaiurka*   Komandorskiye Islands to w-central Aleutian Islands

____   *C. c. adianta*   Central Aleutian Islands south to Washington

____   *C. c. eureka*   Oregon and California

☐ **Spectacled Guillemot** *Cepphus carbo*

Kamchatka and Sea of Okhotsk to Korea, Kuril Is. and n Japan

☐ **Marbled Murrelet** *Brachyramphus marmoratus*

W Aleutian Islands and Alaska to central California

☐ **Long-billed Murrelet** *Brachyramphus perdix*

Kamchatka Peninsula and Sea of Okhotsk to Hokkaido

☐ **Kittlitz's Murrelet** *Brachyramphus brevirostris*

Bering Sea to Gulf of Alaska; winters to Glacier Bay

☐ **Xantus' Murrelet** *Synthliboramphus hypoleucus*

____   *S. h. scrippsi*   Channel Islands and islands off w coast of Baja California

____   *S. h. hypoleucus*   San Benito I. and Guadalupe I. (off Baja California)

☐ **Craveri's Murrelet** *Synthliboramphus craveri*

Islands in Gulf of California; disperses north to s California

☐ **Ancient Murrelet** *Synthliboramphus antiquus*

____   *S. a. antiquus*   E Asia, Aleutians and s Alaska; winters to California

____   *S. a. microrhynchos*   Komandorskiye Islands; winters to Ryukyu Islands

☐ **Japanese Murrelet** *Synthliboramphus wumizusume*

Coasts and islands off e and s Japan and South Korea

☐ **Cassin's Auklet** *Ptychoramphus aleuticus*

____   *P. a. aleuticus*   Aleutian Islands and Alaska to n Baja California

____   *P. a. australis*   S Baja (San Benito to Asunción and San Roque islands)

☐ **Parakeet Auklet** *Aethia psittacula*

N Pacific and Bering Sea; winters to Japan and s California

☐ **Crested Auklet** *Aethia cristatella*

Breeds w Alaska and e Siberia; winters south to Japan

☐ **Whiskered Auklet** *Aethia pygmaea*

Breeds e Siberia and Aleutian Islands; winters south to Japan

☐ **Least Auklet** *Aethia pusilla*

Breeds e Siberia and w Alaska; winters south to n Japan

☐ **Rhinoceros Auklet** *Cerorhinca monocerata*

E Asia and w North America; winters to Baja California

☐ **Atlantic Puffin** *Fratercula arctica*

____	*F. a. naumanni*	N Canada and Greenland to Spitsbergen and n Novaya Zemlya
____	*F. a. arctica*	Baffin I. to Maine, Scandinavia and s Novaya Zemlya
____	*F. a. grabae*	Faeroe Islands, s Scandinavia and British Isles to nw France

☐ **Horned Puffin** *Fratercula corniculata*

E Siberia and nw N America; winters to Japan and s California

☐ **Tufted Puffin** *Fratercula cirrhata*

Coasts and islands of ne Asia to Aleutians and s California

ORDER: PTEROCLIFORMES
FAMILY: PTEROCLIDAE (Sandgrouse—16)

☐ **Tibetan Sandgrouse** *Syrrhaptes tibetanus*

Inhospitable wastes of e Afghanistan to Tibetan plateau

☐ **Pallas' Sandgrouse** *Syrrhaptes paradoxus*

Sandy steppes of central Asia

☐ **Pin-tailed Sandgrouse** *Pterocles alchata*

____	*P. a. alchata*	Spain and s France; formerly Portugal
____	*P. a. caudacutus*	W Sahara to Middle East and w India

☐ **Namaqua Sandgrouse** *Pterocles namaqua*

Dry grasslands of southern Africa

☐ **Chestnut-bellied Sandgrouse** *Pterocles exustus*

____	*P. e. exustus*	Mauritania and Senegambia east to Sudan
____	*P. e. floweri†*	Formerly Egypt. Extinct
____	*P. e. ellioti*	SE Sudan to Eritrea, n Ethiopia and Somalia
____	*P. e. olivascens*	S Ethiopia to Somalia, Kenya and n Tanzania
____	*P. e. erlangeri*	W and s Arabian Peninsula
____	*P. e. hindustan*	SE Iran to Pakistan and India

☐ **Spotted Sandgrouse** *Pterocles senegallus*

Deserts of sub-Saharan Africa and Arabian Pen. to w India

☐ **Black-bellied Sandgrouse** *Pterocles orientalis*

____	*P. o. orientalis*	Fuerteventura I., Iberian Peninsula and Morocco to w Iran
____	*P. o. arenarius*	Kazakstan to s Iran, Afghanistan, and nw China (nw Xinjiang)

☐ **Yellow-throated Sandgrouse** *Pterocles gutturalis*

____	*P. g. saturatior*	Ethiopia to Kenya, Tanzania and extreme n Zambia
____	*P. g. gutturalis*	S Zambia and Botswana to Transvaal and Cape Province

☐ **Crowned Sandgrouse** *Pterocles coronatus*

____	*P. c. coronatus*	Central Sahara to Mediterranean and Morocco east to Red Sea
____	*P. c. vastitas*	Sinai Peninsula and deserts of s Israel and Jordan
____	*P. c. atratus*	S Arabia, Iraq and s Iran to w Pakistan and Afghanistan
____	*P. c. saturatus*	Mountains of interior of Oman
____	*P. c. ladas*	N Pakistan (Kashmir) and adjacent India

☐ **Black-faced Sandgrouse** *Pterocles decoratus*

____	*P. d. ellenbecki*	NE Uganda to n Kenya, s Ethiopia and s Somalia
____	*P. d. decoratus*	Savanna and coastal dunes of se Kenya and e Tanzania
____	*P. d. loverridgei*	W Kenya and w Tanzania

☐ **Madagascar Sandgrouse** *Pterocles personatus*

Arid lowlands of Madagascar

☐ **Lichtenstein's Sandgrouse** *Pterocles lichtensteinii*

____	*P. l. targius*	Sahara and Sahel from Morocco and Mauritania to Chad
____	*P. l. lichtensteinii*	S Israel, Sinai, se Egypt to n Ethiopia, n Somalia and Socotra I.
____	*P. l. sukensis*	SE Sudan and s Ethiopia to central Kenya
____	*P. l. ingramsi*	S Yemen (Hadramaut)
____	*P. l. arabicus*	S Arabia to s Iran, s Afghanistan and Pakistan

☐ **Double-banded Sandgrouse** *Pterocles bicinctus*

____	*P. b. ansorgei*	SW Angola
____	*P. b. bicinctus*	Namibia, Botswana and nw Cape Province
____	*P. b. multicolor*	Mozambique, Malawi and Zambia to Transvaal

☐ **Four-banded Sandgrouse** *Pterocles quadricinctus*

Savanna and thornscrub of sub-Saharan Africa

☐ **Painted Sandgrouse** *Pterocles indicus*

Arid rocky lowlands of e Pakistan and peninsular India

☐ **Burchell's Sandgrouse** *Pterocles burchelli*

SE Angola to Namibia, Botswana and n Cape Province

ORDER: COLUMBIFORMES
FAMILY: COLUMBIDAE (Pigeons and Doves—308)

☐ **Rock Dove** *Columba livia*

____	*C. l. livia*	Western Palearctic
____	*C. l. atlantis*	Madeira, Azores and Cape Verde Islands
____	*C. l. canariensis*	Canary Islands and islands off Morocco
____	*C. l. gymnocyclus*	Mauritania, Mali and Ghana; coastal Senegambia and Guinea
____	*C. l. targia*	Central Sahara to central Sudan
____	*C. l. dakhlae*	Egypt (Dakhla and Kharga oases)
____	*C. l. butleri*	Red Sea Province and Egyptian Sudan
____	*C. l. schimperi*	Nile Valley to Khartoum; Red Sea Hills of e Egypt to n Eritrea
____	*C. l. palaestinae*	Palestine, Sinai and Arabia to Aden and Oman
____	*C. l. gaddi*	Iran to Azerbaijan, Transcaspia, Afghanistan and Uzbekistan
____	*C. l. neglecta*	Mountains of central Asia
____	*C. l. intermedia*	Peninsular India and Sri Lanka
____	*C. l. nigricans*	Mongolia and n China (Shanxi, Jilin and Gansu)

☐ **Hill Pigeon** *Columba rupestris*

____	*C. r. turkestanica*	Altai Mts. to Turkestan, Tibet and n Himalayas
____	*C. r. rupestris*	W Mongolia to Mongolia, e Tibet, s China and Korea

☐ **Snow Pigeon** *Columba leuconota*

____	*C. l. leuconota*	Himalayas from w Afghanistan to Sikkim
____	*C. l. gradaria*	Mts. of e Tibet to sw China (Yunnan) and extreme n Myanmar

☐ **Speckled Pigeon** *Columba guinea*

____	*C. g. guinea*	Senegambia to Ethiopia, Somalia, Uganda, Kenya and Tanzania
____	*C. g. phaeonota*	SW Angola to Zimbabwe and Cape Province

☐ **White-collared Pigeon** *Columba albitorques*

Highlands of Ethiopia and Eritrea

☐ **Stock Pigeon** *Columba oenas*

____	*C. o. oenas*	W Europe and nw Africa to Caspian Sea and Kazakstan
____	*C. o. yarkandensis*	Uzbekistan and Tajikistan to Tien Shan and e Xinjiang

☐ **Pale-backed Pigeon** *Columba eversmanni*

NE Iran to Siberia, nw India and extreme w China

☐ **Somali Pigeon** *Columba oliviae*

Arid coastal hills of n Somalia

☐ **Common Wood-Pigeon** *Columba palumbus*
____ *C. p. azorica*
____ *C. p. maderensis†*
____ *C. p. excelsa*
____ *C. p. palumbus*
____ *C. p. iranica*
____ *C. p. casiotis*

E and central Azores
Formerly mountains of Madeira. Probably extinct
Morocco, Algeria and Tunisia
Europe to w Siberia, e Turkey and Iraq; winters to n Africa
S Transcaspia to Iran
Kazakstan to n Afghanistan, n Pakistan, nw India and Nepal

☐ **Trocaz Pigeon** *Columba trocaz*

Laurel forests of Madeira

☐ **Bolle's Pigeon** *Columba bollii*

W Canary Islands (La Palma, Gomera, El Hierro and Tenerife)

☐ **Afep Pigeon** *Columba unicincta*

Equatorial forests of w and central Africa

☐ **Laurel Pigeon** *Columba junoniae*

W Canary Islands (La Palma, La Gomera and Tenerife)

☐ **Rameron Pigeon** *Columba arquatrix*

Ethiopia to e Zaire, Tanzania and South Africa; w Angola

☐ **Cameroon Pigeon** *Columba sjostedti*

Highland forests of e Nigeria and sw Cameroon

☐ **Maroon Pigeon** *Columba thomensis*

Forests of São Tomé I. (Gulf of Guinea)

☐ **Comoro Pigeon** *Columba polleni*

Mainly high elevation evergreen forests of Comoro Islands

☐ **Speckled Wood-Pigeon** *Columba hodgsonii*

Montane forests of Kashmir to India, w-c China and Myanmar

☐ **White-naped Pigeon** *Columba albinucha*

W Cameroon; e Zaire, w Uganda and w Rwanda

☐ **Ashy Wood-Pigeon** *Columba pulchricollis*

India to w China, Tibet, Myanmar, nw Thailand and Taiwan

☐ **Nilgiri Wood-Pigeon** *Columba elphinstonii*

SW India (Western Ghats)

☐ **Ceylon Wood-Pigeon** *Columba torringtoni*

Sri Lanka

☐ **Pale-capped Pigeon** *Columba punicea*

S Tibet to e India, Myanmar, Thailand and Hainan I. (s China)

☐ **Silvery Wood-Pigeon** *Columba argentina*

Sumatra, Borneo and adjacent islands

☐ **Andaman Wood-Pigeon** *Columba palumboides*

Andaman Islands and Nicobar Islands

☐ **Japanese Wood-Pigeon** *Columba janthina*
____ *C. j. janthina*
____ *C. j. nitens*

Small islands sw of South Korea to Ryukyu Islands
Ogasawara (Bonin Islands) and Iwo (Volcano Islands)

☐ **Metallic Pigeon** *Columba vitiensis*
____ *C. v. griseogularis*
____ *C. v. anthracina*
____ *C. v. metallica*
____ *C. v. halmaheira*
____ *C. v. leopoldi*
____ *C. v. hypoenochroa*
____ *C. v. vitiensis*
____ *C. v. castaneiceps*

Philippines, Sulu Archipelago and islands off n Borneo
Palawan, Calauit and islands off north Borneo
Lesser Sundas
Banggai, Sulas, Kai, Moluccas to New Guinea and Solomons
Vanuatu
New Caledonia, Isle of Pines and Loyalty Islands
Fiji Islands
W Samoa (Savai'i, Apolima, Manono and Upolu)

☐ **White-headed Pigeon** *Columba leucomela*

Coasts and forested islands of e Australia

☐ **Yellow-legged Pigeon** *Columba pallidiceps*

Bismarck Archipelago and Solomon Islands

☐ **White-crowned Pigeon** *Columba leucocephala*

S Florida and offshore islands from West Indies to nw Panama

☐ **Scaly-naped Pigeon** *Columba squamosa*

Greater Antilles, Lesser Antilles and Netherlands Antilles

☐ **Scaled Pigeon** *Columba speciosa*

Tropical s Mexico to Brazil and ne Argentina

☐ **Picazuro Pigeon** *Columba picazuro*
____ *C. p. marginalis* — NE Brazil (Piauí, Bahia and Goiás)
____ *C. p. picazuro* — E Brazil (Pernambuco) to Bolivia and s-central Argentina

☐ **Bare-eyed Pigeon** *Columba corensis*

Arid coastal ne Colombia to n Venezuela and adjacent islands

☐ **Spot-winged Pigeon** *Columba maculosa*
____ *C. m. albipennis* — S Peru to w Bolivia and extreme nw Argentina
____ *C. m. maculosa* — S Bolivia to Paraguay, se Brazil, Uruguay and s-c Argentina

☐ **Band-tailed Pigeon** *Columba fasciata*
____ *C. f. fasciata* — W North America from sw Canada to Nicaragua
____ *C. f. monilis* — San Pedro Mártir of n Baja California
____ *C. f. vioscae* — Mountains of extreme s Baja California (Sierra de la Laguna)
____ *C. f. letonai* — Honduras and El Salvador (including Volcán de San Miguel)
____ *C. f. parva* — N Nicaragua
____ *C. f. crissalis* — Costa Rica and w Panama
____ *C. f. roraima* — *Teupis* of s Venezuela (Mt. Roraima)
____ *C. f. albilinea* — Colombia to Venezuela, nw Brazil, e Bolivia and n Argentina

☐ **Chilean Pigeon** *Columba araucana*

Araucaria woodlands of c and s Chile and adjacent Argentina

☐ **Ring-tailed Pigeon** *Columba caribaea*

Jamaica

☐ **Pale-vented Pigeon** *Columba cayennensis*
____ *C. c. pallidicrissa* — Gulf lowlands of se Mexico to n Colombia
____ *C. c. andersoni* — SE Colombia and e Ecuador to Brazil north of the Amazon
____ *C. c. tobagensis* — Trinidad and Tobago
____ *C. c. cayennensis* — Guyana, Suriname and French Guiana
____ *C. c. sylvestris* — E Peru to Brazil s of the Amazon, Paraguay and n Argentina

☐ **Red-billed Pigeon** *Columba flavirostris*
____ *C. f. restricta* — W Mexico (s Sonora to Sinaloa)
____ *C. f. madrensis* — Tres Marías Islands (off w Mexico)
____ *C. f. flavirostris* — S Texas (Rio Grande Valley) to e Costa Rica
____ *C. f. minima* — Lowlands of Costa Rica (Gulf of Nicoya region)

☐ **Peruvian Pigeon** *Columba oenops*

N Peru (subtropical Marañón Valley) and adjacent s Ecuador

☐ **Plain Pigeon** *Columba inornata*
____ *C. i. inornata* — Cuba, Isle of Pines and Hispaniola
____ *C. i. exigua* — Jamaica
____ *C. i. wetmorei* — Puerto Rico

☐ **Plumbeous Pigeon** *Columba plumbea*
____ *C. p. delicata* — E Colombia to Venezuela, the Guianas, n Brazil and n Bolivia
____ *C. p. chapmani* — NW Ecuador
____ *C. p. pallescens* — Small tributaries of Amazon from Rio Purús to Pará
____ *C. p. baeri* — Central Brazil (Goiás and nw Minas Gerais)
____ *C. p. plumbea* — SE Brazil and Paraguay

☐ **Short-billed Pigeon** *Columba nigrirostris*

Lowland rainforests of se Mexico to nw Colombia (Chocó)

☐ **Ruddy Pigeon** *Columba subvinacea*
_____ *C. s. subvinacea* — Subtropical Costa Rica and Panama
_____ *C. s. berlepschi* — Pacific slope of se Panama to sw Ecuador
_____ *C. s. zuliae* — NE Colombia and w Venezuela
_____ *C. s. peninsularis* — NE Venezuela (Pária Peninsula)
_____ *C. s. purpureotincta* — SE Colombia to Venezuela and the Guianas
_____ *C. s. bogotensis* — Andes of Colombia to ne Bolivia and Amazonian Brazil

☐ **Dusky Pigeon** *Columba goodsoni*
Lowland rainforests of w Colombia to nw Ecuador

☐ **Delegorgue's Pigeon** *Columba delegorguei*
_____ *C. d. sharpei* — SE Sudan to Uganda, Kenya, Tanzania and Zanzibar
_____ *C. d. delegorguei* — Malawi to e Zimbabwe, Mozambique and South Africa
Discontinuously distributed se Sudan to South Africa

☐ **Bronze-naped Pigeon** *Columba iriditorques*
Sierra Leone to nw Angola, Zaire, sw Uganda and Rwanda

☐ **Sao Tome Pigeon** *Columba malherbii*
São Tomé, Príncipe and Pagalu (Gulf of Guinea)

☐ **Lemon Dove** *Columba larvata*
_____ *C. l. hypoleuca* — Sierra Leone to Liberia, se Nigeria, Cameroon, Gabon; Bioko
_____ *C. l. principalis* — Príncipe (Gulf of Guinea)
_____ *C. l. bronzina* — Ethiopia and se Sudan (Boma Hills)
_____ *C. l. larvata* — S Sudan to Uganda, w Tanzania, Malawi and South Africa

☐ **Forest Dove** *Columba simplex*
São Tomé (Gulf of Guinea)

☐ **Pink Pigeon** *Nesoenas mayeri*
Forests of sw Mauritius (on verge of extinction)

☐ **Eurasian Turtle-Dove** *Streptopelia turtur*
_____ *S. t. turtur* — Azores, Canary Is. and Europe to w Siberia and Kazakstan
_____ *S. t. arenicola* — Balearic Islands and nw Africa to Iran and extreme w China
_____ *S. t. hoggara* — S Sahara (Aïr Massif and Hoggar Mountains)
_____ *S. t. rufescens (isabellina)* — Egypt (Dakhla and Kharga oases) and n Sudan (Faiyûm)

☐ **Dusky Turtle-Dove** *Streptopelia lugens*
Montane forests of e Africa and sw Arabia

☐ **Adamawa Turtle-Dove** *Streptopelia hypopyrrha*
Highlands of e Nigeria, n Cameroon and extreme sw Chad

☐ **Oriental Turtle-Dove** *Streptopelia orientalis*
_____ *S. o. meena* — SW Siberia to Iran, Afghanistan, Kashmir and Nepal
_____ *S. o. orientalis* — Central Siberia to China, Korea, Japan and Kuril Islands
_____ *S. o. stimpsoni* — Ryukyu Islands
_____ *S. o. orii* — Taiwan
_____ *S. o. erythrocephala* — Peninsular India
_____ *S. o. agricola* — NE India to Myanmar and s-c China (w Yunnan and Hainan I.)

☐ **Island Collared-Dove** *Streptopelia bitorquata*
_____ *S. b. dusumieri* — Philippines and Sulu Archipelago; vagrant to n Borneo
_____ *S. b. bitorquata* — Java, Bali and Lombok to Sumbawa, Flores, Solor and Timor

☐ **Eurasian Collared-Dove** *Streptopelia decaocto*
_____ *S. d. decaocto* — Europe to Middle East, India, Sri Lanka, w China and Korea
_____ *S. d. xanthocyclus* — Myanmar (Shan States) to s China (Yunnan) and e China

☐ **African Collared-Dove** *Streptopelia roseogrisea*
_____ *S. r. roseogrisea* — SW Mauritania and Senegambia to s Sudan and w Ethiopia
_____ *S. r. arabica* — Coastal Eritrea, Ethiopia and Somalia to Arabia

☐ **White-winged Collared-Dove** *Streptopelia reichenowi*

Borassus palm regions of se Ethiopia and sw Somalia

☐ **African Mourning Dove** *Streptopelia decipiens*

_____	*S. d. shelleyi*	Mauritania and Senegambia to s Niger and central Nigeria
_____	*S. d. logonensis*	Lake Chad basin to s Sudan, e Zaire and n and w Uganda
_____	*S. d. decipiens*	E Sudan (Darfur) to Ethiopia and nw Somalia
_____	*S. d. elegans*	S Ethiopia to s Somalia and e Kenya
_____	*S. d. perspicillata*	W Kenya and central Tanzania
_____	*S. d. ambigua*	E Angola to se Zaire, Zambia, Malawi and Limpopo Valley

☐ **Red-eyed Dove** *Streptopelia semitorquata*

Africa south of the Sahara and sw Arabia

☐ **Ring-necked Dove** *Streptopelia capicola*

_____	*S. c. electa*	W Ethiopia
_____	*S. c. somalica*	E Ethiopia, Somalia and n Kenya south to Uaso Nyiro River
_____	*S. c. tropica*	Cent. Kenya to Angola, Zimbabwe, South Africa and Zanzibar
_____	*S. c. onguati*	SW Angola and n Namibia
_____	*S. c. damarensis*	Namibia, Botswana and sw Zimbabwe
_____	*S. c. capicola*	W Cape Province

☐ **Vinaceous Dove** *Streptopelia vinacea*

Dry savanna of sub-Saharan Africa

☐ **Red Collared-Dove** *Streptopelia tranquebarica*

_____	*S. t. tranquebarica*	Sind, Punjab and w Nepal south through peninsular India
_____	*S. t. humilis*	Tibet to Myanmar, Thailand, SE Asia and n Philippines

☐ **Madagascar Turtle-Dove** *Streptopelia picturata*

_____	*S. p. rostrata*	Seychelles Islands
_____	*S. p. aldabrana*	Amirante Islands
_____	*S. p. copperingi*	Aldabra, Cosmoledo Atoll and Îles Glorieuses
_____	*S. p. comorensis*	Comoro Islands
_____	*S. p. picturata*	Madagascar

☐ **Spotted Dove** *Streptopelia chinensis*

_____	*S. c. suratensis*	Pakistan, Nepal and India to Sri Lanka, Bhutan and Assam
_____	*S. c. chinensis*	Myanmar to e China and Taiwan
_____	*S. c. tigrina*	N India to Malaya, Indochina, Philippines, Gr. and Lesser Sundas

☐ **Laughing Dove** *Streptopelia senegalensis*

_____	*S. s. phoenicophila*	Oases south of Atlas Mts. in Morocco, Algeria and Tunisia
_____	*S. s. aegyptiaca*	Nile Valley (Suez Canal and delta south to Wadi Halfa)
_____	*S. s. sokotrae*	Socotra (off ne Somalia)
_____	*S. s. senegalensis (thome)*	Africa south of the Sahara and Arabia
_____	*S. s. cambayensis*	E Arabia to s Iran, Indian subcontinent, w China and Andamans

☐ **Barred Cuckoo-Dove** *Macropygia unchall*

_____	*M. u. tusalia*	Himalayas (Kashmir to Assam, sw China and Myanmar)
_____	*M. u. minor*	Mts. of se China to Vietnam, Laos, n Thailand and Hainan
_____	*M. u. unchall*	Mts. of Malay Peninsula, Sumatra, Java, Lombok and Flores

☐ **Brown Cuckoo-Dove** *Macropygia phasianella*

E Australia (Cape York Peninsula to e Victoria)

☐ **Dusky Cuckoo-Dove** *Macropygia magna*

_____	*M. m. macassariensis*	SW Sulawesi, Tanakeke and Salayar islands
_____	*M. m. longa*	E Lesser Sundas (Tanahjampea and Kalatoa)
_____	*M. m. magna*	Timor, Wetar and adjacent e Lesser Sundas
_____	*M. m. timorlaoensis*	Tanimbar Islands (Yamdena, Larat and Selaru)

☐ **Slender-billed Cuckoo-Dove** *Macropygia amboinensis*

____	*M. a. sanghirensis*	Sangihe, Siau, Tahulandang, Ruang and Talaud islands
____	*M. a. albicapilla*	Sulawesi, Banggai, Tukangbesi and adjacent islands
____	*M. a. batchianensis*	N Moluccas
____	*M. a. amboinensis*	S Moluccas (Buru, Seram, Ambon and Seram Laut)
____	*M. a. keyensis*	Kai Islands (se Moluccas)
____	*M. a. doreya*	NW New Guinea and w Papuan islands
____	*M. a. maforensis*	Numfor I. (Geelvink Bay off n New Guinea)
____	*M. a. griseinucha*	Meos Num I. (Geelvink Bay off n New Guinea)
____	*M. a. kerstingi*	N New Guinea (Mamberano to Astrolabe Bay) and Yapen I.
____	*M. a. goldiei*	Coastal s New Guinea (Merauke region to Milne Bay)
____	*M. a. meeki*	Manam I. (off ne New Guinea)
____	*M. a. carteretia*	Bismarck Archipelago (except New Hanover) and Lihir Is.
____	*M. a. huskeri*	New Hanover (Bismarck Archipelago)
____	*M. a. cinereiceps*	D'Entrecasteaux Archipelago
____	*M. a. cunctata*	Louisiade Archipelago

☐ **Andaman Cuckoo-Dove** *Macropygia rufipennis*

Andaman and Nicobar islands

☐ **Philippine Cuckoo-Dove** *Macropygia tenuirostris*

Philippines, Taiwan and Lan-yü I.

☐ **Ruddy Cuckoo-Dove** *Macropygia emiliana*

____	*M. e. borneensis*	N Borneo
____	*M. e. hypopercna*	Simeulue I. (off nw Sumatra)
____	*M. e. modiglianii*	Nias I. (off w Sumatra)
____	*M. e. elassa*	Mentawi Islands (Siberut, Sipura and Pagai)
____	*M. e. cinnamomea*	Enggano I. (off w Sumatra)
____	*M. e. emiliana*	Krakatau, Java, Lombok, Sumbawa, Flores and Paloe islands
____	*M. e. megala*	Kangean Islands (off ne Java)

☐ **Black-billed Cuckoo-Dove** *Macropygia nigrirostris*

New Guinea, Bismarck Arch. and D'Entrecasteaux Arch.

☐ **Mackinlay's Cuckoo-Dove** *Macropygia mackinlayi*

____	*M. m. goodsoni*	Admiralty Is., St. Matthias Is. and w New Britain
____	*M. m. krakari*	Karkar I. (Papua New Guinea)
____	*M. m. arossi*	Solomon Islands
____	*M. m. mackinlayi*	Santa Cruz Islands, Banks Group and Vanuatu

☐ **Little Cuckoo-Dove** *Macropygia ruficeps*

____	*M. r. assimilis*	S Myanmar, nw Thailand and extreme sw China (Yunnan)
____	*M. r. engelbachi*	NW Vietnam (w Tonkin and n Laos)
____	*M. r. malayana*	Malay Peninsula
____	*M. r. simalurensis*	Simeulue I. (off Sumatra)
____	*M. r. sumatrana*	Sumatra
____	*M. r. nana*	Borneo and Sibatik I.
____	*M. r. ruficeps*	Java and Bali
____	*M. r. orientalis*	Lombok, Sumbawa, Komodo, Flores, Sumba, Pantar and Timor

☐ **Great Cuckoo-Dove** *Reinwardtoena reinwardtii*

____	*R. r. reinwardtii*	Moluccas
____	*R. r. griseotincta*	W Papuan islands, New Guinea and D'Entrecasteaux Arch.
____	*R. r. brevis*	Biak I. (off n New Guinea)

☐ **Pied Cuckoo-Dove** *Reinwardtoena browni*

Admiralty Islands and Bismarck Archipelago

☐ **Crested Cuckoo-Dove** *Reinwardtoena crassirostris*

Solomon Islands (Bougainville to San Cristobal)

☐ **White-faced Cuckoo-Dove** *Turacoena manadensis*

Sulawesi, Togian, Butung, Banggai and Sula islands

☐ **Slaty Cuckoo-Dove** *Turacoena modesta*

E Lesser Sundas (Timor and Wetar)

☐ **Emerald-spotted Wood-Dove** *Turtur chalcospilos*

Woodland and thornscrub of east and southern Africa

☐ **Black-billed Wood-Dove** *Turtur abyssinicus*

Arid scrub and woodlands of sub-Saharan Africa

☐ **Blue-spotted Wood-Dove** *Turtur afer*

Africa south of the Sahara, Zanzibar and Pemba I.

☐ **Tambourine Dove** *Turtur tympanistria*

Africa south of the Sahara, Bioko and Comoro Islands

☐ **Blue-headed Wood-Dove** *Turtur brehmeri*
____ *T. b. infelix* — Coastal Guinea and Sierra Leone to Cameroon
____ *T. b. brehmeri* — S Cameroon to n Congo, e Zaire and extreme nw Angola

☐ **Namaqua Dove** *Oena capensis*
____ *O. c. capensis* — Africa south of the Sahara, Socotra and Arabia
____ *O. c. aliena* — Madagascar

☐ **Emerald Dove** *Chalcophaps indica*
____ *C. i. indica* — India to Malaysia, Philippines, Indonesia and w Papuan islands
____ *C. i. robinsoni* — Sri Lanka
____ *C. i. natalis* — Christmas I. (Indian Ocean)
____ *C. i. minima* — Numfor, Biak and Mios Num islands (n New Guinea)
____ *C. i. augusta* — Nicobar Islands
____ *C. i. chrysochlora* — E Lesser Sundas, e Australia, New Guinea and adj. islands
____ *C. i. longirostris* — N Australia (n Western Australia and Northern Territory)
____ *C. i. sandwichensis* — Santa Cruz Is., Banks Is., Vanuatu and New Caledonia

☐ **Stephan's Dove** *Chalcophaps stephani*
____ *C. s. wallacei* — Sulawesi and Sula Islands (Taliabu I.)
____ *C. s. stephani* — Kai Is., e New Guinea, Admiralty Is. and Bismarck Arch.
____ *C. s. mortoni* — Solomon Is. (Bougainville to San Cristobal and Santa Anna)

☐ **New Guinea Bronzewing** *Henicophaps albifrons*
____ *H. a. albifrons* — W Papuan islands, New Guinea and Yapen I.
____ *H. a. schelgeli* — Aru Islands

☐ **New Britain Bronzewing** *Henicophaps foersteri*

S Bismarck Archipelago (Umboi, New Britain and Lolobau)

☐ **Common Bronzewing** *Phaps chalcoptera*

Australia and Tasmania

☐ **Brush Bronzewing** *Phaps elegans*
____ *P. e. occidentalis* — SW Australia (Dongara to Point Culver)
____ *P. e. elegans* — SE Queensland to s-central Australia and Tasmania

☐ **Flock Bronzewing** *Phaps histrionica*

NW Australia to w Queensland and nw New South Wales

☐ **Crested Pigeon** *Geophaps lophotes*
____ *G. l. whitlocki* — Arid woodlands and plains of western Australia
____ *G. l. lophotes* — Arid central and e Australia

☐ **Spinifex Pigeon** *Geophaps plumifera*
____ *G. p. ferruginea* — W Australia (De Grey R. to Gascoyne R. and Carnarvon Range)
____ *G. p. plumifera* — Western Australia (Edgar Range) to w Northern Territory
____ *G. p. leucogaster* — Central and eastern Australia

☐ **Squatter Pigeon** *Geophaps scripta*
____ *G. s. peninsulae* — NE Queensland (Cape York Peninsula to Burdekin River)
____ *G. s. scripta* — Central Queensland and extreme n New South Wales

☐ **Partridge Pigeon** *Geophaps smithii*
    ____ *G. s. blaauwi* — NE Western Australia (Kimberley Region)
    ____ *G. s. smithii* — NE Western Australia (Cockatoo Springs) and n N Territory

☐ **Chestnut-quilled Rock-Pigeon** *Petrophassa rufipennis* — W escarpment of Arnhem Land (n Northern Territory)

☐ **White-quilled Rock-Pigeon** *Petrophassa albipennis*
    ____ *P. a. albipennis* — NE Western Australia and n Northern Territory
    ____ *P. a. boothi* — N Northern Territory (Stokes Range to upper Baines River)

☐ **Diamond Dove** *Geopelia cuneata* — Arid interior of Australia

☐ **Zebra Dove** *Geopelia striata* — S Myanmar to Malaysia, Sumatra and Java

☐ **Peaceful Dove** *Geopelia placida*
    ____ *G. p. papua* — Savanna of s New Guinea (Merauke to Port Moresby)
    ____ *G. p. placida* — N and e Australia
    ____ *G. p. clelandi* — N-central western Australia (Pilbara region)

☐ **Barred Dove** *Geopelia maugei* — SE Moluccas and Lesser Sundas

☐ **Bar-shouldered Dove** *Geopelia humeralis*
    ____ *G. h. gregalis* — Lowlands of coastal se New Guinea
    ____ *G. h. humeralis* — Lowlands of n and e Australia
    ____ *G. h. headlandi* — N-central western Australia (Pilbara region)

☐ **Wonga Pigeon** *Leucosarcia melanoleuca* — Rainforests of e Australia (se Queensland to se Victoria)

☐ **Mourning Dove** *Zenaida macroura*
    ____ *Z. m. marginella* — Br. Columbia to Baja California, w US and s-central Mexico
    ____ *Z. m. carolinensis* — E US, Bahamas and Bermuda
    ____ *Z. m. macroura* — Cuba, Isle of Pines, Hispaniola, Puerto Rico and Jamaica
    ____ *Z. m. clarionensis* — Isla Clarión (Revillagigedo Islands off w Mexico)
    ____ *Z. m. turturilla* — Costa Rica and w Panama

☐ **Socorro Dove** *Zenaida graysoni* — Formerly Socorro I. (off w Mexico); small captive population

☐ **Eared Dove** *Zenaida auriculata*
    ____ *Z. a. rubripes* — L Antilles, Trinidad and c Colombia to Venezuela and n Brazil
    ____ *Z. a. hypoleuca* — Arid littoral of w Ecuador and w Peru
    ____ *Z. a. caucae* — W Colombia (Cauca Valley)
    ____ *Z. a. antioquiae* — N-central Andes of Colombia (Antioquia)
    ____ *Z. a. ruficauda* — E Andes of Colombia to w Venezuela (Mérida)
    ____ *Z. a. vinaceorufa* — Netherlands Antilles (Curaçao, Aruba and Bonaire)
    ____ *Z. a. jessieae* — Bank of lower Amazon near Santarém
    ____ *Z. a. marajoensis* — Marajó and Mexiana islands in estuary of the Amazon
    ____ *Z. a. noronha* — NE Brazil (Maranhão, Piauí, Bahia); Fernando de Noronha I.
    ____ *Z. a. virgata* — Bolivia to c Brazil, Uruguay and Argentina to Tierra del Fuego
    ____ *Z. a. auriculata* — Central Chile (Atacama to Llanquihue) and w-c Argentina

☐ **Zenaida Dove** *Zenaida aurita*
    ____ *Z. a. salvadorii* — Coastal n Yucatán Pen., Cozumel, Holbox and Isla Mujeres
    ____ *Z. a. zenaida* — Bahamas, Greater Antilles and Virgin Islands
    ____ *Z. a. aurita* — Lesser Antilles (Anguilla to Grenada)

☐ **Galapagos Dove** *Zenaida galapagoensis*
    ____ *Z. g. galapagoensis* — Drier parts of Galapagos Islands (except range of *exsul*)
    ____ *Z. g. exsul* — Galapagos Islands (Culpepper and Wenman)

☐ **White-winged Dove** *Zenaida asiatica*

____	*Z. a. mearnsi*	Arid s California, N Mex., Arizona, w Mexico; Tres Marías Is.
____	*Z. a. asiatica*	Arid s Texas to Nicaragua; West Indies
____	*Z. a. australis*	W Costa Rica to w Panama

☐ **Pacific Dove** *Zenaida meloda*

Arid tropical sw Ecuador to n Chile (Coquimbo)

☐ **Common Ground-Dove** *Columbina passerina*

____	*C. p. passerina*	Coastal se US (South Carolina to Florida and se Texas)
____	*C. p. pallescens*	Arid sw US to Guatemala and Belize
____	*C. p. socorroensis*	Socorro I. (Revillagigedo Islands off w Mexico)
____	*C. p. neglecta*	Honduras to Costa Rica and Panama
____	*C. p. bahamensis*	Bermuda and Bahamas (except Inagua I.)
____	*C. p. exigua*	Great Inagua I. (s Bahamas) and Mona I. (Puerto Rico)
____	*C. p. insularis*	Cuba, Isle of Pines, Cayman Is., Hispaniola and adj. islands
____	*C. p. jamaicensis*	Jamaica
____	*C. p. navassae*	Navassa I. (off sw Hispaniola)
____	*C. p. portoricensis*	Puerto Rico, Mona, Culebra and Virgin is. (except St. Croix)
____	*C. p. nigrirostris*	St. Croix and n Lesser Antilles
____	*C. p. trochila*	Martinique (Lesser Antilles)
____	*C. p. antillarum*	S Lesser Antilles (St. Lucia and Barbados to Grenada)
____	*C. p. albivitta*	N Colombia, n Venezuela, Netherlands Antilles and Trinidad
____	*C. p. parvula*	Central Colombia (upper Magdalena Valley)
____	*C. p. nana*	W Colombia (Cauca Valley and arid upper Dagua Valley)
____	*C. p. quitensis*	Central Ecuador (Río Guaillabamba to Riobamba)
____	*C. p. griseola*	Extreme s Venezuela to the Guianas and e Brazil

☐ **Plain-breasted Ground-Dove** *Columbina minuta*

____	*C. m. interrupta*	SE Mexico to Belize, Guatemala and Nicaragua
____	*C. m. elaeodes*	Costa Rica to w-central Colombia
____	*C. m. minuta*	E Colombia to Venezuela, Guianas, s Brazil and ne Argentina
____	*C. m. amazilia*	Arid coastal sw Ecuador and Peru (south to Lima)

☐ **Ecuadorian Ground-Dove** *Columbina buckleyi*

Arid littoral of w Ecuador and extreme nw Peru (Tumbes)

☐ **Ruddy Ground-Dove** *Columbina talpacoti*

____	*C. t. eluta*	Coastal w Mexico (n Sinaloa to Chiapas)
____	*C. t. rufipennis*	SE Mexico to Colombia, n Venezuela, Trinidad and Tobago
____	*C. t. caucae*	W Colombia (Cauca Valley)
____	*C. t. talpacoti*	Guianas and Brazil to e Bolivia, Paraguay and c Argentina

☐ **Picui Ground-Dove** *Columbina picui*

____	*C. p. strepitans*	NW Brazil (Maranhão, Piauí, Ceará and Bahia)
____	*C. p. picui*	E Peru to Bolivia, Paraguay, s Argentina, Chile and s Brazil

☐ **Croaking Ground-Dove** *Columbina cruziana*

Arid w Ecuador, Peru and n Chile

☐ **Blue-eyed Ground-Dove** *Columbina cyanopis*

Cerrado of s-central Brazil

☐ **Inca Dove** *Columbina inca*

Semiarid sw US to nw Costa Rica

☐ **Scaled Dove** *Columbina squammata*

____	*C. s. ridgwayi*	Coastal ne Colombia to Venezuela, Margarita I. and Trinidad
____	*C. s. squammata*	C and e Brazil to Bolivia, Paraguay and ne Argentina

☐ **Blue Ground-Dove** *Claravis pretiosa*

SE Mexico (San Luis Potosí) to n Argentina and s Brazil

☐ **Purple-winged Ground-Dove** *Claravis godefrida*

SE Brazil (s Bahia) to e Paraguay and ne Argentina (Misiones)

☐ **Maroon-chested Ground-Dove** *Claravis mondetoura*
____ *C. m. ochoterena* — Mountains of se Mexico (Veracruz to Chiapas)
____ *C. m. salvini* — Guatemala, El Salvador and Honduras
____ *C. m. umbrina* — Costa Rica
____ *C. m. pulchra* — W Panama
____ *C. m. mondetoura* — Andes of Colombia to n Venezuela and e Ecuador
____ *C. m. inca* — Andes of Peru and w-central Bolivia

☐ **Bare-faced Ground-Dove** *Metriopelia ceciliae*
____ *M. c. ceciliae* — Andes of w Peru
____ *M. c. obsoleta* — N Peru (upper Marañón Valley)
____ *M. c. zimmeri* — Andes of extreme s Peru to Bolivia, nw Argentina and n Chile

☐ **Bare-eyed Ground-Dove** *Metriopelia morenoi*

Andes of nw Argentina

☐ **Black-winged Ground-Dove** *Metriopelia melanoptera*
____ *M. m. saturatior* — Andes of sw Colombia and Ecuador
____ *M. m. melanoptera* — Andes of Peru to s Argentina, s Chile and Tierra del Fuego

☐ **Golden-spotted Ground-Dove** *Metriopelia aymara*

Andes of s Peru to nw Argentina and n Chile

☐ **Long-tailed Ground-Dove** *Uropelia campestris*

W-c Brazil (Mato Grosso) and adjacent Bolivia

☐ **White-tipped Dove** *Leptotila verreauxi*
____ *L. v. capitalis* — Tres Marías Islands (off w Mexico)
____ *L. v. angelica* — S Texas and coastal Mexico south to Guerrero and Veracruz
____ *L. v. fulviventris* — SE Mexico and Yucatán Pen. to e Guatemala and Belize
____ *L. v. bangsi* — W Guatemala, El Salvador, Nicaragua and w Honduras
____ *L. v. nuttingi* — W shore of Lake Nicaragua and Isla de Ométepe
____ *L. v. riottei* — Caribbean slope of Costa Rica
____ *L. v. verreauxi* — Extreme sw Nicaragua to Colombia, Venezuela and offshore is.
____ *L. v. zapluta* — Trinidad
____ *L. v. tobagensis* — Tobago
____ *L. v. decolor* — W Andes of Colombia to n Peru (Marañón Valley and Trujillo)
____ *L. v. brasiliensis* — The Guianas and n Brazil south to north bank of the Amazon
____ *L. v. approximans* — NE Brazil (Piauí and Ceará to n Bahia)
____ *L. v. decipiens* — Lowlands of e Peru, e Bolivia and w Brazil s of the Amazon
____ *L. v. chalcauchenia* — S Bolivia to Paraguay, s Brazil, Uruguay and n-c Argentina

☐ **White-faced Dove** *Leptotila megalura*

Andes of Bolivia and nw Argentina

☐ **Gray-fronted Dove** *Leptotila rufaxilla*
____ *L. r. pallidipectus* — Tropical e Colombia and adjacent w Venezuela
____ *L. r. dubusi* — SE Colombia and e Ecuador to *tepuis* of Venezuela and Brazil
____ *L. r. rufaxilla* — Venezuela to Guianas and n Brazil (R. Madeira to n Maranhão)
____ *L. r. hellmayri* — NE Venezuela (Paría Peninsula) and Trinidad
____ *L. r. bahiae* — Central Brazil (s Mato Grosso to Bahia)
____ *L. r. reichenbachii* — Mato Grosso to Espírito Santo, Paraguay and ne Argentina

☐ **Gray-headed Dove** *Leptotila plumbeiceps*
____ *L. p. plumbeiceps* — SE Mexico (s Tamaulipas), w Costa Rica and w Colombia
____ *L. p. notius* — Caribbean slope of w Panama

☐ **Pallid Dove** *Leptotila pallida*

Tropical lowlands of w Colombia and w Ecuador

☐ **Brown-backed Dove** *Leptotila battyi*
____ *L. b. malae* — Pacific slope of Panama (s Veraguas and w Herrera); Cébaco I.
____ *L. b. battyi* — Isla Coiba (off s-central Panama)

☐ **Grenada Dove** *Leptotila wellsi*

Arid scrub of s Grenada (s Lesser Antilles)

☐ **Caribbean Dove** *Leptotila jamaicensis*
____ *L. j. gaumeri*   N Yucatán, Mujeres, Holbox, Cozumel and is. off Honduras
____ *L. j. collaris*   Cayman Islands
____ *L. j. jamaicensis*   Jamaica
____ *L. j. neoxena*   Isla San Andrés (Caribbean Sea off Nicaragua)

☐ **Gray-chested Dove** *Leptotila cassini*
____ *L. c. cerviniventris*   Caribbean lowlands of Guatemala to w Panama))
____ *L. c. rufinucha*   SW Costa Rica to nw Panama (Chiriquí)
____ *L. c. cassini*   Panama (Canal Zone) to n Colombia (Cauca-Magdalena area)

☐ **Ochre-bellied Dove** *Leptotila ochraceiventris*

SW Ecuador (Manabí) to extreme nw Peru (Tumbes and Piura)

☐ **Tolima Dove** *Leptotila conoveri*

E slope of Central Andes of Colombia (Tolima to Huila)

☐ **Purplish-backed Quail-Dove** *Geotrygon lawrencii*

Costa Rica to e Panama (Darién)

☐ **Tuxtla Quail-Dove** *Geotrygon carrikeri*

SE Mexico (Sierra de Tuxtla in se Veracruz)

☐ **Buff-fronted Quail-Dove** *Geotrygon costaricensis*

Humid montane forests of Costa Rica and w Panama

☐ **Russet-crowned Quail-Dove** *Geotrygon goldmani*
____ *G. g. oreas*   E Panama (Cerro Chucantí in e Panamá Province)
____ *G. g. goldmani*   E Panama (e Darién and extreme nw Colombia)

☐ **Sapphire Quail-Dove** *Geotrygon saphirina*
____ *G. s. purpurata*   Humid forests of nw Colombia to w Ecuador
____ *G. s. saphirina*   Trop. e Ecuador to se Peru and extreme w Amazonian Brazil
____ *G. s. rothschildi*   SE Peru (Marcapata Valley)

☐ **Gray-headed Quail-Dove** *Geotrygon caniceps*
____ *G. c. caniceps*   Cuba (on verge of extinction)
____ *G. c. leucometopius*   Dominican Republic (on verge of extinction)

☐ **Crested Quail-Dove** *Geotrygon versicolor*

Montane forests of Jamaica

☐ **Chiriqui Quail-Dove** *Geotrygon chiriquensis*

Humid montane forests of Costa Rica and w Panama

☐ **Olive-backed Quail-Dove** *Geotrygon veraguensis*

Caribbean lowlands of Costa Rica to nw Ecuador

☐ **White-faced Quail-Dove** *Geotrygon albifacies*

Mountains of se Mexico (San Luis Potosí) to nw Nicaragua

☐ **Lined Quail-Dove** *Geotrygon linearis*

Mountains of Colombia, Venezuela, Trinidad and Tobago

☐ **White-throated Quail-Dove** *Geotrygon frenata*
____ *G. f. bourcieri*   Andes of w Colombia and w Ecuador
____ *G. f. erythropareia*   Andes of e Ecuador
____ *G. f. frenata*   Andes of n Peru to central Bolivia
____ *G. f. margaritae*   Andes of s Bolivia to nw Argentina

☐ **Key West Quail-Dove** *Geotrygon chrysia*

Bahamas, Cuba, Isle of Pines, Hispaniola and sw Puerto Rico

☐ **Bridled Quail-Dove** *Geotrygon mystacea*

Puerto Rico and Virgin Is. to Lesser Antilles (s to St. Lucia)

☐ **Violaceous Quail-Dove** *Geotrygon violacea*
____ *G. v. albiventer*   Nicaragua to n Colombia and w Venezuela
____ *G. v. violacea*   Suriname to e Brazil, Bolivia, Paraguay and ne Argentina

☐ **Ruddy Quail-Dove** *Geotrygon montana*

_____ *G. m. montana* — Trop. s Mexico and Gr. Antilles to s Brazil and n Argentina

_____ *G. m. martinica* — Lesser Antilles

☐ **Blue-headed Quail-Dove** *Starnoenas cyanocephala*

Lowlands of Cuba (in danger of extinction)

☐ **Nicobar Pigeon** *Caloenas nicobarica*

_____ *C. n. nicobarica* — Malay Arch. to New Guinea, Philippines and Solomon Islands

_____ *C. n. pelewensis* — Palau Islands

☐ **Luzon Bleeding-heart** *Gallicolumba luzonica*

_____ *G. l. griseolateralis* — N Luzon (n Philippines)

_____ *G. l. luzonica* — N Philippines (central and s Luzon and Polillo)

_____ *G. l. rubiventris* — NE Philippines (Vigo-Gigmoto watershed on Catanduanes)

☐ **Mindanao Bleeding-heart** *Gallicolumba criniger*

_____ *G. c. leytensis* — Philippines (Samar, Leyte and Bohol)

_____ *G. c. criniger* — S Philippines (Mindanao and Dinagat)

_____ *G. c. bartletti* — Basilan I. (se Philippines)

☐ **Mindoro Bleeding-heart** *Gallicolumba platenae*

Forests of Mindoro (central Philippines). Status unknown

☐ **Negros Bleeding-heart** *Gallicolumba keayi*

Forests of Negros (central Philippines). Status unknown

☐ **Sulu Bleeding-heart** *Gallicolumba menagei*

Tawitawi I. (Sulu Archipelago). Status unknown

☐ **Cinnamon Ground-Dove** *Gallicolumba rufigula*

_____ *G. r. rufigula* — W Papuan islands (New Guinea)

_____ *G. r. septentrionalis* — N New Guinea (east to Huon Gulf)

_____ *G. r. helviventris* — Aru Is. and s New Guinea (Waitakwa River to Fly River)

_____ *G. r. alaris* — S New Guinea east to Karimui (Chimbu Province)

_____ *G. r. orientalis* — SE New Guinea (w to Mambare River and Angabunga River)

☐ **Sulawesi Ground-Dove** *Gallicolumba tristigmata*

_____ *G. t. tristigmata* — Humid forests of n and n-central Sulawesi

_____ *G. t. bimaculata* — S Sulawesi

_____ *G. t. auripectus* — S-central and se Sulawesi

☐ **White-bibbed Ground-Dove** *Gallicolumba jobiensis*

_____ *G. j. jobiensis* — New Guinea, Bismarck Arch. and D'Entrecasteaux Arch.

_____ *G. j. chalconota* — Solomon Islands (Guadalcanal and Vella Lavella)

☐ **Caroline Islands Ground-Dove** *Gallicolumba kubaryi*

Montane forests of e Caroline Islands (Truk and Pohnpei)

☐ **Polynesian Ground-Dove** *Gallicolumba erythroptera*

Uninhabited atolls of Tuamotu Archipelago

☐ **White-throated Ground-Dove** *Gallicolumba xanthonura*

Yap (Caroline Islands) and Mariana Islands

☐ **Friendly Ground-Dove** *Gallicolumba stairi*

_____ *G. s. stairi* — Wallis and Futuna Islands and Samoa

_____ *G. s. vitiensis* — Fiji and Tonga (Vava'u, Ha'apai and Nomuka group)

☐ **Santa Cruz Ground-Dove** *Gallicolumba sanctaecrucis*

Santa Cruz Islands (Tinakula and Utupua) and Vanuatu

☐ **Thick-billed Ground-Dove** *Gallicolumba salamonis*

Solomon Islands (Ramos and San Cristobal). Possibly extinct

☐ **Marquesas Ground-Dove** *Gallicolumba rubescens*

Marquesas Islands (Fatuhuku and Hatuta'a)

☐ **Bronze Ground-Dove** *Gallicolumba beccarii*
____ *G. b. beccarii*
____ *G. b. johannae*
____ *G. b. eichhorni*
____ *G. b. admiralitatis*
____ *G. b. intermedia*
____ *G. b. solomonensis*

Mountains of New Guinea
Bismarck Archipelago (Karkar and Nissan)
St. Matthias Islands (Mussau and Emira)
Manus I. (Admiralty Islands)
W Solomon Is. (Bougainville, Gizo and New Georgia Group)
E Solomon Is. (Guadalcanal, San Cristobal, Santa Ana, Rennell)

☐ **Palau Ground-Dove** *Gallicolumba canifrons*

Palau Islands (Babelthuap south to Angaur)

☐ **Wetar Ground-Dove** *Gallicolumba hoedtii*

E Lesser Sundas (Timor and Wetar)

☐ **Thick-billed Ground-Pigeon** *Trugon terrestris*
____ *T. t. terrestris*
____ *T. t. mayri*
____ *T. t. leucopareia*

Salawati I. and nw New Guinea e to Geelvink and Etna bays
N-central New Guinea (Mamberamo River to Humboldt Bay)
S New Guinea (Setekwa River to Milne Bay)

☐ **Pheasant Pigeon** *Otidiphaps nobilis*
____ *O. n. nobilis*
____ *O. n. aruensis*
____ *O. n. cervicalis*
____ *O. n. insularis*

Mountains of w New Guinea, Batanta and Waigeo islands
Aru Islands (New Guinea)
Mts. of e and se New Guinea (Saruwaged, Sepik and Kuper)
Fergusson I. (D'Entrecasteaux Archipelago)

☐ **Western Crowned-Pigeon** *Goura cristata*
____ *G. c. cristata*
____ *G. c. minor*

NW New Guinea (Vogelkop to Etna Bay and Siriwo River)
W Papuan islands (Misool, Salawati, Batanta and Waigeo)

☐ **Southern Crowned-Pigeon** *Goura scheepmakeri*
____ *G. s. sclaterii*
____ *G. s. scheepmakeri*

S New Guinea (Mimika River to Fly River)
Coastal se New Guinea (Hall Sound to Orangerie Bay)

☐ **Victoria Crowned-Pigeon** *Goura victoria*
____ *G. v. victoria*
____ *G. v. beccarii*

Yapen I. and Biak I. (New Guinea)
N New Guinea

☐ **Tooth-billed Pigeon** *Didunculus strigirostris*

Mountains of Western Samoa (Upolu and Savai'i)

☐ **White-eared Dove** *Phapitreron leucotis*
____ *P. l. leucotis*
____ *P. l. nigrorum*
____ *P. l. brevirostris (albifrons)*
____ *P. l. occipitalis*

N Philippines (Catanduanes, Luzon, Mindoro and adj. islands)
Philippines (Cebu, Guimaras, Masbate, Negros, Panay, adj. is.)
Leyte, Mindoro, Bohol, Dinagat, Samar, Mindanao and Siquijor
S Philippines (Basilan) and Sulu Archipelago

☐ **Amethyst Dove** *Phapitreron amethystina*
____ *P. a. amethystina*
____ *P. a. imeldae*
____ *P. a. maculipectus*
____ *P. a. frontalis*

Luzon, Mindanao and adjacent Philippines
Marinduque (n-central Philippines)
Montane forests of Negros (e-central Philippines)
Cebu (e-central Philippines). Probably extinct

☐ **Dark-eared Dove** *Phapitreron cinereiceps*
____ *P. c. brunneiceps*
____ *P. c. cinereiceps*

SE Philippines (Mindanao and Basilan)
Tawitawi (Sulu Archipelago)

☐ **Little Green-Pigeon** *Treron olax*

Lowlands of s Thailand, Malay Peninsula and Greater Sundas

☐ **Pink-necked Pigeon** *Treron vernans*

SE Asia to Philippines and Indonesia

□ **Cinnamon-headed Pigeon** *Treron fulvicollis*
____ *T. f. fulvicollis* — Malay Peninsula, Sumatra and adjacent islands
____ *T. f. melopogenys* — Nias I. (off w Sumatra)
____ *T. f. oberholseri* — Natuna Islands (off nw Borneo)
____ *T. f. baramensis* — N Borneo and adjacent islands off north coast

□ **Orange-breasted Pigeon** *Treron bicincta*
____ *T. b. bicincta* — Indian subcontinent and SE Asia
____ *T. b. leggei* — Sri Lanka
____ *T. b. domvilii* — Hainan (s China)
____ *T. b. javana* — Java and Bali

□ **Pompadour Green-Pigeon** *Treron pompadora*
____ *T. p. pompadora* — India to sw China, Thailand, Laos and s Vietnam
____ *T. p. chloroptera* — Andaman and Nicobar islands
____ *T. p. phayrei* — Myanmar to sw China (Yunnan), Thailand, Laos and s Vietnam
____ *T. p. amadoni* — N Luzon (n Philippines)
____ *T. p. axillaris* — S Luzon, Polillo, Alabat, Catanduanes, Lubang and Mindoro
____ *T. p. canescens* — E Philippines (Mandate to Cebu, Basilan and Mindanao)
____ *T. p. everetti* — Sulu Archipelago (Bongao, Jolo, Sibutu and Tawitawi)
____ *T. p. aromatica* — S Moluccas (Buru), Tanahjampea, Kalao and Kalaotoa islands

□ **Thick-billed Pigeon** *Treron curvirostra*
— Lowlands forests of s Asia and Malay Archipelago

□ **Gray-cheeked Pigeon** *Treron griseicauda*
____ *T. g. sangirensis* — Talaud Islands and Sangihe I.
____ *T. g. wallacei* — Sulawesi, Banggai and Sula islands
____ *T. g. griseicauda* — Java and Bali
____ *T. g. vordermani* — Kangean Islands (Java Sea)

□ **Sumba Green-Pigeon** *Treron teysmannii*
— Lowlands of Sumba I. (w Lesser Sundas)

□ **Flores Green-Pigeon** *Treron floris*
— Lowlands of Lombok, Flores and adjacent w Lesser Sundas

□ **Timor Green-Pigeon** *Treron psittacea*
— Lowlands of e Lesser Sundas (Timor, Roti and Semau)

□ **Large Green-Pigeon** *Treron capellei*
— Malay Peninsula to n Sumatra, Borneo, Java and adj. islands

□ **Yellow-footed Pigeon** *Treron phoenicoptera*
____ *T. p. phillipsi* — Sri Lanka
____ *T. p. chlorigaster* — Peninsular India south of the Gangetic Plain
____ *T. p. phoenicoptera* — E Pakistan and n India to Assam and Bangladesh
____ *T. p. viridifrons* — Extreme sw China (Yunnan) to Myanmar and nw Thailand
____ *T. p. annamensis* — E Thailand to s Laos and s Vietnam

□ **Bruce's Green-Pigeon** *Treron waalia*
— Savanna of sub-Saharan Africa, sw Arabia and Socotra I.

□ **Madagascar Green-Pigeon** *Treron australis*
____ *T. a. griveaudi* — Mohéli (Comoro Islands)
____ *T. a. xenia* — W Madagascar
____ *T. a. australis* — Madagascar (east of the high plateau)

□ **Pemba Green-Pigeon** *Treron pembaensis*
— Pemba I. (off ne Tanzania)

□ **Sao Tome Green-Pigeon** *Treron sanctithomae*
— São Tomé (extirpated on adjacent Ilha das Rôlas)

□ **Yellow-vented Pigeon** *Treron seimundi*
____ *T. s. seimundi* — Mountains of Malay Peninsula
____ *T. s. modestus* — Mountains of Laos and Vietnam (Annam and Cochinchina)

☐ **Pin-tailed Pigeon** *Treron apicauda*

____	*T. a. apicauda*	Foothills of ne India to sw China and s Myanmar (Tenasserim)
____	*T. a. lowei*	Mountains of Thailand, central Laos and central Vietnam
____	*T. a. laotinus*	Mountains of Laos and n Vietnam

☐ **African Green-Pigeon** *Treron calva*

____	*T. c. nudirostris*	Senegal to Gambia and Guinea-Bissau
____	*T. c. sharpei*	Sierra Leone to s Nigeria and n Cameroon
____	*T. c. calva*	E Nigeria to ne Zaire, central Angola and Príncipe I.
____	*T. c. poensis*	Bioko I. (Gulf of Guinea)
____	*T. c. uellensis*	N Zaire to s Sudan and Uganda
____	*T. c. brevicera*	SW Ethiopia to n Tanzania e of Rift Valley (except for coast)
____	*T. c. salvadorii*	Uganda, Rwanda and Burundi to e Zaire
____	*T. c. granviki*	W Kenya and nw Tanzania
____	*T. c. wakefieldii*	Coastal Kenya and nw Tanzania
____	*T. c. granti*	Lowlands of e Tanzania and Zanzibar
____	*T. c. orientalis*	S Tanzania to Mozambique and lower Zambezi Valley
____	*T. c. schalowi*	S Zaire and Zambia to Victoria Falls
____	*T. c. chobiensis*	SW Zimbabwe and n Botswana
____	*T. c. ansorgei*	W Angola (south of Cuanza River)
____	*T. c. vylderi*	NW Namibia (east to Grootfontein)
____	*T. c. damarensis*	NE Namibia and nw Botswana
____	*T. c. delalandii*	Coastal Kenya (Mombasa) to e Cape Province

☐ **Green-spectacled Pigeon** *Treron oxyura*

Montane forests of Sumatra and w Java

☐ **Wedge-tailed Pigeon** *Treron sphenura*

____	*T. s. sphenura*	Mts. of Kashmir to sw China, Myanmar, n Thailand and Laos
____	*T. s. robinsoni*	Mountains of Malay Peninsula and central Vietnam
____	*T. s. korthalsi*	High mountains of Sumatra, Java, Bali and Lombok

☐ **White-bellied Pigeon** *Treron sieboldii*

____	*T. s. sieboldii*	Japan, mountains of Taiwan and e China (Jiangsu and Fujian)
____	*T. s. fopingensis*	Lowlands and foothills of c China (e Sichuan and s Shaanxi)
____	*T. s. murielae*	Extreme sw China to n Thailand, central Vietnam and Hainan

☐ **Whistling Green-Pigeon** *Treron formosae*

____	*T. f. permagnus*	N Ryukyu Islands (Yakushima, Amani-Oshima and Okinawa)
____	*T. f. medioximus*	S Ryukyu Islands (Ishigaki, Iriomote and Yonaguni)
____	*T. f. formosae*	Mountains of Taiwan and Botel Tobago
____	*T. f. filipina*	N Philippines (Batan, Calayan, Camiguin Norte and Sabtang)

☐ **Black-backed Fruit-Dove** *Ptilinopus cinctus*

____	*P. c. baliensis*	Bali
____	*P. c. albocinctus*	Lesser Sundas (Lombok, Sumbawa and Flores)
____	*P. c. everetti*	Lesser Sundas (Pantar and Alor)
____	*P. c. cinctus*	Lesser Sundas (Timor, Wetar and Romang)
____	*P. c. lettiensis*	Lesser Sundas (Leti, Moa, Luang, Sermata and Teun)
____	*P. c. ottonis*	Lesser Sundas (Damar, Babar and Nila)

☐ **Black-banded Fruit-Dove** *Ptilinopus alligator*

N-central Australia (western escarpment of Arnhem Land)

☐ **Red-naped Fruit-Dove** *Ptilinopus dohertyi*

Forests of Sumba (w Lesser Sundas)

☐ **Pink-headed Fruit-Dove** *Ptilinopus porphyreus*

Montane forests of s Sumatra, Java and Bali

☐ **Yellow-breasted Fruit-Dove** *Ptilinopus occipitalis*

____	*P. o. occipitalis*	Lowland forests of n and central Philippines
____	*P. o. incognitus*	Mountains of Mindanao (se Philippines)

☐ **Flame-breasted Fruit-Dove** *Ptilinopus marchei*

Montane forests of Luzon (n Philippines)

☐ **Cream-breasted Fruit-Dove** *Ptilinopus merrilli*
_____ *P. m. faustinoi* N Luzon (n Philippines)
_____ *P. m. merrilli* N Philippines (s Luzon, Polillo and Catanduanes)

☐ **Red-eared Fruit-Dove** *Ptilinopus fischeri*
_____ *P. f. fischeri* Montane forests of n Sulawesi
_____ *P. f. centralis* Montane forests of central and se Sulawesi
_____ *P. f. meridionalis* SW Sulawesi (Lompobattang Massif)

☐ **Jambu Fruit-Dove** *Ptilinopus jambu*

Peninsular Thailand, Malay Pen, Sumatra, Borneo and w Java

☐ **Maroon-chinned Fruit-Dove** *Ptilinopus subgularis*
_____ *P. s. epia* Lowland forests of Sulawesi
_____ *P. s. subgularis* Banggai Islands (Peleng and Banggai)
_____ *P. s. mangoliensis* Sula Islands (Taliabu, Seho and Mangole)

☐ **Black-chinned Fruit-Dove** *Ptilinopus leclancheri*
_____ *P. l. longialis* Lan-yü I. (Taiwan); Batan, Calayan and Camiguin Norte is.
_____ *P. l. leclancheri* Philippines (except Palawan, Basilan and Sulu Archipelago)
_____ *P. l. gironieri* Palawan (sw Philippines)

☐ **Scarlet-breasted Fruit-Dove** *Ptilinopus bernsteinii*
_____ *P. b. bernsteinii* N Moluccas (Halmahera, Ternate and Bacan)
_____ *P. b. micrus* Obi I. (n-central Moluccas)

☐ **Wompoo Fruit-Dove** *Ptilinopus magnificus*
_____ *P. m. alaris* W Papuan islands (Waigeo, Misool, Batanta and Salawati)
_____ *P. m. puella* NW New Guinea (Vogelkop Mountains)
_____ *P. m. interposita* W-central and sw New Guinea
_____ *P. m. septentrionalis* N and ne New Guinea, Yapen, Manam and Karkar islands
_____ *P. m. poliura* SE New Guinea (west to Huon Gulf and Edrich River)
_____ *P. m. assimilis* NE Australia (Cape York Peninsula)
_____ *P. m. keri* NE Australia (Bellenden Ker Range of ne Queensland)
_____ *P. m. magnificus* E Australia (s Queensland and New South Wales)

☐ **Pink-spotted Fruit-Dove** *Ptilinopus perlatus*
_____ *P. p. perlatus* W Papuan islands, nw New Guinea and Yapen I.
_____ *P. p. plumbeicollis* NE New Guinea (Astrolabe Bay to Huon Gulf)
_____ *P. p. zonurus* Aru Islands, s New Guinea and D'Entrecasteaux Archipelago

☐ **Ornate Fruit-Dove** *Ptilinopus ornatus*
_____ *P. o. ornatus* NW New Guinea (Arfak Mountains and coastal Vogelkop)
_____ *P. o. gestroi* New Guinea (west to Cyclops Mountains and Onin Peninsula)

☐ **Tanna Fruit-Dove** *Ptilinopus tannensis*

Vanuatu and Banks Islands

☐ **Orange-fronted Fruit-Dove** *Ptilinopus aurantiifrons*

W Papuan, Yapen, Aru is., New Guinea, D'Entrecasteaux Arch.

☐ **Wallace's Fruit-Dove** *Ptilinopus wallacii*

Lowlands of sw New Guinea, s Moluccas, Kai and Aru islands

☐ **Superb Fruit-Dove** *Ptilinopus superbus*
_____ *P. s. temminckii* Sulawesi and Sula Islands
_____ *P. s. superbus* Moluccas to Bismarck Arch., Solomon Is. and ne Australia

☐ **Many-colored Fruit-Dove** *Ptilinopus perousii*
_____ *P. p. perousii* Samoa (Savai'i, Upolu, Tutuila, Ofu and Tau)
_____ *P. p. mariae* Fiji and Tonga

☐ **Crimson-crowned Fruit-Dove** *Ptilinopus porphyraceus*
_____ *P. p. ponapensis* — Caroline Islands (Truk and Pohnpei)
_____ *P. p. hernsheimi* — Kosrae (e Caroline Islands)
_____ *P. p. porphyraceus (graeffei)* — Small islands of Tonga, Fiji and Niue
_____ *P. p. fasciatus* — Samoa

☐ **Palau Fruit-Dove** *Ptilinopus pelewensis*
Palau Islands (Babelthuap to Angaur)

☐ **Cook Islands Fruit-Dove** *Ptilinopus rarotongensis*
_____ *P. r. rarotongensis* — Rarotonga (Cook Islands)
_____ *P. r. goodwini* — Atiu (s Cook Islands)

☐ **Mariana Fruit-Dove** *Ptilinopus roseicapilla*
Mariana Islands (Saipan, Tinian, Agiguan, Rota and Guam)

☐ **Rose-crowned Fruit-Dove** *Ptilinopus regina*
_____ *P. r. flavicollis* — Lesser Sundas (Flores, Roti, Sawu, Semau and w Timor)
_____ *P. r. roseipileum* — Lesser Sundas (e Timor, Wetar, Romang, Kissar, Moa and Leti)
_____ *P. r. xanthogaster* — Banda, Kai, Damar, Sermata, Babar, Tanimbar and Aru islands
_____ *P. r. ewingii* — N Australia (Kimberley region to n N Territory and Melville I.)
_____ *P. r. regina* — Cape York Pen. to s New S Wales and islands in Torres Strait

☐ **Silver-capped Fruit-Dove** *Ptilinopus richardsii*
_____ *P. r. richardsii* — E Solomon Islands (Ugi and Santa Anna)
_____ *P. r. cyanopterus* — SE Solomon Islands (Rennell and Bellona)

☐ **Gray-green Fruit-Dove** *Ptilinopus purpuratus*
_____ *P. p. chrysogaster* — W Society Islands (Bora Bora, Tahaa, Huahine and Maupiti)
_____ *P. p. frater* — Moorea (e Society Islands)
_____ *P. p. purpuratus* — Tahiti (e Society Islands)

☐ **Makatea Fruit-Dove** *Ptilinopus chalcurus*
Makatea I. (w Tuamotu Archipelago)

☐ **Atoll Fruit-Dove** *Ptilinopus coralensis*
Larger islands in Tuamotu Archipelago (except Makatea)

☐ **Red-bellied Fruit-Dove** *Ptilinopus greyii*
E Solomons to Santa Cruz, Banks, New Caledonia, Isle of Pines

☐ **Rapa Fruit-Dove** *Ptilinopus huttoni*
Rapa I. (Austral Archipelago). Seriously endangered

☐ **White-capped Fruit-Dove** *Ptilinopus dupetithouarsii*
_____ *P. d. viridior* — N Marquesas Islands (Nukuhiva, Uahuka and Uapou)
_____ *P. d. dupetithouarsii* — S Marquesas Is. (Hivaoa, Tahuata, Mohotani and Fatuhiva)

☐ **Red-moustached Fruit-Dove** *Ptilinopus mercierii*
_____ *P. m. tristrami* — Hivaoa (Marquesas Islands). Possibly extinct
_____ *P. m. mercierii†* — Uplands of Nukuhiva (Marquesas Islands). Extinct

☐ **Henderson Island Fruit-Dove** *Ptilinopus insularis*
Henderson I. (Pitcairn Archipelago)

☐ **Coroneted Fruit-Dove** *Ptilinopus coronulatus*
_____ *P. c. trigeminus* — Salawati I. and w coast of Vogelkop Pen. (nw New Guinea)
_____ *P. c. geminus* — N New Guinea (head of Geelvink Bay to Takar) and Yapen I.
_____ *P. c. quadrigeminus* — N New Guinea (Humboldt to Astrolabe Bay) and Manam I.
_____ *P. c. huonensis* — N coastal New Guinea (Huon Bay to Goodenough Bay)
_____ *P. c. coronulatus* — Aru Is. and s coastal New Guinea (Mimika River to Milne Bay)

☐ **Beautiful Fruit-Dove** *Ptilinopus pulchellus*
_____ *P. p. pulchellus* — W Papuan islands and New Guinea
_____ *P. p. decorus* — N New Guinea (east shore of Geelvink Bay to Astrolabe Bay)

☐ **Blue-capped Fruit-Dove** *Ptilinopus monacha*

N Moluccas (Halmahera, Ternate, Bacan and adjacent islands)

☐ **White-breasted Fruit-Dove** *Ptilinopus rivoli*
____ *P. r. prasinorrhous* — Moluccas, Aru Is., w Papuan is. and islands in Geelvink Bay
____ *P. r. bellus* — Mountains of New Guinea, Karkar I. and Goodenough I.
____ *P. r. miquelii* — Yapen I. and Meos Num I. (n New Guinea)
____ *P. r. rivoli* — Bismarck Archipelago
____ *P. r. strophium* — Egum Atoll (Trobriand Islands) and Louisiade Archipelago

☐ **Yellow-bibbed Fruit-Dove** *Ptilinopus solomonensis*
____ *P. s. speciosus* — Numfor, Biak and Traitor's islands (n New Guinea)
____ *P. s. johannis* — Admiralty Islands, St. Matthias Group and New Hanover
____ *P. s. meyeri* — New Britain and satellite islands
____ *P. s. neumanni* — Nissan I. (w Solomon Islands)
____ *P. s. bistictus* — Solomon Islands (Bougainville and Buka)
____ *P. s. vulcanorum* — SW Solomon Islands
____ *P. s. ocularis* — Guadalcanal (se Solomon Islands)
____ *P. s. ambiguus* — Malaita I. (e Solomon Islands)
____ *P. s. solomonensis* — Solomon Islands (San Cristóbal and Ugi)

☐ **Claret-breasted Fruit-Dove** *Ptilinopus viridis*
____ *P. v. viridis* — S Moluccas (Buru, Seram, Ambon and adjacent islands)
____ *P. v. pectoralis* — W Papuan islands and nw New Guinea
____ *P. v. geelvinkiana* — Numfor, Biak and Meos Num islands (n New Guinea)
____ *P. v. salvadorii* — Yapen I. and n New Guinea (Mamberamo River to Madang)
____ *P. v. vicinus* — Trobriand Islands and D'Entrecasteaux Archipelago
____ *P. v. lewisii* — Manus I., Lihir Is., and Nissan I. to w Solomon islands

☐ **White-headed Fruit-Dove** *Ptilinopus eugeniae*

E Solomon Islands (San Cristóbal, Malaupaina and Ugi)

☐ **Orange-bellied Fruit-Dove** *Ptilinopus iozonus*
____ *P. i. iozonus* — Aru Islands
____ *P. i. humeralis* — W Papuan islands and lowlands of nw New Guinea
____ *P. i. jobiensis* — Yapen I., n New Guinea, Manam and adjacent islands
____ *P. i. pseudohumeralis* — Central New Guinea (upper Fly River region)
____ *P. i. finschii* — Huon Peninsula and Fly River to se New Guinea

☐ **Knob-billed Fruit-Dove** *Ptilinopus insolitus*
____ *P. i. insolitus* — Bismarck Archipelago
____ *P. i. inferior* — St. Matthias Group (Mussau and Emira)

☐ **Gray-headed Fruit-Dove** *Ptilinopus hyogaster*

N Moluccas (Morotai, Halmahera, Bacan, Tidore and Ternate)

☐ **Carunculated Fruit-Dove** *Ptilinopus granulifrons*

Obi (n-central Moluccas)

☐ **Black-naped Fruit-Dove** *Ptilinopus melanospila*
____ *P. m. bangueyensis* — S Philippines and islands off n Borneo
____ *P. m. xanthorrhoa* — Talaud Islands, Sangihe I. (Sulawesi) and Doi I. (n Moluccas)
____ *P. m. melanospila* — Sulawesi, Talisei, Bangka, Lembeh and Togian islands
____ *P. m. chrysorrhoa* — Banggai Is., Sula Is. and s Moluccas (Obi and Seram)
____ *P. m. melanauchen* — Matasiri I., Java, Lesser Sundas and islands south of Sulawesi

☐ **Dwarf Fruit-Dove** *Ptilinopus nanus*
____ *P. n. minimus* — W Papuan islands (Waigeo, Batanta, Salawati and Misol)
____ *P. n. nanus* — S New Guinea (Lobo Bay to Port Moresby)

☐ **Negros Fruit-Dove** *Ptilinopus arcanus*

Negros (known from a 1953 specimen from Mt. Canlaon)

☐ **Orange Dove** *Ptilinopus victor*

_____ *P. v. victor* — N Fiji (Vanua Levu, Rabi, Kioa and Taveuni)

_____ *P. v. aureus* — NE Fiji (Qamea and Laucala)

☐ **Golden Dove** *Ptilinopus luteovirens* — W Fiji (Waya Group, Viti Levu, Beqa, Ovalau and Gau)

☐ **Velvet Dove** *Ptilinopus layardi* — Fiji (Kandavu and Ono)

☐ **Cloven-feathered Dove** *Drepanoptila holosericea* — New Caledonia and Isle of Pines

☐ **Madagascar Blue-Pigeon** *Alectroenas madagascariensis* — Humid forests of e Madagascar

☐ **Comoro Blue-Pigeon** *Alectroenas sganzini*

_____ *A. s. minor* — Humid forests of Aldabra

_____ *A. s. sganzini* — Comoro Islands (Grand Comoro, Anjouan and Mayotte)

☐ **Seychelles Blue-Pigeon** *Alectroenas pulcherrima* — Seychelles (Praslin, Mahé, Felicité and Silhouette)

☐ **Pink-bellied Imperial-Pigeon** *Ducula poliocephala* — Highlands of Philippine Islands

☐ **White-bellied Imperial-Pigeon** *Ducula forsteni* — Mts. of Sulawesi and Sula Islands (Taliabu and Mangole)

☐ **Mindoro Imperial-Pigeon** *Ducula mindorensis* — Highlands of Mindoro (central Philippines)

☐ **Gray-headed Imperial-Pigeon** *Ducula radiata* — Montane forests of Sulawesi

☐ **Spotted Imperial-Pigeon** *Ducula carola*

_____ *D. c. carola* — N Philippines (Luzon, Mindoro and Sibuyan)

_____ *D. c. nigrorum* — Philippines (Negros and Siquijor)

_____ *D. c. mindanensis* — S Philippines (Mindoro and Mindanao)

☐ **Green Imperial-Pigeon** *Ducula aenea*

_____ *D. a. sylvatica (andamanica)* — N India to Nepal, Thailand, Indochina and Andaman Islands

_____ *D. a. pusilla* — S India and Sri Lanka

_____ *D. a. nicobarica* — Nicobar Islands

_____ *D. a. mista* — Simeulue I. (off nw Sumatra)

_____ *D. a. babiensis* — Babi and Lasia islands (off se coast of Simeulue I.)

_____ *D. a. consobrina* — Nias I. (off w Sumatra)

_____ *D. a. vicina* — Batu and Mentawi islands (off w Sumatra)

_____ *D. a. aneothorax* — Enggano I. (off w Sumatra)

_____ *D. a. aenea (polia)* — Malay Peninsula, Sumatra and Borneo to Bali and Philippines

_____ *D. a. palawanensis* — Palawan, adjacent s Philippines and Banggai Islands

_____ *D. a. fugaensis* — N Philippines (Calayan, Camiguin Norte and Fuga)

_____ *D. a. nuchalis* — N Luzon (n Philippines)

_____ *D. a. paulina (intermedia, pallidinucha, sulana)* — Sulawesi, Sangihe, Talaud, Togian, Sula and adjacent islands

☐ **White-eyed Imperial-Pigeon** *Ducula perspicillata*

_____ *D. p. perspicillata* — N Moluccas and Kofiau I. (w Papuan islands)

_____ *D. p. neglecta* — S Moluccas (Boano, Seram, Ambon and Saparua)

☐ **Elegant Imperial-Pigeon** *Ducula concinna* — Small islands off Moluccas to e Lesser Sundas

☐ **Pacific Imperial-Pigeon** *Ducula pacifica*

_____ *D. p. sejuncta* — Small islands off n New Guinea, Ninigo Group and Hermit Is.

_____ *D. p. pacifica* — Louisiade Arch. to Solomons, Samoa, Tonga, Niue and Cook Is.

☐ **Red-knobbed Imperial-Pigeon** *Ducula rubricera*

_____ *D. r. rubricera* — Bismarck Archipelago

_____ *D. r. rufigula* — Solomon Islands (except Rennell)

☐ **Micronesian Imperial-Pigeon** *Ducula oceanica*
___ *D. o. monacha* — Palau Islands and Yap I. (w Caroline Islands)
___ *D. o. teraokai* — Truk (Caroline Islands)
___ *D. o. townsendi* — Pohnpei (Caroline Islands)
___ *D. o. oceanica* — Kosrae (e Caroline Islands)
___ *D. o. ratakensis* — Marshall Islands (Wotje, Ailinglaplap, Arno and Jaluit)

☐ **Polynesian Imperial-Pigeon** *Ducula aurorae*
___ *D. a. aurorae* — Makatea I. (Tuamotu Archipelago)
___ *D. a. wilkesii* — Tahiti (Society Islands)

☐ **Marquesas Imperial-Pigeon** *Ducula galeata*
— Nukuhiva I. (Marquesas Islands)

☐ **Spice Imperial-Pigeon** *Ducula myristicivora*
___ *D. m. myristicivora* — Widi I. (off Halmahera) and w Papuan islands (New Guinea)
___ *D. m. geelvinkiana* — Islands in Geelvink Bay (Meos Num, Numfor and Biak)

☐ **Purple-tailed Imperial-Pigeon** *Ducula rufigaster*
___ *D. r. rufigaster* — W Papuan is., Vogelkop and s New Guinea e to Orangerie Bay
___ *D. r. uropygialis* — Yapen I. and n New Guinea (east to Huon Gulf)

☐ **Cinnamon-bellied Imperial-Pigeon** *Ducula basilica*
___ *D. b. basilica* — N Moluccas (Morotai, Halmahera, Ternate, Kasiruta, Bacan)
___ *D. b. obiensis* — Obi I. (central Moluccas)

☐ **Finsch's Imperial-Pigeon** *Ducula finschii*
— Bismarck Archipelago

☐ **Rufescent Imperial-Pigeon** *Ducula chalconota*
___ *D. c. chalconota* — Vogelkop Mountains (nw New Guinea)
___ *D. c. smaragdina* — Montane forests of New Guinea (except Vogelkop)

☐ **Island Imperial-Pigeon** *Ducula pistrinaria*
___ *D. p. rhodinolaema* — Admiralty Is., New Hanover and small is. off n New Guinea
___ *D. p. vanwyckii* — Bismarck Arch. (New Britain, New Ireland and Witu)
___ *D. p. postrema* — Misima I., D'Entrecasteaux and Louisiade archipelagos
___ *D. p. pistrinaria* — Solomon Islands and Lihir Group

☐ **Pink-headed Imperial-Pigeon** *Ducula rosacea*
— Lesser Sundas and islands in Flores Sea and Java Seas

☐ **Christmas Island Imperial-Pigeon** *Ducula whartoni*
— Inland plateau of Christmas I. (e Indian Ocean)

☐ **Gray Imperial-Pigeon** *Ducula pickeringii*
___ *D. p. pickeringii* — Sulu Archipelago and small islands off n and ne Borneo
___ *D. p. langhornei* — Sulu Islands (Bolod and Loran)
___ *D. p. palmasensis* — Miangas and Talaud islands (off Sulawesi)
— Small islands off ne Borneo, n Sulawesi and Sulu Archipelago

☐ **Peale's Imperial-Pigeon** *Ducula latrans*
— Forests of larger Fiji Islands

☐ **Chestnut-bellied Imperial-Pigeon** *Ducula brenchleyi*
— E Solomon Islands (Guadalcanal, Malaita and San Cristobal)

☐ **Baker's Imperial-Pigeon** *Ducula bakeri*
— Banks Group and n Vanuatu

☐ **New Caledonian Imperial-Pigeon** *Ducula goliath*
— Montane forests of New Caledonia and Isle of Pines

☐ **Pinon Imperial-Pigeon** *Ducula pinon*
___ *D. p. pinon* — Aru Islands, w Papuan islands and sw New Guinea
___ *D. p. jobiensis* — Yapen I.; n New Guinea e to Huon Gulf and offshore islands
___ *D. p. rubiensis* — Central and s New Guinea
___ *D. p. salvadorii* — D'Entrecasteaux and Louisiade archipelagos

☐ **Bismarck Imperial-Pigeon** *Ducula melanochroa*

Bismarck Archipelago

☐ **Collared Imperial-Pigeon** *Ducula mullerii*

_____ *D. m. aurantia*

Lowlands of n New Guinea (Geelvink to Astrolabe Bay)

_____ *D. m. mullerii*

Aru Islands, s New Guinea, Boigu and Daru islands

☐ **Zoe Imperial-Pigeon** *Ducula zoeae*

Lowland forests of New Guinea and larger satellite islands

☐ **Mountain Imperial-Pigeon** *Ducula badia*

_____ *D. b. cuprea*

SW India (Western Ghats from Goa to Kerala)

_____ *D. b. insignis*

Himalayan foothills (w Nepal to Sikkim and Bhutan)

_____ *D. b. griseicapilla*

Myanmar to sw China, Hainan, Thailand and Indochina

_____ *D. b. badia*

Malay Pen. and Mergui Arch. to Sumatra, Borneo and w Java

☐ **Dark-backed Imperial-Pigeon** *Ducula lacernulata*

_____ *D. l. lacernulata*

Montane forests of w and central Java

_____ *D. l. williami*

Montane forests of e Java and Bali

_____ *D. l. sasakensis*

W Lesser Sundas (Lombok, Sumbawa and Flores)

☐ **Timor Imperial-Pigeon** *Ducula cineracea*

_____ *D. c. cineracea*

Montane forests of Timor (e Lesser Sundas)

_____ *D. c. schistacea*

Montane forests of Wetar (e Lesser Sundas

☐ **Pied Imperial-Pigeon** *Ducula bicolor*

_____ *D. b. bicolor*

Widespread SE Asia and Malay Archipelago

_____ *D. b. melanura*

Moluccas, Tanimbar and Kai islands

☐ **Torresian Imperial-Pigeon** *Ducula spilorrhoa*

_____ *D. s. subflavescens*

Bismarck Archipelago and Admiralty Islands

_____ *D. s. spilorrhoa*

Aru Islands, New Guinea and adjacent islands to n Australia

☐ **White Imperial-Pigeon** *Ducula luctuosa*

Sulawesi subregion and Sula Islands

☐ **Topknot Pigeon** *Lopholaimus antarcticus*

Coastal e Australia (Queensland to s New South Wales)

☐ **New Zealand Pigeon** *Hemiphaga novaeseelandiae*

_____ *H. n. novaeseelandiae*

Forests of New Zealand and larger offshore islands

_____ *H. n. chathamensis*

Chatham Islands

_____ *H. n. spadicea†*

Formerly Norfolk I. Extinct

☐ **Sombre Pigeon** *Cryptophaps poecilorrhoa*

Humid montane forests of Sulawesi

☐ **Papuan Mountain-Pigeon** *Gymnophaps albertisii*

_____ *G. a. exsul*

Montane forests of Bacan (n Moluccas)

_____ *G. a. albertisii*

Yapen I., New Guinea and Bismarck Archipelago

☐ **Long-tailed Mountain-Pigeon** *Gymnophaps mada*

_____ *G. m. mada*

Montane forests of Buru (s Moluccas)

_____ *G. m. stalkeri*

Montane forests of Seram (s Moluccas)

☐ **Pale Mountain-Pigeon** *Gymnophaps solomonensis*

Solomon Islands (Bougainville to Guadalcanal and Malaita)

ORDER: PSITTACIFORMES
FAMILY: CACATUIDAE (Cockatoos—21)

☐ **Palm Cockatoo** *Probosciger aterrimus*

____	*P. a. stenolophus*	Yapen I. and nw New Guinea
____	*P. a. goliath*	W Papuan islands and w and central New Guinea
____	*P. a. aterrimus*	Aru Is., Misool I., Trans-Fly of s New Guinea and ne Australia

☐ **Red-tailed Black-Cockatoo** *Calyptorhynchus banksii*

____	*C. b. banksii*	Tropical northern Australia
____	*C. b. macrorhynchus*	N-central and ne Australia
____	*C. b. samueli*	W-central to e-central Australia
____	*C. b. naso*	Forests of sw Australia
____	*C. b. graptogyne*	Forests of se South Australia and sw Victoria

☐ **Glossy Black-Cockatoo** *Calyptorhynchus lathami*

____	*C. l. erebus*	E Australia (coastal e-central Queensland)
____	*C. l. lathami*	Inland and coastal e Australia
____	*C. l. halmaturinus*	Kangaroo I. (South Australia)

☐ **Yellow-tailed Black-Cockatoo** *Calyptorhynchus funereus*

____	*C. f. funereus*	E Australia (e-central Queensland to e Victoria)
____	*C. f. whiteae*	E Australia (s Victoria to Eyre Peninsula) and Kangaroo I.
____	*C. f. xanthonotus*	Tasmania and islands in Bass Strait

☐ **Slender-billed Black-Cockatoo** *Calyptorhynchus latirostris*

Woodlands and scrub of sw Australia

☐ **White-tailed Black-Cockatoo** *Calyptorhynchus baudinii*

Extreme sw Australia (south of the Murchison River)

☐ **Gang-gang Cockatoo** *Callocephalon fimbriatum*

New South Wales, Victoria and se South Australia

☐ **Galah** *Eolophus roseicapillus*

____	*E. r. kuhli*	N Australia (Northern Territory)
____	*E. r. roseicapillus*	Western and w-central Australia
____	*E. r. albiceps*	E-central and e Australia south to Tasmania

☐ **Long-billed Corella** *Cacatua tenuirostris*

Woodlands and forests of se Australia

☐ **Western Corella** *Cacatua pastinator*

____	*C. p. derbyi*	Western Australia (Dongara to Moora and Quairading)
____	*C. p. pastinator*	SW Western Australia (Lake Muir and Unicup region)

☐ **Little Corella** *Cacatua sanguinea*

____	*C. s. transfreta*	Lowlands of s New Guinea
____	*C. s. sanguinea*	NW Western Australia and Northern Territory
____	*C. s. westralensis*	Western Australia (Murchison River region)
____	*C. s. gymnopsis*	Inland central and e Australia
____	*C. s. normantoni*	NE Australia (western Cape York Peninsula)

☐ **Tanimbar Cockatoo** *Cacatua goffini*

Coastal lowlands of Tanimbar Islands (e Lesser Sundas)

☐ **Philippine Cockatoo** *Cacatua haematuropygia*

Forests and scrub of Philippine Islands and Palawan

☐ **Yellow-crested Cockatoo** *Cacatua sulphurea*

____	*C. s. sulphurea*	Sulawesi, Muna, Butung, Tanahjampea and adjacent islands
____	*C. s. abbotti*	Masalembu Besar I. (Java Sea)
____	*C. s. parvula*	Lesser Sundas (Sumbawa to Timor)
____	*C. s. citrinocristata*	Sumba (Lesser Sundas)

☐ **Ducorps' Cockatoo** *Cacatua ducorpsii*

E Solomon Islands (Bougainville to Malaita and Guadalcanal)

☐ **Pink Cockatoo** *Cacatua leadbeateri*

Arid and semiarid interior and s coastal Australia

☐ **Sulphur-crested Cockatoo** *Cacatua galerita*
    ____ *C. g. triton*
    ____ *C. g. eleonora*
    ____ *C. g. fitzroyi*
    ____ *C. g. galerita*

New Guinea and adjacent islands
Aru Islands
N Australia (Fitzroy River to Gulf of Carpenteria)
E Australia (Cape York Peninsula to King I. and Tasmania)

☐ **Blue-eyed Cockatoo** *Cacatua ophthalmica*

Bismarck Archipelago (New Britain and New Ireland)

☐ **Salmon-crested Cockatoo** *Cacatua moluccensis*

S Moluccas (Seram, Ambon, Saparua and Haruku)

☐ **White Cockatoo** *Cacatua alba*

N Moluccas (Bacan, Halmahera, Ternate, Tidore, adj. islands)

☐ **Cockatiel** *Nymphicus hollandicus*

Widespread and abundant in interior of Australia

ORDER: PSITTACIFORMES
FAMILY: PSITTACIDAE (Parrots—331)

☐ **Black Lory** *Chalcopsitta atra*
    ____ *C. a. bernsteini*
    ____ *C. a. atra*
    ____ *C. a. insignis*

Misool I. (off w New Guinea)
W New Guinea (w Vogelkop Pen.), Batanta and Salawati is.
W New Guinea (e Vogelkop and Onin Pen.) and Amberpon I.

☐ **Brown Lory** *Chalcopsitta duivenbodei*
    ____ *C. d. duivenbodei*
    ____ *C. d. syringanuchalis*

Coastal n New Guinea (Geelvink Bay to Aitape region)
Coastal lowlands of New Guinea (Aitape to Astrolabe Bay)

☐ **Yellow-streaked Lory** *Chalcopsitta sintillata*
    ____ *C. s. rubrifrons*
    ____ *C. s. sintillata*
    ____ *C. s. chloroptera*

Aru Islands
S New Guinea (Triton Bay to lower Fly River)
Upper Fly River to se Papua New Guinea

☐ **Cardinal Lory** *Chalcopsitta cardinalis*

Lowlands of Solomon Islands and Bismarck Archipelago

☐ **Red-and-blue Lory** *Eos histrio*
    ____ *E. h. challengeri*
    ____ *E. h. talautensis*
    ____ *E. h. histrio*

Miangas I. (off s Sulawesi)
Talaud Islands (Karakelong, Salebabu, Miangas, Kaburuang)
Sangihi, Siau and Ruang islands (n of Sulawesi)

☐ **Violet-necked Lory** *Eos squamata*
    ____ *E. s. riciniata*
    ____ *E. s. obiensis*
    ____ *E. s. squamata*

N Moluccas and Widi I.
N Moluccas (Obi and Bisa)
W Papuan islands and Schilpad I.

☐ **Red Lory** *Eos bornea*
    ____ *E. b. bornea*
    ____ *E. b. cyanonothorus*

S Moluccas and Kai Islands
Buru (s Moluccas)

☐ **Blue-streaked Lory** *Eos reticulata*

Tanimbar Islands (Arafura Sea)

☐ **Black-winged Lory** *Eos cyanogenia*

Islands in Geelvink Bay (off nw New Guinea)

☐ **Blue-eared Lory** *Eos semilarvata*

Montane forests of Seram (s Moluccas)

☐ **Dusky Lory** *Pseudeos fuscata*

New Guinea, Salawati and Yapen islands

☐ **Ornate Lorikeet** *Trichoglossus ornatus*

Sulawesi and larger satellite islands

☐ **Rainbow Lorikeet** *Trichoglossus haematodus*

____	*T. h. mitchellii*	Bali and Lombok
____	*T. h. forsteni*	Sumbawa (Lesser Sundas)
____	*T. h. djampeanus*	Tanahjampea I. (Flores Sea)
____	*T. h. stresemanni*	Kalaotoa I. (Flores Sea)
____	*T. h. fortis*	Sumba (Lesser Sundas)
____	*T. h. weberi*	Flores (Lesser Sundas)
____	*T. h. capistratus*	Timor (Lesser Sundas)
____	*T. h. flavotectus*	E Lesser Sundas (Wetar and Romang)
____	*T. h. rosenbergii*	Biak I. (off n New Guinea)
____	*T. h. intermedius*	N New Guinea (Sepik River to Astrolabe Bay) and Manam I.
____	*T. h. haematodus*	S Moluccas, w Papuan islands and w New Guinea
____	*T. h. nigrogularis (caeruleiceps)*	E Kai Islands, Aru Islands and s New Guinea
____	*T. h. brooki*	Known from two cage birds from Trangan I. (Aru Islands)
____	*T. h. micropteryx*	New Guinea e of Huon Pen.; Kimuta and adjacent islands
____	*T. h. nesophilus*	Admiralty Islands (Ninigo and Hermit groups)
____	*T. h. flavicans*	New Hanover and Admiralty Islands
____	*T. h. massena*	Bismarck Archipelago, Solomon Islands and Vanuatu
____	*T. h. deplanchii*	New Caledonia and Loyalty Islands
____	*T. h. moluccanus*	E Australia (Cape York Pen. to Tasmania and Kangaroo I.)
____	*T. h. rubritorquis*	N Australia (Kimberley region to Gulf of Carpenteria)

☐ **Olive-headed Lorikeet** *Trichoglossus euteles*

Lesser Sundas (Timor and adj. islands from Lomblen to Babar)

☐ **Yellow-and-green Lorikeet** *Trichoglossus flavoviridis*

____	*T. f. meyeri*	Montane forests of Sulawesi
____	*T. f. flavoviridis*	Sula Islands (Taliabu, Seho and Mangole)

☐ **Mindanao Lorikeet** *Trichoglossus johnstoniae*

Montane forests of Mindanao (s Philippines)

☐ **Pohnpei Lorikeet** *Trichoglossus rubiginosus*

Lowlands of Pohnpei (e Caroline Islands)

☐ **Scaly-breasted Lorikeet** *Trichoglossus chlorolepidotus*

Coastal e Australia (nw Queensland to New South Wales)

☐ **Varied Lorikeet** *Psitteuteles versicolor*

N Australia (Kimberley Division to ne Queensland)

☐ **Iris Lorikeet** *Psitteuteles iris*

____	*P. i. iris*	W Timor (e Lesser Sundas)
____	*P. i. rubripileum*	E Timor (e Lesser Sundas)
____	*P. i. wetterensis*	Wetar (e Lesser Sundas)

☐ **Goldie's Lorikeet** *Psitteuteles goldiei*

Mts. of New Guinea (Weyland Mts. to Owen Stanley Range)

☐ **Chattering Lory** *Lorius garrulus*

____	*L. g. morotaianus*	N Moluccas (Morotai and Rau)
____	*L. g. garrulus*	N Moluccas (Halmahera, Widi and Ternate)
____	*L. g. flavopalliatus*	N Moluccas (Kasiruta, Bacan, Obi and Mandiole)

☐ **Purple-bellied Lory** *Lorius hypoinochrous*

____	*L. h. devittatus*	SE New Guinea, Bismarck Archipelago and adjacent islands
____	*L. h. hypoinochrous*	Louisiade Archipelago (Misima and Tagula)
____	*L. h. rosselianus*	Rossel I. (Louisiade Archipelago)

☐ **Purple-naped Lory** *Lorius domicella*

S Moluccas (Seram and Ambon)

☐ **Black-capped Lory** *Lorius lory*

____	*L. l. lory*	W Papuan islands and Vogelkop Peninsula (w New Guinea)
____	*L. l. cyanuchen*	Biak I. (n New Guinea)
____	*L. l. jobiensis*	Yapen I. and Mios Num I. (n New Guinea)
____	*L. l. viridicrissalis*	N New Guinea (Humboldt Bay to Mamberamo River)
____	*L. l. salvadorii*	NE New Guinea (Aitape area to Astrolabe Bay)
____	*L. l. erythrothorax*	S and e New Guinea (except for range of *somu*)
____	*L. l. somu*	Papua New Guinea (Fly River to Purari River)

☐ **White-naped Lory** *Lorius albidinuchus*

New Ireland (Bismarck Archipelago)

☐ **Yellow-bibbed Lory** *Lorius chlorocercus*

E Solomon Islands

☐ **Collared Lory** *Phigys solitarius*

Coastal lowland forests of Fiji Islands

☐ **Blue-crowned Lorikeet** *Vini australis*

Samoa, Lau Arch., Tonga and adjacent islands in s-c Polynesia

☐ **Kuhl's Lorikeet** *Vini kuhlii*

N Line Islands (Rimitara, Kiritimati, Tabuaeran and Teraina)

☐ **Stephen's Lorikeet** *Vini stepheni*

Henderson I. (Pitcairn Islands)

☐ **Blue Lorikeet** *Vini peruviana*

Society Islands, Cook Islands and w Tuamotu Archipelago

☐ **Ultramarine Lorikeet** *Vini ultramarina*

Marquesas Islands (montane forests of Uapou and Nukuhiva)

☐ **Musk Lorikeet** *Glossopsitta concinna*

S Queensland to Victoria, Tasmania and Kangaroo I.

☐ **Little Lorikeet** *Glossopsitta pusilla*

E and se Australia, Tasmania and Kangaroo I.

☐ **Purple-crowned Lorikeet** *Glossopsitta porphyrocephala*

Semiarid lowlands of s Australia and Kangaroo I.

☐ **Palm Lorikeet** *Charmosyna palmarum*

Vanuatu, Duff, Santa Cruz and Banks islands (sw Pacific)

☐ **Red-chinned Lorikeet** *Charmosyna rubrigularis*

Bismarck Arch. (New Britain and New Ireland) and Karkar I.

☐ **Meek's Lorikeet** *Charmosyna meeki*

Montane forests of Solomon Islands (including Bougainvile)

☐ **Blue-fronted Lorikeet** *Charmosyna toxopei*

Buru (s Moluccas)

☐ **Striated Lorikeet** *Charmosyna multistriata*

Mountains of w New Guinea (Snow Mts. to Chimbu Province)

☐ **Pygmy Lorikeet** *Charmosyna wilhelminae*

Mountains of New Guinea (Vogelkop to Owen Stanley Range)

☐ **Red-fronted Lorikeet** *Charmosyna rubronotata*

____	*C. r. rubronotata*	Salawati I. and nw New Guinea (Vogelkop to Adelbert Mts.)
____	*C. r. kordoana*	Biak I. (off nw New Guinea)

☐ **Red-flanked Lorikeet** *Charmosyna placentis*

____	*C. p. intensior*	N Moluccas and Gebe I. (w Papuan islands)
____	*C. p. placentis*	S Moluccas, Aru islands and s New Guinea
____	*C. p. ornata*	W Papuan islands and nw New Guinea
____	*C. p. subplacens*	E New Guinea
____	*C. p. pallidior*	Bismarck Arch. and Solomon Islands (Bougainville and Fead)

☐ **Red-throated Lorikeet** *Charmosyna amabilis*

Fiji (Viti Levu, Vanua Levu, Ovalau and Taveuni)

☐ **Duchess Lorikeet** *Charmosyna margarethae*

Montane forests of Solomon Islands (including Bougainville)

☐ **Fairy Lorikeet** *Charmosyna pulchella*
_____ *C. p. rothschildi* · Cyclops Mountains and montane slopes above Idenburg River
_____ *C. p. pulchella (bella)* · · · · · · · · · · · · · · · · · Montane forests of New Guinea

☐ **Josephine's Lorikeet** *Charmosyna josefinae*
_____ *C. j. josefinae* · Mts. of w New Guinea (Vogelkop to Snow Mountains)
_____ *C. j. cyclopum* · Cyclops Mountains (w New Guinea)
_____ *C. j. sepikiana* · New Guinea (Sepik River and W Highlands to Mt. Bosavi)

☐ **Papuan Lorikeet** *Charmosyna papou*
_____ *C. p. papou* · W New Guinea (montane forests of Vogelkop Peninsula)
_____ *C. p. goliathina* · Weyland Mts. to Eastern Highlands of Papua New Guinea
_____ *C. p. wahnesi* · Mountains of Huon Peninsula (ne New Guinea)
_____ *C. p. stellae* · Mts. of se New Guinea (Herzog Mts. to Owen Stanley Range)

☐ **Plum-faced Lorikeet** *Oreopsittacus arfaki*
_____ *O. a. arfaki* · Vogelkop Mountains (w New Guinea)
_____ *O. a. major* · Snow Mountains (w New Guinea)
_____ *O. a. grandis* · Central mountains of Papua New Guinea

☐ **Yellow-billed Lorikeet** *Neopsittacus musschenbroekii*
_____ *N. m. musschenbroekii* · · · · · · · · · · · · · · · · Vogelkop Mountains (w New Guinea)
_____ *N. m. major* · Snow Mts. to Huon Pen. and Owen Stanley Range

☐ **Orange-billed Lorikeet** *Neopsittacus pullicauda*
_____ *N. p. alpinus* · New Guinea (Snow Mountains to Mt. Capella)
_____ *N. p. socialis* · SE New Guinea (mountains of Huon Pen. and Herzog Mts.)
_____ *N. p. pullicauda* · Mts. of se New Guinea (Mt. Capella to Owen Stanley Range)

☐ **Pesquet's Parrot** *Psittrichas fulgidus*
Patchily distributed mountains of New Guinea

☐ **Kea** *Nestor notabilis*
Mountains of South I. (New Zealand)

☐ **New Zealand Kaka** *Nestor meridionalis*
_____ *N. m. septentrionalis* · · · · · · · · · · · · · · · · · · New Zealand (North I. and adjacent offshore islands)
_____ *N. m. meridionalis* · South I., Stewart I. and larger New Zealand offshore islands

☐ **Kakapo** *Strigops habroptilus*
Nothofagus forests of New Zealand (on verge of extinction)

☐ **Yellow-capped Pygmy-Parrot** *Micropsitta keiensis*
_____ *M. k. keiensis* · Kai Islands and Aru Islands
_____ *M. k. chloroxantha* · W Papuan islands, Vogelkop and Onin peninsulas
_____ *M. k. viridipectus* · S New Guinea (Mimika River to Fly River)

☐ **Geelvink Pygmy-Parrot** *Micropsitta geelvinkiana*
_____ *M. g. geelvinkiana* · Numfor I. (Geelvink Bay off w New Guinea)
_____ *M. g. misoriensis* · Biak I. (Geelvink Bay off n New Guinea)

☐ **Buff-faced Pygmy-Parrot** *Micropsitta pusio*
_____ *M. p. beccarii* · N New Guinea, Manam, Karkar, Bagabag and Rook islands
_____ *M. p. pusio* · SE New Guinea and Bismarck Archipelago
_____ *M. p. harteri* · Fergusson I. (D'Entrecasteaux Archielago)
_____ *M. p. stresemanni* · Louisiade Archipelago (Misima and Tagula)

☐ **Red-breasted Pygmy-Parrot** *Micropsitta bruijnii*
_____ *M. b. pileata* · S Moluccas (Seram and Buru)
_____ *M. b. bruijnii* · Mts. of New Guinea (Vogelkop to Owen Stanley Range)
_____ *M. b. necopinata* · Bismarck Archipelago (New Britain and New Ireland)
_____ *N. b. rosea* · Solomon Is. (Bougainville, Guadalcanal and Kulambangra)

☐ **Meek's Pygmy-Parrot** *Micropsitta meeki*
____ *M. m. meeki* | Admiralty Islands
____ *M. m. proxima* | Bismarck Archipelago (St. Matthias and Squally Islands)

☐ **Finsch's Pygmy-Parrot** *Micropsitta finschii*
____ *M. f. viridifrons* | Bismarck Arch. (New Hanover, New Ireland and Lihir Group)
____ *M. f. nanina* | Solomon Islands (Bougainville, Choiseul and Santa Isabel)
____ *M. f. tristrami* | Vella Lavella, Kulambangra, Rendova and adj. Solomon Is.
____ *M. f. aolae* | E-c Solomon Islands (Russel Is., Guadalcanal and Malaita)
____ *M. f. finschii* | SE Solomon Islands (Ugi, San Cristóbal and Rennell)

☐ **Orange-breasted Fig-Parrot** *Clycopsitta gulielmitertii*
____ *C. g. melanogenia* | Aru Islands
____ *C. g. gulielmitertii* | W New Guinea (Salawati I. and w Vogelkop Peninsula)
____ *C. g. nigrifrons* | N New Guinea
____ *C. g. ramuensis* | NE New Guinea (Ramu River district)
____ *C. g. fuscifrons* | S New Guinea
____ *C. g. amabilis* | NE New Guinea (Huon Peninsula to Milne Bay)
____ *C. g. suavissima* | SE Papua New Guinea

☐ **Double-eyed Fig-Parrot** *Clycopsitta diophthalma*
____ *C. d. diophthalma* | W Papuan islands and w New Guinea
____ *C. d. aruensis* | Aru Islands and extreme s New Guinea
____ *C. d. coccineifrons* | E New Guinea east of Astrolabe Bay and Central Highlands
____ *C. d. virago* | D'Entrecasteaux Archipelago (Goodenough and Fergusson)
____ *C. d. inseparabilis* | Tagula I. (Louisiade Archipelago)
____ *C. d. marshalli* | Cape York Peninsula (extreme n Queensland)
____ *C. d. macleayana* | NE Queensland and Atherton Tableland south to Townsend
____ *C. d. coxeni* | E Australia (se Queensland and ne New South Wales)

☐ **Large Fig-Parrot** *Psittaculirostris desmarestii*
____ *P. d. blythii* | Misool I. (w Papuan Islands)
____ *P. d. occidentalis* | W Vogelkop Peninsula, Salawati and Batanta islands
____ *P. d. desmarestii* | W New Guinea (e regions of Vogelkop Peninsula)
____ *P. d. intermedia* | W New Guinea (Onin Peninsula)
____ *P. d. godmani* | S New Guinea (se Irian Jaya to Fly River)
____ *P. d. cervicalis* | SE New Guinea (Fly River to extreme e Papua New Guinea)

☐ **Edwards' Fig-Parrot** *Psittaculirostris edwardsii*
| Lowlands of ne New Guinea (Humboldt Bay to Huon Gulf)

☐ **Salvadori's Fig-Parrot** *Psittaculirostris salvadorii*
| NW New Guinea (east shore of Geelvink Bay to Cyclops Mts.)

☐ **Guaiabero** *Bolbopsittacus lunulatus*
____ *B. l. lunulatus* | Luzon (n Philippines)
____ *B. l. callainipictus* | Samar (central Philippines)
____ *B. l. intermedius* | N Philippines (Leyte and Panaon)
____ *B. l. mindanensis* | Mindanao (s Philippines)

☐ **Crimson Shining-Parrot** *Prosopeia splendens*
| SW Fiji (Kandavu and Ono)

☐ **Red Shining-Parrot** *Prosopeia tabuensis*
____ *P. t. tabuensis* | Fiji (Vanua Levu, Kioa, Koro and Gau); 'Eua I. (Tonga)
____ *P. t. taviuensis* | Fiji (Taveuni and Ngamea)

☐ **Masked Shining-Parrot** *Prosopeia personata*
| Viti Levu I. (Fiji); extirpated on Ovalau and Mbau

☐ **Horned Parakeet** *Eunymphicus cornutus*
____ *E. c. cornutus* | New Caledonia
____ *E. c. uvaeensis* | Uvéa (Loyalty Islands). Population ±617 birds 1997

☐ **Antipodes Parakeet** *Cyanoramphus unicolor*

Locally in Antipodes Islands

☐ **Red-fronted Parakeet** *Cyanoramphus novaezelandiae*

_____ *C. n. saissetti* — New Caledonia
_____ *C. n. cookii* — Norfolk I.
_____ *C. n. cyanurus* — Kermadec Islands
_____ *C. n. novaezelandiae* — North I., South I., Stewart I. and Auckland Is. (New Zealand)
_____ *C. n. chathamensis* — Chatham Islands
_____ *C. n. hochstetteri* — Antipodes Islands
_____ *C. n. erythrotis†* — Formerly Macquarie I. Extinct

☐ **Yellow-fronted Parakeet** *Cyanoramphus auriceps*

North I., South I., Stewart I. and Auckland Is. (New Zealand)

☐ **Chatham Islands Parakeet** *Cyanoramphus forbesi*

Chatham Islands (Mangere and Little Mangare)

☐ **Malherbe's Parakeet** *Cyanoramphus malherbi*

Nothofagus forests of n South I. (New Zealand)

☐ **Red-capped Parrot** *Purpureicephalus spurius*

Lowlands of extreme sw Australia

☐ **Port Lincoln Parrot** *Barnardius zonarius*

_____ *B. z. semitorquatus* — Extreme w Western Australia
_____ *B. z. occidentalis* — SW Western Australia
_____ *B. z. zonarius* — W Australia to s-c Northern Territory and s-c South Australia

☐ **Mallee Ringneck** *Barnardius barnardi*

_____ *B. b. macgillivrayi* — N Australia (e Northern Territory and adj. nw Queensland)
_____ *B. b. whitei* — South Australia (Flinders Range)
_____ *B. b. barnardi* — Interior of se Australia (except in range of *whitei*)

☐ **Green Rosella** *Platycercus caledonicus*

Tasmania and larger islands in Bass Strait

☐ **Crimson Rosella** *Platycercus elegans*

_____ *P. e. nigrescens* — E Australia (coastal ne Queensland)
_____ *P. e. elegans* — E Australia (se Queensland to se South Australia)
_____ *P. e. melanoptera* — Kangaroo I.

☐ **Yellow Rosella** *Platycercus flaveolus*

Interior se Australia (Murray-Murrumbidgee river systems)

☐ **Adelaide Rosella** *Platycercus adelaidae*

_____ *P. a. subadelaidae* — S South Australia (s Flinders Range)
_____ *P. a. adelaidae* — S South Australia (Mt. Lofty Range to Fleurieu Peninsula)

☐ **Northern Rosella** *Platycercus venustus*

Kimberley Range to Northern Territory/Queensland border

☐ **Eastern Rosella** *Platycercus eximius*

_____ *P. e. cecilae* — E Australia (se Queensland and ne New South Wales)
_____ *P. e. eximius* — SE New South Wales, Victoria and se South Australia
_____ *P. e. diemenensis* — Tasmania

☐ **Pale-headed Rosella** *Platycercus adscitus*

_____ *P. a. adscitus* — E Australia (extreme n Cape York Peninsula south to Cairns)
_____ *P. a. palliceps* — N Queensland south of Mitchell River to n New South Wales

☐ **Western Rosella** *Platycercus icterotis*

_____ *P. i. icterotis* — Coastal areas of extreme sw corner of Australia
_____ *P. i. xanthogenys* — Drier interior of extreme sw corner of Australia

☐ **Mulga Parrot** *Psephotus varius*

Scrub and riverine woodlands of interior s-central Australia

☐ **Red-rumped Parrot** *Psephotus haematonotus*
_____ *P. h. caeruleus* — South Australia (Lake Eyre region) and adjacent Queensland
_____ *P. h. haematonotus* — Scrub and riverine woodlands of interior se Australia

☐ **Hooded Parrot** *Psephotus dissimilis* — N Australia (ne Northern Territory)

☐ **Golden-shouldered Parrot** *Psephotus chrysopterygius* — NE Australia (interior s Cape York Peninsula)

☐ **Bluebonnet** *Northiella haematogaster*
_____ *N. h. haematorrhous* — E Australia (interior s Queensland and n New South Wales)
_____ *N. h. haematogaster* — W and s New South Wales, nw Victoria and se S Australia
_____ *N. h. pallescens* — Inland South Australia
_____ *N. h. narethae* — SE Western Australia to sw South Australia

☐ **Bourke's Parrot** *Neophema bourkii* — Locally in *Acacia* scrub of interior s and central Australia

☐ **Blue-winged Parrot** *Neophema chrysostoma* — SE Australia (sw Queensland to Victoria and Tasmania)

☐ **Elegant Parrot** *Neophema elegans* — Disjunct in sw and se Australia and Kangaroo I.

☐ **Rock Parrot** *Neophema petrophila* — Coasts and islands of w and s Australia

☐ **Orange-bellied Parrot** *Neophema chrysogaster* — Tasmania, islands in Bass Strait and adj. coastal se Australia

☐ **Turquoise Parrot** *Neophema pulchella* — SE Australia (se Queensland to n Victoria)

☐ **Scarlet-chested Parrot** *Neophema splendida* — Interior of s Australia

☐ **Swift Parrot** *Lathamus discolor* — Tasmania and Flinders I.; winters e and se Australia

☐ **Budgerigar** *Melopsittacus undulatus* — Abundant throughout drier parts of Australia

☐ **Ground Parrot** *Pezoporus wallicus*
_____ *P. w. flaviventris* — Coastal sw Australia
_____ *P. w. wallicus* — Tasmania, islands in Bass Strait and coastal se Australia

☐ **Night Parrot** *Geopsittacus occidentalis* — Arid interior of w and c Australia (on verge of extinction)

☐ **Blue-rumped Parrot** *Psittinus cyanurus*
_____ *P. c. cyanurus* — S Thailand to s Myanmar, Malay Pen., Sumatra and Borneo
_____ *P. c. abbotti* — Simeulue and Siumat islands (off w coast of Sumatra)
_____ *P. c. pontius* — Mentawi Is. (Siberut, Sipura, North Pagai and South Pagai)

☐ **Painted Tiger-Parrot** *Psittacella picta*
_____ *P. p. lorentzi* — W New Guinea (Snow Mountains)
_____ *P. p. excelsa* — Mountains of Central Highlands of Papua New Guinea
_____ *P. p. picta* — SE New Guinea (Wharton and Owen Stanley mountains)

☐ **Brehm's Tiger-Parrot** *Psittacella brehmii*
_____ *P. b. brehmii* — NW New Guinea (montane forests of Vogelkop Peninsula)
_____ *P. b. intermixta* — W New Guinea (Snow Mts., Weyland Mts. and Mt. Goliath)
_____ *P. b. harterti* — E New Guinea (mountains of Huon Peninsula)
_____ *P. b. pallida* — Central mountains of Papua New Guinea

☐ **Modest Tiger-Parrot** *Psittacella modesta*
_____ *P. m. modesta* — W New Guinea (Vogelkop Mountains)
_____ *P. m. subcollaris* — W New Guinea (n slope of Snow Mts. e to Hindenburg Range)
_____ *P. m. collaris* — W New Guinea (s slopes of Snow Mountains)

☐ **Madarasz's Tiger-Parrot** *Psittacella madaraszi*

___	*P. m. major*	W New Guinea (Weyland Mts. and n slope of Snow Mts.)
___	*P. m. hallstromi*	Central Highlands and Hindenburg Range of New Guinea
___	*P. m. huonensis*	NE New Guinea (mountains of Huon Peninsula)
___	*P. m. madaraszi*	Mountains of se New Guinea

☐ **Red-cheeked Parrot** *Geoffroyus geoffroyi*

___	*G. g. cyanicollis*	N Moluccas (Morotai, Halmahera and Bacan)
___	*G. g. obiensis*	Central Moluccas (Obi and Bisa)
___	*G. g. rhodops*	S Moluccas (Buru, Seram, Ambon and adjacent islands)
___	*G. g. explorator*	Seram Laut I. (s Moluccas)
___	*G. g. keyensis*	Kai Islands
___	*G. g. floresianus*	W Lesser Sundas (Lombok, Sumbawa, Flores, Besar, Sumba)
___	*G. g. geoffroyi*	E Lesser Sundas (Timor, Samau and Wetar)
___	*G. g. timorlaoensis*	Tanimbar Islands (Arafura Sea)
___	*G. g. pucherani*	W Papuan islands and nw New Guinea east to Etna Bay
___	*G. g. minor*	N New Guinea (Mamberamo River to Astrolabe Bay)
___	*G. g. jobiensis*	Yapen I. and Meos Num I. (n New Guinea)
___	*G. g. mysoriensis*	Biak I. and Numfor I. (n New Guinea)
___	*G. g. orientalis*	NE New Guinea (Huon Peninsula)
___	*G. g. sudestiensis*	Louisiade Archipelago (Misima and Tagula)
___	*G. g. cyanicarpus*	Rossel I. (Louisiade Archchipelago)
___	*G. g. aruensis*	Aru Is., s New Guinea, Louisiade Arch. and n Queensland

☐ **Blue-collared Parrot** *Geoffroyus simplex*

___	*G. s. simplex*	W New Guinea (Vogelkop Mountains)
___	*G. s. buergersi*	Snow Mountains to Owen Stanley Range (New Guinea)

☐ **Singing Parrot** *Geoffroyus heteroclitus*

___	*G. h. heteroclitus*	Bismarck Archipelago and Solomon Islands (except Rennell)
___	*G. h. hyancinthinus*	Rennell (Solomon Islands)

☐ **Luzon Racquet-tail** *Prioniturus montanus*

Mountains of Luzon (n Philippines)

☐ **Mindanao Racquet-tail** *Prioniturus waterstradti*

Mountains of Mindanao (s Philippines)

☐ **Blue-headed Racquet-tail** *Prioniturus platenae*

S Philippines (Balabac, Palawan, Calamian and adj. islands)

☐ **Green Racquet-tail** *Prioniturus luconensis*

N Philippines (lowlands of Luzon and Marinduque)

☐ **Blue-crowned Racquet-tail** *Prioniturus discurus*

___	*P. d. whiteheadi*	Philippines (Negros, Bohol, Samar, Leyte, Masbate and Cebu)
___	*P. d. mindorensis*	Mindoro (n-central Philippines)
___	*P. d. discurus*	Mindanao, Basilan and islands in Sulu Archipelago

☐ **Blue-winged Racquet-tail** *Prioniturus verticalis*

Sulu Archipelago

☐ **Yellowish-breasted Racquet-tail** *Prioniturus flavicans*

Lowlands of n Sulawesi, Bangka, Lembeh and Togian islands

☐ **Golden-mantled Racquet-tail** *Prioniturus platurus*

___	*P. p. talautensis*	Talaud Islands (n Moluccas)
___	*P. p. platurus*	Sulawesi, Togian, Banggai and adjacent islands
___	*P. p. sinerubris*	Sula Islands (Taliabu and Mangole)

☐ **Buru Racquet-tail** *Prioniturus mada*

Montane forests of Buru (s Moluccas)

☐ **Black-lored Parrot** *Tanygnathus gramineus*

Montane forests of Buru (s Moluccas)

☐ **Great-billed Parrot** *Tanygnathus megalorynchos*

____	*T. m. megalorynchos*	Sulawesi and adjacent islands to Moluccas and w Papuan is.
____	*T. m. affinis*	S Moluccas (Buru, Seram, Ambon, Haruku and Seram Laut)
____	*T. m. sumbensis*	Sumba (e Lesser Sundas)
____	*T. m. hellmayri*	E Lesser Sundas (Roti, Semau and sw Timor)
____	*T. m. subaffinis*	Babar and Tanimbar Islands (Yamdena and Larat)

☐ **Blue-naped Parrot** *Tanygnathus lucionensis*

____	*T. l. lucionensis*	N Philippines (Luzon and Mindoro)
____	*T. l. hybridus*	Polillo (n Philippines)
____	*T. l. salvadorii*	S Philippines, Sulu Archipelago and islands off north Borneo
____	*T. l. talautensis*	Talaud Islands (n Moluccas)

☐ **Azure-rumped Parrot** *Tanygnathus sumatranus*

____	*T. s. duponti*	Luzon (n Philippines)
____	*T. s. freeri*	Polillo (n Philippines)
____	*T. s. everetti*	Philippines (Visayan Islands and Mindanao)
____	*T. s. burbidgii*	Sulu Archipelago
____	*T. s. sangirensis*	Sangihi I. and Talaud Islands
____	*T. s. sumatranus*	Sulawesi, Togian, Sula, Muna, Buton is. and Banggai Arch.

☐ **Eclectus Parrot** *Eclectus roratus*

____	*E. r. vosmaeri*	Larger islands in n and central Moluccas
____	*E. r. roratus*	S Moluccas (Buru, Seram, Ambon, Saparua and Haruku)
____	*E. r. cornelia*	Sumba I. (Lesser Sundas)
____	*E. r. riedeli*	Tanimbar Islands (Arafura Sea)
____	*E. r. aruensis*	Aru Islands (New Guinea)
____	*E. r. biaki*	Biak I. (off nw New Guinea)
____	*E. r. polychloros*	Kai and w Papuan is., New Guinea and Bismarck Archipelago
____	*E. r. solomonensis*	Admiralty Islands, Bismarck Arch. and Solomon Islands
____	*E. r. macgillivrayi*	NE Australia (extreme n Queensland)

☐ **Australian King-Parrot** *Alisterus scapularis*

____	*A. s. minor*	N Australia (ne Queensland)
____	*A. s. scapularis*	Coastal e Australia (n Queensland to s Victoria)

☐ **Moluccan King-Parrot** *Alisterus amboinensis*

____	*A. a. hypophonius*	Halmahera I. (n Moluccas)
____	*A. a. sulaensis*	Sula Islands (Taliabu, Seho and Mangole)
____	*A. a. versicolor*	Peleng I. (Banggai Islands)
____	*A. a. buruensis*	Buru (s Moluccas)
____	*A. a. amboinensis*	S Moluccas (Boano, Ambon and Seram)
____	*A. a. dorsalis*	W Papuan islands and nw New Guinea

☐ **Papuan King-Parrot** *Alisterus chloropterus*

____	*A. c. moszkowskii*	N New Guinea (Geelvink Bay to Aitape district)
____	*A. c. callopterus*	Central New Guinea (Weyland Mountains to Fly River)
____	*A. c. chloropterus*	E New Guinea (Huon Gulf to Hall Sound)

☐ **Olive-shouldered Parrot** *Aprosmictus jonquillaceus*

____	*A. j. wetterensis*	Wetar (e Lesser Sundas)
____	*A. j. jonquillaceus*	E Lesser Sundas (Timor and Roti)

☐ **Red-winged Parrot** *Aprosmictus erythropterus*

____	*A. e. coccineopterus*	Trans-Fly lowlands of s New Guinea and n Australia
____	*A. e. erythropterus*	Interior e Australia

☐ **Superb Parrot** *Polytelis swainsonii*

		Interior se Australia (New South Wales and n Victoria)

☐ **Regent Parrot** *Polytelis anthopeplus*

___ *P. a. anthopeplus*	SW Australia
___ *P. a. monarchoides*	Interior western part of se Australia

☐ **Alexandra's Parrot** *Polytelis alexandrae*

Dry eucalyptus forests of interior central and w Australia

☐ **Alexandrine Parakeet** *Psittacula eupatria*

___ *P. e. nipalensis*	E Afghanistan to Pakistan, n India and Bangladesh
___ *P. e. eupatria*	S India and Sri Lanka
___ *P. e. magnirostris*	Andaman Islands
___ *P. e. avensis*	N Myanmar and adjacent ne India
___ *P. e. siamensis*	Thailand to Laos, Cambodia and Vietnam

☐ **Rose-ringed Parakeet** *Psittacula krameri*

___ *P. k. krameri*	Mauritania to Senegal, Guinea, w Uganda and s Sudan
___ *P. k. parvirostris*	E Sudan (Sennar) to Eritrea, Ethiopia, Djibouti and nw Somalia
___ *P. k. borealis*	NW Pakistan to n India, Nepal, se China and c Myanmar
___ *P. k. manillensis*	S peninsular India and Sri Lanka

☐ **Mauritius Parakeet** *Psittacula echo*

Montane forests of Mauritius (on verge of extinction)

☐ **Slaty-headed Parakeet** *Psittacula himalayana*

Himalayas (Afghanistan to n India, Nepal and w Assam)

☐ **Gray-headed Parakeet** *Psittacula finschii*

N India (w Bengal) to s China, Myanmar and Indochina

☐ **Plum-headed Parakeet** *Psittacula cyanocephala*

Indian subcontinent and Sri Lanka

☐ **Blossom-headed Parakeet** *Psittacula roseata*

___ *P. r. roseata*	N India (w Bengal) to Bhutan, Bangladesh and n Myanmar
___ *P. r. juneae*	S Myanmar and Thailand to Laos, Cambodia and Vietnam

☐ **Malabar Parakeet** *Psittacula columboides*

SW India (Western Ghats)

☐ **Layard's Parakeet** *Psittacula calthropae*

Sri Lanka

☐ **Derbyan Parakeet** *Psittacula derbiana*

Extreme sw China to se Tibet and ne Assam

☐ **Red-breasted Parakeet** *Psittacula alexandri*

___ *P. a. fasciata*	N India to Nepal, Myanmar, Thailand, Indochina and Hainan
___ *P. a. abbotti*	Andaman Islands
___ *P. a. cala*	Simeulue I. (off w Sumatra)
___ *P. a. major*	Lasia I. and Babi I. (off Sumatra)
___ *P. a. alexandri*	Java, Bali and extreme s Borneo
___ *P. a. kangeanensis*	Kangean Islands (Java Sea)
___ *P. a. dammermani*	Karimunjawa Islands (Java Sea)

☐ **Nicobar Parakeet** *Psittacula caniceps*

Nicobar Islands

☐ **Long-tailed Parakeet** *Psittacula longicauda*

___ *P. l. tytleri*	Andaman Islands
___ *P. l. nicobarica*	Nicobar Islands
___ *P. l. longicauda*	S Malay Pen., Borneo, Sumatra, Nias, Bangka and Anambas is.
___ *P. l. modesta*	Enggano I. (off sw Sumatra)
___ *P. l. defontainei*	Natuna Islands (off w Borneo)

☐ **Vernal Hanging-Parrot** *Loriculus vernalis*

NE and sw India to s China, SE Asia and Andaman Islands

☐ **Ceylon Hanging-Parrot** *Loriculus beryllinus*

Sri Lanka

☐ **Philippine Hanging-Parrot** *Loriculus philippensis*
____ *L. p. philippensis* — Philippines (Banton, Catanduanes, Luzon, Polillo, Marinduque)
____ *L. p. mindorensis* — Mindoro (Philippines)
____ *L. p. bournsi* — Sibuyan (Philippines)
____ *L. p. regulus* — Guimaras, Masbate, Negros, Panay, Tablas, Ticao and Romblon
____ *L. p. chrysonotus†* — Formerly Cebu (Philippines). Extinct
____ *L. p. worcesteri* — Philippines (Bohol, Leyte and Samar)
____ *L. p. siquijorensis* — Formerly Siquijor (Philippines). Probably extinct
____ *L. p. apicalis* — S Philippines (Mindanao, Basol and Dinagat)
____ *L. p. dohertyi* — Basilan (Philippines)
____ *L. p. bonapartei* — Sulu Archipelago (Bongao, Jolo and Tawitawi)

☐ **Blue-crowned Hanging-Parrot** *Loriculus galgulus* — S Thailand, Malay Pen., Sumatra, Borneo and adjacent islands

☐ **Sulawesi Hanging-Parrot** *Loriculus stigmatus* — Sulawesi and adjacent islands

☐ **Sula Hanging-Parrot** *Loriculus sclateri* — Sula Islands and Banggai Islands

☐ **Moluccan Hanging-Parrot** *Loriculus amabilis* — N Moluccas (Halmahera and Bacan)

☐ **Sangihe Hanging-Parrot** *Loriculus catamene* — Sangihe I. (n of Sulawesi)

☐ **Papuan Hanging-Parrot** *Loriculus aurantiifrons*
____ *L. a. aurantiifrons* — Misool I. (w Papuan islands)
____ *L. a. batavorum* — Waigeo I. and coastal nw New Guinea
____ *L. a. meeki* — E New Guinea, Fergusson I., Goodenough I. and Karkar I.

☐ **Green-fronted Hanging-Parrot** *Loriculus tener* — Bismarck Archipelago

☐ **Pygmy Hanging-Parrot** *Loriculus exilis* — Sulawesi

☐ **Yellow-throated Hanging-Parrot** *Loriculus pusillus* — Java and Bali

☐ **Wallace's Hanging-Parrot** *Loriculus flosculus* — Flores (w Lesser Sundas)

☐ **Gray-headed Lovebird** *Agapornis canus*
____ *A. c. canus* — W and e Madagascar (except range of *ablectanea*)
____ *A. c. ablectanea* — Arid sw Madagascar

☐ **Red-headed Lovebird** *Agapornis pullarius*
____ *A. p. pullarius* — Sierra Leone to Guinea, Sudan, Angola and Zaire; São Tomé I.
____ *A. p. ugandae* — Ethiopia to Uganda, extreme e Zaire, Rwanda and Tanzania

☐ **Black-winged Lovebird** *Agapornis taranta* — Highland forests of Ethiopia

☐ **Black-collared Lovebird** *Agapornis swinderniana*
____ *A. s. swinderniana* — Patchily distributed Liberia, Ivory Coast and Ghana
____ *A. s. zenkeri* — Cameroon to Gabon, s Central African Republic and w Zaire
____ *A. s. emini* — Lowland forests of Zaire and w Uganda

☐ **Rosy-faced Lovebird** *Agapornis roseicollis*
____ *A. r. catumbella* — Subdeserts of sw Angola
____ *A. r. roseicollis* — Subdeserts of Namibia to n Cape Province

☐ **Fischer's Lovebird** *Agapornis fischeri* — N Tanzania (south and east of Lake Victoria)

☐ **Yellow-collared Lovebird** *Agapornis personatus* — Tanzania

☐ **Lilian's Lovebird** *Agapornis lilianae*

S Tanzania to Malawi, Zambia, Zimbabwe and Mozambique

☐ **Black-cheeked Lovebird** *Agapornis nigrigenis*

S Zambia and extreme n Zimbabwe

☐ **Vasa Parrot** *Coracopsis vasa*

____	*C. v. comorensis*	Comoro Islands (Grand Comoro, Mohéli and Anjouan)
____	*C. v. drouhardi*	W and s Madagascar
____	*C. v. vasa*	Savanna and forests of e Madagascar

☐ **Black Parrot** *Coracopsis nigra*

____	*C. n. sibilans*	Comoro Islands (Grand Comoro and Anjouan)
____	*C. n. libs*	Drier areas of w Madagascar
____	*C. n. nigra*	Forests of e Madagascar
____	*C. n. barklyi*	Seychelles (Praslin and Curieuse)

☐ **Gray Parrot** *Psittacus erithacus*

____	*P. e. timneh*	S Guinea to Sierra Leone, Liberia, Mali and w Ivory Coast
____	*P. e. erithacus*	Ivory Coast to Kenya, Tanzania, Príncipe, São Tomé and Bioko

☐ **Brown-necked Parrot** *Poicephalus robustus*

____	*P. r. fuscicollis*	Senegambia to Nigeria and n Angola
____	*P. r. suahelicus*	C Tanzania to ne Transvaal, se Zaire, Angola and Namibia
____	*P. r. robustus*	Extreme se Africa

☐ **Red-fronted Parrot** *Poicephalus gulielmi*

____	*P. g. fantiensis*	Liberia to Ivory Coast and Ghana
____	*P. g. gulielmi*	Cameroon to n Angola e Zaire and w Uganda
____	*P. g. massaicus*	W Kenya and n Tanzania

☐ **Meyer's Parrot** *Poicephalus meyeri*

____	*P. m. meyeri*	N Cameroon to s Chad, n Zaire, s Sudan and Ethiopia
____	*P. m. saturatus*	W Kenya to Uganda, e Zaire, Rwanda, Burunda, nw Tanzania
____	*P. m. matschiei*	SE Zaire to Tanzania, e Angola, n Zambia and n Malawi
____	*P. m. reichenowi*	W Angola
____	*P. m. damarensis*	Extreme s Angola to n Namibia and n-central Botswana
____	*P. m. transvaalensis*	S Zambia to n Mozambique, e Botswana and n South Africa

☐ **Rueppell's Parrot** *Poicephalus rueppellii*

Arid sw Angola to central Namibia

☐ **Brown-headed Parrot** *Poicephalus cryptoxanthus*

____	*P. c. tanganyikae*	SE Kenya to Malawi, n Mozambique, Zanzibar and Pemba I.
____	*P. c. cryptoxanthus*	SE Zimbabwe and Mozambique (s of Save R.) to ne S Africa

☐ **Niam-Niam Parrot** *Poicephalus crassus*

SW Chad to Central African Republic and extreme sw Sudan

☐ **Red-bellied Parrot** *Poicephalus rufiventris*

____	*P. r. pallidus*	Dry thornbush of e Ethiopia and Somalia
____	*P. r. rufiventris*	Central Ethiopia to n Tanzania

☐ **Senegal Parrot** *Poicephalus senegalus*

____	*P. s. senegalus*	Gambia and Guinea-Bissau to s Niger, n Cameroon, sw Chad
____	*P. s. versteri*	NW Ivory Coast to sw Nigeria (south of range of *senegalus*)

☐ **Yellow-fronted Parrot** *Poicephalus flavifrons*

Montane forests of Ethiopia

☐ **Hyacinth Macaw** *Anodorhynchus hyacinthinus*

Interior s Brazil, extreme nw Paraguay and adjacent e Bolivia

☐ **Lear's Macaw** *Anodorhynchus leari*

Caatinga of e Brazil (n Bahia). On verge of extinction

☐ **Spix's Macaw** *Cyanopsitta spixii*

Palm groves of ne Brazil (n Bahia). On verge of extinction

☐ **Blue-and-yellow Macaw** *Ara ararauna*

Tropical e Panama to e Peru, n Bolivia, Paraguay and e Brazil

☐ **Blue-throated Macaw** *Ara glaucogularis*

Chaco of e Bolivia (Beni and Santa Cruz)

☐ **Military Macaw** *Ara militaris*
___ *A. m. mexicana* — Arid w Mexico (Sonora to Isthmus of Tehuántepec)
___ *A. m. militaris* — Tropical Colombia to nw Venezuela, Ecuador and n Peru
___ *A. m. boliviana* — Tropical Bolivia and extreme nw Argentina

☐ **Great Green Macaw** *Ara ambigua*
___ *A. a. ambigua* — E Honduras to nw Colombia
___ *A. a. guayaquilensis* — W Ecuador and adjacent sw Colombia

☐ **Scarlet Macaw** *Ara macao*
___ *A. m. cyanoptera* — SE Mexico to Nicaragua
___ *A. m. macao* — Costa Rica to Colombia, the Guianas, Brazil, Peru and Bolivia

☐ **Red-and-green Macaw** *Ara chloroptera*

Humid e Panama to Brazil, e Peru, ne Bolivia and Paraguay

☐ **Red-fronted Macaw** *Ara rubrogenys*

Andean valleys of central Bolivia

☐ **Chestnut-fronted Macaw** *Ara severa*

Tropical e Panama to the Guianas, n Bolivia and Amaz. Brazil

☐ **Red-bellied Macaw** *Orthopsittaca manilata*

SE Colombia to the Guianas, Trinidad, n Bolivia, Amaz. Brazil

☐ **Blue-headed Macaw** *Propyrrhura couloni*

E Peru to n Bolivia and extreme w Brazil

☐ **Blue-winged Macaw** *Propyrrhura maracana*

E Brazil to Paraguay and extreme ne Argentina

☐ **Golden-collared Macaw** *Propyrrhura auricollis*

NE Bolivia to Paraguay, sw Brazil and n Argentina

☐ **Red-shouldered Macaw** *Diopsittaca nobilis*
___ *D. n. nobilis* — E Venezuela to the Guianas and n Brazil north of the Amazon
___ *D. n. cumanensis* — N Brazil south of lower Amazon to ne Brazil
___ *D. n. longipennis* — SE Peru and ne Bolivia to central and se Brazil

☐ **Thick-billed Parrot** *Rhynchopsitta pachyrhyncha*

Mountains of w Mexico (Sierra Madre Occidental)

☐ **Maroon-fronted Parrot** *Rhynchopsitta terrisi*

Mountains of e Mexico (Sierra Madre Oriental)

☐ **Yellow-eared Parrot** *Ognorhynchus icterotis*

Andes of Colombia and n Ecuador

☐ **Golden Parakeet** *Guarouba guarouba*

NE Brazil (n Maranhão and Pará)

☐ **Blue-crowned Parakeet** *Aratinga acuticaudata*
___ *A. a. koenigi* — NE Colombia and n Venezuela
___ *A. a. neoxena* — Isla Margarita (Venezuela)
___ *A. a. haemorrhous* — Interior ne Brazil
___ *A. a. neumanni* — Highlands of e Bolivia
___ *A. a. acuticaudata* — E Bolivia to Paraguay, s Brazil, w Uruguay and n Argentina

☐ **Green Parakeet** *Aratinga holochlora*
___ *A. h. brewsteri* — Mountains of nw Mexico (Sonora, Sinaloa and Chihuahua)
___ *A. h. holochlora* — Open woodlands and pine forests of s Mexico

☐ **Pacific Parakeet** *Aratinga strenua*

Arid lowlands of se Mexico to n Nicaragua

☐ **Socorro Parakeet** *Aratinga brevipes*

Socorro I. (Revillagigedo Islands off w Mexico)

☐ **Red-throated Parakeet** *Aratinga rubritorquis*

Highlands of e Guatemala to n Nicaragua

☐ **Scarlet-fronted Parakeet** *Aratinga wagleri*

_____ *A. w. wagleri*   N Colombia (south to n Nariño) and extreme nw Venezuela
_____ *A. w. transilis*   Extreme e Colombia to n Venezuela
_____ *A. w. frontata*   W Ecuador and w Peru (south to Arequipa)
_____ *A. w. minor*   C and s central Peru (Marañón Valley south to Ayacucho)

☐ **Mitred Parakeet** *Aratinga mitrata*

_____ *A. m. mitrata*   Andes of central Peru to Bolivia and nw Argentina
_____ *A. m. alticola*   Andes of se Peru (Cuzco)

☐ **Red-masked Parakeet** *Aratinga erythrogenys*

Arid littoral of w Ecuador and nw Peru

☐ **Crimson-fronted Parakeet** *Aratinga finschi*

Humid lowlands of se Nicaragua, Costa Rica and w Panama

☐ **White-eyed Parakeet** *Aratinga leucophthalmus*

_____ *A. l. nicefori*   Known from one specimen from e Colombia (Meta)
_____ *A. l. callogenys*   SE Colombia to e Ecuador, nw Peru and extreme nw Brazil
_____ *A. l. leucophthalmus (propinquus)*   Venezuela to Guianas, Brazil, Bolivia, Paraguay, n Argentina

☐ **Cuban Parakeet** *Aratinga euops*

SW Cuba (Zapata Swamp); formerly Isle of Pines

☐ **Hispaniolan Parakeet** *Aratinga chloroptera*

_____ *A. c. chloroptera*   Hispaniola
_____ *A. c. maugei†*   Formerly Mona I. (off Puerto Rico). Extinct

☐ **Sun Parakeet** *Aratinga solstitialis*

Guyana, Suriname and n Amazonian Brazil

☐ **Jandaya Parakeet** *Aratinga jandaya*

Lowlands of ne Brazil (e Pará and Goiás to Alagoas)

☐ **Golden-capped Parakeet** *Aratinga auricapilla*

_____ *A. a. auricapilla*   E central Brazil (n and central Bahia)
_____ *A. a. aurifrons*   SE Brazil (s Bahia to s Paraná)

☐ **Dusky-headed Parakeet** *Aratinga weddellii*

SE Colombia to n Bolivia and adjacent w Amazonian Brazil

☐ **Brown-throated Parakeet** *Aratinga pertinax*

_____ *A. p. ocularis*   Pacific lowlands of Panama (w Chiriquí to Canal Zone)
_____ *A. p. aeruginosa*   N Colombia to nw Venezuela
_____ *A. p. griseipecta*   NE Colombia (Sinú River Valley)
_____ *A. p. lehmanni*   *Llanos* of e Colombia (possibly adjacent w Venezuela)
_____ *A. p. arubensis*   Aruba (Netherlands Antilles)
_____ *A. p. pertinax*   Curaçao (Netherlands Antilles)
_____ *A. p. xanthogenia*   Bonaire (Netherlands Antilles)
_____ *A. p. tortugensis*   Isla la Tortuga (off n Venezuela)
_____ *A. p. margaritensis*   Isla Margarita and Islas Los Frailes (off n Venezuela)
_____ *A. p. venezuelae*   Generally distributed throughout Venezuela
_____ *A. p. surinama*   NE Venezuela and the Guianas
_____ *A. p. chrysophrys*   *Tepuis* of se Venezuela and adjacent Brazil
_____ *A. p. chrysogenys*   NW Brazil (Rio Negro region)
_____ *A. p. paraensis*   N Amazonian Brazil (Rio Tapajós and Rio Cururu)

☐ **Olive-throated Parakeet** *Aratinga nana*

_____ *A. n. vicinalis*   NE Mexico (Tamaulipas to ne Veracruz)
_____ *A. n. astec*   Caribbean slope of se Mexico to extreme w Panama
_____ *A. n. nana*   Jamaica

☐ **Orange-fronted Parakeet** *Aratinga canicularis*
_____ *A. c. clarae* — W Mexico (Sinaloa to Colima, Durango and Michoacán)
_____ *A. c. eburnirostrum* — SW Mexico (e Michoacán to Guerrero and Oaxaca)
_____ *A. c. canicularis* — Arid tropical w Mexico (Chiapas) to w Costa Rica

☐ **Peach-fronted Parakeet** *Aratinga aurea*
Suriname to s Brazil, se Peru, e Bolivia, Paraguay, n Argentina

☐ **Caatinga Parakeet** *Aratinga cactorum*
_____ *A. c. caixana* — *Caatinga* of ne Brazil (Pará to nw Bahia)
_____ *A. c. cactorum* — Inland *caatinga* of ne Brazil (Bahia and adj. Minas Gerais)

☐ **Nanday Parakeet** *Nandayus nenday*
Pantanal of se Bolivia, sw Brazil, Paraguay and n Argentina

☐ **Golden-plumed Parakeet** *Leptosittaca branickii*
Humid Andes of s Colombia to Ecuador and central Peru

☐ **Burrowing Parrot** *Cyanoliseus patagonus*
_____ *C. p. andinus* — NW Argentina (Salta to San Luis)
_____ *C. p. conlara* — W-central Argentina (San Luis and Córdoba)
_____ *C. p. patagonus* — C to se Argentina; winters to n Argentina and Uruguay
_____ *C. p. bloxami* — Central Chile (Atacama to Valdivia)

☐ **Blue-throated Parakeet** *Pyrrhura cruentata*
Lowlands of se Brazil (Bahia to Rio de Janeiro)

☐ **Blaze-winged Parakeet** *Pyrrhura devillei*
Forests of n Paraguay and sw Brazil (sw Mato Grosso)

☐ **Maroon-bellied Parakeet** *Pyrrhura frontalis*
_____ *P. f. frontalis* — E Brazil (Bahia to Rio de Janeiro and n São Paulo)
_____ *P. f. chiripepe* — SE Brazil to se Paraguay and n Argentina

☐ **Crimson-bellied Parakeet** *Pyrrhura perlata*
Brazil (w Pará, e Amazonas and Mato Grosso) to n Bolivia

☐ **Pearly Parakeet** *Pyrrhura lepida*
_____ *P. l. lepida* — N-central Brazil (ne Pará and nw Maranhão)
_____ *P. l. anerythra* — N-central Brazil (e Pará)
_____ *P. l. coerulescens* — N-central Brazil (w and central Maranhão)

☐ **Green-cheeked Parakeet** *Pyrrhura molinae*
_____ *P. m. phoenicura* — NE Bolivia and w Brazil (w Mato Grosso)
_____ *P. m. molinae* — Highlands of e Bolivia
_____ *P. m. restricta* — Lowlands of e Bolivia (Palmarito)
_____ *P. m. sordida* — Extreme e Bolivia and sw Brazil (s Mato Grosso)
_____ *P. m. australis* — S Bolivia (Tarija) to nw Argentina

☐ **Painted Parakeet** *Pyrrhura picta*
_____ *P. p. eisenmanni* — S-central Panama (Azuero Peninsula)
_____ *P. p. subandina* — NW Colombia (lower Sinú River Valley)
_____ *P. p. caeruleiceps* — W slope of Eastern Andes of n Colombia
_____ *P. p. pantchenkoi* — Sierra de Perijá (Colombia/Venezuela border)
_____ *P. p. picta* — Venezuela to the Guianas and n Amazonian Brazil (Amapá)
_____ *P. p. amazonum* — N-central Brazil (Pará north of the Amazon)
_____ *P. p. microtera* — N-central Brazil south of the Amazon (Pará to n Goiás)
_____ *P. p. lucianii* — NW Brazil (Amazonas) to sw Ecuador, ne Peru and n Bolivia
_____ *P. p. roseifrons* — W Brazil and e Peru (south and east of range of *lucianii*)

☐ **Fiery-shouldered Parakeet** *Pyrrhura egregia*
_____ *P. e. egregia* — *Tepuis* of s Venezuela (Mt. Roraima) and adjacent Guyana
_____ *P. e. obscura* — *Tepuis* of se Venezuela and extreme ne Brazil

☐ **White-eared Parakeet** *Pyrrhura leucotis*

_____ *P. l. emma* — Patchily distributed humid forests of coastal n Venezuela

_____ *P. l. auricularis* — Coastal ne Venezuela (Sucre, Anzoátegui and Monagas)

_____ *P. l. pfrimeri* — Known from the type locality in central Brazil (Goiás)

_____ *P. l. griseipectus* — NE Brazil (Ceará)

_____ *P. l. anca* — Coastal e Brazil (s Bahia to São Paulo)

_____ *P. l. leucotis* — E Brazil (Bahia to São Paulo)

☐ **Santa Marta Parakeet** *Pyrrhura viridicata* — Santa Marta Mountains (ne Colombia)

☐ **Maroon-tailed Parakeet** *Pyrrhura melanura*

_____ *P. m. pacifica* — W slope of Andes of sw Colombia (Nariño) and nw Ecuador

_____ *P. m. chapmani* — Subtropical e slope of Central Andes of s Colombia

_____ *P. m. melanura* — SE Colombia to e Ecuador, ne Peru, s Venezuela and nw Brazil

_____ *P. m. souancei* — S-central Colombia (Macarena Mountains)

_____ *P. m. berlepschi* — E slope of Andes of se Ecuador and n Peru

☐ **El Oro Parakeet** *Pyrrhura orcesi* — Andean foothills of sw Ecuador (El Oro and Azuay)

☐ **Black-capped Parakeet** *Pyrrhura rupicola*

_____ *P. r. rupicola* — Humid forests of e-central Peru

_____ *P. r. sandiae* — Tropical se Peru, n Bolivia and extreme w Amazonian Brazil

☐ **White-necked Parakeet** *Pyrrhura albipectus* — Humid lowlands of se Ecuador

☐ **Flame-winged Parakeet** *Pyrrhura calliptera* — E Andes of Colombia (Boyacá and Cundinamarca)

☐ **Red-eared Parakeet** *Pyrrhura hoematotis*

_____ *P. h. immarginata* — Known only from the type locality in nw Venezuela (Lara)

_____ *P. h. hoematotis* — Montane forests of n Venezuela (Aragua to Miranda)

☐ **Rose-headed Parakeet** *Pyrrhura rhodocephala* — Andes of w Venezuela (Mérida, Táchira, and Trujillo)

☐ **Sulphur-winged Parakeet** *Pyrrhura hoffmanni*

_____ *P. h. hoffmanni* — Highlands of s Costa Rica

_____ *P. h. gaudens* — Mts. of w Panama and Caribbean slope of Bocas del Toro

☐ **Austral Parakeet** *Enicognathus ferrugineus*

_____ *E. f. minor* — S Chile (Colchagua to Aysén) and adj. Andes of sw Argentina

_____ *E. f. ferrugineus* — *Nothofagus* forests of extreme s Chile and s Argentina

☐ **Slender-billed Parakeet** *Enicognathus leptorhynchus* — Lowlands of Chile (Aconcagua to n Aysén and Chiloé I.)

☐ **Monk Parakeet** *Myiopsitta monachus*

_____ *M. m. cotorra* — S Bolivia to Paraguay, s Brazil and nw Argentina

_____ *M. m. monachus* — SE Brazil (Rio Grande do Sul), Uruguay and ne Argentina

_____ *M. m. calita* — W Argentina (Salta to w Córdoba, Mendoza and La Pampa)

☐ **Cliff Parakeet** *Myiopsitta luchsi* — Xeric intermontane valleys of central Bolivia

☐ **Andean Parakeet** *Bolborhynchus orbygnesius* — Andes of Peru and w Bolivia

☐ **Barred Parakeet** *Bolborhynchus lineola*

_____ *B. l. lineola* — Humid montane forests of s Mexico to w Panama

_____ *B. l. tigrinus* — Mountains of nw Venezuela and Colombia to s Peru

☐ **Rufous-fronted Parakeet** *Bolborhynchus ferrugineifrons* — Central Andes of w Colombia (Tolima and Cauca)

☐ **Gray-hooded Parakeet** *Psilopsiagon aymara*

Andes of Bolivia to nw Argentina and n Chile

☐ **Mountain Parakeet** *Psilopsiagon aurifrons*
_____ *P. a. robertsi* — N central Peru (Marañón Valley)
_____ *P. a. aurifrons* — Coastal regions and adj. w slopes of Andes of central Peru
_____ *P. a. margaritae* — Andes of s Peru to Bolivia, n Chile and extreme nw Argentina
_____ *P. a. rubrirostris* — Andes of nw Argentina (Catamarca to Córdoba) and adj. Chile

☐ **Mexican Parrotlet** *Forpus cyanopygius*
_____ *F. c. cyanopygius* — Arid w Mexico (se Sonora to Sinaloa, w Durango and Colima)
_____ *F. c. insularis* — Tres Marías Islands (off w Mexico)

☐ **Green-rumped Parrotlet** *Forpus passerinus*
_____ *F. p. cyanophanes* — Arid tropical n Colombia
_____ *F. p. viridissimus* — NE Colombia to n Venezuela and Trinidad
_____ *F. p. passerinus* — Guyana, Suriname and French Guiana
_____ *F. p. cyanochlorus* — Extreme n Brazil (upper Rio Branco region of Roraima)
_____ *F. p. deliciosus* — Lower Amazonian Brazil

☐ **Blue-winged Parrotlet** *Forpus crassirostris*
_____ *F. c. spengeli* — N Colombia
_____ *F. c. crassirostris (olallae)* — SE Colombia to e Ecuador, ne Peru and w Brazil
_____ *F. c. flavescens* — SE Peru and e Bolivia
_____ *F. c. flavissimus* — NE Brazil (Maranhão, Ceará and Paraíba to n Bahia)
_____ *F. c. vividus* — E and se Brazil to Paraguay and n Argentina

☐ **Spectacled Parrotlet** *Forpus conspicillatus*
_____ *F. c. conspicillatus* — Tropical e Panama to n-central Colombia
_____ *F. c. metae* — E slope of E Andes of Colombia to extreme w Venezuela
_____ *F. c. caucae* — SW Colombia w of Andes (Cauca and Nariño); w Ecuador?

☐ **Dusky-billed Parrotlet** *Forpus sclateri*
_____ *F. s. eidos* — Extreme e Colombia to Venezuela, the Guianas and n Brazil
_____ *F. s. sclateri* — SE Colombia to n Bolivia and Amazonian Brazil

☐ **Pacific Parrotlet** *Forpus coelestis*

Arid littoral of w Ecuador and nw Peru

☐ **Yellow-faced Parrotlet** *Forpus xanthops*

N Peru (dry scrub of upper Marañón Valley)

☐ **Plain Parakeet** *Brotogeris tirica*

E Brazil (Bahia and s Goiás to Rio Grande do Sul)

☐ **Canary-winged Parakeet** *Brotogeris versicolurus*

Lowlands of se Colombia to e Peru and Amazonian Brazil

☐ **Yellow-chevroned Parakeet** *Brotogeris chiriri*
_____ *B. c. behni* — Central and s Bolivia
_____ *B. c. chiriri* — N Bolivia to Paraguay, se Brazil and n Argentina

☐ **Gray-cheeked Parakeet** *Brotogeris pyrrhopterus*

Arid scrub of w Ecuador and extreme nw Peru

☐ **Orange-chinned Parakeet** *Brotogeris jugularis*
_____ *B. j. jugularis* — Tropical sw Mexico to n Colombia and nw Venezuela
_____ *B. j. exsul* — E Colombia and w Venezuela

☐ **Cobalt-winged Parakeet** *Brotogeris cyanoptera*
_____ *B. c. cyanoptera* — SE Colombia to s Venezuela, e Ecuador, e Peru and w-c Brazil
_____ *B. c. gustavi* — N Peru (upper Río Huallaga Valley)
_____ *B. c. beniensis* — N Bolivia (Beni)

☐ **Tui Parakeet** *Brotogeris sanctithomae*
_____ *B. s. sanctithomae* — SE Colombia through Amaz. Brazil to se Peru and ne Bolivia
_____ *B. s. takatsukasae* — Lower Amazon basin of n-central Brazil

☐ **Golden-winged Parakeet** *Brotogeris chrysopterus*
_____ *B. c. chrysopterus* — NE Venezuela to the Guianas and adjacent n Brazil
_____ *B. c. tenuifrons* — N Brazil (upper Rio Negro in Amazonas)
_____ *B. c. solimoensis* — N Brazil (Codajas and Manaus regions)
_____ *B. c. tuipara* — Coastal n Brazil (Rio Tapajós to ne Maranhão)
_____ *B. c. chrysosema* — W Brazil (Rio Madeira to n Mato Grosso)

☐ **Tepui Parrotlet** *Nannopsittaca panychlora* — *Tepuis* of s Venezuela, s Guyana and extreme n Brazil

☐ **Amazonian Parrotlet** *Nannopsittaca dachilleae* — Tropical se Peru and nw Bolivia (probably adjacent w Brazil)

☐ **Lilac-tailed Parrotlet** *Touit batavica* — N Venezuela to the Guianas, Trinidad and Tobago

☐ **Scarlet-shouldered Parrotlet** *Touit huetii* — Patchily distributed n South America to n Bolivia and n Brazil

☐ **Red-fronted Parrotlet** *Touit costaricensis* — Humid foothill forests of se Costa Rica and w Panama

☐ **Blue-fronted Parrotlet** *Touit dilectissima* — Humid e Panama to nw Venezuela and nw Ecuador

☐ **Sapphire-rumped Parrotlet** *Touit purpurata*
_____ *T. p. viridiceps* — SE Colombia to s Venezuela, e Ecuador and ne Peru
_____ *T. p. purpurata* — S Venezuela to the Guianas and n Amazonian Brazil

☐ **Brown-backed Parrotlet** *Touit melanonota* — SE Brazil (s Bahia to Rio de Janeiro and São Paulo)

☐ **Golden-tailed Parrotlet** *Touit surda* — E Brazil (Pernambuco to São Paulo)

☐ **Spot-winged Parrotlet** *Touit stictoptera* — Locally in Andes of s Colombia to Ecuador and ne Peru

☐ **Black-headed Parrot** *Pionites melanocephala*
_____ *P. m. melanocephala* — SE Colombia to Venezuela, the Guianas and n Brazil
_____ *P. m. pallida* — S Colombia to e Ecuador and ne Peru

☐ **White-bellied Parrot** *Pionites leucogaster*
_____ *P. l. xanthomeria* — E Peru and n Bolivia to w Brazil south of the Amazon
_____ *P. l. xanthurus* — Brazil s of the Amazon (R. Purús and R. Juruá to R. Madeira)
_____ *P. l. leucogaster* — N Brazil south of the Amazon (Rio Madeira to Maranhão)

☐ **Vulturine Parrot** *Pionopsitta vulturina* — Humid forests of e Amazonian Brazil south of the Amazon

☐ **Brown-hooded Parrot** *Pionopsitta haematotis*
_____ *P. h. haematotis* — Humid forests of s Caribbean Mexico to w Panama
_____ *P. h. coccincollaris* — E Panama (east of Canal Zone) and nw Colombia

☐ **Rose-faced Parrot** *Pionopsitta pulchra* — Humid forests of w Colombia and nw Ecuador

☐ **Orange-cheeked Parrot** *Pionopsitta barrabandi*
_____ *P. b. barrabandi* — SE Colombia and s Venezuela to Brazil north of the Amazon
_____ *P. b. aurantiigena* — E Ecuador to e Peru, n Bolivia and Brazil south of the Amazon

☐ **Saffron-headed Parrot** *Pionopsitta pyrilia* — Extreme e Panama to n Colombia and nw Venezuela

☐ **Caica Parrot** *Pionopsitta caica* — SE Venezuela to the Guianas and Brazil north of the Amazon

☐ **Pileated Parrot** *Pionopsitta pileata*

Humid forests of se Brazil to e Paraguay and ne Argentina

☐ **Black-winged Parrot** *Hapalopsittaca melanotis*
_____ *H. m. peruviana*
_____ *H. m. melanotis*

Andes of central and s Peru
Andes of Bolivia (La Paz and Cochabamba)

☐ **Rusty-faced Parrot** *Hapalopsittaca amazonina*
_____ *H. a. velezi*
_____ *H. a. amazonina*
_____ *H. a. theresae*

Central Andes of Colombia
E Andes of Colombia
Andes of extreme e Colombia and nw Venezuela

☐ **Indigo-winged Parrot** *Hapalopsittaca fuertesi*

Central Andes of Colombia

☐ **Red-faced Parrot** *Hapalopsittaca pyrrhops*

Andes of sw Ecuador and adjacent nw Peru

☐ **Short-tailed Parrot** *Graydidascalus brachyurus*

SE Colombia to e Ecuador, e Peru and Brazil n of the Amazon

☐ **Blue-headed Parrot** *Pionus menstruus*
_____ *P. m. rubrigularis*
_____ *P. m. menstruus*
_____ *P. m. reichenowi*

Tropical n Costa Rica to w Colombia and w Ecuador
E Colombia to the Guianas, Trinidad, n Brazil and Bolivia
Coastal ne Brazil (Alagoas to Espírito Santo)

☐ **Red-billed Parrot** *Pionus sordidus*
_____ *P. s. antelius*
_____ *P. s. sordidus*
_____ *P. s. ponsi*
_____ *P. s. saturatus*
_____ *P. s. corallinus*
_____ *P. s. mindoensis*

Mountains of ne Venezuela (Anzoátegui, Sucre and Monagas)
Mountains of n Venezuela (Lara and Falcón to Caracas)
Mountains of ne Colombia to Sierra de Perijá (nw Venezuela)
Santa Marta Mountains (ne Colombia)
E Andes of Colombia to e Ecuador, e Peru and n Bolivia
Mountains of w Ecuador

☐ **Scaly-headed Parrot** *Pionus maximiliani*
_____ *P. m. maximiliani*
_____ *P. m. siy*
_____ *P. m. melanobelpharus*
_____ *P. m. lacerus*

NE Brazil (Ceará to Espírito Santo and s Goiás)
SE Bolivia to Paraguay, w Brazil (Mato Grosso), n Argentina
E Paraguay to se Brazil and ne Argentina (Misiones)
NW Argentina (Tucumán, Catamarca and s Salta)

☐ **White-crowned Parrot** *Pionus senilis*

Caribbean slope of se Mexico to w Panama

☐ **Speckle-faced Parrot** *Pionus tumultuosus*
_____ *P. t. seniloides*
_____ *P. t. tumultuosus*

Andes of Colombia to nw Venezuela and extreme n Peru
Andes of Peru and w Bolivia

☐ **Bronze-winged Parrot** *Pionus chalcopterus*

Humid forests of ne Colombia to w Venezuela and nw Peru

☐ **Dusky Parrot** *Pionus fuscus*

Humid ne Colombia to the Guianas and n Amazonian Brazil

☐ **Cuban Parrot** *Amazona leucocephala*
_____ *A. l. bahamensis*
_____ *A. l. leucocephala (palmarum)*
_____ *A. l. caymanensis*
_____ *A. l. hesterna*

Bahamas (Great Inagua, Abaco and Acklins)
Cuba and Isle of Pines
Grand Cayman I.
Cayman Brac I. and (formerly) Little Cayman I.

☐ **Yellow-billed Parrot** *Amazona collaria*

Humid forests of Jamaica

☐ **Hispaniolan Parrot** *Amazona ventralis*

Hispaniola and satellite islands

☐ **Puerto Rican Parrot** *Amazona vittata*
_____ *A. v. vittata*
_____ *A. v. gracilipes*†

Montane forests of e Puerto Rico (critically endangered)
Formerly Culebra I. off e Puerto Rico. Extinct

☐ **Yellow-lored Parrot** *Amazona xantholora*

SE Mexico (Yucatán Peninsula and Cozumel I.) to Belize

☐ **White-fronted Parrot** *Amazona albifrons*
____ *A. a. saltuensis*
____ *A. a. albifrons*
____ *A. a. nana*

Arid nw Mexico (s Sonora and w Durango to Sinaloa)
Arid w Mexico (Nayarit) to sw Guatemala
SE Mexico (extreme se Veracruz) to nw Costa Rica

☐ **Black-billed Parrot** *Amazona agilis*

Jamaica

☐ **Tucuman Parrot** *Amazona tucumana*

Montane forests of se Bolivia and nw Argentina

☐ **Red-spectacled Parrot** *Amazona pretrei*

SE Brazil (Rio Grande do Sul); vagrant to Paraguay, Argentina

☐ **Red-crowned Parrot** *Amazona viridigenalis*

Lowlands of ne Mexico (Nuevo León to n Veracruz)

☐ **Lilac-crowned Parrot** *Amazona finschi*

W Mexico (s Sonora, Chihuahua and Durango to Oaxaca)

☐ **Red-lored Parrot** *Amazona autumnalis*
____ *A. a. autumnalis*
____ *A. a. salvini*
____ *A. a. lilacina*
____ *A. a. diadema*

Caribbean slope of e Mexico to n Nicaragua and Bay Islands
N Nicaragua to sw Colombia and extreme nw Venezuela
W Ecuador (north of Gulf of Guayaquil)
NW Brazil (lower Rio Negro and n bank of the upper Amazon)

☐ **Blue-cheeked Parrot** *Amazona dufresniana*

SE Venezuela (Gran Sabana) to the Guianas and (?) adj. Brazil

☐ **Red-browed Parrot** *Amazona rhodocorytha*

E Brazil (Alagoas and Bahia to Rio de Janeiro and São Paulo)

☐ **Red-tailed Parrot** *Amazona brasiliensis*

SE Brazil (se São Paulo and Paraná)

☐ **Festive Parrot** *Amazona festiva*
____ *A. f. bodini*
____ *A. f. festiva*

E Colombia to Orinoco basin of Venezuela
SE Colombia to e Ecuador, e Peru and w Amazonian Brazil

☐ **Yellow-faced Parrot** *Amazona xanthops*

Interior Brazil (Maranhão) to n Paraguay and e Bolivia

☐ **Yellow-shouldered Parrot** *Amazona barbadensis*

Coastal n Venezuela, Bonaire, La Blanquilla and Margarita is.

☐ **Blue-fronted Parrot** *Amazona aestiva*
____ *A. a. aestiva*
____ *A. a. xanthopteryx*

E Brazil (Maranhão and Pará to Rio Grande do Sul)
Bolivia to sw Brazil, Paraguay and n Argentina

☐ **Yellow-headed Parrot** *Amazona oratrix*
____ *A. o. oratrix*
____ *A. o. tresmariae*
____ *A. o. belizensis*
____ *A. o. caribaea*
____ *A. o. parvipes*
____ *A. o. hondurensis*

Tropical Pacific slope of s Mexico
Tres Marías Islands (off w Mexico)
Belize
Bay Islands off Honduras (Isla Barbareta and Isla Guanaja)
Coastal ne Honduras to ne Nicaragua
N Honduras (Sula Valley)

☐ **Yellow-crowned Parrot** *Amazona ochrocephala*
____ *A. o. panamensis*
____ *A. o. ochrocephala*
____ *A. o. xantholaema*
____ *A. o. nattereri*

Pearl Islands and w Panama to nw Colombia
E Colombia to Venezuela, the Guianas, Trinidad and n Brazil
Ilha de Marajó (off n Brazil)
S Colombia to e Ecuador, e Peru, n Bolivia and w Brazil

☐ **Yellow-naped Parrot** *Amazona auropalliata*

Tropical e Mexico (Oaxaca) to nw Costa Rica

☐ **Kawall's Parrot** *Amazona kawalli*

Amazonian Brazil

☐ **Orange-winged Parrot** *Amazona amazonica*
    ____ *A. a. amazonica* — E Colombia to Venezuela, the Guianas, n Bolivia and e Brazil
    ____ *A. a. tobagensis* — Trinidad and Tobago

☐ **Scaly-naped Parrot** *Amazona mercenaria*
    ____ *A. m. canipalliata* — Andes of Colombia to nw Venezuela and Ecuador
    ____ *A. m. mercenaria* — Andes of n Peru to n Bolivia; single record from Argentina

☐ **Mealy Parrot** *Amazona farinosa*
    ____ *A. f. guatemalae* — Caribbean slope of se Mexico to nw Honduras
    ____ *A. f. virenticeps* — Honduras (Sula Valley) to extreme w Panama
    ____ *A. f. farinosa (inornata, chapmani)* — E Panama to Colombia, the Guianas, ne Bolivia and e Brazil

☐ **Vinaceous Parrot** *Amazona vinacea* — E Brazil (Bahia) to e Paraguay and n Argentina

☐ **St. Lucia Parrot** *Amazona versicolor* — Montane forests of St. Lucia (Lesser Antilles)

☐ **Red-necked Parrot** *Amazona arausiaca* — Montane forests of Dominica (Lesser Antilles)

☐ **St. Vincent Parrot** *Amazona guildingii* — Montane forests of St. Vincent (Lesser Antilles)

☐ **Imperial Parrot** *Amazona imperialis* — Montane forests of Dominica (Lesser Antilles)

☐ **Red-fan Parrot** *Deroptyus accipitrinus*
    ____ *D. a. accipitrinus* — SE Colombia to Venezuela, the Guianas, ne Peru and n Brazil
    ____ *D. a. fuscifrons* — Brazil s of the Amazon (Pará to n Mato Grosso); adj. Bolivia?

☐ **Blue-bellied Parrot** *Triclaria malachitacea* — Lowlands of se Brazil (s Bahia to Rio Grande do Sul)

ORDER: MUSOPHAGIFORMES
FAMILY: MUSOPHAGIDAE (Turacos—23)

☐ **Great Blue Turaco** *Corythaeola cristata* — Lowland rainforests of w and central Africa

☐ **Guinea Turaco** *Tauraco persa*
    ____ *T. p. buffoni* — Senegambia to Liberia
    ____ *T. p. persa* — Ivory Coast to Ghana and Cameroon
    ____ *T. p. phoebus* — S Cameroon to Gabon, n Angola, Congo and nw Zaire

☐ **Livingstone's Turaco** *Tauraco livingstonii*
    ____ *T. l. reichenowi* — Tanzania (Nguru and Uluguru Mts. to Njombe Highlands)
    ____ *T. l. cabanisi* — Coastal lowlands of Tanzania to Mozambique and ne Zululand
    ____ *T. l. livingstonii* — Highlands of Malawi to Mozambique and e Zimbabwe

☐ **Schalow's Turaco** *Tauraco schalowi* — Humid forests of s-central Africa

☐ **Knysna Turaco** *Tauraco corythaix*
    ____ *T. c. phoebus* — Humid forests of Transvaal and nw Swaziland
    ____ *T. c. corythaix* — Natal to w Zululand, s Swaziland and e Cape Province

☐ **Black-billed Turaco** *Tauraco schuettii*
    ____ *T. s. emini* — S Sudan to e Zaire, Uganda, w Kenya, nw Tanzania, Burundi
    ____ *T. s. schuettii* — Zaire east to Ituri basin and south to n Angola

☐ **White-crested Turaco** *Tauraco leucolophus* — Extreme se Nigeria to n Uganda, sw Sudan and w Kenya

☐ **Fischer's Turaco** *Tauraco fischeri*
_____ *T. f. fischeri* — Coastal forests of s Somalia, coastal Kenya and ne Tanzania
_____ *T. f. zanzibaricus* — Zanzibar

☐ **Yellow-billed Turaco** *Tauraco macrorhynchus*
_____ *T. m. macrorhynchus* — Lowland rainforests of Sierra Leone to Ghana
_____ *T. m. verreauxii* — Nigeria to Cameroon, Gabon, Congo and n Angola; Bioko I.

☐ **Bannerman's Turaco** *Tauraco bannermani* — SW Cameroon (Bamenda-Banso highlands)

☐ **Red-crested Turaco** *Tauraco erythrolophus* — Locally in woodlands and savanna of w Angola

☐ **Hartlaub's Turaco** *Tauraco hartlaubi* — Highlands of Kenya, adjacent Uganda and ne Tanzania

☐ **White-cheeked Turaco** *Tauraco leucotis*
_____ *T. l. leucotis* — *Podocarpus* forests of Eritrea, Ethiopia and se Sudan
_____ *T. l. donaldsoni* — S-central Ethiopia south of Rift Valley and extreme w Somalia

☐ **Prince Ruspoli's Turaco** *Tauraco ruspolii* — Juniper forests of s Ethiopia

☐ **Purple-crested Turaco** *Tauraco porphyreolophus*
_____ *T. p. chlorochlamys* — SE Kenya and sw Uganda to Tanzania and n Mozambique
_____ *T. p. porphyreolophus* — Zimbabwe and Mozambique to e Transvaal and Natal

☐ **Ruwenzori Turaco** *Ruwenzorornis johnstoni*
_____ *R. j. johnstoni* — Ruwenzori Mountains (ne Zaire and sw Uganda); e Zaire
_____ *R. j. kivuensis* — Highlands of e Zaire, Rwanda, Burundi and sw Uganda

☐ **Violet Turaco** *Musophaga violacea* — S Senegambia to nw Cameroon, s Chad and Cent. African Rep.

☐ **Ross' Turaco** *Musophaga rossae* — Riparian forests and woodlands of central Africa

☐ **Bare-faced Go-away-bird** *Corythaixoides personatus*
_____ *C. p. personatus* — Rift Valley of Ethiopia
_____ *C. p. leopoldi* — S Uganda to Rwanda, Burundi, sw Kenya, Malawi and Zambia

☐ **Gray Go-away-bird** *Corythaixoides concolor*
_____ *C. c. molybdophanes* — NE Angola to s Zaire, Zambia, s Tanzania and n Mozambique
_____ *C. c. pallidiceps* — W Angola to s Namibia and w Botswana
_____ *C. c. bechuanae (chobiensis)* — S Angola to ne Namibia, Botswana, s Zambia and w Transvaal
_____ *C. c. concolor* — S Malawi and n Mozambique to e Transvaal and e Zululand

☐ **White-bellied Go-away-bird** *Corythaixoides leucogaster* — *Acacia* savanna of Somalia and Ethiopia to ne Tanzania

☐ **Western Plantain-eater** *Crinifer piscator* — *Acacia* savanna of Senegambia to C African Rep. and e Zaire

☐ **Eastern Plantain-eater** *Crinifer zonurus* — *Acacia* savanna of central and east Africa

ORDER: CUCULIFORMES
FAMILY: CUCULIDAE (Cuckoos—138)

☐ **Pied Cuckoo** *Clamator jacobinus*
_____ *C. j. pica* — Sub-Saharan Africa; nw India to Nepal and Myanmar
_____ *C. j. serratus* — South Africa
_____ *C. j. jacobinus* — S India and Sri Lanka

☐ **Levaillant's Cuckoo** *Clamator levaillantii*

Africa south of the Sahara

☐ **Chestnut-winged Cuckoo** *Clamator coromandus*

India to SE Asia; winters to Greater Sundas

☐ **Great Spotted Cuckoo** *Clamator glandarius*

SW Palearctic and Africa south of the Sahara

☐ **Thick-billed Cuckoo** *Pachycoccyx audeberti*
____ *P. a. brazzae* — Sierra Leone to Ghana, Nigeria, Cameroon and w Zaire
____ *P. a. validus* — E Zaire to se Kenya, Tanzania, Mozambique and e Transvaal
____ *P. a. audeberti* — NE Madagascar

☐ **Sulawesi Hawk-Cuckoo** *Cuculus crassirostris*

Mountains of n and central Sulawesi

☐ **Large Hawk-Cuckoo** *Cuculus sparverioides*
____ *C. s. sparverioides* — N Pakistan to India, s China, Myanmar, Thailand and Indochina
____ *C. s. bocki* — Mountains of Malay Peninsula, Sumatra and Borneo

☐ **Common Hawk-Cuckoo** *Cuculus varius*
____ *C. v. varius* — India to Nepal, Bangladesh and Myanmar
____ *C. v. ciceliae* — Sri Lanka

☐ **Moustached Hawk-Cuckoo** *Cuculus vagans*

S Myanmar, Mergui Arch., Malay Pen., Sumatra and Borneo

☐ **Hodgson's Hawk-Cuckoo** *Cuculus fugax*
____ *C. f. nisicolor* — Nepal and e Himalayas to Myanmar, Thailand and Hainan I.
____ *C. f. fugax* — S Thailand, Malay Peninsula and Greater Sundas
____ *C. f. hyperythrus* — NE China to Korea, lower Yangtze Valley and s Japan

☐ **Philippine Hawk-Cuckoo** *Cuculus pectoralis*

Philippine Islands

☐ **Red-chested Cuckoo** *Cuculus solitarius*

Intra-African migrant south of the Sahara

☐ **Black Cuckoo** *Cuculus clamosus*
____ *C. c. gabonensis* — Liberia to Ghana, Nigeria, s Sudan, Uganda and w Kenya
____ *C. c. clamosus* — Highlands of Ethiopia and Somalia to e South Africa

☐ **Indian Cuckoo** *Cuculus micropterus*
____ *C. m. micropterus* — India and Myanmar to SE Asia; winters to Greater Sundas
____ *C. m. concretus* — Vietnam to s Thailand, Malay Pen., Sumatra, Java and Borneo

☐ **Common Cuckoo** *Cuculus canorus*
____ *C. c. bangsi* — Iberian Pen., Balearic Is. and nw Africa; winters in Africa
____ *C. c. canorus* — Europe, Siberia to Kamchatka and Japan; winters to s Africa
____ *C. c. subtelephonus* — Turkestan to s Mongolia; winters to s Asia and Africa
____ *C. c. bakeri* — W China to n India, Nepal, Myanmar, nw Thailand and s China

☐ **African Cuckoo** *Cuculus gularis*

Senegambia to Somalia and South Africa

☐ **Oriental Cuckoo** *Cuculus saturatus*
____ *C. s. saturatus* — S Himalayas to s China and Taiwan; winters to Indonesia
____ *C. s. lepidus (insulindae)* — Malay Peninsula, Greater and Lesser Sundas

☐ **Horsfield's Cuckoo** *Cuculus horsfieldi*

Russia to Siberia, n China, Korea, Japan; winters to Australia

☐ **Lesser Cuckoo** *Cuculus poliocephalus*

South and east Asia; winters pen. India, Sri Lanka and e Africa

☐ **Madagascar Cuckoo** *Cuculus rochii*

Madagascar; winters in e Africa

154

☐ **Pallid Cuckoo** *Cuculus pallidus*

> Australia and Tasmania; winters north to Wallacea

☐ **Dusky Long-tailed Cuckoo** *Cercococcyx mechowi*

> Sierra Leone to nw Angola and e Zaire

☐ **Olive Long-tailed Cuckoo** *Cercococcyx olivinus*

> Liberia to Zaire, w Uganda, nw Zambia and n Angola

☐ **Barred Long-tailed Cuckoo** *Cercococcyx montanus*

____ *C. m. montanus*	Montane forests of sw Uganda, e Zaire and Rwanda
____ *C. m. patulus*	Montane forests of Kenya to s Zaire, Zambia and Mozambique

☐ **Banded Bay Cuckoo** *Cacomantis sonneratii*

____ *C. s. waiti*	Sri Lanka
____ *C. s. sonneratii*	India to Nepal, Myanmar, Thailand and s Indochina
____ *C. s. malayanus*	Malay Peninsula
____ *C. s. schlegeli*	Sumatra, Borneo and Palawan (sw Philippines)
____ *C. s. musicus*	Java

☐ **Plaintive Cuckoo** *Cacomantis merulinus*

____ *C. m. passerinus*	India and Pakistan; winters to Sri Lanka
____ *C. m. querulus*	E Himalayas to s China, Myanmar, Malay Pen. and Indochina
____ *C. m. threnodes*	S Malay Peninsula, Sumatra and Borneo
____ *C. m. lanceolatus*	Java, Sulawesi and Togian Islands
____ *C. m. merulinus*	Philippine Islands

☐ **Brush Cuckoo** *Cacomantis variolosus*

____ *C. v. sepulcralis*	S Thailand, Malay Pen., Gr. and Lesser Sundas and Philippines
____ *C. v. everetti*	Sulu Archipelago (Jolo, Basilan, Tawitawi and adjacent islands)
____ *C. v. virescens*	Sulawesi, Butung, Tukangbesi and Banggai Islands
____ *C. v. infaustus*	N Moluccas to n and central New Guinea
____ *C. v. aeruginosus*	S Moluccas (Buru, Ambon and Seram) and Sula Islands
____ *C. v. oreophilus*	Highlands of e and s New Guinea
____ *C. v. blandus*	Admiralty Islands
____ *C. v. macrocercus*	Bismarck Archipelago (New Britain, New Ireland and Tabar)
____ *C. v. websteri*	New Hanover (Bismarck Archipelago)
____ *C. v. addendus*	Solomon Islands
____ *C. v. variolosus*	N and e Australia; winters to Moluccas and New Guinea

☐ **Moluccan Cuckoo** *Cacomantis heinrichi*

> N Moluccas (Halmahera and Bacan)

☐ **Chestnut-breasted Cuckoo** *Cacomantis castaneiventris*

____ *C. c. arfakianus*	W Papuan islands and nw New Guinea
____ *C. c. weiskei*	Central and e New Guinea
____ *C. c. castaneiventris*	Aru Islands, e coast of Cape York Peninsula and n Queensland

☐ **Fan-tailed Cuckoo** *Cacomantis flabelliformis*

____ *C. f. excitus*	Montane forests of New Guinea
____ *C. f. flabelliformis*	Cape York Pen. to se Australia and Tasmania; sw W Australia
____ *C. f. pyrrophanus*	New Caledonia and Loyalty Islands
____ *C. f. schistaceigularis*	Vanuatu
____ *C. f. simus*	Fiji Islands

☐ **Black-eared Cuckoo** *Chrysococcyx osculans*

> Australia

☐ **Horsfield's Bronze-Cuckoo** *Chrysococcyx basalis*

> Australia and Tasmania; winters to Java

☐ **Shining Bronze-Cuckoo** *Chrysococcyx lucidus*

____ *C. l. harterti*	Solomon Islands (Rennell and Bellona)
____ *C. l. layardi (aeneus)*	New Caledonia, Loyalty Is., Vanuatu, Banks and Santa Cruz is.
____ *C. l. lucidus*	Australia, Tasmania and New Zealand; winters to n Melanesia

☐ **Rufous-throated Bronze-Cuckoo** *Chrysococcyx ruficollis*

Humid montane forests of New Guinea

☐ **White-eared Bronze-Cuckoo** *Chrysococcyx meyeri*

Montane forests of New Guinea and Batanta I.

☐ **Little Bronze-Cuckoo** *Chrysococcyx minutillus*
_____ *C. m. peninsularis* — Extreme s Thailand and Malay Peninsula
_____ *C. m. albifrons* — N Sumatra and w Java
_____ *C. m. cleis* — N and e Borneo
_____ *C. m. aheneus* — SE Borneo and s Philippine Islands
_____ *C. m. jungei* — Sulawesi, Madu I. and Flores
_____ *C. m. rufomerus* — Lesser Sundas (Romang, Kisar, Leti, Moa, Sermata and Damar)
_____ *C. m. ssp.* — Undescribed race from Timor (e Lesser Sundas)
_____ *C. m. crassirostris* — Moluccas (Tayandu, Kai Is.) and Tanimbar Is. (Yamdena, Larat)
_____ *C. m. salvadorii* — Known fom one specimen from Tepa I. (Babar Islands)
_____ *C. m. misoriensis* — Lowlands of coastal n New Guinea and adjacent islands
_____ *C. m. poecilurus* — Lowlands of coastal s New Guinea and adjacent islands
_____ *C. m. minutillus* — Moluccas, Lesser Sundas, n Australia and Melville I.
_____ *C. m. russatus* — NE Australia (n and e Queensland)
_____ *C. m. barnardi* — E Australia (se Queensland to ne New South Wales)

☐ **Asian Emerald Cuckoo** *Chrysococcyx maculatus*

India to s China, SE Asia, Sumatra, Andaman and Nicobar is.

☐ **Violet Cuckoo** *Chrysococcyx xanthorhynchus*
_____ *C. x. xanthorhynchus* — NE India to SE Asia, Greater Sundas and Palawan
_____ *C. x. amethystinus* — Philippine Islands

☐ **Yellow-throated Cuckoo** *Chrysococcyx flavigularis*

Sierra Leone to s Cameroon, sw Sudan, w Uganda and e Zaire

☐ **Klaas' Cuckoo** *Chrysococcyx klaas*

Widespread Africa south of the Sahara and Bioko

☐ **African Emerald Cuckoo** *Chrysococcyx cupreus*
_____ *C. c. cupreus* — Africa south of the Sahara
_____ *C. c. intermedius* — Bioko (Gulf of Guinea)
_____ *C. c. insularum* — São Tomé, Príncipe and Pagalu (Gulf of Guinea)

☐ **Dideric Cuckoo** *Chrysococcyx caprius*

Intra-African migrant Africa south of the Sahara and s Arabia

☐ **Long-billed Cuckoo** *Rhamphomantis megarhynchus*
_____ *R. m. megarhynchus* — Aru Islands and New Guinea
_____ *R. m. sanfordi* — Waigeo I. (off n New Guinea)

☐ **Asian Drongo-Cuckoo** *Surniculus lugubris*
_____ *S. l. dicruroides* — N India to s China and Indochina; winters to Indonesia
_____ *S. l. lugubris* — Coastal sw India, Sri Lanka, Java and Bali
_____ *S. l. brachyurus* — Malaysia, Sumatra, Bangka I., Borneo and sw Philippines
_____ *S. l. musschenbroeki* — Sulawesi, Butung, Halmahera, Bacan and Obi islands

☐ **Philippine Drongo-Cuckoo** *Surniculus velutinus*

Philippine Islands and Sulu Archipelago

☐ **White-crowned Koel** *Caliechthrus leucolophus*

New Guinea and Salawati I.

☐ **Dwarf Koel** *Microdynamis parva*
_____ *M. p. grisecens* — N New Guinea (Humboldt Bay to Kumusi River)
_____ *M. p. parva* — Locally in s New Guinea and D'Entrecasteaux Archipelago

☐ **Black-billed Koel** *Eudynamys melanorhyncha*
_____ *E. m. melanorhyncha* — Sulawesi
_____ *E. m. facialis* — Sula Islands

☐ **Asian Koel** *Eudynamys scolopacea*

____	*E. s. scolopacea*	Nepal to Pakistan, India, Sri Lanka, Laccadives and Maldives
____	*E. s. chinensis*	S China and Indochina; winters to Borneo
____	*E. s. harterti*	Hainan (s China)
____	*E. s. malayana (dolosa)*	NE India to Thailand, Malaya, Sumatra, Borneo and L Sundas
____	*E. s. simalurensis*	Simeulue I. (off w Sumatra)
____	*E. s. frater*	N Philippines (Calayan and Fuga)
____	*E. s. mindanensis*	Philippines, Palawan, Sulu Arch., Sangihe I. and Talaud Islands
____	*E. s. corvina*	N Moluccas (Morotai, Halmahera, Ternate, Tidore and Bacan)
____	*E. s. orientalis*	S Moluccas (Buru, Manipa, Kelang, Seram, Ambon, Watubela)
____	*E. s. picata*	Kai Islands and Sumba to Timor and Roma
____	*E. s. rufiventer*	New Guinea
____	*E. s. salvadorii*	Bismarck Archipelago
____	*E. s. alberti*	Solomon Islands

☐ **Australian Koel** *Eudynamys cyanocephala*

____	*E. c. subcyanocephala*	NW Australia and w Queensland; winters to s Moluccas
____	*E. c. cyanocephala*	N Queensland to n New South Wales; winters to Moluccas

☐ **Long-tailed Koel** *Eudynamys taitensis*

New Zealand; winters to Polynesia and Bismarck Archipelago

☐ **Channel-billed Cuckoo** *Scythrops novaehollandiae*

E Indonesia and Australasian region

☐ **Yellowbill** *Ceuthmochares aereus*

____	*C. a. flavirostris*	Gambia to Nigeria (west of the Niger River)
____	*C. a. aereus*	Nigeria to s Sudan, w Kenya, Zaire, Angola, n Zambia; Bioko I.
____	*C. a. australis*	Ethiopia to Kenya, Tanzania, Mozambique and e South Africa

☐ **Black-bellied Malkoha** *Phaenicophaeus diardi*

____	*P. d. diardi*	S Myanmar, s Thailand, Malay Peninsula and Sumatra
____	*P. d. borneensis*	Borneo

☐ **Chestnut-bellied Malkoha** *Phaenicophaeus sumatranus*

S Myanmar, s Thailand, Malay Pen., Sumatra and Borneo

☐ **Blue-faced Malkoha** *Phaenicophaeus viridirostris*

S peninsular India and Sri Lanka

☐ **Green-billed Malkoha** *Phaenicophaeus tristis*

____	*P. t. tristis*	N India to Nepal, Sikkim, Bhutan, Assam and Bangladesh
____	*P. t. saliens*	N Myanmar to n Thailand, n Indochina and sw China (Yunnan)
____	*P. t. hainanus*	Hainan I. (s China)
____	*P. t. longicaudatus*	S Myanmar, s Thailand, s Indochina and Malaysia
____	*P. t. elongatus*	Sumatra
____	*P. t. kangeangensis*	Kangean Islands (Java Sea)

☐ **Sirkeer Malkoha** *Phaenicophaeus leschenaultii*

____	*P. l. sirkee*	Pakistan and nw India
____	*P. l. infuscatus*	Sub-Himalayas (Kumaon to Nepal, w Assam and Bangladesh)
____	*P. l. leschenaultii*	S India and Sri Lanka

☐ **Raffles' Malkoha** *Phaenicophaeus chlorophaeus*

____	*P. c. chlorophaeus*	S Myanmar to s Thailand, Malay Pen., Sumatra and Borneo
____	*P. c. fuscigularis*	NW Borneo (Sarawak and nw Kalimantan)

☐ **Red-billed Malkoha** *Phaenicophaeus javanicus*

S Myanmar, Malay Peninsula, Greater Sundas and Natuna Is.

☐ **Yellow-billed Malkoha** *Phaenicophaeus calyorhynchus*

____	*P. c. calyorhynchus*	Sulawesi and Togian Islands
____	*P. c. meridionalis*	Central and s Sulawesi
____	*P. c. rufiloris*	Butung I. (off Sulawesi)

☐ **Chestnut-breasted Malkoha** *Phaenicophaeus curvirostris*

____	*P. c. singularis*	S Myanmar to s Thailand, Malay Peninsula and Sumatra
____	*P. c. oeneicaudus*	Mentawi Islands (off sw Sumatra)
____	*P. c. curvirostris*	W and central Java
____	*P. c. deningeri*	E Java and Bali
____	*P. c. microrhinus*	Borneo and Bangka I.
____	*P. c. harringtoni*	S Philippines (Palawan, Balabac, Busuanga, Culion, Calauit)

☐ **Red-faced Malkoha** *Phaenicophaeus pyrrhocephalus*

Sri Lanka

☐ **Red-crested Malkoha** *Phaenicophaeus superciliosus*

____	*P. s. cagayensis*	N Luzon (Cagayan Province)
____	*P. s. superciliosus*	Luzon (south of range of *cagayensis*)

☐ **Scale-feathered Malkoha** *Phaenicophaeus cumingi*

N Philippines (Luzon, Marinduque and Catanduanes)

☐ **Sumatran Ground-Cuckoo** *Carpococcyx viridis*

Lowlands and foothills of sw Sumatra (Basiran Mountains)

☐ **Bornean Ground-Cuckoo** *Carpococcyx radiatus*

Borneo

☐ **Coral-billed Ground-Cuckoo** *Carpococcyx renauldi*

SE Thailand, Laos, Cambodia and Vietnam

☐ **Giant Coua** *Coua gigas*

Thinly distributed in forests and savanna of w and s Madagascar

☐ **Coquerel's Coua** *Coua coquereli*

Humid and dry deciduous forests of w Madagascar

☐ **Red-breasted Coua** *Coua serriana*

Humid forests of ne Madagascar

☐ **Red-fronted Coua** *Coua reynaudii*

Humid forests of n and e Madagascar

☐ **Red-capped Coua** *Coua ruficeps*

____	*C. r. ruficeps*	Lowlands of nw Madagascar
____	*C. r. olivaceiceps*	Lowlands of sw Madagascar

☐ **Running Coua** *Coua cursor*

Semiarid lowland forests of sw Madagascar

☐ **Crested Coua** *Coua cristata*

____	*C. c. cristata*	N and e Madagascar (south to Mahajanga)
____	*C. c. dumonti*	W Madagascar (Mahajanga to Morondava)
____	*C. c. pyropyga*	SW Madagascar (Morondava and Toliara to Amboasary)
____	*C. c. maxima*	SE Madagascar (Tolagnaro region)

☐ **Verreaux's Coua** *Coua verreauxi*

Locally in subdeserts of sw Madagascar

☐ **Blue Coua** *Coua caerulea*

Rainforests of nw and e Madagascar

☐ **Bay Coucal** *Centropus celebensis*

____	*C. c. celebensis*	N Sulawesi and Togian Islands
____	*C. c. rufescens*	Central and s Sulawesi, Labuan Blanda, Muna and Butung is.

☐ **Rufous Coucal** *Centropus unirufus*

N Philippines (Luzon, Polillo and Catanduanes)

☐ **Black-faced Coucal** *Centropus melanops*

____	*C. m. banken*	S Philippines (Bohol, Leyte, Samar and Biliran)
____	*C. m. melanops*	S Philippines (Basilan, Mindanao, Nipa, Dinagat and Siargao)

☐ **Sunda Coucal** *Centropus nigrorufus*

Lowlands of Java

☐ **Buff-headed Coucal** *Centropus milo*
_____ *C. m. albidiventris* — Solomon Is. (Vellalavella, Kulambangra, Gizo and Rendova)
_____ *C. m. milo* — S Solomon Islands (Guadalcanal and Florida Group)

☐ **Goliath Coucal** *Centropus goliath*
— N Moluccas (Morotai, Halmahera, Tidore, Bacan and Obi)

☐ **Violaceous Coucal** *Centropus violaceus*
— Bismarck Archipelago (New Ireland and New Britain)

☐ **Greater Black Coucal** *Centropus menbeki*
_____ *C. m. menbeki* — New Guinea, w Papuan islands and Numfor I.
_____ *C. m. jobiensis* — Yapen I. (Geelvink Bay off n New Guinea)
_____ *C. m. aruensis* — Aru Islands

☐ **Pied Coucal** *Centropus ateralbus*
— Bismarck Archipelago (New Ireland and New Britain)

☐ **Pheasant Coucal** *Centropus phasianinus*
_____ *C. p. mui* — Known from one specimen from Timor (e Lesser Sundas)
_____ *C. p. propinquus* — N New Guinea (Mamberamo River to Astrolabe Bay)
_____ *C. p. nigricans* — SE New Guinea and Yule I.
_____ *C. p. thierfelderi* — S New Guinea and islands in nw Torres Strait
_____ *C. p. melanurus* — N and nw Australia
_____ *C. p. phasianinus* — Coastal e Australia (n Queensland to n New South Wales)

☐ **Kai Coucal** *Centropus spilopterus*
— Kai Islands (se Moluccas)

☐ **Lesser Black Coucal** *Centropus bernsteini*
_____ *C. b. bernsteini* — W and central New Guinea
_____ *C. b. manam* — Manam I. (off ne New Guinea)

☐ **Biak Coucal** *Centropus chalybeus*
— Biak I. (Geelvink Bay off n New Guinea)

☐ **Short-toed Coucal** *Centropus rectunguis*
— Malay Peninsula, Sumatra and Borneo

☐ **Black-hooded Coucal** *Centropus steerii*
— Forests of Mindoro (n-central Philippines)

☐ **Greater Coucal** *Centropus sinensis*
_____ *C. s. sinensis* — Pakistan to n India and s China
_____ *C. s. parroti* — S peninsular India and Sri Lanka
_____ *C. s. intermedius* — Bangladesh to Myanmar, s Thailand, Indochina and Malay Pen.
_____ *C. s. bubutus* — Greater Sundas and adjacent islands to sw Philippines
_____ *C. s. anonymus* — S Philippines (Jolo, Tawitawi, Basilan and Sanga Sanga)
_____ *C. s. kangeanensis* — Kangean Islands (Java Sea)

☐ **Andaman Coucal** *Centropus andamanensis*
— Andaman Islands and adj. Table, Great and Little Coco islands

☐ **Philippine Coucal** *Centropus viridis*
_____ *C. v. major* — Babuyanes Islands (n Philippines)
_____ *C. v. viridis* — Widespread throughout Philippine Islands
_____ *C. v. mindorensis* — N-central Philippines (Mindoro and Semirara)
_____ *C. v. carpenteri* — Batanas Islands north of Luzon (n Batan, Sabtang and Ibuhos)

☐ **Madagascar Coucal** *Centropus toulou*
_____ *C. t. toulou* — Madagascar
_____ *C. t. insularis* — Aldabra
_____ *C. t. assumptionis†* — Formerly Assumption I. Extinct

☐ **Black Coucal** *Centropus grillii*
— Intra-African migrant south of the Sahara

☐ **Green-billed Coucal** *Centropus chlororhynchus*
— Locally in wet zone of sw Sri Lanka

☐ Lesser Coucal *Centropus bengalensis*
____   *C. b. bengalensis*   India and Nepal to Bangladesh, Myanmar and Indochina
____   *C. b. lignator*   S and se China, Hainan I. and Taiwan
____   *C. b. javanensis*   Malay Pen., Sumatra, Java, Borneo, Palawan and Philippines
____   *C. b. sarasinorum*   Sulawesi and Lesser Sundas
____   *C. b. medius*   Moluccas (Indonesia)

☐ Black-throated Coucal *Centropus leucogaster*
____   *C. l. leucogaster*   S Senegal and Guinea-Bissau to se Nigeria
____   *C. l. efulensis*   Lowland forests of sw Cameroon and Gabon
____   *C. l. neumanni*   Locally in ne Zaire (Ituri Forest)

☐ Gabon Coucal *Centropus anselli*

     Lowland swamps of s Cameroon to nw Angola and c Zaire

☐ Blue-headed Coucal *Centropus monachus*
____   *C. m. fischeri (verheyeni)*   Ivory Coast to w Kenya, s Sudan, Ethiopia and n Angola
____   *C. m. monachus*   Ethiopia to central Kenya

☐ Coppery-tailed Coucal *Centropus cupreicaudus*

     Angola to s Zaire, Zambia, Zimbabwe, Tanzania and Malawi

☐ Senegal Coucal *Centropus senegalensis*
____   *C. s. aegyptius*   Lower Egypt (Nile River to El Minya)
____   *C. s. senegalensis*   Senegambia to Somalia and south to Zaire
____   *C. s. flecki*   E Angola to n Botswana, Zambia, Malawi and sw Tanzania

☐ White-browed Coucal *Centropus superciliosus*
____   *C. s. sokotrae*   Socotra I. and sw Arabia
____   *C. s. superciliosus*   E Sudan to Ethiopia, w Somalia, Kenya, ne Uganda, ne Tanzania
____   *C. s. loandae*   Uganda to sw Kenya, n Zimbabwe, Zambia, Botswana, Angola
____   *C. s. burchellii (fasciipygialis)*   E Botswana to s Zimbabwe, Mozambique and South Africa

☐ Dwarf Cuckoo *Coccyzus pumilus*

     Tropical n Colombia to ne Venezuela; one record from n Brazil

☐ Ash-colored Cuckoo *Coccyzus cinereus*

     S Brazil to n Argentina, Paraguay, Bolivia and extreme se Peru

☐ Black-billed Cuckoo *Coccyzus erythropthalmus*

     Breeds e North America; winters to Bolivia

☐ Yellow-billed Cuckoo *Coccyzus americanus*

     Canada to Mexico and West Indies; winters to n Argentina

☐ Pearly-breasted Cuckoo *Coccyzus euleri*

     Locally from n South America to s Brazil and ne Argentina

☐ Mangrove Cuckoo *Coccyzus minor*

     Locally from s Florida to coastal n Brazil

☐ Cocos Island Cuckoo *Coccyzus ferrugineus*

     Cocos I. (off w Costa Rica)

☐ Dark-billed Cuckoo *Coccyzus melacoryphus*

     Venezuela to the Guianas, Brazil, n Argentina and Galapagos

☐ Gray-capped Cuckoo *Coccyzus lansbergi*

     N Colombia and n Venezuela; migrates to w Peru

☐ Great Lizard-Cuckoo *Saurothera merlini*
____   *S. m. bahamensis (andrina)*   Bahamas (Andros, New Providence, and Eleuthera)
____   *S. m. santamariae*   Islands off n-central Cuba
____   *S. m. merlini*   Cuba
____   *S. m. decolor*   Isle of Pines

☐ Puerto Rican Lizard-Cuckoo *Saurothera vieilloti*

     Puerto Rico

☐ Jamaican Lizard-Cuckoo *Saurothera vetula*

     Jamaica

☐ **Hispaniolan Lizard-Cuckoo** *Saurothera longirostris*
____ *S. l. longirostris* — Hispaniola and Saona I.
____ *S. l. petersi* — La Mohotiere I. and Gonâve I. (off w Haiti)

☐ **Chestnut-bellied Cuckoo** *Hyetornis pluvialis*

Jamaica

☐ **Bay-breasted Cuckoo** *Hyetornis rufigularis*

Hispaniola and Gonâve I.

☐ **Squirrel Cuckoo** *Piaya cayana*
____ *P. c. mexicana* — Pacific slope of Mexico (Sinaloa to Isthmus of Tehuántepec)
____ *P. c. thermophila* — E Mexico to e Panama, nw Colombia and offshore islands
____ *P. c. nigricrissa* — W Colombia and w Ecuador to central Peru
____ *P. c. mehleri* — NE Colombia and coastal n Venezuela east to María Peninsula
____ *P. c. mesura* — Colombia east of the Andes and e Ecuador
____ *P. c. circe* — W Venezuela (region south of Lake Maracaibo)
____ *P. c. cayana* — Orinoco Valley of Venezuela to the Guianas and n Brazil
____ *P. c. insulana* — Trinidad
____ *P. c. obscura* — Brazil south of the Amazon (Rio Juruá to Rio Tapajós)
____ *P. c. hellmayri* — Brazil south of the Amazon (Santarém to Amazon delta)
____ *P. c. pallescens* — E Brazil (Piauí, Pernambuco, n Bahia and adjacent e Goiás)
____ *P. c. cabinisi* — S-central Brazil (central Mato Grosso and adjacent Goiás)
____ *P. c. macroura* — SE Brazil to Paraguay, Uruguay and ne Argentina
____ *P. c. mogenseni* — S Bolivia and adjacent nw Argentina

☐ **Black-bellied Cuckoo** *Piaya melanogaster*

Guianas and Venezuela to e Ecuador, Peru and w Brazil

☐ **Little Cuckoo** *Piaya minuta*
____ *P. m. panamensis* — Lowlands of e Panama and n Colombia (west of Gulf of Urabá)
____ *P. m. barinensis* — Extreme e Colombia and adjacent w Venezuela
____ *P. m. gracilis* — Colombia west of the Andes and w Ecuador
____ *P. m. minuta* — E Colombia to Venezuela, the Guianas, Amaz. Brazil and Peru
____ *P. m. chaparensis* — N Bolivia (Río Chaparé region)

☐ **Greater Ani** *Crotophaga major*

E Panama and S America e of Andes to n Argentina; Trinidad

☐ **Smooth-billed Ani** *Crotophaga ani*

Tropical s US to Brazil, n Argentina and West Indies

☐ **Groove-billed Ani** *Crotophaga sulcirostris*

S Baja; s Texas to n Chile, n Argentina, Trinidad and Curaçao

☐ **Guira Cuckoo** *Guira guira*

NE Brazil to Bolivia, Paraguay, Uruguay and central Argentina

☐ **Striped Cuckoo** *Tapera naevia*
____ *T. n. excellens* — Tropical se Mexico to Panama
____ *T. n. naevia* — N S America to Brazil, Argentina, Trinidad and Isla Margarita

☐ **Pheasant Cuckoo** *Dromococcyx phasianellus*

Lowlands of s Mexico to Brazil, Paraguay and ne Argentina

☐ **Pavonine Cuckoo** *Dromococcyx pavoninus*

Tropical South America east of the Andes to ne Argentina

☐ **Lesser Ground-Cuckoo** *Morococcyx erythropygus*
____ *M. e. mexicanus* — Arid w Mexico (Sinaloa to Isthmus of Tehuántepec)
____ *M. e. erythropygus* — S Mexico (Isthmus of Tehuántepec) to n Costa Rica

☐ **Greater Roadrunner** *Geococcyx californianus*

Arid sw US to s Mexico

☐ **Lesser Roadrunner** *Geococcyx velox*

Arid w Mexico (s Sonora to n Nicaragua)

☐ **Scaled Ground-Cuckoo** *Neomorphus squamiger*

Brazil south of the Amazon (lower Rio Tapajós region)

☐ **Rufous-vented Ground-Cuckoo** *Neomorphus geoffroyi*
_____ *N. g. salvini* — Humid lowlands of Nicaragua to Pacific coast of Colombia
_____ *N. g. aequatorialis* — Tropical se Colombia to e Ecuador and n Peru
_____ *N. g. australis* — S Peru and nw Bolivia
_____ *N. g. geoffroyi* — Brazil south of the Amazon (Pará)
_____ *N. g. dulcis* — E Brazil (Espírito Santo to Rio de Janeiro)

☐ **Banded Ground-Cuckoo** *Neomorphus radiolosus*

Humid lowlands of sw Colombia and nw Ecuador

☐ **Rufous-winged Ground-Cuckoo** *Neomorphus rufipennis*

S Venezuela, Guyana and n Brazil (Roraima)

☐ **Red-billed Ground-Cuckoo** *Neomorphus pucheranii*
_____ *N. p. pucheranii* — Amazonian Peru and w Brazil north of the Amazon
_____ *N. p. lepidophanes* — Amazonian Peru and Brazil south of the Amazon

ORDER: STRIGIFORMES
FAMILY: TYTONIDAE (Barn-Owls—16)

☐ **Greater Sooty-Owl** *Tyto tenebricosa*
_____ *T. t. arfaki* — New Guinea and Yapen I.
_____ *T. t. tenebricosa* — SE Australia (Eungella National Park to Victoria)

☐ **Lesser Sooty-Owl** *Tyto multipunctata*

Rainforests of ne Australia (ne Queensland)

☐ **Australian Masked-Owl** *Tyto novaehollandiae*
_____ *T. n. calabyi* — Trans-Fly lowlands of s New Guinea and Daru I.
_____ *T. n. melvillensis* — N Australia (Melville I. and Bathurst I.)
_____ *T. n. galei* — NE Queensland (ne Cape York Peninsula)
_____ *T. n. kimberli* — N Australia (Yampi Peninsula to Atherton tablelands)
_____ *T. n. novaehollandiae (perplexa)* — SW W Australia to Victoria and ne Queensland (Townsville)
_____ *T. n. castanops* — Tasmania, Maria I. and Maatsuyker I.

☐ **New Britain Masked-Owl** *Tyto aurantia*

New Britain (Bismarck Archipelago)

☐ **Lesser Masked-Owl** *Tyto sororcula*
_____ *T. s. cayelii* — S Moluccas (Buru and Seram)
_____ *T. s. sororcula* — Tanimbar Islands (Yamdena and Larat)

☐ **Manus Owl** *Tyto manusi*

Manus I. (Admiralty Islands)

☐ **Taliabu Owl** *Tyto nigrobrunnea*

Taliabu I. (Sula Islands)

☐ **Minahassa Owl** *Tyto inexspectata*

Hill forests of n and n-central Sulawesi

☐ **Sulawesi Owl** *Tyto rosenbergii*
_____ *T. r. rosenbergii* — Rainforests of Sulawesi and Sangihe Island
_____ *T. r. pelengensis* — Peleng I. (Banggai Islands)

☐ **Australasian Grass-Owl** *Tyto longimembris*
_____ *T. l. longimembris (walleri)* — India to Indochina, Sulawesi, Lesser Sundas, n and e Australia
_____ *T. l. chinensis (melli)* — SE China (se Yunnan to Jiangsu) and Vietnam
_____ *T. l. pithecops* — Taiwan
_____ *T. l. amauronota* — Philippine Islands
_____ *T. l. baliem* — W New Guinea
_____ *T. l. papuensis* — Montane grasslands of e New Guinea

☐ **African Grass-Owl** *Tyto capensis*

Wet grasslands of Africa south of the Sahara

☐ **Ashy-faced Owl** *Tyto glaucops*

_____ *T. g. glaucops* — Hispaniola and Tortue I.
_____ *T. g. nigrescens* — Dominica (Lesser Antilles)
_____ *T. g. insularis* — St. Vincent, Bequia, Union, Carriacou and Grenada

☐ **Madagascar Red Owl** *Tyto soumagnei*

E Madagascar (on verge of extinction)

☐ **Barn Owl** *Tyto alba*

_____ *T. a. alba* — W and s Europe; w Canary Islands and North Africa
_____ *T. a. guttata* — Central Europe east to sw European USSR and ne Greece
_____ *T. a. ernesti* — Corsica and Sardinia
_____ *T. a. erlangeri* — Crete and Cyprus to sw Iran, ne Egypt and s Arabian Peninsula
_____ *T. a. schmitzi* — Madeira and Porto Santo I.
_____ *T. a. gracilirostris* — E Canary Islands (Fuerteventura, Lanzarote and Alegranza)
_____ *T. a. detorta* — Cape Verde Islands
_____ *T. a. affinis (hypermetra)* — Sub-Saharan Africa, Zanzibar, Pemba, Madagascar, Comoros
_____ *T. a. poensis* — Bioko (Gulf of Guinea)
_____ *T. a. thomensis* — São Tomé (Gulf of Guinea)
_____ *T. a. stertens* — Indian subcontinent to n Sri Lanka, sw China and s Thailand
_____ *T. a. deroepstorffi* — S Andaman Islands
_____ *T. a. javanica* — Malay Peninsula to Greater Sundas
_____ *T. a. sumbaensis* — Sumba (Lesser Sundas)
_____ *T. a. meeki* — E New Guinea, Manam and Karkar islands
_____ *T. a. delicatula (everetti, kuehni, bellonae, lulu)* — Timor to e Australia, Solomon Is., Loyalty Is., and Samoa
_____ *T. a. crassirostris* — Tanga I. (Bismarck Archipelago)
_____ *T. a. interposita* — N Vanuatu, Santa Cruz Islands and Banks Group
_____ *T. a. pratincola (lucayana)* — S Canada to n Mexico, Bermuda, Bahamas and Hispaniola
_____ *T. a. guatemalae (subandeana)* — W Guatemala to Panama, Pearl Islands and Colombia
_____ *T. a. bondi* — Bay Islands off n Honduras (Roatán and Guanaja)
_____ *T. a. furcata* — Cuba, Cayman Islands and Jamaica
_____ *T. a. niveicauda* — Isle of Pines (off Cuba)
_____ *T. a. bargei* — Netherlands Antilles (Curaçao and Bonaire)
_____ *T. a. punctatissima* — Galapagos Islands
_____ *T. a. contempta* — W Colombia to Venezuela, Ecuador and Peru
_____ *T. a. hellmayri* — Guianas to n Brazil, Margarita I., Trinidad and Tobago
_____ *T. a. tuidara* — Brazil s of the Amazon to Tierra del Fuego and Falkland Is.

☐ **Oriental Bay-Owl** *Phodilus badius*

_____ *P. b. saturatus* — Sikkim and ne India to s China, Myanmar, Thailand, Indochina
_____ *P. b. ripleyi* — SW India (Anaimalai-Nelliamathy Hills)
_____ *P. b. assimilis* — Sri Lanka
_____ *P. b. badius* — Malay Peninsula, Borneo, Sumatra, Java and Nias I.
_____ *P. b. arixuthus* — Bunguran I. (Natuna Islands)
_____ *P. b. parvus* — Belitung I. (off sw Borneo)

☐ **Congo Bay-Owl** *Phodilus prigoginei*

Second specimen in 50 years banded in mts. of e Zaire in 1996

ORDER: STRIGIFORMES
FAMILY: STRIGIDAE (Owls—188)

☐ **White-fronted Scops-Owl** *Otus sagittatus*

S Myanmar, s Thailand and Malay Peninsula

☐ **Andaman Scops-Owl** *Otus balli*

Andaman Islands

☐ **Reddish Scops-Owl** *Otus rufescens*
____ *O. r. malayensis* — S peninsular Thailand and Malay Peninsula
____ *O. r. rufescens* — Sumatra, Bangka I., Java and Borneo

☐ **Sandy Scops-Owl** *Otus icterorhynchus*
____ *O. i. icterorhynchus* — Rainforests of Liberia, Ivory Coast and Ghana
____ *O. i. holerythrus* — S Cameroon to n Congo, n and e Zaire and (?) Gabon

☐ **Sokoke Scops-Owl** *Otus ireneae*
E Kenya (Sokoke Forest) and ne Tanzania (Usambara Mts.)

☐ **Flores Scops-Owl** *Otus alfredi*
Flores (Lesser Sundas)

☐ **Mountain Scops-Owl** *Otus spilocephalus*
____ *O. s. huttoni* — Western Himalayas (n Pakistan to central Nepal)
____ *O. s. spilocephalus* — Himalayas (cent. Nepal to Arunachal Pradesh and Myanmar)
____ *O. s. latouchi* — N Thailand and Laos to se China and Hainan
____ *O. s. hambroecki* — Taiwan
____ *O. s. siamensis* — Mountains of s Thailand to s Vietnam
____ *O. s. vulpes* — Mountains of Malay Peninsula
____ *O. s. vandewateri* — Mountains of Sumatra
____ *O. s. luciae* — Mountains of Borneo

☐ **Rajah Scops-Owl** *Otus brookii*
____ *O. b. solokensis* — Montane forests of Sumatra
____ *O. b. brookii* — Montane forests of Borneo

☐ **Javan Scops-Owl** *Otus angelinae*
Mountains of Java

☐ **Mentawai Scops-Owl** *Otus mentawi*
Mentawi Islands (off w Sumatra)

☐ **Indian Scops-Owl** *Otus bakkamoena*
____ *O. b. plumipes* — W Himalayas (n Pakistan to w Nepal)
____ *O. b. deserticolor* — S Pakistan and (?) se Iran
____ *O. b. gangeticus* — NW India to lowlands of Nepal
____ *O. b. marathae* — Central India
____ *O. b. bakkamoena* — S India and Sri Lanka

☐ **Collared Scops-Owl** *Otus lettia*
____ *O. l. lettia* — E Nepal to Bangladesh, Myanmar, Thailand and Indochina
____ *O. l. erythrocampe* — SE China
____ *O. l. ussuriensis* — Sakhalin I., Ussuriland and ne China
____ *O. l. glabripes* — Taiwan
____ *O. l. umbratilis* — Hainan I. (s China)

☐ **Sunda Scops-Owl** *Otus lempiji*
____ *O. l. condorensis* — S peninsular Thailand (south of Isthmus of Kra)
____ *O. l. lempiji* — Malay Pen., s Sumatra, Bangka, Belitung, Java, Borneo and Bali
____ *O. l. cnephaeus* — S Malay Peninsula
____ *O. l. hypnodes* — N and central Sumatra
____ *O. l. lemurum* — N Borneo
____ *O. l. kangeanus* — Kangean Islands (Java Sea)

☐ **Japanese Scops-Owl** *Otus semitorques*
____ *O. s. semitorques* — S Kuril Islands and Hokkaido south to Yakushima I.
____ *O. s. pryeri* — Hachijo I. (s Izu Is.) and s Ryukyu Is. (Okinawa to Iriomote)

☐ **Wallace's Scops-Owl** *Otus silvicola*
Lesser Sundas (Sumbawa and Flores)

☐ **Palawan Scops-Owl** *Otus fuliginosus*
Palawan (sw Philippines)

☐ **Philippine Scops-Owl** *Otus megalotis*
_____ *O. m. megalotis* — Philippines (Luzon, Catanduanes and Marinduque)
_____ *O. m. everetti* — Philippines (Samar, Biliran, Leyte, Mindando and Basilan)
_____ *O. m. nigrorum* — Negros (Philippines)
_____ *O. m. boholensis* — Bohol (Philippines)

☐ **Mindanao Scops-Owl** *Otus mirus*

Montane rainforests of Mindanao (s Philippines)

☐ **Luzon Scops-Owl** *Otus longicornis*

Montane forests of Luzon (n Philippines)

☐ **Mindoro Scops-Owl** *Otus mindorensis*

Montane forests of Mindoro (Philippines)

☐ **Pallid Scops-Owl** *Otus brucei*
_____ *O. b. brucei* — E Aral Sea to Kyrgystan and Tajikistan
_____ *O. b. obsoletus* — S Turkey to n Syria, n Iraq, Uzbekistan and n Afghanistan
_____ *O. b. semenowi* — S Tajikistan to w China, e Afghanistan and n Pakistan
_____ *O. b. exiguus* — Israel to Iraq, s Iran, Oman, s Afghanistan and w Pakistan

☐ **African Scops-Owl** *Otus senegalensis*
_____ *O. s. senegalensis* — Widespread sub-Saharan Africa
_____ *O. s. pamelae* — S Saudi Arabia
_____ *O. s. socotranus* — Socotra
_____ *O. s. feae* — Pagulu (Gulf of Guinea)
_____ *O. s. nivosus* — SE Kenya (lower Tana River to Lali Hills)

☐ **European Scops-Owl** *Otus scops*
_____ *O. s. scops* — France and Medit. is. to Volga R., n Greece and Transcaucasia
_____ *O. s. pulchellus* — Volga R. to Lake Baikal and south to Altai and Tien Shan Mts.
_____ *O. s. mallorcae* — Iberian Pen., Balearic Is., n Morocco, Algeria and Tunisia
_____ *O. s. cycladum* — S Greece and Crete, s Asia Minor, Israel, s Turkey and Jordan
_____ *O. s. cyprius* — Cyprus
_____ *O. s. turanicus* — Iraq through Iran and s Transcaspia to nw Pakistan

☐ **Oriental Scops-Owl** *Otus sunia*
_____ *O. s. sunia* — N Pakistan to Bangladesh and n India
_____ *O. s. rufipennis* — S India
_____ *O. s. leggei* — Sri Lanka
_____ *O. s. modestus (nicobaricus, distans)* — Assam to Myanmar, Thailand, Indochina; Andaman, Nicobar is.
_____ *O. s. malayanus* — S China (Yunnan to e Guangdong)
_____ *O. s. stictonotus* — SE Siberia to ne China, Sakhalin I. and n Korea
_____ *O. s. japonicus* — Japan

☐ **Flammulated Owl** *Otus flammeolus*

S Br. Columbia to sw US and s Mexico; winters to Guatemala

☐ **Moluccan Scops-Owl** *Otus magicus*
_____ *O. m. morotensis* — N Moluccas (Morotai and Ternate)
_____ *O. m. leucospilus* — N Moluccas (Halmahera, Kasiruta and Bacan)
_____ *O. m. obira* — Obi I. (central Moluccas)
_____ *O. m. magicus* — S Moluccas (Seram and Ambon)
_____ *O. m. bouruensis* — Buru (s Moluccas)
_____ *O. m. albiventris* — Lesser Sundas (Lombok, Sumbawa, Flores, Besar, Lomblen)
_____ *O. m. tempestatis* — Wetar (Lesser Sundas)

☐ **Mantanani Scops-Owl** *Otus mantananensis*
_____ *O. m. romblonis* — Philippines (Romblon, Tablas, Sibuyan, Banton and Semirara)
_____ *O. m. cuyensis* — SW Philippines (Cuyo, Dicabaito and Linapacan)
_____ *O. m. mantananensis* — Mantanani I. (off Borneo); Rasa and Ursula is. (off Palawan)
_____ *O. m. sibutensis (steerei)* — SW Sulu Islands (Sibutu and Tumindao)

☐ **Ryukyu Scops-Owl** *Otus elegans*

____ *O. e. elegans*	Ryukyu Islands (s Japan)
____ *O. e. interpositus*	Daito Islands (s Japanese Archipelago)
____ *O. e. botelensis*	Lan-yü I. (off se Taiwan)
____ *O. e. calayensis*	N Philippines (Batan, Sabtang and Calayan)

☐ **Sulawesi Scops-Owl** *Otus manadensis*

____ *O. m. siaoensis*	Siau I. (off n Sulawesi)
____ *O. m. manadensis*	Sulawesi
____ *O. m. mendeni*	Banggai Islands (Peleng and Labobo)
____ *O. m. sulaensis*	Sula Islands (Taliabu, Seho, Mangole and Sanana)
____ *O. m. kalidupae*	Kaledupa I. (Tukangbesi Islands)

☐ **Sangihe Scops-Owl** *Otus collari*

Sangihe I. (north of Sulawesi)

☐ **Biak Scops-Owl** *Otus beccarii*

Biak I. (off nw New Guinea)

☐ **Seychelles Scops-Owl** *Otus insularis*

Highland forests of Mahé (Seychelles)

☐ **Simeulue Scops-Owl** *Otus umbra*

Simeulue I. (off nw Sumatra)

☐ **Enggano Scops-Owl** *Otus enganensis*

Enggano I. (off sw Sumatra)

☐ **Nicobar Scops-Owl** *Otus alius*

Great Nicobar I. (s Nicobar Islands)

☐ **Pemba Scops-Owl** *Otus pembaensis*

Pemba I. (off n Tanzania)

☐ **Comoro Scops-Owl** *Otus pauliani*

Mt. Karthala on Grand Comoro I. (Comoro Islands)

☐ **Anjouan Scops-Owl** *Otus capnodes*

Anjoun (Comoro Islands)

☐ **Moheli Scops-Owl** *Otus moheliensis*

Mohéli (Comoro Islands)

☐ **Malagasy Scops-Owl** *Otus rutilus*

____ *O. r. mayottensis*	Mayotte (Comoro Islands)
____ *O. r. rutilus*	Madagascar

☐ **Sao Tome Scops-Owl** *Otus hartlaubi*

Highlands of São Tomé (Gulf of Guinea)

☐ **Western Screech-Owl** *Otus kennicottii*

____ *O. k. kennicottii (saturatus)*	Coastal s Alaska to nw Canada and nw California
____ *O. k. bendirei (macfarlanei, brewsteri)*	E Washington and Montana to se California
____ *O. k. aikeni (myochophilus, inyoensis, cineraceus)*	SW US (California) to w Oklahoma, s to n Mexico (Sonora)
____ *O. k. cardonensis (quercinus, clazus, gilmani)*	S California and n Baja California
____ *O. k. xantusi*	Cape district of s Baja California
____ *O. k. yumanensis*	SE California and sw Arizona to n Mexico (nw Sonora)
____ *O. k. suttoni (sortilegus)*	SW Texas to Mexican Plateau
____ *O. k. vinaceus (sinaloensis)*	N Mexico (s Sonora and w Chihuahua to n Sinaloa)

☐ **Balsas Screech-Owl** *Otus seductus*

SW Mexico (s Jalisco and Colima to w Guerrero)

☐ **Pacific Screech-Owl** *Otus cooperi*

____ *O. c. lambi*	Coastal s Mexico (Pacific slope of Oaxaca)
____ *O. c. chiapensis*	Coastal s Mexico (Chiapas)
____ *O. c. cooperi*	Extreme s Chiapas to nw Costa Rica (Guanacaste Peninsula)

☐ **Whiskered Screech-Owl** *Otus trichopsis*

____ *O. t. aspersus (pinosus, ridgwayi, guerrerensis)*	SE Arizona to nw Mexico (Sonora and Chihuahua)
____ *O. t. trichopsis*	Highlands of c Mexico (Durango to Veracruz and Chiapas)
____ *O. t. mesamericanus (pumilus)*	SE Mexico (Chiapas) to n-central Nicaragua

☐ **Eastern Screech-Owl** *Otus asio*

_____ *O. a. maxwelliae (swenki)*	S-central Canada and n-central US
_____ *O. a. naevius*	SE Canada and ne US (south to North Carolina)
_____ *O. a. asio*	Oklahoma to South Carolina and Georgia
_____ *O. a. hasbroucki*	Central Oklahoma to Texas
_____ *O. a. floridanus*	Louisiana to Florida
_____ *O. a. mccallii (semplei)*	S Texas to ne Mexico (Nuevo León and Tamaulipas)

☐ **Tropical Screech-Owl** *Otus choliba*

_____ *O. c. luctisomus*	Costa Rica to nw Colombia; Pearl Islands (Panama)
_____ *O. c. margaritae*	Isla Margarita (off nw Venezuela)
_____ *O. c. duidae*	Duida Mountains (s Venezuela)
_____ *O. c. crucigerus (montanus, kelsoi, alticola, caucae)*	E Colombia to Venezuela, the Guianas, e Peru and ne Brazil
_____ *O. c. suturutus*	Bolivia
_____ *O. c. decussatus (caatingensis)*	S-central and e Brazil
_____ *O. c. choliba (chapadensis)*	S Brazil (s Mato Grosso and São Paulo) to e Paraguay
_____ *O. c. wetmorei (alilucoco)*	W Paraguay and n Argentina
_____ *O. c. uruguaiensis*	SE Brazil to Uruguay and ne Argentina

☐ **Koepcke's Screech-Owl** *Otus koepckeae*

	Disjunct in Andes of nw Peru and w-central Bolivia (La Paz)

☐ **West Peruvian Screech-Owl** *Otus roboratus*

_____ *O. r. pacificus*	SW Ecuador and nw Peru (south to Lambayeque)
_____ *O. r. roboratus*	Extreme s Ecuador and nw Peru (between W and C Andes)

☐ **Bare-shanked Screech-Owl** *Otus clarkii*

	Montane forests of Costa Rica to extreme nw Colombia

☐ **Bearded Screech-Owl** *Otus barbarus*

	Montane forests of s Mexico (Chiapas) and n Guatemala

☐ **Rufescent Screech-Owl** *Otus ingens*

_____ *O. i. venezuelanus*	Andes of n Colombia to nw Venezuela
_____ *O. i. ingens (minimus)*	Andes of n Ecuador to Peru and w-central Bolivia

☐ **Colombian Screech-Owl** *Otus colombianus*

	W slope of Andes of Colombia to nw Ecuador

☐ **Cinnamon Screech-Owl** *Otus petersoni*

	Cloud forests of s Ecuador to n Peru

☐ **Cloud-forest Screech-Owl** *Otus marshalli*

	Cloud forests of central Peru (Pasco and Cuzco)

☐ **Tawny-bellied Screech-Owl** *Otus watsonii*

_____ *O. w. watsonii*	E Colombia to ne Peru, Venezuela, Guianas and Amaz. Brazil
_____ *O. w. usta*	E Peru and s Amaz. Brazil to n Mato Grosso and n Bolivia

☐ **Guatemalan Screech-Owl** *Otus guatemalae*

_____ *O. g. tomlini*	NW Mexico (se Sonora and sw Chihuahua to Sinaloa)
_____ *O. g. hastatus (pettingilli)*	W Mexico (sw Sinaloa to Oaxaca)
_____ *O. g. cassini*	E Mexico (s Tamaulipas and n Veracruz)
_____ *O. g. fuscus*	Mountains of e Mexico (central Veracruz)
_____ *O. g. thompsoni*	Yucatán Peninsula and Cozumel I.
_____ *O. g. guatemalae (peteni)*	Mts. of se Mexico (se Veracruz and ne Oaxaca) to Honduras
_____ *O. g. dacrysistactus*	Mountains of n Nicaragua

☐ **Vermiculated Screech-Owl** *Otus vermiculatus*

_____ *O. v. vermiculatus*	Lowlands of Costa Rica to nw Colombia and n Venezuela
_____ *O. v. roraimae*	*Tepuis* of se Venezuela and adjacent n Brazil
_____ *O. v. napensis (helleri, bolivianus)*	Tropical e Ecuador to Peru and n Bolivia

☐ **Hoy's Screech-Owl** *Otus hoyi*

	Montane forests of s Bolivia and nw Argentina

☐ **Variable Screech-Owl** *Otus atricapillus*

SE Brazil (s Bahia) to se Paraguay and ne Argentina (Misiones)

☐ **Long-tufted Screech-Owl** *Otus sanctaecatarinae*

Foothills of se Brazil, Uruguay and ne Argentina (Misiones)

☐ **Puerto Rican Screech-Owl** *Otus nudipes*
- ____ *O. n. nudipes* — Puerto Rico
- ____ *O. n. newtoni* — Vieques I., Culebra I. and Virgin Islands

☐ **White-throated Screech-Owl** *Otus albogularis*
- ____ *O. a. obscurus* — Sierra de Perijá (Colombia/Venezuela border)
- ____ *O. a. macabrum* — Western and Central Andes of Colombia and Ecuador to n Peru
- ____ *O. a. albogularis* — Eastern Andes of Colombia and n Ecuador
- ____ *O. a. meridensis* — Andes of w Venezuela
- ____ *O. a. aequatorialis* — Andes of e Ecuador
- ____ *O. a. remotus* — Andes of e Peru to w Bolivia (Cochabamba)

☐ **Palau Owl** *Pyrroglaux podarginus*

Lowlands of Palau Islands (w Caroline Islands)

☐ **Cuban Screech-Owl** *Gymnoglaux lawrencii*
- ____ *G. l. exsul* — W Cuba and Isle of Pines
- ____ *G. l. lawrencii* — Central and e Cuba

☐ **Northern White-faced Owl** *Ptilopsis leucotis*

Senegambia to Somalia, n Zaire, n Uganda and central Kenya

☐ **Southern White-faced Owl** *Ptilopsis granti*

SE Gabon to s Zaire, sw Kenya, Namibia and n Cape Province

☐ **Mindanao Eagle-Owl** *Mimizuku gurneyi*

S Philippines (Mindanao, Dinagat and Siargao)

☐ **Great Horned Owl** *Bubo virginianus*
- ____ *B. v. lagophonus* — Central Alaska to ne Oregon and Montana; winters to Texas
- ____ *B. v. saturatus* — Coastal sw Alaska (Cook Inlet) to coastal central California
- ____ *B. v. pacificus* — Coastal California to nw Baja California
- ____ *B. v. elachistus* — S Baja California and Isla Espíritu Santo
- ____ *B. v. subarcticus (occidentalis)* — Mackenzie and nw Br. Col. to Hudson Bay, Wyoming, N Dak.
- ____ *B. v. pallescens* — Deserts of cent. and se Calif. to Kansas and s Mexico (Oaxaca)
- ____ *B. v. heterocnemis* — NE Canada south to Great Lakes region
- ____ *B. v. virginianus* — Minnesota to Nova Scotia, s to Kansas, e Texas and Florida
- ____ *B. v. mayensis* — SE Mexico (Yucatán Peninsula)
- ____ *B. v. mesembrinus* — S Mexico (Isthmus of Tehuántepec) to w Panama
- ____ *B. v. nigrescens* — Andes of Colombia to Ecuador and nw Peru
- ____ *B. v. nacurutu* — E Colombia to the Guianas, ne Brazil, Bolivia and Argentina

☐ **Magellanic Horned Owl** *Bubo magellanicus*

C Peru to w Bolivia, w Argentina, Tierra del Fuego, Cape Horn

☐ **Eurasian Eagle-Owl** *Bubo bubo*
- ____ *B. b. hispanus* — Iberian Peninsula; formerly Atlas Mts. of n Africa (extinct?)
- ____ *B. b. bubo* — Scandinavia and Spain through w Europe to w Russia
- ____ *B. b. ruthenus* — Cent. European Russia to Ural Mts. and lower Volga basin
- ____ *B. b. interpositus* — Turkey and nw Iran to s Ukraine, Romania and Bulgaria
- ____ *B. b. sibiricus (baschkiricus)* — Western foothills of Ural Mountains to Ob River and w Altai
- ____ *B. b. yenisseensis (zaissanensis)* — Central Siberia to n Mongolia
- ____ *B. b. turcomanus (tarimensis)* — Lower Volga R. and Ural R. to nw China and w Mongolia
- ____ *B. b. omissus* — Turkmenistan to extreme w China
- ____ *B. b. hemachalana (tibetanus)* — Pamirs and n Tien Shan south to w Himalayas and w Tibet
- ____ *B. b. nikolskii* — E Iraq to Iran, Afghanistan and w Pakistan
- ____ *B. b. jakutensis* — NE Siberia (Lena River to Sea of Okhotsk)
- ____ *B. b. ussuriensis (dauricus, borissowi)* — SE Siberia to ne China, Sakhalin I., n Hokkaido and s Kuril Is.
- ____ *B. b. kiautschensis (jarlandi, setschuanus, inexpectatus)* — W and central China (s to Yunnan and Sichuan) to Korea
- ____ *B. b. swinhoei* — SE China

☐ **Rock Eagle-Owl** *Bubo bengalensis*

Indian subcontinent to Himalayan foothills and w Myanmar

☐ **Pharaoh Eagle-Owl** *Bubo ascalaphus*

____ *B. a. ascalaphus* — NW Africa and n Egypt to w Iraq

____ *B. a. desertorum* — Sahara to Mauritania, Niger, Ethiopia, Arabia and s Iraq

☐ **Cape Eagle-Owl** *Bubo capensis*

____ *B. c. dillonii* — Highlands of s Eritrea and Ethiopia

____ *B. c. mackinderi* — Kenya and Uganda to Zimbabwe, Mozambique and Malawi

____ *B. c. capensis* — Extreme s Namibia and South Africa

☐ **Spotted Eagle-Owl** *Bubo africanus*

____ *B. a. milesi* — SW Arabia, Yemen and Oman

____ *B. a. africanus* — Gabon to Zaire, s Uganda, central Kenya and s to the Cape

____ *B. a. tanae* — SE Kenya (central and lower Tana River and Lali Hills)

☐ **Grayish Eagle-Owl** *Bubo cinerascens*

Senegambia to Ethiopia, Somalia, n Uganda and n Kenya

☐ **Fraser's Eagle-Owl** *Bubo poensis*

Rainforests of Liberia to w Uganda and nw Angola; Bioko

☐ **Usambara Eagle-Owl** *Bubo vosseleri*

NE Tanzania (Usambara and Uluguru mountains)

☐ **Spot-bellied Eagle-Owl** *Bubo nipalensis*

____ *B. n. nipalensis* — Himalayas to India, sw China (Yunnan), Myanmar and Vietnam

____ *B. n. blighi* — Sri Lanka

☐ **Barred Eagle-Owl** *Bubo sumatranus*

____ *B. s. sumatranus* — S Myanmar, peninsular Thailand, Malay Pen., Sumatra, Bangka I.

____ *B. s. strepitans* — Borneo, Java and Bali

☐ **Shelley's Eagle-Owl** *Bubo shelleyi*

Sierra Leone and Liberia to Cameroon, ne Zaire and Gabon

☐ **Verreaux's Eagle-Owl** *Bubo lacteus*

Savanna and woodlands of Africa south of the Sahara

☐ **Dusky Eagle-Owl** *Bubo coromandus*

____ *B. c. coromandus* — Pakistan to central India, s Nepal, Assam and Bangladesh

____ *B. c. klossii* — Extreme s China to s Myanmar and w Thailand

☐ **Akun Eagle-Owl** *Bubo leucostictus*

Sierra Leone and Liberia to Cameroon, Zaire and nw Angola

☐ **Philippine Eagle-Owl** *Bubo philippensis*

____ *B. p. philippensis* — N Philippines (Luzon and Catanduanes)

____ *B. p. mindanensis* — S Philippines (Mindanao, Samar, Leyte and Bohol)

☐ **Blakiston's Fish-Owl** *Ketupa blakistoni*

____ *K. b. piscivorus* — W Manchuria (west of Great Khingan Mountains)

____ *K. b. doerriesi* — SE Siberia and extreme ne China to Korea

____ *K. b. karafutonis* — Sakhalin I.

____ *K. b. blakistoni* — N Japan (s Kuril Islands and Hokkaido)

☐ **Brown Fish-Owl** *Ketupa zeylonensis*

____ *K. z. semenowi* — Extreme se Turkey to Israel, n Syria and nw India

____ *K. z. leschenault* — India south of Himalayas to Myanmar and Thailand

____ *K. z. zeylonensis* — Sri Lanka

____ *K. z. orientalis* — NE Myanmar to se China, Malay Pen., Indochina and Hainan

☐ **Tawny Fish-Owl** *Ketupa flavipes*

Himalayas to s China, ne Myanmar, s Indochina and Taiwan

☐ **Buffy Fish-Owl** *Ketupa ketupu*
_____ *K. k. aagaardi* — S Assam to s Thailand and Vietnam
_____ *K. k. ketupu* — Malay Pen., Riau Arch., Sumatra, Java, Bali, Borneo and Bangka
_____ *K. k. minor* — Nias I. (off nw Sumatra)
_____ *K. k. pageli* — NW Borneo

☐ **Snowy Owl** *Nyctea scandiaca*

Arctic circumpolar; irregular southern post-breeding irruptions

☐ **Pel's Fishing-Owl** *Scotopelia peli*

Locally in riverine forests of Africa south of the Sahara

☐ **Rufous Fishing-Owl** *Scotopelia ussheri*

Rainforests of Sierra Leone, Liberia, Ivory Coast and Ghana

☐ **Vermiculated Fishing-Owl** *Scotopelia bouvieri*

S Cameroon to Cent. African Rep., Zaire, Gabon and n Angola

☐ **Spotted Wood-Owl** *Strix seloputo*
_____ *S. s. seloputo* — S Myanmar, Malay Pen., Thailand, Sumatra and Java
_____ *S. s. baweana* — Bawean I. (Java Sea off n Java)
_____ *S. s. wiepkeni* — S Philippines (Palawan and Calamian Islands)

☐ **Mottled Wood-Owl** *Strix ocellata*
_____ *S. o. grisescens* — Base of Himalayas (Pakistan to Rajasthan and Bihar)
_____ *S. o. grandis* — W India (Kathiawar Peninsula of s Gujarat)
_____ *S. o. ocellata* — Peninsular India

☐ **Brown Wood-Owl** *Strix leptogrammica*
_____ *S. l. newarensis* — Himalayas (Jammu and Kashmir to ne India)
_____ *S. l. ticehursti (orientalis, shahensis)* — Myanmar to se China, Thailand, n Laos and n Vietnam
_____ *S. l. caligata* — Hainan and Taiwan
_____ *S. l. laotiana* — S Laos and central Vietnam (Annam)
_____ *S. l. indranee (connectens)* — Peninsular India
_____ *S. l. ochrogenys* — Sri Lanka
_____ *S. l. maingayi* — S Myanmar, s Thailand and Malay Peninsula
_____ *S. l. myrtha* — Sumatra
_____ *S. l. nyctiphasma* — Banyak I. (off nw Sumatra)
_____ *S. l. niasensis* — Nias I. (off nw Sumatra)
_____ *S. l. chaseni* — Belitung I. (Java Sea off se Sumatra)
_____ *S. l. vaga* — N Borneo
_____ *S. l. leptogrammica* — Central and s Borneo
_____ *S. l. bartelsi* — Java

☐ **Tawny Owl** *Strix aluco*
_____ *S. a. aluco* — N and e Europe to Ukraine, Crimea, Balkans and Black Sea
_____ *S. a. siberiae* — Ural Mountains to w Siberia
_____ *S. a. sylvatica* — Britain, France, Iberia, s Italy, Greece, w and central Turkey
_____ *S. a. mauritanica* — Morocco, Algeria and Tunisia
_____ *S. a. wilkonskii* — NE Turkey, Caucasus and nw Iran to Turkmenistan
_____ *S. a. sanctinicolai* — Zagros Mountains (ne Iraq and w Iran)
_____ *S. a. harmsi* — Turkestan
_____ *S. a. biddulphi* — Pakistan and nw India
_____ *S. a. nivicola* — Nepal to se China, n Myanmar and n Indochina
_____ *S. a. ma* — NE China and Korea
_____ *S. a. yamadae* — Mountains of s Taiwan

☐ **Hume's Owl** *Strix butleri*

Deserts of Syria, Jordan, Arabia, Sinai Pen. and n Egypt

☐ **Spotted Owl** *Strix occidentalis*
_____ *S. o. caurina* — Temperate forests from s British Columbia to n California
_____ *S. o. occidentalis* — Mountains of s California to n Baja (San Pedro Mártir)
_____ *S. o. lucida* — Mountains of sw US to c Mexico (Michoacán and Guanajuato)

☐ **Barred Owl** *Strix varia*

____	*S. v. varia*	SE Alaska to se Canada and e-central US
____	*S. v. georgica*	SE US (Arkansas to e Texas, the Gulf Coast and s Florida)
____	*S. v. helveola*	S-central Texas
____	*S. v. sartorii*	Mountains of n Mexico (Durango) to Veracruz and Oaxaca

☐ **Fulvous Owl** *Strix fulvescens*

Mountains of s Mexico (e Oaxaca and Chiapas) to El Salvador

☐ **Rusty-barred Owl** *Strix hylophila*

Paraguay to se Brazil (Minas Gerais) and extreme ne Argentina

☐ **Rufous-legged Owl** *Strix rufipes*

____	*S. r. rufipes*	Central Chile and w-central Argentina to Tierra del Fuego
____	*S. r. sanborni*	Chiloe I. (Chile)

☐ **Chaco Owl** *Strix chacoensis*

Chaco of w Paraguay and n Argentina

☐ **Ural Owl** *Strix uralensis*

____	*S. u. liturata*	N Europe to nw Russia, n Poland, Belarus and middle Volga
____	*S. u. uralensis*	E European Russia to Sea of Okhotsk
____	*S. u. macroura (carpathaca)*	Carpathian Mountains to Bulgaria and w Balkans
____	*S. u. yenisseensis*	Central Siberian plateau
____	*S. u. nikolskii (dauurica, tatibanai, coreensis)*	Transbaikalia to Sakhalin, ne China and Korea
____	*S. u. japonica*	Hokkaido (n Japan)
____	*S. u. hondoensis (momiyamae)*	N and central Honshu (Japan)
____	*S. u. fuscescens*	S Honshu south to Kyushu (Japan)

☐ **Père David's Owl** *Strix davidi*

Mountains of central China (se Qinghai and Sichuan)

☐ **Great Gray Owl** *Strix nebulosa*

____	*S. n. nebulosa*	Boreal forests of n North America
____	*S. n. lapponica (elisabethae)*	Boreal forests of n Europe, n Asia and Sakhalin

☐ **African Wood-Owl** *Strix woodfordii*

____	*S. w. nuchalis*	Senegambia to s Sudan, Uganda, n Angola, w Zaire; Bioko
____	*S. w. umbrina*	Ethiopia and se Sudan
____	*S. w. nigricantior*	S Somalia to Kenya, Tanzania, Zanzibar and e Zaire
____	*S. w. woodfordii*	S Angola to s Zaire, Botswana, sw Tanzania and South Africa

☐ **Mottled Owl** *Ciccaba virgata*

____	*C. v. squamulata*	W Mexico (Sonora to Guerrero, Guanajuato and Morelos)
____	*C. v. tamaulipensis*	NE Mexico (s Nuevo León and Tamaulipas)
____	*C. v. centralis*	SE Mexico (Oaxaca and Veracruz) to w Panama
____	*C. v. virgata (minuscula)*	E Panama to Colombia, Venezuela and Ecuador; Trinidad
____	*C. v. macconnelli*	The Guianas and Suriname
____	*C. v. superciliaris*	N-central and ne Amazonian Brazil
____	*C. v. borelliana*	E Paraguay to se Brazil and ne Argentina (Misiones)

☐ **Black-and-white Owl** *Ciccaba nigrolineata*

Lowlands of s Mexico to w Ecuador and extreme nw Peru

☐ **Black-banded Owl** *Ciccaba huhula*

____	*C. h. huhula*	E Colombia to the Guianas, ne Brazil, e Peru and nw Argentina
____	*C. h. albomarginata*	E Paraguay to se Brazil and ne Argentina (Misiones)

☐ **Rufous-banded Owl** *Ciccaba albitarsis*

Andes of Colombia to Venezuela, Ecuador, Peru and Bolivia

☐ **Crested Owl** *Lophostrix cristata*

____	*L. c. stricklandi*	S Mexico (Veracruz) to w Panama and w Colombia
____	*L. c. wedeli*	E Panama to ne Colombia and nw Venezuela
____	*L. c. cristata*	S Colombia to n Bolivia, s Venezuela, Guianas, w Amaz. Brazil

☐ **Maned Owl** *Jubula lettii*

Patchily distributed in humid forests of Liberia to e Zaire

☐ **Spectacled Owl** *Pulsatrix perspicillata*

_____ *P. p. saturata* — S Mexico (Veracruz and Oaxaca) to w Panama (Chiriquí)

_____ *P. p. chapmani* — E Costa Rica and Panama to Colombia, w Ecuador and nw Peru

_____ *P. p. perspicillata* — E Colombia to Venezuela, the Guianas, Brazil and n Bolivia

_____ *P. p. trinitatis* — Trinidad

_____ *P. p. boliviana* — S Bolivia and n Argentina

_____ *P. p. pulsatrix* — Paraguay to e Brazil (Bahia) and ne Argentina (Misiones)

☐ **Tawny-browed Owl** *Pulsatrix koeniswaldiana*

E Paraguay to se Brazil and ne Argentina (Misiones)

☐ **Band-bellied Owl** *Pulsatrix melanota*

_____ *P. m. melanota* — Humid forests of se Colombia to e Ecuador and se Peru

_____ *P. m. philoscia* — *Yungas* of w-central Bolivia

☐ **Northern Hawk Owl** *Surnia ulula*

_____ *S. u. caparoch* — Alaska to Canada, Newfoundland and extreme n US

_____ *S. u. ulula* — N Eurasia

_____ *S. u. tianschanica* — Central Asia to nw and ne China and n Mongolia

☐ **Eurasian Pygmy-Owl** *Glaucidium passerinum*

_____ *G. p. passerinum* — Scandinavia, mts. of Europe to Siberia, Sakhalin and ne China

_____ *G. p. orientale* — Central and e Siberia to Manchuria

☐ **Collared Owlet** *Glaucidium brodiei*

_____ *G. b. brodiei* — Pakistan to s China, se Tibet, n Indochina and Malay Peninsula

_____ *G. b. pardalotum* — Taiwan

_____ *G. b. peritum* — Sumatra

_____ *G. b. borneense* — Borneo

☐ **Pearl-spotted Owlet** *Glaucidium perlatum*

_____ *G. p. perlatum* — Senegambia to w Sudan

_____ *G. p. licua* — E Sudan and Ethiopia to n S Africa, Angola and Namibia

☐ **Northern Pygmy-Owl** *Glaucidium californicum*

_____ *G. c. grinnelli* — Coniferous forests of se Alaska to n California

_____ *G. c. swarthy* — Vancouver I.

_____ *G. c. californicum* — Central British Columbia to sw US and nw Mexico

_____ *G. c. pinicola* — Rocky Mountains (w-central US)

☐ **Mountain Pygmy-Owl** *Glaucidium gnoma*

SE Arizona to highlands of Mexico (Chihuahua to Oaxaca)

☐ **Guatemalan Pygmy-Owl** *Glaucidium cobanense*

Mountains of s Mexico (Chiapas) to Guatemala and Honduras

☐ **Cape Pygmy-Owl** *Glaucidium hoskinsii*

Mountains of s Baja California

☐ **Costa Rican Pygmy-Owl** *Glaucidium costaricanum*

Mountains of central Costa Rica to w Panama

☐ **Cloud-forest Pygmy-Owl** *Glaucidium nubicola*

Pacific slope of Western Andes of Colombia and Ecuador

☐ **Andean Pygmy-Owl** *Glaucidium jardinii*

Mountains of n Colombia to w Venezuela, Ecuador and Peru

☐ **Colima Pygmy-Owl** *Glaucidium palmarum*

_____ *G. p. oberholseri* — NW Mexico (Sonora to Sinaloa)

_____ *G. p. palmarum* — W Mexico (Nayarit to Oaxaca)

_____ *G. p. griscomi* — Central Mexico (sw Morelos and ne Guerrero)

☐ **Tamaulipas Pygmy-Owl** *Glaucidium sanchezi*

NE Mexico (sw Tamaulipas, e San Luis Potosí and n Hidalgo)

☐ **Central American Pygmy-Owl** *Glaucidium griseiceps*
_____ *G. g. occulatum*
_____ *G. g. griseiceps*
_____ *G. g. rarum*

SE Mexico (se Veracruz, n Oaxaca and Chiapas)
Guatemala, Belize and Honduras
Costa Rica and Panama

☐ **Subtropical Pygmy-Owl** *Glaucidium parkeri*

East slope of Andes of Ecuador and Peru

☐ **Yungas Pygmy-Owl** *Glaucidium bolivianum*

E slope of Andes of se Peru, w-c Bolivia and nw Argentina

☐ **Amazonian Pygmy-Owl** *Glaucidium hardyi*

SE Venezuela to the Guianas, Amaz. Brazil, se Peru and Bolivia

☐ **Least Pygmy-Owl** *Glaucidium minutissimum*

E Paraguay to se Brazil and ne Argentina (Misiones)

☐ **Ferruginous Pygmy-Owl** *Glaucidium brasilianum*
_____ *G. b. cactorum*
_____ *G. b. saturatum*
_____ *G. b. ridgwayi*
_____ *G. b. medianum*
_____ *G. b. margaritae*
_____ *G. b. phalaenoides*
_____ *G. b. duidae*
_____ *G. b. olivaceum*
_____ *G. b. ucayalae*
_____ *G. b. brasilianum*
_____ *G. b. pallens*
_____ *G. b. stranecki*

SE Arizona and w Mexico (Sonora to Oaxaca)
S Mexico (Chiapas) and Guatemala
S Texas (lower Rio Grande Valley) to Panama (Canal Zone)
Tropical lowlands of n Colombia
Isla Margarita (Venezuela)
Tropical n Venezuela, Trinidad and the Guianas
Tepuis of s Venezuela (Mt. Duida)
Tepuis of s Venezuela (Mt. Auyan-Tepuí)
E base of Andes of se Colombia to Peru and n Bolivia
S Amazonian Brazil to e Paraguay, Uruguay and ne Argentina
Chaco of e Bolivia, w Paraguay and n Argentina
S Uruguay to central Argentina

☐ **Tucuman Pygmy-Owl** *Glaucidium tucumanum*

Subtropical w Argentina (Salta and Tucumán to Córdoba)

☐ **Peruvian Pygmy-Owl** *Glaucidium peruanum*

Lowlands and foothills of sw Ecuador and w Peru

☐ **Austral Pygmy-Owl** *Glaucidium nanum*

Andes of s Chile and s Argentina; winters to n Argentina

☐ **Cuban Pygmy-Owl** *Glaucidium siju*
_____ *G. s. siju*
_____ *G. s. vittatum*

Cuba
Isle of Pines

☐ **Red-chested Owlet** *Glaucidium tephronotum*
_____ *G. t. tephronotum*
_____ *G. t. pycrafti*
_____ *G. t. medje (elgonense)*

Equatorial forests of Liberia, Ivory Coast and Ghana
Forests of s Cameroon
Congo River basin to Zaire, e Uganda and w Kenya

☐ **Sjostedt's Owlet** *Glaucidium sjostedti*

Lowlands of sw Cameroon to Gabon, n Congo and nw Zaire

☐ **Asian Barred Owlet** *Glaucidium cuculoides*
_____ *G. c. cuculoides*
_____ *G. c. austerum*
_____ *G. c. rufescens*
_____ *G. c. bruegeli*
_____ *G. c. delacouri*
_____ *G. c. deignani*
_____ *G. c. whitelyi*
_____ *G. c. persimile*

Himalayas (ne Pakistan and Kashmir to w Sikkim)
E Sikkim to Bhutan, ne Assam and nw Myanmar
NE India, Bangladesh and n Myanmar
S Myanmar and s Thailand
N Indochina
SE Thailand and s Indochina
Sichuan, Yunnan and se China s of Yangtze to ne Vietnam
Hainan (s China)

☐ **Javan Owlet** *Glaucidium castanopterum*

Java and Bali

☐ **Jungle Owlet** *Glaucidium radiatum*
____ *G. r. radiatum* — Himalayas to Bhutan, India, w Myanmar and Sri Lanka
____ *G. r. malabaricum* — SW peninsular India

☐ **Chestnut-backed Owlet** *Glaucidium castanonotum* — Forests of wet zone of Sri Lanka

☐ **African Barred Owlet** *Glaucidium capense*
____ *G. c. scheffleri* — Extreme s coastal Somalia, e Kenya and ne Tanzania
____ *G. c. ngamiense* — Central Tanzania to e Zaire, Angola, Mozambique and Mafia I.
____ *G. c. capense* — S Mozambique to Natal and e Cape Province

☐ **Chestnut Owlet** *Glaucidium castaneum*
____ *G. c. etchecopari* — Patchily distributed in Liberia and Ivory Coast
____ *G. c. castaneum* — NE Zaire (Semliki Valley) and sw Uganda (Bwamba Forest)

☐ **Albertine Owlet** *Glaucidium albertinum* — Known from 5 specimens from ne Zaire and n Rwanda

☐ **Long-whiskered Owlet** *Xenoglaux loweryi* — Cloud forests of n Peru (Amazonas and San Martín)

☐ **Elf Owl** *Microthene whitneyi*
____ *M. w. whitneyi* — Arid sw US and adjacent nw Mexico (Sonora)
____ *M. w. idonea* — S Texas (lower Rio Grand Valley) to central Mexico
____ *M. w. sanfordi* — Lower Baja California (south of latitude 23°40'N)
____ *M. w. graysoni†* — Formerly Socorro I. (Revillagigedo Is. off w Mexico). Extinct

☐ **Burrowing Owl** *Athene cunicularia*
____ *A. c. hypugaea* — SW Canada to El Salvador
____ *A. c. rostrata* — Isla Clarión (Revillagigedo Islands off w Mexico)
____ *A. c. floridana* — Prairies of central and s Florida, Bahamas, Cuba, Isle of Pines
____ *A. c. troglodytes* — Hispaniola, Gonâve and Beata islands
____ *A. c. amaura†* — Formerly Nevis and Antigua (West Indies). Extinct
____ *A. c. guadeloupensis†* — Formerly Guadeloupe (West Indies). Extinct
____ *A. c. arubensis* — Aruba (Netherlands Antilles)
____ *A. c. brachyptera* — Isla Margarita (off n Venezuela)
____ *A. c. apurensis* — N-central Venezuela
____ *A. c. minor* — S Guyana and adjacent extreme n Brazil (Roraima)
____ *A. c. carrikeri* — E Colombia
____ *A. c. tolimae* — W Colombia (Tolima)
____ *A. c. pichinchae* — W Ecuador (except for arid littoral)
____ *A. c. punensis* — Arid littoral of sw Ecuador and nw Peru
____ *A. c. intermedia* — Coastal w Peru (Paita to Pacasmayo)
____ *A. c. nanodes* — Arid littoral of w Peru (Trujillo to Arequipa)
____ *A. c. juninensis* — Andes of central Peru (Junín) to w Bolivia and nw Argentina
____ *A. c. boliviana* — Bolivia
____ *A. c. grallaria* — E Brazil (Maranhão to Mato Grosso and Paraná)
____ *A. c. partridge* — N Argentina (Corrientes Province)
____ *A. c. cunicularia* — S Bolivia and s Brazil to Paraguay and Tierra del Fuego

☐ **Spotted Owlet** *Athene brama*
____ *A. b. albida* — S Iran and s Pakistan
____ *A. b. indica* — N and central peninsular India
____ *A. b. brama* — Southern India
____ *A. b. pulchra* — Myanmar, extreme sw China, s Laos, Cambodia and s Vietnam

☐ **Forest Owl** *Athene blewitti* — Rediscovered in central India in 1998 after a 100-year absence

☐ **Little Owl** *Athene noctua*
____ *A. n. vidalii* — S Baltic to Iberian Pen., Balearic Is., Poland and nw Russia
____ *A. n. noctua* — Sardinia, Corsica, Italy and Yugoslavia to Carpathian Mts.

____ *A. n. indigena*	Balkans to Turkey, s Russia, Transcaucasia and sw Siberia
____ *A. n. glaux*	N Africa and coastal Israel (north to Haifa)
____ *A. n. saharae (solitudinis)*	Morocco to Tunisia s of Atlas, Libya coast, w Egypt and Arabia
____ *A. n. spilogastra*	Red Sea coast of e Sudan and n Ethiopia
____ *A. n. somaliensis*	E Ethiopia and Somalia
____ *A. n. lilith*	Cyprus: inland Middle East from se Turkey to s Sinai
____ *A. n. bactriana*	Azerbaijan to Iraq, Iran, Afghanistan and Lake Balkhash
____ *A. n. orientalis*	Extreme nw China and adjacent Siberia
____ *A. n. impasta*	W-central China (Kokonor and w Gansu)
____ *A. n. ludlowi*	S-central China and Tibet to n Himalayas
A. n. plumipes	NE China, Mongolia and Ussuriland

☐ **Boreal Owl** *Aegolius funereus*

____ *A. f. funereus*	N Scandinavia to Pyrénées and Urals (except for Caucasus Mts.)
____ *A. f. caucasicus*	N Caucasus Mountains
____ *A. f. pallens*	W Siberia, Tien Shan and s Siberia east to Sakhalin
____ *A. f. magnus*	NE Siberia (Kolyma to Kamchatka Peninsula)
____ *A. f. beickianus*	Extreme nw India (Lahul) to sw China (Qinghai)
____ *A. f. richardsoni*	Central Alaska and n Canada to n US

☐ **Northern Saw-whet Owl** *Aegolius acadicus*

____ *A. a. acadicus*	Mixed woodlands of s Alaska to s Mexico
____ *A. a. brooksi*	Queen Charlotte Islands (off British Columbia)

☐ **Unspotted Saw-whet Owl** *Aegolius ridgwayi*

____ *A. r. tacanensis*	Oak-pine woodlands of s Mexico (Chiapas)
____ *A. r. rostratus*	Locally from Guatemala to nw El Salvador
____ *A. r. ridgwayi*	Costa Rica and w Panama

☐ **Buff-fronted Owl** *Aegolius harrisii*

____ *A. h. harrisii*	Patchily distributed Colombia to Ecuador, Peru and Venezuela
____ *A. h. iheringi*	E Bolivia to Paraguay, e Brazil, Uruguay and ne Argentina
____ *A. h. dabbenei*	W Bolivia and nw Argentina (Tucumán, Salta and Jujuy)

☐ **Rufous Owl** *Ninox rufa*

____ *N. r. humeralis (aruensis)*	New Guinea, Aru Islands and Waigeo I.
____ *N. r. rufa*	Coastal n Australia (Kimberleys and n Northern Territory)
____ *N. r. meesi*	Coastal Cape York Pen. south to Endeavor R. and Mitchell R.
____ *N. r. queenslandica*	Coastal s Queensland (Endeavour River to Rockhamton)

☐ **Powerful Owl** *Ninox strenua*

	E Australia (se Queensland to Victoria and se South Australia)

☐ **Barking Owl** *Ninox connivens*

____ *N. c. rufostrigata*	N Moluccas (Halmahera, Morotai, Bacan and Obi)
____ *N. c. assimilis*	E New Guinea, Manam I. and Karkar I.
____ *N. c. peninsularis (occidentalis)*	Coastal n Australia and islands in Torres Strait
____ *N. c. connivens*	Coastal sw Australia to s Queensland

☐ **Sumba Boobook** *Ninox rudolfi*

	Lowlands of Sumba I. (w Lesser Sundas)

☐ **Andaman Hawk-Owl** *Ninox affinis*

	Andaman Islands and Nicobar Islands

☐ **Morepork** *Ninox novaeseelandiae*

____ *N. n. leucopsis*	Tasmania and islands in Bass Strait
____ *N. n. albaria†*	Lord Howe I. Extinct
____ *N. n. undulata*	Norfolk I.
____ *N. n. novaeseelandiae*	New Zealand and offshore islands

☐ **Southern Boobook** *Ninox boobook*

_____	*N. b. rotiensis*	Roti (Lesser Sundas)
_____	*N. b. fusca*	Timor (e Lesser Sundas)
_____	*N. b. plesseni*	Alor (north of Timor)
_____	*N. b. moae*	Moa, Leti and Romang islands (e of Timor)
_____	*N. b. cinnamomina*	Babar I. (e of Timor)
_____	*N. b. remigialis*	Kai Islands
_____	*N. b. pusilla*	S New Guinea
_____	*N. b. ocellata*	Sawu (Lesser Sundas) and nw Australia
_____	*N. b. lurida*	NE Australia (ne Queensland between Cooktown and Paluma)
_____	*N. b. boobook*	Coastal e Australia (north to s Queensland) and Tasmania

☐ **Brown Hawk-Owl** *Ninox scutulata*

_____	*N. s. ussuriensis*	SE Siberia to se Manchuria and n Korea
_____	*N. s. japonica*	E China, Korea, Japan and Taiwan
_____	*N. s. lugubris*	N India to w Assam and central peninsular India
_____	*N. s. hirsuta*	S India and Sri Lanka
_____	*N. s. obscura*	Andaman Islands and Nicobar Islands
_____	*N. s. burmarnica*	E Assam to s Yunnan, n Malay Pen., Thailand and Indochina
_____	*N. s. palawanensis*	Palawan (sw Philippines)
_____	*N. s. randi*	Philippine Islands and Sulu Archipelago
_____	*N. s. scutulata (malaccensis)*	S Malay Peninsula, Riau Archipelago, Sumatra and Bangka I.
_____	*N. s. javanensis*	W Java
_____	*N. s. borneensis*	Borneo and North Natuna Islands

☐ **White-browed Owl** *Ninox superciliaris*

Forests and semiarid scrub of ne, sw and s Madagascar

☐ **Philippine Hawk-Owl** *Ninox philippensis*

_____	*N. p. philippensis*	Leyte, Luzon, Marinduque, Samar, Polillo and Catanduanes
_____	*N. p. mindorensis*	Mindoro (n Philippines)
_____	*N. p. spilonota*	Philippines (Cebu, Sibuyan, Tablas and Camiguin Sur)
_____	*N. p. proxima (ticaoensis)*	Philippines (Masbate and Ticao)
_____	*N. p. centralis*	Philippines (Guimaras, Negros, Panay and Siquijor)
_____	*N. p. spilocephala*	Philippines (Basilan, Mindanao, Siargao and Dinagat)
_____	*N. p. reyi (everetti)*	Jolo, Tawitawi and adjacent islands in Sulu Archipelago

☐ **Ochre-bellied Hawk-Owl** *Ninox ochracea*

Humid forests of Sulawesi and Butung I.

☐ **Cinnabar Hawk-Owl** *Ninox ios*

NE Sulawesi (Bogani Nani Wartabone National Park)

☐ **Moluccan Hawk-Owl** *Ninox squamipila*

_____	*N. s. hypogramma*	N Moluccas (Halmahera, Ternate and Bacan)
_____	*N. s. hantu*	Buru (s Moluccas)
_____	*N. s. squamipila*	Seram (s Moluccas)
_____	*N. s. forbesi*	Tanimbar Islands (Arafura Sea)

☐ **Christmas Island Hawk-Owl** *Ninox natalis*

Christmas I. (Indian Ocean south of Java)

☐ **Jungle Hawk-Owl** *Ninox theomacha*

_____	*N. t. hoedtii*	Waigeo and Misool islands (off w New Guinea)
_____	*N. t. theomacha*	New Guinea
_____	*N. t. goldii*	D'Entrecasteaux Arch. (Goodenough, Fergusson, Normanby)
_____	*N. t. rosseliana*	Louisiade Archipelago (Tagula and Rossel)

☐ **Manus Hawk-Owl** *Ninox meeki*

Manus (Admiralty Islands)

☐ **Speckled Hawk-Owl** *Ninox punctulata*

Sulawesi, Kabaena, Muna and Butung islands

☐ **Bismarck Hawk-Owl** *Ninox variegata*
_____ *N. v. superior* — New Hanover (Bismarck Archipelago)
_____ *N. v. variegata* — New Ireland (Bismarck Archipelago)

☐ **New Britain Hawk-Owl** *Ninox odiosa* — New Britain (Bismarck Archipelago)

☐ **Solomon Hawk-Owl** *Ninox jacquinoti*
_____ *N. j. eichhorni* — N Solomon Islands (Buka, Bougainville and Choiseul)
_____ *N. j. jacquinoti* — Central Solomon Islands (Santa Isabel and San Jorge)
_____ *N. j. granti* — Guadalcanal (s Solomon Islands)
_____ *N. j. mono* — Mono (nw Solomon Islands)
_____ *N. j. floridae* — Florida Group (central Solomon Islands)
_____ *N. j. malaitae* — Malaita (s Solomon Islands)
_____ *N. j. roseoaxillaris* — S Solomon Islands (Bauro and San Cristóbal)

☐ **Papuan Hawk-Owl** *Uroglaux dimorpha* — Sparsely distributed New Guinea and Yapen I.

☐ **Jamaican Owl** *Pseudoscops grammicus* — Woodlands of Jamaica

☐ **Striped Owl** *Pseudoscops clamator*
_____ *P. c. forbesi* — Tropical s Mexico to Panama
_____ *P. c. clamator* — Colombia to Venezuela, e Peru and central and ne Brazil
_____ *P. c. oberi* — Trinidad and Tobago
_____ *P. c. midas* — E Bolivia to Paraguay, s Brazil, Uruguay and n Argentina

☐ **Stygian Owl** *Asio stygius*
_____ *A. s. lambi* — Highlands of w Mexico (sw Chihuahua to Jalisco)
_____ *A. s. robustus* — S Mexico (Guerrero and Veracruz) to Venezuela and Ecuador
_____ *A. s. siguapa* — Cuba and Isle of Pines
_____ *A. s. noctipetens* — Hispaniola and Gonâve I.
_____ *A. s. stygius* — E Bolivia to n and se Brazil and ne Argentina
_____ *A. s. barberoi* — Paraguay and n Argentina

☐ **Northern Long-eared Owl** *Asio otus*
_____ *A. o. tuftsi* — W Canada to nw Baja, s Texas and n Mexico (Nuevo León)
_____ *A. o. wilsonianus* — S-central and se Canada to s-central US
_____ *A. o. otus* — Europe, Asia and North Africa
_____ *A. o. canariensis* — Canary Islands

☐ **African Long-eared Owl** *Asio abyssinicus*
_____ *A. a. abyssinicus* — Highlands of Eritrea and Ethiopia
_____ *A. a. graueri* — Mt. Kenya and Ruwenzori Mts. to Mt. Kabobo (e Zaire)

☐ **Madagascar Long-eared Owl** *Asio madagascariensis* — Forests of Madagascar

☐ **Short-eared Owl** *Asio flammeus*
_____ *A. f. flammeus* — North America, Europe, n Asia and North Africa
_____ *A. f. ponapensis* — Pohnpei (e Caroline Islands)
_____ *A. f. sandwichensis* — Hawaiian Islands
_____ *A. f. domingensis* — Hispaniola and (?) Cuba
_____ *A. f. portoricensis* — Puerto Rico
_____ *A. f. pallidicaudus* — N Venezuela and Guyana
_____ *A. f. bogotensis* — Andes of Colombia, Ecuador and nw Peru
_____ *A. f. galapagoensis* — Galapagos Islands
_____ *A. f. suinda* — S Peru to Bolivia, se Brazil and Tierra del Fuego
_____ *A. f. sanfordi* — Falkland Islands

☐ **Marsh Owl** *Asio capensis*
____ A. c. tingitanus — NW Morocco
____ A. c. capensis — Patchily distributed Senegambia to Ethiopia and South Africa
____ A. c. hova — Grasslands and marshes of Madagascar

☐ **Fearful Owl** *Nesasio solomonensis*
Solomon Islands (Bougainville, Santa Isabel and Choiseul)

ORDER: CAPRIMULGIFORMES
FAMILY: STEATORNITHIDAE (Oilbird—1)

☐ **Oilbird** *Steatornis caripensis*
Locally from Panama and n S Am. to w Bolivia; Trinidad

ORDER: CAPRIMULGIFORMES
FAMILY: AEGOTHELIDAE (Owlet-Nightjars—9)

☐ **Feline Owlet-Nightjar** *Aegotheles insignis*
Mountains of New Guinea (Vogelkop to se New Guinea)

☐ **Spangled Owlet-Nightjar** *Aegotheles tatei*
S New Guinea (lower elevations of Fly River headwaters)

☐ **Moluccan Owlet-Nightjar** *Aegotheles crinifrons*
N Moluccas (Halmahera, Kasiruta and Bacan)

☐ **Wallace's Owlet-Nightjar** *Aegotheles wallacii*
____ A. w. wallacii — W New Guinea and Aru Islands
____ A. w. gigas — Weyland Mountains (w-central New Guinea)
____ A. w. manni — N coastal mountains of New Guinea (Mt. Menawa and Mt. Turu)

☐ **Archbold's Owlet-Nightjar** *Aegotheles archboldi*
Central New Guinea (Wissel Lakes region)

☐ **Mountain Owlet-Nightjar** *Aegotheles albertisi*
____ A. a. albertisi — Arfak Mountains (nw New Guinea)
____ A. a. wondiwoi — Wandammen Peninsula (New Guinea)
____ A. a. salvadorii — Mountains of New Guinea (Weyland Mts. to se New Guinea)

☐ **New Caledonian Owlet-Nightjar** *Aegotheles savesi*
Known from an 1881 specimen from New Caledonia. Extinct?

☐ **Barred Owlet-Nightjar** *Aegotheles bennettii*
____ A. b. affinis — Arfak Mountains (nw New Guinea)
____ A. b. wiedenfeldi — N New Guinea (Idenburg River to Holnicote Bay)
____ A. b. terborghi — E highlands of Papua New Guinea (Karimui basin region)
____ A. b. bennettii — Coastal se New Guinea (Koembe River to Milne Bay)
____ A. b. plumiferus — D'Entrecasteaux Archipelago (Fergusson and Goodenough)

☐ **Australian Owlet-Nightjar** *Aegotheles cristatus*
____ A. c. cristatus (major, leucogaster) — SE New Guinea and Australia
____ A. c. tasmanicus — Tasmania

ORDER: CAPRIMULGIFORMES
FAMILY: PODARGIDAE (Frogmouths—12)

☐ **Tawny Frogmouth** *Podargus strigoides*
____ P. s. phalaenoides (lilae, gouldi) — N Australia (north of latitude 20°S)
____ P. s. brachypterus — Mainland Australia (west of Great Dividing Range)
____ P. s. strigoides — Australia (east of Great Dividing Range) and Tasmania

☐ **Marbled Frogmouth** *Podargus ocellatus*
    ____ *P. o. ocellatus* — New Guinea, w Papuan is., Aru Is. and islands in Geelvink Bay
    ____ *P. o. intermedius* — Trobriand Islands and D'Entrecasteaux Archipelago
    ____ *P. o. meeki* — Tagula I. (Louisiade Archipelago)
    ____ *P. o. inexpectatus* — N Solomon Islands (Bougainville, Choiseul and Santa Isabel)
    ____ *P. o. marmoratus* — NE Australia (Cape York Peninsula)
    ____ *P. o. plumiferus* — Coastal e Australia (se Queensland to ne New South Wales)

☐ **Papuan Frogmouth** *Podargus papuensis* — New Guinea, Aru, w Papuan is., Solomon Is. and Cape York Pen.

☐ **Large Frogmouth** *Batrachostomus auritus* — S Thailand, Malaysia, Sumatra, Borneo, N Natuna and Labuan is.

☐ **Dulit Frogmouth** *Batrachostomus harterti* — Mountains of n and central Borneo

☐ **Philippine Frogmouth** *Batrachostomus septimus*
    ____ *B. s. microrhynchus* — N Philippines (mountains of Luzon and Catanduanes)
    ____ *B. s. menagei* — Central Philippines (Negros and Panay)
    ____ *B. s. septimus* — Philippines (Basilan, Mindanao, Leyte, Bohol and Samar)

☐ **Gould's Frogmouth** *Batrachostomus stellatus* — Pen. Thailand to Malay Pen., Sumatra, Borneo and adj. islands

☐ **Ceylon Frogmouth** *Batrachostomus moniliger* — Humid forests of sw India and Sri Lanka

☐ **Hodgson's Frogmouth** *Batrachostomus hodgsoni* — NE India to Myanmar, sw China, nw Thailand, Laos and Annam

☐ **Short-tailed Frogmouth** *Batrachostomus poliolophus*
    ____ *B. p. poliolophus* — Montane forests of Sumatra
    ____ *B. p. mixtus* — Montane forests of Borneo

☐ **Javan Frogmouth** *Batrachostomus javensis*
    ____ *B. j. continentalis* — S Myanmar to Thailand, s Laos and central Vietnam
    ____ *B. j. affinis (chaseni)* — SE peninsular Thailand to Sumatra, Borneo and Palawan
    ____ *B. j. javensis* — Lowlands of w and central Java

☐ **Sunda Frogmouth** *Batrachostomus cornutus*
    ____ *B. c. cornutus* — Sumatra, Borneo, Bangka, Belitung and Banggi islands
    ____ *B. c. longicaudatus* — Kangean Islands (ne of Java)

ORDER: CAPRIMULGIFORMES
FAMILY: NYCTIBIIDAE (Potoos—7)

☐ **Great Potoo** *Nyctibius grandis* — Extreme s Mexico to n Bolivia, Paraguay and se Brazil

☐ **Long-tailed Potoo** *Nyctibius aethereus*
    ____ *N. a. chocoensis* — Locally in w Colombia (Chocó)
    ____ *N. a. longicaudatus* — Tropical e Ecuador to Peru and the Guianas
    ____ *N. a. aethereus* — SE Paraguay to se Brazil and ne Argentina

☐ **Northern Potoo** *Nyctibius jamaicensis*
    ____ *N. j. lambi* — Pacific slope of w Mexico
    ____ *N. j. mexicanus* — E and s Mexico to El Salvador, Honduras and Roatán I.
    ____ *N. j. costaricensis* — Pacific slope of Nicaragua, Costa Rica and adj. w Panama
    ____ *N. j. jamaicensis* — Jamaica
    ____ *N. j. abbotti* — Hispaniola and Gonâve I.

☐ **Andean Potoo** *Nyctibius maculosus* — Locally in Andes of e Colombia to w Venezuela and w Bolivia

☐ **Common Potoo** *Nyctibius griseus*

    ____ *N. g. panamensis*   Nicaragua and sw Costa Rica to nw Venezuela and w Ecuador

    ____ *N. g. griseus (cornutus)*   Colombia to Guianas, Trinidad, Tobago, Brazil and n Argentina

☐ **White-winged Potoo** *Nyctibius leucopterus*

    N Amazonian Brazil; e Brazil (Bahia)

☐ **Rufous Potoo** *Nyctibius bracteatus*

    Tropical e Ecuador and e Peru to n Brazil and Guyana

ORDER: CAPRIMULGIFORMES
FAMILY: CAPRIMULGIDAE (Nightjars—89)

☐ **Short-tailed Nighthawk** *Lurocalis semitorquatus*

    ____ *L. s. stonei*   SE Mexico to Guatemala, n Honduras and ne Nicaragua

    ____ *L. s. noctivagus*   Costa Rica to Panama, coastal w Colombia and nw Ecuador

    ____ *L. s. semitorquatus*   NE Colombia to the Guianas, n Brazil, Trinidad and Tobago

    ____ *L. s. schaeferi*   N Venezuela

    ____ *L. s. nattereri*   E Ecuador to e Peru, Brazil s of the Amazon and ne Argentina

☐ **Rufous-bellied Nighthawk** *Lurocalis rufiventris*

    Andes of sw Colombia to w Venezuela, Ecuador, Peru and Bolivia

☐ **Least Nighthawk** *Chordeiles pusillus*

    ____ *C. p. septentrionalis*   E Colombia to s Venezuela, the Guianas and adjacent Brazil

    ____ *C. p. esmeraldae*   SE Colombia to s Venezuela and extreme nw Brazil

    ____ *C. p. xerophilus*   Extreme ne Brazil (Paraíba and Pernambuco)

    ____ *C. p. novaesi*   NE Brazil (Maranhão and Piauí)

    ____ *C. p. pusillus*   E Brazil (Tocantins, Bahia and Goiás)

    ____ *C. p. saturatus*   Extreme e Bolivia and w-central Brazil

☐ **Bahia Nighthawk** *Chordeiles vieilliardi*

    E Brazil (xeric *caatinga* of n Bahia)

☐ **Sand-colored Nighthawk** *Chordeiles rupestris*

    ____ *C. r. xyostictus*   Sandbars and river banks of central Colombia

    ____ *C. r. rupestris*   SE Colombia to Venezuela, c Brazil, ne Peru and c Bolivia

☐ **Lesser Nighthawk** *Chordeiles acutipennis*

    ____ *C. a. texensis*   SW US to central Mexico: winters to n Colombia

    ____ *C. a. micromeris*   N Yucatán Pen., Isla Mujeres and Belize; winters to Panama

    ____ *C. a. littoralis*   S Mexico to Costa Rica

    ____ *C. a. acutipennis*   Tropical n South America to n Bolivia, Paraguay and Brazil

    ____ *C. a. crissalis*   SW Colombia

    ____ *C. a. aequatorialis*   W Colombia, w Ecuador and adjacent nw Peru

    ____ *C. a. exilis*   W Peru to extreme n Chile

☐ **Common Nighthawk** *Chordeiles minor*

    ____ *C. m. minor*   Central and s Canada to n and ne US; winters to n Argentina

    ____ *C. m. hesperis*   SW Canada and w US; winters n South America

    ____ *C. m. sennetti*   S-central Canada and n-central US ; winters to South America

    ____ *C. m. howelli*   W-central and s-central US; winters to South America

    ____ *C. m. henryi*   SW US and n-central Mexico; winters to Colombia

    ____ *C. m. asserriensis*   S-central US to extreme n Mexico (n Tamaulipas)

    ____ *C. m. chapmani*   SE US; winters to Argentina

    ____ *C. m. panamensis*   E Honduras, Belize and Nicaragua to Panama; winters to S Am.

☐ **Antillean Nighthawk** *Chordeiles gundlachii*

    ____ *C. g. vicinus*   S Florida and the Bahamas

    ____ *C. g. gundlachii*   Cuba, Isle of Pines, Jamaica, Hispaniola, Puerto Rico, Virgin Is.

☐ **Nacunda Nighthawk** *Podager nacunda*
_____   *P. n. minor*   Colombia to Venezuela, Trinidad, the Guianas and n Brazil
_____   *P. n. nacunda*   E Peru and Brazil s of Amazon to Paraguay and c Argentina

☐ **Band-tailed Nighthawk** *Nyctiprogne leucopyga*
_____   *N. l. pallida*   Tropical ne Colombia to central Venezuela
_____   *N. l. leucopyga*   E Venezuela to the Guianas and n Brazil
_____   *N. l. exigua*   Tropical e Colombia and s Venezuela
_____   *N. l. latifascia*   Extreme s Venezuela
_____   *N. l. majuscula*   NE Peru to e Bolivia and central Brazil

☐ **Spotted Nightjar** *Eurostopodus argus*
                                           Australia and Tasmania; winters to Aru Is. and Lesser Sundas

☐ **White-throated Nightjar** *Eurostopodus mystacalis*
_____   *E. m. nigripennis*   N and central Solomon Islands
_____   *E. m. exul*   New Caledonia
_____   *E. m. mystacalis (gilberti)*   E Australia; winters to New Guinea

☐ **Diabolical Nightjar** *Eurostopodus diabolicus*
                                           Single 1931 specimen from ne Sulawesi (Kalabat Volcano)

☐ **Papuan Nightjar** *Eurostopodus papuensis*
                                           Lowlands of New Guinea and Salawati I.

☐ **Archbold's Nightjar** *Eurostopodus archboldi*
                                           Highlands of New Guinea

☐ **Malaysian Nightjar** *Eurostopodus temminckii*
                                           S Thailand to Malaysia, Sumatra, Borneo and adjacent islands

☐ **Great Eared-Nightjar** *Eurostopodus macrotis*
_____   *E. m. bourdilloni*   SW India
_____   *E. m. cerviniceps*   Bangladesh and ne India to s China, Indochina and n Malaysia
_____   *E. m. jacobsoni*   Simeulue I. (off nw Sumatra)
_____   *E. m. macrotis*   N and e Philippine Islands
_____   *E. m. macropterus*   Sulawesi, Talaud Is., Sangihe I., Banggai Is. and Sula Is.

☐ **Pauraque** *Nyctidromus albicollis*
_____   *N. a. insularis*   Tres Marías Islands (off w Mexico)
_____   *N. a. merrilli*   Lower Rio Grande Valley to Tamaulipas; winters to Puebla
_____   *N. a. yucatanensis*   Tropical n Mexico to Belize, Cozumel I. and Guatemala
_____   *N. a. intercedens*   S Guatemala to Costa Rica and w Panama
_____   *N. a. gilvus*   Panama and n Colombia
_____   *N. a. albicollis*   E Colombia to Venezuela, Guianas, ne Brazil and n Bolivia
_____   *N. a. derbyanus*   Central and s Brazil to ne Argentina

☐ **Common Poorwill** *Phalaenoptilus nuttallii*
_____   *P. n. nuttallii*   S Br. Columbia to w US and n Mexico; winters to c Mexico
_____   *P. n. californicus*   California (west of the Sierra Nevada) to n Baja
_____   *P. n. hueyi*   Lower Colorado River of California; n Baja and sw Arizona
_____   *P. n. dickeyi*   S Baja California (south of latitude 30°N)
_____   *P. n. adustus*   Extreme s Arizona to n Mexico (central Sonora)

☐ **Least Poorwill** *Siphonorhis brewsteri*
                                           Semiarid lowlands of Hispaniola and Gonâve I.

☐ **Eared Poorwill** *Nyctiphrynus mcleodii*
_____   *N. m. mcleodii*   W Mexico (Chihuahua and s Sonora to Jalisco and Colima)
_____   *N. m. rayi*   Oak-pine woodlands of w-central Mexico (Guerrero)

☐ **Yucatan Poorwill** *Nyctiphrynus yucatanicus*
                                           S Mexico (Yucatán Pen.) to n Belize and Petén of n Guatemala

☐ **Choco Poorwill** *Nyctiphrynus rosenbergi*
                                           W Colombia (Chocó) and extreme nw Ecuador

☐ **Ocellated Poorwill** *Nyctiphrynus ocellatus*

_____   *N. o. lautus*   E Honduras to Nicaragua, Costa Rica and (?) w Panama

_____   *N. o. ocellatus*   Colombia to e Ecuador, Peru, Brazil, Paraguay, ne Argentina

☐ **Chuck-will's-widow** *Caprimulgus carolinensis*

      E US; winters se US to Greater Antilles and n South America

☐ **Rufous Nightjar** *Caprimulgus rufus*

_____   *C. r. minimus*   SE Costa Rica and Panama to Colombia and Venezuela; Coiba I.

_____   *C. r. otiosus*   St. Lucia (Lesser Antilles)

_____   *C. r. rufus (noctivigularus)*   S Venezuela to the Guianas and n-central Brazil

_____   *C. r. rutilus (ornatus, cortapau)*   S Brazil to e Bolivia, Paraguay and ne Argentina

_____   *C. r. saltarius*   NW Argentina and se Bolivia

☐ **Greater Antillean Nightjar** *Caprimulgus cubanensis*

_____   *C. c. cubanensis*   Cuba

_____   *C. c. insulaepinorum*   Isle of Pines and Cayo Coco

☐ **Hispaniolan Nightjar** *Caprimulgus ekmani*

      Hispaniola

☐ **Tawny-collared Nightjar** *Caprimulgus salvini*

      Tropical e Mexico (Nuevo León to Oaxaca and Chiapas)

☐ **Yucatan Nightjar** *Caprimulgus badius*

      Yucatán Pen. and Cozumel I.; winters to Belize and n Honduras

☐ **Silky-tailed Nightjar** *Caprimulgus sericocaudatus*

_____   *C. s. mengeli*   N Peru to nw Bolivia and n Brazil

_____   *C. s. sericocaudatus*   SE Brazil to e Paraguay and ne Argentina

☐ **Buff-collared Nightjar** *Caprimulgus ridgwayi*

_____   *C. r. ridgwayi*   SE Arizona and w Mexico (Sonora to Oaxaca)

_____   *C. r. troglodytes*   Central Guatemala to Honduras and central Nicaragua

☐ **Whip-poor-will** *Caprimulgus vociferus*

_____   *C. v. vociferus*   S Canada and e US; winters to Cuba and w Panama

_____   *C. v. arizonae*   SW US to central Mexico

_____   *C. v. setosus*   E Mexico

_____   *C. v. oaxacae*   SW Mexico

_____   *C. v. chiapensis*   SE Mexico and highlands of Guatemala

_____   *C. v. vermiculatus*   Highlands of Honduras and El Salvador

☐ **Puerto Rican Nightjar** *Caprimulgus noctitherus*

      Dry lowland forests of sw Puerto Rico

☐ **Dusky Nightjar** *Caprimulgus saturatus*

      Montane forests of Costa Rica and w Panama

☐ **Band-winged Nightjar** *Caprimulgus longirostris*

_____   *C. l. ruficervix*   Andes of Colombia to w Venezuela and Ecuador

_____   *C. l. roraimae*   *Tepuis* of s Venezuela

_____   *C. l. atripunctatus*   Andes of Peru to Bolivia, nw Argentina and n Chile

_____   *C. l. decussatus*   Arid littoral of w Peru and extreme n Chile

_____   *C. l. bifasciatus*   Chile and w Argentina

_____   *C. l. longirostris*   SE Brazil to Paraguay, Uruguay and ne Argentina

_____   *C. l. patagonicus*   Central and s Argentina

☐ **White-winged Nightjar** *Caprimulgus candicans*

      Interior of n Bolivia, s-central Brazil and e Paraguay

☐ **Pygmy Nightjar** *Caprimulgus hirundinaceus*

_____   *C. h. cearae*   E Brazil (Ceará to extreme n Bahia)

_____   *C. h. hirundinaceus*   NE Brazil (s Piauí to Bahia and Alagoas)

_____   *C. h. vielliardi*   E Brazil (Espírito Santo)

☐ **Little Nightjar** *Caprimulgus parvulus*
_____   *C. p. heterurus*   N Colombia to central Venezuela
_____   *C. p. parvulus*   E Peru to Brazil s of the Amazon, Uruguay and n Argentina

☐ **Spot-tailed Nightjar** *Caprimulgus maculicaudus*
         Locally from se Mexico to n Bolivia, e Paraguay and se Brazil

☐ **White-tailed Nightjar** *Caprimulgus cayennensis*
_____   *C. c. albicauda*   Savanna of se Costa Rica to nw Colombia
_____   *C. c. apertus*   W Colombia to extreme n Ecuador
_____   *C. c. insularis*   NE Colombia, nw Venezuela, Isla Margarita and adj. islands
_____   *C. c. manati*   Martinique (Lesser Antilles)
_____   *C. c. leopetes*   Trinidad, Tobago, Bocas Islands and Little Tobago
_____   *C. c. cayennensis*   E Colombia to Venezuela, the Guianas and extreme n Brazil

☐ **Scrub Nightjar** *Caprimulgus anthonyi*
         Lowlands of sw Ecuador and nw Peru

☐ **Cayenne Nightjar** *Caprimulgus maculosus*
         Known from a 1917 specimen from French Guiana

☐ **Blackish Nightjar** *Caprimulgus nigrescens*
         E Colombia to s Venezuela, the Guianas, Bolivia and Brazil

☐ **Roraiman Nightjar** *Caprimulgus whitelyi*
         Tepuis of se Venezuela

☐ **Brown Nightjar** *Caprimulgus binotatus*
         Locally from Liberia to n Gabon and central Zaire

☐ **Red-necked Nightjar** *Caprimulgus ruficollis*
_____   *C. r. ruficollis*   Arid Iberian Peninsula and n Morocco
_____   *C. r. desertorum*   NE Morocco, n Algeria and n Tunisia; winters mainly in Mali

☐ **Jungle Nightjar** *Caprimulgus indicus*
_____   *C. i. hazarae*   NE Pakistan to Bangladesh, s China, Myanmar and Malay Pen.
_____   *C. i. indicus*   Peninsular India south of the Himalayas
_____   *C. i. kelaarti*   Sri Lanka
_____   *C. i. jotaka*   SE Siberia to e China, Japan and Korea; winters to Gr. Sundas
_____   *C. i. phalaena*   Palau Islands (w Caroline Islands)

☐ **Eurasian Nightjar** *Caprimulgus europaeus*
_____   *C. e. europaeus*   N and c Europe to n Asia and L. Baikal area; winters to Africa
_____   *C. e. meridionalis*   Mediterranean basin to nw Iran and Caspian Sea
_____   *C. e. sarudnyi*   E side of Caspian Sea (Kazakstan) to Altai Mountains
_____   *C. e. unwini*   Iraq and Iran to w Tien Shan, Turkmenistan and Uzbekistan
_____   *C. e. plumipes*   NW China to w Mongolia
_____   *C. e. dementievi*   NE Mongolia and s Transbaikalia

☐ **Sombre Nightjar** *Caprimulgus fraenatus*
         Ethiopia to nw Somalia, sw Kenya and ne Tanzania

☐ **Rufous-cheeked Nightjar** *Caprimulgus rufigena*
_____   *C. r. damarensis*   Coastal w Angola to Namibia, Botswana and nw South Africa
_____   *C. r. rufigena*   Zimbabwe and s Zambia to South Africa

☐ **Egyptian Nightjar** *Caprimulgus aegyptius*
_____   *C. a. saharae*   Morocco to Nile Delta; winters in western Sahel
_____   *C. a. aegyptius (arenicolor)*   NE Egypt and Arabia to w China, w Pakistan and se Iran

☐ **Nubian Nightjar** *Caprimulgus nubicus*
_____   *C. n. tamaricis*   Israel to Jordan, sw Saudi Arabia and Yemen
_____   *C. n. nubicus*   Central Sudan
_____   *C. n. torridus (taruensis)*   Central Ethiopia to Somalia, Kenya and ne Uganda
_____   *C. n. jonesi*   Socotra

☐ **Sykes' Nightjar** *Caprimulgus mahrattensis*

SE Iran to s Afghanistan, Pakistan and (?) nw India

☐ **Vaurie's Nightjar** *Caprimulgus centralasicus*

W China (known from a 1960 specimen from w Xinjiang)

☐ **Golden Nightjar** *Caprimulgus eximius*
____ *C. e. simplicior* — S Mauritania and n Senegal to central Chad
____ *C. e. eximius* — Central Sudan

☐ **Large-tailed Nightjar** *Caprimulgus macrurus*
____ *C. m. albonotatus* — NE Pakistan and n India to Bhutan and Bangladesh
____ *C. m. bimaculatus (ambiguus, aequabilis, hainanus)* — NE India to s China, Sumatra and Riau Archipelago
____ *C. m. andamanicus* — Andaman Islands
____ *C. m. johnsoni* — S Philippines (Palawan, Busuanga and Culion)
____ *C. m. salvadorii (jungei)* — N Borneo, Labuan, Balambangan, Banguey and s Sula islands
____ *C. m. macrurus* — Java and Bali
____ *C. m. schlegelii (yorki, meeki)* — Wallacea, New Guinea, New Britain and coastal n Australia

☐ **Jerdon's Nightjar** *Caprimulgus atripennis*
____ *C. a. atripennis* — S peninsular India (Western Ghats and Eastern Ghats)
____ *C. a. aequabilis* — Sri Lanka

☐ **Philippine Nightjar** *Caprimulgus manillensis*

Philippine Islands (except Palawan)

☐ **Sulawesi Nightjar** *Caprimulgus celebensis*
____ *C. c. celebensis* — Sulawesi and Butung I.
____ *C. c. jungei* — Sula Islands (Taliabu and Mangole)

☐ **Donaldson-Smith's Nightjar** *Caprimulgus donaldsoni*

Ethiopia and Somalia to se Sudan and ne Tanzania

☐ **Black-shouldered Nightjar** *Caprimulgus nigriscapularis*

Senegambia to se Sudan, w Kenya and sw Zaire

☐ **Fiery-necked Nightjar** *Caprimulgus pectoralis*
____ *C. p. shelleyi* — Angola to s Zaire, se Kenya and sw Tanzania
____ *C. p. fervidus* — S Angola to n Namibia, Botswana, Zimbabwe and ne S Africa
____ *C. p. crepusculans* — SE Zimbabwe to Mozambique, Swaziland and e South Africa
____ *C. p. pectoralis* — S Transvaal, Natal and Cape Province

☐ **Abyssinian Nightjar** *Caprimulgus poliocephalus*

SW Saudi Arabia to Ethiopia, ne Uganda and n Tanzania

☐ **Montane Nightjar** *Caprimulgus ruwenzorii*
____ *C. r. ruwenzorii* — W Angola; sw Uganda to e Zaire
____ *C. r. guttifer* — NE Tanzania; sw Tanzania to n Malawi and ne Zambia
— Ruwenzori Mountain forests of e Zaire and sw Uganda

☐ **Indian Nightjar** *Caprimulgus asiaticus*
____ *C. a. asiaticus* — SE Pakistan to India, s Thailand and s Indochina
____ *C. a. eidos* — Sri Lanka
____ *C. a. siamensis* — N Thailand

☐ **Madagascar Nightjar** *Caprimulgus madagascariensis*
____ *C. m. aldabrensis* — Aldabra
____ *C. m. madagascariensis* — Madagascar and Nosy Boraha

☐ **Swamp Nightjar** *Caprimulgus natalensis*
____ *C. n. natalensis* — E Gambia to Sudan, sw Ethiopia, e Tanzania and n S Africa
____ *C. n. accrae* — Coastal n-central Sierra Leone to w Cameroon

☐ **Plain Nightjar** *Caprimulgus inornatus*

Thornscrub of sub-Saharan Africa and sw Arabian Peninsula

☐ **Star-spotted Nightjar** *Caprimulgus stellatus*

SE Sudan to Ethiopia, Djibouti, Somalia and central Kenya

☐ **Nechisar Nightjar** *Caprimulgus solala*

Described from one wing from a road corpse found in Ethiopia

☐ **Savanna Nightjar** *Caprimulgus affinis*
  _____ *C. a. monticolus*
  _____ *C. a. amoyensis*
  _____ *C. a. stictomus*
  _____ *C. a. griseatus*
  _____ *C. a. mindanensis*
  _____ *C. a. affinis*
  _____ *C. a. propinquus*
  _____ *C. a. undulatus*
  _____ *C. a. kasuidori*
  _____ *C. a. timorensis*

NE Pakistan to India, Myanmar, s Thailand, Cambodia, Vietnam
SE China and n Vietnam
Taiwan
N Philippines
S Philippines (Mindanao); sight record from Jolo (Sulu Arch.)
Greater and Lesser Sundas
N-central and s Sulawesi
W Lesser Sundas (Sumbawa, Komodo and Flores)
Central Lesser Sundas (Sumba and Sawu)
E Lesser Sundas (Alor, Timor, Roti and Kisar)

☐ **Freckled Nightjar** *Caprimulgus tristigma*
  _____ *C. t. sharpei*
  _____ *C. t. pallidogriseus*
  _____ *C. t. tristigma*
  _____ *C. t. lentiginosus*
  _____ *C. t. granosus*

Guinea to Togo, Cameroon and Central African Republic
Nigeria
NE Zaire to s Sudan, Burundi, Ethiopia and n Tanzania
W Angola to Namibia and w Cape Province
SE Zaire to Zambia, s Tanzania and e Cape Province

☐ **Bonaparte's Nightjar** *Caprimulgus concretus*

Lowlands of Sumatra, Borneo and Belitung I.

☐ **Salvadori's Nightjar** *Caprimulgus pulchellus*
  _____ *C. p. pulchellus*
  _____ *C. p. bartelsi*

Sumatra
Java

☐ **Itombwe Nightjar** *Caprimulgus prigoginei*

Single 1955 specimen from e Zaire (Itombwe Forest)

☐ **Collared Nightjar** *Caprimulgus enarratus*

Humid forests of e Madagascar

☐ **Bates' Nightjar** *Caprimulgus batesi*

Congo basin (s Cameroon to n Gabon, e Zaire and w Uganda)

☐ **Long-tailed Nightjar** *Caprimulgus climacurus*
  _____ *C. c. climacurus*
  _____ *C. c. sclateri*
  _____ *C. c. nigricans*

Mauritania to Sudan, w Ethiopia and e Zaire
Guinea to nw Uganda
E Sudan (White Nile region) Nile Valley

☐ **Slender-tailed Nightjar** *Caprimulgus clarus*

SE Sudan to Ethiopia, Djibouti, Somalia and n Tanzania

☐ **Square-tailed Nightjar** *Caprimulgus fossii*
  _____ *C. f. fossii*
  _____ *C. f. welwitschii*
  _____ *C. f. griseoplurus*

Grassy savanna of Gabon and sw Congo
S Zaire to Angola, Natal; Zanzibar and Pemba I.
Kalahari Desert and extreme n South Africa

☐ **Pennant-winged Nightjar** *Macrodipteryx vexillarius*

Brachystegia woodlands of southern Africa

☐ **Standard-winged Nightjar** *Macrodipteryx longipennis*

Senegambia to sw Sudan, n Uganda, Ethiopia and Somalia

☐ **Lyre-tailed Nightjar** *Uropsalis lyra*
  _____ *U. l. lyra*
  _____ *U. l. peruana*
  _____ *U. l. argentina*

Andes of w Colombia to w Venezuela and central Ecuador
Andes of Peru to w Bolivia
Andes of s Bolivia and adjacent n Argentina

☐ **Swallow-tailed Nightjar** *Uropsalis segmentata*
  _____ *U. s. segmentata*
  _____ *U. s. kalinowskii*

Andes of Colombia and n Ecuador
E slope of Andes of central Peru to w Bolivia

☐ **Ladder-tailed Nightjar** *Hydropsalis climacocerca*

____ *H. c. schomburgki*	Riverine habitats of e Venezuela to the Guianas and Suriname
____ *H. c. climacocerca*	Mainly along rivers from se Colombia to n Bolivia
____ *H. c. intercedens*	Central Peru (Obidos region in w Pará)
____ *H. c. pallidior*	N-central Brazil (Santarém region of w Pará)
____ *H. c. canescens*	N-central Brazil (lower Rio Tapajós region of w Pará)

☐ **Scissor-tailed Nightjar** *Hydropsalis torquata*

____ *H. t. torquata*	S Suriname to Amazonian and e Brazil and e Peru
____ *H. t. furcifera*	S Peru to e Bolivia, s Brazil, Uruguay, Paraguay, c Argentina

☐ **Long-trained Nightjar** *Macropsalis forcipata*

SE Brazil and adjacent ne Argentina (Misiones)

☐ **Sickle-winged Nightjar** *Eleothreptus anomalus*

Swamps of se Brazil to s Paraguay and n Argentina

ORDER: APODIFORMES
FAMILY: APODIDAE (Swifts—98)

☐ **Tepui Swift** *Cypseloides phelpsi*

Tepuis of s Venezuela, adj. nw Guyana and n Brazil (Roraima)

☐ **Black Swift** *Cypseloides niger*

____ *C. n. borealis*	Mainly mountains of se Alaska to sw US
____ *C. n. costaricensis*	Highlands of central Mexico to Costa Rica
____ *C. n. niger*	West Indies and Trinidad; Guyana (Merumé Mountains)

☐ **White-chested Swift** *Cypseloides lemosi*

SW Colombia (mountains of upper Cauca Valley)

☐ **Rothschild's Swift** *Cypseloides rothschildi*

Andes of nw Argentina; rarely adj. s Bolivia and Peru (Cuzco)

☐ **Sooty Swift** *Cypseloides fumigatus*

E Bolivia to se Brazil, ne Argentina and adjacent Paraguay

☐ **White-fronted Swift** *Cypseloides storeri*

Mountains of sw Mexico (Jalisco, Guerrero and Michoacán)

☐ **Spot-fronted Swift** *Cypseloides cherriei*

Mts. of Costa Rica; Colombia to w Ecuador and n Venezuela

☐ **White-chinned Swift** *Cypseloides cryptus*

Locally in mts. of nw S America; scattered records C America

☐ **Great Dusky Swift** *Cypseloides senex*

Central and s Brazil to e Paraguay and ne Argentina

☐ **Chestnut-collared Swift** *Streptoprocne rutila*

____ *S. r. griseifrons*	W Mexico (Nayarit to Jalisco, s Durango and w Zacatecas)
____ *S. r. brunnitorques*	SE Mexico to w Bolivia
____ *S. r. rutila*	Venezuela to Guyana and Trinidad

☐ **White-naped Swift** *Streptoprocne semicollaris*

Mts. of w Mexico (Chihuahua to Nayarit, Hidalgo and Morelos)

☐ **White-collared Swift** *Streptoprocne zonaris*

____ *S. z. mexicana*	Highlands of s Mexico to Belize and El Salvador
____ *S. z. bouchellii*	Nicaragua to Panama
____ *S. z. pallidifrons*	Greater Antilles and locally in Lesser Antilles
____ *S. z. subtropicalis*	Mountains of Colombia to w Venezuela (Mérida) and Peru
____ *S. z. altissima*	Andes of Colombia and Ecuador
____ *S. z. minor*	Cordillera of coastal n Venezuela and Trinidad
____ *S. z. albicincta*	Tropical s Venezuela and the Guianas
____ *S. z. kuenzeli*	Andes of Bolivia and nw Argentina
____ *S. z. zonaris*	Lowlands of s Brazil, Bolivia, Paraguay and n Argentina

☐ **Biscutate Swift** *Streptoprocne biscutata*
____   *S. b. seridoensis*   NE Brazil (Seridó region of Paraíba)
____   *S. b. biscutata*   SE Brazil (Minas Gerais) to Paraguay and ne Argentina

☐ **Waterfall Swift** *Hydrochous gigas*

    Mts. of peninsular Malaysia, Borneo, Sumatra and w Java

☐ **Glossy Swiftlet** *Aerodramus esculenta*
____   *A. e. affinis*   Andaman Islands and Nicobar Islands
____   *A. e. elachyptera*   Mergui Archipelago (off Myanmar)
____   *A. e. cyanoptila*   Malay Pen., Sumatra and satellite islands and lowland Borneo
____   *A. e. vanderbilti*   Nias I. (off w Sumatra)
____   *A. e. oberholseri*   Batu Islands and Mentawi Islands (off w Sumatra)
____   *A. e. natalis*   Christmas I. (Indian Ocean south of Java)
____   *A. e. septentrionalis*   Philippines (Calayan, Camiguin Norte, Babuyan, Claro, Fuga)
____   *A. e. isonota*   Luzon (n Philippines)
____   *A. e. marginata*   N and w Philippines (s Luzon to Palawan and Bohol)
____   *A. e. bagobo*   S Philippines (Mindanao, Mindoro and Sulu Archipelago)
____   *A. e. spilura*   N Moluccas
____   *A. e. manadensis*   N Sulawesi, Sangihe, Siau, Talasea and Talaud islands
____   *A. e. esculenta*   S Moluccas, s Sulawesi, Banggai and Sula islands
____   *A. e. minuta*   Salayar, Bonerate, Tanahjampea and Kalao is. (n Flores Sea)
____   *A. e. sumbawae*   W Lesser Sundas (Sumbawa, Sumba, Flores and Besar)
____   *A. e. perneglecta*   Alor, Sawu, Wetar, Kisar, Romang, Damar and Tanimbar is.
____   *A. e. neglecta*   E Lesser Sundas (Roti, Dao, Semau, Timor and Jaco)
____   *A. e. amethystina*   Waigeo I. (off nw New Guinea)
____   *A. e. erwini*   High mountains of w New Guinea
____   *A. e. numforensis*   Numfor I. (off nw New Guinea)
____   *A. e. nitens*   Lowlands of New Guinea and w Papuan islands
____   *A. e. misimae*   Louisiade Archipelago (Misima and Rossel)
____   *A. e. stresemanni*   Admiralty Islands (Manus, Rambutyo, Nauna, Los Negros)
____   *A. e. kakili*   Bismarck Arch. (New Ireland, New Hanover and Dyaul)
____   *A. e. spilogaster*   Bismarck Archipelago (Lihir Group and Tatau Islands)
____   *A. e. hypogrammica*   Bismarck Archipelago (Nissan and Green)
____   *A. e. tametamele*   Bismarck Arch. (New Britain and Witu); Bougainville
____   *A. e. becki*   Central and ne Solomon Islands; single record from Malaita
____   *A. e. makirensis*   San Cristóbal I. (se Solomon Islands)
____   *A. e. desiderata*   Rennell (s Solomon Islands)
____   *A. e. uropygialis*   Vanuatu (Santa Cruz, Torres and Banks Group)
____   *A. e. albidior*   New Caledonia and Loyalty Islands

☐ **Cave Swiftlet** *Aerodramus linchi*
____   *A. l. ripleyi*   Bukit Barisan Mountains (Sumatra)
____   *A. l. dodgei*   High elevations on Mt. Kinabalu (n Borneo)
____   *A. l. linchi*   Java, Madura, Nusa Penida and Bawean islands
____   *A. l. dedii*   Bali and Lombok

☐ **Pygmy Swiftlet** *Aerodramus troglodytes*

    Philippines and Palawan (absent in Sulu Archipelago)

☐ **Seychelles Swiftlet** *Aerodramus elaphrus*

    Seychelles (Mahé, Praslin and La Digue)

☐ **Mascarene Swiftlet** *Aerodramus francicus*

    W Mascarene Islands (Mauritius and Réunion)

☐ **Indian Swiftlet** *Aerodramus unicolor*

    SW pen. India, Sri Lanka and small islands off Malabar coast

☐ **Moluccan Swiftlet** *Aerodramus infuscatus*
____   *A. i. sororum*   Sulawesi, Sangihe, Siau and Taliabu islands
____   *A. i. infuscatus*   N Moluccas (Halmahera, Ternate and Morotai)
____   *A. i. ceramensis*   S Moluccas (Buru, Boano, Seram and Ambon)

☐ **Philippine Swiftlet** *Aerodramus mearnsi*

Lowlands of Philippine Islands

☐ **Mountain Swiftlet** *Aerodramus hirundinaceus*

_____ *A. h. baru* — Yapen I.

_____ *A. h. excelsus* — Central New Guinea (Snow Mountains and Mt. Karstenz)

_____ *A. h. hirundinaceus* — New Guinea, Dampier and Goodenough islands

☐ **White-rumped Swiftlet** *Aerodramus spodiopygius*

_____ *A. s. delichon* — Admiralty Islands (Manus and New Ireland)

_____ *A. s. eichhorni* — Bismarck Archipelago (Mussau I. in St. Matthias group)

_____ *A. s. noonaedanae* — Bismarck Archipelago (New Ireland and New Britain)

_____ *A. s. reichenowi* — Southern and e Solomon Islands

_____ *A. s. desolatus* — Solomon Islands (Duff, Swallow and Santa Cruz)

_____ *A. s. epiensis* — N and central Vanuatu (Banks Group to Epi Islands)

_____ *A. s. ingens* — S Vanuatu

_____ *A. s. leucopygius* — Loyalty Islands and New Guinea

_____ *A. s. assimilis* — Fiji Islands

_____ *A. s. townsendi* — Tonga

_____ *A. s. spodiopygius* — Samoa

☐ **Australian Swiftlet** *Aerodramus terraereginae*

_____ *A. t. terraereginae* — NE Australia (coastal n Queensland)

_____ *A. t. chillagoensis* — S coastal Queensland, Dunk, Family and Hinchinbrook islands

☐ **Himalayan Swiftlet** *Aerodramus brevirostris*

_____ *A. b. brevirostris* — Himalayas to Nepal, ne India, Myanmar and Thailand

_____ *A. b. innominatus* — E-central China to n Vietnam; winters to Malay Peninsula

☐ **Indochinese Swiftlet** *Aerodramus rogersi*

Mountains of e Myanmar, w Thailand, n Laos and Vietnam

☐ **Volcano Swiftlet** *Aerodramus vulcanorum*

Mountains of Java

☐ **Whitehead's Swiftlet** *Aerodramus whiteheadi*

_____ *A. w. whiteheadi* — N Philippines (Mt. Data on n Luzon)

_____ *A. w. origenis* — S Philippines (Mt. Apo on Mindanao)

☐ **Bare-legged Swiftlet** *Aerodramus nuditarsus*

Mountains of central and e New Guinea

☐ **Mayr's Swiftlet** *Aerodramus orientalis*

_____ *A. o. leletensis* — Bismarck Archipelago (Lelet Plateau in central New Ireland)

_____ *A. o. orientalis* — Guadalcanal (Solomon Islands)

☐ **Palawan Swiftlet** *Aerodramus palawanensis*

Palawan (sw Philippines)

☐ **Uniform Swiftlet** *Aerodramus vanikorensis*

_____ *A. v. amelis* — Philippines (Luzon, Mindoro, Cebu, Bohol and Mindanao)

_____ *A. v. aenigma* — Central and se Sulawesi and Muna I.

_____ *A. v. heinrichi* — S Sulawesi

_____ *A. v. moluccarum* — S Moluccas (Seram, Ambon, Banda, Gorong, Tayandu, Kai Is.)

_____ *A. v. waigeuensis* — N Moluccas (Morotai and Halmahera) and w Papuan islands

_____ *A. v. steini* — Biak and Numfor islands (off nw New Guinea)

_____ *A. v. yorki* — Aru Islands, New Guinea and D'Entrecasteaux Archipelago

_____ *A. v. tagulae* — Louisiade Archipelago, Trobriand Islands and Woodlark I.

_____ *A. v. coultasi* — Admiralty Is. (Manus, Rambutyo, Los Negros); St. Matthias Is.

_____ *A. v. pallens* — New Britain, New Ireland, Dyaul I. and New Hanover

_____ *A. v. lihirensis* — Lihir, Feni, Tabar, Nuguria and Hibernian is. (e of New Ireland)

_____ *A. v. lugubris* — Solomon Islands

_____ *A. v. vanikorensis* — Santa Cruz Islands (including Duff and Swallow) and Vanuatu

☐ **Mossy-nest Swiftlet** *Aerodramus salangana*
_____ *A. s. natunae* — N Borneo, Natuna Islands and (?) Sumatra
_____ *A. s. maratua* — Maratua Archipelago (off ne Borneo)
_____ *A. s. aerophilus* — Nias and adjacent islands off w Sumatra
_____ *A. s. salangana* — Java; single Philippine record from Basilan

☐ **Palau Swiftlet** *Aerodramus pelewensis* — Lowlands of Palau Islands (w Caroline Islands)

☐ **Guam Swiftlet** *Aerodramus bartschi* — S Mariana Islands (Saipan, Tinian, Aguijan and Guam)

☐ **Caroline Islands Swiftlet** *Aerodramus inquietus*
_____ *A. i. rukensis* — Central Caroline Islands (Yap and Truk)
_____ *A. i. ponapensis* — Pohnpei (e Caroline Islands)
_____ *A. i. inquietus* — Kosrae (Caroline Islands)

☐ **Atiu Swiftlet** *Aerodramus sawtelli* — Atiu (s Cook Archipelago)

☐ **Polynesian Swiftlet** *Aerodramus leucophaeus* — E Society Islands (Tahiti and Moorea)

☐ **Marquesan Swiftlet** *Aerodramus ocistus*
_____ *A. o. ocistus* — N Marquesas Islands (Eiao, Nukuhiva and Uahuka)
_____ *A. o. gilliardi* — S Marquesas Islands (Uapou, Hivaoa and Tahuata)

☐ **Black-nest Swiftlet** *Aerodramus maximus*
_____ *A. m. maximus* — S Myanmar to s Malay Peninsula, se Vietnam and w Java
_____ *A. m. lowi* — Sumatra, Nias I., and Borneo; one 1887 Palawan specimen
_____ *A. m. tichelmani* — SE Borneo

☐ **Edible-nest Swiftlet** *Aerodramus fuciphagus*
_____ *A. f. inexpectatus* — Andaman and Nicobar islands
_____ *A. f. vestitus* — Sumatra, Belitung I. and Borneo
_____ *A. p. perplexus* — Maratua Archipelago (off e Borneo)
_____ *A. f. fuciphagus* — Java, Kangean Is. and Bali to w L Sundas and Tanahjampea I.
_____ *A. f. dammermani* — Flores (w Lesser Sundas)
_____ *A. f. micans* — E Lesser Sundas (Sumba, Sawu and Timor)

☐ **German's Swiftlet** *Aerodramus germani*
_____ *A. g. germani* — Coasts of Malay Peninsula, n Borneo and s Philippines
_____ *A. g. amechanus* — Anambas Islands (South China Sea)

☐ **Papuan Swiftlet** *Aerodramus papuensis* — N New Guinea (Idenburg River to Huon Peninsula)

☐ **Scarce Swift** *Schoutedenapus myoptilus*
_____ *S. m. poensis* — Bioko (Gulf of Guinea)
_____ *S. m. chapini* — Highlands of e Zaire, Rwanda and sw Uganda
_____ *S. m. myoptilus* — Highlands of Ethiopia to Zimbabwe and w Mozambique

☐ **Schouteden's Swift** *Schoutedenapus schoutedeni* — Known from five specimens (1956-59) from e Zaire

☐ **Philippine Needletail** *Mearnsia picina* — Philippines (Cebu, Leyte, Mindanao, Negros, Biliran, Samar)

☐ **Papuan Needletail** *Mearnsia novaeguineae*
_____ *M. n. buergersi* — N New Guinea (Sepik River area)
_____ *M. n. novaeguineae* — S New Guinea

☐ **Malagasy Spinetail** *Zoonavena grandidieri*
_____ *Z. g. grandidieri* — Madagascar
_____ *Z. g. mariae* — Grand Comoro I. (Comoro Islands)

☐ **Sao Tome Spinetail** *Zoonavena thomensis*

Mountains of São Tomé and Príncipe (Gulf of Guinea)

☐ **White-rumped Needletail** *Zoonavena sylvatica*

India south of the Himalayas to w Myanmar

☐ **Mottled Spinetail** *Telacanthura ussheri*
____ *T. u. ussheri*
____ *T. u. sharpei*
____ *T. u. stictilaema*
____ *T. u. benguellensis*

Senegambia to Nigeria
Cameroon to Gabon, Zaire and Uganda
Coastal s Kenya to n Tanzania, Zanzibar and Pemba I.
W Angola to Mozambique

☐ **Black Spinetail** *Telacanthura melanopygia*

Sierra Leone to s Ghana, Gabon, ne Zaire and ne Angola

☐ **Silver-rumped Needletail** *Rhaphidura leucopygialis*

S Myanmar to Malay Peninsula, Greater Sundas and Bangka I.

☐ **Sabine's Spinetail** *Rhaphidura sabini*

Rainforests of s Guinea to e Zaire, w Uganda and w Kenya

☐ **Cassin's Spinetail** *Neafrapus cassini*

Sierra Leone and Liberia to nw Angola and w Uganda; Bioko

☐ **Bat-like Spinetail** *Neafrapus boehmi*
____ *N. b. boehmi*
____ *N. b. sheppardi*

Angola to s Zaire, w Tanzania and n Zambia
SE Kenya to s Tanzania, Mozambique and ne South Africa

☐ **White-throated Needletail** *Hirundapus caudacutus*
____ *H. c. caudacutus*
____ *H. c. nudipes*

Siberia to Japan and Kuril Islands.; winters to Australia
Himalayas to sw China; winters to India and Myanmar

☐ **Silver-backed Needletail** *Hirundapus cochinchinensis*
____ *H. c. rupchandi*
____ *H. c. cochinchinensis*
____ *H. c. formosanus*

Central Nepal; winters to Malay Peninsula, Sumatra and Java
E Himalayas to SE Asia; winters to Sumatra and Java
Taiwan

☐ **Brown-backed Needletail** *Hirundapus giganteus*
____ *H. g. indicus*
____ *H. g. giganteus*

SW India and Sri Lanka; Bangladesh to SE Asia, Andaman Is.
Malay Peninsula, Greater Sundas and Palawan

☐ **Purple Needletail** *Hirundapus celebensis*

N Sulawesi and Philippines (absent from Palawan)

☐ **Band-rumped Swift** *Chaetura spinicauda*
____ *C. s. fumosa*
____ *C. s. aetherodroma*
____ *C. s. latirostris*
____ *C. s. spinicauda*
____ *C. s. aethalea*

W Costa Rica and w Panama to n Colombia
E Panama to s Ecuador
S Venezuela to Brazilian border and Delta Amacuro
E Venezuela, the Guianas and n Brazil (n Amapá)
Central Brazil south of the Amazon

☐ **Lesser Antillean Swift** *Chaetura martinica*

Guadeloupe, Dominica, Martinique, St. Lucia and St. Vincent

☐ **Gray-rumped Swift** *Chaetura cinereiventris*
____ *C. c. phaeopygos*
____ *C. c. occidentalis*
____ *C. c. schistacea*
____ *C. c. lawrencei*
____ *C. c. guianensis*
____ *C. c. sclateri*
____ *C. c. cinereiventris*

Caribbean slope of e Nicaragua to Panama
W Colombia to w Ecuador and extreme nw Peru
E Colombia to w Venezuela (Mérida and Táchira)
Grenada, Trinidad, Tobago, Isla Margarita and n Venezuela
Tepuis of e Venezuela and w Guyana
S Colombia to s Venezuela, nw Brazil, e Peru and nw Bolivia
E Brazil to Paraguay and ne Argentina (Misiones)

☐ **Pale-rumped Swift** *Chaetura egregia*

E Ecuador to e Peru, n Bolivia and w Amazonian Brazil

☐ **Chimney Swift** *Chaetura pelagica*

E North America; winters to Brazil and n Chile

☐ **Vaux's Swift** *Chaetura vauxi*

_____ *C. v. vauxi*	Locally from se Alaska to sw US; winters to Guatemala
_____ *C. v. tamaulipensis*	E Mexico (sw Tamaulípas and se San Luis Potosí)
_____ *C. v. gaumeri*	SE Mexico (Yucatán Peninsula) and Cozumel I.
_____ *C. v. richmondi*	S Mexico to Costa Rica and extreme w Panama (Chiriquí)
_____ *C. v. ochropygia*	E Panama
_____ *C. v. aphanes*	N Venezuela

☐ **Chapman's Swift** *Chaetura chapmani*

_____ *C. c. chapmani*	Panama to Colombia, Venezuela, Guianas, ne Brazil; Trinidad
_____ *C. c. viridipennis*	Tropical e Peru to e Bolivia and w Amazonian Brazil

☐ **Short-tailed Swift** *Chaetura brachyura*

_____ *C. b. brachyura*	Panama to the Guianas, Trinidad, w-c Brazil and n Bolivia
_____ *C. b. praevelox*	S Lesser Antilles (Grenada, St. Vincent and Tobago)
_____ *C. b. ocypetes*	Locally in sw Ecuador and extreme nw Peru
_____ *C. b. cinereocauda*	N-central Brazil

☐ **Ashy-tailed Swift** *Chaetura andrei*

_____ *C. a. andrei*	Orinoco Valley of e-central Venezuela
_____ *C. a. meridionalis*	Colombia to the Guianas, Brazil, n Paraguay and nw Argentina

☐ **White-throated Swift** *Aeronautes saxatalis*

_____ *A. s. saxatalis*	S British Columbia to Baja Calif. and sw Mexico (Oaxaca)
_____ *A. s. nigrior*	S Mexico (Chiapas) to central Honduras

☐ **White-tipped Swift** *Aeronautes montivagus*

_____ *A. m. montivagus*	Locally in mts. of Colombia to n Venezuela and w Bolivia
_____ *A. m. tatei*	*Tepuis* of s Venezuela and extreme n Brazil

☐ **Andean Swift** *Aeronautes andecolus*

_____ *A. a. parvulus*	Andes of w Peru to extreme n Chile
_____ *A. a. peruvianus*	Andes of se Peru
_____ *A. a. andecolus*	Andes of Bolivia to w Argentina (Río Negro)

☐ **Antillean Palm-Swift** *Tachornis phoenicobia*

_____ *T. p. iradii*	Cuba and Isle of Pines
_____ *T. p. phoenicobia*	Jamaica, Hispaniola, Saona, Beata and Île-á-Vache

☐ **Pygmy Swift** *Tachornis furcata*

_____ *T. f. furcata*	Lowlands of ne Colombia and nw Venezuela
_____ *T. f. nigrodorsalis*	Lowlands of w Venezuela

☐ **Fork-tailed Palm-Swift** *Tachornis squamata*

_____ *T. s. semota*	E Colombia to s Venezuela, e Ecuador, ne Peru and nw Brazil
_____ *T. s. squamata*	Trinidad and the Guianas to Amazonian and e Brazil

☐ **Great Swallow-tailed Swift** *Panyptila sanctihieronymi*

	Mountains of s Mexico to s Honduras and (rarely) n Costa Rica

☐ **Lesser Swallow-tailed Swift** *Panyptila cayennensis*

_____ *P. c. veraecrucis*	Humid lowlands of se Mexico (Veracruz) to n Honduras
_____ *P. c. cayennensis*	S Honduras to n Bolivia and se Brazil; Trinidad and Tobago

☐ **Asian Palm-Swift** *Cypsiurus balasiensis*

_____ *C. b. balasiensis*	Indian subcontinent and Sri Lanka
_____ *C. b. infumatus*	Myanmar to Indochina, Malay Peninsula, Sumatra and Borneo
_____ *C. b. bartelsorum*	Java and Bali
_____ *C. b. pallidior*	Philippine Islands

☐ **African Palm-Swift** *Cypsiurus parvus*

____	*C. p. parvus*	Senegambia to s Sudan, Ethiopia and sw Arabia
____	*C. p. brachypterus*	Sierra Leone to ne Zaire, Angola and Gulf of Guinea islands
____	*C. p. myochrous*	Higher elevations from s Sudan to ne South Africa
____	*C. p. laemostigma*	Coastal lowlands of s Somalia to Mozambique
____	*C. p. hypaenes*	N Namibia and n Botswana
____	*C. p. celer*	Mozambique to Natal
____	*C. p. griveaudi*	Comoro Islands
____	*C. p. gracilis*	Madagascar

☐ **Alpine Swift** *Tachymarptis melba*

____	*T. m. melba*	S Europe to Asia Minor and nw Iran; winters African tropics
____	*T. m. tuneti*	E Morocco to Middle East, Iran, Kazakstan and w Pakistan
____	*T. m. archeri*	N Somalia to sw Arabia and Dead Sea depression
____	*T. m. africanus*	Ethiopia to Cape Province and sw Angola
____	*T. m. maximus*	Ruwenzori Mountains of ne Zaire and Uganda
____	*T. m. marjoriae*	N-central Namibia to nw Cape Province
____	*T. m. willisi*	Madagascar
____	*T. m. nubifuga*	Himalayas; winters in central India
____	*T. m. dorobtatai*	Mountains of w peninsular India
____	*T. m. bakeri*	Sri Lanka

☐ **Mottled Swift** *Tachymarptis aequatorialis*

____	*T. a. lowei*	Sierra Leone to Nigeria
____	*T. a. furensis*	W Sudan (Darfur region)
____	*T. a. aequatorialis (schubotzi, bamendae)*	Eritrea and Ethiopia to Cameroon, Angola and Mozambique
____	*T. a. gelidus*	SW Zimbabwe

☐ **Alexander's Swift** *Apus alexandri*

Cape Verde Islands

☐ **Common Swift** *Apus apus*

____	*A. a. apus*	W Palearctic east to Lake Baikal and Iran; winters to s Africa
____	*A. a. pekinensis*	Iran to Himalayas, Mongolia and n China; winters to s Africa

☐ **Plain Swift** *Apus unicolor*

Madeira and w Canary Islands; winters in n Africa

☐ **Nyanza Swift** *Apus niansae*

____	*A. n. niansae*	Eritrea to Ethiopia, e Uganda, w Kenya and n Tanzania
____	*A. n. somalicus*	N Somalia and adjacent Ethiopia

☐ **Pallid Swift** *Apus pallidus*

____	*A. p. brehmorum*	Madeira, Canary Islands, s Europe to Turkey, coastal n Africa
____	*A. p. illyricus*	Dalmatian coast of Adriatic Sea; winters in Sahel
____	*A. p. pallidus*	Mauritania (Banc d'Arguin), Sahara hills and Egypt to Pakistan

☐ **African Swift** *Apus barbatus*

____	*A. b. glanvillei*	Known from two specimens from Sierra Leone (Rokupr)
____	*A. b. sladeniae*	Locally in se Nigeria, w Cameroon, Bioko I. and w Angola
____	*A. b. serlei*	W Cameroon (Bamenda Plateau)
____	*A. b. roehli*	E Ethiopia to ne Uganda, Kenya, Malawi, e Zaire; ne Angola
____	*A. b. hollidayi*	Victoria Falls area on Zambia/Zimbabwe border
____	*A. b. oreobates*	Zimbabwe and Mozambique (Mt. Gorongoza)
____	*A. b. barbatus*	South Africa

☐ **Forbes-Watson's Swift** *Apus berliozi*

____	*A. b. berliozi*	Socotra
____	*A. b. bensoni*	Coastal e Somalia; winters to coastal Kenya

☐ **Bradfield's Swift** *Apus bradfieldi*
____ *A. b. bradfieldi* | Deserts and arid savanna of sw Angola and Namibia
____ *A. b. deserticola* | South Africa (n Cape Province)

☐ **Madagascar Swift** *Apus balstoni*
____ *A. b. balstoni* | Madagascar
____ *A. b. mayottensis* | Comoro Islands

☐ **Fork-tailed Swift** *Apus pacificus*
____ *A. p. pacificus* | Siberia to Kamchatka, n China and s Japan; winters to Australia
____ *A. p. kanoi* | Southeast Tibet to e China and Taiwan; winters to Indonesia
____ *A. p. leuconyx* | Outer Himalayas and Assam Hills; winters in India
____ *A. p. cooki* | Thailand, Myanmar and Indochina; Hainan I. and Lan-yü I.

☐ **Dark-rumped Swift** *Apus acuticauda*
| Locally in ne India (Khasi Hills)

☐ **Little Swift** *Apus affinis*
____ *A. a. galilejensis* | N and sub-Saharan Africa east to Pakistan
____ *A. a. aerobates* | SW Mauritania to Ethiopia, Somalia, c Angola and S Africa
____ *A. a. bannermani* | Bioko, São Tomé and Príncipe (Gulf of Guinea)
____ *A. a. theresae* | W and s Angola to s Zambia and South Africa
____ *A. a. affinis* | S Somalia to n Mozambique, Pemba I. and Zanzibar to India
____ *A. a. singalensis* | S India and Sri Lanka

☐ **House Swift** *Apus nipalensis*
____ *A. n. nipalensis* | Nepal to se China, Myanmar, Thailand, Indochina, Philippines
____ *A. n. subfurcatus* | Malay Peninsula to Borneo, Sumatra and adjacent islands
____ *A. n. furcatus* | Java and Bali
____ *A. n. kuntzi* | Taiwan

☐ **Horus Swift** *Apus horus*
____ *A. h. horus (toulsoni)* | Widespread intra-African migrant south of the Sahara
____ *A. h. fuscobrunneus* | SW Angola

☐ **White-rumped Swift** *Apus caffer*
| S Iberian Peninsula, central Morocco and sub-Saharan Africa

☐ **Bates' Swift** *Apus batesi*
| Humid forests of w Cameroon to n Gabon and e Zaire

ORDER: APODIFORMES
FAMILY: HEMIPROCNIDAE (Crested Treeswifts—4)

☐ **Crested Treeswift** *Hemiprocne coronata*
| India to sw China, Myanmar and Indochina

☐ **Gray-rumped Treeswift** *Hemiprocne longipennis*
____ *H. l. harterti* | S Myanmar to sw Thailand, Malaysia, Sumatra and Borneo
____ *H. l. perlonga* | Islands off w Sumatra (Simeulue to Enggano)
____ *H. l. longipennis* | Java and Bali to Lombok and Kangean Islands
____ *H. l. wallacii* | Sulawesi, Banggai, Sula and adjacent islands

☐ **Whiskered Treeswift** *Hemiprocne comata*
____ *H. c. comata (stresemanni)* | S Myanmar and pen. Thailand to Sumatra, Borneo and adj. is.
____ *H. c. major (nakamurai)* | Philippine Islands and Sulu Archipelago (absent from Palawan)

☐ **Moustached Treeswift** *Hemiprocne mystacea*

____	*H. m. confirmata*	Moluccas and Aru Islands
____	*H. m. mystacea*	New Guinea and w Papuan islands
____	*H. m. aeroplanes*	Bismarck Archipelago
____	*H. m. macrura*	Admiralty Islands
____	*H. m. woodfordiana*	Solomon Islands, Feni I. and Bougainville
____	*H. m. carbonaria*	San Cristóbal (Solomon Islands)

ORDER: TROCHILIFORMES
FAMILY: TROCHILIDAE (Hummingbirds—335)

☐ **Saw-billed Hermit** *Ramphodon naevius*

Lowlands of se Brazil (s Minas Gerais Santa Catarina)

☐ **White-tipped Sicklebill** *Eutoxeres aquila*

____	*E. a. salvini (munda)*	Humid foothills of e Costa Rica to w Colombia
____	*E. a. heterura*	Western Andes (sw Colombia to w Ecuador)
____	*E. a. aquila*	Eastern Andes (Colombia to n Peru)

☐ **Buff-tailed Sicklebill** *Eutoxeres condamini*

____	*E. c. condamini*	Eastern Andes (se Colombia to n Peru)
____	*E. c. gracilis*	Eastern Andes (Peru to nw Bolivia)

☐ **Hook-billed Hermit** *Glaucis dohrnii*

Coastal se Brazil (Bahia and Espírito Santo)

☐ **Rufous-breasted Hermit** *Glaucis hirsuta*

____	*G. h. insularum*	Grenada, Trinidad and Tobago
____	*G. h. hirsuta*	Panama to w Colombia, Venezuela, Guianas, Brazil, n Bolivia

☐ **Bronzy Hermit** *Glaucis aenea*

E Honduras to w Panama; w Colombia to nw Ecuador

☐ **Band-tailed Barbthroat** *Threnetes ruckeri*

____	*T. r. ventosus*	Tropical e Guatemala and Belize to w Panama
____	*T. r. ruckeri*	N and w Colombia to w Ecuador
____	*T. r. venezuelensis*	NW Venezuela (region sw of Lake Maracaibo)

☐ **Pale-tailed Barbthroat** *Threnetes niger*

____	*T. n. cervinicauda*	E Colombia to e Ecuador, ne Peru and adj. w Amaz. Brazil
____	*T. n. rufigastra*	Central Peru to n Bolivia
____	*T. n. leucurus*	S Venezuela to Suriname, Amazonian Brazil and n Bolivia
____	*T. n. niger*	French Guiana and adjacent Brazil (n Amapá)
____	*T. n. loehkeni*	NE Brazil north of the Amazon (Amapá)
____	*T. n. medianus*	NE Brazil south of the Amazon (e Pará and n Maranhão)

☐ **Broad-tipped Hermit** *Anopetia gounellei*

Lowlands of e Brazil (Piauí, Ceará and Bahia)

☐ **White-whiskered Hermit** *Phaethornis yaruqui*

Tropical Pacific Colombia and w Ecuador

☐ **Green Hermit** *Phaethornis guy*

____	*P. g. coruscus*	Mainly subtropical Costa Rica, Panama and nw Colombia
____	*P. g. emiliae*	Major river valleys of w-central Colombia
____	*P. g. apicalis*	E slope of Andes (n Colombia to nw Venezuela and e Peru)
____	*P. g. guy*	NE Venezuela and Trinidad

☐ **White-bearded Hermit** *Phaethornis hispidus*

E Colombia to s Venezuela, n Bolivia and w Amazonian Brazil

□ **Western Long-tailed Hermit** *Phaethornis longirostris*
___ *P. l. griseoventer* — W Mexico (Nayarit to Colima)
___ *P. l. mexicanus* — SW Mexico (w Guerrero to se Oaxaca)
___ *P. l. longirostris (veracrucis)* — S Mexico (n Oaxaca and Chiapas) to Belize and n Honduras
___ *P. l. cephalus (cassinii)* — E Honduras to nw Colombia
___ *P. l. sussurus* — Santa Marta Mountains (ne Colombia)
___ *P. l. baroni* — W Ecuador and nw Peru

□ **Eastern Long-tailed Hermit** *Phaethornis superciliosus*
___ *P. s. superciliosus* — S Venezuela to the Guianas, Suriname and nw Brazil
___ *P. s. muelleri* — N Brazil south of Amazon (Pará and Maranhão)

□ **Great-billed Hermit** *Phaethornis malaris*
___ *P. m. insolitus* — E Colombia to s Venezuela and adjacent n Brazil
___ *P. m. malaris* — Suriname and French Guiana to adjacent n Brazil (Amapá)
___ *P. m. margarettae* — Coastal e Brazil (Pernambuco to Espírito Santo)
___ *P. m. moorei* — E Colombia to e Ecuador and n Peru
___ *P. m. ochraceiventris* — NE Peru and w Brazil to lower Rio Madeira (s of the Amazon)
___ *P. m. bolivianus* — SE Peru to Bolivia and w Brazil (to west bank of Rio Tapajós)

□ **Tawny-bellied Hermit** *Phaethornis syrmatophorus*
___ *P. s. syrmatophorus* — W Andes of Colombia to sw Ecuador
___ *P. s. columbianus (huallagae)* — E Andes of Colombia to n Peru

□ **Koepcke's Hermit** *Phaethornis koepckeae*
Foothills of e slope of Andes of Peru

□ **Needle-billed Hermit** *Phaethornis philippii*
Trop. e Peru, n Bolivia and w Amaz. Brazil s of the Amazon

□ **Straight-billed Hermit** *Phaethornis bourcieri*
___ *P. b. bourcieri (whitelyi)* — E Colombia to s Venezuela, the Guianas, n Brazil and n Peru
___ *P. b. major* — Brazil south of the Amazon (e bank of lower Rio Tapajós)

□ **Pale-bellied Hermit** *Phaethornis anthophilus*
___ *P. a. hyalinus* — Pearl Islands (Bay of Panama)
___ *P. a. anthophilus (fuliginosus)* — Central Panama to Colombia and n Venezuela

□ **Scale-throated Hermit** *Phaethornis eurynome*
___ *P. e. paraguayensis* — E Paraguay and ne Argentina (Misiones)
___ *P. e. eurynome* — SE Brazil (Bahia to Rio Grande do Sul)

□ **Planalto Hermit** *Phaethornis pretrei*
E Brazil to e Bolivia, e Paraguay and n Argentina

□ **Sooty-capped Hermit** *Phaethornis augusti*
___ *P. a. curiosus* — Santa Marta Mountains (ne Colombia)
___ *P. a. augusti (vicarius)* — Colombia (E Andes and Macarene Mts.) to mts. of n Venezuela
___ *P. a. incanescens* — *Tepuis* of se Venezuela and adjacent Guyana

□ **Buff-bellied Hermit** *Phaethornis subochraceus*
Lowlands of e Bolivia and adjacent Brazil (w Mato Grosso)

□ **Dusky-throated Hermit** *Phaethornis squalidus*
SE Brazil (s Minas Gerais and Espírito Santo to Santa Catarina)

□ **Streak-throated Hermit** *Phaethornis rupurumii*
___ *P. r. rupurumii* — Extreme e Colombia to Venezuela, w Guyana and adj. w Brazil
___ *P. r. amazonicus* — Valley of lower Amazon in n-central Brazil

□ **Little Hermit** *Phaethornis longuemareus*
NE Venezuela to French Guiana; Trinidad

□ **Minute Hermit** *Phaethornis idaliae*
Lowlands of se Brazil (Bahia to Rio de Janeiro)

☐ **Cinnamon-throated Hermit** *Phaethornis nattereri*

E Bolivia and adj. sw Brazil; ne Brazil (Maranhão to Ceará)

☐ **Reddish Hermit** *Phaethornis ruber*
_____ *P. r. episcopus*
_____ *P. r. ruber*
_____ *P. r. nigricinctus*
_____ *P. r. longipennis*

Central and e Venezuela, Guyana and adjacent Brazil
Suriname to French Guiana, Brazil, se Peru and n Bolivia
Extreme e Colombia to sw Venezuela and n Peru
S Peru

☐ **White-browed Hermit** *Phaethornis stuarti*

Foothills of se Peru to central Bolivia

☐ **Black-throated Hermit** *Phaethornis atrimentalis*
_____ *P. a. atrimentalis*
_____ *P. a. riojae*

E Andes of Colombia, Ecuador and n Peru
Central Peru

☐ **Stripe-throated Hermit** *Phaethornis striigularis*
_____ *P. s. saturatus*
_____ *P. s. subrufescens*
_____ *P. s. striigularis*
_____ *P. s. ignobilis*

S Mexico (s Veracruz) to nw Colombia
W Colombia and w Ecuador
N Colombia (Magdalena Valley) and adjacent w Venezuela
N Venezuela

☐ **Gray-chinned Hermit** *Phaethornis griseogularis*
_____ *P. g. griseogularis*
_____ *P. g. zonura*
_____ *P. g. porcullae*

Andes of Colombia to n Peru, s Venezuela and adjacent Brazil
NW Peru (Cajamarca and adjacent Amazonas)
Andes of n Peru (Tumbes, Piura and Lambayeque)

☐ **Tooth-billed Hummingbird** *Androdon aequatorialis*

Humid e Panama to w Colombia (Chocó) and nw Ecuador

☐ **Green-fronted Lancebill** *Doryfera ludovicae*
_____ *D. l. veraguensis*
_____ *D. l. ludovicae (rectirostris, grisea)*

Humid montane forests of Costa Rica and w Panama
Mts. of e Panama to Colombia, w Venezuela and nw Bolivia

☐ **Blue-fronted Lancebill** *Doryfera johannae*
_____ *D. j. johannae*
_____ *D. j. guianensis*

E slope of Andes of se Colombia and e Ecuador to ne Peru
Tepuis of s Venezuela, s Guyana and adjacent n Brazil

☐ **Scaly-breasted Hummingbird** *Phaeochroa cuvierii*
_____ *P. c. roberti*
_____ *P. c. maculicauda*
_____ *P. c. saturatior*
_____ *P. c. cuvierii*
_____ *P. c. berlepschi*

Extreme se Mexico to Belize, Guatemala and ne Costa Rica
Pacific slope of Costa Rica
Coiba I.
E and central Panama
Coastal n Colombia (Cartagena to Barranquilla)

☐ **Wedge-tailed Sabrewing** *Campylopterus curvipennis*
_____ *C. c. curvipennis*
_____ *C. c. pampa*

S Mexico (se San Luis Potosí and sw Tamaulipas to n Oaxaca)
Yucatán Peninsula to n Guatemala, Belize and n Honduras

☐ **Long-tailed Sabrewing** *Campylopterus excellens*

Sierra de Tuxtla (se Mexico)

☐ **Gray-breasted Sabrewing** *Campylopterus largipennis*
_____ *C. l. aequatorialis*
_____ *C. l. largipennis*
_____ *C. l. obscurus*
_____ *C. l. diamantinensis*

E Colombia to Ecuador, Peru, n Bolivia and nw Brazil
E Venezuela, the Guianas and Rio Negro region of nw Brazil
NE Brazil (e Pará and Maranhão)
SE Brazil (Serra Espinhaço in Minas Gerais)

☐ **Rufous Sabrewing** *Campylopterus rufus*

Highlands of s Mexico (Oaxaca and Chiapas) to El Salvador

☐ **Violet Sabrewing** *Campylopterus hemileucurus*
_____ *C. h. hemileucurus*
_____ *C. h. mellitus*

Patchily distributed highlands of s Mexico to s-c Nicaragua
Costa Rica and w Panama

☐ **Rufous-breasted Sabrewing** *Campylopterus hyperythrus*

Tepuis of se Venezuela and adjacent nw Brazil

☐ **White-tailed Sabrewing** *Campylopterus ensipennis*

Mountains of ne Venezuela and Tobago

☐ **Lazuline Sabrewing** *Campylopterus falcatus*

Mountains of Colombia, Venezuela and e Ecuador

☐ **Santa Marta Sabrewing** *Campylopterus phainopeplus*

Santa Marta Mountains (ne Colombia)

☐ **Napo Sabrewing** *Campylopterus villaviscensio*

Foothills of s Colombia to e Ecuador and adjacent ne Peru

☐ **Buff-breasted Sabrewing** *Campylopterus duidae*
_____ *C. d. guaiquinimae* — *Tepuis* of s Venezuela (Mt. Guaiquinima)
_____ *C. d. duidae* — *Tepuis* of s Venezuela (Mt. Duida) and adjacent n Brazil

☐ **Sombre Hummingbird** *Campylopterus cirrochloris*

Forest and scrub of e and central Brazil

☐ **Swallow-tailed Hummingbird** *Eupetomena macrourus*
_____ *E. m. macrourus* — Guianas to n, central and se Brazil and Paraguay
_____ *E. m. simoni* — NE Brazil (s Maranhão, Piauí and Ceará to Minas Gerais)
_____ *E. m. cyanoviridis* — SE Brazil (Serra do Mar in s São Paulo)
_____ *E. m. hirundo* — E Peru (Huiro)
_____ *E. m. bolivianus* — Savanna of nw Bolivia (Beni)

☐ **White-necked Jacobin** *Florisuga mellivora*
_____ *F. m. mellivora* — Tropical s Mexico to n Bolivia and Amazonian Brazil; Trinidad
_____ *F. m. flabellifera* — Tobago (s Lesser Antilles)

☐ **Black Jacobin** *Florisuga fuscus*

E Brazil to Uruguay and ne Argentina

☐ **Brown Violet-ear** *Colibri delphinae*

Belize and Guatemala to the Guianas, Brazil and Bolivia

☐ **Green Violet-ear** *Colibri thalassinus*
_____ *C. t. thalassinus (minor)* — Open mountain slopes of s Mexico to n-central Nicaragua
_____ *C. t. cabanidis* — Highlands of Costa Rica and w Panama
_____ *C. t. cyanotus* — Mountains of Colombia, Venezuela and Ecuador
_____ *C. t. crissalis* — Andes of Peru, Bolivia and extreme nw Argentina

☐ **Sparkling Violet-ear** *Colibri coruscans*
_____ *C. c. germanus (rostratus)* — *Tepuis* of s Venezuela, e Guyana and adjacent n Brazil
_____ *C. c. coruscans* — Mountains of Colombia and Venezuela to nw Argentina

☐ **White-vented Violet-ear** *Colibri serrirostris*

Savanna of e Bolivia to Paraguay, s Brazil and n Argentina

☐ **Green-throated Mango** *Anthracothorax viridigula*

NE Venezuela to the Guianas and n Brazil; Trinidad

☐ **Green-breasted Mango** *Anthracothorax prevostii*
_____ *A. p. prevostii* — E Mexico to Guatemala, Belize and El Salvador
_____ *A. p. gracilirostris* — El Salvador and Honduras to central Costa Rica
_____ *A. p. hendersoni (pinchoti)* — Isla Providéncia and Isla San Andrés (off e Nicaragua)
_____ *A. p. viridicordatus* — Extreme ne Colombia (Guajira Pen.) and coastal n Venezuela
_____ *A. p. iridescens* — W Colombia (Cauca Valley) to w Ecuador and nw Peru

☐ **Black-throated Mango** *Anthracothorax nigricollis*

Panama and Colombia e of Andes to ne Argentina and Brazil

☐ **Veraguan Mango** *Anthracothorax veraguensis*

W Panama (Chiriquí to s Coclé) and adjacent islands

☐ **Antillean Mango** *Anthracothorax dominicus*
_____ *A. d. dominicus* — Hispaniola, Île-á-Vache, Tortue, Gonâve and Beata islands
_____ *A. d. aurulentus* — Puerto Rico, Culebra I., Vieques I. and Virgin Islands

☐ **Green Mango** *Anthracothorax viridis*

☐ **Jamaican Mango** *Anthracothorax mango*
_____ Puerto Rico

☐ **Fiery-tailed Awlbill** *Avocettula recurvirostris*
_____ Jamaica

☐ **Crimson Topaz** *Topaza pella*
_____ SE Venezuela to the Guianas and n-central Brazil; e Ecuador

_____ *T. p. pyra* — SE Colombia to e Ecuador, ne Peru and s Venezuela
_____ *T. p. pamprepta* — E Ecuador (Río Napo and Río Suno region)
_____ *T. p. pella (smaragdula)* — S Venezuela to the Guianas, Suriname and n Brazil (Amapá)
_____ *T. p. microrhyncha* — NE Brazil (south bank of lower Amazon near Belém)

☐ **Purple-throated Carib** *Eulampis jugularis*
_____ Montane forests of Lesser Antilles

☐ **Green-throated Carib** *Eulampis holosericeus*

_____ *E. h. holosericeus* — Puerto Rico, Virgin Is. and Lesser Antilles (except Granada)
_____ *E. h. chlorolaemus* — Grenada

☐ **Ruby-topaz Hummingbird** *Chrysolampis mosquitus*
_____ Trop. e Panama to Colombia, Venezuela, e Bolivia and Brazil

☐ **Antillean Crested Hummingbird** *Orthorhyncus cristatus*

_____ *O. c. exilis* — E Puerto Rico, Virgin Islands and Lesser Antilles to St. Lucia
_____ *O. c. ornatus* — St. Vincent (Lesser Antilles)
_____ *O. c. cristatus* — Barbados (Lesser Antilles)
_____ *O. c. emigrans* — Lesser Antilles (Grenadines and Grenada)

☐ **Violet-headed Hummingbird** *Klais guimeti*

_____ *K. g. merritti* — E Honduras to e Panama
_____ *K. g. guimeti* — E Colombia to Venezuela, Brazil, e Ecuador and n Peru
_____ *K. g. pallidiventris* — E Peru to w-central Bolivia

☐ **Plovercrest** *Stephanoxis lalandi*

_____ *S. l. lalandi* — E Brazil (s Minas Gerais to Espírito Santo and ne São Paulo)
_____ *S. l. loddigesii* — E Paraguay and ne Argentina (Misiones) to s Brazil

☐ **Emerald-chinned Hummingbird** *Abeillia abeillei*

_____ *A. a. abeillei* — Mountains of se Mexico to n Honduras
_____ *A. a. aurea* — Mountains of s Honduras and n Nicaragua

☐ **Tufted Coquette** *Lophornis ornatus*
_____ E Venezuela, Trinidad and the Guianas to n Brazil

☐ **Dot-eared Coquette** *Lophornis gouldii*
_____ Lowlands of n-central Brazil to e Bolivia (Santa Cruz)

☐ **Frilled Coquette** *Lophornis magnificus*
_____ Forests and scrub of e-central Brazil

☐ **Short-crested Coquette** *Lophornis brachylophus*
_____ S Mexico (Sierra Madre del Sur of Guerrero)

☐ **Rufous-crested Coquette** *Lophornis delattrei*

_____ *L. d. lessoni* — Locally from sw Costa Rica to Andes of central Colombia
_____ *L. d. delattrei* — Locally from s Ecuador to e Peru and n Bolivia

☐ **Spangled Coquette** *Lophornis stictolophus*
_____ Andes of e Colombia to w Venezuela and n Peru

☐ **Festive Coquette** *Lophornis chalybeus*

_____ *L. c. verreauxii* — E Colombia to e Ecuador, e Peru, nw Brazil and c Bolivia
_____ *L. c. klagesi* — SE Venezuela
_____ *L. c. chalybeus* — SE Brazil (Espírito Santo, Minas Gerais and Santa Catarina)

☐ **Peacock Coquette** *Lophornis pavoninus*
_____ *L. p. pavoninus* — *Tepuis* of se Venezuela to Guyana (Merumé Mountains)
_____ *L. p. duidae* — *Tepuis* of se Venezuela (Mt. Duida) and adjacent smaller *tepuis*

☐ **Black-crested Coquette** *Lophornis helenae*
Gulf slope of s Mexico (Veracruz) to e Costa Rica

☐ **White-crested Coquette** *Lophornis adorabilis*
Costa Rica to w Panama

☐ **Wire-crested Thorntail** *Popelairia popelairii*
E Colombia to e Ecuador and ne Peru

☐ **Black-bellied Thorntail** *Popelairia langsdorffi*
_____ *P. l. melanosternon* — SE Colombia to s Venezuela, e Ecuador, e Peru and w Brazil
_____ *P. l. langsdorffi* — E Brazil (Bahia, Espírito Santo and Rio de Janeiro)

☐ **Coppery Thorntail** *Popelairia letitiae*
Known from three specimens ca 1852 labeled from "Bolivia"

☐ **Green Thorntail** *Discosura conversii*
Costa Rica to Panama, w Colombia and w Ecuador

☐ **Racket-tailed Coquette** *Discosura longicauda*
Tropical s Venezuela to the Guianas and e Brazil

☐ **Red-billed Streamertail** *Trochilus polytmus*
Jamaica (except range of *scitulus*)

☐ **Black-billed Streamertail** *Trochilus scitulus*
Extreme ne Jamaica (Portland Parish)

☐ **Blue-chinned Sapphire** *Chlorostilbon notatus*
_____ *C. n. notatus (cyanogenys)* — N Colombia to Venezuela, Trinidad, Tobago, Guianas, e Brazil
_____ *C. n. puruensis* — SE Colombia to ne Peru and nw Brazil
_____ *C. n. obsoletus* — NE Peru (lower Río Ucayali near mouth of Río Napo)

☐ **Blue-tailed Emerald** *Chlorostilbon mellisugus*
_____ *C. m. pumilus* — Pacific slope of w Colombia and w Ecuador
_____ *C. m. melanorhynchus* — Andes of sw Colombia (Nariño) and w Ecuador
_____ *C. m. gibsoni* — Colombia (upper Magdalena Valley)
_____ *C. m. chrysogaster* — Lowlands of n Colombia (Cartagena to Santa Marta)
_____ *C. m. nitens* — Arid coast of extreme ne Colombia and nw Venezuela
_____ *C. m. caribaeus* — NE Venezuela, Curaçao, Aruba, Bonaire, Trinidad, Margarita I.
_____ *C. m. duidae* — *Tepuis* of s Venezuela (Mt. Duidae)
_____ *C. m. subfurcatus* — S Venezuela to Guyana and nw Brazil (Rio Branco region)
_____ *C. m. mellisugus* — Suriname, French Guiana and lower Amazonian Brazil
_____ *C. m. phaeopygus (napensis)* — Upper Amazon and tributaries from Colombia to Bolivia
_____ *C. m. peruanus* — E Peru and e Bolivia

☐ **Golden-crowned Emerald** *Chlorostilbon auriceps*
W Mexico (s Sinaloa to Durango, Guerrero and Oaxaca)

☐ **Cozumel Emerald** *Chlorostilbon forficatus*
SE Mexico (Cozumel I. and rarely Isla Mujeres)

☐ **Canivet's Emerald** *Chlorostilbon canivetii*
_____ *C. c. canivetii* — SE Mexico (Tamaulipas) to Belize, n Guatemala and Nicaragua
_____ *C. c. osberti* — SE Mexico (se Chiapas) to Honduras, Holbox, Bay and Hog is.
_____ *C. c. salvini* — Highlands of Pacific slope of nw Costa Rica

☐ **Garden Emerald** *Chlorostilbon assimilis*
Pacific slope of sw Costa Rica and Panama; Coiba and Pearl is.

☐ **Glittering-bellied Emerald** *Chlorostilbon aureoventris*
_____ *C. a. pucherani* — E Brazil (Maranhão and Ceará to Paraná)
_____ *C. a. aureoventris* — E Bolivia to Paraguay and w-central Brazil (Mato Grosso)
_____ *C. a. igneus* — NW Argentina (Jujuy and Chaco to Mendoza and San Luis)
_____ *C. a. berlepschi* — S Brazil (Rio Grande do Sul) to Uruguay and ne Argentina

☐ **Chiribiquete Emerald** *Chlorostilbon olivaresi*

SE Colombia (Sierra de Chiribiquete)

☐ **Cuban Emerald** *Chlorostilbon ricordii*

Cuba, Isle of Pines, Grand Bahama, Great Abaco and Andros

☐ **Hispaniolian Emerald** *Chlorostilbon swainsonii*

Primarily montane forests of Hispaniola

☐ **Puerto Rican Emerald** *Chlorostilbon maugaeus*

Puerto Rico

☐ **Coppery Emerald** *Chlorostilbon russatus*

Highlands of ne Colombia and extreme nw Venezuela

☐ **Narrow-tailed Emerald** *Chlorostilbon stenurus*
_____ *C. s. stenurus*
_____ *C. s. ignotus*

Andes of ne Colombia to nw Venezuela and ne Ecuador
Coastal mts. of n Venezuela to highlands of extreme se Lara

☐ **Green-tailed Emerald** *Chlorostilbon alice*

Mts. of n Venezuela (Falcón to Lara, Sucre and n Monagas)

☐ **Short-tailed Emerald** *Chlorostilbon poortmani*
_____ *C. p. euchloris*
_____ *C. p. poortmani*

Humid montane forests of central Colombia
E slope of Eastern Andes of Colombia and nw Venezuela

☐ **Fiery-throated Hummingbird** *Panterpe insignis*
_____ *P. i. eisenmanni*
_____ *P. i. insignis*

NW Costa Rica (Cordillera de Guanacaste)
N-c Costa Rica (Cordillera de Tilarán) to extreme w Panama

☐ **White-tailed Emerald** *Elvira chionura*

Pacific slope of s Costa Rica to central Panama

☐ **Coppery-headed Emerald** *Elvira cupreiceps*

Highlands of n and central Costa Rica

☐ **Blue-capped Hummingbird** *Eupherusa cyanophrys*

S Mexico (Sierra de Miahuatlán of Oaxaca)

☐ **White-tailed Hummingbird** *Eupherusa poliocerca*

S Mexico (Sierra Madre del Sur from Guerrero to w Oaxaca)

☐ **Stripe-tailed Hummingbird** *Eupherusa eximia*
_____ *E. e. nelsoni*
_____ *E. e. eximia*
_____ *E. e. egregia*

Humid rainforests of se Mexico (Veracruz and Oaxaca)
S Mexico (Chiapas) to Belize and n Nicaragua
Highlands of Costa Rica and w Panama

☐ **Black-bellied Hummingbird** *Eupherusa nigriventris*

Montane forests of central Costa Rica and extreme w Panama

☐ **Rufous-cheeked Hummingbird** *Goethalsia bella*

Highlands of e Panama (Darién) and extreme nw Colombia

☐ **Violet-capped Hummingbird** *Goldmania violiceps*

Highlands of e Panama and extreme nw Colombia

☐ **Dusky Hummingbird** *Cynanthus sordidus*

Mountains of central Mexico (Michoacán to Oaxaca)

☐ **Broad-billed Hummingbird** *Cynanthus latirostris*
_____ *C. l. magicus*
_____ *C. l. latirostris*
_____ *C. l. lawrencei*
_____ *C. l. propinquus*
_____ *C. l. doubledayi (nitidus)*

Arid sw US to nw Mexico (Nayarit)
E Mexico (San Luis Potosí and Tamaulipas to n Veracruz)
Tres Marías Islands (off w Mexico)
Central Mexico (Guanajuato to Michoacán)
S Mexico (Guerrero, Oaxaca and Chiapas)

☐ **Blue-headed Hummingbird** *Cyanophaia bicolor*

Lesser Antilles (mountains of Dominica and Martinique)

☐ **Violet-crowned Woodnymph** *Thalurania colombica*
_____ *T. c. townsendi*
_____ *T. c. venusta*
_____ *T. c. colombica*
_____ *T. c. rostrifera*

Belize and e Guatemala to se Honduras
E Nicaragua to w Panama
N Colombia and nw Venezuela
NW Venezuela (sw Táchira)

☐ **Mexican Woodnymph** *Thalurania ridgwayi*

Pacific slope of w Mexico (s Nayarit, Jalisco and Guerrero)

☐ **Green-crowned Woodnymph** *Thalurania fannyi*

_____ *T. f. fannyi*   E Panama to w Colombia
_____ *T. f. subtropicalis*   W-c Colombia (Cauca Valley and adjacent W and C Andes)
_____ *T. f. verticeps*   Pacific slope of W Andes of sw Colombia and nw Ecuador
_____ *T. f. hypochlora*   Pacific lowlands of Ecuador to extreme n Peru

☐ **Fork-tailed Woodnymph** *Thalurania furcata*

_____ *T. f. refulgens*   NE Venezuela (María Peninsula and Sierra de Cumaná)
_____ *T. f. furcata*   Extreme e Venezuela, Guianas and ne Brazil n of the Amazon
_____ *T. f. fissilis (orenocensis)*   E Venezuela, adjacent extreme w Guyana and ne Brazil
_____ *T. f. nigrofasciata*   SE Colombia to extreme s Venezuela and nw Brazil
_____ *T. f. viridipectus (taczanowskii)*   E slope of Andes and lowlands of e Colombia to ne Peru
_____ *T. f. jelskii*   Tropical e Peru and adjacent Brazil
_____ *T. f. simoni*   Amazonia s of the Amazon in extreme e Peru and w Brazil
_____ *T. f. balzani*   N-central Brazil south of the Amazon
_____ *T. f. furcatoides*   Lower Amazon region of e Brazil south of the Amazon
_____ *T. f. boliviana*   Andean foothills and adj. lowlands of se Peru and ne Bolivia
_____ *T. f. baeri*   NE and central Brazil to se Bolivia and n Argentina
_____ *T. f. eriphile*   SE Brazil, adjacent Paraguay and ne Argentina (Misiones)

☐ **Long-tailed Woodnymph** *Thalurania watertonii*

Coastal e Brazil (e Pará to Pernambuco and Bahia)

☐ **Violet-capped Woodnymph** *Thalurania glaucopis*

SE Brazil to e Paraguay and ne Argentina

☐ **Violet-bellied Hummingbird** *Damophila julie*

_____ *D. j. panamensis*   Humid forests of central Panama (east to Darién)
_____ *D. j. julie*   Tropical n Colombia
_____ *D. j. feliciana*   Tropical sw Colombia to w Ecuador and extreme nw Peru

☐ **Sapphire-throated Hummingbird** *Lepidopyga coeruleogularis*

_____ *L. c. coeruleogularis*   Pacific slope of w Panama (Chiriquí to Canal Zone)
_____ *L. c. confinis*   Caribbean slope of e Panama (Darién) and adj. nw Colombia
_____ *L. c. coelina*   N Colombia (n Chocó to Santa Marta region)

☐ **Sapphire-bellied Hummingbird** *Lepidopyga lilliae*

Coastal n-central Colombia

☐ **Shining-green Hummingbird** *Lepidopyga goudoti*

_____ *L. g. luminosa*   Coastal lowlands of n Colombia
_____ *L. g. goudoti*   N-central Colombia (middle and upper Magdalena Valley)
_____ *L. g. zuliae*   N and w area of Lake Maracaibo basin (Colombia/Venezuela)
_____ *L. g. phaeochroa*   NW Venezuela (south and east area of Lake Maracaibo basin)

☐ **Blue-throated Goldentail** *Hylocharis eliciae*

_____ *H. e. eliciae*   Lowlands of se Mexico and Belize to s Costa Rica
_____ *H. e. earina*   W Panama, Coiba I., Bay of Panama islands and nw Colombia

☐ **Rufous-throated Sapphire** *Hylocharis sapphirina*

E Colombia to Guianas, s Venezuela, se Brazil and ne Argentina

☐ **White-chinned Sapphire** *Hylocharis cyanus*

_____ *H. c. viridiventris*   Colombia to the Guianas, s Venezuela and n Brazil
_____ *H. c. rostrata*   E Peru to ne Bolivia and w Brazil (Mato Grosso)
_____ *H. c. conversa*   E Bolivia to n Paraguay and sw Brazil (Mato Grosso do Sul)
_____ *H. c. cyanus*   Coastal e Brazil (Pernambuco to Rio de Janeiro)
_____ *H. c. griseiventris*   Coastal se Brazil (São Paulo) to ne Argentina (Buenos Aires)

☐ **Gilded Sapphire** *Hylocharis chrysura*

Bolivia to Paraguay, Uruguay, se Brazil and n Argentina

☐ **Blue-headed Sapphire** *Hylocharis grayi*
____   *H. g. humboldtii*   Extreme se Panama to Colombia and nw Ecuador
____   *H. g. grayi*   W Colombia and n Ecuador

☐ **Xantus' Hummingbird** *Hylocharis xantusii*

                                             Arid scrub of s Baja California

☐ **White-eared Hummingbird** *Hylocharis leucotis*
____   *H. l. borealis*   Mountains of se Arizona and n Mexico
____   *H. l. leucotis*   Highland pine forests of central and s Mexico to Guatemala
____   *H. l. pygmaea*   Highlands of El Salvador, Honduras and Nicaragua

☐ **Golden-tailed Sapphire** *Chrysuronia oenone*
____   *C. o. oenone (longirostris)*   E Colombia to e Venezuela, e Ecuador, ne Peru and w Brazil
____   *C. o. josephinae*   Tropical e Amazonian Peru
____   *C. o. alleni*   N Bolivia

☐ **White-throated Hummingbird** *Leucochloris albicollis*

                                             E Bolivia to e Paraguay, n Argentina and se Brazil

☐ **White-tailed Goldenthroat** *Polytmus guainumbi*
____   *P. g. andinus*   E Colombia (south to Meta and Vichada)
____   *P. g. guainumbi*   Venezuela to the Guianas, n Brazil and Trinidad
____   *P. g. thaumantias*   E Bolivia to e Paraguay, c and e Brazil and ne Argentina

☐ **Tepui Goldenthroat** *Polytmus milleri*

                                             Tepuis of s Venezuela and adj. Brazil (Roraima)

☐ **Green-tailed Goldenthroat** *Polytmus theresiae*
____   *P. t. theresiae*   The Guianas and n-c Brazil (Amazonas, Pará and Amapá)
____   *P. t. leucorrhous*   E Colombia to s Venezuela, nw Brazil and ne Peru (Loreto)

☐ **Buffy Hummingbird** *Leucippus fallax*

                                             Coastal n Colombia, Venezuela, La Tortuga I. and Margarita I.

☐ **Tumbes Hummingbird** *Leucippus baeri*

                                             Arid littoral of extreme sw Ecuador and adjacent nw Peru

☐ **Spot-throated Hummingbird** *Leucippus taczanowskii*

                                             W slope of Central Andes of n and central Peru

☐ **Olive-spotted Hummingbird** *Leucippus chlorocercus*

                                             Extreme se Colombia to e Ecuador, ne Peru and nw Brazil

☐ **White-bellied Hummingbird** *Leucippus chionogaster*
____   *A. c. chionogaster*   N and central Peru
____   *A. c. hypoleucus*   SE Peru to Bolivia, Paraguay, nw Argentina and Mato Grosso

☐ **Green-and-white Hummingbird** *Leucippus viridicauda*

                                             E slope of Andes of Peru (s Huánuco to s Puno)

☐ **Many-spotted Hummingbird** *Leucippus hypostictus*

                                             Andes of e Ecuador to se Bolivia and nw Argentina; sw Brazil

☐ **Rufous-tailed Hummingbird** *Amazilia tzacatl*
____   *A. t. tzacatl*   E Mexico (s Tamaulipas) to central Panama
____   *A. t. handleyi*   Isla Escudo de Veraguas (off Caribbean coast of nw Panama)
____   *A. t. fuscicaudata*   N and w Colombia to w Venezuela
____   *A. t. jucunda*   SW Colombia and w Ecuador; Isla Gorgona (off w Colombia)

☐ **Chestnut-bellied Hummingbird** *Amazilia castaneiventris*

                                             W slope of Eastern Andes of n-central Colombia

☐ **Amazilia Hummingbird** *Amazilia amazilia*
____   *A. a. dumerilii*   Pacific slope of Ecuador to n Peru; e slope in Zamora Valley
____   *A. a. leucophaea*   NW Peru
____   *A. a. amazilia*   Arid littoral of w Peru
____   *A. a. caeruleigularis*   Foothills of sw Peru (Nazca Valley in Ica)

☐ **Loja Hummingbird** *Amazilia alticola*

Andes of s Ecuador

☐ **Buff-bellied Hummingbird** *Amazilia yucatanensis*
_____ *A. y. chalconota*   S Texas (lower Rio Grande Valley) to ne Mexico
_____ *A. y. cerviniventris*   S Mexico (Veracruz, Puebla, Oaxaca and Chiapas)
_____ *A. y. yucatanensis*   Yucatán Peninsula, Petén of n Guatemala and n Belize

☐ **Cinnamon Hummingbird** *Amazilia rutila*
_____ *A. r. diluta*   Coastal nw Mexico (Sinaloa and Nayarit)
_____ *A. r. graysoni*   Tres Marías Islands (off w Mexico)
_____ *A. r. rutila*   W Mexico (Jalisco to Oaxaca)
_____ *A. r. corrallirostris*   SE Mexico (Chiapas) to w Costa Rica; Holbox I., Isla Mujeres

☐ **Plain-bellied Emerald** *Agyrtria leucogaster*
_____ *A. l. leucogaster*   E Venezuela to the Guianas and n Brazil
_____ *A. l. bahiae*   E Brazil (Pernambuco to Bahia)

☐ **Versicolored Emerald** *Agyrtria versicolor*
_____ *A. v. millerii*   Tropical e Colombia to s Venezuela, e Peru and n Brazil
_____ *A. v. hollandi*   Tropical se Venezuela and (?) adjacent Guyana
_____ *A. v. nitidifrons*   NE Brazil
_____ *A. v. versicolor*   SE Brazil
_____ *A. v. kubtcheki*   NE Bolivia to e Paraguay, sw Brazil and extreme ne Argentina

☐ **Rondonia Emerald** *Agyrtria rondoniae*

N Bolivia and w-c Brazil (Rondônia)

☐ **White-chested Emerald** *Agyrtria brevirostris*
_____ *A. b. chionopectus*   Trinidad
_____ *A. b. brevirostris*   E Venezuela to Guyana, Suriname and extreme n-c Brazil
_____ *A. b. orienticola*   Coastal French Guiana

☐ **Andean Emerald** *Agyrtria franciae*
_____ *A. f. franciae (veneta)*   Subtropical Andes of nw and central Colombia
_____ *A. f. viridiceps*   Tropical sw Colombia and w Ecuador
_____ *A. f. cyanocollis*   E slope of Andes of n Peru

☐ **White-bellied Emerald** *Agyrtria candida*
_____ *A. c. genini*   Caribbean slope of se Mexico
_____ *A. c. pacifica*   Pacific slope of se Mexico (Chiapas) to s Guatemala
_____ *A. c. candida*   Humid se Mexico (Yucatán Pen.) to Belize and Nicaragua

☐ **Azure-crowned Hummingbird** *Agyrtria cyanocephala*
_____ *A. c. cyanocephala*   Oak-pine woodlands of se Mexico to n-central Nicaragua
_____ *A. c. chlorostephana*   Mosquito coast of e Honduras and ne Nicaragua

☐ **Violet-crowned Hummingbird** *Agyrtria violiceps*
_____ *A. v. ellioti*   Semiarid sw US to w Mexico (Jalisco and Guanajuato)
_____ *A. v. violiceps*   SW Mexico

☐ **Green-fronted Hummingbird** *Agyrtria viridifrons*
_____ *A. v. viridifrons*   S Mexico (e Guerrero to w Oaxaca; e Oaxaca to c Chiapas)
_____ *A. v. wagneri*   S Mexico (central and s Oaxaca)

☐ **Sapphire-spangled Emerald** *Polyerata lactea*
_____ *P. l. zimmeri*   *Tepuis* of se Venezuela (Mt. Auyan-tepui)
_____ *P. l. bartletti*   E Peru to n Bolivia
_____ *P. l. lactea*   Central and s Brazil (s Bahia to São Paulo)

☐ **Glittering-throated Emerald** *Polyerata fimbriata*

____ *P. f. elegantissima* — Extreme ne Colombia to n Venezuela

____ *P. f. distans* — Andes of w Venezuela (Táchira). Probable hybrid

____ *P. f. fimbriata (maculicauda, alia)* — NE Venezuela to Guianas and Brazil north of the Amazon

____ *P. f. apicalis* — Colombia east of the Andes

____ *P. f. fluviatilis* — SE Colombia and e Ecuador

____ *P. f. laeta* — NE Peru

____ *P. f. nigricauda* — E Bolivia and central Brazil south of the Amazon

____ *P. f. tephrocephala* — Coastal se Brazil (Espírito Santo to Rio Grande do Sul)

☐ **Blue-chested Hummingbird** *Polyerata amabilis* — NE Nicaragua to Colombia and Ecuador (west of the Andes)

☐ **Charming Hummingbird** *Polyerata decora* — Pacific slope of sw Costa Rica and extreme w Panama

☐ **Purple-chested Hummingbird** *Polyerata rosenbergi* — Pacific lowlands of w Colombia and nw Ecuador

☐ **Mangrove Hummingbird** *Polyerata boucardi* — W coast of Costa Rica (Gulf of Nicoya to Gulf of Dulce)

☐ **Honduran Emerald** *Polyerata luciae* — Arid interior valleys of n and central Honduras

☐ **Steely-vented Hummingbird** *Saucerottia saucerrottei*

____ *S. s. hoffmanni* — Semiarid w Nicaragua to central Costa Rica

____ *S. s. warscewiczi* — N Colombia and extreme nw Venezuela

____ *S. s. saucerrottei (australis)* — Colombia (W slope of Western Andes and Cauca Valley)

____ *S. s. braccata* — Andes of w Venezuela (Mérida and Trujillo)

☐ **Indigo-capped Hummingbird** *Saucerottia cyanifrons* — Lowlands and foothills of n and central Colombia

☐ **Snowy-bellied Hummingbird** *Saucerottia edward*

____ *S. e. niveoventer* — Extreme sw Costa Rica and w Panama; Isla Coiba

____ *S. e. edward* — Arid tropical Panama (Canal Zone to w Darién)

____ *S. e. collata* — Central Panama

____ *S. e. margaritarum (crosbyi)* — Urabá, Taboga, Taboguilla, Pearl is.; e Panama to sw Darién

☐ **Blue-tailed Hummingbird** *Saucerottia cyanura*

____ *S. c. guatemalae* — Pacific slope of s Mexico (se Chiapas) to s Guatemala

____ *S. c. cyanura* — S Honduras to e El Salvador and nw Nicaragua

____ *S. c. impatiens* — NW and central Costa Rica

☐ **Berylline Hummingbird** *Saucerottia beryllina*

____ *S. b. viola* — Oak-pine woods of nw Mexico (Sonora to Guerrero)

____ *S. b. beryllina* — E and central Mexico (Veracruz to Chiapas)

____ *S. b. lichtensteini* — Montane slopes of s Mexico (w Chiapas)

____ *S. b. sumichrasti* — Coastal mountains of s Mexico (central and s Chiapas)

____ *S. b. devillei* — Highlands of Guatemala to Honduras

☐ **Green-bellied Hummingbird** *Saucerottia viridigaster*

____ *S. v. viridigaster* — E slope of Eastern Andes of Colombia

____ *S. v. iodura* — Andes of w Venezuela (Táchira)

☐ **Copper-tailed Hummingbird** *Saucerottia cupreicauda*

____ *S. c. cupreicauda* — *Tepuis* of s Venezuela, Guyana and extreme n Brazil (Roraima)

____ *S. c. duidae* — *Tepuis* of s Venezuela (Mt. Duidae)

____ *S. c. laireti* — *Tepuis* of s Venezuela (Cerro de la Neblina)

☐ **Copper-rumped Hummingbird** *Saucerottia tobaci*

____ *S. t. tobaci* — Tobago

____ *S. t. erythronotos* — Trinidad

____ *S. t. aliciae* — Arid littoral of ne Venezuela and Isla Margarita

____	*S. t. monticola*	NW Venezuela
____	*S. t. feliciae (apurensis)*	Coastal ranges and arid littoral of n Venezuela
____	*S. t. caudata*	NE Venezuela
____	*S. t. caurensis*	E and se Venezuela (Orinoco Valley to the *tepuis*)

☐ **Snowcap** *Microchera albocoronata*

____	*M. a. parvirostris*	Caribbean slope of s Honduras to s Costa Rica and (?) Panama
____	*M. a. albocoronata*	Atlantic and Pacific slopes of w-central Panama

☐ **Blossomcrown** *Anthocephala floriceps*

____	*A. f. floriceps*	Santa Marta Mountains (ne Colombia)
____	*A. f. berlepschi*	E slope of Central Andes of Colombia (Magdalena Valley)

☐ **White-vented Plumeleteer** *Chalybura buffonii*

____	*C. b. micans*	Central Panama to Pacific slope of nw Colombia
____	*C. b. buffonii*	N-central Colombia (Magdalena Valley) and nw Venezuela
____	*C. b. aenicauda*	N Colombia (Santa Marta region) and n Venezuela
____	*C. b. caeruleogaster*	E slope of Eastern Andes of se Colombia

☐ **Bronze-tailed Plumeleteer** *Chalybura urochrysia*

____	*C. u. melanorrhoa*	Caribbean slope of Nicaragua and Costa Rica
____	*C. u. isaurae (incognita)*	Caribbean slope of w Panama to nw Colombia; e Panama
____	*C. u. urochrysia*	Extreme se Panama to w Colombia and nw Ecuador
____	*C. b. intermedia*	Subtropical sw Ecuador to nw Peru (San Martín)

☐ **Blue-throated Hummingbird** *Lampornis clemenciae*

____	*L. c. bessophilus*	Mts. of sw US to nw Mexico (e Sonora and w Chihuahua)
____	*L. c. clemenciae*	W Texas (Chisos Mountains) to s Mexico (s Oaxaca)

☐ **Amethyst-throated Hummingbird** *Lampornis amethystinus*

____	*L. a. amethystinus*	Mountains of e Mexico (Nayarit to s Tamaulipas and e Oaxaca)
____	*L. a. margaritae (brevirostris)*	Mountains of sw Mexico (Michoacán, Guerrero and w Oaxaca)
____	*L. a. salvini*	Highlands of s Mexico (Chiapas) to Guatemala, El Salvador
____	*L. a. nobilis*	Highlands of Honduras

☐ **Green-throated Mountain-gem** *Lampornis viridipallens*

____	*L. v. amadoni*	S Mexico (Cerro Baúl in Oaxaca)
____	*L. v. ovandensis*	Highlands of s Mexico (Chiapas) and nw Guatemala
____	*L. v. viridipallens (connectans)*	Highlands of Guatemala, n El Salvador and w Honduras
____	*L. v. nubivagus*	Upper tropical El Salvador

☐ **Green-breasted Mountain-gem** *Lampornis sybillae*

Humid montane forests of e Honduras and n-c Nicaragua

☐ **White-bellied Mountain-gem** *Lampornis hemileucus*

Caribbean slope of n-central Costa Rica to w Panama

☐ **White-throated Mountain-gem** *Lampornis castaneoventris*

Montane forests of extreme w Panama

☐ **Purple-throated Mountain-gem** *Lampornis calolaema*

____	*L. c. pectoralis*	Mountains of Nicaragua and nw Costa Rica
____	*L. c. calolaema*	Mountains of Costa Rica and w-central Panama

☐ **Gray-tailed Mountain-gem** *Lampornis cinereicauda*

____	*L. c. cinereicauda*	S Costa Rica (Cordillera de Talamanca)
____	*L. c. homogenes*	Pacific slope of extreme s Costa Rica and w Panama

☐ **Garnet-throated Hummingbird** *Lamprolaima rhami*

Mts. of s Mexico to Guatemala, El Salvador and Honduras

☐ **Ecuadorian Piedtail** *Phlogophilus hemileucurus*

Locally in foothills of s Colombia, e Ecuador and n Peru

☐ **Peruvian Piedtail** *Phlogophilus harterti*

Subtropical se Peru (Huánuco, Pasco, Puno and Cuzco)

☐ **Speckled Hummingbird** *Adelomyia melanogenys*
_____   *A. m. cervina*   W and Central Andes of Colombia
_____   *A. m. melanogenys*   E Andes of Colombia and w Venezuela to s-central Peru
_____   *A. m. connectens*   S Colombia (Huila)
_____   *A. m. debellardiana*   Mts. of Venezuela (Lara, Trujillo, Mérida, Táchira, Perijá)
_____   *A. m. aeneosticta*   Mountains of central and n Venezuela
_____   *A. m. maculata*   Andes of Ecuador and n Peru
_____   *A. m. chlorospila*   Andes of se Peru
_____   *A. m. inornata*   *Yungas* of Bolivia and adj. nw Argentina (Jujuy and Salta)

☐ **Brazilian Ruby** *Clytolaema rubricauda*

SE Brazil (Goiás and Minas Gerais to Rio Grande do Sul)

☐ **Gould's Jewelfront** *Heliodoxa aurescens*

E Colombia to n Bolivia, s Venezuela and w Amaz. Brazil

☐ **Fawn-breasted Brilliant** *Heliodoxa rubinoides*
_____   *H. r. rubinoides*   Central and Eastern Andes of Colombia
_____   *H. r. aequatorialis*   W slope of Andes of Colombia and w Ecuador
_____   *H. r. cervinigularis*   E slope of Andes of e Ecuador and ne Peru

☐ **Violet-fronted Brilliant** *Heliodoxa leadbeateri*
_____   *H. l. leadbeateri*   Coastal mts. of n Venezuela (Falcón to Carabobo and Miranda)
_____   *H. l. parvula*   Andes of Colombia and w Venezuela
_____   *H. l. sagitta*   Andes of e Ecuador and n Peru
_____   *H. l. otero*   Andes of central Peru to nw Bolivia

☐ **Velvet-browed Brilliant** *Heliodoxa xanthogonys*

Tepuis of s Venezuela, Guyana and adjacent n Brazil

☐ **Black-throated Brilliant** *Heliodoxa schreibersii*
_____   *H. s. schreibersii*   SE Colombia to Ecuador, ne Peru and nw Amazonian Brazil
_____   *H. s. whitelyana*   Tropical e Peru

☐ **Pink-throated Brilliant** *Heliodoxa gularis*

Trop. s Colombia to ne Ecuador, ne Peru and extreme nw Brazil

☐ **Rufous-webbed Brilliant** *Heliodoxa branickii*

Andean foothills of e Peru and (?) nw Bolivia

☐ **Empress Brilliant** *Heliodoxa imperatrix*

Pacific slope of sw Colombia to nw Ecuador

☐ **Green-crowned Brilliant** *Heliodoxa jacula*
_____   *H. j. henryi*   Humid montane forests of Costa Rica and w Panama
_____   *H. j. jacula*   Mountains of extreme e Panama and Andes of Colombia
_____   *H. j. jamesoni*   Andes of sw Colombia and w Ecuador

☐ **Magnificent Hummingbird** *Eugenes fulgens*
_____   *E. f. fulgens*   Mts. of s Arizona, New Mexico and Texas to ne Nicaragua
_____   *E. f. spectabilis*   Montane forests of Costa Rica and w Panama

☐ **Scissor-tailed Hummingbird** *Hylonympha macrocerca*

NE Venezuela (mountains of Pária Peninsula)

☐ **Violet-chested Hummingbird** *Sternoclyta cyanopectus*

Andes of w Venezuela and coastal cordillera east to Miranda

☐ **White-tailed Hillstar** *Urochroa bougueri*
_____   *U. b. bougueri*   Andes of sw Colombia and nw Ecuador
_____   *U. b. leucura*   Andes of s Colombia (Nariño) to e Ecuador and ne Peru

☐ **Chestnut-breasted Coronet** *Boissonneaua matthewsii*

Andes of extreme se Colombia, Ecuador and e Peru

☐ **Buff-tailed Coronet** *Boissonneaua flavescens*
_____ *B. f. flavescens*   Andes of Colombia and w Venezuela (Mérida)
_____ *B. f. tinochlora*   Andes of sw Colombia and adjacent nw Ecuador

☐ **Velvet-purple Coronet** *Boissonneaua jardini*

Western Andes of sw Colombia and nw Ecuador

☐ **Shining Sunbeam** *Aglaeactis cupripennis*
_____ *A. c. cupripennis (parvulus, ruficauda)*   Andes of Colombia to Ecuador and central Peru
_____ *A. c. caumatonotus*   Andes of s-c Peru (Junín, Apurímac, Ayacucho and Cuzco)

☐ **White-tufted Sunbeam** *Aglaeactis castelnaudii*
_____ *A. c. regalis*   Andes of central Peru (Huánuco, Pasco and Junín)
_____ *A. c. castelnaudii*   Andes of s Peru (Huancavelica, Ayacucho, Apurímac, Cuzco)

☐ **Purple-backed Sunbeam** *Aglaeactis aliciae*

E slope of Andes of n Peru (La Libertad and Ancash)

☐ **Black-hooded Sunbeam** *Aglaeactis pamela*

Andes of w Bolivia (La Paz and Cochabamba)

☐ **Andean Hillstar** *Oreotrochilus estella*
_____ *O. e. estella*   Andes of sw Peru to w Bolivia, n Chile and nw Argentina
_____ *O. e. bolivianus*   Andes of central Bolivia (Cochabamba)

☐ **Chimborazo Hillstar** *Oreotrochilus chimborazo*
_____ *O. c. jamesoni*   Andes of extreme s Colombia and n Ecuador
_____ *O. c. soederstroemi*   Andes of central Ecuador (Mt. Quilotoa)
_____ *O. c. chimborazo*   Andes of central Ecuador (Mt. Chimborazo and Mt. Azuay)

☐ **Green-headed Hillstar** *Oreotrochilus stolzmanni*

Andes of n and c Peru (Cajamarca, Huánuco); adj. s Ecuador?

☐ **White-sided Hillstar** *Oreotrochilus leucopleurus*

Andes of s Bolivia to s Argentina and s-c Chile (Bío-Bío)

☐ **Black-breasted Hillstar** *Oreotrochilus melanogaster*

Andes of Peru (Junín, Huancavelica, Ancash, Lima, Ayacucho)

☐ **Wedge-tailed Hillstar** *Oreotrochilus adela*

Andes of Bolivia (s La Paz to Potosí and Chuquisaca)

☐ **Mountain Velvetbreast** *Lafresnaya lafresnayi*
_____ *L. l. liriope*   Santa Marta Mountains (ne Colombia)
_____ *L. l. greenewalti*   Andes of w Venezuela (ne Táchira, Mérida and s Trujillo)
_____ *L. l. lafresnayi*   Central and Eastern Andes of Colombia
_____ *L. l. tamae*   Extreme w Venezuela (Páramo de Tamá in s Táchira)
_____ *L. l. saul (orestes)*   Andes of sw Colombia, Ecuador and n Peru
_____ *L. l. rectirostris*   Temperate Andes of n and central Peru

☐ **Bronzy Inca** *Coeligena coeligena*
_____ *C. c. coeligena (zuloagae)*   Coastal mountains of n Venezuela (Lara to Miranda)
_____ *C. c. zuliana*   Sierra de Perijá (Colombia/Venezuela border)
_____ *C. c. columbiana*   E and Central Andes of Colombia and nw Venezuela
_____ *C. c. ferruginea*   W and Central Andes of Colombia
_____ *C. c. obscura*   Andes of extreme s Colombia, Ecuador and Peru
_____ *C. c. boliviana*   Andes of central and se Bolivia

☐ **Brown Inca** *Coeligena wilsoni*

Andes of sw Colombia and w Ecuador

☐ **Black Inca** *Coeligena prunellei*

W slope of Central Andes and Eastern Andes of Colombia

☐ **Gould's Inca** *Coeligena inca*
_____ *C. i. omissa*   Andes of se Peru (Urubamba to Puno)
_____ *C. i. inca*   Andes of Bolivia (La Paz and Cochabamba)

☐ **Collared Inca** *Coeligena torquata*

____	*C. t. conradii*	E Andes of Colombia to nw Venezuela (Trujillo and Mérida)
____	*C. t. torquata*	Andes of Colombia to nw Venezuela (Táchira) and n Peru
____	*C. t. fulgidigula*	Andes of w Ecuador
____	*C. t. margaretae*	Andes of n Peru (Chachapoyas)
____	*C. t. insectivora*	Andes of central Peru
____	*C. t. eisenmanni*	S Peru (Cordillera Vilcabamba)

☐ **White-tailed Starfrontlet** *Coeligena phalerata*

Santa Marta Mountains (ne Colombia)

☐ **Golden Starfrontlet** *Coeligena eos*

Andes of w Venezuela (Trujillo, Barinas, Mérida and Táchira)

☐ **Golden-bellied Starfrontlet** *Coeligena bonapartei*

____	*C. b. consita*	Sierra de Perijá (Colombia/Venezuela border)
____	*C. b. bonapartei*	E Andes of Colombia (Boyacá to Bogotá)
____	*C. b. orina*	N Colombia (single specimen from Páramo de Frontino)

☐ **Blue-throated Starfrontlet** *Coeligena helianthea*

____	*C. h. helianthea*	Andes of ne Colombia (Sierra de Perijá to Bogotá)
____	*C. h. tamai*	W Venezuela (Páramo de Tamá in Táchira)

☐ **Buff-winged Starfrontlet** *Coeligena lutetiae*

Central Andes of Colombia to Ecuador and extreme nw Peru

☐ **Violet-throated Starfrontlet** *Coeligena violifer*

____	*C. v. dichroura*	Andes of s Ecuador (Loja) to Peru (Junín, Huánuco and Lima)
____	*C. v. albicaudata*	Andes of s Peru (Cuzco, Apurímac and Ayacucho)
____	*C. v. osculans*	Andes of se Peru (Cuzco)
____	*C. v. violifer*	Andes of nw Bolivia (La Paz and Cochabamba)

☐ **Rainbow Starfrontlet** *Coeligena iris*

____	*C. i. hesperus*	Andes of s-central Ecuador (Cuenca)
____	*C. i. iris*	Andes of s Ecuador (Loja) to n Peru (Piura)
____	*C. i. aurora*	Andes of n Peru (Cutervo, Cerros de Amachonga)
____	*C. i. fulgidiceps (hypocrita)*	Andes of n Peru (east of Río Marañón in Amazonas)
____	*C. i. flagrans*	Andes of nw Peru (Cajamarca)
____	*C. i. eva*	N Peru (west of Río Marañón in Cajamarca and La Libertad)

☐ **Sword-billed Hummingbird** *Ensifera ensifera*

Andes of w Venezuela to ne Bolivia

☐ **Great Sapphirewing** *Pterophanes cyanopterus*

____	*P. c. cyanopterus*	E Andes of n-c Colombia (Santander and Cundinamarca)
____	*P. c. caeruleus*	C Andes of Colombia (Tolima) to extreme sw Andes (Nariño)
____	*P. c. peruvianus*	Andes of Ecuador, Peru and n Bolivia

☐ **Giant Hummingbird** *Patagona gigas*

____	*P. g. peruviana*	Andes of sw Colombia to n Chile and nw Argentina
____	*P. g. gigas*	Central and s Chile to w-central Argentina

☐ **Green-backed Firecrown** *Sephanoides sephaniodes*

C Chile and Argentina to Tierra del Fuego; Juan Fernandez Is.

☐ **Juan Fernandez Firecrown** *Sephanoides fernandensis*

____	*S. f. fernandensis*	Robinson Crusoe I. (Juan Fernández Islands off Chile)
____	*S. f. leyboldi†*	Alejandro Selkirk I. (Juan Fernández Islands off Chile). Extinct

☐ **Longuemare's Sunangel** *Heliangelus clarisse*

____	*H. c. violiceps*	Sierra de Perijá (Colombia/Venezuela border)
____	*H. c. spencei*	Andes of nw Venezuela (Mérida)
____	*H. c. clarisse*	Eastern Andes of Colombia and adjacent w Venezuela

☐ **Orange-throated Sunangel** *Heliangelus mavors*

Andes of ne Colombia to nw Venezuela (s Lara to Táchira)

☐ **Amethyst-throated Sunangel** *Heliangelus amethysticollis*
_____ *H. a. laticlavius*
_____ *H. a. decolor*
_____ *H. a. amethysticollis*

Andes of s Ecuador and n Peru
E Andes of central Peru (south of Río Marañón)
Andes of s Peru to nw Bolivia

☐ **Gorgeted Sunangel** *Heliangelus strophianus*

Andes of sw Colombia (Nariño) and nw Ecuador

☐ **Tourmaline Sunangel** *Heliangelus exortis*

Andes of Colombia and e slope of Andes of nw Ecuador

☐ **Little Sunangel** *Heliangelus micrastur*
_____ *H. m. micrastur*
_____ *H. m. cutervensis*

Andes of se Ecuador and adjacent n Peru
Andes of nw Peru (Cajamarca)

☐ **Purple-throated Sunangel** *Heliangelus viola*

Andes of s Ecuador and n Peru

☐ **Royal Sunangel** *Heliangelus regalis*

Andes of n Peru (Cajamarca and San Martín)

☐ **Black-breasted Puffleg** *Eriocnemis nigrivestis*

Andes of n Ecuador (Pichincha, Atacazo and Imbabura)

☐ **Glowing Puffleg** *Eriocnemis vestitus*
_____ *E. v. paramillo*
_____ *E. v. vestitus*
_____ *E. v. smaragdinipectus*

N end of Western and Central Andes of Colombia
E Andes of Colombia and nw Venezuela
Central Andes of Colombia, Ecuador and extreme n Peru

☐ **Black-thighed Puffleg** *Eriocnemis derbyi*

Central Andes of Colombia and nw Ecuador

☐ **Turquoise-throated Puffleg** *Eriocnemis godini*

Andes of nw Ecuador and (?) sw Colombia

☐ **Sapphire-vented Puffleg** *Eriocnemis luciani*

Andes of sw Colombia (Nariño) and w Ecuador

☐ **Coppery-bellied Puffleg** *Eriocnemis cupreoventris*

E Andes of Colombia and nw Venezuela (Mérida)

☐ **Coppery-naped Puffleg** *Eriocnemis sapphiropygia*
_____ *E. s. catharina*
_____ *E. s. sapphiropygia*

E Andes of n Peru (Utcubamba Valley)
E Andes of central and s Peru (Pasco and Junín to Puno)

☐ **Golden-breasted Puffleg** *Eriocnemis mosquera*

SW and Central Andes of Colombia to nw Ecuador

☐ **Blue-capped Puffleg** *Eriocnemis glaucopoides*

Andes of s Bolivia and nw Argentina

☐ **Colorful Puffleg** *Eriocnemis mirabilis*

W slope of Western Andes of Colombia (Cauca)

☐ **Emerald-bellied Puffleg** *Eriocnemis alinae*
_____ *E. a. alinae*
_____ *E. a. dybowskii*

S-central and Eastern Andes of Colombia to Ecuador
Eastern Andes of n and central Peru

☐ **Greenish Puffleg** *Haplophaedia aureliae*
_____ *H. a. caucensis*
_____ *H. a. aureliae*
_____ *H. a. russata*

Mts. of se Panama to Western and Central Andes of Colombia
Eastern Andes of Colombia and (?) e slope of Central Andes
E slope of Andes of Ecuador

☐ **Buff-thighed Puffleg** *Haplophaedia assimilis*
_____ *H. a. affinis*
_____ *H. a. assimilis*

Eastern Andes of n and central Peru
Andes of se Peru (Puno) and w Bolivia

☐ **Hoary Puffleg** *Haplophaedia lugens*

Pacific slope of sw Colombia (Nariño) and nw Ecuador

☐ **Purple-bibbed Whitetip** *Urosticte benjamini*

Pacific slope of w Colombia to sw Ecuador and nw Peru

☐ **Rufous-vented Whitetip** *Urosticte ruficrissa*

E slope of Andes in s Colombia and e Ecuador

☐ **Booted Racket-tail** *Ocreatus underwoodii*

____ *O. u. polystictus*	Coastal mountains of n Venezuela (Carabobo to Miranda)
____ *O. u. discifer*	Colombia to nw Venezuela (Zulia to Falcón, Táchira, w Barinas)
____ *O. u. underwoodii*	Eastern Andes of Colombia
____ *O. u. incommodus (ambiguus)*	Western and Central Andes of Colombia
____ *O. u. melanantherus*	Andes of Ecuador
____ *O. u. peruanus*	E Ecuador and ne Peru
____ *O. u. annae*	Andes of central and s Peru
____ *O. u. addae*	*Yungas* of Bolivia (La Paz to Santa Cruz and Chuquisaca)

☐ **Black-tailed Trainbearer** *Lesbia victoriae*

____ *L. v. victoriae (aequatorialis)*	Andes of s Colombia (Nariño) and Ecuador
____ *L. v. juliae*	Andes of n and central Peru
____ *L. v. berlepschi*	Andes of se Peru

☐ **Green-tailed Trainbearer** *Lesbia nuna*

____ *L. n. gouldii*	Andes of Colombia; old record from w Venezuela (Mérida)
____ *L. n. gracilis*	Andes of Ecuador
____ *L. n. pallidiventris*	Andes of n Peru
____ *L. n. eucharis (chlorura)*	Andes of central Peru (Huánuco)
____ *L. n. nuna (boliviana)*	Andes of sw Peru and n Bolivia

☐ **Red-tailed Comet** *Sappho sparganura*

____ *S. s. sparganura*	Andes of n and central Bolivia; accidental s Peru (Puno)
____ *S. s. sapho*	Andes of s Bolivia to w Argentina and n Chile

☐ **Bronze-tailed Comet** *Polyonymus caroli*

Pacific slope of Andes of Peru

☐ **Purple-backed Thornbill** *Ramphomicron microrhynchum*

____ *R. m. andicolum*	Andes of w Venezuela (Mérida)
____ *R. m. microrhynchum*	Andes of Colombia, Ecuador and nw Peru
____ *R. m. albiventre*	Andes of c Peru (Huánuco to Junín, Cuzco and Apurímac)
____ *R. m. bolivianum*	Andes of w Bolivia (Cochabamba)

☐ **Black-backed Thornbill** *Ramphomicron dorsale*

Santa Marta Mountains (ne Colombia)

☐ **Bearded Mountaineer** *Oreonympha nobilis*

____ *O. n. albolimbata*	Andes of w-central Peru (Huancavelica)
____ *O. n. nobilis*	Andes of s Peru (Cuzco and Apurímac)

☐ **Bearded Helmetcrest** *Oxypogon guerinii*

____ *O. g. cyanolaemus*	Santa Marta Mountains (ne Colombia)
____ *O. g. lindenii*	Andes of nw Venezuela (Mérida and Trujillo)
____ *O. g. guerinii*	*Páramo* of E Andes of Colombia (south to Cundinamarca)
____ *O. g. stuebelii*	W Andes of Colombia (Volcán de Ruiz)

☐ **Tyrian Metaltail** *Metallura tyrianthina*

____ *M. t. districta*	Santa Marta Mountains (ne Colombia)
____ *M. t. chloropogon*	Coastal mountains of n Venezuela
____ *M. t. oreopola*	Andes of w Venezuela (Lara, Trujillo and Mérida)
____ *M. t. tyrianthina*	Andes of Colombia, Venezuela (Táchira), Ecuador and n Peru
____ *M. t. quitensis*	Andes of nw Ecuador
____ *M. t. septentrionalis*	Andes of n Peru (west of Río Marañón)
____ *M. t. smaragdinicollis (peruviana)*	Andes of e Peru and n Bolivia

☐ **Perija Metaltail** *Metallura iracunda*

Sierra de Perijá (Colombia/Venezuela border)

☐ **Scaled Metaltail** *Metallura aeneocauda*

____ *M. a. aeneocauda* Andes of se Peru (Cuzco and Puno) to nw Bolivia (La Paz)

____ *M. a. malagae* *Yungas* of Bolivia (Cochabamba and w Santa Cruz)

☐ **Fire-throated Metaltail** *Metallura eupogon*

E Andes of Peru (Huánuco, Junín, Apurímac and Ayacucho)

☐ **Coppery Metaltail** *Metallura theresiae*

____ *M. t. parkeri* Andes of n Peru (Cordillera de Colán)

____ *M. t. theresiae* Andes of n Peru (Amazonas to Huánuco)

☐ **Neblina Metaltail** *Metallura odomae*

Andes of s Ecuador (Loja) and n Peru (Piura and Cajamarca)

☐ **Violet-throated Metaltail** *Metallura baroni*

Páramo of Andes of s-central Ecuador (Azuay)

☐ **Viridian Metaltail** *Metallura williami*

____ *M. w. recisa* Andes of n-c Colombia (Páramo de Frontino in Antioquia)

____ *M. w. williami* Central Andes of Colombia

____ *M. w. primolinus* Eastern Andes of s Colombia (Nariño) and n Ecuador

____ *M. w. atrigularis* Andes of s Ecuador (Cordillera de Chilla in Azuay and Loja)

☐ **Black Metaltail** *Metallura phoebe*

Andes of n Peru (Cajamarca) to extreme n Chile

☐ **Rufous-capped Thornbill** *Chalcostigma ruficeps*

Andes of se Ecuador to e Peru and *yungas* of w Bolivia

☐ **Olivaceous Thornbill** *Chalcostigma olivaceum*

____ *C. o. pallens* Locally in Andes of central Peru

____ *C. o. olivaceum* Locally in Eastern Andes of se Peru and w Bolivia

☐ **Blue-mantled Thornbill** *Chalcostigma stanleyi*

____ *C. s. stanleyi* *Páramo* of Andes of Ecuador

____ *C. s. versigularis* Andes of Peru (east of Río Marañón) to Carpish Mountains

____ *C. s. vulcani* Andes of e Peru (south of Río Huallaga) to w Bolivia

☐ **Bronze-tailed Thornbill** *Chalcostigma heteropogon*

Páramo of ne Colombia to extreme w Venezuela

☐ **Rainbow-bearded Thornbill** *Chalcostigma herrani*

____ *C. h. tolimae* Central Andes of Colombia (Volcán de Tolima)

____ *C. h. herrani* W Andes of s Colombia to extreme n Peru (Piura)

☐ **Mountain Avocetbill** *Opisthoprora euryptera*

C Andes of Colombia to n Peru (Amazonas to La Libertad)

☐ **Gray-bellied Comet** *Taphrolesbia griseiventris*

Andes of nw Peru (s Cajamarca to w Huánuco)

☐ **Long-tailed Sylph** *Aglaiocercus kingi*

____ *A. k. margarethae* Mountains of n-central and coastal Venezuela

____ *A. k. caudatus* Andes of n Colombia and w Venezuela

____ *A. k. emmae* Central and Western Andes of Colombia to nw Ecuador

____ *A. k. kingi* Eastern Andes of Colombia

____ *A. k. mocoa* Central Andes of s Colombia to Ecuador and n Peru

____ *A. k. smaragdinus* E Andes of Peru and *yungas* of w Bolivia

☐ **Violet-tailed Sylph** *Aglaiocercus coelestis*

____ *A. c. coelestis (pseudocoelestis)* Pacific slope of Western Andes of Colombia and n Ecuador

____ *A. c. aethereus* Andes of sw Ecuador

☐ **Venezuelan Sylph** *Aglaiocercus berlepschi*

Mountains of ne Venezuela (Sucre and Monagas)

211

☐ **Hyacinth Visorbearer** *Augastes scutatus*
____   *A. s. scutatus*   High montane forests of se Brazil (central and e Minas Gerais)
____   *A. s. ilseae*   Mid-montane forests of se Brazil (central and e Minas Gerais)
____   *A. s. soaresi*   SE Brazil (Rio Paricicaba basin in s-central Minas Gerais)

☐ **Hooded Visorbearer** *Augastes lumachella*

Locally in ne Brazilian plateaux (Bahia and Minas Gerais)

☐ **Wedge-billed Hummingbird** *Augastes geoffroyi*
____   *A. g. geoffroyi*   Andes of e Colombia to n Venezuela and e Peru
____   *A. g. albogularis*   Western and Central Andes of Colombia and w Ecuador
____   *A. g. chapmani*   Andes of central Bolivia (Cochabamba)

☐ **Purple-crowned Fairy** *Heliothryx barroti*

Gulf slope of se Mexico to sw Ecuador (El Oro)

☐ **Black-eared Fairy** *Heliothryx aurita*
____   *H. a. aurita*   Tropical se Colombia to Venezuela, the Guianas and n Brazil
____   *H. a. phainolaema*   Amazonian Brazil south of the Amazon (Pará and Maranhão)
____   *H. a. auriculata*   Tropical e Peru, n Bolivia, Amazonian and s Brazil

☐ **Horned Sungem** *Heliactin bilopha*

Extreme s Suriname to interior Brazil and adjacent e Bolivia

☐ **Marvelous Spatuletail** *Loddigesia mirabilis*

Andes of n Peru (along east bank of Río Utcubamba)

☐ **Plain-capped Starthroat** *Heliomaster constantii*
____   *H. c. pinicola*   Arid nw Mexico (Sonora to Jalisco)
____   *H. c. leocadiae (surdus)*   Arid tropical w Mexico (Nayarit) to w Guatemala
____   *H. c. constantii*   El Salvador and Nicaragua to sw Costa Rica

☐ **Long-billed Starthroat** *Heliomaster longirostris*
____   *H. l. pallidiceps*   Tropical s Mexico to Nicaragua
____   *H. l. longirostris*   E Costa Rica to Bolivia and Brazil; Trinidad
____   *H. l. albicrissa*   Tropical w Ecuador and nw Peru

☐ **Stripe-breasted Starthroat** *Heliomaster squamosus*

E Brazil (Pernambuco to Bahia, Goiás and São Paulo)

☐ **Blue-tufted Starthroat** *Heliomaster furcifer*

Bolivia to Paraguay, c and s Brazil, Uruguay and n Argentina

☐ **Oasis Hummingbird** *Rhodopis vesper*
____   *R. v. koepckeae*   Arid nw Peru (Cerro Illescas in sw Piura)
____   *R. v. vesper(tertia)*   Arid w Peru to extreme n Chile (Tacna and Tarapacá)
____   *R. v. atacamensis*   Arid n Chile (Atacama)

☐ **Peruvian Sheartail** *Thaumastura cora*

Arid w Peru to extreme n Chile (Arica)

☐ **Sparkling-tailed Hummingbird** *Tilmatura dupontii*

Oak-pine highlands of w Mexico to n Nicaragua

☐ **Slender Sheartail** *Doricha enicura*

Highlands of s Mexico (Chiapas) to w Honduras, El Salvador

☐ **Mexican Sheartail** *Doricha eliza*

Arid s Mexico (Veracruz and Yucatán Pen.); Holbox I.

☐ **Bahama Woodstar** *Calliphlox evelynae*
____   *A. e. evelynae*   Bahamas
____   *A. e. lyrura*   Great Inagua I. (Bahamas)

☐ **Magenta-throated Woodstar** *Calliphlox bryantae*

Highlands of n Costa Rica and w Panama

☐ **Purple-throated Woodstar** *Calliphlox mitchellii*

Tropical e Panama (Darién) to w Colombia and sw Ecuador

☐ **Amethyst Woodstar** *Calliphlox amethystina*

Widespread trop. South America to ne Argentina and s Brazil

☐ **Slender-tailed Woodstar** *Microstilbon burmeisteri*

Arid scrub of e Bolivia and nw Argentina

☐ **Lucifer Hummingbird** *Calothorax lucifer*

Arid mountains of sw US and n Mexico; winters to s Mexico

☐ **Beautiful Hummingbird** *Calothorax pulcher*

Arid scrub of s Mexico (Guerrero and s Puebla to e Oaxaca)

☐ **Vervain Hummingbird** *Mellisuga minima*
____ *M. m. minima*
____ *M. m. vielloti*

Jamaica
Hispaniola, Gonâve, Tortue, Saona, Catalina and Île-á-Vache

☐ **Bee Hummingbird** *Mellisuga helenae*

Cuba and Isle of Pines

☐ **Ruby-throated Hummingbird** *Archilochus colubris*

E Canada and US; winters Mexico to Panama

☐ **Black-chinned Hummingbird** *Archilochus alexandri*

Arid sw British Columbia to nw Mexico; winters to s Mexico

☐ **Anna's Hummingbird** *Calypte anna*

Arid sw British Columbia to nw Baja; winters to n Mexico

☐ **Costa's Hummingbird** *Calypte costae*

Arid sw US to s Baja California and nw Mexico

☐ **Bumblebee Hummingbird** *Atthis heloisa*
____ *A. h. margarethae*
____ *A. h. heloisa*

Mts. of nw Mexico (se Sinaloa and sw Chihuahua to Jalisco)
Highlands of Mexico (c Tamaulipas to Guerrero and Oaxaca)

☐ **Wine-throated Hummingbird** *Atthis ellioti*
____ *A. e. ellioti*
____ *A. e. selasphoroides*

Montane forests of s Mexico (Chiapas) and Guatemala
Humid montane forests of Honduras

☐ **Calliope Hummingbird** *Stellula calliope*

Mts. of Br. Columbia to sw US and n Baja; winters to s Mexico

☐ **Purple-collared Woodstar** *Myrtis fanny*
____ *M. f. fanny*
____ *M. f. megalura*

W and se Ecuador to w Peru (Piura to Arequipa)
N Peru (Cajabamba to La Libertad and extreme nw Huánuco)

☐ **Chilean Woodstar** *Eulidia yarrellii*

Arid s Peru (Tacna and Moquegua) to n Chile (Arica)

☐ **Short-tailed Woodstar** *Myrmia micrura*

Arid scrub of sw Ecuador and nw Peru

☐ **White-bellied Woodstar** *Chaetocercus mulsant*

Andes of Colombia to w Bolivia (Cochabamba)

☐ **Little Woodstar** *Chaetocercus bombus*

Andes of extreme sw Colombia (Nariño) to n Peru

☐ **Gorgeted Woodstar** *Chaetocercus heliodor*
____ *C. h. heliodor*
____ *C. h. cleavesi*

Andes of Colombia and w Ecuador to nw Venezuela (Mérida)
Andes of ne Ecuador

☐ **Santa Marta Woodstar** *Chaetocercus astreans*

Santa Marta Mountains (ne Colombia)

☐ **Esmeraldas Woodstar** *Chaetocercus berlepschi*

Lowlands of w Ecuador (Esmeraldas, Manabí and Guayas)

☐ **Rufous-shafted Woodstar** *Chaetocercus jourdanii*
____ *C. j. jourdanii*
____ *C. j. rosae*
____ *C. j. andinus*

Mountains of ne Venezuela (Cumaná); Trinidad
Mountains of n Venezuela (Zulia to Distrito Federal)
Andes of ne Colombia to w Venezuela (Lara to Táchira)

☐ **Scintillant Hummingbird** *Selasphorus scintilla*

Humid montane forests of Costa Rica and w Panama

☐ **Glow-throated Hummingbird** *Selasphorus ardens*

Mountains of w Panama (Chiriquí and Veraguas)

☐ **Volcano Hummingbird** *Selasphorus flammula*

_____ *S. f. simoni* — Costa Rica (Volcán Poás, Volcán Barba and Cerros de Escazú)
_____ *S. f. flammula* — Costa Rica (Volcán Irazú and Volcán Turrialba)
_____ *S. f. torridus* — Sierra de Talamanca (Costa Rica) and Volcán Barú (w Panama)

☐ **Broad-tailed Hummingbird** *Selasphorus platycercus*

Mountains of sw US to Mexico and Guatemala

☐ **Rufous Hummingbird** *Selasphorus rufus*

Alaska to nw US; winters to s Mexico

☐ **Allen's Hummingbird** *Selasphorus sasin*

_____ *S. s. sasin* — S Oregon to s California; winters to central Mexico
_____ *S. s. sedentarius* — Channel Islands (off s California)

ORDER: COLIIFORMES
FAMILY: COLIIDAE (Mousebirds—6)

☐ **Speckled Mousebird** *Colius striatus*

_____ *C. s. nigricollis*	Nigeria to Cameroon, Gabon and sw Congo
_____ *C. s. striatus*	S Cape Province east to Great Kei River (South Africa)
_____ *C. s. minor*	Natal to sw Zululand, Swaziland, e and n Transvaal
_____ *C. s. integralis*	E Transvaal to Zululand, s Mozambique and se Zimbabwe
_____ *C. s. simulans*	Lower Zambezi valley in Mozambique and Malawi
_____ *C. s. rhodesia*	Highlands of e Zimbabwe and adjacent Mozambique
_____ *C. s. affinis*	Zimbabwe to Malawi, n Mozambique, s and coastal Tanzania
_____ *C. s. mombassicus*	S Somalia to coastal Kenya and ne Tanzania (south to Amani)
_____ *C. s. cinerascens*	W and s Tanzania
_____ *C. s. berlepschi*	N Malawi to ne Zambia and sw Tanzania
_____ *C. s. kikuyensis*	Cent. Kenya and high rainfall areas of peripheral n Tanzania
_____ *C. s. kiwuensis*	Uganda to nw Tanzania, Rwanda and e Zaire
_____ *C. s. congicus*	E Angola to s Zaire and nw Zambia
_____ *C. s. jebelensis*	N border of Uganda and s Sudan
_____ *C. s. leucotis*	E Sudan to w and sw Ethiopia
_____ *C. s. hilgerti*	NE Ethiopia, sw Djibouti and nw Somalia
_____ *C. s. leucophthalmus*	NE Zaire to s Sudan and se Central African Republic

☐ **White-headed Mousebird** *Colius leucocephalus*

_____ *C. l. leucocephalus* — Arid s Somalia, Kenya (except n) and extreme ne Tanzania
_____ *C. l. turneri* — N Kenya (Lake Turkana to Mt. Kenya and Isiolo)

☐ **Red-backed Mousebird** *Colius castanotus*

Euphorbia savanna of Angola; formerly sw Gabon

☐ **White-backed Mousebird** *Colius colius*

Dry savanna of Namibia, Botswana and South Africa

☐ **Blue-naped Mousebird** *Urocolius macrourus*

Semiarid scrub of sub-Saharan Africa

☐ **Red-faced Mousebird** *Urocolius indicus*

_____ *U. i. indicus* — South Africa (s Cape Province east to Great Kei River)
_____ *U. i. pallidus* — Coastal se Tanzania and ne Mozambique
_____ *U. i. lateifrons* — Angola to Namibia and w Botswana
_____ *U. i. mossambicus* — E Angola to Zambia, se Zaire, Malawi and sw Tanzania
_____ *U. i. transvaalensis* — S Mozambique to Zimbabwe, sw Zambia and n Cape Province

ORDER: TROGONIFORMES
FAMILY: TROGONIDAE (Trogons and Quetzals—39)

☐ **Narina Trogon** *Apaloderma narina*
_____ *A. n. narina* — Highlands of Ethiopia to Angola and South Africa
_____ *A. n. littorale* — E Africa (coastal lowlands from Somalia to Natal)
_____ *A. n. brachyurum* — Cameroon and se Nigeria to Uganda
_____ *A. n. constantia* — Sierra Leone and Liberia (Mt. Nimba) to Ghana

☐ **Bare-cheeked Trogon** *Apaloderma aequatoriale*

Lowland rainforests of Cameroon, Gabon and Zaire

☐ **Bar-tailed Trogon** *Apaloderma vittatum*

Montane forests of central and se Africa

☐ **Cuban Trogon** *Priotelus temnurus*
_____ *P. t. temnurus* — Cuba
_____ *P. t. vescus* — Isle of Pines

☐ **Hispaniolan Trogon** *Priotelus roseigaster*

Montane forests of Hispaniola; locally in coastal mangroves

☐ **Black-headed Trogon** *Trogon melanocephalus*
_____ *T. m. melanocephalus* — Gulf-Caribbean slope of e Mexico to ne Costa Rica
_____ *T. m. illaetabilis* — W Costa Rica

☐ **Citreoline Trogon** *Trogon citreolus*
_____ *T. c. citreolus* — Pacific slope of w Mexico (Sinaloa to w Oaxaca)
_____ *T. c. sumichrasti* — Pacific slope of s Mexico (central Oaxaca to Chiapas)

☐ **White-tailed Trogon** *Trogon viridis*
_____ *T. v. chionurus* — Lowlands of e Panama to w Colombia and w Ecuador
_____ *T. v. viridis* — Colombia east of the Andes to n Bolivia and Brazil; Trinidad
_____ *T. v. melanopterus* — Tropical se Brazil (Bahia to São Paulo)

☐ **Baird's Trogon** *Trogon bairdii*

Pacific slope of sw Costa Rica and w Panama

☐ **Violaceous Trogon** *Trogon violaceus*
_____ *T. v. braccatus* — Tropical s Mexico (Oaxaca) to Nicaragua
_____ *T. v. concinnus* — Tropical Costa Rica to w Ecuador
_____ *T. v. caligatus* — E Panama (Darién) to w Venezuela (Maracaibo basin)
_____ *T. v. violaceus* — Venezuela, the Guianas and adjacent n Brazil; Trinidad
_____ *T. v. ramonianus* — Amazonian region of Colombia, Ecuador, Peru and Brazil
_____ *T. v. crissalis* — Brazil (south bank of lower Amazon and its tributaries)

☐ **Mountain Trogon** *Trogon mexicanus*
_____ *T. m. clarus* — Oak-pine woodlands of ne Mexico
_____ *T. m. mexicanus* — Oak-pine woodlands of central Mexico to w Guatemala
_____ *T. m. lutescens* — Highlands of Honduras

☐ **White-eyed Trogon** *Trogon comptus*

Humid forests of w Colombia and nw Ecuador

☐ **Collared Trogon** *Trogon collaris*
_____ *T. c. puella* — Tropical and subtropical central Mexico to w Panama
_____ *T. c. extimus* — Subtropical e Panama (Darién)
_____ *T. c. virginalis* — W Colombia to w Ecuador and nw Peru
_____ *T. c. subtropicalis* — Central Colombia
_____ *T. c. collaris* — E Colombia to Bolivia and s Brazil; Trinidad and Tobago
_____ *T. c. castaneus* — Tropical e Colombia and nw Brazil
_____ *T. c. exopatus* — N Venezuela

☐ **Elegant Trogon** *Trogon elegans*

____	*T. e. canescens*	Oak-pine woodlands of s Arizona to nw Mexico
____	*T. e. goldmani*	Tres Marías Islands (off w Mexico)
____	*T. e. ambiguus*	Extreme s Texas to e and central Mexico
____	*T. e. elegans*	Guatemala (Motagua Valley)
____	*T. e. lubricus*	Nicaragua and nw Costa Rica

☐ **Orange-bellied Trogon** *Trogon aurantiiventris*

____	*T. a. underwoodi*	Humid montane forests of nw Costa Rica
____	*T. a. aurantiiventris*	Humid montane forests of central Costa Rica to w Panama
____	*T. a. flavidior*	W Panama (extreme e Chiriquí on Cerro Flores)

☐ **Masked Trogon** *Trogon personatus*

____	*T. p. sanctaemartae*	Santa Marta Mountains (ne Colombia)
____	*T. p. ptaritepui*	*Tepuis* of s Venezuela
____	*T. p. personatus*	Subtropical mountains of w Venezuela, e Colombia and e Peru
____	*T. p. assimilis*	Subtropical w Ecuador
____	*T. p. temperatus*	Andes of Colombia, Ecuador and Peru
____	*T. p. submontanus*	Foothills of Andes of Bolivia
____	*T. p. duidae*	*Tepuis* of s Venezuela (Mt. Duida)
____	*T. p. roraimae*	Auyan-tepui and Mt. Roraima (Venezuela/Guyana border)

☐ **Black-throated Trogon** *Trogon rufus*

____	*T. r. tenellus*	Tropical se Honduras to extreme nw Colombia
____	*T. r. cupreicauda*	Tropical w Colombia and w Ecuador
____	*T. r. rufus*	E Venezuela to the Guianas and n Brazil (Rio Negro region)
____	*T. r. sulphureus*	Amazonian e Peru and w Brazil
____	*T. r. amazonicus*	NE Brazil (lower Amazon River valley)
____	*T. r. chrysochloros*	S Brazil to Paraguay and ne Argentina

☐ **Surucua Trogon** *Trogon surrucura*

____	*T. s. aurantius*	E Brazil (Minas Gerais to Rio de Janeiro and n São Paulo)
____	*T. s. surrucura*	S Brazil to Paraguay, Uruguay and n Argentina

☐ **Blue-crowned Trogon** *Trogon curucui*

____	*T. c. bolivianus*	E Andes of Colombia to Bolivia and Brazil (e to Rio Tapajós)
____	*T. c. peruvianus*	S-central Colombia
____	*T. c. curucui*	Humid e Brazil (Pará to Goias and Rio de Janeiro)
____	*T. c. behni*	E Bolivia to w Brazil (Mato Grosso), Paraguay and n Argentina

☐ **Black-tailed Trogon** *Trogon melanurus*

____	*T. m. macroura*	E Panama (Canal Zone) to n Colombia
____	*T. m. melanurus*	E Colombia to n Bolivia and n Brazil
____	*T. m. mesurus*	W Ecuador and nw Peru
____	*T. m. eumorphus*	Tropical e Peru
____	*T. m. occidentalis*	Amazonian Brazil

☐ **Slaty-tailed Trogon** *Trogon massena*

____	*T. m. massena*	Humid lowland forests of se Mexico to Nicaragua
____	*T. m. hoffmanni*	Costa Rica and Panama
____	*T. m. australis*	Coastal Pacific Colombia to nw Ecuador

☐ **Lattice-tailed Trogon** *Trogon clathratus*

		Caribbean coast of Costa Rica and w Panama

☐ **Eared Trogon** *Euptilotis neoxenus*

		Montane forests of w Mexico; occasional sw Arizona

☐ **Resplendent Quetzal** *Pharomachrus mocinno*

____	*P. m. mocinno*	Montane forests of s Mexico to n Nicaragua
____	*P. m. costaricensis*	Montane forests of Costa Rica to w Panama

☐ **Crested Quetzal** *Pharomachrus antisianus*

Andes of w Venezuela to w Bolivia

☐ **White-tipped Quetzal** *Pharomachrus fulgidus*
_____ *P. f. festatus*
_____ *P. f. fulgidus*

Santa Marta Mountains (ne Colombia)
Mountains of n Venezuela

☐ **Golden-headed Quetzal** *Pharomachrus auriceps*

Mts. of e Panama to Colombia, nw Venezuela and w Bolivia

☐ **Pavonine Quetzal** *Pharomachrus pavoninus*
_____ *P. p. hargitti*
_____ *P. p. heliactin*
_____ *P. p. pavoninus*
_____ *P. p. viridiceps*

E Colombia and s Venezuela
Subtropical w Ecuador
Upper Amazonia from se Colombia to ne Peru (Río Negro)
Lower Amazonian Brazil (Rio Tapajós)

☐ **Blue-tailed Trogon** *Harpactes reinwardtii*
_____ *H. r. mackloti*
_____ *H. r. reinwardtii*

Montane forests of Sumatra
Montane forests of Java

☐ **Malabar Trogon** *Harpactes fasciatus*
_____ *H. f. malabaricus*
_____ *H. f. fasciatus (parvus)*

Forests of w and s India
Sri Lanka

☐ **Red-naped Trogon** *Harpactes kasumba*
_____ *H. k. kasumba*
_____ *H. k. impavidus*

Lowland forests of Malay Peninsula and Sumatra
Lowlands of Borneo

☐ **Diard's Trogon** *Harpactes diardii*
_____ *H. d. sumatranus*
_____ *H. d. diardii*

Lowland forests of Malay Peninsula and Sumatra
Borneo and Bangka I. (off se Sumatra)

☐ **Philippine Trogon** *Harpactes ardens*
_____ *H. a. herberti*
_____ *H. a. luzoniensis*
_____ *H. a. minor*
_____ *H. a. linae*
_____ *H. a. ardens*

N Philippines (Sierra Madre Mountains of ne Luzon)
N Philippines (Luzon and Marinduque)
Polillo (n Philippines)
Central Philippines (Bohol, Leyte and Samar)
S Philippines (Basilan, Dinagat and Mindanao)

☐ **Whitehead's Trogon** *Harpactes whiteheadi*

Mountains of n Borneo

☐ **Cinnamon-rumped Trogon** *Harpactes orrhophaeus*
_____ *H. o. orrhophaeus*
_____ *H. o. vidua*

Lowlands of Malay Peninsula and Sumatra
Lowlands of nw Borneo

☐ **Scarlet-rumped Trogon** *Harpactes duvaucelii*

Lowland forests of Malay Peninsula, Sumatra and Borneo

☐ **Red-headed Trogon** *Harpactes erythrocephalus*
_____ *H. e. erythrocephalus*
_____ *H. e. helenae*
_____ *H. e. yamakanensis*
_____ *H. e. rosa*
_____ *H. e. intermedius*
_____ *H. e. annamensis*
_____ *H. e. klossi*
_____ *H. e. chaseni*
_____ *H. e. hainanus*
_____ *H. e. flagrans*

Nepal to e Assam, s Myanmar and nw Thailand
SW China (w Yunnan) and n Myanmar
SE China (Fujian and n Guangdong)
Mountains of central China (n Guangxi)
N Laos and n Vietnam
Northeast Thailand and s Indochina
Banthat Mountains (w Cambodia and extreme sw Thailand)
Malay Peninsula
Hainan (s China)
Mountains of Sumatra

☐ **Orange-breasted Trogon** *Harpactes oreskios*

____ *H. o. stellae*	Lowlands of sw China (sw Yunnan), s Myanmar and Indochina
____ *H. o. uniformis*	S Tenasserim, s Malay Peninsula and Sumatra
____ *H. o. oreskios*	Java
____ *H. o. dulitensis*	Mountains of nw Borneo
____ *H. o. nias*	Nias I. (off nw Sumatra)

☐ **Ward's Trogon** *Harpactes wardi*

	Mountains of ne Myanmar and nw Vietnam

ORDER: CORACIIFORMES
FAMILY: ALCEDINIDAE (Kingfishers—93)

☐ **Blyth's Kingfisher** *Alcedo hercules*

	Sikkim to sw China, Myanmar, n Laos, n Vietnam and Hainan

☐ **Common Kingfisher** *Alcedo atthis*

____ *A. a. atthis*	SE Europe and North Africa to nw India
____ *A. a. ispida*	British Isles to w Russia, Iberian and Baltic peninsulas
____ *A. a. bengalensis*	Lake Baikal to Japan, China, Indochina and Indonesia
____ *A. a. taprobana*	S India and Sri Lanka
____ *A. a. floresiana*	Lesser Sundas (Bali to Timor and Wetar)
____ *A. a. hispidoides*	Sulawesi to Moluccas, New Guinea and Bismarck Arch.
____ *A. a. solomonensis*	Bougainville and Solomon Islands (east to San Cristóbal)

☐ **Half-collared Kingfisher** *Alcedo semitorquata*

____ *A. s. heuglini*	Ethiopia
____ *A. s. semitorquata*	S Mozambique and South Africa
____ *A. s. tephria*	Angola to Tanzania and Mozambique

☐ **Shining-blue Kingfisher** *Alcedo quadribrachys*

____ *A. q. quadribrachys*	Senegambia to w-central Nigeria
____ *A. q. guentheri*	Coastal sw Nigeria to extreme s Sudan, Kenya and Zambia

☐ **Blue-eared Kingfisher** *Alcedo meninting*

____ *A. m. coltarti*	Lowlands of Nepal and n India to s Myanmar and Laos
____ *A. m. laubmanni*	E India
____ *A. m. phillipsi*	SW India (Kerala) and Sri Lanka
____ *A. m. scintillans*	Peninsular Myanmar and peninsular Thailand
____ *A. m. rufigaster*	Andaman Islands
____ *A. m. verreauxii*	Malay Peninsula, Sumatra, Borneo and Sulu Archipelago
____ *A. m. proxima*	Pagai Islands (Mentawi Archipelago off w Sumatra)
____ *A. m. subviridis*	Nias I. (off nw Sumatra)
____ *A. m. callima*	Batu Islands (off w Sumatra)
____ *A. m. meninting*	Java and Bali to Lombok, Sulawesi, Sula Is., w Lesser Sundas
____ *A. m. amadoni*	S Philippines (Balabac, Busuanga and Culion)

☐ **Azure Kingfisher** *Alcedo azurea*

____ *A. a. affinis*	N Moluccas (Morotai, Halmahera and Bacan)
____ *A. a. wallaceanus*	Aru Islands
____ *A. a. lessonii*	Lowlands of New Guinea, w Papuan islands and Fergusson I.
____ *A. a. ochrogaster*	N New Guinea and islands in Geelvink Bay
____ *A. a. yamdenae*	Tanimbar Islands (s Banda Sea)
____ *A. a. ruficollaris*	Coastal n Australia and major offshore outlying islands
____ *A. a. azurea*	Coastal e and se Australia
____ *A. a. diemenensis*	Tasmania

☐ **Bismarck Kingfisher** *Alcedo websteri*

Lowlands of Bismarck Archipelago

☐ **Blue-banded Kingfisher** *Alcedo euryzona*

_____ *A. e. peninsulae* — S Myanmar, Malay Peninsula, Sumatra and Borneo
_____ *A. e. euryzona* — Java

☐ **Indigo-banded Kingfisher** *Alcedo cyanopecta*

_____ *A. c. cyanopecta* — Luzon, Marinduque, Masbate, Mindoro, Sibuyan, Polillo, Ticao
_____ *A. c. nigrirostris* — Central Philippines (Cebu, Negros and Panay)

☐ **Silvery Kingfisher** *Alcedo argentata*

_____ *A. a. flumenicola* — Central Philippines (Bohol, Samar and Leyte)
_____ *A. a. argentata* — S Philippines (Basilan, Dinagat and Mindanao)

☐ **Malachite Kingfisher** *Alcedo cristata*

_____ *A. c. galerita* — Africa s of Sahara south to Limpopo River and Mozambique
_____ *A. c. cristata* — S Angola, sw Zambia and Limpopo R. (south to Cape Province)
_____ *A. c. thomensis* — São Tomé (Gulf of Guinea)
_____ *A. c. robertsi* — N Namibia and s Angola to nw Zimbabwe and sw Zambia

☐ **Malagasy Kingfisher** *Alcedo vintsioides*

_____ *A. v. vintsioides* — Madagascar
_____ *A. v. johannae* — Comoro Islands

☐ **White-bellied Kingfisher** *Alcedo leucogaster*

_____ *A. l. bowdleri* — Tropical Guinea to Mali and Ghana
_____ *A. l. leucogaster (batesi)* — Nigeria to s Cameroon, Gabon and nw Angola; Bioko
_____ *A. l. nais* — Príncipe (Gulf of Guinea)
_____ *A. l. leopoldi* — Congo basin (e Congo to s Uganda and nw Zambia)

☐ **Small Blue Kingfisher** *Alcedo coerulescens*

S Sumatra, Java, Bali, Lombok, Sumbawa and Kangean Islands

☐ **Little Kingfisher** *Alcedo pusilla*

_____ *A. p. pusilla* — New Guinea, Kai, Aru, w Papuan is., n Moluccas and Kai Is.
_____ *A. p. laetior* — N New Guinea (Geelvink Bay to Astrolabe Bay)
_____ *A. p. ramsayi* — Coastal n Australia (Anson Bay to Groote Eylandt)
_____ *A. p. halli* — NE Australia (coastal ne Queensland and Hinchinbrook I.)
_____ *A. p. masauji* — Bismarck Arch. (New Britain, New Ireland and New Hanover)
_____ *A. p. bougainvillei* — Solomon Islands (Bougainville, Santa Isabel and Choiseul)
_____ *A. p. halmaherae* — N Moluccas (Halmahera and Bacan)
_____ *A. p. richardsi* — Central Solomon Islands between Vellalavella and Vangunu
_____ *A. p. aolae* — Known from the type specimen from Guadalcanal

☐ **Black-backed Kingfisher** *Ceyx erithacus*

_____ *C. e. erithacus* — India and Sri Lanka to se China, Indochina and Sumatra
_____ *C. e. macrocarus* — Nicobar Islands and (?) Andaman Islands
_____ *C. e. motleyi* — Borneo and adjacent northern offshore islands
_____ *C. e. captus* — Nias I. (off nw Sumatra)
_____ *C. e. jungei* — Batu I. and Simeulue I. (off nw Sumatra)

☐ **Philippine Kingfisher** *Ceyx melanurus*

_____ *C. m. melanurus* — N Philippines (Luzon, Polillo, Alabat and Catanduanes)
_____ *C. m. samarensis* — Central Philippines (Samar and Leyte)
_____ *C. m. mindanensis (platenae)* — S Philippines (Mindanao and Basilan)

☐ **Sulawesi Kingfisher** *Ceyx fallax*

_____ *C. f. sangirensis* — Sangihi I. (ne of Sulawesi)
_____ *C. f. fallax* — Sulawesi and Lembeh I.

☐ **Rufous-backed Kingfisher** *Ceyx rufidorsa*

Malay Peninsula, Greater and Lesser Sundas to w Philippines

☐ **Variable Kingfisher** *Ceyx lepidus*

_____ *C. l. margarethae*	Central and s Philippines
_____ *C. l. wallacii*	Sula Islands (Taliabu, Seho, Mangole and Sanana)
_____ *C. l. uropygialis*	Obi, Bisa, Bacan, Ternate, Halmahera, Tidore and Morotai is.
_____ *C. l. lepidus*	Ambon, Ambelau, Seram, Saparua, Seram Laut, Watubela is.
_____ *C. l. cajeli*	Buru I. (s Moluccas)
_____ *C. l. solitarius*	New Guinea, Aru, w Papuan islands and D'Entrecasteaux Arch.
_____ *C. l. dispar*	Admiralty Islands
_____ *C. l. mulcatus*	Bismarck Arch. (New Hanover, New Ireland and Lihir Islands)
_____ *C. l. sacerdotis*	Bismarck Archipelago (New Britain and Umboi)
_____ *C. l. pallidus*	Solomon Islands (Bougainville and Buka)
_____ *C. l. collectoris*	Solomon Is. (Choiseul, Vellalavella, New Georgia and Rendova)
_____ *C. l. meeki*	Solomon Islands (Choiseul and Santa Isabel)
_____ *C. l. malaitae*	Known from the type specimen from Malaita (Solomon Islands)
_____ *C. l. nigromaxilla*	Guadalcanal (Solomon Islands)
_____ *C. l. gentianus*	San Cristóbal (e Solomon Islands)

☐ **Madagascar Pygmy-Kingfisher** *Ispidina madagascariensis*

_____ *I. m. madagascariensis*	Lowland forests of Madagascar
_____ *I. m. diluta*	SW Madagascar (Sakaraha region)

☐ **African Pygmy-Kingfisher** *Ispidina picta*

_____ *I. p. picta*	Senegambia to Ethiopia, Uganda, s Mozambique and Pemba I.
_____ *I. p. ferruginea*	Rainforests of Sierra Leone to Congo Basin and w Uganda
_____ *I. p. natalensis*	Angola to s Mozambique and South Africa

☐ **Dwarf Kingfisher** *Ispidina lecontei*

Sierra Leone to w Uganda, n Zaire and n Angola

☐ **Banded Kingfisher** *Lacedo pulchella*

_____ *L. p. amabilis*	Lowland forests of s Myanmar, Thailand and s Vietnam
_____ *L. p. deignani*	S Thailand
_____ *L. p. pulchella*	Malay Pen., Sumatra, Java, Riau Arch. and North Natuna Islands
_____ *L. p. melanops*	Borneo and Bangka I.

☐ **Laughing Kookaburra** *Dacelo novaeguineae*

_____ *D. n. minor*	NE Australia (Cape York Peninsula south to Cooktown)
_____ *D. n. novaeguineae*	E and se Australia

☐ **Blue-winged Kookaburra** *Dacelo leachii*

_____ *D. l. superflua*	SW Irian Jaya (Mimika River to Merauke District)
_____ *D. l. intermedia*	S New Guinea (Amazon Bay to Bensbach River)
_____ *D. l. cliftoni*	NW Australia (Hamersley and Pilbara regions)
_____ *D. l. kempi*	Islands in Torres Strait and ne Australia
_____ *D. l. cervina*	Melville I. and adjacent humid coastal Northern Territory
_____ *D. l. leachii*	Northern Territory (Kimberley Division) to se Queensland

☐ **Spangled Kookaburra** *Dacelo tyro*

_____ *D. t. archboldi*	Trans-Fly savanna of s-central New Guinea
_____ *D. t. tyro*	Aru Islands

☐ **Rufous-bellied Kookaburra** *Dacelo gaudichaud*

Lowlands of New Guinea, Aru, Yapen and w Papuan islands

☐ **Shovel-billed Kookaburra** *Clytoceyx rex*

_____ *C. r. rex*	Arfak and Snow mountains to se Papua New Guinea
_____ *C. r. imperator*	Irian Jaya (between Lorentz River and Mt. Goliath)

☐ **Lilac Kingfisher** *Cittura cyanotis*

____	*C. c. sanghirensis*	Rainforests of Sangihi and Siau islands (ne of Sulawesi)
____	*C. c. cyanotis*	Sulawesi and Lembeh I.

☐ **Brown-winged Kingfisher** *Pelargopsis amauropterus*

Coastal areas from e India to Myanmar and pen. Thailand

☐ **Stork-billed Kingfisher** *Pelargopsis capensis*

____	*P. c. capensis*	Nepal to India, Sri Lanka and nw Myanmar
____	*P. c. burmanica*	Myanmar to Thailand, Indochina and south to Isthmus of Kra
____	*P. c. intermedia*	Nicobar Islands
____	*P. c. osmastoni*	Andaman Islands
____	*P. c. malaccensis*	S Malay Peninsula, Riau Archipelago and Lingga Archipelago
____	*P. c. cyanopteryx*	Sumatra, Bangka and Billiton islands
____	*P. c. simalurensis*	Simeulue I. (off nw Sumatra)
____	*P. c. sodalis*	Banyak I. (off nw Sumatra)
____	*P. c. nesoeca*	Nias I. and Batu Islands (off w Sumatra)
____	*P. c. isoptera*	Mentawi Archipelago (Pagai, Siberut and Sipura)
____	*P. c. inominata*	Borneo
____	*P. c. floresiana*	Lesser Sundas (Bali, Lombok, Sumbawa and Flores)
____	*P. c. javana*	Java
____	*P. c. gouldi*	Philippines (Balabac, Culion, Lubang, Mindoro, Palawan, Calauit)
____	*P. c. gigantea (smithi)*	Central and s Philippines

☐ **Black-billed Kingfisher** *Pelargopsis melanorhyncha*

____	*P. m. melanorhyncha*	Sulawesi
____	*P. m. dicrorhyncha*	Peleng I. and Banggai Islands (off Sulawesi)
____	*P. m. eutreptorhyncha*	Sula Islands (e of Sulawesi)

☐ **Ruddy Kingfisher** *Halcyon coromanda*

____	*H. c. major (ochrothorectis)*	Korea, Japan and Ryukyu Is. to s China, Sulawesi, Philippines
____	*H. c. coromanda*	E Himalayas to n Myanmar and sw China; winters to Sumatra
____	*H. c. mizorhina*	Andaman Islands; questionable Nicobar I. specimen
____	*H. c. minor*	Riau Arch., Mentawi Arch., s Malay Pen. and Greater Sundas
____	*H. c. bangsi*	Ryukyu Islands: winters Philippines and Talaud Islands
____	*H. c. linae*	Palawan (sw Philippines)
____	*H. c. claudiae*	Sulu Archipelago (Tawitawi, Bulubuk and Sanga Sanga)
____	*H. c. pelingensis*	Peleng I. (off e Sulawesi)
____	*H. c. rufa*	S Sulawesi, Sangihe, Muna and Butung islands
____	*H. c. sulana*	Sula Islands (e of Sulawesi)

☐ **Chocolate-backed Kingfisher** *Halcyon badia*

____	*H. b. badia*	Sierra Leone to w Uganda, e Zaire and n Angola
____	*H. b. lopezi*	Bioko I. (Gulf of Guinea)

☐ **White-throated Kingfisher** *Halcyon smyrnensis*

____	*H. s. smyrnensis*	Arabian Peninsula to Caucasus Mountains and nw India
____	*H. s. fusca*	W India and Sri Lanka
____	*H. s. saturatior*	Andaman Islands
____	*H. s. perpulchra*	Myanmar to Malay Peninsula and Indochina
____	*H. s. fokiensis*	S and e China; Hainan and Taiwan
____	*H. s. gularis*	Philippine Islands

☐ **Gray-headed Kingfisher** *Halcyon leucocephala*

____	*H. l. acteon*	Cape Verde Islands (Santiago, Fogo and Brava)
____	*H. l. semicaerulea*	Red Sea coast of extreme s Arabian Peninsula
____	*H. l. leucocephala*	Senegambia to Ethiopia, nw Somalia and ne Zaire
____	*H. l. hyacinthina*	S Somalia and coastal Kenya to Mozambique
____	*H. l. pallidiventris*	Congo, Zaire, Rwanda and nw Tanzania to n South Africa

☐ **Black-capped Kingfisher** *Halcyon pileata*

Manchuria, Korea and China to s India, Malaya and Sulu Arch.

☐ **Javan Kingfisher** *Halcyon cyanoventris*

Lowlands of Java and Bali

☐ **Woodland Kingfisher** *Halcyon senegalensis*

_____ *H. s. senegalensis*   Senegambia to Ethiopia and n Tanzania
_____ *H. s. fuscopilea*   Forests of Sierra Leone to s Nigeria and Congo basin
_____ *H. s. cyanoleuca*   NW Tanzania to Angola, Botswana and Natal

☐ **Mangrove Kingfisher** *Halcyon senegaloides*

_____ *H. s. ranivorus*   Coastal Somalia to Tanzania, Zanzibar, Pemba and Mafia islands
_____ *H. s. senegaloides*   Coastal se Africa (Mozambique to South Africa)

☐ **Blue-breasted Kingfisher** *Halcyon malimbica*

_____ *H. m. malimbica*   Riverine woodlands of Cameroon to Uganda and Zambia
_____ *H. m. torquata*   S Senegambia and Guinea-Bissau to extreme w Mali
_____ *H. m. forbesi*   Sierra Leone to e Nigeria and extreme w Cameroon; Bioko I.
_____ *H. m. dryas*   Príncipe I. and (formerly) São Tomé I. (Gulf of Guinea)

☐ **Brown-hooded Kingfisher** *Halcyon albiventris*

_____ *H. a. albiventris*   South Africa
_____ *H. a. vociferans*   Orange Free State and s Natal to s Mozambique
_____ *H. a. orientalis*   Coastal Somalia to n Botswana and Mozambique
_____ *H. a. prentissgrayi*   SE Kenya to Congo, Zaire, Angola and Zambia

☐ **Striped Kingfisher** *Halcyon chelicuti*

_____ *H. c. chelicuti*   S Mauritania and Sengambia to Ethiopia and South Africa
_____ *H. c. eremogiton*   Sahara edge (central Mali) to e Sudan (White Nile region)

☐ **Blue-black Kingfisher** *Todirhamphus nigrocyaneus*

_____ *T. n. nigrocyaneus*   Lowlands of w New Guinea, Salawati and Batanta islands
_____ *T. n. quadricolor*   Yapen I. and n New Guinea (Geelvink Bay to Astrolabe Bay)
_____ *T. n. stictolaema*   S New Guinea (se Irian Jaya to Owen Stanley Range)

☐ **Rufous-lored Kingfisher** *Todirhamphus winchelli*

_____ *T. w. nigrorum*   Bohol, Cebu, Negros, Samar, Siquijor, Leyte, Biliran
_____ *T. w. nesydrionetes*   Central Philippines (Romblon, Sibuyan and Tablas)
_____ *T. w. mindanensis*   Mindanao (s Philippines)
_____ *T. w. winchelli*   Basilan (s Philippines)
_____ *T. w. alfredi*   Sulu Archipelago (Bongao, Jolo, Papahag and Tawitawi)

☐ **Blue-and-white Kingfisher** *Todirhamphus diops*

Halmahera, Ternate, Morotai, Bacan, Obi and adjacent Moluccas

☐ **Lazuli Kingfisher** *Todirhamphus lazuli*

S Moluccas (Ambon, Seram and Haruku)

☐ **Forest Kingfisher** *Todirhamphus macleayii*

_____ *T. m. elizabeth*   E New Guinea
_____ *T. m. macleayi (insularis)*   Tanimbar, Kai and Aru is. to New Guinea and Bismarck Arch.
_____ *T. m. incincta*   E Queensland; winters to e New Guinea and Kai Islands

☐ **New Britain Kingfisher** *Todirhamphus albonotatus*

Coastal lowlands of New Britain (Bismarck Archipelago)

☐ **Ultramarine Kingfisher** *Todirhamphus leucopygius*

Bougainville and Solomon Islands

☐ **Chestnut-bellied Kingfisher** *Todirhamphus farquhari*

Vanuatu (Espíritu Santo, Malo and Malakula)

☐ **Red-backed Kingfisher** *Todirhamphus pyrrhopygia*

Drier inland habitats of Australia

☐ **Flat-billed Kingfisher** *Todirhamphus recurvirostris*

W Samoa (Apolima, Upolu and Savai'i)

☐ **Micronesian Kingfisher** *Todirhamphus cinnamominus*

_____ T. c. miyakoensis — Known from one specimen from Miyako-Jima (Ryukyu Islands)
_____ T. c. cinnamominus† — Formerly Guam (Mariana Is.). Extinct
_____ T. c. pelewensis — Palau Islands (w Caroline Islands)
_____ T. c. reichenbachii — Pohnpei (e Caroline Islands)

☐ **Collared Kingfisher** *Todirhamphus chloris*

_____ T. c. abyssinica — W coast of Red Sea to head of Gulf of Aden
_____ T. c. kalbaensis — S coast of Arabian Peninsula to extreme nw Oman
_____ T. c. vidali — Peninsular India (Ratnagiri District)
_____ T. c. davisoni — Andaman Islands and Cocos Islands (Bay of Bengal)
_____ T. c. occipitalis — Nicobar Islands
_____ T. c. humii — NW India to Malay Pen., Thailand, Myanmar, Mergui Arch.
_____ T. c. armstrongi — S Thailand and Myanmar
_____ T. c. chloroptera — Islands off w Sumatra (except Enggano)
_____ T. c. azela — Enggano I. (off sw Sumatra)
_____ T. c. palmeri — Java, Bali and adjacent islands in Java Sea
_____ T. c. laubmanniana — S Sumatra, Borneo and adjacent islands
_____ T. c. collaris — Philippines, Sulu Archipelago and Palawan
_____ T. c. chloris — Sulawesi to nw New Guinea and Lesser Sundas
_____ T. c. pilbara — W Australia (Exmouth Gulf to mouth of Turner River)
_____ T. c. sordida — S New Guinea, Aru Islands and n Australia
_____ T. c. colona — Islands off se Papua New Guinea and Louisiade Archipelago
_____ T. c. teraokai — Palau Islands (w Caroline Islands)
_____ T. c. owstoni — N Mariana Islands (Asuncion, Pagan, Almagan and Agrihan)
_____ T. c. albicilla — S Mariana Islands (Saipan, Tinian and Aguiguan)
_____ T. c. orii — Rota I. (s Mariana Islands)
_____ T. c. matthiae — St. Matthias Islands (Papua New Guinea)
_____ T. c. stresemanni — French, Umboi, Witu and islands in Dampier Straits
_____ T. c. nusae — Bismarck Archipelago
_____ T. c. novaehiberniae — New Ireland (Bismarck Archipelago)
_____ T. c. bennetti — Nissan I. (e Papua New Guinea)
_____ T. c. tristami — New Britain (Bismarck Archipelago)
_____ T. c. alberti — Buka, Bougainville and Solomon Islands (east to Guadalcanal)
_____ T. c. mala — Malaita (e Solomon Islands)
_____ T. c. sororum — S Solomon Islands (Malaupaina and Malaulalo)
_____ T. c. pavuvu — Pavuvu I. (Russel Group in central Solomon Islands)
_____ T. c. solomonis — Solomon Islands (Uki Ni Masi, San Cristóbal and Santa Anna)
_____ T. c. amoena — Solomon Islands (Rennell and Bellona)
_____ T. c. brachyura — Reef Islands (Fenualoa and Lomlon)
_____ T. c. vicina — Duff Group (e Solomon Islands)
_____ T. c. ornata — E Solomon Islands (Santa Cruz and Tinakula)
_____ T. c. utupuae — Utupua I. (Santa Cruz Group in e Solomon Islands)
_____ T. c. melanodera — Vanikolo I. (Santa Cruz Group in e Solomon Islands)
_____ T. c. torresiana — Torres Group (Toga, Loh and Hiu)
_____ T. c. santoensis — Banks Group to Espíritu Santo and Malo (n Vanuatu)
_____ T. c. juliae — N and central Vanuatu (Maewo and Aoba islands to Efate)
_____ T. c. erromangae — Erromango I. (s Vanuatu)
_____ T. c. tannensis — Tanna I. (s Vanuatu)
_____ T. c. vitiensis — Fiji (Ngau, Ovalau, Koro, Viti Levu, Vanua Levu and Taveuni)
_____ T. c. eximia — Fiji (Kandavu, Ono and Vanua Kula)
_____ T. c. marina — Lau Archipelago (e Fiji)
_____ T. c. sacra — Tonga
_____ T. c. regina — Futuna (Wallis and Futuna, central Polynesia)
_____ T. c. pealei — Tutuila I. (American Samoa)
_____ T. c. manuae — American Samoa (Ofu, Olosega and Tau)

☐ **Sombre Kingfisher** *Todirhamphus funebris*

Halmahera (n Moluccas)

☐ **Talaud Kingfisher** *Todirhamphus enigma*

Talaud Islands (Karakelong and Salebabu)

☐ **Beach Kingfisher** *Todirhamphus saurophaga*

_____ *T. s. saurophaga*

Moluccas to Bismarck Archipelago and Solomon Is;amds

_____ *T. s. admiralitatis (anchoreta)*

Admiralty Islands (Anchorite, Hermit and Ninigo)

☐ **Cinnamon-banded Kingfisher** *Todirhamphus australasia*

_____ *T. a. australasia*

Lesser Sundas (Lombok, Sumba, Timor, Romang and Wetar)

_____ *T. a. dammeriana*

E Lesser Sundas (Moa, Leti, Babar and Damar)

_____ *T. a. odites*

Tanimbar Islands (Yamdena and Larat)

☐ **Sacred Kingfisher** *Todirhamphus sanctus*

_____ *T. s. sanctus*

Australia to Solomon Is. and Philippines; winters to New Guinea

_____ *T. s. vagan (norfolkiensis, adamsi)*

New Zealand, Norfolk, Lord Howe and Kermadec islands

_____ *T. s. canacorum*

New Caledonia and Isle of Pines

_____ *T. s. macmillani*

Loyalty Islands

☐ **Tahiti Kingfisher** *Todirhamphus veneratus*

_____ *T. v. veneratus*

Tahiti (French Polynesia)

_____ *T. v. youngi*

Moorea (French Polynesia)

☐ **Mangaia Kingfisher** *Todirhamphus ruficollaris*

Mangroves of Mangaia I. (s Cook Islands)

☐ **Chattering Kingfisher** *Todirhamphus tuta*

_____ *T. t. tuta*

Borabora, Maupiti, Raiatea, Huahine, Tahaa and Tahiti

_____ *T. t. atiu*

Atiu I. (e Cook Islands)

_____ *T. t. mauke*

Mauke I. (e Cook Islands)

☐ **Marquesas Kingfisher** *Todirhamphus godeffroyi*

S Marquesas Islands (Hivaoa, Tahuata and Fatuhiva)

☐ **Tuamotu Kingfisher** *Todirhamphus gambieri*

_____ *T. g. gambieri†*

Formerly Mangareva I. (e Tuamotu Archipelago). Extinct

_____ *T. g. gertrudae*

Niau I. (nw Tuamotu Archipelago)

☐ **White-rumped Kingfisher** *Caridonax fulgidus*

Lesser Sundas (Lombok, Sumbawa, Flores and Besar)

☐ **Hook-billed Kingfisher** *Melidora macrorrhina*

_____ *M. m. waigiuensis*

Waigeo I. (w Papuan islands)

_____ *M. m. macrorrhina*

New Guinea, Misool, Salawati and Batanta islands

_____ *M. m. jobiensis*

Yapen I. and n New Guinea (Geelvink to Astrolabe Bay)

☐ **Moustached Kingfisher** *Actenoides bougainvillei*

_____ *A. b. bougainvillei*

Bougainville (Solomon Islands)

_____ *A. b. excelsus*

Guadalcanal (Solomon Islands)

☐ **Rufous-collared Kingfisher** *Actenoides concretus*

_____ *A. c. concretus*

S Myanmar, Malay Pen., Sumatra, Bangka and Belitung islands

_____ *A. c. peristephes*

S Myanmar and peninsular Thailand

_____ *A. c. borneanus*

Borneo

☐ **Spotted Kingfisher** *Actenoides lindsayi*

_____ *A. l. lindsayi*

N Philippines (Luzon, Marinduque and Catanduanes)

_____ *A. l. mosleyi*

Forests of Negros (central Philippines)

☐ **Blue-capped Kingfisher** *Actenoides hombroni*

Forests of Mindanao (s Philippines)

☐ **Green-backed Kingfisher** *Actenoides monachus*
_____   *A. m. monachus*   N and central Sulawesi, Manadotua and Lembeh islands
_____   *A. m. capucinus*   E, se and s Sulawesi

☐ **Scaly Kingfisher** *Actenoides princeps*
_____   *A. p. princeps*   Humid montane forests of ne Sulawesi
_____   *A. p. erythrorhamphus*   Humid montane forests of nw and central Sulawesi
_____   *A. p. regalis*   Humid montane forests of se Sulawesi

☐ **Yellow-billed Kingfisher** *Syma torotoro*
_____   *S. t. torotoro*   Forests of w New Guinea and w Papuan islands
_____   *S. t. tentelare*   Aru Islands
_____   *S. t. pseustes*   S New Guinea
_____   *S. t. brevirostris*   S New Guinea
_____   *S. t. meeki*   Lowlands of se New Guinea
_____   *S. t. flavirostris*   NE Australia (Cape York Peninsula)
_____   *S. t. ochracea*   D'Entrecasteaux Archipelago

☐ **Mountain Kingfisher** *Syma megarhyncha*
_____   *S. m. wellsi*   Montane forests of Weyland and Snow mts. (w New Guinea)
_____   *S. m. sellamontis*   Montane forests of e New Guinea
_____   *S. m. megarhyncha*   Montane forests of e New Guinea (except Huon Peninsula)

☐ **Little Paradise-Kingfisher** *Tanysiptera hydrocharis*
      Aru Islands and s New Guinea (Merauke to Fly River)

☐ **Common Paradise-Kingfisher** *Tanysiptera galatea*
_____   *T. g. doris*   Morotai (n Moluccas)
_____   *T. g. emiliae*   Rau (Moluccas)
_____   *T. g. browningi*   Halmahera (n Moluccas)
_____   *T. g. brunhildae*   Doi (Moluccas)
_____   *T. g. sabrina*   Kayoa (n Moluccas)
_____   *T. g. margarethae*   Bacan (n Moluccas)
_____   *T. g. obiensis*   Central Moluccas (Obi and Bisa)
_____   *T. g. acis*   Buru (s Moluccas)
_____   *T. g. boanensis*   Boano (Moluccas)
_____   *T. g. nais*   S Moluccas (Ambon, Manipa, Seram, Manawoka, Gorong)
_____   *T. g. galatea*   NW New Guinea and w Papuan islands
_____   *T. g. meyeri*   N New Guinea (Mamberamo River to Jimi River Valley)
_____   *T. g. minor*   S New Guinea (Digul River to Kumusi River) and Darnley I.
_____   *T. g. vulcani*   Manam I. (off Papua New Guinea)
_____   *T. g. rosseliana*   Rossel I. (Louisiade Archipelago)

☐ **Kofiau Paradise-Kingfisher** *Tanysiptera ellioti*
      Kofiau I. (w Papuan islands)

☐ **Biak Paradise-Kingfisher** *Tanysiptera riedelii*
      Biak I. (off w New Guinea)

☐ **Numfor Paradise-Kingfisher** *Tanysiptera carolinae*
      Numfor I. (off w New Guinea)

☐ **Red-breasted Paradise-Kingfisher** *Tanysiptera nympha*
      Locally in mangroves and forests of New Guinea

☐ **Brown-headed Paradise-Kingfisher** *Tanysiptera danae*
      SE New Guinea (Aroa River to Waria River)

☐ **Buff-breasted Paradise-Kingfisher** *Tanysiptera sylvia*
_____   *T. s. leucura*   Umboi I. (Bismarck Archipelago)
_____   *T. s. nigriceps*   Bismarck Archipelago (New Britain and Duke of York)
_____   *T. s. salvadoriana*   SE New Guinea (Hall Sound to Kemp Welch River)
_____   *T. s. sylvia*   S New Guinea and ne Australia (n Queensland)

☐ **Giant Kingfisher** *Megaceryle maxima*

____	*M. m. maxima*	Senegambia to Ethiopia and South Africa
____	*M. m. gigantea*	Rainforests of Liberia to w Tanzania and n Angola

☐ **Crested Kingfisher** *Megaceryle lugubris*

____	*M. l. continentalis*	W Himalayas (Kashmir to central Bhutan)
____	*M. l. guttulata*	E Himalayas to China, Myanmar and Thailand; Hainan
____	*M. l. pallida*	S Kuril Islands and Hokkaido
____	*M. l. lugubris*	Honshu, Shikoku and Kyushu

☐ **Belted Kingfisher** *Ceryle alcyon*

____	*C. a. caurina*	Alaska to s US; winters to n South America
____	*C. a. alcyon*	Cent. and e Canada to n S America; W Indies; Trinidad; Tobago

☐ **Ringed Kingfisher** *Ceryle torquata*

____	*C. t. torquata*	Extreme s Texas to n Argentina; Trinidad; Isla Margarita
____	*C. t. stictipennis*	Lesser Antilles (Guadeloupe, Martinique and Dominica)
____	*C. t. stellata*	Central Chile and ne Argentina to Tierra del Fuego

☐ **Pied Kingfisher** *Ceryle rudis*

____	*C. r. rudis*	Africa south of the Sahara, Egypt to Iran and Turkey
____	*C. r. leucomelanura*	Kashmir and ne Afghanistan to India and Indochina
____	*C. r. travancoreensis*	Extreme sw India (Cape Comorin to n Kerala)
____	*C. r. insignis*	E China (south of Yangtze River Valley) and Hainan

☐ **Amazon Kingfisher** *Chloroceryle amazona*

____	*C. a. mexicana*	S Mexico to extreme nw Colombia
____	*C. a. amazona*	N South America to n Argentina (mainly east of the Andes)

☐ **Green Kingfisher** *Chloroceryle americana*

____	*C. a. hachisukai*	W-central Texas and nw Mexico
____	*C. a. septentrionalis*	S-central and e Mexico to Guatemala and El Salvador
____	*C. a. isthmica*	Honduras to Panama, Pearl Islands and extreme nw Colombia
____	*C. a. americana (hellmayri)*	Tropical South America (primarily east of the Andes)
____	*C. a. hellmayri*	W Colombia
____	*C. a. bottomeana*	Venezuela (Zulia and Mérida to Distrito Federal and Sucre)
____	*C. a. ecuadorensis*	W Ecuador
____	*C. a. cabanisii*	W Peru and extreme n Chile (west of the Andes)
____	*C. a. croteta*	Trinidad and Tobago
____	*C. a. mathewsii*	Central S America east of the Andes to n Argentina and n Chile

☐ **Green-and-rufous Kingfisher** *Chloroceryle inda*

____	*C. i. inda*	Tropical lowlands of Nicaragua to n Bolivia and Brazil
____	*C. i. chocoensis*	SE Nicaragua to w Ecuador, Venezuela, w Brazil and n Bolivia

☐ **American Pygmy Kingfisher** *Chloroceryle aenea*

____	*C. a. stictoptera*	S Mexico and Yucatán Peninsula to n Costa Rica
____	*C. a. aenea*	Central Costa Rica to n Bolivia and Brazil; Trinidad

ORDER: CORACIIFORMES
FAMILY: TODIDAE (Todies—5)

☐ **Cuban Tody** *Todus multicolor*

Forests and woodlands of Cuba and Isle of Pines

☐ **Broad-billed Tody** *Todus subulatus*

Arid scrub and woodlands of Hispaniola and Gonâve I.

☐ **Narrow-billed Tody** *Todus angustirostris*

Humid montane forests of Hispaniola

☐ **Jamaican Tody** *Todus todus*

Hills and mountains of Jamaica

☐ **Puerto Rican Tody** *Todus mexicanus*

Woodlands and scrub of Puerto Rico

ORDER: CORACIIFORMES
FAMILY: MOMOTIDAE (Motmots—10)

☐ **Tody Motmot** *Hylomanes momotula*

_____ *H. m. chiapensis*	Pacific coast of s Mexico (Chiapas)
_____ *H. m. momotula*	Caribbean slope of s Mexico (Veracruz) to Honduras
_____ *H. m. obscurus*	NW Costa Rica to extreme nw Colombia

☐ **Blue-throated Motmot** *Aspatha gularis*

Oak-pine highlands of s Mexico (Oaxaca) to Honduras

☐ **Russet-crowned Motmot** *Momotus mexicanus*

_____ *M. m. vanrossemi*	NW Mexico (s Sonora to adjacent Chihuahua and Sinaloa)
_____ *M. m. mexicanus*	N-central and central Mexico
_____ *M. m. saturatus*	Southwest Mexico (Oaxaca and Chiapas)
_____ *M. m. castaneiceps*	Arid Guatemala (Zacapa Plains and Motagua Valley)

☐ **Blue-crowned Motmot** *Momotus momota*

_____ *M. m. coeruliceps*	NE Mexico (Nuevo León and Tamaulipas to n Veracruz)
_____ *M. m. goldmani*	Tropical se Mexico (Veracruz) to Petén of n Guatemala
_____ *M. m. exiguus*	Tropical s Mexico (Campeche and Yucatán)
_____ *M. m. lessonii*	Tropical s Mexico (Chiapas) to w Panama
_____ *M. m. conexus*	Panama (Canal Zone) to n Colombia (lower Río Cauca)
_____ *M. m. reconditus*	E Panama to n Colombia (Atrato Valley)
_____ *M. m. spatha*	E Colombia (Serrania Macuira in e Guajira)
_____ *M. m. olivaresi*	E Colombia
_____ *M. m. subrufescens*	Caribbean coast of n Colombia and Venezuela
_____ *M. m. osgoodi*	Humid forests of w Venezuela (Lake Maracaibo region)
_____ *M. m. bahamensis*	Trinidad and Tobago
_____ *M. m. microstephanus*	Colombia and Ecuador (east of Andes) and adjacent nw Brazil
_____ *M. m. momota*	Tropical e Venezuela to the Guianas and n Brazil
_____ *M. m. argenticinctus*	Tropical w Ecuador and nw Peru
_____ *M. m. ignobilis*	E Amazonian Peru and w Brazil
_____ *M. m. nattereri*	Tropical base of Andes of ne Bolivia
_____ *M. m. simplex*	Brazil/Peru border e to Rio Tapajós and s to n Mato Grosso
_____ *M. m. cametensis*	N-central Brazil between Rio Tapajós and Rio Tocantins
_____ *M. m. parensis*	E Brazil (Rio Tocantins to Maranhão and Piauí)
_____ *M. m. pilcomajensis*	S Bolivia to s Brazil and nw Argentina

☐ **Highland Motmot** *Momotus aequatorialis*

_____ *M. a. aequatorialis*	Subtropical Andes of Colombia and e Ecuador
_____ *M. a. chlorolaemus*	Subtropical e Peru

☐ **Rufous Motmot** *Baryphthengus martii*

Caribbean slope of Honduras to n Bolivia and Amaz. Brazil

☐ **Rufous-capped Motmot** *Baryphthengus ruficapillus*

Lowlands of e Brazil to e Paraguay and ne Argentina

☐ **Keel-billed Motmot** *Electron carinatum*

Caribbean slope of se Mexico to ne Costa Rica

□ **Broad-billed Motmot** *Electron platyrhynchum*

_____	*E. p. minor*	E Honduras to n Colombia (lower Cauca Valley)
_____	*E. p. platyrhynchum*	W Colombia and w Ecuador
_____	*E. p. pyrrholaemum*	E Colombia to e Ecuador, e Peru and n Bolivia
_____	*E. p. colombianum*	N Colombia (humid lowlands north of the Andes)
_____	*E. p. orienticola*	W Brazil (Río Purús region)
_____	*E. p. chlorophrys*	Brazil (Mato Grosso, Pará and Goiás)
_____		

□ **Turquoise-browed Motmot** *Eumomota superciliosa*

_____	*E. s. bipartita*	Gulf slope of s Mexico to Pacific slope of Guatemala
_____	*E. s. superciliosa*	SE Mexico (Tabasco, Campeche, n Yucatán and Cozumel I.)
_____	*E. s. vanrossemi*	Arid interior Guatemala (Río Negro and Motagua valleys)
_____	*E. s. sylvestris*	Caribbean lowlands of e Guatemala
_____	*E. s. apiaster*	El Salvador to w Honduras and nw Nicaragua
_____	*E. s. euroaustris*	Arid Caribbean slope of n Honduras
_____	*E. s. australis*	Pacific slope of nw Costa Rica

ORDER: CORACIIFORMES
FAMILY: MEROPIDAE (Bee-eaters—26)

□ **Red-bearded Bee-eater** *Nyctyornis amictus*

Malay Peninsula, Sumatra and Borneo

□ **Blue-bearded Bee-eater** *Nyctyornis athertoni*

_____	*N. a. athertoni*	India to sw China and SE Asia
_____	*N. a. brevicaudata*	Hainan I. (s China)

□ **Purple-bearded Bee-eater** *Meropogon forsteni*

Humid forests of Sulawesi

□ **Black Bee-eater** *Merops gularis*

_____	*M. g. gularis*	Rainforests of Sierra Leone to Nigeria (Cross River)
_____	*M. g. australis*	Nigeria (Cross River) to Uganda and n Angola

□ **Blue-headed Bee-eater** *Merops muelleri*

_____	*M. m. mentalis*	Mali and Sierra Leone to Cameroon (Douala)
_____	*M. m. muelleri*	Congo basin (Cameroon to Kenya and Zaire)

□ **Red-throated Bee-eater** *Merops bulocki*

_____	*M. b. bulocki*	Senegambia to Chad (Chari River) and Central African Republic
_____	*M. b. frenatus*	Sub-Saharan Sudan and adj. Zaire to nw Uganda and w Ethiopia

□ **White-fronted Bee-eater** *Merops bullockoides*

Semiarid tropical savannas of central and s Africa

□ **Little Bee-eater** *Merops pusillus*

_____	*M. p. pusillus*	Savannas from Senegambia to Cameroon, Sudan and ne Zaire
_____	*M. p. ocularis*	E Zaire to n Uganda, s Sudan and Red Sea coast
_____	*M. p. cyanostictus*	E Ethiopia to Somalia and e Kenya
_____	*M. p. meridionalis*	Congo basin to e Zaire, Uganda and w Kenya south to Natal
_____	*M. p. argutus*	SW Angola to sw Zambia and Botswana

□ **Blue-breasted Bee-eater** *Merops variegatus*

_____	*M. v. bangweoloensis*	E Angola to se Zaire, Zambia and extreme w Tanzania
_____	*M. v. loringi*	SE Nigeria and Cameroon to Uganda and Kenya
_____	*M. v. variegatus*	Gabon, Rio Muni and sw Cameroon to Zaire and n Angola
_____	*M. v. lafresnayii*	Ethiopia to Sudan (Boma Hills)

□ **Cinnamon-chested Bee-eater** *Merops oreobates*

Highland forests of e Africa

☐ **Swallow-tailed Bee-eater** *Merops hirundineus*

____ *M. h. chrysolaimus*   Senegal to s Chad and nw Central African Republic
____ *M. h. heuglini*   S Sudan and adjacent Ethiopia, Uganda and Zaire
____ *M. h. furcatus*   S Zaire to Zambia, s Zimbabwe, Mozambique and Tanzania
____ *M. h. hirundineus*   Angola and Namibia to Orange R., Transvaal and Zimbabwe

☐ **Black-headed Bee-eater** *Merops breweri*

Moist forests of entire length of Congo River

☐ **Somali Bee-eater** *Merops revoilii*

Arid thornscrub of e Ethiopia, Somalia and Kenya

☐ **White-throated Bee-eater** *Merops albicollis*

Subdesert steppes of sub-Saharan Africa and sw Arabia

☐ **Green Bee-eater** *Merops orientalis*

____ *M. o. viridissimus*   Savanna of Senegal to Eritrea, Ethiopia and w Sudan
____ *M. o. flavoviridis*   Subdesert steppes of Chad to Red Sea coast of Sudan
____ *M. o. cleopatra*   Nile Valley (Lake Nasser to delta)
____ *M. o. cyanophrys*   Arabian Peninsula
____ *M. o. najdanus*   Central Arabian plateau
____ *M. o. beludschicus*   North end of Persian Gulf to Baluchistan and w India
____ *M. o. orientalis*   Rann of Kutch to Bangladesh and Sri Lanka
____ *M. o. ferrugeiceps*   Assam and Myanmar to Vietnam

☐ **Boehm's Bee-eater** *Merops boehmi*

Humid forests of se Africa (Malawi and adjacent countries)

☐ **Blue-throated Bee-eater** *Merops viridis*

____ *M. v. viridis*   S China, Thailand and Indochina to Sumatra, Borneo and Java
____ *M. v. americanus*   Philippine Islands

☐ **Blue-cheeked Bee-eater** *Merops persicus*

____ *M. p. chrysocercus*   NW Africa (south of Atlas Mts.); Senegambia to Lake Chad
____ *M. p. persicus*   Egypt to Lake Balkhash and Hindu Kush; winters to s Africa

☐ **Madagascar Bee-eater** *Merops superciliosus*

____ *M. s. superciliosus*   East Africa, Comoro Islands and Madagascar
____ *M. s. alternans*   Arid littoral of w Angola and nw Namibia

☐ **Blue-tailed Bee-eater** *Merops philippinus*

India to s China, SE Asia, New Guinea and Indonesia

☐ **Rainbow Bee-eater** *Merops ornatus*

Australia to New Guinea, Solomons, Gr. and Lesser Sundas

☐ **European Bee-eater** *Merops apiaster*

S Palearctic; winters to sub-Saharan Africa and w India

☐ **Chestnut-headed Bee-eater** *Merops leschenaulti*

____ *M. l. leschenaulti*   Sri Lanka and sw India to Thailand, Indochina and Malay Pen.
____ *M. l. andamanensis*   Andaman Islands
____ *M. l. quinticolor*   Java and Bali

☐ **Rosy Bee-eater** *Merops malimbicus*

Humid forests of w and central Africa

☐ **Northern Carmine Bee-eater** *Merops nubicus*

Savanna and grasslands of sub-Saharan Africa

☐ **Southern Carmine Bee-eater** *Merops nubicoides*

Acacia savanna of central and s Africa

ORDER: CORACIIFORMES
FAMILY: CORACIIDAE (Rollers—12)

☐ **European Roller *Coracias garrulus***
_____ *C. g. garrulus*　　　　　　　　N Africa, Europe to Iran and sw Siberia; winters to s Africa
_____ *C. g. semenovi*　　　　　　　　Iraq to w Xinjiang and s Kazakstan; winters to s Africa

☐ **Abyssinian Roller *Coracias abyssinica***

　　　　　　　　　　　　　　　　　Senegambia to Ethiopia, Somalia and Kenya; central Arabia

☐ **Lilac-breasted Roller *Coracias caudata***
_____ *C. c. lorti*　　　　　　　　　Ethiopia south to Lake Turkana, Somalia and ne Kenya
_____ *C. c. caudata*　　　　　　　　Southern and e Africa north to Uganda and Kenya

☐ **Racket-tailed Roller *Coracias spatulata***

　　　　　　　　　　　　　　　　　Tropical sw Angola to ne Tanzania and s Mozambique

☐ **Rufous-crowned Roller *Coracias naevia***
_____ *C. n. naevia*　　　　　　　　Senegambia to Ethiopia, Somalia and n Tanzania
_____ *C. n. mosambica*　　　　　　　Angola and Namibia to Zambia and n South Africa

☐ **Indian Roller *Coracias benghalensis***
_____ *C. b. benghalensis*　　　　　　E Arabia to ne India
_____ *C. b. indica*　　　　　　　　S India and Sri Lanka
_____ *C. b. affinis*　　　　　　　　Bhutan to sw China, Malaysia and Indochina

☐ **Purple-winged Roller *Coracias temminckii***

　　　　　　　　　　　　　　　　　Sulawesi, Lembeh, Bangka, Manterawu, Muna and Butung is.

☐ **Blue-bellied Roller *Coracias cyanogaster***

　　　　　　　　　　　　　　　　　Senegambia to Central African Republic

☐ **Broad-billed Roller *Eurystomus glaucurus***
_____ *E. g. after*　　　　　　　　Senegal to Sudan, coastal w African and n Zaire
_____ *E. g. aethiopicus*　　　　　　Sudan and w Ethiopia
_____ *E. g. suahelicus*　　　　　　S Somalia to central Zaire, ne Zambia, Angola and Natal
_____ *E. g. glaucurus*　　　　　　Madagascar; non-breeding migrant to e Africa

☐ **Blue-throated Roller *Eurystomus gularis***
_____ *E. g. gularis*　　　　　　　Rainforests of Guinea and w Cameroon
_____ *E. g. neglectus*　　　　　　S Nigeria to Uganda and Angola

☐ **Dollarbird *Eurystomus orientalis***
_____ *E. o. abundus*　　　　　　　Himalayas to China, Manchuria and Korea; winters to Indonesia
_____ *E. o. deignani*　　　　　　　N Thailand; winters to Malaysia, Sumatra, Borneo and Java
_____ *E. o. orientalis*　　　　　　S Himalayas to SE Asia, Ryukyu Islands and Indonesian Arch.
_____ *E. o. gigas*　　　　　　　　S Andaman Islands
_____ *E. o. oberholseri*　　　　　　Simeulue I. (off Sumatra)
_____ *E. o. connectens*　　　　　　S Sulawesi, Sula Islands and Lesser Sundas
_____ *E. o. latouchei*　　　　　　NE China
_____ *E. o. waigiouensis*　　　　　New Guinea, w Papuan is., D'Entrecasteaux and Louisiade Arch.
_____ *E. o. pacificus*　　　　　　Australia; winters to New Guinea, s Moluccas and adj. islands
_____ *E. o. crassirostris*　　　　　Bismarck Archipelago
_____ *E. o. solomonensis*　　　　　Feni I. and Solomon Islands

☐ **Purple Roller *Eurystomus azureus***

　　　　　　　　　　　　　　　　　N Moluccas

ORDER: CORACIIFORMES
FAMILY: BRACHYPTERACIIDAE (Ground-Rollers—5)

☐ **Short-legged Ground-Roller** *Brachypteracias leptosomus*

Dense rainforests of central and ne Madagascar

☐ **Scaly Ground-Roller** *Brachypteracias squamigera*

Dense rainforests of central and ne Madagascar

☐ **Pitta-like Ground-Roller** *Atelornis pittoides*

Humid forests of Madagascar

☐ **Rufous-headed Ground-Roller** *Atelornis crossleyi*

Rainforests of central and ne Madagascar

☐ **Long-tailed Ground-Roller** *Uratelornis chimaera*

Subdesert of sw Madagascar

ORDER: CORACIIFORMES
FAMILY: LEPTOSOMATIDAE (Cuckoo-Roller—1)

☐ **Cuckoo-Roller** *Leptosomus discolor*
- ____ *L. d. discolor*   Grand Comoro I.
- ____ *L. d. intermedius*   Anjouan (Comoro Islands)
- ____ *L. d. discolor*   Mayotte I. and Madagascar

ORDER: CORACIIFORMES
FAMILY: UPUPIDAE (Hoopoes—2)

☐ **Eurasian Hoopoe** *Upupa epops*
- ____ *U. e. epops*   W Palearctic to Baluchistan; winters to s India and Africa
- ____ *U. e. major*   Egypt (Nile Valley to Suez Canal)
- ____ *U. e. senegalensis*   Senegambia to Ethiopia, Somalia and Uganda
- ____ *U. e. waibeli*   Chad to Cameroon (Adamawa Plateau), n Uganda and Kenya
- ____ *U. e. africana*   S Zaire to Uganda, Kenya and Cape Province
- ____ *U. e. orientalis*   NW India
- ____ *U. e. ceylonensis*   Central and s India and Sri Lanka
- ____ *U. e. saturata*   E Siberia, Manchuria and n China to extreme sw China
- ____ *U. e. longirostris*   Assam to Malay Peninsula, Indochina and Sumatra

☐ **Madagascar Hoopoe** *Upupa marginata*

Madagascar

ORDER: CORACIIFORMES
FAMILY: PHOENICULIDAE (Woodhoopoes and Scimitar-bills—8)

☐ **Green Woodhoopoe** *Phoeniculus purpureus*
- ____ *P. p. guineensis*   Senegambia to n Ghana, Nigeria, Chad and Central African Rep.
- ____ *P. p. senegalensis*   S Senegal and Gambia to s Ghana
- ____ *P. p. niloticus*   Sudan to w Ethiopia and ne Zaire
- ____ *P. p. marwitzi*   E Uganda and Kenya to central and e Natal
- ____ *P. p. angolensis*   Angola to w Zambia, w Zimbabwe, Namibia and Botswana
- ____ *P. p. purpureus (erythrorhynchos)*   South Africa (Cape Province and Transkei)

☐ **Violet Woodhoopoe** *Phoeniculus damarensis*
- ____ *P. d. damarensis*   Angola and Namibia
- ____ *P. d. granti*   Ethiopia and Kenya

☐ **Black-billed Woodhoopoe** *Phoeniculus somaliensis*

___ *P. s. somaliensis* — SE Ethiopia to w Somalia and ne Kenya

___ *P. s. neglectus* — Arid thornscrub of central Ethiopia

___ *P. s. abyssinicus* — N Ethiopia and Eritrea

☐ **White-headed Woodhoopoe** *Phoeniculus bollei*

___ *P. b. jacksoni* — Humid forests of e Zaire to Sudan and Kenya

___ *P. b. bollei* — Liberia to Central African Republic

___ *P. b. okuensis* — Cameroon (Lake Oku region)

☐ **Forest Woodhoopoe** *Phoeniculus castaneiceps*

___ *P. c. castaneiceps* — Liberia to Nigeria

___ *P. c. brunniceps* — Cameroon to Zaire, Uganda and Kenya

☐ **Black Scimitar-bill** *Rhinopomastus aterrimus*

___ *R. a. aterrimus* — Senegambia to w Sudan

___ *R. a. emini* — Central Sudan to ne Zaire and Uganda

___ *R. a. notatus* — Ethiopia

___ *R. a. anchietae* — Zaire to w Zambia and Angola

☐ **Common Scimitar-bill** *Rhinopomastus cyanomelas*

___ *R. c. cyanomelas* — Angola and Namibia to Transvaal

___ *R. c. shalowi (intermedius)* — Somalia to Zambia and w Natal

☐ **Abyssinian Scimitar-bill** *Rhinopomastus minor*

___ *R. m. minor* — Ethiopia to Somalia and n Kenya

___ *R. m. cabanisi* — Sudan to s Ethiopia, Kenya and Tanzania

ORDER: CORACIIFORMES
FAMILY: BUCEROTIDAE (Hornbills—57)

☐ **White-crested Hornbill** *Tockus albocristatus*

___ *T. a. albocristatus* — Humid forests of Guinea to w Ivory Coast

___ *T. a. macrourus* — E Ivory Coast and Ghana

___ *T. a. cassini* — Nigeria through Congo basin to w Uganda and n Angola

☐ **Black Dwarf Hornbill** *Tockus hartlaubi*

___ *T. h. hartlaubi* — Sierra Leone to Zaire (west of Congo River)

___ *T. h. granti* — Congo basin of Central African Republic to Zaire and Uganda

☐ **Red-billed Dwarf Hornbill** *Tockus camurus*

S Sierra Leone to extreme s Sudan, w Uganda and n Angola

☐ **Monteiro's Hornbill** *Tockus monteiri*

Arid savanna of s Angola and n Namibia

☐ **Red-billed Hornbill** *Tockus erythrorhynchus*

___ *T. e. erythrorhynchus* — Arid savanna of Senegambia to Somalia and south to Tanzania

___ *T. e. rufirostris* — Angola and n Namibia to Mozambique and e South Africa

___ *T. e. damarensis* — Central Namibia (s Damaraland)

☐ **Eastern Yellow-billed Hornbill** *Tockus flavirostris*

Ethiopia and Somalia to n Uganda and ne Tanzania

☐ **Southern Yellow-billed Hornbill** *Tockus leucomelas*

Arid savanna of s-central and s Africa

☐ **Jackson's Hornbill** *Tockus jacksoni*

Arid savanna of ne Uganda and nw Kenya

☐ **Von der Decken's Hornbill** *Tockus deckeni*

Ethiopia and s Somalia to Kenya, ne Uganda and Tanzania

☐ **Crowned Hornbill** *Tockus alboterminatus*

Savanna of e and s Africa, Zanzibar and Pemba I.

☐ **Bradfield's Hornbill** *Tockus bradfieldi*

NW Zimbabwe to sw Zambia, n Botswana and s Angola

☐ **African Pied Hornbill** *Tockus fasciatus*

_____ *T. f. semifasciatus*
_____ *T. f. fasciatus*

Senegambia to just east of Niger River
Nigeria (east of Niger River) to Angola, Zaire and Uganda

☐ **Hemprich's Hornbill** *Tockus hemprichii*

Rocky *Euphorbia* areas of Ethiopia to nw Kenya and Uganda

☐ **African Gray Hornbill** *Tockus nasutus*

_____ *T. n. nasutus (forskalii)*
_____ *T. n. epirhinus (dorsalis)*

Senegambia to Ethiopia, Kenya and Uganda; Arabian Peninsula
S Uganda and se Kenya to n South Africa

☐ **Pale-billed Hornbill** *Tockus pallidirostris*

_____ *T. p. pallidirostris*
_____ *T. p. neumanni*

Angola to s Zaire, Zambia, Mozambique and s Tanzania
E Zambia to Mozambique, Malawi and Tanzania

☐ **Malabar Gray Hornbill** *Ocyceros griseus*

Moist deciduous forests of sw India

☐ **Ceylon Gray Hornbill** *Ocyceros gingalensis*

Moist deciduous forests of Sri Lanka

☐ **Indian Gray Hornbill** *Ocyceros birostris*

NE Pakistan, India and nw Bangladesh

☐ **Malabar Pied-Hornbill** *Anthracoceros coronatus*

Mixed forests of s India and Sri Lanka

☐ **Oriental Pied-Hornbill** *Anthracoceros albirostris*

_____ *A. a. albirostris*
_____ *A. a. convexus*

India to Assam, Nepal, Myanmar, s China and Indochina
S Thailand, Malay Pen., Greater Sundas and adjacent islands

☐ **Black Hornbill** *Anthracoceros malayanus*

Malay Peninsula, Sumatra and Borneo

☐ **Palawan Hornbill** *Anthracoceros marchei*

SW Philippines (Palawan, Balabac, Busuanga and Calauit)

☐ **Sulu Hornbill** *Anthracoceros montani*

Sulu Archipelago (Jolo, Tawitawi and Sanga Sanga)

☐ **Rhinoceros Hornbill** *Buceros rhinoceros*

_____ *B. r. rhinoceros*
_____ *B. r. borneoensis*
_____ *B. r. sylvestris*

Lowlands of s Malay Peninsula and Sumatra
Borneo
Java

☐ **Great Hornbill** *Buceros bicornis*

Lowlands of India to sw China, SE Asia and Sumatra

☐ **Rufous Hornbill** *Buceros hydrocorax*

_____ *B. h. hydrocorax*
_____ *B. h. mindanensis*
_____ *B. h. semigaleatus*

Philippines (Luzon and Marinduque)
Philippines (Mindanao, Basilan, Dinagat and Siargao)
Samar, Leyte, Bohol, Panaon, Buad, Calicoan and Biliran

☐ **Helmeted Hornbill** *Buceros vigil*

Myanmar to s Thailand, Malay Peninsula, Sumatra and Borneo

☐ **Brown Hornbill** *Anorrhinus austeni*

Assam, Myanmar and sw China to Thailand and Indochina

☐ **Rusty-cheeked Hornbill** *Anorrhinus tickelli*

S Myanmar and se Thailand

☐ **Bushy-crested Hornbill** *Anorrhinus galeritus*

S Myanmar, Malay Peninsula, Sumatra, Borneo and Penang I.

☐ **Luzon Hornbill** *Penelopides manillae*

Philippines (Luzon, Marinduque and Catanduanes)`

☐ **Mindoro Hornbill** *Penelopides mindorensis*

Mindoro (central Philippines)

☐ **Tarictic Hornbill** *Penelopides panini*
_____ *P. p. panini*
_____ *P. p. ticaensis*

Panay, Masbate, Guimaras, Negros, Pan de Azucar and Sicogon
Ticao I. (central Philippines)

☐ **Samar Hornbill** *Penelopides samarensis*

Philippines (Samar, Leyte, Calicoan and Bohol)

☐ **Mindanao Hornbill** *Penelopides affinis*
_____ *P. a. affinis*
_____ *P. a. basilanica*

S Philippines (Mindanao, Dinagat and Siargao)
Basilan (s Philippines)

☐ **Sulawesi Hornbill** *Penelopides exarhatus*
_____ *P. e. exarhatus*
_____ *P. e. sanfordi*

N Sulawesi and Lembeh I.
Central and s Sulawesi, Muna, Butung and Togian islands

☐ **White-crowned Hornbill** *Aceros comatus*

Extreme s Myanmar, Malay Peninsula, Sumatra and Borneo

☐ **Rufous-necked Hornbill** *Aceros nipalensis*

Himalayan foothills to sw China and n SE Asia

☐ **Wrinkled Hornbill** *Aceros corrugatus*

Malay Peninsula, Sumatra and Borneo

☐ **Writhe-billed Hornbill** *Aceros waldeni*

Central Philippines (Panay, Guimaras and Negros)

☐ **Writhed Hornbill** *Aceros leucocephalus*

S Philippines (Camiguin, Dinagat and Mindanao)

☐ **Knobbed Hornbill** *Aceros cassidix*

Sulawesi, Lembeh, Togian Islands, Muna and Butung

☐ **Wreathed Hornbill** *Aceros undulatus*

NE India to sw China, SE Asia, Greater Sundas and Andaman Is.

☐ **Narcondam Hornbill** *Aceros narcondami*

Lowland forests of Narcondam I. (Andaman Islands)

☐ **Sumba Hornbill** *Aceros everetti*

Sumba (Lesser Sundas)

☐ **Plain-pouched Hornbill** *Aceros subruficollis*

Myanmar to nw Thailand, Malay Peninsula, Sumatra and Borneo

☐ **Blyth's Hornbill** *Aceros plicatus*
_____ *A. p. ruficollis*
_____ *A. p. plicatus*
_____ *A. p. jungei*
_____ *A. p. dampieri*
_____ *A. p. harterti*

N Moluccas and w New Guinea
S Moluccas (Kelang, Seram and Ambon)
E New Guinea; vagrant to Fergusson I. (D'Entrecasteaux Arch.)
Bismarck Arch. (New Hanover, New Ireland and New Britain)
Solomon Is. (Buka, Bougainville, Fauro and Shortland Islands)

☐ **Trumpeter Hornbill** *Ceratogymna bucinator*

Forests of s-central and se Africa

☐ **Piping Hornbill** *Ceratogymna fistulator*
_____ *C. f. fistulator*
_____ *C. f. sharpii*
_____ *C. f. duboisi*

Mangroves and humid forests of Senegambia to Niger River
Niger River to Cameroon, Gabon and n Angola
Congo basin (n Angola to Central African Republic and Uganda)

☐ **Silvery-cheeked Hornbill** *Ceratogymna brevis*

Montane and coastal forests of Ethiopia to s Mozambique

☐ **Black-and-white-casqued Hornbill** *Ceratogymna subcylindricus*
_____ *C. s. subcylindricus*
_____ *C. s. subquadratus*

Ivory Coast to Nigeria (west of Niger River)
Nigeria (east of Niger River) to w Kenya, Burundi and Angola

☐ **Brown-cheeked Hornbill** *Ceratogymna cylindricus*

Humid forests of Sierra Leone to Ghana

☐ **White-thighed Hornbill** *Ceratogymna albotibialis*

Humid forests of Benin to Angola and Uganda

☐ **Black-casqued Hornbill** *Ceratogymna atrata*

Patchily distributed forests of w and central Africa; Bioko I.

☐ **Yellow-casqued Hornbill** *Ceratogymna elata*

Patchily distributed forests of Senegambia to Cameroon

☐ **Abyssinian Ground-Hornbill** *Bucorvus abyssinicus*

Senegambia to Ethiopia, n Uganda and ne Kenya

☐ **Southern Ground-Hornbill** *Bucorvus leadbeateri*

Savanna of e and s Africa

ORDER: PICIFORMES
FAMILY: GALBULIDAE (Jacamars—18)

☐ **White-eared Jacamar** *Galbalcyrhynchus leucotis*

Colombia east of the Andes to ne Peru and w Amazonian Brazil

☐ **Chestnut Jacamar** *Galbalcyrhynchus purusianus*

Tropical e Peru, n Bolivia and w Amazonian Brazil

☐ **Dusky-backed Jacamar** *Brachygalba salmoni*

Tropical e Panama and nw Colombia

☐ **Pale-headed Jacamar** *Brachygalba goeringi*

Tropical nw Venezuela and adjacent ne Colombia

☐ **Brown Jacamar** *Brachygalba lugubris*
____ *B. l. fulviventris* — E base of Eastern Andes of Colombia (north of the Amazon)
____ *B. l. caquetae* — E base of Eastern Andes of Colombia to e Peru
____ *B. l. lugubris* — E and s Venezuela to the Guianas and n Brazil
____ *B. l. obscuriceps* — Extreme s Venezuela and nw Brazil
____ *B. l. naumburgi* — NE Brazil (Maranhão and Piauí)
____ *B. l. melanosterna* — E Bolivia; central and sw Brazil
____ *B. l. phaeonota* — Central Brazil (known from one specimen from Rio Solimões)

☐ **White-throated Jacamar** *Brachygalba albogularis*

SE Peru to n Bolivia and sw Amazonian Brazil

☐ **Three-toed Jacamar** *Jacamaralcyon tridactyla*

Lowlands of se Brazil (Minas Gerais to Paraná)

☐ **Yellow-billed Jacamar** *Galbula albirostris*
____ *G. a. albirostris* — E Venezuela to the Guianas and n Brazil
____ *G. a. chalcocephala* — E Colombia to Ecuador and ne Peru; w Brazil (upper Rio Negro)

☐ **Blue-cheeked Jacamar** *Galbula cyanicollis*

Humid lowlands of ne Peru and Brazil south of the Amazon

☐ **Rufous-tailed Jacamar** *Galbula ruficauda*
____ *G. r. melanogenia* — Lowlands of s Mexico to w Ecuador
____ *G. r. ruficauda* — C Colombia to the Guianas and n Brazil; Trinidad and Tobago
____ *G. r. pallens* — Arid tropical n Colombia
____ *G. r. brevirostris* — NW Venezuela (tropical Lake Maracaibo region)
____ *G. r. rufoviridis* — Brazil south of Amazon to n Bolivia, Paraguay and ne Argentina
____ *G. r. heterogyna* — Bolivia east of the Andes and sw Brazil (w Mato Grosso)

☐ **Green-tailed Jacamar** *Galbula galbula*

E Colombia to s Venezuela, the Guianas and n Brazil

☐ **Coppery-chested Jacamar** *Galbula pastazae*

Foothills of se Colombia to e Ecuador and w Amazonian Brazil

☐ **Bluish-fronted Jacamar** *Galbula cyanescens*

Riverine forests of e Peru to n Bolivia and w Amazonian Brazil

☐ **White-chinned Jacamar** *Galbula tombacea*

_____ G. t. tombacea	Amazonian Colombia to e Ecuador, e Peru and w Brazil
_____ G. t. mentalis	Central and w Amazonian Brazil

☐ **Purplish Jacamar** *Galbula chalcothorax*

	S Colombia to n Bolivia and sw Amazonian Brazil

☐ **Bronzy Jacamar** *Galbula leucogastra*

_____ G. l. leucogastra	S Venezuela to the Guianas and w Amazonian Brazil
_____ G. l. viridissima	Central Brazil (Rio Tapajós area)

☐ **Paradise Jacamar** *Galbula dea*

_____ G. d. dea	Venezuela to Guianas and Brazil n of Amazon (e of Rio Negro)
_____ G. d. amazonum	N Bolivia (Río Beni) and Brazil s of the Amazon (east to Pará)
_____ G. d. brunneiceps	E Peru and w Brazil
_____ G. d. phainopepla	W Brazil south of the Amazon (west of Rio Madeira)

☐ **Great Jacamar** *Jacamerops aurea*

_____ J. a. penardi	Caribbean slope of Costa Rica to w Colombia
_____ J. a. aurea	E Colombia to Venezuela and the Guianas
_____ J. a. ridgwayi	Lower Amazonian Brazil (Rio Negro and Rio Tapajós eastward)
_____ J. a. isidori	E Ecuador to e Peru, w Brazil and n Bolivia

ORDER: PICIFORMES
FAMILY: BUCCONIDAE (Puffbirds—33)

☐ **White-necked Puffbird** *Notharchus macrorhynchos*

_____ N. m. hyperrynchus	Semiarid s Mexico to nw South America
_____ N. m. cryptoleucus	Pacific lowlands of El Salvador and nw Nicaragua
_____ N. m. macrorhynchos	Guianas and Brazil north of the Amazon
_____ N. m. paraensis	Lower Amazon east of Rio Tapajós (Pará and Maranhão)
_____ N. m. swainsoni	SE Brazil to e Paraguay and ne Argentina

☐ **Black-breasted Puffbird** *Notharchus pectoralis*

	Humid forests of e Panama to w Colombia and nw Ecuador

☐ **Brown-banded Puffbird** *Notharchus ordii*

	S Venezuela to n Amazonian Brazil, se Peru and n Bolivia

☐ **Pied Puffbird** *Notharchus tectus*

_____ N. t. subtectus	E Panama to central Colombia and sw Ecuador
_____ N. t. picatus	E Ecuador and e Peru
_____ N. t. tectus	S Venezuela to Guianas and Amazonian Brazil (e to Maranhão)

☐ **Chestnut-capped Puffbird** *Bucco macrodactylus*

_____ B. m. macrodactylus	E Colombia to Venezuela, n Bolivia and w Amazonian Brazil
_____ B. m. caurensis	S Venezuela (Río Caura region)

☐ **Spotted Puffbird** *Bucco tamatia*

_____ B. t. pulmentum	E Colombia to e Ecuador, e Peru and adjacent nw Brazil
_____ B. t. tamatia	Extreme e Colombia, Venezuela, Guianas and adj. n Brazil
_____ B. t. inexpectatus	N-c Brazil (north bank of the Amazon west of Rio Negro)
_____ B. t. punctuliger	C Brazil (s bank of the Amazon between Rio Purús and Rio Madeira)
_____ B. t. hypneleus	Right bank of lower Amazon (e of Rio Tapajós) and delta islands
_____ B. t. interior	SW Brazil (n and w Mato Grosso)

☐ **Sooty-capped Puffbird** *Bucco noanamae*

	Humid forests of nw Colombia

☐ **Collared Puffbird** *Bucco capensis*

_____ B. c. dugandi	SE Colombia to Ecuador and central Peru
_____ B. c. capensis	S Venezuela to the Guianas, Amazonian Brazil and e Peru

☐ **Barred Puffbird** *Nystalus radiatus*

Humid forests of w Panama to w Ecuador

☐ **White-eared Puffbird** *Nystalus chacuru*

_____ *N. c. uncirostris* — SE Peru and e Bolivia
_____ *N. c. chacuru* — Campos of s Brazil, Paraguay and ne Argentina

☐ **Striolated Puffbird** *Nystalus striolatus*

_____ *N. s. striolatus* — E Ecuador to e Peru, Bolivia and sw Amazonian Brazil
_____ *N. s. torridus* — E Brazil south of the Amazon (Pará)

☐ **Spot-backed Puffbird** *Nystalus maculatus*

_____ *N. m. maculatus* — E Brazil (south of the Amazon) to Minas Gerais and Bahia
_____ *N. m. parvirostris* — Central Brazil (Goiás, Minas Gerais and se Mato Grosso)
_____ *N. m. pallidigula* — SW Brazil (w Mato Grosso)
_____ *N. m. striatipectus* — Lowlands of e Bolivia to Paraguay and n Argentina

☐ **Russet-throated Puffbird** *Hypnelus ruficollis*

_____ *H. r. ruficollis* — N Colombia and w Venezuela (w Lake Maracaibo region)
_____ *H. r. decolor* — NE Colombia (Guajira Peninsula) and nw Venezuela (Falcón)
_____ *H. r. striaticollis* — NW Venezuela
_____ *H. r. coloratus* — W Venezuela (humid region south of Lake Maracaibo)
_____ *H. r. bicinctus* — N Venezuela and Orinoco Valley below Caicara
_____ *H. r. stoicus* — Isla Margarita

☐ **White-chested Puffbird** *Malacoptila fusca*

_____ *M. f. fusca* — SE Colombia to e Peru, the Guianas and w Amazonian Brazil
_____ *M. f. venezuelae* — S Venezuela

☐ **Semicollared Puffbird** *Malacoptila semicincta*

Humid lowlands of se Peru, sw Brazil and n Bolivia

☐ **Crescent-chested Puffbird** *Malacoptila striata*

_____ *M. s. minor* — Humid lowlands of e Brazil (Maranhão)
_____ *M. s. striata* — SE Brazil (s Bahia and e Minas Gerais to Santa Catarina)

☐ **Black-streaked Puffbird** *Malacoptila fulvogularis*

_____ *M. f. substriata* — Colombia (trade skins and 1 specimen from Llanos de Meta)
_____ *M. f. huilae* — N Colombia (Magdalena Valley)
_____ *M. f. fulvogularis* — Andean foothills of s Colombia to w Bolivia

☐ **Rufous-necked Puffbird** *Malacoptila rufa*

_____ *M. r. rufa* — E Ecuador to e Peru and w Brazil (s of Amazon to Rio Madeira)
_____ *M. r. brunnescens* — Humid forests of Amazonian Brazil

☐ **White-whiskered Puffbird** *Malacoptila panamensis*

_____ *M. p. inornata* — Tropical s Mexico to n Nicaragua
_____ *M. p. fuliginosa* — Tropical se Nicaragua to w Panama
_____ *M. p. panamensis* — Tropical sw Costa Rica to nw Colombia
_____ *M. p. poliopis* — Tropical sw Colombia and w Ecuador
_____ *M. p. magdalenae* — Tropical n Colombia (Magdalena Valley)

☐ **Moustached Puffbird** *Malacoptila mystacalis*

Humid forests of Venezuela and Colombia

☐ **Lanceolated Monklet** *Micromonacha lanceolata*

_____ *M. l. austinsmithi* — E Costa Rica and w Panama
_____ *M. l. lanceolata* — W Colombia to e Ecuador, e Peru and adj. w Amazonian Brazil

☐ **Fulvous-chinned Nunlet** *Nonnula sclateri*

Lowlands of se Peru to n Bolivia and sw Amazonian Brazil

☐ **Rusty-breasted Nunlet** *Nonnula rubecula*

____ *N. r. duidae*	*Tepuis* of s Venezuela (Mt. Duida)
____ *N. r. interfluvialis*	*Tepuis* of s Venezuela and adjacent n Brazil
____ *N. r. cineracea*	W Brazil and adjacent ne Peru
____ *N. r. simplex*	NE Brazil (Pará)
____ *N. r. rubecula*	SE Brazil to e Paraguay and ne Argentina

☐ **Brown Nunlet** *Nonnula brunnea*

Humid lowlands of se Colombia, e Ecuador and ne Peru

☐ **Gray-cheeked Nunlet** *Nonnula frontalis*

Lowlands of central Panama to nw Colombia

☐ **Rufous-capped Nunlet** *Nonnula ruficapilla*

____ *N. r. pallescens*	Littoral of ne Colombia
____ *N. r. rufipectus*	NE Peru (north of the Amazon)
____ *N. r. ruficapilla*	E Peru (Marañón, Huallaga and Ucayali valleys) and adj. Brazil
____ *N. r. nattereri*	SW Brazil (w Mato Grosso)
____ *N. r. inundata*	E Brazil (Pará) on left bank of Rio Tocantins near Jacundá

☐ **Chestnut-headed Nunlet** *Nonnula amaurocephala*

Humid forests of w Amazonian Brazil

☐ **White-faced Nunbird** *Hapaloptila castanea*

Locally in Andean foothills of s Colombia to n Peru

☐ **Black Nunbird** *Monasa atra*

Humid forests of Guianas, s Venezuela and n Brazil

☐ **Black-fronted Nunbird** *Monasa nigrifrons*

____ *M. n. nigrifrons*	Lowlands of se Colombia to n Bolivia and Brazil
____ *M. n. canescens*	Tropical Bolivia e of Andes

☐ **White-fronted Nunbird** *Monasa morphoeus*

____ *M. m. grandior*	Caribbean slope of Nicaragua to nw Panama
____ *M. m. fidelis*	E Panama (Cerro Azul and Río Chepo)
____ *M. m. pallescens*	E Panama and nw Colombia
____ *M. m. sclateri*	N Colombia (lower Cauca and Magdalena valleys)
____ *M. m. peruana*	SE Colombia to e Peru and nw Brazil
____ *M. m. morphoeus*	Amazonian Brazil south of the Amazon and se Brazil
____ *M. m. boliviana*	NE Bolivia along Río Beni and Río Coroico

☐ **Yellow-billed Nunbird** *Monasa flavirostris*

Humid forests of Colombia to e Peru and w Amazonian Brazil

☐ **Swallow-wing** *Chelidoptera tenebrosa*

____ *C. t. tenebrosa*	E Colombia to the Guianas, n Bolivia and central Brazil
____ *C. t. brasiliensis*	E and se Brazil (Alagoas to São Paulo)
____ *C. t. pallida*	Tropical w Venezuela

ORDER: PICIFORMES
FAMILY: CAPITONIDAE (Barbets—83)

☐ **Fire-tufted Barbet** *Psilopogon pyrolophus*

Upland forests of Malay Peninsula and Sumatra

☐ **Great Barbet** *Megalaima virens*

____ *M. v. marshallorum*	NW Himalayas (Kashmir to Simla)
____ *M. v. magnifica*	Assam and hills of n Myanmar
____ *M. v. clamator*	Upper Myanmar (Hpimaw Hills and Shweli/Salween divide)
____ *M. v. virens*	E and s China to s Myanmar, n Thailand, Laos and n Annam

☐ **Red-vented Barbet** *Megalaima lagrandieri*
____ *M. l. rothschildi* | N Vietnam and n Laos
____ *M. l. lagrandieri* | S Laos to central and s Annam and Vietnam

☐ **Brown-headed Barbet** *Megalaima zeylanica*
____ *M. z. kangrae* | W Himalayas (Kangra to Garhwal)
____ *M. z. inornata* | W India (Mt. Abu and Godavari River south to Cannanore)
____ *M. z. caniceps* | Central and e India
____ *M. z. zeylanica* | S India and Sri Lanka

☐ **Lineated Barbet** *Megalaima lineata*
____ *M. l. hodgsoni* | W Himalayas to Malay Peninsula and Indochina
____ *M. l. lineata* | Java and Bali

☐ **White-cheeked Barbet** *Megalaima viridis*

Lowlands and foothills of sw India

☐ **Green-eared Barbet** *Megalaima faiostricta*

Extreme s China to Thailand, Laos and Vietnam

☐ **Brown-throated Barbet** *Megalaima corvina*

Forests of w and central Java

☐ **Gold-whiskered Barbet** *Megalaima chrysopogon*
____ *M. c. laeta* | S Thailand and Malay Peninsula
____ *M. c. chrysopogon* | Sumatra
____ *M. c. chrysopsis* | Borneo

☐ **Red-crowned Barbet** *Megalaima rafflesii*
____ *M. r. malayensis* | S Myanmar and Malay Peninsula
____ *M. r. rafflesii* | Sumatra and Bangka I.
____ *M. r. billitonis* | Mentawi Archipelago (Billiton and Mendanau)
____ *M. r. borneensis* | Borneo

☐ **Red-throated Barbet** *Megalaima mystacophanos*
____ *M. m. mystacophanos* | S Myanmar, Malay Peninsula and Sumatra
____ *M. m. humii* | Borneo
____ *M. m. ampala* | Batu Islands (off w Sumatra)

☐ **Black-banded Barbet** *Megalaima javensis*

Java and Bali

☐ **Yellow-fronted Barbet** *Megalaima flavifrons*

Sri Lanka

☐ **Golden-throated Barbet** *Megalaima franklinii*
____ *M. f. franklinii* | Himalayas (Nepal and Sikkim to Yunnan and n Vietnam)
____ *M. f. ramsayi* | Mountains of s Myanmar to n and w Thailand
____ *M. f. auricularis* | Mountains of s Laos and s Vietnam
____ *M. f. trangensis* | Mountains of peninsular Thailand
____ *M. f. minor* | Mountains of Malay Peninsula

☐ **Black-browed Barbet** *Megalaima oorti*
____ *M. o. oorti* | Montane forests of Malay Peninsula and Sumatra
____ *M. o. annamensis* | S Indochina (Langbian and Bolavens plateaux)
____ *M. o. nuchalis* | Taiwan
____ *M. o. faber* | Hainan (s China)
____ *M. o. sini* | Montane forests of se China (Guangxi)

☐ **Blue-throated Barbet** *Megalaima asiatica*
____ *M. a. asiatica* | Kashmir to Assam and central Myanmar
____ *M. a. rubescens* | Assam (south of the Brahmaputra River) and nw Myanmar
____ *M. a. davisoni* | S Myanmar to s China and n Indochina
____ *M. a. chersonesus* | Mountains of peninsular Thailand

☐ **Mountain Barbet** *Megalaima monticola*

Mountains of n Borneo

☐ **Moustached Barbet** *Megalaima incognita*

____ *M. i. incognita*	S Myanmar
____ *M. i. euroa (elbeli)*	S peninsular Thailand and Indochina

☐ **Yellow-crowned Barbet** *Megalaima henricii*

____ *M. h. henricii*	Peninsular Thailand, Malay Peninsula and Sumatra
____ *M. h. brachyrhyncha*	Borneo

☐ **Flame-fronted Barbet** *Megalaima armillaris*

____ *M. a. armillaris*	W and central Java
____ *M. a. baliensis*	E Java and Bali

☐ **Golden-naped Barbet** *Megalaima pulcherrima*

Mountains of n Borneo

☐ **Blue-eared Barbet** *Megalaima australis*

____ *M. a. cyanotis*	Himalayas to Indochina
____ *M. a. stuarti*	Peninsular Myanmar and Thailand
____ *M. a. duvaucelii*	Malay Peninsula, Sumatra, Bangka I. and Borneo
____ *M. a. gigantorhinus*	Nias I. (off nw Sumatra)
____ *M. a. tanamassae*	Batu Islands (off w Sumatra)
____ *M. a. australis*	Java
____ *M. a. hebereri*	Bali

☐ **Bornean Barbet** *Megalaima eximia*

____ *M. e. eximia*	Mountains of n Borneo
____ *M. e. cyanea*	N Borneo (Mt. Kinabalu)

☐ **Crimson-fronted Barbet** *Megalaima rubricapilla*

____ *M. r. malabarica*	Lowlands and foothills of sw India
____ *M. r. rubricapilla*	Lowlands and foothills of Sri Lanka

☐ **Coppersmith Barbet** *Megalaima haemacephala*

____ *M. h. indica*	NW India to Malay Peninsula and Indochina
____ *M. h. delica*	Sumatra
____ *M. h. rosea*	Java and Bali
____ *M. h. haemacephala*	N Philippines (Luzon and Mindoro)
____ *M. h. intermedia*	Philippines (Guimaras, Negros, Panay, Calagayan, Pan de Azucar)
____ *M. h. celestinoi*	Philippines (Samar, Leyte, Biliran and Catanduanes)
____ *M. h. mindanensis*	Mindanao (s Philippines)
____ *M. h. cebuensis*	Cebu (central Philippines)
____ *M. h. homochroa*	Philippines (Masbate, Romblon and Tablas); possibly Palawan

☐ **Brown Barbet** *Calorhamphus fuliginosus*

____ *C. f. hayii*	Peninsular Myanmar and Thailand, Malay Peninsula and Sumatra
____ *C. f. tertius*	N Borneo
____ *C. f. fuliginosus*	Borneo (except northern part)

☐ **Naked-faced Barbet** *Gymnobucco calvus*

____ *G. c. calvus*	Lowland forests of Sierra Leone to Gabon
____ *G. c. congicus*	W Congo and lower Congo River (w Zaire and nw Angola)
____ *G. c. vernayi*	W-central Angola (Mt. Moco)

☐ **Bristle-nosed Barbet** *Gymnobucco peli*

Ivory Coast to s Cameroon, Gabon, w Zaire and n Angola

☐ **Sladen's Barbet** *Gymnobucco sladeni*

Forests of central and e Zaire

☐ **Gray-throated Barbet** *Gymnobucco bonapartei*

____	*G. b. bonapartei*	S Cameroon to Gabon, Congo, n Angola and w Zaire
____	*G. b. cinereiceps*	Central African Rep. to n Zaire, s Sudan, w Kenya and Tanzania

☐ **White-eared Barbet** *Stactolaema leucotis*

____	*S. l. kilimensis*	Locally in highlands of central Kenya and ne Tanzania
____	*S. l. leucogrammicus*	Highlands of s-central Tanzania (Uluguru Mts. to Mahenge)
____	*S. l. leucotis*	E Zimbabwe to Malawi, Mozambique and Natal

☐ **Anchieta's Barbet** *Stactolaema anchietae*

____	*S. a. rex*	W-central Angola
____	*S. a. anchietae*	Highlands of s-central Angola to w Zambia
____	*S. a. katangae*	E Angola to Zaire and Zambia

☐ **Whyte's Barbet** *Stactolaema whytii*

____	*S. w. terminatum*	S Tanzania (Iringa region)
____	*S. w. stresemanni*	SW Tanzania and ne Zambia
____	*S. w. sowerbyi*	E and ne Zimbabwe and adjacent Mozambique
____	*S. w. whytii*	S Malawi, immediately adjacent Mozambique and s-c Tanzania
____	*S. w. angoniensis*	E Zambia and Malawi (west of Shire River)
____	*S. w. buttoni*	N-central Zambia (along Zaire border)

☐ **Green Barbet** *Stactolaema olivacea*

____	*S. o. olivacea*	E Kenya (Tana River) to e Tanzania
____	*S. o. howelli*	E Tanzania (Udzungwa Mountains and Mahenge)
____	*S. o. woodwardi*	SE Tanzania (Rondo Plateau) and Zululand (Ngoye Forest)
____	*S. o. rungweensis*	SW Tanzania to n Malawi (Misuku Hills)
____	*S. o. belcheri*	S Malawi (Mt. Thyolo) and n Mozambique (Mt. Namuli)

☐ **Speckled Tinkerbird** *Pogoniulus scolopaceus*

____	*P. s. scolopaceus*	Sierra Leone and s Guinea to se Nigeria
____	*P. s. stellatus*	Bioko (Gulf of Guinea)
____	*P. s. flavisquamatus*	S Cameroon to extreme w Kenya and n Angola

☐ **Western Tinkerbird** *Pogoniulus coryphaeus*

____	*P. c. coryphaeus*	SE Nigeria (Obudu Plateau) and adjacent sw Cameroon
____	*P. c. hildamariae*	Zaire to Rwanda and sw Uganda
____	*P. c. angolensis*	NW Angola (Mt. Moco and Mombolo highlands)

☐ **Moustached Tinkerbird** *Pogoniulus leucomystax*

Montane forests of Kenya and Tanzania to Malawi

☐ **Green Tinkerbird** *Pogoniulus simplex*

Coastal forests of se Kenya to s Mozambique

☐ **Red-rumped Tinkerbird** *Pogoniulus atroflavus*

Senegambia to w Uganda, Congo R. mouth and Ruwenzori Mts.

☐ **Yellow-throated Tinkerbird** *Pogoniulus subsulphureus*

____	*P. s. chrysopygius*	Guinea and Sierra Leone to Ghana
____	*P. s. flavimentum*	Togo and s Nigeria to Uganda and e Zaire
____	*P. s. subsulphureus*	Bioko (Gulf of Guinea)

☐ **Yellow-rumped Tinkerbird** *Pogoniulus bilineatus*

____	*P. b. leucolaima*	Senegambia to s Sudan, Uganda, se Zaire and n Angola
____	*P. b. poensis*	Bioko (Gulf of Guinea)
____	*P. b. mfumbiri*	Highlands of extreme sw Uganda to w Tanzania and Zambia
____	*P. b. jacksoni*	Highlands of e Uganda, c Kenya, Rwanda and n Tanzania
____	*P. b. fischeri*	Coastal Kenya and Tanzania, Zanzibar and Mafia I.
____	*P. b. bilineatus*	SE Tanzania to Mozambique and e South Africa

☐ **White-chested Tinkerbird** *Pogoniulus makawai*

1964 specimen from nw Zambia (possible aberrant *P. bilineatus*)

☐ **Yellow-fronted Tinkerbird** *Pogoniulus chrysoconus*

____	*P. c. chrysoconus*	Senegambia to Ethiopia and nw Tanzania
____	*P. c. xanthostictus*	Ethiopia
____	*P. c. extoni*	Angola to Zaire, Tanzania, Namibia and ne Cape Province

☐ **Red-fronted Tinkerbird** *Pogoniulus pusillus*

____	*P. p. uropygialis*	N and central Ethiopia and n Somalia
____	*P. p. affinis*	SE Sudan to se Ethiopia, s Somalia, Kenya, Uganda, Tanzania
____	*P. p. pusillus*	Mozambique to e Cape Province

☐ **Yellow-spotted Barbet** *Buccanodon duchaillui*

Sierra Leone to s Sudan, Zaire, Uganda and w Kenya

☐ **Hairy-breasted Barbet** *Tricholaema hirsuta*

____	*T. h. hirsuta*	Sierra Leone to Ghana
____	*T. h. flavipunctata*	S Nigeria and Cameroon to n and central Gabon
____	*T. h. angolensis*	S Gabon to Zaire, Cabinda and n Angola
____	*T. h. ansorgii*	E Cameroon to e Zaire, s Sudan, Uganda and w Kenya

☐ **Red-fronted Barbet** *Tricholaema diademata*

____	*T. d. diademata*	S Sudan to Ethiopia, n Somalia and Kenya
____	*T. d. massaica*	Central Kenya to central and sw Tanzania

☐ **Miombo Barbet** *Tricholaema frontata*

Angola to sw Tanzania, n Malawi and Zambia

☐ **Pied Barbet** *Tricholaema leucomelas*

____	*T. l. centralis*	Angola to sw Zambia, w Zimbabwe and South Africa
____	*T. l. leucomelas*	South Africa (central and sw Cape Province)
____	*T. l. affinis*	E Zimbabwe and sw Mozambique to e Cape Province

☐ **Spot-flanked Barbet** *Tricholaema lachrymosa*

____	*T. l. lachrymosa*	Extreme ne Zaire to s Sudan, n Kenya and nw Tanzania
____	*T. l. radcliffei*	Lake Victoria basin

☐ **Black-throated Barbet** *Tricholaema melanocephala*

____	*T. m. melanocephala*	N and central Ethiopia and ne Somalia
____	*T. m. stigmatothorax*	S Ethiopia to Kenya and central Tanzania
____	*T. m. blandi*	N Somalia (except nw corner)
____	*T. m. flavibuccalis*	Tanzania (Serengeti National Park)

☐ **Banded Barbet** *Lybius undatus*

____	*L. u. thiogaster*	Highlands of Eritrea and ne Ethiopia
____	*L. u. undatus*	Highlands of nw to central Ethiopia
____	*L. u. leucogenys*	Highlands of sw and s-central Ethiopia
____	*L. u. salvadori*	Highlands of se Ethiopia

☐ **Vieillot's Barbet** *Lybius vieilloti*

____	*L. v. buchanani*	S Mauritania and Mali to Niger, n Nigeria and Chad
____	*L. v. rubescens*	Senegambia and Sierra Leone to n Zaire
____	*L. v. vieilloti*	Sudan (Khartoum) to nw Zaire and n Ethiopia

☐ **White-headed Barbet** *Lybius leucocephalus*

____	*L. l. leucocephalus*	S Sudan to ne Zaire, Uganda, nw Tanzania and w-c Kenya
____	*L. l. adamauae*	N Nigeria to s Chad, Central African Republic and nw Zaire
____	*L. l. albicauda*	Extreme s Kenya and n Tanzania
____	*L. l. senex*	Highlands of central and se Kenya
____	*L. l. lynesi*	Central and s-central Tanzania
____	*L. l. leucogaster*	Highlands of sw Angola

☐ **Chaplin's Barbet** *Lybius chaplini*

Miombo woodlands of s-central Zambia

☐ **Red-faced Barbet** *Lybius rubrifacies*

Acacia belt of sw Uganda to e Rwanda and nw Tanzania

☐ **Black-billed Barbet** *Lybius guifsobalito*

E Sudan to w Ethiopia, ne Zaire, Uganda and w Kenya

☐ **Black-collared Barbet** *Lybius torquatus*

____ *L. t. zombae*	S-central Malawi and central Mozambique to se Tanzania
____ *L. t. pumilio*	E Zaire to n Zambia, w Tanzania and nw Mozambique
____ *L. t. irroratus*	Coastal Kenya (Lamu and Tana River) to central Tanzania
____ *L. t. congicus*	N Angola to nw Zambia and s-central Zaire
____ *L. t. vivacens*	S-central and w Mozambique to e Zimbabwe and s Malawi
____ *L. t. bocagei*	S Angola to n Namibia, n Botswana and sw Zambia
____ *L. t. torquatus*	SE Botswana to e Cape Province, Swaziland and Natal

☐ **Brown-breasted Barbet** *Lybius melanopterus*

Savanna of s Somalia to se Malawi and n Mozambique

☐ **Black-backed Barbet** *Lybius minor*

____ *L. m. minor*	S Gabon and w Zaire to w Angola
____ *L. m. macclounii*	S-c and se Zaire to c Angola, n Zambia, Malawi and Tanzania

☐ **Double-toothed Barbet** *Lybius bidentatus*

____ *L. b. bidentatus*	Guinea-Bissau and Sierra Leone to w Zaire and n Angola
____ *L. b. aequatorialis*	Central African Rep. to e Ethiopia, w Kenya and nw Tanzania

☐ **Bearded Barbet** *Lybius dubius*

Sahel (Senegambia to central Central African Republic)

☐ **Black-breasted Barbet** *Lybius rolleti*

E Sahel (s Chad to s Sudan, nw Uganda and Cent. African Rep.)

☐ **Yellow-billed Barbet** *Trachyphonus purpuratus*

____ *T. p. goffinii*	Sierra Leone and s Guinea to Ghana
____ *T. p. togoensis*	E Ghana to sw Nigeria
____ *T. p. purpuratus*	SE Nigeria and s Cameroon to n Angola and central Zaire
____ *T. p. elgonensis*	S Sudan and w Kenya to e Zaire and s Uganda

☐ **Crested Barbet** *Trachyphonus vaillantii*

____ *T. v. suahelicus*	N-c Angola and Zaire to Tanzania, Angola and w Mozambique
____ *T. v. vaillantii*	E Botswana to s Zimbabwe, s Mozambique and e Cape Province

☐ **Yellow-breasted Barbet** *Trachyphonus margaritatus*

____ *T. m. margaritatus*	Mali, Niger and ne Nigeria to Chad, Sudan and e Ethiopia
____ *T. m. somalicus*	E Ethiopia to Djibouti and n Somalia

☐ **Red-and-yellow Barbet** *Trachyphonus erythrocephalus*

____ *T. e. shelleyi*	Somalia and Ethiopia (Ogaden Depression) to ne Kenya
____ *T. e. versicolor*	SE Sudan and central Ethiopia to ne Uganda and n Kenya
____ *T. e. erythrocephalus*	Central Kenya to ne Tanzania

☐ **D'Arnaud's Barbet** *Trachyphonus darnaudii*

____ *T. d. darnaudii*	SE Sudan to ne Uganda, sw Ethiopia and w-central Kenya
____ *T. d. boehmi*	Ethiopia to s Somalia, e Kenya and ne Tanzania
____ *T. d. emini*	Tanzania (Singida area and Dar es Salaam to Uhehe region)
____ *T. d. usambiro*	SW Kenya to Tanzania (Tabora region)

☐ **Scarlet-crowned Barbet** *Capito aurovirens*

Forests of se Colombia to e Peru and w Amazonian Brazil

☐ **Unnamed Barbet** *Capito sp. nov.*

New species discovered 1997 in ne Peru. Awaiting publication

☐ **Spot-crowned Barbet** *Capito maculicoronatus*

_____   *C. m. maculicoronatus*   W Panama (Veraguas to Canal Zone)

_____   *C. m. pirrensis*   E Panama (Pacific slope of Darién) and adjacent nw Colombia

_____   *C. m. melas*   Caribbean slope of e Panama

_____   *C. m. rubrilateralis*   Tropical w Colombia (south to Buenaventura)

☐ **Orange-fronted Barbet** *Capito squamatus*

Humid forests of w Ecuador and adjacent sw Colombia

☐ **White-mantled Barbet** *Capito hypoleucus*

_____   *C. h. hypoleucus*   Humid forests of central Colombia

_____   *C. h. carrikeri*   N-central Colombia

_____   *C. h. extinctus*   Central Colombia

☐ **Black-girdled Barbet** *Capito dayi*

Humid forests of w Amazonian Brazil

☐ **Five-colored Barbet** *Capito quinticolor*

Pacific sw Colombia and extreme nw Ecuador

☐ **Black-spotted Barbet** *Capito niger*

_____   *C. n. niger*   Guianas and ne Brazil north of the Amazon

_____   *C. n. punctatus*   Tropical e base of Andes from Colombia to Peru

_____   *C. n. intermedius*   Venezuela (Maipures region of upper Río Orinoco)

_____   *C. n. aurantiicinctus*   S Venezuela (mouth of Río Caura south to Mt. Duida)

_____   *C. n. auratus*   NW Peru (tropical zone of lower Río Ucayali)

_____   *C. n. orosae*   NW Brazil (Rio Eirú)

_____   *C. n. amazonicus*   Amazonian Brazil (São Paulo de Olivença to Rio Purús)

_____   *C. n. transilens*   NW Brazil (upper Rio Negro)

_____   *C. n. nitidior*   N Brazil (near junction of Rio Solimões and Putumayo)

_____   *C. n. hypochondriacus*   N-central Brazil (Manacapurú)

_____   *C. n. novaolindae*   NW Brazil (Nova Olinda)

_____   *C. n. arimae*   NW Brazil (right bank of Rio Purús from Amazon to Arimã)

_____   *C. n. insperatus*   Tropical se Peru to n Bolivia and w Brazil

☐ **Brown-chested Barbet** *Capito brunneipectus*

Lowlands of n-central Brazil (w Pará)

☐ **Lemon-throated Barbet** *Eubucco richardsoni*

_____   *E. r. richardsoni*   Tropical e Colombia, e Ecuador and e Peru (n of Río Marañón)

_____   *E. r. nigriceps*   NW Peru (Pebas region)

_____   *E. r. auranticollis*   E Peru s of R. Marañón and w Brazil s of Amazon to R. Madeira

_____   *E. r. coccineus*   Central Peru (Junín)

☐ **Red-headed Barbet** *Eubucco bourcierii*

_____   *E. b. salvini*   Highlands of Costa Rica and w Panama

_____   *E. b. anomalus*   Subtropical and upper tropical e Panama

_____   *E. b. occidentalis*   Subtropical Western Andes of Colombia

_____   *E. b. bourcierii*   E slope of Central Andes and w slope of E Andes of Colombia

_____   *E. b. aequatorialis*   Subtropical w slope of Andes of Ecuador and n Peru

_____   *E. b. orientalis*   Subtropical e slope of Andes of Ecuador

☐ **Scarlet-hooded Barbet** *Eubucco tucinkae*

Humid Andes of e Peru, n Bolivia and w Amazonian Brazil

☐ **Versicolored Barbet** *Eubucco versicolor*

_____   *E. v. steerii*   Andes of n Peru

_____   *E. v. glaucogularis*   Andes of central Peru

_____   *E. v. versicolor*   Andes of s Peru and nw Bolivia

☐ **Toucan Barbet** *Semnornis ramphastinus*

_____   *S. r. caucae*   W Andes of sw Colombia

_____   *S. r. ramphastinus*   Andes of w Ecuador

☐ **Prong-billed Barbet** *Semnornis frantzii*

	Humid montane forests of Costa Rica and w Panama

ORDER: PICIFORMES
FAMILY: RAMPHASTIDAE (Toucans—41)

☐ **Emerald Toucanet** *Aulacorhynchus prasinus*

____ A. p. wagleri	Mountains of sw Mexico (Guerrero and w Oaxaca)
____ A. p. prasinus	SE Mexico (Veracruz, adjacent San Luis Potosí and Oaxaca)
____ A. p. stenorhabdus	Subtropical s Mexico to w Guatemala and n El Salvador
____ A. p. virescens	Petén of n Guatemala, Belize, Honduras and n Nicaragua
____ A. p. volcanius	El Salvador (Volcán San Miguel)
____ A. p. maxillaris	Highlands of Costa Rica and w Panama
____ A. p. caeruleogularis	Highlands of e-central Panama (Chiriquí and Veraguas)
____ A. p. cognatus	Mountains of e Panama (Darién)
____ A. p. griseigularis	N end of W Andes and w slope of Central Andes of Colombia
____ A. p. phaeolaemus	Subtropical Western Andes of Colombia
____ A. p. lautus	Santa Marta Mountains (ne Colombia)
____ A. p. albivitta	E and Central Andes of Colombia, e Ecuador and w Venezuela
____ A. p. cyanolaemus	Subtropical Andes of se Ecuador and n Peru
____ A. p. dimidiatus	Andes of n Peru (Huánuco)
____ A. p. atrogularis	Andes of e Peru and n Bolivia

☐ **Groove-billed Toucanet** *Aulacorhynchus sulcatus*

____ A. s. sulcatus	Coastal cordillera of n Venezuela
____ A. s. erythrognathus	Andes of ne Venezuela (Cumaná)
____ A. s. calorhynchus	Santa Marta Mts. (ne Colombia) and Sierra de Perijá (w Venezuela)

☐ **Chestnut-tipped Toucanet** *Aulacorhynchus derbianus*

____ A. d. derbianus	E Ecuador to e Peru and n Bolivia
____ A. d. nigrirostris	Central Peru
____ A. d. duidae	*Tepuis* of s Venezuela (Mt. Duida)
____ A. d. whitelianus	*Tepuis* of s Venezuela and adjacent Guyana
____ A. d. osgoodi	S Guyana (Acari Mountains)

☐ **Crimson-rumped Toucanet** *Aulacorhynchus haematopygus*

____ A. h. sexnotatus	Subtropical sw Colombia (Nariño) and Andes of w Ecuador
____ A. h. haematopygus	Andes of Colombia and Sierra de Perijá (w Venezuela)

☐ **Yellow-browed Toucanet** *Aulacorhynchus huallagae*

	Humid mountains of n Peru (La Libertad)

☐ **Blue-banded Toucanet** *Aulacorhynchus coeruleicinctis*

	Andes of e Peru and w Bolivia

☐ **Lettered Aracari** *Pteroglossus inscriptus*

	SE Colombia to n Bolivia and Amaz. Brazil south of the Amazon

☐ **Green Aracari** *Pteroglossus viridis*

____ P. v. humboldti	SE Colombia to n Bolivia and w Brazil
____ P. v. didymus	Range unknown; specimen from Upper Amazonia
____ P. v. viridis	S Venezuela to the Guianas and Brazil north of the Amazon

☐ **Red-necked Aracari** *Pteroglossus bitorquatus*

____ P. b. sturmii	Amazonian Brazil (Rio Madeira) to e Bolivia
____ P. b. reichenowi	S bank of lower Amazon (Rio Tapajós to Rio Tocantins)
____ P. b. bitorquatus	Lower Amazon east of Rio Tocantins and adjacent n Maranhão

☐ **Ivory-billed Aracari** *Pteroglossus azara*

____ P. a. flavirostris	E Colombia and Ecuador to s Venezuela and nw Brazil
____ P. a. azara	W Brazil between lower Rio Negro and Rio Solimões

☐ **Brown-mandibled Aracari** *Pteroglossus mariae*

E Peru to n Bolivia and w Amazonian Brazil s of the Amazon

☐ **Chestnut-eared Aracari** *Pteroglossus castanotis*

____ *P. c. castanotis* Tropical e Colombia to e Ecuador, e Peru and nw Brazil
____ *P. c. australis* Tropical e Bolivia to w and se Brazil and ne Argentina

☐ **Black-necked Aracari** *Pteroglossus aracari*

____ *P. a. roraimae* S and e Venezuela to Guyana and Suriname
____ *P. a. atricollis* French Guiana and Brazil north of the Amazon
____ *P. a. aracari* Amazonian Brazil south of the Amazon
____ *P. a. vergens* E Brazil (Minas Gerais, São Paulo, Paraná and Santa Catarina)

☐ **Collared Aracari** *Pteroglossus torquatus*

____ *P. t. torquatus* Tropical s Mexico to w Panama
____ *P. t. erythrozonus* SE Mexico to Belize and Petén of n Guatemala
____ *P. t. nuchalis* Tropical n Colombia and coastal n Venezuela
____ *P. t. pectoralis* NW Venezuela (Maracaibo basin)
____ *P. t. erythropygius* W Ecuador (Chandron Valley to Esmeraldas)

☐ **Fiery-billed Aracari** *Pteroglossus frantzii*

Pacific slope of Costa Rica and w Panama

☐ **Stripe-billed Aracari** *Pteroglossus sanguineus*

Humid forests of w Colombia and nw Ecuador

☐ **Pale-mandibled Aracari** *Pteroglossus erythropygius*

Pacific lowlands of w Ecuador

☐ **Many-banded Aracari** *Pteroglossus pluricinctus*

S Venezuela to ne Peru and nw Amazonian Brazil

☐ **Curl-crested Aracari** *Pteroglossus beauharnaesii*

E Peru to n Bolivia and w Amazonian Brazil s of the Amazon

☐ **Saffron Toucanet** *Baillonius bailloni*

Humid forests of se Brazil to ne Argentina and e Paraguay

☐ **Plate-billed Mountain-Toucan** *Andigena laminirostris*

Andes of sw Colombia and w Ecuador

☐ **Gray-breasted Mountain-Toucan** *Andigena hypoglauca*

____ *A. h. hypoglauca* Central Andes of Colombia
____ *A. h. lateralis* Temperate Andes of e Ecuador and e Peru

☐ **Hooded Mountain-Toucan** *Andigena cucullata*

Andes of se Peru and w Bolivia

☐ **Black-billed Mountain-Toucan** *Andigena nigrirostris*

____ *A. n. occidentalis* Subtropical Western Andes of Colombia
____ *A. n. spilorhynchus* Central Andes of s Colombia and ne Ecuador
____ *A. n. nigrirostris* Subtropical Eastern Andes of Colombia and nw Venezuela

☐ **Yellow-eared Toucanet** *Selenidera spectabilis*

Humid forests of e Honduras to nw Ecuador

☐ **Golden-collared Toucanet** *Selenidera reinwardtii*

____ *S. r. reinwardtii* Tropical se Colombia to e Ecuador and ne Peru
____ *S. r. langsdorffi* Tropical e Peru and w Amazonian Brazil

☐ **Tawny-tufted Toucanet** *Selenidera nattereri*

Locally in s Venezuela, the Guianas and nw Amazonian Brazil

☐ **Guianan Toucanet** *Selenidera culik*

S Venezuela to the Guianas and nw Amazonian Brazil

☐ **Spot-billed Toucanet** *Selenidera maculirostris*

____ *S. m. hellmayri* Amazonian Brazil s of Amazon (Rio Madeira to Rio Tapajós)
____ *S. m. maculirostris* SE Brazil (Bahia) to ne Argentina

☐ **Gould's Toucanet** *Selenidera gouldii*

Locally in lowlands of extreme ne Bolivia; ne Brazil

☐ **Keel-billed Toucan** *Ramphastos sulfuratus*

___ *R. s. sulfuratus* — Lowlands of s Mexico to n Guatemala and Belize

___ *R. s. brevicarinatus* — SE Guatemala to n Colombia and nw Venezuela

☐ **Choco Toucan** *Ramphastos brevis*

Pacific slope of w Colombia and w Ecuador

☐ **Citron-throated Toucan** *Ramphastos citreolaemus*

Humid forests of nw Venezuela and n Colombia

☐ **Yellow-ridged Toucan** *Ramphastos culminatus*

Lowlands of w Venezuela to n Bolivia and w Amazonian Brazil

☐ **Channel-billed Toucan** *Ramphastos vitellinus*

___ *R. v. vitellinus (aurantiirostris)* — Venezuela to the Guianas and Brazil n of the Amazon; Trinidad

___ *R. v. ariel* — Tropical Brazil south of the Amazon

___ *R. v. pintoi* — SE Brazil (s Goiás and w São Paulo)

___ *R. v. theresae* — NE Brazil (Piauí and Maranhão)

☐ **Red-breasted Toucan** *Ramphastos dicolorus*

Humid forests of se Brazil to e Paraguay and ne Argentina

☐ **Chestnut-mandibled Toucan** *Ramphastos swainsonii*

Humid forests of n Honduras to w Ecuador

☐ **Black-mandibled Toucan** *Ramphastos ambiguus*

___ *R. a. ambiguus* — Northern section of upper Amazon basin

___ *R. a. abbreviatus* — E slope of Andes of Colombia to w Venezuela and e Peru

☐ **Red-billed Toucan** *Ramphastos tucanus*

S Venezuela to the Guianas and n Amazonian Brazil

☐ **Cuvier's Toucan** *Ramphastos cuvieri*

___ *R. c. cuvieri (inca)* — SE Colombia to n Bolivia and Amazonian Brazil

___ *R. c. oblitus* — Amazonian Brazil (Rio Tapajós to Rio Tocantins)

☐ **Toco Toucan** *Ramphastos toco*

___ *R. t. toco* — The Guianas and ne Brazil

___ *R. t. albogularis* — E and s Brazil to Paraguay, n Bolivia and n Argentina

---

ORDER: PICIFORMES
FAMILY: INDICATORIDAE (Honeyguides—17)

☐ **Spotted Honeyguide** *Indicator maculatus*

___ *I. m. maculatus* — Humid forests of Gambia to s Nigeria

___ *I. m. stictothorax* — S Cameroon to s Sudan, Cabinda, e Zaire and sw Uganda

☐ **Scaly-throated Honeyguide** *Indicator variegatus*

Savanna and riparian woodlands of e and s Africa

☐ **Greater Honeyguide** *Indicator indicator*

Africa south of the Sahara

☐ **Malaysian Honeyguide** *Indicator archipelagicus*

Malay Peninsula, Sumatra and Borneo

☐ **Lesser Honeyguide** *Indicator minor*

___ *I. m. senegalensis* — Senegambia and Guinea to n Cameroon, Chad and w Sudan

___ *I. m. riggenbachi* — Cameroon to sw Sudan, w Uganda and ne Zaire

___ *I. m. diadematus* — Ethiopia and n Somalia to central Sudan

___ *I. m. damarensis* — S Angola to central Namibia

___ *I. m. teitensis* — Sudan and Somalia to Namibia, Zimbabwe and Mozambique

___ *I. m. minor* — Border of se Botswana, Lesotho, Swaziland and South Africa

☐ **Thick-billed Honeyguide** *Indicator conirostris*

_____ *I. c. ussheri*   Liberia to Ghana

_____ *I. c. conirostris*   Nigeria to Kenya, Zaire and Angola

☐ **Willcock's Honeyguide** *Indicator willcocksi*

_____ *I. w. ansorgei*   Locally in humid forests of Guinea-Bissau

_____ *I. w. willcocksi*   Mt. Nimba to s Nigeria, s Cameroon, Zaire and Uganda

_____ *I. w. hutsoni*   Central Nigeria to n Cameroon, Cent. African Rep. and sw Sudan

☐ **Least Honeyguide** *Indicator exilis*

_____ *I. e. exilis*   Senegambia to Angola, Zambia and Zaire

_____ *I. e. poensis*   Humid forests of Bioko (Gulf of Guinea)

_____ *I. e. pachyrhynchus*   SW Sudan and w Uganda to Kenya, e Zaire and nw Tanzania

☐ **Dwarf Honeyguide** *Indicator pumilio*

    Montane forests of e Zaire, Rwanda, Burundi and w Uganda

☐ **Pallid Honeyguide** *Indicator meliphilus*

    E Uganda to w Kenya, n Tanzania; c Angola and Mozambique

☐ **Yellow-rumped Honeyguide** *Indicator xanthonotus*

_____ *I. x. xanthonotus*   Himalayas (e Afghanistan to ne Myanmar)

_____ *I. x. fulvus*   NE Myanmar (Naga Hills)

☐ **Lyre-tailed Honeyguide** *Melichneutes robustus*

    Guinea to Cent. African Rep., s Uganda, e Zaire and nw Angola

☐ **Yellow-footed Honeyguide** *Melignomon eisentrauti*

    Forests of ne Liberia and sw Cameroon

☐ **Zenker's Honeyguide** *Melignomon zenkeri*

    S Cameroon to ne Zaire, Central African Rep. and sw Uganda

☐ **Cassin's Honeyguide** *Prodotiscus insignis*

_____ *P. i. insignis*   SE Nigeria to Angola, se Sudan, Uganda and central Kenya

_____ *P. i. flavodorsalis*   Sierra Leone to sw Nigeria

☐ **Green-backed Honeyguide** *Prodotiscus zambesiae*

_____ *P. z. zambesiae*   Angola to sw Tanzania and Mozambique

_____ *P. z. ellenbecki*   Ethiopia to Kenya and ne Tanzania

☐ **Wahlberg's Honeyguide** *Prodotiscus regulus*

_____ *P. r. regulus*   Sudan to Angola and South Africa

_____ *P. r. camerunensis*   Guinea to Central African Republic

ORDER: PICIFORMES
FAMILY: PICIDAE (Woodpeckers—217)

☐ **Eurasian Wryneck** *Jynx torquilla*

_____ *J. t. torquilla*   W Europe to SE Asia and Japan; winters to tropical Africa

_____ *J. t. tschusii*   Italy, Sicily, Sardinia, Corsica and coastal Yugoslavia

_____ *J. t. mauretanica*   NE Algeria and adjacent Tunisia

_____ *J. t. himalayana*   NW India (Kashmir); winters to s India

☐ **Rufous-necked Wryneck** *Jynx ruficollis*

_____ *J. r. ruficollis*   SE Gabon to s Zaire, Uganda, Kenya, n Angola and S Africa

_____ *J. r. pulchricollis*   SE Nigeria and Cameroon to s Sudan and nw Uganda

_____ *J. r. aequatorialis*   Highlands of w and central Ethiopia

☐ **Orinoco Piculet** *Picumnus pumilus*

    Extreme e Colombia, adjacent sw Venezuela and nw Brazil

☐ **Speckled Piculet** *Picumnus innominatus*

____ *P. i. innominatus*	W Himalayas (n Pakistan to Assam)
____ *P. i. malayorum*	India to extreme sw China, Indochina, Sumatra and Borneo
____ *P. i. chinensis*	W and s China

☐ **Bar-breasted Piculet** *Picumnus aurifrons*

____ *P. a. aurifrons*	Central Brazil (Mato Grosso to Rio Tapajós)
____ *P. a. transfasciatus*	E-central Brazil (Rio Tapajós to Rio Tocantins)
____ *P. a. borbae*	Central Brazil (lower Rio Tapajós to lower Rio Madeira)
____ *P. a. wallacii*	W-central Brazil (lower Rio Madeira to Rio Purús)
____ *P. a. purusianus*	W Brazil (upper Rio Purús)
____ *P. a. flavifrons*	W Brazil (Rio Solimões) to e Peru
____ *P. a. juruanus*	W Brazil (upper Rio Juruá) to e Peru (Río Ucayali)

☐ **Lafresnaye's Piculet** *Picumnus lafresnayi*

____ *P. l. lafresnayi*	Tropical se Colombia to e Ecuador and Peru
____ *P. l. punctifrons*	Tropical e Peru
____ *P. l. taczanowskii*	NE Peru (Huambo-Inayabamba-Huánuco region)
____ *P. l. pusillus*	W Amazonian Brazil (Rio Negro and Rio Solimões region)

☐ **Golden-spangled Piculet** *Picumnus exilis*

____ *P. e. salvini*	E Venezuela (Delta Amacuro)
____ *P. e. clarus*	E-central Venezuela (e Bolívar)
____ *P. e. undulatus*	*Tepuis* of se Venezuela, s Guyana and n Brazil
____ *P. e. buffoni*	E Guyana to ne Brazil (Rio Amapá)
____ *P. e. pernambucensis*	Coastal e Brazil (Pernambuco and Alagoas)
____ *P. e. alegriae*	Coastal forests of ne Brazil (Maranhão)
____ *P. e. exilis*	E Brazil (Bahia to Espírito Santo)

☐ **Ecuadorian Piculet** *Picumnus sclateri*

____ *P. s. parvistriatus*	Arid scrub of w Ecuador (Manabi to Guayas)
____ *P. s. sclateri*	Arid scrub of sw Ecuador and adjacent nw Peru
____ *P. s. porcullae*	Arid scrub of n Peru (central Piura to n Lambayeque)

☐ **Scaled Piculet** *Picumnus squamulatus*

____ *P. s. squamulatus*	N and e Colombia (except for range of *roehli*)
____ *P. s. roehli*	NE Colombia (Boyacá and Santa Marta region) to n Venezuela
____ *P. s. obsoletus*	Extreme ne Venezuela (Sucre)

☐ **White-bellied Piculet** *Picumnus spilogaster*

____ *P. s. orinocensis*	Extreme e Venezuela
____ *P. s. spilogaster*	The Guianas and n Brazil
____ *P. s. pallidus*	Known from a few specimens from ne Brazil (e Pará)

☐ **Guianan Piculet** *Picumnus minutissimus*

Guianas and adjacent n Brazil (ne Pará)

☐ **Spotted Piculet** *Picumnus pygmaeus*

NE Brazil (Maranhão to s Bahia and n Minas Gerais)

☐ **Speckle-chested Piculet** *Picumnus steindachneri*

Montane ne Peru (Río Huallaga region of San Martín)

☐ **White-barred Piculet** *Picumnus cirratus*

____ *P. c. macconnelli*	NE Brazil (e Amazonian basin)
____ *P. c. confusus*	Guyana and French Guiana
____ *P. c. jelskii*	Andean slopes of e Peru
____ *P. c. cirratus*	S Brazil (Minas Gerais and Espírito Santo) to e Paraguay
____ *P. c. pilcomayensis*	E and w Paraguay to se Bolivia and n Argentina
____ *P. c. tucumanus*	N Argentina (w Salta to La Rioja)
____ *P. c. thamnophiloides*	Andes of s Bolivia (Chuquisaca) to extreme n Argentina

☐ **Varzea Piculet** *Picumnus varzeae*

Amazonian Brazil (Rio Madeira to extreme w Pará)

☐ **Ocellated Piculet** *Picumnus dorbygnianus*
____ *P. d. jelskii* — Andes of e Peru, Bolivia and extreme nw Argentina
____ *P. d. dorbygnianus* — Andes of Bolivia and extreme nw Argentina

☐ **Ochre-collared Piculet** *Picumnus temminckii*

Lowlands of se Brazil to ne Argentina and e Paraguay

☐ **White-wedged Piculet** *Picumnus albosquamatus*
____ *P. a. albosquamatus* — N Bolivia to w Brazil (Mato Grosso) and adjacent Paraguay
____ *P. a. guttifer* — Brazil (e Mato Grosso to Pará, Maranhão, Goiás and Minas Gerais)

☐ **Rusty-necked Piculet** *Picumnus fuscus*

Riverine forests of n Bolivia and sw Brazil (Mato Grosso)

☐ **Rufous-breasted Piculet** *Picumnus rufiventris*
____ *P. r. rufiventris* — Humid forests of se Colombia and e Ecuador
____ *P. r. grandis* — E Peru (Huánuco and Junín)
____ *P. r. brunneifrons* — N Bolivia (Cochabamba)

☐ **Tawny Piculet** *Picumnus fulvescens*

Lowlands of ne Brazil (Pernambuco and adjacent Alagoas)

☐ **Ochraceous Piculet** *Picumnus limae*

Lowlands of e Brazil (Ceará, Alagoas and w Paraíba)

☐ **Mottled Piculet** *Picumnus nebulosus*

SE Brazil to ne Argentina, Uruguay and (?) e Paraguay

☐ **Plain-breasted Piculet** *Picumnus castelnau*

E slope of Andes of se Colombia, e Ecuador and ne Peru

☐ **Fine-barred Piculet** *Picumnus subtilis*

Foothills of se Peru (Cuzco and Madre de Dios)

☐ **Olivaceous Piculet** *Picumnus olivaceus*
____ *P. o. dimotus* — Lowlands of e Guatemala to Nicaragua
____ *P. o. flavotinctus* — Costa Rica to extreme e Panama
____ *P. o. olivaceus* — N Colombia
____ *P. o. harterti* — SW Colombia and w Ecuador; single record from nw Peru
____ *P. o. eisenmanni* — E Colombia (Sierra de Perijá) and nw Venezuela (Zulia)
____ *P. o. tachirensis* — E Andes of Colombia and adjacent w Venezuela (Táchira)

☐ **Grayish Piculet** *Picumnus granadensis*
____ *P. g. antioquensis* — Foothills of n Andes of Colombia (Antioquia)
____ *P. g. granadensis* — N Colombia (middle Cauca Valley to Patía Valley)

☐ **Chestnut Piculet** *Picumnus cinnamomeus*
____ *P. c. cinnamomeus* — Caribbean lowlands of n Colombia and Magdalena Valley
____ *P. c. perijanus* — NW Venezuela (n portions of Lake Maracaibo basin)
____ *P. c. persaturatus* — Central Colombia (Serranía de San Jerónimo)
____ *P. c. venezuelensis* — W Venezuela (s and e areas of Lake Maracaibo)

☐ **African Piculet** *Sasia africana*

S Cameroon to e Zaire, sw Uganda and n Angola

☐ **Rufous Piculet** *Sasia abnormis*
____ *S. a. abnormis* — S Myanmar, Malay Pen., Greater Sundas and offshore islands
____ *S. a. magnirostris* — Nias I. (off nw Sumatra)

☐ **White-browed Piculet** *Sasia ochracea*
____ *S. o. ochracea* — Foothills of Himalayas (nw India to s Vietnam)
____ *S. o. reichenowi* — S Myanmar and adjacent sw Thailand
____ *S. o. kinneari* — S China (Yunnan and Quangxi) and adjacent n Vietnam

☐ **Antillean Piculet** *Nesoctites micromegas*
____ *N. m. micromegas* — Hispaniola
____ *N. m. abbotti* — Gonâve I. (off w Haiti)

☐ **White Woodpecker** *Melanerpes candidus*
Woodlands of South America east of the Andes to n Argentina

☐ **Lewis' Woodpecker** *Melanerpes lewis*
Oak-pine woodlands of w North America; winters to n Mexico

☐ **Guadeloupe Woodpecker** *Melanerpes herminieri*
Woodlands of Guadeloupe (Lesser Antilles)

☐ **Puerto Rican Woodpecker** *Melanerpes portoricensis*
Puerto Rico and Vieques I.

☐ **Red-headed Woodpecker** *Melanerpes erythrocephalus*
____ *M. e. erythrocephalus* — E North America (s-central Canada to e US)
____ *M. e. caurinus* — Great Plains to central Colorado and w Nebraska

☐ **Acorn Woodpecker** *Melanerpes formicivorus*
____ *M. f. bairdi* — Oak-pine woodlands of Oregon to n Baja California
____ *M. f. angustifrons* — Cape region of s Baja California
____ *M. f. formicivorus (aculeatus)* — SW US to central Mexico
____ *M. f. albeolus* — S Mexico (e Chiapas) to ne Guatemala and Belize
____ *M. f. lineatus* — S Mexico (Chiapas) to Guatemala and n Nicaragua
____ *M. f. striatipectus* — Nicaragua to w Panama
____ *M. f. flavigula* — Andes of Colombia

☐ **Golden-naped Woodpecker** *Melanerpes chrysauchen*
____ *M. c. chrysauchen* — Humid sw Costa Rica and adjacent w Panama
____ *M. c. pulcher* — N Colombia (central Magdalena Valley)

☐ **Black-cheeked Woodpecker** *Melanerpes pucherani*
Humid forests of se Mexico to w Ecuador

☐ **Yellow-tufted Woodpecker** *Melanerpes cruentatus*
Guianas and s Venezuela to e Bolivia and Amazonian Brazil

☐ **Yellow-fronted Woodpecker** *Melanerpes flavifrons*
Humid se Brazil to ne Argentina and e Paraguay

☐ **White-fronted Woodpecker** *Melanerpes cactorum*
Arid scrub of se Peru to n Argentina, Paraguay and sw Brazil

☐ **Hispaniolan Woodpecker** *Melanerpes striatus*
Forests and woodlands of Hispaniola

☐ **Jamaican Woodpecker** *Melanerpes radiolatus*
Forests and woodlands of Jamaica

☐ **Golden-cheeked Woodpecker** *Melanerpes chrysogenys*
____ *M. c. chrysogenys* — Coastal lowlands of nw Mexico (Sinaloa and Nayarit)
____ *M. c. flavinuchus* — SW Mexico (Jalisco to Oaxaca)

☐ **Gray-breasted Woodpecker** *Melanerpes hypopolius*
Semiarid sw Mexico (Guerrero and Morelos to Oaxaca)

☐ **Yucatan Woodpecker** *Melanerpes pygmaeus*
____ *M. p. rubricomus* — Yucatán Peninsula and adjacent Belize to ne Guatemala
____ *M. p. pygmaeus* — Cozumel I.
____ *M. p. tysoni* — Guanaja I. (off n Honduras)

☐ **Red-crowned Woodpecker** *Melanerpes rubricapillus*
____ *M. r. rubricapillus* — SW Costa Rica to Colombia, Venezuela, Suriname and Tobago
____ *M. r. subfusulus* — Coiba I. (Panama)
____ *M. r. seductus* — San Miguel del Rey I. (Panama)

☐ **Hoffmann's Woodpecker** *Melanerpes hoffmannii*
Arid scrub and savanna of s Honduras to Costa Rica

☐ **Gila Woodpecker** *Melanerpes uropygialis*

____ *M. u. uropygialis*	Arid lowlands of sw US to central Mexico
____ *M. u. cardonensis*	N Baja California
____ *M. u. brewsteri*	S Baja California
____ *M. u. fuscescens*	NW Mexico (s Sonora)

☐ **Golden-fronted Woodpecker** *Melanerpes aurifrons*

____ *M. a. aurifrons*	Lowlands of sw Oklahoma and Texas to s-central Mexico
____ *M. a. polygrammus*	Arid sw Mexico (sw Oaxaca and w Chiapas)
____ *M. a. grateloupensis*	E Mexico (Tamaulipas and San Luís Potosí to Veracruz)
____ *M. a. dubius*	S Mexico (Tabasco) to n Guatemala and Belize
____ *M. a. leei*	Cozumel I. (off e Mexico)
____ *M. a. turneffensis*	Turneffe Islands (off Belize)
____ *M. a. santacruzi*	S Chiapas and Guatemala to El Salvador and n Nicaragua
____ *M. a. pauper*	Coastal ne Honduras
____ *M. a. insulanus*	Utila I. (off n Honduras)
____ *M. a. canescens*	Roatán I. and Barbareta I. (off n Honduras)

☐ **Red-bellied Woodpecker** *Melanerpes carolinus*

E North America (s Canada to Texas and Florida Keys)

☐ **West Indian Woodpecker** *Melanerpes superciliaris*

____ *M. s. nyeanus*	Great Bahama and San Salvador
____ *M. s. blakei*	Abaco I. (Bahamas)
____ *M. s. superciliaris*	Cuba, Cantiles Keys and adjacent islands
____ *M. s. murceus*	Isle of Pines, Cayo Largo and Cayo Real
____ *M. s. caymanensis*	Grand Cayman I.

☐ **Williamson's Sapsucker** *Sphyrapicus thyroideus*

____ *S. t. thyroideus*	Mts. of s British Columbia to s California; winters to n Mexico
____ *S. t. nataliae*	SE British Columbia to Rocky Mts. and Great Basin ranges

☐ **Yellow-bellied Sapsucker** *Sphyrapicus varius*

N America; winters to Panama, West Indies and Neth. Antilles

☐ **Red-naped Sapsucker** *Sphyrapicus nuchalis*

SW Canada to sw US; winters to n Mexico and s Baja California

☐ **Red-breasted Sapsucker** *Sphyrapicus ruber*

____ *S. r. ruber*	Coastal s Alaska to w Oregon
____ *S. r. daggetti*	S Oregon to Sierra Nevada of s California and Nevada

☐ **Cuban Woodpecker** *Xiphidiopicus percussus*

____ *X. p. percussus*	Cuba
____ *X. p. insulaepinorum*	Isle of Pines
____ *X. p. gloriae*	Cantiles Keys (Cuba)

☐ **Fine-spotted Woodpecker** *Campethera punctuligera*

____ *C. p. punctuligera*	SW Mauritania to Senegambia, Chad and Central African Rep.
____ *C. p. balia*	S Sudan and ne Zaire

☐ **Nubian Woodpecker** *Campethera nubica*

____ *C. n. nubica*	Sudan to Ethiopia, Kenya, nw Zaire and sw Tanzania
____ *C. n. pallida*	S Somalia

☐ **Bennett's Woodpecker** *Campethera bennettii*

____ *C. b. bennettii*	E-central Namibia to se Zaire, w Tanzania and south to Natal
____ *C. b. capricorni*	S Angola to n Namibia, n Botswana and sw Zambia

☐ **Reichenow's Woodpecker** *Campethera scriptoricauda*

Central and e Tanzania to se Malawi and n Mozambique

252

☐ **Golden-tailed Woodpecker** *Campethera abingoni*
_____ *C. a. chrysura* — Senegal to s Sudan, ne Zaire and w Uganda
_____ *C. a. kavirondensis* — E Rwanda to n Tanzania and sw Kenya
_____ *C. a. suahelica* — S Tanzania to Zambia, e Transvaal and n Swaziland
_____ *C. a. abingoni* — E Zaire to Angola, nw Zambia, ne Namibia and n Transvaal
_____ *C. a. anderssoni* — SW Angola to Namibia, sw Botswana and n Cape Province
_____ *C. a. constricta* — Natal to Zululand, s Swaziland and s Mozambique

☐ **Mombasa Woodpecker** *Campethera mombassica*
— S Somalia to coastal Kenya and ne Tanzania

☐ **Knysna Woodpecker** *Campethera notata*
— Coastal e South Africa (s Natal to Cape Province)

☐ **Little Green Woodpecker** *Campethera maculosa*
— Lowland forests of Guinea-Bissau to central Ghana

☐ **Green-backed Woodpecker** *Campethera cailliautii*
_____ *C. c. permista* — E Ghana to sw Sudan, sw Uganda, nw Angola and central Zaire
_____ *C. c. nyansae* — E Rwanda to nw Tanzania, sw Kenya and n Namibia
_____ *C. c. cailliautii* — S Somalia through coastal Kenya to ne Tanzania and Zanzibar
_____ *C. c. loveridgei* — Central Tanzania to e Zimbabwe and Mozambique

☐ **Tullberg's Woodpecker** *Campethera tullbergi*
_____ *C. t. tullbergi* — Mountains of Nigeria and Cameroon; Bioko
_____ *C. t. taeniolaema* — Zaire to Rwanda, Uganda, Burundi, w Tanzania and w Kenya
_____ *C. t. hausburgi* — Highlands of Kenya (east of Rift Valley)

☐ **Buff-spotted Woodpecker** *Campethera nivosa*
_____ *C. n. nivosa* — Senegambia to Gabon, w Zaire, nw Zambia and Angola
_____ *C. n. poensis* — Bioko (Gulf of Guinea)
_____ *C. n. herberti* — Central African Rep. to w Kenya, Sudan, Uganda and e Zaire
_____ *C. n. maxima* — Known from two specimens from n Ivory Coast

☐ **Brown-eared Woodpecker** *Campethera caroli*
_____ *C. c. arizelus* — Guinea-Bissau and Sierra Leone to Liberia
_____ *C. c. caroli* — Nigeria and Cameroon to Angola, Kenya and nw Tanzania

☐ **Ground Woodpecker** *Geocolaptes olivaceus*
_____ *G. o. olivaceus* — South Africa (central and w Cape Province)
_____ *G. o. prometheus* — S Africa (e Cape Province to Transvaal, Natal and Swaziland)

☐ **Little Gray Woodpecker** *Dendropicos elachus*
— Sahel (Senegambia to Chad and w-central Sudan)

☐ **Speckle-breasted Woodpecker** *Dendropicos poecilolaemus*
— Extreme se Nigeria to sw Sudan, Uganda and w Kenya

☐ **Abyssinian Woodpecker** *Dendropicos abyssinicus*
— Savanna and juniper highlands of Ethiopia

☐ **Cardinal Woodpecker** *Dendropicos fuscescens*
_____ *D. f. fuscescens* — N-c Namibia through South Africa to s Transvaal and w Natal
_____ *D. f. intermedius* — Natal and Transvaal to Mozambique (lower Zambesi River)
_____ *D. f. centralis* — NW Angola to n Namibia, s Zaire, w Tanzania and Zimbabwe
_____ *D. f. hartlaubi* — Coastal s Kenya to Tanzania, Malawi and e Zambia
_____ *D. f. lafresnayi* — Senegambia and Sierra Leone to Nigeria
_____ *D. f. sharpii* — Cameroon to s Sudan, w Zaire and n Angola
_____ *D. f. lepidus* — E Zaire and highlands of Ethiopia to Uganda and nw Tanzania
_____ *D, f, massaicus* — S Ethiopia, inland and w Kenya and n-central Tanzania
_____ *D. f. hemprichii* — Ethiopia to Somalia, Kenya to ne Tanzania

☐ **Gabon Woodpecker** *Dendropicos gabonensis*
_____ *D. g. gabonensis* — S Cameroon to Zaire, Uganda and Cabinda
_____ *D. g. reichenowi* — S Nigeria and extreme sw Cameroon

☐ **Melancholy Woodpecker** *Dendropicos lugubris*

Sierra Leone to Liberia, Ghana and sw Nigeria

☐ **Stierling's Woodpecker** *Dendropicos stierlingi*

Woodlands of s Tanzania to n Mozambique and s Malawi

☐ **Bearded Woodpecker** *Dendropicos namaquus*

____ *D. n. namaquus*	Central African Rep. to s Sudan, e Zaire, Tanzania and Angola
____ *D. n. schoensis*	Ethiopia to Somalia and n Kenya
____ *D. n. coalescens*	S Mozambique to South Africa

☐ **Fire-bellied Woodpecker** *Dendropicos pyrrhogaster*

Sierra Leone and Guinea to s-central Nigeria

☐ **Golden-crowned Woodpecker** *Dendropicos xantholophus*

SW Cameroon to s Sudan, Uganda, w Kenya and nw Angola

☐ **Elliot's Woodpecker** *Dendropicos elliotii*

____ *D. e. elliotii*	Humid forests of Cameroon to Gabon, Zaire and Uganda
____ *D. e. gabela*	NW Angola
____ *D. e. johnstoni*	Montane forests of Cameroon and Nigeria; Bioko

☐ **Gray Woodpecker** *Dendropicos goertae*

____ *D. g. abessinicus*	E Sudan to w Ethiopia
____ *D. g. goertae*	Senegambia to s Sudan, w Kenya and nw Tanzania
____ *D. g. koenigi*	Sahel of Sahara (e Mali to Niger, Chad and w Sudan)
____ *D. g. meriodionalis*	S-central Zaire (possibly this race from s Gabon to nw Angola)

☐ **Gray-headed Woodpecker** *Dendropicos spodocephalus*

____ *D. s. rhodeogaster*	Highlands of central Kenya to n-central Tanzania
____ *D. s. spodocephalus*	Highlands of central and s Ethiopia

☐ **Olive Woodpecker** *Dendropicos griseocephalus*

____ *D. g. ruwenzori*	Namibia to Zaire, Uganda, Tanzania, Zimbabwe and Malawi
____ *D. g. kilimensis*	Humid montane forests of Tanzania
____ *D. g. griseocephalus*	Natal and e Transvaal to Cape Province

☐ **Brown-backed Woodpecker** *Dendropicos obsoletus*

____ *D. o. obsoletus*	Senegambia to w Sudan and Uganda
____ *D. o. heuglini*	E Sudan to n Ethiopia
____ *D. o. ingens*	Central and s Ethiopia to ne Uganda, Kenya and Tanzania
____ *D. o. crateri*	Tanzania (Nou Forest, Crater Highlands and Ngorongoro Crater)

☐ **Sulawesi Woodpecker** *Dendrocopos temminckii*

Sulawesi, Butung I. and Togian Islands

☐ **Philippine Woodpecker** *Dendrocopos maculatus*

____ *D. m. validirostris*	Philippines (Catanduanes, Lubang, Luzon, Marinduque, Mindoro)
____ *D. m. leytensis*	Central Philippines (Bohol, Leyte, Calicoan and Samar)
____ *D. m. maculatus*	Philippines (Cebu, Guimaras, Negros, Panay and Gigantes)
____ *D. m. fulvifasciatus*	S Philippines (Basilan, Mindanao and Dinagat)
____ *D. m. ramsayi*	Sulu Arch. (Bongao, Jolo, Tawitawi, Sanga Sanga and Sibutu)
____ *D. m. siasiensis*	Siasi I. (Sulu Arch.)
____ *D. m. menagei*	Sibuyan (s Philippines)

☐ **Brown-capped Woodpecker** *Dendrocopos nanus*

____ *D. n. nanus*	N and central peninsular India
____ *D. n. cinereigula*	S India (Madras and Kerala)
____ *D. n. gymnophthalmus*	Sri Lanka

☐ **Sunda Woodpecker** *Dendrocopos moluccensis*

____ *D. m. moluccensis*	Malay Peninsula to Borneo, Sumatra and Java
____ *D. m. grandis*	Lesser Sundas (Lombok, Lomblen, Sumbawa, Flores, Besar, Alor)

☐ Gray-capped Woodpecker *Dendrocopos canicapillus*

____	*D. c. doerriesi*	E Siberia to Korea and e Manchuria
____	*D. c. scintilliceps*	N China (Liaoning to Sichuan, Hubei and Zhejiang)
____	*D. c. kaleensis*	Extreme sw China to n Myanmar, n Vietnam and Taiwan
____	*D. c. swinhoei*	Hainan I. (s China)
____	*D. c. semicoronatus*	E Nepal to n India, w Assam, Sikkim and Bhutan
____	*D. c. mitchelli*	W Nepal to nw India and n Pakistan
____	*D. c. canicapillus*	E Assam to central and s Myanmar, Thailand and Laos
____	*D. c. delacouri*	S Vietnam and Cambodia
____	*D. c. auritus*	Malay Peninsula and s Thailand
____	*D. c. volzi*	Mountains of Sumatra
____	*D. c. aurantiventris*	Mountains of Borneo

☐ Pygmy Woodpecker *Dendrocopos kizuki*

____	*D. k. ijimae*	N Korea and e Manchuria to Sakhalin, s Kuril Is. and Hokkaido
____	*D. k. seebohmi*	Korea, Cheju-Do Islands and Honshu
____	*D. k. amamii*	N Ryukyu Islands (Amami-O-Shima and Tokuno-Shima)
____	*D. k. kizuki*	N China, s Japan, Okinawa, Iriomote and Izu Islands

☐ Lesser Spotted Woodpecker *Dendrocopos minor*

____	*D. m. comminutus*	England and Wales
____	*D. m. hortorum*	N France and Netherlands to Austria and n Yugoslavia
____	*D. m. buturlini*	S France to n Spain, Italy and Balkan Peninsula
____	*D. m. minor*	Scandinavian Peninsula to w USSR and Ural Mountains
____	*D. m. amurensis*	Ural Mountains to Kamchatka Peninsula
____	*D. m. kamtschatkensis*	Siberia east to Sea of Okhotsk and n Mongolia
____	*D. m. colchicus*	Caucasus and Transcaucasia
____	*D. m. danfordi*	Asia Minor
____	*D. m. hyrcanus*	S Caspian lowlands
____	*D. m. quadrifasciatus*	Azerbaijan (Lenkoran region)
____	*D. m. morgani*	Zagros Mountains and nw Iran
____	*D. m. ledouci*	NW Africa (Morocco, Algeria and Tunisia)

☐ Brown-fronted Woodpecker *Dendrocopos auriceps*

Montane oak-pine forests of Afghanistan to e Nepal

☐ Fulvous-breasted Woodpecker *Dendrocopos macei*

____	*D. m. westermanni*	W Nepal to nw India and Pakistan
____	*D. m. macei*	Central Nepal to n Myanmar
____	*D. m. longipennis*	Myanmar to s Vietnam
____	*D. m. andamanensis*	Andaman Islands
____	*D. m. analis*	Sumatra, Java and Bali

☐ Stripe-breasted Woodpecker *Dendrocopos atratus*

NE India to sw China, nw Thailand and Laos

☐ Yellow-crowned Woodpecker *Dendrocopos mahrattensis*

____	*D. m. mahrattensis*	India to Myanmar, Thailand and s Laos
____	*D. m. pallescens*	Pakistan and nw India

☐ Arabian Woodpecker *Dendrocopos dorae*

Acacia *wadis* of w Saudi Arabia to w Aden and Yemen

☐ Rufous-bellied Woodpecker *Dendrocopos hyperythrus*

____	*D. h. marshalli*	NW India and adjacent Pakistan
____	*D. h. hyperythrus*	NE India to n Thailand, w Yunnan, se Tibet and Xinjiang
____	*D. h. subrufinus*	Manchuria and Korea; winters to s China and n Indochina
____	*D. h. annamensis*	S Vietnam and adjacent s Laos

☐ Darjeeling Woodpecker *Dendrocopos darjellensis*

Humid montane forests of India to sw China and n SE Asia

☐ Crimson-breasted Woodpecker *Dendrocopos cathpharius*

____	*D. c. cathpharius*	E Himalayas (Nepal to n Assam)
____	*D. c. ludlowi*	SE Tibet
____	*D. c. pyrrhothorax*	Hills south of Brahmaputra River and adjacent n Myanmar
____	*D. c. tenebrosus*	N Myanmar to Thailand, Laos, n Vietnam and Yunnan
____	*D. c. pernyii*	W China (nw Yunnan, Sichuan and Xinjiang north to Gansu)
____	*D. c. innixus*	E-central China (central Hubei)

☐ Middle Spotted Woodpecker *Dendrocopos medius*

____	*D. m. medius*	Europe to Spain and Greece, extreme w Turkey and w USSR
____	*D. m. caucasicus*	N Turkey to Caucasus and Transcaucasia
____	*D. m. anatoliae*	W and s Turkey to n Iraq
____	*D. m. sanctijohannis*	Zagros Mountains (sw Iran)

☐ White-backed Woodpecker *Dendrocopos leucotos*

____	*D. l. leucotos*	N, central and e Europe to ne Asia, Korea and Sakhalin
____	*D. l. uralensis*	Ural Mountains to central Siberia
____	*D. l. lilfordi*	S Europe to Asia Minor, Caucasus and Transcaucasia
____	*D. l. tangi*	W China (Sichuan)
____	*D. l. subcirris*	S Kuril Islands and Hokkaido
____	*D. l. stejnegeri*	N-central Honshu
____	*D. l. namiyei*	S Honshu, Kyushu, Shikoku and Cheju-Do Islands
____	*D. l. takahashii*	Ullung I. (South Korea)
____	*D. l. owstoni*	Amami-O-Shima I. (n Ryukyus)
____	*D. l. fohkiensis*	Mountains of se China (Fujian)
____	*D. l. insularis*	Taiwan

☐ Great Spotted Woodpecker *Dendrocopos major*

____	*D. m. major*	N Europe and Scandinavia to Siberia and Amur River basin
____	*D. m. anglicus*	British Isles
____	*D. m. pinetorum*	Central Europe (Netherlands to Alps and Carpathian Mountains)
____	*D. m. italiae*	Mainland Italy, Sicily and extreme nw Yugoslavia
____	*D. m. parroti*	Corsica
____	*D. m. harterti*	Sardinia
____	*D. m. hispanus*	Iberian Peninsula
____	*D. m. candidus*	SE Europe (s Yugoslavia to s Ukraine)
____	*D. m. tenuirostris*	Crimean Peninsula, Caucasus and Transcaucasia
____	*D. m. canariensis*	Tenerife (Canary Islands)
____	*D. m. paphlagoniae*	N Asia Minor
____	*D. m. thanneri*	Gran Canaria I. (Canary Islands)
____	*D. m. mauritanus*	Morocco
____	*D. m. numidus*	N Algeria and Tunisia
____	*D. m. poelzami*	SE Transcaucasia (Lenkoran) to n Iran and s Caspian region
____	*D. m. brevirostris*	W Siberia and n Mongolia
____	*D. m. kamtschaticus*	Kamchatka Peninsula and n coast of Sea of Okhotsk
____	*D. m. japonicus*	E Manchuria, Sakhalin, Kuril Islands, Korea and n Japan
____	*D. m. cabanisi*	S Manchuria to e China, e Myanmar and Indochina; Hainan
____	*D. m. stresemanni*	W China and n Myanmar

☐ Syrian Woodpecker *Dendrocopos syriacus*

____	*D. s. syriacus*	SE Europe, Turkey and sw Iran to Israel and Jordan
____	*D. s. transcaucasicus*	Transcaucasia to Armenia and n Iran
____	*D. s. milleri*	SE Iran

☐ White-winged Woodpecker *Dendrocopos leucopterus*

Aral Sea to Lake Balkhash, ne Afghanistan and extreme w China

☐ Sind Woodpecker *Dendrocopos assimilis*

Arid woodlands and desert scrub of se Iran to Pakistan

☐ **Himalayan Woodpecker** *Dendrocopos himalayensis*
_____ *D. h. albescens* — W Himalayas (Himachal Pradesh to ne Afghanistan)
_____ *D. h. himalayensis* — Himalayas of w Nepal and adjacent nw India

☐ **Striped Woodpecker** *Picoides lignarius*
Arid highlands of Bolivia to s Chile and s Argentina

☐ **Checkered Woodpecker** *Picoides mixtus*
_____ *P. m. mixtus* — N Argentina (Paraná R. drainage and Buenos Aires Province)
_____ *P. m. berlepschi* — Central Argentina (Córdoba south to Neuquén and Río Negro)
_____ *P. m. malleator* — *Chaco* of n Argentina, Paraguay and se Bolivia
_____ *P. m. cancellatus* — Interior e Brazil to extreme e Paraguay

☐ **Ladder-backed Woodpecker** *Picoides scalaris*
_____ *P. s. cactophilus* — Arid sw US to central Mexico
_____ *P. s. eremicus* — N Baja California
_____ *P. s. lucasanus* — S Baja California
_____ *P. s. graysoni* — Tres Marías Islands (off w Mexico)
_____ *P. s. sinaloensis* — W Mexico (s Sonora to Guerrero, sw Puebla and central Oaxaca)
_____ *P. s. scalaris* — S Mexico (Veracruz and Chiapas)
_____ *P. s. parvus* — SE Mexico (Yucatán Peninsula)
_____ *P. s. leucoptilurus* — Belize and Guatemala to ne Nicaragua

☐ **Nuttall's Woodpecker** *Picoides nuttallii*
Chaparral and oak woodlands of n California to nw Baja

☐ **Downy Woodpecker** *Picoides pubescens*
_____ *P. p. pubescens* — Coastal e US (North Carolina to Florida and e Texas)
_____ *P. p. medianus* — C Alaska to Newfoundland and c US (east of Rocky Mountains)
_____ *P. p. leucurus* — Rocky Mountains (se Alaska to sw US)
_____ *P. p. glacialis* — Coastal se Alaska
_____ *P. p. gairdnerii* — Coastal w British Columbia to nw California
_____ *P. p. turati* — Interior Washington, Oregon and California

☐ **Hairy Woodpecker** *Picoides villosus*
_____ *P. v. septentrionalis* — W North America (Alaska to n New Mexico)
_____ *P. v. sitkensis* — Coastal se Alaska and n British Columbia
_____ *P. v. picoideus* — Queen Charlotte Islands (off British Columbia)
_____ *P. v. harrisi* — Coastal s British Columbia to nw California
_____ *P. v. hyloscopus* — W California south to n Baja California
_____ *P. v. orius* — Cascade Mts. of Br. Columbia to se California and w Texas
_____ *P. v. icastus* — SE Arizona and New Mexico through w Mexico to Jalisco
_____ *P. v. villosus* — E North America to s-central US
_____ *P. v. terraenovae* — Newfoundland
_____ *P. v. audubonii* — S-central US to e Texas
_____ *P. v. jardinii* — Central Mexico to Jalisco, Guerrero and Oaxaca
_____ *P. v. sanctorum* — S Mexico (Chiapas) to w Panama
_____ *P. v. piger* — Bahamas (Abaco, Mores and Grand Bahama)
_____ *P. v. maynardi* — Bahamas (Andros and New Providence)

☐ **Strickland's Woodpecker** *Picoides stricklandi*
_____ *P. s. arizonae* — SE Arizona to nw Mexico (n Sinaloa and adjacent Durango)
_____ *P. s. fraterculus* — W Mexico (s Sinaloa and adjacent Durango to Michoacán)
_____ *P. s. stricklandi* — Oak-pine woodlands of se Mexico

☐ **Red-cockaded Woodpecker** *Picoides borealis*
Patchily distributed pine forests of se US

☐ **White-headed Woodpecker** *Picoides albolarvatus*
_____ *P. a. albolarvatus* — Montane coniferous forests of British Columbia to sw US
_____ *P. a. gravirostris* — S California (mountains of Los Angeles and San Diego region)

☐ Three-toed Woodpecker *Picoides tridactylus*

____	*P. t. tridactylus*	N Europe to n Mongolia, Manchuria and Sakhalin
____	*P. t. crissoleucus*	N *taiga* of Ural Mountains to Sea of Okhotsk
____	*P. t. albidior*	Kamchatka Peninsula
____	*P. t. alpinus*	Mountains of Europe to ne Korea and Hokkaido
____	*P. t. funebris*	Tibet and sw China
____	*P. t. dorsalis*	Rocky Mountains of w US
____	*P. t. fasciatus*	Alaska and Yukon south to Oregon
____	*P. t. bacatus*	Alberta, Labrador and Newfoundland s to Minnesota and ne US

☐ Black-backed Woodpecker *Picoides arcticus*

Boreal forests of n North America

☐ Scarlet-backed Woodpecker *Veniliornis callonotus*

____	*V. c. callonotus*	Arid extreme sw Colombia and nw Ecuador
____	*V. c. major*	Arid w Ecuador and nw Peru

☐ Yellow-vented Woodpecker *Veniliornis dignus*

____	*V. d. dignus*	Andes of Colombia and w Venezuela
____	*V. d. baezae*	Andes of Ecuador
____	*V. d. valdizani*	Andes of Peru

☐ Bar-bellied Woodpecker *Veniliornis nigriceps*

____	*V. n. equifasciatus*	Andes of Colombia and Ecuador
____	*V. n. pectoralis*	Andes of s Ecuador and Peru
____	*V. n. nigriceps*	Andes of w Bolivia

☐ Smoky-brown Woodpecker *Veniliornis fumigatus*

____	*V. f. oleagineus*	Lowlands and foothills of e Mexico
____	*V. f. sanguinolentus*	Central and s Mexico to w Panama
____	*V. f. reichenbachi*	E Panama to e Ecuador and n Venezuela
____	*V. f. fumigatus*	Upper Amazonia
____	*V. f. obscuratus*	E slope of Andes of nw Peru to nw Argentina (Jujuy)

☐ Little Woodpecker *Veniliornis passerinus*

____	*V. p. olivinus*	S Brazil to Paraguay, Bolivia and n Argentina
____	*V. p. taenionotus*	E Brazil
____	*V. p. tapajoensis*	Central Brazil
____	*V. p. insignis*	W-central Brazil
____	*V. p. diversus*	N Brazil
____	*V. p. passerinus*	Guianas and ne Brazil
____	*V. p. modestus*	NE Venezuela
____	*V. p. fidelis*	E Colombia to w Venezuela
____	*V. p. agilis*	E Ecuador to n Bolivia and w Brazil

☐ Dot-fronted Woodpecker *Veniliornis frontalis*

Humid Andean slopes of s Bolivia and nw Argentina

☐ White-spotted Woodpecker *Veniliornis spilogaster*

SE Brazil to e Paraguay, Uruguay and ne Argentina

☐ Blood-colored Woodpecker *Veniliornis sanguineus*

Humid coastal lowland forests and mangroves of the Guianas

☐ Red-rumped Woodpecker *Veniliornis kirkii*

____	*V. k. neglectus*	Savanna and woodlands of sw Costa Rica and w Panama
____	*V. k. cecilii*	E Panama to w Colombia and w Ecuador
____	*V. k. kirkii*	Trinidad and Tobago; Paría Peninsula of ne Venezuela
____	*V. k. continentalis*	N and w Venezuela
____	*V. k. monticola*	*Tepuis* of se Venezuela (Mt. Roraima)

☐ Choco Woodpecker *Veniliornis chocoensis*

Humid forests of nw Colombia to nw Ecuador

☐ **Golden-collared Woodpecker** *Veniliornis cassini*

Humid forests of s Venezuela, the Guianas and n Brazil

☐ **Red-stained Woodpecker** *Veniliornis affinis*

____ *V. a. orenocensis*	E Colombia to s Venezuela and n Brazil
____ *V. a. hilaris*	E Ecuador through e Peru to n Bolivia and w Brazil
____ *V. a. ruficeps*	Central and e Brazil
____ *V. a. affinis*	E Brazil

☐ **Yellow-eared Woodpecker** *Veniliornis maculifrons*

Lowlands of se Brazil (s Bahia to Rio de Janeiro)

☐ **Rufous-winged Woodpecker** *Piculus simplex*

Caribbean slope of Honduras to w Panama

☐ **Stripe-cheeked Woodpecker** *Piculus callopterus*

Humid lowlands and foothills on both slopes of Panama

☐ **Lita Woodpecker** *Piculus litae*

Humid lowlands of w Colombia and nw Ecuador

☐ **White-throated Woodpecker** *Piculus leucolaemus*

Humid e Ecuador to n Bolivia and w Amazonian Brazil

☐ **Yellow-throated Woodpecker** *Piculus flavigula*

____ *P. f. flavigula*	E Colombia to Venezuela, the Guianas and n Amazonian Brazil
____ *P. f. magnus*	SE Colombia to n Bolivia and ne Brazil
____ *P. f. erythropis*	E Brazil
____ *P. f. ssp. nov.*	SW Colombia west of the Andes (possible valid species)

☐ **Golden-green Woodpecker** *Piculus chrysochloros*

____ *P. c. aurosus*	Tropical e Panama
____ *P. c. xanthochlorus*	NE Colombia and nw Venezuela
____ *P. c. capistratus*	Central Colombia to nw Brazil and Suriname
____ *P. c. guianensis*	French Guiana
____ *P. c. paracensis*	NE Brazil
____ *P. c. laemostictus*	W Brazil
____ *P. c. hypochryseus*	W Brazil to n Bolivia
____ *P. c. chrysochloros*	Central and s Brazil to Bolivia and n Argentina
____ *P. c. polyzonus*	SE Brazil

☐ **Yellow-browed Woodpecker** *Piculus aurulentus*

Lowlands of se Brazil to ne Argentina and e Paraguay

☐ **Golden-olive Woodpecker** *Piculus rubiginosus*

____ *P. r. aeruginosus*	Lowlands and mountains of e Mexico
____ *P. r. yucatanensis*	SE Mexico (Oaxaca) to Panama
____ *P. r. alleni*	Santa Marta Mountains (ne Colombia)
____ *P. r. buenavistae*	Andean slopes of e Colombia and e Ecuador
____ *P. r. tobagensis*	Tobago
____ *P. r. trinitatis*	Trinidad
____ *P. r. meridensis*	NW Venezuela
____ *P. r. deltanus*	E Venezuela (Delta Amacuro)
____ *P. r. guianae*	E Venezuela and adjacent Guyana
____ *P. r. paraquensis*	Mountains of s-central Venezuela
____ *P. r. rubiginosus*	Mountains of n-central and ne Venezuela
____ *P. r. viridissimus*	*Tepuis* of s Venezuela (high plateau of Auyan-tepui)
____ *P. r. nigriceps*	Acari Mountains (Guyana and Suriname)
____ *P. r. gularis*	Colombia (Central and Western Andes and Cauca Valley)
____ *P. r. rubripileus*	Extreme sw Colombia to w Ecuador and nw Peru
____ *P. r. coloratus*	N-central Peru
____ *P. r. chrysogaster*	Central Peru
____ *P. r. canipileus*	N and se Bolivia
____ *P. r. tucumanus*	S Bolivia to nw Argentina

☐ **Gray-crowned Woodpecker** *Piculus auricularis*

Pacific slope of Mexico (s Sonora to central Oaxaca)

☐ **Crimson-mantled Woodpecker** *Piculus rivolii*

____ *P. r. rivolii*	Andes of e-central Colombia to w Venezuela
____ *P. r. meridae*	Andes of w Venezuela
____ *P. r. quindiuna*	Andes of n-central Colombia
____ *P. r. brevirostris*	Andes of sw Colombia to central Peru
____ *P. r. atriceps*	Andes of se Peru and s Bolivia

☐ **Black-necked Woodpecker** *Colaptes atricollis*

____ *C. a. atricollis*	Xeric w slopes of Andes of Peru
____ *C. a. peruvianus*	N Peru (xeric slopes of Marañón Valley)

☐ **Spot-breasted Woodpecker** *Colaptes punctigula*

____ *C. p. striatigularis*	Tropical e Panama to w-central Colombia
____ *C. p. ujhelyii*	N Colombia
____ *C. p. zuliae*	NW Venezuela
____ *C. p. punctipectus*	Venezuela (expect for range of *zuliae*)
____ *C. p. punctigula*	Suriname and French Guyana
____ *C. p. guttatus*	Amazonian Brazil and n Bolivia

☐ **Green-barred Woodpecker** *Colaptes melanochloros*

____ *C. m. melanochloros*	SE Brazil to Paraguay and extreme ne Argentina
____ *C. m. nattereri*	NE Brazil to n Bolivia
____ *C. m. nigroviridis*	S Bolivia to e Paraguay and n Argentina
____ *C. m. leucofrenatus*	S Brazil to ne Argentina

☐ **Golden-breasted Woodpecker** *Colaptes melanolaimus*

Arid scrub of e Bolivia to w-central Argentina

☐ **Northern Flicker** *Colaptes auratus*

____ *C. a. cafer*	W North America and Mexico
____ *C. a. auratus*	N and e North America
____ *C. a. mexicanoides*	Highlands of s Mexico (Chiapas) to Nicaragua
____ *C. a. chrysocaulosus*	Cuba and Grand Cayman I.

☐ **Gilded Flicker** *Colaptes chrysoides*

____ *C. c. mearnsi*	Arid se California and nw Baja California
____ *C. c. tenebrosus*	NW Mexico
____ *C. c. brunnescens*	Central Baja California
____ *C. c. chrysoides*	S Baja California

☐ **Fernandina's Flicker** *Colaptes fernandinae*

Locally in palm groves of Cuba

☐ **Chilean Flicker** *Colaptes pitius*

Humid forests and scrub of Chile and s Argentina

☐ **Andean Flicker** *Colaptes rupicola*

____ *C. r. cinereicapillus*	Andean grasslands of n Peru
____ *C. r. puna*	Central and s Peru
____ *C. r. rupicola*	Bolivia to n Chile and nw Argentina

☐ **Campo Flicker** *Colaptes campestris*

____ *C. c. campestris*	S Suriname to e and s Brazil
____ *C. c. campestroides*	S Paraguay to Uruguay and n Argentina

☐ **Cinnamon Woodpecker** *Celeus loricatus*

____ *C. l. diversus*	Humid forests of Nicaragua to w Panama
____ *C. l. mentalis*	Panama to extreme nw Colombia
____ *C. l. loricatus*	W Colombia and nw Ecuador
____ *C. l. innotatus*	Colombia (Magdalena Valley and adjacent w slopes of E Andes)

☐ **Rufous Woodpecker** *Celeus brachyurus*
____	*C. b. humei*	NW India to extreme w Nepal
____	*C. b. jerdonii*	Central and s peninsular India and Sri Lanka
____	*C. b. phaioceps*	N India and central Nepal to Myanmar and Thailand
____	*C. b. squamigularis*	S pen. Thailand to Sumatra, Bangka, Belitung and Nias islands
____	*C. b. brachyurus*	Java
____	*C. b. badiosus*	Borneo and n Natuna Islands
____	*C. b. fokiensis*	S China and n Vietnam
____	*C. b. holroydi*	Hainan I. (s China)
____	*C. b. annamensis*	Laos, Cambodia and s Vietnam

☐ **Scaly-breasted Woodpecker** *Celeus grammicus*
____	*C. g. grammicus*	Humid forests of s Venezuela to n Bolivia and w Brazil
____	*C. g. verreauxi*	Tropical e Ecuador and adjacent ne Peru
____	*C. g. subcervinus*	W Amazonian Brazil and Mato Grosso
____	*C. g. latifasciatus*	SE Peru to n Bolivia and w Brazil (upper Rio Madeira)

☐ **Waved Woodpecker** *Celeus undatus*
____	*C. u. undatus*	E Venezuela to the Guianas and ne Brazil
____	*C. u. amacurensis*	NE Venezuela (Delta Amacuro)
____	*C. u. multifasciatus*	N Amazonian Brazil (Pará east to Rio Tocantins)

☐ **Chestnut-colored Woodpecker** *Celeus castaneus*

Gulf-Caribbean slope of s Mexico to w Panama

☐ **Chestnut Woodpecker** *Celeus elegans*
____	*C. e. leotaudi*	Trinidad
____	*C. e. hellmayri*	E Venezuela to Guyana and Suriname
____	*C. e. deltanus*	NE Venezuela (Delta Amacuro)
____	*C. e. elegans*	French Guiana, adj. Suriname and ne Brazil north of the Amazon
____	*C. e. jumana*	E Colombia to sw Venezuela, n Bolivia and s Amazonian Brazil
____	*C. e. citreopygius*	E Ecuador and e Peru

☐ **Pale-crested Woodpecker** *Celeus lugubris*
____	*C. l. lugubris*	Dry lowlands of e Bolivia and sw Brazil (w Mato Grosso)
____	*C. l. kerri*	Paraguay and s Mato Grosso to extreme n Argentina

☐ **Blond-crested Woodpecker** *Celeus flavescens*
____	*C. f. ochraceus*	Lower Amazonian and e Brazil south to e Bahia
____	*C. f. intercedens*	E Brazil (w Bahia south to Minas Gerais)
____	*C. f. flavescens*	E Brazil (Rio de Janeiro) to Paraguay and ne Argentina

☐ **Cream-colored Woodpecker** *Celeus flavus*
____	*C. f. flavus*	Guianas to s Venezuela and Amazonian Brazil
____	*C. f. tectricialis*	NE Brazil (Maranhão)
____	*C. f. subflavus*	E Brazil (Bahia and Espírito Santo)
____	*C. f. peruvianus*	Tropical e Peru and n Bolivia

☐ **Rufous-headed Woodpecker** *Celeus spectabilis*
____	*C. s. spectabilis*	Lowlands of e Ecuador and adjacent ne Peru
____	*C. s. exsul*	Tropical se Peru and n Bolivia
____	*C. s. obrieni*	E Brazil (w Piauí)

☐ **Ringed Woodpecker** *Celeus torquatus*
____	*C. t. torquatus*	E Venezuela to the Guianas and ne Brazil (Pará)
____	*C. t. occidentalis*	S Venezuela to w and c Amazonian Brazil, e Peru and e Bolivia
____	*C. t. tinnunculus*	E Brazil (Bahia and Espírito Santo)
____	*C. t. peteroyensi*	E Brazil (e Pará and w Maranhão)

☐ **Helmeted Woodpecker** *Dryocopus galeatus*

Humid forests of se Brazil to Paraguay and ne Argentina

☐ **Lineated Woodpecker** *Dryocopus lineatus*

____	*D. l. scapularis*	W Mexico (s Sonora to Oaxaca)
____	*D. l. similis*	E Mexico (Tamaulipas) to Costa Rica
____	*D. l. lineatus*	Costa Rica to w Colombia and e Peru
____	*D. l. fuscipennis*	Arid littoral of w Ecuador and nw Peru
____	*D. l. erythrops*	SE Brazil to e Paraguay and ne Argentina

☐ **Pileated Woodpecker** *Dryocopus pileatus*

____	*D. p. abieticola*	Canada to w and ne US
____	*D. p. pileatus*	Central, e and se US

☐ **Black-bodied Woodpecker** *Dryocopus schulzi*

Dry forests of se Bolivia to w Paraguay and n Argentina

☐ **White-bellied Woodpecker** *Dryocopus javensis*

____	*D. j. hodgsonii*	Peninsular India
____	*D. j. feddeni*	Thailand, Myanmar and Indochina
____	*D. j. javensis*	S Thailand and Malay Pen. to Gr. Sundas and offshore islands
____	*D. j. parvus*	Simeulue I. (off nw Sumatra)
____	*D. j. forresti*	Montane forests of n Myanmar and adjacent sw China
____	*D. j. richardsi*	Korea
____	*D. j. confusus*	Luzon (n Philippines)
____	*D. j. pectoralis*	Philippines (Leyte, Samar, Panaon, Calicoan and Bohol)
____	*D. j. philippinensis*	Philippines (Panay, Negros, Masbate and Guimaras)
____	*D. j. mindorensis*	Mindoro (Philippines)
____	*D. j. cebuensis†*	Formerly Cebu (central Philippines). Extinct
____	*D. j. multilunatus*	S Philippines (Basilan and Mindanao)
____	*D. j. suluensis*	Sulu Archipelago
____	*D. j. hargitti*	Palawan (sw Philippines)

☐ **Andaman Woodpecker** *Dryocopus hodgei*

High evergreen forests of Andaman Islands

☐ **Black Woodpecker** *Dryocopus martius*

____	*D. m. martius*	Coniferous and beech forests of Eurasia
____	*D. m. khamensis*	Tibet and sw China

☐ **Powerful Woodpecker** *Campephilus pollens*

____	*C. p. pollens*	Andes of w Venezuela to Ecuador
____	*C. p. peruviana*	Andes of n Peru

☐ **Crimson-bellied Woodpecker** *Campephilus haematogaster*

____	*C. h. splendens*	Humid forests of Panama to w Ecuador
____	*C. h. haematogaster*	Humid forests of e Colombia to e Peru

☐ **Red-necked Woodpecker** *Campephilus rubricollis*

____	*C. r. rubricollis*	Guianas and s Venezuela to Amazon River and Ecuador
____	*C. r. trachelopyrus*	NE Peru to n Bolivia (La Paz)
____	*C. r. olallae*	Brazil south of the Amazon to Bolivia (Cochabamba)

☐ **Robust Woodpecker** *Campephilus robustus*

Lowlands of se Brazil to e Paraguay and ne Argentina

☐ **Crimson-crested Woodpecker** *Campephilus melanoleucos*

____	*C. m. malherbii*	W Panama to n and w Colombia
____	*C. m. melanoleucos*	S America east of the Andes to ne Argentina and Brazil

☐ **Guayaquil Woodpecker** *Campephilus gayaquilensis*

Arid Pacific lowlands of sw Colombia to nw Peru

☐ **Pale-billed Woodpecker** *Campephilus guatemalensis*

____ *C. g. nelsoni*	Lowlands of w Mexico (s Sonora to Oaxaca)
____ *C. g. regius*	Lowlands of ne Mexico (south to Veracruz)
____ *C. g. guatemalensis*	Lowlands of s Mexico (Veracruz) to w Panama

☐ **Cream-backed Woodpecker** *Campephilus leucopogon*

Dry woodlands of s Bolivia to n Argentina and s Brazil

☐ **Magellanic Woodpecker** *Campephilus magellanicus*

Nothofagus forests of s Argentina and s Chile

☐ **Ivory-billed Woodpecker** *Campephilus principalis*

____ *C. p. principalis*†	Formerly se US. Extinct ca 1948
____ *C. p. bairdii*	Formerly Cuba (last recorded 1987). Probably extinct

☐ **Imperial Woodpecker** *Campephilus imperialis*

Sierra Madre Occidental of w Mexico. Probably extinct

☐ **Banded Woodpecker** *Picus mineaceus*

____ *P. m. perlutus*	S Myanmar and peninsular Thailand
____ *P. m. malaccensis*	Malay Peninsula, Sumatra and Borneo
____ *P. m. niasensis*	Nias I. (off nw Sumatra)
____ *P. m. mineaceus*	Java

☐ **Lesser Yellownape** *Picus chlorolophus*

____ *P. c. chlorolophus*	E Nepal to n Vietnam
____ *P. c. simlae*	N India (Himachal Pradesh) to w Nepal
____ *P. c. annamensis*	SE Thailand to s Vietnam
____ *P. c. chlorigaster*	Central and s India
____ *P. c. wellsi*	Sri Lanka
____ *P. c. citrinocristatus*	N Vietnam
____ *P. c. longipennis*	Hainan
____ *P. c. rodgersi*	Highlands of w Malaysia
____ *P. c. vanheysti*	Highlands of Sumatra

☐ **Crimson-winged Woodpecker** *Picus puniceus*

____ *P. p. observandus*	Lowlands of Malay Peninsula, Sumatra, Borneo and Bangka I.
____ *P. p. soligae*	Nias I. (off nw Sumatra)
____ *P. p. puniceus*	Java

☐ **Greater Yellownape** *Picus flavinucha*

____ *P. f. flavinucha*	NW India to sw China and n Vietnam
____ *P. f. styani*	Hainan and immediately adjacent mainland China
____ *P. f. ricketti*	N Vietnam
____ *P. f. pierrei*	SE Thailand to Cambodia and s Vietnam
____ *P. f. mystacalis*	N Sumatra
____ *P. f. korinchi*	SW Sumatra
____ *P. f. wrayi*	Highlands of Malaysia

☐ **Checker-throated Woodpecker** *Picus mentalis*

____ *P. m. humei*	Malay Peninsula, Sumatra, Borneo and Bangka I.
____ *P. m. mentalis*	Evergreen and moss forests of w Java

☐ **Streak-breasted Woodpecker** *Picus viridanus*

Lowlands of Myanmar, peninsular Thailand and n Malaysia

☐ **Laced Woodpecker** *Picus vittatus*

SE Asia, Sumatra, Java, Bali and Kangean Islands

☐ **Streak-throated Woodpecker** *Picus xanthopygaeus*

Indian subcontinent to sw China and SE Asia

☐ **Scaly-bellied Woodpecker** *Picus squamatus*

____ *P. s. squamatus*	Extreme e Iran to ne Afghanistan and Sikkim
____ *P. s. flavirostris*	Afghanistan and w Pakistan

☐ **Japanese Woodpecker** *Picus awokera*
_____ *P. a. awokera* — Japan (Honshu, Tobishima, Awashima and Sado)
_____ *P. a. horii* — Japan (Shikoku, Kyushu and Tsushima)
_____ *P. a. takatsukasae* — Japan (Tanegashima and Yakushima)

☐ **Green Woodpecker** *Picus viridis*
_____ *P. v. viridis* — Europe south to France, Alps, n Yugoslavia and Romania
_____ *P. v. karelini* — SE Europe to Asia Minor, n Iran and sw Turkmenistan
_____ *P. v. innominatus* — Zagros Mountains (sw Iran)
_____ *P. v. sharpei* — Iberian Peninsula north to the Pyrénées

☐ **Levaillant's Woodpecker** *Picus vaillantii* — Mountains of Morocco, Algeria and Tunisia

☐ **Red-collared Woodpecker** *Picus rabieri* — Forests of n Vietnam, e Laos and extreme s Yunnan

☐ **Black-headed Woodpecker** *Picus erythropygius*
_____ *P. e. erythropygius* — SE Thailand to Laos, Cambodia and Vietnam
_____ *P. e. nigrigenis* — Myanmar and w Thailand

☐ **Gray-faced Woodpecker** *Picus canus*
_____ *P. c. canus* — Europe and w Siberia to Altai Mountains and Lake Baikal
_____ *P. c. biedermanni* — C Asia (Tarbagatay, Altai and Sayan mountains to s Transbaikal)
_____ *P. c. jessoensis* — E Siberia to n China, Korea, Sakhalin and Hokkaido
_____ *P. c. guerini* — China (central Sichuan to Yangtze River basin)
_____ *P. c. sobrinus* — SE China and ne Vietnam
_____ *P. c. tancolo* — Hainan and Taiwan
_____ *P. c. kogo* — W China (Shaanxi to Qinghai and n Sichuan)
_____ *P. c. sordidior* — W China (w Sichuan, se Tibet and Yunnan) to ne Myanmar
_____ *P. c. hessei* — Nepal and n India to Myanmar, Thailand and Vietnam
_____ *P. c. sanguiniceps* — Himalayas (nw India to Pakistan and extreme w Nepal)
_____ *P. c. robinsoni* — Malaysia (Gunang Tahan and Cameron Highlands)
_____ *P. c. dedemi* — Highlands of Sumatra

☐ **Olive-backed Woodpecker** *Dinopium rafflesii*
_____ *D. r. rafflesii* — S Myanmar, peninsular Thailand, Malay Peninsula and Sumatra
_____ *D. r. dulitense* — Borneo

☐ **Himalayan Flameback** *Dinopium shorii*
_____ *D. s. shorii* — Himalayas (nw India to n Bangladesh); w India (Western Ghats)
_____ *D. s. anguste* — Myanmar and adjacent ne India (Assam)

☐ **Common Flameback** *Dinopium javanense*
_____ *D. j. malabaricum* — Wet woodlands of w India
_____ *D. j. intermedium* — Bangladesh and Assam to Myanmar, sw China and Indochina
_____ *D. j. javanense* — W Malaysia, Sumatra, w Java and Borneo
_____ *D. j. exsul* — E Java and Bali
_____ *D. j. raveni* — Eraban I. and adjacent ne Borneo
_____ *D. j. everetti* — S Philippines (Balabac, Palawan and Calamian)

☐ **Black-rumped Flameback** *Dinopium benghalense*
_____ *D. b. benghalense* — N India to Assam
_____ *D. b. dilutum* — Pakistan
_____ *D. b. puncticolle* — Central and s India; n Sri Lanka
_____ *D. b. psarodes* — Central and s Sri Lanka

☐ **White-naped Woodpecker** *Chrysocolaptes festivus*
_____ *C. f. festivus* — Lowlands and hills of India
_____ *C. f. tantus* — Sri Lanka

☐ **Greater Flameback** *Chrysocolaptes lucidus*

____	*C. l. guttacristatus*	NW India and Nepal to sw China (Yunnan) and Indochina
____	*C. l. socialis*	Coastal w India
____	*C. l. stricklandi*	Sri Lanka
____	*C. l. chersonesus*	Malaysia, Singapore, Sumatra, w and c Java
____	*C. l. andrewsi*	NE Borneo
____	*C. l. strictus*	E Java
____	*C. l. kangeanensis*	Coastal e Java, Bali and Kangean Islands
____	*C. l. haematribon*	N Philippines (Luzon, Catanduanes and Marinduque)
____	*C. l. xanthocephalus*	Philippines (Negros, Guimaras, Panay, Masbate and Ticao)
____	*C. l. rufopunctatus*	Philippines (Bohol, Leyte, Samar, Biliran and Panaon)
____	*C. l. grandis*	Polillo I. (Philippines)
____	*C. l. erythrocephalus*	Philippines (Balabac, Palawan, Busuanga and Calamian Is.)
____	*C. l. lucidus*	S Philippines (Zamboanga Pen. of w Mindando and Basilan)
____	*C. l. montanus*	Mindanao (except Zamboanga Peninsula)

☐ **Pale-headed Woodpecker** *Gecinulus grantia*

____	*G. g. grantia*	E Himalayas (Nepal to n Myanmar and nw Thailand)
____	*G. g. indochinensis*	SW China (Yunnan) to Laos and Vietnam
____	*G. g. viridanus*	SE China (Fujian and n Guangdong)

☐ **Bamboo Woodpecker** *Gecinulus viridis*

Lowlands of e Myanmar, adjacent Thailand, n Laos and Malaya

☐ **Okinawa Woodpecker** *Sapheopipo noguchii*

Okinawa (Yambaru Moutains). On verge of extinction

☐ **Maroon Woodpecker** *Blythipicus rubiginosus*

Malay Peninsula, Sumatra and Borneo

☐ **Bay Woodpecker** *Blythipicus pyrrhotis*

____	*B. p. pyrrhotis*	Mountains of ne India and Nepal to Myanmar and Indochina
____	*B. p. sinensis*	SE China (Guizhou and Guangxi to Fujian)
____	*B. p. annamensis*	Highlands of s Vietnam
____	*B. p. hainanus*	Mountains of Hainan (s China)
____	*B. p. cameroni*	Highlands of Malaysia

☐ **Orange-backed Woodpecker** *Reinwardtipicus validus*

____	*R. v. xanthopygius*	S Myanmar, s Thailand, Malay Peninsula, Sumatra and Borneo
____	*R. v. validus*	Java

☐ **Buff-rumped Woodpecker** *Meiglyptes tristis*

____	*M. t. grammithorax*	S Myanmar and Thailand to Sumatra, Borneo and adj. islands
____	*M. t. tristis*	Java

☐ **Black-and-buff Woodpecker** *Meiglyptes jugularis*

Humid forests of Myanmar, Thailand and Indochina

☐ **Buff-necked Woodpecker** *Meiglyptes tukki*

____	*M. t. tukki*	Malay Peninsula, Sumatra, n Borneo and adjacent islands
____	*M. t. percnerpes*	S Borneo
____	*M. t. batu*	Batu Islands (off w Sumatra)
____	*M. t. pulonis*	Banggi I. (off n Borneo)
____	*M. t. infuscatus*	Nias I. (off nw Sumatra)

☐ **Gray-and-buff Woodpecker** *Hemicircus concretus*

____	*H. c. sordidus*	S Myanmar, pen. Thailand to Sumatra, Borneo and adj. islands
____	*H. c. concretus*	W and central Java

☐ **Heart-spotted Woodpecker** *Hemicircus canente*

Humid forests of India, Myanmar, Thailand and Indochina

☐ **Ashy Woodpecker** *Mulleripicus fulvus*

    ____   *M. f. fulvus*   N Sulawesi, Bangka, Lembeh, Manterawu and Togian islands

    ____   *M. f. wallacei*   S Sulawesi, Muna and Butung islands

☐ **Sooty Woodpecker** *Mulleripicus funebris*

    ____   *M. f. funebris*   Philippines (central and s Luzon, Catanduanes and Marinduque)

    ____   *M. f. mayri*   N Luzon (Philippines)

    ____   *M. f. parkesi*   Polillo (Philippines)

    ____   *M. f. fuliginosus*   Philippines (Samar, Leyte and Mindanao)

☐ **Great Slaty Woodpecker** *Mulleripicus pulverulentus*

    ____   *M. p. harterti*   India and Nepal to sw China and Indochina

    ____   *M. p. pulverulentus*   Malaysia to Borneo, Sumatra, Java and Palawan

Part II

Order: Passeriformes

Perching Birds

FAMILY: EURYLAIMIDAE (Broadbills—15)

☐ **African Broadbill** *Smithornis capensis*

____ *S. c. delacouri*	Sierra Leone to Ghana
____ *S. c. camerunensis*	Cameroon to Gabon and Central African Republic
____ *S. c. medianus*	Highlands of s Kenya and n Tanzania
____ *S. c. suahelicus*	Coastal s Kenya to Tanzania and Mozambique
____ *S. c. meinertzhageni*	Highlands of ne Zaire, Uganda and w Kenya
____ *S. c. albigularis*	Angola to Zaire, n Zambia, w Tanzania and n Malawi
____ *S. c. conjunctus*	Caprivi Strip and middle Zambezi Valley to nw Mozambique
____ *S. c. cryptoleucus*	S Malawi and se Tanzania to ne Transvaal and Mozambique
____ *S. c. capensis*	South Africa (coastal Natal and s Zululand)

☐ **Gray-headed Broadbill** *Smithornis sharpei*

____ *S. s. zenkeri*	S Cameroon and n Gabon
____ *S. s. sharpei*	Bioko (Gulf of Guinea)
____ *S. s. eurylaemus*	E Zaire

☐ **Rufous-sided Broadbill** *Smithornis rufolateralis*

____ *S. r. rufolateralis*	Liberia to w Zaire
____ *S. r. budongoensis*	Central Zaire to w Uganda

☐ **Grauer's Broadbill** *Pseudocalyptomena graueri*

	Itombwe Mountains of e Zaire and sw Uganda

☐ **Dusky Broadbill** *Corydon sumatranus*

____ *C. s. laoensis*	N Myanmar to n Thailand, Laos, Cambodia and Vietnam
____ *C. s. sumatranus*	Malay Peninsula, s Thailand, Sumatra and Penang I.
____ *C. s. brunnescens*	Borneo and North Natuna Islands

☐ **Black-and-red Broadbill** *Cymbirhynchus macrorhynchos*

____ *C. m. malaccensis*	N Myanmar to s Thailand, Malay Peninsula and s Vietnam
____ *C. m. affinis*	W Myanmar (s Arakan to Rangoon)
____ *C. m. macrorhynchos*	Borneo
____ *C. m. lemniscatus*	Sumatra

☐ **Banded Broadbill** *Eurylaimus javanicus*

____ *E. j. javanicus*	Java
____ *E. j. harterti*	Myanmar and Malay Peninsula to Sumatra and Riau Archipelago
____ *E. j. brookei*	Borneo and North Natuna Islands

☐ **Black-and-yellow Broadbill** *Eurylaimus ochromalus*

____ *E. o. ochromalus*	N Myanmar to Thailand, Sumatra, Borneo and adjacent islands
____ *E. o. mecistus*	Tuangku I. (Banyak Islands off nw Sumatra)
____ *E. o. kalamantan*	Borneo (Saribas District of Sarawak)

☐ **Wattled Broadbill** *Eurylaimus steerii*

____ *E. s. steerii*	Philippines (Basilan, Malamaui and Mindanao (Zamboanga Pen.)
____ *E. s. mayri*	S Philippines (Dinagat, Siargao and Mindanao)

☐ **Visayan Broadbill** *Eurylaimus samarensis*

	Central Philippines (Leyte, Samar and Bohol)

☐ **Long-tailed Broadbill** *Psarisomus dalhousiae*

____ *P. d. dalhousiae*	Himalayas to ne India, Myanmar, sw China and Vietnam
____ *P. d. psittacinus*	Malay Peninsula and Sumatra
____ *P. d. borneensis*	NW Borneo
____ *P. d. cyanicauda*	Thailand, Cambodia and s Annam

☐ **Silver-breasted Broadbill** *Serilophus lunatus*

____	*S. l. lunatus*	SW China (sw Yunnan) to Myanmar and adjacent nw Thailand
____	*S. l. rubropygius*	Nepal to ne India and Myanmar
____	*S. l. stolidus*	N Myanmar and peninsular Thailand
____	*S. l. elisabethae*	NE Myanmar to se China, e Thailand and Indochina
____	*S. l. impavidus*	S Laos (Bolavens Plateau)
____	*S. l. rothschildi*	Malay Peninsula and extreme s peninsular Thailand
____	*S. l. intensus*	Sumatra
____	*S. l. polionotus*	Mountains of Hainan (s China)

☐ **Green Broadbill** *Calyptomena viridis*

____	*C. v. viridis*	Borneo, Sumatra, Nias, Batu, Lingga and n Natuna islands
____	*C. v. continentis*	N Myanmar and Thailand to Malay Peninsula and Singapore
____	*C. v. siberu*	Siberut, Pagai and Mentawai islands (off Sumatra)

☐ **Hose's Broadbill** *Calyptomena hosii*

Patchily distributed submontane forests of n Borneo

☐ **Whitehead's Broadbill** *Calyptomena whiteheadi*

Montane forests of Borneo

FAMILY: PHILEPITTIDAE (Asities or False-Sunbirds—4)

☐ **Velvet Asity** *Philepitta castanea*

Humid montane slopes of e Madagascar

☐ **Schlegel's Asity** *Philepitta schlegeli*

Patchily distributed dense forests of w Madagascar

☐ **Sunbird Asity** *Neodrepanis coruscans*

Highland forests of e Madagascar

☐ **Yellow-bellied Asity** *Neodrepanis hypoxanthus*

Rain forests of e-central Madagascar

FAMILY: FURNARIIDAE (Ovenbirds—240)

☐ **Campo Miner** *Geobates poecilopterus*

S-c Brazil (Minas Gerais to São Paulo) and adjacent ne Bolivia

☐ **Coastal Miner** *Geositta peruviana*

____	*G. p. paytae*	Arid littoral of Peru (Tumbes to Ancash)
____	*G. p. peruviana*	Arid littoral of central Peru (Lima)
____	*G. p. rostrata*	Arid littoral of s-central Peru (Ica)

☐ **Grayish Miner** *Geositta maritima*

Arid littoral of Peru (Ancash) to n Chile (Atacama)

☐ **Common Miner** *Geositta cunicularia*

____	*G. c. juninensis*	Highlands of Peru (Junín and Huancavelica)
____	*G. c. titicacae*	High plateau of s Peru to extreme n Chile and nw Argentina
____	*G. c. georgei*	*Lomas* of coastal s Peru
____	*G. c. frobeni*	Arid Andes of s Peru (Arequipa and Tacna)
____	*G. c. deserticolor*	Arid littoral of sw Peru (Arequipa) to n Chile (Atacama)
____	*G. c. fissirostris*	Central Chile (s Atacama to Llanquihué)
____	*G. c. hellmayri*	W Argentina
____	*G. c. cunicularia*	Extreme s Brazil to Uruguay, Argentina and Tierra del Fuego

☐ **Puna Miner** *Geositta punensis*

Andes of extreme s Peru to w Bolivia, n Chile and nw Argentina

☐ **Short-billed Miner** *Geositta antarctica*

Breeds s Chile and s Argentina; winters north to Mendoza

☐ **Dark-winged Miner** *Geositta saxicolina*

Andes of central Peru (w Junín, Huancavelica, Lima and Pasco)

☐ **Rufous-banded Miner** *Geositta rufipennis*

Andes of w Bolivia, central Chile and w Argentina

☐ **Creamy-rumped Miner** *Geositta isabellina*

Andes of central Chile and adjacent w Argentina

☐ **Thick-billed Miner** *Geositta crassirostris*

W slope of Andes of Peru (Lima south to Arequipa)

☐ **Slender-billed Miner** *Geositta tenuirostris*
____ *G. t. tenuirostris* — Andes of n Ecuador to nw Argentina and extreme n Chile
____ *G. t. kalimayae* — Andes of n Ecuador (w slopes of Volcán Iliniza)

☐ **Scale-throated Earthcreeper** *Upucerthia dumetaria*
____ *U. d. hypoleuca* — Andes of extreme s Peru to sw Bolivia, n Chile and w Argentina
____ *U. d. hallinani* — N Chile and nw Argentina (Jujuy)
____ *U. d. saturatior* — Central Chile (Aconcagua to Valdivia)
____ *U. d. dumetaria* — Central Argentina to Tierra del Fuego

☐ **Plain-breasted Earthcreeper** *Upucerthia jelskii*

Andes of central Peru to extreme n Chile and nw Argentina

☐ **Buff-breasted Earthcreeper** *Upucerthia validirostris*

Andes of extreme s Bolivia (Potosí) and nw Argentina

☐ **White-throated Earthcreeper** *Upucerthia albigula*

W slope of Andes of sw Peru and extreme n Chile (Arica)

☐ **Striated Earthcreeper** *Upucerthia serrana*
____ *U. s. serrana* — Andes of Peru (Cajamarca to Lima)
____ *U. s. huancavelicae* — Andes of sw Peru (Huancavelica)

☐ **Straight-billed Earthcreeper** *Upucerthia ruficauda*
____ *U. r. montana* — *Puna* of s Peru (Arequipa and Tacna)
____ *U. r. ruficauda* — *Puna* of w Bolivia to n Chile and nw Argentina
____ *U. r. famatinae* — N Argentina

☐ **Rock Earthcreeper** *Upucerthia andaecola*

Andes of w Bolivia to nw Argentina and adjacent n Chile

☐ **Chaco Earthcreeper** *Ochetorhynchus certhioides*
____ *O. c. estebani* — *Chaco* of se Bolivia, w Paraguay and adjacent n Argentina
____ *O. c. luscinia* — *Chaco* of w Argentina (La Rioja and Mendoza)
____ *O. c. certhioides* — *Chaco* of n and central Argentina

☐ **Bolivian Earthcreeper** *Ochetorhynchus harterti*

Andes of s Bolivia (Cochabamba, w Santa Cruz and Chuquisaca)

☐ **Band-tailed Earthcreeper** *Eremobius phoenicurus*

S Argentina (Neuquén to s Santa Cruz) and extreme s Chile

☐ **Crag Chilia** *Chilia melanura*
____ *C. m. atacamae* — Mountains of n-central Chile (Atacama and Coquimbo)
____ *C. m. melanura* — Mountains of central Chile (south to Colchagua)

☐ **Blackish Cinclodes** *Cinclodes antarcticus*
____ *C. a. antarcticus* — Tierra del Fuego and Cape Horn Archipelago
____ *C. a. maculirostris* — Falkland Islands

☐ **Chilean Seaside Cinclodes** *Cinclodes nigrofumosus*

Rocky coast of Chile (Arica south to Valdivia)

☐ **Peruvian Seaside Cinclodes** *Cinclodes taczanowskii*

Rocky coasts of Peru (Ancash south to Tacna)

☐ **Dark-bellied Cinclodes** *Cinclodes patagonicus*
____ *C. p. chilensis* — Central Chile and w Argentina; Chiloé I.
____ *C. p. patagonicus* — S Chile and s Argentina to Tierra del Fuego and adjacent islands

☐ **Gray-flanked Cinclodes** *Cinclodes oustaleti*

_____ *C. o. oustaleti*   Central and s Chile and adjacent Argentina; Chiloé I.

_____ *C. o. baeckstroemii*   Juan Fernández Islands (off Chile)

_____ *C. o. hornensis*   Tierra del Fuego and Cape Horn Archipelago

☐ **Olrog's Cinclodes** *Cinclodes olrogi*

Andes of n-central Argentina (w Córdoba and ne San Luis)

☐ **Bar-winged Cinclodes** *Cinclodes fuscus*

_____ *C. f. oreobates*   Santa Marta Mts., Central and Eastern Andes of n Colombia

_____ *C. f. paramo*   Andes of sw Colombia (Nariño)

_____ *C. f. heterurus*   Andes of w Venezuela (Mérida, Trujillo and Lara)

_____ *C. f. albidiventris*   Andes of Ecuador

_____ *C. f. longipennis*   Andes of n Peru (La Libertad, Cajamarca and Huánuco)

_____ *C. f. rivularis*   Andes of Peru (Junin to Puno)

_____ *C. f. albiventris*   Andes of s Peru, Bolivia, n Chile and nw Argentina

_____ *C. f. riojanus*   Andes of ne Argentina (La Rioja)

_____ *C. f. rufus*   Andes of central Argentina

_____ *C. f. yzurietae*   Andes of s Argentina

_____ *C. f. fuscus*   Extreme se Brazil to Uruguay, s Chile and s Argentina

☐ **Comechingones Cinclodes** *Cinclodes comechingonus*

Andes of n-central Argentina (w Córdoba to e Tucumán)

☐ **Stout-billed Cinclodes** *Cinclodes excelsior*

_____ *C. e. colombiana*   N Colombia (Santa Marta Mountains and Nevado de Tolima)

_____ *C. e. excelsior*   Andes of sw Colombia and Andes of Ecuador

☐ **Royal Cinclodes** *Cinclodes aricomae*

Andes of s Peru and extreme w Bolivia (La Paz)

☐ **Long-tailed Cinclodes** *Cinclodes pabsti*

SE Brazil (se Santa Catarina and adjacent ne Rio Grande do Sul)

☐ **White-winged Cinclodes** *Cinclodes atacamensis*

_____ *C. a. atacamensis*   Andes of Peru to w Bolivia, n Chile and n Argentina

_____ *C. a. schocolatinus*   Central Argentina (Sierra de Córdoba and ne San Luis)

☐ **White-bellied Cinclodes** *Cinclodes palliatus*

Andes of central Peru (Junín, Lima and Huancavelica)

☐ **Pale-legged Hornero** *Furnarius leucopus*

_____ *F. l. longirostris*   Arid coastal n Colombia and nw Venezuela

_____ *F. l. endoecus*   Colombia (Magdalena Valley) and w Venezuela (Zulia)

_____ *F. l. leucopus*   Interior s Guyana and adjacent n Brazil

_____ *F. l. cinnamomeus*   SW Ecuador and nw Peru

_____ *F. l. tricolor*   Amazonian Peru, adjacent w Brazil and n Bolivia (Beni)

_____ *F. l. assimilis*   E and s Brazil to se Bolivia (Santa Cruz)

☐ **Bay Hornero** *Furnarius torridus*

Along Amazon R. (s Colombia, ne Ecuador, ne Peru and w Brazil)

☐ **Tail-banded Hornero** *Furnarius figulus*

_____ *F. f. pileatus*   Lower Amazonian Brazil

_____ *F. f. figulus*   E Brazil (south to Minas Gerais and Espírito Santo)

☐ **Lesser Hornero** *Furnarius minor*

Amazonian Brazil, s Colombia, e Ecuador and ne Peru

☐ **Rufous Hornero** *Furnarius rufus*

_____ *F. r. albogularis*   SE Brazil (Goiás and Bahia to São Paulo)

_____ *F. r. commersoni*   W Brazil (Mato Grosso) and adjacent Bolivia

_____ *F. r. schuhmacheri*   N and e Bolivia (La Paz and Beni to Tarija)

_____ *F. r. paraguayae*   Paraguay and n Argentina

_____ *F. r. rufus*   S Brazil and Uruguay to central Argentina

☐ **Crested Hornero** *Furnarius cristatus*

Chaco of se Bolivia to w Paraguay and n Argentina

☐ **Des Murs' Wiretail** *Sylviorthorhynchus desmursii*

Central and s Chile and adjacent Argentina

☐ **Thorn-tailed Rayadito** *Aphrastura spinicauda*

____ *A. s. spinicauda* — Central Chile and adjacent w Argentina south to Tierra del Fuego
____ *A. s. bullocki* — Mocha I. (Chile)
____ *A. s. fulva* — Chiloé I. (Chile)

☐ **Masafuera Rayadito** *Aphrastura masafuerae*

Alejandro Selkirk I. (Juan Fernández Islands off Chile)

☐ **Andean Tit-Spinetail** *Leptasthenura andicola*

____ *L. a. extima* — Santa Marta Mountains (ne Colombia)
____ *L. a. exterior* — E Andes of Colombia (Boyacá)
____ *L. a. andicola* — Central Andes of Colombia and Ecuador
____ *L. a. certhia* — Andes of w Venezuela (Mérida and Trujillo)
____ *L. a. peruviana* — Andes of Peru to n Bolivia (La Paz)

☐ **Streaked Tit-Spinetail** *Leptasthenura striata*

____ *L. s. superciliaris* — W slope of coastal cordillera of Peru (Ancash to Lima)
____ *L. s. albigularis* — Andes of w Peru (Huancavelica)
____ *L. s. striata* — Andes of sw Peru (Arequipa and Tacna) to n Chile (Tarapacá)

☐ **Rusty-crowned Tit-Spinetail** *Leptasthenura pileata*

____ *L. p. latistriata* — Andes of w Peru (Ayacucho)
____ *L. p. cajabambae* — Andes of Peru (Cajamarca to Junín and Huancavelica)
____ *L. p. pileata* — Cordillera of w Peru (Lima)

☐ **White-browed Tit-Spinetail** *Leptasthenura xenothorax*

Andes of s Peru (Apurímac and Cuzco)

☐ **Striolated Tit-Spinetail** *Leptasthenura striolata*

SE Brazil (Paraná south to n Rio Grande do Sul)

☐ **Plain-mantled Tit-Spinetail** *Leptasthenura aegithaloides*

____ *L. a. grisescens* — Coastal arid s Peru and n Chile
____ *L. a. berlepschi* — Altiplano of s Peru, Bolivia, n Chile and nw Argentina
____ *L. a. aegithaloides* — Lowlands of Chile (s Coquimbo to n Aysén)
____ *L. a. pallida* — Lowlands of w and s Argentina to Tierra del Fuego

☐ **Tufted Tit-Spinetail** *Leptasthenura platensis*

S Paraguay; extreme sw Brazil, Uruguay and Argentina

☐ **Brown-capped Tit-Spinetail** *Leptasthenura fuliginiceps*

____ *L. f. fuliginiceps* — Andes of w Bolivia (north to La Paz)
____ *L. f. paranensis* — Andes of w Argentina and mountains of Córdoba and San Luis

☐ **Araucaria Tit-Spinetail** *Leptasthenura setaria*

SE Brazil (Rio de Janeiro to Rio Grande do Sul) to ne Argentina

☐ **Tawny Tit-Spinetail** *Leptasthenura yanacensis*

Locally in Andes of n Peru and w Bolivia

☐ **Wren-like Rushbird** *Phleocryptes melanops*

____ *P. m. brunnescens* — Coastal w Peru (Trujillo to Pisco)
____ *P. m. juninensis* — Central Peru (Lago de Junín region)
____ *P. m. schoenobaenus* — Highlands of s Peru, w Bolivia and nw Argentina
____ *P. m. loaensis* — N Chile (Tarapacá)
____ *P. m. melanops* — S Brazil to c Chile, c Argentina, Paraguay and Uruguay

☐ **Curve-billed Reedhaunter** *Limnornis curvirostris*

Extreme s Brazil to s Uruguay and e Argentina

☐ **Straight-billed Reedhaunter** *Limnornis rectirostris*

Extreme s Brazil to s Uruguay and e Argentina

☐ **Bay-capped Wren-Spinetail** *Spartonoica maluroides*

Extreme s Brazil to Uruguay and central Argentina

☐ **Chotoy Spinetail** *Schoeniophylax phryganophila*
_____ *S. p. phryganophila*   N and e Bolivia to s Brazil, Uruguay, Paraguay and n Argentina
_____ *S. p. petersi*   Interior e Brazil (n Minas Gerais and w Bahia)

☐ **White-whiskered Spinetail** *Poecilurus candei*
_____ *P. c. candei*   Arid Caribbean littoral of n Colombia and w Venezuela
_____ *P. c. atrigularis*   N Colombia (Magdalena Valley)
_____ *P. c. venezuelensis*   NE Colombia (Guajira Peninsula) and arid nw Venezuela

☐ **Hoary-throated Spinetail** *Poecilurus kollari*

Locally in campos of n Brazil (Roraima) and (?) adjacent Guyana

☐ **Ochre-cheeked Spinetail** *Poecilurus scutatus*
_____ *P. s. scutatus*   E and central Brazil
_____ *P. s. whitii*   E Bolivia to sw Brazil (Mato Grosso) and nw Argentina
_____ *P. s. teretiala*   E Brazil (Serra dos Carajás in s Pará)

☐ **Russet-bellied Spinetail** *Synallaxis zimmeri*

W slope of Andes of central Peru (Ancash)

☐ **Bahia Spinetail** *Synallaxis whitneyi*

E Brazil (Serra de Ouricana in s Bahia)

☐ **Rufous-breasted Spinetail** *Synallaxis erythrothorax*
_____ *S. e. furtiva*   Lowlands of se Mexico (Veracruz, Oaxaca and Tabasco)
_____ *S. e. erythrothorax*   SE Mexico (Yucatán Peninsula) to nw Honduras
_____ *S. e. pacifica*   Pacific lowlands of s Mexico (Chiapas) to El Salvador

☐ **Rufous Spinetail** *Synallaxis unirufa*
_____ *S. u. unirufa*   Andes of Colombia and e Ecuador
_____ *S. u. munotztebari*   Sierra de Perijá (e Colombia) and Andes of w Venezuela
_____ *S. u. meridana*   Extreme e Colombia and Andes of w Venezuela
_____ *S. u. ochrogaster*   Andes of Peru south to Cordillera Vilcabamba (n Cuzco)

☐ **Black-throated Spinetail** *Synallaxis castanea*

Coastal mountains of n Venezuela (Aragua to Distrito Federal)

☐ **Rusty-headed Spinetail** *Synallaxis fuscorufa*

Santa Marta Mountains (ne Colombia)

☐ **Azara's Spinetail** *Synallaxis azarae*
_____ *S. a. elegantior*   E Andes of Colombia and w Venezuela
_____ *S. a. media*   W and Central Andes of Colombia and n Ecuador
_____ *S. a. ochracea*   Subtropical sw Ecuador and nw Peru
_____ *S. a. fruticicola*   N Peru (La Libertad, Cajamarca, San Martín and Amazonas)
_____ *S. a. infumata*   N-central Peru (San Martín, Huánuco and Junín)
_____ *S. a. urubambae*   SE Peru (Cuzco)
_____ *S. a. carabayae*   Andes of se Peru (Puno) and n Bolivia (La Paz)
_____ *S. a. azarae*   Andes of n Bolivia (Cochabamba)
_____ *S. a. samaipatae*   Andes of s Bolivia (Santa Cruz, Chuquisaca and Tarija)
_____ *S. a. superciliosa*   Andes of nw Argentina (Jujuy and Tucumán)

☐ **Apurimac Spinetail** *Synallaxis courseni*

Andes of s Peru (Bosque de Ampay region of Apurímac)

☐ **Silvery-throated Spinetail** *Synallaxis subpudica*

E Andes of n Colombia (Boyacá and Cundinamarca)

☐ **Sooty-fronted Spinetail** *Synallaxis frontalis*
_____ *S. f. frontalis*   E and central Brazil to Paraguay, Uruguay and n Argentina
_____ *S. f. fuscipennis*   E Bolivia and nw Argentina

☐ **Cinereous-breasted Spinetail** *Synallaxis hypospodia*

Locally from se Peru and n Bolivia to central and ne Brazil

☐ **Pale-breasted Spinetail** *Synallaxis albescens*

____	*S. a. latitabunda*	SW Costa Rica
____	*S. a. hypoleuca*	Pacific coast of s Panama and nw Colombia
____	*S. a. insignis*	Andes of Colombia
____	*S. a. occipitalis*	E Colombia and nw Venezuela
____	*S. a. littoralis*	Caribbean littoral of n Colombia
____	*S. a. perpallida*	NE Colombia (Guajira Peninsula) and nw Venezuela
____	*S. a. nesiotis*	Santa Marta Mts. (ne Colombia) to n Venezuela; Isla Margarita
____	*S. a. trinitatis*	E Venezuela and Trinidad
____	*S. a. josephinae*	S Venezuela, Guyana, Suriname and adjacent n Brazil
____	*S. a. inaequalis*	French Guiana
____	*S. a. griseonota*	Central Brazil (lower Rio Tapajós region)
____	*S. a. albescens*	Central and e Brazil to e Paraguay and ne Argentina
____	*S. a. australis*	E Bolivia to w Paraguay and nw Argentina

☐ **Chicli Spinetail** *Synallaxis spixi*

SE Brazil to e Paraguay, Uruguay and ne Argentina

☐ **Dark-breasted Spinetail** *Synallaxis albigularis*

____	*S. a. rodolphei*	S Colombia
____	*S. a. albigularis*	SE Colombia to e Ecuador, e Peru and w Amazonian Brazil

☐ **Slaty Spinetail** *Synallaxis brachyura*

____	*S. b. nigrofumosa*	Caribbean slope of Honduras to Panama
____	*S. b. chapmani*	SW Costa Rica to extreme nw Peru (Tumbes)
____	*S. b. caucae*	Tropical and subtropical Colombia (Cauca Valley)
____	*S. b. brachyura*	Magdalena Valley and n Western Andes of Colombia

☐ **Rufous-capped Spinetail** *Synallaxis ruficapilla*

E Paraguay to se Brazil and ne Argentina (Misiones)

☐ **Pinto's Spinetail** *Synallaxis infuscata*

NE Brazil (ne Maranhão, e Pernambuco and adjacent Alagoas)

☐ **Cabanis' Spinetail** *Synallaxis cabanisi*

____	*S. c. cabanisi*	E base of Andes of Peru (north to Huánuco)
____	*S. c. fulviventris*	E base of Andes of Bolivia (south to s Beni and Cochabamba)

☐ **Dusky Spinetail** *Synallaxis moesta*

____	*S. m. moesta*	Tropical and subtropical Eastern Andes of Colombia
____	*S. m. obscura*	Tropical se Colombia
____	*S. m. brunneicaudalis*	E Ecuador and ne Peru (San Martín and Loreto)

☐ **MacConnell's Spinetail** *Synallaxis macconnelli*

Tepuis of s Venezuela, adjacent Brazil, Guyana and Suriname

☐ **Plain-crowned Spinetail** *Synallaxis gujanensis*

____	*S. g. columbiana*	Tropical and subtropical Eastern Andes of Colombia
____	*S. g. gujanensis*	Venezuela to the Guianas and n Brazil
____	*S. g. huallagae*	NE Peru (Loreto)
____	*S. g. canipileus*	SE Peru (Cuzco and Puno)
____	*S. g. inornata*	Brazil south of the Amazon and adjacent Bolivia
____	*S. g. certhiola*	Bolivia (Beni, La Paz and Santa Cruz)
____	*S. g. simoni*	Central Brazil (along Rio Araguaia in Goiás)

☐ **White-lored Spinetail** *Synallaxis albilora*

E Bolivia (e Santa Cruz) to interior sw Brazil and n Paraguay

☐ **Maranon Spinetail** *Synallaxis maranonica*

S Ecuador (Zamora-Chinchipe) to nw Peru (n Cajamarca)

☐ **White-bellied Spinetail** *Synallaxis propinqua*

River islands in Amazon basin (Guianas to Bolivia)

☐ **Gray-bellied Spinetail** *Synallaxis cinerascens*

E Paraguay to se Brazil, n Uruguay and ne Argentina

☐ **Black-faced Spinetail** *Synallaxis tithys*

Arid tropical sw Ecuador to extreme nw Peru (Tumbes)

☐ **Ruddy Spinetail** *Synallaxis rutilans*

_____ *S. r. caquetensis* — Tropical se Colombia to e Ecuador and ne Peru
_____ *S. r. confinis* — NW Brazil (between Rio Negro and Rio Solimões)
_____ *S. r. dissors* — E Colombia to the Guianas and Brazil north of the Amazon
_____ *S. r. amazonica* — E Peru to n Bolivia and w Amazonian Brazil
_____ *S. r. rutilans* — Brazil s of the Amazon (Rio Tapajós to Rio Tocantins)
_____ *S. r. omissa* — Brazil south of the Amazon (Rio Tocantins to n Maranhão)
_____ *S. r. tertia* — NE Bolivia (n La Paz) and adjacent w Brazil (Mato Grosso)

☐ **Chestnut-throated Spinetail** *Synallaxis cherriei*

_____ *S. c. napoensis* — Extreme s Ecuador to se Colombia and e Peru (San Martín)
_____ *S. c. cherriei* — S Amazonian Brazil

☐ **Stripe-breasted Spinetail** *Synallaxis cinnamomea*

_____ *S. c. cinnamomea* — E Andes of Colombia to nw Venezuela (Sierra de Perijá)
_____ *S. c. carri* — Trinidad
_____ *S. c. terrestris* — Tobago
_____ *S. c. aveledoi* — W Venezuela (Falcón, Lara and n Táchira)
_____ *S. c. bolivari* — Coastal cordillera of n Venezuela
_____ *S. c. striatipectus* — Mountains of ne Venezuela (Sucre, Anzoátegui and Monagas)
_____ *S. c. pariae* — Subtropical mountains of ne Venezuela (Paría Peninsula)

☐ **Red-shouldered Spinetail** *Synallaxis hellmayri*

Arid ne Brazil (Piauí, n Bahia and w Pernambuco)

☐ **Necklaced Spinetail** *Synallaxis stictothorax*

_____ *S. s. stictothorax* — Arid littoral of sw Ecuador and Isla Puná
_____ *S. s. maculata* — Arid nw Peru (Tumbes, Lambayeque, Piura and La Libertad)

☐ **Chinchipe Spinetail** *Synallaxis chinchipensis*

NW Peru (upper Marañón and Chinchipe valleys)

☐ **Great Spinetail** *Siptornopsis hypochondriacus*

NW Peru (upper arid Río Marañón Valley)

☐ **White-browed Spinetail** *Hellmayrea gularis*

_____ *H. g. gularis* — Andes of Colombia to n Ecuador and w Venezuela
_____ *H. g. brunneidorsalis* — Sierra de Perijá (Colombia/Venezuela border)
_____ *H. g. cinereiventris* — Andes of w Venezuela (Mérida and Trujillo)
_____ *H. g. rufiventris* — Andes of central Peru (Junín)

☐ **Creamy-crested Spinetail** *Cranioleuca albicapilla*

_____ *C. a. albicapilla* — Andes of Peru (Junín, Huancavelica, Apurímac and Ayacucho)
_____ *C. a. albigula* — Andes of se Peru (Cuzco)

☐ **Light-crowned Spinetail** *Cranioleuca albiceps*

_____ *C. a. albiceps* — Andes of extreme s Peru (s Puno) and w Bolivia (La Paz)
_____ *C. a. discolor* — Andes of Bolivia (Cochabamba and Santa Cruz)

☐ **Marcapata Spinetail** *Cranioleuca marcapatae*

_____ *C. m. marcapatae* — Andes of se Peru (Cuzco)
_____ *C. m. weskei* — SE Peru (cloud forests of Cordillera Vilcabamba in Cuzco)

☐ **Baron's Spinetail** *Cranioleuca baroni*

_____ *C. b. baroni* — Andes of Peru (Amazonas and Cajamarca)
_____ *C. b. capitalis* — Andes of Peru (Huánuco)
_____ *C. b. zaratensis* — Andes of s Peru (Pasco and Lima)

☐ **Line-cheeked Spinetail** *Cranioleuca antisiensis*
_____ *C. a. antisiensis* Andes of sw Ecuador (Azuay, El Oro and Loja)
_____ *C. a. furcata* Andes of nw Peru (San Martín)
_____ *C. a. palamblae* Andes of nw Peru (south to n Cajamarca and Lambayeque)

☐ **Ash-browed Spinetail** *Cranioleuca curtata*
_____ *C. c. curtata* Subtropical Eastern Andes of Colombia
_____ *C. c. cisandina* Subtrop. Magdalena Valley of central Colombia to n Peru
_____ *C. c. debilis* Andes of Peru (Junín) to w Bolivia

☐ **Streak-capped Spinetail** *Cranioleuca hellmayri*

Santa Marta Mountains (ne Colombia)

☐ **Tepui Spinetail** *Cranioleuca demissa*

Tepuis of s Venezuela, adjacent Guyana and n Brazil (n Roraima)

☐ **Pallid Spinetail** *Cranioleuca pallida*

Mts. of se Brazil (Brasília to Espírito Santo and se São Paulo)

☐ **Red-faced Spinetail** *Cranioleuca erythrops*
_____ *C. e. rufigenis* Highlands of Costa Rica and w Panama (Chiriquí)
_____ *C. e. griseigularis* W Andes and w slope of Central Andes of Colombia
_____ *C. e. erythrops* Andes of w Ecuador (sw Manabí and w Guayas)

☐ **Gray-headed Spinetail** *Cranioleuca semicinerea*
_____ *C. s. semicinerea* NE Brazil (Ceará, Alagoas, s Bahia and n Minas Gerais)
_____ *C. s. goyana* E Brazil (s-central Goiás)

☐ **Crested Spinetail** *Cranioleuca subcristata*
_____ *C. s. fuscivertex* Sierra de Perijá (Colombia/Venezuela border)
_____ *C. s. subcristata* E Andes of Colombia and mountains of n Venezuela

☐ **Olive Spinetail** *Cranioleuca obsoleta*

E Paraguay to se Brazil (São Paulo) and ne Argentina

☐ **Stripe-crowned Spinetail** *Cranioleuca pyrrhophia*
_____ *C. p. rufipennis* Known from type locality in La Paz, Bolivia
_____ *C. p. striaticeps* E Bolivia (Cochabamba, Santa Cruz and Chuquisaca)
_____ *C. p. pyrrhophia* S Bolivia to Uruguay, Paraguay, n Argentina and extreme s Brazil

☐ **Sulphur-bearded Spinetail** *Cranioleuca sulphurifera*

S Brazil (Rio Grande do Sul) to Uruguay and e Argentina

☐ **Rusty-backed Spinetail** *Cranioleuca vulpina*
_____ *C. v. alopecias* Extreme e Colombia to w Venezuela and n Brazil
_____ *C. v. apurensis* SW Venezuela (w Apure)
_____ *C. v. reiseri* NE Brazil (Piauí, Pernambuco and Bahia)
_____ *C. v. vulpina* Brazil (Rio Araguaia to Mato Grosso and São Paulo)
_____ *C. v. vulpecula* Tropical e Ecuador to ne Peru, w Brazil and ne Bolivia
_____ *C. v. foxi* W Bolivia (Río Chaparé/Río Mamoré junction)

☐ **Speckled Spinetail** *Cranioleuca gutturata*

S Colombia to n Bolivia, the Guianas and n Amazonian Brazil

☐ **Scaled Spinetail** *Cranioleuca muelleri*

Lower Amazonian Brazil and Mexiana I.

☐ **Bolivian Spinetail** *Cranioleuca henricae*

Andes of n Bolivia (Río La Paz drainage system)

☐ **Coiba Spinetail** *Cranioleuca dissita*

Coiba I. (off Pacific coast of Panama)

☐ **Pink-legged Graveteiro** *Acrobatornis fonsecai*

E Brazil (cocoa-growing region of se Bahia)

☐ **Red-and-white Spinetail** *Certhiaxis mustelina*

Extreme se Colombia to e Peru and Amazonian Brazil

☐ **Yellow-chinned Spinetail** *Certhiaxis cinnamomea*

____	*C. c. fuscifrons*	N Colombia (Río Atrato to Santa Marta region)
____	*C. c. marabina*	NW Venezuela (Zulia)
____	*C. c. valenciana*	Venezuela (Carabobo and Aragua to Apure and Barinas)
____	*C. c. orenocensis*	E Venezuela (lower Orinoco Valley)
____	*C. c. cinnamomea*	NE Venezuela to the Guianas, Trinidad and ne Brazil
____	*C. c. pallida*	Brazil north of the Amazon (Rio Negro to Rio Tapajós)
____	*C. c. cearensis*	E Brazil (Maranhão, Ceará, Piauí, Pernambuco and Bahia)
____	*C. c. russeola*	W Bolivia to se Brazil, Paraguay and n Argentina

☐ **Ochre-browed Thistletail** *Schizoeaca coryi*

Andes of w Venezuela (n Táchira, Mérida and Trujillo)

☐ **Perija Thistletail** *Schizoeaca perijana*

Sierra de Perijá (Colombia/Venezuela border)

☐ **White-chinned Thistletail** *Schizoeaca fuliginosa*

____	*S. f. fumigata*	Central and Western Andes of Colombia
____	*S. f. fuliginosa*	Andes of e Colombia, extreme w Venezuela and n Ecuador
____	*S. f. peruviana*	Andes of n Peru (Amazonas and San Martín)
____	*S. f. ayacuchensis*	Andes of Peru (Ayacucho)
____	*S. f. plengei*	Andes of Peru (Cordillera Carpish in Huánuco)

☐ **Mouse-colored Thistletail** *Schizoeaca griseomurina*

Andes of s Ecuador and extreme n Peru

☐ **Eye-ringed Thistletail** *Schizoeaca palpebralis*

Andes of central Peru (Junín)

☐ **Vilcabamba Thistletail** *Schizoeaca vilcabambae*

____	*S. v. vilcabambae*	S Peru (Cordillera Vilcabamba in Cuzco)
____	*S. v. ayacuchensis*	Andes of s Peru (Ayacucho)

☐ **Puna Thistletail** *Schizoeaca helleri*

Andes of s Peru (s Cuzco and Puno)

☐ **Black-throated Thistletail** *Schizoeaca harterti*

Andes of w Bolivia (La Paz, Cochabamba and w Santa Cruz)

☐ **Itatiaia Thistletail** *Oreophylax moreirae*

High mountains of se Brazil (s Espírito Santo to ne São Paulo)

☐ **Creamy-breasted Canastero** *Asthenes dorbignyi*

____	*A. d. consobrina*	Andes of nw Bolivia (La Paz)
____	*A. d. dorbignyi*	Andes of Bolivia and nw Argentina

☐ **Dark-winged Canastero** *Asthenes arequipae*

Andes of w Peru (Lima and Ayacucho) to w Bolivia and n Chile

☐ **Pale-tailed Canastero** *Asthenes huancavelicae*

____	*A. h. usheri*	Arid Andes of s-central Peru (Ancash to Apurímac)
____	*A. h. huancavelicae*	Arid Andes of sw Peru (Huancavelica)

☐ **Berlepsch's Canastero** *Asthenes berlepschi*

Andes of w Bolivia (Nevado Illampu region in La Paz)

☐ **Steinbach's Canastero** *Asthenes steinbachi*

Andes of w Argentina (w Salta to Mendoza)

☐ **Lesser Canastero** *Asthenes pyrrholeuca*

____	*A. p. affinis*	Central Argentina and Chile; winters to Bolivia and Paraguay
____	*A. p. pyrrholeuca*	NW Argentina
____	*A. p. sordida*	Chile (Aconcagua to Aysén); w Argentina (Lake Nahuel Huapí)
____	*A. p. flavogularis*	E and s Argentina (Buenos Aires to Santa Cruz)

☐ **Short-billed Canastero** *Asthenes baeri*

____	*A. b. chacoensis*	NW Paraguay (Puerto Casado)
____	*A. b. baeri*	W Paraguay to extreme se Brazil, Uruguay and central Argentina

278

☐ **Patagonian Canastero** *Asthenes patagonica*

S Argentina (Mendoza south to n Santa Cruz)

☐ **Dusky-tailed Canastero** *Asthenes humicola*
_____ *A. h. goodalli* | Andes of n Chile (sw Antofogasta)
_____ *A. h. humicola* | N and central Chile (Atacama to n Maule)
_____ *A. h. polysticta* | S Chile (s Maule, Concepción and Malleco)

☐ **Canyon Canastero** *Asthenes pudibunda*
_____ *A. p. neglecta* | Andes of w Peru (Ancash)
_____ *A. p. pudibunda* | *Polylepis* zone of Peru (La Libertad to Tacna)

☐ **Rusty-fronted Canastero** *Asthenes ottonis*

Andes of central Peru (Huancavelica to Cuzco)

☐ **Iquico Canastero** *Asthenes heterura*

Andes of w Bolivia (La Paz and Cochabamba)

☐ **Cordilleran Canastero** *Asthenes modesta*
_____ *A. m. proxima* | Central and se Peru (Junín and Cuzco)
_____ *A. m. modesta* | *Puna* of s Peru to w Bolivia, n Chile and nw Argentina
_____ *A. m. rostrata* | Andes of n Bolivia (Cochabamba)
_____ *A. m. serrana* | Central Argentina (south to Santa Cruz)
_____ *A. m. australis* | Andes of Chile (Atacama to Colchagua) and adjacent Argentina

☐ **Cactus Canastero** *Asthenes cactorum*
_____ *A. c. cactorum* | Pacific slope of Andes of w Peru (Lima, Ica and Arequipa)
_____ *A. c. lachayensis* | Central coast of Peru (Lomas de Lachay)

☐ **Cipo Canastero** *Asthenes luizae*

Interior se Brazil (Serra do Cipó in Minas Gerais)

☐ **Streak-throated Canastero** *Asthenes humilis*
_____ *A. h. cajamarcae* | Arid temperate w Andes of Peru (Cajamarca)
_____ *A. h. humilis* | Arid Andes of Peru (Ancash to Junín and Huancavelica)
_____ *A. h. robusta* | Andes of se Peru (Puno) and w Bolivia (La Paz)

☐ **Streak-backed Canastero** *Asthenes wyatti*
_____ *A. w. wyatti* | Arid Andes of n Colombia (Santander)
_____ *A. w. sanctaemartae* | Santa Marta Mountains (ne Colombia)
_____ *A. w. mucuchiesi* | Andes of nw Venezuela (Mérida)
_____ *A. w. perijanus* | Sierra de Perijá (Colombia/Venezuela border)
_____ *A. w. aequatorialis* | W Andes of central Ecuador
_____ *A. w. azuay* | Andes of s Ecuador (Azuay)
_____ *A. w. graminicola* | Andes of Peru (Junín, Cuzco, Huancavelica and Puno)

☐ **Puna Canastero** *Asthenes sclateri*
_____ *A. s. punensis* | Andes of extreme se Peru (Puno) and w Bolivia (La Paz)
_____ *A. s. cuchacanchae* | Andes of sw Bolivia (Cochabamba and Potosí)
_____ *A. s. lilloi* | Andes of nw Argentina (Tucumán, Catamarca and La Rioja)
_____ *A. s. sclateri* | Andes of n-central Argentina (Sierra de Córdoba)

☐ **Austral Canastero** *Asthenes anthoides*

Extreme s Chile and s Argentina to Tierra del Fuego and Staten I.

☐ **Hudson's Canastero** *Asthenes hudsoni*

Extreme s Brazil to Uruguay and e Argentina (s to Río Negro)

☐ **Scribble-tailed Canastero** *Asthenes maculicauda*

Locally in Andes of s Peru (Puno) to w Bolivia and nw Argentina

☐ **Junin Canastero** *Asthenes virgata*

Very local in Andes of central and s Peru

☐ **Line-fronted Canastero** *Asthenes urubambensis*
_____ *A. u. huallagae* | Andes of n Peru (La Libertad to Huánuco and Pasco)
_____ *A. u. urubambensis* | Andes of se Peru (Cuzco) to n Bolivia (La Paz and Cochabamba)

☐ **Many-striped Canastero** *Asthenes flammulata*
_____ *A. f. multostriata* — E Andes of Colombia
_____ *A. f. quindiana* — Central Andes of Colombia (Nevado de Tolima)
_____ *A. f. flammulata* — Andes of s Colombia (Nariño) and adjacent Ecuador
_____ *A. f. pallida* — Andes of n Peru (La Libertad and Cajamarca)
_____ *A. f. taczanowskii* — Andes of n central Peru (La Libertad to Junín)

☐ **Orinoco Softtail** *Thripophaga cherriei*
N Venezuela (upper Orinoco River in nw Amazonas)

☐ **Striated Softtail** *Thripophaga macroura*
Locally in e Brazil (s Bahia to Espírito Santo and n Rio de Janeiro)

☐ **Plain Softtail** *Phacellodomus fusciceps*
_____ *P. f. dimorpha* — Locally in ne Ecuador and ne Peru; se Peru (Pasco south to Puno)
_____ *P. f. obidensis* — E Amazonian Brazil (mouth of Rio Madeira to Rio Tapajós)
_____ *P. f. fusciceps* — N Bolivia (Beni, La Paz and Cochabamba)

☐ **Russet-mantled Softtail** *Phacellodomus berlepschi*
N Peru (Cordillera de Colán)

☐ **Common Thornbird** *Phacellodomus rufifrons*
_____ *P. r. inornatus* — *Llanos* of ne Colombia and Venezuela
_____ *P. r. castilloi* — S Venezuela (n Bolívar)
_____ *P. r. peruvianus* — NW Peru (Río Marañón Valley) and adjacent s Ecuador
_____ *P. r. specularis* — NE Brazil (Pernambuco)
_____ *P. r. rufifrons* — E Brazil (Piauí, Bahia and Minas Gerais)
_____ *P. r. fargoi* — SW Brazil (Mato Grosso) and n Paraguay
_____ *P. r. sincipitalis* — Bolivia (Santa Cruz and Tarija) and nw Argentina

☐ **Little Thornbird** *Phacellodomus sibilatrix*
Chaco of w Paraguay to s Bolivia, w Uruguay and n Argentina

☐ **Streak-fronted Thornbird** *Phacellodomus striaticeps*
_____ *P. s. griseipectus* — Andes of s Peru (Cuzco, Apurímac and Puno)
_____ *P. s. striaticeps* — Andes of w Bolivia and nw Argentina

☐ **Greater Thornbird** *Phacellodomus ruber*
N Brazil to n Bolivia, Paraguay and n Argentina

☐ **Freckle-breasted Thornbird** *Phacellodomus striaticollis*
SE Brazil (e Paraná) to Uruguay and ne Argentina

☐ **Spot-breasted Thornbird** *Phacellodomus maculipectus*
Andes of s Bolivia and nw Argentina (south to La Rioja)

☐ **Chestnut-backed Thornbird** *Phacellodomus dorsalis*
N Peru (upper Marañón Valley)

☐ **Red-eyed Thornbird** *Phacellodomus erythrophthalmus*
_____ *P. e. erythrophthalmus* — Coastal e Brazil (s Bahia to São Paulo)
_____ *P. e. ferrugineigula* — Coastal se Brazil (São Paulo to s Rio Grande do Sul)

☐ **Canebrake Groundcreeper** *Clibanornis dendrocolaptoides*
E Paraguay to se Brazil and ne Argentina

☐ **Firewood-gatherer** *Anumbius annumbi*
Savanna of Paraguay to s Brazil, Uruguay and central Argentina

☐ **Lark-like Brushrunner** *Coryphistera alaudina*
_____ *C. a. campicola* — *Chaco* of se Bolivia and adjacent w Paraguay
_____ *C. a. alaudina* — S Bolivia to n Argentina and extreme s Brazil

☐ **Rufous Cacholote** *Pseudoseisura cristata*
_____ *P. c. cristata* — Arid ne Brazil (Pernambuco, Piauí, Bahia and Minas Gerais)
_____ *P. c. unirufa* — N Bolivia, *chaco* of n Paraguay and sw Brazil (Mato Grosso)

☐ **Brown Cacholote** *Pseudoseisura lophotes*
SE Bolivia to w Paraguay, s Brazil, Uruguay and n Argentina

☐ **White-throated Cacholote** *Pseudoseisura gutturalis*

W and central Argentina

☐ **Orange-fronted Plushcrown** *Metopothrix aurantiacus*

Tropical se Colombia to n Bolivia and w Amazonian Brazil

☐ **Equatorial Graytail** *Xenerpestes singularis*

Locally in foothills of e Ecuador and n Peru

☐ **Double-banded Graytail** *Xenerpestes minlosi*
____ *X. m. minlosi* — Tropical e Panama and Caribbean lowlands of Colombia
____ *X. m. umbraticus* — Pacific lowlands of Colombia

☐ **Spectacled Prickletail** *Siptornis striaticollis*

Locally in Andes of s Colombia to extreme n Peru

☐ **Rusty-winged Barbtail** *Premnornis guttuligera*
____ *P. g. guttuligera* — Andes of Colombia and Ecuador to s Peru
____ *P. g. venezuelana* — Andes of extreme nw Venezuela (sw Táchira)

☐ **Spotted Barbtail** *Premnoplex brunnescens*
____ *P. b. brunneicauda* — Subtropical highlands of Costa Rica and w Panama
____ *P. b. distinctus* — Subtropical mountains of central Panama (Veraguas)
____ *P. b. mnionophilus* — Mountains of Panama (w San Blas)
____ *P. b. albescens* — Subtropical mountains of e Panama (Cerro Tacarcuna)
____ *P. b. coloratus* — Subtropical Sierra Marta Mountains (ne Colombia)
____ *P. b. brunnescens* — Andes of Colombia, Venezuela, Ecuador and n Peru
____ *P. b. stictonotus* — SE Peru (Puno) and w Bolivia (La Paz and Cochabamba)
____ *P. b. rostratus* — Mts. of n Venezuela (Lara, Aragua, Carabobo and Miranda)

☐ **White-throated Barbtail** *Premnoplex tatei*
____ *P. t. tatei* — Mountains of n Venezuela (Sucre, Anzoátegui and n Monagas)
____ *P. t. pariae* — NE Venezuela (mountains of Paría Peninsula)

☐ **Roraiman Barbtail** *Roraimia adusta*
____ *R. a. obscurodorsalis* — *Tepuis* of se Venezuela (Bolívar and Amazonas)
____ *R. a. duidae* — *Tepuis* of s Venezuela (Mt. Duida)
____ *R. a. adusta* — *Tepuis* of e Venezuela, adjacent w Guyana and extreme n Brazil

☐ **Ruddy Treerunner** *Margarornis rubiginosus*
____ *M. r. rubiginosus* — Highlands of Costa Rica and w Panama (w Chiriquí)
____ *M. r. boultoni* — Highlands of central Panama (e Chiriquí and Veraguas)

☐ **Fulvous-dotted Treerunner** *Margarornis stellatus*

W Andes of Colombia and nw Ecuador

☐ **Beautiful Treerunner** *Margarornis bellulus*

Humid montane forests of e Panama (Mt. Pirre)

☐ **Pearled Treerunner** *Margarornis squamiger*
____ *M. s. perlatus* — Andes of Colombia to n Peru and w Venezuela
____ *M. s. peruvianus* — Andes of Peru (Cajamarca to Huánuco, Junín and Cuzco)
____ *M. s. squamiger* — Andes of se Peru (Puno) and w Bolivia (La Paz and Cochabamba)

☐ **White-throated Treerunner** *Pygarrhichas albogularis*

Central Chile and adjacent Argentina south to Tierra del Fuego

☐ **Great Xenops** *Megaxenops parnaguae*

Arid *caatinga* of interior ne and e-central Brazil

☐ **Rufous-tailed Xenops** *Xenops milleri*

SE Colombia to s Venezuela, Guianas, e Peru and Amaz. Brazil

☐ **Slender-billed Xenops** *Xenops tenuirostris*
____ *X. t. acutirostris* — SE Colombia to s Venezuela, e Ecuador and ne Peru
____ *X. t. hellmayri* — French Guiana, Suriname and extreme n Brazil (Roraima)
____ *X. t. tenuirostris* — S Venezuela to e Peru, n Bolivia and Amazonian Brazil

☐ **Plain Xenops** *Xenops minutus*

_____ *X. m. mexicanus*	Tropical s Mexico to Honduras
_____ *X. m. ridgwayi*	Tropical Nicaragua to Costa Rica and w Panama
_____ *X. m. littoralis*	Tropical e Panama to w Ecuador (El Oro)
_____ *X. m. neglectus*	N Colombia and n Venezuela
_____ *X. m. remoratus*	Tropical e Colombia to s Venezuela and n Brazil
_____ *X. m. ruficaudus*	Extreme e Colombia to Venezuela, the Guianas and n Brazil
_____ *X. m. olivaceus*	Lowlands of ne Colombia
_____ *X. m. obsoletus*	Tropical e Ecuador to e Peru, n Bolivia and w Brazil
_____ *X. m. genibarbis*	N Brazil south of the Amazon (Rio Madeira to Maranhão)
_____ *X. m. minutus*	E Brazil (Pernambuco) to e Paraguay and ne Argentina

☐ **Streaked Xenops** *Xenops rutilans*

_____ *X. r. septentrionalis*	Highlands of Costa Rica and w Panama
_____ *X. r. heterurus*	E Panama to ne Ecuador and Venezuela; Trinidad
_____ *X. r. incomptus*	E Panama (Darién)
_____ *X. r. perijanus*	Sierra de Perijá (Colombia/Venezuela border)
_____ *X. r. phelpsi*	Santa Marta Mountains (ne Colombia)
_____ *X. r. guayae*	Tropical w Ecuador and extreme nw Peru (Piura)
_____ *X. r. peruvianus*	Tropical e Ecuador and e Peru
_____ *X. r. purusianus*	Brazil south of the Amazon (Rio Purús, Madeira and Tapajós)
_____ *X. r. connectens*	E Bolivia and nw Argentina
_____ *X. r. chapadensis*	SW Brazil (Mato Grosso) and n Bolivia (Río Beni)
_____ *X. r. rutilans*	SE Brazil to e Paraguay and ne Argentina

☐ **Sharp-billed Treehunter** *Heliobletus contaminatus*

E Paraguay to se Brazil (Espírito Santo) and ne Argentina

☐ **White-browed Foliage-gleaner** *Anabacerthia amaurotis*

SE Paraguay to se Brazil (s Espírito Santo) and ne Argentina

☐ **Montane Foliage-gleaner** *Anabacerthia striaticollis*

_____ *A. s. striaticollis*	Subtropical Andes of Colombia and Venezuela
_____ *A. s. anxia*	Santa Marta Mountains (ne Colombia)
_____ *A. s. perijana*	Sierra de Perijá (Colombia/Venezuela border)
_____ *A. s. venezuelana*	Coastal cordillera of n Venezuela
_____ *A. s. montana*	Subtropical e Ecuador and e Peru
_____ *A. s. yungae*	Andes of se Peru (Cuzco and Puno) and w Bolivia

☐ **Scaly-throated Foliage-gleaner** *Anabacerthia variegaticeps*

_____ *A. v. variegaticeps*	S Mexico (Guerrero and Veracruz) to w Panama
_____ *A. v. temporalis*	W slope of Western Andes of Colombia and Ecuador

☐ **Streaked Tuftedcheek** *Pseudocolaptes boissonneautii*

_____ *P. b. boissonneautii*	Andes of Colombia and n Ecuador
_____ *P. b. striaticeps*	Coastal cordillera of n Venezuela
_____ *P. b. meridae*	Andes of w Venezuela (Táchira, Mérida and Trujillo)
_____ *P. b. oberholseri*	S Colombia
_____ *P. b. orientalis*	Andes of s Ecuador
_____ *P. b. intermedianus*	W Andes of Peru (Piura)
_____ *P. b. pallidus*	Andes of nw Peru (Cajamarca)
_____ *P. b. medianus*	Andes of n Peru (Cajamarca to La Libertad)
_____ *P. b. auritus*	Andes of central Peru (Huánuco, Cuzco and Puno)
_____ *P. b. carabayae*	Andes of se Peru (Puno) and w Bolivia

☐ **Buffy Tuftedcheek** *Pseudocolaptes lawrencii*

_____ *P. l. lawrencii*	Highlands of Costa Rica and w Panama (w Chiriquí)
_____ *P. l. panamensis*	Highlands of central Panama (e Chiriquí and Veraguas)

☐ **Pacific Tuftedcheek** *Pseudocolaptes johnsoni*

W slope of Western Andes of sw Colombia and w Ecuador

□ **Flammulated Treehunter** *Thripadectes flammulatus*
_____ *T. f. flammulatus*   Andes of Colombia, Ecuador and extreme n Peru
_____ *T. f. bricenoi*   Andes of w Venezuela (Mérida)

□ **Buff-throated Treehunter** *Thripadectes scrutator*

E slope of Andes of Peru and w Bolivia (Cochabamba)

□ **Striped Treehunter** *Thripadectes holostictus*
_____ *T. h. striatidorsus*   Andes of sw Colombia (Nariño) and w Ecuador
_____ *T. h. holostictus*   Andes of Colombia to sw Venezuela, e Ecuador and n Peru
_____ *T. h. moderatus*   Subtropical e Peru (Junín and Cuzco) and w Bolivia

□ **Black-billed Treehunter** *Thripadectes melanorhynchus*
_____ *T. m. striaticeps*   E Andes of Colombia (single record from w Meta)
_____ *T. m. melanorhynchus*   E slope of Andes of Ecuador and e Peru (south to Puno)

□ **Streak-capped Treehunter** *Thripadectes virgaticeps*
_____ *T. v. sclateri*   W Andes of Colombia (Cauca and Nariño)
_____ *T. v. magdalenae*   N Colombia (subtropical Magdalena Valley in Huila)
_____ *T. v. klagesi*   Coastal mountains of n Venezuela (Carabobo to Distrito Federal)
_____ *T. v. tachirensis*   Andes of w Venezuela (sw Lara and Táchira)
_____ *T. v. virgaticeps*   Subtropical nw Ecuador (south to Pichincha)
_____ *T. v. sumaco*   Subtropical e Ecuador (w Napo)

□ **Uniform Treehunter** *Thripadectes ignobilis*

Humid Western Andes of Colombia and w Ecuador (s to El Oro)

□ **Streak-breasted Treehunter** *Thripadectes rufobrunneus*

Central highlands of Costa Rica and w Panama

□ **Lineated Foliage-gleaner** *Syndactyla subalaris*
_____ *S. s. lineata*   Subtropical Costa Rica and w Panama
_____ *S. s. tacarcunae*   Mountains of e Panama (Darién)
_____ *S. s. subalaris*   Western and Central Andes of Colombia and w Ecuador
_____ *S. s. striolata*   Eastern Andes of Colombia and Andes of w Venezuela
_____ *S. s. mentalis*   Subtropical e Ecuador
_____ *S. s. colligata*   Subtropical nw Peru (Cajamarca)
_____ *S. s. ruficrissa*   Subtropical central Peru (Junín)

□ **Guttulated Foliage-gleaner** *Syndactyla guttulata*
_____ *S. g. guttulata*   Mountains of n Venezuela (Yaracuy to Distrito Federal)
_____ *S. g. pallida*   Mountains of ne Venezuela (Anzoátegui, Sucre and n Monagas)

□ **Buff-browed Foliage-gleaner** *Syndactyla rufosuperciliata*
_____ *S. r. similis*   Andes of extreme s Ecuador and n Peru (Cajamarca)
_____ *S. r. cabanisi*   E slope of Andes of Peru and Bolivia
_____ *S. r. oleaginea*   SE Bolivia and ne Argentina
_____ *S. r. rufosuperciliata*   SE Brazil (Minas Gerais to São Paulo and Paraná)
_____ *S. r. acrita*   S Brazil to Paraguay, Uruguay and ne Argentina

□ **Rufous-necked Foliage-gleaner** *Syndactyla ruficollis*
_____ *S. r. celicae*   Andes of extreme sw Ecuador (Loja)
_____ *S. r. ruficollis*   Andes of nw Peru (Piura, Cajamarca and Lambayeque)

□ **Pale-browed Treehunter** *Cichlocolaptes leucophrus*

E Brazil (s Bahia to ne Santa Catarina)

□ **Point-tailed Palmcreeper** *Berlepschia rikeri*

SE Colombia to e Peru, nw Bolivia, Guianas and Amaz. Brazil

□ **Peruvian Recurvebill** *Simoxenops ucayalae*

Tropical se Peru, extreme nw Bolivia and Amazonian Brazil

□ **Bolivian Recurvebill** *Simoxenops striatus*

Yungas of w Bolivia (La Paz, Cochabamba and w Santa Cruz)

☐ **Striped Woodhaunter** *Hyloctistes subulatus*

____	*H. s. nicaraguae*	Caribbean lowlands of e Nicaragua
____	*H. s. virgatus*	Lowlands of Costa Rica and w Panama
____	*H. s. assimilis*	Extreme e Panama (Darién) to w Colombia and w Ecuador
____	*H. s. cordobae*	NW Colombia
____	*H. s. lemae*	S Venezuela (Amazonas and Bolívar)
____	*H. s. subulatus*	Tropical se Colombia to n Bolivia and w Amazonian Brazil

☐ **Chestnut-winged Hookbill** *Ancistrops strigilatus*

____	*A. s. strigilatus*	W Amazonia from se Colombia to nw Bolivia and w Brazil
____	*A. s. cognitus*	Central Brazil (lower Rio Tapajós)

☐ **Chestnut-winged Foliage-gleaner** *Philydor erythropterus*

____	*P. e. erythropterus*	SE Colombia to s Venezuela, n Bolivia and w Amazonian Brazil
____	*P. e. diluvialis*	N-central Brazil (lower Rio Tapajós)

☐ **Rufous-rumped Foliage-gleaner** *Philydor erythrocercus*

____	*P. e. subfulvus*	Tropical se Colombia to e Ecuador and n Peru
____	*P. e. erythrocercus*	Guianas and Brazil north of the Amazon (east of Rio Negro)
____	*P. e. ochrogaster*	Central and se Peru and Bolivia
____	*P. e. lyra*	Tropical e Peru, n Bolivia and Brazil south of the Amazon
____	*P. e. suboles*	W Brazil (north bank of Rio Solimões)

☐ **Rufous-tailed Foliage-gleaner** *Philydor ruficaudatus*

____	*P. r. ruficaudatus*	Tropical se Colombia to n Bolivia and w Amazonian Brazil
____	*P. r. flavipectus*	S Venezuela to the Guianas and n Amazonian Brazil

☐ **Buff-fronted Foliage-gleaner** *Philydor rufus*

____	*P. r. panerythrus*	Highlands of Costa Rica to Eastern Andes of Colombia
____	*P. r. riveti*	W Andes of Colombia and nw Ecuador (Pichincha and El Oro)
____	*P. r. columbianus*	Coastal cordillera of n Venezuela
____	*P. r. cuchiverus*	Subtropical s Venezuela (Bolívar)
____	*P. r. bolivianus*	E Peru and Bolivia (La Paz and Santa Cruz)
____	*P. r. chapadensis*	SW Brazil (Mato Grosso)
____	*P. r. rufus*	E Brazil (Goiás and Bahia) to e Paraguay and ne Argentina

☐ **Ochre-breasted Foliage-gleaner** *Philydor lichtensteini*

	E Paraguay to e and se Brazil and ne Argentina (Misiones)

☐ **Russet-mantled Foliage-gleaner** *Philydor dimidiatus*

____	*P. d. dimidiatus*	SW Brazil (s Mato Grosso)
____	*P. d. baeri*	SE Brazil (Goiás) to extreme ne Paraguay (Concepción)

☐ **Cinnamon-rumped Foliage-gleaner** *Philydor pyrrhodes*

	SE Colombia to s Venezuela, Guianas, n Bolivia, e Amaz. Brazil

☐ **Slaty-winged Foliage-gleaner** *Philydor fuscipennis*

____	*P. f. fuscipennis*	Lowlands of Panama (Veraguas, Coclé, Colón and Canal Zone)
____	*P. f. erythronotus*	Lowlands of e Panama to nw Colombia and w Ecuador

☐ **Black-capped Foliage-gleaner** *Philydor atricapillus*

	E Paraguay to se Brazil (s Bahia) and ne Argentina

☐ **Alagoas Foliage-gleaner** *Philydor novaesi*

	Montane forests of ne Brazil (Alagoas)

☐ **White-collared Foliage-gleaner** *Anabazenops fuscus*

	SE Brazil (Minas Gerais and Espírito Santo to e Santa Catarina)

☐ **Crested Foliage-gleaner** *Anabazenops dorsalis*

	SE Colombia to extreme nw Bolivia and w Amazonian Brazil

☐ **Chestnut-crowned Foliage-gleaner** *Automolus rufipileatus*

____	*A. r. consobrinus*	Tropical e Colombia to the Guianas, n Bolivia and w Brazil
____	*A. r. rufipileatus*	Brazil south of the Amazon (Rio Purús to n Maranhão)

☐ **White-eyed Foliage-gleaner** *Automolus leucophthalmus*
_____ *A. l. lammi* — E Brazil (Paraíba, Pernambuco and Alagoas)
_____ *A. l. leucophthalmus* — E Brazil (Bahia to Rio Grande do Sul)
_____ *A. l. sulphurascens* — S Brazil (se Mato Grosso) to e Paraguay and ne Argentina

☐ **White-throated Foliage-gleaner** *Automolus roraimae*
_____ *A. r. paraquensis* — *Tepuis* of s Venezuela (Mt. Paraque, Parú and Ptari-tepui)
_____ *A. r. duidae* — *Tepuis* of s Venezuela (Mt. Duidae and Mt. Yaví)
_____ *A. r. albigularis* — Subtropical mountains of se Venezuela (Gran Sabana)
_____ *A. r. roraimae* — *Tepuis* of extreme n Brazil (Mt. Roraima)

☐ **Buff-throated Foliage-gleaner** *Automolus ochrolaemus*
_____ *A. o. cervinigularis* — Gulf-Caribbean slope of s Mexico to Belize and Nicaragua
_____ *A. o. amusos* — Tropical se Guatemala to Honduras
_____ *A. o. hypophaeus* — Caribbean slope of e Nicaragua to nw Panama
_____ *A. o. exsertus* — Pacific slope of sw Costa Rica to w Panama (Chiriquí)
_____ *A. o. pallidigularis* — E Panama to Colombia and nw Ecuador
_____ *A. o. turdinus* — Tropical n and w Amazon basin
_____ *A. o. ochrolaemus* — Tropical e Peru to n Bolivia and w Brazil
_____ *A. o. auricularis* — NE Bolivia (Rio Beni) and w Brazil (Rio Purús to Rio Tapajós)

☐ **Olive-backed Foliage-gleaner** *Automolus infuscatus*
_____ *A. i. infuscatus* — Tropical se Colombia to e Ecuador, e Peru and nw Bolivia
_____ *A. i. badius* — E Colombia to s Venezuela and nw Brazil
_____ *A. i. cervicalis* — E Venezuela to Guyana, Suriname and Brazil (n of the Amazon)
_____ *A. i. perusianus* — W Brazil (Rio Purús to Rio Solimões)
_____ *A. i. paraensis* — Brazil south of the Amazon (Rio Madeira to Rio Capím)

☐ **Brown-rumped Foliage-gleaner** *Automolus melanopezus*
— SE Colombia to se Peru, extreme nw Bolivia and w Amaz. Brazil

☐ **Ruddy Foliage-gleaner** *Automolus rubiginosus*
_____ *A. r. guerrerensis* — Subtropical sw Mexico (Guerrero and w Oaxaca)
_____ *A. r. rubiginosus* — Subtropical e Mexico (Veracruz)
_____ *A. r. veraepacis* — Subtropical n Guatemala (Alta Verapaz)
_____ *A. r. umbrinus* — Subtropical s Mexico (Chiapas) to n Nicaragua
_____ *A. r. fumosus* — Subtropical w Panama (Chiriquí)
_____ *A. r. saturatus* — Tropical e Panama and nw Colombia (Antioquia)
_____ *A. r. sasaimae* — N Colombia (upper tropical Magdalena Valley)
_____ *A. r. nigricauda* — W Colombia (Baudó Mountains) to w Ecuador
_____ *A. r. rufipectus* — Santa Marta Mountains (ne Colombia)
_____ *A. r. cinnamomeigula* — Tropical base of Eastern Andes of Colombia
_____ *A. r. caquetae* — SE Colombia (Caquetá and Putumayo)
_____ *A. r. venezuelanus* — *Tepuis* of s Venezuela
_____ *A. r. obscurus* — S Venezuela, the Guianas and n Amazonian Brazil
_____ *A. r. brunnescens* — E Ecuador (Río Suno region) and adjacent ne Peru
_____ *A. r. moderatus* — Tropical ne Peru (San Martín and Loreto)
_____ *A. r. watkinsi* — SE Peru (Huánuco) to w Bolivia (La Paz)

☐ **Chestnut-capped Foliage-gleaner** *Hylocryptus rectirostris*
— Campos of interior e and s-central Brazil to ne Paraguay

☐ **Henna-hooded Foliage-gleaner** *Hylocryptus erythrocephalus*
_____ *H. e. erythrocephalus* — SW Ecuador (Loja) and nw Peru (south to Lambayeque)
_____ *H. e. palamblae* — W Andes of Peru (Piura)

☐ **Short-billed Leaftosser** *Sclerurus rufigularis*
_____ *S. r. fulvigularis* — SE Colombia to s Venezuela, the Guianas and n Brazil
_____ *S. r. brunnescens (furfurosus)* — Amazonian Brazil (north of Rio Solimões)
_____ *S. r. rufigularis* — S Amazonian Brazil to ne Peru and n Bolivia

☐ **Tawny-throated Leaftosser** *Sclerurus mexicanus*

_____ S. m. mexicanus	Tropical se Mexico (Veracruz and Chiapas) to Honduras
_____ S. m. pullus	Costa Rica to w Panama; e Panama (Mt. Tacarcuna)
_____ S. m. andinus	Tropical e Panama to Colombia
_____ S. m. obscurior	W Andes of Colombia and w Ecuador
_____ S. m. peruvianus	Tropical w Amazon basin
_____ S. m. macconnelli	S Venezuela to the Guianas and e Amazonian Brazil
_____ S. m. bahiae	E Brazil (Alagoas to ne São Paulo)

☐ **Gray-throated Leaftosser** *Sclerurus albigularis*

_____ S. a. canigularis	Montane forests of Costa Rica and w Panama (Chiriquí)
_____ S. a. propinquus	Santa Marta Mountains (ne Colombia)
_____ S. a. albigularis	Tropical e Colombia to Venezuela, Trinidad and Tobago
_____ S. a. kunanensis	NE Venezuela (Paría Peninsula)
_____ S. a. zamorae	E Ecuador, e Peru and sw Amazonian Brazil
_____ S. a. kempffi	NE Bolivia (Serrania Huanchaca)
_____ S. a. albicollis	N Bolivia (south to w Santa Cruz)

☐ **Black-tailed Leaftosser** *Sclerurus caudacutus*

_____ S. c. caudacutus	The Guianas
_____ S. c. insignis	S Venezuela (Amazonas and Bolívar) and adjacent n Brazil
_____ S. c. brunneus	Tropical se Colombia to Peru and w Amazonian Brazil
_____ S. c. olivascens	E Peru (Ayacucho) to extreme n Bolivia (Pando)
_____ S. c. pallidus	N Brazil south of the Amazon (Rio Madeira to Rio Capím)
_____ S. c. umbretta	Coastal e Brazil (Alagoas to Espírito Santo)

☐ **Rufous-breasted Leaftosser** *Sclerurus scansor*

_____ S. s. cearensis	NE Brazil (Ceará and n Bahia)
_____ S. s. scansor	E Brazil (Goiás) to e Paraguay and ne Argentina

☐ **Scaly-throated Leaftosser** *Sclerurus guatemalensis*

_____ S. g. guatemalensis	Tropical s Mexico (Veracruz) to e Panama
_____ S. g. salvini	W Colombia (Chocó) to w Ecuador (south to Guayas)
_____ S. g. ennosiphyllus	Colombia (Río Magdalena Valley in Santander)

☐ **Sharp-tailed Streamcreeper** *Lochmias nematura*

_____ L. n. nelsoni	Extreme e Panama (Darién)
_____ L. n. sororia	Andes of Colombia to ne Peru; coastal mts. of n Venezuela
_____ L. n. chimantae	Mountains of se Venezuela (Gran Sabana)
_____ L. n. castanonota	*Tepuis* of s Venezuela (Bolívar and Amazonas)
_____ L. n. obscurata	E-central Peru and w Bolivia
_____ L. n. nematura	SE Brazil to e Paraguay, Uruguay and ne Argentina

FAMILY: DENDROCOLAPTIDAE (Woodcreepers—51)

☐ **Tyrannine Woodcreeper** *Dendrocincla tyrannina*

_____ D. t. tyrannina	Andes of Colombia to e Peru (Cordillera Vilcabamba)
_____ D. t. hellmayri	Andes of e Colombia and w Venezuela (sw Táchira)

☐ **Thrush-like Woodcreeper** *Dendrocincla turdina*

	E Paraguay to se Brazil (Bahia) and ne Argentina (Misiones)

☐ **Tawny-winged Woodcreeper** *Dendrocincla anabatina*

_____ D. a. anabatina	Gulf-Caribbean slope of se Mexico to extreme w Panama
_____ D. a. typhla	Tropical se Mexico (Yucatán and Campeche)

☐ **Plain-brown Woodcreeper** *Dendrocincla fuliginosa*

____	*D. f. ridgwayi*	Tropical Honduras to w Colombia and w Ecuador
____	*D. f. lafresnayei*	N and e Colombia and adjacent nw Venezuela
____	*D. f. phaeochroa*	Tropical e Colombia to e Ecuador and e Peru
____	*D. f. meruloides*	Coastal n Venezuela, Trinidad and Tobago
____	*D. f. deltana*	Orinoco River delta
____	*D. f. barinensis*	W-central Venezuela
____	*D. f. fuliginosa*	E Venezuela to the Guianas and adjacent n Brazil
____	*D. f. neglecta*	W Amazonian Brazil
____	*D. f. rufoolivacea*	Lower Amazon (Rio Tapajós to n Maranhão)
____	*D. f. taunayi*	NE Brazil (Pernambuco)
____	*D. f. brumaii*	Central Brazil
____	*D. f. atritrostris*	N and e Bolivia to sw Brazil (Mato Grosso)

☐ **White-chinned Woodcreeper** *Dendrocincla merula*

____	*D. m. bartletti*	SE Colombia to s Venezuela, e Peru and w Brazil
____	*D. m. merula*	The Guianas and adjacent n Brazil
____	*D. m. obidensis*	Lower Amazonian Brazil (Faro and Obidos regions)
____	*D. m. olivascens*	Brazil south of the Amazon (Rio Madeira to Rio Tapajós)
____	*D. m. castanoptera*	Brazil south of the Amazon (Rio Tapajós to Rio Tocantins)
____	*D. m. badia*	Brazil south of the Amazon (Rio Tocantins to Rio Guamá)
____	*D. m. remota*	E-central Bolivia (Santa Cruz)

☐ **Ruddy Woodcreeper** *Dendrocincla homochroa*

____	*D. h. homochroa*	S Mexico to Guatemala and Honduras
____	*D. h. acedesta*	SW Nicaragua and w Costa Rica to extreme w Panama
____	*D. h. ruficeps*	E Panama to nw Venezuela (Lara, Mérida, Barinas and Apure)
____	*D. h. meridionalis*	Sierra de Perijá (Colombia/Venezuela border)

☐ **Long-tailed Woodcreeper** *Deconychura longicauda*

____	*D. l. typica*	SE Honduras to w Panama
____	*D. l. darienensis*	E Panama (Darién)
____	*D. l. minor*	Tropical n Colombia
____	*D. l. longicauda*	The Guianas and Brazil north of the Amazon
____	*D. l. connectens*	NW Amazonian Brazil to e Ecuador and Peru
____	*D. l. zimmeri*	E Brazil (Pará)
____	*D. l. pallida*	SE Peru to n Bolivia and w Brazil (Mato Grosso)

☐ **Spot-throated Woodcreeper** *Deconychura stictolaema*

SE Colombia to the Guianas, ne Peru and Amazonian Brazil

☐ **Olivaceous Woodcreeper** *Sittasomus griseicapillus*

____	*S. g. jaliscensis*	SW Mexico (Jalisco)
____	*S. g. sylvioides*	SE Mexico (Veracruz) to Costa Rica
____	*S. g. gracileus*	SE Mexico (Yucatán Peninsula) and coastal Belize
____	*S. g. levis*	W Panama (Chiriquí) to n Colombia
____	*S. g. veraguensis*	E Panama (Veraguas and Azuero Peninsula)
____	*S. g. aequatorialis*	W Ecuador (Esmeraldas) to nw Peru (Tumbes)
____	*S. g. perijanus*	Subtropical Sierra de Perijá (Colombia/Venezuela border)
____	*S. g. griseus*	Mountains of Venezuela and Tobago
____	*S. g. amazonus*	Tropical e Colombia and Ecuador to Amazonian Brazil
____	*S. g. axillaris*	Tropical e Venezuela and extreme n Brazil
____	*S. g. viridis*	Bolivia (La Paz, Beni, Cochabamba and Santa Cruz)
____	*S. g. viridior*	E Bolivia (Santa Cruz)
____	*S. g. transitivus*	W Brazil (ne Mato Grosso)
____	*S. g. griseicapillus*	W Brazil to Paraguay, n Argentina and s Bolivia
____	*S. g. reiseri*	NE Brazil (Maranhão and Piauí to n Goiás and w Bahia)
____	*S. g. olivaceus*	E Brazil (coastal se Bahia)
____	*S. g. sylviellus*	SE Brazil to extreme ne Argentina and se Paraguay

☐ **Wedge-billed Woodcreeper** *Glyphorynchus spirurus*

_____	*G. s. pectoralis*	S Mexico (Veracruz) to Nicaragua
_____	*G. s. sublestus*	Costa Rica to w Ecuador and w Venezuela
_____	*G. s. pallidus*	Panama
_____	*G. s. subrufescens*	W Colombia (Río Atrato and Río San Juan valleys)
_____	*G. s. integratus*	NE Colombia (Bolívar and middle Magdalena Valley)
_____	*G. s. rufigularis*	Tropical e Colombia to s Venezuela, n Ecuador and w Brazil
_____	*G. s. amacurensis*	NE Venezuela (Delta Amacuro)
_____	*G. s. coronobscurus*	S Venezuela
_____	*G. s. spirurus*	E Venezuela, the Guianas and adjacent n Brazil
_____	*G. s. castelnaudii*	Tropical e Ecuador, e Peru and w Amazonian Brazil
_____	*G. s. albigularis*	SE Peru (Puno) to n Bolivia (Beni and Cochabamba)
_____	*G. s. inornatus*	Amazonian Brazil (Rio Madeira to Tapajós and Mato Grosso)
_____	*G. s. cuneatus*	Amazonian Brazil (Rio Tapajós to n Maranhão)

☐ **Scimitar-billed Woodcreeper** *Drymornis bridgesii*

S Bolivia to c Argentina, Uruguay, w Paraguay and sw Brazil

☐ **Long-billed Woodcreeper** *Nasica longirostris*

E Colombia to sw Venezuela, n Bolivia, Amaz. Brazil and Fr. Guiana

☐ **Cinnamon-throated Woodcreeper** *Dendrexetastes rufigula*

_____	*D. r. devillei*	W Amazonian basin (se Colombia to ne Bolivia)
_____	*D. r. rufigula*	The Guianas and n Brazil
_____	*D. r. monileger*	W Brazil (Rio Madeira to Amazonas/Mato Grosso border)
_____	*D. r. paraensis*	NE Brazil (south of the Amazon in Pará)

☐ **Bar-bellied Woodcreeper** *Hylexetastes stresemanni*

_____	*H. s. insignis*	W Amazonian Brazil (Rio Uaupés region)
_____	*H. s. stresemanni*	NW Brazil (lower Rio Negro to Rio Solimões)
_____	*H. s. undulatus*	Tropical se Peru to extreme nw Bolivia and w Brazil

☐ **Red-billed Woodcreeper** *Hylexetastes perrotii*

SE Venezuela to the Guianas and Brazil north of the Amazon

☐ **Uniform Woodcreeper** *Hylexetastes uniformis*

Central Amazonian Brazil to ne Bolivia

☐ **Brigida's Woodcreeper** *Hylexetastes brigidai*

Brazil (Pará and Mato Grosso)

☐ **White-throated Woodcreeper** *Xiphocolaptes albicollis*

_____	*X. a. bahiae*	NE Brazil (e and central Bahia)
_____	*X. a. albicollis*	SE Brazil (Goiás and Bahia) to e Paraguay and ne Argentina

☐ **Moustached Woodcreeper** *Xiphocolaptes falcirostris*

_____	*X. f. falcirostris*	E Brazil (Maranhão, Piauí, Ceará, w and n Bahia)
_____	*X. f. franciscanus*	E Brazil (known from one specimen from Minas Gerais)
_____	*X. f. villanovae*	E Brazil (ne Bahia)

☐ **Great Rufous Woodcreeper** *Xiphocolaptes major*

_____	*X. m. remoratus*	SW Brazil (Mato Grosso)
_____	*X. m. castaneus*	S Brazil to Bolivia and nw Argentina (south to n Santa Fe)
_____	*X. m. major*	W and central Paraguay to n Argentina
_____	*X. m. esterani*	N Argentina (Tucumán)

☐ **Strong-billed Woodcreeper** *Xiphocolaptes promeropirhynchus*

_____	*X. p. omiltemensis*	SW Mexico (Sierra Madre del Sur of Guerrero)
_____	*X. p. sclateri*	SE Mexico (Veracruz and Oaxaca)
_____	*X. p. emigrans*	S Mexico (Chiapas) to n Nicaragua
_____	*X. p. costaricensis*	Highlands of Costa Rica
_____	*X. p. panamensis*	Mountains of s Panama (e Veraguas)
_____	*X. p. rostratus*	N Colombia (Bolívar)

____ *X. p. sanctaemartae*	N Colombia (Santa Marta Mts.) and w Venezuela (Sierra de Perijá)
____ *X. p. virgatus*	W slope of Central Andes of Colombia to Rio Magdalena
____ *X. p. macarenae*	W-central Colombia
____ *X. p. promeropirhynchus*	Central and E Andes of Colombia and Andes of w Venezuela
____ *X. p. procerus*	Coastal mountains of n Venezuela
____ *X. p. tenebrosus*	*Tepuis* of s Venezuela (Chimantá Tepui and Mt. Roraima)
____ *X. p. neblinae*	*Tepuis* of s Venezuela
____ *X. p. ignotus*	Andes of Ecuador
____ *X. p. crassirostris*	SW Ecuador (El Oro and Loja) to n Peru
____ *X. p. compressirostris*	Temperate n Peru (Cajamarca, Amazonas and San Martín)
____ *X. p. phaeopygus*	Temperate central Peru (Junín)
____ *X. p. solivagus*	E Cordillera of Peru (Junín)
____ *X. p. lineatocephalus*	SE Peru (Cuzco) to central Bolivia
____ *X. p. orenocensis*	Venezuela to e Ecuador, e Peru and adjacent w Brazil
____ *X. p. berlepschi*	Tropical e Peru and w Brazil (south of the Amazon)
____ *X. p. paraensis*	Brazil (Rio Madeira south of the Amazon to Santarém)
____ *X. p. obsoletus*	N and e Bolivia (La Paz, Cochabamba and Santa Cruz)

☐ **Northern Barred-Woodcreeper** *Dendrocolaptes sanctithomae*

____ *D. s. scheffleri*	Pacific coast of sw Mexico (Guerrero and Oaxaca)
____ *D. s. sanctithomae*	S Mexico (Veracruz) to Nicaragua
____ *D. s. legtersi*	SE Mexico (e Yucatán Peninsula)
____ *D. s. nigrirostris*	Costa Rica and Panama
____ *D. s. hesperius*	SW Costa Rica and adjacent w Panama
____ *D. s. colombianus*	W Colombia to nw Ecuador
____ *D. s. hyleorus*	NE Colombia (Magdalena and Santander)
____ *D. s. punctipectus*	Sierra de Perijá (Colombia/Venezuela border)

☐ **Amazonian Barred-Woodcreeper** *Dendrocolaptes certhia*

____ *D. c. certhia*	S Venezuela to the Guianas and Brazil north of the Amazon
____ *D. c. radiolatus*	SE Colombia to ne Peru and nw Brazil
____ *D. c. juruanus*	E Peru to e Bolivia and w Amazonian Brazil
____ *D. c. polyzonus*	N Bolivia (La Paz, Cochabamba and Santa Cruz)
____ *D. c. ridgwayi*	N Brazil south of the Amazon (Rio Tapajós to Rio Tocantins)
____ *D. c. medius*	N Brazil south of the Amazon (Rio Tocantins to Maranhão)
____ *D. c. concolor*	N Brazil south of the Amazon (Rio Madeira to Rio Tocantins)

☐ **Hoffmann's Woodcreeper** *Dendrocolaptes hoffmannsi*

	Central Amazonian Brazil south of the Amazon

☐ **Black-banded Woodcreeper** *Dendrocolaptes picumnus*

____ *D. p. puncticollis*	Highlands of s Mexico (Chiapas) to Honduras
____ *D. p. costaricensis*	Highlands of Costa Rica and w Panama
____ *D. p. veraguensis*	Highlands of s Panama (Veraguas)
____ *D. p. multistrigatus*	Andes of Colombia and w Venezuela
____ *D. p. seilerni*	Santa Marta Mountains (ne Colombia) and coastal n Venezuela
____ *D. p. picumnus*	E Venezuela to the Guianas and Brazil north of the Amazon
____ *D. p. validus*	Tropical w Amazon basin
____ *D. p. transfasciatus*	Central Brazil (near junction of Rio Tapajós and the Amazon)
____ *D. p. olivaceus*	Bolivia (La Paz, Cochabamba and Santa Cruz)
____ *D. p. pallescens*	SW Brazil (w Mato Grosso) to s Bolivia and Paraguay
____ *D. p. extimus*	E Paraguay (Rio Alto Paraná region)
____ *D. p. casaresi*	NW Argentina (Jujuy, Salta and Tucumán)

☐ **Planalto Woodcreeper** *Dendrocolaptes platyrostris*

____ *D. p. intermedius*	NE Brazil (Pará and Bahia to e Paraguay)
____ *D. p. platyrostris*	SE Brazil (Goiás to e Paraguay and ne Argentina)

☐ **Straight-billed Woodcreeper** *Xiphorhynchus picus*

____ *X. p. extimus*	Pacific slope of s Panama
____ *X. p. dugandi*	N Colombia (Chocó, Bolívar, Atlántico and Santa Marta Mts.)
____ *X. p. picirostris*	NE Colombia (e Santa Marta Mountains) to w Venezuela
____ *X. p. saturatior*	Tropical e Colombia to w Venezuela (Maracaibo region)
____ *X. p. borreroi*	SW Colombia
____ *X. p. choicus*	N Venezuela (e Falcón to Miranda)
____ *X. p. parguanae*	NW Venezuela
____ *X. p. longirostris*	Isla Margarita (Venezuela)
____ *X. p. altirostris*	Trinidad
____ *X. p. phalara*	S Venezuela
____ *X. p. deltans*	NE Venezuela (Delta Amacuro)
____ *X. p. picus*	E Colombia to Venezuela, the Guianas, Brazil n of the Amazon
____ *X. p. duidae*	*Tepuis* of s Venezuela and adjacent Brazil
____ *X. p. peruvianus*	E Peru, adjacent w Brazil and n Bolivia (Beni and Santa Cruz)
____ *X. p. kienerii*	W Brazil (Rio Solimões to w Mato Grosso)
____ *X. p. rufescens*	Central Brazil (Rio Tapajós to Rio Madeira)
____ *X. p. bahiae*	NE Brazil (Piauí, Ceará and Maranhão to Goiás and Bahia)

☐ **Zimmer's Woodcreeper** *Xiphorhynchus necopinus*

	Lowlands of Amazonian Brazil (unknown in life)

☐ **Striped Woodcreeper** *Xiphorhynchus obsoletus*

____ *X. o. palliatus*	Tropical se Colombia to ne Bolivia and w Brazil (Rio Juruá)
____ *X. o. notatus*	E Colombia to s Venezuela and nw Brazil
____ *X. o. obsoletus*	E Venezuela to the Guianas and Amazonian Brazil
____ *X. o. caicarae*	NE Venezuela (Delta Amacuro)

☐ **Ocellated Woodcreeper** *Xiphorhynchus ocellatus*

____ *X. o. napensis*	Tropical se Colombia to e Ecuador and ne Peru
____ *X. o. lineatocapillus*	E Venezuela (known from one specimen)
____ *X. o. ocellatus*	Extreme e Colombia to ne Peru, s Venezuela and nw Brazil
____ *X. o. perplexus*	NE Peru and adjacent w Brazil (along Rio Solimões)
____ *X. o. chunchotambo*	Tropical e Peru (Loreto, Amazonas, Huánuco and Junín)
____ *X. o. brevirostris*	Tropical se Peru and ne Bolivia

☐ **Spix's Woodcreeper** *Xiphorhynchus spixii*

____ *X. s. ornatus*	Tropical se Colombia to e Ecuador and ne Peru
____ *X. s. insignis*	E-central Peru (upper Rio Ucayali and Rio Marañón)
____ *X. s. juruanus*	SE Peru to ne Bolivia and w Brazil
____ *X. s. spixii*	Brazil south of the Amazon (Rio Tapajós to Rio Guaporé)
____ *X. s. elegans*	Brazil south of the Amazon (Rio Guaporé to Rio Purús)

☐ **Buff-throated Woodcreeper** *Xiphorhynchus guttatus*

____ *X. g. confinis*	E Guatemala and n Honduras
____ *X. g. costaricensis*	SE Honduras to Nicaragua, Costa Rica and w Panama
____ *X. g. marginatus*	E Panama (Chiriquí, Veraguas and Azuero Peninsula)
____ *X. g. nanus*	E Panama to n Colombia and w Venezuela
____ *X. g. rosenbergi*	W Colombia (upper tropical Cauca Valley)
____ *X. g. demonstratus*	E Colombia and nw Venezuela
____ *X. g. jardinei*	NE Venezuela (Sucre and Monagas)
____ *X. g. margaritae*	Isla Margarita (Venezuela)
____ *X. g. polystictus*	E Colombia to the Guianas and n Brazil
____ *X. g. connectens*	Brazil north of the Amazon (Rio Negro eastward)
____ *X. g. eytoni*	Brazil south of the Amazon (Rio Madeira to Ceará)
____ *X. g. guttatoides*	Tropical w Amazonian basin
____ *X. g. vicinalis*	Brazil south of the Amazon (Rio Madeira to Rio Tapajós)
____ *X. g. dorbignyanus*	NE Bolivia and sw Brazil
____ *X. g. guttatus*	Coastal e Brazil (Pernambuco to Rio de Janeiro)

☐ **Chestnut-rumped Woodcreeper** *Xiphorhynchus pardalotus*

____	*X. p. caurensis*	SE Venezuela and w Guyana
____	*X. p. pardalotus*	Guianas and e Amazonian Brazil north of the Amazon

☐ **Cocoa Woodcreeper** *Xiphorhynchus susurrans*

E Guatemala to Colombia, n Venezuela, Trinidad and Tobago

☐ **Ivory-billed Woodcreeper** *Xiphorhynchus flavigaster*

____	*X. f. tardus*	Tropical nw Mexico (extreme se Sonora)
____	*X. f. mentalis*	W Mexico (Sinaloa and Durango to Jalisco and Michoacán)
____	*X. f. flavigaster*	SW Mexico (Guerrero and w Oaxaca)
____	*X. f. saltuarius*	NE Mexico (s Tamaulipas, San Luis Potosí and n Veracruz)
____	*X. f. yucatanensis*	SE Mexico (Yucatán Peninsula and Meco I.)
____	*X. f. eburneirostris*	SE Mexico (Veracruz) to nw Costa Rica
____	*X. f. ultimus*	NW Costa Rica (Nicoya Peninsula)

☐ **Black-striped Woodcreeper** *Xiphorhynchus lachrymosus*

____	*X. l. lachrymosus*	E Nicaragua to Pacific coast of Colombia and nw Ecuador
____	*X. l. alarum*	Tropical n Colombia (Sinú, Cauca and Magdalena valleys)

☐ **Spotted Woodcreeper** *Xiphorhynchus erythropygius*

____	*X. e. erythropygius*	Subtropical s Mexico (Veracruz, Guerrero and Oaxaca)
____	*X. e. parvus*	Subtropical s Mexico (Chiapas) to n-central Nicaragua
____	*X. e. punctigula*	Tropical se Nicaragua to w Panama (Veraguas)
____	*X. e. insolitus*	E Panama and nw Colombia (Atrato and Truando rivers)
____	*X. e. aequatorialis*	Tropical Pacific Colombia and w Ecuador

☐ **Olive-backed Woodcreeper** *Xiphorhynchus triangularis*

____	*X. t. triangularis*	Andes of Colombia to n Peru and w Venezuela
____	*X. t. hylodromus*	Mts. of n Venezuela (Yaracuy, Carabobo, Aragua and Miranda)
____	*X. t. intermedius*	Mountains of central Peru (Junín)
____	*X. t. bangsi*	Mountains of Bolivia (La Paz, Cochabamba and Santa Cruz)

☐ **White-striped Woodcreeper** *Lepidocolaptes leucogaster*

____	*L. l. umbrosus*	W Mexico (se Sonora to Durango, Nayarit and Jalisco)
____	*L. l. leucogaster*	SW Mexico (Colima to Oaxaca, Puebla and Veracruz)

☐ **Streak-headed Woodcreeper** *Lepidocolaptes souleyetii*

____	*L. s. guerrerensis*	W Mexico (Sierra Madre del Sur of Guerrero)
____	*L. s. insignis*	Tropical se Mexico (Veracruz) to n Honduras
____	*L. s. compressus*	S Mexico (Chiapas) to w Panama
____	*L. s. lineaticeps*	Tropical e Panama to n Colombia and w Venezuela
____	*L. s. littoralis*	Tropical n Colombia to the Guianas, Trinidad and adj. n Brazil
____	*L. s. uaireni*	Extreme se Venezuela (along Rio Uairén in Bolívar)
____	*L. s. esmeraldae*	Tropical sw Colombia (Nariño) and adjacent w Ecuador
____	*L. s. souleyetii*	Tropical sw Ecuador and nw Peru (south to Lambayeque)

☐ **Narrow-billed Woodcreeper** *Lepidocolaptes angustirostris*

____	*L. a. griseiceps*	Suriname (known from type location near Sipaliwini)
____	*L. a. coronatus*	N Brazil (Maranhão and Piauí to Goiás and nw Bahia)
____	*L. a. bahiae*	NE Brazil (Piauí, Ceará and Bahia)
____	*L. a. bivittatus*	E Bolivia and Brazilian plateau
____	*L. a. hellmayri*	Subtropical Andes of Bolivia (Cochabamba and Santa Cruz)
____	*L. a. certhiolus*	Central Bolivia, *chaco* of Paraguay and nw Argentina
____	*L. a. dabbenei*	SW Paraguay and n Argentina
____	*L. a. angustirostris*	E Paraguay to sw Brazil (sw Mato Grosso) and n Argentina
____	*L. a. praedatus*	W Uruguay to ne and central Argentina (San Luis and La Pampa)

☐ **Spot-crowned Woodcreeper** *Lepidocolaptes affinis*

____	*L. a. lignicida*	E Mexico (near Ciudad Victoria in w Tamaulipas)
____	*L. a. affinis*	Subtropical s Mexico to n Nicaragua
____	*L. a. neglectus*	Subtropical Costa Rica and w Panama

☐ **Montane Woodcreeper** *Lepidocolaptes lacrymiger*

____	*L. l. sanctaemartae*	Subtropical Santa Marta Mountains (ne Colombia)
____	*L. l. sneiderni*	Andes of Colombia
____	*L. l. lacrymiger*	E Andes of Colombia and Sierra de Perijá of adjacent Venezuela
____	*L. l. lafresnayi*	Subtropical coastal cordillera of n Venezuela
____	*L. l. aequatorialis*	Subtropical Andes of sw Colombia (Nariño) and Ecuador
____	*L. l. frigidus*	E slope of Andes of sw Colombia (Nariño)
____	*L. l. warscewiczi*	Subtropical Peru (Cajamarca and Amazonas to Junín)
____	*L. l. carabayae*	Subtropical se Peru (Cuzco and Puno)
____	*L. l. bolivianus*	Subtropical Bolivia (La Paz, Cochabamba and Santa Cruz)

☐ **Scaled Woodcreeper** *Lepidocolaptes squamatus*

____	*L. s. wagleri*	NE Brazil (Piauí)
____	*L. s. squamatus*	E Brazil (Bahia, Minas Gerais, Rio de Janeiro and n São Paulo)
____	*L. s. falcinellus*	SE Brazil to ne Argentina and se Paraguay (Rio Alto Paraná)

☐ **Lesser Woodcreeper** *Lepidocolaptes fuscus*

____	*L. f. atlanticus*	E Brazil (Ceará and Pernambuco)
____	*L. f. brevirostris*	Arid ne Brazil (n Bahia)
____	*L. f. tenuirostris*	E Brazil (Bahia to Espírito Santo north of Rio Doce)
____	*L. f. fuscus*	SE Brazil (Rio de Janeiro) to e Paraguay and ne Argentina

☐ **Lineated Woodcreeper** *Lepidocolaptes albolineatus*

____	*L. a. albolineatus*	E Venezuela (Bolívar) to the Guianas and n Brazil
____	*L. a. duidae*	S Venezuela (Amazonas) and nw Brazil
____	*L. a. fuscicapillus*	Amazonian Ecuador to Peru, e Bolivia and adjacent Mato Grosso
____	*L. a. madeirae*	W Amazonian Brazil south of the Amazon
____	*L. a. layardi*	E Amazonian Brazil south of the Amazon

☐ **Greater Scythebill** *Campylorhamphus pucherani*

Locally in Western Andes of Colombia to se Peru (Cuzco)

☐ **Red-billed Scythebill** *Campylorhamphus trochilirostris*

____	*C. t. brevipennis*	Tropical e Panama (Canal Zone to Darién) and w Colombia
____	*C. t. venezuelensis*	Tropical n Colombia and n Venezuela
____	*C. t. thoracicus*	Tropical sw Colombia (Nariño) and w Ecuador
____	*C. t. zarumillanus*	NW Peru (Tumbes and Piura)
____	*C. t. napensis*	Tropical e Ecuador and e Peru
____	*C. t. notabilis*	W Brazil south of the Amazon (Rio Purús to Rio Madeira)
____	*C. t. snethlageae*	Central Amazonian Brazil
____	*C. t. major*	NE Brazil (Piauí and Ceará)
____	*C. t. omissus*	E Brazil (e Goiás, n Minas Gerais and w and n Bahia)
____	*C. t. trochilirostris*	NE Brazil (se Bahia)
____	*C. t. devius*	Tropical n Bolivia (La Paz and Cochabamba)
____	*C. t. lafresnayanus*	E Bolivia to sw Brazil (w Mato Grosso) and *chaco* of n Paraguay
____	*C. t. hellmayri*	N Argentina

☐ **Brown-billed Scythebill** *Campylorhamphus pusillus*

____	*C. p. borealis*	Costa Rica and w Panama
____	*C. p. olivaceus*	Central Panama (Veraguas)
____	*C. p. tachirensis*	Andes of extreme e Colombia and w Venezuela (Táchira)
____	*C. p. pusillus*	Subtropical Andes of Colombia to w Ecuador and n Peru

☐ **Black-billed Scythebill** *Campylorhamphus falcularius*

SE Brazil (s Bahia) to e Paraguay and ne Argentina

☐ **Curve-billed Scythebill** *Campylorhamphus procurvoides*

_____ *C. p. sanus*	E Colombia to ne Peru, Venezuela, w Guyana and n Brazil
_____ *C. p. procurvoides*	French Guiana and adjacent n Brazil
_____ *C. p. probatus*	Amazonian Brazil (Rio Madeira to Rio Tapajós)
_____ *C. p. multostriatus*	Amazonian Brazil (Rio Tapajós to Rio Tocantins)

FAMILY: THAMNOPHILIDAE (Typical Antbirds—207)

☐ **Fasciated Antshrike** *Cymbilaimus lineatus*

_____ *C. l. fasciatus*	SE Honduras and Nicaragua to nw Ecuador
_____ *C. l. intermedius*	Tropical e Colombia to n Bolivia and Amazonian Brazil
_____ *C. l. lineatus*	SE Venezuela to the Guianas and ne Brazil north of the Amazon

☐ **Bamboo Antshrike** *Cymbilaimus sanctaemariae*

SE Peru to nw Bolivia (Pando) and sw Amazonian Brazil

☐ **Spot-backed Antshrike** *Hypoedaleus guttatus*

_____ *H. g. leucogaster*	SE Brazil (Bahia, Minas Gerais and Espírito Santo)
_____ *H. g. guttatus*	SE Brazil (Goiás) to e Paraguay and ne Argentina

☐ **Giant Antshrike** *Batara cinerea*

_____ *B. c. excubitor*	E slope of Andes of Bolivia (Santa Cruz)
_____ *B. c. argentina*	S Bolivia (n Tarija) and nw Argentina (south to Tucumán)
_____ *B. c. cinerea*	SE Brazil (Rio de Janeiro) to w Paraguay and ne Argentina

☐ **Tufted Antshrike** *Mackenziaena severa*

SE Brazil (Espírito Santo) to ne Argentina and extreme e Paraguay

☐ **Large-tailed Antshrike** *Mackenziaena leachii*

SE Brazil (Minas Gerais) to ne Argentina and e Paraguay

☐ **Black-throated Antshrike** *Frederickena viridis*

SE Venezuela to the Guianas and ne Brazil north of the Amazon

☐ **Undulated Antshrike** *Frederickena unduligera*

_____ *F. u. fulva*	SE Colombia to e Ecuador and nw Bolivia
_____ *F. u. diversa*	E and se Peru (Loreto, San Martín and Madre de Dios)
_____ *F. u. unduligera*	W Amazonian Brazil (upper Rio Negro)
_____ *F. u. pallida*	Brazil (Lago Sampaio region of Rio Madeira)

☐ **Great Antshrike** *Taraba major*

_____ *T. m. melanocrissus*	Tropical se Mexico to w Panama
_____ *T. m. obscurus*	SW Costa Rica to coastal nw Colombia and n Cauca Valley
_____ *T. m. transandeanus*	Extreme sw Colombia to w Ecuador and extreme nw Peru
_____ *T. m. granadensis*	Tropical n Colombia and nw Venezuela
_____ *T. m. semifasciatus*	E Colombia to s Venezuela, the Guianas, n and e Brazil
_____ *T. m. duidae*	*Tepuis* of se Venezuela (Mt. Duida)
_____ *T. m. melanurus*	W Amazon basin (se Colombia to Peru and w Brazil)
_____ *T. m. borbae*	Brazil south of the Amazon (Rio Purús to Rio Madeira)
_____ *T. m. stagurus*	NE Brazil (west to Maranhão and south to Minas Gerais)
_____ *T. m. major*	E Bolivia to s Brazil, Paraguay, Uruguay and ne Argentina

☐ **Collared Antshrike** *Sakesphorus bernardi*

_____ *S. b. bernardi*	Arid tropical sw Ecuador (Guayaquil) and Isla Puná
_____ *S. b. piurae*	Tropical sw Ecuador to nw Peru (Tumbes and Piura)
_____ *S. b.. cajamarcae*	Coastal w Peru (Cajamarca and La Libertad)
_____ *S. b. shumbae*	N Peru (Rio Marañón drainage in Cajamarca)

☐ **Black-crested Antshrike** *Sakesphorus canadensis*
_____ *S. c. pulchellus* — N Colombia and nw Venezuela
_____ *S. c. phainoleucus* — NE Colombia (Guajira Peninsula) and nw Venezuela
_____ *S. c. loretoyacuensis* — SE Colombia to ne Peru and n Amazonian Brazil
_____ *S. c. intermedius* — Venezuela and extreme n Brazil (Rio Surumú)
_____ *S. c. fumosus* — S Venezuela (upper Orinoco River and Caño Casiquiare)
_____ *S. c. trinitatis* — NE Venezuela, Trinidad and Guyana
_____ *S. c. canadensis* — Suriname and French Guiana

☐ **Silvery-cheeked Antshrike** *Sakesphorus cristatus*

Arid ne Brazil (Piauí and Ceará to extreme n Minas Gerais)

☐ **Black-backed Antshrike** *Sakesphorus melanonotus*

Caribbean ne Colombia and nw Venezuela

☐ **Band-tailed Antshrike** *Sakesphorus melanothorax*

Suriname, French Guiana and lower Amazonian Brazil

☐ **Glossy Antshrike** *Sakesphorus luctuosus*
_____ *S. l. luctuosus* — Lower Amazonian Brazil (Rio Madeira to Rio Tocantins)
_____ *S. l. araguayae* — Central Brazil (s Goiás and Mato Grosso)

☐ **White-bearded Antshrike** *Biatas nigropectus*

SE Brazil (s Minas Gerais) to ne Argentina

☐ **Barred Antshrike** *Thamnophilus doliatus*
_____ *T. d. intermedius* — E Mexico (Tamaulipas) to e Costa Rica
_____ *T. d. yucatanensis* — SE Mexico (Yucatán Peninsula) and Petén of n Guatemala
_____ *T. d. pacificus* — Pacific slope of Honduras to w Panama (Chiriquí)
_____ *T. d. eremnus* — Isla Coiba (Panama)
_____ *T. d. nigricristatus* — Pacific slope of Panama and n Colombia
_____ *T. d. nesiotes* — Pearl Islands (Gulf of Panama)
_____ *T. d. albicans* — N Colombia (upper Magdalena Valley)
_____ *T. d. nigrescens* — N Colombia (ne Norte de Santander) and nw Venezuela
_____ *T. d. tobagensis* — Tobago
_____ *T. d. fraterculus* — E Colombia, n Venezuela, Trinidad and Isla Margarita
_____ *T. d. doliatus* — E Venezuela to the Guianas and n Brazil
_____ *T. d. subradiatus* — Tropical e Peru and w Brazil (east to lower Rio Negro)
_____ *T. d. signatus* — NE Bolivia and sw Amazonian Brazil
_____ *T. d. difficilis* — E Brazil (Maranhão and Goiás to Mato Grosso)
_____ *T. d. capistratus* — E Brazil (Ceará, Pernambuco, Piauí and Bahia)
_____ *T. d. radiatus* — E Bolivia (n Santa Cruz) to s Brazil and n Argentina
_____ *T. d. cadwaladeri* — S Bolivia (Rio Pilcomayo region)

☐ **Chapman's Antshrike** *Thamnophilus zarumae*
_____ *T. z. zarumae* — Subtropical sw Ecuador (El Oro and Loja) and nw Peru (Piura)
_____ *T. z. palamblae* — NW Peru (Piura and Lambayeque)

☐ **Bar-crested Antshrike** *Thamnophilus multistriatus*
_____ *T. m. brachyurus* — W Colombia (Cauca Valley) and w slope of Western Andes
_____ *T. m. selvae* — W slope of Western Andes of Colombia (upper Río San Juan)
_____ *T. m. multistriatus* — E slope of Western Andes, Central and E Andes of Colombia
_____ *T. m. oecotonophilus* — NE Colombia and extreme w Venezuela (Sierra de Perijá)

☐ **Chestnut-backed Antshrike** *Thamnophilus palliatus*
_____ *T. p. similis* — E slope of Andes of central Peru (Huánuco and Junín)
_____ *T. p. puncticeps* — SE Peru (Cuzco and Puno) to n Bolivia and s Amazonian Brazil
_____ *T. p. palliatus* — Coastal e Brazil (Paraíba to Rio de Janeiro)

☐ **Lined Antshrike** *Thamnophilus tenuepunctatus*
_____ *T. t. tenuepunctatus* — E slope of Eastern Andes of Colombia
_____ *T. t. tenuifasciatus* — SE Colombia (Putumayo) and e Ecuador
_____ *T. t. berlepschi* — SE Ecuador (Zamora) and n Peru (San Martín)

☐ **Black-hooded Antshrike** *Thamnophilus bridgesi*

Pacific slope of sw Costa Rica and w Panama (e to Azuero Pen.)

☐ **Black Antshrike** *Thamnophilus nigriceps*

_____ *T. n. nigriceps* Tropical e Panama (Darién) and nw Colombia
_____ *T. n. magdalenae* Colombia (Río Magdalena Valley)

☐ **Cocha Antshrike** *Thamnophilus praecox*

Tropical e Ecuador (upper Río Napo)

☐ **Blackish-gray Antshrike** *Thamnophilus nigrocinereus*

_____ *T. n. cinereoniger* Upper Orinoco region of Colombia and Venezuela; nw Brazil
_____ *T. n. kulczynskii* French Guiana
_____ *T. n. nigrocinereus* NE Brazil (lower Amazon River and estuary islands)
_____ *T. n. tschudii* W Brazil (Rio Madeira and Rio Mamoré)
_____ *T. n. huberi* N Brazil (banks and islands of Rio Tapajós)

☐ **Castelnau's Antshrike** *Thamnophilus cryptoleucus*

SE Colombia to e Ecuador, ne Peru and w Amazonian Brazil

☐ **White-shouldered Antshrike** *Thamnophilus aethiops*

_____ *T. a. wetmorei* SE Colombia (north to w Meta)
_____ *T. a. aethiops* E Ecuador and ne Peru
_____ *T. a. polionotus* S and e Venezuela and nw Brazil
_____ *T. a. kapouni* E and se Peru, n Bolivia and w Brazil (Rio Solimões)
_____ *T. a. juruanus* W Brazil (south of Rio Solimões from Rio Juruá to Rio Purús)
_____ *T. a. injunctus* Brazil south of the Amazon (Rio Madeira to Rio Purús)
_____ *T. a. punctuliger* Central Brazil north of the Amazon
_____ *T. a. atriceps* Brazil south of the Amazon (Rio Tapajós to Rio Xingú)
_____ *T. a. incertus* NE Brazil (Rio Tocantins to Maranhão)
_____ *T. a. distans* Coastal ne Brazil (Pernambuco and Alagoas)

☐ **Uniform Antshrike** *Thamnophilus unicolor*

_____ *T. u. grandior* Colombia to e Ecuador and n Peru (Cajamarca and San Martín)
_____ *T. u. unicolor* Subtropical w Ecuador (south to El Oro and Loja)
_____ *T. u. caudatus* Andes of n Peru (south to Pasco)

☐ **Upland Antshrike** *Thamnophilus aroyae*

Lower Andean slopes of extreme se Peru (Puno) and w Bolivia

☐ **Plain-winged Antshrike** *Thamnophilus schistaceus*

_____ *T. s. capitalis* Tropical w Amazon basin (se Colombia to ne Peru)
_____ *T. s. dubius* S Ecuador and n Peru (south of Rio Marañón)
_____ *T. s. schistaceus* Tropical se Peru to n Bolivia and w Amazonian Brazil
_____ *T. s. heterogynus* W Amazonian Brazil (Rio Solimões, Rio Purús and Rio Madeira)
_____ *T. s. inornatus* Brazil south of the Amazon (lower Rio Madeira to Rio Tocantins)

☐ **Mouse-colored Antshrike** *Thamnophilus murinus*

_____ *T. m. murinus* E Colombia and e Ecuador to the Guianas and nw Brazil
_____ *T. m. cayennensis* French Guiana and Brazil (north bank of the Amazon at Faro)
_____ *T. m. canipennis* E Peru and Amazonian Brazil (east to Rio Madeira)

☐ **Western Slaty-Antshrike** *Thamnophilus atrinucha*

_____ *T. a. atrinucha* S Belize and se Guatemala to w Ecuador and nw Venezuela
_____ *T. a. gorgonae* Gorgona I. (off s Colombia)

☐ **Guianan Slaty-Antshrike** *Thamnophilus punctatus*

_____ *T. p. interpositus* W Venezuela south of the Andes and adjacent Colombia (Arauca)
_____ *T. p. punctatus* Extreme e Venezuela to the Guianas and Brazil n of the Amazon

☐ **Peruvian Slaty-Antshrike** *Thamnophilus leucogaster*

_____ *T. l. leucogaster* NW Peru (middle Marañón Valley in Cajamarca and Amazonas)
_____ *T. l. huallagae* NE Peru (w slope of middle Río Huallaga Valley in San Martín)

☐ **Natterer's Slaty-Antshrike** *Thamnophilus stictocephalus*
_____ *T. s. stictocephalus*   Locally in central Brazil (south of the Amazon)
_____ *T. s. parkeri*   Bolivia (plateau of Serranía de Huanchaca in ne Santa Cruz)

☐ **Bolivian Slaty-Antshrike** *Thamnophilus sticturus*

Bolivia (Cochabamba and Santa Cruz); sw Brazil (sw Mato Grosso)

☐ **Planalto Slaty-Antshrike** *Thamnophilus pelzelni*

Plateau region of central and e Brazil

☐ **Sooretama Slaty-Antshrike** *Thamnophilus ambiguus*

Coastal se Brazil (s Bahia and Espírito Santo to Rio de Janeiro)

☐ **Streak-backed Antshrike** *Thamnophilus insignis*
_____ *T. i. insignis*   S Venezuela (Gran Sabana in Bolívar and Amazonas)
_____ *T. i. nigrifrontalis*   *Tepuis* of s Venezuela (Mt. Paraque, Mt. Duida and Auyan-tepui)

☐ **Amazonian Antshrike** *Thamnophilus amazonicus*
_____ *T. a. cinereiceps*   Extreme e Colombia to w Venezuela and n Peru
_____ *T. a. amazonicus*   Tropical s Colombia to n Bolivia and w Brazil (se Mato Grosso)
_____ *T. a. divaricatus*   E Venezuela to the Guianas and ne Amazonian Brazil
_____ *T. a. paraensis*   Brazil (east of Rio Tocantins to Maranhão south of the Amazon)
_____ *T. a. obscurus*   Amazonian Brazil south of the Amazon (n and e of *amazonicus*)
_____ *T. a. huallagae*   N Peru (Río Huallaga region of San Martín)

☐ **Variable Antshrike** *Thamnophilus caerulescens*
_____ *T. c. subandinus*   E Peru (La Libertad, Amazonas and San Martín)
_____ *T. c. melanochrous*   Central and s Peru (Junín, Cuzco and Puno)
_____ *T. c. aspersiventer*   N Bolivia (La Paz and Cochabamba)
_____ *T. c. connectens*   E Bolivia (Santa Cruz)
_____ *T. c. dinellii*   Central and s Bolivia to nw Argentina and extreme nw Paraguay
_____ *T. c. paraguayensis*   N Paraguay and adjacent w Brazil (s Mato Grosso)
_____ *T. c. gilvigaster*   SE Brazil to Uruguay and ne Argentina
_____ *T. c. caerulescens*   S Brazil (Minas Gerais) to e Paraguay and ne Argentina
_____ *T. c. albonotatus*   Mountains of se Brazil on Minas Gerais/Espírito Santo border
_____ *T. c. ochraceiventer*   E Brazil (s Goiás)
_____ *T. c. pernambucensis*   E Brazil (Pernambuco)
_____ *T. c. cearensis*   E Brazil (Ceará)

☐ **Rufous-winged Antshrike** *Thamnophilus torquatus*

Lowlands of e Bolivia to e and central Brazil

☐ **Rufous-capped Antshrike** *Thamnophilus ruficapillus*
_____ *T. r. jaczewskii*   N Peru (Amazonas and Cajamarca)
_____ *T. r. marcapatae*   SE Peru (Cuzco and Puno)
_____ *T. r. subfasciatus*   *Yungas* of Bolivia (Cochabamba and La Paz)
_____ *T. r. cochabambae*   S Bolivia and nw Argentina
_____ *T. r. ruficapillus*   SE Brazil to ne Argentina, e Paraguay and Uruguay

☐ **Spot-winged Antshrike** *Pygiptila stellaris*
_____ *P. s. maculipennis*   SE Colombia to n Bolivia
_____ *P. s. occipitalis*   E Colombia to n Venezuela, Suriname and n Brazil
_____ *P. s. purusiana*   W Amazonian Brazil
_____ *P. s. stellaris*   Brazil south of the Amazon and nw Mato Grosso

☐ **Pearly Antshrike** *Megastictus margaritatus*

SE Colombia to s Venezuela, e Peru and w Amazonian Brazil

☐ **Black Bushbird** *Neoctantes niger*

W Amazonian Brazil to se Colombia, e Ecuador and e Peru

☐ **Recurve-billed Bushbird** *Clytoctantes alixii*

Caribbean lowlands of n Colombia and extreme w Venezuela

☐ **Rondonia Bushbird** *Clytoctantes atrogularis*

Locally in sw Amazonian Brazil (e Rondônia)

☐ **Speckled Antshrike** *Xenornis setifrons*

E Panama and nw Colombia (n and central Chocó)

☐ **Russet Antshrike** *Thamnistes anabatinus*

_____ *T. a. anabatinus*	Gulf Caribbean slope of se Mexico to Belize and Honduras
_____ *T. a. saturatus*	Humid tropical Nicaragua to w Panama
_____ *T. a. coronatus*	Central and e Panama (Veraguas to Darién)
_____ *T. a. intermedius*	Tropical w Colombia and w Ecuador (south to El Oro)
_____ *T. a. aequatorialis*	Tropical se Colombia and e Ecuador
_____ *T. a. gularis*	W Venezuela (Táchira)
_____ *T. a. rufescens*	Peru south of the Río Marañón (Amazonas) to w Bolivia

☐ **Spot-breasted Antvireo** *Dysithamnus stictothorax*

SE Brazil (e Minas Gerais to Paraná) and ne Argentina

☐ **Plain Antvireo** *Dysithamnus mentalis*

_____ *D. m. septentrionalis*	S Mexico (Campeche) to w Panama
_____ *D. m. suffusus*	E Panama (Darién) and lower Cauca Valley of Colombia
_____ *D. m. extremus*	W slope of Central Andes of Colombia
_____ *D. m. semicinereus*	Santa Marta Mountains (ne Colombia)
_____ *D. m. viridis*	NE Colombia and nw Venezuela (Zulia and Táchira)
_____ *D. m. cumbreanus*	N Venezuela
_____ *D. m. andrei*	E Venezuela (n Orinoco delta) and Trinidad
_____ *D. m. oberi*	Tobago
_____ *D. m. ptaritepui*	Subtropical *tepuis* of s Venezuela (Amazonas and Bolívar)
_____ *D. m. spodionotus*	*Tepuis* of s and e Venezuela
_____ *D. m. aequatorialis*	Subtropical w Ecuador and nw Peru (Tumbes and Piura)
_____ *D. m. napensis*	Subtropical e Ecuador
_____ *D. m. tambillanus*	N Peru (Cajamarca, San Martín and Huánuco)
_____ *D. m. olivaceus*	Central Peru (Chanchamayo Valley)
_____ *D. m. tavarae*	SE Peru (Puno) and w Bolivia
_____ *D. m. emiliae*	NE Brazil (Pará, n Maranhão, Ceará and Pernambuco)
_____ *D. m. affinis*	Central Brazil (Mato Grosso and s Goiás)
_____ *D. m. mentalis*	SE Brazil (Bahia) to e Paraguay and ne Argentina

☐ **Streak-crowned Antvireo** *Dysithamnus striaticeps*

Extreme se Honduras, e Nicaragua and Costa Rica

☐ **Spot-crowned Antvireo** *Dysithamnus puncticeps*

_____ *D. p. puncticeps*	Humid lowlands of se Costa Rica to n Colombia
_____ *D. p. intensus*	E Panama (Darién lowlands) and w Colombia
_____ *D. p. flemmingi*	SW Colombia and nw Ecuador (south to Pichincha)

☐ **Rufous-backed Antvireo** *Dysithamnus xanthopterus*

SE Brazil (Rio de Janeiro to Paraná)

☐ **White-streaked Antvireo** *Dysithamnus leucostictus*

_____ *D. l. leucostictus*	E slope of Eastern Andes of Colombia, Ecuador and n Peru
_____ *D. l. tucuyensis*	Coastal mountains of n Venezuela (Monagas to Lara)

☐ **Plumbeous Antvireo** *Dysithamnus plumbeus*

SE Brazil (s Bahia to e Minas Gerais and n Rio de Janeiro)

☐ **Bicolored Antvireo** *Dysithamnus occidentalis*

_____ *D. o. occidentalis*	Andes of sw Colombia (Farallones de Cali National Park)
_____ *D. o. punctitectus*	E slope of Andes of Ecuador (w Napo, Morona-Santiago, Carchi)

☐ **Saturnine Antshrike** *Thamnomanes saturninus*

_____ *T. s. huallagae*	Extreme ne Peru (Loreto) and w Amazonian Brazil
_____ *T. s. saturninus*	W-central Brazil and extreme ne Bolivia (ne Santa Cruz)

☐ **Dusky-throated Antshrike** *Thamnomanes ardesiacus*

_____ *T. a. ardesiacus*	SE Colombia to e Ecuador and e Peru north of the Amazon
_____ *T. a. obidensis*	S Venezuela to the Guianas and n Amazonian Brazil

☐ **Cinereous Antshrike** *Thamnomanes caesius*

    ____ *T. c. glaucus*   E Colombia to the Guianas and Brazil north of the Amazon

    ____ *T. c. intermedius*   Central Peru (along Rio Ucayali to mouth of Rio Urubamba)

    ____ *T. c. persimilis*   Brazil south of the Amazon (Rio Purús to Rio Tapajós)

    ____ *T. c. hoffmannsi*   Brazil south of the Amazon (Rio Tapajós to n Maranhão)

    ____ *T. c. caesius*   E Brazil (Paraíba to Bahia and Rio de Janeiro)

☐ **Bluish-slate Antshrike** *Thamnomanes schistogynus*

Tropical e Peru, n Bolivia and sw Amazonian Brazil

☐ **Pygmy Antwren** *Myrmotherula brachyura*

    ____ *M. b. ignota*   Central and e Panama to nw Colombia and nw Ecuador

    ____ *M. b. brachyura*   Tropical e Colombia to n Bolivia and Amazonian Brazil

☐ **Short-billed Antwren** *Myrmotherula obscura*

SE Colombia to ne Peru and locally in w Amazonian Brazil

☐ **Sclater's Antwren** *Myrmotherula sclateri*

E Peru, n Bolivia and Amazonian Brazil south of the Amazon

☐ **Klages' Antwren** *Myrmotherula klagesi*

Amazonian Brazil near mouth of Rio Tapajós and Rio Negro

☐ **Yellow-throated Antwren** *Myrmotherula ambigua*

Extreme e Colombia, sw Venezuela and nw Amazonian Brazil

☐ **Cherrie's Antwren** *Myrmotherula cherriei*

NE Colombia, sw Venezuela and n Amazonian Brazil

☐ **Pacific Streaked-Antwren** *Myrmotherula pacifica*

Panama (Veraguas) to coastal Pacific Colombia and Ecuador

☐ **Amazonian Streaked-Antwren** *Myrmotherula multostriata*

E Colombia to n Bolivia and Brazil south of the Amazon

☐ **Guianan Streaked-Antwren** *Myrmotherula surinamensis*

S Venezuela to the Guianas and n Amazonian Brazil

☐ **Stripe-chested Antwren** *Myrmotherula longicauda*

    ____ *M. l. soderstromi*   E base of Andes of s Colombia and Ecuador (on Rio Napo)

    ____ *M. l. pseudoaustralis*   N Peru (San Martín and Huánuco) and adjacent Ecuador

    ____ *M. l. longicauda*   E Peru (Loreto, Ucayali and Junín)

    ____ *M. l. australis*   SE Peru (Cuzco and Puno) to w Bolivia

☐ **Plain-throated Antwren** *Myrmotherula hauxwelli*

    ____ *M. h. suffusa*   SE Colombia to e Ecuador and ne Peru

    ____ *M. h. hauxwelli*   E Peru (drainage of Rio Huallaga) and w Brazil

    ____ *M. h. clarior*   Brazil s of the Amazon (Rio Madeira to Rio Xingú) to n Bolivia

    ____ *M. h. hellmayri*   NE Brazil south of the Amazon (Rio Xingú to n Maranhão)

☐ **Rufous-bellied Antwren** *Myrmotherula guttata*

S Venezuela to the Guianas and ne Amazonian Brazil

☐ **Star-throated Antwren** *Myrmotherula gularis*

SE Brazil (Espírito Santo to Paraná and ne Rio Grande do Sul)

☐ **Brown-bellied Antwren** *Myrmotherula gutturalis*

S Venezuela to the Guianas and ne Amazonian Brazil

☐ **Checker-throated Antwren** *Myrmotherula fulviventris*

    ____ *M. f. costaricensis*   S Honduras to w Panama (Almirante Bay)

    ____ *M. f. fulviventris*   E Panama to Colombia (lower Cauca Valley) and w Ecuador

    ____ *M. f. salmoni*   Colombia (Bolívar, Santander and Antioquia)

☐ **White-eyed Antwren** *Myrmotherula leucophthalma*

    ____ *M. l. dissita*   E Peru (Ucayali) to n Bolivia (La Paz and n Santa Cruz)

    ____ *M. l. leucophthalma*   W-central Amazonian Brazil (except range of *phaeonota*)

    ____ *M. l. phaeonota*   Brazil s of the Amazon (lower Rio Madeira to lower Rio Tapajós)

    ____ *M. l. sordida*   Brazil south of the Amazon (Rio Tapajós to Rio Tocantins)

☐ **Brown-backed Antwren** *Myrmotherula fjeldsaai*

Lower tropical e Ecuador and immediately adjacent Peru

☐ **Stipple-throated Antwren** *Myrmotherula haematonota*

____	*M. h. pyrrhonota*	Tropical se Colombia to s Venezuela and nw Brazil
____	*M. h. haematonota*	Tropical ne Peru (Loreto) and adjacent se Ecuador
____	*M. h. amazonica*	W and central Amazonian Brazil

☐ **Foothill Antwren** *Myrmotherula spodionota*

____	*M. s. spodionota*	E slope of Andes of s Colombia south to n Peru (n Amazonas)
____	*M. s. sororia*	E Peru (south of Río Marañón from San Martín to Madre de Dios)

☐ **Ornate Antwren** *Myrmotherula ornata*

____	*M. o. ornata*	Coastal e Colombia (Intendencia de Meta)
____	*M. o. saturata*	Tropical se Colombia to e Ecuador and ne Peru (Loreto)
____	*M. o. atrogularis*	NE Peru (drainage of Río Huallaga and Río Ucayali)
____	*M. o. meridionalis*	SE Peru (Madre de Dios and Puno) to n Bolivia
____	*M. o. hoffmannsi*	Amazonian Brazil south of the Amazon

☐ **Rufous-tailed Antwren** *Myrmotherula erythrura*

____	*M. e. erythrura*	SE Colombia to e Peru (Loreto) and adjacent nw Brazil
____	*M. e. septentrionalis*	E Peru (Loreto to Puno) and w Amazonian Brazil

☐ **White-flanked Antwren** *Myrmotherula axillaris*

____	*M. a. albigula*	S Mexico (Chiapas) to w Colombia and w Ecuador
____	*M. a. melaena*	E Colombia to e Peru, s Venezuela and n Amazonian Brazil
____	*M. a. heterozyga*	E Peru (upper Río Ucayali drainage) and adjacent w Brazil
____	*M. a. axillaris*	NW Venezuela to the Guianas and n Brazil; Trinidad
____	*M. a. fresnayana*	SE Peru (Puno) and Bolivia
____	*M. a. luctuosa*	E Brazil (Pernambuco and Bahia to Rio de Janeiro)

☐ **Rio de Janeiro Antwren** *Myrmotherula fluminensis*

	SE Brazil (known from a 1988 specimen from Serra dos Órgãos)

☐ **Slaty Antwren** *Myrmotherula schisticolor*

____	*M. s. schisticolor*	S Mexico (Chiapas) to w Ecuador (south to Loja)
____	*M. s. sanctaemartae*	NE Colombia (Santa Marta Mts.) and mountains of n Venezuela
____	*M. s. interior*	Andean slopes from e Colombia to s Peru (Puno)

☐ **Rio Suno Antwren** *Myrmotherula sunensis*

____	*M. s. sunensis*	Extreme se Colombia to extreme ne Peru and w Amazonian Brazil
____	*M. s. yessupi*	Locally in central Peru (Huánuco and Pasco)

☐ **Long-winged Antwren** *Myrmotherula longipennis*

____	*M. l. longipennis*	SE Colombia to the Guianas and Brazil north of the Amazon
____	*M. l. zimmeri*	Tropical e Ecuador and ne Peru (mouth of Rio Curaray)
____	*M. l. garbei*	E Peru, w Amazonian Brazil and extreme nw Bolivia
____	*M. l. transitiva*	Amazonian Brazil (Rio Madeira to Rio Paraná)
____	*M. l. ochrogyna*	Brazil south of the Amazon (Rio Madeira to Rio Tapajós)
____	*M. l. paraensis*	Brazil south of the Amazon (Rio Tapajós to Rio Guamá)

☐ **Salvadori's Antwren** *Myrmotherula minor*

	SE Brazil (n Espírito Santo to central São Paulo)

☐ **Ihering's Antwren** *Myrmotherula iheringi*

____	*M. i. heteroptera*	SE Peru (Madre de Dios) to central Brazil (Rio Madeira)
____	*M. i. iheringi*	Amazonian Brazil (Rio Madeira to Rio Tapajós)

☐ **Ashy Antwren** *Myrmotherula grisea*

	Andean foothills of w Bolivia

☐ **Plain-winged Antwren** *Myrmotherula behni*

____	*M. b. behni*	E slope of Andes of Colombia to e Ecuador (Morona-Santiago)
____	*M. b. yavii*	S Venezuela (Bolívar and Amazonas) and extreme n Brazil
____	*M. b. inornata*	*Tepuis* of se Venezuela and adjacent Guyana
____	*M. b. camanii*	S Venezuela

☐ **Unicolored Antwren** *Myrmotherula unicolor*

SE Brazil (n Rio de Janeiro to extreme n Rio Grande do Sul)

☐ **Alagoas Antwren** *Myrmotherula snowi*

NE Brazil (Alagoas near Murici on Rio Pedra Branca)

☐ **Band-tailed Antwren** *Myrmotherula urosticta*

SE Brazil (se Bahia to n Rio de Janeiro)

☐ **Gray Antwren** *Myrmotherula menetriesii*
    ____ *M. m. pallida*
    ____ *M. m. cinereiventris*
    ____ *M. m. menetriesii*
    ____ *M. m. berlepschi*
    ____ *M. m. omissa*

E Colombia to s Venezuela and nw Brazil
E Venezuela to the Guianas and Brazil north of the lower Amazon
E Peru south of the Amazon to n Bolivia and w Amazonian Brazil
Central Brazil (Rio Madeira to Rio Tapajós)
NE Brazil (Rio Tapajós to nw Maranhão)

☐ **Leaden Antwren** *Myrmotherula assimilis*

River islands of the Amazon and its major tributaries

☐ **Banded Antwren** *Dichrozona cincta*
    ____ *D. c. cincta*
    ____ *D. c. stellata*
    ____ *D. c. zononota*

SE Colombia to extreme sw Venezuela and nw Brazil
E Ecuador and w Brazil (Rio Juruá to Rio Purús)
E Peru, Amazonian Brazil north of the Amazon and n Bolivia

☐ **Stripe-backed Antbird** *Myrmorchilus strigilatus*
    ____ *M. s. strigilatus*
    ____ *M. s. suspicax*

E Brazil (Piauí, Ceará and Pernambuco to n Minas Gerais)
SE Bolivia to w Brazil (w Mato Grosso), w Paraguay, n Argentina

☐ **Ash-throated Antwren** *Herpsilochmus parkeri*

E slope of Andes of n-central Peru (San Martín)

☐ **Creamy-bellied Antwren** *Herpsilochmus motacilloides*

E slope of Andes of Peru (Junín to n Cuzco)

☐ **Black-capped Antwren** *Herpsilochmus atricapillus*

NE Brazil to e Bolivia, nw Paraguay and nw Argentina

☐ **Pileated Antwren** *Herpsilochmus pileatus*

NE Brazil (Bahia, Ceará, Maranhão and Pará)

☐ **Spot-tailed Antwren** *Herpsilochmus sticturus*

S Venezuela to the Guianas and n Amazonian Brazil

☐ **Dugand's Antwren** *Herpsilochmus dugandi*

Locally in se Colombia, e Ecuador and ne Peru

☐ **Todd's Antwren** *Herpsilochmus stictocephalus*

Extreme e Venezuela to the Guianas and extreme n Brazil

☐ **Ancient Antwren** *Herpsilochmus gentryi*

Sandy soil forests in extreme se Ecuador and n Peru

☐ **Spot-backed Antwren** *Herpsilochmus dorsimaculatus*

Extreme e Colombia, s Venezuela and n Brazil

☐ **Roraiman Antwren** *Herpsilochmus roraimae*

Tepuis of s Venezuela, adjacent Guyana and n Brazil (Roraima)

☐ **Pectoral Antwren** *Herpsilochmus pectoralis*

Locally in ne Brazil (Maranhão, Rio Grande do Norte and Bahia)

☐ **Large-billed Antwren** *Herpsilochmus longirostris*

Brazilian plateau (Piauí to Mato Grosso do Sul) and ne Bolivia

☐ **Yellow-breasted Antwren** *Herpsilochmus axillaris*
    ____ *H. a. senex*
    ____ *H. a. aequatorialis*
    ____ *H. a. puncticeps*
    ____ *H. a. axillaris*

Tropical and subtropical Western Andes of sw Colombia
E slope of Andes of se Colombia and e Ecuador
E slope of Andes of n Peru (Loreto to Huánuco)
E slope of Andes of s Peru (Junín, Cuzco and Puno)

☐ **Rufous-winged Antwren** *Herpsilochmus rufimarginatus*
    ____ *H. r. exiguus*
    ____ *H. r. frater*
    ____ *H. r. scapularis*
    ____ *H. r. rufimarginatus*

Pacific slope of e Panama (e Darién)
Colombia and Venezuela to Bolivia and e Brazil (Maranhão)
E Brazil (Pernambuco to Espírito Santo and Minas Gerais)
SE Brazil (Rio de Janeiro) to e Paraguay and ne Argentina

☐ **Dot-winged Antwren** *Microrhopias quixensis*

_____	*M. q. boucardi*	Tropical s Mexico to sw Honduras
_____	*M. q. virgata*	Nicaragua and Costa Rica to w Panama
_____	*M. q. consobrina*	E Panama to w Colombia and w Ecuador
_____	*M. q. microsticta*	The Guianas
_____	*M. q. quixensis*	E Ecuador and ne Peru (south to n bank of Rio Marañón)
_____	*M. q. intercedens*	N Peru (lower Río Ucayali and adjacent s bank of the Amazon)
_____	*M. q. nigriventris*	Central Peru (San Martín, Junín and Cuzco)
_____	*M. q. albicauda*	SE Peru (Madre de Dios and Puno)
_____	*M. q. bicolor*	Amazonian Brazil (west bank of Rio Tapajós) to n Bolivia
_____	*M. q. emiliae*	Amazonian Brazil (east of Rio Tapajós)

☐ **Parana Antwren** *Stymphalornis acutirostris*

Marshes in se Brazil (Paraná)

☐ **Narrow-billed Antwren** *Formicivora iheringi*

Interior e Brazil (central Bahia to Minas Gerais)

☐ **White-fringed Antwren** *Formicivora grisea*

_____	*F. g. alticincta*	Pearl Islands (Bay of Panama)
_____	*F. g. hondae*	N Colombia (Magdalena Valley)
_____	*F. g. fumosa*	E Colombia and w Venezuela
_____	*F. g. intermedia*	NE Colombia, nw Venezuela, Margarita and Chachacare islands
_____	*F. g. tobagensis*	Tobago
_____	*F. g. orenocensis*	S Venezuela (middle and lower Orinoco Valley)
_____	*F. g. rufiventris*	Extreme e Colombia and s Venezuela
_____	*F. g. grisea*	Guianas to lower Amazon, ne Brazil (Pernambuco) and n Bolivia
_____	*F. g. deluzae*	SE Brazil (Rio de Janeiro)
_____	*F. g. ssp.*	Undescribed race from ne Bolivia (e Beni and ne Santa Cruz)

☐ **Black-bellied Antwren** *Formicivora melanogaster*

_____	*F. m. melanogaster*	Brazil (Mato Grosso and s Maranhão) to e Bolivia and n Paraguay
_____	*F. m. bahiae*	Plateau of e Brazil (Piauí, Ceará and n Bahia)

☐ **Serra Antwren** *Formicivora serrana*

_____	*F. s. serrana*	Mountains of se Brazil (s Espírito Santo)
_____	*F. s. interposita*	SE Brazil (n Rio de Janeiro and adjacent s Minas Gerais)

☐ **Restinga Antwren** *Formicivora littoralis*

Coastal beaches of se Brazil (Rio de Janeiro)

☐ **Black-hooded Antwren** *Formicivora erythronotos*

Locally in lowlands of se Brazil (Rio de Janeiro)

☐ **Rusty-backed Antwren** *Formicivora rufa*

_____	*F. r. urubambae*	E Peru (San Martín and Cuzco)
_____	*F. r. chapmani*	S Suriname and e Brazil (Rio Tapajós to Maranhão and Piuaí)
_____	*F. r. rufa*	Amazonian Brazil to n and e Bolivia and e Paraguay

☐ **Ferruginous Antbird** *Drymophila ferruginea*

SE Brazil (se Bahia to e Santa Catarina)

☐ **Bertoni's Antbird** *Drymophila rubricollis*

SE Brazil to extreme e Paraguay and ne Argentina

☐ **Rufous-tailed Antbird** *Drymophila genei*

SE Brazil (Minas Gerais, Espírito Santo and Rio de Janeiro)

☐ **Ochre-rumped Antbird** *Drymophila ochropyga*

SE Brazil (Espírito Santo and Minas Gerais to São Paulo)

☐ **Striated Antbird** *Drymophila devillei*

_____	*D. d. devillei*	Locally in extreme s Colombia, e Ecuador, e Peru and n Bolivia
_____	*D. d. subochracea*	Bamboo patches in s Amazonian Brazil

☐ **Dusky-tailed Antbird** *Drymophila malura*

SE Brazil to ne Argentina and se Paraguay

☐ **Long-tailed Antbird** *Drymophila caudata*
    ____   *D. c. hellmayri*   Santa Marta Mountains of ne Colombia and n end of E Andes
    ____   *D. c. klagesi*   Mountains of n Venezuela (east to Pária Peninsula)
    ____   *D. c. aristeguietana*   Sierra de Perijá (Colombia/Venezuela border)
    ____   *D. c. caudata*   Subtropical Andes of Colombia to w Bolivia (La Paz)

☐ **Scaled Antbird** *Drymophila squamata*

SE Brazil (Alagoas to e Santa Catarina and e Minas Gerais)

☐ **Streak-capped Antwren** *Terenura maculata*

SE Brazil (se Bahia) to ne Argentina and e Paraguay

☐ **Orange-bellied Antwren** *Terenura sicki*

E Brazil (Alagoas and ne Pernambuco)

☐ **Rufous-rumped Antwren** *Terenura callinota*
    ____   *T. c. callinota*   Foothill forests of Costa Rica to n Peru (Cajamarca)
    ____   *T. c. peruviana*   Foothills of e Peru (San Martín to Cuzco)
    ____   *T. c. guianensis*   S Guyana (Acari Mountains) and adjacent s Suriname
    ____   *T. c. venezuelana*   Sierra de Perijá (Colombia/Venezuela border)

☐ **Chestnut-shouldered Antwren** *Terenura humeralis*
    ____   *T. h. humeralis*   E Ecuador to e Peru and w Brazil (south of Rio Solimões)
    ____   *T. h. transfluvialis*   W Amazonian Brazil and extreme nw Bolivia

☐ **Yellow-rumped Antwren** *Terenura sharpei*

Foothill forests of se Peru (Puno) and w Bolivia

☐ **Ash-winged Antwren** *Terenura spodioptila*
    ____   *T. s. signata*   SE Colombia to nw Brazil (upper Rio Negro)
    ____   *T. s. spodioptila*   S Venezuela to the Guianas and nw Brazil
    ____   *T. s. elaopteryx*   French Guiana and ne Brazil (north of the lower Amazon)
    ____   *T. s. meridionalis*   Brazil south of the Amazon (near e bank of lower Rio Tapajós)

☐ **Gray Antbird** *Cercomacra cinerascens*
    ____   *C. c. cinerascens*   Tropical e Colombia to ne Peru, s Venezuela and nw Brazil
    ____   *C. c. immaculata*   E Venezuela to the Guianas and Brazil north of the Amazon
    ____   *C. c. sclateri*   E Peru to ne Bolivia and w Amazonian Brazil
    ____   *C. c. iterata*   Brazil south of the Amazon

☐ **Rio de Janeiro Antbird** *Cercomacra brasiliana*

SE Brazil (s Bahia and e Minas Gerais to Rio de Janeiro)

☐ **Dusky Antbird** *Cercomacra tyrannina*
    ____   *C. t. crepera*   SE Mexico to Caribbean slope of w Panama (Veraguas)
    ____   *C. t. rufiventris*   E Panama to w Ecuador (Chimborazo)
    ____   *C. t. tyrannina*   E Colombia to s Venezuela and nw Brazil
    ____   *C. t. vicina*   North end of Eastern Andes of Colombia and w Venezuela
    ____   *C. t. saturatior*   E Venezuela to the Guianas and ne Amazonian Brazil

☐ **Willis' Antbird** *Cercomacra laeta*
    ____   *C. l. laeta*   SE Amazonian Brazil (Rio Tocantins to Pará and adj. Maranhão)
    ____   *C. l. waimiri*   NE Brazil (vicinity of Manaus and e Roraima)
    ____   *C. t. sabinoi*   Extreme ne Brazil (Pernambuco and Alagoas)

☐ **Parker's Antbird** *Cercomacra parkeri*

Central Andes of Colombia

☐ **Blackish Antbird** *Cercomacra nigrescens*
    ____   *C. n. nigrescens*   Suriname and French Guiana
    ____   *C. n. aequatorialis*   E Ecuador and n Peru (Amazonas and San Martín)
    ____   *C. n. notata*   Central Peru (Huánuco and Junín)
    ____   *C. n. fuscicauda*   SE Peru to n Bolivia and w Amazonian Brazil
    ____   *C. n. approximans*   Brazil s of the Amazon (Rio Purús to Rio Tapajós, Mato Grosso)
    ____   *C. n. ochrogyna*   Brazil (n Mato Grosso along Rio Araguaia)

☐ **Bananal Antbird** *Cercomacra ferdinandi*

Central Brazil (Bananal I. in w Goiás and adjacent Mato Grosso)

☐ **Black Antbird** *Cercomacra serva*
_____ C. s. serva
_____ C. s. hypomelaena

Extreme se Colombia, e Ecuador and ne Peru (Loreto)
E Peru (Huánuco) to n Bolivia and w Amazonian Brazil

☐ **Jet Antbird** *Cercomacra nigricans*
_____ C. n. nigricans
_____ C. n. atrata

E Panama (including Pearl Islands) to w Ecuador and n Venezuela
NW Colombia

☐ **Rio Branco Antbird** *Cercomacra carbonaria*

Extreme n Brazil (along Rio Branco) and adjacent Guyana

☐ **Mato Grosso Antbird** *Cercomacra melanaria*

Tropical n Bolivia to sw Brazil (Mato Grosso) and n Paraguay

☐ **Manu Antbird** *Cercomacra manu*

Locally in se Peru, nw Bolivia and s Amazonian Brazil

☐ **White-backed Fire-eye** *Pyriglena leuconota*
_____ P. l. pacifica
_____ P. l. castanoptera
_____ P. l. picea
_____ P. l. similis
_____ P. l. marcapatensis
_____ P. l. hellmayri
_____ P. l. maura
_____ P. l. interposita
_____ P. l. leuconota
_____ P. l. pernambucensis

Humid tropical w Ecuador
Subtropical e Colombia to e Ecuador and n Peru (Cajamarca)
Subtropical n Peru (Loreto, Huánuco and Junín)
Brazil south of the Amazon (Rio Tapajós to Rio Xingú)
SE Peru (Cuzco and Puno)
Bolivia (Beni, La Paz, Cochabamba and Santa Cruz)
SE Bolivia to sw Brazil (Mato Grosso) and ne Paraguay
E-central Brazil (Rio Anapú)
E Brazil (Rio Tapajós in e Pará to n Maranhão)
NE Brazil (Pernambuco and Alagoas)

☐ **White-shouldered Fire-eye** *Pyriglena leucoptera*

SE Brazil (Bahia) to ne Argentina and e Paraguay

☐ **Fringe-backed Fire-eye** *Pyriglena atra*

Lowlands of coastal e Brazil (central Bahia)

☐ **Slender Antbird** *Rhopornis ardesiaca*

Highlands of e Brazil (se Bahia)

☐ **White-browed Antbird** *Myrmoborus leucophrys*
_____ M. l. erythrophrys
_____ M. l. leucophrys
_____ M. l. griseigula
_____ M. l. angustirostris
_____ M. l. koenigorum

E slope of Eastern Andes of Colombia
W Venezuela to e Peru, n Bolivia and w Brazil
Brazil s of the Amazon to n Bolivia and w Brazil (w Mato Grosso)
S Venezuela to the Guianas and Brazil north of the Amazon
Central Peru (upper Río Huallaga Valley in Huánuco)

☐ **Ash-breasted Antbird** *Myrmoborus lugubris*
_____ M. l. berlepschi
_____ M. l. stictopterus
_____ M. l. femininus
_____ M. l. lugubris

NE Peru to ne Ecuador and Amazonian Brazil s of Rio Solimões
Amazonian Brazil (north of Rio Solimões)
Brazil south of the Amazon (along lower Rio Madeira)
Central Brazil (along both banks of the Amazon)

☐ **Black-faced Antbird** *Myrmoborus myotherinus*
_____ M. m. elegans
_____ M. m. napensis
_____ M. m. myotherinus
_____ M. m. incanus
_____ M. m. ardesiacus
_____ M. m. proximus
_____ M. m. ochrolaema
_____ M. m. sororius

E slope of Andes of Colombia to s Venezuela and nw Brazil
E Ecuador and ne Peru (north of the Amazon)
Peru south of the Amazon to ne Bolivia and sw Brazil
W-central Brazil (along north bank of Rio Solimões)
W Brazil (Rio Solimões to Rio Negro)
W Brazil (south of Rio Solimões to lower Rio Madeira)
Brazil south of the Amazon (Rio Madeira to Belém)
Central Brazil (upper Rio Madeira to Mato Grosso)

☐ **Black-tailed Antbird** *Myrmoborus melanurus*

Tropical ne Peru (Río Ucayali drainage of Loreto and n Ucayali)

☐ **Warbling Antbird** *Hypocnemis cantator*

_____	*H. c. flavescens*	Tropical e Colombia to s Venezuela and nw Brazil
_____	*H. c. notaea*	Gran Sabana of se Venezuela, Guyana and extreme n Brazil
_____	*H. c. cantator*	Suriname to French Guiana and Brazil north of the Amazon
_____	*H. c. saturata*	Tropical se Colombia to e Ecuador and ne Peru (Loreto)
_____	*H. c. peruviana*	Trop. e Peru south of the Amazon and w Amazonian Brazil
_____	*H. c. subflava*	Tropical e Peru (Junín and Ayacucho)
_____	*H. c. collinsi*	Tropical se Peru (Puno) and n Bolivia
_____	*H. c. implicata*	Brazil south of Rio Solimões (Rio Purús to Parintins)
_____	*H. c. striata*	Brazil south of the Amazon (Rio Tapajós to Rio Xingú)
_____	*H. c. affinis*	Brazil south of the Amazon (Rio Xingú to Rio Tocantins)
_____	*H. c. ochrogyna*	NE Bolivia (Beni) and sw Brazil (nw Mato Grosso)

☐ **Yellow-browed Antbird** *Hypocnemis hypoxantha*

_____	*H. h. hypoxantha*	SE Colombia to e Ecuador and ne Peru (north of Río Marañón)
_____	*H. h. ochraceiventris*	S Venezuela to the Guianas and Amazonian Brazil

☐ **Black-chinned Antbird** *Hypocnemoides melanopogon*

_____	*H. m. occidentalis*	E and s Colombia to Venezuela and nw Brazil
_____	*H. m. melanopogon*	The Guianas and n Amazonian Brazil
_____	*H. m. minor*	Brazil south of Rio Solimões (Rio Purús to Rio Madeira)

☐ **Band-tailed Antbird** *Hypocnemoides maculicauda*

_____	*H. m. maculicauda*	E Peru to n Bolivia and w Amazonian Brazil south of the Amazon
_____	*H. m. orientalis*	Brazil south of the Amazon east to Maranhão and n Mato Grosso

☐ **Black-and-white Antbird** *Myrmochanes hemileucus*

	Amazon river islands (se Colombia to n Bolivia and w Brazil)

☐ **Bare-crowned Antbird** *Gymnocichla nudiceps*

_____	*G. n. chiroleuca*	Caribbean slope of e Guatemala and Belize to se Costa Rica
_____	*G. n. erratilis*	SW Costa Rica and w Panama (Chiriquí and Veraguas)
_____	*G. n. nudiceps*	E Panama and nw Colombia (Río Atrato)
_____	*G. n. sanctamartae*	N Colombia (Santa Marta region and Magdalena Valley)

☐ **Silvered Antbird** *Sclateria naevia*

_____	*S. n. naevia*	NE Venezuela to the Guianas and n Brazil; Trinidad
_____	*S. n. diaphora*	Venezuela (valleys of the Río Caura and Río Mocho)
_____	*S. n. argentata*	E Colombia to n Bolivia, s Venezuela and w Amazonian Brazil
_____	*S. n. toddi*	Brazil south of the Amazon (Serra de Parintins to Rio Xingú)

☐ **Black-headed Antbird** *Percnostola rufifrons*

_____	*P. r. rufifrons*	Guianas and Brazil (north bank of Amazon east of Rio Tocantins)
_____	*P. r. subcristata*	Brazil north of the Amazon (lower Rio Negro to Oriximiná)
_____	*P. r. minor*	E Colombia to s Venezuela, e Peru and nw Amazonian Brazil
_____	*P. r. jensoni*	E Peru (north bank of Amazon east of confluence with Río Napo)

☐ **Slate-colored Antbird** *Percnostola schistacea*

	SE Colombia to e Ecuador, e Peru and w Amazonian Brazil

☐ **Spot-winged Antbird** *Percnostola leucostigma*

_____	*P. l. subplumbea*	E Colombia to e Ecuador and ne Peru (south to Río Ucayali)
_____	*P. l. obscura*	Lower subtropical Gran Sabana of s Venezuela
_____	*P. l. saturata*	SE Venezuela (Mt. Roraima)
_____	*P. l. leucostigma*	S Venezuela to the Guianas and n Amazonian Brazil
_____	*P. l. infuscata*	S Venezuela (upper Río Orinoco) to w Brazil north of Rio Solimões
_____	*P. l. intensa*	Subtropical Peru (Huánuco and Junín)
_____	*P. l. brunneiceps*	SE Peru (Cuzco and Puno) and adjacent n Bolivia
_____	*P. l. humaythae*	Brazil south of Rio Solimões (Rio Juruá to Rio Madeira)
_____	*P. l. rufifacies*	Brazil south of the Amazon (Rio Madeira to Rio Tocantins)

☐ **Caura Antbird** *Percnostola caurensis*
_____   *P. c. caurensis*   S Venezuela (w Bolívar and Amazonas)
_____   *P. c. australis*   Extreme s Venezuela and adjacent n Brazil (nw Amazonas)

☐ **White-lined Antbird** *Percnostola lophotes*

     SE Peru (Ucayali to Puno) and nw Bolivia

☐ **Stub-tailed Antbird** *Myrmeciza berlepschi*

     Tropical w Colombia and nw Ecuador (Esmeraldas)

☐ **White-bellied Antbird** *Myrmeciza longipes*
_____   *M. l. panamensis*   Arid tropical e Panama and n Colombia
_____   *M. l. longipes*   E Colombia and n Venezuela; Trinidad
_____   *M. l. boucardi*   Colombia (upper Magdalena Valley)
_____   *M. l. griseipectus*   SE Colombia to s Venezuela, the Guianas and lower Amaz. Brazil

☐ **Chestnut-backed Antbird** *Myrmeciza exsul*
_____   *M. e. exsul*   Caribbean lowlands of Honduras to e Panama
_____   *M. e. maculifer*   E Panama (Darién) to w Colombia and w Ecuador (south to El Oro)

☐ **Ferruginous-backed Antbird** *Myrmeciza ferruginea*
_____   *M. f. ferruginea*   Extreme e Venezuela to the Guianas and ne Amazonian Brazil
_____   *M. f. eluta*   Brazil south of the Amazon (Rio Tapajós to Rio Madeira)

☐ **Scalloped Antbird** *Myrmeciza ruficauda*
_____   *M. r. soror*   NE Brazil (Pernambuco)
_____   *M. r. ruficauda*   E Brazil (Paraíba to Espírito Santo)

☐ **White-bibbed Antbird** *Myrmeciza loricata*

     SE Brazil (Bahia to Rio de Janeiro and São Paulo)

☐ **Squamate Antbird** *Myrmeciza squamosa*

     SE Brazil (Rio de Janeiro to n Rio Grande do Sul)

☐ **Dull-mantled Antbird** *Myrmeciza laemosticta*
_____   *M. l. laemosticta*   Caribbean slope of Costa Rica and w Panama
_____   *M. l. palliata*   E Panama (Darién) and nw Colombia
_____   *M. l. bolivari*   Colombia (near Quimarí in sw Bolívar)
_____   *M. l. venezuelae*   NW Venezuela (east to Mérida and Táchira)

☐ **Esmeraldas Antbird** *Myrmeciza nigricauda*

     Lowlands of w Colombia and w Ecuador (south to El Oro)

☐ **Yapacana Antbird** *Myrmeciza disjuncta*

     Tropical forests of sw Venezuela and extreme e Colombia

☐ **Gray-bellied Antbird** *Myrmeciza pelzelni*

     Extreme e Colombia to sw Venezuela and extreme nw Brazil

☐ **Chestnut-tailed Antbird** *Myrmeciza hemimelaena*
_____   *M. h. hemimelaena*   Tropical se Colombia to n Bolivia and w Amazonian Brazil
_____   *M. h. pallens*   S Amazonian Brazil (Rio Madeira to Rio Xingú and n Mato Grosso)

☐ **Plumbeous Antbird** *Myrmeciza hyperythra*

     SE Colombia to n Bolivia and w Amazonian Brazil

☐ **White-shouldered Antbird** *Myrmeciza melanoceps*

     SE Colombia to ne Peru and w Amazonian Brazil

☐ **Goeldi's Antbird** *Myrmeciza goeldii*

     SE Peru to extreme nw Bolivia and extreme sw Amazonian Brazil

☐ **Sooty Antbird** *Myrmeciza fortis*
_____   *M. f. fortis*   SE Colombia to extreme nw Bolivia and w Amazonian Brazil
_____   *M. f. incanescens*   Brazil (known only from the type locality on Rio Solimões)

☐ **Immaculate Antbird** *Myrmeciza immaculata*
_____   *M. i. zeledoni*   Caribbean slope of Costa Rica and w Panama
_____   *M. i. immaculata*   Central and E Andes of Colombia to w Ecuador and w Venezuela
_____   *M. i. brunnea*   Mountains of nw Venezuela

☐ **Gray-headed Antbird** *Myrmeciza griseiceps*

Andes of sw Ecuador and nw Peru

☐ **Black-throated Antbird** *Myrmeciza atrothorax*
_____ *M. a. metae* — Tropical Eastern Andes of Colombia
_____ *M. a. atrothorax* — S Venezuela to the Guianas and n Amazonian Brazil
_____ *M. a. stictothorax* — E Amazonian Brazil (lower Rio Tapajós)
_____ *M. a. tenebrosa* — NE Peru n of the Amazon and w Brazil north of Rio Solimões
_____ *M. a. maynana* — N Peru (south of Río Marañón and west of Río Huallaga)
_____ *M. a. obscurata* — Peru south of the Amazon and w Brazil (upper Rio Juruá)
_____ *M. a. griseiventris* — Bolivia (Beni, La Paz and Cochabamba)
_____ *M. a. melanura* — E Bolivia (Santa Cruz) and sw Brazil (Mato Grosso)

☐ **White-plumed Antbird** *Pithys albifrons*
_____ *P. a. brevibarba* — E Colombia to ne Peru (Loreto) and w Amazonian Brazil
_____ *P. a. albifrons* — S Venezuela to the Guianas and n Amazonian Brazil
_____ *P. a. peruviana* — E Peru south to Cordillera Vilcabamba (Cuzco)

☐ **White-masked Antbird** *Pithys castanea*

Known from a 1937 specimen from n Peru (nw Loreto)

☐ **Rufous-throated Antbird** *Gymnopithys rufigula*
_____ *G. r. pallida* — S Venezuela (Orinoco Valley)
_____ *G. r. pallidigula* — *Tepuis* of s Venezuela (Bolívar and Amazonas)
_____ *G. r. rufigula* — E Venezuela to the Guianas and n Amazonian Brazil

☐ **Bicolored Antbird** *Gymnopithys leucaspis*
_____ *G. l. olivascens* — Tropical Honduras to w Panama
_____ *G. l. bicolor* — E Panama and nw Colombia (east to Sinú Valley)
_____ *G. l. daguae* — Tropical w Colombia (upper Río Atrato to Río San Juan)
_____ *G. l. aequatorialis* — Tropical sw Colombia (Nariño) and w Ecuador
_____ *G. l. ruficeps* — Tropical central Colombia (Antioquia)
_____ *G. l. leucaspis* — Tropical e Colombia
_____ *G. l. castanea* — Tropical e Ecuador and ne Peru (Loreto)
_____ *G. l. peruana* — N Peru (Marañón Valley)
_____ *G. l. lateralis* — NW Amazonian Brazil

☐ **Lunulated Antbird** *Gymnopithys lunulata*

Locally in tropical e Ecuador and ne Peru

☐ **White-throated Antbird** *Gymnopithys salvini*
_____ *G. s. maculata* — E Peru (south of the Amazon) and w Amazonian Brazil
_____ *G. s. salvini* — N Bolivia (south to La Paz and Cochabamba) and adjacent Brazil

☐ **Wing-banded Antbird** *Myrmornis torquata*
_____ *M. t. stictoptera* — Caribbean lowlands of e Nicaragua to nw Colombia
_____ *M. t. torquata* — E Colombia to the Guianas, ne Peru and Amazonian Brazil

☐ **Hairy-crested Antbird** *Rhegmatorhina melanosticta*
_____ *R. m. melanosticta* — Extreme se Colombia (Putumayo) and e Ecuador
_____ *R. m. brunneiceps* — N Peru (San Martín)
_____ *R. m. purusiana* — E Peru and w Amazonian Brazil (east to Rio Madeira)
_____ *R. m. badia* — SE Peru (Puno), n Bolivia (La Paz and Beni) and adjacent Brazil

☐ **Chestnut-crested Antbird** *Rhegmatorhina cristata*

SE Colombia and extreme nw Brazil (upper Rio Uaupés)

☐ **White-breasted Antbird** *Rhegmatorhina hoffmannsi*

Central Amazonian Brazil to w Mato Grosso

☐ **Harlequin Antbird** *Rhegmatorhina berlepschi*

E Amazonian Brazil (near west bank of lower Rio Tapajós)

☐ **Bare-eyed Antbird** *Rhegmatorhina gymnops*

E Amazonian Brazil (Rio Tapajós to Rio Xingú and Mato Grosso)

☐ **Spotted Antbird** *Hylophylax naevioides*
____ *H. n. capnitis* — E Honduras to w Panama
____ *H. n. naevioides* — E Panama to w Ecuador (south to e Guayas)
____ *H. n. subsimilis* — Pacific lowlands of w Colombia

☐ **Spot-backed Antbird** *Hylophylax naevia*
____ *H. n. theresae* — SE Colombia to n Bolivia and w Amazonian Brazil
____ *H. n. consobrina* — S Venezuela to the Guianas and nw Amazonian Brazil
____ *H. n. naevia* — *Tepuis* of s Venezuela (Bolívar) and the Guianas
____ *H. n. peruviana* — N Peru (San Martín and Huánuco)
____ *H. n. obscura* — N Brazil (north bank of Rio Solimões)
____ *H. n. ochracea* — N Brazil south of the Amazon (Rio Tapajós to Rio Tocantins)

☐ **Dot-backed Antbird** *Hylophylax punctulata*
____ *H. p. punctulata* — S Venezuela to e Ecuador, n Bolivia and Amazonian Brazil
____ *H. p. subochracea* — Brazil south of the Amazon (Rio Madeira to Rio Xingú)

☐ **Scale-backed Antbird** *Hylophylax poecilinota*
____ *H. p. poecilinota* — S Venezuela to the Guianas and Brazil north of the Amazon
____ *H. p. duidae* — E Colombia to s Venezuela and nw Amazonian Brazil
____ *H. p. lepidonota* — SE Colombia to e Ecuador and e Peru (south to Ayacucho)
____ *H. p. griseiventris* — SE Peru (Madre de Dios) to n Bolivia and w Brazil (Mato Grosso)
____ *H. p. gutturalis* — W Brazil (south of Rio Solimões and on upper Rio Juruá)
____ *H. p. nigrigula* — Brazil south of the Amazon (Rio Parintins to Rio Tapajós)
____ *H. p. vidua* — Brazil south of the Amazon (Rio Xingú to n Maranhão)

☐ **Black-spotted Bare-eye** *Phlegopsis nigromaculata*
____ *P. n. nigromaculata* — SE Colombia to n Bolivia and sw Brazil (Mato Grosso)
____ *P. n. bowmani* — N Brazil south of the Amazon (Rio Madeira to Rio Xingú)
____ *P. n. confinis* — N Brazil south of the Amazon (Rio Xingú to Rio Tocantins)
____ *P. n. paraensis* — N Brazil south of the Amazon (Rio Tocantins to n Maranhão)

☐ **Reddish-winged Bare-eye** *Phlegopsis erythroptera*
____ *P. e. erythroptera* — SE Colombia to extreme nw Bolivia, s Venezuela and nw Brazil
____ *P. e. ustulata* — E Peru and w Amazonian Brazil (south of Rio Solimões)

☐ **Pale-faced Antbird** *Skutchia borbae*
____ Central Amazonian Brazil (Rio Tapajós to Rio Madeira)

☐ **Ocellated Antbird** *Phaenostictus mcleannani*
____ *P. m. saturatus* — Tropical e Honduras to extreme w Panama
____ *P. m. mcleannani* — Panama (Veraguas to Canal Zone)
____ *P. m. chocoanus* — Tropical e Panama and nw Colombia
____ *P. m. pacificus* — SW Colombia (Nariño) to nw Ecuador (Esmeraldas)

FAMILY: FORMICARIIDAE (Antthrushes and Antpittas—62)

☐ **Rufous-capped Antthrush** *Formicarius colma*
____ *F. c. colma* — E Colombia to s Venezuela, the Guianas and n Brazil
____ *F. c. nigrifrons* — E Ecuador to e Peru , n Bolivia and w Amazonian Brazil
____ *F. c. amazonicus* — Brazil south of the Amazon (Rio Madeira to nw Maranhão)
____ *F. c. ruficeps* — Coastal e Brazil (Pernambuco to Rio Grande do Sul)

☐ **Black-headed Antthrush** *Formicarius nigricapillus*
____ *F. n. nigricapillus* — Caribbean slope of e Costa Rica and w Panama
____ *F. n. destructus* — Tropical Pacific Colombia and w Ecuador

☐ **Black-faced Antthrush** *Formicarius analis*

____	*F. a. monileger*	Caribbean slope of s Mexico and e Guatemala
____	*F. a. pallidus*	SE Mexico (Yucatán Peninsula) and Petén of Guatemala
____	*F. a. intermedius*	Belize and Honduras
____	*F. a. umbrosus*	Lowlands of e Nicaragua to w Panama
____	*F. a. hoffmanni*	Lowlands of sw Costa Rica to sw Panama (Chiriquí)
____	*F. a. panamensis*	E Panama (Choclé and Darién) and adjacent nw Colombia
____	*F. a. virescens*	Tropical w base of Santa Marta Mountains (ne Colombia)
____	*F. a. saturatus*	N Colombia to nw Venezuela; Trinidad
____	*F. a. griseoventris*	Sierra de Perijá (Colombia/Venezuela border)
____	*F. a. connectens*	E Colombia (Meta and Vaupes southward)
____	*F. a. zamorae*	Tropical e Ecuador to ne Peru and w Brazil (n of Rio Solimões)
____	*F. a. olivaceus*	Tropical n Peru (lower Huallaga and Marañón valleys)
____	*F. a. crissalis*	SE Venezuela (Bolívar) to the Guianas and adjacent n Brazil
____	*F. a. analis*	Amazonian Peru to w Brazil and n and e Bolivia

☐ **Rufous-fronted Antthrush** *Formicarius rufifrons*

SE Peru (Madre de Dios), adjacent Brazil and Bolivia

☐ **Rufous-breasted Antthrush** *Formicarius rufipectus*

____	*F. r. rufipectus*	Caribbean slope of e Costa Rica and w Panama
____	*F. r. carrikeri*	E Panama (Darién) to W and C Andes of Colombia and Ecuador
____	*F. r. lasallei*	Mountains of nw Venezuela (Táchira and Zulia)
____	*F. r. thoracicus*	Subtropical e Ecuador and e Peru (south to Cuzco)

☐ **Striated Antthrush** *Chamaeza nobilis*

____	*C. n. rubida*	SE Colombia to e Ecuador and ne Peru (Loreto)
____	*C. n. nobilis*	E Peru to nw Bolivia and w Amazonian Brazil
____	*C. n. fulvipectus*	Central Amazonian Brazil (Santarém)

☐ **Short-tailed Antthrush** *Chamaeza campanisona*

____	*C. c. colombiana*	E slope of Andes of Colombia (w Meta and Macarena Mountains)
____	*C. c. punctigula*	E Ecuador (Napo and Pastaza) to n Peru (Cajamarca)
____	*C. c. venezuelana*	Mountains of n Venezuela (east to Distrito Federal and Aragua)
____	*C. c. yavii*	*Tepuis* of south-central Venezuela (Cerro Yaví)
____	*C. c. obscura*	Subtropical mountains of e Venezuela (Bolívar)
____	*C. c. fulvescens*	*Tepuis* of se Venezuela (Mt. Roraima) and adjacent Guyana
____	*C. c. olivacea*	Tropical e-central Peru (south to Madre de Dios)
____	*C. c. berlepschi*	SE Peru (Marcapata Valley in Cuzco)
____	*C. c. huachamacarii*	Tropical s Peru (Puno)
____	*C. c. boliviana*	Bolivia (La Paz, Cochabamba and Santa Cruz)
____	*C. c. campanisona*	SE Brazil (Bahia) to ne Argentina and e Paraguay

☐ **Brazilian Antthrush** *Chamaeza ruficauda*

Coastal se Brazil (Minas Gerais to n Rio Grande do Sul)

☐ **Schwartz's Antthrush** *Chamaeza turdina*

____	*C. t. turdina*	W slope of Central Andes of Colombia (in Valle above Palmira)
____	*C. t. chionogaster*	Mountains of n Venezuela (Yaracuy to Miranda)

☐ **Such's Antthrush** *Chamaeza meruloides*

SE Brazil (Minas Gerais to ne Santa Catarina)

☐ **Barred Antthrush** *Chamaeza mollissima*

____	*C. m. mollissima*	Locally in Andes of Colombia and Ecuador
____	*C. m. yungae*	Locally in Andes of Peru (Piura and Cuzco) and w Bolivia

☐ **Black-crowned Antpitta** *Pittasoma michleri*

____	*P. m. zeledoni*	Caribbean slope of Costa Rica and w Panama
____	*P. m. michleri*	E Panama and extreme nw Colombia (Chocó)

☐ **Rufous-crowned Antpitta** *Pittasoma rufopileatum*
_____ *P. r. rosenbergi*   W Andes of Colombia and Baudó Mountains (south to Chocó)
_____ *P. r. harterti*   Lowlands and foothills of Colombia (Cauca and w Nariño)
_____ *P. r. rufopileatum*   Pacific lowlands of nw Ecuador

☐ **Undulated Antpitta** *Grallaria squamigera*
_____ *G. s. squamigera*   Andes of Colombia, Ecuador and w Venezuela
_____ *G. s. canicauda*   Andes of e Peru to w Bolivia (La Paz and Cochabamba)

☐ **Giant Antpitta** *Grallaria gigantea*
_____ *G. g. lehmanni*   E slope of Central Andes of Colombia (Magdalena Valley)
_____ *G. g. hylodroma*   W slope of Andes of Ecuador (Pichincha)
_____ *G. g. gigantea*   E slope of Andes of Ecuador (Napo and Tungurahua)

☐ **Great Antpitta** *Grallaria excelsa*
_____ *G. e. excelsa*   Sierra de Perijá (Colombia/Venezuela border)
_____ *G. e. phelpsi*   Mountains of n Venezuela (Colonia Tovar in Aragua)

☐ **Variegated Antpitta** *Grallaria varia*
_____ *G. v. cinereiceps*   Tropical s Venezuela and nw Brazil (upper Rio Negro)
_____ *G. v. varia*   The Guianas and n Brazil (south to north bank of lower Amazon)
_____ *G. v. distincta*   Brazil on south bank of Amazon (Rio Madeira to Rio Tapajós)
_____ *G. v. intercedens*   E Brazil (Pernambuco and Bahia)
_____ *G. v. imperator*   SE Brazil to e Paraguay and ne Argentina

☐ **Scaled Antpitta** *Grallaria guatimalensis*
_____ *G. g. ochraceiventris*   Highlands of sw Mexico (Jalisco, Guerrero and Morelos)
_____ *G. g. guatimalensis*   Subtropical s Mexico to n Nicaragua
_____ *G. g. princeps*   Subtropical Costa Rica and w Panama
_____ *G. g. chocoensis*   Mountains of e Panama (Darién) and nw Colombia (Chocó)
_____ *G. g. carmelitae*   Santa Marta Mts. (ne Colombia) to nw Venezuela (Mérida)
_____ *G. g. regulus*   Tropical e Ecuador and Peru (south to Cuzco)
_____ *G. g. aripoensis*   Central parts of Northern Range of Trinidad
_____ *G. g. roraimae*   *Tepuis* of s Venezuela and n Brazil (Serra do Curupira)

☐ **Moustached Antpitta** *Grallaria alleni*
                                  Central Andes of Colombia and n Ecuador

☐ **Tachira Antpitta** *Grallaria chthonia*
                                  Andes of sw Venezuela (sw Táchira)

☐ **Plain-backed Antpitta** *Grallaria haplonota*
_____ *G. h. haplonota*   Mountains of n Venezuela (Lara, Carabobo, Aragua and Miranda)
_____ *G. h. pariae*   NE Venezuela (subtropical mountains of Paría Peninsula)
_____ *G. h. parambae*   Tropical nw Ecuador (Imbabura, Pichincha and El Oro)
_____ *G. h. chaplinae*   E slope of Andes of Ecuador (Napo and Morona-Santiago)

☐ **Ochre-striped Antpitta** *Grallaria dignissima*
                                  Extreme se Colombia (w Putumayo) to e Ecuador and ne Peru

☐ **Elusive Antpitta** *Grallaria eludens*
                                  Lowlands of e Peru (Ucayali, Madre de Dios), adj. Brazil (Acre)

☐ **Santa Marta Antpitta** *Grallaria bangsi*
                                  Santa Marta Mountains (ne Colombia)

☐ **Chestnut-crowned Antpitta** *Grallaria ruficapilla*
_____ *G. r. ruficapilla*   Andes of Colombia and n Ecuador
_____ *G. r. perijana*   Sierra de Perijá (Colombia/Venezuela border)
_____ *G. r. avilae*   Coastal cordillera of n Venezuela and Andes of Lara
_____ *G. r. nigrolineata*   Andes of w Venezuela (Táchira, Mérida and Trujillo)
_____ *G. r. connectens*   Subtropical Andes of sw Ecuador
_____ *G. r. albiloris*   S Ecuador (Loja) and nw Peru (south to Lambayeque)
_____ *G. r. interior*   Central Cordillera of n Peru (Amazonas and San Martín)

☐ **Cundinamarca Antpitta** *Grallaria kaestneri*

Cloud forests of Eastern Andes of Colombia (Cundinamarca)

☐ **Watkins' Antpitta** *Grallaria watkinsi*

Lowlands and Andes of sw Ecuador and nw Peru (Tumbes)

☐ **Stripe-headed Antpitta** *Grallaria andicola*

Andes of Peru and extreme w Bolivia (La Paz)

☐ **Bicolored Antpitta** *Grallaria rufocinerea*

Locally in Central and Eastern Andes of Colombia

☐ **Chestnut-naped Antpitta** *Grallaria nuchalis*
_____ *G. n. ruficeps*
_____ *G. n. obsoleta*
_____ *G. n. nuchalis*

Colombia (Central Andes and w slope of Eastern Andes)
W slope of Andes of nw Ecuador (Imbabura and Pichincha)
E slope of Andes of Ecuador and extreme n Peru (Piura)

☐ **Jocotoco Antpitta** *Grallaria ridgelyi*

Andes of s Ecuador (upper Río Chinchipe drainage)

☐ **Pale-billed Antpitta** *Grallaria carrikeri*

E slope of Andes of n Peru (Amazonas and La Libertad)

☐ **Yellow-breasted Antpitta** *Grallaria flavotincta*

W slope of Western Andes of Colombia and nw Ecuador

☐ **White-bellied Antpitta** *Grallaria hypoleuca*
_____ *G. h. hypoleuca*
_____ *G. h. castanea*

W slope of Eastern Andes of Colombia
Central Andes of Colombia to extreme n Peru (Piura)

☐ **Rusty-tinged Antpitta** *Grallaria przewalskii*

E slope of Andes of n Peru (Amazonas to e La Libertad)

☐ **Bay Antpitta** *Grallaria capitalis*

E slope of Andes of Peru (Junín, Pasco and Huánuco)

☐ **Red-and-white Antpitta** *Grallaria erythroleuca*

E slope of Andes of se Peru (Cuzco)

☐ **White-throated Antpitta** *Grallaria albigula*

Andes of s Peru and w Bolivia to extreme nw Argentina

☐ **Gray-naped Antpitta** *Grallaria griseonucha*
_____ *G. g. tachirae*
_____ *G. g. griseonucha*

Andes of w Venezuela (ne Táchira)
Andes of w Venezuela (e Mérida)

☐ **Rufous Antpitta** *Grallaria rufula*
_____ *G. r. spatiator*
_____ *G. r. saltuensis*
_____ *G. r. rufula*
_____ *G. r. cajamarcae*
_____ *G. r. obscura*
_____ *G. r. occabambae*
_____ *G. r. cochabambae*

Santa Marta Mountains (ne Colombia)
Sierra de Perijá (Colombia/Venezuela border)
Andes of Colombia to w Venezuela (Táchira) and Ecuador
Andes of n Peru (Cajamarca)
Andes of central Peru (Huánuco and Junín)
Andes of se Peru (Cuzco)
Andes of w Bolivia (La Paz and Cochabamba)

☐ **Chestnut Antpitta** *Grallaria blakei*

Andes of central Peru (Amazonas, Huánuco and Pasco)

☐ **Rufous-faced Antpitta** *Grallaria erythrotis*

Andes of w Bolivia (La Paz, Cochabamba and w Santa Cruz)

☐ **Tawny Antpitta** *Grallaria quitensis*
_____ *G. q. quitensis*
_____ *G. q. alticola*
_____ *G. q. atuensis*

Central Andes of Colombia and Andes of Ecuador
E Andes of Colombia (Boyacá and Cundinamarca)
Andes of n Peru (Piura to e La Libertad)

☐ **Brown-banded Antpitta** *Grallaria milleri*

W slope of Central Andes of Colombia (Caldas and Quindío)

☐ **Spotted Antpitta** *Hylopezus macularius*
_____ *H. m. diversus*
_____ *H. m. macularius*
_____ *H. m. paraensis*

Extreme se Colombia to s Venezuela and ne Peru (Loreto)
S Venezuela to the Guianas and adjacent n Brazil
Amazonian Brazil (south to Rondônia and east to e Pará)

☐ **Streak-chested Antpitta** *Hylopezus perspicillatus*
_____ *H. p. intermedius*   Caribbean slope of ne Honduras to w Panama
_____ *H. p. lizanoi*   Pacific slope of sw Costa Rica and w Panama
_____ *H. p. perspicillatus*   E Panama and nw Colombia
_____ *H. p. periophthammicus*   Tropical Pacific coast of Colombia and w Ecuador
_____ *H. p. pallidior*   Colombia (lower Cauca, upper Sinú and Magdalena valleys)

☐ **Masked Antpitta** *Hylopezus auricularis*

N Bolivia (Riberalta area of Beni)

☐ **Fulvous-bellied Antpitta** *Hylopezus dives*
_____ *H. d. dives*   Caribbean slope of ne Honduras to Costa Rica
_____ *H. d. flammulatus*   Caribbean slope of w Panama
_____ *H. d. barbacoae*   Lowlands of e Panama and w Colombia; adjacent nw Ecuador?

☐ **White-lored Antpitta** *Hylopezus fulviventris*
_____ *H. f. caquetae*   Amazon lowlands of extreme se Colombia (north to w Caquetá)
_____ *H. f. fulviventris*   Tropical e Ecuador (Napo and Pastaza) and extreme n Peru

☐ **Amazonian Antpitta** *Hylopezus berlepschi*
_____ *H. b. yessupi*   SE Peru (north to Junín)
_____ *H. p. berlepschi*   N Bolivia and Amazonian Brazil south of the Amazon

☐ **White-browed Antpitta** *Hylopezus ochroleucus*

Interior ne Brazil (Piauí and Ceará to s Bahia)

☐ **Speckle-breasted Antpitta** *Hylopezus nattereri*

SE Brazil (Rio de Janeiro) to ne Argentina and e Paraguay

☐ **Thrush-like Antpitta** *Myrmothera campanisona*
_____ *M. c. modesta*   Tropical Eastern Andes of se Colombia
_____ *M. c. dissors*   E Colombia to s Venezuela and nw Amazonian Brazil
_____ *M. c. campanisona*   SE Venezuela to the Guianas and adjacent n Brazil
_____ *M. c. signata*   Tropical e Ecuador and ne Peru (Loreto)
_____ *M. c. minor*   Tropical e Peru to extreme n Bolivia and w Amazonian Brazil
_____ *M. c. subcanescens*   N Brazil south of the Amazon (Rio Madeira to Rio Tapajós)

☐ **Tepui Antpitta** *Myrmothera simplex*
_____ *M. s. guaiquinimae*   *Tepuis* of se Venezuela (Bolívar)
_____ *M. s. duidae*   *Tepuis* of s Venezuela (Amazonas)
_____ *M. s. simplex*   *Tepuis* of se Venezuela (Gran Sabana) and extreme n Brazil

☐ **Ochre-breasted Antpitta** *Grallaricula flavirostris*
_____ *G. f. costaricensis*   Mountains of Costa Rica and w Panama (east to Veraguas)
_____ *G. f. brevis*   E Panama (upper slopes of Mt. Pirre)
_____ *G. f. ochraceiventris*   Locally in Western Andes of Colombia
_____ *G. f. flavirostris*   Subtropical Eastern Andes of Colombia and e Ecuador
_____ *G. f. mindoensis*   Subtropical n Ecuador (Pichincha)
_____ *G. f. zarumae*   Subtropical sw Ecuador (El Oro)
_____ *G. f. similis*   Subtropical Andes of e Peru
_____ *G. f. boliviana*   Andes of n Bolivia (La Paz and Cochabamba)

☐ **Rusty-breasted Antpitta** *Grallaricula ferrugineipectus*
_____ *G. f. rara*   E Andes of Colombia and nw Venezuela (Sierra de Perijá)
_____ *G. f. ferrugineipectus*   Santa Marta Mts. (ne Colombia) and mountains of n Venezuela
_____ *G. f. leymebambae*   Andes of Peru and w Bolivia (La Paz)

☐ **Scallop-breasted Antpitta** *Grallaricula loricata*

Coastal mountains of n Venezuela (Yaracuy to Distrito Federal)

☐ **Hooded Antpitta** *Grallaricula cucullata*
_____ *G. c. cucullata*   Central and Western Andes of Colombia

☐ **Peruvian Antpitta** *Grallaricula peruviana*

E slope of Andes of se Ecuador and extreme n Peru

☐ **Ochre-fronted Antpitta** *Grallaricula ochraceifrons*

Andes of n Peru (San Martín and Amazonas)

☐ **Slate-crowned Antpitta** *Grallaricula nana*

_____ *G. n. occidentalis*	Western and Central Andes of Colombia
_____ *G. n. nana*	E Andes of Colombia, Ecuador, n Peru and w Venezuela
_____ *G. n. olivascens*	Coastal mountains of n Venezuela (Aragua and Distrito Federal)
_____ *G. n. cumanensis*	Coastal mts. of n Venezuela (Anzoátegui, Sucre and Monagas)
_____ *G. n. pariae*	NE Venezuela (subtropical mountains of Paría Peninsula)
_____ *G. n. kukenamensis*	*Tepuis* of se Venezuela (e Bolívar) and (?) adjacent Guyana

☐ **Crescent-faced Antpitta** *Grallaricula lineifrons*

Locally in Andes of s Colombia and Ecuador

FAMILY: CONOPOPHAGIDAE (Gnateaters—8)

☐ **Rufous Gnateater** *Conopophaga lineata*

_____ *C. l. lineata*	E Brazil (Pernambuco, s Bahia, Goiás and e Mato Grosso)
_____ *C. l. cearae*	E Brazil (Ceará, n Pernambuco and Bahia)
_____ *C. l. vulgaris*	SE Brazil to e Paraguay and ne Argentina

☐ **Chestnut-belted Gnateater** *Conopophaga aurita*

_____ *C. a. inexpectata*	SE Colombia and adjacent nw Brazil
_____ *C. a. aurita*	The Guianas and Brazil north of the Amazon
_____ *C. a. occidentalis*	Tropical e Ecuador and ne Peru (Loreto)
_____ *C. a. australis*	E Peru south of the Amazon and w Amazonian Brazil
_____ *C. a. snethlageae*	Central Brazil south of the Amazon
_____ *C. a. pallida*	Brazil on left bank of Rio Tocantins

☐ **Hooded Gnateater** *Conopophaga roberti*

NE Brazil (Pará to Ceará and s Piauí)

☐ **Ash-throated Gnateater** *Conopophaga peruviana*

E Ecuador to e Peru, nw Bolivia and w Amazonian Brazil

☐ **Slaty Gnateater** *Conopophaga ardesiaca*

_____ *C. a. saturata*	E slope of Andes of s Peru (north to Cuzco)
_____ *C. a. ardesiaca*	Andes of Bolivia (south to s Tarija)

☐ **Chestnut-crowned Gnateater** *Conopophaga castaneiceps*

_____ *C. c. chocoensis*	Colombia (Western and Central Andes and Baudó Mountains)
_____ *C. c. castaneiceps*	Subtropical Central and E Andes of Colombia and ne Ecuador
_____ *C. c. chapmani*	SE Ecuador (Zamora) and ne Peru (Cajamarca and San Martín)
_____ *C. c. brunneinucha*	Andes of central Peru (Huánuco, Junín and Cuzco)

☐ **Black-cheeked Gnateater** *Conopophaga melanops*

_____ *C. m. perspicillata*	E Brazil (Paraíba, Pernambuco and Bahia)
_____ *C. m. melanops*	SE Brazil (Espírito Santo to e Santa Catarina)

☐ **Black-bellied Gnateater** *Conopophaga melanogaster*

N Bolivia (Beni) and Amazonian Brazil south of the Amazon

FAMILY: RHINOCRYPTIDAE (Tapaculos—56)

☐ **Black-throated Huet-huet** *Pteroptochos tarnii*

S Chile and adjacent sw Argentina

□ **Chestnut-throated Huet-huet** *Pteroptochos castaneus*

S-central Chile (Colchagua to Ñuble and Concepción)

□ **Moustached Turca** *Pteroptochos megapodius*
____ *P. m. atacamae*   Arid n Chile (Atacama)
____ *P. m. megapodius*   Central Chile (Coquimbo to Concepción)

□ **White-throated Tapaculo** *Scelorchilus albicollis*
____ *S. a. atacamae*   Semiarid n Chile (Atacama to n Coquimbo)
____ *S. a. albicollis*   Central Chile (s Coquimbo to Curicó)

□ **Chucao Tapaculo** *Scelorchilus rubecula*
____ *S. r. rubecula*   S Chile (Colchagua to Aysén) and adjacent w Argentina
____ *S. r. mochae*   Mocha I. (off Chile)

□ **Crested Gallito** *Rhinocrypta lanceolata*
____ *R. l. lanceolata*   *Chaco* of extreme s Bolivia to central Argentina
____ *R. l. saturata*   W Paraguay (Puerto Casado region)

□ **Sandy Gallito** *Teledromas fuscus*

Semiarid w Argentina (w Salta to Neuquén and Río Negro)

□ **Rusty-belted Tapaculo** *Liosceles thoracicus*
____ *L. t. dugandi*   Tropical se Colombia to w Brazil (Rio Tocantins)
____ *L. t. erithacus*   Tropical e Ecuador and e Peru (south to Río Urubamba)
____ *L. t. thoracicus*   SE Peru and w Amazonian Brazil

□ **Collared Crescent-chest** *Melanopareia torquata*
____ *M. t. torquata*   *Cerrado* of interior e Brazil
____ *M. t. rufescens*   *Cerrado* of central Brazil, e Bolivia and extreme ne Paraguay

□ **Olive-crowned Crescent-chest** *Melanopareia maximiliani*
____ *M. m. maximiliani*   W Bolivia (*yungas* of La Paz)
____ *M. m. argentina*   *Chaco* of w Bolivia, w Paraguay and n Argentina

□ **Elegant Crescent-chest** *Melanopareia elegans*
____ *M. e. elegans*   Arid sw Ecuador (north to Manabí and extreme s Pichincha)
____ *M. e. paucalensis*   Arid e Peru (La Libertad, Piura and Cajamarca)

□ **Maranon Crescent-chest** *Melanopareia maranonica*

Extreme s Ecuador and n-central Peru (Río Marañón Valley)

□ **Spotted Bamboowren** *Psilorhamphus guttatus*

SE Brazil (Minas Gerais) to ne Argentina and (?) adj. Paraguay

□ **Slaty Bristlefront** *Merulaxis ater*

SE Brazil (s Bahia and Espírito Santo to e Paraná)

□ **Stresemann's Bristlefront** *Merulaxis stresemanni*

Coastal e Brazil (known from two specimens from Bahia)

□ **Ochre-flanked Tapaculo** *Eugralla paradoxa*

S-central Chile (Maule to Chiloé) and adjacent Argentina

□ **Ash-colored Tapaculo** *Myornis senilis*

Andes of Colombia, Ecuador and n Peru (Carpish Mountains)

□ **Unicolored Tapaculo** *Scytalopus unicolor*

Andes of n Peru (Cajamarca and La Libertad)

□ **Blackish Tapaculo** *Scytalopus latrans*
____ *S. l. latrans*   Andes of Colombia to w Venezuela, e Ecuador and n Peru
____ *S. l. subcinereus*   Andes of sw Ecuador and Peru (south to Lambayeque)
____ *S. l. intermedius*   Andes of n Peru (Utcubamba drainage of Amazonas)

□ **Trilling Tapaculo** *Scytalopus parvirostris*

Andes of Peru and Bolivia

☐ **Large-footed Tapaculo** *Scytalopus macropus*

E slope of Andes of e Peru (Amazonas to Junín)

☐ **Rufous-vented Tapaculo** *Scytalopus femoralis*

E slope of Andes of e Peru (Amazonas to Junín)

☐ **Long-tailed Tapaculo** *Scytalopus micropterus*

Andes of Colombia to Ecuador and n Peru

☐ **Bolivian Tapaculo** *Scytalopus bolivianus*

Andes of s Peru and w Bolivia

☐ **White-crowned Tapaculo** *Scytalopus atratus*
____ *S. a. atratus*
____ *S. a. confusus*

E slope of Andes of Colombia (w Casanare)
E Andes of Colombia and e Ecuador to s Peru (Cuzco)

☐ **Perija Tapaculo** *Scytalopus nigricans*

Sierra de Perijá (Colombia/Venezuela border) and (?) adj. Táchira

☐ **Santa Marta Tapaculo** *Scytalopus sanctaemartae*

Santa Marta Mountains (ne Colombia)

☐ **Pale-throated Tapaculo** *Scytalopus panamensis*

E Panama (Cerro Tacarcuna) and extreme nw Colombia (Chocó)

☐ **Narino Tapaculo** *Scytalopus vicinior*

Andes of sw Colombia and nw Ecuador

☐ **Silvery-fronted Tapaculo** *Scytalopus argentifrons*
____ *S. a. argentifrons*
____ *S. a. chiriquensis*

Humid montane forests of Costa Rica and extreme w Panama
Montane forests of w Panama (Chiriquí and Veraguas)

☐ **Brown-rumped Tapaculo** *Scytalopus latebricola*

Santa Marta Mountains (ne Colombia)

☐ **Merida Tapaculo** *Scytalopus meridanus*

Andes of w Venezuela and (?) adjacent e Colombia

☐ **Colombian Tapaculo** *Scytalopus infasciatus*

E slope of Central Andes of Colombia (Cundinamarca)

☐ **Caracas Tapaculo** *Scytalopus caracae*

Coastal mountains of n Venezuela

☐ **Spillman's Tapaculo** *Scytalopus spillmanni*

Andes of s Colombia to central Ecuador

☐ **Zimmer's Tapaculo** *Scytalopus zimmeri*

Andes of s Bolivia

☐ **Puna Tapaculo** *Scytalopus simonsi*

Andes of s Peru and Bolivia

☐ **Vilcabamba Tapaculo** *Scytalopus urubambae*

Eastern Andes of Peru (Cuzco)

☐ **Neblina Tapaculo** *Scytalopus altirostris*

Eastern Andes of Peru (Amazonas to Huánuco)

☐ **Ancash Tapaculo** *Scytalopus affinis*

Western Andes of Peru (Cajamarca and Ancash)

☐ **Paramo Tapaculo** *Scytalopus canus*

Páramo of Andes of n Colombia to n Peru

☐ **Magellanic Tapaculo** *Scytalopus magellanicus*

Andes of central Chile and Argentina to Tierra del Fuego

☐ **Matorral Tapaculo** *Scytalopus griseicollis*

Andes of Colombia and w Venezuela to nw Argentina

☐ **White-browed Tapaculo** *Scytalopus superciliaris*

Andes of nw Argentina

☐ **Dusky Tapaculo** *Scytalopus fuscus*

Andes of central Chile (Atacama to Río Bío-Bío)

☐ **Tschudi's Tapaculo** *Scytalopus acutirostris*

Andes of n and central Peru

☐ **Mouse-colored Tapaculo** *Scytalopus speluncae*

Mountains of se Brazil to ne Argentina and (?) se Paraguay

☐ **Brasilia Tapaculo** *Scytalopus novacapitalis*

Locally in interior southern Brazil

☐ **Bahia Tapaculo** *Scytalopus psychopompus*

Coastal lowlands of e Brazil (se Bahia)

☐ **Wetland Tapaculo** *Scytalopus iraiensis*

SW Brazil (recently discovered in marshes 20 km east of Curitiba)

☐ **White-breasted Tapaculo** *Scytalopus indigoticus*

E Brazil (Minas Gerais to extreme ne Rio Grande do Sul)

☐ **Diademed Tapaculo** *Scytalopus schulenbergi*

E slope of Andes of s Peru and n Bolivia

☐ **Choco Tapaculo** *Scytalopus chocoensis*

E Panama (Cerro Pirre) to nw Ecuador

☐ **Ecuadorian Tapaculo** *Scytalopus robbinsi*

Andes of sw Ecuador (Azuay and El Oro)

☐ **Chusquea Tapaculo** *Scytalopus parkeri*

Andes of s Ecuador to extreme n Peru

☐ **Ocellated Tapaculo** *Acropternis orthonyx*

_____ *A. o. orthonyx* — Andes of e Colombia and nw Venezuela
_____ *A. o. infuscata* — Andes of e Ecuador and extreme n Peru (Piura and Amazonas)

FAMILY: PHYTOTOMIDAE (Plantcutters—3)

☐ **Peruvian Plantcutter** *Phytotoma raimondii*

Coastal nw Peru (Tumbes south to n Lima)

☐ **White-tipped Plantcutter** *Phytotoma rutila*

_____ *P. r. angustirostris* — Highlands of w Bolivia and nw Argentina
_____ *P. r. rutila* — *Chaco* of w Paraguay, w Uruguay, n Argentina and extreme s Brazil

☐ **Rufous-tailed Plantcutter** *Phytotoma rara*

Central and s Chile and Argentina; accidental Falkland Islands

FAMILY: COTINGIDAE (Cotingas—68)

☐ **Black-necked Red-Cotinga** *Phoenicircus nigricollis*

SE Colombia to sw Venezuela, ne Peru and w and c Amaz. Brazil

☐ **Guianan Red-Cotinga** *Phoenicircus carnifex*

Extreme s Venezuela to the Guianas and lower Amazonian Brazil

☐ **Shrike-like Cotinga** *Laniisoma elegans*

_____ *L. e. venezuelensis* — Locally from tropical ne Colombia to nw Venezuela
_____ *L. e. buckleyi* — E slope of Andes of e Ecuador and e Peru
_____ *L. e. elegans* — Tropical se Brazil (Espírito Santo to e Paraná)
_____ *L. e. cadwaladeri* — Tropical nw Bolivia (La Paz)

☐ **Speckled Mourner** *Laniocera rufescens*

_____ *L. r. rufescens* — Gulf lowlands of s Mexico to nw Colombia (Chocó)
_____ *L. r. griseigula* — Tropical n Colombia (Córdoba, Antioquia and Santander)
_____ *L. r. tertia* — Tropical sw Colombia and nw Ecuador (Esmeraldas)

☐ **Cinereous Mourner** *Laniocera hypopyrra*

E Colombia to Venezuela, e Brazil, n Bolivia and Amaz. Brazil

☐ **Swallow-tailed Cotinga** *Phibalura flavirostris*

_____ *P. f. flavirostris* — SE Brazil (Goiás) to e Paraguay and ne Argentina
_____ *P. f. boliviana* — Foothills of w Bolivia (La Paz)

☐ **Black-and-gold Cotinga** *Tijuca atra*

SE Brazil (Rio de Janeiro, s Minas Gerais to extreme e São Paulo)

☐ **Gray-winged Cotinga** *Tijuca condita*

Cloud forests of se Brazil in Rio de Janeiro (Serra dos Órgãos)

☐ **Hooded Berryeater** *Carpornis cucullatus*	
	SE Brazil (Espírito Santo to Rio Grande do Sul)
☐ **Black-headed Berryeater** *Carpornis melanocephalus*	
	Coastal se Brazil (Alagoas and e Bahia to ne Paraná)
☐ **Red-crested Cotinga** *Ampelion rubrocristata*	
	Andes of Colombia to w Venezuela and w Bolivia
☐ **Chestnut-crested Cotinga** *Ampelion rufaxilla*	
_____ *A. r. antioquiae*	Subtropical Andes of w Colombia
_____ *A. r. rufaxilla*	E slope of Andes of Ecuador, Peru and w Bolivia
☐ **Chestnut-bellied Cotinga** *Doliornis remseni*	
	Eastern Andes of Ecuador and extreme n Peru
☐ **Bay-vented Cotinga** *Doliornis sclateri*	
	Andes of Peru (San Martín, La Libertad, Huánuco, Pasco and Junín)
☐ **White-cheeked Cotinga** *Zaratornis stresemanni*	
	Polylepis woodlands of Peru (La Libertad to Ayacucho)
☐ **Green-and-black Fruiteater** *Pipreola riefferii*	
_____ *P. r. occidentalis*	Andes of sw Colombia and w Ecuador
_____ *P. r. riefferii*	Andes of e Colombia to nw Venezuela (Táchira) and e Ecuador
_____ *P. r. melanolaema*	Andes of w Venezuela (north to s Lara)
_____ *P. r. confusa*	Andes of e Ecuador to Andes of Peru (n Amazonas)
_____ *P. r. chachapoyas*	Subtropical Central Andes of n Peru (San Martín)
_____ *P. r. tallmanorum*	Andes of central Peru (Huánuco)
☐ **Band-tailed Fruiteater** *Pipreola intermedia*	
_____ *P. i. intermedia*	Subtropical Andes of Peru (La Libertad to Junín)
_____ *P. i. signata*	Andes of se Peru (Cuzco and Puno) to w Bolivia
☐ **Barred Fruiteater** *Pipreola arcuata*	
_____ *P. a. arcuata*	Andes of Colombia, w Venezuela, Ecuador, n Peru and w Bolivia
_____ *P. a. viridicauda*	Andes of central Peru (Junín) to w Bolivia
☐ **Golden-breasted Fruiteater** *Pipreola aureopectus*	
_____ *P. a. decora*	Santa Marta Mountains (ne Colombia)
_____ *P. a. aureopectus*	Subtropical Andes of e Colombia and w Venezuela
_____ *P. a. festiva*	Coastal mountains of n Venezuela
☐ **Orange-breasted Fruiteater** *Pipreola jucunda*	
	W slope of Western Andes of Colombia and w Ecuador
☐ **Black-chested Fruiteater** *Pipreola lubomirskii*	
	Andes of s Colombia to extreme n Peru (Cajamarca)
☐ **Masked Fruiteater** *Pipreola pulchra*	
	Andes of e Peru (Amazonas to Cordillera Vilcabamba of Cuzco)
☐ **Fiery-throated Fruiteater** *Pipreola chlorolepidota*	
	Andean foothills of se Colombia to Ecuador and c Peru (Pasco)
☐ **Scarlet-breasted Fruiteater** *Pipreola frontalis*	
_____ *P. f. squamipectus*	Andes of se Ecuador (w Napo) and n Peru (San Martín)
_____ *P. f. frontalis*	Andes of se Peru (Huánuco) to w Bolivia
☐ **Handsome Fruiteater** *Pipreola formosa*	
_____ *P. f. formosa*	Coastal cordillera of n Venezuela
_____ *P. f. rubidior*	Mts. of ne Venezuela (Anzoátegui, Monagas and Sucre)
_____ *P. f. pariae*	NE Venezuela (Paría Peninsula)
☐ **Red-banded Fruiteater** *Pipreola whitelyi*	
_____ *P. w. kathleenae*	*Tepuis* of s Venezuela (se Bolívar)
_____ *P. w. whitelyi*	*Tepuis* of w Guyana (Mt. Twek-quay) and adj. n Brazil (Roraima)

☐ **Scaled Fruiteater** *Ampelioides tschudii*

Andes of Colombia and w Venezuela to w Bolivia (La Paz)

☐ **Buff-throated Purpletuft** *Iodopleura pipra*

Locally in humid coastal se Brazil

☐ **White-browed Purpletuft** *Iodopleura isabellae*
　　___ *I. i. isabellae*
　　___ *I. i. paraensis*

SE Colombia to e Ecuador, e Peru, n Bolivia and n Brazil
NE Brazil (Rio Tocantins to Pará and Goiás)

☐ **Dusky Purpletuft** *Iodopleura fusca*

SE Venezuela to the Guianas and extreme n Brazil (Roraima)

☐ **Kinglet Calyptura** *Calyptura cristata*

SE Brazil. Rediscovered in 1998 after a 100-year absence

☐ **Gray-tailed Piha** *Lipaugus subalaris*

E slope of Andes of s Colombia, e Ecuador and e Peru

☐ **Olivaceous Piha** *Lipaugus cryptolophus*
　　___ *L. c. mindoensis*
　　___ *L. c. cryptolophus*

Andes of sw Colombia and w Ecuador
Andes of e Colombia, e Ecuador and e Peru (south to Huánuco)

☐ **Dusky Piha** *Lipaugus fuscocinereus*

Andes of Colombia to Ecuador and extreme n Peru (Piura)

☐ **Scimitar-winged Piha** *Lipaugus uropygialis*

S Peru (Cordillera Apolobamba of Puno) and w Bolivia

☐ **Screaming Piha** *Lipaugus vociferans*

E Colombia to s Venezuela, Guianas, n Bolivia, Amaz. and e Brazil

☐ **Rufous Piha** *Lipaugus unirufus*
　　___ *L. u. unirufus*
　　___ *L. u. castaneotinctus*

Gulf lowlands of s Mexico to n Colombia
Tropical sw Colombia to nw Ecuador

☐ **Cinnamon-vented Piha** *Lipaugus lanioides*

SE Brazil (Espírito Santo and Minas Gerais to ne Santa Catarina)

☐ **Rose-collared Piha** *Lipaugus streptophorus*

Tepuis of s Venezuela, adjacent w Guyana and extreme n Brazil

☐ **Purple-throated Cotinga** *Porphyrolaema porphyrolaema*

Tropical se Colombia to se Peru and w Amazonian Brazil

☐ **Lovely Cotinga** *Cotinga amabilis*

Gulf lowlands of s Mexico (Veracruz) to se Costa Rica

☐ **Turquoise Cotinga** *Cotinga ridgwayi*

Pacific slope of sw Costa Rica to w Panama (w Chiriquí)

☐ **Blue Cotinga** *Cotinga nattererii*

Central Panama to Colombia, nw Ecuador and w Venezuela

☐ **Plum-throated Cotinga** *Cotinga maynana*

Lowlands of se Colombia to n Bolivia and w Amazonian Brazil

☐ **Purple-breasted Cotinga** *Cotinga cotinga*

E Colombia to s Venezuela, Guianas, n and e Amazonian Brazil

☐ **Banded Cotinga** *Cotinga maculata*

SE Brazil (s Bahia and Minas Gerais to Rio de Janeiro)

☐ **Spangled Cotinga** *Cotinga cayana*

S Venezuela and the Guianas to n Bolivia and Amazonian Brazil

☐ **Pompadour Cotinga** *Xipholena punicea*

E Colombia to s Venezuela, Guianas, ne Bolivia and Amaz. Brazil

☐ **White-tailed Cotinga** *Xipholena lamellipennis*

Lower Amazonian Brazil (Rio Tapajós to n Maranhão)

☐ **White-winged Cotinga** *Xipholena atropurpurea*

Coastal e Brazil (Paraíba to n Rio de Janeiro)

☐ **Black-tipped Cotinga** *Carpodectes hopkei*

Humid lowlands of e Panama to w Colombia and nw Ecuador

☐ **Yellow-billed Cotinga** *Carpodectes antoniae*

Pacific lowlands of sw Costa Rica and extreme w Panama

☐ **Snowy Cotinga** *Carpodectes nitidus*

Caribbean slope of n Honduras to extreme w Panama

☐ **Black-faced Cotinga** *Conioptilon mcilhennyi*

Tropical se Peru (s Ucayali and s Madre de Dios)

☐ **Bare-necked Fruitcrow** *Gymnoderus foetidus*

S Venezuela and the Guianas to n Bolivia and Amazonian Brazil

☐ **Crimson Fruitcrow** *Haematoderus militaris*

Extreme s Venezuela to the Guianas and n Amazonian Brazil

☐ **Purple-throated Fruitcrow** *Querula purpurata*

Trop. Costa Rica to n Bolivia, the Guianas and Amazonian Brazil

☐ **Red-ruffed Fruitcrow** *Pyroderus scutatus*
____ P. s. occidentalis   Andes of w Colombia and nw Ecuador
____ P. s. granadensis   E Andes of Colombia and w Venezuela
____ P. s. orenocensis   Upper tropical Venezuela (ne Bolívar) and n Guyana
____ P. s. masoni   Subtropical e Peru (s Amazonas to Junín)
____ P. s. scutatus   Tropical se Brazil to e Paraguay and ne Argentina

☐ **Long-wattled Umbrellabird** *Cephalopterus penduliger*

W Andes of sw Colombia and w Ecuador (south to El Oro)

☐ **Amazonian Umbrellabird** *Cephalopterus ornatus*

S Venezuela to Guyana, n Bolivia and Amazonian Brazil

☐ **Bare-necked Umbrellabird** *Cephalopterus glabricollis*

Humid highlands of Costa Rica and w Panama

☐ **Capuchinbird** *Perissocephalus tricolor*

S Venezuela to the Guianas and ne Amazonian Brazil

☐ **Three-wattled Bellbird** *Procnias tricarunculata*

Humid montane forests of Nicaragua to w Panama

☐ **White Bellbird** *Procnias alba*
____ P. a. alba   SE Venezuela to the Guianas and e Amazonian Brazil
____ P. a. wallacei   NE Brazil (Belém area of e Pará)

☐ **Bearded Bellbird** *Procnias averano*
____ P. a. carnobarba   NE Colombia to n Venezuela, w Guyana and adj. Brazil; Trinidad
____ P. a. averano   NE Brazil (Maranhão and Piauí to Pernambuco and Alagoas)

☐ **Bare-throated Bellbird** *Procnias nudicollis*

SE Brazil (Alagoas) to e Paraguay and ne Argentina (Misiones)

☐ **Guianan Cock-of-the-rock** *Rupicola rupicola*

E Colombia to s Venezuela, the Guianas and n Amazonian Brazil

☐ **Andean Cock-of-the-rock** *Rupicola peruviana*
____ R. p. sanguinolenta   Andes of w Colombia and nw Ecuador
____ R. p. aequatorialis   Andes of e Colombia to w Venezuela, e Ecuador and e Peru
____ R. p. peruviana   Andes of central Peru (San Martín to Junín)
____ R. p. saturata   Andes of se Peru (Cuzco and Puno) and w Bolivia

FAMILY: PIPRIDAE (Manakins—52)

☐ **Jet Manakin** *Chloropipo unicolor*

E slope of Andes from e Ecuador (Napo) to s Peru (Puno)

☐ **Olive Manakin** *Chloropipo uniformis*
____ C. u. duidae   *Tepuis* of s Venezuela (s Bolívar and Amazonas)
____ C. u. uniformis   *Tepuis* of w Guyana and extreme n Brazil (Roraima)

☐ **Green Manakin** *Chloropipo holochlora*
____ C. h. suffusa   Extreme e Panama (Darién) and adjacent nw Colombia
____ C. h. litae   Tropical w Colombia to nw Ecuador (south to Pichincha)
____ C. h. holochlora   Tropical se Colombia, e Ecuador and e Peru (south to Junín)
____ C. h. viridior   Foothills of se Peru (Cuzco and nw Puno)

☐ **Yellow-headed Manakin** *Chloropipo flavicapilla*

Western and Central Andes of Colombia and ne Ecuador

☐ **White-collared Manakin** *Manacus candei*

Gulf lowlands of s Mexico to e Costa Rica

☐ **Orange-collared Manakin** *Manacus aurantiacus*
____ *M. a. aurantiacus*
____ *M. a. viridiventris*

Pacific slope of s Costa Rica and w Panama (east to Azuero Pen.)
W and n Colombia and nw Ecuador

☐ **Golden-collared Manakin** *Manacus vitellinus*
____ *M. v. cerritus*
____ *M. v. vitellinus*

Lowlands of nw Panama (w Bocas del Toro)
Lowlands of Panama and w Colombia (south to sw Cauca)

☐ **White-bearded Manakin** *Manacus manacus*
____ *M. m. milleri*
____ *M. m. abditivus*
____ *M. m. flaveolus*
____ *M. m. bangsi*
____ *M. m. interior*
____ *M. m. trinitatis*
____ *M. m. umbrosus*
____ *M. m. manacus*
____ *M. m. leucochlamys*
____ *M. m. maximus*
____ *M. m. expectatus*
____ *M. m. longibarbatus*
____ *M. m. purissimus*
____ *M. m. gutturosus*
____ *M. m. purus*
____ *M. m. subpurus*

Tropical n Colombia (Sinú, Cauca and Magdalena valleys)
Santa Marta, lower Cauca and middle Magdalena valleys
N Colombia (tropical upper Magdalena Valley)
Tropical sw Colombia and extreme nw Ecuador
Colombia (e of the Andes) to e Ecuador, n Peru and nw Brazil
Trinidad
Tropical s Venezuela (Amazonas)
S Venezuela to the Guianas and n Brazil
Tropical nw Ecuador (Esmeraldas, Manabí and Guayas)
Tropical sw Ecuador (El Oro and w Loja)
Tropical ne Peru (Loreto) and adjacent w Brazil
Lower Amazonian Brazil (Rio Xingú to Rio Tocantins)
E Brazil (Rio Tocantins to se Pará and n Maranhão)
SE Brazil (Alagoas) to e Paraguay and ne Argentina
N Brazil (Rio Madeira to Rio Tapajós and sw Pará)
S-central Brazil (se Amazonas, e Guaporé and nw Mato Grosso)

☐ **White-throated Manakin** *Corapipo gutturalis*

S Venezuela to the Guianas and ne Amazonian Brazil

☐ **White-ruffed Manakin** *Corapipo altera*
____ *C. a. altera*
____ *C. a. heteroleuca*

E Honduras (Olancho) to nw Costa Rica
Tropical sw Costa Rica to nw Colombia (Chocó)

☐ **White-bibbed Manakin** *Corapipo leucorrhoa*

Foothills of w Colombia and nw Venezuela

☐ **Lance-tailed Manakin** *Chiroxiphia lanceolata*

SW Costa Rica to n Colombia, n Venezuela and Isla Margarita

☐ **Long-tailed Manakin** *Chiroxiphia linearis*
____ *C. l. linearis*
____ *C. l. fastuosa*

Pacific lowlands of s Mexico (Oaxaca) and Guatemala
El Salvador to w Nicaragua and nw Costa Rica

☐ **Blue-backed Manakin** *Chiroxiphia pareola*
____ *C. p. atlantica*
____ *C. p. napensis*
____ *C. p. pareola*
____ *C. p. regina*

Tobago
Tropical se Colombia (east of the Andes) to e Ecuador and e Peru
E Venezuela, the Guianas, n and e Amazonian Brazil
Tropical ne Peru (south of the Amazon) and w Amazonian Brazil

☐ **Yungas Manakin** *Chiroxiphia boliviana*

SE Peru (Cuzco, s Madre de Dios and Puno) and w Bolivia

☐ **Blue Manakin** *Chiroxiphia caudata*

Lowlands of se Brazil (s Bahia) to e Paraguay and ne Argentina

☐ **Crimson-hooded Manakin** *Pipra aureola*
____ *P. a. aureola*
____ *P. a. auranticollis*
____ *P. a. flavicollis*
____ *P. a. borbae*

Tropical ne Venezuela to the Guianas and ne Brazil
Brazil on Rio Tapajós in w Pará and adj. n bank of the Amazon
Lower Amazonian Brazil in e Amazonas and w Pará
Brazil along lower and middle Rio Madeira in e Amazonas

☐ **Band-tailed Manakin** *Pipra fasciicauda*

_____	*P. f. calamae*	Brazil (Rio Madeira in n Guaporé and nw Mato Grosso)
_____	*P. f. saturata*	E slope of Central Andes of Peru (San Martín and s Loreto)
_____	*P. f. purusiana*	Tropical e Peru (south to Cuzco) and adjacent w Amazonian Brazil
_____	*P. f. fasciicauda*	Tropical se Peru (Puno) and ne Bolivia
_____	*P. f. scarlatina*	N Bolivia to se Brazil, e Paraguay and ne Argentina

☐ **Wire-tailed Manakin** *Pipra filicauda*

_____	*P. f. subpallida*	Tropical e Colombia and nw Venezuela
_____	*P. f. filicauda*	E Ecuador to ne Peru, s Venezuela and w Amazonian Brazil

☐ **White-crowned Manakin** *Pipra pipra*

_____	*P. p. anthracina*	Caribbean slope of Costa Rica and w Panama
_____	*P. p. bolivari*	NW Colombia (upper Sinú Valley)
_____	*P. p. coracina*	E Andes of Colombia, e Ecuador and n Peru
_____	*P. p. minimus*	W slope of Western Andes of Colombia (Cauca)
_____	*P. p. unica*	Subtropical Colombia (Antioquia and Huila)
_____	*P. p. pipra*	Extreme e Colombia to Venezuela, the Guianas and n Brazil
_____	*P. p. discolor*	Tropical ne Peru (along Río Napo in ne Loreto)
_____	*P. p. occulta*	E slope of Central Andes of Peru (San Martín and Huánuco)
_____	*P. p. pygmaea*	Tropical e Peru (lower Río Huallaga in Loreto)
_____	*P. p. microlopha*	Tropical e Peru (south of Río Marañón) and w Amazonian Brazil
_____	*P. p. comata*	Tropical e Peru (s Pasco, Junín and n Cuzco)
_____	*P. p. separabilis*	Amazonian Brazil (Rio Tapajós to Belém)
_____	*P. p. cephaleucos*	Coastal se Brazil (s Bahia to Rio de Janeiro)

☐ **Blue-crowned Manakin** *Pipra coronata*

_____	*P. c. velutina*	Humid sw Costa Rica to w Panama
_____	*P. c. minuscula*	E Panama to nw Ecuador (south to Pichincha)
_____	*P. c. caquetae*	Tropical se Colombia (east of Andes in w Meta and w Caquetá)
_____	*P. c. carbonata*	SE Colombia to n Peru, s Venezuela and n Amazonian Brazil
_____	*P. c. coronata*	Tropical e Ecuador to ne Peru and w Amazonian Brazil
_____	*P. c. exquisita*	Tropical e Peru (s Loreto to Junín)
_____	*P. c. caelestipileata*	SE Peru (Puno) and adjacent w Amazonian Brazil
_____	*P. c. regalis*	Tropical n Bolivia south to Cochabamba

☐ **Golden-headed Manakin** *Pipra erythrocephala*

_____	*P. e. erythrocephala*	E Panama to the Guianas and Brazil north of the Amazon; Trinidad
_____	*P. e. berlepschi*	Tropical se Colombia to ne Peru and w Amazonian Brazil
_____	*P. e. flammiceps*	E Colombia (Santander)

☐ **Red-capped Manakin** *Pipra mentalis*

_____	*P. m. mentalis*	Gulf lowlands of se Mexico to e Costa Rica; Isla de Mujeres
_____	*P. m. ignifera*	Tropical w Costa Rica and w Panama
_____	*P. m. minor*	Extreme e Panama to w Colombia and nw Ecuador

☐ **Red-headed Manakin** *Pipra rubrocapilla*

Tropical e Peru to n Bolivia, s Amazonian and e Brazil

☐ **Round-tailed Manakin** *Pipra chloromeros*

Lowlands and foothills of e Peru and n Bolivia

☐ **Scarlet-horned Manakin** *Pipra cornuta*

Tepuis of s Venezuela, w Guyana and extreme n Brazil

☐ **Opal-crowned Manakin** *Pipra iris*

_____	*P. i. iris*	E Amazonian Brazil (Belém region of e Pará to n Maranhão)
_____	*P. i. eucephala*	Brazil south of the Amazon (east bank of lower Rio Tapajós)

☐ **Blue-rumped Manakin** *Pipra isidorei*

_____	*P. i. isidorei*	E slope of Andes of Colombia (w Meta) and e Ecuador
_____	*P. i. leucopygia*	Andean foothills of n Peru (San Martín and n Huánuco)

☐ **Golden-crowned Manakin** *Pipra vilasboasi*

E Amazian Brazil (near headwaters of Rio Tapajós in sw Pará)

☐ **Snow-capped Manakin** *Pipra nattereri*

Extreme ne Bolivia and central Amazonian Brazil

☐ **Cerulean-capped Manakin** *Pipra coeruleocapilla*

E slope of Andes of s Peru (s Huánuco to Puno)

☐ **Tepui Manakin** *Lepidothrix suavissima*

Tepuis of s Venezuela to n Guyana and extreme n Brazil

☐ **White-fronted Manakin** *Lepidothrix serena*

Guyana (Acari Mountains) and n Amazonian Brazil

☐ **Helmeted Manakin** *Antilophia galeata*

Tableland of interior s Brazil to ne Bolivia and ne Paraguay

☐ **Golden-winged Manakin** *Masius chrysopterus*

_____ *M. c. bellus*   W slope of W Andes to w side of Central Andes of Colombia
_____ *M. c. pax*   Subtropical se Colombia (e Nariño) and e Ecuador
_____ *M. c. coronulatus*   W Andes of Colombia (sw Cauca and Nariño) and w Ecuador
_____ *M. c. chrysopterus*   Central and Eastern Andes of Colombia and nw Venezuela
_____ *M. c. peruvianus*   Subtropical n Peru (n Cajamarca and n San Martín)

☐ **Pin-tailed Manakin** *Ilicura militaris*

SE Brazil (Espírito Santo to Paraná and e Santa Catarina)

☐ **Fiery-capped Manakin** *Machaeropterus pyrocephalus*

_____ *M. p. pallidiceps*   S Venezuela (nw Bolívar) and extreme n Brazil (Roraima)
_____ *M. p. pyrocephalus*   E Peru (San Martín) to n Bolivia and w Amazonian Brazil

☐ **Striped Manakin** *Machaeropterus regulus*

_____ *M. r. antioquiae*   Eastern Andes of w and central Colombia
_____ *M. r. striolatus*   Tropical e Colombia to e Ecuador, ne Peru and w Amaz. Brazil
_____ *M. r. obscurostriatus*   Tropical nw Venezuela (Mérida)
_____ *M. r. zulianus*   Tropical w Venezuela (w Zulia, Táchira and n Barinas)
_____ *M. r. aureopectus*   Tropical se Venezuela (ne Amazonas and se Bolívar)
_____ *M. r. regulus*   Coastal se Brazil (Bahia to Rio de Janeiro)

☐ **Club-winged Manakin** *Machaeropterus deliciosus*

W slope of Andes of sw Colombia and w Ecuador

☐ **Black Manakin** *Xenopipo atronitens*

E Colombia to s Venezuela, ne Bolivia and s Amazonian Brazil

☐ **Yellow-crested Manakin** *Heterocercus flavivertex*

E Colombia to sw Venezuela and n Amazonian Brazil

☐ **Orange-crested Manakin** *Heterocercus aurantiivertex*

Locally in e Ecuador and adjacent ne Peru (sw Loreto)

☐ **Flame-crested Manakin** *Heterocercus linteatus*

S Amazonian Brazil to ne Peru and extreme ne Bolivia

☐ **Saffron-crested Tyrant-Manakin** *Neopelma chrysocephalum*

E Colombia to s Venezuela, the Guianas and n Amazonian Brazil

☐ **Sulphur-bellied Tyrant-Manakin** *Neopelma sulphureiventer*

Tropical e Peru to n Bolivia and adjacent w Amazonian Brazil

☐ **Pale-bellied Tyrant-Manakin** *Neopelma pallescens*

Lower Amazonian Brazil; central and e Brazil to ne Bolivia

☐ **Wied's Tyrant-Manakin** *Neopelma aurifrons*

_____ *N. a. aurifrons*   Coastal se Brazil (s Bahia, Espírito Santo and Minas Gerais)
_____ *N. a. chrysolophum*   SE Brazil (s Minas Gerais, Rio de Janeiro and e São Paulo)

☐ **Dwarf Tyrant-Manakin** *Tyranneutes stolzmanni*

E Colombia to s Venezuela, n Bolivia and Amazonian Brazil

☐ **Tiny Tyrant-Manakin** *Tyranneutes virescens*

SE Venezuela to the Guianas and ne Amazonian Brazil

☐ **Black-capped Piprites** *Piprites pileatus*

☐ **Gray-headed Piprites** *Piprites griseiceps*

Locally from se Brazil (Rio de Janeiro) to ne Argentina

☐ **Wing-barred Piprites** *Piprites chloris*

Caribbean lowlands of e Guatemala to Costa Rica

____ P. c. antioquiae	Central Andes of Colombia (Antioquia)
____ P. c. perijanus	Sierra de Perijá (e Colombia) and Andes of w Venezuela
____ P. c. tschudii	Tropical se Colombia to central Peru and nw Brazil
____ P. c. chlorion	Tropical se Venezuela, the Guianas and n Brazil
____ P. c. grisescens	N Brazil (e Pará)
____ P. c. bolivianus	Tropical n Bolivia and sw Amazonian Brazil
____ P. c. chloris	SE Brazil (Espírito Santo) to e Paraguay and ne Argentina

FAMILY: TYRANNIDAE (Tyrant Flycatchers—425)

☐ **White-lored Tyrannulet** *Ornithion inerme*

S Venezuela to the Guianas, n Bolivia, Amazonian and e Brazil

☐ **Yellow-bellied Tyrannulet** *Ornithion semiflavum*

Humid lowlands of s Mexico (Oaxaca) to ne Costa Rica

☐ **Brown-capped Tyrannulet** *Ornithion brunneicapillum*

____ O. b. brunneicapillum	Caribbean slope of Costa Rica to w Colombia and nw Ecuador
____ O. b. dilutum	Santa Marta Mountains (ne Colombia) to nw Venezuela

☐ **Northern Beardless-Tyrannulet** *Camptostoma imberbe*

____ C. i. ridgwayi	SE Arizona to sw New Mexico and w Mexico
____ C. i. imberbe	S Texas to n Costa Rica
____ C. i. thyellophila	Cozumel I. (off Yucatán Peninsula of e Mexico)

☐ **Southern Beardless-Tyrannulet** *Camptostoma obsoletum*

____ C. o. flaviventre	Pacific coast of sw Costa Rica and Panama
____ C. o. orphnum	Coiba and Cébaco islands (Panama)
____ C. o. major	Pearl Islands (Panama)
____ C. o. caucae	Colombia (Western Andes, Cauca and Magdalena valleys)
____ C. o. bogotensis	E Colombia (Bogotá and Meta)
____ C. o. pusillum	Caribbean coast of n Colombia and nw Venezuela
____ C. o. napaeum	Extreme s-central Venezuela to the Guianas and n Brazil
____ C. o. venezuelae	Tropical n and central Venezuela; Trinidad
____ C. o. maranonicum	N Peru (middle Marañón Valley)
____ C. o. olivaceum	SE Colombia to e Ecuador, ne Peru and w Brazil (w Amazonas)
____ C. o. sclateri	Tropical w Ecuador and extreme nw Peru (Tumbes and n Piura)
____ C. o. griseum	Arid littoral of w Peru (Lambayeque to Lima)
____ C. o. bolivianum	Central Bolivia to nw Argentina (Tucumán)
____ C. o. cinerascens	E Brazil (Maranhão to Ceará and Mato Grosso) and w Bolivia
____ C. o. obsoletum	SE Brazil to Uruguay, Paraguay and n Argentina

☐ **Mouse-colored Tyrannulet** *Phaeomyias murina*

____ P. m. eremonoma	Pacific lowlands of Panama (Chiriquí to e Panama Province)
____ P. m. incomta	Colombia to Venezuela, the Guianas and n Brazil; Trinidad
____ P. m. tumbezana	Arid tropical sw Ecuador to nw Peru (south to ne Lambayeque)
____ P. m. inflava	Arid tropical nw Peru (Lambayeque to n Lima)
____ P. m. maranonica	N Peru (arid tropical Marañón Valley)
____ P. m. wagae	Tropical e Peru to nw Bolivia and w Amazonian Brazil
____ P. m. ignobilis	S Bolivia to Paraguay and nw Argentina (south to La Rioja)
____ P. m. murina	Southern, e and se Brazil

☐ **Cocos Island Flycatcher** *Nesotriccus ridgwayi*

Cocos I. (off Costa Rica)

☐ **Yellow Tyrannulet** *Capsiempis flaveola*

____ *C. f. semiflava*	Tropical s Nicaragua to e-central Panama; Coiba I.
____ *C. f. leucophrys*	Colombia (Magdalena Valley) to nw Venezuela
____ *C. f. cerulus*	Extreme e Colombia to ne Ecuador and Venezuela
____ *C. f. amazonus*	The Guianas and n Brazil (Amazonas, w Pará and Amapá)
____ *C. f. magnirostris*	SW Ecuador (Pichincha to El Oro)
____ *C. f. flaveola*	SE Brazil to ne Bolivia, e Paraguay, ne Argentina and se Peru

☐ **Yellow-crowned Tyrannulet** *Tyrannulus elatus*

Tropical sw Costa Rica to n Bolivia and Amazonian Brazil

☐ **Forest Elaenia** *Myiopagis gaimardii*

____ *M. g. macilvainii*	Tropical e Panama and Caribbean coast of Colombia
____ *M. g. trinitatis*	Trinidad
____ *M. g. bogotensis*	Tropical ne Colombia and n Venezuela
____ *M. g. guianensis*	Extreme e Colombia to se Venezuela, the Guianas and n Brazil
____ *M. g. gaimardii*	Tropical s Ecuador to e Peru, n Bolivia and sw Brazil
____ *M. g. subcinereus*	Central and e Brazil

☐ **Gray Elaenia** *Myiopagis caniceps*

____ *M. c. absita*	Extreme e Panama (Darién)
____ *M. c. parambae*	Tropical w Colombia and nw Ecuador (south to w Cañar)
____ *M. c. cinerea*	E Colombia to e Ecuador, ne Peru, s Venezuela and nw Brazil
____ *M. c. caniceps*	Tropical se Brazil to Paraguay, s Bolivia and n Argentina

☐ **Pacific Elaenia** *Myiopagis subplacens*

W Ecuador (w Esmeraldas and Manabí) to nw Peru

☐ **Yellow-crowned Elaenia** *Myiopagis flavivertex*

S Venezuela to the Guianas, ne Peru and w Amazonian Brazil

☐ **Jamaican Elaenia** *Myiopagis cotta*

Jamaica

☐ **Greenish Elaenia** *Myiopagis viridicata*

____ *M. v. jaliscensis*	Tropical w Mexico (Sinaloa and Durango to Guerrero)
____ *M. v. minima*	Tres Marías Islands (off w Mexico)
____ *M. v. placens*	Tropical se Mexico (Tamaulipas) to Honduras; Cozumel I.
____ *M. v. pacifica*	Pacific lowlands of s Mexico (Chiapas) to w Honduras
____ *M. v. accola*	Tropical Nicaragua to Panama, n Colombia and w Venezuela
____ *M. v. pallens*	Colombia (Cundinamarca, Huila and Santa Marta region)
____ *M. v. restricta*	Tropical s Venezuela
____ *M. v. zuliae*	Sierra de Perijá (Colombia/Venezuela border)
____ *M. v. implacens*	Tropical sw Colombia (Nariño) and w Ecuador
____ *M. v. viridicata*	SE Peru to e Bolivia, e Paraguay, n Argentina, e and se Brazil

☐ **Gray-and-white Tyrannulet** *Pseudelaenia leucospodia*

____ *P. l. cinereifrons*	Arid scrub of sw Ecuador (Guayas); Isla Puná and Isla La Plata
____ *P. l. leucospodia*	Arid scrub of nw Peru (Tumbes to La Libertad)

☐ **Caribbean Elaenia** *Elaenia martinica*

____ *E. m. remota*	Cozumel, Isla de Mujeres and Holbox I. (off e Mexico)
____ *E. m. chinchorrensis*	Great Key I. off Quintana Roo (e Mexico)
____ *E. m. cinerascens*	Isla San Andrés and Isla Providéncia (Caribbean Sea)
____ *E. m. caymanensis*	Cayman Islands
____ *E. m. riisii*	Virgin Islands, Antigua I. and Netherlands Antilles
____ *E. m. martinica*	Lesser Antilles (south to Grenada)
____ *E. m. barbadensis*	Barbados

☐ **Large Elaenia** *Elaenia spectabilis*

Extreme se Colombia to n Argentina and Brazil

☐ **Yellow-bellied Elaenia** *Elaenia flavogaster*
_____ *E. f. subpagana*   S Mexico (Oaxaca and Veracruz) to Costa Rica; Coiba I.
_____ *E. f. pallididorsalis*   Panama; Cébaco I. and Pearl Islands
_____ *E. f. flavogaster*   Colombia to the Guianas, Brazil, Paraguay, Argentina; Trinidad
_____ *E. f. semipagana*   Tropical w Ecuador (El Oro and Loja) and nw Peru; Isla Puná

☐ **Noronha Elaenia** *Elaenia ridleyana*

Ilha Fernando de Noronha (off ne Brazil)

☐ **White-crested Elaenia** *Elaenia albiceps*
_____ *E. a. griseigularis*   Andes of sw Colombia (Nariño) to Ecuador and nw Peru
_____ *E. a. diversa*   Central Andes of Peru (Cajamarca to Huánuco)
_____ *E. a. urubambae*   Subtropical se Peru (Cuzco)
_____ *E. a. modesta*   Arid tropical w Peru (La Libertad) to nw Chile
_____ *E. a. albiceps*   Extreme se Peru (Puno) and nw Bolivia
_____ *E. a. chilensis*   Andes of Bolivia to Tierra del Fuego; winters north to Brazil

☐ **Small-billed Elaenia** *Elaenia parvirostris*

S Brazil to Bolivia and c Argentina; winters n to Colombia

☐ **Slaty Elaenia** *Elaenia strepera*

Andes of s Bolivia and nw Argentina; winters n to Venezuela

☐ **Olivaceous Elaenia** *Elaenia mesoleuca*

SE Brazil (Goiás) to e Paraguay and ne Argentina

☐ **Mottle-backed Elaenia** *Elaenia gigas*

Tropical se Colombia to e Ecuador, e Peru and w Bolivia

☐ **Brownish Elaenia** *Elaenia pelzelni*

River islands of Amazon system

☐ **Plain-crested Elaenia** *Elaenia cristata*
_____ *E. c. cristata*   Venezuela and Guianas to Amaz. and e Brazil and ne Bolivia
_____ *E. c. alticola*   *Tepuis* of s Venezuela (se Bolívar) and adjacent n Brazil

☐ **Rufous-crowned Elaenia** *Elaenia ruficeps*

SE Colombia to the Guianas, s Venezuela and n Amaz. Brazil

☐ **Lesser Elaenia** *Elaenia chiriquensis*
_____ *E. c. chiriquensis*   NW Costa Rica to Panama; Coiba, Cébaco and Pearl islands
_____ *E. c. brachyptera*   Pacific slope of sw Colombia (Nariño) and nw Ecuador
_____ *E. c. albivertex*   Colombia to the Guianas, Brazil and n Argentina; Trinidad

☐ **Mountain Elaenia** *Elaenia frantzii*
_____ *E. f. ultima*   Mountains of Guatemala, El Salvador, Honduras and Nicaragua
_____ *E. f. frantzii*   Mountains of Costa Rica and w Panama (Chiriquí and Veraguas)
_____ *E. f. pudica*   Andes of Colombia and coastal mountains of n Venezuela
_____ *E. f. browni*   N Colombia (Santa Marta Mountains and Sierra de Perijá)

☐ **Highland Elaenia** *Elaenia obscura*
_____ *E. o. obscura*   E slope of Andes of s Ecuador to Bolivia and nw Argentina
_____ *E. o. sordida*   SE Brazil (Rio de Janeiro) to e Paraguay and ne Argentina

☐ **Great Elaenia** *Elaenia dayi*
_____ *E. d. tyleri*   *Tepuis* of s Venezuela (Duida, Huachamacare and Parú)
_____ *E. d. auyantepui*   *Tepuis* of s Venezuela (Auyan-tepui)
_____ *E. d. dayi*   *Tepuis* of s Venezuela (Roraima, Kukenamk and Ptari-tepui)

☐ **Sierran Elaenia** *Elaenia pallatangae*
_____ *E. p. pallatangae*   Andes of s Colombia and Ecuador
_____ *E. p. davidwillardi*   *Tepuis* of s Venezuela
_____ *E. p. olivina*   *Tepuis* of s Venezuela, adjacent Guyana and extreme n Brazil
_____ *E. p. intensa*   Andes of Peru
_____ *E. p. exsul*   Andes of Bolivia (La Paz and Cochabamba)

☐ **Greater Antillean Elaenia** *Elaenia fallax*
_____   *E. f. fallax*   Humid montane forests of Jamaica
_____   *E. f. cherriei*   Humid montane forests of Hispaniola

☐ **Torrent Tyrannulet** *Serpophaga cinerea*
_____   *S. c. grisea*   Rocky mountain streams of Costa Rica and w Panama
_____   *S. c. cinerea*   Mountain streams of Colombia and Venezuela to w Bolivia

☐ **Sooty Tyrannulet** *Serpophaga nigricans*

      SE Bolivia to c Argentina, e Paraguay, Uruguay and s Brazil

☐ **River Tyrannulet** *Serpophaga hypoleuca*
_____   *S. h. hypoleuca*   SE Colombia to e Ecuador, e Peru, n Bolivia and w Amaz. Brazil
_____   *S. h. venezuelana*   Tropical Venezuela (Apure, Anzoátegui and n Bolívar)
_____   *S. h. pallida*   Amazonian Brazil south of the Amazon

☐ **White-crested Tyrannulet** *Serpophaga subcristata*
_____   *S. s. straminea*   SE Brazil (s Piauí and Bahia) to Uruguay
_____   *S. s. subcristata*   E Bolivia to sw Brazil (Mato Grosso), Paraguay and c Argentina

☐ **White-bellied Tyrannulet** *Serpophaga munda*

      W Bolivia to w Paraguay, extreme sw Brazil and w Argentina

☐ **Ochre-bellied Flycatcher** *Mionectes oleagineus*
_____   *M. o. assimilis*   Tropical s Mexico to e Costa Rica and Panama (Bocas del Toro)
_____   *M. o. obscurus*   Arid tropical El Salvador
_____   *M. o. dyscolus*   Tropical w Costa Rica and w Panama (Chiriquí)
_____   *M. o. lutescens*   Pacific slope of Panama (Chiriquí and Veraguas); Isla Coiba
_____   *M. o. parcus*   Tropical e Panama to n Colombia and nw Venezuela
_____   *M. o. chloronotus*   Tropical e Colombia to n Peru, s Venezuela and w Brazil
_____   *M. o. pacificus*   Tropical sw Colombia (Nariño) to w Ecuador (w Loja)
_____   *M. o. abdominalis*   Tropical n Venezuela (Distrito Federal and Miranda)
_____   *M. o. pallidiventris*   Tropical ne Venezuela; Trinidad and Tobago
_____   *M. o. intensus*   Trop. se Venezuela (s Bolívar and Amazonas) and adj. Guyana
_____   *M. o. dorsalis*   *Tepuis* of se Venezuela (Gran Sabana of Bolívar)
_____   *M. o. hauxwelli*   Tropical e Ecuador and ne Peru north of the Amazon
_____   *M. o. wallacei*   Tropical Guianas to Suriname and ne Brazil
_____   *M. o. maynana*   Tropical e Peru (Amazonas and San Martín) to n Bolivia
_____   *M. o. oleagineus*   Coastal se Brazil (Bahia to Rio de Janeiro)

☐ **Streak-necked Flycatcher** *Mionectes striaticollis*
_____   *M. s. columbianus*   Andes of e Colombia and e Ecuador
_____   *M. s. selvae*   W slope of Western Andes of Colombia (Caldas)
_____   *M. s. viridiceps*   Extreme tropical sw Colombia (w Nariño) and w Ecuador
_____   *M. s. palamblae*   Andes of n Peru (Piura south to Huánuco)
_____   *M. s. poliocephalus*   Andes of Peru (Pasco and Junín)
_____   *M. s. striaticollis*   Andes of se Peru (Cuzco) to w Bolivia

☐ **Olive-striped Flycatcher** *Mionectes olivaceus*
_____   *M. o. olivaceus*   Lowlands and foothills of Costa Rica and w Panama
_____   *M. o. hederaceus*   E Panama to w Colombia, Ecuador and w Bolivia
_____   *M. o. galbinus*   Santa Marta Mountains (ne Colombia)
_____   *M. o. pallidus*   E Andes of Colombia (Magdalena and n Meta)
_____   *M. o. meridae*   Andes of extreme ne Colombia and adjacent nw Venezuela
_____   *M. o. venezuelanus*   Coastal cordillera of n Venezuela; Trinidad

☐ **Gray-hooded Flycatcher** *Mionectes rufiventris*

      SE Brazil (Espírito Santo) to e Paraguay and ne Argentina

☐ **MacConnell's Flycatcher** *Mionectes macconnelli*

____	*M. m. mercedesfosteri*	E Andes of Venezuela
____	*M. m. roraimae*	S Venezuela to the Guianas and e Amazonian Brazil
____	*M. m. macconnelli*	Tropical e Venezuela to extreme ne Brazil (Amapá)
____	*M. m. peruanus*	SE Peru (s Ucayali to Puno)
____	*M. m. amazonus*	Tropical n Bolivia and w Amazonian Brazil

☐ **Rufous-breasted Flycatcher** *Leptopogon rufipectus*

____	*L. r. rufipectus*	Andes of Colombia to e Ecuador and extreme n Peru (Piura)
____	*L. r. venezuelanus*	Andes of ne Colombia and extreme w Venezuela (Táchira)

☐ **Inca Flycatcher** *Leptopogon taczanowskii*

E slope of Andes of Peru (Amazonas to Cuzco)

☐ **Sepia-capped Flycatcher** *Leptopogon amaurocephalus*

____	*L. a. pileatus*	Tropical s Mexico to Guatemala, Belize and Honduras
____	*L. a. faustus*	Tropical Nicaragua to Costa Rica and Panama
____	*L. a. idius*	Coiba I. (Panama)
____	*L. a. diversus*	Santa Marta and Magdalena valleys of n Colombia and w Zulia
____	*L. a. orinocensis*	Tropical w and sw Venezuela
____	*L. a. obscuritergum*	S Venezuela (Bolívar and Amazonas) to e Brazil (Amapá)
____	*L. a. peruvianus*	Tropical e Colombia to n Bolivia
____	*L. a. amaurocephalus*	Tropical se Brazil to e Paraguay, n Argentina and e Bolivia

☐ **Slaty-capped Flycatcher** *Leptopogon superciliaris*

____	*L. s. hellmayri*	Humid montane forests of Costa Rica and w Panama
____	*L. s. transandinus*	E Panama (Darién), W Andes of Colombia and w Ecuador
____	*L. s. poliocephalus*	Upper tropical central and e-central Colombia
____	*L. s. superciliaris*	Upper trop. se Colombia, e Ecuador and n Peru s to Junín
____	*L. s. venezuelensis*	Coastal cordillera of n Venezuela; n Brazil
____	*L. s. pariae*	NE Venezuela (Paría Peninsula); Trinidad
____	*L. s. albidiventer*	SE Peru (Cuzco and Puno) and *yungas* of w Bolivia

☐ **Bronze-olive Pygmy-Tyrant** *Pseudotriccus pelzelni*

____	*P. p. berlepschi*	Mountains of extreme e Panama and adjacent nw Colombia
____	*P. p. annectens*	Andes of sw Colombia and nw Ecuador (south to El Oro)
____	*P. p. pelzelni*	E Colombia (Meta) and e Ecuador (Napo-Pastaza)
____	*P. p. peruvianus*	Andes of e Peru (San Martín to Cuzco)

☐ **Hazel-fronted Pygmy-Tyrant** *Pseudotriccus simplex*

E slope of Andes of s Peru (Puno) and w Bolivia

☐ **Rufous-headed Pygmy-Tyrant** *Pseudotriccus ruficeps*

Andes of Colombia to w Bolivia (La Paz and Cochabamba)

☐ **Marble-faced Bristle-Tyrant** *Phylloscartes ophthalmicus*

____	*P. o. ophthalmicus*	Andes of Colombia to nw Venezuela, e Ecuador and n Peru
____	*P. o. purus*	Coastal cordillera of n Venezuela (Yaracuy to Distrito Federal)
____	*P. o. ottonis*	Andes of se Peru (Puno) and w Bolivia

☐ **Venezuelan Bristle-Tyrant** *Phylloscartes venezuelanus*

Coastal cordillera of n Venezuela (Carabobo to Distrito Federal)

☐ **Antioquia Bristle-Tyrant** *Phylloscartes lanyoni*

Central Andes of n Colombia (Antioquia and e Caldas)

☐ **Spectacled Bristle-Tyrant** *Phylloscartes orbitalis*

Andes of extreme s Colombia to Ecuador, Peru and w Bolivia

☐ **Variegated Bristle-Tyrant** *Phylloscartes poecilotis*

____	*P. p. poecilotis*	Andes of n Colombia to w Venezuela, e Ecuador and s Peru
____	*P. p. pifanoi*	Sierra de Perijá (Colombia/Venezuela border)

☐ **Southern Bristle-Tyrant** *Phylloscartes eximius*

SE Brazil (Espírito Santo) to e Paraguay and ne Argentina

☐ **Black-fronted Tyrannulet** *Phylloscartes nigrifrons*

Tepuis of s Venezuela (s Bolívar and Amazonas)

☐ **Chapman's Bristle-Tyrant** *Phylloscartes chapmani*
    ____ *P. c. chapmani*
    ____ *P. c. duidae*

Tepuis of s Venezuela (s Bolívar and ne Amazonas)
Tepuis of se Venezuela (Cerro de la Neblina) and (?) adj. Brazil

☐ **Ecuadorian Tyrannulet** *Phylloscartes gualaquizae*

E slope of Andes of e Ecuador and n Peru (San Martín)

☐ **Rufous-lored Tyrannulet** *Phylloscartes flaviventris*

Coastal mts. of n Venezuela and Andes s to Peru and n Bolivia

☐ **Cinnamon-faced Tyrannulet** *Phylloscartes parkeri*

Andean foothills of central and se Peru and adjacent n Bolivia

☐ **Minas Gerais Tyrannulet** *Phylloscartes roquettei*

Known from a 1926 specimen from e Brazil (n Minas Gerais)

☐ **Sao Paulo Tyrannulet** *Phylloscartes paulistus*

SE Brazil (Espírito Santo) to e Paraguay and ne Argentina

☐ **Oustalet's Tyrannulet** *Phylloscartes oustaleti*

SE Brazil (Espírito Santo to e Santa Catarina)

☐ **Restinga Tyrannulet** *Phylloscartes kronei*

Coastal se Brazil (se São Paulo to ne Santa Catarina)

☐ **Serra do Mar Tyrannulet** *Phylloscartes difficilis*

Coastal mts. of se Brazil (Espírito Santo to n Rio Grande do Sul)

☐ **Alagoas Tyrannulet** *Phylloscartes ceciliae*

Highlands of ne Brazil (Alagoas)

☐ **Mottle-cheeked Tyrannulet** *Phylloscartes ventralis*
    ____ *P. v. angustirostris*
    ____ *P. v. tucumanus*
    ____ *P. v. ventralis*

E slope of Andes of Peru (San Martín) to n Bolivia
Andes of nw Argentina (Jujuy to Tucumán and Catamarca)
SE Brazil (Minas Gerais) to Uruguay, e Paraguay, ne Argentina

☐ **Bahia Tyrannulet** *Phylloscartes beckeri*

Montane forests of se Brazil (s Bahia near Boa Nova)

☐ **Yellow-green Tyrannulet** *Phylloscartes flavovirens*

Pacific lowlands of Panama (Canal Zone to e Darién)

☐ **Olive-green Tyrannulet** *Phylloscartes virescens*

Lowlands of Guianas and adjacent n Brazil (Amazonas)

☐ **Rufous-browed Tyrannulet** *Phylloscartes superciliaris*
    ____ *P. s. superciliaris*
    ____ *P. s. palloris*
    ____ *P. s. griseocapillus*

Mountains of Costa Rica to w Panama (Veraguas)
E Panama (Darién) and adjacent Colombia (Chocó)
Sierra de Perijá (Colombia/Venezuela border) and se Ecuador

☐ **Bay-ringed Tyrannulet** *Phylloscartes sylviolus*

SE Brazil (Espírito Santo) to e Paraguay and ne Argentina

☐ **Planalto Tyrannulet** *Phyllomyias fasciatus*
    ____ *P. f. cearae*
    ____ *P. f. fasciatus*
    ____ *P. f. brevirostris*

E Brazil (Ceará and e Pernambuco)
E Brazil (Maranhão to se Mato Grosso and s Goiás)
SE Brazil (Minas Gerais) to e Paraguay and ne Argentina

☐ **White-fronted Tyrannulet** *Phyllomyias zeledoni*
    ____ *P. z. zeledoni*
    ____ *P. z. leucogenys*
    ____ *P. z. wetmorei*
    ____ *P. z. viridiceps*
    ____ *P. z. bunites*

Mountains of Costa Rica and w Panama
E Colombia to e Ecuador and se Peru
Sierra de Perijá (Colombia/Venezuela border)
Coastal mountains of n Venezuela (Carabobo to Miranda)
Tepuis of s Venezuela in Bolívar (Cerro Chimantá-tepui)

☐ **Rough-legged Tyrannulet** *Phyllomyias burmeisteri*

E slope of Andes of e Bolivia, n Argentina, e Paraguay, se Brazil

☐ **Greenish Tyrannulet** *Phyllomyias virescens*

SE Brazil (Espírito Santo) to e Paraguay and ne Argentina

☐ **Reiser's Tyrannulet** *Phyllomyias reiseri*

____ *P. r. urichi* — Extreme ne Venezuela (Sucre, Monagas and Anzoátegui)

____ *P. r. reiseri* — Interior e Brazil (Piauí) to ne Paraguay

☐ **Sclater's Tyrannulet** *Phyllomyias sclateri*

____ *P. s. subtropicalis* — E slope of Andes of se Peru (Cuzco and Puno)

____ *P. s. sclateri* — Andean foothills of Bolivia to nw Argentina (s to Tucumán)

☐ **Gray-capped Tyrannulet** *Phyllomyias griseocapilla* — SE Brazil (Minas Gerais and Espírito Santo to Santa Catarina)

☐ **Sooty-headed Tyrannulet** *Phyllomyias griseiceps*

____ *P. g. cristatus* — Lowlands of e Panama to n Colombia and n Venezuela

____ *P. g. caucae* — Colombia (upper Cauca Valley in Caldas and Tolima)

____ *P. g. griseiceps* — W Ecuador (w Esmeraldas south to El Oro and w Loja)

____ *P. g. pallidiceps* — SE Venezuela to Guyana, Amazonian Brazil, e Ecuador, e Peru

☐ **Plumbeous-crowned Tyrannulet** *Phyllomyias plumbeiceps* — Andes of Colombia to s Peru (Cuzco)

☐ **Black-capped Tyrannulet** *Phyllomyias nigrocapillus*

____ *P. n. flavimentum* — Santa Marta Mountains (ne Colombia)

____ *P. n. nigrocapillus* — Andes of Colombia and Ecuador to s Peru (Cuzco)

____ *P. n. aureus* — Andes of w Venezuela (n Táchira to s Lara)

☐ **Ashy-headed Tyrannulet** *Phyllomyias cinereiceps* — Andes of Colombia to Ecuador and s Peru (Puno)

☐ **Tawny-rumped Tyrannulet** *Phyllomyias uropygialis* — Andes of Colombia and w Venezuela to w Bolivia (s to Tarija)

☐ **Paltry Tyrannulet** *Zimmerius vilissimus*

____ *Z. v. vilissimus* — S Mexico (Chiapas) to El Salvador

____ *Z. v. parvus* — Honduras to Panama and extreme nw Colombia (Chocó)

☐ **Venezuelan Tyrannulet** *Zimmerius improbus*

____ *Z. i. improbus* — Andes of n Colombia and Sierra de Perijá (w Venezuela)

____ *Z. i. tamae* — Santa Marta Mountains (ne Colombia)

____ *Z. i. petersi* — Coastal cordillera of n Venezuela (s Lara east to Miranda)

☐ **Bolivian Tyrannulet** *Zimmerius bolivianus*

____ *Z. b. viridissimus* — Andes of se Peru (Huánuco to Puno)

____ *Z. b. bolivianus* — Andes of w Bolivia (La Paz and Cochabamba)

☐ **Red-billed Tyrannulet** *Zimmerius cinereicapillus* — Foothills of e Ecuador and e Peru (south to Madre de Dios)

☐ **Slender-footed Tyrannulet** *Zimmerius gracilipes*

____ *Z. g. gracilipes* — SE Colombia to s Venezuela, the Guianas and ne Brazil

____ *Z. g. acer* — NE Brazil (Alagoas)

____ *Z. g. gilvus* — E Ecuador to e Peru, n Bolivia and Amazonian Brazil

☐ **Peruvian Tyrannulet** *Zimmerius viridiflavus* — E slope of Andes of Peru (Huánuco to Junín)

☐ **Golden-faced Tyrannulet** *Zimmerius chrysops*

____ *Z. c. minimus* — Santa Marta Mountains (ne Colombia)

____ *Z. c. cumanensis* — Coastal mts. of Venezuela (Anzoátegui, Sucre and Monagas)

____ *Z. c. albigularis* — SW Colombia (Nariño) and w Ecuador (south to sw Guayas)

____ *Z. c. flavidifrons* — SW Ecuador (se Guayas to w Loja and El Oro)

____ *Z. c. chrysops* — S Colombia to Ecuador, n Peru and nw Venezuela

☐ **Amazonian Scrub-Flycatcher** *Sublegatus obscurior* — E Colombia to s Venezuela, Guianas, n Bolivia, Amaz. Brazil

☐ **Northern Scrub-Flycatcher** *Sublegatus arenarum*

____ *S. a. arenarum*	Pacific lowlands of sw Costa Rica to w Panama
____ *S. a. atrirostris*	E Panama to ne Colombia; Pearl, Coiba and Cébaco islands
____ *S. a. glaber*	Coastal n Venezuela, the Guianas and Suriname; Trinidad
____ *S. a. pallens*	Islas Los Roques, Isla Margarita and Netherlands Antilles
____ *S. a. tortugensis*	Isla La Tortuga (Venezuela)
____ *S. a. orinocensis*	Extreme e Colombia, Orinoco Valley of s Venezuela, adj. Brazil

☐ **Southern Scrub-Flycatcher** *Sublegatus modestus*

____ *S. m. modestus*	Tropical e Peru to e Brazil (Maranhão, Pernambuco and Paraná)
____ *S. m. brevirostris*	E Bolivia to Paraguay, Uruguay and central Argentina

☐ **Suiriri Flycatcher** *Suiriri suiriri*

____ *S. s. affinis*	*Chaco* of Suriname; e Brazil (Pará) to nw Bolivia
____ *S. s. bahiae*	E Brazil (Paraíba, Pernambuco, ne Bahia and e Piauí)
____ *S. s. suiriri*	SW Brazil to Paraguay, Uruguay, Bolivia and n Argentina

☐ **White-throated Tyrannulet** *Mecocerculus leucophrys*

____ *M. l. montensis*	Santa Marta Mountains (ne Colombia)
____ *M. l. notatus*	W and central Andes of Colombia (south to Cauca)
____ *M. l. setophagoides*	E Andes of Colombia (Santander to Cundinamarca)
____ *M. l. rufomarginatis*	S Colombia (Nariño) to w Ecuador and nw Peru (Piura)
____ *M. l. gularis*	Subtropical nw Venezuela (Zulia and Táchira to Lara)
____ *M. l. palliditergum*	Coastal cordillera of n Venezuela (Yaracuy to Miranda)
____ *M. l. nigriceps*	Subtropical ne Venezuela (Sucre and Monagas)
____ *M. l. chapmani*	*Tepuis* of s Venezuela
____ *M. l. roraimae*	Subtropical central Venezuela (Amazonas and Bolívar)
____ *M. l. parui*	*Tepuis* of s Venezuela (Cerro Parú in Amazonas)
____ *M. l. brunneomarginatus*	Andes of Peru (La Libertad and Cajamarca to Cuzco)
____ *M. l. pallidior*	Humid temperate Western Andes of Peru (w Ancash)
____ *M. l. leucophrys*	Temperate Andes of se Peru to Bolivia and nw Argentina

☐ **White-tailed Tyrannulet** *Mecocerculus poecilocercus*

Andes of Colombia to Ecuador and s Peru (Cuzco)

☐ **Buff-banded Tyrannulet** *Mecocerculus hellmayri*

E slope of Andes of s Peru (Puno) to w Bolivia and nw Argentina

☐ **Rufous-winged Tyrannulet** *Mecocerculus calopterus*

Andes of Ecuador and nw Peru (s to Lambayeque and La Libertad)

☐ **Sulphur-bellied Tyrannulet** *Mecocerculus minor*

Andes of Colombia and w Venezuela to e Peru (Huánuco)

☐ **White-banded Tyrannulet** *Mecocerculus stictopterus*

____ *M. s. stictopterus*	Andes of Colombia, Ecuador and n Peru
____ *M. s. albocaudatus*	Andes of nw Venezuela (Trujillo, Mérida and Táchira)
____ *M. s. taeniopterus*	Andes of e Peru to w Bolivia (La Paz and Cochabamba)

☐ **Slender-billed Tyrannulet** *Inezia tenuirostris*

Arid ne Colombia to nw Venezuela (Zulia, Falcón and n Lara)

☐ **Plain Tyrannulet** *Inezia inornata*

SE Peru to nw Argentina, Paraguay, sw and Amazonian Brazil

☐ **Pale-tipped Tyrannulet** *Inezia subflava*

____ *I. s. intermedia*	Caribbean lowlands of n Colombia and nw Venezuela
____ *I. s. obscura*	Extreme e Colombia to s Venezuela and nw Brazil
____ *I. s. caudata*	S Venezuela to the Guianas and extreme n Brazil
____ *I. s. subflava*	Amazonian Brazil and ne Bolivia (ne Beni and ne Santa Cruz)

☐ **Lesser Wagtail-Tyrant** *Stigmatura napensis*

____ *S. n. napensis*	Amazon system is. (se Colombia, e Ecuador, ne Peru and w Brazil)
____ *S. n. bahiae*	River islands in e Brazil (Pernambuco and Bahia)

☐ **Greater Wagtail-Tyrant** *Stigmatura budytoides*
____   *S. b. budytoides*   S Bolivia (Cochabamba south to Tarija)
____   *S. b. inzonata*   SE Bolivia to w Paraguay and n Argentina
____   *S. b. flavocinerea*   Central Argentina
____   *S. b. gracilis*   NE Brazil (Pernambuco and n Bahia)

☐ **Agile Tit-Tyrant** *Uromyias agilis*

Andes of Colombia to extreme w Venezuela and Ecuador

☐ **Unstreaked Tit-Tyrant** *Uromyias agraphia*
____   *U. a. plengei*   E Peru (Cordillera de Colán in Amazonas)
____   *U. a. squamigera*   Central Peru (Carpish Mountains in e La Libertad and Huánuco)
____   *U. a. agraphia*   SE Peru (Cordillera Vilcanota and Urubamba Valley of Cuzco)

☐ **Ash-breasted Tit-Tyrant** *Anairetes alpinus*
____   *A. a. alpinus*   Andes of Peru (n Ancash. Apurímac and Cuzco)
____   *A. a. bolivianus*   *Yungas* of w Bolivia (La Paz)

☐ **Black-crested Tit-Tyrant** *Anairetes nigrocristatus*

Andes of extreme s Ecuador and w Peru (south to Pasco)

☐ **Pied-crested Tit-Tyrant** *Anairetes reguloides*
____   *A. r. albiventris*   Arid littoral of w Peru (Ancash to Ica and w Ayacucho)
____   *A. r. reguloides*   Arid sw Peru (s Ayacucho) to extreme n Chile (Tarapacá)

☐ **Yellow-billed Tit-Tyrant** *Anairetes flavirostris*
____   *A. f. huancabambae*   Western and Central Andes of nw Peru south to Huánuco
____   *A. f. arequipae*   Andes of sw Peru (Lima) to nw Chile
____   *A. f. cuzcoensis*   Andes of se Peru (Cuzco)
____   *A. f. flavirostris*   Andes of s Peru (Puno) to Bolivia, n Chile and w Argentina

☐ **Juan Fernandez Tit-Tyrant** *Anairetes fernandezianus*

Robinson Crusoe I. (Juan Fernández Islands off s Chile)

☐ **Tufted Tit-Tyrant** *Anairetes parulus*
____   *A. p. aequatorialis*   Andes of s Colombia to n Argentina (Salta and Jujuy)
____   *A. p. patagonicus*   W Argentina (s Mendoza to n Santa Cruz)
____   *A. p. parulus*   Andes of Chile and sw Argentina to Tierra del Fuego

☐ **Many-colored Rush-Tyrant** *Tachuris rubrigastra*
____   *T. r. libertatis*   Marshes of coastal w Peru (La Libertad to n Ica)
____   *T. r. alticola*   Andes of se Peru to w Bolivia and nw Argentina
____   *T. r. rubrigastra*   SE Brazil to Paraguay, Uruguay, n Argentina and w Chile
____   *T. r. loaensis*   N Chile (Antofagasta)

☐ **Sharp-tailed Tyrant** *Culicivora caudacuta*

E Bolivia to s-central Brazil, e Paraguay and ne Argentina

☐ **Bearded Tachuri** *Polystictus pectoralis*
____   *P. p. bogotensis*   W Colombia (Cauca Valley and Cundinamarca)
____   *P. p. brevipennis*   NE Colombia to s Venezuela, the Guianas and extreme n Brazil
____   *P. p,. pectoralis*   S Brazil to e Bolivia, Uruguay, Paraguay and n Argentina

☐ **Gray-backed Tachuri** *Polystictus superciliaris*

SE Brazil (central Bahia to Minas Gerais and n São Paulo)

☐ **Crested Doradito** *Pseudocolopteryx sclateri*

S Venezuela to Guyana, ne Argentina and s Brazil; Trinidad

☐ **Dinelli's Doradito** *Pseudocolopteryx dinellianus*

Locally in n Argentina; winters to s Bolivia and w Paraguay

☐ **Subtropical Doradito** *Pseudocolopteryx acutipennis*

Andes of Colombia to nw Argentina (south to La Rioja)

☐ **Warbling Doradito** *Pseudocolopteryx flaviventris*

Extreme s Brazil to e Bolivia, Uruguay, Argentina and c Chile

☐ **Tawny-crowned Pygmy-Tyrant** *Euscarthmus meloryphus*
    _____ *E. m. paulus* — NE Colombia (Santa Marta region) and n Venezuela
    _____ *E. m. fulviceps* — Tropical sw Ecuador and w Peru (south to La Libertad)
    _____ *E. m. meloryphus* — SE Brazil to n Uruguay, e Bolivia, e Paraguay and n Argentina

☐ **Rufous-sided Pygmy-Tyrant** *Euscarthmus rufomarginatus*
    _____ *E. r. savannophilus* — Savanna of s Suriname (Sipaliwini)
    _____ *E. r. rufomarginatus* — E Brazil (Maranhão and Piauí) to ne Bolivia and ne Paraguay

☐ **White-bellied Pygmy-Tyrant** *Myiornis albiventris* — E slope of Andes of Peru (Huánuco) to w Bolivia (Santa Cruz)

☐ **Eared Pygmy-Tyrant** *Myiornis auricularis* — SE Brazil (se Bahia) to e Paraguay and ne Argentina

☐ **Black-capped Pygmy-Tyrant** *Myiornis atricapillus* — Humid lowlands of Costa Rica to w Colombia and nw Ecuador

☐ **Short-tailed Pygmy-Tyrant** *Myiornis ecaudatus*
    _____ *M. e. miserabilis* — E Colombia to the Guianas, Suriname and n Brazil; Trinidad
    _____ *M. e. ecaudatus* — Amazonian Brazil to e Peru and n Bolivia

☐ **Scale-crested Pygmy-Tyrant** *Lophotriccus pileatus*
    _____ *L. p. luteiventris* — Highlands of Costa Rica to e Panama (Darién)
    _____ *L. p. santaeluciae* — Andes of Colombia and nw Venezuela (Zulia to Táchira)
    _____ *L. p. squamaecrista* — Andes of Colombia and w Ecuador
    _____ *L. p. pileatus* — Andes of e Ecuador and Peru (south to n Cuzco)
    _____ *L. p. hypochlorus* — Andes of se Peru (Cuzco and Puno)

☐ **Double-banded Pygmy-Tyrant** *Lophotriccus vitiosus*
    _____ *L. v. affinis* — SE Colombia to ne Peru and nw Amazonian Brazil
    _____ *L. v. guianensis* — The Guianas and ne Brazil (Amapá and Pará); Mato Grosso?
    _____ *L. v. congener* — W Amazonian Brazil (Rio Juruá in sw Amazonas)
    _____ *L. v. vitiosus* — E Peru (e San Martín, s Loreto and Huánuco)

☐ **Long-crested Pygmy-Tyrant** *Lophotriccus eulophotes* — Extreme sw Amaz. Brazil, adj. se Peru and extreme nw Bolivia

☐ **Helmeted Pygmy-Tyrant** *Lophotriccus galeatus* — E Colombia to s Venezuela, the Guianas and n Amaz. Brazil

☐ **Pale-eyed Pygmy-Tyrant** *Lophotriccus pilaris*
    _____ *L. p. wilcoxi* — Arid tropical Pacific coast of Panama
    _____ *L. p. pilaris* — N Colombia and adjacent Venezuela (Zulia and Táchira)
    _____ *L. p. venezuelensis* — N Venezuela south to n Amazonas and n Bolívar
    _____ *L. p. griseiceps* — E Colombia to Venezuela, w Guyana and extreme n Brazil

☐ **Northern Bentbill** *Oncostoma cinereigulare* — Lowlands of s Mexico (Veracruz) to w Panama

☐ **Southern Bentbill** *Oncostoma olivaceum* — Tropical e Panama and n Colombia (east to Santa Marta region)

☐ **Rufous-crowned Tody-Tyrant** *Poecilotriccus ruficeps*
    _____ *P. r. melanomystax* — Central Andes of Colombia (Antioquia to Tolima)
    _____ *P. r. ruficeps* — E Andes of Colombia, ne Ecuador and w Venezuela (Táchira)
    _____ *P. r. rufigenis* — Andes of w Colombia and w Ecuador (south to Chimborazo)
    _____ *P. r. peruvianus* — Andes of extreme n Peru (Piura and Cajamarca)

☐ **Slate-headed Tody-Tyrant** *Poecilotriccus sylvia*
    _____ *P. s. schistaceiceps* — Gulf slope of s Mexico (Veracruz) to Panama (Canal Zone)
    _____ *P. s. superciliare* — Tropical n Colombia (Cauca and Magdalena valleys)
    _____ *P. s. griseolum* — Extreme e Colombia to nw Venezuela (east to n Bolívar)
    _____ *P. s. sylvia* — Guianas and n Brazil (along Rio Branco)
    _____ *P. s. schulzi* — NE Brazil (se Pará to n Piauí)

☐ **Black-and-white Tody-Tyrant** *Poecilotriccus capitalis*

SE Colombia to e Ecuador, ne Peru and sw Brazil (Rondônia)

☐ **White-cheeked Tody-Tyrant** *Poecilotriccus albifacies*

SE Peru (s Madre de Dios and adjacent ne Cuzco)

☐ **Black-chested Tyrant** *Taeniotriccus andrei*
____ *T. a. andrei* — Tropical se Venezuela and nw Amazonian Brazil
____ *T. a. klagesi* — E Amazonian Brazil (along Rio Tapajós and Rio Xingú)

☐ **Snethlage's Tody-Tyrant** *Hemitriccus minor*
____ *H. m. minor* — E Brazil (lower Rio Xingú and Rio Tocantins to central Pará)
____ *H. m. pallens* — W-central Brazil (Amazonas) east to Rio Negro and Rio Madeira
____ *H. m. minima* — Central Amazonian Brazil to extreme ne Bolivia

☐ **Boat-billed Tody-Tyrant** *Hemitriccus josephinae*

S Guyana to Suriname, French Guiana and n Brazil (Amapá)

☐ **Flammulated Bamboo-Tyrant** *Hemitriccus flammulatus*
____ *H. f. flammulatus* — Tropical e Peru, adjacent sw Brazil and *yungas* of n Bolivia
____ *H. f. olivascens* — Tropical n Bolivia (south to n Santa Cruz)

☐ **Drab-breasted Bamboo-Tyrant** *Hemitriccus diops*

SE Brazil (se Bahia) to e Paraguay and ne Argentina

☐ **Brown-breasted Bamboo-Tyrant** *Hemitriccus obsoletus*
____ *H. o. obsoletus* — Mountains of se Brazil (Rio de Janeiro and São Paulo)
____ *H. o. zimmeri* — Mountains of se Brazil (Paraná and Rio Grande do Sul)

☐ **White-eyed Tody-Tyrant** *Hemitriccus zosterops*
____ *H. z. zosterops* — S Colombia to s Venezuela, the Guianas and nw Brazil
____ *H. z. flaviviridis* — N Peru (central Amazonas and n San Martín)
____ *H. z. griseipectus* — SE Peru (Cuzco) to n Bolivia and central Amazonian Brazil
____ *H. z. naumburgae* — NE Brazil (Paraíba to Alagoas)

☐ **Zimmer's Tody-Tyrant** *Hemitriccus minimus*

E Amazonian Brazil to ne Bolivia (n Beni and ne Santa Cruz)

☐ **Eye-ringed Tody-Tyrant** *Hemitriccus orbitatus*

Lowlands of se Brazil (s Minas Gerais to ne Rio Grande do Sul)

☐ **Johannes' Tody-Tyrant** *Hemitriccus iohannis*

SE Colombia to e Peru, n Bolivia and w Amazonian Brazil

☐ **Stripe-necked Tody-Tyrant** *Hemitriccus striaticollis*
____ *H. s. striaticollis* — NE Colombia and ne Peru to n Bolivia, central and e Brazil
____ *H. s. griseiceps* — W-central Brazil (lower Rio Tapajós in e Pará)

☐ **Hangnest Tody-Tyrant** *Hemitriccus nidipendulus*
____ *H. n. nidipendulus* — E-central Brazil (Bahia)
____ *H. n. paulistus* — SE Brazil (Espírito Santo and Minas Gerais to São Paulo)

☐ **Yungas Tody-Tyrant** *Hemitriccus spodiops*

Yungas of Bolivia (La Paz, Cochabamba and s Beni)

☐ **Pearly-vented Tody-Tyrant** *Hemitriccus margaritaceiventer*
____ *H. m. impiger* — Arid tropical ne Colombia and n Venezuela; Isla Margarita
____ *H. m. septentrionalis* — S Colombia (arid tropical upper Magdalena Valley)
____ *H. m. duidae* — *Tepuis* of s Venezuela (Mt. Duida)
____ *H. m. auyantepui* — Subtropical *tepuis* of se Venezuela (se Bolívar)
____ *H. m. breweri* — Subtropical se Venezuela (Jaua massif)
____ *H. m. rufipes* — Tropical Peru east of the Andes (Cuzco) to nw Bolivia
____ *H. m. margaritaceiventer* — E Bolivia to n Argentina, e Paraguay and w Brazil
____ *H. m. wuchereri* — E Brazil (Maranhão to Ceará, Pernambuco and Bahia)

☐ **Pelzeln's Tody-Tyrant** *Hemitriccus inornatus*

NW Brazil (known from an 1831 specimen from Rio Içana)

☐ **Black-throated Tody-Tyrant** *Hemitriccus granadensis*

____	*H. g. lehmanni*	Santa Marta Mountains (ne Colombia)
____	*H. g. granadensis*	Andes of Colombia and ne Ecuador
____	*H. g. andinus*	E Andes of Colombia and w Venezuela (Táchira)
____	*H. g. intensus*	Sierra de Perijá (Colombia/Venezuela border)
____	*H. g. federalis*	Montane forests of coastal n Venezuela (Distrito Federal)
____	*H. g. pyrrhops*	Andes of se Ecuador and Peru (south to Cuzco)
____	*H. g. caesius*	Andes of se Peru (Puno) and adjacent n Bolivia

☐ **Buff-throated Tody-Tyrant** *Hemitriccus rufigularis*

Foothills on e slope of Andes in Ecuador, Peru and w Bolivia

☐ **Cinnamon-breasted Tody-Tyrant** *Hemitriccus cinnamomeipectus*

S Ecuador (Cordillera del Cóndor) to n Peru (San Martín)

☐ **Buff-breasted Tody-Tyrant** *Hemitriccus mirandae*

Lowlands of e Brazil (Ceará, Pernambuco and Alagoas)

☐ **Kaempfer's Tody-Tyrant** *Hemitriccus kaempferi*

SE Brazil (e Santa Catarina)

☐ **Fork-tailed Tody-Tyrant** *Hemitriccus furcatus*

SE Brazil (Rio de Janeiro, s Minas Gerais and ne São Paulo)

☐ **Buff-cheeked Tody-Flycatcher** *Todirostrum senex*

W Brazil (known from an 1830 specimen from Amazonas)

☐ **Ruddy Tody-Flycatcher** *Todirostrum russatum*

Tepuis of se Venezuela and n Brazil (Cerro Uei-tepui in Roraima)

☐ **Ochre-faced Tody-Flycatcher** *Todirostrum plumbeiceps*

____	*T. p. obscurum*	E slope of Andes of se Peru (Puno) to n Bolivia
____	*T. p. viridiceps*	S Bolivia to nw Argentina (Jujuy and Salta)
____	*T. p. plumbeiceps*	SE Brazil (São Paulo) to e Paraguay and ne Argentina
____	*T. p. cinereipectum*	SE Brazil (Espírito Santo and se Minas Gerais); Alagoas

☐ **Rusty-fronted Tody-Flycatcher** *Todirostrum latirostre*

____	*T. l. mituense*	SE Colombia (Mitú region of Vaupés)
____	*T. l. caniceps*	Tropical se Colombia to e Ecuador and e Peru
____	*T. l. latirostre*	Central Brazil (Rio Juruá to Rio Purús in Amazonas)
____	*T. l. mixtum*	SE Peru (n Puno) to n Bolivia
____	*T. l. ochropterum*	S Brazil (n São Paulo) to e Bolivia and w Brazil (Mato Grosso)
____	*T. l. austroriparium*	E Brazil (right bank of Rio Tapajós near Santarém in w Pará)
____	*T. l. senectum*	Amazonian Brazil (ne Amazonas and nw Pará)

☐ **Smoky-fronted Tody-Flycatcher** *Todirostrum fumifrons*

____	*T. f. penardi*	Suriname to French Guiana and lower Amazonian Brazil
____	*T. f. fumifrons*	Coastal ne Brazil (Paraíba to ne Bahia)

☐ **Spotted Tody-Flycatcher** *Todirostrum maculatum*

____	*T. m. signatum*	SE Colombia to ne Ecuador, e Peru, n Bolivia and w Brazil
____	*T. m. amacurense*	Extreme e Venezuela and n Guyana; Trinidad
____	*T. m. maculatum*	French Guiana to Suriname and ne Amazonian Brazil
____	*T. m. diversum*	Central Amazonian Brazil
____	*T. m. annectens*	N-central Brazil (Rio Branco to Rio Negro)

☐ **Yellow-lored Tody-Flycatcher** *Todirostrum poliocephalum*

Lowlands of se Brazil (s Minas Gerais to e Santa Catarina)

☐ **Short-tailed Tody-Flycatcher** *Todirostrum viridanum*

Coastal nw Venezuela (Zulia and Falcón)

☐ **Black-headed Tody-Flycatcher** *Todirostrum nigriceps*

Caribbean slope of Costa Rica to w Ecuador and nw Venezuela

☐ **Painted Tody-Flycatcher** *Todirostrum pictum*

S Venezuela to the Guianas and n Brazil (east of Rio Negro)

☐ **Golden-winged Tody-Flycatcher** *Todirostrum calopterum*

SE Colombia (Putumayo) to e Ecuador and ne Peru (Loreto)

☐ **Black-backed Tody-Flycatcher** *Todirostrum pulchellum*

Humid foothills of se Peru (Cuzco and Puno)

☐ **Common Tody-Flycatcher** *Todirostrum cinereum*

_____ *T. c. virididorsale*	Tropical s Mexico (Veracruz and n Oaxaca)
_____ *T. c. finitimum*	Tropical s Mexico (Tabasco and Chiapas) to nw Costa Rica
_____ *T. c. wetmorei*	Tropical central and e Costa Rica and Panama
_____ *T. c. sclateri*	SW Colombia (Nariño) to w Ecuador and nw Peru
_____ *T. c. cinereum*	Tropical s Colombia to s Venezuela, the Guianas and n Brazil
_____ *T. c. peruanum*	E Ecuador and e Peru (south to Cuzco)
_____ *T. c. coloreum*	SE Brazil (Espírito Santo) to n Paraguay and n Bolivia
_____ *T. c. cearae*	NE Brazil (e Pará to Piauí, Ceará, Alagoas and n Bahia)

☐ **Yellow-browed Tody-Flycatcher** *Todirostrum chrysocrotaphum*

_____ *T. c. guttatum*	SE Colombia to ne Peru, extreme sw Venezuela and nw Brazil
_____ *T. c. neglectum*	E Peru to n Bolivia and sw Brazil
_____ *T. c. chrysocrotaphum*	E Peru (south of Río Marañón) and w Amazonian Brazil
_____ *T. c. similis*	NE Brazil (along lower Rio Tapajós in w Pará)
_____ *T. c. illigeri*	NE Brazil (along Rio Tapajós from w Pará to n Maranhão)

☐ **Ringed Antpipit** *Corythopis torquata*

_____ *C. t. sarayacuensis*	SE Colombia to e Ecuador and ne Peru
_____ *C. t. torquata*	E Peru (Amazonas, Huánuco and Junín) and w Amaz. Brazil
_____ *C. t. anthoides*	S Venezuela to the Guianas and n Amazonian Brazil
_____ *C. t. subtorquata*	N Bolivia (south to La Paz, Cochabamba and w Santa Cruz)

☐ **Southern Antpipit** *Corythopis delalandi*

S Brazil to e Bolivia, e Paraguay and ne Argentina

☐ **Brownish Flycatcher** *Cnipodectes subbrunneus*

_____ *C. s. panamensis*	Lowlands of e Panama (Bocas del Toro) to n Colombia
_____ *C. s. subbrunneus*	W Colombia (Chocó) south to w Ecuador
_____ *C. s. minor*	SE Colombia to e Ecuador, e Peru, nw Bolivia and w Amaz. Brazil

☐ **Large-headed Flatbill** *Ramphotrigon megacephala*

_____ *R. m. pectoralis*	SE Colombia (Meta and Putamayo) to e Ecuador and s Venezuela
_____ *R. m. venezuelensis*	NW Venezuela (Barinas, Yaracuy, w Apure and Amazonas)
_____ *R. m. boliviana*	Tropical e Peru (Loreto) to n Bolivia and w Amazonian Brazil
_____ *R. m. megacephala*	SE Brazil (e Minas Gerais) to se Paraguay and ne Argentina

☐ **Dusky-tailed Flatbill** *Ramphotrigon fuscicauda*

Extreme se Colombia to n Bolivia and sw Brazil (Mato Grosso)

☐ **Rufous-tailed Flatbill** *Ramphotrigon ruficauda*

SE Colombia to s Venezuela, Guianas, n Bolivia, Amaz. Brazil

☐ **Eye-ringed Flatbill** *Rhynchocyclus brevirostris*

_____ *R. b. brevirostris*	S Mexico (e Oaxaca and Veracruz) to w Panama
_____ *R. b. pallidus*	Pacific coast of s Mexico (Guerrero to Oaxaca)
_____ *R. b. hellmayri*	Mountains of e Panama (Darién) and extreme nw Colombia

☐ **Pacific Flatbill** *Rhynchocyclus pacificus*

W Colombia (Chocó) to nw Ecuador (south to s Pichincha)

☐ **Olivaceous Flatbill** *Rhynchocyclus olivaceus*

_____ *R. o. bardus*	Tropical e Panama and n Colombia (Chocó to Bolívar)
_____ *R. o. mirus*	NE Colombia (lower Atrato Valley)
_____ *R. o. tamborensis*	Colombia (Rio Lebrija region of Santander)
_____ *R. o. jelambianus*	Venezuela (Sucre to Carabobo, Mérida, Tachirá and Zulia)
_____ *R. o. flavus*	Tropical ne Colombia and n Venezuela
_____ *R. o. aequinoctialis*	SE Colombia to e Ecuador, e Peru and n Bolivia
_____ *R. o. guianensis*	S Venezuela to the Guianas and n Amazonian Brazil
_____ *R. o. sordidus*	Brazil south of the Amazon (Rio Tapajós to n Maranhão)
_____ *R. o. olivaceus*	SE Brazil (e Pernambuco to Rio de Janeiro)

☐ **Fulvous-breasted Flatbill** *Rhynchocyclus fulvipectus*

Andes of Colombia and extreme w Venezuela to w Bolivia

☐ **Yellow-olive Flycatcher** *Tolmomyias sulphurescens*

____	*T. s. cinereiceps*	Tropical s Mexico (Oaxaca) to Costa Rica
____	*T. s. flavoolivaceus*	W Panama (Chiriquí and Darién) to Colombia (sw Bolívar)
____	*T. s. asemus*	W Colombia (Cauca and Magdalena valleys)
____	*T. s. confusus*	E Andes of Colombia to sw Venezuela and ne Ecuador
____	*T. s. exortivus*	Santa Marta region of n Colombia to n Venezuela
____	*T. s. berlepschi*	Trinidad
____	*T. s. cherriei*	S Venezuela to the Guianas and n Amazonian Brazil
____	*T. s. duidae*	*Tepuis* of se Venezuela and adjacent nw Brazil
____	*T. s. aequatorialis*	W Ecuador and nw Peru (Tumbes and Piura)
____	*T. s. peruvianus*	SE Ecuador (Loja) and n Peru (south to Junín)
____	*T. s. insignis*	NE Peru (Loreto) and adjacent w Amazonian Brazil
____	*T. s. mixtus*	NE Brazil (e Pará to nw Maranhão)
____	*T. s. inornatus*	Subtropical se Peru (n Puno)
____	*T. s. pallescens*	E Brazil (Minas Gerais) to n Bolivia and n Argentina
____	*T. s. grisescens*	Paraguay and n Argentina (e Chaco, Formosa and n Santa Fe)
____	*T. s. sulphurescens*	SE Brazil to e Paraguay and ne Argentina

☐ **Yellow-margined Flycatcher** *Tolmomyias assimilis*

____	*T. a. flavotectus*	E Costa Rica to w Colombia and nw Ecuador (south to Guayas)
____	*T. a. neglectus*	E Colombia to sw Venezuela and nw Amazonian Brazil
____	*T. a. obscuriceps*	SE Colombia (Meta) to ne Peru north of the Amazon (Loreto)
____	*T. a. examinatus*	SE Venezuela to the Guianas and ne Brazil (Pará and Amapá)
____	*T. a. paraensis*	NE Brazil (e Pará and nw Maranhão)
____	*T. a. assimilis*	Amazonian Brazil (e Amazonas to Rio Tapajós in w Pará)
____	*T. a. clarus*	Tropical Peru north of Río Marañón (south to n Puno)
____	*T. a. calamae*	Tropical n Bolivia and sw Brazil (se Amazonas)

☐ **Gray-crowned Flycatcher** *Tolmomyias poliocephalus*

____	*T. p. poliocephalus*	SE Colombia to e Peru, s Venezuela and w Amazonian Brazil
____	*T. p. klagesi*	Tropical e Venezuela (n Amazonas to Delta Amacuro)
____	*T. p. sclateri*	Tropical Guianas, Amazonian and e Brazil and nw Bolivia

☐ **Orange-eyed Flycatcher** *Tolmomyias traylori*

Tropical s Colombia and ne Peru north of the Amazon

☐ **Yellow-breasted Flycatcher** *Tolmomyias flaviventris*

____	*T. f. aurulentus*	N Colombia (n Bolívar and Guajira Peninsula) to nw Venezuela
____	*T. f. collingwoodi*	E Colombia to the Guianas and ne Brazil; Trinidad and Tobago
____	*T. f. viridiceps*	SE Colombia to e Ecuador, e Peru and upper Amazonian Brazil
____	*T. f. dissors*	SW Venezuela (Amazonas) and lower Amazonian Brazil
____	*T. f. zimmeri*	N-central Peru (San Martín to Junín)
____	*T. f. subsimilis*	SE Peru (n Puno) to nw Bolivia and sw Brazil
____	*T. f. flaviventris*	E Brazil (Maranhão to Espírito Santo and Mato Grosso)

☐ **Cinnamon-crested Spadebill** *Platyrinchus saturatus*

____	*P. s. saturatus*	E Colombia to s Venezuela, the Guianas and n Amaz. Brazil
____	*P. s. pallidiventris*	Brazil on s bank of the Amazon (Rio Tapajós to n Maranhão)

☐ **Stub-tailed Spadebill** *Platyrinchus cancrominus*

____	*P. c. cancrominus*	Tropical s Mexico to e Nicaragua
____	*P. c. timothei*	SE Mexico (Yucatán Peninsula) to Petén of n Guatemala
____	*P. c. dilutus*	El Salvador to w Nicaragua and nw Costa Rica

☐ **Yellow-throated Spadebill** *Platyrinchus flavigularis*

____	*P. f. flavigularis*	Andes of Colombia and w Venezuela to se Peru (Cuzco)
____	*P. f. vividus*	Sierra de Perijá (Colombia/Venezuela border)

☐ **Golden-crowned Spadebill** *Platyrinchus coronatus*
_____ *P. c. superciliaris* — Caribbean slope of Honduras to Colombia and nw Ecuador
_____ *P. c. coronatus* — Extreme se Colombia to n Bolivia, s Venezuela and w Brazil
_____ *P. c. gumia* — SE Venezuela to the Guianas and n Amazonian Brazil

☐ **White-throated Spadebill** *Platyrinchus mystaceus*
_____ *P. m. neglectus* — E Costa Rica to e Colombia and extreme nw Venezuela
_____ *P. m. perijanus* — Subtropical Sierra de Perijá (Colombia/Venezuela border)
_____ *P. m. insularis* — N Venezuela; Trinidad and Tobago
_____ *P. m. imatacae* — S Venezuela (Sierra de Imataca in Bolívar)
_____ *P. m. ventralis* — S Venezuela (Cerro de la Neblina) and adjacent Brazil
_____ *P. m. duidae* — *Tepuis* of se Venezuela and adjacent n Brazil
_____ *P. m. ptaritepui* — *Tepuis* of se Venezuela (se Bolívar)
_____ *P. m. albogularis* — Colombia (Western Andes and Cauca Valley) to w Ecuador
_____ *P. m. zamorae* — Andes of e Ecuador and n Peru (south to Junín)
_____ *P. m. mystaceus* — SE Brazil to e Paraguay and ne Argentina
_____ *P. m. partridgei* — *Yungas* of Bolivia (Cochabamba and Santa Cruz)
_____ *P. m. bifasciatus* — S Brazil (central Mato Grosso to central Goiás)
_____ *P. m. cancromus* — E Brazil (Maranhão to Ceará, n Bahia and e Paraná)
_____ *P. m. niveigularis* — Coastal ne Brazil (Paraíba to Alagoas)

☐ **White-crested Spadebill** *Platyrinchus platyrhynchos*
_____ *P. p. platyrhynchos* — Extreme e Colombia to s Venezuela, the Guianas and n Brazil
_____ *P. p. senex* — E Ecuador to e Peru (Loreto), nw Bolivia and extreme w Brazil
_____ *P. p. nattereri* — W Brazil (Rio Purús to Rio Madeira and Rio Jiparaná)
_____ *P. p. amazonicus* — Amazonian Brazil (Rio Tapajós east to Pará)

☐ **Russet-winged Spadebill** *Platyrinchus leucoryphus*
SE Brazil (Espírito Santo) to e Paraguay and ne Argentina

☐ **Royal Flycatcher** *Onychorhynchus coronatus*
_____ *O. c. mexicanus* — Gulf lowlands of se Mexico (Veracruz) to e Panama (Darién)
_____ *O. c. fraterculus* — NE Colombia to e Venezuela (w Zulia and w Barinas)
_____ *O. c. castelnaui* — SE Colombia to n Bolivia and w Brazil (Amazonas)
_____ *O. c. coronatus* — E Venezuela to the Guianas and n Amazonian Brazil
_____ *O. c. occidentalis* — W Ecuador (Esmeraldas) to extreme n Peru (Tumbes)
_____ *O. c. swainsoni* — SE Brazil (Minas Gerais, Rio de Janeiro, Sao Paulo and Paraná)

☐ **Ornate Flycatcher** *Myiotriccus ornatus*
_____ *M. o. ornatus* — W slope of Eastern and Central Andes of Colombia
_____ *M. o. stellatus* — Western Andes of Colombia and Ecuador
_____ *M. o. phoenicurus* — Eastern Andes of se Colombia to e Ecuador and n Peru
_____ *M. o. aureiventris* — Andes of se Peru (Huánuco to Puno)

☐ **Flavescent Flycatcher** *Myiophobus flavicans*
_____ *M. f. flavicans* — Andes of Colombia to Ecuador and Peru (north of Río Marañón)
_____ *M. f. perijanus* — NW Venezuela (Sierra de Perijá and Páramo de Tamá)
_____ *M. f. venezuelanus* — Mts. of n Venezuela (Táchira to Distrito Federal and Miranda)
_____ *M. f. caripensis* — Coastal cordillera of ne Venezuela (Monagas and Sucre)
_____ *M. f. superciliosus* — Central Andes of Peru (s Amazonas to Cuzco)

☐ **Orange-crested Flycatcher** *Myiophobus phoenicomitra*
_____ *M. p. litae* — W slope of Andes of Colombia (s Chocó) and Ecuador
_____ *M. p. phoenicomitra* — E slope of Andes of e Ecuador to n Peru (San Martín)

☐ **Roraiman Flycatcher** *Myiophobus roraimae*
_____ *M. r. roraimae* — SE Colombia to e Ecuador, s Venezuela, w Guyana and w Brazil
_____ *M. r. sadiecoatsi* — *Tepuis* of s Venezuela (Bolívar and Amazonas)
_____ *M. r. rufipennis* — Locally in se Peru (San Martín to Puno)

☐ **Unadorned Flycatcher** *Myiophobus inornatus*

E slope of Andes of s Peru (Cuzco) to w Bolivia

☐ **Handsome Flycatcher** *Myiophobus pulcher*

_____ *M. p. pulcher*	W Andes of sw Colombia and nw Ecuador (south to Pichincha)
_____ *M. p. bellus*	Central and Eastern Andes of Colombia and ne Ecuador
_____ *M. p. oblitus*	Andes of se Peru (Cuzco and n Puno)

☐ **Orange-banded Flycatcher** *Myiophobus lintoni*

E slope of Andes of s Ecuador to extreme n Peru (Piura)

☐ **Ochraceous-breasted Flycatcher** *Myiophobus ochraceiventris*

E slope of Andes of e Peru (Amazonas) to w Bolivia (La Paz)

☐ **Bran-colored Flycatcher** *Myiophobus fasciatus*

_____ *M. f. furfurosus*	SW Costa Rica and w Panama; Pearl Islands
_____ *M. f. fasciatus*	Colombia to n Venezuela, the Guianas and adj. Brazil; Trinidad
_____ *M. f. crypterythrus*	Tropical sw Colombia to w Ecuador and extreme nw Peru
_____ *M. f. rufescens*	Arid w Peru (La Libertad) to extreme n Chile (Tarapacá)
_____ *M. f. saturatus*	E Peru (San Martín to central Cuzco)
_____ *M. f. auriceps*	SE Peru (Cuzco) to n Bolivia, n Argentina and w Paraguay
_____ *M. f. flammiceps*	E Brazil (e Pará) to Uruguay, e Paraguay and ne Argentina

☐ **Olive-chested Flycatcher** *Myiophobus cryptoxanthus*

Tropical e Ecuador and ne Peru (San Martín)

☐ **Ruddy-tailed Flycatcher** *Terenotriccus erythrurus*

_____ *T. e. fulvigularis*	Tropical se Mexico to Colombia, w Ecuador and Venezuela
_____ *T. e. signatus*	E Colombia to ne Peru (north of Río Marañón)
_____ *T. e. venezuelensis*	Extreme e Colombia to s Venezuela and nw Brazil
_____ *T. e. brunneifrons*	E Peru (south of Río Marañón) to n Bolivia and sw Brazil
_____ *T. e. erythrurus*	S Venezuela (Bolívar) to the Guianas and ne Brazil
_____ *T. e. perusianus*	Amazonian Brazil (middle Rio Purús)
_____ *T. e. amazonus*	Amazonian Brazil (Rio Purús to Rio Tapajós)
_____ *T. e. hellmayri*	NE Brazil (along lower Rio Tocantins east to Maranhão)

☐ **Tawny-breasted Flycatcher** *Myiobius villosus*

_____ *M. v. villosus*	E Panama (Cerro Tacarcuna) to w Colombia and w Ecuador
_____ *M. v. schaeferi*	E Andes of n Colombia and extreme w Venezuela (Táchira)
_____ *M. v. clarus*	Foothills of e Ecuador and e Peru (south to Junín)
_____ *M. v. peruvianus*	Foothills of se Peru (Puno) and nw Bolivia (La Paz)

☐ **Sulphur-rumped Flycatcher** *Myiobius sulphureipygius*

_____ *M. s. sulphureipygius*	Tropical se Mexico to Honduras
_____ *M. s. aureatus*	S Honduras to w Colombia and w Ecuador

☐ **Whiskered Flycatcher** *Myiobius barbatus*

_____ *M. b. semiflavus*	E-central Colombia (Nechí region of Antioquia)
_____ *M. b. barbatus*	SE Colombia to n Peru, s Venezuela, the Guianas and n Brazil
_____ *M. b. amazonicus*	E Peru (south of Río Marañón) east to Rio Madeira (Brazil)
_____ *M. b. insignis*	NE Brazil (south of the Amazon from Rio Tapajós to Pará)

☐ **Yellow-rumped Flycatcher** *Myiobius mastacalis*

SE Brazil (s Goiás, Paraíba and Bahia to Santa Catarina)

☐ **Black-tailed Flycatcher** *Myiobius atricaudus*

_____ *M. a. atricaudus*	Tropical sw Costa Rica to Panama and w Colombia
_____ *M. a. portovelae*	W Ecuador and extreme nw Peru (Tumbes)
_____ *M. a. modestus*	E Venezuela (n Bolívar)
_____ *M. a. adjacens*	S Colombia (Putumayo) to e Ecuador, e Peru and w Brazil
_____ *M. a. connectens*	NE Brazil (Rio Tapajós to n Maranhão)
_____ *M. a. snethlagei*	NE Brazil (Maranhão, Piauí, Ceará and w Bahia to se Goiás)
_____ *M. a. ridgwayi*	SE Brazil (Espírito Santa and s Minas Gerais to ne Paraná)

☐ **Cinnamon Tyrant** *Neopipo cinnamomea*
_____ *N. c. helenae* — Extreme s Venezuela to the Guianas and n Brazil (Amapá)
_____ *N. c. cinnamomea* — Extreme e Colombia to e Ecuador, e Peru and w Amaz. Brazil

☐ **Cinnamon Flycatcher** *Pyrrhomyias cinnamomea*
_____ *P. c. assimilis* — Santa Marta Mountains (ne Colombia)
_____ *P. c. pyrrhoptera* — Andes of Colombia to nw Venezuela, Ecuador and n Peru
_____ *P. c. vieillotioides* — Coastal mountains of nw Venezuela (Lara to Miranda)
_____ *P. c. spadix* — Coastal mountains of ne Venezuela (Anzoátegui to w Sucre)
_____ *P. c. pariae* — NE Venezuela (Cerro Azul and Cerro Humo on París Peninsula)
_____ *P. c. cinnamomea* — Subtropical e Peru (San Martín) to nw Argentina

☐ **Cliff Flycatcher** *Hirundinea ferruginea*
_____ *H. f. sclateri* — E Andes of Colombia to w Venezuela and e Peru (s to Cuzco)
_____ *H. f. ferruginea* — Extreme e Colombia to se Venezuela, the Guianas and nw Brazil
_____ *H. f. bellicosa* — S and e Brazil to e Paraguay, Uruguay and ne Argentina
_____ *H. f. pallidior* — N and e Bolivia to w Paraguay and nw Argentina

☐ **Fuscous Flycatcher** *Cnemotriccus fuscatus*
_____ *C. f. cabanisi* — N Colombia to e Venezuela; Trinidad and Tobago
_____ *C. f. fuscatior* — Tropical e Peru (lower Río Napo) to sw Venezuela and w Brazil
_____ *C. f. duidae* — S Venezuela (s Amazonas) and nw Brazil (Rio Negro)
_____ *C. f. fumosus* — The Guianas and ne Brazil (upper Rio Branco)
_____ *C. f. bimaculatus* — S and se Brazil to Paraguay, n Argentina and n Bolivia
_____ *C. f. beniensis* — N Bolivia (confluence of Río Madre de Dios and Río Beni)
_____ *C. f. fuscatus* — Coastal se Brazil (Bahia to ne Argentina)

☐ **Euler's Flycatcher** *Lathrotriccus euleri*
_____ *L. e. johnstonei†* — Grenada (Lesser Antilles). Extinct
_____ *L. e. lawrencei* — Extreme e Colombia to n Venezuela and Suriname; Trinidad
_____ *L. e. bolivianus* — E Ecuador to n Bolivia, s Venezuela and Amazonian Brazil
_____ *L. e. argentinus* — E Bolivia to Paraguay and n Argentina; winters to e Brazil
_____ *L. e. euleri* — SE Brazil to ne Argentina; winters to Peru, Bolivia and Brazil

☐ **Gray-breasted Flycatcher** *Lathrotriccus griseipectus*
— Arid tropical sw Ecuador and nw Peru

☐ **Tawny-chested Flycatcher** *Aphanotriccus capitalis*
— E Nicaragua to n Costa Rica (south to Puerto Limón)

☐ **Black-billed Flycatcher** *Aphanotriccus audax*
— Tropical e Panama and n Colombia

☐ **Belted Flycatcher** *Xenotriccus callizonus*
— Highlands of s Mexico (Chiapas), Guatemala and El Salavdor

☐ **Pileated Flycatcher** *Xenotriccus mexicanus*
— Highlands of central Mexico (Michoacan to central Oaxaca)

☐ **Tufted Flycatcher** *Mitrephanes phaeocercus*
_____ *M. p. tenuirostris* — Mountains of w Mexico (Sonora and Chihuahua to Jalisco)
_____ *M. p. phaeocercus* — Mountains of e Mexico (Tamaulipas to e Oaxaca)
_____ *M. p. burleighi* — Mountains of s Mexico (Jalisco to sw Oaxaca)
_____ *M. p. nicaraguae* — Mountains of s Mexico (Chiapas) to ne Nicaragua
_____ *M. p. aurantiiventris* — Highlands of Costa Rica and w Panama (Chiriquí)
_____ *M. p. vividus* — Mountains of central Panama to eastern Darién
_____ *M. p. eminulus* — E Panama (Cerro Pirre) and adjacent nw Colombia (Chocó)
_____ *M. p. berlepschi* — NW Colombia (Atrato Valley) to nw Ecuador (Esmeraldas)

☐ **Olive Flycatcher** *Mitrephanes olivaceus*
— E slope of Andes of ne Peru (Piura) to w Bolivia

☐ **Olive-sided Flycatcher** *Contopus cooperi*
— Breeds temperate North America; winters south to Bolivia

338

☐ **Greater Pewee** *Contopus pertinax*

____ *C. p. pallidiventris* — Oak-pine forests of s Arizona and n Mexico; winters to Belize

____ *C. p. pertinax* — S Mexico (Jalisco and Veracruz) to Guatemala

____ *C. p. minor* — Highlands of Belize, Honduras, El Salvador and n Nicaragua

☐ **Dark Pewee** *Contopus lugubris*

Montane forests of Costa Rica and extreme w Panama (Chiriquí)

☐ **Smoke-colored Pewee** *Contopus fumigatus*

____ *C. f. ardosiacus* — Colombia to ne Venezuela, e Ecuador and ne Peru

____ *C. f. cineraceus* — Subtropical n Venezuela (Yaracuy to Miranda)

____ *C. f. duidae* — *Tepuis* of s Venezuela (s Bolívar and Amazonas), adj. Guyana

____ *C. f. zarumae* — SW Ecuador (Nariño) to n Peru (sw Cajamarca)

____ *C. f. fumigatus* — SE Peru (Puno) and w Bolivia (La Paz and Cochabamba)

____ *C. f. brachyrhynchus* — SE Bolivia (Santa Cruz and Tarija) to nw Argentina (Tucumán)

☐ **Ochraceous Pewee** *Contopus ochraceus*

Montane forests of Costa Rica and extreme w Panama (Chiriquí)

☐ **Western Wood-Pewee** *Contopus sordidulus*

____ *C. s. saturatus* — Alaska to California; winters to n South America

____ *C. s. siccicola* — S British Columbia (e of the Cascades) to Idaho and Montana

____ *C. s. amplus* — E Alaska to Wyoming, South Dakota; winters to n S America

____ *C. s. veliei* — SW US to n Mexico; winters to Panama

____ *C. s. peninsulae* — S Baja California; winters to nw South America

____ *C. s. griscomi* — SW Mexico; winters to n South America

____ *C. s. sordidulus* — S Mexico (Guerrero); winters to Colombia and Ecuador

☐ **Eastern Wood-Pewee** *Contopus virens*

Breeds e North America; winters to n Bolivia and w Brazil

☐ **Tropical Pewee** *Contopus cinereus*

____ *C. c. brachytarsus* — Tropical se Mexico (Oaxaca and Veracruz) to Panama

____ *C. c. rhizophorus* — Arid Pacific littoral of w Costa Rica (Guanacaste)

____ *C. c. aithalodes* — Isla Coiba (Panama)

____ *C. c. bogotensis* — N Colombia to n Venezuela and nw Brazil; Trinidad

____ *C. c. surinamensis* — S Venezuela to the Guianas and ne Brazil

____ *C. c. punensis* — Andes of Ecuador to s Peru (Ica and Madre de Dios); Isla Puná

____ *C. c. pallescens* — E Brazil (Maranhão) to ne Paraguay, Bolivia and nw Argentina

____ *C. c. cinereus* — SE Brazil (Bahia to Paraná) to e Paraguay and ne Argentina

☐ **Blackish Pewee** *Contopus nigrescens*

____ *C. n. nigrescens* — E slope of Andes of Ecuador (Napo-Pastaza and Santiago-Zamora)

____ *C. n. canescens* — E Peru (s to Cuzco); s Guyana (Acari Mts.) and e Amaz. Brazil

☐ **Cuban Pewee** *Contopus caribaeus*

____ *C. c. bahamensis* — Grand Bahama, Abaco, Andros, New Providence and Eleuthera

____ *C. c. caribaeus* — Cuba and Isle of Pines

____ *C. c. morenoi* — S Cuba (Zapata Swamp) and adjacent offshore cays

____ *C. c. nerlyi* — Islands off s Camagüey (Cuba)

☐ **Jamaican Pewee** *Contopus pallidus*

Jamaica

☐ **Hispaniolan Pewee** *Contopus hispaniolensis*

____ *C. h. hispaniolensis* — Hispaniola

____ *C. h. tacitus* — Gonâve I. (Haiti)

☐ **Lesser Antillean Pewee** *Contopus latirostris*

____ *C. l. blancoi* — Montane forests of Puerto Rico

____ *C. l. brunneicapillus* — Montane forests of Dominica, Guadeloupe and Martinique

____ *C. l. latirostris* — Montane forests of St. Lucia

☐ **White-throated Pewee** *Contopus albogularis*

☐ **Yellow-bellied Flycatcher** *Empidonax flaviventris*

☐ **Acadian Flycatcher** *Empidonax virescens*

☐ **Alder Flycatcher** *Empidonax alnorum*

☐ **Willow Flycatcher** *Empidonax traillii*
_____ *E. t. brewsteri*
_____ *E. t. adastus*
_____ *E. t. extimus*
_____ *E. t. traillii*

☐ **White-throated Flycatcher** *Empidonax albigularis*
_____ *E. a. timidus*
_____ *E. a. albigularis*
_____ *E. a. australis*

☐ **Least Flycatcher** *Empidonax minimus*

☐ **Hammond's Flycatcher** *Empidonax hammondii*

☐ **Gray Flycatcher** *Empidonax wrightii*

☐ **Dusky Flycatcher** *Empidonax oberholseri*

☐ **Pine Flycatcher** *Empidonax affinis*
_____ *E. a. pulverius*
_____ *E. a. trepidus*
_____ *E. a. affinis*
_____ *E. a. bairdi*
_____ *E. a. vigensis*

☐ **Pacific-slope Flycatcher** *Empidonax difficilis*
_____ *E. d. difficilis*
_____ *E. d. insulicola*
_____ *E. d. cineritius*

☐ **Cordilleran Flycatcher** *Empidonax occidentalis*
_____ *E. o. hellmayri*
_____ *E. o. occidentalis*

☐ **Yellowish Flycatcher** *Empidonax flavescens*
_____ *E. f. imperturbatus*
_____ *E. f. salvini*
_____ *E. f. flavescens*

☐ **Buff-breasted Flycatcher** *Empidonax fulvifrons*
_____ *E. f. pygmaeus*
_____ *E. f. fulvifrons*
_____ *E. f. rubicundus*
_____ *E. f. brodkorbi*
_____ *E. f. fusciceps*

☐ **Black-capped Flycatcher** *Empidonax atriceps*

☐ **Eastern Phoebe** *Sayornis phoebe*

Suriname to French Guiana and extreme ne Brazil (Amapá)

Breeds e Canada and US; winters Mexico to Panama

Breeds e US; winters Nicaragua to Ecuador and Venezuela

Breeds Alaska to ne US; winters Colombia to Bolivia

Pacific northwest (s British Columbia) to Sierra Nevada
Great Basin and central Rocky Mts. south to Utah and Colorado
Breeds s Calif. e to New Mexico and (?) formerly w Texas
Great Plains to ne US and se Canada; winters to nw S America

Highlands of nw Mexico (Chihuahua to s Durango)
Highlands of e Mexico to Guatemala, El Salvador and Honduras
Highlands of Nicaragua to w Panama (Chiriquí)

Breeds Canada and US; winters n Mexico to Panama

Breeds w North America; winters to Nicaragua

Breeds w North America; winters to s Mexico

Breeds w North America; winters to s Mexico

Oak-pine forests of nw Mexico (Sinaloa to Jalisco)
N Mexico (Coahuila and Tamaulipas); winters to Guatemala
Pine forests of Mexican plateau (Michoacán to Puebla)
Pine forests of s Mexico (Guerrero, Oaxaca and Chiapas)
Oak-pine forests of e Mexico (Veracruz)

W North America (se Alaska to n Baja); winters to s Mexico
Channel Islands off s California
Cape district of Baja California

Woodlands of sw Canada to n Mexico; winters to s Mexico
Highlands of Mexico

S Mexico (Sierra de Tuxtla in se Veracruz)
Highlands of se Mexico (Oaxaca) to Nicaragua
Highlands of Costa Rica and w Panama (east to Veraguas)

SW US and nw Mexico (Sonora to Coahuila)
Mountains of ne Mexico (Tamaulipas and San Luis Potosí)
Mexico (Chihuahua and Durango to Guerrero and Veracruz)
S Mexico (Río Molino area of s Oaxaca)
SE Mexico (Chiapas) to Guatemala and Honduras

Mountains of Costa Rica and w Panama

Breeds e Canada and US; winters to se Mexico

☐ **Black Phoebe** *Sayornis nigricans*

_____	*S. n. semiatra*	W US (Oregon) to Baja California and w Mexico (Nayarit)
_____	*S. n. nigricans*	Highlands of ne Mexico (Tamaulipas to n Chiapas)
_____	*S. n. aquatica*	S Mexico (highlands of s Chiapas) to Guatemala and Nicaragua
_____	*S. n. amnicola*	Highlands of Costa Rica and w Panama (Chiriquí)
_____	*S. n. angustirostris*	E Panama to Colombia, Ecuador, s Peru and n Venezuela
_____	*S. n. latirostris*	Andes of Bolivia and nw Argentina

☐ **Say's Phoebe** *Sayornis saya*

_____	*S. s. saya*	Arid scrub of w North America (Alaska to n Mexico)
_____	*S. s. quiescens*	Northern half of Baja California and Isla de Cedros
_____	*S. s. pallida*	S Mexico (Jalisco and Zacatecas to Hidalgo and Oaxaca)

☐ **Vermilion Flycatcher** *Pyrocephalus rubinus*

_____	*P. r. flammeus*	Arid sw US to Baja California and nw Mexico (Nayarit)
_____	*P. r. mexicanus*	Arid sw Texas to Guerrero, Oaxaca, Puebla and Veracruz
_____	*P. r. blatteus*	SE Mexico (s Veracruz) to Guatemala and Honduras
_____	*P. r. pinicola*	Lowland pine savanna of ne Nicaragua
_____	*P. r. nanus*	Galapagos Islands (except Chatham I.)
_____	*P. r. dubius*	Chatham I. (Galapagos Islands)
_____	*P. r. saturatus*	NE Colombia to n Venezuela, Guyana and n Brazil
_____	*P. r. piurae*	Colombia (west of Eastern Andes) to w Ecuador and nw Peru
_____	*P. r. ardens*	N Peru (Cajamarca, Amazonas and extreme e Piura)
_____	*P. r. obscurus*	W Peru (Lima)
_____	*P. r. cocachacrae*	SW Peru (Ica to Tacna) and adjacent n Chile
_____	*P. r. major*	SE Peru (Cuzco and Puno)
_____	*P. r. rubinus*	Extreme se Brazil to se Bolivia, Paraguay, Uruguay, ne Argentina

☐ **Crowned Chat-Tyrant** *Silvicultrix frontalis*

_____	*S. f. albidiadema*	Eastern Andes of Colombia (north to Norte de Santander)
_____	*S. f. frontalis*	Central Andes of Colombia and w Andes of n Ecuador
_____	*S. f. orientalis*	E Andes of Ecuador to n Peru
_____	*S. f. spodionota*	Andes of Peru (Junín, Ayacucho and Cordillera Vilcabamba)
_____	*S. f. boliviana*	Andes of Peru (Huánuco and Cuzco) to w Bolivia

☐ **Jelski's Chat-Tyrant** *Silvicultrix jelskii*

	Andes of sw Ecuador and nw Peru (s to Lima and Huánuco)

☐ **Yellow-bellied Chat-Tyrant** *Silvicultrix diadema*

_____	*S. d. jesupi*	Santa Marta Mountains (ne Colombia)
_____	*S. d. rubellula*	NE Colombia (Sierra de Perijá) and nw Venezuela (Zulia)
_____	*S. d. tovarensis*	Coastal cordillera of n Venezuela (Aragua and Distrito Federal)
_____	*S. d. diadema*	E Andes of Colombia and extreme sw Venezuela (Táchira)
_____	*S. d. meridana*	Andes of w Venezuela (Táchira, Mérida and Trujillo)
_____	*S. d. gratiosa*	Andes of Colombia and n Ecuador (south to Pichincha)
_____	*S. d. cajamarcae*	Andes of n Peru (Piura and Cajamarca)

☐ **Golden-browed Chat-Tyrant** *Silvicultrix pulchella*

_____	*S. p. similis*	E slope of Andes of Peru (s Amazonas to Junín)
_____	*S. p. pulchella*	Andes of se Peru (Cuzco and Ayacucho) to w Bolivia

☐ **Slaty-backed Chat-Tyrant** *Ochthoeca cinnamomeiventris*

_____	*O. c. cinnamomeiventris*	Andes of Colombia to n Ecuador and sw Venezuela
_____	*O. c. nigrita*	Andes of w Venezuela (Mérida, w Barinas and Táchira)
_____	*O. c. angustifasciata*	Andes of n Peru (s Amazonas, San Martín and Cajamarca)
_____	*O. c. thoracica*	Andes of se Peru (Pasco) to w Bolivia (Cochabamba)

☐ **Piura Chat-Tyrant** *Ochthoeca piurae*

	Locally in Andes of nw Peru (Piura to Ancash)

☐ **D'Orbigny's Chat-Tyrant** *Ochthoeca oenanthoides*
_____ *O. o. polionota* — Andes of Peru (north to La Libertad and w Huánuco)
_____ *O. o. oenanthoides* — Andes of Bolivia to extreme n Chile and nw Argentina

☐ **Rufous-breasted Chat-Tyrant** *Ochthoeca rufipectoralis*
_____ *O. r. poliogastra* — Santa Marta Mountains (ne Colombia)
_____ *O. r. rubicundula* — Sierra de Perijá (Colombia/Venezuela border)
_____ *O. r. obfuscata* — Central and W Andes of Colombia to Peru (nw San Martín)
_____ *O. r. rufopectus* — Eastern Andes of Colombia (south to Bogotá)
_____ *O. r. centralis* — Andes of Peru (s La Libertad, Ancash and Huánuco)
_____ *O. r. tectricialis* — W slope of Eastern Andes of Peru (Pasco to Cuzco)
_____ *O. r. rufipectoralis* — Andes of se Peru (Cuzco and Puno) to w Bolivia

☐ **Brown-backed Chat-Tyrant** *Ochthoeca fumicolor*
_____ *O. f. fumicolor* — E Andes of Colombia and w Venezuela (w Táchira)
_____ *O. f. ferruginea* — Central and Western Andes of Colombia (Antioquia)
_____ *O. f. superciliosa* — Andes of w Venezuela (Trujillo, Mérida and e Táchira)
_____ *O. f. brunneifrons* — Central and Western Andes of Colombia to central Peru
_____ *O. f. berlepschi* — Andes of se Peru (Cuzco and Puno) to w Bolivia

☐ **White-browed Chat-Tyrant** *Ochthoeca leucophrys*
_____ *O. l. dissors* — N Peru (upper Marañón Valley)
_____ *O. l. interior* — Andes of central Peru (Huánuco and Pasco)
_____ *O. l. urubambae* — Andes of s Peru (Junín to ne Ayacucho and Cuzco)
_____ *O. l. leucometopa* — W slope of Andes of Peru (Ancash) to extreme nw Chile
_____ *O. l. leucophrys* — Andes of w Bolivia
_____ *O. l. tucumana* — Andes of nw Argentina (Salta to San Juan)

☐ **Tumbes Tyrant** *Ochthoeca salvini*

Arid nw Peru (Tumbes to La Libertad)

☐ **Patagonian Tyrant** *Colorhamphus parvirostris*

S Chile (Valdivia) and adj. Argentina south to Tierra del Fuego

☐ **Drab Water-Tyrant** *Ochthornis littoralis*

S Guyana to s Venezuela, n Bolivia and Amazonian Brazil

☐ **Red-rumped Bush-Tyrant** *Cnemarchus erythropygius*
_____ *C. e. orinomus* — Santa Marta Mountains and Eastern Andes of n Colombia
_____ *C. e. erythropygius* — Andes of s Colombia to Ecuador, e Peru and w Bolivia

☐ **Streak-throated Bush-Tyrant** *Myiotheretes striaticollis*
_____ *M. s. striaticollis* — Andes of Colombia to w Venezuela, Ecuador and central Peru
_____ *M. s. pallidus* — Andes of e Peru (Cuzco) to n Bolivia and nw Argentina

☐ **Santa Marta Bush-Tyrant** *Myiotheretes pernix*

Santa Marta Mountains (ne Colombia)

☐ **Smoky Bush-Tyrant** *Myiotheretes fumigatus*
_____ *M. f. olivaceus* — Sierra de Perijá (Colombia/Venezuela border)
_____ *M. f. fumigatus* — Andes of Colombia and n Ecuador
_____ *M. f. lugubris* — Andes of w Venezuela (Táchira, Trujillo and Mérida)
_____ *M. f. cajamarcae* — Andes of s Ecuador (Cañar) and Peru (south to Cuzco)

☐ **Rufous-bellied Bush-Tyrant** *Myiotheretes fuscorufus*

E slope of Andes of s Peru (Pasco) to w Bolivia

☐ **Fire-eyed Diucon** *Xolmis pyrope*
_____ *X. p. pyrope* — Andes of central Chile and adj. Argentina to Tierra del Fuego
_____ *X. p. fortis* — Chiloe I. (Chile)

☐ **Gray Monjita** *Xolmis cinerea*
_____ *X. c. cinerea* — Suriname; Amazonian and e Brazil, Uruguay and ne Argentina
_____ *X. c. pepoaza* — SE Peru (Madre de Dios) to e Bolivia, Paraguay and n Argentina

☐ **Black-crowned Monjita** *Xolmis coronata*

S Argentina; winters to s Bolivia, Paraguay and extreme s Brazil

☐ **White-rumped Monjita** *Xolmis velata*

Savanna and campos of e Brazil, ne Paraguay and e Bolivia

☐ **White Monjita** *Xolmis irupero*
  _____ *X. i. nivea*
  _____ *X. i. irupero*

E Brazil (Ceará and Pernambuco to Bahia and Minas Gerais)
SE Brazil to Paraguay, Uruguay, Bolivia and n Argentina

☐ **Rusty-backed Monjita** *Xolmis rubetra*

W Argentina (Mendoza to Santa Cruz); winters to w Uruguay

☐ **Salinas Monjita** *Xolmis salinarum*

Arid *salinas* of nw Argentina

☐ **Black-and-white Monjita** *Heteroxolmis dominicana*

SE Brazil (Paraná) to Paraguay, Uruguay and ne Argentina

☐ **Chocolate-vented Tyrant** *Neoxolmis rufiventris*

Extreme s Argentina and Chile; winters n to extreme se Brazil

☐ **Black-billed Shrike-Tyrant** *Agriornis montana*
  _____ *A. m. solitaria*
  _____ *A. m. insolens*
  _____ *A. m. intermedia*
  _____ *A. m. montana*
  _____ *A. m. maritima*
  _____ *A. m. leucura*

Andes of Colombia and Ecuador
Andes of Peru
Andes of w Bolivia (La Paz and Oruro) to n Chile (Tarapacá)
Andes of e and s Bolivia and nw Argentina (south to La Rioja)
Andes of n Chile (Tarapacá to Coquimbo)
Andes of central Chile and s Argentina

☐ **White-tailed Shrike-Tyrant** *Agriornis andicola*
  _____ *A. a. andicola*
  _____ *A. a. albicauda*

Andes of Ecuador (north to Imbabura)
Andes of Peru to w Bolivia, n Chile and nw Argentina

☐ **Great Shrike-Tyrant** *Agriornis livida*
  _____ *A. l. livida*
  _____ *A. l. fortis*

Coast and mountains of Chile (Atacama to Valdivia)
S Chile (Aysén) and s Argentina to Tierra del Fuego

☐ **Gray-bellied Shrike-Tyrant** *Agriornis microptera*
  _____ *A. m. andecola*
  _____ *A. m. microptera*

Andes of s Peru to Bolivia, nw Argentina and n Chile
Andes of s Argentina; winters to w Paraguay and s Uruguay

☐ **Lesser Shrike-Tyrant** *Agriornis murina*

S Argentina; winters north to w Paraguay and s Bolivia

☐ **Rufous-webbed Tyrant** *Polioxolmis rufipennis*
  _____ *P. r. rufipennis*
  _____ *P. r. bolivianus*

Andes of Peru to extreme nw Argentina and (?) adjacent n Chile
Andes of central Bolivia

☐ **Spot-billed Ground-Tyrant** *Muscisaxicola maculirostris*
  _____ *M. m. niceforoi*
  _____ *M. m. rufescens*
  _____ *M. m. maculirostris*

Eastern Andes of Colombia (Boyacá and Cundinamarca)
Andes of Ecuador (Pichincha to Azuay)
Andes of Peru to w Bolivia, w Argentina and Chile

☐ **Little Ground-Tyrant** *Muscisaxicola fluviatilis*

SE Colombia to e Ecuador, e Peru, n Bolivia and sw Amaz. Brazil

☐ **Dark-faced Ground-Tyrant** *Muscisaxicola macloviana*
  _____ *M. m. mentalis*
  _____ *M. m. macloviana*

S Argentina and Chile; winters on coast to n Peru and Uruguay
Falkland Islands

☐ **Cinnamon-bellied Ground-Tyrant** *Muscisaxicola capistrata*

Breeds s Chile and s Argentina; winters north in Andes to s Peru

☐ **Rufous-naped Ground-Tyrant** *Muscisaxicola rufivertex*
  _____ *M. r. occipitalis*
  _____ *M. r. pallidiceps*
  _____ *M. r. rufivertex*

Andes of Peru and n Bolivia (La Paz and Cochabamba)
Andes of sw Peru to nw Argentina and n Chile
Andes of s Chile and s Argentina; winters north to Antofagasta

☐ **Puna Ground-Tyrant** *Muscisaxicola juninensis*

Andes of Peru (Junín and Lima) to n Chile and nw Argentina

☐ **White-browed Ground-Tyrant** *Muscisaxicola albilora*

Andes of c and s Chile and adj. Argentina; winters to s Ecuador

☐ **Plain-capped Ground-Tyrant** *Muscisaxicola alpina*
_____ *M. a. columbiana*
_____ *M. a. quesadea*
_____ *M. a. alpina*
_____ *M. a. grisea*

Central Andes of Colombia (Nevado del Ruiz to Cauca)
E Andes of Colombia (Boyacá and Cundinamarca)
Páramo of Ecuador
Páramo of Peru and w Bolivia (La Paz to Cochabamba)

☐ **Cinereous Ground-Tyrant** *Muscisaxicola cinerea*
_____ *M. c. cinerea*
_____ *M. c. argentina*

Andes of s Peru (Puno) to w Bolivia, n Chile and n Argentina
Andes of nw Argentina (Jujuy to Catamarca and Tucumán)

☐ **White-fronted Ground-Tyrant** *Muscisaxicola albifrons*

Andes of s Peru (Ancash) to w Bolivia and extreme n Chile

☐ **Ochre-naped Ground-Tyrant** *Muscisaxicola flavinucha*
_____ *M. f. flavinucha*
_____ *M. f. brevirostris*

Andes of Chile and Argentina; winters to n Peru (La Libertad)
S Chile (Aysén) south to Tierra del Fuego

☐ **Black-fronted Ground-Tyrant** *Muscisaxicola frontalis*

Andes of Chile and Argentina; winters n to s Peru (Arequipa)

☐ **Short-tailed Field-Tyrant** *Muscigralla brevicauda*

Arid sw Ecuador to extreme n Chile (Arica)

☐ **Andean Negrito** *Lessonia oreas*

Andes of Peru (Huánuco) to n Chile and nw Argentina

☐ **Austral Negrito** *Lessonia rufa*

C Chile and Argentina to Tierra del Fuego; winters to se Brazil

☐ **Cinereous Tyrant** *Knipolegus striaticeps*

E Bolivia to n Argentina, w Paraguay and extreme sw Brazil

☐ **Hudson's Black-Tyrant** *Knipolegus hudsoni*

Central Argentina; winters to Bolivia, sw Brazil and se Peru

☐ **Amazonian Black-Tyrant** *Knipolegus poecilocercus*

S Venezuela and w Guyana to e Ecuador and Amazonian Brazil

☐ **Andean Tyrant** *Knipolegus signatus*
_____ *K. s. signatus*
_____ *K. s. cabanisi*

E slope of Andes of Peru (Cajamarca to Junín)
Andes of se Peru (Cuzco) to w Bolivia and n Argentina

☐ **Blue-billed Black-Tyrant** *Knipolegus cyanirostris*

SE Brazil to Uruguay, e Paraguay and ne Argentina

☐ **Rufous-tailed Tyrant** *Knipolegus poecilurus*
_____ *K. p. poecilurus*
_____ *K. p. venezuelanus*
_____ *K. p. paraquensis*
_____ *K. p. salvini*
_____ *K. p. peruanus*

Andes of Colombia and w Venezuela
Coastal cordillera of n Venezuela (Distrito Federal)
Subtropical s Venezuela (Cerro Paraque area of Amazonas)
Tepuis of s Venezuela, Guyana and extreme n Brazil
Andes of se Ecuador, e Peru and n Bolivia

☐ **Riverside Tyrant** *Knipolegus orenocensis*
_____ *K. o. orenocensis*
_____ *K. o. xinguensis*
_____ *K. o. sclateri*

Extreme se Colombia and Orinoco system of Venezuela
E Brazil (Rio Xingú, Rio Tapajós and Rio Araguaia)
Tropical ne Peru (Loreto) and central Amazonian Brazil

☐ **White-winged Black-Tyrant** *Knipolegus aterrimus*
_____ *K. a. heterogyna*
_____ *K. a. anthracinus*
_____ *K. a. aterrimus*
_____ *K. a. franciscanus*

N Peru (Marañón Valley in Cajamarca, La Libertad and Ancash)
Andes of Peru (Ayacucho, Cuzco, Puno) and w Bolivia (La Paz)
Andes of e Bolivia, w Argentina and *chaco* of Paraguay
E-central Brazil (Minas Gerais and Rio São Francisco in Bahia)

☐ **Velvety Black-Tyrant** *Knipolegus nigerrimus*

E Brazil (ne Bahia and Alagoas to ne Rio Grande do Sul)

☐ **Crested Black-Tyrant** *Knipolegus lophotes*

S-central and se Brazil to Uruguay and ne Paraguay

☐ **Spectacled Tyrant** *Hymenops perspicillatus*
_____ *H. p. perspicillatus*
_____ *H. p. andina*

SW Brazil to Uruguay, Paraguay and n Argentina
C Chile and c Argentina; winters to n Bolivia and sw Brazil

☐ **Pied Water-Tyrant** *Fluvicola pica*

E Panama to Venezuela, the Guianas, extreme n Brazil; Trinidad

☐ **Black-backed Water-Tyrant** *Fluvicola albiventer*

Amazonian and e Brazil to e Bolivia, Paraguay and n Argentina

☐ **Masked Water-Tyrant** *Fluvicola nengeta*
_____ *F. n. atripennis*
_____ *F. n. nengeta*

SW Ecuador to nw Peru (Tumbes)
E Brazil (Maranhão to Minas Gerais and ne São Paulo)

☐ **White-headed Marsh-Tyrant** *Arundinicola leucocephala*

Colombia to the Guianas, s Brazil and n Argentina; Trinidad

☐ **Cock-tailed Tyrant** *Alectrurus tricolor*

Locally in e Bolivia, ne Argentina, ne Paraguay and s Brazil

☐ **Strange-tailed Tyrant** *Alectrurus risora*

Locally in e Paraguay, s Brazil, Uruguay and n Argentina

☐ **Streamer-tailed Tyrant** *Gubernetes yetapa*

E Bolivia to Paraguay, s-central and se Brazil and ne Argentina

☐ **Yellow-browed Tyrant** *Satrapa icterophrys*

Extreme se Peru to n Argentina, e and s Brazil; Venezuela

☐ **Long-tailed Tyrant** *Colonia colonus*
_____ *C. c. leuconotus*
_____ *C. c. fuscicapillus*
_____ *C. c. poecilonotus*
_____ *C. c. niveiceps*
_____ *C. c. colonus*

Tropical ne Honduras to Panama, w Colombia and nw Ecuador
S slope of Andes of Colombia, n Ecuador and extreme ne Peru
Tropical se Venezuela (e Bolívar) to the Guianas and Suriname
Tropical e Peru (San Martín) to n Bolivia
SE Brazil (s Maranhão) to e Paraguay and ne Argentina

☐ **Cattle Tyrant** *Machetornis rixosus*
_____ *M. r. flavigularis*
_____ *M. r. obscurodorsalis*
_____ *M. r. rixosus*

Caribbean coast of n Colombia and n Venezuela
Llanos of e Colombia and sw Venezuela
Interior e Brazil to e Bolivia, Paraguay, Uruguay and n Argentina

☐ **Shear-tailed Gray Tyrant** *Muscipipra vetula*

SE Brazil (Minas Gerais) to e Paraguay and ne Argentina

☐ **Rufous-tailed Attila** *Attila phoenicurus*

Amazonian and se Brazil to e Paraguay and ne Argentina

☐ **Cinnamon Attila** *Attila cinnamomeus*

S Venezuela and the Guianas to n Bolivia and Amazonian Brazil

☐ **Ochraceous Attila** *Attila torridus*

Extreme sw Colombia to w Ecuador and nw Peru (Tumbes)

☐ **Citron-bellied Attila** *Attila citriniventris*

Extreme s Venezuela to ne Peru (Loreto) and w Amaz. Brazil

☐ **Bright-rumped Attila** *Attila spadiceus*
_____ *A. s. pacificus*
_____ *A. s. cozumelae*
_____ *A. s. guameri*
_____ *A. s. flammulatus*
_____ *A. s. salvadorensis*
_____ *A. s. citreopygus*
_____ *A. s. sclateri*
_____ *A. s. caniceps*
_____ *A. s. parvirostris*
_____ *A. s. parambae*
_____ *A. s. spadiceus*
_____ *A. s. uropygialis*

Coastal nw Mexico (extreme s Sonora to w Oaxaca)
Cozumel I. (off Yucatán Peninsula of e Mexico)
Tropical n Yucatán Pen.; Holbox I., Meco I. and Isla Mujeres
Tropical se Mexico (Veracruz) to El Salvador
Tropical El Salvador to nw Nicaragua
Tropical se Honduras and Nicaragua to w Panama
Tropical e Panama and nw Colombia (upper Sinú Valley)
Trop. n Colombia (middle Magdalena and lower Sinú valleys)
Santa Marta Mountains (ne Colombia) and nw Venezuela
W Colombia (Río Atrato to Nariño) and nw Ecuador
E Colombia to the Guianas, ne Peru, n Bolivia, n Brazil; Trinidad
SE Brazil (Alagoas and Bahia to Rio de Janeiro)

☐ **Dull-capped Attila** *Attila bolivianus*
_____ *A. b. nattereri* — Extreme se Colombia to ne Peru and w Amazonian Brazil
_____ *A. b. bolivianus* — Tropical sw Brazil (Amazonas and Mato Grosso) and n Bolivia

☐ **Gray-hooded Attila** *Attila rufus*
_____ *A. r. hellmayri* — Tropical e Brazil (central Bahia)
_____ *A. r. rufus* — Tropical se Brazil (Minas Gerais to Rio Grande do Sul)

☐ **Rufous Casiornis** *Casiornis rufa*
SE Peru to e Bolivia, Paraguay, n Argentina, Amaz. and e Brazil

☐ **Ash-throated Casiornis** *Casiornis fusca*
Caatinga and scrub of ne Brazil

☐ **Sirystes** *Sirystes sibilator*
_____ *S. s. albogriseus* — E Panama (Veraguas) to nw Colombia and nw Ecuador
_____ *S. s. albocinereus* — SE Colombia to e Ecuador, e Peru, n Bolivia and w Brazil
_____ *S. s. subcanescens* — S Suriname and ne Brazil
_____ *S. s. sibilator* — E Brazil (Goiás and Bahia) to e Paraguay and ne Argentina
_____ *S. s. atimastus* — SW Brazil (Mato Grosso)

☐ **Rufous Mourner** *Rhytipterna holerythra*
_____ *R. h. holerythra* — Gulf lowlands of se Mexico (Veracruz) to n Colombia
_____ *R. h. rosenbergi* — W Colombia (s Chocó and Nariño) to nw Ecuador

☐ **Grayish Mourner** *Rhytipterna simplex*
_____ *R. s. frederici* — Colombia (e of Andes) to the Guianas, n Bolivia and Amaz. Brazil
_____ *R. s. simplex* — SE Brazil (Alagoas to São Paulo and Rio de Janeiro)

☐ **Pale-bellied Mourner** *Rhytipterna immunda*
E Colombia to Suriname, French Guiana and Amazonian Brazil

☐ **Rufous Flycatcher** *Myiarchus semirufus*
Arid coastal nw Peru (Tumbes to n Lima)

☐ **Yucatan Flycatcher** *Myiarchus yucatanensis*
_____ *M. y. yucatanensis* — E Mexico (Yucatán Peninsula) to n Guatemala and n Belize
_____ *M. y. lanyoni* — Cozumel I. (off Yucatán Peninsula of e Mexico)

☐ **Sad Flycatcher** *Myiarchus barbirostris*
Open woodlands and montane forests of Jamaica

☐ **Dusky-capped Flycatcher** *Myiarchus tuberculifer*
_____ *M. t. olivascens* — SW US and nw Mexico; winters to Oaxaca
_____ *M. t. lawrenceii* — E Mexico (Nuevo León) to highlands of Guatemala
_____ *M. t. querulus* — SW Mexico (s Sinaloa to Oaxaca)
_____ *M. t. tresmariae* — Tres Marías Islands (off w Mexico)
_____ *M. t. platyrhynchus* — Cozumel I. (off Yucatán Peninsula of e Mexico)
_____ *M. t. manens* — SE Mexico (s Yucatán Peninsula)
_____ *M. t. connectens* — Guatemala to n Nicaragua
_____ *M. t. littoralis* — Pacific coast of se Honduras to nw Costa Rica
_____ *M. t. nigricapillus* — Extreme se Nicaragua to Costa Rica and w Panama
_____ *M. t. brunneiceps* — Tropical e Panama and w Colombia
_____ *M. t. pallidus* — N Colombia to n and w Venezuela
_____ *M. t. tuberculifer* — E Colombia to Suriname and Amaz. Brazil; se Brazil; Trinidad
_____ *M. t. nigriceps* — SW Colombia to w Ecuador and nw Peru
_____ *M. t. atriceps* — E slope of Andes of Ecuador to e Peru, Bolivia and nw Argentina

☐ **Swainson's Flycatcher** *Myiarchus swainsoni*
_____ *M. s. phaeonotus* — S Venezuela and the Guianas to lower Amazonian Brazil
_____ *M. s. pelzelni* — SE Peru to n Bolivia and e Brazil (Mato Grosso to Pará)
_____ *M. s. ferocior* — SE Bolivia to w Paraguay and c Argentina; winters to Colombia
_____ *M. s. swainsoni* — SE Brazil to e Paraguay and ne Argentina; winters to Trinidad

☐ **Venezuelan Flycatcher** *Myiarchus venezuelensis*

Caribbean lowlands of n Colombia and n Venezuela; Tobago

☐ **Panama Flycatcher** *Myiarchus panamensis*
____ *M. p. actiosus* — Pacific coast of nw Costa Rica
____ *M. p. panamensis* — Pacific slope of sw Costa Rica to sw Colombia and nw Venezuela

☐ **Short-crested Flycatcher** *Myiarchus ferox*
____ *M. f. brunnescens* — *Llanos* of e Colombia to Venezuela and Guyana
____ *M. f. ferox* — Tropical se Colombia to n Bolivia, the Guianas and n Brazil
____ *M. f. australis* — S Brazil to e Bolivia, e Paraguay and ne Argentina

☐ **Pale-edged Flycatcher** *Myiarchus cephalotes*
____ *M. c. caribbaeus* — Mountains of n Venezuela (Trujillo and Lara to Sucre)
____ *M. c. cephalotes* — Andes of Colombia and w Venezuela to w Bolivia

☐ **Sooty-crowned Flycatcher** *Myiarchus phaeocephalus*
____ *M. p. phaeocephalus* — Arid w Ecuador and nw Peru (south to Lambayeque))
____ *M. p. interior* — E slope of Andes of nw Peru and adjacent Ecuador

☐ **Apical Flycatcher** *Myiarchus apicalis*

Arid scrub of Colombia (west of the Eastern Andes)

☐ **Ash-throated Flycatcher** *Myiarchus cinerascens*
____ *M. c. cinerascens* — Semiarid w US and w Mexico; winters to n Costa Rica
____ *M. c. pertinax* — S Baja California (south of latitude 29°)

☐ **Nutting's Flycatcher** *Myiarchus nuttingi*
____ *M. n. inquietus* — Semiarid w Mexico (Sonora to Chiapas) and central Mexico
____ *M. n. nuttingi* — Arid interior montane valleys of Chiapas to nw Costa Rica
____ *M. n. flavidior* — Pacific lowlands of s Mexico (Chiapas) to nw Costa Rica

☐ **Great Crested Flycatcher** *Myiarchus crinitus*

Breeds se Canada to Gulf States; winters to nw South America

☐ **Brown-crested Flycatcher** *Myiarchus tyrannulus*
____ *M. t. magister* — SW US through w Mexico to Oaxaca; Tres Marías Islands
____ *M. t. cooperi* — S Texas through e Mexico to Guatemala, Belize and Honduras
____ *M. t. cozumelae* — Cozumel I. (off Yucatán Peninsula of e Mexico)
____ *M. t. insularum* — Utila, Roatán and Bonaca islands (off Honduras)
____ *M. t. brachyurus* — Pacific coast of El Salvador to nw Costa Rica
____ *M. t. tyrannulus* — E Colombia to the Guianas, n Argentina and n Brazil; Trinidad
____ *M. t. bahiae* — N and e Brazil (Amapá to São Paulo) and ne Argentina

☐ **Grenada Flycatcher** *Myiarchus nugator*

S Lesser Antilles (St. Vincent, the Grenadines and Grenada)

☐ **Galapagos Flycatcher** *Myiarchus magnirostris*

Galapagos Islands

☐ **Rufous-tailed Flycatcher** *Myiarchus validus*

Wooded hills and mountains of Jamaica

☐ **La Sagra's Flycatcher** *Myiarchus sagrae*
____ *M. s. lucaysiensis* — Bahamas
____ *M. s. sagrae* — Cuba, Isle of Pines and Grand Cayman I.

☐ **Stolid Flycatcher** *Myiarchus stolidus*
____ *M. s. dominicensis* — Hispaniola, Gonâve, Tortue, Beata and Grand Cayemite islands
____ *M. s. stolidus* — Jamaica

☐ **Lesser Antillean Flycatcher** *Myiarchus oberi*
____ *M. o. oberi* — Lesser Antilles (Dominica and Guadeloupe)
____ *M. o. sanctaeluciae* — St. Lucia (Lesser Antilles)
____ *M. o. berlepschii* — Lesser Antilles (St. Kitts, Barbuda and Nevis)
____ *M. o. sclateri* — Martinique (Lesser Antilles)

☐ **Puerto Rican Flycatcher** *Myiarchus antillarum*

Puerto Rico, Vieques I., Culebra I. and Virgin Islands

☐ **Flammulated Flycatcher** *Deltarhynchus flammulatus*

Pacific lowlands of w Mexico (Sinaloa to w Chiapas)

☐ **Lesser Kiskadee** *Philohydor lictor*
____ *P. l. panamensis* — E Panama to n Colombia
____ *P. l. lictor* — E Colombia to the Guianas, e Bolivia, Amazonian and e Brazil

☐ **Great Kiskadee** *Pitangus sulphuratus*
____ *P. s. texanus* — S Texas (Rio Grande Valley) to se Mexico (Veracruz)
____ *P. s. derbianus* — Arid w Mexico (s Sonora to Isthmus of Tehuántepec)
____ *P. s. guatimalensis* — SE Mexico (Nuevo León) to central Panama
____ *P. s. trinitatis* — Extreme e Colombia to e Venezuela and nw Brazil; Trinidad
____ *P. s. caucensis* — W and s Colombia (sw Bolívar, Cauca and Magdalena valleys)
____ *P. s. rufipennis* — Coastal n Colombia and n Venezuela
____ *P. s. sulphuratus* — Tropical se Colombia to se Peru, the Guianas and n Brazil
____ *P. s. maximiliani* — Amazonian Brazil to e Bolivia and *chaco* of Paraguay
____ *P. s. bolivianus* — Highlands of e Bolivia (Cochabamba to Tarija)
____ *P. s. argentinus* — Extreme se Brazil to e Paraguay, Uruguay and central Argentina

☐ **Boat-billed Flycatcher** *Megarynchus pitangua*
____ *M. p. tardiusculus* — Foothills of nw Mexico (s Sinaloa to Nayarit)
____ *M. p. caniceps* — SW Mexico (s Jalisco)
____ *M. p. mexicanus* — E Mexico (Tamaulipas) to nw Colombia; Cébaco I. (Panama)
____ *M. p. deserticola* — Central Guatemala (valley of Río Negro)
____ *M. p. pitangua* — Tropical n and central South America to n Argentina; Trinidad
____ *M. p. chrysogaster* — Pacific slope of w Ecuador and nw Peru (Tumbes and n Piura)

☐ **Rusty-margined Flycatcher** *Myiozetetes cayanensis*
____ *M. c. hellmayri* — E Panama to Colombia, e Ecuador and extreme nw Venezuela
____ *M. c. rufipennis* — E Colombia to n Venezuela and e Ecuador
____ *M. c. cayanensis* — S Venezuela, the Guianas and Amazonian Brazil to n Bolivia
____ *M. c. erythropterus* — SE Brazil (e Minas Gerais to Rio de Janeiro)

☐ **Social Flycatcher** *Myiozetetes similis*
____ *M. s. primulus* — W Mexico (s Sonora to n Sinaloa)
____ *M. s. hesperis* — W Mexico (s Sinaloa to s Zacatecas, sw Puebla and Oaxaca)
____ *M. s. texensis* — E Mexico (s Tamaulipas) to n Costa Rica
____ *M. s. columbianus* — Tropical sw Costa Rica to n Colombia and n Venezuela
____ *M. s. similis* — E Colombia to n Bolivia, Venezuela and n Amazonian Brazil
____ *M. s. grandis* — W Ecuador (Esmeraldas) to extreme nw Peru (Tumbes)
____ *M. s. pallidiventris* — E Brazil (Pará) to e Paraguay and ne Argentina

☐ **Gray-capped Flycatcher** *Myiozetetes granadensis*
____ *M. g. granadensis* — Caribbean slope of e Honduras to central highlands of Panama
____ *M. g. occidentalis* — E Panama (Darién) to w Ecuador and extreme nw Peru (Tumbes)
____ *M. g. obscurior* — E Colombia to s Venezuela, n Bolivia and w Amazonian Brazil

☐ **Dusky-chested Flycatcher** *Myiozetetes luteiventris*
____ *M. l. luteiventris* — SE Colombia to se Venezuela, n Bolivia and w Amaz. Brazil
____ *M. l. septentrionalis* — Suriname (Marowijne area) and adjacent Brazil (Amapá)

☐ **White-ringed Flycatcher** *Conopias albovittata*
____ *C. a. albovittata* — Lowlands of e Honduras to w Colombia and nw Ecuador
____ *C. a. distincta* — Lower Caribbean slopes of Costa Rica

☐ **Three-striped Flycatcher** *Conopias trivirgata*
____ *C. t. berlepschi* — S Venezuela (Bolívar) to ne Peru and lower Amazonian Brazil
____ *C. t. trivirgata* — SE Brazil (se Bahia to Paraná) to e Paraguay and ne Argentina

☐ **Yellow-throated Flycatcher** *Conopias parva*

E Colombia to s Venezuela, the Guianas and n Brazil

☐ **Lemon-browed Flycatcher** *Conopias cinchoneti*
_____ *C. c. icterophrys*
_____ *C. c. cinchoneti*

Andes of Colombia to nw Venezuela (Sierra de Perijá)
Andes of e Ecuador and e Peru (south to Cuzco)

☐ **Golden-bellied Flycatcher** *Myiodynastes hemichrysus*

Montane forests of Costa Rica and w Panama (e to Veraguas)

☐ **Golden-crowned Flycatcher** *Myiodynastes chrysocephalus*
_____ *M. c. minor*
_____ *M. c. cinerascens*
_____ *M. c. chrysocephalus*

Extreme e Panama (Darién) and Colombia south to Ecuador
Andes of n Colombia and coastal cordillera of n Venezuela
E slope of Andes of Peru to Bolivia and nw Argentina

☐ **Baird's Flycatcher** *Myiodynastes bairdii*

Arid sw Ecuador to nw Peru (Lima)

☐ **Streaked Flycatcher** *Myiodynastes maculatus*
_____ *M. m. insolens*
_____ *M. m. difficilis*
_____ *M. m. nobilis*
_____ *M. m. chapmani*
_____ *M. m. maculatus*
_____ *M. m. tobagensis*
_____ *M. m. solitarius*

Gulf slope of Mexico to Honduras; winters to n South America
Costa Rica to Colombia and Venezuela; Coiba I. and Cébaco I.
Caribbean coast of ne Colombia to w slope of Sierra de Perijá
Pacific Colombia (Chocó) to nw Peru (Piura)
Venezuela and the Guianas to ne Peru and n Amazonian Brazil
N Venezuela and Guyana; Trinidad and Tobago
S Peru to Paraguay, Uruguay, central Argentina and Brazil

☐ **Sulphur-bellied Flycatcher** *Myiodynastes luteiventris*

SE Arizona to Costa Rica; winters e Ecuador to n Bolivia

☐ **Piratic Flycatcher** *Legatus leucophaius*
_____ *L. l. variegatus*
_____ *L. l. leucophaius*

Tropical se Mexico (San Luis Potosí) to Honduras
Nicaragua to n Argentina and s Brazil; Trinidad and Tobago

☐ **White-bearded Flycatcher** *Phelpsia inornata*

Llanos of Venezuela

☐ **Variegated Flycatcher** *Empidonomus varius*
_____ *E. v. rufinus*
_____ *E. v. varius*

E Venezuela to the Guianas, n and w Amazonian Brazil
SE Brazil to Paraguay, Uruguay, n Argentina, e Peru, e Bolivia

☐ **Crowned Slaty Flycatcher** *Griseotyrannus aurantioatrocristatus*
_____ *G. a. pallidiventris*
_____ *G. a. aurantioatrocristatus*

E Brazil (Rio Tapajós to n Goiás and Piauí)
Bolivia to n Argentina and s Brazil; winters n to w Amazonia

☐ **Sulphury Flycatcher** *Tyrannopsis sulphurea*

S Venezuela and Guianas to n Bolivia and Amaz. Brazil; Trinidad

☐ **Snowy-throated Kingbird** *Tyrannus niveigularis*

Extreme sw Colombia to w Ecuador and nw Peru (s to Ancash)

☐ **White-throated Kingbird** *Tyrannus albogularis*

S Venezuela and the Guianas to n Bolivia and Amazonian Brazil

☐ **Tropical Kingbird** *Tyrannus melancholicus*
_____ *T. m. satrapa*
_____ *T. m. despotes*
_____ *T. m. melancholicus*

S Arizona to n Colombia and n Venezuela; Trinidad and Tobago
NE Brazil (Amapá, Maranhão and Ceará to Bahia)
Tropical n South America to central Argentina and Brazil

☐ **Couch's Kingbird** *Tyrannus couchii*

Extreme s Texas to n Guatemala and Belize

☐ **Cassin's Kingbird** *Tyrannus vociferans*
_____ *T. v. vociferans*
_____ *T. v. xenopterus*

Arid w US to central Mexico; winters to Honduras
Highlands of sw Mexico (Guerrero)

☐ **Thick-billed Kingbird** *Tyrannus crassirostris*
_____ *T. c. pompalis*
_____ *T. c. crassirostris*

Extreme se Arizona south along w coast of Mexico to Colima
SW Mexico (Guerrero to Oaxaca); winters to Guatemala

☐ **Western Kingbird** *Tyrannus verticalis*

Breeds w North America; winters s Mexico to Costa Rica

☐ **Eastern Kingbird** *Tyrannus tyrannus*

E North America; winters mainly w Amazon basin

☐ **Gray Kingbird** *Tyrannus dominicensis*

_____ *T. d. dominicensis*

_____ *T. d. vorax*

Coastal se US to Colombia and Venezuela; Trinidad; Neth. Ant.

Lesser Antilles; winters to Trinidad and the Guianas

☐ **Loggerhead Kingbird** *Tyrannus caudifasciatus*

_____ *T. c. bahamensis*

_____ *T. c. caudifasciatus*

_____ *T. c. flavescens*

_____ *T. c. caymanensis*

_____ *T. c. jamaicensis*

_____ *T. c. taylori*

_____ *T. c. gabbii*

Grand Bahama, Abaco, Andros and New Providence islands

Cuba

Isle of Pines

Cayman Islands

Jamaica

Puerto Rico and Vieques I.

Hispaniola

☐ **Giant Kingbird** *Tyrannus cubensis*

Cuba and Isle of Pines; formerly Great Inagua and Caicos islands

☐ **Scissor-tailed Flycatcher** *Tyrannus forficatus*

Breeds s-central US; winters to w Panama

☐ **Fork-tailed Flycatcher** *Tyrannus savana*

_____ *T. s. monachus*

_____ *T. s. sanctaemartae*

_____ *T. s. circumdatus*

_____ *T. s. savana*

S Mexico (Veracruz) to Colombia, the Guianas and n Brazil

Caribbean coast of n Colombia and nw Venezuela (Guajira Pen.)

Lower Amazonian Brazil (west to Manaus area)

Central and s S America and Falkland Is.; winters to West Indies

☐ **Sapayoa** *Sapayoa aenigma*

Tropical central Panama to Colombia and extreme nw Ecuador

☐ **Greater Schiffornis** *Schiffornis major*

_____ *S. m. major*

_____ *S. m. duidae*

Tropical se Colombia to n Bolivia and Amazonian Brazil

Tropical se Venezuela (s Amazonas)

☐ **Thrush-like Schiffornis** *Schiffornis turdinus*

_____ *S. t. veraepacis*

_____ *S. t. dumicola*

_____ *S. t. panamensis*

_____ *S. t. acrolophites*

_____ *S. t. rosenbergi*

_____ *S. t. stenorhynchus*

_____ *S. t. olivaceus*

_____ *S. t. aeneus*

_____ *S. t. amazonus*

_____ *S. t. wallacii*

_____ *S. t. steinbachi*

_____ *S. t. intermedius*

_____ *S. t. turdinus*

Gulf-Caribbean slope of se Mexico to s Costa Rica

Tropical w Panama (Chiriquí, Veraguas and n Coclé)

Tropical e Panama and nw Colombia

E Panama (Cerro Mali and Tacarcuna), adj. Colombia (Chocó)

Trop. w Colombia (Chocó to Nariño) and w Ecuador (s to Loja)

Tropical ne Colombia and n Venezuela

Tropical se Venezuela (Bolívar) and adjacent Guyana

E Andes of Ecuador and adjacent n Peru (Piura and Cajamarca)

S Venezuela to e Peru and w Amazonian Brazil

Tropical French Guiana, Suriname and ne Brazil

Upper tropical se Peru (Junín) to n Bolivia

Campos of e Brazil (Alagoas and Paraíba)

SE Brazil (s Bahia, e Minas Gerais and e Espírito Santo)

☐ **Greenish Schiffornis** *Schiffornis virescens*

SE Brazil (s Bahia) to e Paraguay and ne Argentina

☐ **White-naped Xenopsaris** *Xenopsaris albinucha*

_____ *X. a. minor*

_____ *X. a. albinucha*

Locally in w and c Venezuela and extreme n Brazil (Roraima)

Interior ne Brazil to e Bolivia, w Paraguay and n Argentina

☐ **Chestnut-crowned Becard** *Pachyramphus castaneus*

_____ *P. c. saturatus*

_____ *P. c. intermedius*

_____ *P. c. parui*

_____ *P. c. amazonus*

_____ *P. c. castaneus*

Trop. se Colombia to e Ecuador, n Peru and w Amazonian Brazil

Tropical n Venezuela (Falcón to Sucre and Monagas)

Tropical s Venezuela (Cerro Parú in Amazonas)

Lower Amazonian Brazil (e Amazonas and Pará)

SE Brazil (Bahia and se Goiás) to e Paraguay and ne Argentina

☐ **Green-backed Becard** *Pachyramphus viridis*
_____ *P. v. griseigularis* — SE Venezuela (e Bolívar) and lower Amazonian Brazil
_____ *P. v. viridis* — E Bolivia to n Argentina, e Uruguay, Paraguay and e Brazil

☐ **Yellow-cheeked Becard** *Pachyramphus xanthogenys*
_____ *P. x. xanthogenys* — E slope of Andes of e Ecuador (south to Zamora-Chinchipe)
_____ *P. x. peruanus* — E slope of Andes of central Peru (Huánuco and Junín)

☐ **Barred Becard** *Pachyramphus versicolor*
_____ *P. v. costaricensis* — Humid montane forests of Costa Rica and w Panama (Chiriquí)
_____ *P. v. versicolor* — E and Central Andes of Colombia to w Venezuela and Ecuador
_____ *P. v. meridionalis* — E slope of Andes of s Ecuador to e Peru and w Bolivia

☐ **Cinnamon Becard** *Pachyramphus cinnamomeus*
_____ *P. c. fulvidior* — SE Mexico (Oaxaca and Chiapas) to extreme w Panama
_____ *P. c. cinnamomeus* — Tropical e Panama to Colombia and Ecuador (south to El Oro)
_____ *P. c. magdalenae* — N Colombia to nw Venezuela (Maracaibo basin)
_____ *P. c. badius* — W Venezuela (s Táchira)

☐ **White-winged Becard** *Pachyramphus polychopterus*
_____ *P. p. similis* — Caribbean slope of Guatemala to extreme n Colombia (Chocó)
_____ *P. p. cinereiventris* — N Colombia (east to Santa Marta region)
_____ *P. p. dorsalis* — Tropical and subtropical sw Colombia and nw Ecuador
_____ *P. p. tenebrosus* — Tropical se Colombia (Caquetá) to e Ecuador and ne Peru
_____ *P. p. tristis* — NE Colombia to Guianas and ne Brazil; Trinidad and Tobago
_____ *P. p,. nigriventris* — Trop. se Colombia (Meta) to s Venezuela, n Bolivia, w Brazil
_____ *P. p. polychopterus* — E Brazil (Piauí and Ceará to Alagoas and Bahia)
_____ *P. p. spixii* — S Brazil to Paraguay, Uruguay, e Bolivia and n Argentina

☐ **Gray-collared Becard** *Pachyramphus major*
_____ *P. m. uropygialis* — W Mexico (Sonora, Sinaloa, Durango, Michoacán and Guerrero)
_____ *P. m. major* — E Mexico (Nuevo León and San Luis Potosí to Chiapas)
_____ *P. m. matudai* — Pacific slope of s Mexico (Chiapas) and n Guatemala
_____ *P. m. itzensis* — SE Mexico (Campeche, Yucatán, Quintana Roo) and Belize
_____ *P. m. australis* — Guatemala to n-central Nicaragua

☐ **Black-and-white Becard** *Pachyramphus albogriseus*
_____ *P. a. ornatus* — Costa Rica to w Panama (Chiriquí and Veraguas)
_____ *P. a. coronatus* — Santa Marta Mts. (n Colombia) and nw Venezuela (Zulia)
_____ *P. a. albogriseus* — Subtropical E Andes of n Colombia (Boyacá) and n Venezuela
_____ *P. a. guayaquilensis* — W Ecuador (Guayaquil basin) and Isla Puná
_____ *P. a. salvini* — E slope of Andes of e Ecuador and Peru (south to Ayacucho)

☐ **Black-capped Becard** *Pachyramphus marginatus*
_____ *P. m. nanus* — Colombia to the Guianas, n Bolivia and Amazonian Brazil
_____ *P. m. marginatus* — Coastal e Brazil (Pernambuco to se São Paulo)

☐ **Glossy-backed Becard** *Pachyramphus surinamus*
Suriname, French Guiana and lower Amazonian Brazil

☐ **Cinereous Becard** *Pachyramphus rufus*
_____ *P. r. rufus* — E Panama to Colombia, the Guianas, Amazonian and e Brazil
_____ *P. r. juruanus* — SE Ecuador to e Peru (Loreto) and w Brazil (sw Amazonas)

☐ **Slaty Becard** *Pachyramphus spodiurus*
Pacific lowlands of w Ecuador and extreme nw Peru

☐ **Pink-throated Becard** *Pachyramphus minor*
S Venezuela and the Guianas to e Bolivia and Amazonian Brazil

☐ **Jamaican Becard** *Pachyramphus niger*
Wooded hills of Jamaica

☐ **Rose-throated Becard** *Pachyramphus aglaiae*

____ P. a. albiventris	SE Arizona and w Mexico (south to Guerrero and Zacatecas)
____ P. a. gravis	S Texas and ne Mexico (Tamaulipas to San Luis Potosí)
____ P. a. yucatanensis	SE Mexico (Yucatán, Campeche and Quintana Roo)
____ P. a. insularis	Tres Marías Islands (off w Mexico)
____ P. a. aglaiae	Coastal s Mexico (Guerrero to Oaxaca)
____ P. a. sumichrasti	Lowlands of se Mexico (Veracruz) to w Guatemala
____ P. a. hypophaeus	Belize and Honduras to w-central Costa Rica
____ P. a. latirostris	Pacific slope of n El Salvador to nw Costa Rica

☐ **One-colored Becard** *Pachyramphus homochrous*

____ P. h. homochrous	Tropical central Panama to nw Peru (Tumbes and Piura)
____ P. h. quimarinus	NW Colombia (Sinú Valley)
____ P. h. canescens	Caribbean coast of n Colombia and nw Venezuela

☐ **Crested Becard** *Pachyramphus validus*

____ P. v. audax	S Peru (Ayacucho) to Bolivia and nw Argentina
____ P. v. validus	Tropical e Bolivia to ne Argentina, Paraguay and e Brazil

☐ **Black-tailed Tityra** *Tityra cayana*

____ T. c. cayana	E Colombia to n Bolivia, the Guianas and n Brazil; Trinidad
____ T. c. braziliensis	E Brazil (Maranhão) to e Paraguay and ne Argentina

☐ **Masked Tityra** *Tityra semifasciata*

____ T. s. hannumi	Arid tropical nw Mexico (se Sonora and ne Sinaloa)
____ T. s. griseiceps	Pacific coast of Mexico (Sinaloa and w Durango to Oaxaca)
____ T. s. personata	Arid tropical e Mexico (Tamaulipas to n Nicaragua)
____ T. s. costaricensis	SE Honduras to Nicaragua, Costa Rica and w Panama
____ T. s. columbiana	Tropical e Panama to Colombia and w Venezuela
____ T. s. nigriceps	Tropical sw Colombia (Nariño) and nw Ecuador
____ T. s. semifasciata	Amazonian Brazil south of the Amazon
____ T. s. fortis	SE Colombia to se Peru, n Bolivia and w Amazonian Brazil

☐ **Black-crowned Tityra** *Tityra inquisitor*

____ T. i. fraserii	Tropical se Mexico (San Luis Potosí) to central Panama
____ T. i. albitorques	Tropical e Panama to nw Bolivia and w Amazonian Brazil
____ T. i. buckleyi	Tropical se Colombia (Caquetá) and e Ecuador (Napo-Pastaza)
____ T. i. erythrogenys	Tropical e Colombia to Venezuela, the Guianas and n Brazil
____ T. i. pelzelni	Tropical ne Bolivia, Mato Grosso and Brazil s of the Amazon
____ T. i. inquisitor	Tropical se Brazil (s Piauí) to e Paraguay and ne Argentina

FAMILY: OXYRUNCIDAE (Sharpbill—1)

☐ **Sharpbill** *Oxyruncus cristatus*

____ O. c. frater	Discontinuously distributed Costa Rica and w Panama
____ O. c. brooksi	Mountains of e Panama
____ O. c. hypoglaucus	Mountains of Guyana, Suriname and se Venezuela
____ O. c. phelpsi	Mountains of Venezuela (Bolívar and Amazonas) and adj. Guyana
____ O. c. tocantinsi	Central Brazil (Goiás to Pará and Amapá)
____ O. c. cristatus	Disjunct ranges in se Brazil, s Paraguay, e Bolivia and e Peru

FAMILY: PITTIDAE (Pittas—32)

☐ **Eared Pitta** *Pitta phayrei*

SW China (s Yunnan) to n Myanmar, Thailand and Indochina

☐ **Blue-naped Pitta** *Pitta nipalensis*
____ *P. n. nipalensis* — S Himalayas (central Nepal to ne India and nw Myanmar)
____ *P. n. hendeei* — SW China (se Yunnan) to Vietnam and n Laos

☐ **Blue-rumped Pitta** *Pitta soror*
____ *P. s. soror* — Vietnam (s Annam and Cochinchina)
____ *P. s. annamensis* — Vietnam (central Annam and s Laos)
____ *P. s. petersi* — Vietnam (n Annam, se Tonkin and central Laos)
____ *P. s. tonkinensis* — SE China (Guangxi) to central Tonkin
____ *P. s. flynnstonei* — SW Cambodia and se Thailand
____ *P. s. douglasi* — S China (Seven Finger Mountains of Hainan)

☐ **Rusty-naped Pitta** *Pitta oatesi*
____ *P. o. oatesi* — Myanmar to sw Thailand
____ *P. o. castaneiceps* — SW China (s Yunnan) to central Laos and nw Tonkin
____ *P. o. bolovenensis* — S-central Laos (Bolavens Plateau)
____ *P. o. deborah* — Malay Peninsula

☐ **Schneider's Pitta** *Pitta schneideri*

Mountains of n Sumatra (critically endangered)

☐ **Giant Pitta** *Pitta caerulea*
____ *P. c. caerulea* — N Myanmar to Thailand, Malay Peninsula and Sumatra
____ *P. c. hosei* — Borneo

☐ **Blue Pitta** *Pitta cyanea*
____ *P. c. cyanea* — Himalayas (ne India to sw China, Myanmar, Thailand, Indochina)
____ *P. c. aurantiaca* — Mountains of Cambodia and se Thailand
____ *P. c. willoughbyi* — Mountains of central Laos to s Annam

☐ **Banded Pitta** *Pitta guajana*
____ *P. g. irena* — Peninsular Thailand to n Myanmar and Malay Peninsula
____ *P. g. guajana* — E Java and Bali
____ *P. g. affinis* — W Java
____ *P. g. schwaneri* — Borneo

☐ **Bar-bellied Pitta** *Pitta elliotii*

Lowland forests of Cambodia, Laos and Vietnam

☐ **Gurney's Pitta** *Pitta gurneyi*

Peninsular Thailand and n Myanmar (critically endangered)

☐ **Blue-headed Pitta** *Pitta baudii*

Primary lowland forests of Borneo

☐ **Hooded Pitta** *Pitta sordida*
____ *P. s. cucullata* — Foothills of ne India to sw China (Yunnan) and Indochina
____ *P. s. abbotti* — Nicobar Islands
____ *P. s. sordida* — Philippine Islands (except Palawan)
____ *P. s. palawanensis* — S Philippines (Palawan, Culion, Balabac, Calauit and Busuanga)
____ *P. s. bangkana* — Bangka and Belitung islands (off Borneo)
____ *P. s. muelleri* — Greater Sundas, Labuan and Sibutu islands
____ *P. s. sanghirana* — Sangihe I. (ne of Sulawesi)
____ *P. s. forsteni* — N Sulawesi (Minahassa Peninsula)
____ *P. s. goodfellowi* — Aru Islands (New Guinea)
____ *P. s. novaeguineae* — W Papuan islands, New Guinea and Karkar I.
____ *P. s. mefoorana* — Numfor I. (off nw New Guinea)
____ *P. s. rosenbergii* — Biak I. (off nw New Guinea)

☐ **Ivory-breasted Pitta** *Pitta maxima*
____ *P. m. maxima* — N Moluccas (Halmahera, Bacan, Kasiruta and Obi)
____ *P. m. morotainsis* — Morotai I. (n Moluccas)

☐ **Superb Pitta** *Pitta superba*

Manus I. (Bismarck Archipelago)

☐ **Azure-breasted Pitta** *Pitta steerii*
____ *P. s. coelestis* — Philippines (Samar, Leyte and Bohol)
____ *P. s. steerii* — Mindanao (s Philippines)

☐ **Whiskered Pitta** *Pitta kochi*

Mountains of n Luzon (n Philippines)

☐ **Red-bellied Pitta** *Pitta erythrogaster*
____ *P. e. erythrogaster* — Philippine Islands
____ *P. e. propinqua* — SW Philippines (Palawan and Balabac)
____ *P. e. thompsoni* — S Philippines (Culion and Calauit)
____ *P. e. inspeculata* — Talaud Islands (Karekelong, Salebabu and Kaburuang)
____ *P. e. caeruleitorques* — Sangihe I. (ne of Sulawesi)
____ *P. e. palliceps* — Siau and Tahulandang islands (Celebes Sea)
____ *P. e. celebensis* — Sulawesi, Manterawu I. and Togian Islands
____ *P. e. rufiventris* — Morotai, Halmahera, Kasiruta, Bacan, Moti, Damar and Obi islands
____ *P. e. cyanonota* — Ternate (n Moluccas)
____ *P. e. rubrinucha* — Buru (s Moluccas)
____ *P. e. piroensis* — Seram (s Moluccas)
____ *P. e. bernsteini* — Gebe I. (east of Halmahera)
____ *P. e. kuehni* — Kai and adjacent islands in Banda Sea
____ *P. e. macklotii* — New Guinea and ne Australia (Cape York Peninsula)
____ *P. e. habenichti* — N New Guinea (Weyland Mountains to Astrolabe Bay)
____ *P. e. loriae* — SE New Guinea
____ *P. e. oblita* — Papua New Guinea (upper montane Aroa River region)
____ *P. e. meeki* — Rossel I. (Louisiade Archipelago)
____ *P. e. finschii* — D'Entrecasteaux Archipelago (Fergusson and Goodenough)
____ *P. e. aruensis* — Aru Islands (off sw New Guinea)
____ *P. e. gazellae* — Bismarck Archipelago (New Britain and Rooke I.)
____ *P. e. novaehibernicae* — New Ireland (Bismarck Archipelago)
____ *P. e. extima* — New Hanover (Bismarck Archipelago)
____ *P. e. splendida* — Tabar I. (e of New Ireland)

☐ **Sula Pitta** *Pitta dohertyi*

Banggai Is. (Peleng, Banggai) and Sula Is. (Taliabu, Seho, Mangole)

☐ **Blue-banded Pitta** *Pitta arcuata*

Primary submontane forests of Borneo

☐ **Garnet Pitta** *Pitta granatina*
____ *P. g. granatina* — Borneo
____ *P. g. coccinea* — Malay Peninsula, s peninsular Thailand, n Myanmar and Sumatra

☐ **Black-headed Pitta** *Pitta ussheri*

Lowlands of n Borneo

☐ **Black-crowned Pitta** *Pitta venusta*

W Sumatra (Barisan Mountains and Karo highlands)

☐ **African Pitta** *Pitta angolensis*
____ *P. a. angolensis* — S Cameroon to Gabon, nw Angola and w Zaire
____ *P. a. pulih* — Sierra Leone and Guinea to w Cameroon
____ *P. a. longipennis* — Intratropical migrant (Uganda and Kenya to e South Africa)

☐ **Green-breasted Pitta** *Pitta reichenowi*

Rainforests of Congo basin and adjacent w Uganda

☐ **Indian Pitta** *Pitta brachyura*

Widespread Indian subcontinent

☐ **Fairy Pitta** *Pitta nympha*

____ *P. n. nympha*	S Japan to Korea and ne China; winters to SE Asia and Borneo
____ *P. n. melli*	SE China (Guangxi and Guangdong)

☐ **Blue-winged Pitta** *Pitta moluccensis*

SW China to SE Asia and Borneo; winters to Greater Sundas

☐ **Mangrove Pitta** *Pitta megarhyncha*

Coastal Bangladesh to Sumatra and Riau Archipelago

☐ **Elegant Pitta** *Pitta elegans*

____ *P. e. hutzi*	Known from 2 specimens from Nusa Penida I. (east of Bali)
____ *P. e. elegans*	Sangihe I., Sula Islands and n Moluccas
____ *P. e. virginalis*	Tanahjampea, Kalaotoa and Kalao islands (off Sulawesi)
____ *P. e. vigorsii*	Seram, Watubela, Banda, Tayandu, Kai and Tanimbar islands
____ *P. e. concinna*	Lombok, Sumbawa, Flores, Adonara, Lomblen and Alor islands
____ *P. e. maria*	Lesser Sundas (Sumba and s Flores)

☐ **Noisy Pitta** *Pitta versicolor*

____ *P. v. simillima*	NE Australia (e Cape York Peninsula and islands in Torres Straits)
____ *P. v. intermedia*	NE Australia (Cairns District of n Queensland)
____ *P. v. versicolor*	S Queensland, New South Wales and adjacent islands

☐ **Black-faced Pitta** *Pitta anerythra*

____ *P. a. anerythra*	Santa Isabel (Solomon Islands)
____ *P. a. nigrifrons*	Choiseul (Solomon Islands)
____ *P. a. pallida*	Bougainville (Papua New Guinea)

☐ **Rainbow Pitta** *Pitta iris*

Northern Territory, Melville I. and nw Australia

FAMILY: ATRICHORNITHIDAE (Scrub-birds—2)

☐ **Rufous Scrub-bird** *Atrichornis rufescens*

E Australia (extreme se Queensland and ne New South Wales)

☐ **Noisy Scrub-bird** *Atrichornis clamosus*

Extreme sw Western Australia (Two People Bay environs)

FAMILY: MENURIDAE (Lyrebirds—2)

☐ **Albert's Lyrebird** *Menura alberti*

Humid e Australia (se Queensland and ne New South Wales)

☐ **Superb Lyrebird** *Menura novaehollandiae*

____ *M. n. edwardi*	E Australia (se Queensland)
____ *M. n. novaehollandiae*	E Australia (New South Wales to Victoria)

FAMILY: ACANTHISITTIDAE (New Zealand Wrens—3)

☐ **Rifleman** *Acanthisitta chloris*

____ *A. c. granti*	North, Great and Little Barrier islands (New Zealand)
____ *A. c. chloris*	South, Stewart and Codfish islands (New Zealand)
____ *A. c. citrina*	SW South I. (New Zealand)

☐ **Bush Wren** *Xenicus longipes*

____ *X. l. stokesii†*	North I. (New Zealand). Extinct ca 1850
____ *X. l. longipes*	Montane forests of South I. (New Zealand). Possibly extinct
____ *X. l. variabilis*	Small islands off Stewart I. (New Zealand). Possibly extinct

☐ **South Island Wren** *Xenicus gilviventris*

High mountains of South I. (New Zealand)

FAMILY: ALAUDIDAE (Larks—91)

☐ **Monotonous Lark** *Mirafra passerina*

SW Angola to s Zambia, n Namibia, Zimbabwe, n Cape Province

☐ **Singing Bushlark** *Mirafra cantillans*
  ____ M. c. marginata — S Sudan to Eritrea, ne Ethiopia, Somalia and Kenya
  ____ M. c. chadensis — Senegal and Mali to Sudan and w Ethiopia
  ____ M. c. simplex — W Arabia
  ____ M. c. cantillans — N India

☐ **Australasian Bushlark** *Mirafra javanica*
  ____ M. j. williamsoni — S China to central Myanmar, Thailand and Indochina
  ____ M. j. beaulieui — S Vietnam
  ____ M. j. philippensis — N Philippines (Luzon and Mindoro)
  ____ M. j. mindanensis — S Philippines (Mindanao)
  ____ M. j. javanica — S Borneo, Java, Bali and Lombok
  ____ M. j. parva — Lesser Sundas (Sumbawa, Komodo, Padar, Rinca, Flores, Sumba)
  ____ M. j. timorensis — E Lesser Sundas (Sawu and Timor)
  ____ M. j. sepikiana — N New Guinea (upper Sepik River area)
  ____ M. j. aliena — NE New Guinea (Morobe District)
  ____ M. j. halli — NW Australia (Roebuck Bay area)
  ____ M. j. subrufescens — NW Australia (Port Hedland and De Grey River to Fitzroy River)
  ____ M. j. soderbergi — W Northern Territory (Daly River to South Alligator River)
  ____ M. j. melvillensis — Melville I. (Northern Territory)
  ____ M. j. rufescens — E Northern Territory (Gulf of Carpenteria) to n Queensland
  ____ M. j. horsfieldii — Central and s Queensland to New South Wales and Victoria
  ____ M. j. woodwardi — Midwestern Australia (Minilya River to Roebourne)
  ____ M. j. secunda — South Australia

☐ **Latakoo Lark** *Mirafra cheniana*

Botswana to Zimbabwe and interior ne South Africa

☐ **White-tailed Lark** *Mirafra albicauda*

W Chad to s Sudan, Ethiopia, Kenya and Tanzania

☐ **Madagascar Lark** *Mirafra hova*

Grasslands of Madagascar

☐ **Kordofan Lark** *Mirafra cordofanica*

Senegambia to Mauritania, Niger and Sudan (Darfur and Kordofan)

☐ **Williams' Lark** *Mirafra williamsi*

Black lava deserts of n Kenya (Marsabit region)

☐ **Friedmann's Lark** *Mirafra pulpa*

SW Ethiopia and n Kenya

☐ **Red-winged Lark** *Mirafra hypermetra*
  ____ M. h. kidepoensis — S Sudan and ne Uganda
  ____ M. h. kathangorensis — Extreme se Sudan
  ____ M. h. gallarum — E and s Ethiopia
  ____ M. h. hypermetra — Somalia to Kenya and n Tanzania

☐ **Somali Long-billed Lark** *Mirafra somalica*

Red soil deserts of n Somalia

☐ **Ash's Lark** *Mirafra ashi*

Arid coastal s Somalia

☐ **Angola Lark** *Mirafra angolensis*
  ____ M. a. angolensis — N and w-central Angola
  ____ M. a. antonii (minyanyae) — E Angola to s Zaire and nw Zambia
  ____ M. a. marungensis — SE Zaire (Marungu Plateau)

356

☐ **Rufous-naped Lark Mirafra africana**

____ M. a. henrici	Guinea to Liberia
____ M. a. batesi	Niger to Nigeria
____ M. a. bamendae	W Cameroon
____ M. a. stresemanni	N Cameroon (Ngaoundéré)
____ M. a. kurrae	Sudan (Kurra and Darfur provinces)
____ M. a. ruwenzoria	E Zaire to sw Uganda
____ M. a. tropicalis	S Uganda to w Kenya and n Tanzania
____ M. a. sharpei	Somalia (Silo Plain, Tuyo Plain and Bankisah)
____ M. a. athi	Central Kenya (Nairobi and Nakuru) to ne Tanzania
____ M. a. harterti	E Kenya (Ukamba)
____ M. a. occidentalis	W Angola (Huila escarpment north to Kisama)
____ M. a. gomesi	E Angola (Macondo) to nw Zambia (Kabompo)
____ M. a. kaballii	NE Angola (Luiacana) and w Zambia (Balovale)
____ M. a. pallida	Namibia (Windhoek north to Kaokoveld and Ovamboland)
____ M. a. ghansiensis	Namibia and w Botswana
____ M. a. malbranti	Central and s Zaire (Djambala, Petianga and Kasai)
____ M. a. chapini	S Zaire and nw Zambia
____ M. a. nigrescens	NE Zambia (Lundazi) and s Tanzania (Ukinga and Njombe)
____ M. a. transvaalensis	SE Botswana to Zimbabwe, Tanzania, Malawi and South Africa
____ M. a. nyikae	Nyika Plateau (e Zambia and Malawi)
____ M. a. isolata	Malawi (Mangochi District)
____ M. a. grisescens	W Zambia to nw Zimbabwe and n Botswana
____ M. a. africana	S Natal to e Cape Province

☐ **Flappet Lark Mirafra rufocinnamomea**

____ M. r. serlei	SE Nigeria
____ M. r. tigrina	W Cameroon to n Zaire
____ M. r. furensis	W Sudan (w Darfur)
____ M. r. sobatensis	E Sudan (confluence of White Nile and Sobat rivers)
____ M. r. torrida	SE Sudan to s Ethiopia, Uganda, central Kenya and Tanzania
____ M. r. rufocinnamomea	NW and central Ethiopia
____ M. r. omoensis	SW Ethiopia (Omo to Madji and Baro rivers)
____ M. r. kawirondensis	E Zaire to w Uganda and w Kenya
____ M. r. fischeri	E Angola to s Somalia, e Kenya, Tanzania and n Mozambique
____ M. r. schoutedeni	Gabon to Central African Republic, w Zaire and ne Angola
____ M. r. lwenarum	N Zambia (Balovale)
____ M. r. smithersi	Zambia to Zimbabwe, ne Botswana and n Transvaal
____ M. r. mababiensis	W Zambia to central Botswana
____ M. r. pintoi	E Transvaal to ne Natal, Swaziland and s Mozambique

☐ **Clapper Lark Mirafra apiata**

____ M. a. jappi	Zambia (Kalabo and Luanginga River)
____ M. a. reynoldsi	N Botswana to Zambia (between Zambezi and Kwando rivers)
____ M. a. nata	NE Botswana (Makgadikgadi Pan)
____ M. a. deserti	N Namibia to w and central Botswana
____ M. a. apiata	Namaqualand to sw Cape Province
____ M. a. marjoriae	South Africa (Cape Peninsula to Knysna)
____ M. a. hewitti	N Cape Province to Transvaal, Lesotho and sw Botswana

☐ **Collared Lark Mirafra collaris**

	Arid acacia of se Ethiopia, Somalia and ne Kenya

☐ **Indian Bushlark Mirafra erythroptera**

____ M. e. furva	NW India (Kathiawar Peninsula)
____ M. e. sindiana	N India
____ M. e. erythroptera	Central and s peninsular India

☐ **Gillett's Lark Mirafra gilletti**

	Acacia savanna of e Ethiopia to Somalia and n Kenya

357

☐ **Fawn-colored Lark** *Mirafra africanoides*

_____	*M. a. intercedens*	S Ethiopia to sw Somalia, Kenya, Tanzania and ne Uganda
_____	*M. a. macdonaldi*	S Ethiopia (Yavello region)
_____	*M. a. alopex*	SE Ethiopia and nw Somalia
_____	*M. a. trapnelli*	E Angola to w Zambia (west of Zambezi River)
_____	*M. a. makarikari*	SE Angola to n Namibia, w Zambia, w Zimbabwe and c Botswana
_____	*M. a. harei (omaruru, isseli, rubidior)*	NW Namibia
_____	*M. a. sarwensis*	NE Namibia and w Botswana
_____	*M. a. africanoides (transvaalensis)*	S Botswana to Namibia and Cape Province
_____	*M. a. austin-robertsi*	E Botswana to w Zimbabwe, w Transvaal and ne Cape Province
_____	*M. a. vincenti*	Central Zimbabwe to Mozambique

☐ **Rufous-winged Bushlark** *Mirafra assamica*

_____	*M. a. assamica*	N India to Nepal, Sikkim, Bhutan and Assam
_____	*M. a. affinis*	S India (Mysore and s Orissa south) and Sri Lanka
_____	*M. a. microptera*	Central Myanmar
_____	*M. a. subsessor*	N Thailand (Chiang Mai plain)
_____	*M. a. erythrocephala (marionae)*	S Myanmar and s Thailand to s Indochina

☐ **Rusty Lark** *Mirafra rufa*

_____	*M. r. nigriticola*	E Mali to n Togo and Niger
_____	*M. r. rufa*	Chad to w Sudan (Darfur)
_____	*M. r. lynesi*	Central Sudan (Kordofan)

☐ **Pink-breasted Lark** *Mirafra poecilosterna*

Savanna of s Ethiopia to Kenya, e Uganda and n Tanzania

☐ **Degodi Lark** *Mirafra degodiensis*

SE Ethiopia

☐ **Sabota Lark** *Mirafra sabota*

_____	*M. s. plebeja*	Coastal n Angola (Cabinda)
_____	*M. s. ansorgei*	Coastal Angola (Moçamedes to Novo Redondo)
_____	*M. s. sabota*	Coastal Angola to Namibia, Botswana, Natal and Cape Province
_____	*M. s. naevia*	NW Namibia
_____	*M. s. waibeli*	N Namibia (Etosha and Ovamboland) to n Botswana
_____	*M. s. herero*	S and e Namibia to nw Cape Province
_____	*M. s. sabotoides*	W Zimbabwe to s Botswana and nw Transvaal
_____	*M. s. suffusca*	SW Zimbabwe to s Mozambique, ne Natal, e Transvaal, Swaziland
_____	*M. s. bradfieldi*	South Africa (n, central and e Cape Province)

☐ **Rufous-rumped Lark** *Pinarocorys erythropygia*

Arid thornscrub of sub-Saharan Africa

☐ **Dusky Lark** *Pinarocorys nigricans*

_____	*P. n. occidentalis*	Angola to s Zaire (Kwango and Kasai)
_____	*P. n. nigricans*	S Zaire (Shaba) to n Zambia and w Tanzania

☐ **Archer's Lark** *Heteromirafra archeri*

Highlands of nw Somalia

☐ **Sidamo Lark** *Heteromirafra sidamoensis*

Known from two specimens from s Ethiopia

☐ **Rudd's Lark** *Heteromirafra ruddi*

High altitude grasslands of e South Africa

☐ **Cape Lark** *Certhilauda curvirostris*

_____	*C. c. bradshawi*	S Namibia and n Cape Province
_____	*C. c. falcirostris*	South Africa (nw Cape Province)
_____	*C. c. curvirostris*	South Africa (s and w Cape Province)

☐ **Algulhas Lark** *Certhilauda brevirostris*

South Africa (Algulhas Plain of coastal w Cape Province)

☐ **Eastern Long-billed Lark *Certhilauda semitorquata***

____ *C. s. transvaalensis*	South Africa (Central Transvaal to n Natal and n Cape Province)
____ *C. s. semitorquata*	South Africa (s Transvaal to Natal and e Cape Province)
____ *C. s. algida*	South Africa (e Cape Province)
____ *C. s. daviesi*	South Africa (ne South Africa to e Cape Province)

☐ **Karoo Long-billed Lark *Certhilauda subcoronata***

____ *C. s. damarensis*	W-central Namibia
____ *C. s. subcoronata*	Karoo Plains of s Namibia and w Cape Province
____ *C. s. gilli*	South Africa (s-central Cape Province)

☐ **Benguela Lark *Certhilauda benguelensis***

____ *C. b. benguelensis*	Extreme coastal sw Angola and n Namibia
____ *C. b. kaokensis*	Brandberg Mountains (s Angola and n Namibia)

☐ **Short-clawed Lark *Certhilauda chuana***

E Botswana to Transvaal and w Orange Free State

☐ **Dune Lark *Certhilauda erythrochlamys***

Arid coastal Namibia to nw South Africa (Walvis Bay)

☐ **Karoo Lark *Certhilauda albescens***

____ *C. a. cavei*	Coastal sw Namibia to nw South Africa
____ *C. a. albescens*	SW Cape Province (Cape Town to Berg River)
____ *C. a. codea*	Coastal South Africa (Saldanha Bay to Port Nolloth)
____ *C. a. guttata*	Cape Province (Clanwilliam to Little Namaqualand)
____ *C. a. karruensis*	Cape Province (Calvinia and Williston to Oudtshoorn)

☐ **Barlow's Lark *Certhilauda barlowi***

Coastal sw Africa (Luderitz to Oranjemund)

☐ **Ferruginous Lark *Certhilauda burra***

Kalahari Desert (ne Namibia and sw Botswana)

☐ **Spike-heeled Lark *Chersomanes albofasciata***

____ *C. a. obscurata*	SW, central and e Angola
____ *C. a. boweni*	NW Namibia (Cunene to Swakopmund, Usakos and Karibib)
____ *C. a. erikssoni*	N Namibia (Ovamboland and Outjo)
____ *C. a. arenaria*	S Namibia to n Cape Province (Van Wyksvlei)
____ *C. a. kalahariae (bathoeni)*	W and s Botswana to n Cape Province (Stella and Vryburg)
____ *C. a. barlowi*	E Botswana
____ *C. a. beesleyi*	Tanzania
____ *C. a. albofasciata (baddeleyi)*	S Botswana to e Cape Province
____ *C. a. garrula (bushmanensis, meinertzhageni)*	South Africa (w and n Cape Province)
____ *C. a. macdonaldi*	South Africa (s and e Karoo)
____ *C. a. alticola (subpallida)*	South Africa (s and central Transvaal)

☐ **Black-eared Sparrow-Lark *Eremopterix australis***

Grassy plains of s Namibia to s Botswana and n South Africa

☐ **Chestnut-backed Sparrow-Lark *Eremopterix leucotis***

____ *E. l. melanocephala*	Senegambia to Nile River
____ *E. l. leucotis*	E and s Sudan to Eritrea and Ethiopia
____ *E. l. madaraszi*	NE Uganda to Kenya and n Tanzania; n Malawi and Mozambique
____ *E. l. smithii*	Zambia to s Malawi, Zimbabwe, e Botswana and South Africa
____ *E. l. hoeschi*	S Angola to n Namibia, ne Botswana and w Zimbabwe

☐ **Black-crowned Sparrow-Lark *Eremopterix nigriceps***

____ *E. n. nigriceps*	Cape Verde Islands
____ *E. n. albifrons*	S Morocco to Mauritania, Mali, Chad and w Sudan
____ *E. n. melanauchen*	E Sudan to Ethiopia, Somalia, s Iraq, s Iran, s Pakistan and nw India
____ *E. n. forbeswatsoni*	Arabia and Socotra I.
____ *E. n. affinis*	Peninsular India and Sri Lanka

☐ **Gray-backed Sparrow-Lark** *Eremopterix verticalis*

____ E. v. damarensis	Coastal Angola to Namibia, Zambia and nw Botswana
____ E. v. harti	Zambia (Liuwa Plain, Kalabo, Senanga and Siloana Plains)
____ E. v. khama	NE Botswana (Makgadikgadi) to Zambia and Zimbabwe
____ E. v. verticalis	Zambia to Botswana, w Transvaal, Zimbabwe and Cape Province

☐ **Chestnut-headed Sparrow-Lark** *Eremopterix signata*

____ E. s. signata	Extreme se Sudan to se Ethiopia and Somalia
____ E. s. harrisoni	SE Sudan to nw Kenya (west of Lake Turkana)

☐ **Fischer's Sparrow-Lark** *Eremopterix leucopareia*

NE Uganda to Kenya, Tanzania, n Zambia and Malawi

☐ **Ashy-crowned Sparrow-Lark** *Eremopterix grisea*

Grasslands and stony plains of Indian subcontinent

☐ **Bar-tailed Lark** *Ammomanes cincturus*

____ A. c. cincturus	Cape Verde Islands
____ A. c. arenicolor	Deserts of North Africa to Sinai Peninsula and Arabia
____ A. c. pallens	Mali to Sudan
____ A. c. zarudnyi	Deserts of e Iran to s Afghanistan and s Pakistan

☐ **Rufous-tailed Lark** *Ammomanes phoenicurus*

____ A. p. phoenicurus	N India (Rann of Kutch to e Bengal)
____ A. p. testaceus	Dry regions of peninsular India

☐ **Desert Lark** *Ammomanes deserti*

____ A. d. geyri (janetti, bensoni)	Mauritania to se Algeria (Ahaggar Mts.) and Niger (Aïr Massif)
____ A. d. payni (monodi)	Morocco south of the Great Atlas Mountains and sw Algeria
____ A. d. algeriensis (mirei)	Algeria to Tunisia and w Libya
____ A. d. whitakeri	W Algerian Sahara to Libya and n Chad (Tibesti)
____ A. d. mya	Central Algerian Sahara (between 27°N and 30°N)
____ A. d. isabellinus	Egypt west of the Nile Valley and Dakhla Oasis
____ A. d. deserti	S Libya and Egypt east of the Nile to Red Sea
____ A. d. kollmanspergeri	NE Chad to w Sudan (Darfur)
____ A. d. erythrochrous	N Chad (Ndjamena) to n Sudan (Dongola to Kordofan)
____ A. d. samharensis	Red Sea coast of e Sudan, Eritrea and Ethiopia
____ A. d. assabensis	Ethiopia and nw Somalia
____ A. d. akeleyi	Highlands of n Somalia
____ A. d. annae	Black lava deserts of Jordan and extreme s Syria
____ A. d. coxi	Syria and n Iraq (e to Samarra and Al Fallujah)
____ A. d. parvirostris	W Turkmenistan
____ A. d. azizi	NE Saudi Arabia (Al Hufuf region)
____ A. d. darica	Zagros Mountains (sw Iran)
____ A. d. saturatus	Black lava deserts of s Arabia (n Hijaz to Aden)
____ A. d. taimuri	Oman (Muscat region)
____ A. d. insularis	Bahrain I. (Persian Gulf)
____ A. d. cheesmani	Iraq (e of the Tigres River) to w Iran (w of Zagros Mts.)
____ A. d. iranicus	Iran to Baluchistan, s Afghanistan and w Pakistan
____ A. d. orientalis	NE Iran to n Afghanistan and Turkestan
____ A. d. phoenicuroides	SE Afghanistan to Pakistan and nw India

☐ **Gray's Lark** *Ammomanes grayi*

____ A. g. hoeschi	Sandy deserts of extreme sw Angola to n Namibia (Cape Cross)
____ A. g. grayi	W Namibia (Cape Cross to southern edge of Namib Desert)

☐ **Greater Hoopoe-Lark** *Alaemon alaudipes*

____ A. a. boavistae	Cape Verde Islands
____ A. a. alaudipes	Deserts of North Africa (Morocco, Algeria and Tunisia)
____ A. a. desertorum	Coastal Sudan (Port Sudan) to nw Somalia and Aden
____ A. a. doriae	E Arabia to Iraq, Iran and nw India

☐ **Lesser Hoopoe-Lark** *Alaemon hamertoni*

_____	A. h. hamertoni	Deserts of n Somalia (south of latitude 7°N)
_____	A. h. tertia	Deserts of n Somalia (west of longitude 47°E)
_____	A. h. altera	Deserts of n Somalia (longitude 47°E to 49°E)

☐ **Thick-billed Lark** *Ramphocoris clotbey*

Stony deserts of nw Africa to Jordan and nw Arabia

☐ **Calandra Lark** *Melanocorypha calandra*

_____	M. c. calandra	Mediterranean basin to e Turkey, nw Iran, Transcaucasia and Urals
_____	M. c. hebraica	Israel to w Jordan, w Syria and adjacent s Turkey
_____	M. c. psammochroa	Transcaspia and Turkestan to Iran and Afghanistan

☐ **Bimaculated Lark** *Melanocorypha bimaculata*

_____	M. b. bimaculata	NE Turkey to s Transcaucasia and Iran; winters to s Sudan
_____	M. b. rufescens	S Turkey to Syria, Lebanon and Iraq; winters to ne Ethiopia
_____	M. b. torquata	E Iran to Afghanistan, nw India and w China (w Xinjiang)

☐ **Tibetan Lark** *Melanocorypha maxima*

_____	M. m. holdereri	W China (sw Xinjiang to w Gansu, Qinghai and sw Tibet)
_____	M. m. flavescens	W-central China in Gansu (Humboldt spur of w Nan Shan Mts.)
_____	M. m. maxima	W China (Xinjiang to Sichuan) to s Tibet and Sikkim

☐ **Mongolian Lark** *Melanocorypha mongolica*

High steppes of Mongolia and n China; winters to central China

☐ **White-winged Lark** *Melanocorypha leucoptera*

Arid steppes of central Eurasia

☐ **Black Lark** *Melanocorypha yeltoniensis*

Steppes of s Russia and sw Siberia; winters to Black Sea region

☐ **Greater Short-toed Lark** *Calandrella brachydactyla*

_____	C. b. brachydactyla	Mediterranean environs and islands
_____	C. b. hungarica	Hungary
_____	C. b. rubiginosa	N Africa (Morocco, Algeria and Tunisia); Malta
_____	C. b. woltersi	NW Syria and adjacent s Turkey
_____	C. b. hermonensis	Sinai Peninsula to extreme s Turkey and e Syria
_____	C. b. eremica	SW Arabia
_____	C. b. artemisiana	Asia Minor, Transcaucasia and nw Iran
_____	C. b. longipennis (orientalis)	Caucasus to Ukraine, n Mongolia and ne China; winters to e Africa
_____	C. b. dukhunensis	Tibet to ne China

☐ **Blanford's Lark** *Calandrella blanfordi*

_____	C. b. blanfordi	Highlands of Ethiopia
_____	C. b. erlangeri (fuertesi)	Central Ethiopia
_____	C. b. daroodensis	N and central Somalia

☐ **Hume's Lark** *Calandrella acutirostris*

_____	C. a. acutirostris	Mountains of ne Iran to n Afghanistan, e Turkestan and w China
_____	C. a. tibetana	Himalayas of n Pakistan to n India and e Tibet; winters to India

☐ **Lesser Short-toed Lark** *Calandrella rufescens*

_____	C. r. rufescens	Tenerife (Canary Islands)
_____	C. r. polatzeki	Canary Islands (Gran Canaria, Fuerteventura and Lanzarote)
_____	C. r. apetzii	S Iberian Peninsula
_____	C. r. minor	North Africa to n Sinai and s Turkey
_____	C. r. nicolli	N Egypt (northern Nile Delta)
_____	C. r. aharonii	High plateau of cent. Turkey; winters to Syrian Desert and Jordan
_____	C. r. pseudobaetica	Highlands of Armenia and sw shores of Caspian Sea
_____	C. r. persica	S Iraq and Iran to se Afghanistan
_____	C. r. heinei	SE Russia n to Volga basin and sw Siberia; winters to Asia Minor

☐ **Red-capped Lark** *Calandrella cinerea*

____ C. c. williamsi	Kenya (Naivasha, Kinangop, Athi and Kapiti plains)
____ C. c. saturatior	Kenya to Uganda, Tanzania, Angola, Zambia, Malawi, Zimbabwe
____ C. c. spleniata (ongumensis)	W Namibia (margins of Namib Desert)
____ C. c. cinerea (witputzi)	Namibia to w Orange Free State and South Africa
____ C. c. millardi	S Botswana
____ C. c. anderssoni	Transvaal to Natal and e Cape Province

☐ **Asian Short-toed Lark** *Calandrella cheleensis*

____ C. c. cheleensis	E Transbaikalia and n Mongolia to ne China
____ C. c. leucophaea	Turkestan (south of Kyzyl Kum Desert); winters to Asia Minor
____ C. c. kukunoorensis	SW Mongolia (Lake Kokonor basin)
____ C. c. seebohmi	NW Mongolia and w China (Xinjiang e to Khotan River)
____ C. c. biecki	W China (s Gobi Desert to nw Gansu)
____ C. c. stegmanni	Arid w China (ne Gansu)
____ C. c. tangutica	Mountains of w China (s Kokonor) to ne Tibet

☐ **Sand Lark** *Calandrella raytal*

____ C. r. raytal	Coastal se Iran to Afghanistan, n India and s Myanmar
____ C. r. krishnarkumarsinhji	NW India (Kathiawar Peninsula)
____ C. r. adamsi	Coastal nw India

☐ **Somali Short-toed Lark** *Calandrella somalica*

____ C. s. megaensis	S Ethiopia
____ C. s. somalica	E Ethiopia to n Somalia
____ C. s. perconfusa	Central and w plateau of n Somalia
____ C. s. athensis	Kenya and ne Tanzania

☐ **Pink-billed Lark** *Spizocorys conirostris*

____ S. c. damarensis	NW Namibia (Swakop River to Ovamboland)
____ S. c. barlowi	S Namibia to s Botswana and nw Cape Province
____ S. c. harti	SW Zambia (Matabele Plain)
____ S. c. makawai	Extreme sw Zambia (Liuwa and Mutala plains)
____ S. c. crypta	NE Botswana (Makgadikgadi Pan)
____ S. c. conirostris	S Transvaal to e Orange Free State and interior Natal
____ S. c. transiens	E Transvaal to e and n Cape Province

☐ **Botha's Lark** *Spizocorys fringillaris*

High altitude grasslands of se Transvaal and Orange Free State

☐ **Sclater's Lark** *Spizocorys sclateri*

Deserts of s Namibia and Cape Province

☐ **Obbia Lark** *Spizocorys obbiensis*

Deserts of coastal Somalia (Obbia to Hal Hambo)

☐ **Masked Lark** *Spizocorys personata*

____ S. p. personata	E Ethiopia (Ogaden Peninsula)
____ S. p. yavelloensis	S Ethiopia and n Kenya (Didi Galgalla Desert)
____ S. p. intensa	N-central Kenya (Isiolo and Chanler's Falls)

☐ **Dunn's Lark** *Eremalauda dunni*

____ E. d. dunni	S edge of Sahara (Mauritania to Mali, Chad and central Sudan)
____ E. d. eremodites	SW Arabia

☐ **Stark's Lark** *Eremalauda starki*

Extreme sw Angola to Namibia, sw Botswana and w Cape Prov.

☐ **Dupont's Lark** *Chersophilus duponti*

____ C. d. duponti	Iberian Peninsula, Morocco, n Algeria and nw Tunisia
____ C. d. margaritae	Algeria (s slopes of Atlas Mts.) to se Tunisia, n Libya and nw Egypt

☐ **Crested Lark** *Galerida cristata*

____	*G. c. cristata*	Central Europe to Crimean Peninsula and n Morocco
____	*G. c. pallida*	Iberian Peninsula
____	*G. c. kleinschmidti*	NW Morocco (south to Rabat and Azrou and east to Er Rif)
____	*G. c. neumanni*	Italy (Toscana to Rome area)
____	*G. c. apuliae*	S and southeast Italy
____	*G. c. meridionalis*	S Yugoslavia to mainland Greece, Ionian Is., Crete and w Turkey
____	*G. c. cypriaca*	Kárpathos, Rhodes and Cyprus
____	*G. c. tenuirostris*	NE Yugoslavia to e Hungary, Romania, Crimea and Caucasus
____	*G. c. caucasica*	Caucasus to ne Turkey, Taurus Mountains and e Aegean islands
____	*G. c. riggenbachi*	W Morocco (Casablanca to Sous Valley)
____	*G. c. carthaginis*	Coastal nw Africa (ne Morocco to Tunisia)
____	*G. c. randonii*	E Morocco to Algeria (Hauts Plateaux)
____	*G. c. balsaci*	Coastal Mauritania
____	*G. c. macrorhyncha*	Mauritania (Atar area) to Atlas Saharien and n Algerian Sahara
____	*G. c. arenicola*	NE Algerian Sahara to s Tunisia and Libya
____	*G. c. helenae*	SE Algeria and immediately adjacent sw Libya
____	*G. c. brachyura*	NE Libya to Egyptian Red Sea coast, Saudi Arabia and s Iraq
____	*G. c. festae*	Libya (Benghazi to Tobruk)
____	*G. c. nigricans*	Egypt (Nile Delta north of barrage, east to Dumyat)
____	*G. c. maculata*	Egypt (Nile Valley from Cairo to Aswan and El Faiyum)
____	*G. c. halfae*	Egypt (Nile Valley south of Aswan) to n Sudan (Wadi Halfa)
____	*G. c. cinnamomea*	Lebanon (Mt. Carmel and Haifa to Beirut)
____	*G. c. zion*	Highlands of n Jerusalem to Lebanon, Syria and s Turkey
____	*G. c. subtaurica*	Central Turkey to nw Iran, s Caspian region and w Turkmenistan
____	*G. c. magna*	Kazakstan to lower Ural R., Lake Balkhash and extreme w China
____	*G. c. leautungensis*	Manchuria and n China
____	*G. c. coreensis*	Korea
____	*G. c. lynesi*	Mountains of nw India (Kashmir)
____	*G. c. chendoola*	Mountains of n India
____	*G. c. senegallensis*	Senegambia to Guinea, Sierra Leone and Niger
____	*G. c. jordansi*	Niger (nw of Agadès)
____	*G. c. alexanderi (zalingei)*	Nigeria to w Sudan
____	*G. c. isabellina*	Sudan (Kordofan to Nile Valley)
____	*G. c. altirostris*	Sudan (Dongola and Berber to Red Sea) to Eritrea
____	*G. c. somaliensis*	N Somalia, se Ethiopia and n Kenya

☐ **Thekla Lark** *Galerida theklae*

____	*G. t. theklae*	S France, Iberian Peninsula and Balearic Islands
____	*G. t. erlangeri*	N Morocco (Tangier to Algerian border)
____	*G. t. ruficolor*	Morocco (s to High Atlas) to coastal n Algeria and n Tunisia
____	*G. t. aguirrei*	Morocco (s from Anti-Atlas) to coastal n Mauritania
____	*G. t. superflua*	E Morocco (w to Moulouya River) to n Algeria and e Tunisia
____	*G. t. carolinae (deichleri)*	Algeria (n Sahara) to Tunisia, Libya and nw Egypt
____	*G. t. harrarensis*	NW Ethiopia (Jigjigga and Harrar)
____	*G. t. praetermissa*	Highlands and coastal Ethiopia
____	*G. t. huei*	S Ethiopia (Bale Mountains)
____	*G. t. huriensis*	SE Ethiopia and n Kenya
____	*G. t. ellioti*	Somalia
____	*G. t. mullablensis*	S Somalia (Mallable)

☐ **Malabar Lark** *Galerida malabarica*

	Arid w peninsular India

☐ **Sun Lark** *Galerida modesta*

____	*G. m. nigrita*	Senegambia to Sierra Leone and Mali
____	*G. m. modesta (giffardi)*	Burkina Faso to n Nigeria, n Cameroon, Chad and w Sudan
____	*G. m. strumpelli*	Cameroon (Foumban, Tibati and Ngaoundéré)
____	*G. m. bucolica*	N Zaire to w Uganda

☐ **Tawny Lark** *Galerida deva*

Semiarid central plateau of India

☐ **Long-billed Lark** *Galerida magnirostris*

_____ *G. m. harei*	Namaqualand and Karoo to e Cape Prov. and Orange Free State
_____ *G. m. magnirostris*	South Africa (sw Cape Province)
_____ *G. m. montivaga*	South Africa (Lesotho and sw Natal)

☐ **Short-tailed Lark** *Pseudalaemon fremantlii*

_____ *P. f. fremantlii*	SE Ethiopia and Somalia
_____ *P. f. megaensis*	S Ethiopia to n Kenya
_____ *P. f. delamerei*	S Kenya to n Tanzania

☐ **Wood Lark** *Lullula arborea*

_____ *L. a. arborea*	N Europe to Portugal, n Spain, n Italy, n Yugoslavia and Ukraine
_____ *L. a. pallida*	S Europe to Crimea, Caucasus, Iran and Turkmenistan

☐ **Sky Lark** *Alauda arvensis*

_____ *A. a. arvensis*	Azores; Europe from Wales to Norway, Ural Mountains and Alps
_____ *A. a. scotica*	Ireland, nw England, Scotland and Faeroe Islands
_____ *A. a. guillelmi*	N Portugal and nw Spain
_____ *A. a. sierrae*	Central and s Portugal to s Spain
_____ *A. a. harterti*	Mountains of nw Africa
_____ *A. a. cantarella*	S Europe to Balkans, Crimea and Iran; winters to N Africa
_____ *A. a. armenicus*	Transcaucasia and e Turkey to sw Iran (Zagros and Elburz mts.)
_____ *A. a. dulcivox*	SE Russia to Yenisey basin and Afghanistan; winters to nw India
_____ *A. a. kiborti*	S Siberia to n Mongolia, Manchuria and Korea; winters e China
_____ *A. a. intermedia*	SE Siberia to lower Amur River and ne Manchuria; winters e China
_____ *A. a. pekinensis*	NE Siberia to Sea of Okhotsk, Kamchatka Pen. and Kuril Is.
_____ *A. a. lonnbergi*	Shantar and Sakhalin islands (Sea of Okhotsk); winters to Japan

☐ **Japanese Skylark** *Alauda japonica*

Major islands in Japanese Archipelago; winters to Ryukyu Islands

☐ **Oriental Skylark** *Alauda gulgula*

_____ *A. g. inconspicua*	Transcaspia to Turkmenistan, e Iran, Afghanistan and nw India
_____ *A. g. lhamarum*	Pamir Mountains and w Himalayas (Kashmir to n Punjab)
_____ *A. g. weigoldi*	E China (Shandong to s Shaanxi and central Sichuan)
_____ *A. g. coelivox*	SE China (Fujian, Guangdong and Guangxi)
_____ *A. g. inopinata*	W China (n Gansu) to Nepal, se Tibet and n Myanmar
_____ *A. g. vernayi*	Extreme se Tibet to Bhutan, n Myanmar and sw China (w Yunnan)
_____ *A. g. australis*	S India (Nilgiri and Palni hills, Cochin and Travancore)
_____ *A. g. gulgula*	E India to Sri Lanka and s Myanmar
_____ *A. g. coelivox*	SE China (Fujian, Guangdong and Guangxi) to n Vietnam
_____ *A. g. herberti*	Central and s Thailand to s Indochina
_____ *A. g. sala*	S China (Hainan and adjacent Leizhou Bandao Peninsula)
_____ *A. g. wattersi*	Taiwan and Pescadores Islands
_____ *A. g. wolfei*	Philippine Islands

☐ **Razo Skylark** *Alauda razae*

Razo (Cape Verde Islands)

☐ **Horned Lark** *Eremophila alpestris*

_____ *E. a. arcticola*	N Alaska to mountains of British Columbia and n Washington
_____ *E. a. alpina*	Arctic-alpine summits of nw US (Mt. Rainier and Mt. St. Helens)
_____ *E. a. hoyti*	Arctic coast of North America to s Canada; winters to n US
_____ *E. a. alpestris*	Arctic ne Canada to Newfoundland; winters to coastal se US
_____ *E. a. leucolaema*	S Canada to sw US and nw Texas; winters to nw Mexico
_____ *E. a. enthymia*	Great Plains of central Canada to central US; winters to n Mexico
_____ *E. a. praticola*	SE Canada to central and e-central US
_____ *E. a. strigata*	Humid coastal belt of sw Br. Col. and nw US w of the Cascades
_____ *E. a. merrilli*	E slope of Cascades and adj. lowlands from Br. Col. to ne Calif.
_____ *E. a. lamprochroma*	SE Oregon to sw Idaho, ne California and w Nevada

____ E. a. utahensis	S-central Idaho to e-central Nevada and w-central Utah
____ E. a. sierrae	Mountains of ne California (s Cascades and n Sierra Nevada)
____ E. a. rubea	Central California (Sacramento Valley)
____ E. a. actia	Coastal range of s California (Humboldt Co.) to n Baja California
____ E. a. insularis	Channel Islands (off s California)
____ E. a. ammophila	Deserts of sw Nevada and se California; winters to nw Mexico
____ E. a. leucansiptila	Colorado Desert (sw Nevada, w Arizona, ne Baja and nw Sonora)
____ E. a. occidentalis	N and cent. Arizona to n-cent. New Mexico; winters to n Mexico
____ E. a. adusta	S Arizona (s of Tucson) to extreme sw New Mexico and n Sonora
____ E. a. giraudi	Coastal prairie region of se Texas to e Mexico (ne Tamaulipas)
____ E. a. enertera	W-central Baja California and coastal islands s of Magdalena Bay
____ E. a. aphrasta	NW Mexico (Chihuahua and Durango)
____ E. a. lactea	NE Mexico (Coahuila)
____ E. a. diaphora	NE Mexico (se Coahuila to s Tamaulipas, Hidalgo and ne Puebla)
____ E. a. chrysolaema	S Mexican Plateau (Jalisco to Michoacán, Puebla and Veracruz)
____ E. a. oaxacae	S Mexico (e Oaxaca)
____ E. a. peregrina	Colombia (savanna of Bogotá)
____ E. a. flava	N Palearctic region
____ E. a. balcanica	Mountains of se Europe (Yugoslavia, Bulgaria and n Greece)
____ E. a. atlas	High plateaux of Morocco
____ E. a. bicornis	W Turkey (Taurus Mountains) to Lebanon and Palestine
____ E. a. penicillata	Mountains of Asia Minor, the Caucasus and w Iran
____ E. a. albigula	Mountains of n and e Iran to Pamirs, Afghanistan and w China
____ E. a. brandti	Steppes of central Asia to mountains of w Mongolia and n China
____ E. a. longirostris	NW Himalayas
____ E. a. teleschowi	Mountains of w China (extreme se Xinjiang)
____ E. a. khamensis	SW China (Kham region of w and s Sichuan)
____ E. a. przewalskii	W China (nw Qinghai)
____ E. a. nigrifrons	W China (Kokonor to w Gansu)
____ E. a. argalea	W China (extreme sw Xinjiang) to nw India (Kashmir to Ladakh)
____ E. a. elwesi	W China (s Qinghai and s Tibet) to n Sikkim

☐ **Temminck's Lark** *Eremophila bilopha*

Deserts of North Africa to n Arabia and sw Iraq

FAMILY: HIRUNDINIDAE (Swallows—90)

☐ **African River Martin** *Pseudochelidon eurystomina*

Large rivers of Zaire; winters to coastal Gabon

☐ **White-eyed River Martin** *Pseudochelidon sirintarae*

Last recorded ca 1980 from central Thailand. Probably extinct

☐ **Brown-chested Martin** *Progne tapera*

____ P. t. tapera	Trop. e Colombia to Bolivia, the Guianas and Amazonian Brazil
____ P. t. fusca	SE Brazil to Paraguay, e Bolivia, Uruguay and n Argentina

☐ **Purple Martin** *Progne subis*

____ P. s. subis	S Canada to highlands of central Mexico; winters to Brazil
____ P. s. arboricola	Mountains of w North America
____ P. s. hesperia	SW Arizona to nw Mexico (Sonora), s Baja Calif. and Isla Tiburón

☐ **Cuban Martin** *Progne cryptoleuca*

Cuba and Isle of Pines; casual in s Florida

☐ **Caribbean Martin** *Progne dominicensis*

West Indies (except Cuba and Isle of Pines); Tobago

☐ **Sinaloa Martin** *Progne sinaloae*

Sierra Madre Occidental of w Mexico; winter range unknown

□ **Gray-breasted Martin** *Progne chalybea*

    ____ *P. c. chalybea* · N Mexico to n Argentina and Brazil

    ____ *P. c. macrorhamphus* · E Bolivia and e Brazil to Paraguay, Uruguay and ne Argentina

□ **Southern Martin** *Progne elegans*

Bolivia to Paraguay and Argentina; winters north to Colombia

□ **Galapagos Martin** *Progne modesta*

Galapagos Islands

□ **Peruvian Martin** *Progne murphyi*

Coastal Peru (Piura south to Ica), rarely to n Chile (Arica)

□ **Tree Swallow** *Tachycineta bicolor*

Breeds Alaska to s US; winters to n South America

□ **Mangrove Swallow** *Tachycineta albilinea*

Lowlands of n Mexico to Panama

□ **Tumbes Swallow** *Tachycineta stolzmanni*

Coastal nw Peru (Tumbes to La Libertad)

□ **White-winged Swallow** *Tachycineta albiventer*

Guianas and Venezuela to Brazil, n Argentina and Brazil; Trinidad

□ **White-rumped Swallow** *Tachycineta leucorrhoa*

Bolivia to Paraguay, se Brazil and n Argentina; winters to s Peru

□ **Chilean Swallow** *Tachycineta meyeni*

Breeds s Chile and Argentina; winters n to Bolivia and Brazil

□ **Golden Swallow** *Tachycineta euchrysea*

    ____ *T. e. euchrysea* · Mountains of Jamaica

    ____ *T. e. sclateri* · Mountains of Hispaniola

□ **Violet-green Swallow** *Tachycineta thalassina*

    ____ *T. t. lepida* · Alaska to central Baja and nw Mexico (Chihuahua and Coahuila)

    ____ *T. t. brachyptera* · Mts. of central and s Baja; coastal w Mexico (Sonora to Sinaloa)

    ____ *T. t. thalassina* · Mexican plateau (s Chihuahua to Oaxaca)

□ **Bahama Swallow** *Tachycineta cyaneoviridis*

Pine forests of n Bahamas; winters in Bahamas and e Cuba

□ **Blue-and-white Swallow** *Pygochelidon cyanoleuca*

    ____ *P. c. cyanoleuca* · Highlands of Costa Rica to Venezuela, Brazil and n Argentina

    ____ *P. c. peruviana* · Coastal Peru (La Libertad to Arequipa)

    ____ *P. c. patagonica* · Central Chile and Argentina to Tierra del Fuego

□ **Brown-bellied Swallow** *Notiochelidon murina*

    ____ *N. m. murina* · Andes of Colombia to s Peru (Arequipa and Cuzco)

    ____ *N. m. meridensis* · Andes of w Venezuela (Mérida and Trujillo)

    ____ *N. m. cyanodorsalis* · Cordillera of w Bolivia and possibly adjacent Peru (Puno)

□ **Pale-footed Swallow** *Notiochelidon flavipes*

Andes of Colombia and w Venezuela to w Bolivia

□ **Black-capped Swallow** *Notiochelidon pileata*

Highlands of s Mexico (Chiapas) to w Honduras

□ **White-banded Swallow** *Atticora fasciata*

Guianas and s Venezuela to n Bolivia and Amazonian Brazil

□ **Black-collared Swallow** *Atticora melanoleuca*

Rapids on rivers of Guianas, s Venezuela and Amazonian Brazil

□ **White-thighed Swallow** *Neochelidon tibialis*

    ____ *N. t. minima* · Extreme e Panama (Darién) to w Colombia and w Ecuador

    ____ *N. t. griseiventris* · S Colombia to se Venezuela, n Bolivia and w Amazonian Brazil

    ____ *N. t. tibialis* · SE Brazil (Espírito Santo to Rio de Janeiro and São Paulo)

□ **Andean Swallow** *Stelgidopteryx andecola*

    ____ *S. a. andecola* · Andes of s Peru (Cuzco, Puno and Arequipa) to n Bolivia and Chile

    ____ *S. a. oroyae* · *Puna* of central Peru

☐ **Tawny-headed Swallow** *Stelgidopteryx fucata*

Venezuela and n Brazil; Brazil s of the Amazon to n Argentina

☐ **Northern Rough-winged Swallow** *Stelgidopteryx serripennis*

_____ *S. s. serripennis* SE Alaska to Arizona, New Mexico, e Texas and Gulf States
_____ *S. s. psammochrous* S California to Baja, s Texas and s Mexico (Oaxaca)
_____ *S. s. fulvipennis* S Mexico (Oaxaca and Veracruz) to highlands of Costa Rica
_____ *S. s. ridgwayi* SE Mexico (Yucatán Peninsula)
_____ *S. s. stuarti* S Veracruz, Oaxaca and Chiapas to Belize and Guatemala

☐ **Southern Rough-winged Swallow** *Stelgidopteryx ruficollis*

_____ *S. r. uropygialis* Caribbean lowlands of Honduras and Nicaragua to nw Peru
_____ *S. r. decolor* Pacific coast of Costa Rica and Panama
_____ *S. r. aequalis* N Colombia to e and s Venezuela
_____ *S. r. ruficollis* SE Colombia to the Guianas, Brazil and n Argentina

☐ **White-backed Swallow** *Cheramoeca leucosternus*

Arid interior of Australia

☐ **Bank Swallow** *Riparia riparia*

_____ *R. r. riparia* Breeds widely in Holarctic regions; winters in tropics
_____ *R. r. ijimae* Kamchatka Pen. and Kuril Is. to Amur River and Hokkaido
_____ *R. r. diluta* Kirghiz Steppes and Altai Mts. to Iran, n India and se China
_____ *R. r. shelleyi* Lower Egypt and Suez Canal region
_____ *R. r. eilata* S Israel

☐ **Plain Martin** *Riparia paludicola*

_____ *R. p. mauretanica* · W Morocco (Oued Oum R'bia and Oued Sous)
_____ *R. p. paludibula* Senegambia to Sudan and ne Ethiopia
_____ *R. p. schoensis* Highlands of Ethiopia
_____ *R. p. newtoni* Mountains of e Nigeria and w Cameroon (Bamenda highlands)
_____ *R. p. ducis* E Zaire (Kivu) to Uganda, Kenya and central Tanzania
_____ *R. p. paludicola* Angola to Zambia, s Tanzania and South Africa
_____ *R. p. cowani* Madagascar
_____ *R. p. chinensis* Afghanistan and Pakistan to n India, Myanmar and SE Asia
_____ *R. p. tantilla* N Philippines (Luzon and [?] Negros)

☐ **Congo Martin** *Riparia congica*

Zaire (middle and lower Congo River and lower Ubangi River)

☐ **Banded Martin** *Riparia cincta*

_____ *R. c. erlangeri* Ethiopia and Sudan (upper White Nile River)
_____ *R. c. suahelica* S Sudan to Kenya, Uganda, Zambia, Zimbabwe, Mozambique
_____ *R. c. parvula* N Angola to sw Zaire and nw Zambia; winters to Cameroon
_____ *R. c. xerica* Kalahari of n Botswana and Namibia to Angola and w Zambia
_____ *R. c. cincta* Zimbabwe and Kwazulu-Natal to Cape Province

☐ **Mascarene Martin** *Phedina borbonica*

_____ *P. b. borbonica* Mauritius and Réunion (w Mascarene Islands)
_____ *P. b. madagascariensis* Madagascar and Pemba I.; wanders to e Africa

☐ **Brazza's Martin** *Phedina brazzae*

Locally along rivers of sw Zaire and ne Angola (Lunda)

☐ **Cliff Swallow** *Petrochelidon pyrrhonota*

_____ *P. p. pyrrhonota* N Am. w of Rockies (s Canada to nw Baja); winters to Argentina
_____ *P. p. hypopolia* Alaska and w Canada to s California, Nevada and Utah
_____ *P. p. tachina* SW Utah to Arizona, New Mexico and s Texas
_____ *P. p. melanogaster* Extreme s Arizona to Mexican plateau and s Mexico (Oaxaca)

☐ **Chestnut-collared Swallow** *Petrochelidon rufocollaris*

_____ *P. r. aequatorialis* Pacific coast of s Ecuador (Loja and Guayaquil)
_____ *P. r. rufocollaris* Pacific coast of n and central Peru (south to Lima)

☐ **Cave Swallow** *Petrochelidon fulva*
_____ *P. f. pelodoma* — N Arizona to New Mexico, s Texas and ne Mexico (Tamaulipas)
_____ *P. f. citata* — S Mexico (n Yucatán Peninsula and interior valley of Chiapas)
_____ *P. f. cavicola* — Cuba and Isle of Pines
_____ *P. f. poeciloma* — Jamaica
_____ *P. f. fulva* — Hispaniola and Gonâve I.
_____ *P. f. puertoricensis* — Puerto Rico

☐ **Gray-rumped Swallow** *Hirundo griseopyga*
_____ *H. g. melbina* — Liberia and Guinea-Bissau to Gabon and lower Congo River
_____ *H. g. griseopyga* — S Ethiopia and Sudan to Kenya, Uganda and n South Africa
_____ *H. g. andrewi* — Recorded only on migration in Kenya; probably breeds in Ethiopia

☐ **Eurasian Crag-Martin** *Hirundo rupestris*
_____ *H. r. rupestris* — S Palearctic to central Asia; winters to Arabia and India
_____ *H. r. theresae* — Atlas Mountains (s Morocco)

☐ **Pale Crag-Martin** *Hirundo obsoleta*
_____ *H. o. presaharica* — Atlas Saharien Mountains (Mauritania to Morocco and Algeria)
_____ *H. o. spatzi* — S-central Algeria to sw Libya, Chad and Mali
_____ *H. o. buchanani* — S-central Sahara (Aïr Massif of n Niger)
_____ *H. o. obsoleta* — E Sudan (Nile Valley) to Egypt, Turkey and Iran
_____ *H. o. arabica* — E Sudan (Red Sea Province) to n Somalia, sw Arabia and Socotra
_____ *H. o. perpallida* — S Iraq and ne Arabia
_____ *H. o. pallida* — E Iran to Afghanistan and nw India
North Africa across s-central Eurasia to sw India (w Gujarat)

☐ **Rock Martin** *Hirundo fuligula*
_____ *H. f. birwae* — Senegambia to Nigeria
_____ *H. f. pusilla* — S Mali to w and central Sudan, Eritrea and Ethiopia
_____ *H. f. rufigula* — N Nigeria to Chad, s Sudan, Ethiopia, Uganda and n Tanzania
_____ *H. f. fusciventris* — S Sudan to s Ethiopia, Zambia, Malawi and n Mozambique
_____ *H. f. bansoensis* — Sierra Leone to Nigeria and Cameroon
_____ *H. f. anderssoni* — SW Angola to Namibia and sw Cape Province
_____ *H. f. pretoriae* — E South Africa (Kwazulu-Natal to Transvaal and Cape Province)
_____ *H. f. fuligula* — SE Botswana and e Cape Province
_____ *H. f. peloplasta* — Central and e Iran to Afghanistan and Pakistan

☐ **Dusky Crag-Martin** *Hirundo concolor*
_____ *H. c. concolor* — Himalayan foothills (nw India to w Bengal)
_____ *H. c. sintaungensis* — SW China (s Yunnan) to e Myanmar, n Thailand and Indochina

☐ **Barn Swallow** *Hirundo rustica*
_____ *H. r. erythrogaster* — Alaska and Canada to s Mexico; winters to s Argentina
_____ *H. r. rustica* — Europe, Asia and Iraq to Yenisey basin, w China and N Africa
_____ *H. r. savignii* — Egyptian delta (south to Luxor)
_____ *H. r. transitiva* — Lebanon to s Syria and Israel
_____ *H. r. tytleri* — S Siberia to n Mongolia
_____ *H. r. gutturalis* — E Himalayas to ne Myanmar, Japan, Korea; winters to Indonesia

☐ **Red-chested Swallow** *Hirundo lucida*
_____ *H. l. clara* — Southern edge of Sahara (Mali and Burkina Faso to w Nigeria)
_____ *H. l. lucida* — Senegal to Ghana, Togo and extreme w Nigeria
_____ *H. l. rothschildi* — Central and sw Ethiopia
_____ *H. l. subalaris* — E Zaire (lower and upper valley of the Congo River)

☐ **Ethiopian Swallow** *Hirundo aethiopica*
_____ *H. a. aethiopica* — Senegambia to se Sudan, w Kenya, Uganda and Tanzania
_____ *H. a. amadoni* — E Ethiopia and Somalia to e Kenya

☐ **Angola Swallow** *Hirundo angolensis*
_____ *H. a. arcticincta* — Uganda to w Kenya and nw Tanzania
_____ *H. a. angolensis* — Angola and Gabon to se Zaire, Tanzania, n Zambia and Malawi

☐ **White-throated Swallow** *Hirundo albigularis*
_____ *H. a. ambigua* — Angola to se Zaire, Botswana, Zambia and Malawi
_____ *H. a. albigularis* — Zimbabwe and Mozambique to South Africa

☐ **Hill Swallow** *Hirundo domicola*
SE peninsular India (Nilgiri Hills to s Kerala) and Sri Lanka

☐ **Pacific Swallow** *Hirundo tahitica*
_____ *H. t. abbotti* — Malaysia, w Sumatra, Borneo, Philippines and adjacent islands
_____ *H. t. mallopega* — Andaman Islands, e Sumatra and Java
_____ *H. t. namiyei* — Ryukyu Islands and Taiwan
_____ *H. t. javanica* — Sulawesi, Moluccas and Lesser Sundas
_____ *H. t. frontalis* — New Guinea
_____ *H. t. ambiens* — New Britain (Bismarck Archipelago)
_____ *H. t. subfusca* — Melanesia, Fiji, Tonga and Polynesia
_____ *H. t. tahitica* — Society Islands

☐ **Welcome Swallow** *Hirundo neoxena*
_____ *H. n. carteri* — W Australia and Bernier I.
_____ *H. n. parsonsi* — NE Australia (ne Queensland)
_____ *H. n. neoxena* — S Queensland to Victoria, e South Australia and Tasmania

☐ **Wire-tailed Swallow** *Hirundo smithii*
_____ *H. s. smithii* — Widespread Africa south of the Sahara
_____ *H. s. filifera* — Afghanistan and Baluchistan to India, Myanmar and Indochina

☐ **White-throated Blue Swallow** *Hirundo nigrita*
Sierra Leone to s Zaire, Gabon and n Angola

☐ **Black-and-rufous Swallow** *Hirundo nigrorufa*
Savanna of Angola to s Zaire and n Zambia

☐ **Blue Swallow** *Hirundo atrocaerulea*
_____ *H. a. lynesi* — Mountains of Tanzania to Malawi; winters to Kenya
_____ *H. a. atrocaerulea* — Mountains of s Zimbabwe to Kwazulu-Natal

☐ **Pied-winged Swallow** *Hirundo leucosoma*
Savanna of w Africa (Senegambia to extreme w Cameroon)

☐ **White-tailed Swallow** *Hirundo megaensis*
Arid highlands of s Ethiopia (Sidamo Province)

☐ **Pearl-breasted Swallow** *Hirundo dimidiata*
_____ *H. d. marwitzi* — Angola to Zaire, Zambia, Zimbabwe, sw Tanzania and Malawi
_____ *H. d. dimidiata* — Zimbabwe to Transvaal, Orange Free State and Cape Province

☐ **Greater Striped-Swallow** *Hirundo cucullata*
Breeds southern Africa; winters north to central Kenya

☐ **Lesser Striped-Swallow** *Hirundo abyssinica*
_____ *H. a. abyssinica* — E Sudan to Eritrea, Ethiopia and Somalia
_____ *H. a. unitatis* — S Sudan to Kenya, w Uganda and e Cape Province
_____ *H. a. puella* — Senegambia to ne Nigeria and n Cameroon
_____ *H. a. maxima* — SE Nigeria and s Cameroon to sw Central African Republic
_____ *H. a. bannermani* — NE Central African Republic to sw Sudan (Darfur Province)
_____ *H. a. ampliformes* — S Angola to n Namibia, w Zambia and nw Zimbabwe

☐ **Rufous-chested Swallow** *Hirundo semirufa*
_____ *H. s. gordoni* — Senegal to s Sudan, n Angola, sw Kenya and nw Tanzania
_____ *H. s. semirufa* — Botswana to Malawi, Mozambique and e Cape Province

☐ **Mosque Swallow** *Hirundo senegalensis*

____	*H. s. senegalensis*	Mauritania and Senegambia to s Chad and s Sudan
____	*H. s. saturatior*	S Ghana to Gabon, Ethiopia, Uganda and Kenya
____	*H. s. monteiri*	Angola to Zaire, Zambia, Malawi and Mozambique

☐ **Red-rumped Swallow** *Hirundo daurica*

____	*H. d. daurica*	S Siberia to Amur River, n Mongolia and Transbaikalia
____	*H. d. japonica*	Korea, e and central China and Japan
____	*H. d. gephyra*	W China
____	*H. d. nipalensis*	Central Himalayas to sw China (Yunnan), n India and n Myanmar
____	*H. d. erythropygia*	N India (base of Himalayas to Nilgiri)
____	*H. d. hyperythra*	Sri Lanka
____	*H. d. rufula*	Iberian Peninsula to N Africa, Iran, Afghanistan and nw India
____	*H. d. domicella*	Senegambia to s Sudan and extreme nw Uganda
____	*H. d. disjuncta*	Sierra Leone (Birwa Plateau in Tingi Mountains)
____	*H. d. kumboensis*	Cameroon (Bamenda highlands)
____	*H. d. emini*	S Sudan to e Zaire, Uganda, Kenya, Tanzania and Malawi
____	*H. d. melanocrissa*	Highlands of Ethiopia

☐ **Striated Swallow** *Hirundo striolata*

____	*H. s. mayri*	NW India to n Myanmar and nw Thailand
____	*H. s. stanfordi*	NE Myanmar to sw China (s Yunnan), n Thailand and n Laos
____	*H. s. vernayi*	Thailand/Tenasserim border and w Thailand
____	*H. s. badia*	Malay Peninsula (Thailand to Selangor State)
____	*H. s. striolata*	Greater and Lesser Sundas to the Philippines and Taiwan

☐ **Red Sea Swallow** *Hirundo perdita*

Known from one specimen from Red Sea coast of e Sudan

☐ **Preuss' Swallow** *Hirundo preussi*

Guinea-Bissau, Sierra Leone and Mali to Cameroon and ne Zaire

☐ **Red-throated Swallow** *Hirundo rufigula*

Gabon and s-central Zaire to Gabon, Angola and nw Zambia

☐ **South African Swallow** *Hirundo spilodera*

S Zimbabwe and South Africa; winters to lower Congo basin

☐ **Tree Martin** *Hirundo nigricans*

____	*H. n. timoriensis*	Lesser Sundas (Timor, Alor and Flores); winters to Solomon Islands
____	*H. n. nigricans*	S New Guinea; Queensland to e South Australia and Tasmania
____	*H. n. neglecta*	W and n Australia

☐ **Streak-throated Swallow** *Hirundo fluvicola*

NE Afghanistan to n Pakistan and peninsular India

☐ **Fairy Martin** *Hirundo ariel*

Australia and Tasmania; ranges to New Guinea

☐ **Forest Swallow** *Hirundo fuliginosa*

Lowland forests of e Nigeria, s Cameroon and Gabon

☐ **House Martin** *Delichon urbica*

____	*D. u. urbica*	Europe to central Asia, w and se Africa
____	*D. u. meridionalis*	Mediterranean basin to North Africa, Iran and n India
____	*D. u. lagopoda*	Siberia to Mongolia and Manchuria; winters to s China, Thailand

☐ **Asian Martin** *Delichon dasypus*

____	*D. d. dasypus*	Siberia to Kuril Is., Japan; winters to Greater Sundas, Philippines
____	*D. d. cashmiriensis*	Himalayas (se Afghanistan to India and w China)
____	*D. d. nigrimentalis*	SE China (Fujian and Guangxi) and Taiwan

☐ **Nepal Martin** *Delichon nipalensis*

____	*D. n. nipalensis*	Himalayas (Garhwal to ne India, Bangladesh and w Myanmar)
____	*D. n. cuttingi*	N Myanmar to extreme sw China (Yunnan) and n Tonkin

☐ **Square-tailed Sawwing** *Psalidoprocne nitens*
_____ *P. n. nitens* — Guinea to Cameroon, Gabon and extreme w Zaire
_____ *P. n. centralis* — NW Zaire (Tshuapa to Semliki Valley)

☐ **Mountain Sawwing** *Psalidoprocne fuliginosa*
Mountains of se Nigeria and sw Cameroon; Bioko

☐ **White-headed Sawwing** *Psalidoprocne albiceps*
_____ *P. a. albiceps* — S Sudan to w Kenya, e Zaire, Tanzania, Zambia and Malawi
_____ *P. a. suffusa* — N Angola to extreme sw Zaire

☐ **Shari Sawwing** *Psalidoprocne chalybea*
Extreme se Nigeria to Cameroon, Central African Rep. and Zaire

☐ **Petit's Sawwing** *Psalidoprocne petiti*
SE Nigeria and sw Cameroon to Cabinda and lower Congo River

☐ **Mangbettu Sawwing** *Psalidoprocne mangbettorum*
Extreme ne Zaire to extreme sw Sudan

☐ **Ethiopian Sawwing** *Psalidoprocne oleaginea*
SW Ethiopia (Maji region)

☐ **Brown Sawwing** *Psalidoprocne antinorii*
_____ *P. a. antinorii* — Highlands of ne, s and e-central Ethiopia (s to Lake Turkana)
_____ *P. a. blanfordi* — Highlands of w-central Ethiopia

☐ **Blue Sawwing** *Psalidoprocne pristoptera*
Highlands of Eritrea to n Ethiopia and Somalia

☐ **Eastern Sawwing** *Psalidoprocne orientalis*
SW Gabon to Cabinda, s Zaire, Tanzania and w Mozambique

☐ **Black Sawwing** *Psalidoprocne holomelas*
_____ *P. h. holomelas* — Highlands of Kenya and Tanzania to South Africa
_____ *P. h. ruwenzori* — Ruwenzori Mountains (e Zaire and sw Uganda)
_____ *P. h. massaica* — Uluguru Mountains and Usambara Mountains (Tanzania)

☐ **Fanti Sawwing** *Psalidoprocne obscura*
Senegambia to e Nigeria, sw Cameroon and Central African Rep.

FAMILY: MOTACILLIDAE (Wagtails and Pipits—62)

☐ **Forest Wagtail** *Dendronanthus indicus*
E Siberia to Manchuria, Korea and n China; winters to Gr. Sundas

☐ **White Wagtail** *Motacilla alba*
_____ *M. a. alba* — Iceland to Faeroes, continental Europe, s Urals and Asia Minor
_____ *M. a. yarrellii* — Britain, Ireland and adj. coastal w continental Europe
_____ *M. a. subpersonata* — Morocco
_____ *M. a. persica* — Iran (s slopes of Elburz and Zagros mountains east to Kirman)
_____ *M. a. dukhunensis* — SE Russia to central Siberia, Altai Mts., Kazakstan and n Iran
_____ *M. a. personata* — Central Siberia to nw Mongolia, n Iran, Afghanistan and n India
_____ *M. a. baicalensis* — SE Siberia to Mongolia, Transbaicalia, n Gobi and nw Manchuria
_____ *M. a. ocularis* — NE Siberia to Chukotsk Pen. and Kamchatka; winters to SE Asia

☐ **Black-backed Wagtail** *Motacilla lugens*
_____ *M. l. lugens* — S Kamchatka to Japanese Arch.; winters to s China and India
_____ *M. l. leucopsis* — S Mongolia to n and e China and e Amurland
_____ *M. l. alboides* — W Himalayas (Kashmir to sw China, n Myanmar and s Tibet)

☐ **Japanese Wagtail** *Motacilla grandis*
Breeds Japanese Islands; winters to China, Korea and Taiwan

☐ **White-browed Wagtail** *Motacilla madaraspatensis*
Sandy river banks of n Pakistan and India

☐ **African Pied Wagtail** *Motacilla aguimp*
____	*M. a. vidua*	Sierra Leone to s Sudan, Ethiopia, Kenya and South Africa
____	*M. a. aguimp*	Namibia to Orange Free State, Lesotho and sw Transvaal

☐ **Cape Wagtail** *Motacilla capensis*
____	*M. c. simplicissima*	Angola to se Zaire, Zambia, Caprivi Strip, Botswana and Zimbabwe
____	*M. c. capensis (bradfieldi)*	Namibia to Zimbabwe and Mozambique
____	*M. c. wellsi*	Highlands of e Zaire to Uganda and Kenya

☐ **Madagascar Wagtail** *Motacilla flaviventris*

Open country and streams throughout Madagascar

☐ **Citrine Wagtail** *Motacilla citreola*
____	*M. c. citreola*	NE Russia to Siberia, Mongolia and Manchuria; winters to India
____	*M. c. werae*	Russian and Siberian steppes to e Iran, Afghanistan and India
____	*M. c. calcarata*	E Iran to n Afghanistan, Tibet, s China and Myanmar

☐ **Yellow Wagtail** *Motacilla flava*
____	*M. f. flavissima*	Britain and adj. continental coast of nw Europe; winters to Africa
____	*M. f. thunbergi*	Norway to Sweden, s Finland and n Siberia
____	*M. f. flava*	S Scandinavia to central Europe and east to Ural Mountains
____	*M. f. cinereocapilla*	Italy, Sicily, Corsica, Sardinia, nw Yugoslavia; winters to Africa
____	*M. f. iberia*	SW France, Iberian Peninsula and nw Africa
____	*M. f. pygmaea*	Egypt
____	*M. f. feldegg*	Balkans to Turkey, Iraq, Iran and Afghanistan; winters to e Africa
____	*M. f. melanogrisea*	Volga Delta and e Caspian shores to Tarbagatay Mts. and Ili basin
____	*M. f. lutea*	Lower Volga River basin to Kazakstan
____	*M. f. beema*	Russia to w Siberia, n Kazakstan and Altai; winters to s Africa
____	*M. f. taivana*	E Siberia to Sea of Okhotsk and Sakhalin; winters to Indonesia
____	*M. f. leucocephala*	NW Mongolia to w China (nw Xinjiang) and adjacent USSR
____	*M. f. plexa*	N Siberia (Taymyr Peninsula to Kolyma River basin)
____	*M. f. simillima*	Coastal ne Sea of Okhotsk to n Kuril Islands; winters to Indonesia
____	*M. f. angarensis*	E Siberia to w Transbaicalia and n Mongolia; winters to Myanmar
____	*M. f. zaissanensis*	Steppes of central Asia; winters to India
____	*M. f. macronyx*	Ussuriland to ne Mongolia and c Manchuria; winters to Malaysia
____	*M. f. tschutschensis*	Chukotsk Pen., Nunivak I. and w Alaska; winters to e China, Java

☐ **Gray Wagtail** *Motacilla cinerea*
____	*M. c. patriciae*	Azores
____	*M. c. schmitzi*	Madeira
____	*M. c. canariensis*	Canary Islands
____	*M. c. cinerea*	Europe to North Africa, Caucasus and Iran
____	*M. c. melanope*	Ural Mountains and Afghanistan east to middle Amur River
____	*M. c. robusta*	NE Asia to Japan, e China and Korea; winters to Indonesia

☐ **Mountain Wagtail** *Motacilla clara*
____	*M. c. chapini*	Sierra Leone to Gabon, Zaire and w Uganda
____	*M. c. torrentium*	E Uganda to Kenya, Rwanda, Angola and South Africa
____	*M. c. clara*	Ethiopia

☐ **Golden Pipit** *Tmetothylacus tenellus*

Arid scrub of se Sudan to Ethiopia, Somalia, Kenya and n Tanzania

☐ **Yellow-throated Longclaw** *Macronyx croceus*

Widespread grasslands of sub-Saharan Africa

☐ **Fuelleborn's Longclaw** *Macronyx fuellebornii*
____	*M. f. fuellebornii*	Grasslands and *brachystegia* woodlands of extreme s Tanzania
____	*M. f. ascensi*	Grasslands and *brachystegia* woodlands of central Africa

☐ **Abyssinian Longclaw** *Macronyx flavicollis*

High grasslands of Ethiopia

☐ **Orange-throated Longclaw** *Macronyx capensis*
____ *M. c. colletti (latimerae, stabilior)* | E Zimbabwe to s Mozambique, Transvaal and Orange Free State
____ *M. c. capensis* | S and sw Cape Province

☐ **Rosy-throated Longclaw** *Macronyx ameliae*
Moist grasslands of ne, central and se Africa

☐ **Pangani Longclaw** *Macronyx aurantiigula*
Arid savanna of s Somalia to ne Tanzania

☐ **Grimwood's Longclaw** *Macronyx grimwoodi*
Wet grasslands of e Angola to sw Zaire and extreme nw Zambia

☐ **Sharpe's Pipit** *Macronyx sharpei*
Grassy highlands of Kenya

☐ **Yellow-breasted Pipit** *Anthus chloris*
S Transvaal to w Natal, Orange Free State, Lesotho, e Cape Prov.

☐ **Striped Pipit** *Anthus lineiventris*
Rocky montane areas of central, e and s Africa

☐ **Yellow-tufted Pipit** *Anthus crenatus*
South Africa (montane slopes of e Cape Province to w Swaziland)

☐ **Mountain Pipit** *Anthus hoeschi*
South Africa (Drakensberg Mountains of s Lesotho)

☐ **Oriental Pipit** *Anthus rufulus*
____ *A. r. rufulus* | Pakistan to India, s China, Myanmar, Thailand and Indochina
____ *A. r. waitei* | Pakistan and nw India (Uttar Pradesh)
____ *A. r. malayensis* | S Myanmar to Malay Pen., Sumatra, Java, Riau Arch. and Borneo
____ *A. r. lugubris* | Widespread throughout Philippine Islands and Palawan
____ *A. r. albidus* | S Sulawesi and Lesser Sundas
____ *A. r. medius* | E Lesser Sundas (Sawu, Timor, Kisar, Leti, Moa and Sermata)

☐ **Australasian Pipit** *Anthus novaeseelandiae*
____ *A. n. exiguous* | Grasslands of c New Guinea (Mt. Hagen to upper Watut River)
____ *A. n. rogersi* | N Australia (Northern Territory to Gulf of Carpenteria)
____ *A. n. subaustralis* | Interior Queensland and S Australia to western Australia
____ *A. n. bilbali* | SW Australia
____ *A. n. australis* | Queensland to Victoria and e South Australia
____ *A. n. bistriatus* | Tasmania and islands in Bass Strait
____ *A. n. reischeki* | North I. (New Zealand); casual to Kermadec Islands
____ *A. n. novaeseelandiae* | South I. (New Zealand)
____ *A. n. chathamensis* | Chatham Islands
____ *A. n. aucklandicus* | Auckland Islands
____ *A. n. steindachneri* | Antipodes Islands

☐ **Plain-backed Pipit** *Anthus leucophrys*
____ *A. l. ansorgei* | S Mauritania to Senegambia and Guinea-Bissau
____ *A. l. zenkeri* | S Mali to s Sudan, n Zaire, w Uganda, w Kenya and nw Tanzania
____ *A. l. gouldii* | Sierra Leone to Liberia and Ivory Coast
____ *A. l. omoensis* | Extreme e Sudan and Ethiopia
____ *A. l. saphiroi* | SE Ethiopia (n Ogaden-Harar) to nw Somalia
____ *A. l. goodsoni* | Central and sw Kenya to extreme n Tanzania
____ *A. l. tephridorsus* | S Angola to sw Zambia, ne Namibia and nw Botswana
____ *A. l. bohndorffi* | Angola to s Zaire, Zambia, n Malawi and Tanzania
____ *A. l. leucophrys (enunciator)* | Mozambique to Swaziland, Lesotho and South Africa

☐ **Long-tailed Pipit** *Anthus longicaudatus*
Breeding range unknown; winters in South Africa (Kimberly area)

☐ **Richard's Pipit** *Anthus richardi*
____ *A. r. richardi* | W Siberia; winters to India, Thailand and n Indochina
____ *A. r. dauuricus* | W Transbaicalia and n Mongolia
____ *A. r. centralasiae* | Kazakstan (Tien Shan Mts.) to w China (Nan Shan Mts.)
____ *A. r. sinensis* | Extreme e Siberia to s China; winters to Malaya and Sumatra

☐ **Buffy Pipit** *Anthus vaalensis*

_____	*A. v. neumanni*	Plateau of Angola
_____	*A. v. namibicus*	NE and central Namibia
_____	*A. v. chobiensis*	NE Namibia to s Zaire, sw Tanzania, Malawi and Mozambique
_____	*A. v. exasperatus*	Salt pans of ne Botswana; wanders to Zimbabwe
_____	*A. v. vaalensis (daviesi)*	S Botswana to South Africa

☐ **African Pipit** *Anthus cinnamomeus*

_____	*A. c. lynesi*	SE Nigeria to Cameroon and w Sudan (Darfur)
_____	*A. c. camaroonensis*	Cameroon (Mt. Cameroon and Mt. Manenguba)
_____	*A. c. itombwensis*	E Zaire (Itombwe Highlands and Mt. Kabobo)
_____	*A. c. stabilis*	Central and se Sudan
_____	*A. c. cinnamomeus*	Highlands of w and se Ethiopia
_____	*A. c. annae*	Eritrea to Ethiopia, Djibouti and Somalia
_____	*A. c. lacuum*	Kenya to se Uganda and central Tanzania
_____	*A. c. lichenya*	NE Angola to s Zaire, w Uganda, w Tanzania and Mozambique
_____	*A. c. bocagei*	Angola to Botswana, Zimbabwe, s Mozambique and n Cape Prov.
_____	*A. c. grotei*	Salt pans of n Namibia and n Botswana
_____	*A. c. spurium*	NE Namibia to n Botswana, s Malawi and s Mozambique
_____	*A. c. eximius*	Yemen

☐ **Long-legged Pipit** *Anthus pallidiventris*

_____	*A. p. pallidiventris*	Cameroon and Equatorial Guinea to Gabon and nw Angola
_____	*A. p. esobe*	Central Zaire (upper Congo River)

☐ **Malindi Pipit** *Anthus melindae*

_____	*A. m. mallablensis*	Somalia (ne of Mogadishu in Mallable region)
_____	*A. m. melindae*	Coastal s Somalia and se Kenya (s to Mombassa)

☐ **Tawny Pipit** *Anthus campestris*

_____	*A. c. campestris*	Europe to North Africa and Asia; winters to Africa and India
_____	*A. c. griseus*	E Iran to sw Kazakstan
_____	*A. c. kastcshenkoi*	W Siberia to n India

☐ **Blyth's Pipit** *Anthus godlewskii*

S Siberia to Mongolia, China, Tibet and ne India

☐ **Long-billed Pipit** *Anthus similis*

_____	*A. s. bannermani*	Sierra Leone to sw Mali, Nigeria and Cameroon
_____	*A. s. asbenaicus*	Central Niger (Aïr Massif)
_____	*A. s. moco*	Central Angola (Mt. Moco region)
_____	*A. s. schoutedeni (chorsophilus)*	Angolan plateau to ne Namibia, s Zaire and w Zambia
_____	*A. s. palliditinctus*	Desert edges of extreme sw Angola and nw Namibia
_____	*A. s. leucocraspedon*	SW Angola to s Namibia, sw Botswana and nw Cape Province
_____	*A. s. nivescens*	NE Sudan (Red Sea Hills) to Eritrea, Djibouti and n Somalia
_____	*A. s. jebelmarrae*	W Sudan (Darfur) and central Sudan
_____	*A. s. hararensis*	Highlands of Ethiopia
_____	*A. s. chyuluensis*	Kenya to n Tanzania
_____	*A. s. dewittei (hallae)*	Highlands of se Zaire to Rwanda, Burundi and sw Uganda
_____	*A. s. nyassae (winterbottomi)*	E Zambia to sw Tanzania, Malawi and adjacent nw Mozambique
_____	*A. s. frondicolus*	NE Botswana to Zimbabwe plateau and adjacent Mozambique
_____	*A. s. nicholsoni*	SE Botswana to s Transvaal, w Orange Free State and n Cape Prov.
_____	*A. s. petricolus*	Lesotho and South Africa (south of *nicholsoni*)
_____	*A. s. arabicus*	SW Arabian Peninsula
_____	*A. s. sokotrae*	Socotra
_____	*A. s. captus*	Hills of Lebanon, Syria and Israel; winters in Jordan Valley
_____	*A. s. decaptus*	Afghanistan to Pakistan and nw India
_____	*A. s. jerdoni*	Himalayas of e Afghanistan to Sikkim; winters to Myanmar
_____	*A. s. similis*	S India (Nilgiri and Palni hills)
_____	*A. s. travancoriensis*	Extreme s India (Ashambu Hills in Travancore)
_____	*A. s. yamethini*	Foothills of central Myanmar

☐ **Berthelot's Pipit** *Anthus berthelotii*
_____ *A. b. berthelotii* — Canary Islands
_____ *A. b. madeirensis* — Madeira, Selvagem and Porto Santo islands

☐ **Short-tailed Pipit** *Anthus brachyurus*
_____ *A. b. leggei (eludens)* — SE Gabon to Angola, Zaire, w Uganda and Zambia to e S Africa
_____ *A. b. brachyurus* — Grasslands of s Mozambique and e South Africa

☐ **Bush Pipit** *Anthus caffer*
_____ *A. c. australoabyssinicus* — Highlands of extreme s Ethiopia
_____ *A. c. blayneyi* — Highlands of Kenya and Tanzania
_____ *A. c. mzimbaensis* — N Zambia to ne Botswana, Zimbabwe plateau and w Malawi
_____ *A. c. caffer* — SE Botswana to sw Zimbabwe, Transvaal, w Swaziland, n Natal
_____ *A. c. traylori* — S Mozambique, adjacent e Transvaal and extreme ne Natal

☐ **Sokoke Pipit** *Anthus sokokensis*

— Coastal forests of se Kenya and ne Tanzania

☐ **Tree Pipit** *Anthus trivialis*
_____ *A. t. trivialis* — Europe to Asia Minor, w Siberia and s Caspian Sea
_____ *A. t. schueteri* — Mountains of nw China to Tien Shan Mts. and e Afghanistan
_____ *A. t. haringtoni* — NW Himalayas (Kashmir to Garhwal)

☐ **Olive-backed Pipit** *Anthus hodgsoni*
_____ *A. h. yunnanensis* — NE Eurasia; winters to India, Myanmar, Philippines and Borneo
_____ *A. h. hodgsoni* — NW China to Himalayas, Korea and Japan; winters to SE Asia
_____ *A. h. berezowskii* — W China (Xinjiang to se Tibet and Yunnan); winters to India

☐ **Pechora Pipit** *Anthus gustavi*
_____ *A. g. gustavi* — N Eurasia; winters to China, Philippines and Indonesia
_____ *A. g. commandorensis* — Komandorskiye Islands
_____ *A. g. menzbieri* — S Ussuriland

☐ **Meadow Pipit** *Anthus pratensis*
_____ *A. p. whistleri* — Ireland and w Scotland
_____ *A. p. pratensis* — SE Greenland to Europe and w Siberia; winters to N Africa, Iran

☐ **Red-throated Pipit** *Anthus cervinus*

— Tundra of n Palearctic, Alaska; winters to Africa and Indonesia

☐ **Rosy Pipit** *Anthus roseatus*

— E Afghanistan to se Tibet and sw China; winters to SE Asia

☐ **Rock Pipit** *Anthus petrosus*
_____ *A. p. petrosus* — Rocky coasts of British Isles, nw France and Channel Islands
_____ *A. p. meinertzhageni* — Outer Hebrides
_____ *A. p. kleinschmidti* — Faeroes, Shetlands, Fair Isle, Orkneys and St. Kilda I.
_____ *A. p. littoralis* — Fenno-Scandia and nw Russia; winters to s Spain and Morocco

☐ **Water Pipit** *Anthus spinoletta*
_____ *A. s. spinoletta* — Mts. of central and sw Europe (Iberia to Balkans and nw Turkey)
_____ *A.. s. coutellii* — E Turkey to Caucasus, n Iran and Turkmenistan
_____ *A. s. blakistoni* — NE Afghanistan to Transbaicalia and Nan Shan Mountains

☐ **Upland Pipit** *Anthus sylvanus*

— Himalayas (e Afghanistan to Nepal and se China)

☐ **American Pipit** *Anthus rubescens*
_____ *A. r. rubescens* — NE Siberia to Kamchatka Pen.; n North Am.; winters to Mexico
_____ *A. r. japonicus* — E Siberia (s of *rubescens*); winters to s China, India and Myanmar
_____ *A. r. pacificus* — Aleutian Islands to w Canada and nw US; winters to s Mexico
_____ *A. r. alticola* — Mts. of sw US (Utah, Colorado, n Arizona and n New Mexico)

☐ **Nilgiri Pipit** *Anthus nilghiriensis*

Montane grasslands of sw India (w Tamil Nadu and Kerala)

☐ **Correndera Pipit** *Anthus correndera*
_____ *A. c. calcaratus* — Arid *páramo* of Peru (Junín, Cuzco and Puno)
_____ *A. c. catamarcae* — *Páramo* of Bolivia (Potosí) to n Chile and extreme nw Argentina
_____ *A. c. chilensis* — S Chile and s Argentina
_____ *A. c. correndera* — Coastal se Brazil to Uruguay, Paraguay and n Argentina
_____ *A. c. grayi* — Falkland Islands

☐ **South Georgia Pipit** *Anthus antarcticus*

Grasslands of South Georgia I.

☐ **Sprague's Pipit** *Anthus spragueii*

Prairies and plains of North America; winters to s Mexico

☐ **Short-billed Pipit** *Anthus furcatus*
_____ *A. f. brevirostris* — *Puna* of Andes of Peru and Bolivia
_____ *A. f. furcatus* — Extreme se Brazil to Paraguay, Uruguay and n Argentina

☐ **Hellmayr's Pipit** *Anthus hellmayri*
_____ *A. h. hellmayri* — Andes of s Peru (Puno) to Bolivia and nw Argentina (Tucumán)
_____ *A. h. dabbenei* — Andes of w Argentina (w Neuquén and w Chubut) and adj. Chile
_____ *A. h. brasilianus* — SE Brazil (São Paulo, Rio de Janeiro) to Uruguay and n Argentina

☐ **Paramo Pipit** *Anthus bogotensis*
_____ *A. b. bogotensis* — E Andes of Colombia and Ecuador
_____ *A. b. meridae* — Andes of nw Venezuela (Mérida, Táchira and Trujillo)
_____ *A. b. immaculatus* — Andes of s Peru (Junín) to n Bolivia (La Paz and Cochabamba)
_____ *A. b. shiptoni* — Andes of s Bolivia (Cochabamba) to nw Argentina (Tucumán)

☐ **Yellowish Pipit** *Anthus lutescens*
_____ *A. l. parvus* — Savanna of w Panama
_____ *A. l. lutescens* — Savanna of e Colombia to Venezuela, Guianas, Brazil, Argentina
_____ *A. l. peruvianus* — Coastal n Peru (Lambayeque) to extreme n Chile (Tacna)

☐ **Chaco Pipit** *Anthus chacoensis*

Locally in *chaco* of e Paraguay and n Argentina

☐ **Ochre-breasted Pipit** *Anthus nattereri*

Locally in se Brazil, se Paraguay and ne Argentina

☐ **Alpine Pipit** *Anthus gutturalis*
_____ *A. g. wallastoni* — High alpine grasslands of w-central New Guinea
_____ *A. g. rhododendri* — Alpine grasslands of e-central New Guinea and Huon Peninsula
_____ *A. g. gutturalis* — High alpine grasslands of se New Guinea

FAMILY: CAMPEPHAGIDAE (Cuckoo-shrikes—82)

☐ **Ground Cuckoo-shrike** *Coracina maxima*
_____ *C. m. pallida* — Drier parts of interior n Australia
_____ *C. m. maxima* — Drier parts of interior s Australia

☐ **Large Cuckoo-shrike** *Coracina macei*
_____ *C. m. macei* — India south of the Himalayas (Garhwal to Travancore)
_____ *C. m. nipalensis* — Lower Himalayas of India to Nepal, Sikkim and w Assam
_____ *C. m. rexpineti* — SE China (Fujian, Guangdong and Yunnan) to n Laos and Taiwan
_____ *C. m. layardi* — Sri Lanka
_____ *C. m. andamana* — Andaman Islands
_____ *C. m. siamensis* — SW China (se Yunnan) to Myanmar, pen. Thailand, s Indochina
_____ *C. m. larutensis* — N Malaysia
_____ *C. m. larvivora* — Hainan (s China)

□ **Sunda Cuckoo-shrike** *Coracina larvata*

_____	*C. l. melanocephala*	Mountains of Sumatra
_____	*C. l. normani*	Mountains of Borneo
_____	*C. l. larvata*	Mountains of Java

□ **Javan Cuckoo-shrike** *Coracina javensis*

Malay Peninsula, Java and Bali

□ **Slaty Cuckoo-shrike** *Coracina schistacea*

Banggai and Sula islands (off Sulawesi)

□ **Wallacean Cuckoo-shrike** *Coracina personata*

_____	*C. p. pollens*	Kai Islands (Kai Kecil, Kai Besar and Add)
_____	*C. p. floris*	Lesser Sundas (Sumbawa, Komodo, Rinca, Besar and Flores)
_____	*C. p. alfrediana*	Lesser Sundas (Lomblen and Alor)
_____	*C. p. sumbensis*	Sumba (Lesser Sundas)
_____	*C. p. personata*	Lesser Sundas (Roti, Semau, Timor, Wetar, Leti, Moa, Sermata)
_____	*C. p. unimoda*	Tanimbar Islands (Yamdena, Larat and Loetoe)

□ **Melanesian Cuckoo-shrike** *Coracina caledonica*

_____	*C. c. bougainvillei*	Bougainville (Solomon Islands)
_____	*C. c. kulambangrae*	Kulambangra (Solomon Islands)
_____	*C. c. welchmani*	Santa Isabel (Solomon Islands)
_____	*C. c. amadonis*	Guadalcanal (Solomon Islands)
_____	*C. c. thilenii*	Vanuatu (Espíritu Santo, Malo and Malakula)
_____	*C. c. seiuncta*	Erromango (Vanuatu)
_____	*C. c. lifuensis*	Lifou (Loyalty Islands)
_____	*C. c. caledonica*	New Caledonia

□ **Black-faced Cuckoo-shrike** *Coracina novaehollandiae*

_____	*C. n. melanops*	Australia; winters to New Guinea and Solomon Islands
_____	*C. n. lettiensis*	Lesser Sundas (Leti, Moa and Sermata)
_____	*C. n. subpallida*	Central and w Australia; winters to Kai Islands
_____	*C. n. novaehollandiae*	Tasmania and Flinders I.; winters to New Guinea

□ **Stout-billed Cuckoo-shrike** *Coracina caeruleogrisea*

_____	*C. c. strenua*	Mountains of w and central New Guinea and Yapen Island
_____	*C. c. caeruleogrisea*	Aru Islands and Trans-Fly lowlands of s New Guinea
_____	*C. c. adamsoni*	SE New Guinea (Astrolabe Bay to Hall Sound)

□ **Bar-bellied Cuckoo-shrike** *Coracina striata*

_____	*C. s. dobsoni*	Andaman Islands
_____	*C. s. sumatrensis*	S peninsular Thailand, Malaysia, Sumatra and Borneo
_____	*C. s. bungurensis*	Anambas and Natunas islands (South China Sea)
_____	*C. s. simalurensis*	Simeulue I. (off Sumatra)
_____	*C. s. babiensis*	Babi I. (off Sumatra)
_____	*C. s. kannegieteri*	Nias I. (off Sumatra)
_____	*C. s. enganensis*	Enggano I. (off Sumatra)
_____	*C. s. vordermani*	Kangean Islands (Java Sea)
_____	*C. s. striata*	Philippines (Luzon, Polillo and Lubang)
_____	*C. s. mindorensis*	Philippines (Mindoro, Libagao and Tablas)
_____	*C. s. panayensis*	Philippines (Guimaras, Masbate, Panay, Ticao and Negros)
_____	*C. s. boholensis*	Philippines (Bohol, Leyte, Panaon, Calicoan and Samar)
_____	*C. s. cebuensis*	Cebu (Philippines). Probably extinct
_____	*C. s. kochii*	S Philippines (Mindanao, Nipa and Basilan)
_____	*C. s. difficilis*	S Philippines (Palawan, Busuanga and Balabac)
_____	*C. s. guillemardi*	Sulu Archipelago

□ **Pied Cuckoo-shrike** *Coracina bicolor*

Sulawesi, Sangihe, Manterawu, Bangka, Muna, Butung, Togian is.

☐ **Moluccan Cuckoo-shrike** *Coracina atriceps*
_____ *C. a. magnirostris*
_____ *C. a. atriceps*

N Moluccas (Ternate, Halmahera, Bacan and Kasiruta)
Seram (s Moluccas)

☐ **Buru Cuckoo-shrike** *Coracina fortis*

Forests of Buru (s Moluccas)

☐ **Cerulean Cuckoo-shrike** *Coracina temminckii*
_____ *C. t. temminckii*
_____ *C. t. rileyi*
_____ *C. t. tonkeana*

Montane forests of n Sulawesi
Montane forests of central and se Sulawesi
Montane forests of e Sulawesi

☐ **Yellow-eyed Cuckoo-shrike** *Coracina lineata*
_____ *C. l. axillaris*
_____ *C. l. maforensis*
_____ *C. l. sublineata*
_____ *C. l. nigrifrons*
_____ *C. l. ombriosa*
_____ *C. l. pusilla*
_____ *C. l. malaitae*
_____ *C. l. makirae*
_____ *C. l. gracilis*
_____ *C. l. lineata*

Mountains of central New Guinea and Waigeo I.
Numfor I. (New Guinea)
Bismarck Archipelago (New Ireland and New Britain)
Solomon Islands (Bougainville, Choiseul and Santa Isabel)
Solomon Is. (Kulambangra, New Georgia Group and Rendova)
Guadalcanal (Solomon Islands)
Malaita (Solomon Islands)
San Cristóbal (Solomon Islands)
Rennell (Solomon Islands)
Coastal e Queensland (Cairns) to New South Wales

☐ **Boyer's Cuckoo-shrike** *Coracina boyeri*
_____ *C. b. boyeri*
_____ *C. b. subalaris*

Misool, Yapen, Salawati islands and w New Guinea
S New Guinea

☐ **White-rumped Cuckoo-shrike** *Coracina leucopygia*

Lowlands of Sulawesi and adjacent islands

☐ **White-bellied Cuckoo-shrike** *Coracina papuensis*
_____ *C. p. melanolora*
_____ *C. p. papuensis*
_____ *C. p. intermedia*
_____ *C. p. oriomo*
_____ *C. p. angustifrons*
_____ *C. p. louisiadensis*
_____ *C. p. ingens*
_____ *C. p. sclateri*
_____ *C. p. perpallida*
_____ *C. p. elegans*
_____ *C. p. eyerdami*
_____ *C. p. timorlaoensis*
_____ *C. p. hypoleuca*
_____ *C. p. stalkeri*
_____ *C. p. robusta*

N Moluccas
Yapen, Batanta, Salawati islands and w New Guinea
S New Guinea (Mimika River to Lorentz River)
Lowlands of se New Guinea and ne Australia (n Queensland)
SE New Guinea (Huon Gulf to Hall Sound)
Tagula I. (Louisiade Archipelago)
Admiralty Islands (Manus and Los Negros)
Bismarck Archipelago
Solomon Is. (Bougainville, Choiseul, Santa Isabel and Florida)
Solomon Is. (New Georgia Group, Rendova and Guadalcanal)
Malaita (Solomon Islands)
Tanimbar Islands (Banda Sea)
Kai, Tanimbar and Aru Islands to n Australia and Melville I.
N and central Queensland (Cooktown to Inkerman)
Coastal central Queensland to Victoria and se South Australia

☐ **Hooded Cuckoo-shrike** *Coracina longicauda*
_____ *C. l. grisea*
_____ *C. l. longicauda*

Jayawijaya Mountains (central New Guinea)
Central Highlands and mts. of Huon Peninsula (ne New Guinea)

☐ **Halmahera Cuckoo-shrike** *Coracina parvula*

Halmahera (n Moluccas)

☐ **Pygmy Cuckoo-shrike** *Coracina abbotti*

High montane forests of n, central and se Sulawesi

☐ **New Caledonian Cuckoo-shrike** *Coracina analis*

New Caledonia

☐ **White-breasted Cuckoo-shrike** *Coracina pectoralis*

Brachystegia woodlands of Africa south of the Sahara

☐ **Blue Cuckoo-shrike** *Coracina azurea*

Sierra Leone to Gabon, Zaire and sw Uganda; Bioko I.

☐ **Gray Cuckoo-shrike** *Coracina caesia*

_____ *C. c. pura*   Sudan and Ethiopia to Uganda and Malawi
_____ *C. c. preussi*   Humid montane forests of se Nigeria, Cameroon and Bioko I.
_____ *C. c. caesia*   Zimbabwe and Mozambique to e South Africa

☐ **Grauer's Cuckoo-shrike** *Coracina graueri*

Montane forests of e Zaire and adjacent sw Uganda

☐ **Ashy Cuckoo-shrike** *Coracina cinerea*

_____ *C. c. cucullata*   Comoro Islands (Grand Comoro and Mohéli)
_____ *C. c. cinerea*   Coastal n and e Madagascar
_____ *C. c. pallida*   Arid central, w and sw Madagascar

☐ **Mauritius Cuckoo-shrike** *Coracina typica*

Native forests of Mauritius (w Mascarene Islands)

☐ **Reunion Cuckoo-shrike** *Coracina newtoni*

Forests of nw Réunion (w Mascarene Islands)

☐ **Cicadabird** *Coracina tenuirostris*

_____ *C. t. edithae*   S Sulawesi
_____ *C. t. emancipata*   Tanahjampea I. (Flores Sea)
_____ *C. t. kalaotuae*   Kalaotoa I. (Flores Sea)
_____ *C. t. pererrata*   Tukangbesi Islands (Kaledupa and Tomea)
_____ *C. t. pelingi*   Banggai Islands (Peleng and Banggai)
_____ *C. t. grayi*   N Moluccas (Morotai, Halmahera, Ternate, Tidore and Bacan)
_____ *C. t. obiensis*   S Moluccas (Obi and Bisa)
_____ *C. t. timoriensis*   E Lesser Sundas (Lomblen and Timor)
_____ *C. t. aruensis*   Aru Islands and Trans-Fly lowlands of s New Guinea
_____ *C. t. nehrkorni*   Waigeo I. (New Guinea)
_____ *C. t. muelleri*   Kofiau and Misool is., New Guinea and D'Entrecasteaux Arch.
_____ *C. t. numforana*   Numfor I. (New Guinea)
_____ *C. t. meyeri*   Biak I. (New Guinea)
_____ *C. t. tagulana*   Louisiade Archipelago (Tagula and Misima)
_____ *C. t. timoriensis*   E Lesser Sundas (Timor and Lomblen)
_____ *C. t. rooki*   Umboi (Bismarck Archipelago)
_____ *C. t. remota*   Bismarck Arch. (New Ireland, New Hanover and Duke of York)
_____ *C. t. heinrothi*   New Britain (Bismarck Archipelago)
_____ *C. t. matthiae*   St. Matthias Islands (Bismarck Archipelago)
_____ *C. t. ultima*   Bismarck Archipelago (Lihir and Tanga)
_____ *C. t. admiralitatis*   Admiralty Islands
_____ *C. t. rostrata*   Rossel (Solomon Islands)
_____ *C. t. erythropygia*   Solomon Islands (Guadalcanal, Malaita, Florida and Savo)
_____ *C. t. salomonis*   San Cristóbal (Solomon Islands)
_____ *C. t. saturatior*   N and central Solomon Islands
_____ *C. t. nisoria*   Solomon Islands (Pavuvu and Russell Group)
_____ *C. t. monacha*   Palau Islands (Caroline Islands)
_____ *C. t. nesiotis*   Yap (Caroline Islands)
_____ *C. t. insperata*   Pohnpei (Caroline Islands)
_____ *C. t. melvillensis*   NW Australia, Northern Territory and n Queensland
_____ *C. t. tenuirostris*   Queensland to New South Wales and Victoria

☐ **Blackish Cuckoo-shrike** *Coracina coerulescens*

_____ *C. c. coerulescens*   N Philippines (lowlands of Luzon and Catanduanes)
_____ *C. c. deschauenseei*   Marinduque (n Philippines)
_____ *C. c. altera†*   Formerly Cebu (central Philippines). Extinct

☐ **Sumba Cuckoo-shrike** *Coracina dohertyi*

Lesser Sundas (Sumbawa, Flores and Sumba)

☐ **Sula Cuckoo-shrike** *Coracina sula*

Lowlands of Sula Islands (Talibau, Seho, Mangole and Sanana)

☐ **Kai Cuckoo-shrike** *Coracina dispar*

Lowlands of Kai Islands (s Ceram Sea)

☐ **Black-bibbed Cuckoo-shrike** *Coracina mindanensis*

____ C. m. lecroyae	Luzon (n Philippines)
____ C. m. elusa	Mindoro (Philippines)
____ C. m. ripleyi	Philippines (Bohol, Samar, Biliran and Leyte)
____ C. m. mindanensis	S Philippines (Mindanao and Basilan)
____ C. m. everetti	Sulu Archipelago (Bongao, Jolo, Lapac and Tawitawi)

☐ **Sulawesi Cuckoo-shrike** *Coracina morio*

____ C. m. talautensis	Talaud Islands (Salebabu, Karakelong and Kaburuang)
____ C. m. salvadorii	Sangihe I. (off n Sulawesi)
____ C. m. morio	Sulawesi, Lembeh, Muna, Tomea, Kabaena and Butung islands

☐ **Pale-gray Cuckoo-shrike** *Coracina ceramensis*

____ C. c. ceramensis	S Moluccas (Seram, Buru and Boano)
____ C. c. hoogerwerfi	Obi (s Moluccas)

☐ **Papuan Cuckoo-shrike** *Coracina incerta*

Montane forests of New Guinea, Yapen and w Papuan islands

☐ **Gray-headed Cuckoo-shrike** *Coracina schisticeps*

____ C. s. schisticeps	Misool I. and Salawati I. and nw New Guinea
____ C. s. reichenowi	N New Guinea (Geelvink Bay to Sepik River Valley)
____ C. s. poliopsa	S New Guinea (Kapare River to Astrolabe Mountains)
____ C. s. vittata	D'Entrecasteaux Archipelago (Fergusson and Goodenough)

☐ **New Guinea Cuckoo-shrike** *Coracina melas*

____ C. m. waigeuensis	Waigeo I. (New Guinea)
____ C. m. tommasonis	Yapen I. (New Guinea)
____ C. m. melas	Salawati I. and w New Guinea
____ C. m. meeki	E New Guinea
____ C. m. goodsoni	Aru Islands (New Guinea)
____ C. m. batantae	Batanta I. (New Guinea)

☐ **Black-bellied Cuckoo-shrike** *Coracina montana*

____ C. m. montana	Montane forests of New Guinea
____ C. m. bicinia	Montane forests in Sepik River region of New Guinea

☐ **Solomon Islands Cuckoo-shrike** *Coracina holopolia*

____ C. h. holopolia	Bougainville, Choiseul, Buka, Guadalcanal and Santa Isabel
____ C. h. pygmaea	Solomon Islands (Kulambangra and Vangunu)
____ C. h. tricolor	Malaita (Solomon Islands)

☐ **McGregor's Cuckoo-shrike** *Coracina mcgregori*

Mountains of Mindanao (s Philippines)

☐ **Indochinese Cuckoo-shrike** *Coracina polioptera*

____ C. p. jabouillei	N Vietnam
____ C. p. indochinensis	Myanmar to central Thailand, central Laos and s Vietnam
____ C. p. polioptera	S Myanmar to s Thailand, Cambodia and s Laos

☐ **White-winged Cuckoo-shrike** *Coracina ostenta*

Central Philippines (Guimaras, Negros and Panay)

☐ **Black-winged Cuckoo-shrike** *Coracina melaschistos*

____ C. m. melaschistos	N Pakistan, Himalayas and ne Indian subcontinent
____ C. m. avensis	W China to central and s Myanmar, n Thailand and n Vietnam
____ C. m. intermedia	Central and s China and Taiwan; winters to Indochina
____ C. m. saturata	N Vietnam and Hainan; winters to Indochina

☐ **Lesser Cuckoo-shrike** *Coracina fimbriata*

_____	C. f. neglecta	S Myanmar and peninsular Thailand
_____	C. f. culminata	S Malay Peninsula
_____	C. f. schierbrandii	Sumatra and Borneo
_____	C. f. compta	Simeulue and Siberut islands (off w Sumatra)
_____	C. f. fimbriata	Java and Bali

☐ **Black-headed Cuckoo-shrike** *Coracina melanoptera*

_____	C. m. melanoptera	N India (n Punjab and United Provinces); winters to Myanmar
_____	C. m. sykesi	S India and Sri Lanka

☐ **Golden Cuckoo-shrike** *Campochaera sloetii*

_____	C. s. sloetii	W New Guinea (Arfak Mountains to Idenberg River)
_____	C. s. flaviceps	SE New Guinea (Mimika River to Port Moresby)

☐ **Black-and-white Triller** *Lalage melanoleuca*

_____	L. m. melanoleuca	N Philippines (Luzon and Mindoro)
_____	L. m. minor	S Philippines (Samar, Leyte and Mindanao)

☐ **Pied Triller** *Lalage nigra*

_____	L. n. davisoni	Nicobar Islands
_____	L. n. nigra	Malay Peninsula, Sumatra, Java and offshore islands
_____	L. n. chilensis	Borneo and Philippine Islands

☐ **White-rumped Triller** *Lalage leucopygialis*

Sulawesi subregion and Sula Islands

☐ **White-shouldered Triller** *Lalage sueurii*

E Java, Bali, Sulawesi subregion and Lesser Sundas

☐ **White-winged Triller** *Lalage tricolor*

Arid regions of Australia and Port Moresby area of New Guinea

☐ **Rufous-bellied Triller** *Lalage aurea*

N Moluccas (Morotai, Ternate, Halmahera, Bacan, Kasiruta, Obi)

☐ **White-browed Triller** *Lalage moesta*

Tanimbar Islands (Arafura Sea)

☐ **Varied Triller** *Lalage leucomela*

_____	L. l. keyensis	Kai Islands (Kai Kecil, Kai Besar and Add)
_____	L. l. polygrammica	Aru Islands and e New Guinea
_____	L. l. obscurior	D'Entrecasteaux Archipelago
_____	L. l. trobriandi	Trobriand Islands
_____	L. l. pallescens	Louisiade Archipelago (Misima and Tagula)
_____	L. l. falsa	Bismarck Archipelago (New Britain, Umboi and Duke of York)
_____	L. l. karu	New Ireland (Bismarck Archipelago)
_____	L. l. albidior	New Hanover (Bismarck Archipelago)
_____	L. l. ottomeyeri	Lihir Islands (Bismarck Archipelago)
_____	L. l. tabarensis	Tabar I. (Bismarck Archipelago)
_____	L. l. conjuncta	St. Matthias I. (Bismarck Archipelago)
_____	L. l. sumunae	Dyaul I. (Bismarck Archipelago)
_____	L. l. rufiventer	Northern Territory and Melville I.
_____	L. l. yorki	NE Australia (Cape York Peninsula of n Queensland)
_____	L. l. leucomela	E Australia (coastal e Queensland and n New South Wales)

☐ **Black-browed Triller** *Lalage atrovirens*

_____	L. a. atrovirens	Misool, Salawati and Waigeo islands and n New Guinea
_____	L. a. leucoptera	Biak I. (n New Guinea)

☐ **Samoan Triller** *Lalage sharpei*

_____	L. s. sharpei	Highlands of Upolu (Western Samoa)
_____	L. s. tenebrosa	Highlands of Savai'i (Western Samoa)

☐ **Polynesian Triller** *Lalage maculosa*

☐	*L. m. modesta*	N and central Vanuatu
____	*L. m. ultima*	Efate (Vanuatu)
____	*L. m. melanopygia*	Santa Cruz (Vanuatu)
____	*L. m. vanikorensis*	Vanikoro (Santa Cruz Islands, Vanuatu)
____	*L. m. soror*	Kandavu (Fiji)
____	*L. m. pumila*	Viti Levu (Fiji)
____	*L. m. mixta*	Central and nw Fiji Islands
____	*L. m. woodi*	Vanua Levu (Fiji)
____	*L. m. rotumae*	Rotuma (Fiji)
____	*L. m. nesophila*	Lau Archipelago (Fiji)
____	*L. m. vauana*	Vavua Group (Fiji)
____	*L. m. tabuensis*	Tonga Islands (w Pacific Ocean)
____	*L. m. keppeli*	Keppel and Boscawen islands
____	*L. m. futunae*	Wallis and Futuna Islands (Futuna and Horne)
____	*L. m. whitmeei*	Cook Islands (Niue and Savage)
____	*L. m. maculosa*	Western Samoa (Upolu and Savai'i)

☐ **Long-tailed Triller** *Lalage leucopyga*

____	*L. l. affinis*	Solomon Islands (San Cristóbal and Ugi)
____	*L. l. deficiens*	Solomon Islands (Torres I. and Banks Group)
____	*L. l. albiloris*	Central and n Vanuatu
____	*L. l. simillima*	S Vanuatu and Loyalty Islands
____	*L. l. montrosieri*	New Caledonia
____	*L. l. leucopyga*	Norfolk I.

☐ **Petit's Cuckoo-shrike** *Campephaga petiti*

SE Nigeria and Cameroon to ne Zaire, w Uganda and w Kenya

☐ **Black Cuckoo-shrike** *Campephaga flava*

Angola to Kenya, Tanzania, Mozambique and South Africa

☐ **Red-shouldered Cuckoo-shrike** *Campephaga phoenicea*

Senegambia to s Sudan, Ethiopia, w Kenya and n Angola

☐ **Purple-throated Cuckoo-shrike** *Campephaga quiscalina*

____	*C. q. quiscalina*	Guinea and Sierra Leone to Cameroon, Zambia and n Angola
____	*C. q. martini*	E Zaire to Uganda and central Kenya
____	*C. q. munzneri*	Highlands of e Tanzania

☐ **Ghana Cuckoo-shrike** *Campephaga lobata*

E Sierra Leone to Liberia, Ivory Coast and s Ghana

☐ **Oriole Cuckoo-shrike** *Campephaga oriolina*

S Cameroon to sw Central African Republic, e Zaire and Gabon

☐ **Rosy Minivet** *Pericrocotus roseus*

____	*P. r. roseus*	Himalayas (Afghanistan to sw China, Myanmar and n India)
____	*P. r. stanfordi*	S China to s Thailand and s Laos

☐ **Brown-rumped Minivet** *Pericrocotus cantonensis*

Breeds central and se China; winters to Thailand and Indochina

☐ **Ashy Minivet** *Pericrocotus divaricatus*

NE Asia; winters to Philippines and Indonesia

☐ **Small Minivet** *Pericrocotus cinnamomeus*

____	*P. c. peregrinus*	Himalayas and n India
____	*P. c. pallidus*	Pakistan (Indus River valley from Rann of Kutch to Punjab)
____	*P. c. malabaricus*	W India (Western Ghats from Belgaum to Kerala)
____	*P. c. cinnamomeus*	S peninsular India and Sri Lanka
____	*P. c. vividus*	Andaman Islands
____	*P. c. thai*	Myanmar to n Thailand and Laos
____	*P. c. sacerdos*	Cambodia and s Vietnam
____	*P. c. separatus*	S Myanmar (Mergui District) and s peninsular Thailand
____	*P. c. saturatus*	Java and Bali

☐ **Ryukyu Minivet** *Pericrocotus tegimae*

S Kyushu and Ryukyu Islands (s Japan)

☐ **Fiery Minivet** *Pericrocotus igneus*
_____ *P. i. igneus*
_____ *P. i. trophis*

Myanmar, Malaya, Sumatra, Borneo and adj. islands; Palawan
Simeulue I. (off Sumatra)

☐ **Flores Minivet** *Pericrocotus lansbergei*

W Lesser Sundas (Sumbawa and Flores)

☐ **White-bellied Minivet** *Pericrocotus erythropygius*
_____ *P. e. erythropygius*
_____ *P. e. albifrons*

Peninsular India (Punjab and Rajasthan to Bihar and Mysore)
Plains of central Myanmar

☐ **Long-tailed Minivet** *Pericrocotus ethologus*
_____ *P. e. favillaceus*
_____ *P. e. laetus*
_____ *P. e. ethologus*
_____ *P. e. yvettae (mariae)*
_____ *P. e. ripponi*
_____ *P. e. annamensis*

Himalayas of Afghanistan and Kashmir to Nepal
E Nepal to Sikkim, Bengal and w Assam (Khasi Hills)
S China and extreme ne India; winters to n Indochina
Myanmar and adjacent sw China (Yunnan)
SW China (Yunnan), e Myanmar (s Shan States) and nw Thailand
Laos (Langbian Plateau)

☐ **Short-billed Minivet** *Pericrocotus brevirostris*
_____ *P. b. brevirostris*
_____ *P. b. affinis*
_____ *P. b. neglectus*
_____ *P. b. anthoides*

E Himalayas to se Tibet, Nepal and w Assam
SW China (s Sichuan to w Yunnan) to e Assam and nw Myanmar
N Thailand to n Tenasserim and n Laos
SW China (se Yunnan, Guangxi and Guangdong) to n Vietnam

☐ **Sunda Minivet** *Pericrocotus miniatus*

Highlands of Sumatra and Java

☐ **Scarlet Minivet** *Pericrocotus flammeus*
_____ *P. f. speciosus*
_____ *P. f. flammeus*
_____ *P. f. fohkiensis*
_____ *P. f. fraterculus*
_____ *P. f. elegans*
_____ *P. f. semiruber*
_____ *P. f. flammifer*
_____ *P. f. xanthogaster*
_____ *P. f. andamanensis*
_____ *P. f. minythomelas*
_____ *P. f. modiglianii*
_____ *P. f. insulanus*
_____ *P. f. novus*
_____ *P. f. leytensis*
_____ *P. f. johnstoniae (gonzalesi)*
_____ *P. f. marchesae*
_____ *P. f. siebersi*
_____ *P. f. exul*

Himalayas (Kashmir to e Assam); winters to n India
Peninsular India and Sri Lanka
SE China (Hunan, Fujian, Guangdong and Guangxi)
Hainan (s China)
SW China (nw Yunnan) to ne India, n Myanmar and n Indochina
SE India (E Ghats) to s Myanmar, Thailand and n Indochina
S Myanmar to sw Thailand and n Malay Peninsula
S Malaya, Sumatra, Bangka and Belitung islands
Andaman Islands
Simeulue I. (off Sumatra)
Enggano I. (off Sumatra)
Borneo
N Philippines (Luzon and Negros)
Central Philippines (Samar and Leyte)
Mindanao (s Philippines)
Jolo Group (Sulu Archipelago)
Java and Bali
Lombok (Lesser Sundas)

☐ **Gray-chinned Minivet** *Pericrocotus solaris*
_____ *P. s. solaris*
_____ *P. s. rubrolimbatus*
_____ *P. s. montpellieri*
_____ *P. s. griseogularis*
_____ *P. s. deignani*
_____ *P. s. nassovicus*
_____ *P. s. montanus*
_____ *P. s. cinereigula*

E Himalayas (Nepal to nw Myanmar)
S Myanmar and n Thailand
SW China (nw and central Yunnan)
SE China to n Indochina and Taiwan
Laos (Langbian Plateau)
Mountains of se Thailand and w Cambodia
Mountains of Malaya and w Sumatra
Mountains of n Borneo

☐ **Bar-winged Flycatcher-shrike** *Hemipus picatus*

_____	*H. p. capitalis*	Himalayas to n Myanmar, sw China, n Thailand and n Indochina
_____	*H. p. picatus*	Peninsular India to s Myanmar, s Thailand and s Indochina
_____	*H. p. intermedius*	Peninsular Thailand to nw Malaysia, Sumatra and ne Borneo
_____	*H. p. leggei*	Sri Lanka

☐ **Black-winged Flycatcher-shrike** *Hemipus hirundinaceus*

Malaysia, Sumatra, Borneo, Java, Bali and adjacent islands

FAMILY: PYCNONOTIDAE (Bulbuls—130)

☐ **Crested Finchbill** *Spizixos canifrons*

_____	*S. c. canifrons*	S Assam (south of the Brahmaputra) to hills of w Myanmar
_____	*S. c. ingrami*	E Myanmar to sw China (Yunnan), nw Thailand and n Indochina

☐ **Collared Finchbill** *Spizixos semitorques*

_____	*S. s. semitorques*	Mountains of s China to n Vietnam (nw Tonkin)
_____	*S. s. cinereicapillus*	Taiwan

☐ **Straw-headed Bulbul** *Pycnonotus zeylanicus*

Myanmar to Malay Peninsula, Sumatra, Nias I., Java and Borneo

☐ **Striated Bulbul** *Pycnonotus striatus*

_____	*P. s. striatus*	Himalayas of Nepal to sw China, Assam and w Myanmar
_____	*P. s. arctus*	NE Assam (Mishmi Hills)
_____	*P. s. paulus*	Myanmar to sw China, n Thailand, n Laos and n Vietnam

☐ **Cream-striped Bulbul** *Pycnonotus leucogrammicus*

Highland forests of w Sumatra

☐ **Spot-necked Bulbul** *Pycnonotus tympanistrigus*

Foothills of w Sumatra

☐ **Black-and-white Bulbul** *Pycnonotus melanoleucus*

Peninsular Thailand, Malaysia, Sumatra, Siberut I. and Borneo

☐ **Gray-headed Bulbul** *Pycnonotus priocephalus*

SW pen. India (s Maharashtra and Goa to w Mysore and Kerala)

☐ **Black-headed Bulbul** *Pycnonotus atriceps*

_____	*P. a. atriceps*	NE India to sw China, SE Asia, Bali, Borneo and Palawan
_____	*P. a. fuscoflavescens*	Andaman Islands
_____	*P. a. hyperemnus*	Sumatra, Simeulue, Nias, Mentawai, Bangka and Belitung islands
_____	*P. a. baweanus*	Bawean I. (Java Sea)
_____	*P. a. hodiernus*	Maratua Islands (Celebes Sea)

☐ **Black-crested Bulbul** *Pycnonotus melanicterus*

_____	*P. m. flaviventris*	Himalayas (Punjab) to ne India, n Myanmar and sw China
_____	*P. m. gularis*	Hills of sw India (w Mysore to Kerala and Tamil Nadu)
_____	*P. m. melanicterus*	Sri Lanka
_____	*P. m. vantynei*	S Myanmar to n Thailand, n Laos, Tonkin and n Annam
_____	*P. m. xanthops*	SE Myanmar to n Thailand
_____	*P. m. negatus*	S Myanmar and adjacent sw Thailand
_____	*P. m. auratus*	N plateau of ne Thailand and adjacent w Laos
_____	*P. m. johnsoni*	S plateau of Thailand to s Laos, Cambodia and Vietnam
_____	*P. m. elbeli*	Islets off coast of se Thailand
_____	*P. m. caecilii*	N Malay Peninsula
_____	*P. m. dispar*	Sumatra and Java
_____	*P. m. montis*	Highlands of n Borneo

☐ **Styan's Bulbul** *Pycnonotus taivanus*

Coastal lowland forests of e and s Taiwan

☐ **Scaly-breasted Bulbul** *Pycnonotus squamatus*

____	*P. s. weberi*	S Myanmar to peninsular Thailand, Malaya and Sumatra
____	*P. s. squamatus*	W and central Java
____	*P. s. borneensis*	Borneo

☐ **Gray-bellied Bulbul** *Pycnonotus cyaniventris*

____	*P. c. cyaniventris*	S Myanmar to Thailand, Malaya, Sumatra and Sipoura I.
____	*P. c. paroticalis*	Borneo

☐ **Red-whiskered Bulbul** *Pycnonotus jocosus*

____	*P. j. fuscicaudatus*	W India (Tapiti River to Kerala and n Madras)
____	*P. j. abuensis*	W India (n Bombay to sw Rajasthan)
____	*P. j. pyrrhotis*	Valley of Nepal and n India (e Punjab to Bihar)
____	*P. j. emeria*	Lowlands of e India to Myanmar and sw Thailand
____	*P. j. whistleri*	Andaman Islands
____	*P. j. monticolus*	E Himalayas from Sikkim to n Myanmar and sw China (Yunnan)
____	*P. j. pattani*	Thailand to n Malaysia and s Indochina
____	*P. j. hainanensis*	N Vietnam and se China (s Guangdong); Naochow I.
____	*P. j. jocosus*	S China (Guizhou to Guangxi, e Guangdong and Hong Kong)

☐ **Brown-breasted Bulbul** *Pycnonotus xanthorrhous*

____	*P. x. xanthorrhous*	Himalayas of Tibet to ne Myanmar, sw China and n Vietnam
____	*P. x. andersoni*	S China (Sichuan to n Guangdong and nw Fujian)

☐ **Light-vented Bulbul** *Pycnonotus sinensis*

____	*P. s. hoyi*	Middle Yangtze River Valley (Sichuan, Hubei and Hunan)
____	*P. s. sinensis*	S China (lower Yangtze River Valley and maritime provinces)
____	*P. s. hainanus*	S China (sw Guangdong and s Guangxi); n Vietnam; Hainan
____	*P. s. formosae*	Taiwan
____	*P. s. orii*	S Ryukyu Islands (Yonaguni and Ishigaki)

☐ **Common Bulbul** *Pycnonotus barbatus*

____	*P. b. barbatus*	Morocco, Algeria and Tunisia
____	*P. b. inornatus*	Senegal to Ghana, n Niger, n Nigeria, n Cameroon and w Chad
____	*P. b. gabonensis*	Central Nigeria and central Cameroon to Gabon and s Congo
____	*P. b. arsinoe*	E Chad to Egypt and Sudan (s to Darfur, Kordofan, Nile Valley)
____	*P. b. schoanus*	Eritrea and e Ethiopia to extreme se Sudan (Boma Hills)
____	*P. b. somaliensis*	Djibouti to nw Somalia and se Ethiopia
____	*P. b. spurius*	S Ethiopia (s Bale to n Sidamo-Borama)
____	*P. b. dodsoni*	S Somalia and adjacent Ethiopia to n Kenya
____	*P. b. tricolor (minor, fayi, ngami)*	E Cameroon to Zaire, s Sudan, Angola, Namibia and Zambia
____	*P. b. layardi (micrus, tenebrior, naumanni)*	SE Kenya to e Tanzania, Zambia, ne Botswana and S Africa

☐ **Black-fronted Bulbul** *Pycnonotus nigricans*

____	*P. n. nigricans (grisescentior)*	Arid s Angola to Namibia, s Botswana and n Transvaal
____	*P. n. superior*	S Transvaal to Lesotho, Orange Free State and ne Cape Province

☐ **Cape Bulbul** *Pycnonotus capensis*

South Africa (s and sw Cape Province)

☐ **White-spectacled Bulbul** *Pycnonotus xanthopygos*

Coastal s Turkey to Near East, Sinai Peninsula and Arabia

☐ **White-eared Bulbul** *Pycnonotus leucotis*

E Iraq to s Iran, n Arabia, s Afghanistan and w India

☐ **White-cheeked Bulbul** *Pycnonotus leucogenys*

____	*P. l. mesoptamiae*	Iraq, Arabia and s Iran (valleys of the Tigris and Euphrates)
____	*P. l. dactylus*	Persian Gulf coast of e Saudi Arabia
____	*P. l. leucotis*	Lowlands of s Iran to Afghanistan and arid nw India
____	*P. l. humii*	NW Pakistan
____	*P. l. leucogenys*	Himalayas of ne Afghanistan to e Assam (n of the Brahmaputra)

☐ **Red-vented Bulbul** *Pycnonotus cafer*
- ____ *P. c. intermedius* — Himalayas (w Pakistan to w Uttar Pradesh)
- ____ *P. c. humayuni* — W Pakistan (Salt Range) to nw India
- ____ *P. c. bengalensis* — E Himalayas (e Uttar Pradesh) to ne India, Nepal and Bhutan
- ____ *P. c. wetmorei* — NE peninsular India
- ____ *P. c. primrosei* — S Assam (south of the Brahmaputra) and West Bengal
- ____ *P. c. pusillus* — S India (Bombay, Madhya Pradesh and Andhra to Kerala)
- ____ *P. c. cafer* — Sri Lanka
- ____ *P. c. stanfordi* — N Myanmar to extreme sw China (w Yunnan)
- ____ *P. c. melanchimus* — S-central Myanmar (Mandalay to Rangoon)

☐ **Sooty-headed Bulbul** *Pycnonotus aurigaster*
- ____ *P. a. chrysorrhoides* — S China (Fujian, e Guandong and Hong Kong)
- ____ *P. a. resurrectus* — S China (Guandong and Naochow I.); n Vietnam
- ____ *P. a. dolichurus* — Central Vietnam (Quangtri and Thuathien provinces)
- ____ *P. a. latouchei* — SW China to n Thailand, n Laos and n Vietnam
- ____ *P. a. klossi* — SE Myanmar to n Thailand
- ____ *P. a. schauenseei* — S Myanmar to sw Thailand
- ____ *P. a. thais* — S Thailand
- ____ *P. a. germani* — SE Thailand to s Indochina
- ____ *P. a. aurigaster* — Java and Bali; introduced Singapore, Sumatra and s Sulawesi

☐ **Puff-backed Bulbul** *Pycnonotus eutilotus*
- S Myanmar, Malaya, Sumatra, Bangka I. and Borneo

☐ **Blue-wattled Bulbul** *Pycnonotus nieuwenhuisii*
- ____ *P. n. inexpectatus* — Rediscovered in 1996 after 60 year absence in nw Sumatra
- ____ *P. n. nieuwenhuisii* — Known from a 1901 specimen from ne Borneo

☐ **Yellow-wattled Bulbul** *Pycnonotus urostictus*
- ____ *P. u. ilokensis* — N Luzon (n Philippines)
- ____ *P. u. urostictus* — N Philippines (Luzon and Polillo); formerly Catanduanes
- ____ *P. u. atricaudatus* — Philippines (Bohol, Samar, Panaon, Biliran and Leyte)
- ____ *P. u. philippensis* — S Philippines (Dinagat, Siargao and Mindanao)
- ____ *P. u. basilanicus* — S Philippiness (Basilan and Zamboanga area of Mindanao)

☐ **Orange-spotted Bulbul** *Pycnonotus bimaculatus*
- ____ *P. b. snouckaerti* — Mountains of nw Sumatra
- ____ *P. b. barat* — Mountains of sw Sumatra, w and central Java
- ____ *P. b. bimaculatus* — Mountains of e Java and Bali

☐ **Stripe-throated Bulbul** *Pycnonotus finlaysoni*
- ____ *P. f. davisoni* — S Myanmar (delta of the Irrawaddy River)
- ____ *P. f. eous* — SE Myanmar to sw China (s Yunnan), Thailand and s Indochina
- ____ *P. f. finlaysoni* — Malay Peninsula (s Myanmar and Isthmus of Kra to Malacca)

☐ **Yellow-throated Bulbul** *Pycnonotus xantholaemus*
- Thornscrub of s India

☐ **Yellow-eared Bulbul** *Pycnonotus penicillatus*
- Highlands of Sri Lanka

☐ **Flavescent Bulbul** *Pycnonotus flavescens*
- ____ *P. f. flavescens* — Hills of s Assam (south of the Brahmaputra) to w Myanmar
- ____ *P. f. vividus* — NE Myanmar to sw China (Yunnan), Thailand and n Indochina
- ____ *P. f. sordidus* — S Indochina
- ____ *P. f. leucos* — N Borneo (Mt. Kinabalu to Mt. Mulu and Mt. Murud)

☐ **White-browed Bulbul** *Pycnonotus luteolus*
- ____ *P. l. luteolus* — Arid scrub of coastal s peninsular India
- ____ *P. l. insulae* — Lowlands of Sri Lanka

□ **Yellow-vented Bulbul** *Pycnonotus goiavier*

____	*P. g. jambu*	Lowlands of se Thailand to s Indochina
____	*P. g. personatus*	Malay Peninsula, Riau Arch., Sumatra, Bangka and Belitung is.
____	*P. g. analis*	Java and Bali; probably introduced to Lombok and s Sulawesi
____	*P. g. gourdini*	Borneo and Maratua Islands
____	*P. g. goiavier*	N and central Philippine Islands
____	*P. g. samarensis*	Philippines (Bohol, Cebu, Leyte, Samar, Ticao and Biliran)
____	*P. g. suluensis*	S Philippines (Mindanao, Basilan, Camiguin Sur and Sulu Arch.)

□ **Olive-winged Bulbul** *Pycnonotus plumosus*

____	*P. p. plumosus*	Malay Peninsula, Riau Arch., e Sumatra and Java
____	*P. p. porphyreus*	W Sumatra, Nias, Batu, Banyak and Mentawi islands
____	*P. p. billitonis*	W and s Borneo and Belitung I.
____	*P. p. hutzi*	N and e Borneo
____	*P. p. chiroplethis*	Anambas Islands (South China Sea)
____	*P. p. hachisukae*	Banggai and adjacent islands off ne Borneo; Cagayan Sulu
____	*P. p. cinereifrons*	SW Philippines (Palawan, Culion and Busuanga)
____	*P. p. sibergi*	Bawean I. (Java Sea)

□ **Streak-eared Bulbul** *Pycnonotus blanfordi*

____	*P. b. blanfordi*	Central and s Myanmar
____	*P. b. conradi*	Thailand to n Malaysia and s Indochina
____	*P. b. robinsoni*	Central Malaysia

□ **Cream-vented Bulbul** *Pycnonotus simplex*

____	*P. s. simplex*	S Thailand to Malaya, Sumatra, Riau, Lingga, Nias and Batu is.
____	*P. s. prillwitzi*	Java
____	*P. s. perplexus*	N and e Borneo; Balembangan I.
____	*P. s. oblitus*	S and w Borneo; Bangka, Belitung and South Natuna islands
____	*P. s. halizonus*	Anambas Islands and North Natuna Islands

□ **Red-eyed Bulbul** *Pycnonotus brunneus*

____	*P. b. brunneus*	Lowlands of Malay Peninsula, Sumatra, Borneo and adj. islands
____	*P. b. zapolius*	Anambas Islands (South China Sea)

□ **Spectacled Bulbul** *Pycnonotus erythropthalmos*

____	*P. e. erythropthalmos*	Malay Peninsula, Belitung I., Sumatra and adjacent w islands
____	*P. e. salvadorii*	Borneo

□ **Cameroon Mountain Greenbul** *Andropadus montanus*

Montane forests of Nigeria and Cameroon

□ **Shelley's Greenbul** *Andropadus masukuensis*

____	*A. m. kakamegae*	E Zaire to Uganda, w Kenya and w Tanzania
____	*A. m. roehli*	Highlands of e Tanzania
____	*A. m. masukuensis*	SW Tanzania (Rungwe Mts.) to n Malawi (Masuku Mts.)

□ **Little Greenbul** *Andropadus virens*

____	*A. v. erythropterus*	Lowlands of Gambia to s Nigeria
____	*A. v. virens*	Cameroon to Gabon, Angola, s Sudan and w Kenya; Bioko
____	*A. v. holochlorus*	Lowland forests of w Uganda
____	*A. v. hallae*	Single specimen from e Zaire (probable melanistic *A. v. virens*)
____	*A. v. zombensis*	Gabon to se Zaire, e Kenya, Tanzania and Mozambique; Mafia I.
____	*A. v. marwitzi*	Coastal se Kenya (Usambara, Kilimanjaro and Vanga-Rabia areas)
____	*A. v. zanzibaricus*	Zanzibar (Tanzania)

□ **Gray Greenbul** *Andropadus gracilis*

____	*A. g. extremus*	Sierra Leone to sw Nigeria
____	*A. g. gracilis*	SE Nigeria to s Cameroon, Gabon, nw Angola and central Zaire
____	*A. g. ugandae*	E Zaire to Uganda and w Kenya

☐ **Ansorge's Greenbul** *Andropadus ansorgei*

_____ *A. a. ansorgei* — Sierra Leone to Gabon, n Angola, n Zaire and w Uganda

_____ *A. a. kavirondensis* — W Kenya (n Kavirondo to Mt. Elgon area)

☐ **Plain Greenbul** *Andropadus curvirostris*

_____ *A. c. leoninus* — Sierra Leone to central Ghana

_____ *A. c. curvirostris* — S Ghana to n Angola, s Sudan, Uganda and w Kenya; Bioko

☐ **Slender-billed Greenbul** *Andropadus gracilirostris*

_____ *A. g. gracilirostris* — Guinea to extreme s Sudan, w Zaire, w Kenya and Angola

_____ *A. g. percivali* — Highlands of central Kenya to extreme w Tanzania

☐ **Sombre Greenbul** *Andropadus importunus*

_____ *A. i. insularis (somaliensis, subalaris, fricki)* — S Somalia to Kenya and n Tanzania; Manda I.

_____ *A. i. hypoxanthus (loquax)* — S Tanzania to Malawi, Zambia, e Zimbabwe and Mozambique

_____ *A. i. oleaginus* — S Mozambique to n Kwazulu-Natal and ne Transvaal

_____ *A. i. importunus (errolius, noomei)* — Natal to s Zululand, Transvaal, Swaziland and Cape Province

☐ **Yellow-whiskered Greenbul** *Andropadus latirostris*

_____ *A. l. congener* — Senegal to sw Nigeria

_____ *A. l. latirostris* — S Nigeria to n Angola, e Zaire, Kenya and Tanzania; Bioko

☐ **Western Mountain-Greenbul** *Andropadus tephrolaemus*

_____ *A. t. bamendae* — Mountains of se Nigeria and adjacent w Cameroon

_____ *A. t. tephrolaemus* — SW Cameroon (Mt. Cameroon); Bioko

☐ **Eastern Mountain-Greenbul** *Andropadus nigriceps*

_____ *A. n. kikuyuensis* — Mountains of e Zaire to w Uganda and central Kenya

_____ *A. n. nigriceps* — Mountains of s Kenya (Nguruman Hills) to n Tanzania

_____ *A. n. kungwensis* — W Tanzania (Mt. Kungwe area)

_____ *A. n. usambarae* — SE Kenya (Taita Hills) to ne Tanzania (s Pare, w Usambara mts.)

_____ *A. n. neumanni* — NE Tanzania (Uluguru Mountains)

_____ *A. n. chlorigula* — E Tanzania (Nguru Mts. and highlands of Iranga District)

_____ *A. n. fusciceps* — Mts. of sw Tanzania, ne Zambia, Malawi and ne Mozambique

☐ **Stripe-cheeked Greenbul** *Andropadus milanjensis*

_____ *A. m. striifacies* — Highlands of se Kenya to n Tanzania (Kilimanjaro to Iringa)

_____ *A. m. olivaceiceps* — Highlands of sw Tanzania to n Malawi and n Mozambique

_____ *A. m. milanjensis* — Malawi (Mt. Milanje) to w Mozambique and Zimbabwe

☐ **Golden Greenbul** *Calyptocichla serina* — Sierra Leone to Gabon, Angola and ne Zaire; Bioko

☐ **Honeyguide Greenbul** *Baeopogon indicator*

_____ *B. i. leucurus (togoensis)* — Sierra Leone to Liberia, Ivory Coast, Ghana and Togo

_____ *B. i. indicator (chlorosaturata)* — S Nigeria to e Zaire, s Sudan, Uganda, w Kenya and nw Zambia

☐ **Sjostedt's Greenbul** *Baeopogon clamans* — Locally in Cameroon, Equatorial Guinea, w Gabon and ne Zaire

☐ **Spotted Greenbul** *Ixonotus guttatus* — Liberia to s Cameroon, Gabon, Zaire, w Uganda, nw Tanzania

☐ **Simple Greenbul** *Chlorocichla simplex* — Guinea-Bissau to ne Angola, e Zaire and extreme s Sudan

☐ **Yellow-throated Greenbul** *Chlorocichla flavicollis*

_____ *C. f. flavicollis* — Senegal to e Nigeria and n Cameroon

_____ *C. f. adamauae* — N Cameroon (Adamawa Plateau)

_____ *C. f. simplicicolor* — E Cameroon (Uam region)

_____ *C. f. soror* — N-central Cameroon to Gabon, Zaire, s Sudan and Ethiopia

_____ *C. f. flavigula (pallidigula)* — Angola to Zaire, w Uganda, w Kenya, Zambia and nw Tanzania

☐ **Yellow-necked Greenbul** *Chlorocichla falkensteini*
_____ *C. f. viridescentior* — S Cameroon (River Ja region)
_____ *C. f. falkensteini* — S Central African Republic to Rio Muni, sw Zaire and n Angola

☐ **Yellow-bellied Greenbul** *Chlorocichla flaviventris*
_____ *C. f. centralis* — Somalia to Kenya, e Tanzania and n Mozambique
_____ *C. f. occidentalis (zambesiae, ortiva)* — W Tanzania to Zaire, Angola, Botswana, Transvaal, Mozambique
_____ *C. f. flaviventris* — Natal and n Mozambique

☐ **Joyful Greenbul** *Chlorocichla laetissima*
_____ *C. l. laetissima* — Montane forests of e Zaire to s Sudan, Uganda and nw Kenya
_____ *C. l. schoutedeni* — Montane forests of se Zaire to sw Tanzania and ne Zambia

☐ **Prigogine's Greenbul** *Chlorocichla prigoginei*
— Submontane forests of e Zaire (Lendu Plateau and Butembo)

☐ **Swamp Greenbul** *Thescelocichla leucopleura*
— Sierra Leone to Cameroon, e Zaire and w Uganda

☐ **Leaf-love** *Phyllastrephus scandens*
_____ *P. s. scandens* — Senegal to n Nigeria and n Cameroon
_____ *P. s. orientalis (acedis, upembae)* — S Cameroon to s Zaire, s Sudan and extreme w Tanzania

☐ **Cabanis' Greenbul** *Phyllastrephus cabanisi*
_____ *P. c. cabanisi* — Highlands of w Angola to s Zaire, Zambia and sw Tanzania
_____ *P. c. sucosus* — E Zaire to s Sudan, Uganda, w Kenya and nw Tanzania
_____ *P. c. nandensis* — W Kenya (n Nandi Hills)
_____ *P. c. ngurumanensis* — SW Kenya (Nguruman Hills)

☐ **Fischer's Greenbul** *Phyllastrephus fischeri*
— Extreme se Somalia to Kenya, Tanzania and n Mozambique

☐ **Placid Greenbul** *Phyllastrephus placidus*
— N Kenya to Tanzania, Zambia, s Malawi and ne Mozambique

☐ **Terrestrial Brownbul** *Phyllastrephus terrestris*
_____ *P. t. suahelicus (bensoni)* — E Kenya to e Tanzania and n Mozambique
_____ *P. t. intermedius (katangae) (robertsi)* — S Angola to s Zaire, Zambia, e Zululand and s Mozambique
_____ *P. t. terrestris* — W Zululand, Swaziland, Transvaal and Natal to Cape Province

☐ **Northern Brownbul** *Phyllastrephus strepitans*
— Extreme s Sudan to n Uganda, s Ethiopia, Kenya and e Tanzania

☐ **Pale-olive Greenbul** *Phyllastrephus fulviventris*
— Riparian vegetation of extreme w Zaire, Cabinda and w Angola

☐ **Gray-olive Greenbul** *Phyllastrephus cerviniventris*
— S Kenya to Tanzania, Zambia, s Zaire, Malawi and Mozambique

☐ **Baumann's Greenbul** *Phyllastrephus baumanni*
— Lowland forests of Sierra Leone and Liberia to s Nigeria

☐ **Toro Olive-Greenbul** *Phyllastrephus hypochloris*
— Forests of ne Zaire to extreme se Sudan, Uganda and w Kenya

☐ **Cameroon Olive-Greenbul** *Phyllastrephus poensis*
— Montane forests of se Nigeria and sw Cameroon; Bioko

☐ **Sassi's Greenbul** *Phyllastrephus lorenzi*
— Primary forests of e Zaire

☐ **Yellow-streaked Bulbul** *Phyllastrephus flavostriatus*
_____ *P. f. tenuirostris* — Coastal se Kenya to Tanzania and ne Mozambique
_____ *P. f. kungwensis* — W Tanzania (Kungwe-Mahari Mountains)
_____ *P. f. uzungwensis* — E Tanzania (Udzungwa Mountains)
_____ *P. f. alfredi* — SW Tanzania to e Zambia and n Malawi
_____ *P. f. graueri* — E Zaire (highlands west of lakes Kivu, Edward and Albert)
_____ *P. f. olivaceogriseus* — Highlands of e Zaire (nw of Lake Tanganyika) to sw Uganda
_____ *P. f. vincenti* — Highlands of se Malawi and adjacent n Mozambique
_____ *P. f. flavostriatus (distans, dendrophilus, dryobates)* — E Zimbabwe and Mozambique (s of Zambezi River) to Natal

☐ **Gray-headed Greenbul** *Phyllastrephus poliocephalus*

Montane rainforests of se Nigeria and sw Cameroon

☐ **Tiny Greenbul** *Phyllastrephus debilis*
_____ *P. d. rabai*   Lowlands of coastal se Kenya to se Tanzania (Rufiji River)
_____ *P. d. albigula*   E Tanzania (Nguru and Usambara mountains)
_____ *P. d. debilis*   SE Tanzania to e Zimbabwe and s Mozambique

☐ **White-throated Greenbul** *Phyllastrephus albigularis*
_____ *P. a. albigularis*   SW Senegal to Cameroon, Gabon, s Sudan and Uganda
_____ *P. a. viridiceps*   NW Angola

☐ **Icterine Greenbul** *Phyllastrephus icterinus*

Sierra Leone to Gabon, Zaire and extreme w Uganda; Bioko

☐ **Liberian Greenbul** *Phyllastrephus leucolepis*

Humid forests of se Liberia

☐ **Xavier's Greenbul** *Phyllastrephus xavieri*
_____ *P. x. serlei*   Lowlands and foothills of Mt. Cameroon
_____ *P. x. xavieri (sethsmithi)*   Cameroon to n Zaire, w Uganda and nw Tanzania

☐ **Long-billed Greenbul** *Phyllastrephus madagascariensis*
_____ *P. m. madagascariensis*   Forests of e Madagascar
_____ *P. m. inceleber*   Forests of n and w Madagascar

☐ **Spectacled Greenbul** *Phyllastrephus zosterops*
_____ *P. z. fulvescens*   Humid forests of extreme n Madagascar (Mt. d'Ambre)
_____ *P. z. andapae*   NE Madagascar (Andapa region)
_____ *P. z. zosterops*   E Madagascar
_____ *P. z. ankafanae*   Highlands of se Madagascar (Fianarantsoa region)

☐ **Appert's Greenbul** *Phyllastrephus apperti*

SW Madagascar (Zombitse and Vohibasia forests)

☐ **Dusky Greenbul** *Phyllastrephus tenebrosus*

Rainforests of e-central Madagascar

☐ **Gray-crowned Greenbul** *Phyllastrephus cinereiceps*

Rainforests of e Madagascar

☐ **Common Bristlebill** *Bleda syndactyla*
_____ *B. s. syndactyla (multicolor)*   Sierra Leone to Gabon, nw Angola, w Zaire and Zambia
_____ *B. s. woosnami*   E Zaire to s Sudan, Kenya, Uganda and Zambia
_____ *B. s. nandensis*   W Kenya (Nandi Hills)

☐ **Green-tailed Bristlebill** *Bleda eximia*
_____ *B. e. eximia*   Guinea to Sierra Leone and Ghana
_____ *B. e. notata*   S Nigeria to Central African Republic; Bioko
_____ *B. e. ugandae*   NE Zaire to s Sudan and Uganda

☐ **Gray-headed Bristlebill** *Bleda canicapilla*
_____ *B. c. moreli*   Senegal and Gambia
_____ *B. c. canicapilla*   Guinea-Bissau to Nigeria

☐ **Yellow-spotted Nicator** *Nicator chloris*

Senegal to Zaire, Uganda, extreme s Sudan and w Tanzania

☐ **Eastern Nicator** *Nicator gularis*

S Somalia to Kenya, Tanzania, Zambia, Mozambique and Natal

☐ **Yellow-throated Nicator** *Nicator vireo*

S Cameroon to Gabon, n Angola and extreme w Uganda

☐ **Red-tailed Greenbul** *Criniger calurus*
_____ *C. c. verreauxi*   Senegambia to sw Nigeria
_____ *C. c. calurus*   S Nigeria (Benin) to extreme w Zaire (lower Congo); Bioko
_____ *C. c. emini*   W-central Zaire to ne Angola, Uganda and Tanzania

☐ **Western Bearded-Greenbul** *Criniger barbatus*

_____ *C. b. barbatus* Sierra Leone to Togo
_____ *C. b. ansorgeanus* S Nigeria (lower Niger River delta)

☐ **Eastern Bearded-Greenbul** *Criniger chloronotus*

SE Nigeria to e Zaire, n Angola and extreme w Uganda

☐ **Yellow-bearded Greenbul** *Criniger olivaceus*

Senegambia to Ghana and Ivory Coast

☐ **White-bearded Greenbul** *Criniger ndussumensis*

SE Nigeria and Cameroon to Gabon, Angola and n Zaire

☐ **Finsch's Bulbul** *Alophoixus finschii*

Lowlands of s peninsular Thailand, Malaya, Sumatra and Borneo

☐ **White-throated Bulbul** *Alophoixus flaveolus*

_____ *A. f. flaveolus* Himalayas (Nepal to ne Myanmar)
_____ *A. f. burmanicus* SW China (w Yunnan) to se Myanmar to w Thailand

☐ **Puff-throated Bulbul** *Alophoixus pallidus*

_____ *A. p. griseiceps* Pegu Yoma Mountains (Myanmar)
_____ *A. p. robinsoni* S Myanmar (Amherst District of Tenasserim)
_____ *A. p. henrici* SW China (w Yunnan to s Guangxi) to n Thailand, n Indochina
_____ *A. p. pallidus* Hainan (s China)
_____ *A. p. isani* NW part of eastern plateau of Thailand
_____ *A. p. annamensis* Central Indochina
_____ *A. p. khmerensis* S Laos to Cambodia and s Vietnam

☐ **Ochraceous Bulbul** *Alophoixus ochraceus*

_____ *A. o. hallae* S Vietnam
_____ *A. o. cambodianus* SE Thailand and sw Cambodia (Chaine de l'Éléphant)
_____ *A. o. ochraceus* S Myanmar to sw Thailand
_____ *A. o. sordidus* Malay Peninsula and Mergui Archipelago
_____ *A. o. sacculatus* Highlands of s Malaysia (n Perak to Negri Sembilan and Pahang)
_____ *A. o. sumatranus* Highlands of w Sumatra
_____ *A. o. fowleri* Highlands of n Borneo (Sarawak)
_____ *A. o. ruficrissus* Highlands of ne Borneo

☐ **Gray-cheeked Bulbul** *Alophoixus bres*

_____ *A. b. tephrogenys* S Myanmar, Malay Peninsula and lowlands of e Sumatra
_____ *A. b. bres* W and central Java
_____ *A. b. balicus* E Java and Bali
_____ *A. b. gutteralis* Borneo
_____ *A. b. frater* SW Philippines (Balabac, Busuanga, Calamianes and Palawan)

☐ **Yellow-bellied Bulbul** *Alophoixus phaeocephalus*

_____ *A. p. phaeocephalus* Malay Pen., Sumatra, Bangka, Belitung and North Natuna Is.
_____ *A. p. connectens* NE Borneo
_____ *A. p. sulphuratus* Central Borneo
_____ *A. p. diardi* W Borneo

☐ **Golden Bulbul** *Alophoixus affinis*

_____ *A. a. platenae* Sangihe I. (off Sulawesi)
_____ *A. a. aureus* Togian Islands (off Sulawesi)
_____ *A. a. harterti* Banggai Islands (Peleng, Banggai, Labobo and Banda)
_____ *A. a. longirostris* Sula Islands (Taliabu, Mangole and Sanana)
_____ *A. a. chloris* N Moluccas (Morotai, Halmahera, Bacan and Kasiruta)
_____ *A. a. lucasi* Obi (n Moluccas)
_____ *A. a. mystacalis* Buru (s Moluccas)
_____ *A. a. affinis* Seram (s Moluccas)
_____ *A. a. flavicaudus* Ambon (s Moluccas)

☐ **Hook-billed Bulbul** *Setornis criniger*

Lowland forests of Borneo, e Sumatra and Bangka I.

☐ **Hairy-backed Bulbul** *Tricholestes criniger*
____ *T. c. criniger* — Malay Peninsula, Tioman I. and e Sumatra
____ *T. c. sericeus* — W Sumatra, Batu Islands, Lingga Archipelago and Musala I.
____ *T. c. viridis* — Borneo and North Natuna Islands

☐ **Olive Bulbul** *Iole virescens*

Forests of Bangladesh and ne India to Myanmar and w Thailand

☐ **Gray-eyed Bulbul** *Iole propinqua*
____ *I. p. propinqua* — E Myanmar to sw China, n Thailand, n Laos and n Vietnam
____ *I. p. lekhakuni* — S Myanmar to sw Thailand
____ *I. p. simulator* — SE Thailand to s Laos, Cambodia and n Vietnam
____ *I. p. cinnamomeoventris* — Malay Pen. (Mergui District and Isthmus of Kra to Trang)
____ *I. p. aquilonis* — S China (sw Guangxi) and n Vietnam
____ *I. p. innectens* — S Vietnam

☐ **Buff-vented Bulbul** *Iole olivacea*

Malay Peninsula, Sumatra, Borneo and adjacent islands

☐ **Yellow-browed Bulbul** *Iole indica*
____ *I. i. ictericus* — W India (w Ghats from s Maharashtra to Belgaum and Goa)
____ *I. i. indica* — SW India and Sri Lanka
____ *I. i. guglielmi* — Sri Lanka

☐ **Sulphur-bellied Bulbul** *Ixos palawanensis*

Mountains of Palawan (sw Philippines)

☐ **Philippine Bulbul** *Ixos philippinus*
____ *I. p. philippinus* — Philippines (Luzon, Samar, Leyte, Marinduque and Bohol)
____ *I. p. parkesi* — Burian (Philippines)
____ *I. p. guimarasensis* — Philippines (Guimaras, Masbate, Panay, Negros, Ticao, Verde)
____ *I. p. mindorensis* — Philippines (Mindoro and Semirara)
____ *I. p. saturatior* — Mindanao, Cebu, Bohol, Biliran, Leyte, Panaon and Samar

☐ **Streak-breasted Bulbul** *Ixos siquijorensis*
____ *I. s. cinereiceps* — Philippines (Romblon and Tablas)
____ *I. s. monticola†* — Cebu (Philippines). Extinct
____ *I. s. siquijorensis* — Siquijor (Philippines)

☐ **Brown-eared Bulbul** *Ixos amaurotis*
____ *I. a. hensoni* — Breeds sw Hokkaido; winters to s Korea, n Japan and se China
____ *I. a. matchiae* — S Japan (Hachijo-jima, Tanegashima and Yakushima)
____ *I. a. amaurotis* — Central Japanese is. (Honshu to Kyushu); Cheju-Do I. (Korea)
____ *I. a. squamiceps* — Bonin Islands (Mukojima, Chichijima and Hahajima)
____ *I. a. magnirostris* — Volcano Islands (Japan)
____ *I. a. borodinonis* — Daito Islands (Japan)
____ *I. a. ogawae* — N Ryukyu Islands (Amami-O-Shima and Tokuno-Shima)
____ *I. a. pryeri* — Central Ryukyu Islands (Ihiya, Okinawa, Zamami and Kume)
____ *I. a. insignis* — Miyako-Jima (s Ryukyu Islands)
____ *I. a. stejnegeri* — Ryukyu Islands (Ishigaki, Iriomote and Yonaguni)
____ *I. a. nagamichii* — S Taiwan and Lan-yü I.
____ *I. a. batanensis* — Philippines (Babuyan Claro, Batan, Ivojos and Sabtang)
____ *I. a. fugensis* — Philippines (Calayan, Fuga and Dalupiri)
____ *I. a. camiguiensis* — Camiguin Norte (n Philippines)

☐ **Yellowish Bulbul** *Ixos everetti*
____ *I. e. everetti* — Philippines (Dinagat, Mindanao, Panaon, Biliran and Siargao)
____ *I. e. samarensis* — Philippines (Samar and Leyte)
____ *I. e. haynaldi* — Sulu Arch. (Bongao, Jolo, Sibutu, Tawitawi and Sanga Sanga)
____ *I. e. catarmanensis* — Camiguin Sur (s Philippines)

☐ **Zamboanga Bulbul** *Ixos rufigularis*

S Philippines (Basilan and Zamboanga Pen. of w Mindanao)

☐ **Streaked Bulbul** *Ixos malaccensis*

Malay Pen., s Vietnam, Sumatra, Borneo and adjacent islands

☐ **Ashy Bulbul** *Hemixos flavala*

_____	*H. f. flavala*	E Himalayas (Garhwal to Nepal, w Yunnan and sw Myanmar)
_____	*H. f. cannipennis*	S China (Fujian, Guangdong and Guangxi) to n Vietnam
_____	*H. f. castanota*	Hainan (s China)
_____	*H. f. bourdellei*	SW China (s Yunnan) to e Thailand and n Laos
_____	*H. f. remota*	S Laos (Bolavens and Langbian plateaux)
_____	*H. f. hildebrandti*	N Myanmar to nw Thailand
_____	*H. f. davisoni*	Central Myanmar to sw Thailand
_____	*H. f. cinerea*	Malay Peninsula and Sumatra
_____	*H. f. connectens*	Highlands of n Borneo

☐ **Chestnut Bulbul** *Hemixos castanonotus*

_____	*H. c. canipennis*	S China (Hunan, Guangxi, Fujian and Guangdong)
_____	*H. c. castanonotus*	N Vietnam (Tonkin) and Hainan

☐ **Mountain Bulbul** *Hypsipetes mcclellandii*

_____	*H. m. mcclellandii*	E Himalayas (w Uttar Pradesh to e Assam)
_____	*H. m. ventralis*	SW Myanmar (Chin Hills and Arakan Yoma Mountains)
_____	*H. m. tickelli*	E Myanmar (n Shan States) to nw Thailand
_____	*H. m. similis*	NE Myanmar (Kachin) to sw China (Yunnan) and n Indochina
_____	*H. m. holtii*	S China (Sichuan to Fujian and Guandong)
_____	*H. m. loquax*	N and e Thailand to s Laos (Bolavens Plateau)
_____	*H. m. griseiventer*	Laos (Langbian Plateau)
_____	*H. m. canescens*	SE Thailand (Khao Kuap region)
_____	*H. m. peracensis*	Peninsular Thailand to n Malaysia (Selangor and Pahang)

☐ **Sunda Bulbul** *Hypsipetes virescens*

_____	*H. v. sumatranus*	Montane forests of w Sumatra
_____	*H. v. virescens*	Montane forests of Java

☐ **Madagascar Bulbul** *Hypsipetes madagascariensis*

_____	*H. m. madagascariensis*	Madagascar
_____	*H. m. grotei*	Isles Glorieuses (Indian Ocean off Réunion)
_____	*H. m. parvirostris*	Comoro Islands
_____	*H. m. rostratus*	Aldabra

☐ **Black Bulbul** *Hypsipetes leucocephalus*

_____	*H. l. psaroides*	Himalayas of n Afghanistan to e Assam and se Tibet
_____	*H. l. nigrescens*	E Assam (s of the Brahmaputra) to w Myanmar
_____	*H. l. ganeesa*	SW India (Western Ghats)
_____	*H. l. humii*	Sri Lanka
_____	*H. l. ambiens*	NE Myanmar to sw China (w Yunnan in Irrawaddy watershed)
_____	*H. l. concolor*	E Myanmar to sw China, e Thailand, Laos and s Vietnam
_____	*H. l. sinensis*	E Myanmar to sw China; winters to Thailand and s Laos
_____	*H. l. stresemanni*	SW China (Likiang Mts. of nw Yunnan) to Thailand and s Laos
_____	*H. l. leucothorax*	E China (Sichuan to Shaanxi and Hebei); winters to s Laos
_____	*H. l. leucocephalus*	Maritime provinces of se China
_____	*H. l. perniger*	Hainan (s China)
_____	*H. l. nigerrimus*	Taiwan

☐ **Seychelles Bulbul** *Hypsipetes crassirostris*

Seychelles (Mahé, Praslin and Félicité)

☐ **Comoro Bulbul** *Hypsipetes parvirostris*

Comoro Islands (highlands of Grand Comoro and Mohéli)

☐ **Reunion Bulbul** *Hypsipetes borbonicus*

Evergreen forests of Réunion (w Mascarene Islands)

☐ **Mauritius Bulbul** *Hypsipetes olivaceus*

Maccabe forest of sw Mauritius (w Mascarene Islands)

☐ **Nicobar Bulbul** *Hypsipetes nicobariensis*

Forests of Nicobar Islands

☐ **White-headed Bulbul** *Hypsipetes thompsoni*

Montane forests of s Myanmar to nw Thailand

☐ **Black-collared Bulbul** *Neolestes torquatus*

Savanna of Gabon to Angola, se Zaire and nw Zambia

FAMILY: REGULIDAE (Kinglets—6)

☐ **Golden-crowned Kinglet** *Regulus satrapa*

____	*R. s. olivaceus*	SE Alaska to Oregon (w of Cascades); winters to s California
____	*R. s. amoenus*	Kenai Pen. and central Yukon to Rocky Mts.; winters to sw US
____	*R. s. satrapa*	Labrador and Newfoundland to e US; winters to Gulf Coast
____	*R. s. apache*	Mountains of s Arizona; winters to s Texas and New Mexico
____	*R. s. aztecus*	Mts. of Mexico (Michoacán to Hidalgo, Puebla and Guerrero)
____	*R. s. clarus*	Mountains of s Mexico (Chiapas) and s Guatemala

☐ **Ruby-crowned Kinglet** *Regulus calendula*

____	*R. c. grinnelli*	Coastal Alaska and British Columbia; winters to s California
____	*R. c. calendula*	N and e Canada to ne US; winters to Guatemala, Cuba, Bahamas
____	*R. c. obscurus*	Guadalupe I. (off w Mexico)

☐ **Goldcrest** *Regulus regulus*

____	*R. r. regulus (anglorum, interni)*	Europe to Asia Minor and w Siberia; winters to Mediterranean
____	*R. r. azoricus*	São Miguel I. (Azores)
____	*R. r. sanctaemariae*	Santa Maria I. (Azores)
____	*R. r. inermis*	W Azores (Flores, Faial, Pico, São Jorge and Terciera)
____	*R. r. buturlini*	Crimea, Caucasus and Azerbaijan; winters to n Iran
____	*R. r. hyrcanus*	E Turkey (Elburz Mountains) to n Iran (s Caspian District)
____	*R. r. coatsi*	W Siberia to Altai Mountains; winters to s Nan Shan Mountains
____	*R. r. tristis*	Mountains of central Asia; winters to Transcaspia and w Iran
____	*R. r. himalayensis*	Himalayas of Afghanistan to Pakistan and Nepal
____	*R. r. sikkimensis*	Himalayas of Nepal to se Tibet and w China
____	*R. r. japonensis*	Mountains of Manchuria to n and e China, Korea and Japan
____	*R. r. yunnanensis*	Mts. of w China (s Gansu and Shaanxi to Sichuan and Yunnan)

☐ **Canary Islands Kinglet** *Regulus teneriffae*

Coniferous and mixed forests of Canary Islands

☐ **Flamecrest** *Regulus goodfellowi*

Montane forests of central Taiwan

☐ **Firecrest** *Regulus ignicapillus*

____	*R. i. madeirensis*	Madeira (e Atlantic Ocean)
____	*R. i. ignicapillus*	England and w Europe to Mediterranean and Asia Minor
____	*R. i. balearicus*	Balearic Islands and North Africa (Morocco to n Tunisia)

FAMILY: CHLOROPSEIDAE (Leafbirds—8)

☐ **Philippine Leafbird** *Chloropsis flavipennis*

Philippines (Cebu, Leyte and Mindanao)

☐ **Yellow-throated Leafbird** *Chloropsis palawanensis*

Philippines (Balabac, Busuanga, Palawan and Calamian)

☐ **Greater Green Leafbird** *Chloropsis sonnerati*

____	C. s. zosterops	Myanmar, peninsular Thailand, Malaysia, Sumatra and Borneo
____	C. s. parvirostris	Nias I. (off Sumatra)
____	C. s. sonnerati	Java

☐ **Lesser Green Leafbird** *Chloropsis cyanopogon*

____	C. c. cyanopogon	S Myanmar, n pen. Thailand, Malaysia, Sumatra and Borneo
____	C. c. septentrionalis	S peninsular Thailand

☐ **Blue-winged Leafbird** *Chloropsis cochinchinensis*

____	C. c. jerdoni	Peninsular India and Sri Lanka
____	C. c. kinneari	SW China (s Yunnan) to e Thailand and n Indochina
____	C. c. cochinchinensis	SE Thailand and s Indochina
____	C. c. serithai	Peninsular Thailand south to Isthmus of Kra
____	C. c. moluccensis	S Thailand and Malay Peninsula
____	C. c. icterocephala	Sumatra
____	C. c. natunensis	Natuna Islands (China Sea)
____	C. c. viridinucha	Borneo
____	C. c. billitonis	Belitung I. (off Borneo)
____	C. c. nigricollis	Java

☐ **Golden-fronted Leafbird** *Chloropsis aurifrons*

____	C. a. aurifrons	Himalayas and ne India to Myanmar
____	C. a. frontalis	Peninsular India
____	C. a. insularis	SW India (Travancore) and Sri Lanka
____	C. a. pridii	SW China (s Yunnan) to s Myanmar, n Thailand and n Laos
____	C. a. inornata	Central and se Thailand to Cambodia and s Vietnam
____	C. a. incompta	SW Thailand and s Indochina
____	C. a. media	Sumatra

☐ **Orange-bellied Leafbird** *Chloropsis hardwickii*

____	C. h. hardwickii	E Himalayas to sw China, Myanmar, n Thailand and n Vietnam
____	C. h. melliana	S China (Guangxi, Fujian and Guangdong) to n Vietnam
____	C. h. lazulina	Hainan (s China)
____	C. h. malayana	Malay Peninsula

☐ **Blue-masked Leafbird** *Chloropsis venusta*

Foothills of Sumatra

FAMILY: AEGITHINIDAE (Ioras—4)

☐ **Common Iora** *Aegithina tiphia*

____	A. t. multicolor	S India and Sri Lanka
____	A. t. deignani	Peninsular India to n and central Myanmar
____	A. t. humei	Central India (south of the Ganges River)
____	A. t. tiphia	NE India (Kumaon to Bengal and Assam)
____	A. t. septentrionalis	Pakistan and nw India (Punjab)
____	A. t. philipi	SW China to central Myanmar, n Thailand, Laos and n Vietnam
____	A. t. cambodiana	Cambodia to se Thailand and s Vietnam
____	A. t. horizoptera	S Myanmar to Thailand, Malaysia, Sumatra and adj. islands
____	A. t. scapularis	Java and Bali
____	A. t. viridis	S Borneo
____	A. t. aequanimis	N Borneo, adjacent northern islands and Palawan

☐ **White-tailed Iora** *Aegithina nigrolutea*

Lowlands of n Pakistan and nw India

☐ **Green Iora** *Aegithina viridissima*

____	*A. v. viridissima*	S Myanmar, peninsular Thailand, Malaya, Sumatra and Borneo
____	*A. v. thapsina*	Anambas Islands (South China Sea)

☐ **Great Iora** *Aegithina lafresnayei*

____	*A. l. lafresnayei*	S Thailand and Malaysia
____	*A. l. innotata*	SW China (s Yunnan) to Myanmar, Thailand and n Indochina
____	*A. l. xanthotis*	Cambodia and s Indochina

FAMILY: PTILOGONATIDAE (Silky-flycatchers—4)

☐ **Black-and-yellow Silky-flycatcher** *Phainoptila melanoxantha*

Montane forests of Costa Rica and w Panama (e to Veraguas)

☐ **Gray Silky-flycatcher** *Ptilogonys cinereus*

____	*P. c. otofuscus*	Sierra Madre Occidental of w Mexico
____	*P. c. cinereus*	Highlands of central and e Mexico
____	*P. c. pallescens*	Highlands of sw Mexico (e Michoacán and Guerrero)
____	*P. c molybdophanes*	Highlands of s Mexico (Chiapas) and w Guatemala

☐ **Long-tailed Silky-flycatcher** *Ptilogonys caudatus*

Mountains of Costa Rica and w Panama (Volcán de Chiriquí)

☐ **Phainopepla** *Phainopepla nitens*

____	*P. n. lepida*	Arid sw US to Baja and nw Mexico (Sonora and Chihuahua)
____	*P. n. nitens*	S Texas to s Mexican plateau

FAMILY: BOMBYCILLIDAE (Waxwings—3)

☐ **Bohemian Waxwing** *Bombycilla garrulus*

____	*B. g. pallidiceps*	NW North America; highly nomadic in winter
____	*B. g. garrulus*	Fenno-Scandia to w Siberia; winters to central Europe
____	*B. g. centralasiae*	Central Siberia to Sea of Okhotsk; winters to s China and Japan

☐ **Cedar Waxwing** *Bombycilla cedrorum*

North America; winters to n S America and Greater Antilles

☐ **Japanese Waxwing** *Bombycilla japonica*

SE Siberia and n Manchuria; winters to s China and Ryukyu Is.

FAMILY: HYPOCOLIIDAE (Hypocolius—1)

☐ **Hypocolius** *Hypocolius ampelinus*

Iraq (Tigris-Euphrates valleys) to Turkmenia; winters Saudi Arabia

FAMILY: DULIDAE (Palmchat—1)

☐ **Palmchat** *Dulus dominicus*

Hispaniola, Gonâve I. and Saona I.

FAMILY: CINCLIDAE (Dippers—5)

☐ **White-throated Dipper** *Cinclus cinclus*

_____	*C. c. hibernicus*	Ireland, Outer Hebrides and w coast of Scotland
_____	*C. c. gularis*	Orkney Islands, c and e Scotland, w and c England and Wales
_____	*C. c. cinclus*	Fenno-Scandia to south coast of White Sea and e Prussia
_____	*C. c. aquaticus*	Central and s Europe to Balkan Peninsula
_____	*C. c. minor*	Mountains of Morocco, Tunisia and Algeria
_____	*C. c. olympicus†*	Formerly Cyprus. Extinct
_____	*C. c. caucasicus*	Caucasus Mountains to nw Iran; winters to Iraq and Pakistan
_____	*C. c. rufiventris*	Coastal w Syria (Lebanon Mountains)
_____	*C. c. persicus*	SW Iran (Zagros and Bakhtiari mountains)
_____	*C. c. uralensis*	Ural Mountains
_____	*C. c. leucogaster*	Mountains of central Asia
_____	*C. c. cashmeriensis*	Himalayas (w Kashmir to Sikkim)
_____	*C. c. przewalskii*	Mountains of s Tibet and w China

☐ **Brown Dipper** *Cinclus pallasii*

_____	*C. p. tenuirostris*	Mountains of central Asia and Himalayas
_____	*C. p. dorjei*	Mts. of e Sikkim, Assam, e Tibet, n Myanmar and n Thailand
_____	*C. p. pallasii*	Mountains of ne Asia, Japan, w China, n Thailand, n Vietnam
_____	*C. p. marila*	NE India (Khasi Hills)

☐ **American Dipper** *Cinclus mexicanus*

_____	*C. m. unicolor*	Aleutian Islands to Alaska, w Canada and w US
_____	*C. m. mexicanus*	Highlands of n and central Mexico
_____	*C. m. anthonyi*	Mountains of s Mexico (Chiapas) to Guatemala and Honduras
_____	*C. m. ardesiacus*	Mountains of Costa Rica and w Panama

☐ **White-capped Dipper** *Cinclus leucocephalus*

_____	*C. l. rivularis*	Santa Marta Mountains (ne Colombia)
_____	*C. l. leuconotus*	Mountains of Colombia to w Venezuela and Ecuador
_____	*C. l. leucocephalus*	Mountains of Peru and Bolivia

☐ **Rufous-throated Dipper** *Cinclus schulzi*

	E slope of Andes of extreme nw Argentina and se Bolivia

FAMILY: TROGLODYTIDAE (Wrens—79)

☐ **Black-capped Donacobius** *Donacobius atricapillus*

_____	*D. a. brachypterus*	Tropical e Panama (Darién) to n Colombia
_____	*D. a. nigrodorsalis*	SE Colombia to e Ecuador and se Peru (Madre de Dios)
_____	*D. a. atricapillus*	Venezuela to Guianas, Amazonian and e Brazil and ne Argentina
_____	*D. a. albovittatus*	E Bolivia (Beni, Cochabamba and Santa Cruz); adjacent Brazil?

☐ **White-headed Wren** *Campylorhynchus albobrunneus*

_____	*C. a. albobrunneus*	Humid lowlands of central and e Panama
_____	*C. a. harterti*	E Panama (Darién) and w Colombia

☐ **Band-backed Wren** *Campylorhynchus zonatus*

_____	*C. z. zonatus*	E Mexico (e San Luis Potosí and n Veracruz to n Puebla)
_____	*C. z. restrictus*	S Mexico (s Veracruz and n Oaxaca) to Belize and Guatemala
_____	*C. z. vulcanius*	S Mexico (Chiapas) to Nicaragua
_____	*C. z. costaricensis*	Caribbean slope of Costa Rica and w Panama
_____	*C. z. curvirostris*	N Colombia (tropical base of Santa Marta Mountains)
_____	*C. z. brevirostris*	N Colombia to nw Ecuador

☐ **Gray-barred Wren** *Campylorhynchus megalopterus*
_____ *C. m. megalopterus*   Coniferous forests of Mexican plateau
_____ *C. m. nelsoni*   Mountains of s Mexico (sw Veracruz and Oaxaca)

☐ **Giant Wren** *Campylorhynchus chiapensis*

             Humid Pacific lowlands of s Mexico (Chiapas)

☐ **Rufous-naped Wren** *Campylorhynchus rufinucha*
_____ *C. r. humilis*   Arid lowlands of sw Mexico (Colima to Chiapas)
_____ *C. r. rufinucha*   Lowlands of e Mexico (Veracruz and adjacent Oaxaca)
_____ *C. r. nigricaudatus*   S Mexico (coastal Chiapas) to w Guatemala
_____ *C. r. castaneus*   Interior of Guatemala to Honduras and Nicaragua
_____ *C. r. capistratus*   Pacific coast of El Salvador to Nicaragua and nw Costa Rica
_____ *C. r. nicoyae*   SW Costa Rica (Nicoya Peninsula)

☐ **Spotted Wren** *Campylorhynchus gularis*

             Oak-pine woodlands of w and central Mexico

☐ **Boucard's Wren** *Campylorhynchus jocosus*

             Arid oak-pine forests of s Mexican plateau

☐ **Yucatan Wren** *Campylorhynchus yucatanicus*

             Arid coastal lowlands of se Mexico (n Yucatán Peninsula)

☐ **Cactus Wren** *Campylorhynchus brunneicapillus*
_____ *C. b. couesi (anthonyi)*   Arid sw US to n Baja, nw Mexico and extreme n Tamaulipas
_____ *C. b. sandigense*   Arid San Diego County (s California)
_____ *C. b. bryanti*   Pacific slope of w Baja California between 31° and 29°
_____ *C. b. parus*   Coastal central Baja California between 28°50' and 25°05'
_____ *C. b. seri*   Isla Tiburón (Sea of Cortés)
_____ *C. b. affinis*   S Baja California
_____ *C. b. brunneicapillus*   NW Mexico (Sonora to nw Sinaloa)
_____ *C. b. guttatus*   Central plateau of Mexico

☐ **Bicolored Wren** *Campylorhynchus griseus*
_____ *C. g. albicilius*   Tropical n Colombia to nw Venezuela
_____ *C. g. bicolor*   Colombia (upper Magdalena Valley)
_____ *C. g. minor*   Tropical e Colombia to n Venezuela
_____ *C. g. pallidus*   S Venezuela (Amazonas)
_____ *C. g. griseus*   E Venezuela (n Amazonas) to w Guyana and extreme n Brazil

☐ **Thrush-like Wren** *Campylorhynchus turdinus*
_____ *C. t. aenigmaticus*   Extreme sw Colombia (Nariño)
_____ *C. t. hypostictus*   E Colombia to Ecuador, Peru, Bolivia, Brazil s of the Amazon
_____ *C. t. turdinus*   E-central Brazil (Maranhão to Goiás, Bahia and Espírito Santo)
_____ *C. t. unicolor*   Tropical e Bolivia to sw Brazil (Mato Grosso) and e Paraguay

☐ **Stripe-backed Wren** *Campylorhynchus nuchalis*
_____ *C. n. pardus*   Arid tropical n Caribbean Colombia
_____ *C. n. brevipennis*   Coastal n Venezuela
_____ *C. n. nuchalis*   Central Venezuela
_____

☐ **Fasciated Wren** *Campylorhynchus fasciatus*
_____ *C. f. pallescens*   Arid sw Ecuador to nw Peru (Tumbes, Piura and Lambayeque)
_____ *C. f. fasciatus*   Arid w Peru (s Piura to Huánuco and n Lima)

☐ **Gray-mantled Wren** *Odontorchilus branickii*
_____ *O. b. branickii*   Trop. and subtrop. e Colombia, Ecuador, Peru and n Bolivia
_____ *O. b. minor*   N Ecuador (Imbabura)

☐ **Tooth-billed Wren** *Odontorchilus cinereus*

             Humid lowlands of Amazonian Brazil south of the Amazon

□ **Rock Wren** *Salpinctes obsoletus*

_____ *S. o. obsoletus*	SW Canada and w US to n and central Mexico
_____ *S. o. guadeloupensis*	Guadalupe I. (off w Mexico)
_____ *S. o. tenuirostris*	San Benito Islands (off s Baja California)
_____ *S. o. exsul*	San Benedicto I. (Revillagigedo Islands off s Baja California)
_____ *S. o. neglectus*	Highlands of se Mexico (Chiapas) to Guatemala and Honduras
_____ *S. o. guttatus*	Highlands of El Salvador to Nicaragua and Costa Rica

□ **Canyon Wren** *Catherpes mexicanus*

_____ *C. m. pallidior*	W North America (s Canada to Wyoming and central California)
_____ *C. m. conspersus (griseus, punctulatus)*	W US to Baja California and nw Mexico
_____ *C. m. albifrons*	SW Texas to n Mexico (Coahuila and Nuevo León)
_____ *C. m. meliphonus*	NW Mexico
_____ *C. m. mexicanus*	Mexico (se Sonora to central plateau and sw Chiapas)
_____ *C. m. croizati*	SE Mexico
_____ *C. m . cantator*	S Mexico

□ **Slender-billed Wren** *Hylorchilus sumichrasti*

Lowlands of s Mexico (Veracruz and adjacent n Oaxaca)

□ **Nava's Wren** *Hylorchilus navai*

Lowlands of s Mexico (Chiapas and extreme e Veracruz)

□ **Rufous Wren** *Cinnycerthia unirufa*

_____ *C. u. unirufa*	Andes of ne Colombia (Cundinamarca to Magdalena)
_____ *C. u. unibrunnea*	Central Andes of Colombia to Ecuador and extreme n Peru
_____ *C. u. chakei*	Andes of nw Venezuela

□ **Sharpe's Wren** *Cinnycerthia olivascens*

_____ *C. o. bogotensis*	W slope of Eastern Andes of Colombia
_____ *C. o. olivascens*	Central and Western Andes of Colombia to n Peru (Amazonas)

□ **Peruvian Wren** *Cinnycerthia peruana*

Eastern Andes of Peru (Amazonas to Ayacucho)

□ **Fulvous Wren** *Cinnycerthia fulva*

_____ *C. f. fitzpatrick*	E Peru (Cordillera Vilcabamba of Cuzco)
_____ *C. f. fulva*	Eastern Andes of Peru (Cuzco)
_____ *C. f. gravesi*	Andes of s Peru (Puno) to n Bolivia (Cochabamba and La Paz)

□ **Black-throated Wren** *Thryothorus atrogularis*

_____ *T. a. atrogularis*	Caribbean slope of Nicaragua to Costa Rica and w Panama
_____ *T. a. xerampelinus*	Pacific slope of e Panama (Darién)

□ **Sooty-headed Wren** *Thryothorus spadix*

Humid foothill forests of e Panama to w Colombia

□ **Black-bellied Wren** *Thryothorus fasciatoventris*

_____ *T. f. melanogaster*	Pacific lowlands of sw Costa Rica to w Panama
_____ *T. f. albigularis*	E Panama (Canal Zone) to w Colombia (Chocó)
_____ *T. f. fasciatoventris*	Tropical n Colombia to Río Magdalena Valley

□ **Inca Wren** *Thryothorus eisenmanni*

Andes of s Peru (Cuzco)

□ **Whiskered Wren** *Thryothorus mystacalis*

_____ *T. m. saltuensis*	W slope of Western Andes of Colombia (Chocó to Cauca)
_____ *T. m. yananchae*	SW Colombia (upper tropical valley of Río Guáitara in Nariño)
_____ *T. m. mystacalis*	Andes of w Ecuador south to El Oro (locally to sea level)
_____ *T. m. macrurus*	E slope of Central Andes and w slope of E Andes of Colombia
_____ *T. m. amaurogaster*	Subtropical e slope of Eastern Andes of Colombia
_____ *T. m. consobrinus*	N Venezuela (Sierra de Perijá and mts. of Zulia, Lara and Mérida)
_____ *T. m. ruficaudatus*	Coastal cordillera of n Venezuela
_____ *T. m. tachirensis*	Foothills and Andes of nw Venezuela (Táchira)

☐ **Plain-tailed Wren** *Thryothorus euophrys*

_____ *T. e. euophrys*	Andes of extreme s Colombia (w Nariño) and n Ecuador
_____ *T. e. longipes*	Temperate e slope of Andes of Ecuador
_____ *T. e. atriceps*	Subtropical Andes of nw Peru (Piura)
_____ *T. e. schulenbergi*	E slope of Andes of n Peru (Amazonas)

☐ **Moustached Wren** *Thryothorus genibarbis*

_____ *T. g. genibarbis*	N-central and Amazonian Brazil
_____ *T. g. juruanus*	W Amazonian Brazil to se Peru (Ucayali) and nw Bolivia
_____ *T. g. intercedens*	Central Brazil (Goiás to Minas Gerais and Mato Grosso)
_____ *T. g. bolivianus*	Lowlands of Bolivia (La Paz, Cochabamba and Santa Cruz)

☐ **Coraya Wren** *Thryothorus coraya*

_____ *T. c. griseipectus*	SE Colombia to e Ecuador, w Amaz. Brazil and n Peru (Loreto)
_____ *T. c. caurensis*	Extreme e Colombia to s Venezuela and n Brazil
_____ *T. c. barrowcloughiana*	*Tepuis* of s Venezuela (Mt. Roraima and Mt. Cuquenam)
_____ *T. c. ridgwayi*	Mountains of e Venezuela (Gran Sabana) to w Guyana
_____ *T. c. obscurus*	*Tepuis* of se Venezuela in Bolívar (Auyan-tepui)
_____ *T. c. coraya*	The Guianas to Suriname and adjacent n Brazil
_____ *T. c. herberti*	N Brazil s of the Amazon (Rio Tocantins to Rio Tapajós)
_____ *T. c. albiventris*	E Peru (e slope of Andes in San Martín)
_____ *T. c. amazonicus*	Tropical e Peru south of Río Marañón (Loreto and Huánuco)
_____ *T. c. cantator*	Subtropical mountains of se Peru (Junín and Cuzco)

☐ **Happy Wren** *Thryothorus felix*

_____ *T. f. sonorae*	Pacific slope of nw Mexico (s Sonora to n Sinaloa)
_____ *T. f. pallidus*	W Mexico (Sinaloa and w Durango to Jalisco and Michoacán)
_____ *T. f. lawrencii*	María Madre I. (Tres Marías Islands off w Mexico)
_____ *T. f. magdalenae*	María Magdalena I. (Tres Marías Islands off w Mexico)
_____ *T. f. felix*	S Mexico (se Jalisco to Michoacán, Guerrero and w Oaxaca)
_____ *T. f. grandis*	S Mexico (upper Río Balsas drainage to sw Puebla, n Guerrero)

☐ **Spot-breasted Wren** *Thryothorus maculipectus*

_____ *T. m. microstictus*	E Mexico (e Nuevo León, San Luis Potosí and Tamaulipas)
_____ *T. m. maculipectus*	Gulf-Caribbean slope of ne Mexico (Veracruz to n Oaxaca)
_____ *T. m. umbrinus*	S Mexico (Chiapas) to Guatemala, e Nicaragua and n Costa Rica
_____ *T. m. canobrunneus*	SE Mexico (Yucatán Pen.) to Belize and Petén of Guatemala

☐ **Rufous-breasted Wren** *Thryothorus rutilus*

_____ *T. r. hyperythrus*	Pacific slope of sw Costa Rica to e Panama (Río Chepó in Darién)
_____ *T. r. laetus*	N Colombia (Santa Marta Mts.) to nw Venezuela (Sierra de Perijá)
_____ *T. r. hypospodius*	E slope of Eastern Andes of Colombia (Boyacá to Meta)
_____ *T. r. interior*	W slope of Eastern Andes of Colombia in s Magdalena Valley
_____ *T. r. columbianus*	Central Andes of Colombia (Valle)
_____ *T. r. intensus*	Andes of nw Venezuela (Trujillo, Mérida and Táchira)
_____ *T. r. rutilus*	Mountains of n Venezuela; Trinidad
_____ *T. r. tobagensis*	Tobago
_____ *T. r. paucimaculatus*	Tropical w Ecuador (Guayas) to nw Peru (Piura)

☐ **Speckle-breasted Wren** *Thryothorus sclateri*

	S-central Colombia; sw Ecuador to nw Peru

☐ **Riverside Wren** *Thryothorus semibadius*

	Pacific lowlands of sw Costa Rica and extreme w Panama

☐ **Bay Wren** *Thryothorus nigricapillus*

_____ *T. n. costaricensis*	Caribbean lowlands of e Nicaragua, Costa Rica and nw Panama
_____ *T. n. castaneus*	Panama (Veraguas to Canal Zone and adjacent Darién)
_____ *T. n. schottii*	Pacific slope of e Panama (Darién) and adjacent nw Colombia
_____ *T. n. reditus*	NE Panama (Caribbean slope of extreme e Darién)
_____ *T. n. connectens*	SW Colombia (Cauca and Nariño)
_____ *T. n. nigricapillus*	Tropical w Ecuador (Esmeraldas to El Oro)

☐ **Stripe-breasted Wren** *Thryothorus thoracicus*

Caribbean lowlands of e Nicaragua to w Panama

☐ **Stripe-throated Wren** *Thryothorus leucopogon*

____ *T. l. grisescens* — Caribbean coast of e Panama
____ *T. l. leucopogon* — Pacific coast of e Panama (Darién), w Colombia and nw Ecuador

☐ **Banded Wren** *Thryothorus pleurostictus*

____ *T. p. nisorius* — W Mexico (Michoacán, Guerrero, Morelos, México and Puebla)
____ *T. p. oaxacae* — SW Mexico (coastal central Guerrero to Oaxaca)
____ *T. p. acaciarum* — S Mexico (Chiapas)
____ *T. p. oblitus* — Pacific lowlands of e Chiapas to Guatemala and w El Salvador
____ *T. p. pleurostictus* — Guatemala (Gualán region of Zacapa)
____ *T. p. lateralis* — Lowlands of El Salvador and w Honduras
____ *T. p. ravus* — Pacific lowlands of Nicaragua to nw Costa Rica

☐ **Carolina Wren** *Thryothorus ludovicianus*

____ *T. l. ludovicianus* — S Canada to Texas and se US
____ *T. l. miamensis* — Peninsular Florida
____ *T. l. nesophilus* — Florida
____ *T. l. burleighi* — Cat I., Ship I. and Horn I. (off Mississippi)
____ *T. l. lomitensis* — Texas (lower Rio Grande Valley) and ne Mexico (n Tamaulipas)
____ *T. l. berlandieri* — Mts. of e Mexico (e Coahuila, Nuevo León and sw Tamaulipas)
____ *T. l. tropicalis* — Tropical ne Mexico (e San Luis Potosí)
____ *T. l. albinucha* — SE Mexico (Yucatán Peninsula) to Petén of n Guatemala
____ *T. l. subfulvus* — Arid interior of Guatemala to nw Nicaragua

☐ **Rufous-and-white Wren** *Thryothorus rufalbus*

____ *T. r. transfinis* — Extreme s Mexico (Pacific slope of sw Chiapas)
____ *T. r. rufalbus* — Highlands of Guatemala and El Salvador
____ *T. r. sylvus* — W Honduras
____ *T. r. castanonotus* — Pacific slope of Nicaragua to Costa Rica and w Panama
____ *T. r. skutchi* — E Panama
____ *T. r. cumanensis* — Caribbean coast of n Colombia to ne Venezuela (Paría Peninsula)
____ *T. r. minlosi* — Tropical e Colombia to nw Venezuela

☐ **Sinaloa Wren** *Thryothorus sinaloa*

____ *T. s. cinereus* — NW Mexico (se Sonora, sw Chihuahua and n Sinaloa)
____ *T. s. sinaloa* — W Mexico (c Sinaloa to w Durango, Nayarit, Jalisco and Colima)
____ *T. s. russeus* — SW Mexico (coastal Guerrero to extreme sw Oaxaca)

☐ **Plain Wren** *Thryothorus modestus*

____ *T. m. modestus* — S Mexico (Oaxaca and Chiapas) to Guatemala and n Nicaragua
____ *T. m. roberti* — Caribbean lowlands of Honduras
____ *T. m. vanrossemi* — Caribbean lowlands of El Salvador
____ *T. m. zeledoni* — E Nicaragua to e Costa Rica and nw Panama (w Bocas del Toro)
____ *T. m. elutus* — W Panama (Chiriquí to Canal Zone)

☐ **Buff-breasted Wren** *Thryothorus leucotis*

____ *T. l. galbraithii* — E Panama and nw Colombia (n Chocó and n Antioquia)
____ *T. l. conditus* — Pearl Islands (Gulf of Panama)
____ *T. l. leucotis* — N Colombia (w slope of Santa Marta Mts.) to Magdalena Valley
____ *T. l. collinus* — N Colombia (n Guajira Peninsula in Serranía de Macuira)
____ *T. l. venezuelanus* — N tropical Colombia and nw Venezuela
____ *T. l. zuliensis* — E Colombia (Norte de Santander) to w Venezuela
____ *T. l. peruanus* — SE Colombia to e Ecuador, e Peru, n Bolivia and w Amaz. Brazil
____ *T. l. bogotensis* — *Llanos* of e Colombia to central Venezuela
____ *T. l. hypoleucus* — *Llanos* of n central Venezuela
____ *T. l. albipectus* — NE Venezuela to the Guianas, ne Brazil and n Mato Grosso
____ *T. l. rufiventris* — E Brazil (s Maranhão to Piauí, Goiás, Minas Gerais and São Paulo)

☐ **Niceforo's Wren** *Thryothorus nicefori*

W slope of Eastern Andes of n Colombia

☐ **Superciliated Wren** *Thryothorus superciliaris*
____ *T. s. superciliaris* Arid coastal Ecuador (Manabi to Guayas); Isla Puná
____ *T. s. baroni* Arid s Ecuador (El Oro) to nw Peru (Ancash)

☐ **Fawn-breasted Wren** *Thryothorus guarayanus*

N Bolivia and adjacent sw Brazil (sw Mato Grosso)

☐ **Long-billed Wren** *Thryothorus longirostris*
____ *T. l. bahiae* Lowlands of ne Brazil (Ceará to Pernambuco, Piauí and n Bahia)
____ *T. l. longirostris* Coastal e Brazil (Rio de Janeiro to São Paulo and Santa Catarina)

☐ **Gray Wren** *Thryothorus griseus*

W Amazonian Brazil (sw Amazonas)

☐ **Bewick's Wren** *Thryomanes bewickii*
____ *T. b. calophonus* SW British Columbia to w Washington and w Oregon
____ *T. b. drymoecus* SW Oregon to California (Sacramento and n San Joaquin valleys)
____ *T. b. atrestus* S-central Oregon to ne California and w-central Nevada
____ *T. b. marinensis* Coastal California (Del Norte County to Marin County)
____ *T. b. spilurus (drymoecus)* Coastal California (San Francisco to Santa Cruz County)
____ *T. b. eremophilus* Mountains of se California to Wyoming and nw Mexico
____ *T. b. leucophrys†* San Clemente I. (off s California). Extinct
____ *T. b. charienturus (nesophilus, catalinae, correctus)* Channel Islands, sw California and w slope of s Sierra Nevada
____ *T. b. cerroensis* W-central Baja California (30° to 26°N) and Isla Cedros
____ *T. b. magdalenensis* S Baja California south of 26ºN
____ *T. b. brevicauda†* Formerly Guadeloupe I. (off Baja California). Extinct ca 1903
____ *T. b. bewickii* N-central US to Kansas, Nebraska and Mississippi
____ *T. b. altus* E US (Appalachian Mts. to Alabama and South Carolina)
____ *T. b. cryptus* Kansas and Oklahoma to s Texas and ne Mexico (n Tamaulipas)
____ *T. b. pulichi* S Texas (Rio Grande Valley)
____ *T. b. sadai* N Mexico
____ *T. b. muriunus* Central plateau of Mexico
____ *T. b. mexicanus* SE Mexican plateau (s Puebla, w Veracruz and Oaxaca)

☐ **Socorro Wren** *Thryomanes sissonii*

Socorro I. (Revillagigedo Islands off w Mexico)

☐ **Zapata Wren** *Ferminia cerverai*

SW Cuba (dense vegetation of Zapata Swamp)

☐ **Winter Wren** *Troglodytes troglodytes*
____ *T. t. islandicus* Iceland
____ *T. t. borealis* Faeroe Islands (n Atlantic Ocean)
____ *T. t. zetlandicus* Shetland Islands (Scotland)
____ *T. t. hebridensis* Outer Hebrides Islands
____ *T. t. fridariensis* Fair Isle (Scotland)
____ *T. t. hirtensis* St. Kilda I. (Scotland)
____ *T. t. indigenus* Ireland, Inner Hebrides, Orkneys, Scotland and England
____ *T. t. troglodytes* Continental Europe and Asia Minor
____ *T. t. kabylorum* Balearic Islands, s Spain and nw Africa
____ *T. t. koenigi* Corsica and Sardinia
____ *T. t. cypriotes* Crete, Rhodes, Cyprus and Levant
____ *T. t. hyrcanus* Crimean Peninsula to Caucasus Mts., n Iraq and Iran
____ *T. t. juniperi* NW Libya
____ *T. t. zagrossiensis* Zagros Mountains (sw Iran)
____ *T. t. tianschanicus* NE Iran and s Transcaspia to n Afghanistan and Turkestan
____ *T. t. pallescens* Kamchatka Peninsula and Komandorskiye Islands
____ *T. t. kurilensis* N Kuril Islands (Shasukotan and Ushichi)
____ *T. t. fumigatus* S Kuril Islands, Japan and n Izu Islands
____ *T. t. mosukei* Izu Islands and Borodino Islands
____ *T. t. ogawae* S Japanese Archipelago (Tanegashima and Yakushima)
____ *T. t. taivanus* Taiwan

_____ *T. t. dauricus* — Transbaicalia to Sakhalin, Manchuria and Korea
_____ *T. t. idius* — Central China (Gansu to Shaanxi, w Liaoning and Guangdong)
_____ *T. t. szetschuanus* — SW China
_____ *T. t. talifuensis* — W China (s Sichuan to w Yunnan) and ne Myanmar
_____ *T. t. subpallidus* — Himalayas of Afghanistan
_____ *T. t. neglectus* — W Himalayas (Gilgit to w Nepal)
_____ *T. t. nipalensis* — Himalayas of Nepal to ne Assam and se Tibet
_____ *T. t. magrathi* — NW India (Safed Koh Mountains)
_____ *T. t. alascensis* — Pribilof Islands (St. George, St. Paul and Otter)
_____ *T. t. kiskensis* — W Aleutians (Kiska, Little Kiska, Amchitka, Ogliuga)
_____ *T. t. meligerus* — W Aleutians (Attu, Agattu, Alaid, Nitzi and Buldir)
_____ *T. t. ochroleucus* — Alaska
_____ *T. t. tanagensis* — Central Aleutians (Andreanof Islands)
_____ *T. t. seguamensis* — Central Aleutians (Seguam, Amutka and Yunaska)
_____ *T. t. stevensoni* — W Alaska Peninsula, Amak and Amagat islands
_____ *T. t. petrophilus* — E Aleutians (Fox Islands group)
_____ *T. t. semidiensis* — SE Alaska (Chowiet and Aghiyuk islands)
_____ *T. t. helleri* — S Alaska (Kodiak, Afognak and Raspberry islands)
_____ *T. t. pacificus* — SE Alaska and sw Yukon to w Canada and nw US
_____ *T. t. hiemalis* — Central and s Canada to e Texas and central Florida
_____ *T. t. pullus* — Appalachian Mts. (e W Virginia and w Virginia to ne Georgia)
_____ *T. t. muiri* — Coastal n California (south to Marin County)
_____ *T. t. obscurior* — Coastal central Calif. (San Francisco to San Luis Obispo Co.)

☐ **House Wren** *Troglodytes aedon*

_____ *T. a. parkmanii* — SW Canada to central and w US and n Baja California
_____ *T. a. aedon* — SE Canada and e US
_____ *T. a. baldwini* — S-central Canada to s US
_____ *T. a. cahooni* — Mountains of se Arizona to nw Mexico (n Jalisco)
_____ *T. a. compositus* — Mountains of e Mexico (Coahuila and Nuevo León to Puebla)
_____ *T. a. brunneicollis* — W Mexico (Nayarit to Colima, Guerrero, Morelos and Oaxaca)
_____ *T. a. intermedius* — S Mexico (se Oaxaca and e Tabasco) to Costa Rica
_____ *T. a. beani* — E Mexico (Cozumel I. off Quintana Roo)
_____ *T. a. inquietus* — Panama and Pearl Islands
_____ *T. a. carychrous* — Coiba I. (Panama)
_____ *T. a. rufescens* — Dominica (Lesser Antilles)
_____ *T. a. martinicensis* — Martinique (Lesser Antilles)
_____ *T. a. mesoleucus* — St. Lucia (Lesser Antilles)
_____ *T. a. guadelupensis* — Guadeloupe (Lesser Antilles)
_____ *T. a. musicus* — St. Vincent (Lesser Antilles)
_____ *T. a. atopus* — N Colombia (Caribbean lowlands and Magdalena Valley)
_____ *T. a. striatulus* — W and Central Andes of Colombia and Andes of w Venezuela
_____ *T. a. columbae* — Subtropical and temperate Eastern Andes of Colombia
_____ *T. a. albicans* — Colombia (Nariño) to the Guianas, n Peru and Brazil; Trinidad Tobago
_____ *T. a. togabensis* — Arid littoral of w Peru (Cajamarca to n Ica)
_____ *T. a. audax* — *Puna* of n Peru to w Bolivia (La Paz)
_____ *T. a. puna* — Trop. and subtrop. e slope of Andes of Peru (Amazonas to Puno)
_____ *T. a. carabayae* — Coastal s Peru (Arequipa) to n Chile (Tarapacá)
_____ *T. a. tecellatus* — N Chile (Antofagasta, Atacama and n Coquimbo)
_____ *T. a. atacamensis* — Central and s Brazil to e Paraguay and ne Argentina (Misiones)
_____ *T. a. musculus* — Extreme s Brazil to Uruguay and ne Argentina
_____ *T. a. bonairiae* — S Chile and s Argentina to Tierra del Fuego
_____ *T. a. chilensis*

☐ **Cobb's Wren** *Troglodytes cobbi*

Falkland Islands

☐ **Clarion Wren** *Troglodytes tanneri*

Isla Clarión (Revillagigedo Islands off w Mexico)

☐ **Rufous-browed Wren** *Troglodytes rufociliatus*

____ *T .r. chiapensis*	Highlands of s Mexico (Chiapas)
____ *T. r. rufociliatus*	Highlands of e Guatemala and n El Salvador
____ *T. r. nannoides*	Highlands of w El Salvador (Volcán de Santa Ana)
____ *T. r. rehni*	Highlands of Honduras to nw Nicaragua

☐ **Ochraceous Wren** *Troglodytes ochraceus*

____ *T. o. ochraceus*	Highlands of Costa Rica
____ *T. o. ligea*	Highlands of w Panama (Chiriquí)

☐ **Santa Marta Wren** *Troglodytes monticola*

Santa Marta Mountains (ne Colombia)

☐ **Mountain Wren** *Troglodytes solstitialis*

____ *T. s. festinus*	E Panama (known from a single specimen from Mt. Pirre)
____ *T. s. solitarius*	Andes of Colombia and w Venezuela
____ *T. s. solstitialis*	Andes of s Colombia to Ecuador and n Peru (Cajamarca)
____ *T. s. macrourus*	Andes of e-central Peru (s Amazonas to Cuzco)
____ *T. s. frater*	Andes of extreme se Peru (Puno) to Bolivia
____ *T. s. auricularis*	Andes of nw Argentina (south to Tucumán and Catamarca)

☐ **Tepui Wren** *Troglodytes rufulus*

____ *T. r. rufulus*	*Tepuis* of se Venezuela and adjacent n Brazil
____ *T. r. fulvigularis*	*Tepuis* of se Venezuela (Ptari-tepui, Sororopón and Auyan-tepui)
____ *T. r. yavii*	*Tepuis* of se Venezuela (Cerro Yaví and Cerro Sarisariñama)
____ *T. r. duidae*	*Tepuis* of s Venezuela (Duida, Parú and Paraque)
____ *T. r. wetmorei*	*Tepuis* of se Venezuela (Cerro de la Neblina)
____ *T. r. marahuacae*	*Tepuis* of se Venezuela (Amazonas)

☐ **Sedge Wren** *Cistothorus platensis*

____ *C. p. stellaris*	E Canada to e US; winters Florida to ne Mexico
____ *C. p. tinnulus*	W Mexico (Michoacán)
____ *C. p. potosinus*	E Mexico (San Luis Potosí)
____ *C. p. jalapensis*	E Mexico (Veracruz)
____ *C. p. warneri*	S Mexico (w Chiapas)
____ *C. p. elegans*	Highlands of se Mexico (Veracruz) to Guatemala
____ *C. p. russelli*	Pine ridge region of Belize
____ *C. p. graberi*	SE Honduras to ne Nicaragua
____ *C. p. lucidus*	Subtropical s Costa Rica to w Panama (Chiriquí)
____ *C. p. alticola*	Mountains of n Colombia to n Venezuela and n Guyana
____ *C. p. tamae*	E Andes of Colombia and w Venezuela (Táchira)
____ *C. p. tolimae*	Central Andes of Colombia (Tolima and Caldas)
____ *C. p. aequatorialis*	Central and Western Andes of s Colombia to Ecuador and Peru
____ *C. p. graminicola*	Andes of central Peru (Junín to Cuzco)
____ *C. p. minimus*	Andes of s Peru (Puno)
____ *C. p. boliviae*	Andes of nw Bolivia (La Paz and Santa Clara)
____ *C. p. polyglottus*	SE Brazil (Goiás and Minas Gerais) to Paraguay and ne Argentina
____ *C. p. tucumanus*	NW Argentina (Jujuy to Catamarca and Tucumán)
____ *C. p. platensis*	Central and e Argentina
____ *C. p. hornensis*	S Argentina (Neuquén) and Chile (Coquimbo) to Tierra del Fuego
____ *C. p. falklandicus*	Falkland Islands

☐ **Apolinar's Wren** *Cistothorus apolinari*

E Andes of Colombia (Boyacá and Cundinamarca)

☐ **Paramo Wren** *Cistothorus meridae*

Andes of nw Venezuela (Trujillo and Mérida)

☐ **Marsh Wren** *Cistothorus palustris*

____ *C. p. browningi*	Coastal marshes of British Columbia
____ *C. p. paludicola*	SW Br. Columbia to sw California; winters to n Baja, nw Sonora
____ *C. p. plesius (pulverius)*	SW Canada to Rocky Mountains, e California and sw Texas
____ *C. p. laingi*	W-central Canada to Montana; winters to s Mexico

____ *C. p. iliacus*	W-central Canada to w-central US; winters to Gulf Coast
____ *C. p. dissaeptus*	S-central Canada to n-central US
____ *C. p. clarkae*	Coastal s California (Los Angeles Co. to San Diego County)
____ *C. p. aestuarinus*	Inland valleys of s California, s Nevada, Arizona and sw Arizona
____ *C. p. deserticola*	Deserts of s California
____ *C. p. palustris*	Coastal marshes of New England to Virginia
____ *C. p. waynei*	Coastal marshes of se Virginia to North Carolina
____ *C. p. griseus*	Coastal marshes of South Carolina to e-central Florida
____ *C. p. marianae*	Coastal marshes of sw Alabama to sw Florida
____ *C. p. thryophilus*	Coastal marshes of Mississippi to Louisiana and s Texas
____ *C. p. tolucensis*	Central Mexico (Río Lerma marshes to Hidalgo and w Puebla)

☐ **White-bellied Wren** *Uropsila leucogastra*

____ *U. l. leucogastra*	Gulf lowlands of e Mexico (e San Luis Potosí to n Oaxaca)
____ *U. l. centralis*	Central Mexico
____ *U. l. restricta*	S Mexico
____ *U. l. pacifica*	Coastal lowlands of sw Mexico (Colima and Guerrero)
____ *U. l. musica*	Coastal plain of s Mexico (ne Oaxaca, Tabasco and n Chiapas)
____ *U. l. brachyura*	Yucatán Pen. to Petén of Guatemala, Belize and nw Honduras

☐ **Timberline Wren** *Thryorchilus browni*

____ *T. b. ridgwayi*	Mountains of Costa Rica (Volcán Turialba and Volcán Irazú)
____ *T. b. basultoi*	Mountains of sw Costa Rica (Cerros de Dota)
____ *T. b. browni*	Mountains of w Panama (Volcán Barú in w Chiriquí)

☐ **White-breasted Wood-Wren** *Henicorhina leucosticta*

____ *H. l. decolorata*	SE Mexico
____ *H. l. prostheleuca*	Trop. e Mexico (San Luis Potosí) to Belize and w Guatemala
____ *H. l. tropaea*	Caribbean coast of Guatemala to nw Panama
____ *H. l. smithei*	Petén of Guatemala
____ *H. l. costaricensis*	Central Costa Rica (Cartago Province)
____ *H. l. pittieri*	SW Costa Rica and w Panama
____ *H. l. alexandri*	Panama
____ *H. l. darienensis*	Tropical e Panama and nw Colombia (south to Chocó)
____ *H. l. albilateralis*	Upper tropical and subtropical central Colombia
____ *H. l. eucharis*	Upper trop. and lower subtropical Colombia (Río Dagua Valley)
____ *H. l. inornata*	Pacific lowlands of s Colombia to Ecuador (Pichincha)
____ *H. l. hauxwelli*	E slope of Andes of s Colombia to e Ecuador and central Peru
____ *H. l. leucosticta*	S Venezuela, Guyana, Suriname and n Brazil (upper Rio Negro)

☐ **Gray-breasted Wood-Wren** *Henicorhina leucophrys*

____ *H. l. festiva*	W Mexico (cloud forests of w Michoacán and Guerrero)
____ *H. l. mexicana*	E Mexico (San Luis Potosí to Puebla, Veracruz and n Oaxaca)
____ *H. l. castanea*	S Mexico (Chiapas) to n Guatemala
____ *H. l. capitalis*	S Mexico (w Chiapas) to w Guatemala and El Salvador
____ *H. l. composita*	Subtropical highlands of s-central Honduras
____ *H. l. minuscula*	S Mexico
____ *H. l. collina*	Highlands of Costa Rica and w Panama (Chiriquí and Veraguas)
____ *H. l. anachoreta*	Temp. and upper subtrop. Santa Marta Mountains (ne Colombia)
____ *H. l. bangsi*	Subtrop. and upper trop. Santa Marta Mountains (ne Colombia)
____ *H. l. tamae*	E slope of E Andes of Colombia to Andes of nw Venezuela
____ *H. l. leucophrys*	Andes of Colombia to Ecuador and Peru
____ *H. l. brunneiceps*	W Andes of Colombia to extreme n Ecuador (Imbabura)
____ *H. l. hilaris*	Subtropical mountains of sw Ecuador
____ *H. l. manastarae*	Subtropical mts. of nw Venezuela (Alto Río Negro in Zulia)
____ *H. l. sanluisensis*	NW Venezuela
____ *H. l. venezuelensis*	Subtropical coastal cordillera of n Venezuela (Lara to Miranda)
____ *H. l. meridana*	W Venezuela
____ *H. l. boliviana*	Subtrop. mts. of w Bolivia (Cochabamba, La Paz and Santa Cruz)

□ **Bar-winged Wood-Wren** *Henicorhina leucoptera*

Andes of n Peru and immediately adjacent Ecuador

□ **Nightingale Wren** *Microcerculus philomela*

Humid s Mexico (n Chiapas) to central Costa Rica

□ **Scaly-breasted Wren** *Microcerculus marginatus*

_____ *M. m. luscinia*	Foothills of s Costa Rica and Panama
_____ *M. m. taeniatus*	N Colombia to n Venezuela and Ecuador (s to Guayas)
_____ *M. m. marginatus*	E Colombia to n Bolivia and Amazonian Brazil

□ **Flutist Wren** *Microcerculus ustulatus*

_____ *M. u. duidae*	Mts. of s Venezuela (Duida, Yaví, Paraque and Sierra de Curupira)
_____ *M. u. lunatipectus*	*Tepuis* of s Venezuela (Amazonas and Bolívar)
_____ *M. u. obscurus*	*Tepuis* of se Venezuela (Ptari-tepui, Uei-tepui, Sororopán-tepui)
_____ *M. u. ustulatus*	*Tepuis* of se Venezuela, n Brazil and w Guyana (Mt. Twek-quay)

□ **Wing-banded Wren** *Microcerculus bambla*

_____ *M. b. albigularis*	Tropical e Ecuador and w Amazonian Brazil; se Peru
_____ *M. b. caurensis*	Tropical s Venezuela (Amazonas and s Bolívar)
_____ *M. b. bambla*	Trop. se Venezuela (Auyan-tepui) to the Guianas and ne Brazil

□ **Song Wren** *Cyphorhinus phaeocephalus*

_____ *C. p. richardsoni*	Caribbean lowlands of se Honduras to Nicaragua
_____ *C. p. infuscatus*	Caribbean lowlands of Costa Rica and extreme nw Panama
_____ *C. p. lawrencii*	Lowlands of e Panama to nw Colombia
_____ *C. p. propinquus*	Tropical lowlands of n Colombia
_____ *C. p. chocoanus*	Pacific lowlands of w Colombia (Chocó)
_____ *C. p. phaeocephalus*	Pacific lowlands of sw Colombia to w Ecuador (s to El Oro)

□ **Chestnut-breasted Wren** *Cyphorhinus thoracicus*

_____ *C. t. dichrous*	Central and Western Andes of Colombia to Peru (San Martín)
_____ *C. t. thoracicus*	Trop. and subtrop. e slope of Andes of se Peru (Huánuco to Puno)

□ **Musician Wren** *Cyphorhinus aradus*

_____ *C. a. transfluvialis*	SE Colombia (Caquetá) to n Brazil (Rio Negro)
_____ *C. a. salvini*	SE Colombia (Putumayo) to e Ecuador and ne Peru (Loreto)
_____ *C. a. urbanoi*	Trop. and lower subtrop. s Venezuela (Gran Sabana in e Bolívar)
_____ *C. a. aradus*	S Venezuela (Gran Sabana) to the Guianas and adjacent ne Brazil
_____ *C. a. faroensis*	N Brazil (north bank of Amazon in Faro and Obidos areas)
_____ *C. a. griseolateralis*	N Amazonian Brazil
_____ *C. a. interpositus*	Brazil south of the Amazon (Rio Madeira to Rio Tapajós)
_____ *C. a. modulator*	Tropical e Peru, n Bolivia and w Amazonian Brazil

FAMILY: MIMIDAE (Mockingbirds and Thrashers—35)

□ **Gray Catbird** *Dumetella carolinensis*

S Br. Columbia to Gulf States; winters to West Indies and Panama

□ **Black Catbird** *Melanoptila glabrirostris*

Coastal e Mexico (Yucatán Pen. and adj. islands) to n Guatemala

□ **Bahama Mockingbird** *Mimus gundlachii*

_____ *M. g. gundlachii*	Bahamas, cays off n Cuba, Great Inagua and Caicos islands
_____ *M. g. hillii*	Arid coastal lowlands of s Jamaica

□ **Northern Mockingbird** *Mimus polyglottos*

_____ *M. p. leucopterus*	SW Canada to s Baja California and sw Mexico (Oaxaca)
_____ *M. p. polyglottos*	E Canada to central, e and se US
_____ *M. p. orpheus*	Bahamas and Greater Antilles

☐ **Tropical Mockingbird** *Mimus gilvus*
____ *M. g. gracilis* — S Mexico (Oaxaca) to Guatemala, Honduras and El Salvador
____ *M. g. leucophaeus* — Humid tropical se Mexico, Cozumel I., Isla Mujeres and Belize
____ *M. g. antillarum* — Martinique, St. Lucia, St. Vincent, the Grenadines and Grenada
____ *M. g. tobagensis* — Trinidad and Tobago
____ *M. g. rostratus* — Netherlands Antilles and adjacent islands off n coast of Venezuela
____ *M. g. magnirostris* — Isla San Andrés (w Caribbean Sea)
____ *M. g. tolimensis* — W and central Colombia
____ *M. g. melanopterus* — Coastal n Colombia to Venezuela, Guyana and extreme n Brazil
____ *M. g. gilvus* — French Guiana and Suriname
____ *M. g. antelius* — Coastal e Brazil (Pará to Rio de Janeiro)

☐ **Chalk-browed Mockingbird** *Mimus saturninus*
____ *M. s. saturninus* — S Suriname and n Brazil (Amapá to se Pará)
____ *M. s. arenaceus* — NE Brazil (Paraíba, Alagoas and Bahia)
____ *M. s. frater* — N Bolivia to ne and sw Brazil (Mato Grosso)
____ *M. s. modulator* — SE Bolivia to s Brazil, Uruguay, Paraguay and n Argentina

☐ **Patagonian Mockingbird** *Mimus patagonicus*
Central and s Argentina and s Chile

☐ **Brown-backed Mockingbird** *Mimus dorsalis*
Arid montane scrub of Bolivia and extreme nw Argentina

☐ **White-banded Mockingbird** *Mimus triurus*
Central Argentina and Bolivia (Beni); winters to sw Brazil

☐ **Long-tailed Mockingbird** *Mimus longicaudatus*
____ *M. l. platensis* — Isla La Plata (off w Ecuador)
____ *M. l. albogriseus* — Arid sw Ecuador (Manabi to s Loja) and extreme n Peru (Piura)
____ *M. l. longicaudatus* — W Peru (La Libertad to Ica)
____ *M. l. maranonicus* — N Peru (upper Marañón Valley)

☐ **Chilean Mockingbird** *Mimus thenca*
Coastal Chile (Atacama to Valdivia)

☐ **Galapagos Mockingbird** *Nesomimus parvulus*
____ *N. p. parvulus* — Main Galapagos Islands except extreme eastern islands
____ *N. p. barringtoni* — Barrington (Galapagos Islands)
____ *N. p. personatus* — Galapagos Islands (Abingdon, Bindloe, James and Jervis)
____ *N. p. wenmani* — Wenman (Galapagos Islands)
____ *N. p. hulli* — Culpepper (Galapagos Islands)
____ *N. p. bauri* — Tower (Galapagos Islands)

☐ **Charles Mockingbird** *Nesomimus trifasciatus*
Galapagos Islands (Champion and Gardner)

☐ **Hood Mockingbird** *Nesomimus macdonaldi*
Hood and adjacent se Galapagos Islands

☐ **San Cristobal Mockingbird** *Nesomimus melanotis*
San Cristóbal (Galapagos Islands)

☐ **Sage Thrasher** *Oreoscoptes montanus*
Arid s British Columbia to Baja California and central Mexico

☐ **Socorro Mockingbird** *Mimodes graysoni*
Socorro I. (Revillagigedo Islands off w Mexico). ±100 pairs 1992

☐ **Brown Thrasher** *Toxostoma rufum*
____ *T. r. rufum* — SE Canada to Gulf States (mainly east of Rocky Mountains)
____ *T. r. longicauda* — S-central Canada to e Colorado and Kansas; winters to se US

☐ **Long-billed Thrasher** *Toxostoma longirostre*
____ *T. l. sennetti* — Arid s Texas to ne Mexico
____ *T. l. longirostre* — E Mexico (ne Querétaro to n Puebla and central Veracruz)

☐ **Cozumel Thrasher** *Toxostoma guttatum*
Cozumel I. (se Mexico off Quintana Roo)

☐ **Gray Thrasher** *Toxostoma cinereum*
____ *T. c. mearnsi* — Desert scrub of w Baja California (latitude 31°N to 28°N)
____ *T. c. cinereum* — Cape District of s Baja California (south of latitude 28°N)

☐ **Bendire's Thrasher** *Toxostoma bendirei*
____ *T. b. bendirei* — Arid sw US to nw Mexico (n Sonora)
____ *T. b. candidum* — Sonoran Desert of w Mexico (w Sonora)
____ *T. b. rubricatum* — Central and s interior of se Sonora and coast near Isla Tiburón

☐ **Ocellated Thrasher** *Toxostoma ocellatum*
____ *T. o. ocellatum* — Highlands of c Mexico (San Luis Potosí to Hidalgo and México)
____ *T. o. villai* — Oak-pine highlands of s Mexico (Puebla to Oaxaca)

☐ **Curve-billed Thrasher** *Toxostoma curvirostre*
____ *T. c. palmeri* — Arid s Arizona to w Mexico (central Sonora)
____ *T. c. celsum* — SE Arizona to w Texas and n Mexico (ne Sonora to w Coahuila)
____ *T. c. oberholseri* — S Texas to ne Mexico (e Coahuila, Nuevo León and Tamaulipas)
____ *T. c. maculatum* — NW Mexico (s Sonora to n Sinaloa and sw Chihuahua)
____ *T. c. insularum* — Islands in Sea of Cortés (San Estéban and Tiburón)
____ *T. c. occidentale* — NW Mexico (s Sinaloa, Nayarit, nw Jalisco and w Durango)
____ *T. c. curvirostre* — S Mexico (se Jalisco to Guerrero, México, Puebla and Oaxaca)

☐ **California Thrasher** *Toxostoma redivivum*
____ *T. r. sonomae* — Chaparral belt of n California (south to Monterey)
____ *T. r. redivivum* — Chaparral belt of s California and nw Baja

☐ **Crissal Thrasher** *Toxostoma crissale*
____ *T. c. coloradense* — Arid s California and Arizona to ne Baja and nw Sonora
____ *T. c. crissale* — Arid sw US to w Texas and n Mexico (Sonora to nw Coahuila)
____ *T. c. trinitatis* — N Baja California (Valle de La Trinidad)
____ *T. c. dumosum* — N Mexico (Zacatecas, s Coahuila, San Luis Potosí and Hidalgo)

☐ **Le Conte's Thrasher** *Toxostoma lecontei*
____ *T. l. lecontei* — Arid sw US to n Baja California and nw Mexico
____ *T. l. macmillanorum* — Inland central California (s San Joaquin Valley)

☐ **Vizcaino Thrasher** *Toxostoma arenicola*
Vizcaino desert of central Baja California (29°N to 26°N)

☐ **White-breasted Thrasher** *Ramphocinclus brachyurus*
____ *R. b. brachyurus* — Martinique (Lesser Antilles)
____ *R. b. sanctaeluciae* — St. Lucia (Lesser Antilles)

☐ **Blue Mockingbird** *Melanotis caerulescens*
____ *M. c. longirostris* — Tres Marías Islands (off w Mexico)
____ *M. c. caerulescens* — Oak-pine zone of w Mexico (s Sonora to Isthmus of Tehuántepec)

☐ **Blue-and-white Mockingbird** *Melanotis hypoleucus*
Humid highlands of s Mexico (Chiapas) to w Honduras

☐ **Gray Trembler** *Cinclocerthia gutturalis*
____ *C. g. gutturalis* — Martinique (Lesser Antilles)
____ *C. g. macrorhyncha* — St. Lucia (Lesser Antilles)

☐ **Brown Trembler** *Cinclocerthia ruficauda*
____ *C. r. pavida* — Lesser Antilles (Montserrat and adjacent nw Leeward Islands)
____ *C. r. tremula* — Guadeloupe (Lesser Antilles)
____ *C. r. ruficauda* — Dominica (Lesser Antilles)
____ *C. r. tenebrosa* — St. Vincent (Lesser Antilles)

☐ **Scaly-breasted Thrasher** *Margarops fuscus*

_____	*M. f. atlanticus*	Barbados
_____	*M. f. hypenemus*	N Lesser Antilles
_____	*M. f. schwartzi*	St. Lucia (Lesser Antilles)
_____	*M. f. vincenti*	St. Vincent (Lesser Antilles)
_____	*M. f. fuscus*	Lesser Antilles (Dominica to Grenada)

☐ **Pearly-eyed Thrasher** *Margarops fuscatus*

_____	*M. f. fuscatus*	S Bahamas, Hispaniola, Puerto Rico, Lesser and Neth. Antilles
_____	*M. f. densirostris*	Lesser Antilles (Guadeloupe, Dominica and Martinique)
_____	*M. f. klinikowskii*	St. Lucia (Lesser Antilles)
_____	*M. f. bonairensis*	Bonaire and Horquilla (Los Hermanos Archipelago off Venezuela)

FAMILY: PRUNELLIDAE (Accentors—13)

☐ **Alpine Accentor** *Prunella collaris*

_____	*P. c. collaris*	Mountains of Europe to Carpathians, n Yugoslavia and nw Africa
_____	*P. c. subalpina*	Mountains of se Europe to Crete and w Turkey
_____	*P. c. montana*	Caucasus Mountains to n Iraq and s Iran
_____	*P. c. rufilata*	Tajikistan to n Afghanistan, w China (w Xinjiang) and se Tibet
_____	*P. c. whymperi*	W Himalayas (Kashmir to Garhwal and Kumaon)
_____	*P. c. nipalensis*	E Himalayas to sw China (e Xinjiang to n Yunnan) and se Tibet
_____	*P. c. tibetana (berezowski)*	NW China (n Xinjiang, s Qinghai and Gansu) to e Tibet
_____	*P. c. erythropygia*	Altai Mts. to n China, Sea of Okhotsk, Korea and Japan
_____	*P. c. fennelli*	Mountains of Taiwan

☐ **Himalayan Accentor** *Prunella himalayana*

Mountains of central Asia to Afghanistan, s Tibet and nw India

☐ **Robin Accentor** *Prunella rubeculoides*

_____	*P. r. rubeculoides*	Himalayas of n Pakistan to Nepal, Sikkim and se Tibet
_____	*P. r. fusca*	Mountains of e Tibet and w China (Xinjiang, Gansu and Shaanxi)

☐ **Rufous-breasted Accentor** *Prunella strophiata*

_____	*P. s. jerdoni*	Mountains of e Afghanistan to n India (Kashmir and Kumaon)
_____	*P. s. strophiata*	Himalayas of Nepal to se Tibet, sw China and n Myanmar

☐ **Siberian Accentor** *Prunella montanella*

_____	*P. m. montanella*	Ural Mountains to Altai, Lake Baikal and Sikhote Alin Mountains
_____	*P. m. badia*	NE Siberia (lower Lena River to Sea of Okhotsk)

☐ **Radde's Accentor** *Prunella ocularis*

Mountains of Turkey, Armenia, n Georgia and Iran

☐ **Yemen Accentor** *Prunella fagani*

High mountains of Yemen; winters to s Arabia

☐ **Brown Accentor** *Prunella fulvescens*

_____	*P. f. fulvescens*	Tien Shan Mountains to Afghanistan and Pakistan
_____	*P. f. dahurica*	Altai Mountains to Mongolia
_____	*P. f. dresseri*	Mountains of w China (sw Xinjiang to w Gansu and n Tibet)
_____	*P. f. nanschanica*	Montane forests of w China on Qinghai/Gansu border
_____	*P. f. khamensis*	Mts. of w China (Xinjiang to s Qinghai, Gansu and ne Tibet)
_____	*P. f. sushkini*	Treeline mountain slopes of s Tibet

☐ **Black-throated Accentor** *Prunella atrogularis*

_____	*P. a. atrogularis*	N Ural Mountains; winters to Afghanistan and Iran
_____	*P. a. huttoni (lucens)*	Russian Altai (Dzhungarski Mts.); winters to Pakistan, ne India

☐ **Mongolian Accentor** *Prunella koslowi*

Mts. of Mongolia and immediately adjacent n China (Ningxia)

☐ **Dunnock** *Prunella modularis*

____	*P. m. hebridium*	Ireland, Outer Hebrides, Inner Hebrides and w Scotland
____	*P. m. occidentalis*	E Scotland, England, Wales and w France
____	*P. m. modularis*	N and cent. Europe; winters to w Mediterranean is. and N Africa
____	*P. m. mabbotti*	SW France to Pyrénées, Iberian Peninsula and Apennine Mts.
____	*P. m. meinertzhageni*	S Yugoslavia and Bulgaria
____	*P. m. fuscata*	Mountains of Crimean Peninsula
____	*P. m. euxina*	N Turkey to w Caucasus Mountains
____	*P. m. obscura*	Caucasus and e Turkey to n Iran; winters to mts. of Lebanon

☐ **Japanese Accentor** *Prunella rubida*

____	*P. r. rubida*	S Kuril Islands, Shikoku and Hokkaido
____	*P. r. fervida*	Honshu (Japan); winters to Kyushu

☐ **Maroon-backed Accentor** *Prunella immaculata*

Nepal to se Tibet and sw China; winters to ne Myanmar

FAMILY: TURDIDAE (Thrushes—175)

☐ **Rufous Flycatcher-Thrush** *Neocossyphus fraseri*

____	*N. f. rubicunda*	Nigeria to Central African Republic, w Zaire, Gabon and Angola
____	*N. f. vulpina*	S Sudan to Uganda, ne Zaire, nw Zambia and nw Tanzania
____	*N. f. fraseri*	Bioko (Gulf of Guinea)

☐ **Finsch's Flycatcher-Thrush** *Neocossyphus finschii*

Lowlands of Sierra Leone and Liberia to Ghana and s Nigeria

☐ **Red-tailed Ant-Thrush** *Neocossyphus rufus*

____	*N. r. gabunensis*	Lowlands of se Cameroon to Gabon, ne Zaire and w Uganda
____	*N. r. rufus*	Coastal n Kenya to n Tanzania (Tana River to Mikindani); Zanzibar

☐ **White-tailed Ant-Thrush** *Neocossyphus poensis*

____	*N. p. poensis*	Sierra Leone to Cameroon, Gabon and s Congo; Bioko
____	*N. p. praepectoralis*	N Angola to Central African Republic, w Zaire and Uganda
____	*N. p. kakamegoes*	W Kenya (Kakamega Forest)
____	*N. p. nigridorsalis*	W Kenya (n Nandi Hills)
____	*N. p. pallidigularis*	NW Angola (Canzele)

☐ **Forest Rock-Thrush** *Pseudocossyphus sharpei*

Humid e-central plateau of Madagascar

☐ **Benson's Rock-Thrush** *Pseudocossyphus bensoni*

Montane rocky areas of sw Madagascar (Isalo Massif)

☐ **Littoral Rock-Thrush** *Pseudocossyphus imerinus*

____	*P. i. erythronotus*	Arid littoral of n Madagascar
____	*P. i. salomonseni*	Coastal lowlands of e Madagascar
____	*P. i. imerinus*	Coastal lowlands of se Madagascar

☐ **Cape Rock-Thrush** *Monticola rupestris*

SE Botswana to s Mozambique, Swaziland and Cape Province

☐ **Sentinel Rock-Thrush** *Monticola explorator*

____	*M. e. explorator*	Lowlands of Natal to Transvaal and sw Cape Province
____	*M. e. tenebriformis*	Swaziland (Lebombo Mts.); winters north to s Mozambique

☐ **Short-toed Rock-Thrush** *Monticola brevipes*

____	*M. b. niveiceps*	W Angola (Huila escarpment)
____	*M. b. brevipes (leucocapilla)*	S Angola to Namibia, Botswana and Cape Province
____	*M. b. pretoriae*	Mountains of se Botswana to w Transvaal

☐ **Miombo Rock-Thrush** *Monticola angolensis*
_____ *M. a. angolensis (niassae)*   Angola to s Zaire, Rwanda, Zambia and Tanzania
_____ *M. a. hylophila*   S Zambia to Zimbabwe, w Malawi and w Mozambique

☐ **Rufous-tailed Rock-Thrush** *Monticola saxatilis*

Rocky regions of s Palearctic region; winters to e Africa

☐ **Little Rock-Thrush** *Monticola rufocinereus*
_____ *M. r. rufocinereus*   Mts. of se Sudan to Ethiopia, e Uganda, w Kenya and ne Tanzania
_____ *M. r. sclateri*   W Saudi Arabia

☐ **Blue-capped Rock-Thrush** *Monticola cinclorhynchus*

Mts. of e Afghanistan, n Pakistan and India; winters to Myanmar

☐ **White-throated Rock-Thrush** *Monticola gularis*

SE Siberia to ne China and Korea; winters to SE Asia

☐ **Chestnut-bellied Rock-Thrush** *Monticola rufiventris*

Pakistan to se Tibet, sw China, Myanmar, n Laos and n Vietnam

☐ **Blue Rock-Thrush** *Monticola solitarius*
_____ *M. s. solitarius*   S Europe, nw Africa and Middle East; winters to central Africa
_____ *M. s. longirostris*   N Iraq and Iran to Pakistan; winters to n India and ne Africa
_____ *M. s. pandoo*   Central Asia and Himalayas; winters to Malaysia and Indonesia
_____ *M. s. philippensis*   SE Siberia to China, Japan and Lan-yü I.; winters to Indonesia
_____ *M. s. madoci*   Malay Peninsula and Sumatra

☐ **Ceylon Whistling-Thrush** *Myophonus blighi*

Mountain ravines of Sri Lanka

☐ **Shiny Whistling-Thrush** *Myophonus melanurus*

Montane moss forests of Sumatra

☐ **Sunda Whistling-Thrush** *Myophonus glaucinus*
_____ *M. g. glaucinus*   Montane forests of Java and Bali
_____ *M. g. castaneus*   Foothill forests of Sumatra
_____ *M. g. borneensis*   Foothill and montane forests of Borneo

☐ **Malayan Whistling-Thrush** *Myophonus robinsoni*

Moist montane forests of central Malaya

☐ **Malabar Whistling-Thrush** *Myophonus horsfieldii*

Swift flowing rocky streams of peninsular India

☐ **Formosan Whistling-Thrush** *Myophonus insularis*

Mountain streams of Taiwan

☐ **Blue Whistling-Thrush** *Myophonus caeruleus*
_____ *M. c. temminckii*   Central Asia to n India, Pakistan, se Tibet and Myanmar
_____ *M. c. eugenei*   NE Assam to s Myanmar, n Thailand, sw China and Indochina
_____ *M. c. caeruleus*   W China (Sichuan); winters to s China and n Indochina
_____ *M. c. crassirostris*   Peninsular and extreme se Thailand to n Malaysia
_____ *M. c. dichrorhynchus*   Central and s Malaysia; foothills of w Sumatra
_____ *M. c. flavirostris*   Foothill and montane forests of Java

☐ **Geomalia** *Geomalia heinrichi*

Mountains of Sulawesi

☐ **Slaty-backed Thrush** *Zoothera schistacea*

E Lesser Sundas (Yamdena and Larat)

☐ **Moluccan Thrush** *Zoothera dumasi*
_____ *Z. d. dumasi*   Mid-mountain forests of Buru (s Moluccas)
_____ *Z. d. joiceyi*   Mid-mountain forests of Seram (s Moluccas)

☐ **Chestnut-capped Thrush** *Zoothera interpres*
_____ *Z. i. interpres*   S Thailand, Malaysia, Greater and Lesser Sundas and s Philippines
_____ *Z. i. leucolaema*   Enggano I. (off w Sumatra)

☐ **Chestnut-backed Thrush** *Zoothera dohertyi*

Lesser Sundas (Lombok, Sumbawa, Sumba, Flores and w Timor)

☐ **Rusty-backed Thrush** *Zoothera erythronota*
_____ *Z. e. erythronota* | Lowland forests of Sulawesi
_____ *Z. e. mendeni* | Peleng I. (Banggai Islands)
_____ *Z. e. subspecies?* | Taliabu I. (Sula Islands)

☐ **Pied Thrush** *Zoothera wardii*

Himalayas of n India from Nepal to Assam; winters to Sri Lanka

☐ **Ashy Thrush** *Zoothera cinerea*

N Philippines (Luzon and Mindoro)

☐ **Orange-banded Thrush** *Zoothera peronii*
_____ *Z. p. peronii* | E Lesser Sundas (Roti and w Timor)
_____ *Z. p. audacis* | E Lesser Sundas (e Timor, Wetar, Romang, Damar and Babar)

☐ **Orange-headed Thrush** *Zoothera citrina*
_____ *Z. c. citrina* | W Pakistan to n Myanmar; winters to Sri Lanka
_____ *Z. c. cyanotus* | Peninsular India (north to Gujarat and Andhra)
_____ *Z. c. innotata* | S Myanmar to s China and Indochina; winters to Malaysia
_____ *Z. c. melli* | SE China (Fujian and n Guangdong)
_____ *Z. c. courtoisi* | E China (Anhui Province)
_____ *Z. c. aurimacula* | S Vietnam and Hainan
_____ *Z. c. andamanensis* | Andaman Islands
_____ *Z. c. albogularis* | Nicobar Islands
_____ *Z. c. gibsonhilli* | Central Malay Peninsula (s Myanmar to s Thailand)
_____ *Z. c. aurata* | Mountains of n Borneo
_____ *Z. c. rubecula* | W Java
_____ *Z. c. orientis* | E Java and Bali

☐ **Everett's Thrush** *Zoothera everetti*

High mountains of n Borneo (Sarawak and Sabah)

☐ **Siberian Thrush** *Zoothera sibirica*
_____ *Z. s. sibirica* | NE Asia; winters to SE Asia, Sumatra and Java
_____ *Z. s. davisoni* | Sakhalin I. and n Japan; winters to s China, SE Asia and Sumatra

☐ **Abyssinian Ground-Thrush** *Zoothera piaggiae*
_____ *Z. p. piaggiae* | Ethiopia to se Sudan, n Kenya, sw Uganda and mts. of e Zaire
_____ *Z. p. hadii* | SE Sudan (Imatong and Dongotona mountains)
_____ *Z. p. ruwenzorii* | Ruwenzori Mountains (Zaire/Uganda border)
_____ *Z. p. kilimensis* | Kenya (east of Rift Valley) to n Tanzania (Mt. Kilimanjaro)
_____ *Z. p. rowei* | N Tanzania (Loliondo and Magaidu forests)

☐ **Kivu Ground-Thrush** *Zoothera tanganjicae*

Montane forests of e Zaire, Rwanda, n Burundi and sw Uganda

☐ **Crossley's Ground-Thrush** *Zoothera crossleyi*
_____ *Z. c. crossleyi* | Montane forests of se Nigeria, Cameroon, Congo and w Zaire
_____ *Z. c. pilettei* | NE Zaire (Semliki Vallei and w slope of Itombwe highlands)

☐ **Orange Ground-Thrush** *Zoothera gurneyi*
_____ *Z. g. otomitra* | Angola (Mt. Moco) to Zaire, Tanzania and n Malawi
_____ *Z. g. chuka* | Mt. Kenya and Kikuyu escarpment
_____ *Z. g. raineyi (chyulu)* | Montane forests of se Kenya (Taita and Chyulu Hills)
_____ *Z. g. disruptans* | Central Malawi to Mozambique, e Zimbabwe and n Transvaal
_____ *Z. g. gurneyi* | South Africa (Natal and e Cape Province)

☐ **Black-eared Ground-Thrush** *Zoothera cameronensis*
_____ *Z. c. cameronensis* | Lowland forests of Cameroon and Gabon
_____ *Z. c. graueri* | Lowlands forests of ne Zaire and w Uganda

☐ **Gray Ground-Thrush** *Zoothera princei*
_____ *Z. p. princei* | Dense lowland forests of Liberia to Ivory Coast and Ghana
_____ *Z. p. batesi* | Coastal s Cameroon to Gabon, ne Zaire and extreme w Uganda

☐ **Oberlaender's Ground-Thrush** *Zoothera oberlaenderi*

Lowlands of e Zaire and w Uganda (Bwamba Forest)

☐ **Spotted Ground-Thrush** *Zoothera guttata*

_____ *Z. g. maxis* — S Sudan
_____ *Z. g. fischeri* — Coastal e Kenya and Tanzania
_____ *Z. g. lippensi* — E Zaire
_____ *Z. g. belcheri* — S Malawi (Mt. Thyolo)
_____ *Z. g. guttata* — S Malawi to Natal and Cape Province
_____ *Z. g. nateliens* — South Africa (Cape Province)

☐ **Spot-winged Thrush** *Zoothera spiloptera*

Montane forests of Sri Lanka

☐ **Sunda Thrush** *Zoothera andromedae*

Patchily distributed Philippines to Sumatra, Java, Lesser Sundas

☐ **Plain-backed Thrush** *Zoothera mollissima*

_____ *Z. m. whiteheadi* — W Himalayas (n Pakistan to w Nepal)
_____ *Z. m. mollissima* — E Himalayas to se Tibet; winters to Myanmar and Indochina
_____ *Z. m. griseiceps* — SW China (Sichuan and Yunnan) to n Vietnam (Tonkin)

☐ **Long-tailed Thrush** *Zoothera dixoni*

Himalayas to sw China and se Tibet; winters to SE Asia

☐ **Scaly Thrush** *Zoothera dauma*

_____ *Z. d. aurea* — Siberia to Manchuria and Korea; winters to s China and Indochina
_____ *Z. d. toratugumi* — Manchuria and Japan; winters in Taiwan and Lan-yü I.
_____ *Z. d. dauma* — Pakistan to Myanmar, s China and Thailand; winters to s India
_____ *Z. d. neilgherriensis* — S peninsular India (Mysore, Madras and Kerala)
_____ *Z. d. imbricata* — Highlands of Sri Lanka
_____ *Z. d. hancii* — Peninsular Thailand to s Vietnam; s Ryukyu Islands and Taiwan

☐ **Amami Thrush** *Zoothera major*

Amami-O-Shima (n Ryukyu Islands)

☐ **Horsfield's Thrush** *Zoothera horsfieldi*

Mountains of Sumatra, Java, Bali, Lombok and Sumbawa

☐ **Fawn-breasted Thrush** *Zoothera machiki*

Tanimbar Islands (Yamdena and Larat)

☐ **Olive-tailed Thrush** *Zoothera lunulata*

_____ *Z. l. cuneata* — Locally in mountains of New Guinea and n Queensland
_____ *Z. l. lunulata* — New South Wales, Victoria, South Australia and Kangaroo I.
_____ *Z. l. macrorhyncha* — Tasmania

☐ **Russet-tailed Thrush** *Zoothera heinei*

E Australia (e Queensland to New South Wales)

☐ **New Britain Thrush** *Zoothera talaseae*

Bismarck Archipelago (New Britain and Umboi) and Bougainville

☐ **San Cristobal Thrush** *Zoothera margaretae*

_____ *Z. m. margaretae* — Mountains of San Cristóbal (Solomon Islands)
_____ *Z. m. turipavae* — Mountains of Guadalcanal (Solomon Islands)

☐ **Long-billed Thrush** *Zoothera monticola*

_____ *Z. m. monticola* — Himalayas of n India to Nepal and ne Myanmar
_____ *Z. m. atrata* — N Vietnam (nw Tonkin)

☐ **Dark-sided Thrush** *Zoothera marginata*

Nepal to n India, sw China, Myanmar, Thailand and n Indochina

☐ **Sulawesi Thrush** *Cataponera turdoides*

_____ *C. t. abditiva* — N-central Sulawesi
_____ *C. t. tenebrosa* — S-central Sulawesi (Latimojong Mountains)
_____ *C. t. turdoides* — S Sulawesi (Lompobattang Mountains)
_____ *C. t. heinrichi* — SE Sulawesi (Mekonga Mountains)

☐ **Tristan Thrush** *Nesocichla eremita*
_____ *N. e. eremita*   Tristan da Cunha I. (Atlantic Ocean)
_____ *N. e. gordoni*   Inaccessible I. (Atlantic Ocean)
_____ *N. e. procax*   Nightingale I. (Atlantic Ocean)

☐ **Forest Thrush** *Cichlherminia lherminieri*
_____ *C. l. lherminieri*   Guadeloupe (Lesser Antilles)
_____ *C. l. lawrencii*   Montserrat (Lesser Antilles)
_____ *C. l. dominicensis*   Dominica (Lesser Antilles)
_____ *C. l. sanctaeluciae*   St. Lucia (Lesser Antilles)

☐ **Eastern Bluebird** *Sialia sialis*
_____ *S. s. sialis*   S-central and e Canada to se US; winters to n Mexico and Cuba
_____ *S. s. grata*   S peninsular Florida
_____ *S. s. episcopus*   S coastal Texas (Rockport) to e Mexico (s Tamaulipas)
_____ *S. s. fulva*   Mts. of s-c Arizona to s Mexico (Guerrero); winters to Guatemala
_____ *S. s. guatemalae*   Mts. of se Mexico (s Tamaulipas to Chiapas) and Guatemala
_____ *S. s. meridionalis* Mountains of El Salvador to ne Nicaragua

☐ **Western Bluebird** *Sialia mexicana*
_____ *S. m. occidentalis* S British Columbia to s California and w Nevada
_____ *S. m. bairdi*   SW US to nw Mexico (Sonora and Chihuahua)
_____ *S. m. anabelae*   Mountains of n Baja Calif. (Sierra Juárez and San Pedro Mártir)
_____ *S. m. amabilis*   Sierra Madre Occidental of Mexico (s Chihuahua to Zacatecas)
_____ *S. m. mexicana*   Plateau of ne Mexico (Coahuila to Nuevo León and Tamaulipas)
_____ *S. m. australis*   S plateau of Mexico (Jalisco to Morelos, Puebla and Veracruz)

☐ **Mountain Bluebird** *Sialia currucoides*
                          W North America (Alaska to c Mexico); winters to Baja Calif.

☐ **Townsend's Solitaire** *Myadestes townsendi*
_____ *M. t. townsendi*   Central Alaska to w US, Baja California and nw Mexico
_____ *M. t. calophonus*   N Mexico (s Chihuahua to Durango, Jalisco and Zacatecas)

☐ **Brown-backed Solitaire** *Myadestes occidentalis*
_____ *M. o. cinereus*   Mts. of Mexico (se Sonora to Sinaloa, Chihuahua and Durango)
_____ *M. o. occidentalis* Mts. of w Mexico (Nayarit to Guerrero, w Oaxaca and Morelos)
_____ *M. o. insularis*   Tres Marías Islands (off w Mexico)
_____ *M. o. deignani*   Mountains of s Mexico (Oaxaca and s Chiapas)
_____ *M. o. oberholseri* Mts. of s Mexico to Guatemala, El Salvador and central Honduras

☐ **Cuban Solitaire** *Myadestes elisabeth*
_____ *M. e. elisabeth*   Locally in mountains of Cuba
_____ *M. e. retrusus†*   Formerly Isle of Pines (Cuba). Extinct

☐ **Rufous-throated Solitaire** *Myadestes genibarbis*
_____ *M. g. solitarius*   Montane forests of Jamaica
_____ *M. g. montanus*   Montane forests of Hispaniola
_____ *M. g. dominicanus*   Montane forests of Dominica
_____ *M. g. genibarbis*   Montane forests of Martinique
_____ *M. g. sanctaeluciae* Montane forests of St. Lucia
_____ *M. g. sibilans*   Montane forests of St. Vincent

☐ **Black-faced Solitaire** *Myadestes melanops*
                          Mountains of Costa Rica and w Panama (e to Veraguas)

☐ **Varied Solitaire** *Myadestes coloratus*
                          Highlands of extreme e Panama (Darién) and adj. nw Colombia

☐ **Slate-colored Solitaire** *Myadestes unicolor*
_____ *M. u. unicolor*   Humid montane forests of s Mexico to Guatemala and n Honduras
_____ *M. u. pallens*   Humid montane forests of n-central Nicaragua

☐ **Andean Solitaire** *Myadestes ralloides*
_____ *M. r. plumbeiceps*   W and central Andes of Colombia and w Ecuador
_____ *M. r. candelae*   N-central Colombia (Magdalena Valley)
_____ *M. r. venezuelensis*   E Andes of Colombia to n Venezuela, e Ecuador and n Peru
_____ *M. r. ralloides*   Central Peru (La Libertad and Huánuco) to n Bolivia

☐ **Kamao** *Myadestes myadestinus*

    Kauai (Alakai Swamp)

☐ **Olomao** *Myadestes lanaiensis*
_____ *M. l. rutha*   Montane forests of Molokai (Mt. Olokui). On verge of extinction
_____ *M. l. lanaiensis†*   Formerly Lanai. Extinct

☐ **Omao** *Myadestes obscurus*

    Highlands of Hawaii

☐ **Puaiohi** *Myadestes palmeri*

    Kauai (Alakai Swamp)

☐ **Rufous-brown Solitaire** *Cichlopsis leucogenys*
_____ *C. l. chubbi*   W slope of Andes of sw Colombia (w Valle) and nw Ecuador
_____ *C. l. peruvianus*   E slope of Andes of central Peru (Junín and Huánuco)
_____ *C. l. gularis*   Tepuis of se Venezuela (Bolívar) and adjacent Guyana
_____ *C. l. leucogenys*   Coastal se Brazil (s Bahia and Espírito Santo)

☐ **White-eared Solitaire** *Entomodestes leucotis*

    E slope of Andes of Peru and w Bolivia (La Paz and Cochabamba)

☐ **Black Solitaire** *Entomodestes coracinus*

    W slope of Western Andes of Colombia (Chocó) and nw Ecuador

☐ **Orange-billed Nightingale-Thrush** *Catharus aurantiirostris*
_____ *C. a. aenopennis*   Highlands of nw Mexico (n Sinaloa to sw Chihuahua)
_____ *C. a. clarus*   N central Mexico (s Sinaloa to w Puebla and sw Tamaulipas)
_____ *C. a. melpomene*   S Mexico (Veracruz, ne Puebla, Oaxaca and Chiapas)
_____ *C. a. bangsi*   Guatemala to El Salvador and Honduras
_____ *C. a. costaricensis*   Nicaragua to nw Costa Rica
_____ *C. a. russatus*   Mountains of sw Costa Rica and w Panama
_____ *C. a. griseiceps*   Mountains of w Panama (e Chiriquí and Veraguas)
_____ *C. a. insignis*   N Colombia (upper Magdalena Valley)
_____ *C. a. aurantiirostris*   Mountains of ne Colombia and nw Venezuela
_____ *C. a. sierrae*   Santa Marta Mountains (ne Colombia)
_____ *C. a. inornatus*   W slope of e Andes of Colombia (Santander)
_____ *C. a. phaeoplurus*   Central Colombia (Cauca, upper Patía and Guáitara valleys)
_____ *C. a. birchalli*   Mountains of ne Venezuela (Sucre); Trinidad
_____ *C. a. barbaritoi*   W Venezuela (Sierra de Perijá and valley of upper Río Negro)

☐ **Slaty-backed Nightingale-Thrush** *Catharus fuscater*
_____ *C. f. hellmayri*   Mountains of Costa Rica and w Panama (Chiriquí and Veraguas)
_____ *C. f. mirabilis*   Extreme e Panama (Mt. Pirre)
_____ *C. f. sanctaemartae*   Santa Marta Mountains (ne Colombia)
_____ *C. f. fuscater*   E Panama (Mt. Tacarcuna); e Andes of Venezuela to Ecuador
_____ *C. f. opertaneus*   W Andes of Colombia (Antioquia)
_____ *C. f. caniceps*   Andes of n and central Peru
_____ *C. f. mentalis*   Andes of extreme se Peru (Puno) and nw Bolivia (La Paz)

☐ **Russet Nightingale-Thrush** *Catharus occidentalis*
_____ *C. o. olivascens*   Mts. of nw Mexico (extreme s Sonora, n Sinaloa, w Chihuahua)
_____ *C. o. durangensis*   Mountains of nw Mexico (nw Durango)
_____ *C. o. lambi*   Mountains of e Mexico (n Puebla)
_____ *C. o. fulvescens*   Mts. of central Mexico (Jalisco to s Tamaulipas and w Puebla)
_____ *C. o. occidentalis*   Mts. of se Mexico (e San Luis Potosí to Puebla and s Oaxaca)

☐ **Black-billed Nightingale-Thrush** *Catharus gracilirostris*

____ *C. g. gracilirostris*	Humid montane forests of Costa Rica
____ *C. g. accentor*	Humid montane forests of w Panama

☐ **Ruddy-capped Nightingale-Thrush** *Catharus frantzii*

____ *C. f. frantzii*	Mountains of w Jalisco to c Michoacán, c México and Morelos
____ *C. f. confusus*	Mts. of se San Luis Potosí to ne Hidalgo, ne Puebla and n Oaxaca
____ *C. f. nelsoni*	Mountains of s Mexico (sw Guerrero to se Oaxaca)
____ *C. f. chiapensis*	Mountains of s Mexico (central Chiapas)
____ *C. f. juancitonis*	Mountains of s Mexico (s Chiapas) to Guatemala and Honduras
____ *C. f. waldroni*	Mountains of n Nicaragua
____ *C. f. frantzii*	Mountains of Costa Rica
____ *C. f. wetmorei*	Mountains of w Panama (Chiriquí)

☐ **Black-headed Nightingale-Thrush** *Catharus mexicanus*

____ *C. m. mexicanus*	Mountains of e Mexico (Tamaulipas to Veracruz and w Chiapas)
____ *C. m. cantator*	Highlands of s Mexico (Chiapas) to e Guatemala and Honduras
____ *C. m. fumosus*	Highlands of Nicaragua to Costa Rica and w Panama

☐ **Spotted Nightingale-Thrush** *Catharus dryas*

____ *C. d. harrisoni*	Highlands of se Mexico (Oaxaca)
____ *C. d. ovandensis*	Highlands of s Mexico (Chiapas)
____ *C. d. dryas*	W Guatemala (Sierra de las Minas) to Honduras; w Ecuador
____ *C. d. maculatus*	E slope of Andes of Colombia to e Ecuador, e Peru and n Bolivia
____ *C. d. ecuadoreanus*	Andes of w Ecuador
____ *C. d. blakei*	Andes of extreme n Argentina (Jujuy and Salta))

☐ **Veery** *Catharus fuscescens*

____ *C. f. fuscescens*	E Canada and e US; winters to Amazonian Brazil
____ *C. f. fuliginosa*	SW Newfoundland to s-central Quebec; winters to South America
____ *C. f. salicicola*	W Canada and w US; winters to w Brazil (Mato Grosso)
____ *C. f. subpallidus*	N Washington to ne Oregon, w Montana and Colorado

☐ **Gray-cheeked Thrush** *Catharus minimus*

____ *C. m. minimus*	NE Siberia and Canada; winters to n South America
____ *C. m. aliciae*	SE Canada; winters to West Indies

☐ **Bicknell's Thrush** *Catharus bicknelli*

	Newfoundland and adj. Canada to ne US; winters in Hispaniola

☐ **Swainson's Thrush** *Catharus ustulatus*

____ *C. u. almae*	S Alaska and w Canada; winters to Gulf Coast of s US
____ *C. u. ustulatus*	Coastal se Alaska to s Oregon; winters to w Mexico
____ *C. u. oedicus*	N Washington to s California; winters to s Mexico
____ *C. u. swainsoni*	E Canada to e US; winters to West Indies and n Argentina

☐ **Hermit Thrush** *Catharus guttatus*

____ *C. g. guttatus*	Alaskan Peninsula to sw Canada; winters to central Mexico
____ *C. g. nanus (verecundus)*	Coastal se Alaska and w Br. Columbia; winters to Baja California
____ *G. g. vaccinius*	Vancouver I.; winters to coastal central California
____ *C. g. slevini (oromelus, jewetti)*	Washington and Oregon to c California; winters to nw Mexico
____ *C. g. sequoiensis*	Sierra Nevada of California and w Nevada; winters to n Mexico
____ *C. g. polionotus*	E Washington to e-central California, Nevada and sw Utah
____ *C. g. auduboni*	Rocky Mts. of sw US to New Mexico; winters to Guatemala
____ *C. g. faxoni*	Yukon and n Canada to e US; winters to Florida
____ *C. g. crymophilus*	Newfoundland; winters to se US

☐ **Wood Thrush** *Hylocichla mustelina*

	Breeds e North America; winters s Texas to Panama

☐ **Pale-eyed Thrush** *Platycichla leucops*

	Andes of Colombia to w Bolivia; *tepuis* and mts. of w Venezuela

☐ **Yellow-legged Thrush** *Platycichla flavipes*

_____ *P. f. venezuelensis*	N Colombia to n and w Venezuela
_____ *P. f. melanopleura*	NE Venezuela, Isla Margarita and Trinidad
_____ *P. f. xanthoscelus*	Tobago
_____ *P. f. polionota*	S Venezuela (Bolívar) and Guyana
_____ *P. f. flavipes*	SE Brazil (s Bahia) to ne Paraguay and ne Argentina

☐ **Groundscraper Thrush** *Psophocichla litsipsirupa*

_____ *P. l. simensis*	Highlands of Eritrea and Ethiopia
_____ *P. l. stierlingi*	N Angola to se Zaire, w Tanzania, w Malawi and Mozambique
_____ *P. l. pauciguttatus*	S Angola to n Namibia and nw Botswana
_____ *P. l. litsipsirupa*	C Namibia to Botswana, Zimbabwe, Mozambique and S Africa

☐ **Yemen Thrush** *Turdus menachensis*

	Mountains of sw Arabian Peninsula

☐ **Olive Thrush** *Turdus olivaceus*

_____ *T. o. ludoviciae*	Mountains of n Somalia
_____ *T. o. oldeani*	Mountains of n-central Tanzania
_____ *T. o. roehli*	Mountains of ne Tanzania (Pare and Usambara mountains)
_____ *T. o. helleri*	SE Kenya (Taita Hills and Mt. Kasigau)
_____ *T. o. deckeni*	N Tanzania (Longido and Ketumbeine to Mt. Kilimanjaro)
_____ *T. o. abyssinicus*	Highlands of Ethiopia, se Sudan, n Uganda, Kenya and n Tanzania
_____ *T. o. baraka*	Mountains of e Zaire and w Uganda (Ruwenzori Mountains)
_____ *T. o. bambusicola*	Highlands of Burundi, Rwanda, sw Uganda, nw Tanzania, e Zaire
_____ *T. o. nyikae*	Tanzania (Nguru and Uluguru mts.), n Malawi and ne Zambia
_____ *T. o. miljanensis*	Mountains of s Malawi and Mozambique
_____ *T. o. swynnertoni*	Montane forests of e Zimbabwe and adjacent Mozambique
_____ *T. o. culminans*	Natal (Drakensberg to Nkandhla, Qudeni and Ngorne forests)
_____ *T. o. transvaalensis*	N and e Transvaal and w Swaziland
_____ *T. o. smithi*	S Namibia to se Botswana, sw Transvaal and n Cape Province
_____ *T. o. pondoensis*	Natal and Swaziland to Transkei and e Cape Province
_____ *T. o. olivaceus*	South Africa (sw Cape Province)

☐ **Olivaceous Thrush** *Turdus olivaceofuscus*

_____ *T. o. olivaceofuscus*	São Tomé (Gulf of Guinea)
_____ *T. o. xanthorhynchus*	Príncipe (Gulf of Guinea)

☐ **Comoro Thrush** *Turdus bewsheri*

_____ *T. b. comorensis*	Grand Comoro I.
_____ *T. b. moheliensis*	Mohéli (Comoro Islands)
_____ *T. b. bewsheri*	Anjouan (Comoro Islands)

☐ **Kurrichane Thrush** *Turdus libonyanus*

_____ *T. l. verreauxi*	S Zaire to Angola, n Namibia, Zambia, w Zimbabwe, n Botswana
_____ *T. l. libonyanus*	E Botswana to Transvaal and n Cape Province
_____ *T. l. peripheris*	S Mozambique (Maputo) to Natal and se Swaziland
_____ *T. l. tropicalis*	SE Zaire to Tanzania, Malawi, Zimbabwe and Mozambique

☐ **African Thrush** *Turdus pelios*

_____ *T. p. chiguancoides*	Senegal to Gambia, Guinea, Sierra Leone, Liberia and n Ghana
_____ *T. p. saturatus*	W Ghana to Cameroon, w Congo and Gabon
_____ *T. p. pelios*	E Cameroon to Chad, s Sudan, Eritrea and Ethiopia
_____ *T. p. adamauae*	N Cameroon (Adamawa Plateau)
_____ *T. p. nigrilorum*	Highlands of Mt. Cameroon
_____ *T. p. poensis*	Bioko (Gulf of Guinea)
_____ *T. p. centralis*	N Zaire to s Sudan, sw Ethiopia, Uganda, Kenya and Tanzania
_____ *T. p. graueri*	Extreme e Zaire to Rwanda, Burundi and w Tanzania
_____ *T. p. bocagei*	W Angola (Benguela highlands) to w Zaire
_____ *T. p. stormsi*	SE Zaire (Shaba) to ne Angola and nw Zambia

☐ **African Bare-eyed Thrush** *Turdus tephronotus*

Arid lowlands of Ethiopia and Somalia to Kenya and ne Tanzania

☐ **Gray-backed Thrush** *Turdus hortulorum*

Breeds e Siberia, Manchuria and n Korea; winters to SE Asia

☐ **Tickell's Thrush** *Turdus unicolor*

Himalayas of Kashmir to Nepal; winters to s peninsular India

☐ **Black-breasted Thrush** *Turdus dissimilis*

Mountains of Assam to sw China, n Myanmar and n SE Asia

☐ **Japanese Thrush** *Turdus cardis*

Central China and Japan; winters to s China and Indochina

☐ **White-collared Blackbird** *Turdus albocinctus*

Himalayas of n India to se Tibet, sw China and nw Myanmar

☐ **Ring Ouzel** *Turdus torquatus*
_____ *T. t. torquatus* — Scandinavia, Britain, Ireland and coastal w France
_____ *T. t. alpestris* — Mts. of central and s Europe; winters to Asia Minor and N Africa
_____ *T. t. amicorum* — Caucasus and e Turkey to n Iran; winters to s Iran

☐ **Gray-winged Blackbird** *Turdus boulboul*

Himalayas of w Pakistan to n Myanmar, s China and n SE Asia

☐ **Eurasian Blackbird** *Turdus merula*
_____ *T. m. merula* — W Europe
_____ *T. m. azorensis* — Azores
_____ *T. m. cabrerae* — Madeira and w Canary Islands
_____ *T. m. mauritanicus* — North Africa (Morocco to Tunisia)
_____ *T. m. aterrimus (insularum)* — SE Europe to Crete, Rhodes, Caucasus, Transcaucasia and n Iran
_____ *T. m. syriacus* — S Turkey to Syria, n Iraq and s Iran
_____ *T. m. intermedius* — C Asia to ne Afghanistan, Pamirs and Xinjiang; winters to s Iraq
_____ *T. m. maximus* — W Pakistan and India to Sikkim, Bhutan and se Tibet
_____ *T. m. sowerbyi* — SW China (Sichuan)
_____ *T. m. mandarinus* — W-central China (Guizhou)
_____ *T. m. nigropileus* — W Ghats (Gujarat to Mysore) and Nilgiri Plateau of s central India
_____ *T. m. spencei* — E Ghats (Madhya Pradesh to Seshachalam Hills) of e India
_____ *T. m. simillimus* — SW India (Mysore and w Madras)
_____ *T. m. bourdilloni* — SW India (Kerala)
_____ *T. m. kinnisii* — Hills of Sri Lanka

☐ **Island Thrush** *Turdus poliocephalus*
_____ *T. p. erythropleurus* — Christmas I. (Indian Ocean)
_____ *T. p. loeseri* — Mountains of n Sumatra
_____ *T. p. indrapurae* — Mountains of sw Sumatra
_____ *T. p. biesenbachi* — W Java (Mt. Papandajan region)
_____ *T. p. fumidus* — W Java (Mt. Gedeh region)
_____ *T. p. stresemanni* — W Java (Mt. Lawoe region)
_____ *T. p. javanicus* — Central Java
_____ *T. p. whiteheadi* — Mountains of e Java
_____ *T. p. seebohmi* — N Borneo (Mt. Kinabalu and Trus Madi)
_____ *T. p. niveiceps* — Mountains of Taiwan and Lan-yü I.
_____ *T. p. thomassoni* — Mountains of n Luzon (n Philippines)
_____ *T. p. mayonensis* — Mountains of s Luzon (n Philippines)
_____ *T. p. mindorensis* — Mountains of Mindoro (Philippines)
_____ *T. p. nigrorum* — Mountains of Negros (Philippines)
_____ *T. p. malindangensis* — S Philippines (Mt. Malindang region of nw Mindanao)
_____ *T. p. katanglad* — S Philippines (Mt. Katanglad region of central Mindanao)
_____ *T. p. kelleri* — S Philippines (Mt. Apo and adjacent mountains of se Mindanao)
_____ *T. p. hygroscopus* — S-central Sulawesi (Latimojong Mountains)
_____ *T. p .celebensis* — SW Sulawesi (Bonthain Peak and Wawa Kareng)
_____ *T. p. schlegelii* — E Lesser Sundas (Mount Mutis on w Timor)
_____ *T. p. sterlingi* — E Lesser Sundas (Munt Ramelan on e Timor)
_____ *T. p. deningeri* — S Moluccas (Mt. Binaia on Seram)
_____ *T. p. versteegi* — W New Guinea (Jayawijaya Mountains)

_____	_T. p. carbonarius_	New Guinea (Bismarck Mountains)
_____	_T. p. keysseri_	NE New Guinea (Saruwaged Mountains of Huon Peninsula)
_____	_T. p. papuensis_	Mountains of se New Guinea
_____	_T. p. tolokiwae_	Tolokiwa I. (Bismarck Archipelago)
_____	_T. p. heinrothi_	St. Matthias I. (Bismarck Archipelago)
_____	_T. p. canescens_	Goodenough I. (D'Entrecasteaux Archipelago)
_____	_T. p. bougainvillei_	Bougainville (Solomon Islands)
_____	_T. p. kulambangrae_	Kulambangra (Solomon Islands)
_____	_T. p. sladeni_	Guadalcanal (Solomon Islands)
_____	_T. p. rennellianus_	Rennell (Solomon Islands)
_____	_T. p. vanikorensis_	Vanuatu (Vanikoro, Santa Cruz and Espíritu Santo)
_____	_T. p. placens_	Banks Group (Ureparapara and Vanua Lava)
_____	_T. p. whitneyi_	Gau I. (Banks Group)
_____	_T. p. malekulae_	Vanuatu (Pentecost, Malakulu and Ambrim)
_____	_T. p. becki_	Vanuatu (Paama, Lopevi, Epi and Mai)
_____	_T. p. efatensis_	Vanuatu (Efate and Nguna)
_____	_T. p. albifrons_	Erromango (Vanuatu)
_____	_T. p. xanthopus_	New Caledonia
_____	_T. p. pritzbueri_	Loyalty Islands (Tanna and Lifu)
_____	_T. p. mareensis_	Maré (Loyalty Islands).
_____	_T. p. poliocephalus_	Norfolk I.
_____	_T. p. layardi_	Fiji (Viti Levu, Ovalau, Yasawa and Koro)
_____	_T. p. ruficeps_	Kandavu (Fiji)
_____	_T. p. vitiensis_	Vanua Levu (Fiji)
_____	_T. p. hades_	Ngau (Fiji)
_____	_T. p. tempesti_	Taveuni (Fiji)
_____	_T. p. samoensis_	Western Samoa (Savai'i and Upolu)

☐ **Chestnut Thrush** _Turdus rubrocanus_

_____	_T. r. rubrocanus_	Himalayas of Afghanistan to Nepal, Sikkim and Bhutan
_____	_T. r. gouldi_	Himalayas of se Tibet to sw China and n Myanmar

☐ **White-backed Thrush** _Turdus kessleri_

Himalayas of w China (Gansu to Sichuan); winters to n India

☐ **Gray-sided Thrush** _Turdus feae_

Mountains of ne China (Liaoning); winters to India and Myanmar

☐ **Eyebrowed Thrush** _Turdus obscurus_

Siberia, Mongolia and Japan; winters to Indonesia and Philippines

☐ **Pale Thrush** _Turdus pallidus_

NE Siberia to Kuril Is. and Japan; winters to SE Asia and Sumatra

☐ **Brown-headed Thrush** _Turdus chrysolaus_

_____	_T. c. orii_	Kuril Islands; winters to main Japanese islands and Ryukyu Is.
_____	_T. c. chrysolaus_	Sakhalin I. (Russia) to n Japan; winters to s China and Philippines

☐ **Izu Thrush** _Turdus celaenops_

Izu Islands and Yakushima (Ryukyu Islands)

☐ **Dark-throated Thrush** _Turdus ruficollis_

_____	_T. r. atrogularis_	E Russia to w Siberia; winters to n India and China
_____	_T. r. ruficollis_	E Siberia to n Manchuria; winters to w China, Myanmar, ne India

☐ **Dusky Thrush** _Turdus naumanni_

_____	_T. n. eunomus_	N Siberia to Kamchatka; winters to Japan, s China and Myanmar
_____	_T. n. naumanni_	C Siberia to n Manchuria, Amurland, Sakhalin; winters to Korea

☐ **Fieldfare** _Turdus pilaris_

N Palearctic; winters to n Africa, Mediterranean and Near East

☐ **Redwing** _Turdus iliacus_

_____	_T. i. coburni_	Iceland and Faeroes; winters to nw Europe
_____	_T. i. iliacus_	N Europe to central Asia; winters to North Africa and Near East

☐ **Song Thrush** *Turdus philomelos*

_____	*T. p. herbridensis*	Outer Hebrides and Isle of Skye
_____	*T. p. clarkei*	British Isles and w Europe; winters to n Mediterranean basin
_____	*T. p. philomelos*	N and e Europe to central Asia; winters to North Africa and Iran
_____	*T. p. nataliae*	Sayan Mountains to Lake Baikal and n Iran; winters to s Iran

☐ **Chinese Thrush** *Turdus mupinensis*

W China (s Gansu to Shaanxi, Hubei, Sichuan and nw Yunnan)

☐ **Mistle Thrush** *Turdus viscivorus*

_____	*T. v. viscivorus*	Western Palearctic (except range of *deichleri*) to w Siberia
_____	*T. v. deichleri*	Northwest Africa, Corsica and Sardinia
_____	*T. v. bonapartei*	E Siberia to central Asia and the Himalayas; winters to n India

☐ **Red-legged Thrush** *Turdus plumbeus*

_____	*T. p. plumbeus*	N Bahamas
_____	*T. p. schistaceus*	E Cuba
_____	*T. p. rubripes*	Central and w Cuba and Isle of Pines; formerly Swan I.
_____	*T. p. coryi*	Cayman Brac (Greater Antilles)
_____	*T. p. ardosiaceus*	Hispaniola, Puerto Rico, Gonâve I. and Tortue I.
_____	*T. p. albiventris*	Dominica (Lesser Antilles)

☐ **Chiguanco Thrush** *Turdus chiguanco*

_____	*T. c. conradi*	Andes of s Ecuador and central Peru
_____	*T. c. chiguanco*	Coastal Peru; nw Bolivia (La Paz)
_____	*T. c. anthracinus*	W Bolivia to ne Chile (Atacama) and w Argentina

☐ **Sooty Robin** *Turdus nigrescens*

Mountains of Costa Rica and w Panama (extreme w Chiriquí)

☐ **Great Thrush** *Turdus fuscater*

_____	*T. f. opertaneus*	NW Colombia
_____	*T. f. cacozelus*	Santa Marta Mountains (ne Colombia)
_____	*T. f. clarus*	Sierra de Perijá (Colombia/Venezuela border)
_____	*T. f. quindio*	Central and Western Andes of Colombia to n Ecuador
_____	*T. f. gigas*	E Andes of Colombia to w Venezuela (Mérida and Táchira to Lara)
_____	*T. f. gigantodes*	S Ecuador to n Peru (Junín)
_____	*T. f. ockendeni*	Andes of se Peru (Cuzco and Puno)
_____	*T. f. fuscater*	Andes of w Bolivia (La Paz and Cochabamba)

☐ **Black Robin** *Turdus infuscatus*

Humid montane forests of s Mexico to nw Honduras

☐ **Glossy-black Thrush** *Turdus serranus*

_____	*T. s. cumanensis*	NE Venezuela (Anzoátegui, Sucre and Monagas)
_____	*T. s. atrosericeus*	NE Colombia (Páramo de Tamá) to Andes of n Venezuela
_____	*T. s. fuscobrunneus*	Mountains of central and s Colombia to Ecuador
_____	*T. s. serranus*	Mountains of Peru, Bolivia and nw Argentina (Salta and Jujuy)

☐ **Andean Slaty-Thrush** *Turdus nigriceps*

E slope of Andes of n Peru to Bolivia and nw Argentina

☐ **Eastern Slaty-Thrush** *Turdus subalaris*

S Brazil (Goiás, Mato Grosso, Paraná) to Paraguay, ne Argentina

☐ **Black-hooded Thrush** *Turdus olivater*

_____	*T. o. sanctaemartae*	Santa Marta Mountains (ne Colombia)
_____	*T. o. olivater*	E Colombia and coastal mountains of n Venezuela
_____	*T. o. caucae*	SW Colombia (Cauca Valley)
_____	*T. o. paraquensis*	*Tepuis* of s Venezuela (Cerro Paraque)
_____	*T. o. kemptoni*	*Tepuis* of s Venezuela (Cerro de la Neblina)
_____	*T. o. duidae*	*Tepuis* of s Venezuela (Mt. Duida)
_____	*T. o. roraimae*	*Tepuis* of s Venezuela (s Bolívar), s Guyana and adjacent n Brazil
_____	*T. o. ptaritepui*	*Tepuis* of se Venezuela (Mt. Ptari-tepui)

□ **Plumbeous-backed Thrush** *Turdus reevei*

Arid scrub of sw Ecuador and nw Peru

□ **Maranon Thrush** *Turdus maranonicus*

N Peru (upper Marañón Valley) and adjacent Ecuador

□ **Chestnut-bellied Thrush** *Turdus fulviventris*

E Andes of Colombia to nw Venezuela and extreme n Peru

□ **Rufous-bellied Thrush** *Turdus rufiventris*

____ *T. r. juensis* — NE Brazil (Piauí and Ceará to Pernambuco and w Bahia)
____ *T. r. rufiventris* — S Brazil (s Bahia) to Uruguay, Paraguay, Bolivia and n Argentina

□ **Austral Thrush** *Turdus falcklandii*

____ *T. f. pembertoni* — S-central Argentina (Río Negro and Neuquén)
____ *T. f. magellanicus* — S Chile and s Argentina to Tierra del Fuego; Juan Fernández Is.
____ *T. f. falcklandii* — Falkland Islands

□ **Pale-breasted Thrush** *Turdus leucomelas*

____ *T. l. albiventer* — N Colombia to Venezuela, the Guianas and n Brazil
____ *T. l. cautor* — NE Colombia (Guajira Peninsula)
____ *T. l. leucomelas* — S Brazil to e Paraguay, n Bolivia, ne Argentina; e Peru (San Martín)

□ **Creamy-bellied Thrush** *Turdus amaurochalinus*

E Peru to central Argentina, Paraguay, Uruguay and Brazil

□ **Mountain Robin** *Turdus plebejus*

____ *T. p. differens* — Mountains of se Mexico (extreme se Chiapas) and Guatemala
____ *T. p. rafaelensis* — Mountains of El Salvador and Nicaragua
____ *T. p. plebejus* — Mts. of Costa Rica and w Panama (Bocas del Toro and Chiriquí)

□ **Black-billed Thrush** *Turdus ignobilis*

____ *T. i. ignobilis* — E and Central Andes of Colombia
____ *T. i. goodfellowi* — Colombia (Cauca Valley and west slope of Western Andes)
____ *T. i. debilis* — E Colombia to w Venezuela, nw Brazil, e Peru and n Bolivia
____ *T. i. murinus* — SE Venezuela (Amazonas and Bolívar) and Guyana
____ *T. i. arthuri* — SE Venezuela (Mt. Duida), adjacent Guyana and French Guiana

□ **Lawrence's Thrush** *Turdus lawrencii*

Tropical s Venezuela to n Bolivia and w Amazonian Brazil

□ **Cocoa Thrush** *Turdus fumigatus*

____ *T. f. personus* — Lesser Antilles (St. Vincent and Grenada)
____ *T. f. aquilonalis* — Coastal ne Colombia to n Venezuela; Trinidad
____ *T. f. orinocensis* — E Colombia (e Vichada and Meta) and w Venezuela
____ *T. f. fumigatus* — The Guianas to n and e Brazil, Mato Grosso and e Bolivia

□ **Pale-vented Thrush** *Turdus obsoletus*

____ *T. o. obsoletus* — Caribbean slope of Costa Rica to Panama and nw Colombia
____ *T. o. parambanus* — Pacific coast of Colombia and w Ecuador
____ *T. o. colombianus* — E slope of Western Andes of Colombia

□ **Hauxwell's Thrush** *Turdus hauxwelli*

S Venezuela to se Colombia, n Bolivia and w Amazonian Brazil

□ **Clay-colored Robin** *Turdus grayi*

____ *T. g. tamaulipensis* — Tropical e Mexico (s Tamaulipas to Yucatán Pen. and n Chiapas)
____ *T. g. microrhynchus* — E Mexico (Santa María del Río region of San Luis Potosí)
____ *T. g. grayi* — E Mexico (Sierra Madre Oriental) to Guatemala
____ *T. g. megas* — W Guatemala to Nicaragua
____ *T. g. casius* — Costa Rica to nw Colombia (nw Chocó)
____ *T. g. incomptus* — Coastal n Colombia (Barranquilla to Santa Marta Peninsula)

□ **Bare-eyed Thrush** *Turdus nudigenis*

____ *T. n. nudigenis* — S Lesser Antilles; Trinidad; Colombia to Guianas and n Brazil
____ *T. n. extimus* — N Brazil (s bank of lower Amazon in Santarém region)

☐ **Ecuadorian Thrush** *Turdus maculirostris*

Coastal w Ecuador (Esmeraldas) to extreme nw Peru (Tumbes)

☐ **Unicolored Thrush** *Turdus haplochrous*

Rare and local in n Bolivia (Beni and Santa Cruz)

☐ **White-eyed Thrush** *Turdus jamaicensis*

Montane forests and wooded hills of Jamaica

☐ **White-throated Thrush** *Turdus assimilis*
____ *T. a. calliphthongus* — Highlands of nw Mexico (se Sonora to ne Sinaloa and Chihuahua)
____ *T. a. lygrus* — W Mexico (s Sinaloa to w Oaxaca and sw Chiapas)
____ *T. a. assimilis* — E Mexico (s Tamaulipas to e México, n Oaxaca and w Veracruz)
____ *T. a. oaxacae* — Highlands of Oaxaca
____ *T. a. leucauchen* — S Mexico (s Veracruz) to Honduras
____ *T. a. rubicundus* — Pacific slope of w Guatemala and El Salvador
____ *T. a. atrotinctus* — Caribbean highlands of e Nicaragua
____ *T. a. oblitus* — Highlands of n and central Costa Rica
____ *T. a. cnephosus* — Highlands of sw Costa Rica to w Panama (Chiriquí and Veraguas)
____ *T. a. coibensis* — Coiba I. (w Panama)
____ *T. a. daguae* — E Panama (Darién) to w Colombia and nw Ecuador

☐ **White-necked Thrush** *Turdus albicollis*
____ *T. a. phaeopygoides* — NE Colombia to n Venezuela; Trinidad and Tobago
____ *T. a. phaeopygus* — Extreme e Colombia to the Guianas and n Amazonian Brazil
____ *T. a. spodiolaemus* — E Ecuador to e Peru, n Bolivia and w Brazil
____ *T. a. contemptus* — *Yungas* of Bolivia (La Paz, Santa Cruz and Tarija)
____ *T. a. crotopezus* — E Brazil (Bahia, Espírito Santo and Alagoas)
____ *T. a. albicollis* — SE Brazil (Rio de Janeiro to Rio Grande do Sul)
____ *T. a. paraguayensis* — SW Brazil (Mato Grosso) to Paraguay and ne Argentina

☐ **Rufous-backed Robin** *Turdus rufopalliatus*
____ *T. r. rufopalliatus* — Arid w Mexico (Sonora to w Puebla and Oaxaca)
____ *T. r. graysoni* — Tres Marías Islands and adjacent coastal Nayarit (w Mexico)

☐ **Rufous-collared Robin** *Turdus rufitorques*

Highlands of s Mexico (Chiapas) to central Honduras

☐ **American Robin** *Turdus migratorius*
____ *T. m. migratorius* — N Alaska and n Canada to central US; winters e Mexico and Cuba
____ *T. m. caurinus* — SE Alaska and w Canada to nw Oregon; winters to California
____ *T. m. nigrideus* — E Canada (n Quebec and Labrador) to Gulf Coast of US
____ *T. m. achrusterus* — S-central US; winters to se Mexico
____ *T. m. propinquus* — E British Columbia to sw US and sw Mexico; winters to Guatemala
____ *T. m. philippsi* — E Mexico (sw Tamaulipas to Puebla, Guerrero and Oaxaca)
____ *T. m. confinis* — Mountains of s Baja California (Sierra de la Laguna)

☐ **La Selle Thrush** *Turdus swalesi*
____ *T. s. dodae* — Humid montane forests of central Dominican Republic
____ *T. s. swalesi* — Humid forests of Haiti (Morne La Selle)

☐ **White-chinned Thrush** *Turdus aurantius*

Wooded hills and mountains of Jamaica

☐ **Varied Thrush** *Ixoreus naevius*
____ *I. n. naevius* — SE Alaska to coastal nw California; winters to s California
____ *I. n. meruloides* — N Alaska and nw Canada to nw US; winters to w-central US
____ *I. n. carlottae* — Queen Charlotte Islands (off sw Canada)

☐ **Aztec Thrush** *Ridgwayia pinicola*

Oak-pine forests of w and central Mexico (Sonora to Oaxaca)

☐ **Fruit-hunter** *Chlamydochaera jefferyi*

Patchily distributed mountains of n Borneo (Sabah)

☐ **Rusty-bellied Shortwing** *Brachypteryx hyperythra*

NE India (Sikkim to Arunachal Pradesh) to sw China (Yunnan)

☐ **Gould's Shortwing** *Brachypteryx stellata*

____ *B. s. stellata*	Himalayas (Nepal to Bhutan, se Tibet, sw China and ne Myanmar)
____ *B. s. fusca*	Mountains of n Vietnam (nw Tonkin)

☐ **White-bellied Shortwing** *Brachypteryx major*

____ *B. m. major*	Peninsular India (Nilgiri Hills of Mysore and w Madras)
____ *B. m. albiventris*	Peninsular India (sw Madras to Kerala)

☐ **Lesser Shortwing** *Brachypteryx leucophrys*

____ *B. l. nipalensis*	Himalayas of n India to sw China (Yunnan) and Myanmar
____ *B. l. carolinae*	S China to n Thailand and n Indochina
____ *B. l. langbianensis*	Mountains of s Laos (Langbian Plateau) and s Vietnam
____ *B. l. wrayi*	Mountains of Malaysia
____ *B. l. leucophrys*	Mts. of Sumatra, Java, Bali, Lombok, Sumbawa, Alor and Timor

☐ **White-browed Shortwing** *Brachypteryx montana*

____ *B. m. cruralis*	E Himalayas to n Myanmar and w China; winters to n Indochina
____ *B. m. sinensis*	Mountains of se China (nw Fujian and Guangxi)
____ *B. m. goodfellowi*	Mountains of Taiwan
____ *B. m. poliogyna*	Mountains of n Luzon (n Philippines)
____ *B. m. andersoni*	Mountains of s Luzon (n Philippines)
____ *B. m. mindorensis*	Highlands of Mindoro (Philippines)
____ *B. m. brunneiceps*	Mountains of Negros (Philippines)
____ *B. m. mindanensis*	S Philippines (Mt. Apo and Mt. Matutum on Mindanao)
____ *B. m. malindangensis*	S Philippines (Mt. Malindang region of nw Mindanao)
____ *B. m. sillimani*	Mountains of s Palawan (s Philippines)
____ *B. m. erythrogyna*	Mountains of n Borneo
____ *B. m. saturata*	Mountains of Sumatra
____ *B. m. montana*	Mountains of Java
____ *B. m. floris*	Mountains of Flores (w Lesser Sundas)

☐ **Great Shortwing** *Heinrichia calligyna*

____ *H. c. simplex*	Tentolo-Matinan Mountains (ne peninsula of Sulawesi)
____ *H. c. calligyna*	Mount Latimojong (s central Sulawesi)
____ *H. c. picta*	Mekonga Mountains (se Sulawesi)

☐ **Rufous Rock-jumper** *Chaetops frenatus*

	South Africa (Western and Eastern Cape Province)

☐ **Orange-breasted Rock-jumper** *Chaetops aurantius*

	Rocky montane slopes of Lesotho, Natal and e Cape Province

☐ **Brown-chested Alethe** *Alethe poliocephala*

____ *A. p. poliocephala*	Sierra Leone to Ghana
____ *A. p. hallae*	Angola (Gabela escarpment of Cuanza Sul)
____ *A. p. giloensis*	S Sudan
____ *A. p. carruthersi*	Extreme s Sudan to ne Zaire, Uganda and w Kenya
____ *A. p. compsonota*	Nigeria and Cameroon to nw Angola (Quicolungo); Bioko
____ *A. p. vandewhegei*	Rwanda and Burundi
____ *A. p. nandensis*	W Kenya (Nandi Hills)
____ *A. p. kungwensis*	W Tanzania (Kungwe-Mahari Mountains)
____ *A. p. ufipae*	SW Tanzania (Ufipa Plateau) and se Zaire

☐ **Red-throated Alethe** *Alethe poliophrys*

____ *A. p. poliophrys*	Montane forests of ne Zaire, Rwanda, Burundi and sw Uganda
____ *A. p. kaboboensis*	Montane forests of e Zaire (Mt. Kabobo)

☐ **Cholo Alethe** *Alethe choloensis*

____ *A. c. choloensis*	Montane forests of s Malawi (east of Rift Valley)
____ *A. c. namuli*	NW Mozambique (Namuli massif)

☐ **White-chested Alethe** *Alethe fuelleborni*

Mountains of e Tanzania to n Malawi and s-central Mozambique

☐ **Fire-crested Alethe** *Alethe diademata*

_____	*A. d. diademata*	Senegambia to Sierra Leone, Liberia, Ghana and Togo
_____	*A. d. castanea*	S Nigeria to Cameroon, Gabon and Zaire; Bioko
_____	*A. d. woosnami*	E Zaire to sw Sudan, w Uganda and nw Tanzania

FAMILY: CISTICOLIDAE (Cisticolas and Allies—111)

☐ **Red-faced Cisticola** *Cisticola erythrops*

_____	*C. e. erythrops*	Senegambia to Central African Republic
_____	*C. e. sylvia*	NE Zaire and s Sudan to central Tanzania and s Zaire
_____	*C. e. nyasa*	Extreme se Zaire to s Tanzania, n Botswana and Natal
_____	*C. e. lepe*	Angola
_____	*C. e. pyrrhomitrus*	SE Sudan to Ethiopia
_____	*C. e. niloticus*	Sudan (upper Blue Nile)

☐ **Singing Cisticola** *Cisticola cantans*

_____	*C. c. concolor*	N Nigeria to s Sudan
_____	*C. c. adamauae*	Cameroon to Congo and nw Zaire
_____	*C. c. belli*	Central African Republic to ne Zaire, Uganda and nw Tanzania
_____	*C. c. cantans*	S Eritrea to s Ethiopia
_____	*C. c. muenzneri*	Kenya and n Tanzania (south to Nguru Mountains)
		S Tanzania (Uluguru Mountains) to Zimbabwe

☐ **Whistling Cisticola** *Cisticola lateralis*

_____	*C. l. lateralis*	Senegambia to Nigeria and Cameroon
_____	*C. l. antinorii*	Central African Republic to w Kenya
_____	*C. l. modesta (vincenti)*	Gabon to n Angola and s Zaire

☐ **Chattering Cisticola** *Cisticola anonymus*

Nigeria to Cameroon, Gabon, Congo, Zaire and nw Angola

☐ **Trilling Cisticola** *Cisticola woosnami*

_____	*C. w. woosnami*	NE Zaire to Uganda, Burundi and n Tanzania (south to Iringa)
_____	*C. w. lufira*	SW Tanzania (Kigoma and Rukwa)

☐ **Bubbling Cisticola** *Cisticola bulliens*

_____	*C. b. septentrionalis*	Cabinda and lower Congo River to n Angola (south to Gabela)
_____	*C. b. bulliens*	S Angola (Benguela escarpment)

☐ **Chubb's Cisticola** *Cisticola chubbi*

_____	*C. c. adametzi*	SE Nigeria to Cameroon
_____	*C. c. discolor*	S Cameroon (Mt. Cameroon)
_____	*C. c. chubbi*	Zaire to Rwanda, Burundi, Uganda and Kenya
_____	*C. c. marungensis*	SE Zaire (Marungu Plateau)

☐ **Hunter's Cisticola** *Cisticola hunteri*

High mountains of w Kenya, Uganda and n Tanzania

☐ **Black-lored Cisticola** *Cisticola nigriloris*

Highlands of n Malawi, ne Zambia and s Tanzania

☐ **Rock-loving Cisticola** *Cisticola aberrans*

_____	*C. a. admiralis*	Guinea to Sierra Leone, Mali and s Ghana
_____	*C. a. petrophilus*	N Nigeria to w Cameroon, ne Zaire and sw Sudan
_____	*C. a. bailunduensis*	Central Angola
_____	*C. a. emini (teitensis)*	S Kenya to n Tanzania
_____	*C. a. nyika*	SW Tanzania to Zambia, Malawi, Zimbabwe and Mozambique
_____	*C. a. lurio*	Malawi (east of Rift Valley) and adjacent nw Mozambique
_____	*C. a. aberrans*	Botswana to Transvaal, w Swaziland and Natal
_____	*C. a. minor*	Lowlands of s Mozambique to Natal and e Cape Province

☐ **Boran Cisticola** *Cisticola bodessa*
_____ *C. b. bodessa* — Juniper woodlands of s Sudan to Eritrea, s Ethiopia and n Kenya
_____ *C. b. kaffensis* — W Ethiopia (Kaffa Province)

☐ **Rattling Cisticola** *Cisticola chiniana*
_____ *C. c. simplex* — S Sudan to n Uganda
_____ *C. c. fricki* — S Ethiopia to n Kenya
_____ *C. c. humilis* — W Kenya and ne Uganda; n Tanzania (Loliondo region)
_____ *C. c. ukamba* — Highlands of e Kenya and ne Tanzania
_____ *C. c. victoria* — Lake Victoria basin (sw Kenya and adjacent Tanzania)
_____ *C. c. heterophrys* — Coastal Kenya and Tanzania
_____ *C. c. fischeri* — N-central Tanzania (south to Tabora region)
_____ *C. c. keithi* — S-central Tanzania (Dodoma to Iringa)
_____ *C. c. mbeya* — S Tanzania (Mbeya to Chimala)
_____ *C. c. emendatus* — SE Tanzania to n Mozambique, Malawi and extreme e Zambia
_____ *C. c. procerus* — Extreme s Malawi (Chiromo) and n Mozambique (Tete)
_____ *C. c. chiniana (vulpiniceps)* — Zimbabwe to w Mozambique, Transvaal and se Botswana
_____ *C. c. fortis* — N Angola to Zambia, s Congo, Gabon and s Zaire
_____ *C. c. frater* — Central Namibia
_____ *C. c. bensoni* — S Zambia
_____ *C. c. smithersi* — W Zimbabwe to nw Botswana, sw Zambia, n Namibia and s Angola
_____ *C. c. campestris* — S coastal Mozambique to Swaziland and Natal

☐ **Ashy Cisticola** *Cisticola cinereolus*
_____ *C. c. cincereolus* — NE Ethiopia and s Somalia
_____ *C. c. schillingsi* — S Ethiopia and extreme se Sudan to n Tanzania

☐ **Red-pate Cisticola** *Cisticola ruficeps*
_____ *C. r. guinea* — Senegal to Nigeria and Cameroon (Adamawa Plateau)
_____ *C. r. ruficeps* — Chad to s Sudan (Kordofan and Bahr-el-Ghazal)
_____ *C. r. scotopterus* — Central Sudan (White and Blue Nile valleys) to Eritrea
_____ *C. r. mongalla* — S Sudan (upper White Nile) to n Uganda

☐ **Dorst's Cisticola** *Cisticola dorsti*
Grassy steppes of nw Nigeria, n Cameroon and s Chad

☐ **Gray Cisticola** *Cisticola rufilatus*
_____ *C. r. rufilatus* — S Angola and n Namibia to Botswana, Zimbabwe and n Cape Prov.
_____ *C. r. ansorgei (venustula)* — E Angola to s Zaire, n Zambia and Malawi
_____ *C. r. vicinior* — Plateau of Zimbabwe

☐ **Red-headed Cisticola** *Cisticola subruficapillus*
_____ *C. s. newtoni* — SW Angola to Namibia (Kaokoveld)
_____ *C. s. windhoekensis* — Central Namibia (Waterberg Mts. to Naukluft Mts.)
_____ *C. s. karasensis* — S Namibia (Great Namaqualand) to nw Cape Province
_____ *C. s. namaqua* — NW Cape Prov. (Oliphants River to Orange River and w Karoo)
_____ *C. s. subruficapillus* — SW Cape Province (east to Knysna and Oliphants)
_____ *C. s. jamesi* — SE Cape Prov. (Port Elizabeth to e Karoo and Orange Free State)

☐ **Wailing Cisticola** *Cisticola lais*
_____ *C. l. namba* — Highlands of w Angola
_____ *C. l. distinctus* — Highlands of e Uganda and central Kenya
_____ *C. l. semifasciatus* — S Tanzania (Iringa Plateau) to Malawi, Zambia, n Mozambique
_____ *C. l. mashona* — S Mozambique to Zimbabwe, n Transvaal and Swaziland
_____ *C. l. oreobates* — Central Mozambique (Mt. Gorongoza)
_____ *C. l. monticola* — S Transvaal
_____ *C. l. lais* — SE Transvaal to Natal, e Orange Free State, Lesotho, e Cape Prov.
_____ *C. l. maculatus* — S Cape Province (east to Port Elizabeth)

☐ **Tana River Cisticola** *Cisticola restrictus*
NE Kenya (lower Tana River basin)

Cisticolas and Allies

☐ Churring Cisticola *Cisticola njombe*
_____ C. n. njombe | Highlands of s Tanzania
_____ C. n. mariae | NE Zambia and w Malawi (Nyika Plateau)

☐ Winding Cisticola *Cisticola galactotes*
_____ C. g. amphilectus (griseus) | Senegal to Ghana, coastal Nigeria and w Congo basin
_____ C. g. zalingei | N Nigeria to s Sudan (Darfur)
_____ C. g. marginatus | S Sudan (upper White Nile) to n Uganda
_____ C. g. lugubris | Ethiopia
_____ C. g. haematocephalus | Coastal s Somalia to Kenya and n Tanzania
_____ C. g. nyansae | Central and e Zaire to Uganda and w Kenya
_____ C. g. suahelicus (isodactylus) | Central Tanzania to se Zaire, n Zambia, Malawi and Mozambique
_____ C. g. galactotes | SE Zimbabwe and South Africa
_____ C. g. luapula | N Zambia (Lake Mweru and Lake Bangweulu basin)
_____ C. g. schoutedeni | W Zambia
_____ C. g. stagnans | Caprivi Strip and adjacent s Zambia and w Zimbabwe

☐ Chirping Cisticola *Cisticola pipiens*
_____ C. p. pipiens | W Angola
_____ C. p. congo | E Angola to Zambia, Zaire, Tanzania and Burundi
_____ C. p. arundicola | SE Angola (Cuando Cubango) to Botswana and Zimbabwe

☐ Carruthers' Cisticola *Cisticola carruthersi*
Zaire to Uganda, w Kenya, Rwanda, Burundi and nw Tanzania

☐ Tinkling Cisticola *Cisticola tinniens*
_____ C. t. perpullus | Angola to s Zaire and nw Zambia
_____ C. t. oreophilus | Highlands of w and central Kenya
_____ C. t. shiwae | NE Zambia to se Zaire and extreme sw Tanzania
_____ C. t. dyleffi | Mountains nw of Lake Tanganyika (west of Ruzizi Valley)
_____ C. t. tinniens | Zimbabwe to South Africa

☐ Stout Cisticola *Cisticola robustus*
_____ C. r. santae | Highlands of e Nigeria and w Cameroon
_____ C. r. schraderi | Central Eritrea and adjacent n Ethiopia (Adigrat)
_____ C. r. robustus | N Ethiopian plateau and Harrar
_____ C. r. omo | S Ethiopian plateau
_____ C. r. nuchalis (ambigua) | NE Zaire to Kenya and n Tanzania
_____ C. r. angolensis | S Zaire (w Shaba) to nw Zambia and Angola
_____ C. r. awemba | SE Zaire (e Shaba) to sw Tanzania and ne Zambia

☐ Croaking Cisticola *Cisticola natalensis*
_____ C. n. strangei (valida, kapitensis, littoralis) | Senegal to Cabinda, Sudan, Rwanda, Burundi, Uganda and Kenya
_____ C. n. tonga | Sudan (White Nile and Blue Nile regions)
_____ C. n. inexpectatus | Highlands of Ethiopia
_____ C. n. argenteus | S Ethiopia and se Somalia to n Kenya
_____ C. n. natalensis (vigilax) | Interior Tanzania to se Zambia, Mozambique and South Africa
_____ C. n. holubi | Extreme n Botswana, extreme w Zimbabwe and adj. s Zambia
_____ C. n. katanga | SW Tanzania, adj. n Malawi, ne Zambia, se Zaire and ne Angola

☐ Piping Cisticola *Cisticola fulvicapillus*
_____ C. f. dispar | W Zaire to central plateau of Angola and nw Zambia
_____ C. f. hallae | S Angola to sw Zambia, nw Zimbabwe, n Botswana, n Namibia
_____ C. f. muelleri | NW Zambia to e Tanzania, Mozambique and ne Zimbabwe
_____ C. f. dexter | Plateau of Zimbabwe to Transvaal and extreme e Botswana
_____ C. f. lebombo | Mozambique to Transvaal, n Zululand, Swaziland and w Natal
_____ C. f. ruficapillus | Highlands of Transvaal to w Orange Free State and ne Cape Prov.
_____ C. f. fulvicapillus | Interior e Cape Prov. to Drakensberg escarpment and w Lesotho
_____ C. f. dumicola | W Zululand to Natal, coastal Transkei and e Cape Province
_____ C. f. silberbaueri | South Africa (winter rainfall area of sw Cape Province)

☐ **Aberdare Cisticola** *Cisticola aberdare*

W-central Kenya (Aberdare Mountains)

☐ **Tabora Cisticola** *Cisticola angusticaudus*

SE Uganda to sw Kenya, Rwanda, Tanzania, se Zaire and Zambia

☐ **Slender-tailed Cisticola** *Cisticola melanurus*

Locally in ne Angola, s Zaire and extreme w Zambia

☐ **Siffling Cisticola** *Cisticola brachypterus*

____ C. b. brachypterus	Gambia to Central African Republic, Sudan, n Zaire and n Angola
____ C. b. zedlitzi	Eritrea and Ethiopian plateau
____ C. b. reichenowi	Extreme s Somalia to coastal Kenya and Tanzania
____ C. b. loanda	SE Zaire to w Zambia and interior Angola
____ C. b. hypoxanthus	NE Zaire to n Uganda and se Sudan
____ C. b. ankole	S Uganda to Rwanda, Burundi, adjacent e Zaire and nw Tanzania
____ C. b. katonae	Interior of Kenya and n Tanzania
____ C. b. kericho	SW Kenya (Kericho)
____ C. b. isabellinus (tenebricosus)	Central Tanzania to Mozambique, Zimbabwe and e Zambia

☐ **Rufous Cisticola** *Cisticola rufus*

Grasslands of Gambia to Lake Chad and Central African Republic

☐ **Foxy Cisticola** *Cisticola troglodytes*

____ C. t. troglodytes	Central African Republic to s Sudan (White Nile) and w Kenya
____ C. t. ferrugineus	W Ethiopia and adjacent e Sudan (Blue Nile)

☐ **Tiny Cisticola** *Cisticola nanus*

SE Sudan to Ethiopia, Somalia, Kenya and n Tanzania

☐ **Zitting Cisticola** *Cisticola juncidis*

____ C. j. cisticola	Coastal w France to Iberian Pen., Balearic Islands and nw Africa
____ C. j. juncidis	S France to Corsica, Sardinia, Balkans, Turkey, Syria and Israel
____ C. j. neurotica	Cyprus, Levant, Iraq and w Iran
____ C. j. uropygialis (perrenia)	Senegal to s Nigeria, Sudan, Rwanda and n Tanzania; Mafia I.
____ C. j. terrestris	Rio Muni to central Zaire, Burundi and s Tanzania
____ C. j. cursitans	E Afghanistan to Pakistan, Nepal, n Myanmar, India, Sri Lanka
____ C. j. salamalii	SW India (Kerala)
____ C. j. omalura	Sri Lanka
____ C. j. malaya	S Myanmar to Thailand, Malaysia, Sumatra and w Java
____ C. j. brunniceps	Japan (Honshu to Ryukyu, Izu and Cheju-Do is.) to n Philippines
____ C. j. tinnabulans	S China to Indochina, Hainan, Taiwan and Philippines
____ C. j. nigrostriata	SW Philippines (Culion and Palawan)
____ C. j. fuscicapilla	E Java, Kangean Islands and Lesser Sundas
____ C. j. constans	Sulawesi, Togian Is., Muna I., Tukangbesi Is. and Peleng I.
____ C. j. normani	Coastal s New Guinea and w Queensland
____ C. j. leanyeri	Coastal Northern Territory to Gulf of Carpenteria
____ C. j. laveryi	Coastal e Queensland

☐ **Socotra Cisticola** *Cisticola haesitatus*

Socotra I.

☐ **Madagascar Cisticola** *Cisticola cherinus*

Grasslands of Madagascar and Aldabra

☐ **Desert Cisticola** *Cisticola aridulus*

____ C. a. aridulus	Mali, Niger and n Nigeria to s Sudan
____ C. a. lavandulae	Coastal Eritrea to Ethiopia and Somalia
____ C. a. tanganyika	Kenya and Tanzania
____ C. a. lobito	Coastal Angola
____ C. a. traylori	E Angola and extreme w Zambia
____ C. a. eremicus	S Angola to n Namibia, s Zambia, Zimbabwe and n Botswana
____ C. a. perplexus	N Zambia (Banmgweulu swamps)
____ C. a. kalahari	Central Namibia to s Botswana and South Africa
____ C. a. caliginus	Natal to Swaziland, s Mozambique and adjacent ne Transvaal

□ **Cloud Cisticola** *Cisticola textrix*

____	*C. t. bulubulu*	Highlands of s Angola
____	*C. t. anselli*	Highlands of e Angola and nw Zambia
____	*C. t. marleyi*	S Mozambique to ne Zululand and coastal Natal
____	*C. t. major*	Transvaal to w Natal, w Swaziland and e Cape Province
____	*C. t. textrix*	S Cape Province (Cape Town to Port Elizabeth)

□ **Black-necked Cisticola** *Cisticola eximius*

____	*C. e. occidens*	S Senegal to Sierra Leone, s Mali and Nigeria
____	*C. e. winneba*	Coastal Ghana (Winneba)
____	*C. e. eximius*	N Zaire to Ethiopia, extreme w Kenya and s Central African Rep.

□ **Cloud-scraping Cisticola** *Cisticola dambo*

____	*C. d. dambo*	NE Angola to s Zaire and nw Zambia
____	*C. d. kasai*	S Zaire (nw Kasai)

□ **Pectoral-patch Cisticola** *Cisticola brunnescens*

____	*C. b. mbangensis*	N Cameroon (Adamawa Plateau)
____	*C. b. brunnescens*	Ethiopia and nw Somalia
____	*C. b. wambera*	NW Ethiopia (Wambera Plateau)
____	*C. b. nakuruensis*	Highlands of Kenya and n Tanzania (west of Rift Valley)
____	*C. b. hindii*	Highlands of Kenya and n Tanzania (east of Rift Valley)
____	*C. b. lynesi*	Highlands of w Cameroon

□ **Pale-crowned Cisticola** *Cisticola cinnamomeus*

____	*C. c. midcongo*	SE Gabon (Teke Plateau)
____	*C. c. cinnamomeus*	S Tanzania to se Zaire, Zambia, Zimbabwe, Botswana, Angola
____	*C. c. egregius (taciturnus)*	S Mozambique to South Africa

□ **Wing-snapping Cisticola** *Cisticola ayresii*

____	*C. a. gabun*	Gabon to Congo and nw Zaire
____	*C. a. imatong*	S Sudan (Imatong Mountains)
____	*C. a. entebbe*	Extreme e Zaire to Rwanda, Uganda, nw Tanzania and w Kenya
____	*C. a. itombwensis*	Mountains ne of Lake Tanganyika
____	*C. a. mauensis*	Highlands of Kenya
____	*C. a. ayresii*	S Tanzania to se Zaire, e Zambia, Mozambique and South Africa

□ **Golden-headed Cisticola** *Cisticola exilis*

____	*C. e. tytleri*	Foothills of Nepal to ne India, n Myanmar and sw China (Yunnan)
____	*C. e. erythrocephala*	S India (s Mysore, w Tamil Nadu and Kerala)
____	*C. e. equicaudata*	E Myanmar to central Thailand, Cambodia and s Vietnam
____	*C. e. courtoisi*	SE China (se Yunnan to s Hunan, Jiangxi and Fujian)
____	*C. e. volitans*	Taiwan
____	*C. e. semirufa*	Philippine Islands and Sulu Archipelago
____	*C. l. rustica*	Sulawesi subregion and s Moluccas
____	*C. e. lineocapilla*	Java, Bali, Lesser Sundas and n Australia (Northern Territory)
____	*C. e. diminuta*	New Guinea to Solomon Islands and ne Australia (n Queensland)
____	*C. e. polionota*	Bismarck Archipelago
____	*C. e. alexandrae*	NW Australia to w Queensland
____	*C. e. exilis*	S Queensland to Victoria, se South Australia and n Tasmania

□ **White-browed Chinese Warbler** *Rhopophilus pekinensis*

____	*R. p. albosuperciliaris*	NW China (Xinjiang) from Tarim Basin to Lop Nor
____	*R. p. leptorhynchus*	N-central China (ne Qinghai, Shaanxi and Gansu)
____	*R. p. pekinensis*	S Manchuria to Korea and ne China

□ **Socotra Warbler** *Incana incanus*

	Socotra (off e Somalia)

□ **Streaked Scrub-Warbler** *Scotocerca inquieta*

____	*S. i. saharae (harterti)*	Morocco to Tunisia, Algeria and Libya
____	*S. i. theresae*	Mauritania and s Morocco
____	*S. i. inquieta*	Deserts of e Egypt and n Arabia
____	*S. i. grisea*	W Saudi Arabia (Taif Plateau), e South Yemen and Oman
____	*S. i. buryi*	SW Saudi Arabia, North Yemen and Hadramaut
____	*S. i. striata*	Iran to Baluchistan, Pakistan and nw India
____	*S. i. platyura*	Transcaspia to s Uzbekistan, n Turkmenistan and w Tajikistan
____	*S. i. montana*	Mts. of s Turkmenistan to w Tajikistan and n Afghanistan

□ **Rufous-vented Prinia** *Prinia burnesii*

Elephant and *sarkhan* grass of Pakistan to nw India (w Punjab)

□ **Swamp Prinia** *Prinia cinerascens*

Wet grasslands of ne India (Assam) and n Bangladesh

□ **Striated Prinia** *Prinia criniger*

____	*P. c. striatula*	Foothills of ne Afghanistan and w Pakistan
____	*P. c. criniger*	Foothills of Pakistan and Kashmir to Arunachal Pradesh
____	*P. c. catharia*	NE India (Assam) to s China and w Myanmar (Chin Hills)
____	*P. c. parvirostris*	SW China (se Yunnan)
____	*P. c. parumstriata*	Coastal provinces of se China and Yangtze River drainage
____	*P. c. striata*	Taiwan

□ **Brown Prinia** *Prinia polychroa*

____	*P. p. bangsi*	S China (se Yunnan and w Jiangxi) and Taiwan
____	*P. p. cooki*	Central Myanmar to e Thailand, Laos and Cambodia
____	*P. p. rocki*	Laos (Langbian Plateau)
____	*P. p. polychroa*	Java

□ **Hill Prinia** *Prinia atrogularis*

____	*P. a. atrogularis*	E Nepal to Sikkim, Bhutan, se Tibet and Arunachal Pradesh
____	*P. a. khasiana*	NE India (Assam) to Bangladesh, w Myanmar and s China
____	*P. a. erythropleura*	Myanmar (s Shan States, Kayah and Tenasserim) to n Thailand
____	*P. a. superciliaris*	Hills of e Myanmar to s China (Yunnan), n Laos and n Vietnam
____	*P. a. waterstradti*	Highlands of e Malaysia (Gunong Tahan)
____	*P. a. klossi*	High plateaus of s Laos and s Vietnam
____	*P. a. dysancrita*	Hills of w Sumatra

□ **Gray-crowned Prinia** *Prinia cinereocapilla*

Himalayan foothills of n India (Kashmir to Bhutan and s Assam)

□ **Rufous-fronted Prinia** *Prinia buchanani*

Thornscrub of India and Pakistan (Indus River plain)

□ **Rufescent Prinia** *Prinia rufescens*

____	*P. r. rufescens*	Nepal to Bhutan, se Tibet, s China, Bangladesh, Myanmar and India
____	*P. r. beavani*	SE Myanmar to sw Thailand and n Indochina (Laos and Vietnam)
____	*P. r. peninsularis*	S Myanmar and peninsular Thailand (Isthmus of Kra to Trang)
____	*P. r. objurgans*	SE Thailand
____	*P. r. extrema*	S Peninsular Thailand and Malay Peninsula
____	*P. r. dalatensis*	S Vietnam

□ **Gray-breasted Prinia** *Prinia hodgsonii*

____	*P. h. rufula*	Kashmir to Assam, sw China (nw Yunnan) and n Myanmar
____	*P. h. hodgsonii*	India to w Myanmar
____	*P. h. albogularis*	SW peninsular India (E Ghats to s Mysore and Kerala)
____	*P. h. leggei*	Sri Lanka
____	*P. h. erro*	E Myanmar (Shan States) to Thailand and s Indochina
____	*P. h. confusa*	S China (s Sichuan and w Yunnan) to ne Laos and n Vietnam

□ **Bar-winged Prinia** *Prinia familiaris*

____	*P. f. prinia*	Lowlands of Sumatra, w Java and Karimunjawa Islands
____	*P. f. familiaris*	E Java and Bali

☐ **Graceful Prinia** *Prinia gracilis*

____	*P. g. akyildizi*	Coastal s Turkey (Antalya to Adana)
____	*P. g. irakensis*	NE Syria to Iraq and sw Iran (foothills of Zagros Mountains)
____	*P. g. palestinae*	E Sinai to s Israel, Lebanon, Syria, Jordan and nw Arabia
____	*P. g. deltae*	Egypt (Nile Delta) to Sinai and w Israel
____	*P. g. gracilis*	Nile Valley (Cairo to n Sudan) and n Egypt (El Faiyum)
____	*P. g. natronensis*	N Egypt (Wadi el Natrun)
____	*P. g. yemenensis*	Coastal Arabia and Yemen (Mecca to Aden and Hadramaut)
____	*P. g. carlo*	S Sudan to Eritrea, Ethiopia, Djibouti and s Somalia
____	*P. g. hufufae*	E Saudi Arabia (Hufuf Oasis) and Bahrain
____	*P. g. carpenteri*	Coastal Oman
____	*P. g. lepida*	S coastal Iran to Afghanistan, Pakistan and n India
____	*P. g. stevensi*	S Nepal to ne India (Assam and Arunachal Pradesh)

☐ **Jungle Prinia** *Prinia sylvatica*

____	*P. s. insignis*	NW India (Rann of Kutch and Gujarat to w Rajasthan)
____	*P. s. gangetica*	*Terai* of Nepal to n India and Bangladesh
____	*P. s. mahendrae*	NE India (Orissa)
____	*P. s. sylvatica*	Peninsular India (north to Madhya Pradesh and Mahjarashtra)
____	*P. s. valida*	Sri Lanka

☐ **Yellow-bellied Prinia** *Prinia flaviventris*

____	*P. f. sindiana*	Pakistan (Indus River system) to nw India
____	*P. f. flaviventris*	Nepal to Bhutan, ne India, Bangladesh and n Myanmar
____	*P. f. delacouri*	SE Myanmar to central Thailand and Indochina
____	*P. f. sonitans*	SE China (n Guangxi, Guangdong, Fujian), Hainan and Taiwan
____	*P. f. rafflesi*	S Myanmar, peninsular Thailand, Malaya, Sumatra and Java
____	*P. f. halistona*	Nias I. (off Sumatra)
____	*P. f. latrunculus*	Borneo

☐ **Ashy Prinia** *Prinia socialis*

____	*P. s. stewarti*	N Pakistan (upper Indus River) to Nepal and n India
____	*P. s. inglisi*	NE India to Sikkim, Bhutan, Assam and Bangladesh
____	*P. s. socialis*	Peninsular India
____	*P. s. brevicauda*	Sri Lanka

☐ **Tawny-flanked Prinia** *Prinia subflava*

____	*P. s. subflava*	Senegal to s Sudan, adj. Uganda, s-central Ethiopia and s Eritrea
____	*P. s. pallescens*	Mali to Sudan, Ethiopia and nw Eritrea
____	*P. s. melanorhyncha*	Sierra Leone to Cameroon, n Zaire, Kenya and nw Tanzania
____	*P. s. graueri*	E Zaire (Kivu) to Rwanda and highlands of Angola
____	*P. s. affinis*	E Zaire to sw Tanzania, Zambia, e Botswana and s Mozambique
____	*P. s. bechulanae (ovampensis)*	SW Angola to n Namibia, n Botswana, sw Zambia, w Zimbabwe
____	*P. s. mutatrix*	S Tanzania to Malawi, e Zambia, e Zimbabwe and Mozambique
____	*P. s. kasokae*	W Zambia (west of Zambezi River) and adjacent e Angola
____	*P. s. tenella*	Coastal e Africa (Somalia to s Tanzania)
____	*P. s. pondoensis*	S Mozambique to Natal, e Swaziland and e Cape Province

☐ **Plain Prinia** *Prinia inornata*

____	*P. s. terricolor*	E Baluchistan to Pakistan and nw India
____	*P. s. inornata*	Central and peninsular India (south to s Madras)
____	*P. s. franklinii*	S India (sw Mysore, Kerala and hills of w and s Madras)
____	*P. s. insularis*	Sri Lanka
____	*P. s. fusca*	Nepal to Sikkim, Bhutan, Assam and Bangladesh
____	*P. s. extensicauda*	S China to n Laos, n Vietnam and Hainan
____	*P. s. blanfordi*	Myanmar and n Thailand
____	*P. s. herberti*	S Myanmar and s Thailand to s Laos, Cambodia and s Vietnam
____	*P. s. flavirostris*	Taiwan

☐ **Pale Prinia** *Prinia somalica*
- ____ *P. s. erlangeri* — SE Sudan to Ethiopia, Uganda, Kenya and Somalia
- ____ *P. s. somalica* — Extreme n Somalia

☐ **River Prinia** *Prinia fluviatilis*

Locally in Niger, Chad and n Cameroon (status unknown)

☐ **Black-chested Prinia** *Prinia flavicans*
- ____ *P. f. ansorgei* — Coastal Angola and Namibia (Namib Desert to Walvis Bay)
- ____ *P. f. bihe* — Angola highlands to Zambia
- ____ *P. f. flavicans* — Namibia to Botswana and nw Cape Province
- ____ *P. f. nubilosa* — E Botswana to sw Zambia, sw Zimbabwe and Transvaal
- ____ *P. f. ortleppi* — SW Transvaal to w Orange Free State and ne Cape Province

☐ **Karoo Prinia** *Prinia maculosa*
- ____ *P. m. maculosa* — S Namibia to s Orange Free State and Cape Province
- ____ *P. m. psammophila* — SW Namibia to w Cape Province
- ____ *P. m. exultans* — South Africa (Lesotho, adjacent ne Cape Province and w Natal)

☐ **Drakensberg Prinia** *Prinia hypoxantha*

Transvaal to Natal, Lesotho and e Cape Province

☐ **Namaqua Prinia** *Prinia substriata*
- ____ *P. s. confinis* — S Namibia (arid lower Orange River)
- ____ *P. s. substriata* — Orange Free State, Karoo and s Little Namaqualand

☐ **Sao Tome Prinia** *Prinia molleri*

São Tomé (Gulf of Guinea)

☐ **Roberts' Prinia** *Prinia robertsi*

Highland forests of e Zimbabwe and adjacent sw Mozambique

☐ **Sierra Leone Prinia** *Prinia leontica*

Montane ravines of e Sierra Leone, s Guinea and sw Ivory Coast

☐ **White-chinned Prinia** *Prinia leucopogon*
- ____ *P. l. leucopogon* — E Nigeria to middle Ubangi River and w side of Lake Tanganyika
- ____ *P. l. reichenowi* — Zaire to Uganda, Rwanda, Burundi, Kenya and Tanzania

☐ **Banded Prinia** *Prinia bairdii*
- ____ *P. b. bairdii* — SE Nigeria to Cabinda, ne Zaire and w Uganda
- ____ *P. b. heinrichi* — NW Angola (Cuanza Norte)
- ____ *P. b. obscura* — Highlands of e Zaire to w Uganda, Rwanda and Burundi
- ____ *P. b. melanops* — Kenya (west of Rift Valley)

☐ **Red-winged Prinia** *Prinia erythroptera*
- ____ *P. e. erythroptera* — Senegal to s Mali and n Cameroon
- ____ *P. e. jodoptera* — Central and s Cameroon to s Sudan
- ____ *P. e. major* — Ethiopia
- ____ *P. e. rhodoptera* — Kenya to Mozambique

☐ **Rufous-eared Warbler** *Malcorus pectoralis*
- ____ *M. p. etoshae* — N Namibia (Etosha Pan to n Damaraland)
- ____ *M. p. ocularius* — Namibia to Botswana, sw Transvaal and n Cape Province
- ____ *M. p. pectoralis* — South Africa (w Cape Province to sw Orange Free State)

☐ **Red-winged Gray Warbler** *Drymocichla incana*

E Nigeria and Cameroon to se Sudan and nw Uganda

☐ **Green Longtail** *Urolais epichlora*
- ____ *U. e. epichlora* — Montane forests of Nigeria (Obudu Plateau) and sw Cameroon
- ____ *U. e. cinderella* — S Cameroon (Mt. Oku to Bamenda highlands)
- ____ *U. e. mariae* — Bioko (Gulf of Guinea)

☐ **Cricket Longtail** *Spiloptila clamans*

Mauritania and Senegal to Mali, central Sudan and n Ethiopia

☐ **Black-collared Apalis** *Apalis pulchra*

____	*A. p. pulchra*	Mts. of se Nigeria and Cameroon; se Sudan to Uganda and Kenya
____	*A. p. murphyi*	Extreme e Zaire (Marungu Plateau)

☐ **Ruwenzori Apalis** *Apalis ruwenzori*

Montane forests of e Zaire, sw Uganda, Rwanda and Burundi

☐ **Bar-throated Apalis** *Apalis thoracica*

____	*A. t. fuscigularis*	SE Kenya (Taita Hills)
____	*A. t. griseiceps (iringae)*	SE Kenya (Chyulu Hills) and highlands of Tanzania
____	*A. t. pareensis*	N Tanzania (South Pare Mountains)
____	*A. t. uluguru*	NE Tanzania (Uluguru Mountains)
____	*A. t. murina*	NE Tanzania to n Malawi and adjacent Zambia
____	*A. t. youngi*	SW Tanzania to ne Malawi and adjacent Zambia
____	*A. t. whitei*	E Zambia to s Malawi and adjacent Mozambique (Zobue)
____	*A. t. flavigularis*	SE Malawi (e of Nyasa-Shire Rift) and adjacent Mozambique
____	*A. t. quarta*	NE Zimbabwe (Mt. Nyangani) and Mozambique (Mt. Gorongoza)
____	*A. t. arnoldi*	E Zimbabwe and adjacent Mozambique
____	*A. t. lynesi*	N Mozambique (Mt. Namuli)
____	*A. t. rhodesiae*	Zimbabwe plateau and ne Botswana
____	*A. t. flaviventris*	SE Botswana to n and w Transvaal
____	*A. t. spelonkensis*	E and n Transvaal
____	*A. t. lebomboensis*	NE Zululand (Lebombo Mts.) to e Swaziland and s Mozambique
____	*A. t. venusta (darglensis)*	Zululand to Natal, e Griqualand and Great Kei River
____	*A. t. drakensbergensis*	South Africa (Drakensberg Mountains to w Swaziland)
____	*A. t. thoracica*	SE Cape Province (Great Kei and Gamtoos River to Umtata)
____	*A. t. claudei*	S Cape Province (Knysna to Humansdorp and Beaufort West)
____	*A. t. capensis*	S and sw Cape Province (Paarl to Oudtshoorn and Mossel Bay)
____	*A. t. grisopyga*	Coastal w Cape Province (Lamberts Bay to Cape Town)

☐ **Black-capped Apalis** *Apalis nigriceps*

____	*A. n. nigriceps*	Sierra Leone to Gabon and Central African Republic; Bioko
____	*A. n. collaris*	E Zaire to sw Uganda

☐ **Black-throated Apalis** *Apalis jacksoni*

____	*A. j. bambuluensis*	Highlands of Nigeria and Cameroon
____	*A. j. minor (albimentalis)*	Lowlands of Cameroon and Zaire
____	*A. j. jacksoni*	Zaire to Angola, Sudan, Uganda and Kenya

☐ **White-winged Apalis** *Apalis chariessa*

____	*A. c. macphersoni*	Montane forests of se Kenya to n Mozambique
____	*A. c. chariessa*	Kenya (lower Tana River)

☐ **Masked Apalis** *Apalis binotata*

SW Cameroon to ne Gabon, e Zaire, e Uganda and nw Tanzania

☐ **Black-faced Apalis** *Apalis personata*

____	*A. p. personata*	Montane forests of e Zaire, w Uganda, Rwanda and Burundi
____	*A. p. marungensis*	SE Zaire (Marungu Plateau)

☐ **Yellow-breasted Apalis** *Apalis flavida*

____	*A. f. caniceps*	Gambia to n Angola and w Kenya
____	*A. f. flavocincta (malensis)*	SE Sudan to n Uganda, s Ethiopia, Somalia, Kenya, ne Tanzania
____	*A. f. viridiceps*	N Somalia, adjacent Ethiopia and n Kenya
____	*A. f. abyssinica*	Highlands of sw Ethiopia
____	*A. f. pugnax*	Highlands of s Kenya
____	*A. f. golzi*	SE Kenya (Taita Hills) to interior Tanzania and Rwanda
____	*A. f. flavida*	W Angola to n Namibia, n Botswana and sw Zambia
____	*A. f. neglecta (renata, lucidigula, niassae, tenerrima)*	E Angola to se Kenya, Tanzania, Mozambique and n Natal
____	*A. f. florisuga*	Central Natal to South Africa

☐ **Rudd's Apalis** *Apalis ruddi*

_____ *A. r. caniviridis* — S Malawi

_____ *A. r. ruddi* — Coastal Mozambique (Save River to lower Incomati River)

_____ *A. r. fumosa* — Mozambique (Maputo District) to coastal Natal

☐ **Sharpe's Apalis** *Apalis sharpii*

Humid forests of Sierra Leone, Ivory Coast and Ghana

☐ **Buff-throated Apalis** *Apalis rufogularis*

_____ *A. r. sanderi* — SW Nigeria (Lagos to Ife and Niger River)

_____ *A. r. rufogularis* — E Nigeria to Cameroon, Gabon and Central African Rep.; Bioko

_____ *A. r. angolensis* — NW Angola

_____ *A. r. brauni* — W Angola (Cuanza Sul escarpment)

_____ *A. r. argentea (eidos)* — E Zaire to Rwanda, Burundi and w Tanzania

_____ *A. r. nigrescens* — SW Sudan to Zaire, Zambia, ne Angola, Uganda and nw Tanzania

_____ *A. r. kigezi* — SW Uganda (Bwindi-Impenetrable Forest)

☐ **Bamenda Apalis** *Apalis bamendae*

Montane forests of w Cameroon and Adamawa Plateau

☐ **Gosling's Apalis** *Apalis goslingi*

Montane forests of s Cameroon to Gabon, ne Angola and Zaire

☐ **Chestnut-throated Apalis** *Apalis porphyrolaema*

_____ *A. p. kaboboensis* — Montane forests of e Zaire (Mt. Kabobo)

_____ *A. p. affinis* — Mountains of sw Uganda

_____ *A. p. porphyrolaema* — Montane forests of Kenya to n Tanzania

☐ **Chapin's Apalis** *Apalis chapini*

_____ *A. c. strausae* — SW Tanzania to ne Zambia and w Malawi

_____ *A. c. chapini* — Montane forests of e Tanzania (Uluguru Mountains)

☐ **Black-headed Apalis** *Apalis melanocephala*

_____ *A. m. melanocephala* — S Somalia to coastal Kenya and coastal ne Tanzania

_____ *A. m. nigrodorsalis* — Highlands of Kenya

_____ *A. m. moschi* — S Kenya (Taita Hills) and highlands of e Tanzania

_____ *A. m. muhuluensis* — SE Tanzania (Mahenge and Songea)

_____ *A. m. adjacens* — SE Malawi

_____ *A. m. fuliginosa* — SE Malawi (Mulanje and Thyolo mountains)

_____ *A. m. lightoni* — W Mozambique to se Zimbabwe

_____ *A. m. tenebricosa* — N Mozambique (Njesi Plateau, Mt. Chiperoni and Mt. Namuli)

_____ *A. m. addenda* — S Mozambique

☐ **Chirinda Apalis** *Apalis chirindensis*

_____ *A. c. vumbae* — Zimbabwe (Nyanga Highlands to Bvumba Mountains)

_____ *A. c. chirindensis* — W-central Mozambique (Mt. Gorongoza) and adj. e Zimbabwe

☐ **Gray Apalis** *Apalis cinerea*

_____ *A. c. funebris* — Montane forests of Nigeria and Cameroon

_____ *A. c. sclateri* — Mt. Cameroon; Bioko (Gulf of Guinea)

_____ *A. c. grandis* — W Angola

_____ *A. c. cinerea* — Zaire to s Sudan, ne Uganda, Rwanda, Kenya and nw Tanzania

☐ **Brown-headed Apalis** *Apalis alticola*

_____ *A. a. alticola* — SW Kenya to Tanzania, n Malawi, s Zaire and n Zambia

_____ *A. a. dowsetti* — S Zaire (Marungu Plateau)

☐ **Karamoja Apalis** *Apalis karamojae*

_____ *A. k. karamojae* — Mountains of n Uganda

_____ *A. k. stronachi* — Highlands of ne Tanzania (Nzega district)

☐ **Red-faced Apalis** *Apalis rufifrons*

____	*A. r. rufifrons*	Chad to n Sudan, ne Ethiopia, Djibouti and nw Somalia
____	*A. r. smithi*	S Sudan to se Ethiopia, Somalia, Uganda, Kenya and Tanzania
____	*A. r. rufidorsalis*	SE Kenya (Tsavo)

☐ **Oriole Warbler** *Hypergerus atriceps*

Gallery forests and palms of Senegal to Central African Republic

☐ **Gray-capped Warbler** *Eminia lepida*

SE Sudan to n Zaire, Rwanda, Burundi, Uganda, Kenya, Tanzania

☐ **Green-backed Camaroptera** *Camaroptera brachyura*

____	*C. b. brevicaudata*	Senegal and Sierra Leone to c Sudan and lowlands of Ethiopia
____	*C. b. tincta*	Liberia to w Kenya, nw Angola, nw Zambia and w Tanzania
____	*C. b. abessinica*	S Sudan to ne Zaire, Ethiopia, n Uganda, n Kenya and w Somalia
____	*C. b. insulata*	Ethiopia (Ghere region and Kaffa Province)
____	*C. b. erlangeri (albiventris)*	S Somalia to coastal Kenya and ne Tanzania
____	*C. b. aschani*	Highlands of Kenya to extreme sw Uganda and e Zaire (Kivu)
____	*C. b. griseigula*	W Kenya to e Uganda and n Tanzania
____	*C. b. pileata*	S Kenya to se Tanzania; Mafia I. and Zanzibar
____	*C. b. fugglescouchmani*	E Tanzania to Zambia and Malawi
____	*C. b. bororensis*	S Tanzania to s Malawi and n Mozambique
____	*C. b. harterti*	Escarpment of se Gabon and nw Angola
____	*C. b. intercalata*	S Zaire (Shaba) to w Tanzania, e Angola and e Zambia
____	*C. b. sharpei (noomei)*	S Angola to Namibia, Zambia, Malawi, Zimbabwe, w Transvaal
____	*C. b. transitiva*	SE Botswana to Zimbabwe
____	*C. b. beirensis (marleyi)*	Mozambique (n of Save River) to e Zimbabwe and ne Zululand
____	*C. b. brachyura*	Natal and w Zululand to South Africa
____	*C. b. constans*	E Zululand to e Swaziland, Transvaal, se Zimbabwe, Mozambique

☐ **Yellow-browed Camaroptera** *Camaroptera superciliaris*

Guinea and Sierra Leone to Zaire, Uganda and nw Angola

☐ **Olive-green Camaroptera** *Camaroptera chloronota*

____	*C. c. kelsalli*	Senegal to Ghana
____	*C. c. chloronota*	Togo to s Cameroon, Gabon and Congo
____	*C. c. granti*	Bioko (Gulf of Guinea)
____	*C. c. toroensis*	Central African Rep. to sw Sudan, Uganda, w Kenya and Tanzania
____	*C. c. kamitugaensis*	E Zaire (Itombwe region)

☐ **Miombo Camaroptera** *Calamonastes undosus*

____	*C. u. cinereus*	Congo to w Zaire, Angola and nw Zambia
____	*C. u. katangae*	S Zaire (Shaba) to n Zambia
____	*C. u. huilae*	W-central Angola
____	*C. u. stierlingi (buttoni, neglectus)*	SE Angola to ne Namibia, s Zambia, e Tanzania and Mozambique
____	*C. u. undosus*	Kenya to Rwanda and Tanzania
____	*C. u. olivascens*	S coastal Tanzania to Malawi and coastal Mozambique
____	*C. u. irwini*	Extreme e Zambia to Botswana, Zimbabwe and Mozambique
____	*C. u. pintoi*	Transvaal to Swaziland, Natal and Zululand

☐ **Gray Wren-Warbler** *Calamonastes simplex*

SE Sudan to Ethiopia, Somalia, Kenya, ne Uganda, ne Tanzania

☐ **Barred Camaroptera** *Calamonastes fasciolatus*

____	*C. f. pallidior*	SW Angola
____	*C. f. fasciolatus*	Central Namibia to Botswana, Zimbabwe and n Cape Province
____	*C. f. europhilus*	SE Botswana to Zimbabwe (s Matabeleland) and Transvaal

☐ **Kopje Warbler** *Euryptila subcinnamomea*

____	*E. s. petrophila*	Namibia and extreme nw Cape Province
____	*E. s. subcinnamomea*	South Africa (Cape Province)

FAMILY: SYLVIIDAE (Old World Warblers—279)

☐ **Chestnut-headed Tesia** *Tesia castaneocoronata*

_____ *T. c. castaneocoronata*	E Himalayas to Bangladesh, n Myanmar, s Tibet and nw Thailand
_____ *T. c. ripleyi*	SE Tibet to sw China (Sichuan and Yunnan)
_____ *T. c. abadiei*	N Vietnam (nw Tonkin)

☐ **Javan Tesia** *Tesia superciliaris*

Montane forests of Java

☐ **Slaty-bellied Tesia** *Tesia olivea*

NE India to s China, Myanmar, nw Thailand, n Laos and Tonkin

☐ **Gray-bellied Tesia** *Tesia cyaniventer*

Nepal to s China (w Yunnan and Guangxi), SE Asia and Java

☐ **Russet-capped Tesia** *Tesia everetti*

_____ *T. e. sumbawana*	Sumbawa (w Lesser Sundas)
_____ *T. e. everetti*	Flores (w Lesser Sundas)

☐ **Timor Stubtail** *Urosphena subulata*

_____ *U. s. subulata*	E Lesser Sundas (Timor and Wetar)
_____ *U. s. advena*	Babar (e Lesser Sundas)

☐ **Bornean Stubtail** *Urosphena whiteheadi*

Mountains of n Borneo (Kinabalu to Liang Kubung)

☐ **Asian Stubtail** *Urosphena squameiceps*

Breeds ne Asia; winters to SE Asia and Taiwan

☐ **Manchurian Bush-Warbler** *Cettia canturians*

E Siberia to Manchuria, China and Korea; winters to s China

☐ **Pale-footed Bush-Warbler** *Cettia pallidipes*

_____ *C. p. pallidipes*	Himalayan foothills to n Myanmar
_____ *C. p. laurentei*	S China; winters to nw Thailand, n Laos and n Vietnam
_____ *C. p. osmastoni*	Andaman Islands

☐ **Japanese Bush-Warbler** *Cettia diphone*

_____ *C. d. borealis*	Manchuria to Korea and s China; winters to Taiwan
_____ *C. d. viridis*	S Sakhalin and s Kuril Islands; winters to se China
_____ *C. d. cantans*	Main Japanese islands south to Cheju-Do Islands
_____ *C. d. riukiuensis*	Ryukyu Islands
_____ *C. d. restricta*	Daito Islands
_____ *C. d. diphone*	S Izu Islands, Bonin Islands and Volcano Islands

☐ **Philippine Bush-Warbler** *Cettia seebohmi*

Montane forests of n Luzon (n Philippines)

☐ **Palau Bush-Warbler** *Cettia annae*

Palau Islands (Babelthaup, Koror, Garakayo, Peleliu and Ngabad)

☐ **Shade Warbler** *Cettia parens*

Montane forests of San Cristóbal I. (s Solomon Islands)

☐ **Fiji Bush-Warbler** *Cettia ruficapilla*

_____ *C. r. ruficapilla*	Kandavu (Fiji Islands)
_____ *C. r. badiceps*	Viti Levu (Fiji Islands)
_____ *C. r. castaneoptera*	Vanua Levu (Fiji Islands)
_____ *C. r. funebris*	Taveuni (Fiji Islands)

☐ **Tanimbar Bush-Warbler** *Cettia carolinae*

Yamdena (Tanimbar Islands)

☐ **Brownish-flanked Bush-Warbler** *Cettia fortipes*

_____ *C. f. pallida*	NE Himalayas (Kashmir to w Nepal)
_____ *C. f. fortipes*	Himalayas of e Nepal to Bhutan, se Tibet, ne India and Myanmar
_____ *C. f. davidiana*	Mountains of s China to n Laos and n Vietnam
_____ *C. f. robustipes*	Mountains of Taiwan

☐ **Sunda Bush-Warbler** *Cettia vulcania*

_____ C. v. sepiaria	Mountains of n Sumatra
_____ C. v. flaviventris	Mountains of central and s Sumatra
_____ C. v. vulcania	Java, Bali, Lombok and Sumbawa
_____ C. v. oreophila	N Borneo (Mt. Kinabalu)
_____ C. v. banksi	Mountains of n Borneo (Sabah and Sarawak)
_____ C. v. palawana	Mountains of Palawan (sw Philippines)
_____ C. v. everetti	Timor (e Lesser Sundas)

☐ **Chestnut-crowned Bush-Warbler** *Cettia major*

_____ C. m. major	Himalayas of Nepal to ne India, se Tibet, Myanmar and sw China
_____ C. m. vafer	NE India (Meghalaya and Cachar hills of Assam)

☐ **Aberrant Bush-Warbler** *Cettia flavolivacea*

_____ C. f. flavolivacea	Himalayas of Garhwal to Nepal, Arunachal Pradesh and se Tibet
_____ C. f. intricata	NE Myanmar to nw Thailand and sw China (s Shanxi, e Sichuan)
_____ C. f. dulcivox	S China (s Sichuan to s Yunnan)
_____ C. f. stresemanni	NE India (Garo and Khasi hills of Assam)
_____ C. f. weberi	W Myanmar (Chin Hills)
_____ C. f. alexanderi	Extreme ne India (Manipur) and adjacent Myanmar
_____ C. f. oblita	N Laos and n Vietnam

☐ **Yellowish-bellied Bush-Warbler** *Cettia acanthizoides*

_____ C. a. acanthizoides	Himalayas of n India to s Tibet, s China and e Myanmar
_____ C. a. brunnescens	SE Tibet (Tsangpo Valley)
_____ C. a. concolor	Mountains of Taiwan

☐ **Gray-sided Bush-Warbler** *Cettia brunnifrons*

_____ C. b. whistleri	NW Himalayas (Kashmir to Garhwal)
_____ C. b. brunnifrons	E Himalayas (Garhwal to Nepal, Sikkim, Bhutan and se Tibet)
_____ C. b. muroides	S Tibet to s China (Sichuan and Yunnan west of Mekong River)
_____ C. b. umbratica	N Myanmar to extreme ne India (Assam) and sw China

☐ **Cetti's Warbler** *Cettia cetti*

_____ C. c. cetti	S Europe to Asia Minor and North Africa
_____ C. c. orientalis	Turkey to Crimea, n Iran (Zagros Mts.) and n Afghanistan
_____ C. c. albiventris	Iran to Kazakstan, Afghanistan, Pakistan and w Xinjiang

☐ **African Bush-Warbler** *Bradypterus baboecala*

_____ B. b. centralis	Nigeria to s Cameroon, ne Zaire, Burundi, Rwanda, sw Uganda
_____ B. b. chadensis	W Chad
_____ B. b. sudanensis	S Sudan
_____ B. b. abyssinicus	Ethiopia
_____ B. b. elgonensis	Highlands of w and central Kenya and se Uganda
_____ B. b. tongensis (moreaui)	SE Kenya to Tanzania, Zambia, Malawi, Mozambique and Natal
_____ B. b. benguellensis	W Angola
_____ B. b. msiri (bedfordi)	E Angola to Zambia, se Zaire (Shaba) and ne Botswana
_____ B. b. transvaalensis	C Zimbabwe to w Swaziland, Transvaal, Lesotho and w Natal
_____ B. b. baboecala	S South Africa (east to Great Kei River)

☐ **Ja River Scrub-Warbler** *Bradypterus grandis*

	Swamps and reedbeds of s Cameroon and Gabon

☐ **White-winged Scrub-Warbler** *Bradypterus carpalis*

	Lowland papyrus swamps of ne Zaire, Uganda and Rwanda

☐ **Grauer's Scrub-Warbler** *Bradypterus graueri*

	Highland papyrus swamps of e Zaire and adjacent Rwanda

☐ **Bamboo Scrub-Warbler** *Bradypterus alfredi*

_____ B. a. alfredi	W Ethiopia to w Uganda and w Zaire
_____ B. a. kungwensis	W Tanzania and nw Zambia

☐ **Knysna Scrub-Warbler** *Bradypterus sylvaticus*

_____ *B. s. pondoensis* — Coastal scrub of e Cape Province (Natal to Transkei)

_____ *B. s. sylvaticus* — South Africa (Cape Peninsula to Port Elizabeth)

☐ **Cameroon Scrub-Warbler** *Bradypterus lopezi*

_____ *B. l. camerunensis* — Mt. Cameroon

_____ *B. l. lopezi* — Bioko (Gulf of Guinea)

_____ *B. l. barakae* — Zaire, Rwanda and sw Uganda

_____ *B. l. boultoni* — Angola

_____ *B. l. mariae* — Kenya to ne Tanzania

_____ *B. l. usambarae* — S Kenya (Taita Hills) to sw Tanzania, n Malawi, n Mozambique

_____ *B. l. ufipae* — SW Tanzania to se Zaire and n Zambia

_____ *B. l. granti* — Malawi (south of Nyika) to n Mozambique (Mt. Chiperone)

☐ **African Scrub-Warbler** *Bradypterus barratti*

_____ *B. b. priesti* — E Zimbabwe and adjacent s Mozambique

_____ *B. b. barratti* — SW Mozambique to e Transvaal, Swaziland, n Zululand, n Natal

_____ *B. b. cathkinensis* — Drakensberg Mts. (e Griqualand to Natal/Transvaal border)

_____ *B. b. godfreyi (wilsoni)* — Natal and Cape Province

☐ **Bangwa Scrub-Warbler** *Bradypterus bangwaensis*

E Nigeria (Obudu Plateau) and adjacent s Cameroon

☐ **Cinnamon Bracken-Warbler** *Bradypterus cinnamomeus*

_____ *B. c. cinnamomeus* — Ethiopia to Kenya, Uganda, Burundi, Rwanda and n Tanzania

_____ *B. c. cavei* — SE Sudan

_____ *B. c. mildbreadi* — Ruwenzori Mountains (Zaire/Uganda border)

_____ *B. c. nyassae* — N Tanzania to se Zaire, ne Zambia and Malawi

☐ **Victorin's Scrub-Warbler** *Bradypterus victorini*

Mountains of South Africa (s Cape Province)

☐ **Spotted Bush-Warbler** *Bradypterus thoracicus*

_____ *B. t. suschkini* — N Altai Mountains to sw Transbaikalia and ne Baikal

_____ *B. t. davidi* — SE Transbaikalia and w Amurland to Manchuria and n Liaoning

_____ *B. t. kashmirensis* — NW Himalayas (Kashmir to Kumaon)

_____ *B. t. thoracicus* — W Himalayas (Nepal to Assam), se Tibet and sw China

_____ *B. t. przewalskii* — Mountains of w China to se Tibet and n Myanmar

_____ *B. t. shanensis* — Mountains of n Myanmar; winters to lowlands of Thailand

☐ **Long-billed Bush-Warbler** *Bradypterus major*

_____ *B. m. major* — Mountains of Uzbekistan and Xinjiang to w Himalayas (Kashmir)

_____ *B. m. innae* — Extreme w China (Kunlun Shan Mountains)

☐ **Chinese Bush-Warbler** *Bradypterus tacsanowskius*

E Siberia to se Tibet and s China; winters to n Indochina

☐ **Russet Bush-Warbler** *Bradypterus seebohmi*

_____ *B. s. idoneus* — SE Tibet to n Thailand and s Vietnam

_____ *B. s. melanorhynchus* — Mountains of se China (n Guangdong, nw Fujian and Taiwan)

_____ *B. s. seebohmi* — Mountains of n Luzon (n Philippines)

_____ *B. s. montis* — Mountains of e Java

_____ *B. s. timoriensis* — Mountains of Timor (e Lesser Sundas)

☐ **Brown Bush-Warbler** *Bradypterus luteoventris*

_____ *B. l. luteoventris* — Himalayas of e Nepal to ne India (Assam), se Tibet and sw China

_____ *B. l. ticehursti* — S Myanmar and n Thailand

☐ **Ceylon Bush-Warbler** *Bradypterus palliseri*

Dwarf bamboo montane forests of Sri Lanka

☐ **Friendly Bush-Warbler** *Bradypterus accentor*

Montane forests of n Borneo (Mt. Kinabalu and Mt. Trus Madi)

☐ **Long-tailed Bush-Warbler** *Bradypterus caudatus*
_____ *B. c. caudatus* — Mountains of n Luzon (n Philippines)
_____ *B. c. malindangensis* — Mt. Malindang on nw Mindanao (s Philippines)
_____ *B. c. unicolor* — Mt. Apo on s-central Mindanao (s Philippines)

☐ **Chestnut-backed Bush-Warbler** *Bradypterus castaneus*
_____ *B. c. castaneus* — Mountains of Sulawesi
_____ *B. c. disturbans* — Buru (s Moluccas)
_____ *B. c. musculus* — Seram (s Moluccas)

☐ **Brown Emu-tail** *Dromaeocercus brunneus* — Humid rainforests of e Madagascar

☐ **Gray Emu-tail** *Dromaeocercus seebohmi* — Humid grassy swamps of e Madagascar

☐ **Black-capped Rufous-Warbler** *Bathmocercus cerviniventris* — Sierra Leone to se Guinea, Liberia, Ivory Coast and Ghana

☐ **Black-faced Rufous-Warbler** *Bathmocercus rufus*
_____ *B. r. rufus* — S Cameroon to Gabon and Central African Republic
_____ *B. r. vulpinus (jacksoni)* — E Zaire to extreme s Sudan, Uganda, Kenya and Tanzania

☐ **Mrs. Moreau's Warbler** *Sceptomycter winifredae* — Montane forests of e Tanzania (Uluguru Mountains)

☐ **Aldabra Brush-Warbler** *Nesillas aldabrana* — Formerly Aldabra (Comoro Islands). Possibly extinct

☐ **Anjouan Brush-Warbler** *Nesillas longicaudata* — Forest undergrowth of Anjouan (Comoro Islands)

☐ **Madagascar Brush-Warbler** *Nesillas typica*
_____ *N. t. moheliensis* — Mohéli (Comoro Islands)
_____ *N. t. obscura* — NW Madagascar
_____ *N. t. typica* — Central and e Madagascar
_____ *N. t. lantzi* — Subdesert of sw Madagascar

☐ **Grand Comoro Brush-Warbler** *Nesillas brevicaudata* — Forest undergrowth of Grand Comoro I.

☐ **Moheli Brush-Warbler** *Nesillas mariae* — Forests of Mohéli (Comoro Islands)

☐ **Thamnornis** *Thamnornis chloropetoides* — Subdesert of sw Madagascar

☐ **Moustached Grass-Warbler** *Melocichla mentalis*
_____ *M. m. mentalis* — Senegambia to Gabon, s Zaire, Angola, Zambia and n Malawi
_____ *M. m. amaurourus (atricauca, chyulu, granviki)* — S Sudan to sw Ethiopia, Kenya, Tanzania and Zambia
_____ *M. m. orientalis* — E Kenya to s Tanzania, s Malawi, Zambia, Zimbabwe, Mozambique
_____ *M. m. incanus* — NE Tanzania (Mt. Meru)
_____ *M. m. luangwae* — Zambia

☐ **Damara Rock-jumper** *Achaetops pycnopygius* — Rocky regions of sw Angola and n Namibia

☐ **Cape Grassbird** *Sphenoeacus afer*
_____ *S. a. excisus* — E Zimbabwe and adjacent sw Mozambique
_____ *S. a. natalensis* — Kwazulu-Natal to w Swaziland, n Lesotho and Transvaal
_____ *S. a. intermedius* — Lesotho to Transkei and Port Elizabeth
_____ *S. a. afer* — SW Cape Province

☐ **Lanceolated Warbler** *Locustella lanceolata* — E Palearctic; winters to s Asia, Greater Sundas and Philippines

☐ **Grasshopper Warbler** *Locustella naevia*
_____ *L. n. naevia* — Europe to e Russia and Crimea Pen.; winters to n and w Africa
_____ *L. n. obscurior* — Caucasus to Georgia and n Armenia; winters to ne Africa
_____ *L. n. straminea* — W Siberia to w China (Tien Shan Mountains of w Xinjiang)
_____ *L. n. mongolica* — Kazakstan to Afghanistan and w Mongolia; winters to n India

☐ **Pallas' Warbler** *Locustella certhiola*
_____ *L. c. rubescens*   N Siberia to Sea of Okhotsk and Kamchatka; winters to s India
_____ *L. c. sparsimstriata*   S Siberia to n Altai Mts., Sayan Mts. and Transbaicalia
_____ *L. c. certhiola (minor)*   S Siberia to Manchuria and Sea of Japan; winters to India
_____ *L. c. centralasiae*   SE Siberia to ne China; winters to Andaman and Nicobar is.

☐ **Middendorff's Warbler** *Locustella ochotensis*
_____ *L. o. subcerthiola*   Kamchatka Peninsula and n Kuril Islands; winters to Philippines
_____ *L. o. ochotensis*   E Siberia to n Japan; winters to Philippines, Borneo and Sulawesi

☐ **Pleske's Warbler** *Locustella pleskei*
E Siberia to Korea, Kyushu and Izu Islands; winters in s China

☐ **Eurasian River Warbler** *Locustella fluviatilis*
Central and e Europe to w Siberia; winters in e Africa

☐ **Savi's Warbler** *Locustella luscinioides*
_____ *L. l. luscinioides*   Central and e Europe to Iberian Pen. and N Africa; winters to Sudan
_____ *L. l. sarmatica*   Ukraine and Sea of Azov to Volga and s Urals; winters ne Africa
_____ *L. l. fusca*   Turkey and Jordan to central Asia; winters to Sudan and Ethiopia

☐ **Gray's Warbler** *Locustella fasciolata*
NE Asia; winters to Philippines, East Indies and w New Guinea

☐ **Sakhalin Warbler** *Locustella amnicola*
Sakhalin, s Kuril Islands and Hokkaido; winters in Philippines

☐ **Moustached Warbler** *Acrocephalus melanopogon*
_____ *A. m. melanopogon*   Mediterranean basin (Europe and North Africa)
_____ *A. m. mimica*   W Turkey to s Russia, Iraq, Iran and Afghanistan
_____ *A. m. albiventris*   Russia (e coast of Sea of Azov to lower Don River)

☐ **Aquatic Warbler** *Acrocephalus paludicola*
Mainly open marshes of w Palearctic; winters in Africa

☐ **Sedge Warbler** *Acrocephalus schoenobaenus*
Palearctic region; winters to s Africa

☐ **Streaked Reed-Warbler** *Acrocephalus sorghophilus*
Breeds ne China (Liaoning to Hubei); winters in Philippines

☐ **Black-browed Reed-Warbler** *Acrocephalus bistrigiceps*
_____ *A. b. bistrigiceps*   E Siberia to n China and n Manchuria; winters to s Asia
_____ *A. b. tangorum*   N Manchuria; winters to s China and Thailand

☐ **Paddyfield Warbler** *Acrocephalus agricola*
_____ *A. a. septima*   S Ukraine and w Kazakstan; winters to se Iran and w India
_____ *A. a. capistrata (brevipennis)*   SW Siberia to Kazakstan, Mongolia, Afghanistan and ne Iran
_____ *A. a. agricola*   Breeding range unknown; winters in Indian subcontinent

☐ **Blunt-winged Warbler** *Acrocephalus concinens*
_____ *A. c. haringtoni*   Mountains of n Afghanistan to nw India (Kashmir) and Pakistan
_____ *A. c. stevensi*   Plains of Brahmaputra River (Assam) and adjacent Myanmar
_____ *A. c. concinens*   N and central China; winters to s Myanmar and s Thailand

☐ **Eurasian Reed-Warbler** *Acrocephalus scirpaceus*
_____ *A. s. scirpaceus*   NW Africa and Europe east to Crimea and Volga River
_____ *A. s. fuscus*   E Mediterranean and Caspian to Kazakstan; winters to s Africa

☐ **African Reed-Warbler** *Acrocephalus baeticatus*
_____ *A. b. guiersi*   N Senegal
_____ *A. b. cinnamomeus (fraterculus, hopsoni)*   Senegal to s Sudan, Ethiopia and Somalia south to Mozambique
_____ *A. b. hallae*   SW Angola to Namibia, sw Botswana, sw Zambia and Malawi
_____ *A. b. avicenniae*   Mangroves of coastal Sudan, Eritrea, Somalia and w Arabia
_____ *A. b. suahelicus*   Coastal Tanzania to Mozambique and Natal
_____ *A. b. baeticatus*   N Botswana to Transvaal, Natal, e and s Cape Province

☐ **Blyth's Reed-Warbler** *Acrocephalus dumetorum*

E Palearctic; winters in India and Sri Lanka

☐ **Marsh Warbler** *Acrocephalus palustris*

Europe to central Russia; winters to coastal se Africa (Natal)

☐ **Great Reed-Warbler** *Acrocephalus arundinaceus*
___ *A. a. arundinaceus*
___ *A. a. zarudnyi*

Europe to w Siberia, Turkey, n Iran and nw Africa; winters Africa
N Iraq and Iran to s Afghanistan, Altai, nw Mongolia and w China

☐ **Oriental Reed-Warbler** *Acrocephalus orientalis*

SE Siberia to n China; winters s Asia, Indonesia and Philippines

☐ **Clamorous Reed-Warbler** *Acrocephalus stentoreus*
___ *A. s. stentoreus*
___ *A. s. brunnescens*
___ *A. s. amyae*
___ *A. s. meridionalis*
___ *A. s. harterti*
___ *A. s. celebensis*
___ *A. s. siebersi*
___ *A. s. lentecaptus*
___ *A. s. sumbae*

Egypt to Sinai Peninsula, Levant and Jordan
Arabia and Iran to Mongolia and India; winters to India
Plains of Brahmaputra River (Assam) to Myanmar and sw China
Sri Lanka
Philippines (Luzon, Mindoro, Leyte, Bohol and Mindanao)
S Sulawesi
W Java
SE Borneo, Java and w Lesser Sundas (Lombok and Sumbawa)
Buru I. (s Moluccas) and e Lesser Sundas (Sumba and Timor)

☐ **Large-billed Reed-Warbler** *Acrocephalus orinus*

Known from a 1905 specimen from n India (Himachal Pradesh)

☐ **Basra Reed-Warbler** *Acrocephalus griseldis*

S Iraq (Tigris and Euphrates valleys); winters Kenya to Malawi

☐ **Australian Reed-Warbler** *Acrocephalus australis*
___ *A. a. toxopei*
___ *A. a. carterae*
___ *A. a. australis*
___ *A. a. gouldi*

New Guinea, Bismarck Archipelago and Solomon Islands
NW Australia
E Australia (s Queensland to Victoria and Tasmania)
SW Australia

☐ **Nightingale Reed-Warbler** *Acrocephalus luscinia*
___ *A. l. luscinia*
___ *A. l. yamashinae*
___ *A. l. nijoi*

Mariana Islands (Guam, Agrihan, Alamagan and Saipan)
Pagan (n Mariana Islands)
Aguijan (n Mariana Islands)

☐ **Caroline Reed-Warbler** *Acrocephalus syrinx*

Caroline Is. (Woleai, Lamotrek, Truk, Pohnpei, Nukuoro, Kosrae)

☐ **Nauru Reed-Warbler** *Acrocephalus rehsei*

Nauru I. (Melanesia)

☐ **Millerbird** *Acrocephalus familiaris*
___ *A. f. kingi*
___ *A. f. familiaris†*

Nihoa (w Hawaiian Islands)
Laysan (w Hawaiian Islands). Extirpated ca 1923

☐ **Christmas Island Warbler** *Acrocephalus aequinoctialis*
___ *A. a. aequinoctialis*
___ *A. a. pistor*

Kiritimati (n Line Islands in central Pacific)
N Line Islands (Teraina and Tabuaeran)

☐ **Tahiti Reed-Warbler** *Acrocephalus caffer*
___ *A. c. caffer*
___ *A. c. garretti*
___ *A. c. longirostris*

Tahiti (Society Islands)
Huahine (Society Islands). Possibly extinct
Moorea (Society Islands).

☐ **Tuamotu Reed-Warbler** *Acrocephalus atyphus*
___ *A. a. atyphus*
___ *A. a. ravus*
___ *A. a. palmarum*
___ *A. a. niauensis*
___ *A. a. eremus*
___ *A. a. flavidus*

Islands in nw Tuamotu Archipelago
Islands in se Tuamotu Archipelago
Anaa I. (Tuamotu Archipelago)
Niau I. (Tuamotu Archipelago)
Makatea I. (Tuamotu Archipelago)
Napuka I. (Tuamotu Archipelago)

☐ **Rimitara Reed-Warbler** *Acrocephalus rimitarae*

Rimitara (Tubuai Islands)

☐ **Pitcairn Reed-Warbler** *Acrocephalus vaughani*

Pitcairn I. (s Polynesia)

☐ **Henderson Island Reed-Warbler** *Acrocephalus taiti*

Henderson I. (sw Pitcairn Islands)

☐ **Marquesan Reed-Warbler** *Acrocephalus mendanae*

____ *A. m. percernis*	Nukuhiva I. (Marquesas Islands)
____ *A. m. consobrinus*	Motane I. (Marquesas Islands)
____ *A. m. mendanae*	Marquesas Islands (Hivaoa and Tahuata)
____ *A. m. fatuhivae*	Fatuhiva I. (Marquesas Islands)
____ *A. m. idae*	Uahuka I. (Marquesas Islands)
____ *A. m. dido*	Uapou I. (Marquesas Islands)
____ *A. m. aquilonis*	Eiao I. (Marquesas Islands)
____ *A. m. postremus*	Hatutu I. (Marquesas Islands)

☐ **Cook Islands Reed-Warbler** *Acrocephalus kerearako*

____ *A. k. kaoko*	Mitiaro I. (Cook Islands)
____ *A. k. kerearako*	Mangaia I. (Cook Islands)

☐ **Greater Swamp-Warbler** *Acrocephalus rufescens*

____ *A. r. senegalensis*	Senegal
____ *A. r. rufescens*	Ghana to Nigeria, Cameroon, Cabinda and nw Zaire; Bioko
____ *A. r. chadensis*	Lake Chad environs
____ *A. r. ansorgei (niloticus, foxi)*	S Sudan to Uganda, e Zaire, w Kenya, n Botswana and nw Angola

☐ **Cape Verde Swamp-Warbler** *Acrocephalus brevipennis*

Santiago (Cape Verde Is.). Extirpated on São Nicolau and Brava

☐ **Lesser Swamp-Warbler** *Acrocephalus gracilirostris*

____ *A. g. neglectus*	W Chad
____ *A. g. jacksoni*	S Sudan to w Kenya, Uganda and adjacent Zaire
____ *A. g. tsanae*	NW Ethiopia (Lake Tana)
____ *A. g. leptorhynchus*	Ethiopia to Kenya, Zambia, Zimbabwe, e Transvaal, coastal Natal
____ *A. g. parvus*	Highlands of sw Ethiopia to Kenya, n Tanzania, Rwanda, Burundi
____ *A. g. cunensis*	SW Angola to n Namibia, n Botswana, sw Zambia, w Zimbabwe
____ *A. g. winterbottomi*	N and nw Zambia to e Angola and sw Tanzania
____ *A. g. gracilirostris (zuluensis)*	S Mozambique to se Zimbabwe, Transvaal and South Africa

☐ **Madagascar Swamp-Warbler** *Acrocephalus newtoni*

Aquatic habitats of Madagascar

☐ **Thick-billed Warbler** *Acrocephalus aedon*

____ *A. a. aedon*	S Siberia to w Mongolia; winters to Myanmar, Thailand, Indonesia
____ *A. a. stegmanni*	E Siberia to Mongolia; winters to se China, Thailand and Indochina

☐ **Rodrigues Brush-Warbler** *Acrocephalus rodericanus*

Rodrigues (e Mascarene Islands). Seriously endangered

☐ **Seychelles Brush-Warbler** *Acrocephalus sechellensis*

Cousin (Seychelles Islands)

☐ **Booted Warbler** *Hippolais caligata*

____ *H. c. caligata*	Central and e Russia; winters to India and Sri Lanka
____ *H. c. annectens*	Altai Mountains to nw Mongolia; winters to n India

☐ **Sykes' Warbler** *Hippolais rama*

Arabia to Turkestan and w China; winters in s India and Sri Lanka

☐ **Olivaceous Warbler** *Hippolais pallida*

____ *H. p. opaca*	Iberian Peninsula, Morocco, Tunisia, Algeria and Libya
____ *H. p. elaeica*	SE Europe to Iran and sw Asia; winters to ne Africa
____ *H. p. pallida*	Egypt; winters to s Sudan and Ethiopia
____ *H. p. reiseri*	Algerian Sahara, s Morocco, Mauritania and Libya
____ *H. p. laeneni*	Niger, Chad and Nigeria to w Sudan

☐ **Upcher's Warbler** *Hippolais languida*

S-central Asia; winters in ne Africa and s Arabia

☐ **Olive-tree Warbler** *Hippolais olivetorum*

Balkan Peninsula and Asia Minor; winters in e and se Africa

☐ **Melodious Warbler** *Hippolais polyglotta*

SW Palearctic; winters in savanna of w Africa

☐ **Icterine Warbler** *Hippolais icterina*

Central Europe to w Siberia and n Iran; winters to s Africa

☐ **African Yellow Warbler** *Chloropeta natalensis*
_____ *C. n. batesi* — Nigeria to n Zaire and sw Sudan
_____ *C. n. massaica* — SE Sudan and Ethiopia to e Zaire, Uganda, Kenya and s Tanzania
_____ *C. n. major* — Gabon and Angola to s Zaire and n Zambia
_____ *C. n. natalensis* — S Zambia and s Tanzania to e South Africa

☐ **Mountain Yellow Warbler** *Chloropeta similis*

Mountains of e Zaire to se Sudan, Kenya, Tanzania and n Malawi

☐ **Papyrus Yellow Warbler** *Chloropeta gracilirostris*
_____ *C. g. gracilirostris* — E Zaire to Kenya, w Uganda and Burundi
_____ *€. g. bensoni* — NE Zambia (mouth of Luapula River)

☐ **Fairy Warbler** *Stenostira scita*
_____ *S. s. scita* — W Cape Province; winters to s Namibia
_____ *S. s. rudebecki* — Lesotho; winters to Transvaal
_____ *S. s. saturatior* — S Africa (Great and Little Karoo); winters to Orange Free State

☐ **Buff-bellied Warbler** *Phyllolais pulchella*

E Nigeria to Chad, s Sudan, Ethiopia, Zaire, Kenya and n Tanzania

☐ **African Tailorbird** *Orthotomus metopias*
_____ *O. m. metopias (pallidus)* — Montane forests of e Tanzania to nw Mozambique (Njesi Plateau)
_____ *O. m. altus* — E Tanzania (Uluguru Mountains)

☐ **Long-billed Tailorbird** *Orthotomus moreaui*
_____ *O. m. moreaui* — NE Tanzania (Usambara Mountains)
_____ *O. m. sousae* — W-central Mozambique (Njesi Plateau)

☐ **Mountain Tailorbird** *Orthotomus cuculatus*
_____ *O. c. coronatus* — Mts. of e Nepal to ne India, sw China, n Thailand, Laos, Vietnam
_____ *O. c. thais* — Mountains of peninsular Thailand (south of Isthmus of Kra)
_____ *O. c. cuculatus* — Sumatra, Java and Bali
_____ *O. c. cinereicollis* — Mts. of ne Borneo (Kinabalu to Mulu and Tama Abu Range)
_____ *O. c. philippinus* — N Luzon (n Philippines)
_____ *O. c. viridicollis* — Mountains of Palawan (sw Philippines)
_____ *O. c. riedeli* — N Sulawesi
_____ *O. c. stentor* — N-central and se Sulawesi
_____ *O. c. meisei* — S-central Sulawesi (Latimojong Mountains)
_____ *O. c. hedymeles* — S Sulawesi (Mt. Lompobatang) and Taliabu I. (Sula Islands)
_____ *O. c. batjanensis* — Mountains of Bacan I. (n Moluccas)
_____ *O. c. dumasi* — S Moluccas (Buru and Seram)
_____ *O. c. everetti* — Flores (w Lesser Sundas)

☐ **Common Tailorbird** *Orthotomus sutorius*
_____ *O. s. guzuratus* — Himalayan foothills (Pakistan to peninsular India)
_____ *O. s. patia* — *Terai* of Nepal to ne India and Myanmar
_____ *O. s. luteus* — NE India (ne Assam) to n Myanmar
_____ *O. s. sutorius* — Plains and foothills of Sri Lanka
_____ *O. s. fernandonis* — Central highlands of Sri Lanka
_____ *O. s. inexpectatus* — SE Tibet to s China (w and s Yunnan) and Thailand
_____ *O. s. longicauda* — S China to Myanmar, n Laos, Vietnam and Hainan
_____ *O. s. maculicollis* — Malaysia
_____ *O. s. edela* — Java

☐ **Rufous-headed Tailorbird** *Orthotomus heterolaemus*

Mountains of Mindanao (s Philippines)

☐ **Dark-necked Tailorbird** *Orthotomus atrogularis*
_____ *O. a. nitidus* — NE India (Assam) to Myanmar, s China, Thailand and Indochina
_____ *O. a. atrogularis* — Malaysia to Sumatra, Bangka I., Belitung I. and Borneo
_____ *O. a. humphreysi* — N and e Borneo
_____ *O. a. anambensis* — Tioman, Natuna and Anambas islands (South China Sea)
_____ *O. a. chloronotos* — N Luzon (n Philippines)

☐ **Philippine Tailorbird** *Orthotomus castaneiceps*
_____ *O. c. castaneiceps* — Philippines (Masbate, Panay, Guimaras, Bantayan and Ticao)
_____ *O. c. rabori* — Negros (Philippines)

☐ **Rufous-fronted Tailorbird** *Orthotomus frontalis*
_____ *O. f. frontalis* — S Philippines (Samar, Leyte, Dinagat, Bohol and Mindanao)
_____ *O. f. mearnsi* — Basilan (s Philippines)

☐ **Gray-backed Tailorbird** *Orthotomus derbianus*
_____ *O. d. derbianus* — Luzon (n Philippines); single specimen from Palawan
_____ *O. d. nilesi* — Catanduanes (n Philippines)

☐ **Rufous-tailed Tailorbird** *Orthotomus sericeus*
_____ *O. s. hesperius* — Myanmar to Thailand, Malaysia, Sumatra, Riau and Lingga archs.
_____ *O. s. sericeus* — Borneo
_____ *O. s. rubicundulus* — Sirhassen I. (South Natuna Islands)
_____ *O. s. nuntius* — SW Philippines (Balabac, Palawan, Cagayan Sulu and Sulu Arch.)

☐ **Ashy Tailorbird** *Orthotomus ruficeps*
_____ *O. r. cineraceus* — S Myanmar to Malaysia, Indochina, Sumatra and adjacent islands
_____ *O. r. baeus* — Nias and Pagai islands (off w Sumatra)
_____ *O. r. concinnus* — Siberut and Sipoura islands (off w Sumatra)
_____ *O. r. ruficeps* — Coastal mangroves of Java
_____ *O. r. palliolatus* — Kangean and Karimunjawa islands (Java Sea)
_____ *O. r. baweanus* — Bawean I. (Java Sea)
_____ *O. r. borneoensis* — Borneo
_____ *O. r. cagayanensis* — Cagayan Sulu (sw Philippines)

☐ **Olive-backed Tailorbird** *Orthotomus sepium*
_____ *O. s. sundaicus* — Panaitan I. (off w Java)
_____ *O. s. sepium* — Lowlands of Java, Bali, Madura and Lombok

☐ **Yellow-breasted Tailorbird** *Orthotomus samarensis*

Philippines (Bohol, Leyte and Samar)

☐ **White-browed Tailorbird** *Orthotomus nigriceps*

S Philippines (Mindanao, Dinagat and Siargao)

☐ **White-eared Tailorbird** *Orthotomus cinereiceps*
_____ *O. c. obscurior* — Mindanao (s Philippines)
_____ *O. c. cinereiceps* — Basilan (s Philippines)

☐ **White-tailed Warbler** *Poliolais lopezi*
_____ *P. l. manengubae* — SE Nigeria and s Cameroon (Mt. Manenguba and Mt. Kupé)
_____ *P. l. alexanderi* — Mt. Cameroon
_____ *P. l. lopezi* — Bioko (Gulf of Guinea)

☐ **Grauer's Warbler** *Graueria vittata*

Dense montane forests of e Zaire, sw Uganda and w Rwanda

☐ **Salvadori's Eremomela** *Eremomela salvadorii*

E Zaire to se Gabon, central plateau of Angola and w Zambia

☐ **Yellow-vented Eremomela** *Eremomela flavicrissalis*

S Ethiopia to s Somalia, ne Uganda and se Kenya

☐ **Yellow-bellied Eremomela** *Eremomela icteropygialis*

_____ *E. i. alexanderi*	Senegambia to Sudan (Darfur and Kordofan)
_____ *E. i. griseoflava (karamojensis, crawfurdi)*	Ethiopia to Somalia, e Uganda, Rwanda, w Kenya and Tanzania
_____ *E. i. abdominalis*	Kenya to n Tanzania
_____ *E. i. polioxantha*	S Zaire to Tanzania, sw Zimbabwe, e Transvaal and Mozambique
_____ *E. i. puellula*	SW Angola
_____ *E. i. icteropygialis*	Namibia and w Botswana
_____ *E. i. helenorae (viriditincta)*	Caprivi Strip to Zimbabwe, sw Zambia and w Mozambique
_____ *E. i. perimacha*	S Botswana to w Transvaal and nw Cape Province)
_____ *E. i. saturatior (sharpei)*	South Africa (Orange Free State to Cape Province)

☐ **Senegal Eremomela** *Eremomela pusilla*

Senegambia to Cameroon, sw Chad and nw Central African Rep.

☐ **Green-backed Eremomela** *Eremomela canescens*

_____ *E. c. canescens*	Central African Rep. to Chad, s Sudan, Uganda and w Kenya
_____ *E. c. elegans*	Sudan (Darfur and Kordofan to Sennar)
_____ *E. c. abyssinica*	Eritrea to Ethiopia and Sudan
_____ *E. c. elgonensis*	W Kenya (Mt. Elgon to s Nandi Hills)

☐ **Greencap Eremomela** *Eremomela scotops*

_____ *E. s. pulchra (extrema)*	SE Gabon to Angola, Zaire, Zambia, w Malawi, Transvaal, Natal
_____ *E. s. congensis (angolensis)*	Congo to nw Zaire and n Angola
_____ *E. s. citriniceps*	Uganda to w Kenya and w Tanzania
_____ *E. s. kikuyuensis*	Highlands of central Kenya
_____ *E. s. scotops (chlorolchlamys, occipitalis)*	E Kenya to Tanzania, Botswana, Zimbabwe, Mozambique, Natal

☐ **Yellow-rumped Eremomela** *Eremomela gregalis*

_____ *E. g. damarensis*	Namibia (Oösop region on Swakop River)
_____ *E. g. gregalis (albigularis)*	Arid *karoo* of s Namibia and nw Cape Province

☐ **Rufous-crowned Eremomela** *Eremomela badiceps*

_____ *E. b. fantiensis*	Sierra Leone to w Nigeria
_____ *E. b. badiceps*	Nigeria to n Angola and w Uganda; Bioko
_____ *E. b. latukae*	S Sudan

☐ **Turner's Eremomela** *Eremomela turneri*

_____ *E. t. kalindei*	E-central Zaire and extreme sw Uganda (Nyondo Forest)
_____ *E. t. turneri*	W Kenya (Mt. Elgon, Kakamega Forest and s Nandi Hills)

☐ **Black-necked Eremomela** *Eremomela atricollis*

Brachystegia woodlands of Angola to se Zaire and Zambia

☐ **Burnt-neck Eremomela** *Eremomela usticollis*

_____ *E. u. rensi*	S Zambia to s Malawi and Mozambique (north of Save River)
_____ *E. u. usticollis (baumgarti)*	S Angola to Namibia, Zimbabwe, Mozambique and South Africa

☐ **Rand's Warbler** *Randia pseudozosterops*

Rainforests of e Madagascar

☐ **Dark Newtonia** *Newtonia amphichroa*

Humid highland forests of e Madagascar

☐ **Common Newtonia** *Newtonia brunneicauda*

_____ *N. b. brunneicauda*	Wooded areas of Madagascar
_____ *N. b. monticola*	Central Madagascar (Mt. Ankarata)

☐ **Archbold's Newtonia** *Newtonia archboldi*

Subdesert of sw Madagascar

☐ **Red-tailed Newtonia** *Newtonia fanovanae*

Locally in rainforests of e Madagascar

☐ **Cryptic Warbler** *Cryptosylvicola randriansoloi*

Rainforests of e Madagascar

☐ **Green Crombec** *Sylvietta virens*

_____ *S. v. flaviventris*	Senegambia to sw Nigeria
_____ *S. v. virens*	SE Nigeria to Cameroon, Gabon and central Zaire
_____ *S. v. tando (meridionalis)*	Congo to s Zaire and nw Angola
_____ *S. v. baraka*	E Zaire to Kenya

☐ **Lemon-bellied Crombec** *Sylvietta denti*

_____ *S. d. hardyi*	Sierra Leone to Ghana (race in Gambia and Nigeria unknown)
_____ *S. d. denti*	S Cameroon to Zaire

☐ **White-browed Crombec** *Sylvietta leucophrys*

_____ *S. l. leucophrys*	W Kenya and w Uganda (Kibale Forest and Ruwenzori Mts.)
_____ *S. l. chloronota (arileuca)*	SW Uganda (Kigezi) to e Zaire and w Tanzania
_____ *S. l. chapini*	E Zaire (Lendu Plateau)

☐ **Northern Crombec** *Sylvietta brachyura*

_____ *S. b. brachyura*	Senegambia and Sierra Leone to Sudan and n Eritrea
_____ *S. b. carnapi (dilutior)*	Cameroon to Uganda and w Kenya
_____ *S. b. leucopsis*	S Eritrea to Ethiopia, se Sudan, Somalia, Kenya and Tanzania

☐ **Short-billed Crombec** *Sylvietta philippae*

	Acacia steppes of nw Somalia and adjacent Ethiopia

☐ **Red-capped Crombec** *Sylvietta ruficapilla*

_____ *S. r. rufigenis*	Lower Congo inland to Kasai
_____ *S. r. schoutedeni*	E Zaire (Lake Tanganyika to Marungu and Mt. Kabobo)
_____ *S. r. gephyra*	S Zaire (w Shaba) to Zambia and Zimbabwe
_____ *S. r. chubbi*	S Zaire (se Shaba) to Malawi and n Mozambique
_____ *S. r. makayii*	Interior of n Angola
_____ *S. r. ruficapilla*	Central Angola to s Zaire (sw Shaba)

☐ **Red-faced Crombec** *Sylvietta whytii*

_____ *S. w. loringi (abayensis)*	Sudan and Ethiopia to n Uganda, w Kenya and ne Tanzania
_____ *S. w. jacksoni*	S and e Uganda to sw Kenya, w Tanzania and n Malawi
_____ *S. w. minima*	Coastal e Kenya and Tanzania
_____ *S. w. whytii (nemorivaga)*	Coastal s Tanzania to Mozambique, Zimbabwe and s Malawi

☐ **Somali Crombec** *Sylvietta isabellina*

	Dry acacia steppes of Ethiopia, Somalia and n Kenya

☐ **Cape Crombec** *Sylvietta rufescens*

_____ *S. r. adelphe*	Zaire to Zambia and n Malawi
_____ *S. r. ansorgei*	Coastal Angola (Benguela to Luanda)
_____ *S. r. flecki (mossamedes, ochrocara)*	S Angola to e Namibia, e Botswana, sw Zambia and Zimbabwe
_____ *S. r. pallida*	SE Zambia to Mozambique, Zimbabwe, Malawi and Transvaal
_____ *S. r. rufescens*	S Botswana to sw Transvaal and w Cape Province
_____ *S. r. diverga*	S Transvaal to Orange Free State and e Cape Province
_____ *S. r. resurga*	Natal

☐ **Neumann's Warbler** *Hemitesia neumanni*

	Montane forests of e Zaire, sw Uganda and w Rwanda

☐ **Kemp's Longbill** *Macrosphenus kempi*

_____ *M. k. kempi*	Sierra Leone to sw Nigeria
_____ *M. k. flammeus*	SE Nigeria and w Cameroon

☐ **Yellow Longbill** *Macrosphenus flavicans*

_____ *M. f. flavicans*	SE Nigeria to Cameroon, Angola and w Zaire; Bioko
_____ *M. f. hypochondriacus*	E Zaire to Uganda, Central African Rep. and extreme sw Sudan

☐ **Gray Longbill** *Macrosphenus concolor*

	S Guinea and Sierra Leone to extreme ne Angola and sw Uganda

☐ **Pulitzer's Longbill** *Macrosphenus pulitzeri*

Escarpment of w Angola (Vila Nova do Seles to Chingoroi area)

☐ **Kretschmer's Longbill** *Macrosphenus kretschmeri*
_____ *M. k. kretschmeri* — Extreme se Kenya to central Tanzania
_____ *M. k. griseiceps* — SE Tanzania to ne Mozambique

☐ **Bocage's Longbill** *Amaurocichla bocagei*

Locally in forests of s São Tomé

☐ **Green Hylia** *Hylia prasina*
_____ *H. p. prasina* — Senegambia to Angola, Zaire, s Sudan, w Kenya and nw Tanzania
_____ *H. p. poensis* — Bioko (Gulf of Guinea)

☐ **White-browed Tit-Warbler** *Leptopoecile sophiae*
_____ *L. s. sophiae* — Mountains of central Asia to Pakistan and nw India
_____ *L. s. stoliczkae* — S-central Asia to w Gobi Desert
_____ *L. s. major* — Kazakstan (e Tien Shan Mountains) to w China (Xinjiang)
_____ *L. s. obscura* — SE Tibet to s China (se Xinjiang, Sichuan and s Gansu)

☐ **Crested Tit-Warbler** *Leptopoecile elegans*

Coniferous forests of n-central China to Tibet and Sichuan

☐ **Red-faced Woodland-Warbler** *Phylloscopus laetus*
_____ *P. l. laetus* — E Zaire (Lendu Plateau and Ruwenzori Mountains) to Burundi
_____ *P. l. schoutedeni* — E Zaire (Mt. Kabobo)

☐ **Laura's Wood-Warbler** *Phylloscopus laurae*
_____ *P. l. laurae* — W Angola (Mt. Moco)
_____ *P. l. eustacei* — SE Zaire to nw Zambia and sw Tanzania

☐ **Yellow-throated Wood-Warbler** *Phylloscopus ruficapillus*
_____ *P. r. minullus* — SE Kenya and e Tanzania
_____ *P. r. ochrogularis* — W Tanzania (Kungwe-Mahale Mountains)
_____ *P. r. johnstoni* — Malawi to nw Mozambique, ne Zambia and s Tanzania
_____ *P. r. alacris* — E Zimbabwe and w Mozambique (Mt. Gorongoza)
_____ *P. r. quelimanensis* — N Mozambique (Mt. Namuli)
_____ *P. r. ruficapillus (ochraceiceps)* — South Africa (e Transvaal and Natal)
_____ *P. r. voelckeri* — South Africa (e and s Cape Province)

☐ **Uganda Wood-Warbler** *Phylloscopus budongoensis*

Primary forests of Gabon to ne Zaire, Uganda and w Kenya

☐ **Brown Woodland-Warbler** *Phylloscopus umbrovirens*
_____ *P. u. yemenensis* — SW Arabian Peninsula
_____ *P. u. umbrovirens* — Eritrea to Ethiopia and nw Somalia
_____ *P. u. omoensis* — W and s Ethiopia
_____ *P. u. williamsi* — N Somalia (Erigave district)
_____ *P. u. mackensianus* — S Sudan to e Uganda and central Kenya
_____ *P. u. dorcadichrous* — SE Kenya to n Tanzania
_____ *P. u. alpinus* — Ruwenzori Mountains (Zaire/Rwanda border)
_____ *P. u. wilhelmi* — E Zaire to Rwanda and sw Uganda (Kivu Volcanoes)
_____ *P. u. fugglescouchmani* — E Tanzania (Uluguru Mountains)

☐ **Black-capped Woodland-Warbler** *Phylloscopus herberti*
_____ *P. h. camerunensis* — Highlands of se Nigeria and w Cameroon
_____ *P. h. herberti* — Bioko (Gulf of Guinea)

☐ **Willow Warbler** *Phylloscopus trochilus*
_____ *P. t. acredula* — Scandinavia to Siberia (Yenisey River); winters to w Africa
_____ *P. t. trochilus* — S Sweden to s Poland and Romania; winters to w Africa
_____ *P. t. yakutensis* — E Siberia (Taymyr Peninsula to Anadyr River); winters to s Africa

☐ **Common Chiffchaff** *Phylloscopus collybita*
_____ *P. c. canariensis*   Canary Is. (La Palma, Hierro, Gomera, Tenerife and Gran Canaria)
_____ *P. c. exsul*   Lanzarote (ne Canary Islands)
_____ *P. c. abietinus (brevirostris)*   Scandinavia to Urals, Caucasus, Transcaucasia and n Iran
_____ *P. c. collybita*   Denmark to Pyrénées, Poland and Romania; winters to n Africa
_____ *P. c. brehmii*   Iberian Peninsula to sw France; n Morocco and n Algeria
_____ *P. c. tristis*   Ural Mountains to ne Iran, n India and Bangladesh

☐ **Mountain Chiffchaff** *Phylloscopus sindianus*
_____ *P. s. lorenzii*   SW Asia (e Turkey to Caucasus, Transcaucasia and ne Iran)
_____ *P. s. sindianus*   Extreme w China (sw Xinjiang) to n Pakistan and n India

☐ **Plain Leaf-Warbler** *Phylloscopus neglectus*

     Oak-juniper woodlands of Iran to Afghanistan and Kashmir

☐ **Bonelli's Warbler** *Phylloscopus bonelli*
_____ *P. b. bonelli*   W and central Europe; winters to sahel of n Africa
_____ *P. b. orientalis*   Balkans, Turkey and Levant; winters to Sudan

☐ **Wood Warbler** *Phylloscopus sibilatrix*

     Breeds Europe and Russia; winters in tropical Africa

☐ **Dusky Warbler** *Phylloscopus fuscatus*
_____ *P. f. fuscatus*   Siberia to Mongolia and w China; winters to India and Indochina
_____ *P. f. robustus*   N China (south of Gobi Desert) to n Sichuan; winters to Indochina
_____ *P. f. weigoldi*   Mts. of s Tibet to e Himalayas and sw China; winters to ne India

☐ **Smoky Warbler** *Phylloscopus fuligiventer*
_____ *P. f. fuligiventer*   Himalayas of Nepal to Sikkim, Bhutan, sw Tibet and ne India
_____ *P. f. tibetanus*   SE Tibet to s China (sw Xinjiang); winters to ne India

☐ **Tickell's Leaf-Warbler** *Phylloscopus affinis*

     Mts. of n India to s China, se Tibet, Myanmar and Thailand

☐ **Buff-throated Warbler** *Phylloscopus subaffinis*

     Alpine scrub of central and s China to se Tibet

☐ **Sulphur-bellied Warbler** *Phylloscopus griseolus*

     Alpine scrub of s Asia; winters in India

☐ **Yellow-streaked Warbler** *Phylloscopus armandii*
_____ *P. a. armandii*   Mts. of Mongolia to e China; winters to Myanmar and n Laos
_____ *P. a. perplexus*   SE Tibet to n Myanmar and sw China (Sichuan, Hubei, Yunnan)

☐ **Radde's Warbler** *Phylloscopus schwarzi*

     Breeds ne Asia; winters in SE Asia

☐ **Buff-barred Warbler** *Phylloscopus pulcher*
_____ *P. p. kangrae*   Montane oak-rhododendron forests of nw Himalayas
_____ *P. p. pulcher*   Nepal to Tibet, sw China and n Myanmar; winters to n Thailand

☐ **Ashy-throated Warbler** *Phylloscopus maculipennis*
_____ *P. m. virens*   N India (Kashmir and n Punjab to Arunachal Pradesh)
_____ *P. m. maculipennis*   E Himalayas to se Tibet, sw China, n Myanmar and n Indochina

☐ **Pale-rumped Warbler** *Phylloscopus chloronotus*

     Himalayas of Pakistan to se Tibet, ne India and s-central China

☐ **Lemon-rumped Warbler** *Phylloscopus proregulus*
_____ *P. p. proregulus (kansuensis)*   Coniferous forests and *taiga* of e Asia; winters to Indochina
_____ *P. p. simlaensis*   NW Himalayas (Afghanistan to w Nepal)

☐ **Gansu Leaf-Warbler** *Phylloscopus kansuensis*

     Mountains of w China (Qinghai and Gansu)

☐ **Chinese Leaf-Warbler** *Phylloscopus sichuanensis*

     Mountains of central China (Sichuan, Liaoning and Shanxi)

☐ **Brooks' Leaf-Warbler** *Phylloscopus subviridis*

Coniferous forests of Turkestan, ne Afghanistan and n India

☐ **Inornate Warbler** *Phylloscopus inornatus*

_____ *P. i. inornatus*   Ural Mts. to Sea of Okhotsk, Mongolia, Manchuria and Korea
_____ *P. i. humei*   Sayan and Altai Mts. to nw Himalayas; winters to SE Asia
_____ *P. i. mandellii*   S Tibet to Sikkim, Myanmar and sw China; winters to n Thailand

☐ **Arctic Warbler** *Phylloscopus borealis*

_____ *P. b. talovka*   Scandinavia to s Siberia and nw Mongolia; winters to Philippines
_____ *P. b. borealis*   NE Siberia to Chukotsk Pen.; winters to se China and Philippines
_____ *P. b. transbaicalicus* E Siberia to n Mongolia; winters to SE Asia
_____ *P. b. xanthodryas*   Sea of Okhotsk to Kamchatka Pen., Kuril Is., Hokkaido and Honshu
_____ *P. b. hylebata*   E Amurland to n Manchuria, Ussuriland and North Korea
_____ *P. b. kennikotti*   W Alaska; winters in Philippines

☐ **Greenish Warbler** *Phylloscopus trochiloides*

_____ *P. t. viridanus*   NE Europe to central Asia and Afghanistan; winters to s India
_____ *P. t. trochiloides*   Himalayas to Tibet and w China; winters n India to Indochina
_____ *P. t. ludlowi*   W Himalayas (Gilgit and Kashmir to Kumaon); winters to s India
_____ *P. t. obscuratus*   NW China to Tibet; winters to Myanmar, Thailand and Indochina

☐ **Green Warbler** *Phylloscopus nitidus*

Caucasus to n Turkey, n Iran and nw Afghanistan; winters s India

☐ **Two-barred Warbler** *Phylloscopus plumbeitarsus*

S Siberia to Mongolia and Manchuria; winters to SE Asia

☐ **Pale-legged Leaf-Warbler** *Phylloscopus tenellipes*

Breeds river valleys of ne Asia; winters in SE Asia

☐ **Sakhalin Leaf-Warbler** *Phylloscopus borealoides*

Sakhalin, Kuril Islands and Hokkaido (n Japan)

☐ **Large-billed Leaf-Warbler** *Phylloscopus magnirostris*

Kashmir to s Tibet and s China; winters to India and Myanmar

☐ **Tytler's Leaf-Warbler** *Phylloscopus tytleri*

Coniferous forests of Pakistan and n India; winters to Myanmar

☐ **Western Crowned Leaf-Warbler** *Phylloscopus occipitalis*

Mountains of e Afghanistan and Kashmir; winters in India

☐ **Eastern Crowned Leaf-Warbler** *Phylloscopus coronatus*

Siberia and n China; winters in SE Asia and Greater Sundas

☐ **Ijima's Leaf-Warbler** *Phylloscopus ijimae*

Izu Islands (s Japanese Archipelago); winters in n Philippines

☐ **Blyth's Leaf-Warbler** *Phylloscopus reguloides*

_____ *P. r. kashmiriensis*   Himalayas of nw India (Kashmir to Garhwal)
_____ *P. r. reguloides*   Himalayas of ne India to Nepal, s Tibet and s China (sw Sichuan)
_____ *P. r. assamensis*   NE India (Assam) to n Myanmar and sw China (nw Yunnan)
_____ *P. r. claudiae*   Mts. of w China to e Tibet; winters to s China and SE Asia
_____ *P. r. fokiensis*   S China (w Hubei, Guizhou, Guangxi, nw Fujian and Anhui)
_____ *P. r. goodsoni*   Breeding range unknown; winters on Hainan (s China)
_____ *P. r. ticehursti*   S Vietnam (Langbian Plateau)

☐ **Hainan Leaf-Warbler** *Phylloscopus hainanus*

Hainan (s China)

☐ **Emei Leaf-Warbler** *Phylloscopus emeiensis*

SW China (Mt. Emei Shan in Sichuan)

☐ **White-tailed Leaf-Warbler** *Phylloscopus davisoni*

_____ *P. d. davisoni*   Extreme sw China to e Myanmar, n Thailand, n Laos and Tonkin
_____ *P. d. disturbans*   S China (Sichuan to se Yunnan, n Guizhou and se Hunan)
_____ *P. d. ogilviegranti*   SE China (nw Fujian and adjacent Guangdong)
_____ *P. d. intensior*   SE Thailand (Trat Province) to mountains of n Cambodia
_____ *P. d. klossi*   Mountains of s Laos and s Vietnam

☐ **Yellow-vented Warbler** *Phylloscopus cantator*

____	*P. c. cantator*	Mts. of Sikkim and ne India to Myanmar; winters to nw Thailand
____	*P. c. pernotus*	N Laos

☐ **Sulphur-breasted Warbler** *Phylloscopus ricketti*

Mountains of s China; winters to Laos and s Vietnam

☐ **Lemon-throated Warbler** *Phylloscopus cebuensis*

____	*P. c. luzonensis*	N and central Luzon (n Philippines)
____	*P. c. sorsogoensis*	S Luzon (s Philippines)
____	*P. c. cebuensis*	Philippines (Cebu and Negros)

☐ **Mountain Warbler** *Phylloscopus trivirgatus*

____	*P. t. parvirotris*	Malaya
____	*P. t. trivirgatus*	Sumatra, Java, Bali, Lombok, Sumbawa and nw Borneo
____	*P. t. kinabaluensis*	Mountains of ne Borneo (Mt. Kinabalu)
____	*P. t. sarawacensis*	Mountains of w Borneo (Poi Mountains of w Sarawak)
____	*P. t. benguetensis*	N Luzon (n Philippines)
____	*P. t. nigrorum*	Philippines (s Luzon, Negros and Mindoro)
____	*P. t. diuatae*	Diuata Mountains of ne Mindanao (s Philippines)
____	*P. t. mindanensis*	Mindanao (Mt. Apo and Mt. Mayo)
____	*P. t. malindangensis*	Mindanao (Mt. Malindang and Zamboanga Peninsula)
____	*P. t. flavostriatus*	Mindanao (Mt. Katanglad and mts. of Misamis Oriental Prov.)
____	*P. t. peterseni*	Mountains of Palawan (sw Philippines)

☐ **Sulawesi Leaf-Warbler** *Phylloscopus sarasinorum*

____	*P. s. nesophilus*	Mountains of n Sulawesi
____	*P. s. sarasinorum*	Mountains of s Sulawesi

☐ **Timor Leaf-Warbler** *Phylloscopus presbytes*

____	*P. p. floris*	Flores (w Lesser Sundas)
____	*P. p. presbytes*	Timor (e Lesser Sundas)

☐ **Island Leaf-Warbler** *Phylloscopus poliocephalus*

____	*P. p. henrietta*	N Moluccas (Halmahera and Ternate)
____	*P. p. waterstradti*	Moluccas (Bacan and Obi)
____	*P. p. everetti*	Buru (s Moluccas)
____	*P. p. ceramensis*	S Moluccas (Seram and Ambon)
____	*P. p. avicola*	Kai Besar I. (Kai Islands)
____	*P. p. maforensis*	Numfor I. (n New Guinea)
____	*P. p. misoriensis*	Biak I. (n New Guinea)
____	*P. p. poliocephalus*	NW New Guinea (Tamrau, Arfak and Wandammen mountains)
____	*P. p. albigularis*	W-central New Guinea (Weyland Mountains)
____	*P. p. paniaiae*	W-central New Guinea (Wissel Lakes region)
____	*P. p. cyclopum*	N New Guinea (Cyclops Mountains)
____	*P. p. giulianettii*	New Guinea (Snow, Sepik, Saruwaged and Herzog mountains)
____	*P. p. hamlini*	Goodenough I. (D'Entrecasteaux Archipelago)
____	*P. p. matthiae*	St. Matthias I. (Bismarck Archipelago)
____	*P. p. moorhousei*	Bismarck Archipelago (New Britain and Umboi)
____	*P. p. leletensis*	New Ireland (Bismarck Archipelago)
____	*P. p. becki*	Solomon Islands (Guadalcanal, Santa Isabel and Malaita)
____	*P. p. bougainvillei*	Bougainville (Solomon Islands)
____	*P. p. pallescens*	Kulambangra (Solomon Islands)

☐ **Philippine Leaf-Warbler** *Phylloscopus olivaceus*

S Philippines (Samar, Leyte, Mindanao, Negros) and Sulu Arch.

☐ **San Cristobal Leaf-Warbler** *Phylloscopus makirensis*

San Cristóbal (s Solomon Islands)

☐ **Kulambangra Leaf-Warbler** *Phylloscopus amoenus*

Montane forests of Kulambangra (central Solomon Islands)

□ Golden-spectacled Warbler *Seicercus burkii*

_____	S. b. whistleri	W Himalayas (Pakistan to Kashmir and Kumaon); winters s India
_____	S. b. burkii	Nepal to ne India and se Tibet; winters to peninsular India
_____	S. b. tephrocephalus	N Myanmar to sw China and n Thailand; winters to Indochina
_____	S. b. distinctus	S China (Yunnan) to se Tibet and n Vietnam; winters to s Vietnam
_____	S. b. valentini	E Tibet to central and sw China; winters to s Yunnan

□ Gray-hooded Warbler *Seicercus xanthoschistos*

_____	S. x. xanthoschistos	W Himalayas (nw Pakistan to Kashmir, Nepal and se Tibet)
_____	S. x. jerdoni	E Himalayas (e Nepal to Sikkim, Bhutan and Arunachal Pradesh)
_____	S. x. tephrodiras	NE India (Assam, Nagaland and Manipur) to Myanmar
_____	S. x. flavogularis	NE India (Abor and Mishmi hills) to n Myanmar

□ White-spectacled Warbler *Seicercus affinis*

_____	S. a. affinis	Nepal to ne India, n Myanmar, sw China, n Laos and s Vietnam
_____	S. a. intermedius	Mts. of se China (nw Fujian); winters to sw China and Indochina

□ Gray-cheeked Warbler *Seicercus poliogenys*

	Montane forests of n India to sw China, Myanmar and Indochina

□ Chestnut-crowned Warbler *Seicercus castaniceps*

_____	S. c. castaneiceps	E Himalayas (Nepal to Sikkim, Bhutan and ne India)
_____	S. c. collinsi	Myanmar (s Shan States) to nw Thailand
_____	S. c. laurentei	SW China (se Yunnan)
_____	S. s. sinensis	S China (Shaanxi, Sichuan, nw Fujian) to n Laos and n Vietnam
_____	S. c. stresemanni	S Laos (Bolavens Plateau)
_____	S. c. youngi	Mountains of peninsular Thailand (south of Isthmus of Kra)
_____	S. c. annamensis	Mountains of Vietnam (Langbian and Da Lat plateaux)
_____	S. c. butleri	Mountains of Malay Peninsula
_____	S. c. muelleri	W Sumatra (Barisan Mountains)

□ Yellow-breasted Warbler *Seicercus montis*

_____	S. m. davisoni	High mountains of s Malay Peninsula
_____	S. m. inornatus	Mountains of Sumatra
_____	S. m. montis	Mountains of Borneo (Kinabalu to Poi Range)
_____	S. m. xanthopygius	Mountains of Palawan (sw Philippines)
_____	S. m. floris	Mountains of Flores (w Lesser Sundas)
_____	S. m. paulinae	Mountains of Timor (e Lesser Sundas)

□ Sunda Warbler *Seicercus grammiceps*

_____	S. g. sumatrensis	Mountains of Sumatra
_____	S. g. grammiceps	Mountains of Java and Bali

□ Rufous-faced Warbler *Abroscopus albogularis*

_____	A. a. albogularis	Nepal to Sikkim, ne India, Bangladesh, Yunnan and w Myanmar
_____	A. a. fulvifacies	S China to n Laos and n Vietnam; Hainan
_____	A. a. hugonis	NW Thailand

□ Yellow-bellied Warbler *Abroscopus superciliaris*

_____	A. s. flaviventris	Central Nepal to Sikkim, Bhutan, ne India and Bangladesh
_____	A. s. superciliaris	S China (Yunnan) to Myanmar, w Thailand and nw Laos
_____	A. s. drasticus	NE India (Arunachal Pradesh) to n Myanmar; winters sw Thailand
_____	A. s. smythiesi	Myanmar (central Irrawaddy basin from Pakokkuu to Prome)
_____	A. s. euthymus	N and central Vietnam
_____	A. s. bambusarum	Peninsular Thailand (Isthmus of Kra to Phangnga)
_____	A. s. sakaiorum	Malay Peninsula (s Thailand to Negeri Sembilan)
_____	A. s. papilio	Sumatra
_____	A. s. schwaneri	Borneo
_____	A. s. vordermani	Java

☐ **Black-faced Warbler** *Abroscopus schisticeps*

_____	*A. s. schisticeps*	Central Nepal to Sikkim and ne India (Darjiling)
_____	*A. s. flavimentalis*	SE Tibet to ne India and Myanmar (Chin Hills and Mt. Victoria)
_____	*A. s. ripponi*	S China (Sichuan and Yunnan) to e Myanmar and n Vietnam

☐ **Broad-billed Warbler** *Tickellia hodgsoni*

_____	*T. h. hodgsoni*	Nepal to ne India and w Myanmar
_____	*T. h. tonkinensis*	SW China (se Yunnan) to n Laos and nw Tonkin

☐ **Yellow-bellied Hyliota** *Hyliota flavigaster*

_____	*H. f. flavigaster*	Senegal to s Sudan, w Ethiopia, Kenya and Tanzania
_____	*H. f. barbozae (marginalis)*	Lake Victoria to Angola, Zambia, Malawi and n Mozambique

☐ **Southern Hyliota** *Hyliota australis*

_____	*H. a. slatini*	W Cameroon; ne Zaire to w Uganda and w Kenya
_____	*H. a. inornata (pallidipectus)*	Angola to s Zaire (Shaba), Zambia, Malawi and n Mozambique
_____	*H. a. australis (rhodesiae)*	Zimbabwe and Mozambique

☐ **Usambara Hyliota** *Hyliota usambarae*

NE Tanzania (Rubu River to Usambara Mountains)

☐ **Violet-backed Hyliota** *Hyliota violacea*

_____	*H. v. nehrkorni*	Liberia to Ghana and Togo
_____	*H. v. violacea*	Lowlands of Nigeria and Cameroon to Gabon and e Zaire

☐ **Marsh Grassbird** *Megalurus pryeri*

_____	*M. p. sinensis*	Reedbeds of ne China (e Liaoning and ne Hebei); winters se China
_____	*M. p. pryeri*	Honshu (Japan)

☐ **Tawny Grassbird** *Megalurus timoriensis*

_____	*M. t. tweeddalei*	Philippines (Luzon, Panay, Tablas, Marinduque, Ticao, Negros)
_____	*M. t. mindorensis*	Mindoro (Philippines)
_____	*M. t. alopex*	Philippines (Bohol, Cebu and Leyte)
_____	*M. t. crex*	S Philippines (Mindanao and Camiguin Sur)
_____	*M. t. celebensis*	N-central Sulawesi
_____	*M. t. amboinensis*	Ambon (s Moluccas)
_____	*M. t. inquirendus*	Sumba (Lesser Sundas)
_____	*M. t. timoriensis*	Timor (e Lesser Sundas)
_____	*M. t. alisteri*	Romang (e Lesser Sundas) and Yamdena (Tanimbar Islands)
_____	*M. t. stresemanni*	NW New Guinea (Lake Giji, Arfak Mts. and Wissel Lakes)
_____	*M. t. mayri*	N New Guinea (Lake Sentani, Humboldt Bay to Astrolabe Bay)
_____	*M. t. wahgiensis*	Central Highlands of New Guinea
_____	*M. t. montanus*	Central Highlands of New Guinea (Mt. Hagen and Mt. Wilhelm)
_____	*M. t. macrurus*	SE New Guinea
_____	*M. t. harterti*	E New Guinea (Huon Peninsula)
_____	*M. t. alpinus*	Alpine grasslands of Snow Mountains to se New Guinea
_____	*M..t. muscalis*	S New Guinea (Middle Fly River region)
_____	*M. t. interscapularis*	Bismarck Arch. (New Britain, New Ireland and New Hanover)
_____	*M. t. oweni*	E Australia (se Queensland and e New South Wales)

☐ **Little Grassbird** *Megalurus gramineus*

_____	*M. g. papuensis*	W New Guinea (Wissel Lakes region)
_____	*M. g. gramineus*	S Queensland to s Australia, Tasmania, King I. and Flinders I.

☐ **Striated Grassbird** *Megalurus palustris*

_____	*M. p. tokiao*	Pakistan to India, s China, s Myanmar, Thailand and Indochina
_____	*M. p. forbesi*	Philippines (Luzon, Mindoro, Panay, Samar and Mindanao)
_____	*M. p. palustris*	Borneo and Java

☐ **Fly River Grassbird** *Megalurus albolimbatus*

SE New Guinea (Fly River lowlands)

451

☐ **Fernbird** *Megalurus punctatus*
____   *M. p. vealeae*   North I. (New Zealand)
____   *M. p. punctatus*   South I. (New Zealand)
____   *M. p. stewartianus*   Stewart I. (New Zealand)
____   *M. p. wilsoni*   Codfish I. (New Zealand)
____   *M. p. caudatus*   Snares I. (New Zealand)

☐ **Brown Songlark** *Cincloramphus cruralis*

Widespread Australia (except for tropical north)

☐ **Rufous Songlark** *Cincloramphus mathewsi*

Savanna of Australia

☐ **Spinifex-bird** *Eremiornis carteri*

Spinifex grass of interior n Australia

☐ **Buff-banded Bushbird** *Buettikoferella bivittata*

Lowland scrub of Timor (e Lesser Sundas)

☐ **New Caledonian Grassbird** *Megalurulus mariei*

Grasslands and open heath of New Caledonia

☐ **Bismarck Thicketbird** *Megalurulus grosvenori*

Known from 2 specimens from New Britain (Bismarck Arch.)

☐ **Bougainville Thicketbird** *Megalurulus llaneae*

Mountains of Bougainville (n Solomon Islands)

☐ **Guadalcanal Thicketbird** *Megalurulus whitneyi*
____   *M. w. whitneyi*   Mountains of Espíritu Santo (Vanuatu)
____   *M. w. turipavae*   Mountains of Guadalcanal (se Solomon Islands)

☐ **Rusty Thicketbird** *Megalurulus rubiginosus*

Scrub of New Britain (Bismarck Archipelago)

☐ **Long-legged Warbler** *Trichocichla rufa*
____   *T. r. rufa*   Viti Levu (Fiji Islands). Possibly extinct
____   *T. r. cluniei*   Vanua Levu (Fiji Islands). Possibly extinct

☐ **Bristled Grassbird** *Chaetornis striatus*

Grasslands of Indian subcontinent

☐ **Rufous-rumped Grassbird** *Graminicola bengalensis*
____   *G. b. bengalensis*   W Nepal to n India, Bangladesh and n Myanmar
____   *G. b. sinica*   S China (e Guangxi and Guangdong)
____   *G. b. striata*   S Myanmar to central Thailand, n Vietnam and Hainan

☐ **Broad-tailed Grassbird** *Schoenicola platyura*

Grasslands of sw India (Western Ghats from Mysore to Kerala)

☐ **Fan-tailed Grassbird** *Schoenicola brevirostris*
____   *S. b. alexinae*   Guinea to Ethiopia and n Malawi
____   *S. b. brevirostris*   Malawi to South Africa

☐ **Wrentit** *Chamaea fasciata*
____   *C. f. phaea*   Coastal nw Oregon (Columbia River to California border)
____   *C. f. rufula*   Chaparral of coastal n California (Del Norte to Marin counties)
____   *C. f. intermedia*   Chaparral belt of central California (San Francisco region)
____   *C. f. fasciata*   Coastal s California (Monterey to San Luis Obispo counties)
____   *C. f. henshawi*   Chaparral belt of interior s Oregon to s California (San Diego)
____   *C. f. canicauda*   Chaparral belt of nw Baja California

☐ **Yemen Warbler** *Sylvia buryi*

Acacia scrub of s Yemen and sw Saudi Arabia

☐ **Blackcap** *Sylvia atricapilla*
____   *S. a. gularis (atlantis)*   Cape Verde Islands and Azores
____   *S. a. heineken*   SW Spain, Portugal, Madeira and Canary Islands
____   *S. a. atricapilla*   Europe to w Siberia and nw Africa; winters to s Africa
____   *S. a. pauluccii (koenigi)*   Corsica, Sardinia, Balearic Islands, Tunisia, Italy and Sicily
____   *S. a. dammholzi*   Caucasus, Transcaucasia and n Iran; winters to ne Africa

☐ **Garden Warbler** *Sylvia borin*
_____ *S. b. borin* — Br. Isles to Scandinavia, s Urals and Caucasus; winters to s Africa
_____ *S. b. woodwardi (pallida)* — N European Russia and w Siberia; winters to s Africa

☐ **Greater Whitethroat** *Sylvia communis*
_____ *S. c. communis* — W Europe and Scandinavia to North Africa; winters to n Africa
_____ *S. c. volgensis* — E Europe to w Siberia
_____ *S. c. icterops* — W Siberia to Iran and Asia Minor; winters to e Africa
_____ *S. c. rubicola* — NW China and w Mongolia to Kazakstan; winters to s Africa

☐ **Lesser Whitethroat** *Sylvia curruca*
_____ *S. c. curruca* — W Europe to Caucasus and w Siberia; winters to central Africa
_____ *S. c. blythi (affinis)* — E Siberia to n Altai and n Mongolia
_____ *S. c. halimodendri* — Plains of lower Volga to e Kazakstan (Lake Zaysan) and w Altai
_____ *S. c. caucasica* — Mountains of Balkan Peninsula to w Iran and Caucasus Mountains
_____ *S. c. telengitica* — Deserts of Soviet Altai to w and s Mongolia
_____ *S. c. jaxartica (snigirewskii)* — Plains of s Transcaspia

☐ **Small Whitethroat** *Sylvia minula*
_____ *S. m. margelanica* — Uzbekistan and Kyrgyzstan to w China (Tien Shan Mountains)
_____ *S. m. minula* — Deserts of w China (Xinjiang to n Qinghai)
_____ *S. m. chuancheica* — Deserts of w China (basin of Huang Po River to Ningxia)

☐ **Hume's Whitethroat** *Sylvia althaea*
Mts. of e Iran to Afghanistan and n India; winters to s India

☐ **Desert Warbler** *Sylvia nana*
_____ *S. n. deserti* — Deserts of nw Africa to e Libya
_____ *S. n. nana* — Caspian Sea to Mongolia and w China; winters to ne Africa, India
_____ *S. n. theresae* — Breeding area unknown; winters in Pakistan

☐ **Barred Warbler** *Sylvia nisoria*
_____ *S. n. nisoria* — S Scandinavia and Europe to Ural Mountains; winters to e Africa
_____ *S. n. merzbacheri* — W Siberia to n Iran, Afghanistan and w China; winters to e Africa

☐ **Orphean Warbler** *Sylvia hortensis*
_____ *S. h. hortensis* — SW Europe and North Africa; winters s Mauritania to w Sudan
_____ *S. h. crassirostris* — SE Europe to Levant, Turkey, Caucasus and North Africa
_____ *S. h. jerdoni (balchanica)* — Iraq and Iran to Kazakstan and Pakistan; winters to n India

☐ **Red Sea Warbler** *Sylvia leucomelaena*
_____ *S. l. blanfordi* — Red Sea coast of Egypt, ne Sudan and Eritrea
_____ *S. l. somaliensis* — Djibouti and n Somalia
_____ *S. l. leucomelaena* — W Saudi Arabia to North Yemen, w South Yemen and Oman
_____ *S. l. negevensis* — Arava Valley (Israel-Jordan border)

☐ **Rueppell's Warbler** *Sylvia rueppelli*
Rocky slopes of e Mediterranean region; winters in ne Africa

☐ **Subalpine Warbler** *Sylvia cantillans*
_____ *S. c. cantillans* — S Europe to Italy, Corsica and Sardinia; winters Senegal to Chad
_____ *S. c. inornata* — Morocco to Tunisia and (?) nw Libya; winters Senegal to w Niger
_____ *S. c. albistriata* — Balkan Peninsula to w Turkey; winters Sahara oases and Arabia

☐ **Sardinian Warbler** *Sylvia melanocephala*
_____ *S. m. leucogastra* — Canary Islands
_____ *S. m. melanocephala (pasiphae)* — S Europe, Mediterranean islands, w Turkey and North Africa
_____ *S. m. norrisae†* — Formerly Egypt (Faiyum region). Extinct
_____ *S. m. momus* — Syria, Israel, Jordan and Sinai Peninsula; winters to ne Africa

☐ **Cyprus Warbler** *Sylvia melanothorax*
Arid scrub of Cyprus; winters to Near East and ne Egypt

☐ **Ménétries' Warbler** *Sylvia mystacea*

____	*S. m. mystacea*	Transcaucasia and ne Turkey to lower Volga; winters to ne Africa
____	*S. m. rubescens (semenowi)*	Lebanon and se Turkey to Iraq and sw Iran; winters to ne Africa
____	*S. m. turcmenica*	E Iran to n Afghanistan and w Tajikistan; winters ne Africa

☐ **Spectacled Warbler** *Sylvia conspicillata*

____	*S. c. orbitalis*	Madeira, Canary Islands and Cape Verde Islands
____	*S. c. conspicillata*	W Mediterranean basin and nw Africa; winters to Senegal and Niger

☐ **Tristram's Warbler** *Sylvia deserticola*

____	*S. d. maroccana*	Morocco and w Algeria (Haut and Moyen Atlas mountains)
____	*S. d. ticehursti*	Atlas Mountains of Morocco (Ouarzazarte region)
____	*S. d. deserticola*	Algeria (Atlas Saharien and Aurès) and adjacent Tunisia

☐ **Dartford Warbler** *Sylvia undata*

____	*S. u. dartfordiensis*	S England, w France, nw Spain and n Portugal
____	*S. u. undata*	Medit. France, Corsica, Sardinia, Sicily, Balearic Is. and Italy
____	*S. u. toni*	Iberian Peninsula and coastal Morocco, Algeria, Tunisia

☐ **Marmora's Warbler** *Sylvia sarda*

____	*S. s. balearica*	Coastal s Spain and Balearic Islands; winters to nw Africa
____	*S. s. sarda*	Corsica, Sardinia, Montecristo, Pantelleria, Giannutri and Zembra

☐ **Layard's Warbler** *Parisoma layardi*

____	*P. l. layardi*	Namibia to nw Cape Province, Namaqualand and middle Orange R.
____	*P. l. aridicola*	Highlands of Namibia, Damaraland and n Cape Province
____	*P. l. barnesi*	Highlands of Lesotho and ne Cape Province; w Cape Province
____	*P. l. subsolanum*	Highlands of sw Cape Province to Orange Free State

☐ **Rufous-vented Warbler** *Parisoma subcaeruleum*

____	*P. s. ansorgei*	Coastal sw Angola
____	*P. s. cinerascens*	Namibia
____	*P. s. subcaeruleum*	Botswana to Cape Province and Orange Free State
____	*P. s. orpheanum*	Zimbabwe to Transvaal, Natal, w Zululand and Lesotho

☐ **Brown Warbler** *Parisoma lugens*

____	*P. l. lugens*	Ethiopia
____	*P. l. griseiventris*	S Ethiopia (Bale Mountains)
____	*P. l. jacksoni*	Sudan and Uganda to Kenya, n Tanzania, e Zaire and Malawi
____	*P. l. prigoginei*	E Zaire (Itombwe Mountains)
____	*P. l. clara*	Tanzania (Matengo Highlands)

☐ **Banded Warbler** *Parisoma boehmi*

____	*P. b. somalicum*	Ethiopia and Somalia
____	*P. b. marsabit*	N-central Kenya
____	*P. b. boehmi*	S Kenya and Tanzania

FAMILY: POLIOPTILIDAE (Gnatcatchers—15)

☐ **Collared Gnatwren** *Microbates collaris*

____	*M. c. collaris*	SE Colombia to the Guianas, Suriname and adjacent nw Brazil
____	*M. c. paraguensis*	S Venezuela (Bolívar and Amazonas)
____	*M. c. perlatus*	N Amazonian Brazil and ne Peru (Loreto and n San Martín)

☐ **Tawny-faced Gnatwren** *Microbates cinereiventris*

____	*M. c. semitorquatus*	Caribbean slope of se Nicaragua to w Panama
____	*M. c. magdalenae*	Caribbean slope of extreme e Panama to n Colombia
____	*M. c. cinereiventris*	Pacific coast of Colombia to sw Ecuador (Guayas)
____	*M. c. peruvianus*	Trop. se Colombia (Nariño) to e Ecuador and se Peru (Puno)

☐ **Long-billed Gnatwren** *Ramphocaenus melanurus*

____	*R. m. rufiventris*	Trop. se Mexico (Oaxaca) to Panama, Colombia and e Ecuador
____	*R. m. ardeleo*	SE Mexico (Yucatán Peninsula) and Petén of n Guatemala
____	*R. m. sanctaemarthae*	Caribbean coast of n Colombia to nw Venezuela (Zulia)
____	*R. m. griseodorsalis*	W-central Colombia (Antioquia south to Valle)
____	*R. m. pallidus*	NE Colombia e of Andes to n Venezuela (e Falcón to Miranda)
____	*R. m. trinitatis*	Tropical e Colombia (Meta) to ne Venezuela; Trinidad
____	*R. m. albiventris*	S Venezuela (e Bolívar) to the Guianas and ne Brazil
____	*R. m. duidae*	Tropical ne Ecuador to s Venezuela (Amazonas and Bolívar)
____	*R. m. badius*	SE Ecuador to ne Peru (north of Río Marañón)
____	*R. m. obscurus*	Tropical e Peru (Loreto) to n Bolivia (La Paz)
____	*R. m. amazonum*	E Peru (right bank of upper Río Ucayali) and adjacent nw Brazil
____	*R. m. sticturus*	SW Brazil (Mato Grosso)
____	*R. m. austerus*	E Brazil (e Pará and n Maranhão)
____	*R. m. melanurus*	Coastal ne Brazil (Pernambuco to São Paulo)

☐ **Blue-gray Gnatcatcher** *Polioptila caerulea*

____	*P. c. caerulea*	E and c US to Gulf Coast; winters to ne Mexico and West Indies
____	*P. c. amoenissima*	SW Oregon to n Baja and n Mexico; winters to s Mexico
____	*P. c. obscura*	S Baja California (28°N to Cape District)
____	*P. c. gracilis*	Foothills of nw Mexico (se Sonora)
____	*P. c. nelsoni*	S Mexico (Guerrero to Oaxaca and s Chiapas)
____	*P. c. deppei*	E Mexico (San Luis Potosí to Veracruz, Tabasco and n Chiapas)
____	*P. c. mexicana*	SE Mexico (Yucatán Peninsula)
____	*P. c. cozumelae*	Cozumel I. (off e Mexico)

☐ **Cuban Gnatcatcher** *Polioptila lembeyei*

Semiarid coastal scrub of e Cuba and Cayo Coco

☐ **California Gnatcatcher** *Polioptila californica*

SW California to s Baja, Santa Margarita I. and Espírito Santo I.

☐ **Black-tailed Gnatcatcher** *Polioptila melanura*

____	*P. m. lucida*	Arid sw US to ne Baja California and nw Mexico (Durango)
____	*P. m. melanura*	W Nevada to Texas and e Mexico (Tamaulipas, San Luis Potosí)
____	*P. m. pontilis*	Central Baja California from latitude 30°N to 27°N
____	*P. m. margaritae*	S Baja California; Santa Margarita I. and Espírito Santo I.
____	*P. m. curtata*	Isla Tiburón (Sea of Cortés)

☐ **Black-capped Gnatcatcher** *Polioptila nigriceps*

____	*P. n. restricta*	Extreme s Arizona to nw Mexico (Sonora and Chihuahua))
____	*P. n. nigriceps*	Arid w Mexico (n Sinaloa to Durango, Jalisco and Colima)

☐ **White-lored Gnatcatcher** *Polioptila albiloris*

____	*P. a. vanrossemi*	Arid w and s Mexico (Michoacán and Guerrero to s Chiapas)
____	*P. a. albiventris*	SE Mexico (extreme n Yucatán Peninsula)
____	*P. a. albiloris*	Interior of Guatemala to nw Costa Rica

☐ **Maranon Gnatcatcher** *Polioptila maranonica*

W Peru (Río Marañón Valley from Piura south to Lima)

☐ **Guianan Gnatcatcher** *Polioptila guianensis*

____	*P. g. facilis*	S Venezuela (Amazonas) to extreme ne Brazil (upper Rio Negro)
____	*P. g. guianensis*	Guyana, Suriname and French Guiana
____	*P. g. paraensis*	E Brazil (Manaus area and from lower Rio Tapajós to Belém)

☐ **Tropical Gnatcatcher** *Polioptila plumbea*

_____ *P. p. brodkorbi*	Lowlands of se Mexico (s Veracruz) to e Nicaragua
_____ *P. p. superciliaris*	SE Mexico (Quintana Roo and Campeche) to Panama
_____ *P. p. cinericia*	Panama (Coiba and Pearl islands)
_____ *P. p. bilineata*	N Colombia to w Peru (n Lima)
_____ *P. p. plumbeiceps*	E slope of Andes of n Colombia to n Venezuela; Isla Margarita
_____ *P. p. anteocularis*	N Colombia (upper Magdalena Valley)
_____ *P. p. daguae*	Colombia (upper Río Dagua and upper Río Patía)
_____ *P. p. innotata*	Extreme e Colombia to s Venezuela and extreme n Brazil
_____ *P. p. plumbea*	The Guianas and ne Brazil (Rio Tapajós to n Maranhão)
_____ *P. p. maior*	Trop. e Peru (upper Río Marañón) from Piura to La Libertad
_____ *P. p. parvirostris*	Trop. e Peru (upper Amazon, Río Huallaga and Río Marañón)
_____ *P. p. atricapilla*	NE Brazil (Maranhão to Piauí, Ceará, Pernambuco and Bahia)

☐ **Creamy-bellied Gnatcatcher** *Polioptila lactea*

Lowlands of se Brazil to e Paraguay and ne Argentina

☐ **Slate-throated Gnatcatcher** *Polioptila schistaceigula*

Tropical forests of e Panama to nw Ecuador

☐ **Masked Gnatcatcher** *Polioptila dumicola*

_____ *P. d. berlepschi*	Interior e Brazil (n Goiás, se Pará to Mato Grosso) and e Bolivia
_____ *P. d. dumicola*	Extreme s Brazil to Bolivia, Paraguay, Uruguay and n Argentina
_____ *P. d. saturata*	Highlands of Bolivia (Cochabamba)

FAMILY: MUSCICAPIDAE (Old World Flycatchers—270)

☐ **Silverbird** *Empidornis semipartitus*

S Sudan to n Ethiopia, Uganda. w Kenya and w Tanzania

☐ **Pale Flycatcher** *Bradornis pallidus*

_____ *B. p. pallidus*	Senegambia to n Zaire, s Sudan and w Ethiopia
_____ *B. p. parvus*	SW Ethiopia to e Sudan, e Zaire and nw Uganda
_____ *B. p. bowdleri*	Eritrea to central Ethiopia
_____ *B. p. bafirawari*	S Ethiopia and ne Kenya
_____ *B. p. duyerali*	NE Ethiopia (Duyer Ali) to central Somalia (El Bur)
_____ *B. p. subalaris*	Coastal e Kenya to ne Tanzania
_____ *B. p. erlangeri*	S Somalia (Bardera and Serenli to Hanole)
_____ *B. p. modestus (nigeriae)*	Guinea to se Mali and Central African Republic
_____ *B. p. murinus*	Congo to Angola, w Kenya, n Botswana and nw Zimbabwe
_____ *B. p. aquaemontis*	Central Namibia (Waterberg Plateau)
_____ *B. p. griseus*	SE Kenya to c Tanzania, e Zambia, e Zimbabwe and n Malawi
_____ *B. p. divisus*	SE Zambia to Mozambique, n Transvaal and ne Swaziland
_____ *B. p. sibilans*	Mozambique (south of Sul do Save) to n Natal

☐ **Chat Flycatcher** *Bradornis infuscatus*

_____ *B. i. benguellensis*	Arid coastal sw Angola (Benguela) to nw Namibia (Kaokoveld)
_____ *B. i. namaquensis*	Namibia
_____ *B. i. placidus*	Botswana to w Transvaal, nw Orange Free State and n Cape Prov.
_____ *B. i. seimundi*	South Africa (n Cape Province to sw Orange Free State)
_____ *B. i. infuscatus*	SW Namibia to sw Cape Province

☐ **Mariqua Flycatcher** *Bradornis mariquensis*

_____ *B. m. acaciae*	Savanna of s Angola to sw Botswana and n Cape Province
_____ *B. m. mariquensis*	S Botswana to w Zimbabwe and w Transvaal
_____ *B. m. territinctus*	NE Namibia and nw Botswana

☐ **African Gray Flycatcher** *Bradornis microrhynchus*

____	*B. m. neumanni*	SE Sudan to s Ethiopia, central Somalia, n Kenya and ne Uganda
____	*B. m. pumilus*	Central Ethiopia to n Somalia
____	*B. m. burae*	E Kenya to se Somalia
____	*B. m. microrhynchus*	SW Kenya to w Tanzania and ne Zambia
____	*B. m. taruensis*	SE Kenya

☐ **Angola Slaty-Flycatcher** *Melaenornis brunneus*

____	*M. b. brunneus*	Northern end of western escarpment of Angola
____	*M. b. bailunduensis*	Angola (Mt. Moco and central highlands)

☐ **White-eyed Slaty-Flycatcher** *Melaenornis fischeri*

____	*M. f. fischeri*	Mountains of se Sudan to Uganda, Kenya and ne Tanzania
____	*M. f. toruensis*	Highlands of sw Uganda and e Zaire to Rwanda and Burundi
____	*M. f. nyikensis (ufipae)*	E Zaire (Marungu Highlands) to Tanzania and Malawi
____	*M. f. semicinctus*	Highlands of e Zaire (west of Lake Albert)

☐ **Abyssinian Slaty-Flycatcher** *Melaenornis chocolatinus*

____	*M. c. chocolatinus*	High plateau of s Eritrea to w and central Ethiopia
____	*M. c. reichenowi*	Highlands of w Ethiopia (Wallegha to Gimirra)

☐ **Northern Black-Flycatcher** *Melaenornis edolioides*

____	*M. e. edolioides*	Savanna of Senegambia to Mali, Sierra Leone and Cameroon
____	*M. e. lugubris*	E Cameroon to w Ethiopia, nw Zaire, Uganda, w Kenya, Tanzania
____	*M. e. schistaceus*	Eritrea and e Ethiopia to n Kenya (Moyale)

☐ **Southern Black-Flycatcher** *Melaenornis pammelaina*

____	*M. p. ater*	SE Botswana to Malawi, e Zimbabwe, Mozambique, e S Africa
____	*M. p. pammelaina*	S Tanzania to se Malawi and Mozambique (n of Sul do Save)
____	*M. p. diabolicus*	S Angola to n Namibia and nw Botswana
____	*M. p. tropicalis*	Zaire to Uganda,, Rwanda, Kenya and w Tanzania
____	*M. p. poliogygna*	Angola to Caprivi Strip, Zimbabwe, nw Malawi and sw Tanzania

☐ **Yellow-eyed Black-Flycatcher** *Melaenornis ardesiacus*

Mountains of e Zaire to Rwanda, Burundi and sw Uganda

☐ **Nimba Flycatcher** *Melaenornis annamarulae*

Humid forests of e Sierra Leone to Liberia and s Ivory Coast

☐ **African Forest-Flycatcher** *Fraseria ocreata*

____	*F. o. kelsalli*	Humid forests of Sierra Leone
____	*F. o. prosphora*	Liberia to Ghana
____	*F. o. ocreata*	Nigeria and Cameroon to Angola, Zaire and w Uganda; Bioko

☐ **White-browed Forest-Flycatcher** *Fraseria cinerascens*

____	*F. c. cinerascens*	Senegal and Gambia to Ghana
____	*F. c. ruthae*	S Nigeria to Cameroon, Zaire and Cabinda

☐ **Fiscal Flycatcher** *Sigelus silens*

SE Botswana and South Africa; winters to Mozambique

☐ **Buru Jungle-Flycatcher** *Rhinomyias addita*

Forests of Buru (s Moluccas)

☐ **Flores Jungle-Flycatcher** *Rhinomyias oscillans*

____	*R. o. oscillans*	Sumbawa (w Lesser Sundas)
____	*R. o. stresemanni*	Sumba (w Lesser Sundas)

☐ **Brown-chested Jungle-Flycatcher** *Rhinomyias brunneata*

____	*R. b. brunneata*	Breeds se China; winters to Malaysia, Thailand and Nicobar Is.
____	*R. b. nicobarica*	S China (Guangxi); winters to Nicobar Islands

☐ **Gray-chested Jungle-Flycatcher** *Rhinomyias umbratilis*

S pen. Thailand, Malaysia, Sumatra, Borneo, Java; N Natuna Is.

☐ **Fulvous-chested Jungle-Flycatcher** *Rhinomyias olivacea*
_____ *R. o. olivacea* — N Myanmar, peninsular Thailand, Sumatra, Java and Borneo
_____ *R. o. perolivacea* — North Natuna Islands

☐ **Chestnut-tailed Jungle-Flycatcher** *Rhinomyias ruficauda*
_____ *R. r. samarensis* — Philippines (Leyte, Samar and e Mindanao)
_____ *R. r. boholensis* — Bohol (Philippines)
_____ *R. r. zamboanga* — W Mindanao (s Philippines)
_____ *R. r. ruficauda* — Basilan (s Philippines)
_____ *R. r. ocularis* — Sulu Archipelago (Pangamican and Tawitawi)
_____ *R. r. ruficrissa* — N Borneo (Mt. Kinabalu)
_____ *R. r. isola* — Montane forests of Sarawak (n Borneo)

☐ **Henna-tailed Jungle-Flycatcher** *Rhinomyias colonus*
_____ *R. c. subsolanus* — E Sulawesi
_____ *R. c. pelingensis* — Peleng I. (Banggai Islands off Sulawesi)
_____ *R. c. colonus* — Sula Islands (Taliabu, Seho, Mangole and Sanana)

☐ **Eyebrowed Jungle-Flycatcher** *Rhinomyias gularis*

Mountains of n Borneo (Mt. Kinabalu and adjacent mountains)

☐ **Rusty-flanked Jungle-Flycatcher** *Rhinomyias insignis*

Montane forests of n Luzon (n Philippines)

☐ **Negros Jungle-Flycatcher** *Rhinomyias albigularis*

Philippines (lowlands of Negros and Guimaras)

☐ **Mindanao Jungle-Flycatcher** *Rhinomyias goodfellowi*

Montane forests of Mt. Apo on Mindanao (s Philippines)

☐ **Spotted Flycatcher** *Muscicapa striata*
_____ *M. s. striata* — Europe to N Africa, Siberia and Asia Minor; winters to s Africa
_____ *M. s. neumanni* — E Siberia to Caucasus, s China and s Asia; winters to e Africa
_____ *M. s. balearica* — Balearic Islands; winters to w and sw Africa
_____ *M. s. tyrrhenica* — Corsica and Sardinia
_____ *M. s. sarudnyi* — Cacausus Mts. to n Iran and Afghanistan; winters to East Africa
_____ *M. s. inexpectata* — Crimean Peninsula
_____ *M. s. mongola* — SE Altai to n Mongolia to se Transbaikalia

☐ **Gambaga Flycatcher** *Muscicapa gambagae*

Semiarid s Mali to Ghana, Kenya, Somalia and sw Arabia

☐ **Gray-spotted Flycatcher** *Muscicapa griseisticta*

SE Siberia to ne China; winters to New Guinea and Philippines

☐ **Siberian Flycatcher** *Muscicapa sibirica*
_____ *M. s. sibirica* — SE Siberia to Japan; winters to Indochina and Greater Sundas
_____ *M. s. gulmergi* — W Himalayas (e Afghanistan to Kashmir and Garhwal)
_____ *M. s. cacabata* — E Himalayas to se Tibet and ne India; winters to s Thailand
_____ *M. s. rothschildi* — Mts. of w China to n Myanmar; winters to Malaysia and Indochina

☐ **Asian Brown Flycatcher** *Muscicapa dauurica*

Siberia to Japan, s China and India; winters to Greater Sundas

☐ **Brown-streaked Flycatcher** *Muscicapa williamsoni*
_____ *M. w. williamsoni* — S Myanmar to pen. Thailand, Malaya, s Vietnam and Sumatra
_____ *M. w. siamensis* — N plateau of Thailand and Vietnam
_____ *M. w. umbrosa* — NE Borneo (Sabah)

☐ **Ash-breasted Flycatcher** *Muscicapa randi*

N Philippines (Luzon and Negros)

☐ **Sumba Brown Flycatcher** *Muscicapa segregata*

Sumba (Lesser Sundas)

☐ **Rusty-tailed Flycatcher** *Muscicapa ruficauda*

Uzbekistan, Tajikistan and e Afghanistan to n India and Nepal

☐ **Brown-breasted Flycatcher** *Muscicapa muttui*

NE India to s China and n Vietnam; winters to Sri Lanka

☐ **Ferruginous Flycatcher** *Muscicapa ferruginea*

Nepal to n India, s China and Taiwan; winters to Indochina

☐ **Ussher's Flycatcher** *Muscicapa ussheri*

Sierra Leone to Ghana and Nigeria

☐ **Sooty Flycatcher** *Muscicapa infuscata*

____ *M. i. infuscata (chapini)* — Nigeria to nw Angola, Central African Republic and w Zaire
____ *M. i. minuscula* — NE Zaire to Uganda, nw Zambia and n Tanzania

S Nigeria to n Angola, Zaire, extreme s Sudan and nw Zambia

☐ **Boehm's Flycatcher** *Muscicapa boehmi*

Angola to Zaire, Zambia, sw Tanzania and n Mozambique

☐ **Swamp Flycatcher** *Muscicapa aquatica*

____ *M. a. aquatica* — Gambia to sw Sudan and n Zaire
____ *M. a. infulata (ruandae)* — S Sudan to e Zaire, w Kenya, nw Tanzania and ne Zambia
____ *M. a. lualabae* — SE Zaire (swamps along Lualaba River)
____ *M. a. grimwoodi* — S Zambia (Kabwe district, Suye Lake and Lukanga Swamp)

☐ **Olivaceous Flycatcher** *Muscicapa olivascens*

Sierra Leone to Liberia, Ivory Coast, Cameroon and e Zaire

☐ **Chapins' Flycatcher** *Muscicapa lendu*

____ *M. l. lendu* — Mts. of ne Zaire to sw Uganda and w Kenya (Kakamega Forest)
____ *M. l. itombwensis* — E Zaire (Itombwe Mountains)

☐ **African Dusky Flycatcher** *Muscicapa adusta*

____ *M. a. obscura (poensis, albiventris, kumboensis, okuensis)* — Highlands of Cameroon; Bioko (Gulf of Guinea)
____ *M. a. pumila (grotei, subtilis, interposita, chyulu)* — Mountains of s Sudan to Cameroon, Uganda and n Tanzania
____ *M. a. minima* — Highlands of Eritrea and ne Ethiopia
____ *M. a. marsabit* — N Kenya (Mt. Marsabit region)
____ *M. a. murina (roehli)* — Mountains of se Kenya (Taita Hills) to nw Tanzania
____ *M. a. fuelleborni* — Highlands of s and central Tanzania
____ *M. a. subadusta (angolensis)* — Angola to s Zaire, nw Zambia, Zimbabwe and Mozambique
____ *M. a. mesica* — Zimbabwe (except for eastern highlands)
____ *M. a. fuscula* — Coastal Transkei to Swaziland, Natal and e Cape Province
____ *M. a. adusta* — N and e Transvaal to Natal, Swaziland and Cape Province

☐ **Little Gray Flycatcher** *Muscicapa epulata*

Lowlands of se Guinea to Liberia, Gabon and ne Zaire

☐ **Yellow-footed Flycatcher** *Muscicapa sethsmithi*

S Nigeria and Cameroon to Gabon, Zaire and w Uganda; Bioko

☐ **Dusky-blue Flycatcher** *Muscicapa comitata*

____ *M. c. aximensis* — Sierra Leone and se Guinea to s Nigeria
____ *M. c. camerunensis* — Mt. Cameroon
____ *M. c. comitata (stuhlmanni)* — Cameroon to nw Angola, Zaire, Uganda and sw Sudan

☐ **Tessmann's Flycatcher** *Muscicapa tessmanni*

Lowlands of Ivory Coast to s Cameroon and ne Zaire

☐ **Cassin's Flycatcher** *Muscicapa cassini*

Sierra Leone to Angola, w Uganda and extreme n Zambia

☐ **Ashy Flycatcher** *Muscicapa caerulescens*

____ *M. c. nigrorum* — SE Guinea to Sierra Leone, Ghana and Togo
____ *M. c. brevicauda* — SE Nigeria to nw Angola, e Zaire, s Sudan and Uganda
____ *M. c. cinereola* — S Somalia to e Kenya and e Tanzania
____ *M. c. impavida* — S Zaire to sw Angola, Namibia, w Tanzania and n Mozambique
____ *M. c. vulturna* — S Malawi to s Zimbabwe, e Transvaal and n Swaziland
____ *M. c. caerulescens* — Extreme s Mozambique to Natal and e Cape Province

☐ **Gray-throated Tit-Flycatcher** *Myioparus griseigularis*

____ *M. g. parelii* — Liberia (Mt. Nimba) to Ivory Coast and Ghana
____ *M. g. griseigularis* — SE Nigeria to nw Angola, e Zaire, w Uganda and nw Tanzania

☐ **Gray Tit-Flycatcher** *Myioparus plumbeus*

____ *M. p. plumbeus*   Senegambia to nw Angola, s Ethiopia, Uganda and nw Tanzania
____ *M. p. orientalis*   Lowlands of e Kenya to e Tanzania, Mozambique and Natal
____ *M. p. catoleucum (grandior)*   Angola plateau to Namibia, s Zaire, Botswana, Malawi and Natal

☐ **Grand Comoro Flycatcher** *Humblotia flavirostris*

Grand Comoro I. (Mt. Karthala)

☐ **European Pied Flycatcher** *Ficedula hypoleuca*

____ *F. h. hypoleuca*   British Isles and n Europe to w Siberia; winters to tropical Africa
____ *F. h. iberiae*   Iberian Peninsula; winters in west Africa
____ *F. h. tomensis* (syn. *sibirica*)   *Taiga* of w Siberia (Ural Mts. to Yenisey R.); winters to e Africa
____ *F. h. speculigera*   Morocco (south to Middle Atlas Mts.), n Algeria and n Tunisia

☐ **Collared Flycatcher** *Ficedula albicollis*

E France to Balkans and Ukraine; winters in tropical and s Africa

☐ **Semicollared Flycatcher** *Ficedula semitorquata*

Montane forests of Balkan Pen. to nw Iran; winters in e Africa

☐ **Korean Flycatcher** *Ficedula zanthopygia*

Mountains of ne Asia; winters in SE Asia and Greater Sundas

☐ **Narcissus Flycatcher** *Ficedula narcissina*

____ *F. n. elisae*   Mts. of ne China (n Liaoning); winters to s China and Hainan
____ *F. n. narcissina*   Sakhalin to Japan; winters to Philippines and Borneo
____ *F. n. owstoni*   S Ryukyu Islands

☐ **Mugimaki Flycatcher** *Ficedula mugimaki*

SE Siberia, Sakhalin and ne China; winters to SE Asia, Indonesia

☐ **Slaty-backed Flycatcher** *Ficedula hodgsonii*

Himalayas (Nepal to n Myanmar and sw China); winters SE Asia

☐ **Rufous-gorgeted Flycatcher** *Ficedula strophiata*

____ *F. s. strophiata*   Himalayas to s China and n Thailand; winters to n Indochina
____ *F. s. fuscogularis*   S Laos (Langbian Plateau)

☐ **Red-breasted Flycatcher** *Ficedula parva*

____ *F. p. parva*   N Europe to s Urals, Balkans and s Caspian; winters to s Asia
____ *F. p. albicilla*   Siberia to Kamchatka Pen. and n Mongolia; winters to Borneo

☐ **Kashmir Flycatcher** *Ficedula subrubra*

Himalayas of n India (Kashmir); winters to s India and Sri Lanka

☐ **Snowy-browed Flycatcher** *Ficedula hyperythra*

____ *F. h. hyperythra*   E Himalayas to s China, Myanmar, nw Thailand and n Vietnam
____ *F. h. annamensis*   S China (sw Yunnan) and n Laos (Langbian Plateau)
____ *F. h. sumatrana*   Malay Peninsula, Sumatra and Borneo
____ *F. h. mjobergi*   W Borneo (Poi Mountains)
____ *F. h. vulcani*   Java, Bali and w Lesser Sundas (Lombok, Sumbawa and Flores)
____ *F. h. innexa*   Taiwan
____ *F. h. luzoniensis*   Luzon (n Philippines)
____ *F. h. mindorensis*   Mindoro (Philippines)
____ *F. h. calayensis*   Calayan (Philippines)
____ *F. h. nigrorum*   Negros (Philippines)
____ *F. h. montigena*   Mountains of central Mindanao (s Philippines)
____ *F. h. daggayana*   N. Mindanao (s Philippines)
____ *F. h. malindangensis*   Mt. Malindang region of nw Mindanao I. (s Philippines)
____ *F. h. rara*   Palawan (sw Philippines)
____ *F. h. annalisa*   N peninsula of Sulawesi
____ *F. h. jugosae*   Central and s Sulawesi and Taliabu I. (Sula Islands)
____ *F. h. pallidipectus*   Bacan (s Moluccas)
____ *F. h. alifura*   Buru (s Moluccas)
____ *F. h. negroides*   Seram (s Moluccas)
____ *F. h. clarae*   Timor (e Lesser Sundas)
____ *F. h. audacis*   Babar (e Lesser Sundas)

☐ **White-gorgeted Flycatcher** *Ficedula monileger*
_____ *F. m. monileger* — Himalayas of Nepal to Bhutan and ne India (Arunachal Pradesh)
_____ *F. m. leucops* — NE India to s China (Yunnan), Myanmar, Thailand and n Vietnam
_____ *F. m. gularis* — Myanmar (Arakan Yoma Mountains)

☐ **Rufous-browed Flycatcher** *Ficedula solitaris*
_____ *F. s. submonileger* — Mountains of se Myanmar to peninsular Thailand and s Vietnam
_____ *F. s. malayana* — Mountains of Malay Peninsula
_____ *F. s. solitaris* — Mountains of Sumatra

☐ **Rufous-chested Flycatcher** *Ficedula dumetoria*
_____ *F. d. muelleri* — Peninsular Thailand, Malaysia, Sumatra and Borneo
_____ *F. d. dumetoria* — Java, Bali and w Lesser Sundas (Lombok, Sumbawa and Flores)
_____ *F. d. riedeli* — Tanimbar Islands (Larat and Yamdena)

☐ **Rufous-throated Flycatcher** *Ficedula rufigula*

Lowland rainforests of Sulawesi

☐ **Cinnamon-chested Flycatcher** *Ficedula buruensis*
_____ *F. b. buruensis* — Buru (s Moluccas)
_____ *F. b. ceramensis* — Seram (s Moluccas)
_____ *F. b. siebersi* — Kai Besar (Kai Islands)

☐ **Little Slaty Flycatcher** *Ficedula basilanica*
_____ *F. b. samarensis* — Central Philippines (Leyte and Samar)
_____ *F. b. basilanica* — S Philippines (Basilan, Dinagat and Mindanao)

☐ **Sumba Flycatcher** *Ficedula harterti*

Lowlands of Sumba (w Lesser Sundas)

☐ **Palawan Flycatcher** *Ficedula platenae*

Lowlands of Palawan (sw Philippines)

☐ **Russet-tailed Flycatcher** *Ficedula crypta*

Submontane forests of Mindanao (s Philippines)

☐ **Furtive Flycatcher** *Ficedula disposita*

Submontane forests of Luzon (n Philippines)

☐ **Lompobattang Flycatcher** *Ficedula bonthaina*

SW Sulawesi (Lompobattang massif)

☐ **Little Pied Flycatcher** *Ficedula westermanni*
_____ *F. w. collini* — Himalayas (Nepal to Sikkim); winters to plains of India
_____ *F. w. australorientis* — Himalayas (Bhutan to s China, n Myanmar, Thailand, Indochina)
_____ *F. w. langbianis* — S Laos (Langbian Plateau) and Vietnam
_____ *F. w. westermanni* — S Thailand, Malaysia, Sumatra, Borneo, Sulawesi and Mindanao
_____ *F. w. hasselti* — S Sumatra, Java, Bali, Lombok, Sumbawa, Flores and s Sulawesi
_____ *F. w. mayri* — E Lesser Sundas (Timor and Wetar)
_____ *F. w. rabori* — N Philippines (Luzon, Negros and Panay)
_____ *F. w. palawanensis* — Mountains of s Palawan (sw Philippines)

☐ **Ultramarine Flycatcher** *Ficedula superciliaris*
_____ *F. s. superciliaris* — Himalayas (n Pakistan to Nepal and Sikkim); winters to c India
_____ *F. s. aestigma* — Himalayas (Bhutan to se Tibet, sw China, Myanmar and n India)

☐ **Slaty-blue Flycatcher** *Ficedula tricolor*
_____ *F. t. tricolor* — Himalayas (Kashmir to central Nepal)
_____ *F. t. minuta* — Himalayas (e Nepal to se Tibet) and ne India (Arunachal Pradesh)
_____ *F. t. cerviniventris* — N India (Manipur Hills) to Myanmar (Chin Hills)
_____ *F. t. diversa* — Mountains of s-central China; winters to n Indochina

☐ **Black-and-rufous Flycatcher** *Ficedula nigrorufa*

Mountains of sw India (w Maharashtra south to Kerala)

☐ **Sapphire Flycatcher** *Ficedula sapphira*

_____ *F. s. sapphira*	Himalayas (e Nepal to se Tibet, sw China and ne India)
_____ *F. s. tienchuanensis*	Mountains of w-central China (Sichuan to s Shaanxi)
_____ *F. s. laotiana*	Mountains of nw Thailand, n Laos and n Vietnam

☐ **Black-banded Flycatcher** *Ficedula timorensis*

Timor (e Lesser Sundas)

☐ **Blue-and-white Flycatcher** *Cyanoptila cyanomelana*

_____ *C. c. cumatilis*	NE Asia; winters to Philippines, Indochina and Greater Sundas
_____ *C. c. cyanomelana*	Japan and Korea; winters to Myanmar, Thailand and Gr. Sundas

☐ **Verditer Flycatcher** *Eumyias thalassina*

_____ *E. t. thalassina*	N Pakistan to s China and Indochina; winters to pen. India
_____ *E. t. thalassoides*	Peninsular Thailand, Malaya, Sumatra and (rarely) Borneo

☐ **Dull-blue Flycatcher** *Eumyias sordida*

Forested uplands of Sri Lanka

☐ **Island Flycatcher** *Eumyias panayensis*

_____ *E. p. septentrionalis*	Montane forests of n, central and se Sulawesi
_____ *E. p. meriodionalis*	Montane forests of s Sulawesi
_____ *E. p. sanghirensis*	Talaud Islands., Sangihe, Siau, Tahulandang, Ruang and Biaro is.
_____ *E. p. subspecies?*	Taliabu (Sula Islands)
_____ *E. p. obiensis*	Montane forests of Obi (s Moluccas)
_____ *E. p. harterti*	Montane forests of Seram (s Moluccas)
_____ *E. p. nigrimentalis*	N Philippines (montane forests of Luzon and Mindoro)
_____ *E. p. panayensis*	Central Philippines (montane forests of Negros and Panay)
_____ *E. p. nigriloris*	S Philippines (montane forests of Mindanao)

☐ **Nilgiri Flycatcher** *Eumyias albicaudata*

Foothill forests of sw peninsular India (Mysore south to Kerala)

☐ **Indigo Flycatcher** *Eumyias indigo*

_____ *E. i. ruficrissa*	High montane forests of Sumatra
_____ *E. i. indigo*	High montane forests of Java
_____ *E. i. cerviniventris*	High montane forests of Borneo

☐ **Large Niltava** *Niltava grandis*

_____ *N. g. grandis*	Himalayas (Nepal to n Myanmar, s China and n Indochina)
_____ *N. g. griseiventris*	S China (se Yunnan)
_____ *N. g. decipiens*	Peninsular Thailand to Malaysia and Sumatra
_____ *N. g. decorata*	S Laos (Langbian Plateau)

☐ **Small Niltava** *Niltava macgrigoriae*

_____ *N. m. macgrigoriea*	Himalayas of Nepal to s China and ne India (Darjiling)
_____ *N. m. signata*	E Himalayas to Bhutan, n Myanmar, nw Thailand and Indochina

☐ **Fujian Niltava** *Niltava davidi*

Central and s China; winters to se Thailand and Indochina

☐ **Rufous-bellied Niltava** *Niltava sundara*

_____ *N. s. whistleri*	W Himalayas from Pakistan to n India (Kumaon)
_____ *N. s. sundara*	E Himalayas to se Tibet, s China (n Yunnan) and n Laos
_____ *N. s. denotata*	SW China to n Myanmar; winters to n Thailand and n Laos

☐ **Rufous-vented Niltava** *Niltava sumatrana*

Mountains of Malay Peninsula and Sumatra

☐ **Vivid Niltava** *Niltava vivida*

_____ *N. v. oatesi*	SE Tibet to sw China, ne India, Myanmar and n Vietnam
_____ *N. v. vivida*	Taiwan

☐ **Matinan Flycatcher** *Cyornis sanfordi*

Mountains of n Sulawesi

☐ **Blue-fronted Flycatcher** *Cyornis hoevelli*

Montane forests of central and se Sulawesi

☐ **Timor Blue-Flycatcher** *Cyornis hyacinthinus*
_____ *C. h. hyacinthinus* — E Lesser Sundas (Roti, Semau and Timor)
_____ *C. h. kuehni* — Wetar (e Lesser Sundas)

☐ **White-tailed Flycatcher** *Cyornis concretus*
_____ *C. c. cyanea* — Mountains of ne India to s China, Myanmar and n Thailand
_____ *C. c. concretus* — Mountains of s Malay Peninsula and Sumatra
_____ *C. c. everetti* — Mountains of n Borneo

☐ **Rueck's Blue-Flycatcher** *Cyornis ruckii*

Known from four specimens ca 1919 from ne Sumatra

☐ **Blue-breasted Flycatcher** *Cyornis herioti*
_____ *C. h. herioti* — N Philippines (mountains of n and central Luzon)
_____ *C. h. camarinensis* — N Philippines (mountains of s Luzon and Catanduanes)

☐ **Hainan Blue-Flycatcher** *Cyornis hainanus*

Mts. of s China to s Myanmar, Thailand and Indochina; Hainan

☐ **White-bellied Blue-Flycatcher** *Cyornis pallipes*

Uplands of sw India (w Maharashtra to Kerala)

☐ **Pale-chinned Blue-Flycatcher** *Cyornis poliogenys*
_____ *C. p. poliogenys* — Himalayas (central Nepal to ne India, Bhutan and w Myanmar)
_____ *C. p. cachariensis* — E Himalayas (Assam) to nw Myanmar and s China (nw Yunnan)
_____ *C. p. laurentei* — SW China (se Yunnan)
_____ *C. p. vernayi* — E India (Eastern Ghats from n Orissa to Andhra Pradesh)

☐ **Pale Blue-Flycatcher** *Cyornis unicolor*
_____ *C. u. unicolor* — Himalayas (Garhwal) to n India, n Myanmar, s China and n Laos
_____ *C. u. diaoluoensis* — Hainan (s China)
_____ *C. u. harterti* — Malay Pen. (south of Isthmus of Kra), Sumatra, Java and Borneo

☐ **Blue-throated Flycatcher** *Cyornis rubeculoides*
_____ *C. r. rubeculoides* — Kashmir to n India and n Myanmar; winters to Sri Lanka
_____ *C. r. dialilaema* — E Myanmar to n and sw Thailand
_____ *C. .r. rogersi* — Myanmar (Arakan Yoma and lower Chindwin River area)
_____ *C. r. glaucicomans* — S China (Sichuan, Guizhou, w Hubei and Shaanxi)
_____ *C. r. klossi* — E Thailand to s Laos and s Vietnam

☐ **Hill Blue-Flycatcher** *Cyornis banyumas*
_____ *C. b. magnirostris* — Himalayas (Nepal to Bangladesh); winters to pen. Thailand
_____ *C. b. whitei* — NE Myanmar to s China, ne Thailand, n Laos and n Vietnam
_____ *C. b. lekhakuni* — Eastern plateau of Thailand
_____ *C. b. deignani* — SE Thailand
_____ *C. b. coerulifrons* — Malay Peninsula (south of Isthmus of Kra)
_____ *C. b. liga* — E Java
_____ *C. b. banyumas* — Central Java
_____ *C. b. coeruleatus* — Borneo

☐ **Long-billed Blue-Flycatcher** *Cyornis caerulatus*
_____ *C. c. albiventer* — Lowland forests of Sumatra
_____ *C. c. rufifrons* — Lowland forests of w Borneo
_____ *C. c. caerulatus* — Lowland forests of n, e and s Borneo

☐ **Malaysian Blue-Flycatcher** *Cyornis turcosus*
_____ *C. t. rupatensis* — Lowland forests of Malaysia, Sumatra and w Borneo
_____ *C. t. turcosus* — Lowland forests of central and e Borneo

☐ **Palawan Blue-Flycatcher** *Cyornis lemprieri*

SW Philippines (Balabac, Calamian and Palawan)

☐ **Bornean Blue-Flycatcher** *Cyornis superbus*

Montane forests of Borneo

☐ **Tickell's Blue-Flycatcher** *Cyornis tickelliae*

_____	*C. t. tickelliae*	India to sw China (s Yunnan), n Myanmar and Bangladesh
_____	*C. t. jerdoni*	Sri Lanka
_____	*C. t. sumatrensis*	S peninsular Thailand to Malaysia and ne Sumatra
_____	*C. t. indochina*	S Myanmar to Thailand and Indochina
_____	*C. t. lampra*	Anambas Islands (South China Sea)

☐ **Mangrove Blue-Flycatcher** *Cyornis rufigastra*

_____	*C. r. rufigastra*	Coastal lowlands of s Thailand, Malaya, Sumatra and Borneo
_____	*C. r. lepidula*	Karimunjawa Islands (Java Sea)
_____	*C. r. rhizohorae*	W Java and Sebesi I. (Sunda Strait)
_____	*C. r. karimatensis*	Karimata I. (off sw Borneo)
_____	*C. r. blythi*	N Philippines (Luzon and Polillo)
_____	*C. r. marinduqensis*	Philippines (Marinduque)
_____	*C. r. mindorensis*	Philippines (Mindoro)
_____	*C. r. philippensis* (includes *litoralis*)	Central and s Philippines, Palawan and Sulu Archipelago

☐ **Sulawesi Blue-Flycatcher** *Cyornis omissus*

_____	*C. o. omissus*	Sulawesi
_____	*C. o. peromissa*	Salayar I. (Flores Sea)
_____	*C. o. djampeanus*	Tanahjampea I. (Flores Sea)
_____	*C. o. kalaoensis*	Kalao I. (Flores Sea)

☐ **Pygmy Blue-Flycatcher** *Muscicapella hodgsoni*

_____	*M. h. hodgsoni*	Himalayas of Nepal to ne India, Bhutan, Myanmar and Thailand
_____	*M. h. sondaica*	Mountains of Thailand, Malaya, Sumatra and Borneo

☐ **Gray-headed Canary-flycatcher** *Culicicapa ceylonensis*

_____	*C. c. calochrysea*	Pakistan to n India, s China, Myanmar, Malaysia and Indochina
_____	*C. c. ceylonensis*	S India and Sri Lanka to Sumatra, Java, Borneo and Palawan
_____	*C. c. sejuncta*	W Lesser Sundas (Lombok and Flores)
_____	*C. c. connectens*	Sumba (w Lesser Sundas)

☐ **Citrine Canary-flycatcher** *Culicicapa helianthea*

_____	*C. h. septentrionalis*	N Philippines (nw Luzon)
_____	*C. h. zimmeri*	Philippines (Luzon and Catanduanes)
_____	*C. h. panayensis*	Panay, Negros, Cebu, Leyte, Mindanao, Biliran and Palawan
_____	*C. h. mayri*	Sulu Archipelago (Bongao and Tawitawi)
_____	*C. h. helianthea*	Sulawesi, Salayar, Banggai and Sula islands

☐ **Dohrn's Flycatcher** *Horizorhinus dohrni*

Príncipe (Gulf of Guinea)

☐ **White-starred Robin** *Pogonocichla stellata*

_____	*P. s. ruwenzorii* (*friedmanni*)	NE Zaire (Kivu region) to sw Uganda, Rwanda and Burundi
_____	*P. s. guttifer*	Mt. Kilimanjaro (n Tanzania)
_____	*P. s. elgonensis*	Mt. Elgon region on Kenya/Uganda border
_____	*P. s. pallidiflava*	S Sudan (Imatong Mountains)
_____	*P. s. macarthuri*	SE Kenya (Chyulu Mountains)
_____	*P. s. helleri*	Kenya (Taita Hills) and Tanzania (Pare Mountains)
_____	*P. s. orientalis*	Tanzania to Zambia, Malawi and central Mozambique
_____	*P. s. transvaalensis* (*lebombo*)	Highlands of e Zimbabwe, ne Transvaal and Mozambique
_____	*P. s. stellata*	Zululand and Natal to Orange Free State and s Cape Province
_____	*P. s. intensa*	Sudan to Kenya and n Tanzania

☐ **Swynnerton's Robin** *Swynnertonia swynnertoni*

_____	*S. s. rodgersi*	E Tanzania (Udzungwa Mountains)
_____	*S. s. swynnertoni* (*umbratica*)	Mountains of e Zimbabwe and w Mozambique

☐ **Forest Robin** *Stiphrornis erythrothorax*

____ S. e. erythrothorax	Sierra Leone to s Nigeria
____ S. e. gabonensis	Coastal Cameroon and Gabon; Bioko (Gulf of Guinea)
____ S. e. xanthogaster (mabirae)	E Cameroon to e Zaire, w Uganda and extreme s Sudan

☐ **Bocage's Akalat** *Sheppardia bocagei*

____ S. b. granti	Mountains of se Nigeria and w Cameroon
____ S. b. poensis (insulana)	Bioko (Gulf of Guinea)
____ S. b. kaboboensis	E Zaire (Mt. Kabobo)
____ S. b. schoutedeni	E Zaire (mountains west of Lake Edward to Kivu))
____ S. b. bocagei	Western highlands of Angola
____ S. b. kungwensis	W Tanzania (Kungwe-Mahari Mountains)
____ S. b. ilyai	W Tanzania (east of Mt. Kungwe)
____ S. b. chapini	SE Zaire and n-central Zambia

☐ **Lowland Akalat** *Sheppardia cyornithopsis*

____ S. c. houghtoni	Lowlands of Guinea to Sierra Leone, Liberia and Ivory Coast
____ S. c. cyornithopsis	Lowland forests of s Cameroon and Gabon
____ S. c. lopezi	Lowland forests of e Zaire to w Uganda and nw Tanzania

☐ **Equatorial Akalat** *Sheppardia aequatorialis*

____ S. a. aequatorialis	Mts. of e Zaire to sw Uganda, w Rwanda, Burundi and w Kenya
____ S. a. acholiensis	S Sudan (Imatong Mountains)

☐ **Sharpe's Akalat** *Sheppardia sharpei*

____ S. s. usambarae	Tanzania (Usambara Mountains and Nguru Mountains)
____ S. s. sharpei	Montane forests of sw Tanzania to Zambia and n Malawi

☐ **East Coast Akalat** *Sheppardia gunningi*

____ S. g. sokokensis	Coastal and riverine forests of se Kenya to e Tanzania
____ S. g. bensoni	Lowlands of nw Malawi
____ S. g. gunningi	SE Mozambique

☐ **Gabela Akalat** *Sheppardia gabela*

	Angola (humid montane forests of Gabela escarpment)

☐ **Usambara Akalat** *Sheppardia montana*

	NE Tanzania (w Usambara Mountains)

☐ **Iringa Akalat** *Sheppardia lowei*

	Dry montane forests of s-central Tanzania

☐ **European Robin** *Erithacus rubecula*

____ E. r. melophilus	British Isles and Scandinavia
____ E. r. rubecula	W Europe, nw Morocco, Azores, Madeira and w Canary Islands
____ E. r. superbus	Central Canary Islands (Teneriffe and Gran Canaria)
____ E. r. witherbyi (sardus)	S Spain, Corsica, Sardinia, ne Morocco, Algeria and Tunisia
____ E. r. balcanicus	Balkan Peninsula to w Turkey
____ E. r. valens	Crimean Peninsula
____ E. r. hyrcanus	SE Transcaucasia to n Iran
____ E. r. tataricus	W Siberia (Ural Mountains to Semipalatinsk); winters to Iran

☐ **Japanese Robin** *Erithacus akahige*

____ E. a. akahige	S Kuril and Sakhalin is. to n Japanese Arch.; winters to s China
____ E. a. rishirensis	Rishiri I. (off nw Hokkaido)
____ E. a. tanensis	S Japanese Arch. (Izu, Tanegashima and Yakushima islands)

☐ **Ryukyu Robin** *Erithacus komadori*

____ E. k. komadori	Ryukyu Is. (Tanega-Shima, Amami-O-Shima, Tokuno-Shima)
____ E. k. namiyei	Okinawa (central Ryukyu Islands)
____ E. k. subrufus	S Ryukyu Islands (Ishigaki, Iriomote and Yonaguni)

465

☐ **Rufous-tailed Robin** *Luscinia sibilans*

Breeds s Siberia to Sea of Okhotsk; winters s China to SE Asia

☐ **Thrush Nightingale** *Luscinia luscinia*

N Eurasia; winters to e and s Africa

☐ **Common Nightingale** *Luscinia megarhynchos*

_____ *L. m. megarhynchos* W Europe, N Africa and Asia Minor; winters in tropical Africa
_____ *L. m. africana* Caucasus and e Turkey to sw Iran and Iraq; winters to E Africa
_____ *L. m. hafizi* Aral Sea to Mongolia; winters coastal e Africa

☐ **Siberian Rubythroat** *Luscinia calliope*

Siberia to Japan; winters to SE Asia, Philippines and Palau Is.

☐ **White-tailed Rubythroat** *Luscinia pectoralis*

_____ *L. p. pectoralis* Mountains of Turkestan to Afghanistan (Pamirs) and n Pakistan
_____ *L. p. confusus* E Himalayas (Nepal to Bhutan); winters to ne India
_____ *L. p. ballioni* W China (w Xinjiang from Tien Shan to Kashgar)
_____ *L. p. tschebaiewi* E Ladakh to nw China (Gansu), se Tibet and extreme n Myanmar

☐ **Bluethroat** *Luscinia svecica*

_____ *L. s. svecica (gaetkei, robusta)* Scandinavia across Siberia to w Alaska; winters N Africa, s Asia
_____ *L. s. namnetum* Western France
_____ *L. s. cyanecula* Central Europe and Spain; winters to North Africa
_____ *L. s. volgae* NE Ukraine to middle Volga River
_____ *L. s. magna* Caucasus area, e Turkey and Iran; winters to Sudan and Ethiopia
_____ *L. s. luristanica* Armenia to sw Iran; winters to Iraq and the Sudan
_____ *L. s. pallidogularis (saturatior, altaica)* SW Siberia to Turkmenistan, Altai Mts. and upper Yenisey
_____ *L. s. tianschanica* Pamir Mountains and Tien Shan Mountains
_____ *L. s. abbotti* W Pakistan and nw India
_____ *L. s. przewalskii* Inner Mongolia to w China (Qinghai) and s Tibet
_____ *L. s. kobdensis* W China (Xinjiang)

☐ **Rufous-headed Robin** *Luscinia ruficeps*

N-central China (Tsingling Mountains of Shaanxi and Sichuan)

☐ **Black-throated Blue Robin** *Luscinia obscura*

W cent. China (se Gansu, sw Shaanxi, n Sichuan and n Yunnan)

☐ **Firethroat** *Luscinia pectardens*

Mts. of se Tibet to w-central China; winters to ne Myanmar

☐ **Indian Blue Robin** *Luscinia brunnea*

_____ *L. b. brunnea* Himalayas (Pakistan to Bhutan and se Tibet); winters to Sri Lanka
_____ *L. b. wickhami* Myanmar (Chin Hills)

☐ **Siberian Blue Robin** *Luscinia cyane*

_____ *L. c. cyane* S Siberia (Altai Mts. to Sea of Okhotsk); winters to Indonesia
_____ *L. c. bochaiensis* E Siberia to ne China, Korea and Japan; winters to Malaysia

☐ **Red-flanked Bluetail** *Tarsiger cyanurus*

_____ *T. c. cyanurus* N Russia to n Japan; winters to s China, Taiwan and Gr. Sundas
_____ *T. c. pallidior* Afghanistan to Nepal; winters to Myanmar, Thailand and Laos
_____ *T. c. rufilatus* Nepal to ne India and sw China; winters to Indochina

☐ **Golden Bush-Robin** *Tarsiger chrysaeus*

_____ *T. c. whistleri* N Pakistan to Kashmir and nw India
_____ *T. c. chrysaeus* Nepal to ne India, n Myanmar and w China; winters to n Vietnam

☐ **White-browed Bush-Robin** *Tarsiger indicus*

_____ *T. i. indicus* Himalayas (Nepal to Bhutan, se Tibet and Assam)
_____ *T. i. yunnanensis* SW China (Yunnan); winters to n Myanmar and n Tonkin
_____ *T. i. formosanus* Mountains of Taiwan

☐ **Rufous-breasted Bush-Robin** *Tarsiger hyperythrus*

Himalayas (ne India, se Tibet and s China); winters to Myanmar

☐ **Collared Bush-Robin** *Tarsiger johnstoniae*

Mountains of Taiwan

☐ **White-throated Robin** *Irania gutturalis*

Turkey to Iraq, Iran and s Turkestan; winters in East Africa

☐ **White-bellied Robin-Chat** *Cossyphicula roberti*
_____ *C. r. roberti* — Montane forests of se Nigeria and w Cameroon; Bioko
_____ *C. r. rufescentior* — Montane forests of e Zaire, Rwanda and sw Uganda

☐ **Mountain Robin-Chat** *Cossypha isabellae*
_____ *C. i. batesi* — Montane forests of se Nigeria
_____ *C. i. isabellae* — Montane forests of Mt. Cameroon

☐ **Archer's Robin-Chat** *Cossypha archeri*
_____ *C. a. archeri (albimentalis)* — Montane forests of e Zaire to Rwanda, Burundi and sw Uganda
_____ *C. a. kimbutui* — Montane forests of se Zaire (Mt. Kabobo)

☐ **Olive-flanked Robin-Chat** *Cossypha anomala*
_____ *C. a. grotei* — Highlands of e Tanzania
_____ *C. a. mbuluensis* — N-central Tanzania (Mbulu region)
_____ *C. a. macclounii* — S Tanzania (Tukuyu District) to n Malawi (Viphya Plateau)
_____ *C. a. anomala* — N-central Malawi (Mt. Mulanje region)
_____ *C. a. gurue* — Montane forests of n-central Mozambique

☐ **Cape Robin-Chat** *Cossypha caffra*
_____ *C. c. iolaema* — Mts. of extreme s Sudan to Kenya, Zambia and Mozambique
_____ *C. c. kivuensis* — E Zaire (Kivu highlands) and sw Uganda
_____ *C. c. drakensbergi* — Natal-Transvaal border to e Transvaal
_____ *C. c. vespera* — Highlands of e Zimbabwe
_____ *C. c. namaquensis* — S Namibia to Orange Free State and w Transvaal
_____ *C. c. caffra* — Natal to Swaziland and Cape Province

☐ **White-throated Robin-Chat** *Cossypha humeralis*

E Botswana to s Mozambique, e Transvaal and n Natal

☐ **Blue-shouldered Robin-Chat** *Cossypha cyanocampter*
_____ *C. c. cyanocampter* — Guinea to Mali, Sierra Leone, Cameroon and Gabon
_____ *C. c. bartteloti (pallidiventris)* — NE Zaire to s Sudan, Uganda and w Kenya

☐ **Gray-winged Robin-Chat** *Cossypha polioptera*

Sierra Leone to se Sudan, w Kenya, nw Tanzania and ne Angola

☐ **Rueppell's Robin-Chat** *Cossypha semirufa*
_____ *C. s. semirufa* — SE Sudan (Boma Hills) to Eritrea, Ethiopia and n Kenya
_____ *C. s. donaldsoni* — E and se Ethiopia (Harrar and e Gallaland)
_____ *C. s. intercedens* — S-central highlands of Kenya to n Tanzania (Mt. Kilimanjaro)

☐ **White-browed Robin-Chat** *Cossypha heuglini*
_____ *C. h. heuglini* — Zaire to s Sudan, s Ethiopia, Angola, Zimbabwe and e Transvaal
_____ *C. h. subrufescens* — Gabon to n Angola and extreme w Zaire
_____ *C. h. intermedia* — Coastal e Somalia to e Kenya, Tanzania and n Natal

☐ **Red-capped Robin-Chat** *Cossypha natalensis*
_____ *C. n. larischi* — Nigeria to n Angola
_____ *C. n. intensa (garguensis) (tennenti)* — S Somalia and Sudan to Angola, e Transvaal and Mozambique
_____ *C. n. natalensis* — Coastal Natal to e Cape Province

☐ **Chorister Robin-Chat** *Cossypha dichroa*
_____ *C. d. dichroa* — Forests of e and s South Africa and w Swaziland
_____ *C. d. mimica* — NE Transvaal (Zoutpansberg and Woodbush)

☐ **White-headed Robin-Chat** *Cossypha heinrichi*

Savanna and forests of nw Angola and adjacent w Zaire

467

☐ **Snowy-crowned Robin-Chat** *Cossypha niveicapilla*
____ *C. n. niveicapilla* — Senegal to s Sudan, sw Ethiopia, Uganda, Kenya and Tanzania
____ *C. n. melanonota* — Lake Victoria basin

☐ **White-crowned Robin-Chat** *Cossypha albicapilla*
____ *C. a. albicapilla* — Senegal to Guinea
____ *C. a. giffardi* — Ghana to Nigeria, s Chad and n Cameroon
____ *C. a. omoensis* — Extreme se Sudan to sw Ethiopia

☐ **Angola Cave-Chat** *Xenocopsychus ansorgei* — Rocky caves and gorges of w Angola

☐ **Collared Palm-Thrush** *Cichladusa arquata* — Coastal Kenya to Mozambique, Caprivi Strip and se Angola

☐ **Rufous-tailed Palm-Thrush** *Cichladusa ruficauda* — Scrub and palms of s Gabon to coastal Angola and n Namibia

☐ **Spotted Morning-Thrush** *Cichladusa guttata*
____ *C. g. guttata* — S Sudan to w Uganda, Zaire and nw Kenya (w of Lake Turkana)
____ *C. g. intercalans* — SW Ethiopia to Kenya, Tanzania to e Zaire
____ *C. g. rufipennis* — Littoral of s Somalia to e Kenya and e Tanzania (Dar-es-Salaam)

☐ **Forest Scrub-Robin** *Cercotrichas leucosticta*
____ *C. l. leucosticta* — Ghana
____ *C. l. colstoni* — Sierra Leone (Kambui Hills) and Liberia
____ *C. l. collsi* — Central African Republic to ne Zaire and w Uganda
____ *C. l. reichenowi* — N Angola (Huila escarpment)

☐ **Bearded Scrub-Robin** *Cercotrichas quadrivirgata*
____ *C. q. quadrivirgata* — S Somalia to Kenya, Tanzania, Botswana, Zambia and ne S Africa
____ *C. q. greenwayi* — Zanzibar and Mafia I. (off Tanzania)

☐ **Miombo Scrub-Robin** *Cercotrichas barbata* — Angola to Zaire, Burundi, Zambia, sw Tanzania, n Mozambique

☐ **Brown Scrub-Robin** *Cercotrichas signata*
____ *C. s. tongensis (reclusa) (oatleyi)* — Extreme s Mozambique to e Swaziland and n Natal
____ *C. s. signata* — South Africa (Transvaal and s Natal to se Cape Province)

☐ **Brown-backed Scrub-Robin** *Cercotrichas hartlaubi* — Locally in s Cameroon; nw Angola to w Kenya and nw Tanzania

☐ **Red-backed Scrub-Robin** *Cercotrichas leucophrys*
____ *C. l. leucoptera* — S Sudan to ne Uganda, s Ethiopia, n Somalia and n Kenya
____ *C. l. zambesiana* — S Sudan to e Kenya, n Mozambique and e Zambia
____ *C. l. eluta* — S Somalia (Juba River area) and adjacent ne Kenya
____ *C. l. brunneiceps* — Central Kenya to ne Tanzania (w of Kilimanjaro to Loliondo)
____ *C. l. vulpina* — S central Kenya to extreme ne Tanzania
____ *C. l. sclateri* — Central Tanzania
____ *C. l. munda* — Congo River to central Angola and Zaire (Katanga)
____ *C. l. ovamboensis* — S Angola to sw Zambia, n Botswana, n Namibia, w Zimbabwe
____ *C. l. leucophrys* — S Zimbabwe and Transvaal to s Cape Province

☐ **Rufous-tailed Scrub-Robin** *Cercotrichas galactotes*
____ *C. g. galactotes* — W Mediterranean basin and North Africa; winters to s Sahara
____ *C. g. syriacus* — E Mediterranean basin and Middle East; winters to e Africa
____ *C. g. familiaris* — S Caucasus to Iran and Pakistan; winters to s Arabia

☐ **Kalahari Scrub-Robin** *Cercotrichas paena*
____ *C. p. benguellensis* — SW Angola (Benguela Province)
____ *C. p. damarensis* — Namibia
____ *C. p. paena* — Botswana to Zimbabwe, w Transvaal and n Cape Province
____ *C. p. oriens* — W Orange Free State to s Transvaal and s Zimbabwe

□ **African Scrub-Robin** *Cercotrichas minor*

____	*C. m. minor*	Senegambia to Sudan, Eritrea, Ethiopia and n Somalia
____	*C. m. hamertoni*	E Somalia (Beira and Wagar mountains)

□ **Karoo Scrub-Robin** *Cercotrichas coryphaeus*

____	*C. c. coryphaeus*	S Namibia to Botswana and w Cape Province
____	*C. c. cinerea*	SE Namibia to sw Cape Province
____	*C. c. eurina*	Orange Free State to Lesotho

□ **Black Scrub-Robin** *Cercotrichas podobe*

____	*C. p. podobe*	Mauritania to Chad, Sudan, Eritrea, Ethiopia and n Somalia
____	*C. p. melanoptera*	W Saudi Arabia, Yemen and Aden

□ **Herero Chat** *Namibornis herero*

Rocky bush country of extreme sw Angola to w Namibia

□ **Madagascar Magpie-Robin** *Copsychus albospecularis*

____	*C. a. albospecularis*	N Madagascar
____	*C. a. inexpectatus*	E Madagascar
____	*C. a. pica*	W Madagascar
____	*C. a. winterbottomi*	SW Madagascar

□ **Oriental Magpie-Robin** *Copsychus saularis*

____	*C. s. saularis*	Lowlands of Pakistan to n and w India
____	*C. s. ceylonensis*	SE India and Sri Lanka
____	*C. s. erimelas*	NE India to Myanmar, Thailand and Indochina
____	*C. s. andamanensis*	Andaman Islands
____	*C. s. prosthopellus*	S China (Sichuan to mouth of Yangtze River and Hainan)
____	*C. s. musicus*	Peninsular Thailand, Malaysia and Sumatra
____	*C. s. nesiotes*	SE Sumatra, Rhio Archipelago, Belitung and Bangka islands
____	*C. s. zacneus*	Simeulue I. (off Sumatra)
____	*C. s. nesiarchus*	Nias I. (off Sumatra)
____	*C. s. masculus*	Batu Islands (Pini, Tello and Tana Massa)
____	*C. s. pagiensis*	Mentawi Archipelago, Siberut and Sipoura islands (off Sumatra)
____	*C. s. javensis*	W Java
____	*C. s. amoenus*	E Java and Bali
____	*C. s. problematicus*	SW and w Borneo
____	*C. s. adamsi*	N Borneo, Banggi and adjacent islands
____	*C. s. pluto*	E Borneo and Maratua Islands
____	*C. s. deuteronymus*	N Philippines (Luzon, Lubang and Palaui)
____	*C. s. mindanensis*	S Philippines and Sulu Archipelago

□ **White-rumped Shama** *Copsychus malabaricus*

____	*C. m. malabaricus*	S peninsular India
____	*C. m. leggei*	Sri Lanka
____	*C. m. indicus*	Nepal to Assam and ne India
____	*C. m. albiventris*	Andaman Islands
____	*C. m. interpositus*	SW China to Myanmar, Thailand, Indochina and Mergui Arch.
____	*C. m. minor*	Hainan (s China)
____	*C. m. mallopercnus*	Malay Peninsula, Riau Archipelago and Lingga Archipelago
____	*C. m. tricolor*	Sumatra, w Java, Banka, Belitung and Karimata islands
____	*C. m. mirabilis*	Prinsen I. (Sunda Strait)
____	*C. m. melanurus*	Islands off nw Sumatra
____	*C. m. opisthopelus*	Islands off sw Sumatra
____	*C. m. javanus*	Central Java
____	*C. m. omissus*	E Java
____	*C. m. ochroptilus*	Anambas Islands (South China Sea)
____	*C. m. abbotti*	Bangka and Belitung islands (off Borneo)
____	*C. m. eumesus*	Natuna Islands (off Borneo)
____	*C. m. suavis*	Borneo (except northern part)
____	*C. m. nigricauda*	Kangean Islands and Matasiri I. (Java Sea)

☐ **Seychelles Magpie-Robin** *Copsychus sechellarum*

Frégate (Seychelles). Seriously endangered

☐ **White-crowned Shama** *Copsychus stricklandii*
_____ *C. s. stricklandii*
_____ *C. s. barbouri*

Lowlands of n Borneo, Labuan, Balembangan and Banggi islands
Maratua Islands (off n Borneo)

☐ **White-browed Shama** *Copsychus luzoniensis*
_____ *C. l. luzonensis*
_____ *C. l. parvimaculatus*
_____ *C. l. shemleyi*
_____ *C. l. superciliaris*

N Philippines (Luzon and Catanduanes)
Polillo (Philippines)
Marinduque (Philippines)
Philippines (Ticao, Masbate, Panay and Negros)

☐ **White-vented Shama** *Copsychus niger*

S Philippines (Balabac, Busuanga, Culion, Bantac and Palawan)

☐ **Black Shama** *Copsychus cebuensis*

Cebu (s-central Philippines)

☐ **Rufous-tailed Shama** *Trichixos pyrropyga*

S Peninsular Thailand, Malaya, Sumatra and Borneo

☐ **Indian Robin** *Saxicoloides fulicata*
_____ *S. f. cambaiensis*
_____ *S. f. erythrura*
_____ *S. f. intermedia*
_____ *S. f. fulicata*
_____ *S. f. leucoptera*

Pakistan to n and w India and lowlands of Nepal
NE India (plains of Bihar and West Bengal)
Central India (Bombay to Hyderabad and Krishna River)
S India (Bombay to Mysore and Kerala)
Lowlands of Sri Lanka

☐ **Ala Shan Redstart** *Phoenicurus alaschanicus*

Montane coniferous forests of n China to ne Tibet

☐ **Rufous-backed Redstart** *Phoenicurus erythronota*

Montane forests of central Asia; winters to Iran and n India

☐ **Blue-capped Redstart** *Phoenicurus caeruleocephalus*

Montane juniper and pine forests of s Asia

☐ **Black Redstart** *Phoenicurus ochruros*
_____ *P. o. gibraltariensis*
_____ *P. o. aterrimus*
_____ *P. o. ochruros*
_____ *P. o. semirufus*
_____ *P. o. phoenicuroides*
_____ *P. o. rufiventris*
_____ *P. o. xerophilus*

W and central Europe to Crimea and North Africa
Iberian Peninsula
Mountains of e Turkey to n Iran; winters to Iraq
Hills of Syria and Lebanon; winters to Israel and Sinai Peninsula
Tien Shan Mts. to n Mongolia; winters to ne Africa and India
Himalayas (Tibet to nw China); winters to India and n Myanmar
W China (Astin Tagh Mountains to w Gansu and Qinghai)

☐ **Common Redstart** *Phoenicurus phoenicurus*
_____ *P. p. phoenicurus*
_____ *P. p. samamisicus*

Europe and North Africa to central Asia; winters to trop. Africa
Crimea and Caucasus to w Afghanistan; winters to ne Africa

☐ **Hodgson's Redstart** *Phoenicurus hodgsoni*

Himalayas of w-central China; winters to India and Myanmar

☐ **White-throated Redstart** *Phoenicurus schisticeps*

Nepal to s Tibet and w-central China; winters to Myanmar

☐ **Daurian Redstart** *Phoenicurus auroreus*
_____ *P. a. auroreus*
_____ *P. a. leucopterus*

S Siberia to Mongolia; winters to Japan and Ryukyu Islands
W China to se Tibet and nw Thailand; winters to n Myanmar

☐ **Moussier's Redstart** *Phoenicurus moussieri*

Bare plateaux of s Morocco, n Algeria and n Tunisia

☐ **White-winged Redstart** *Phoenicurus erythrogaster*
_____ *P. e. erythrogaster*
_____ *P. e. grandis*

Caucasus Mountains to s Caspian region of Iran
Central Asia to se Tibet, s China, Pakistan and n India

☐ **Blue-fronted Redstart** *Phoenicurus frontalis*

Himalayas of s Asia; winters to SE Asia

☐ **White-capped Redstart** *Chaimarrornis leucocephalus*

Himalayas of s Asia; winters to SE Asia

☐ **Plumbeous Redstart** *Rhyacornis fuliginosus*
    ____ *R. f. fuliginosus*

Himalayas (Pakistan to Myanmar, se Tibet, w China, n Vietnam)
    ____ *R. f. affinis*
Taiwan

☐ **Luzon Redstart** *Rhyacornis bicolor*

Rocky streams of n Luzon (n Philippines)

☐ **White-bellied Redstart** *Hodgsonius phaenicuroides*
    ____ *H. p. phaenicuroides*

Himalayas of Pakistan to se Tibet, sw China and n Myanmar
    ____ *H. p. ichangensis*
Himalayas of w China; winters to n Vietnam and Laos

☐ **White-tailed Robin** *Cinclidium leucurum*
    ____ *C. l. leucurum*

Mts. of Nepal to Myanmar, sw China, Indochina and Malaysia
    ____ *C. l. cambodianum*
S Cambodia (Chaine de l'Éléphant)
    ____ *C. l. montium*
Mountains of Taiwan

☐ **Sunda Robin** *Cinclidium diana*
    ____ *C. d. sumatranum*

Mountains of n and w-central Sumatra
    ____ *C. d. diana*
Mountains of Java

☐ **Blue-fronted Robin** *Cinclidium frontale*
    ____ *C. f. frontale*

Himalayan foothills of e Nepal, Sikkim and sw China
    ____ *C. f. orientale*
Mountains of nw Thailand, n Vietnam (Tonkin) and Laos

☐ **Grandala** *Grandala coelicolor*

Alpine meadows of Kashmir to se Tibet, Myanmar and w China

☐ **Little Forktail** *Enicurus scouleri*
    ____ *E. s. scouleri*

Mountains of se Russia to the Himalayas, n India and sw China
    ____ *E. s. fortis*
Mountain streams of Taiwan

☐ **Sunda Forktail** *Enicurus velatus*
    ____ *E. v. sumatranus*

Rocky mountain streams of Sumatra
    ____ *E. v. velatus*
Rocky mountain streams of Java

☐ **Chestnut-naped Forktail** *Enicurus ruficapillus*

S Myanmar to s Thailand, Malaya, Sumatra and Borneo

☐ **Black-backed Forktail** *Enicurus immaculatus*

Rocky streams of n India to Myanmar, sw China, nw Thailand

☐ **Slaty-backed Forktail** *Enicurus schistaceus*

Rocky mountain streams of n India to s China and SE Asia

☐ **White-crowned Forktail** *Enicurus leschenaulti*
    ____ *E. l. indicus*

Himalayas of ne India to Myanmar, n Thailand and Indochina
    ____ *E. l. sinensis*
W and s China; Hainan
    ____ *E. l. frontalis*
Malaysia, Sumatra, Nias I. and lowlands of Borneo
    ____ *E. l. chaseni*
Tanahmasa I. (Batu Islands off w Sumatra)
    ____ *E. l. leschenaulti*
Java and Bali
    ____ *E. l. borneensis*
Mountains of n Borneo

☐ **Spotted Forktail** *Enicurus maculatus*
    ____ *E. m. maculatus*

Himalayas of n Afghanistan to Kashmir, Nepal and s Tibet
    ____ *E. m. guttatus*
Himalayas of extreme e Nepal to sw China and Myanmar
    ____ *E. m. bacatus*
Mts. of s China (se Yunnan and nw Fujian) to n Vietnam
    ____ *E. m. robinsoni*
South Vietnam (Da Lat Plateau)

☐ **Purple Cochoa** *Cochoa purpurea*

Montane forests of n India to sw China, Myanmar and Indochina

☐ **Green Cochoa** *Cochoa viridis*

Montane forests of n India to sw China, Myanmar and Indochina

☐ **Sumatran Cochoa** *Cochoa beccarii*

Highlands of w Sumatra (unreported since mid 1940's)

☐ **Javan Cochoa** *Cochoa azurea*

Mountains of w and central Java

☐ **Whinchat** *Saxicola rubetra*

W Palearctic; winters tropical and s Africa

☐ **White-browed Bushchat** *Saxicola macrorhyncha*

Arid plains of s Afghanistan, e Pakistan and nw India

☐ **White-throated Bushchat** *Saxicola insignis*

Rocky alpine meadows of central Asia; winters to n India

☐ **Canary Islands Chat** *Saxicola dacotiae*
____ *S. d. dacotiae* — Fuerteventura (Canary Islands)
____ *S. d. murielae†* — Formerly Canary Is. (Montaña Clara and Allegranza). Extinct

☐ **Common Stonechat** *Saxicola torquata*
____ *S. t. hibernans* — Britain, Ireland, coastal w France and w coast of Iberian Pen.
____ *S. t. rubicola* — W and s Europe and North Africa; winters to Middle East
____ *S. t. variegata* — Steppes of lower Volga and mouth of Ural River to e Caucasus
____ *S. t. armenica* — Mountains of e Turkey to Transcaucasia and Iran
____ *S. t. maura* — E Russia to central Asia; winters to Iran, Iraq and n India
____ *S. t. stejnegeri* — E Siberia to Japan and Korea; winters to s China and Indochina
____ *S. t. indica* — Himalayas (Kashmir to Sikkim and Assam); winters to India
____ *S. t. przewalskii (yunnanensis)* — Mountains of w China; winters to Myanmar and n India

☐ **African Stonechat** *Saxicola axillaris*
____ *S. a. moptana* — Inner Niger delta, s Mali and Senegal delta
____ *S. a. nebularum* — Highlands of Sierra Leone, Guinea, Liberia and w Ivory Coast
____ *S. a. salax* — SE Nigeria to Gabon, lower Congo and Angola; Bioko
____ *S. a. axillaris* — Highlands of e Zaire to Rwanda, Uganda, Kenya and n Tanzania
____ *S. a. jebelmarrae* — W Sudan (Darfur region)
____ *S. a .albofasciata* — Highlands of Ethiopia, s Sudan and ne Uganda
____ *S. a. stonei* — Angola to w Tanzania, s Mozambique and n Cape Province
____ *S. a. clanceyi* — Coastal w Namibia to nw Cape Province
____ *S. a. promiscua* — Highlands of s Tanzania to Malawi, Mozambique, e Zimbabwe
____ *S. a. oreobates* — Highlands of Lesotho; winters to e Zimbabwe
____ *S. a. felix* — Mountains of sw Arabia
____ *S. a. voeltzkowi* — Grand Comoro I.
____ *S. a. sibilla* — Madagascar

☐ **Reunion Stonechat** *Saxicola tectes*

Réunion (w Mascarene Islands)

☐ **White-tailed Stonechat** *Saxicola leucura*

E Pakistan to Nepal, n India and Myanmar

☐ **Pied Bushchat** *Saxicola caprata*
____ *S. c. rossorum* — Transcaspia to e Iran, Afghanistan and n Kashmir
____ *S. c. bicolor* — Pakistan to Baluchistan and Kashmir; winters to central India
____ *S. c. burmanica* — Central India to sw China, Myanmar, n Thailand and Indochina
____ *S. c. nilgiriensis* — S India (w Madras and Kerala)
____ *S. c. atrata* — Sri Lanka
____ *S. c. caprata* — N Philippines (Luzon, Lubang and Mindoro)
____ *S. c. randi* — Philippines (Negros, Bohol, Masbate, Ticao, Cebu, Siquijor)
____ *S. c. anderseni* — S Philippines (Mindanao, Camiguin Sur, Leyte and Biliran)
____ *S. c. fruticola* — Java, Bali. Lombok, Sumbawa, Flores, Lomblen and Alor
____ *S. c. pyrrhonota* — Lesser Sundas (Kisar, Wetar, Sawu, Semau, Roti and Timor)
____ *S. c. francki* — Sumba (Lesser Sundas)
____ *S. c. cognata* — Babar (Lesser Sundas)
____ *S. c. albonotata* — Sulawesi, Salayar and Butung islands
____ *S. c. aethiops* — N New Guinea and New Britain (Bismarck Archipelago)
____ *S. c. belensis* — Central mts. of New Guinea (Wissel Lakes to Snow Mountains)
____ *S. c. wahgiensis* — Central highlands of New Guinea to Huon Pen. and se mountains

☐ **Jerdon's Bushchat** *Saxicola jerdoni*
_____ *S. j. harringtoni* — Afghanistan to Nepal, Myanmar, s China and n Indochina
_____ *S. j. jerdoni* — S Tibet to sw China (s Yunnan)

☐ **Gray Bushchat** *Saxicola ferrea*
— N Pakistan to s Tibet, se China, Myanmar and n Indochina

☐ **Timor Bushchat** *Saxicola gutturalis*
_____ *S. g. gutturalis* — E Lesser Sundas (Timor and Roti)
_____ *S. g. luctuosa* — Semau (e Lesser Sundas)

☐ **Buff-streaked Chat** *Oenanthe bifasciata*
— Rocky montane areas of Natal to Transvaal and Cape Province

☐ **White-tailed Wheatear** *Oenanthe leucopyga*
_____ *O. l. aegra* — Rocky deserts of Mauritania to Tunisia
_____ *O. l. leucopyga* — Rocky deserts of Mali to Chad, Sudan, Eritrea and Ethiopia
_____ *O. l. ernesti* — Deserts of e Egypt to Dead Sea, Saudi Arabia, Iraq and sw Iran

☐ **Hooded Wheatear** *Oenanthe monacha*
— Rocky desert ravines of ne Sudan and Egypt to s Pakistan

☐ **Hume's Wheatear** *Oenanthe alboniger*
— Bare rocky hills of e Arabia to s Iran, Afghanistan and Pakistan

☐ **Black Wheatear** *Oenanthe leucura*
_____ *O. l. leucura* — Iberian Peninsula to coastal s France, Italy, Sardinia and Sicily
_____ *O. l. syenitica* — Extreme nw Mauritania to Morocco, Tunisia, Algeria and Libya

☐ **Mountain Wheatear** *Oenanthe monticola*
_____ *O. m. albipileata* — Coastal Angola (Benguela escarpment)
_____ *O. m. nigricauda* — Angola (highlands of Huambo and s Cuanza Sul)
_____ *O. m. atmorii* — N Namibia (south to Damaraland)
_____ *O. m. monticola (griseiceps)* — S Botswana and Transvaal to Swaziland and Natal

☐ **Somali Wheatear** *Oenanthe phillipsi*
— Mountains of se Ethiopia and n Somalia

☐ **Northern Wheatear** *Oenanthe oenanthe*
_____ *O. o. leucorhoa* — NE Canada to Greenland and Iceland; winters to w Africa
_____ *O. o. oenanthe* — British Isles to Mediterranean and Siberia; winters to c Africa
_____ *O. o. libanotica* — S Spain and Balearic Is. to Iran, Kazakstan and Mongolia
_____ *O. o. seebohmi* — Morocco to ne Algeria; winters to Mauritania

☐ **Mourning Wheatear** *Oenanthe lugens*
_____ *O. l. halophila* — N Sahara (e Morocco to n Libya and nw Egypt)
_____ *O. l. lugens* — Egypt (east of the Nile) to Israel, Syria, Jordan and n Iraq
_____ *O. l. lugentoides* — W Arabia (Taif to Yemen)
_____ *O. l. boscaweni* — S Arabia (Hadramaut)
_____ *O. l. vauriei* — NE Somalia
_____ *O. l. lugubris* — Highlands of n and central Ethiopia
_____ *O. l. schalowi* — Highlands of s Kenya to ne Tanzania
_____ *O. l. persica* — S Iran; wanders to s Egypt, n Sudan and s Israel

☐ **Finsch's Wheatear** *Oenanthe finschii*
_____ *O. f. finschii* — Turkey to Israel, n Arabia and s Iran; winters to Cyprus and Egypt
_____ *O. f. barnesi* — E Turkey to e Caucasus, n Iran, Afghanistan and w Pakistan

☐ **Variable Wheatear** *Oenanthe picata*
— Iran to n Baluchistan and Pakistan; winters to s Iran and n India

☐ **Red-rumped Wheatear** *Oenanthe moesta*
_____ *O. m. moesta* — Extreme nw Mauritania to Morocco and coastal nw Egypt
_____ *O. m. brooksbanki* — S Syria to Jordan, nw Saudi Arabia and sw Iraq

☐ **Pied Wheatear** *Oenanthe pleschanka*

Stony s-central Eurasia; winters Arabia and Iran to ne Africa

☐ **Cyprus Wheatear** *Oenanthe cypriaca*

Stony areas of Cyprus; winters in ne Africa

☐ **Black-eared Wheatear** *Oenanthe hispanica*
- ____ *O. h. hispanica* — S Europe and North Africa; winters Senegal to Mali
- ____ *O. h. melanoleuca (xanthomeleana)* — SE Europe to Caspian and Iran; winters to ne and w Africa

☐ **Red-tailed Wheatear** *Oenanthe xanthoprymna*
- ____ *O. x. chrysopygia* — E Turkey to n Iran and s Russia; winters to Arabia and Iraq
- ____ *O. x. xanthoprymna* — Mts. of sw Iran; winters Sinai and coastal Egypt to Sudan
- ____ *O. x. kingi* — Afghanistan and Baluchistan; winters to Pakistan and w India

☐ **Desert Wheatear** *Oenanthe deserti*
- ____ *O. d. homochroa* — Deserts of North Africa (Western Sahara to w Egypt)
- ____ *O. d. deserti* — Levant
- ____ *O. d. atrogularis* — Transcaucasia and Iran to Afghanistan and Mongolia
- ____ *O. d. oreophila* — W China to Kashmir and Tibet; winters to Pakistan and ne Africa

☐ **Capped Wheatear** *Oenanthe pileata*
- ____ *O. p. neseri* — S Angola and n Namibia to w Botswana
- ____ *O. p. livingstonii* — E Angola to Zaire, Kenya, Tanzania, Malawi and Mozambique
- ____ *O. p. pileata* — S Namibia and South Africa

☐ **Isabelline Wheatear** *Oenanthe isabellina*

S-central Eurasia; winters ne Africa, Arabia and India

☐ **Red-breasted Wheatear** *Oenanthe bottae*
- ____ *O. b. bottae* — Highlands of sw Arabia (Mecca to Yemen)
- ____ *O. b. frenata* — Highlands of Eritrea and Ethiopia

☐ **Heuglin's Wheatear** *Oenanthe heuglini*

Mauritania to Mali, Cameroon, Sudan, Ethiopia and nw Kenya

☐ **Sicklewing Chat** *Cercomela sinuata*
- ____ *C. s. ensifera* — S Namibia to Transvaal, Orange Free State and n Cape Province
- ____ *C. s. hyernephela* — South Africa (arid regions of Lesotho); winters to Natal
- ____ *C. s. sinuata* — South Africa (s Cape Province)

☐ **Karoo Chat** *Cercomela schlegelii*
- ____ *C. s. benguellensis* — Coastal sw Angola (Benguella escarpment)
- ____ *C. s. schlegelii* — Coastal Namibia (w Damaraland to Erongo Mountains)
- ____ *C. s. namaquensis* — S Namibia to nw Cape Province
- ____ *C. s. kobosensis* — Namibia (Great Namaqualand)
- ____ *C. s. pollux* — South Africa (w Orange Free State and Cape Province)

☐ **Tractrac Chat** *Cercomela tractrac*
- ____ *C. t. hoeschi* — Coastal deserts of sw Angola and nw Namibia
- ____ *C. t. albicans* — Coastal n Namibia (w Damaraland and n Great Namaqualand)
- ____ *C. t. barlowi* — Namibia (central and s Great Namaqualand)
- ____ *C. t. nebulosa* — Coastal sand dunes of sw Namibia and w South Africa
- ____ *C. t. tractrac* — South Africa (Karoo to Aliwal)

☐ **Familiar Chat** *Cercomela familiaris*
- ____ *C. f. falkensteini* — Ghana to sw Sudan, n Ethiopia, Uganda and Kenya
- ____ *C. f. omoensis* — SE Sudan (Boma Hills) to sw Ethiopia
- ____ *C. f. modesta* — NE Angola to Malawi, Zambia, Zimbabwe and Mozambique
- ____ *C. f. angolensis* — W Angola to n Namibia
- ____ *C. f. galtoni* — E Namibia to w Botswana and n Cape Province
- ____ *C. f. hellmayri* — SE Botswana to Zimbabwe, Transvaal and Orange Free State
- ____ *C. f. actuosa* — Drakensberg, Transkei, w Natal and Lesotho
- ____ *C. f. familiaris* — S Mozambique to Natal and s Cape Province

☐ **Brown-tailed Chat** *Cercomela scotocerca*

____	*C. s. furensis*	W Sudan (Darfur)
____	*C. s. scotocerca*	Red Sea coast of e Sudan to n Ethiopia
____	*C. s. turkana*	SW Ethiopia to nw Kenya and Uganda
____	*C. s. spectatrix*	Ethiopia (Awash Valley) and n Somalia
____	*C. s. validior*	Somalia (Run region)

☐ **Indian Chat** *Cercomela fusca*

Rocky hills and cliffs of ne Pakistan and n India

☐ **Sombre Chat** *Cercomela dubia*

Montane deserts of central Ethiopia and nw Somalia

☐ **Blackstart** *Cercomela melanura*

____	*C. m. ultima*	Mali and s Niger
____	*C. m. airensis*	E Niger (Aïr Massif) to Chad and w Sudan (Kordafan)
____	*C. m. lypura*	W coast of Red Sea from se Egypt to e Sudan and Eritrea
____	*C. m. aussae*	E Ethiopia (Donakil Depression), Djibouti and adjacent Somalia
____	*C. m. melanura*	Dead Sea depression of Egypt and Jordan to Saudi Arabia
____	*C. m. neumanni*	W Saudi Arabia to Yemen, Aden and Hadramaut

☐ **Moorland Chat** *Cercomela sordida*

____	*C. s. sordida*	High altitude moorlands of Ethiopia
____	*C. s. rudolfi*	N Kenya (Mt. Elgon moorlands) and adjacent e Uganda
____	*C. s. ernesti*	N Kenya (Mt. Kenya and Aberdare Mountains)
____	*C. s. olimotiensis*	High altitude moorlands of n Tanzania (Crater Highlands)
____	*C. s. hypospodia*	N Tanzania (Mt. Kilimanjaro moorlands)

☐ **Congo Moorchat** *Myrmecocichla tholloni*

Gabon to s Angola, Central African Republic and w Zaire

☐ **Northern Anteater-Chat** *Myrmecocichla aethiops*

____	*M. a. aethiops*	Senegambia to Chad, n Nigeria and n Cameroon
____	*M. a. sudanensis*	W Sudan (Darfur and Kordofan)
____	*M. a. cryptoleuca*	Highlands of n Kenya to n Tanzania

☐ **Southern Anteater-Chat** *Myrmecocichla formicivora*

Namibia to Botswana and South Africa

☐ **Sooty Chat** *Myrmecocichla nigra*

Nigeria to Angola, extreme s Sudan, Tanzania and Zambia

☐ **Rueppell's Chat** *Myrmecocichla melaena*

High plateau of Eritrea and n Ethiopia

☐ **White-fronted Black-Chat** *Myrmecocichla albifrons*

____	*M. a. frontalis*	Extreme s Mauritania to Senegal, Nigeria, Chad and Cameroon
____	*M. a. limbata*	E Cameroon to Central African Republic (Ubangi-Shari region)
____	*M. a. clericalis*	S Sudan (west of the Nile) to ne Zaire and n Uganda
____	*M. a. albifrons*	Eritrea and n Ethiopia
____	*M. a. pachyrhyncha*	SW Ethiopia

☐ **White-headed Black-Chat** *Myrmecocichla arnotti*

____	*M. a. harterti*	Angola
____	*M. a. arnotti*	SW Zaire to Namibia, Zambia, Tanzania, Malawi and n Transvaal

☐ **Mocking Cliff-Chat** *Thamnolaea cinnamomeiventris*

____	*T. c. bambarae*	Mali (Mandingo Mountains)
____	*T. c. coronata*	Togo and se Burkina Faso to n Cameroon and w Sudan (Darfur)
____	*T. c. kordofanensis*	Central Sudan (Kordofan and Nuba Hills)
____	*T. c. albiscapulata*	S Ethiopia
____	*T. c. subrufipennis*	Extreme se Sudan to sw Ethiopia, Zambia and Malawi
____	*T. c. odica*	E Zimbabwe
____	*T. c. cinnamomeiventris*	E Transvaal to Orange Free State, Natal and e Cape Province
____	*T. c. autochthones*	S Mozambique to e Transvaal, e Swaziland and n Natal

☐ **White-winged Cliff-Chat** *Thamnolaea semirufa*

Highlands of Eritrea and Ethiopia

☐ **Boulder Chat** *Pinarornis plumosus*

SE Zambia to Botswana, s Malawi, Zimbabwe and Mozambique

FAMILY: PLATYSTEIRIDAE (Wattle-eyes—31)

☐ **African Shrike-flycatcher** *Megabyas flammulatus*
____ *M. f. flammulatus* — Sierra Leone to Cameroon, Gabon and w Zaire; Bioko
____ *M. f. aequatorialis (carolathi)* — NW Angola to Zaire, Uganda, w Kenya and extreme s Sudan

☐ **Black-and-white Shrike-flycatcher** *Bias musicus*
____ *B. m. musicus (feminina, pallidiventris)* — Sierra Leone to n Angola, Zaire, Uganda and nw Tanzania
____ *B. m. changamwensis* — Kenya to e Tanzania
____ *B. m. clarens* — S Malawi to e Zimbabwe and Mozambique

☐ **Ward's Flycatcher** *Pseudobias wardi*

Rainforests of e Madagascar

☐ **Brown-throated Wattle-eye** *Platysteira cyanea*
____ *P. c. cyanea* — Senegal to Gabon, Angola, Central African Republic and Zaire
____ *P. c. aethiopica* — SE Sudan (Boma) and Ethiopia
____ *P. c. nyansae* — S Sudan to n Zaire, Kenya, Uganda and nw Tanzania

☐ **White-fronted Wattle-eye** *Platysteira albifrons*

Lowlands and escarpment of w Angola and adjacent sw Zaire

☐ **Black-throated Wattle-eye** *Platysteira peltata*
____ *P. p. cryptoleuca* — Somalia to e Zimbabwe and n Mozambique; Mafia I.
____ *P. p. mentalis* — Angola to s Zaire, Zambia, Uganda, Kenya and w Tanzania
____ *P. p. peltata* — Zambia to Malawi, Mozambique, e Zimbabwe and e Africa

☐ **Banded Wattle-eye** *Platysteira laticincta*

Bamenda Mountains (w Cameroon)

☐ **Chestnut Wattle-eye** *Platysteira castanea*
____ *P. c. hormophora* — Sierra Leone to Togo
____ *P. c. castanea* — S Nigeria to se Sudan, Uganda, Kenya, n Tanzania, n Angola

☐ **White-spotted Wattle-eye** *Platysteira tonsa*

Forests of s Ivory Coast to Nigeria, Gabon and n Zaire

☐ **Red-cheeked Wattle-eye** *Platysteira blissetti*

Humid forests of Guinea and s Sierra Leone to s Cameroon

☐ **Black-necked Wattle-eye** *Platysteira chalybea*

Humid forests of s Cameroon and Gabon; Bioko

☐ **Jameson's Wattle-eye** *Platysteira jamesoni*

E Zaire to Uganda, se Sudan, w Kenya and nw Tanzania

☐ **Yellow-bellied Wattle-eye** *Platysteira concreta*
____ *P. c. concreta* — Sierra Leone to Ghana
____ *P. c. ansorgei* — Escarpment of w Angola (Cuanza Norte to n Huila)
____ *P. c. graueri (kumbaensis, harterti, silvae)* — Nigeria to Gabon, Zaire and w Kenya
____ *P. c. kungwensis* — Extreme w Tanzania (Mt. Nkungwe and Mt. Mahari)

☐ **Boulton's Batis** *Batis margaritae*
____ *B. m. margaritae* — W-central Angola (Mt. Moco)
____ *B. m. kathleenae* — Mountains of nw Zambia and adjacent extreme se Zaire

☐ **Short-tailed Batis** *Batis mixta*
____ *B. m. ultima* — Coastal se Kenya
____ *B. m. mixta* — Highlands of s Kenya to n Tanzania and n Malawi

476

☐ **Ruwenzori Batis** *Batis diops*

E Zaire to w Uganda, Rwanda, Burundi and nw Tanzania

☐ **Cape Batis** *Batis capensis*
____ *B. c. reichenowi*
____ *B. c. sola*
____ *B. c. dimorpha*
____ *B. c. erythrophthalma*
____ *B. c. kennedyi*
____ *B. c. hollidayi*
____ *B. c. capensis*

SE Tanzania (Mikindani to Lindi)
N Malawi (Mwantjati to Nyika)
Mountains of s Malawi and adjacent Mozambique
E highlands of Zimbabwe and adjacent w Mozambique
SW Zimbabwe (Mopoto Hills region)
Zululand, Swaziland and Mozambique (Lebombo Range)
S Natal to Orange Free State and Cape Province

☐ **Woodward's Batis** *Batis fratrum*

S Malawi to e Zimbabwe, Mozambique and Natal

☐ **Chinspot Batis** *Batis molitor*
____ *B. m. pintoi*
____ *B. m. puella*
____ *B. m. palliditergum*
____ *B. m. molitor*

Angola to sw Zaire and nw Zambia
E Zaire to Uganda, w Kenya and w Tanzania
S Zaire to Namibia, Botswana, Malawi and n Cape Province
S Mozambique to e Cape Province

☐ **Pale Batis** *Batis soror*

Lowlands of se Kenya to Malawi and Mozambique; Zanzibar

☐ **Pririt Batis** *Batis pririt*
____ *B. p. affinis*
____ *B. p. pririt*

Arid coastal sw Angola to n Namibia and w Botswana
Central Botswana to sw Transvaal and w Cape Province

☐ **Senegal Batis** *Batis senegalensis*

Senegambia to s Mauritania, s Niger and Cameroon

☐ **Gray-headed Batis** *Batis orientalis*
____ *B. o. bella (somaliensis)*
____ *B. o. orientalis*
____ *B. o. chadensis*
____ *B. o. lynesi*

N Eritrea and e Ethiopia to Djibouti, n Somalia and n Kenya
Central Eritrea to n Ethiopia
NE Nigeria to Zaire, Chad, Sudan and w Ethiopia
N Sudan (e Red Sea Province)

☐ **Black-headed Batis** *Batis minor*
____ *B. m. erlangeri (congoensis, nyansae, batesi)*
____ *B. m. minor*
____ *B. m. suahelicus*

Ethiopian Plateau and Somalia to Cameroon and Angola
S Somalia
Kenya and Tanzania

☐ **Pygmy Batis** *Batis perkeo*

Arid s Ethiopia, Sudan, Somalia, Kenya to extreme ne Tanzania

☐ **Verreaux's Batis** *Batis minima*

Humid forests of s Cameroon and w Gabon

☐ **Ituri Batis** *Batis ituriensis*

Humid forests of Zaire and adjacent w Uganda

☐ **Fernando Po Batis** *Batis poensis*

Bioko (Gulf of Guinea)

☐ **West African Batis** *Batis occulta*

Humid forests of Sierra Leone to s Cameroon and Gabon

☐ **Angola Batis** *Batis minulla*

Forests of se Gabon to w Angola, Cabinda and adjacent Zaire

☐ **White-tailed Shrike** *Lanioturdus torquatus*

Angola to escarpment of central Namibia

FAMILY: RHIPIDURIDAE (Fantails—43)

☐ **Yellow-bellied Fantail** *Rhipidura hypoxantha*

E Himalayas to se Tibet, s China, Myanmar, Thailand, Tonkin

☐ **Blue Fantail** *Rhipidura superciliaris*
_____ *R. s. superciliaris* — Philippines (Basilan and Zamboanga Peninsula of n Mindanao)
_____ *R. s. apo* — Philippines (se Mindanao)
_____ *R. s. samarensis* — Philippines (Bohol, Leyte and Samar)

☐ **Blue-headed Fantail** *Rhipidura cyaniceps*
_____ *R. c. pinicola* — Philippines (highlands of n Luzon)
_____ *R. c. cyaniceps* — Philippines (Luzon and Catanduanes)
_____ *R. c. sauli* — Philippines (Tablas)
_____ *R. c. albiventris* — Philippines (Guimaras, Masbate, Negros, Panay and Ticao)

☐ **Rufous-tailed Fantail** *Rhipidura phoenicura*

Montane forests of Java

☐ **Black-and-cinnamon Fantail** *Rhipidura nigrocinnamomea*
_____ *R. n. hutchinsoni* — Philippines (montane forests of n Mindanao)
_____ *R. n. nigrocinnamomea* — Philippines (montane forests of se Mindanao)

☐ **White-throated Fantail** *Rhipidura albicollis*
_____ *R. a. canescens* — W Himalayas (Pakistan and Kashmir to w Nepal)
_____ *R. a. albicollis* — Himalayas (w Nepal and Sikkim)
_____ *R. a. orissae* — NE India
_____ *R. a. stanleyi* — E Himalayas to Assam and Myanmar
_____ *R. a. vernayi* — SE India
_____ *R. a. celsa* — SE Tibet to s China, Hainan, w Thailand and n Indochina
_____ *R. a. atrata* — S Thailand to Malaya and Sumatra
_____ *R. a. sarawacensis* — N Borneo (Poi Mountains)
_____ *R. a. kinabalu* — Mountains of n Borneo (Kinabalu to Murud and Mulu)
_____ *R. a. cinerascens* — S Indochina

☐ **Spot-breasted Fantail** *Rhipidura albogularis*

S and c India (north to Rajasthan, Madhya Pradesh and Orissa)

☐ **White-bellied Fantail** *Rhipidura euryura*

Montane forests of Java

☐ **White-browed Fantail** *Rhipidura aureola*
_____ *R. a. aureola* — N India
_____ *R. a. compressirostris* — S peninsular India and Sri Lanka
_____ *R. a. burmanica* — Assam to w Yunnan, Myanmar, pen. Thailand and Indochina

☐ **Northern Fantail** *Rhipidura rufiventris*
_____ *R. r. obiensis* — Obi I. (n Moluccas)
_____ *R. r. bouruensis* — Buru I. (s Moluccas)
_____ *R. r. cinerea* — S Moluccas (Seram, Ambon and Boano)
_____ *R. r. finitima* — Tayandu Islands (Taam, Kilsuin and Kur)
_____ *R. r. perneglecta* — Watubela Islands (s Moluccas)
_____ *R. r. assimilis* — Kai Islands (Kai Kecil, Kai Besar)
_____ *R. r. tenkatei* — Roti (e Lesser Sundas)
_____ *R. r. rufiventris* — E Lesser Sundas (Semau, Timor and Jaco)
_____ *R. r. pallidiceps* — Wetar (e Lesser Sundas)
_____ *R. r. buttikoferi* — E Lesser Sundas (Sermata, Moa, Leti, Romang and Damar)
_____ *R. r. gularis* — New Guinea, Yapen and w Papuan islands
_____ *R. r. kordensis* — Biak I. (New Guinea)
_____ *R. r. vidua* — Kofiau I. (New Guinea)
_____ *R. r. nigromentalis* — Louisiade Archipelago (Tagula and Misima)
_____ *R. r. gigantea* — Bismarck Archipelago (Lihir and Tabar Groups)
_____ *R. r. tangenensis* — Bismarck Archipelago (Boang and Tanga)
_____ *R. r. mussai* — St. Matthias Islands (Bismarck Archipelago)

_____ *R. r. setosa* — Bismarck Archipelago (New Ireland, New Hanover and Dyaul)
_____ *R. r. finschii* — Bismarck Archipelago (New Britain and Duke of York)
_____ *R. r. niveiventris* — Admiralty Islands
_____ *R. r. tenkatei* — Roti I. (e Lesser Sundas)
_____ *R. r. isura* — Coastal n Western Australia
_____ *R. r. superciliosa* — Northern Territory to Queensland (south to Townsville)

☐ **Pied Fantail** *Rhipidura javanica*
_____ *R. j. longicauda* — SE Asia to Sumatra, Borneo and adjacent islands
_____ *R. j. javanica* — Java and Bali; single record from Lombok
_____ *R. j. nigritorquis* — Philippine Islands and Sulu Archipelago

☐ **Spotted Fantail** *Rhipidura perlata*
— S peninsular Thailand, Malaya, Sumatra and Borneo

☐ **Willie-wagtail** *Rhipidura leucophrys*
_____ *R. l. picata* — N Western Australia and Northern Territory to Queensland
_____ *R. l. leucophrys* — E Australia, n Tasmania, King I. and Furneaux Group
_____ *R. l. melaleuca* — Moluccas, New Guinea, Bismarck Arch. and Solomon Islands

☐ **Brown-capped Fantail** *Rhipidura diluta*
_____ *R. d. sumbawensis* — Sumbawa (w Lesser Sundas)
_____ *R. d. diluta* — W Lesser Sundas (Flores and Lomblen)

☐ **Cinnamon-tailed Fantail** *Rhipidura fuscorufa*
— Tanimbar Is. (Larat, Yamdena, Lutu, Mutu, Selaru) and Babar

☐ **White-winged Fantail** *Rhipidura cockerelli*
_____ *R. c. cockerelli* — Solomon Islands (Guadalcanal)
_____ *R. c. coultasi* — Solomon Islands (Malaita)
_____ *R. c. septentrionalis* — Solomon Islands (Buka, Bougainville and Shortland)
_____ *R. c. interposita* — Solomon Islands (Choiseul and Santa Isabel)
_____ *R. c. floridana* — Solomon Islands (Florida and Tulagi)
_____ *R. c. lavellae* — Solomon Islands (Vellalavella and Ranongga)
_____ *R. c. albina* — Solomon Islands (Kulambangra and Rendova)

☐ **Friendly Fantail** *Rhipidura albolimbata*
_____ *R. a. albolimbata* — Mountains of nw New Guinea to Huon Peninsula
_____ *R. a. lorentzi* — Snow Mountains and Central Highlands of New Guinea

☐ **Chestnut-bellied Fantail** *Rhipidura hyperythra*
_____ *R. h. hyperythra* — Aru Islands (New Guinea)
_____ *R. h. mulleri* — Yapen I. and w New Guinea (Astrolabe Bay to Lake Kutubu)
_____ *R. h. castaneothorax* — SE New Guinea (Saruwaged Mtns. to Angabunga River)

☐ **Sooty Thicket-Fantail** *Rhipidura threnothorax*
_____ *R. t. threnothorax* — New Guinea, Aru, Waigeo, Salawati and Misool islands
_____ *R. t. fumosa* — Yapen I. (New Guinea)

☐ **Black Thicket-Fantail** *Rhipidura maculipectus*
— Lowlands of New Guinea, Aru, Batanta and Salawati islands

☐ **White-bellied Thicket-Fantail** *Rhipidura leucothorax*
_____ *R. l. leucothorax* — NW New Guinea (Astrolabe Bay to Port Moresby)
_____ *R. l. clamosa* — Karimui Basin and adjacent e-central New Guinea
_____ *R. l. episcopalis* — SE New Guinea (Kapa Kapa to Astrolabe Bay)

☐ **Black Fantail** *Rhipidura atra*
_____ *R. a. atra* — Mountains of New Guinea and Waigeo I.
_____ *R. a. vulpes* — N New Guinea (Cyclops Mountains)

☐ **Mangrove Fantail** *Rhipidura phasiana*
— SE New Guinea (Trans-Fly lowlands) and n Australia

☐ **Brown Fantail** *Rhipidura drownei*

_____ *R. d. drownei* | Montane forests of Bougainville (Solomon Islands)
_____ *R. d. ocularis* | Montane forests of Guadalcanal (Solomon Islands)

☐ **Dusky Fantail** *Rhipidura tenebrosa*

Mountains of San Cristóbal (Solomon Islands)

☐ **Rennell Fantail** *Rhipidura rennelliana*

Forests of Rennell (se Solomon Islands)

☐ **Gray Fantail** *Rhipidura fuliginosa*

_____ *R. f. bulgeri* | New Caledonia and Lifou I.
_____ *R. f. brenchleyi* | Vanuatu and Banks Islands; San Cristóbal (s Solomon Islands)
_____ *R. f. preissi* | S Western Australia
_____ *R. f. albicauda* | Arid interior of Australia
_____ *R. f. alisteri* | Queensland to Victoria and South Australia
_____ *R. f. albiscapa* | Tasmania and islands in Bass Strait; winters to se Australia
_____ *R. f. placabilis* | North I. (New Zealand)
_____ *R. f. fuliginosa* | Stewart I. and South I. (New Zealand)
_____ *R. f. penitus* | Chatham Islands
_____ *R. f. pelzelni* | Norfolk I.
_____ *R. f. cervina*† | Formerly Lord Howe I. Extinct

☐ **Streaked Fantail** *Rhipidura spilodera*

_____ *R. s. spilodera* | Vanuatu and Banks Group
_____ *R. s. layardi* | Fiji (Ovalau and Viti Levu)
_____ *R. s. erythronota* | Fiji (Yanganga and Vanua Levu)
_____ *R. s. rufilateralis* | Taveuni (Fiji)
_____ *R. s. verreauxi* | New Caledonia, Lifou and Maré islands

☐ **Kandavu Fantail** *Rhipidura personata*

Dense riparian thickets of Kandavu (sw Fiji)

☐ **Samoan Fantail** *Rhipidura nebulosa*

_____ *R. n. nebulosa* | Mountains of Upolu (Western Samoa)
_____ *R. n. altera* | Mountains of Savai'i (Western Samoa)

☐ **Dimorphic Fantail** *Rhipidura brachyrhyncha*

_____ *R. b. brachyrhyncha* | NW New Guinea (Arfak Mountains)
_____ *R. b. devisi* | Mountains of se New Guinea and Huon Peninsula

☐ **Rusty-flanked Fantail** *Rhipidura teysmanni*

_____ *R. t. toradja* | Mountains of n, central and se Sulawesi
_____ *R. t. teysmanni* | Mt. Lompobatang (sw Sulawesi)
_____ *R. t. sulaensis* | Taliabu I. (Sula Islands)

☐ **Cinnamon-backed Fantail** *Rhipidura superflua*

Montane forests of Buru (s Moluccas)

☐ **Streaky-breasted Fantail** *Rhipidura dedemi*

Seram (s Moluccas)

☐ **Long-tailed Fantail** *Rhipidura opistherythra*

Tanimbar Islands (Larat, Yamdena and Maru)

☐ **Palau Fantail** *Rhipidura lepida*

Palau Islands (Babelthuap to Peleliu)

☐ **Rufous-backed Fantail** *Rhipidura rufidorsa*

_____ *R. r. rufidorsa* | NW New Guinea, Misool and Yapen islands
_____ *R. r. kumusi* | N coast of se New Guinea (Kumusi River to Collingwood Bay)
_____ *R. r. kubuna* | S coast of se New Guinea

☐ **Matthias Fantail** *Rhipidura matthiae*

St. Matthias Group (n Bismarck Archipelago)

☐ **Bismarck Fantail** *Rhipidura dahli*

____ *R. d. dahli* — Mountains of New Britain (Bismarck Archipelago)

____ *R. d. antonii* — Mountains of New Ireland (Bismarck Archipelago)

☐ **Malaita Fantail** *Rhipidura malaitae*

Montane forests of Malaita (se Solomon Islands)

☐ **Manus Fantail** *Rhipidura semirubra*

Manus, San Miguel, Tong and adjacent Admiralty Islands

☐ **Rufous Fantail** *Rhipidura rufifrons*

____ *R. r. celebensis*	Tanahjampea and Lalao islands (Flores Sea)
____ *R. r. mimosae*	Kalaotoa I. (Flores Sea)
____ *R. r. torrida*	N Moluccas (Halmahera, Ternate, Bacan and Obi)
____ *R. r. squamata*	Banda, Seram Laut, Tayandu Is. and Kai Is.
____ *R. r. sumbensis*	Sumba (Lesser Sundas)
____ *R. r. semicollaris*	Flores to Timor and adjacent Lesser Sundas
____ *R. r. elegantula*	E Lesser Sundas (Leti, Moa, Romang, Damar and Babar)
____ *R. r. hamadryas*	Tanimbar Islands (Arafura Sea)
____ *R. r. henrici*	Aru Islands
____ *R. r. streptophora*	S New Guinea
____ *R. r. louisiadensis*	D'Entrecasteaux and Louisiade archipelagos
____ *R. r. uraniae*	Guam (Mariana Islands)
____ *R. r. saipanensis*	Mariana Islands (Saipan and Tinian)
____ *R. r. mariae*	Mariana Islands (Agiguan and Rota)
____ *R. r. versicolor*	Yap (Caroline Islands)
____ *R. r. melaenolaema*	Vanikoro (Santa Cruz Islands)
____ *R. r. agilis*	Santa Cruz Group (Solomon Islands)
____ *R. r. utupuae*	Utupua (Solomon Islands)
____ *R. r. commoda*	Bougainville, Choiseul and adjacent Solomon Islands
____ *R. r. rufofronta*	Guadalcanal (Solomon Islands)
____ *R. r. granti*	Central Solomon Islands
____ *R. r. russata*	San Cristóbal (Solomon Islands)
____ *R. r. brunnea*	Malaita (Solomon Islands)
____ *R. r. kuperi*	Santa Anna (Solomon Islands)
____ *R. r. ugiensis*	Ugi (Solomon Islands)
____ *R. r. dryas*	N Western Australia, Northern Territory and Melville I.
____ *R. r. rufifrons*	E Australia (Queensland to Victoria)

☐ **Pohnpei Fantail** *Rhipidura kubaryi*

Pohnpei (e Caroline Islands)

FAMILY: MONARCHIDEA (Monarch Flycatchers—98)

☐ **Chestnut-capped Flycatcher** *Erythrocercus mccallii*

____ *E. m. nigeriae*	Dense forests of Sierra Leone to Guinea and sw Nigeria
____ *E. m. mccallii*	SE Nigeria to Cameroon, Gabon and Zaire
____ *E. m. congicus*	E and s Zaire to w Uganda

☐ **Yellow Flycatcher** *Erythrocercus holochlorus*

Coastal s Somalia to se Kenya and ne Tanzania

☐ **Livingstone's Flycatcher** *Erythrocercus livingstonei*

____ *E. l. thomsoni*	S Tanzania to Malawi and n Mozambique
____ *E. l. livingstonei*	Zambia to Zimbabwe and nw Mozambique
____ *E. l. francisi*	S Malawi and Mozambique (south to Limpopo River)

☐ **African Blue-Flycatcher** *Elminia longicauda*

____ *E. l. longicauda*	Senegal to Gambia and Nigeria
____ *E. l. teresita*	Cameroon to s Sudan, w Kenya, nw Tanzania and Angola

☐ **White-tailed Blue-Flycatcher** *Elminia albicauda*

Angola to sw Uganda, Tanzania and n Mozambique

☐ **Dusky Crested-Flycatcher** *Elminia nigromitrata*
_____ *E. n. colstoni* — Liberia to Nigeria
_____ *E. n. nigromitrata* — Cameroon to s Sudan, Kenya, Uganda and Tanzania

☐ **White-bellied Crested-Flycatcher** *Elminia albiventris*
_____ *E. a. albiventris* — Montane forests of se Nigeria and s Cameroon; Bioko
_____ *E. a. toroensis* — Montane forests of e Zaire, Rwanda and sw Uganda

☐ **White-tailed Crested-Flycatcher** *Elminia albonotata*
_____ *E. a. albonotata* — Zaire to s Ethiopia, Kenya, Tanzania, n Malawi and Zambia
_____ *E. a. subcaerulea* — E Tanzania to Malawi and Mozambique (north of the Zambezi)
_____ *E. a. swynnertoni* — E Zimbabwe and Mozambique (south of the Zambezi)

☐ **Blue-headed Crested-Flycatcher** *Trochocercus nitens*
_____ *T. n. reichenowi* — Guinea and Sierra Leone to Togo
_____ *T. n. nitens* — Nigeria and Cameroon to Gabon, n Angola, e Zaire and s Sudan

☐ **African Crested-Flycatcher** *Trochocercus cyanomelas*
_____ *T. c. vivax* — Uganda and w Tanzania to s Zaire and Zambia
_____ *T. c. bivittatus* — Somalia to Kenya, e Tanzania and Zanzibar
_____ *T. c. megalolophus* — Malawi and n Mozambique to Zimbabwe and n Natal
_____ *T. c. segregus* — E Transvaal to Natal and w Zululand
_____ *T. c. cyanomelas* — South Africa (w Transkei to sw Cape Province)

☐ **Short-crested Monarch** *Hypothymis helenae*
_____ *H. h. personata* — N Philippines (Camiguin Norte)
_____ *H. h. helenae* — N Philippines (Luzon, Samar and Polillo)
_____ *H. h. agusanae* — S Philippines (Mindando, Dinagat and Siargao)

☐ **Black-naped Monarch** *Hypothymis azurea*
_____ *H. a. styani* — India and Nepal to s China and Indochina; Hainan
_____ *H. a. oberholseri* — Taiwan
_____ *H. a. forrestia* — Mergui Archipelago (s Myanmar)
_____ *H. a. montana* — N and central Thailand
_____ *H. a. galerita* — Peninsular Thailand
_____ *H. a. prophata* — S Thailand, Malaysia, Sumatra and Borneo
_____ *H. a. tytleri* — Andaman Islands and Cocos Islands (Bay of Bengal)
_____ *H. a. ceylonensis* — Sri Lanka
_____ *H. a. idiochroa* — Car Nicobar I.
_____ *H. a. nicobarica* — Nicobar Islands
_____ *H. a. opisthocyanea* — Anambas Islands (South China Sea)
_____ *H. a. javana* — Java and Bali
_____ *H. a. penidae* — Penida I. (Lesser Sundas)
_____ *H. a. karimatensis* — Karimata I. (off w Borneo)
_____ *H. a. gigantoptera* — Natunas Islands (South China Sea)
_____ *H. a. aeria* — Maratua Islands (off Borneo)
_____ *H. a. consobrina* — Simeulue I. (off Sumatra)
_____ *H. a. leucophila* — Mentawi Archipelago (off Sumatra)
_____ *H. a. richmondi* — Enggano I. (Sumatra)
_____ *H. a. abbotti* — Babi and Masia islands (Malaysia)
_____ *H. a. symmixta* — Lesser Sundas
_____ *H. a. azurea* — Philippine Islands
_____ *H. a. catarmanensis* — S Philippines (Camiguin Sur)

☐ **Pale-blue Monarch** *Hypothymis puella*
_____ *H. p. puella* — Sulawesi and adjacent islands
_____ *H. p. blasii* — Banggai and Sula islands

☐ **Celestial Monarch** *Hypothymis coelestis*

Philippine Islands

☐ **Cerulean Paradise-Flycatcher** *Eutrichomyias rowleyi*

Rediscovered 1995 on Sangihe I. after considered extinct

☐ **Black-headed Paradise-Flycatcher** *Terpsiphone rufiventer*

_____ *T. r. rufiventer*	Senegal and Gambia to Guinea-Bissau and w Guinea
_____ *T. r. nigriceps*	Sierra Leone to Togo and sw Benin
_____ *T. r. fagani*	Benin and sw Nigeria
_____ *T. r. tricolor*	Bioko (Gulf of Guinea)
_____ *T. r. smithii*	Pagalu (Gulf of Guinea)
_____ *T. r. neumanni*	SE Nigeria to s Cameroon, Gabon, Cabinda and n Angola
_____ *T. r. schubotzi*	SE Cameroon and sw Central African Republic
_____ *T. r. mayombe*	Congo and w Zaire (Lukolela, Mayombe and Ubangi)
_____ *T. r. somereni*	Forests of w Uganda
_____ *T. r. emini*	SE Uganda to extreme w Kenya and nw Tanzania
_____ *T. r. ignea*	E Central African Rep. to s Zaire, ne Angola and nw Zambia

☐ **Bedford's Paradise-Flycatcher** *Terpsiphone bedfordi*

E Zaire (ne Ituri and region west of Itombwe and Kahuzi Mts.)

☐ **Rufous-vented Paradise-Flycatcher** *Terpsiphone rufocinerea*

SE Nigeria and s Cameroon to Gabon to n Angola

☐ **Bates' Paradise-Flycatcher** *Terpsiphone batesi*

_____ *T. b. batesi*	S Cameroon, Rio Muni and Gabon to e Zaire
_____ *T. b. bannermani*	N Angola to Zaire (lower Congo River) and Congo

☐ **African Paradise-Flycatcher** *Terpsiphone viridis*

_____ *T. v. viridis*	Senegal and Gambia to Sierra Leone
_____ *T. v. speciosa*	S Cameroon to e Zaire, s Sudan and Gabon
_____ *T. v. ferretti*	Mali and Ivory Coast to ne Zaire, Sudan, Kenya and Tanzania
_____ *T. v. restricta*	Lake Victoria region of w Kenya and Uganda
_____ *T. v. kivuensis*	SW Uganda to e Zaire, Rwanda, Burundi and nw Tanzania
_____ *T. v. suahelica*	Highlands of w Kenya and Tanzania
_____ *T. v. ungujaensis*	E Tanzania to Zambia; Zanzibar, Pemba I. and Mafia I.
_____ *T. v. plumbeiceps*	S Angola to w Zaire, sw Tanzania and ne South Africa
_____ *T. v. granti*	Natal to sw Cape Province; winters to s Tanzania
_____ *T. v. harterti*	S Arabian peninsula

☐ **Sao Tome Paradise-Flycatcher** *Terpsiphone atrochalybeia*

São Tomé (Gulf of Guinea)

☐ **Madagascar Paradise-Flycatcher** *Terpsiphone mutata*

_____ *T. m. mutata*	Forests of e Madagascar
_____ *T. m. singetra*	Forests of w Madagascar
_____ *T. m. pretiosa*	Mayotte (Indian Ocean)
_____ *T. m. vulpina*	Anjouan (Comoro Islands)
_____ *T. m. voeltzkowiana*	Mohéli (Comoro Islands)
_____ *T. m. comoroensis*	Grand Comoro I.

☐ **Seychelles Paradise-Flycatcher** *Terpsiphone corvina*

Forests of La Digue (Seychelles)

☐ **Mascarene Paradise-Flycatcher** *Terpsiphone bourbonnensis*

_____ *T. m. bourbonnensis*	Réunion (Mascarene Islands)
_____ *T. m. desolata*	Mauritius (Mascarene Islands)

☐ **Japanese Paradise-Flycatcher** *Terpsiphone atrocaudata*

_____ *T. a. atrocaudata*	Japan (Honshu, Shikoku and Kyushu); winters to SE Asia
_____ *T. a. illex*	Ryukyu Islands and Taiwan
_____ *T. a. periophthalmica*	Philippines (Luzon, Batan, Mindoro and Palawan)

☐ **Blue Paradise-Flycatcher** *Terpsiphone cyanescens*

SW Philippines (Calamian Group and Palawan)

☐ Rufous Paradise-Flycatcher *Terpsiphone cinnamomea*

____	*T. c. unirufa*	N Philippines (Luzon to Negros)
____	*T. c. cinnamomea*	S Philippines (Mindanao, Basilan and islands in Sulu Arch.)
____	*T. c. talautensis*	Talaud Islands (Karakelong, Salebabu and Kaburuang)

☐ Asian Paradise-Flycatcher *Terpsiphone paradisi*

____	*T. p. leucogaster*	Mountains of Afghanistan, Pakistan and w India
____	*T. p. paradisi*	Central and s India; winters to Sri Lanka
____	*T. p. ceylonensis*	Sri Lanka
____	*T. p. incei*	China, Manchuria and Japan; winters to Malaysia and Sumatra
____	*T. p. saturatior*	E Himalayas, Assam and Bangladesh; winters to Malaysia
____	*T. p. myanmare*	Central and s Myanmar
____	*T. p. indochinensis*	S China (s Yunnan) to s Thailand and Indochina
____	*T. p. affinis*	Malaya, Sumatra, Riau and Lingga arch., Bangka, Belitung is.
____	*T. p. nicobarica*	Andaman and Nicobar islands
____	*T. p. madzoedi*	N Sumatra
____	*T. p. australis*	S Sumatra and Java
____	*T. p. borneensis*	Borneo
____	*T. p. procera*	Simeulue I. (off Sumatra)
____	*T. p. insularis*	Nias I. (off Sumatra)
____	*T. p. sumbaensis*	Sumba (w Lesser Sundas)
____	*T. p. floris*	W Lesser Sundas (Sumbawa, Alor, Besar, Lomblen and Flores)

☐ Elepaio *Chasiempis sandwichensis*

____	*C. s. sandwichensis*	Drier areas of Hawaii (Hawaiian Islands)
____	*C. s. bryani*	*Mamame-naio* forests on Mauna Kea (Hawaii)
____	*C. s. ridgwayi*	Wetter areas of Hawaii (Hawaiian Islands)
____	*C. s. sclateri*	Kauai (Hawaiian Islands)
____	*C. s. gayi*	Oahu (Hawaiian Islands)

☐ Rarotonga Monarch *Pomarea dimidiata*

Forest undergrowth of Rarotonga (sw Cook Islands)

☐ Tahiti Monarch *Pomarea nigra*

____	*P. n. nigra*	Highlands of Tahiti (Society Islands)
____	*P. n. pomarea†*	Formerly highlands of Maupiti I. (Society Islands). Extinct

☐ Iphis Monarch *Pomarea iphis*

____	*P. i. iphis*	Uahuka (n Marquesas Islands)
____	*P. i. fluxa†*	Formerly Eioa (n Marquesas Islands). Extinct

☐ Marquesas Monarch *Pomarea mendozae*

Marquesas (Nukuhiva, Uapou, Hivaoa, Tahuata and Motane)

☐ Fatuhiva Monarch *Pomarea whitneyi*

Fatuhiva (s Marquesas Islands)

☐ Ogea Monarch *Mayrornis versicolor*

Forests of Ogea Levu (se Fiji)

☐ Slaty Monarch *Mayrornis lessoni*

____	*M. l. lessoni*	Northwest Fiji Islands and Lau Archipelago
____	*M. l. orientalis*	E Fiji Islands

☐ Vanikoro Monarch *Mayrornis schistaceus*

Vanikoro (Santa Cruz Islands)

☐ Buff-bellied Monarch *Neolalage banksiana*

Vanuatu and Banks Group (se Melanesia)

☐ Southern Shrikebill *Clytorhynchus pachycephaloides*

____	*C. p. pachycephaloides*	New Caledonia
____	*C. p. grisescens*	Vanuatu, Banks and Torres groups (se Melanesia)

☐ Rennell Shrikebill *Clytorhynchus hamlini*

Rennell (se Solomon Islands)

☐ **Fiji Shrikebill** *Clytorhynchus vitiensis*

____	*C. v. powelli*	American Samoa (Tau, Ofu, Olosega and Manua)
____	*C. v. compressirostris*	Fiji (Kandavu, Ono and Vanuakula)
____	*C. v .vitiensis*	W Fiji Islands
____	*C. v. buensis*	Fiji (Vanua Levu and Kioa)
____	*C. v. layardi*	Taveuni (Fiji)
____	*C. v. pontifex*	W Fiji Islands (Ngamea and Rambi)
____	*C. v. wiglesworthi*	Rotuma I. (Fiji)
____	*C. v. vatuana*	N Lau Archipelago (e Fiji Islands)
____	*C. v. nesiotes*	S Lau Archipelago (e Fiji Islands)
____	*C. v. heinei*	Central Tonga Islands
____	*C. v. fortunae*	Futuna and Alifi islands (Wallis and Futuna Group)
____	*C. v. keppeli*	Keppel and Boscawen islands (between Tonga and Samoa)

☐ **Black-throated Shrikebill** *Clytorhynchus nigrogularis*

____	*C. n. nigrogularis*	Mountains of larger Fiji Islands
____	*C. n. sanctaecrucis*	Mountains of Santa Cruz Group (Solomon Islands)

☐ **Truk Monarch** *Metabolus rugensis*

Truk (e Caroline Islands)

☐ **Black Monarch** *Monarcha axillaris*

____	*M. a. axillaris*	NW New Guinea (Arfak, Weyland and Wandammen mts.)
____	*M. a. fallax*	Mountains of se New Guinea and Goodenough I.

☐ **Rufous Monarch** *Monarcha rubiensis*

Lowlands of w New Guinea (absent from Vogelkop Peninsula)

☐ **Island Monarch** *Monarcha cinerascens*

____	*M. c. commutatus*	Sangihe and Siau islands (north of Sulawesi)
____	*M. c. jabobii*	Talaud Islands (Moluccas)
____	*M. c. disjunctus*	Lesser Sundas
____	*M. c. intercedens*	Sulawesi, Tukangbesi, Peleng, Banggai and Sula islands
____	*M. c. cinerascens*	Lesser Sundas (Timor, Wetar and Romang)
____	*M. c. kisserensis*	Lesser Sundas (Kisar, Damar, Kai and Tanimbar Islands)
____	*M. c. harterti*	N and s Moluccas
____	*M. c. brunneus*	Great Banda I. (s Moluccas)
____	*M. c. inornatus*	NW New Guinea, Aru, Waigeo, Salawati and Misool islands
____	*M. c. steini*	Numfor I. (New Guinea)
____	*M. c. geelvinkianus*	Yapen and Biak islands (New Guinea)
____	*M. c. fuscescens*	Islands in Geelvink Bay (n New Guinea)
____	*M. c. nigrirostris*	Coastal n New Guinea (Dagua to Huon Gulf)
____	*M. c. fulviventris*	Ninigo, Hermit, Anchorite and Admiralty islands
____	*M. c. perpallidus*	St. Matthias Group and w Bismarck Archipelago
____	*M. c. impediens*	E Bismarck Archipelago to Solomon Islands
____	*M. c. rosselianus*	D'Entrecasteaux, Bismarck and Louisiade archipelagos

☐ **Black-winged Monarch** *Monarcha frater*

____	*M. f. frater*	Vogelkop Mountains (nw New Guinea)
____	*M. f. kunupi*	Weyland Mountains (central New Guinea)
____	*M. f. periophthalmicus*	Mountains of e and se New Guinea
____	*M. f. canescens*	N Queensland (tip of Cape York Pen. to McIlwraith Range)

☐ **Black-faced Monarch** *Monarcha melanopsis*

E Australia (ne Queensland to Victoria); winters to New Guinea

☐ **Bougainville Monarch** *Monarcha erythrostictus*

Rainforests of Bougainville (Solomon Islands)

☐ **Chestnut-bellied Monarch** *Monarcha castaneiventris*

____	*M. c. castaneiventris*	Solomons (Guadalcanal, Malaita, Santa Isabel, Florida, Choiseul)
____	*M. c. obscurior*	Rossel (Solomon Islands)
____	*M. c. megarhyncha*	San Cristóbal (Solomon Islands)
____	*M. c. ugiensis*	Ugi (Solomon Islands)

☐ **White-capped Monarch** *Monarcha richardsii*

Forests of central Solomon Islands

☐ **White-naped Monarch** *Monarcha pileatus*
_____ *M. p. pileatus*
_____ *M. p. buruensis*

Halmahera (n Moluccas)
Buru (n Moluccas)

☐ **Loetoe Monarch** *Monarcha castus*

Tanimbar Is. (Larat, Yamdena, Selaru); Tayandu Is. (Kilsuin)

☐ **White-eared Monarch** *Monarcha leucotis*

Coastal ne Australia (e Queensland to ne New South Wales)

☐ **Spot-winged Monarch** *Monarcha guttulus*

New Guinea, w Papuan islands and Louisiade Archipelago

☐ **Black-bibbed Monarch** *Monarcha mundus*

E Lesser Sundas (Babar, Damar, Larat, Yamdena and Selaru)

☐ **Spectacled Monarch** *Monarcha trivirgatus*
_____ *M. t. bimaculatus*
_____ *M. t. diadematus*
_____ *M. t. boanensis*
_____ *M. t. nigrimentum*
_____ *M. t. wellsi*
_____ *M. t. trivirgatus*
_____ *M. t. bernsteini*
_____ *M. t. albiventris*
_____ *M. t. gouldi*
_____ *M. t. melanopterus*

N Moluccas (Morotai, Halmahera and Bacan)
N Moluccas (Obi and Bisa)
Boano I. (s Moluccas)
S Moluccas (Seram and Ambon)
Seram Laut Is. (Gorong, Manawoka) and Watubela Is. (Kasiui)
Lesser Sundas
Salawati I. (New Guinea)
S New Guinea and ne Australia (n Queensland)
N Queensland (Cooktown) to e-central New South Wales
Louisiade Archipelago

☐ **Flores Monarch** *Monarcha sacerdotum*

SW Flores (w Lesser Sundas)

☐ **White-tipped Monarch** *Monarcha everetti*

Tanahjampea I. (Flores Sea)

☐ **Black-tipped Monarch** *Monarcha loricatus*

Lowlands of Buru (s Moluccas)

☐ **Black-chinned Monarch** *Monarcha boanensis*

Boano I. (s Moluccas)

☐ **White-tailed Monarch** *Monarcha leucurus*

Kai Islands (Kai Kecil, Kai Besar and Baer)

☐ **Black-backed Monarch** *Monarcha julianae*

Known from a 1959 specimen from Kofiau I. (New Guinea)

☐ **Hooded Monarch** *Monarcha manadensis*

Patchily distributed lowland forests of New Guinea

☐ **Biak Monarch** *Monarcha brehmii*

Biak I. off nw New Guinea

☐ **Manus Monarch** *Monarcha infelix*
_____ *M. i. infelix*
_____ *M. i. coultasi*

Manus I. (n Bismarck Archipelago)
Rambutyo I. (n Bismarck Archipelago)

☐ **White-breasted Monarch** *Monarcha menckei*

Mussau I. (St. Matthias Group in Bismarck Archipelago)

☐ **Black-tailed Monarch** *Monarcha verticalis*
_____ *M. v. ateralbus*
_____ *M. v. verticalis*

Dyaul I. (Bismarck Archipelago)
New Britain, New Ireland and adj. islands in Bismarck Arch.

☐ **Kulambangra Monarch** *Monarcha browni*
_____ *M. b. browni*
_____ *M. b. ganongae*
_____ *M. b. nigrotectus*
_____ *M. b. meeki*

Kulambangra (New Georgia Group of Solomon Islands)
Ranongga (New Georgia Group of Solomon Islands)
Vellalavella (New Georgia Group of Solomon Islands)
Rendova and Tetipari (New Georgia Group of Solomon Islands)

☐ **White-collared Monarch** *Monarcha viduus*

San Cristóbal (s Solomon Islands)

☐ **Black-and-white Monarch** *Monarcha barbatus*
_____ M. b. barbatus   Solomons (Bougainville, Guadalcanal, Choiseul and Santa Isabel)
_____ M. b. malaitae   Malaita (Solomon Islands)

☐ **Yap Monarch** *Monarcha godeffroyi*

Forests of Yap (nw Caroline Islands)

☐ **Tinian Monarch** *Monarcha takatsukasae*

Mariana Islands (Tinian and Agiguan)

☐ **Golden Monarch** *Monarcha chrysomela*
_____ M. c. aurantiacus   N New Guinea (Geelvink to Astrolabe Bay and Ramu River)
_____ M. c. melanonotus   NW New Guinea and w Papuan islands
_____ M. c. kordensis   Biak and Misool islands (New Guinea)
_____ M. c. nitida   E and se New Guinea and Louisiade Archipelago
_____ M. c. aruensis   S New Guinea and Aru Islands
_____ M. c. pulcherrima   Dyaul I. (Bismarck Archipelago)
_____ M. c. chrysomela   Bismarck Archipelago (New Hanover and New Ireland)
_____ M. c. whitneyorum   Lihir Group (Bismarck Archipelago)
_____ M. c. tabarensis   Tabar Group (Bismarck Archipelago)

☐ **Frilled Monarch** *Arses telescophthalmus*
_____ A. t. telescophthalmus   NW New Guinea, Salawati and Misool islands
_____ A. t. batantae   Batanta and Waigeo islands (New Guinea)
_____ A. t. aruensis   Aru Islands (New Guinea)
_____ A. t. lauterbachi   N coast of se New Guinea (Milne Bay to Huon Peninsula)
_____ A. t. harterti   S New Guinea (Mimika River to Purari River)
_____ A. t. henkei   Coastal se New Guinea (Hall Sound to Orangerie Bay)
_____ A. t. lorealis   NE Australia (Cape York Peninsula of n Queensland)

☐ **Rufous-collared Monarch** *Arses insularis*

Lowlands of n New Guinea and Yapen I.

☐ **Pied Monarch** *Arses kaupi*

Rainforests of ne Queensland (Cooktown to Townsville)

☐ **Guam Flycatcher** *Myiagra freycineti*

Guam (s Mariana Islands). On verge of extinction

☐ **Palau Flycatcher** *Myiagra erythrops*

Mangroves and lowlands of Palau (w Caroline Islands)

☐ **Pohnpei Flycatcher** *Myiagra pluto*

Pohnpei (e Caroline Islands)

☐ **Oceanic Flycatcher** *Myiagra oceanica*

Truk (w Caroline Islands)

☐ **Biak Flycatcher** *Myiagra atra*

Numfor and Biak islands (New Guinea)

☐ **Moluccan Flycatcher** *Myiagra galeata*
_____ M. g. galeata   N Moluccas (Obi, Bacan, Ternate, Halmahera, Bisa, Morotai)
_____ M. g. buruensis   Buru (s Moluccas)
_____ M. g. seramensis   S Moluccas (Seram, Ambon and Boano)
_____ M. g. goramensis   Seram Laut and Kai Islands (Kai Cecil)

☐ **Leaden Flycatcher** *Myiagra rubecula*
_____ M. r. papuana   Savanna of s New Guinea
_____ M. r. sciurorum   Louisiade and D'Entrecasteaux archipelagos
_____ M. r. rubecula   S Queensland to Victoria; winters to s New Guinea
_____ M. r. concinna   N Western Australia, N Territory, Melivile I. and n Queensland
_____ M. r. yorki   Queensland (Cape York to Burnett River) and Fraser I.

☐ **Steel-blue Flycatcher** *Myiagra ferrocyanea*
_____ M. f. ferrocyanea   Solomon Islands (Santa Isabel, Choiseul and Guadalcanal)
_____ M. f. feminina   Kulambangra (New Georgia Group in Solomon Islands)
_____ M. f. cinerea   Bougainville (Solomon Islands)
_____ M. f. malaitae   Malaita (Solomon Islands)

☐ **Ochre-headed Flycatcher** *Myiagra cervinicauda*

Lowlands of San Cristóbal (s Solomon Islands)

☐ **Melanesian Flycatcher** *Myiagra caledonica*

____	*M. c. caledonica*	New Caledonia
____	*M. c. melanura*	Maré (Loyalty Islands) and Vanuatu (Tanna and Erromanga)
____	*M. c. viridinitens*	Loyalty Islands (Lifou and Ovéa)
____	*M. c. marinae*	N and central Vanuatu, Banks and Torres groups
____	*M. c. occidentalis*	Rennell (se Solomon Islands)

☐ **Vanikoro Flycatcher** *Myiagra vanikorensis*

____	*M. v. vanikorensis*	Vanikoro (Santa Cruz Islands)
____	*M. v. rufiventris*	W Fiji Islands
____	*M. v. kandavensis*	Kandavu and adjacent w Fiji Islands
____	*M. v. dorsalis*	S-central Fiji Islands and n Lau Archipelago
____	*M. v. townsendi*	S Lau Archipelago (Fiji)

☐ **Samoan Flycatcher** *Myiagra albiventris*

Western Samoa (Savai'i and Upolu)

☐ **Blue-crested Flycatcher** *Myiagra azureocapilla*

____	*M. a. azureocapilla*	Fiji (montane forests of Taveuni)
____	*M. a. castaneigularis*	Fiji (montane forests of Vanua Levu and Kambara)
____	*M. a. whitneyi*	Fiji (montane forests of Viti Levu)

☐ **Broad-billed Flycatcher** *Myiagra ruficollis*

____	*M. r. ruficollis*	Lesser Sundas and small islands in Flores Sea
____	*M. r. fulviventris*	Tanimbar Islands (Larat, Yamdena and Selaru)
____	*M. r. mimikae*	New Guinea; coastal n Australia (W Australia to n Queensland)

☐ **Satin Flycatcher** *Myiagra cyanoleuca*

SE Australia and Tasmania; winters to New Guinea region

☐ **Restless Flycatcher** *Myiagra inquieta*

____	*M. i. nana*	Trans-Fly of se New Guinea, n W Australia and N Territory
____	*M. i. westralensis*	S Western Australia
____	*M. i. inquieta*	Queensland to Victoria and South Australia

☐ **Shining Flycatcher** *Myiagra alecto*

____	*M. a. alecto*	N Moluccas
____	*M. a. longirostris*	Tanimbar Islands (Arafura Sea)
____	*M. a. chalybeocephala*	New Guinea, w Papuan islands and Bismarck Archipelago
____	*M. a. manumudani*	Manam I. (New Guinea)
____	*M. a. wardelli*	Trans-Fly of se New Guinea and n Queensland
____	*M. a. lucida*	Louisiade Archipelago and D'Entrecasteaux Archipelago
____	*M. a. rufolateralis*	Coastal n Australia, Melville I. and Groote Eylandt
____	*M. a. tormenti*	Western Australia (Derby region)

☐ **Dull Flycatcher** *Myiagra hebetior*

____	*M. h. hebetior*	St. Matthias Group (Bismarck Archipelago)
____	*M. h. eichhorni*	Bismarck Arch. (New Hanover, New Ireland and New Britain)
____	*M. h. cervinicolor*	Dyaul I. (Bismarck Archipelago)

☐ **Silktail** *Lamprolia victoriae*

____	*L. v. victoriae*	Fiji (mountains of Taveuni)
____	*L. v. kleinschmidti*	Fiji (mountains of Vanua Levu)

☐ **Black-breasted Boatbill** *Machaerirhynchus nigripectus*

____	*M. n. nigripectus*	NW New Guinea (Vogelkop Mountains)
____	*M. n. saturatus*	Montane forests of central New Guinea
____	*M. n. harterti*	Mountains of Huon Peninsula and se New Guinea

☐ **Yellow-breasted Boatbill** *Machaerirhynchus flaviventer*

____ *M. f. albifrons*	Waigeo I. (New Guinea)
____ *M. f. albigula*	W Papuan islands and w New Guinea
____ *M. f. novus*	N coast of se New Guinea
____ *M. f. xanthogenys*	Aru Islands and s New Guinea (Mimika River to Milne Bay)
____ *M. f. secundus*	Cairns-Atherton region of n Queensland
____ *M. f. flaviventer*	Queensland south to Archer River and Hinchinbrook I.

FAMILY: PETROICIDAE (Australasian Robins—44)

☐ **Greater Ground-Robin** *Amalocichla sclateriana*

____ *A. s. occidentalis*	Snow Mountains (w New Guinea)
____ *A. s. sclateriana*	Owen Stanley Mountains (se New Guinea)

☐ **Lesser Ground-Robin** *Amalocichla incerta*

____ *A. i. incerta*	Arfak Mountains of w New Guinea
____ *A. i. olivascentior*	Wandamman and Weyland to Snow Mts. (w New Guinea)
____ *A. i. brevicauda*	Mountains of e and se New Guinea

☐ **Torrent Flycatcher** *Monachella muelleriana*

____ *M. m. muelleriana*	Swift flowing streams of New Guinea
____ *M. m. coultasi*	New Britain (Bismarck Archipelago)

☐ **Jacky-winter** *Microeca fascinans*

____ *M. f. zimmeri*	Papua New Guinea (Port Moresby area)
____ *M. f. pallida*	N Australia (Northern Territory and n Queensland)
____ *M. f. fascinans*	E Australia (s Queensland to se South Australia)
____ *M. f. barcoo*	Central Australia (Cooper Creek to w New South Wales)
____ *M. f. assimilis*	SW Australia to sw Northern Territory and w Victoria

☐ **Golden-bellied Flyrobin** *Microeca hemixantha*

	Tanimbar Islands (Larat, Yamdena and Lutu)

☐ **Lemon-bellied Flycatcher** *Microeca flavigaster*

____ *M. f. tarara*	E New Guinea
____ *M. f. laeta*	New Guinea (Wandamman and Victor Emanual mountains)
____ *M. f. terraereginae*	SE New Guinea and ne Queensland
____ *M. f. flavigaster*	Coastal Northern Territory, Melville I. and Groote Eylandt
____ *M. f. tormenti*	NW Australia (King Sound to Napier Broome Bay)

☐ **Yellow-legged Flycatcher** *Microeca griseoceps*

____ *M. g. occidentalis*	Mountains of nw New Guinea
____ *M. g. griseoceps*	Mountains of se New Guinea and n Queensland

☐ **Olive Flyrobin** *Microeca flavovirescens*

____ *M. f. flavovirescens*	S New Guinea (Wassi Kussa to Fly River) and Aru Islands
____ *M. f. cuicui*	New Guinea, Yapen I. and w Papuan islands

☐ **Canary Flycatcher** *Microeca papuana*

	Montane forests of New Guinea

☐ **Garnet Robin** *Eugerygone rubra*

____ *E. r. rubra*	NW New Guinea (Arfak Mountains)
____ *E. r. saturatior*	Mountains of central and se New Guinea

☐ **Alpine Robin** *Petroica bivittata*

____ *P. b. caudata*	Central New Guinea (Snow and Nassau mountains)
____ *P. b. bivittata*	High mountains of se New Guinea

☐ **Snow Mountain Robin** *Petroica archboldi*

New Guinea (Mt. Wilhelmina and Mt. Carstensz)

☐ **Scarlet Robin** *Petroica multicolor*

____	*P. m. pusilla*	Western Samoa (Upolu and Savai'i)
____	*P. m. feminina*	Vanuatu (Efate and Mai)
____	*P. m. similis*	Vanuatu (Tanna and Aneityum)
____	*P. m. cognata*	Vanuatu (Erromanga I.)
____	*P. m. ambrynensis*	Vanuatu and Banks Group
____	*P. m. soror*	Vanua Lava (Banks Group)
____	*P. m. kleinschmidti*	Fiji (Viti Levu and Vanua Levu)
____	*P. m. taveunensis*	Taveuni (Fiji)
____	*P. m. becki*	Kandavu (Fiji)
____	*P. m. polymorpha*	San Cristóbal (Solomon Islands)
____	*P. m. septentrionalis*	Bougainville (Solomon Islands)
____	*P. m. kulambangrae*	Kulambangra (Solomon Islands)
____	*P. m. dennisi*	Guadalcanal (Solomon Islands)
____	*P. m. campbelli*	SW Western Australia e to Esperance Bay
____	*P. m. boodang*	SE Queensland to Victoria, se South Australia and Tasmania
____	*P. m. multicolor*	Norfolk I.

☐ **Tomtit** *Petroica macrocephala*

____	*P. m. toitoi*	North I. and adjacent offshore islands (New Zealand)
____	*P. m. macrocephala*	South I. and Stewart Island (New Zealand)
____	*P. m. marrineri*	Auckland Islands
____	*P. m. chathamensis*	Chatham Islands
____	*P. m. dannefaerdi*	Snares Islands

☐ **Red-capped Robin** *Petroica goodenovii*

Scrub and *mulga* of interior of Australia

☐ **Flame Robin** *Petroica phoenicea*

SE Australia, Tasmania and islands in Bass Strait

☐ **Rose Robin** *Petroica rosea*

Coastal se Queensland to s Victoria and se South Australia

☐ **Pink Robin** *Petroica rodinogaster*

SE New S Wales, s Victoria, extreme se S Australia; Tasmania

☐ **New Zealand Robin** *Petroica australis*

____	*P. a. longipes*	North I., Little Barrier I. and Kapiti I. (New Zealand)
____	*P. a. australis*	South I. (New Zealand)
____	*P. a. rakiura*	Stewart I. (New Zealand)

☐ **Chatham Robin** *Petroica traversi*

Chatham Islands (Mangere I. and South East I). Endangered

☐ **Hooded Robin** *Melanodryas cucullata*

____	*M. c. picata*	N Western Australia to central Queensland; Melville I.
____	*M. c. cucullata*	SW Australia to Victoria and New South Wales; Tasmania

☐ **Dusky Robin** *Melanodryas vittata*

Tasmania and islands in Bass Strait

☐ **White-faced Robin** *Tregellasia leucops*

____	*T. l. leucops*	NW New Guinea (mountains of Vogelkop Peninsula)
____	*T. l. mayri*	New Guinea (Wandammen and Weyland mountains)
____	*T. l. nigroorbitalis*	New Guinea (Nassau and Snow mountains)
____	*T. l. heurni*	New Guinea (Weyland Mts. and upper Mamberano River)
____	*T. l. nigriceps*	New Guinea (Victor Emanuel and Snow mountains)
____	*T. l. melanogenys*	N New Guinea (Cyclops Mountains to Aicora River)
____	*T. l. wahgiensis*	Mountains of e New Guinea
____	*T. l. albifacies*	Mountains of se New Guinea
____	*T. l. auricularis*	Lowlands of s New Guinea (Orimo River region)
____	*T. l. albigularis*	Lowlands of ne Queensland (Cape York Pen. to Chester River)

☐ **Pale-yellow Robin** *Tregellasia capito*

_____	*T. c. nana*	E Australia (coastal ne Queensland and Hinchinbrook I.)
_____	*T. c. capito*	E Australia (coastal se Queensland and ne New South Wales)

☐ **Yellow Robin** *Eopsaltria australis*

_____	*E. a. magnirostris*	E Australia (ne Queensland)
_____	*E. a. chrysorrhoa*	S Queensland e of Great Dividing Range and nw New S Wales
_____	*E. a. coomooboolaroo*	Carnarvon Range and Duaringa (interior s-central Queensland)
_____	*E. a. australis*	E Australia (extreme s Queensland and e New South Wales)
_____	*E. a. austina*	E Australia (interior of central and n New South Wales)
_____	*E. a. viridior*	E Australia (se South Australia to Victoria)
_____	*E. a. rosinae*	South Australia

☐ **Gray-breasted Robin** *Eopsaltria griseogularis*

Casuarina of sw Australia

☐ **Yellow-bellied Robin** *Eopsaltria flaviventris*

Forests of New Caledonia

☐ **White-breasted Robin** *Eopsaltria georgiana*

Coastal acacia scrub of sw Western Australia

☐ **Mangrove Robin** *Eopsaltria pulverulenta*

_____	*E. p. pulverulenta*	Coastal lowlands of New Guinea
_____	*E. p. leucura*	Aru Islands and ne Australia (ne Queensland)
_____	*E. p. cinereiceps*	Coastal n Western Australia
_____	*E. p. alligator*	N Australia (coastal Northern Territory to ne Queensland)

☐ **Black-chinned Robin** *Poecilodryas brachyura*

_____	*P. b. brachyura*	W New Guinea (Vogelkop, Wandammen and Weyland mts.)
_____	*P. b. albotaeniata*	New Guinea (Geelvink Bay region) and Yapen I.
_____	*P. b. dumasi*	N New Guinea (Humboldt Bay to Sepik River)

☐ **Black-sided Robin** *Poecilodryas hypoleuca*

_____	*P. h. steini*	Waigeo I. (New Guinea)
_____	*P. h. hypoleuca*	W New Guinea to Port Moresby area and w Papuan islands
_____	*P. h. hermani*	N New Guinea (Mamberamo River to upper Watut River)

☐ **White-browed Robin** *Poecilodryas superciliosa*

_____	*P. s. cerviniventris*	Coastal nw Australia (Fitzroy River to Gulf of Carpentaria)
_____	*P. s. superciliosa*	N Queensland (Cape York to Rockhampton)

☐ **Olive-yellow Robin** *Poecilodryas placens*

Patchily distributed New Guinea and Batanta I.

☐ **Black-throated Robin** *Poecilodryas albonotata*

_____	*P. a. albonotata*	W New Guinea (Vogelkop Mountains)
_____	*P. a. griseiventris*	Central Highlands of New Guinea
_____	*P. a. correcta*	New Guinea (mountains of Huon Peninsula and se peninsula)

☐ **White-winged Robin** *Peneothello sigillatus*

_____	*P. s. quadrimaculatus*	W New Guinea (Nassau and Snow mountains)
_____	*P. s. saruwagedi*	New Guinea (mountains of Huon Peninsula)
_____	*P. s. hagenensis*	C New Guinea (highlands of Mt. Hagen and Star Mountains)
_____	*P. s. sigillatus*	Central Highlands and mountains of se New Guinea

☐ **Smoky Robin** *Peneothello cryptoleucus*

_____	*P. c. cryptoleucus*	NW New Guinea (Tamrau and Arfak mountains)
_____	*P. c. albidior*	New Guinea (Weyland, Gauttier and Nassau mountains)
_____	*P. c. maximus*	W New Guinea (Kumawa Mountains)

☐ **White-rumped Robin** *Peneothello bimaculatus*

_____	*P. b. bimaculatus*	Mountains of nw New Guinea
_____	*P. b. vicarius*	Mountains of se New Guinea and Huon Peninsula

☐ **Blue-gray Robin** *Peneothello cyanus*

____	*P. c. cyanus*	NW New Guinea (Vogelkop Mountains)
____	*P. c. atricapillus*	Mountains of ne and central New Guinea
____	*P. c. subcyanus*	Central highlands and mts. of se New Guinea and Huon Pen.

☐ **Ashy Robin** *Heteromyias albispecularis*

____	*H. a. albispecularis*	NW New Guinea (Tamrau and Arfak mountains)
____	*H. a. atricapillus*	NE New Guinea (mountains of Huon Peninsula)
____	*H. a. rothschildi*	New Guinea (Weyland and Snow mountains)
____	*H. a. centralis*	Central Highlands of New Guinea
____	*H. a. armiti*	Herzog Mountains and mountains of se New Guinea

☐ **Gray-headed Robin** *Heteromyias cinereifrons*

Coastal highlands of ne Queensland (Cooktown to Townsville)

☐ **Green-backed Robin** *Pachycephalopsis hattamensis*

____	*P. h. hattamensis*	NW New Guinea (Tamrau and Arfak mountains)
____	*P. h. ernesti*	NW New Guinea (Wandammen Mountains)
____	*P. h. axillaris*	New Guinea (Weyland, Nassau and Snow mountains)
____	*P. h. insulanus*	Mountains of New Guinea
____	*P. h. lecroyae*	Mountains of e-central New Guinea

☐ **White-eyed Robin** *Pachycephalopsis poliosoma*

____	*P. p. idenburgi*	N slopes of central ranges of n New Guinea
____	*P. p. hypopolia*	NE New Guinea (mountains of Huon Peninsula)
____	*P. p. albigularis*	New Guinea (Weyland and Victor Emanuel mountains)
____	*P. p. balim*	Central New Guinea (valleys of the Bele and Balim rivers)
____	*P. p. approximans*	Central New Guinea (south slopes of Snow Mountains)
____	*P. p. hunsteini*	New Guinea (mountains along upper Sepik River)
____	*P. p. poliosoma*	Herzog Mountains and mountains of se New Guinea

☐ **Northern Scrub-Robin** *Drymodes superciliaris*

____	*D. s. beccarii*	NW New Guinea (Arfak and Wandammen mountains)
____	*D. s. nigriceps*	New Guinea (Cyclops Mts. and n slope of Snow Mountains)
____	*D. s. brevirostris*	S and se New Guinea and Aru Islands
____	*D. s. colcloughi*	Coastal Northern Territory
____	*D. s. superciliaris*	Cape York Peninsula of n Queensland (south to Coen River)

☐ **Southern Scrub-Robin** *Drymodes brunneopygia*

____	*D. b. brunneopygia*	Interior New South Wales, Victoria and e South Australia
____	*D. b. pallidus*	S and w South Australia

FAMILY: PACHYCEPHALIDAE (Whistlers and Allies—57)

☐ **Whitehead** *Mohoua albicilla*

Little and Great Barrier is., s North, Arid and Kapiti islands

☐ **Yellowhead** *Mohoua ochrocephala*

Forests of South I. and Stewart I. (New Zealand)

☐ **Pipipi** *Mohoua novaeseelandiae*

Forests of South I. and Stewart I. (New Zealand)

☐ **Crested Shrike-tit** *Falcunculus frontatus*

____	*F. f. leucogaster*	SW Australia
____	*F. f. whitei*	Northern Territory and nw Western Australia
____	*F. f. frontatus*	N Queensland to Victoria and se South Australia

☐ **Crested Bellbird** *Oreoica gutturalis*

____	*O. g. pallescens*	Dry interior of nw Australia and Tasmania
____	*O. g. gutturalis*	Dry interior of southern two-thirds of Australia

☐ **Mottled Whistler** *Rhagologus leucostigma*

____ *R. l. leucostigma* — NW New Guinea (Arfak and Tamrau mountains)
____ *R. l. novus* — N New Guinea (Weyland and Nassau mountains)
____ *R. l. obscurus* — Mountains of central and se New Guinea and Huon Peninsula

☐ **Dwarf Whistler** *Pachycare flavogrisea*

____ *P. f. flavogrisea* — W New Guinea (Vogelkop and Wandammen mountains)
____ *P. f. subaurantia* — Mountains of central New Guinea
____ *P. f. randi* — New Guinea (Snow Mountains in Idenburg River area)
____ *P. f. subpallida* — SE New Guinea (Herzog and Saruwaged mountains)

☐ **Olive-flanked Whistler** *Hylocitrea bonensis*

____ *H. b. bonensis* — Mountains of n, central and se Sulawesi
____ *H. b. bonthaina* — S Sulawesi (Mt. Lompobattang)

☐ **Maroon-backed Whistler** *Coracornis raveni*

Mountains of Sulawesi

☐ **Rufous-naped Whistler** *Aleadryas rufinucha*

____ *A. r. rufinucha* — NW New Guinea (Volgelkop Mountains)
____ *A. r. niveifrons* — Mountains of central New Guinea
____ *A. r. lochmia* — NE New Guinea (mountains of Huon Peninsula)
____ *A. r. gamblei* — Herzog Mountains and mountains of se New Guinea

☐ **Olive Whistler** *Pachycephala olivacea*

____ *P. o. macphersoniana* — Mountains of extreme s Queensland and n New South Wales
____ *P. o. olivacea* — Coastal New South Wales to se South Australia and Tasmania

☐ **Red-lored Whistler** *Pachycephala rufogularis*

SW New South Wales to se S Australia and nw Victoria

☐ **Gilbert's Whistler** *Pachycephala inornata*

____ *P. i. gilbertii* — SW Australia (east to Nullarbor Plain)
____ *P. i. inornata* — SE Australia (n Victoria and New South Wales)

☐ **Mangrove Whistler** *Pachycephala grisola*

India to Myanmar, Andaman Is., Greater Sundas and Palawan

☐ **Green-backed Whistler** *Pachycephala albiventris*

N Philippines (Luzon and Mindoro)

☐ **White-vented Whistler** *Pachycephala homeyeri*

Central and s Philippines and Sulu Archipelago

☐ **Island Whistler** *Pachycephala phaionotus*

Moluccas, Kai, Aru and w Papuan islands

☐ **Rusty Whistler** *Pachycephala hyperythra*

____ *P. h. hyperythra* — W New Guinea (Vogelkop Mountains)
____ *P. h. sepikiana* — New Guinea (Sepik Mts. to mts. south of Mamberamo River)
____ *P. h. reichenowi* — NE New Guinea (Saruwaged Mountains)
____ *P. h. salvadorii* — Mountains of se New Guinea

☐ **Brown-backed Whistler** *Pachycephala modesta*

____ *P. m. modesta* — Herzog Mountains and mountains of se New Guinea
____ *P. m. hypoleuca* — New Guinea (Sepik and Saruwaged mountains)
____ *P. m. telefolminensis* — Central New Guinea (Victor Emanuel and Hindenburg mts.)

☐ **Bornean Whistler** *Pachycephala hypoxantha*

____ *P. h. hypoxantha* — Mountains of n Borneo (Kinabalu to n Sarawak)
____ *P. h. sarawacensis* — N Borneo (Poi Mountains)

☐ **Sulphur-bellied Whistler** *Pachycephala sulfuriventer*

Montane forests of Sulawesi

☐ **Vogelkop Whistler** *Pachycephala meyeri*

NW New Guinea (Arfak, Tamrau and [?] Foya Mountains)

☐ **Yellow-bellied Whistler** *Pachycephala philippinensis*

____ *P. p. fallax*	Calayan (n Philippines)
____ *P. p. illex*	Camiguin Norte (n Philippines)
____ *P. p. philippinensis*	N Philippines (Luzon and Catanduanes)
____ *P. p. siquijorensis*	Siquijor (Philippines)
____ *P. p. apoensis*	Philippines (Dinagat, Samar, Leyte, Biliran and Mindanao)
____ *P. p. basilanica*	Basilan (Philippines)
____ *P. p. boholensis*	Bohol (Philippines)

☐ **Gray-headed Whistler** *Pachycephala griseiceps*

____ *P. g. rufipennis*	Kai Islands (Kai Kecil and Kai Besar)
____ *P. g. gagiensis*	Gagi I. (New Guinea)
____ *P. g. waigeuensis*	Waigeo and Gebe islands (New Guinea)
____ *P. g. miosnomensis*	Meos Num I. (New Guinea)
____ *P. g. griseiceps*	Aru Islands and ne New Guinea
____ *P. g. jobiensis*	N New Guinea and Yapen I.
____ *P. g. perneglecta*	S New Guinea
____ *P. g. dubia*	SE New Guinea and D'Entrecasteaux Archipelago
____ *P. g. sudestensis*	Tagula I. (Louisiade Archipelago)
____ *P. g. peninsulae*	NE Queensland s to Rockingham Bay; Hinchinbrook I.

☐ **Fawn-breasted Whistler** *Pachycephala orpheus*

E Lesser Sundas (Semau, Timor, Jaco and Wetar)

☐ **Gray Whistler** *Pachycephala simplex*

N Australia (coastal N Territory, Melville I. and Groote Eylandt)

☐ **Golden Whistler** *Pachycephala pectoralis*

____ *P. p. javana*	E Java and Bali
____ *P. p. teysmanni*	Salayar I. (Flores Sea)
____ *P. p. everetti*	Tanahjampea, Kalaotoa and Madu islands (Flores Sea)
____ *P. p. pelengensis*	Banggai Islands (Peleng and Banggai)
____ *P. p. clio*	Sula Islands (Taliabu, Seho, Mangole and Sanana))
____ *P. p. mentalis*	N Moluccas (Bacan, Halmahera and Morotai)
____ *P. p. tidorensis*	N Moluccas (Tidore and Ternate)
____ *P. p. obiensis*	S Moluccas (Obi and Bisa)
____ *P. p. buruensis*	Buru (s Moluccas)
____ *P. p. macrorhynchus*	S Moluccas (Ambon and Seram)
____ *P. p. fulvotincta*	E Lesser Sundas
____ *P. p. fulviventris*	Sumba (Lesser Sundas)
____ *P. p. calliope*	E Lesser Sundas (Roti, Timor, Semau and Wetar)
____ *P. p. compar*	E Lesser Sundas (Leti and Moa)
____ *P. p. par*	Romang (e Lesser Sundas)
____ *P. p. dammeriana*	Damar (e Lesser Sundas)
____ *P. p. sharpei*	Babar (Lesser Sundas)
____ *P. p. fuscoflava*	Tanimbar Islands (Larat and Yamdena)
____ *P. p. queenslandica*	N Queensland
____ *P. p. ashbyi*	S Queensland and extreme n New South Wales
____ *P. p. pectoralis*	New South Wales
____ *P. p. youngi*	E Victoria
____ *P. p. fuliginosa*	W Victoria, South Australia and Kangaroo I.
____ *P. p. occidentalis*	Southwestern Australia
____ *P. p. glaucura*	Tasmania and islands in Bass Strait
____ *P. p. tabarensis*	Tabar I. (Papua New Guinea)
____ *P. p. ottomeyeri*	Lihir Islands (Bismarck Archipelago)
____ *P. p. goodsoni*	Admiralty Islands (Bismarck Archipelago)
____ *P. p. citreogaster*	Bismarck Arch. (New Hanover, New Britain and New Ireland)
____ *P. p. sexuvaria*	St. Matthias Islands (Bismarck Archipelago)
____ *P. p. fergussonis*	Fergusson I. (D'Entrecasteaux Archipelago)
____ *P. p. collaris*	Louisiade Archipelago
____ *P. p. rosseliana*	Rossel I. (Louisiade Archipelago)

____	*P. p. misimae*	Misima I. (Louisiade Archipelago)
____	*P. p. whitneyi*	Shortland I. (Solomon Islands)
____	*P. p. bougainvillei*	Solomon Islands (Buka and Bougainville)
____	*P. p. orioloides*	Solomon Islands (Choiseul, Santa Isabel and Florida)
____	*P. p. cinnamomea*	Solomon Islands (Guadalcanal and Beagle)
____	*P. p. sanfordi*	Malaita (Solomon Islands)
____	*P. p. pavuvu*	Pavuvu Islands (Solomon Islands)
____	*P. p. centralis*	E New Georgia Group (Solomon Islands)
____	*P. p. feminina*	Rennell (se Solomon Islands)
____	*P. p. melanoptera*	S New Georgia Group (Solomon Islands)
____	*P. p. melanonota*	Solomon Islands (Ranongga and Vellalavella)
____	*P. p. christophori*	Solomon Islands (Santa Anna and San Cristóbal)
____	*P. p. utupuae*	Utupua I. (Solomon Islands)
____	*P. p. littayei*	Loyalty Islands (New Caledonia, Lifou and Maré)
____	*P. p. cucullata*	Aneityum (Vanuatu)
____	*P. p. chlorura*	Erromango (Vanuatu)
____	*P. p. intacta*	Vanuatu and Banks Group
____	*P. p. vanikorensis*	Vanikoro and Santa Cruz Islands
____	*P. p. ornata*	N Santa Cruz Islands
____	*P. p. kandavensis*	Kandavu Islands (Fiji)
____	*P. p. lauana*	S Lau Archipelago (Fiji)
____	*P. p. vitiensis*	Ngau (Fiji)
____	*P. p. koroana*	Karo (Fiji)
____	*P. p. torquata*	Taveuni (Fiji)
____	*P. p. ambigua*	Fiji (Rambi and Kioa)
____	*P. p. graeffii*	Fiji (Wala and Viti Levu)
____	*P. p. optata*	Fiji (Ovalu and se Viti Levu)
____	*P. p. aurantiiventris*	Fiji (Yanganga and Vanua Levu)
____	*P. p. bella*	Vanua Lava (Banks Group)
____	*P. p. contempta*	Lord Howe I.
____	*P. p. xanthoprocta*	Norfolk I.

☐ **Sclater's Whistler** *Pachycephala soror*

____	*P. s. soror*	NW New Guinea (Vogelkop Mountains)
____	*P. s. klossi*	Mountains of central and e New Guinea
____	*P. s. bartoni*	Mountains of se New Guinea and Goodenough I.
____	*P. s. octogenarii*	New Guinea (Kumawa Mountains)
____	*P. s. remota*	Mountains of Goodenough I. (D'Entrecasteaux Archipelago)

☐ **Lorentz's Whistler** *Pachycephala lorentzi*

New Guinea (Snow, Victor Emanuel and Hindenburg mts.)

☐ **Black-tailed Whistler** *Pachycephala melanura*

____	*P. m. balim*	N New Guinea (Balim and Bele valleys)
____	*P. m. dahli*	Islands off se New Guinea and Bismarck Archipelago
____	*P. m. bynoei*	Western Australia (North West Cape to De Grey River)
____	*P. m. hilli*	NW Australia (Napier Broome Bay and Hecla I.)
____	*P. m. melanura*	NW Australia (King Sound and Roebuck Bay)
____	*P. m. violatae*	Coastal nw W Australia (King Sound to N.W. Cape); Melville I.
____	*P. m. spinicauda*	N Australia (n Queensland and islands in Torres Straits)

☐ **New Caledonian Whistler** *Pachycephala caledonica*

Forests of New Caledonia

☐ **Samoan Whistler** *Pachycephala flavifrons*

W Samoa (Savai'i and Upolu)

☐ **Tongan Whistler** *Pachycephala jacquinoti*

Low scrub of Vava'u (n Tonga)

☐ **Regent Whistler** *Pachycephala schlegelii*

____	*P. s. schlegelii*	New Guinea (Vogelkop and Wandammen mountains)
____	*P. s. obscurior*	Mountains of central and e New Guinea
____	*P. s. cyclopum*	New Guinea (Cyclops Mountains)

☐ **Bare-throated Whistler** *Pachycephala nudigula*
_____ *P. n. ilsa* — Montane forests of Sumbawa (Lesser Sundas)
_____ *P. n. nudigula* — Montane forests of Flores (Lesser Sundas)

☐ **Hooded Whistler** *Pachycephala implicata*
_____ *P. i. implicata* — Montane forests of Guadalcanal (Solomon Islands)
_____ *P. i. richardsi* — Montane forests of Bougainville (Solomon Islands)

☐ **Golden-backed Whistler** *Pachycephala aurea*
— Locally from Weyland and Snow Mountains to se New Guinea

☐ **Drab Whistler** *Pachycephala griseonota*
_____ *P. g. lineolata* — Sula Islands (Taliabu, Seho and Sanana)
_____ *P. g. cinerascens* — N Moluccas (Morotai, Halmahera, Ternate, Tidore and Bacan)
_____ *P. g. johni* — Obi (n Moluccas)
_____ *P. g. examinata* — Buru (s Moluccas)
_____ *P. g. griseonota* — Seram (s Moluccas)
_____ *P. g. kuehni* — Kai Islands (Kai Kecil and Kai Besar)

☐ **Wallacean Whistler** *Pachycephala arctitorquis*
_____ *P. a. tianduana* — Tayandu Islands (Banda Sea)
_____ *P. a. kebirensis* — E Lesser Sundas (Moa, Romang, Babar, Wedan and Damar)
_____ *P. a. arctitorquis* — Tanimbar Islands (Yamdena, Larat, Lutu and Mutu)

☐ **Black-headed Whistler** *Pachycephala monacha*
— Mountains of central New Guinea and Aru Islands

☐ **White-bellied Whistler** *Pachycephala leucogastra*
_____ *P. l. dorsalis* — Mountains of central and e New Guinea
_____ *P. l. leucogastra* — Coastal se New Guinea (Hall Sound to Port Moresby)
_____ *P. l. meeki* — Rossel (Louisiade Archipelago)

☐ **Rufous Whistler** *Pachycephala rufiventris*
_____ *P. r. falcata* — Melville I. and adjacent Northern Territory
_____ *P. r. colletti* — N Western Australia and Northern Territory
_____ *P. r. pallida* — Gulf of Carpenteria (Normanton to Georgetown)
_____ *P. r. dulcior* — NE Australia (n Queensland from Cape York to Townsville)
_____ *P. r. rufiventris* — E Australia (central Queensland to Victoria)
_____ *P. r. maudeae* — Central Australia
_____ *P. r. xanthetraea* — New Caledonia

☐ **White-breasted Whistler** *Pachycephala lanioides*
_____ *P. l. carnaroni* — Western Australia (Shark Bay region)
_____ *P. l. bulleri* — Coastal Western Australia
_____ *P. l. lanioides* — N Western Australia (Kimberley District)
_____ *P. l. fretorum* — W Australia (Northern Territory and nw Queensland); Melville I.

☐ **Sooty Shrike-Thrush** *Colluricincla umbrina*
_____ *C. u. atra* — N New Guinea
_____ *C. u. umbrina* — S New Guinea

☐ **Rufous Shrike-Thrush** *Colluricincla megarhyncha*
_____ *C. m. affinis* — Waigeo I. (New Guinea)
_____ *C. m. batantae* — Batanta I. (New Guinea)
_____ *C. m. misoliensis* — Misool I. (New Guinea)
_____ *C. m. aruensis* — Aru Islands (New Guiinea)
_____ *C. m. obscura* — Yapen I. (New Guinea)
_____ *C. m. melanorhyncha* — Biak I. (New Guinea)
_____ *C. m. idenburgi* — N New Guinea (slopes south of Idenburg River)
_____ *C. m. hybrida* — N New Guinea (Humboldt Bay to Mamberamo River)
_____ *C. m. tappenbecki* — NE New Guinea (Astrolabe Bay to lower Sepik River)
_____ *C. m. maeandrina* — NE New Guinea (upper Sepik River and Victor Emanuel Mts.)

____	*C. m. megarhyncha*	W New Guinea (Vogelkop to Onin Peninsula)
____	*C. m. ferruginea*	Head of Geelvink Bay (nw New Guinea)
____	*C. m. nea*	Herzog Mts., s coast of Huon Gulf and upper Watut River
____	*C. m. madaraszi*	NE New Guinea (Huon Peninsula)
____	*C. m. goodsoni*	S New Guinea (Merauke District)
____	*C. m. wuroi*	S New Guinea (Oriomo River to Morehead River)
____	*C. m. palmeri*	S New Guinea (Trans-Fly lowlands)
____	*C. m. despecta*	S coast of se New Guinea (Milne Bay to Hall Sound)
____	*C. m. superflua*	N coast of se New Guinea (Collingwood Bay to Aicora River)
____	*C. m. fortis*	D'Entrecasteaux Archipelago
____	*C. m. trobriandi*	Trobriand Islands (Solomon Sea)
____	*C. m. discolor*	Tagula I. (Louisiade Archipelago)
____	*C. m. parvula*	N Australia (Northern Territory, Melville I. and Groote Eylandt)
____	*C. m. conigravi*	Western Australia (Kimberley District)
____	*C. m. griseata*	Islands off Cape York Peninsula
____	*C. m. normani*	NE Australia (Cape York Peninsula and n Queensland)
____	*C. m. parvissima*	E Australia (Cairns District of n Queensland)
____	*C. m. gouldii*	E Australia (c and s Queensland from Bowen to Moreton Bay)
____	*C. m. rufogaster*	E Australia (n New South Wales)

☐ **Sangihe Shrike-Thrush** *Colluricincla sanghirensis*

Sangihe I. (north of Sulawesi)

☐ **Bower's Shrike-Thrush** *Colluricincla boweri*

NE Australia (montane rainforests of Cape York Peninsula)

☐ **Sandstone Shrike-Thrush** *Colluricincla woodwardi*

____	*C. w. woodwardi*	Locally in ne Western Australia and Northern Territory
____	*C. w. assimilis*	W Australia (Kimberley Division to extreme nw Queensland)

☐ **Gray Shrike-Thrush** *Colluricincla harmonica*

____	*C. h. tachycrypta*	Coastal se New Guinea
____	*C. h. roebucki*	N Western Australia (Roebuck Bay area)
____	*C. h. parryi*	Western Australia (Kimberley Division)
____	*C. h. julietae*	Interior of n Western Australia
____	*C. h. kolichisi*	Western Australia
____	*C. h. brunnea*	Northern Territory, Melville I. and Groote Eylandt
____	*C. h. superciliosa*	N Queensland (Gulf of Carpentaria to Cape York)
____	*C. h. pallescens*	N Australia (Queensland from Cairns District to Rockhampton)
____	*C. h. harmonica*	E Australia (s Queensland to e Victoria)
____	*C. h. halmaturina*	SW New South Wales to se South Australia and Kangaroo I.
____	*C. h. anda*	South Australia (near Queensland border)
____	*C. h. whitei*	Interior South Australia and Eyre Peninsula
____	*C. h. rufiventris*	W and central Australia
____	*C. h. strigata*	Tasmania and islands in Bass Strait

☐ **Morningbird** *Colluricincla tenebrosa*

Palau Islands (Babelthuap to Peleliu)

☐ **Hooded Pitohui** *Pitohui dichrous*

____	*P. d. dichrous*	Mountains of n New Guinea and Yapen I.
____	*P. d. monticola*	Mountains of central New Guinea

☐ **White-bellied Pitohui** *Pitohui incertus*

Lowlands of s New Guinea (Lorentz River to upper Fly River)

☐ **Rusty Pitohui** *Pitohui ferrugineus*

____	*P. f. leucorhynchus*	Waigeo I. (New Guinea)
____	*P. f. fuscus*	Batanta I. (New Guinea)
____	*P. f. brevipennis*	Aru Islands (New Guinea)
____	*P. f. ferrugineus*	NW New Guinea, Misool and Salawati islands
____	*P. f. holerythrus*	N New Guinea and Yapen I.
____	*P. f. clarus*	SE New Guinea

☐ **Crested Pitohui** *Pitohui cristatus*

____	*P. c. cristatus*	W New Guinea (Arfak Mountains)
____	*P. c. arthuri*	New Guinea (Orimo River, Cyclops and Sepik mountains)
____	*P. c. kodonophonos*	Mountains and lowlands of se New Guinea

☐ **Variable Pitohui** *Pitohui kirhocephalus*

____	*P. k. kirhocephalus*	Coastal ne New Guinea (Vogelkop to Geelvink Bay)
____	*P. k. salvadorii*	NW New Guinea (Geelvink Bay region)
____	*P. k. dohertyi*	NW New Guinea (islands and peninsulas of Wandammen area)
____	*P. k. rubiensis*	NW New Guinea (head of Geelvink Bay)
____	*P. k. tibialis*	NW New Guinea (western half of Vogelkop Peninsula)
____	*P. k. stramineipectus*	SW New Guinea (Triton Bay region)
____	*P. k. decipiens*	SW New Guinea (Onin Peninsula)
____	*P. k. adiensis*	Adi Island (off s coast of Onin Peninsula, sw New Guinea)
____	*P. k. carolinae*	SW New Guinea (Etna Bay region)
____	*P. k. brunneivertex*	W New Guinea (se coast of Geelvink Bay)
____	*P. k. jobiensis*	Kurudu I. and Yapen I. (New Guinea)
____	*P. k. meyeri*	Coastal n New Guinea (Mamberamo River to Tami River)
____	*P. k. senex*	N New Guinea (upper Sepik Valley)
____	*P. k. brunneicaudus*	N New Guinea (lower Sepik River to upper Ramu River)
____	*P. k. nigripectus*	S New Guinea
____	*P. k. meriodionalis*	SE New Guinea (Chads Bay to Yule I.)
____	*P. k. brunneiceps*	S New Guinea (Fly River to Gulf of Papua)
____	*P. k. aruensis*	Aru Islands (New Guinea)
____	*P. k. uropygialis*	Salawati and Misool islands (New Guinea)
____	*P. k. pallidus*	Sagewin and Batanta islands (New Guinea)
____	*P. k. cervineiventris*	Waigeo and Gemien islands (New Guinea)

☐ **Black Pitohui** *Pitohui nigrescens*

____	*P. n. nigrescens*	NW New Guinea (Arfak and Tamrau mountains)
____	*P. n. wandamensis*	New Guinea (Wandammen Peninsula)
____	*P. n. buergersi*	New Guinea (Sepik, Hindenburg and Hagen mountains)
____	*P. n. meeki*	Central New Guinea (Weyland, Nassau and Snow mountains)
____	*P. n. harterti*	NE New Guinea (Saruwaged Mountains of Huon Peninsula)
____	*P. n. schistaceus*	Herzog Mountains and mountains of se New Guinea

☐ **Wattled Ploughbill** *Eulacestoma nigropectus*

____	*E. n. clara*	Central Highlands of New Guinea
____	*E. n. nigropectus*	Mountains of se New Guinea

FAMILY: PICATHARTIDAE (Rockfowl—2)

☐ **White-necked Rockfowl** *Picathartes gymnocephalus*

Locally in Guinea, Liberia, Sierra Leone, Ivory Coast and Ghana

☐ **Gray-necked Rockfowl** *Picathartes oreas*

Forests of se Nigeria to s Cameroon and ne Gabon; Bioko

FAMILY: TIMALIIDAE (Babblers—265)

☐ **Malia** *Malia grata*

____	*M. g. recondita*	Montane forests of peninsular n Sulawesi
____	*M. g. stresemanni*	Central and se peninsular Sulawesi
____	*M. g. grata*	S Sulawesi (Mt. Lompobattang)

☐ **Ashy-headed Laughingthrush** *Garrulax cinereifrons*

Humid forests of sw Sri Lanka

☐ **Sunda Laughingthrush** *Garrulax palliatus*
_____ *G. p. palliatus* — Montane forests of w Sumatra
_____ *G. p. schistochlamys* — Montane forests of n Borneo

☐ **Rufous-fronted Laughingthrush** *Garrulax rufifrons*
_____ *G. r. rufifrons* — Montane forests of w Java
_____ *G. r. slamatensis* — Central Java (Mt. Slamet area)

☐ **Masked Laughingthrush** *Garrulax perspicillatus*

Lowland scrub of s China to Indochina

☐ **White-throated Laughingthrush** *Garrulax albogularis*
_____ *G. a. whistleri* — Kashmir to Pakistan and nw India (Uttar Pradesh)
_____ *G. a. albogularis* — Himalayas (w Nepal to e Bhutan)
_____ *G. a. eous* — SW China (Qinghai, s Shaanxi, s Sichuan, n Yunnan) to nw Tonkin
_____ *G. a. ruficeps* — Montane forests of Taiwan

☐ **White-crested Laughingthrush** *Garrulax leucolophus*
_____ *G. l. leucolophus* — W Himalayas to Nepal, Sikkim, Bhutan and Assam (Mishmi Hills)
_____ *G. l. patkaicus* — S Assam (s of the Brahmaputra) to n Myanmar and nw Yunnan
_____ *G. l. belangeri* — S Myanmar and sw Thailand (valley of Mekong River)
_____ *G. l. diardi* — SE Myanmar to sw Yunnan, peninsular Thailand and Indochina
_____ *G. l. bicolor* — Mountains of w Sumatra

☐ **Lesser Necklaced Laughingthrush** *Garrulax monileger*
_____ *G. m. monileger* — Himalayas from Nepal to ne Myanmar and s China (sw Yunnan)
_____ *G. m. badius* — NE Assam (Mishmi Hills)
_____ *G. m. stuarti* — SE Myanmar to nw Thailand
_____ *G. m. fuscatus* — Central Myanmar to sw Thailand
_____ *G. m. mouhoti* — SE Thailand to Cambodia and s Vietnam
_____ *G. m. pasquieri* — Central Vietnam (Thuatien and Quangtri provinces)
_____ *G. m. schauenseei* — E Myanmar to sw Yunnan, ne plateau of Thailand and n Laos
_____ *G. m. tonkinensis* — S China (Guangxi and se Yunnan) to n Vietnam
_____ *G. m. melli* — SE China (Fujian and Hunan to n Guangdong)
_____ *G. m. schmackeri* — Hainan (s China)

☐ **Greater Necklaced Laughingthrush** *Garrulax pectoralis*
_____ *G. p. pectoralis* — Himalayas of Nepal to s China (s Yunnan w of the Mekong R.)
_____ *G. p. melanotis* — Himalayas (Sikkim to Assam, n Myanmar and s China)
_____ *G. p. pingi* — S China (w Yunnan south of range of *melanotis*)
_____ *G. p. subfusus* — SE Myanmar to w Thailand and nw Laos
_____ *G. p. robini* — S China (s Yunnan e of the Mekong) to n Vietnam and ne Laos
_____ *G. p. picticollis* — E China (Anhui to Shaanxi, Fujian and Hunan to Guangdong)
_____ *G. p. semitorquatus* — Hainan (s China)

☐ **Black Laughingthrush** *Garrulax lugubris*
_____ *G. l. lugubris* — Highlands of Malay Peninsula and w Sumatra
_____ *G. l. calvus* — Highlands of ne Borneo

☐ **Striated Laughingthrush** *Garrulax striatus*
_____ *G. s. striatus* — NW Himalayas (East Punjab to Kumaon)
_____ *G. s. vibex* — Himalayas (w and central Nepal to s Tibet)
_____ *G. s. sikkimensis* — Himalayas (e Nepal to se Tibet, sw China, Sikkim and Bhutan)
_____ *G. s. cranbrooki* — Bhutan to Assam, w Myanmar and s China (nw Yunnan)

☐ **White-necked Laughingthrush** *Garrulax strepitans*
_____ *G. s. strepitans* — Myanmar to sw China (sw Yunnan), w Thailand and nw Laos
_____ *G. s. terrarius* — SE Thailand

☐ **Black-hooded Laughingthrush** *Garrulax milleti*

Montane forests of central and s Annam (status unknown)

☐ **Gray Laughingthrush** *Garrulax maesi*
_____ *G. m. grahami*
_____ *G. m. maesi*
_____ *G. m. varennei*
_____ *G. m. castanotis*

SW China (sw Sichuan to se Guangxi and ne Yunnan)
Mountains of sw China (Guangxi) and n Tonkin
NE and central Laos (Chiang Khwang and Thakkek provinces)
Hainan (s China)

☐ **Rufous-necked Laughingthrush** *Garrulax ruficollis*

Mixed forests of e Nepal to sw China, ne India and Myanmar

☐ **Chestnut-backed Laughingthrush** *Garrulax nuchalis*

Lowlands of ne India (Arunachal Pradesh) to n Myanmar

☐ **Black-throated Laughingthrush** *Garrulax chinensis*
_____ *G. c. lochmius*
_____ *G. c. chinensis*
_____ *G. c. propinquus*
_____ *G. c. germaini*
_____ *G. c. monachus*

S China (sw Yunnan) to se Myanmar, n Thailand and n Laos
S China (se Yunnan, s Guangxi and s Guangdong) to n Laos
S Myanmar to sw Thailand
S Vietnam (Phantiet and Phanrang provinces)
Hainan (s China)

☐ **White-cheeked Laughingthrush** *Garrulax vassali*

Montane forests of s Annam and s Laos

☐ **Yellow-throated Laughingthrush** *Garrulax galbanus*
_____ *G. g. galbanus*
_____ *G. g. courtoisi*
_____ *G. g. simaoensis*

SE Assam (Manipur and Lushai Hills) to w Myanmar
E-central China (n Jiangxi Province)
S China (Yunnan)

☐ **Wynaad Laughingthrush** *Garrulax delesserti*

SW India (W Ghats from Goa to Kerala and w Tamil Nadu)

☐ **Rufous-vented Laughingthrush** *Garrulax gularis*

E Bhutan to ne India, n Myanmar and n Laos

☐ **Père David's Laughingthrush** *Garrulax davidi*
_____ *G. d. chinganicus*
_____ *G. d. davidi*
_____ *G. d. experrectus*
_____ *G. d. concolor*

N Manchuria (Khingan Mountains)
N China (Inner Mongolia to Gansu, e Qinghai and Liaoning)
N Gansu (north spur of Nan Shan Mountains)
N Sichuan (Sungpan region)

☐ **Sukatschev's Laughingthrush** *Garrulax sukatschewi*

SW China (montane forests of s Gansu and adjacent Sichuan)

☐ **Moustached Laughingthrush** *Garrulax cineraceus*
_____ *G. c. cineraceus*
_____ *G. c. strenuus*
_____ *G. c. cinereiceps*

S Assam (s of the Brahmaputra) to w Myanmar (Chin Hills)
NE Myanmar to s China (se Sichuan and nw Yunnan)
S China (w Sichuan to Anhui, Guandong and Zhejiang)

☐ **Rufous-chinned Laughingthrush** *Garrulax rufogularis*
_____ *G. r. occidentalis*
_____ *G. r. grosvenori*
_____ *G. r. rufogularis*
_____ *G. r. assamensis*
_____ *G. r. rufitinctus*
_____ *G. r. rufiberbis*
_____ *G. r. intensior*

W Himalayas (Pakistan to nw Uttar Pradesh)
Himalayas of w Nepal
Himalayas (Nepal to Bhutan and n Assam)
NE Assam
Assam south of the Brahmaputra (Khasi Hills)
N Myanmar
N Vietnam (Tonkin)

☐ **Spotted Laughingthrush** *Garrulax ocellatus*
_____ *G. o. griseicauda*
_____ *G. o. ocellatus*
_____ *G. o. maculipectus*
_____ *G. o. artemisiae*

Himalayas from nw India (nw Uttar Pradesh) to w Nepal
Himalayas (central Nepal to Bhutan and se Tibet)
S China (nw Yunnan) to ne Myanmar
S China (s Gansu to Sichuan and ne Yunnan)

☐ **Barred Laughingthrush** *Garrulax lunulatus*

S-central China (s Gansu, s Shaanxi and w Sichuan)

☐ **Biet's Laughingthrush** *Garrulax bieti*

Mountains of s China (sw Sichuan and nw Yunnan)

☐ **Giant Laughingthrush** *Garrulax maximus*

Mts. of se Tibet to s China (s Gansu, w Sichuan and nw Yunnan)

☐ **Gray-sided Laughingthrush** *Garrulax caerulatus*

____ *G. c. caerulatus*   Himalayas from Nepal to Bhutan and Assam (n of Brahmaputra)
____ *G. c. subcaerulatus*   S Assam south of the Brahmaputra (Khasi Hills)
____ *G. c. livingstoni*   E Assam (Naga Hills and Manipur) to nw Myanmar
____ *G. c. kaurensis*   N Myanmar (Kachin State)
____ *G. c. latifrons*   NE Myanmar (Myitkyina District) and adj. s China (nw Yunnan)

☐ **Rusty Laughingthrush** *Garrulax poecilorhynchus*

____ *G. p. ricinus*   Mts. of s China (Gansu to s Sichuan and extreme nw Yunnan)
____ *G. p. berthemyi*   Mountains of se China (s Anhui to Zhejiang and nw Fujian)
____ *G. p. poecilorhynchus*   Mountains of Taiwan

☐ **Chestnut-capped Laughingthrush** *Garrulax mitratus*

____ *G. m. major*   Highlands of Malay Pen. (n Perak to s Selangor and Pahang)
____ *G. m. mitratus*   Highlands of w Sumatra
____ *G. m. damnatus*   Mountains of e Sarawak (Mt. Dulit, Mt. Derian, Kelabit Plateau)
____ *G. m. treacheri*   N Borneo (Mt. Kinabalu)
____ *G. m. griswoldi*   Highlands of central Borneo (Schwaner and Müller mountains)

☐ **Spot-breasted Laughingthrush** *Garrulax merulinus*

____ *G. m. merulinus*   S China (w Yunnan) to n Myanmar and s Assam
____ *G. m. obscurus*   S China (se Yunnan) to n Laos and nw Tonkin
____ *G. m. annamensis*   Laos (Langbian Plateau)

☐ **Hwamei** *Garrulax canorus*

____ *G. c. canorus*   S China (Yangtze Valley) to Tonkin, n Annam and n Laos
____ *G. c. owstoni*   Mountains of Hainan (s China)
____ *G. c. taewanus*   Taiwan

☐ **White-browed Laughingthrush** *Garrulax sannio*

____ *G. s. albosuperciliaris*   NE India (Naga Hills and Manipur in e Assam)
____ *G. s. comis*   S China (Yunnan) to ne Myanmar, n Laos, n Annam and Tonkin
____ *G. s. sannio*   S China (Guangxi, Guandong, Fujian, Jiangxi, Hunan) to Tonkin
____ *G. s. oblectans*   W central China (sw Hubei, n Guizhou and Sichuan)

☐ **Rufous-breasted Laughingthrush** *Garrulax cachinnans*

SW Peninsular India (Nilgiri Hills in w Tamil Nadu)

☐ **Gray-breasted Laughingthrush** *Garrulax jerdoni*

____ *G. j. jerdoni*   Hill forests of sw India (Western Ghats in Coorg region)
____ *G. j. fairbanki*   S India (Palni and Anaimalai hills and n Kerala)
____ *G. j. meridionalis*   Hill forests of sw India (s Kerala)

☐ **Streaked Laughingthrush** *Garrulax lineatus*

____ *G. l. bilkevitchi*   Tajikistan and e Afghanistan to nw Pakistan
____ *G. l. gilgit*   NE Pakistan (Gilgit region of Kashmir)
____ *G. l. lineatus*   Himalayas (central Kashmir to nw Uttar Pradesh and sw Tibet)
____ *G. l. setafer*   Nepal to Sikkim and w Bengal (Darjiling)
____ *G. l. imbricatus*   Bhutan and se Tibet

☐ **Striped Laughingthrush** *Garrulax virgatus*

Mountains of ne India (Assam) and sw Myanmar (Chin Hills)

☐ **Scaly Laughingthrush** *Garrulax subunicolor*

____ *G. s. subunicolor*   Himalayas (Nepal to Sikkim, Bhutan, e Assam and se Tibet)
____ *G. s. griseatus*   Extreme ne Myanmar (Kachin State) to s China (nw Yunnan)
____ *G. s. fooksi*   Mountains of nw Tonkin

☐ **Brown-capped Laughingthrush** *Garrulax austeni*

____ *G. a. austeni* — Montane forests of s Assam (south of the Brahmaputra)
____ *G. a. victoriae* — W Myanmar (Mt. Victoria)

☐ **Blue-winged Laughingthrush** *Garrulax squamatus*

Montane forests of Nepal to sw China, Myanmar and nw Tonkin

☐ **Elliot's Laughingthrush** *Garrulax elliotii*

____ *G. e. przewalskii* — Montane forests of s-central China (Gansu and e Qinghai)
____ *G. e. elliotii* — Mts. of s China (s Shaanxi, w Hubei, Sichuan and nw Yunnan)

☐ **Variegated Laughingthrush** *Garrulax variegatus*

____ *G. v. similis* — Himalayas (e Afghanistan to w Pakistan and w Kashmir)
____ *G. v. variegatus* — Himalayas of nw India (Himachal Pradesh) to Nepal

☐ **Prince Henry's Laughingthrush** *Garrulax henrici*

Semiarid montane scrub of w China (sw Xinjiang and se Tibet)

☐ **Black-faced Laughingthrush** *Garrulax affinis*

____ *G. a. affinis* — Mountains of w and central Nepal
____ *G. a. bethelae* — Himalayas from e Nepal to e Bhutan and se Tibet
____ *G. a. oustaleti* — S China (nw Yunnan) to ne Assam and ne Myanmar
____ *G. a. muliensis* — SW China (Yangtze River Valley of se Qinghai and nw Yunnan)
____ *G. a. blythii* — Mountains of w-central China (n Sichuan in Moupin region)
____ *G. a. saturatus* — N Tonkin (Fan Si Pan Mountains)

☐ **White-whiskered Laughingthrush** *Garrulax morrisonianus*

Montane forests of Taiwan

☐ **Chestnut-crowned Laughingthrush** *Garrulax erythrocephalus*

____ *G. e. erythrocephalus* — Himalayas of w India (Himachal Pradesh to Uttar Pradesh)
____ *G. e. kali* — W and central Nepal
____ *G. e. nigrimentum* — Himalayas of Sikkim, Bhutan and se Tibet
____ *G. e. imprudens* — Hill forests of Assam (north and east of the Brahmaputra)
____ *G. e. chrysopterus* — Hill forests of s Assam (south of the Brahmaputra)
____ *G. e. godwini* — Hill forests of se Assam (Barail Mountains)
____ *G. e. erythrolaema* — E Manipur and sw Myanmar (Chin Hills and Arakan Yoma Mts.)
____ *G. e. woodi* — NE Myanmar (Kachin and N Shan States) and adj. sw Yunnan
____ *G. e. connectens* — Mountains of nw Tonkin and ne Laos
____ *G. e. subconnectens* — Mountains of ne Thailand (Doi Phu Kha)
____ *G. e. schistaceus* — Mountains of e Myanmar and nw Thailand
____ *G. e. melanostigma* — SE Myanmar (s Shan States) to high mountains of nw Thailand
____ *G. e. ramsayi* — S Myanmar (Karenni State and Tavoy District)
____ *G. e. peninsulae* — High mountains of peninsular Thailand and Malay Peninsula

☐ **Golden-winged Laughingthrush** *Garrulax ngoclinhensis*

Western highlands of Vietnam (Mount Ngoc Linh)

☐ **Collared Laughingthrush** *Garrulax yersini*

S Laos (Langbian Plateau). Status unknown

☐ **Red-winged Laughingthrush** *Garrulax formosus*

____ *G. f. formosus* — SW China (sw Sichuan, ne Yunnan and s Guangxi)
____ *G. f. greenwayi* — N Tonkin (Fan Si Pan Mountains)

☐ **Red-tailed Laughingthrush** *Garrulax milnei*

____ *G. m. sharpei* — E Myanmar to s China (s Yunnan), nw Thailand and n Indochina
____ *G. m. vitryi* — S Laos (Bolavens Plateau)
____ *G. m. sinianus* — SE China (Guizhou and Guangxi)
____ *G. m. milnei* — Mountains of se China (nw Fujian)

☐ **Gray-faced Liocichla** *Liocichla omeiensis*

Mountains of sw China (central Sichuan on Mt. Omei Shan)

☐ **Steere's Liocichla** *Liocichla steerii*

Montane forests of Taiwan

☐ **Red-faced Liocichla** *Liocichla phoenicea*

_____	*L. p. phoenicea*	Himalayas from Nepal to Bhutan and Assam (Mishmi Hills)
_____	*L. p. bakeri*	S Assam (s of the Brahmaputra) to nw Myanmar and nw Yunnan
_____	*L. p. ripponi*	E Myanmar (Kachin State to s Shan States) and nw Thailand
_____	*L. p. wellsi*	S China (se Yunnan) to n Laos and n Tonkin

☐ **Spot-throat** *Modulatrix stictigula*

_____	*M. s. stictigula*	NE Tanzania (Usambara and Nguru mountains)
_____	*M. s. pressa*	E Tanzania (Ukaguru Mts.) to n Malawi (Masuku Mts.)

☐ **Dapple-throat** *Arcanator orostruthus*

_____	*A. o. armani*	NE Tanzania (Usambara Mountains)
_____	*A. o. sanjei*	NE Tanzania (Udzungwa Mountains)
_____	*A. o. orostruthus*	N Mozambique (Mt. Namuli)

☐ **White-chested Babbler** *Trichastoma rostratum*

_____	*T. r. rostratum*	Malay Pen., Sumatra, Belitung I., Riau and Lingga archipelagos
_____	*T. r. macropterum*	Borneo and Banggai I.

☐ **Sulawesi Babbler** *Trichastoma celebense*

_____	*T. c. celebense*	N peninsular Sulawesi, Bangka, Lembeh and Manterawu islands
_____	*T. c. rufofuscum*	N-central, s-central and se Sulawesi and Butung I.
_____	*T. c. finschi*	S Sulawesi
_____	*T. c. togianense*	Togian Islands

☐ **Ferruginous Babbler** *Trichastoma bicolor*

Lowlands of Malay Peninsula, Sumatra, Bangka I. and Borneo

☐ **Bagobo Babbler** *Trichastoma woodi*

S Philippines (montane forests of Mindanao)

☐ **Abbott's Babbler** *Malacocincla abbotti*

_____	*M. a. abbotti (rufescentior)*	S Myanmar to Thailand, nw Malay Pen. and Mergui Archipelago
_____	*M. a. krishnarajui*	E India (Eastern Ghats in n Andhra Pradesh)
_____	*M. a. williamsoni*	Thailand (e part of sw plateau) and nw Cambodia
_____	*M. a. obscurius*	Coastal se Thailand (Chon Buri Province to Trat); Ko Kut I.
_____	*M. a. altera*	Central Laos and central Vietnam
_____	*M. a. olivacea*	Peninsular Thailand and Malay Peninsula to e Sumatra
_____	*M. a. sirense*	Borneo, Matasiri and Belitung islands
_____	*M. a. baweana*	Bawean I. (Java Sea)

☐ **Horsfield's Babbler** *Malacocincla sepiarium*

_____	*M. s. tardinata*	Malay Peninsula (Pattani to Selangor and Pahang)
_____	*M. s. liberalis*	Highlands of nw Sumatra
_____	*M. s. barussana*	Highlands of sw Sumatra
_____	*M. s. sepiarium*	W and central Java
_____	*M. s. minus*	E Java and Bali
_____	*M. s. harterti*	N and e Borneo
_____	*M. s. rufiventris*	W and s Borneo

☐ **Short-tailed Babbler** *Malacocincla malaccensis*

_____	*M. m. malaccensis*	Malay Pen., Sumatra, Anambas, N Natuna, Lingga and Riau arch.
_____	*M. m. saturata*	W Borneo, Bangka and Belitung islands
_____	*M. m. poliogenys*	E Borneo
_____	*M. m. feriata*	Extreme ne Sarawak (Mt. Mulu)

☐ **Ashy-headed Babbler** *Malacocincla cinereiceps*

S Philippines (Balabac and Palawan)

☐ **Brown-capped Babbler** *Pellorneum fuscocapillum*

_____	*P. f. babaulti*	Arid lowlands of n and e Sri Lanka
_____	*P. f. fuscocapillum*	Wet zone of sw Sri Lanka
_____	*P. f. scortillum*	Humid forests of sw Sri Lanka

☐ **Marsh Babbler** *Pellorneum palustre*

NE India (Arunachal Pradesh to Cachar, Khasi, Chittagong Hills)

☐ **Buff-breasted Babbler** *Pellorneum tickelli*

____	*P. t. assamense*	NE India (Arunachal Pradesh to Bangladesh and Manipur)
____	*P. t. grisescens*	SW Myanmar (Arakan Yoma Mountains)
____	*P. t. fulvum*	S China (sw Yunnan) to ne Myanmar, n Thailand and Indochina
____	*P. t. annamense*	Central and s Vietnam to s Laos (Bolavens Plateau)
____	*P. t. tickelli*	Central and s Malay Peninsula and adjacent Thailand
____	*P. t. buettikoferi*	S Sumatra and Belitung I.

☐ **Temminck's Babbler** *Pellorneum pyrrogenys*

____	*P. p. pyrrogenys*	W Java
____	*P. p. besuki*	E Java
____	*P. p. erythrote*	W Sarawak (Mt. Poi and Mt. Penrissen)
____	*P. p. longstaffi*	Montane forests of Sarawak
____	*P. p. canicapillum*	Highlands of n Borneo

☐ **Spot-throated Babbler** *Pellorneum albiventre*

____	*P. a. ignotum*	Hill forests of ne Assam (Mishmi Hills)
____	*P. a. albiventre (nagaense)*	Bhutan/Assam border to w Myanmar (Chin Hills)
____	*P. a. cinnamomeum*	Central Myanmar to nw Thailand, s Laos and s Annam
____	*P. a. pusillum*	Eastern regions of n Laos and w Tonkin

☐ **Puff-throated Babbler** *Pellorneum ruficeps*

____	*P. r. olivaceum*	SW India (Kerala)
____	*P. r. ruficeps*	Coastal lowlands and hills of w and central India
____	*P. r. punctatum*	W Himalayas (Kangra to Garhwal)
____	*P. r. mandellii*	Nepal to Sikkim, Bhutan and ne India (Darjiling District)
____	*P. r. chamelum*	S Assam south of the Brahmaputra (Garo Hills to Naga Hills)
____	*P. r. pectorale*	NE Assam (Mishmi Hills)
____	*P. r. ripleyi*	NE Assam south of the Brahmaputra (Lakhimpur District)
____	*P. r. vocale*	NE India (valley of central Manipur)
____	*P. r. victoriae*	N Myanmar (Chin Hills)
____	*P. r. stageri*	NE Myanmar (Myitkyina and Bhamo districts)
____	*P. r. shanense*	Central Myanmar (N and S Shan States) to s China (sw Yunnan)
____	*P. r. hilarum*	Arid zone of central Myanmar
____	*P. r. minus*	S Myanmar (lower Irrawaddy River)
____	*P. r. subochraceum*	S Myanmar and adjacent sw Thailand
____	*P. r. insularum*	S Myanmar (Mergui Archipelago)
____	*P. r. acrum*	Central plains of Thailand and n Malay Peninsula
____	*P. r. chthonium*	N plateau of Thailand
____	*P. r. indictinctum*	Mekong River drainage of n plateau of Thailand
____	*P. r. oreum*	S China (s Yunnan between Mekong and Salween river)
____	*P. r. vividum*	S Yunnan (Red River Valley) to extreme n Tonkin and c Annam
____	*P. r. elbeli*	Northwest part of e plateau of Thailand
____	*P. r. ubonense*	E part of e plateau of Thailand and adjacent s Laos
____	*P. r. deignani*	S Vietnam
____	*P. r. dilloni*	S Indochina
____	*P. r. euroum*	Central plains of Thailand (e of Chao Phaya) to w Cambodia
____	*P. r. smithi*	Islets off coastal se Thailand and Cambodia

☐ **Black-capped Babbler** *Pellorneum capistratum*

____	*P. c. nigrocapitatum*	Malay Peninsula to Singapore, North Natuna Is. and Belitung I.
____	*P. c. nyctilampis*	Sumatra and Bangka I.
____	*P. c. capistratoides*	W and s Borneo
____	*P. c. morrelli*	N and e Borneo and Banggai Islands
____	*P. c. capistratum*	Java

☐ **Palawan Babbler** *Malacopteron palawanense*

SW Philippines (Balabac and Palawan)

☐ **Moustached Babbler** *Malacopteron magnirostre*
_____ *M. m. magnirostre (flavum)* S Myanmar and s Thailand to Sumatra and adjacent islands
_____ *M. m. cinereocapillum* N Borneo

☐ **Sooty-capped Babbler** *Malacopteron affine*
_____ *M. a. affine* SE peninsular Thailand to Malaya, Singapore and Sumatra
_____ *M. a. notatum* Banyak I. (off Sumatra)
_____ *M. a. phoeniceum* Borneo

☐ **Scaly-crowned Babbler** *Malacopteron cinereum*
_____ *M. c. indochinense* SE Thailand to Cambodia and s Laos
_____ *M. c. cinereum* Malay Peninsula to Sumatra, Borneo and adjacent islands
_____ *M. c. niasense* Nias I. (off Sumatra)
_____ *M. c. rufifrons* Java
_____ *M. c. bungurense* North Natuna Islands (off n Borneo)

☐ **Rufous-crowned Babbler** *Malacopteron magnum*
_____ *M. m. magnum* S Myanmar, Malay Pen., Sumatra, Borneo and North Natuna Is.
_____ *M. m. saba* NE Borneo

☐ **Gray-breasted Babbler** *Malacopteron albogulare*
_____ *M. a. albogulare* Malay Peninsula, ne Sumatra, Batu Islands and Lingga Arch.
_____ *M. a. moultoni* NW Borneo

☐ **Blackcap Illadopsis** *Illadopsis cleaveri*
_____ *I. c. johnsoni* Humid forests of Sierra Leone to Liberia
_____ *I. c. cleaveri* Ghana
_____ *I. c. marchanti* S Nigeria
_____ *I. c. batese* SE Nigeria to Cameroon, Cent. African Rep., Gabon and Congo
_____ *I. c. poense* Bioko (Gulf of Guinea)

☐ **Scaly-breasted Illadopsis** *Illadopsis albipectus*
_____ *I. a. barakae* E Zaire (east of Ituri River) to Uganda, s Sudan and sw Kenya
_____ *I. a. albipectus* N Angola to e Zaire (west of Ituri River)

☐ **Rufous-winged Illadopsis** *Illadopsis rufescens*
  Patchily distributed forests of Sierra Leone to Ghana and Togo

☐ **Puvel's Illadopsis** *Illadopsis puveli*
_____ *I. p. puveli* Guinea to Sierra Leone
_____ *I. p. strenuipes* S Nigeria to Cameroon and ne Zaire

☐ **Pale-breasted Illadopsis** *Illadopsis rufipennis*
_____ *I. r. extremis* E Sierra Leone to Ivory Coast and Ghana
_____ *I. r. rufipennis* S Nigeria to Cameroon, Zaire, Gabon, Uganda, sw Kenya, s Sudan
_____ *I. r. bocagei* Bioko (Gulf of Guinea)
_____ *I. r. distans* NE Tanzania and Zanzibar I.

☐ **Brown Illadopsis** *Illadopsis fulvescens*
_____ *I. f. gularis* Sierra Leone to Ivory Coast and Ghana
_____ *I. f. moloneyanum* E Ghana and Togo
_____ *I. f. iboensis* SW Nigeria
_____ *I. f. fulvescens* Cameroon to w Zaire
_____ *I. f. ugandae* N Zaire to Uganda
_____ *I. f. dilutius* N Angola

☐ **Mountain Illadopsis** *Illadopsis pyrrhoptera*
_____ *I. p. kivuense* Mts. of e Zaire to Rwanda, Burundi, w Uganda and w Tanzania
_____ *I. p. pyrrhoptera* Montane forests of w Kenya to w Tanzania and n Malawi

☐ **African Hill Babbler** *Illadopsis abyssinica*

_____	*I. a. monachus*	Montane forests of sw Cameroon
_____	*I. a. atriceps*	Cameroon to ne Zaire and w Uganda
_____	*I. a. claudi*	Montane forests of Bioko (Gulf of Guinea)
_____	*I. a. abyssinica (poliothorax, loima, hildegardae)*	Highlands of w Ethiopia to se Sudan, Kenya and sw Tanzania
_____	*I. a. ansorgei*	Highlands of w-central Angola to se Zaire and w Tanzania
_____	*I. a. stierlingi*	Highlands of Tanzania to n Malawi

☐ **Gray-chested Illadopsis** *Kakamega poliothorax*

SE Nigeria to s Cameroon, e Zaire and w Kenya; Bioko

☐ **Thrush Babbler** *Ptyrticus turdinus*

_____	*P. t. harterti*	Grasslands of central Cameroon
_____	*P. t. turdinus*	SW Sudan to ne Zaire
_____	*P. t. upembae*	SE Zaire to n Zambia

☐ **Large Scimitar-Babbler** *Pomatorhinus hypoleucos*

_____	*P. h. hypoleucos*	NE India (Assam) to Bangladesh and w Myanmar
_____	*P. h. tickelli*	S China (s Yunnan) to s Myanmar, Thailand and n Indochina
_____	*P. h. brevirostris*	S Indochina
_____	*P. h. wrayi*	Malay Peninsula
_____	*P. h. hainanus*	Hainan (s China)

☐ **Spot-breasted Scimitar-Babbler** *Pomatorhinus erythrocnemis*

_____	*P. e. ferrugilatus*	Montane forests of Kashmir to central Nepal
_____	*P. e. haringtoni*	Himalayas (Sikkim to Bhutan)
_____	*P. e. mcclellandi*	Assam south of the Brahmaputra to w Myanmar (Chin Hills)
_____	*P. e. odicus*	Mts. of ne Myanmar to s China (Yunnan), n Laos and nw Tonkin
_____	*P. e. decarlei*	Mountains of sw China (Qinghai, s Sichuan and nw Yunnan)
_____	*P. e. dedekeni*	Mountains of sw China (e Qinghai to nw Yunnan)
_____	*P. e. gravivox*	Mountains of sw China (nw Sichuan to s Gansu and s Shaanxi)
_____	*P. e. sowerbyi*	Central China (central Shaanxi)
_____	*P. e. cowensae*	S China (e Sichuan to sw Hubei and n Guizhou)
_____	*P. e. swinhoei*	E China (Anhui to ne Jiangxi and Fujian)
_____	*P. e. abbreviatus*	SE China (s Hunan, Guangxi and n Guandgong)
_____	*P. e. erythrocnemis*	Taiwan

☐ **Rusty-cheeked Scimitar-Babbler** *Pomatorhinus erythrogenys*

Himalayas of central Myanmar and nw Thailand

☐ **Indian Scimitar-Babbler** *Pomatorhinus horsfieldii*

_____	*P. h. obscurus*	NW India (Aravalli Mountains of Rajasthan)
_____	*P. h. horsfieldii*	W India (Western Ghats from Satpura Range to Goa)
_____	*P. h. maderaspatensis*	E central India (Eastern Ghats from Andhra to Salem District)
_____	*P. h. travancoreensis*	SW India (Western Ghats from North Kanara to Kerala)
_____	*P. h. melanurus*	Sri Lanka

☐ **White-browed Scimitar-Babbler** *Pomatorhinus schisticeps*

_____	*P. s. leucogaster*	Himalayas (Himachal Pradesh to nw Uttar Pradesh)
_____	*P. s. schisticeps*	Himalayas (w Nepal to Bhutan, Assam and nw Myanmar)
_____	*P. s. salimalii*	NE Assam (Mishmi Hills)
_____	*P. s. cryptanthus*	NE Assam (Lakhimpur District) and (?) adjacent ne Myanmar
_____	*P. s. mearsi*	W Myanmar (lower Chindwin District to Arakan Yoma Mts.)
_____	*P. s. ripponi*	E Myanmar to n Thailand and adjacent nw Laos
_____	*P. s. nuchalis*	W Myanmar (Southern Shan State and Karenni State)
_____	*P. s. difficilis*	Mountains of nw Thailand and s Myanmar (Amherst District)
_____	*P. s. olivaceus*	Lowlands of s Myanmar and peninsular Thailand
_____	*P. s. humilis*	E Thailand (Nan Province) to s Laos and central Vietnam
_____	*P. s. klossi*	SE Thailand and sw Cambodia
_____	*P. s. annamensis*	S Vietnam (Langbian Plateau)
_____	*P. s. fastidiosus*	Malay Peninsula (s Myanmar and Isthmus of Kra to Trang)

☐ **Chestnut-backed Scimitar-Babbler** *Pomatorhinus montanus*

____	*P. m. occidentalis*	Malay Peninsula, Sumatra and Bangka I.
____	*P. m. montanus*	W and central Java
____	*P. m. ottolanderi*	E Java and Bali
____	*P. m. bornensis*	Borneo

☐ **Streak-breasted Scimitar-Babbler** *Pomatorhinus ruficollis*

____	*P. r. ruficollis*	W and central Nepal
____	*P. r. godwini*	E Himalayas (e Nepal to Sikkim, Bhutan, se Tibet and n Assam)
____	*P. r. bakeri*	Hill forests of se Assam (s of the Brahmaputra) to w Myanmar
____	*P. r. bhamoensis*	N Myanmar (Bhamo District)
____	*P. r. similis*	NE Myanmar to s China (nw Yunnan)
____	*P. r. albipectus*	S China (sw Yunnan) and adjacent n Laos
____	*P. r. beaulieui*	N Laos
____	*P. r. laurentei*	S China (Kunming region of Yunnan)
____	*P. r. reconditus (laurenti)*	S China (se Yunnan to n Vietnam)
____	*P. r. stridulus*	Hill forests of se China (Guandong, Fujian and Jiangxi)
____	*P. r. intermedius*	Central China (se Hubei, Hunan, Guangxi and Guizhou)
____	*P. r. eidos*	SW China (s Sichuan)
____	*P. r. nigrostellatus*	Hainan (s China)
____	*P. r. musicus*	Taiwan

☐ **Red-billed Scimitar-Babbler** *Pomatorhinus ochraceiceps*

____	*P. o. stenorhynchus*	NE Assam (Mishmi Hills) to n Myanmar
____	*P. o. austeni*	Hill forests of e Assam (Naga Hills to Barail Mts. and Manipur)
____	*P. o. ochraceiceps*	Myanmar to mountains of n Thailand, Tonkin and n Laos
____	*P. o. alius*	Plateau of ne Thailand to s Indochina

☐ **Coral-billed Scimitar-Babbler** *Pomatorhinus ferruginosus*

____	*P. f. ferruginosus*	Himalayas (e Nepal to e Assam north of the Brahmaputra)
____	*P. f. formosus*	Hill forests of Assam (south of the Brahmaputra and Manipur)
____	*P. f. phayrei*	Hill forests of sw Myanmar (Chin Hills and Arakan Yoma Mts.)
____	*P. f. stanfordi*	NE Myanmar (Kachin State)
____	*P. f. mariae*	Central Myanmar
____	*P. f. albogularis*	E Myanmar to nw Thailand
____	*P. f. orientalis*	N Indochina (Tonkin and n Laos)

☐ **Slender-billed Scimitar-Babbler** *Xiphirhynchus superciliaris*

____	*X. s. superciliaris*	Himalayas (e Nepal to Sikkim and Bhutan)
____	*X. s. intextus*	Hill forests of s Assam (s and e of the Brahmaputra)
____	*X. s. forresti*	Mountains of ne Myanmar and sw China (nw Yunnan)
____	*X. s. rothschildi*	Montane forests of n Vietnam (Fan Si Pan Mountains)

☐ **Short-tailed Scimitar-Babbler** *Jabouilleia danjoui*

____	*J. d. danjoui*	Central Vietnam (Langbian Plateau)
____	*J. d. parvirostris*	Central Vietnam (Col des Nuages)

☐ **Long-billed Wren-Babbler** *Rimator malacoptilus*

____	*R. m. malacoptilus*	E Himalayas (Sikkim to e Assam and ne Myanmar)
____	*R. m. pasquieri*	N Vietnam (Fan Si Pan Mountains)
____	*R. m. albostriatus*	Highlands of w Sumatra

☐ **Bornean Wren-Babbler** *Ptilocichla leucogrammica*

Patchily distributed lowlands of Borneo

☐ **Striated Wren-Babbler** *Ptilocichla mindanensis*

____	*P. m. minuta*	N Philippines (Leyte and Samar)
____	*P. m. fortichi*	Central Philippines (Bohol)
____	*P. m. mindanensis*	S Philippines (Mindanao)
____	*P. m. basilanica*	S Philippines (Basilan)

☐ **Falcated Wren-Babbler** *Ptilocichla falcata*

SW Philippines (Balabac and Palawan)

☐ **Striped Wren-Babbler** *Kenopia striata*

S peninsular Thailand, Malay Peninsula, Sumatra and Borneo

☐ **Large Wren-Babbler** *Napothera macrodactyla*
_____ *N. m. macrodactyla* SW Peninsular Thailand and Malay Peninsula
_____ *N. m. beauforti* NE Sumatra
_____ *N. m. lepidopleura* Java

☐ **Rusty-breasted Wren-Babbler** *Napothera rufipectus*

Montane forests of w Sumatra

☐ **Black-throated Wren-Babbler** *Napothera atrigularis*

Patchily distributed forests of Borneo

☐ **Marbled Wren-Babbler** *Napothera marmorata*
_____ *N. m. grandior* Montane forests of central Malaya (Selangor/Pahang border)
_____ *N. m. marmorata* Highlands of w Sumatra

☐ **Limestone Wren-Babbler** *Napothera crispifrons*
_____ *N. c. crispifrons* Limestone hills of n Thailand to s Myanmar
_____ *N. c. calcicola* Limestone hills of central Thailand (Sathani Hin Lap)
_____ *N. c. annamensis* Limestone hills of n Indochina

☐ **Streaked Wren-Babbler** *Napothera brevicaudata*
_____ *N. b. striata* Hill forests of s Assam (s of the Brahmaputra) to sw Myanmar
_____ *N. b. venningi* S China (w Yunnan) to ne Myanmar
_____ *N. b. brevicaudata* N Thailand south to s Myanmar
_____ *N. b. stevensi* S China (sw Guangxi) and n Indochina
_____ *N. b. griseigularis* SE Thailand and sw Cambodia
_____ *N. b. proxima* Central Vietnam and s Laos
_____ *N. b. rufiventer* S Vietnam (Langbian Plateau)
_____ *N. b. leucosticta* N Malay Peninsula

☐ **Mountain Wren-Babbler** *Napothera crassa*

High mountains of n Borneo (ne Sarawak and n Sabah)

☐ **Luzon Wren-Babbler** *Napothera rabori*
_____ *N. r. rabori* N Philippines (Ilicos Norte and Cagayan provinces of Luzon)
_____ *N. r. mesoluzonica* N Philippines (Laguna Province of Luzon)
_____ *N. r. sorsogonensis* N Philippines (Sorsogon and Camarines Sur provinces of Luzon)

☐ **Eyebrowed Wren-Babbler** *Napothera epilepidota*
_____ *N. e. guttaticollis* Hill forests of n Assam (north of the Brahmaputra)
_____ *N. e. roberti* Hill forests of s Assam (s of the Brahmaputra) to nw Myanmar
_____ *N. e. bakeri* Central Myanmar (Southern Shan and Karenni states)
_____ *N. e. davisoni* N Thailand south to s Myanmar
_____ *N. e. amyea* N Indochina
_____ *N. e. delacouri* S China (s Yunnan and Yao Shan region of Guangxi)
_____ *N. e. hainana* Hainan (s China)
_____ *N. e. clara* S Vietnam (Langbian Plateau)
_____ *N. e. granti* N Malay Peninsula
_____ *N. e. diluta (lucilleae)* Highlands of n and w Sumatra
_____ *N. e. mendeni* Highlands of sw Sumatra
_____ *N. e. epilepidota* Highlands of w and central Java
_____ *N. e. exsul* Highlands of n Borneo

☐ **Scaly-breasted Wren-Babbler** *Pnoepyga albiventer*
_____ *P. a. pallidior* Himalayas (East Punjab to w Nepal)
_____ *P. a. albiventer* Himalayas of Nepal to Assam, n Myanmar, s China and n Tonkin

☐ **Immaculate Wren-Babbler** *Pnoepyga immaculata*

Himalayas of Nepal; winters in *terai* lowlands

☐ **Pygmy Wren-Babbler** *Pnoepyga pusilla*
____ *P. p. pusilla*
____ *P. p. formosana*
____ *P. p. annamensis*
____ *P. p. harterti*
____ *P. p. lepida*
____ *P. p. rufa*
____ *P. p. everetti*
____ *P. p. timorensis*

Nepal to Assam, n Myanmar, se Tibet, sw China and n Thailand
Highlands of Taiwan
S Indochina (Langbian Plateau) and s Laos (Bolavens Plateau)
Highlands of Malay Peninsula
Highlands of w Sumatra
Highlands of Java
Highlands of Flores (e Lesser Sundas)
Highlands of Timor (e Lesser Sundas)

☐ **Rufous-throated Wren-Babbler** *Spelaeornis caudatus*

Mountains of e Nepal to Sikkim, Darjiling and Bhutan

☐ **Mishmi Wren-Babbler** *Spelaeornis badeigularis*

NE India (known from a 1948 specimen from Mishmi Hills)

☐ **Bar-winged Wren-Babbler** *Spelaeornis troglodytoides*
____ *S. t. sherriffi*
____ *S. t. souliei*
____ *S. t. rocki*
____ *S. t. troglodytoides*
____ *S. t. halsueti*

E Bhutan
SE Tibet to s China (nw Yunnan) and ne Myanmar
S China (nw Yunnan east of the Mekong River)
W-central China (Qinghai to nw Sichuan)
W-central China (Tsingling Mts. in s Shaanxi and adj. Gansu)

☐ **Spotted Wren-Babbler** *Spelaeornis formosus*

Humid forests of Sikkim to se China and w Myanmar

☐ **Long-tailed Wren-Babbler** *Spelaeornis chocolatinus*
____ *S. c. chocolatinus*
____ *S. c. oatesi*
____ *S. c. reptatus*
____ *S. c. kinneari*

Hill forests of Assam (south of the Brahmaputra) and Manipur
N Myanmar (Mt. Victoria)
NE Myanmar to s China (sw Yunnan)
N Vietnam (nw Tonkin)

☐ **Tawny-breasted Wren-Babbler** *Spelaeornis longicaudatus*

Oak-rhododendron forests of ne India (Assam and Manipur)

☐ **Wedge-billed Wren-Babbler** *Sphenocichla humei*
____ *S. h. humei*
____ *S. h. roberti*

Himalayas from Sikkim to n Assam (n of the Brahmaputra)
Hill forests of s Assam (s of the Brahmaputra) to ne Myanmar

☐ **Common Jery** *Neomixis tenella*
____ *N. t. tenella*
____ *N. t. decaryi*
____ *N. t. orientalis*
____ *N. t. debilis*

Savanna of n Madagascar
Savanna of w Madagascar
Humid forests of central and s Madagascar
Arid subdesert of sw Madagascar

☐ **Green Jery** *Neomixis viridis*
____ *N. v. delacouri*
____ *N. v. viridis*

Humid highland forests of ne Madagascar
Humid highland forests of se Madagascar

☐ **Stripe-throated Jery** *Neomixis striatigula*
____ *N. s. sclateri*
____ *N. s. pallidior*
____ *N. s. striatigula*

Humid forests of ne Madagascar
Arid subdesert of sw Madagascar
Humid forests of se Madagascar

☐ **Wedge-tailed Jery** *Hartertula flavoviridis*

Rainforests of e Madagascar (Sianaka Forest s to Vondrozo)

☐ **Deignan's Babbler** *Stachyris rodolphei*

Montane bamboo forests of nw Thailand (Doi Luang Chiang)

☐ **Buff-chested Babbler** *Stachyris ambigua*
____ *S. a. ambigua*
____ *S. a. planicola*
____ *S. a. adjuncta*
____ *S. a. insuspecta*

Himalayas (Sikkim to Bhutan and Assam s of the Brahmaputra)
NE Myanmar (Kachin State) to nw Yunnan (Salween Valley)
N and e Thailand to n Laos and nw Tonkin
S Laos (Bolavens Plateau)

☐ **Rufous-fronted Babbler** *Stachyris rufifrons*

_____ *S. r. pallescens* — Hill forests of sw Myanmar (Chin Hills and Arakan Yoma Mts.)
_____ *S. r. rufifrons* — SE Myanmar to w Thailand
_____ *S. r. obscura* — S Myanmar (Mergui District) and central peninsular Thailand
_____ *S. r. poliogaster* — W Malaya (s Perak to Johore) to Sumatra
_____ *S. r. sarawacensis* — N Borneo (Mt. Poi in w Sarawak)

☐ **Rufous-capped Babbler** *Stachyris ruficeps*

_____ *S. r. ruficeps* — E Himalayas (Sikkim to Bhutan and n Assam n of Brahmaputra)
_____ *S. r. rufipectus* — Hill forests of ne Assam to nw Myanmar
_____ *S. r. davidi* — Central and s China (Yangtze River Valley) to n Indochina
_____ *S. r. bhamoensis* — NE Myanmar (Kachin and N Shan States) to nw Yunnan
_____ *S. r. goodsoni* — Hainan (s China)
_____ *S. r. praecognita* — Taiwan
_____ *S. r. pagana* — S Vietnam

☐ **Black-chinned Babbler** *Stachyris pyrrhops* — Himalayas (Kashmir to central Nepal)

☐ **Golden Babbler** *Stachyris chrysaea*

_____ *S. c. chrysaea* — Nepal to Sikkim, Assam, Bhutan, sw China and n Myanmar)
_____ *S. c. binghami* — SE Assam to sw Myanmar (Chin Hills and Arakan Yoma Mts.)
_____ *S. c. aurata* — S Myanmar (s Shan State) to extreme n Thailand and n Indochina
_____ *S. c. assimilis* — Central Myanmar (west of the Salween River) to nw Thailand
_____ *S. c. chrysops* — Hills of Malay Peninsula
_____ *S. c. frigida* — Highlands of w Sumatra

☐ **Pygmy Babbler** *Stachyris plateni*

_____ *S. p. pygmaea* — Philippines (Leyte and Samar)
_____ *S. p. plateni* — S Philippines (Mindanao)

☐ **Golden-crowned Babbler** *Stachyris dennistouni* — N Philippines (Sierra Madre Mountains of n Luzon)

☐ **Black-crowned Babbler** *Stachyris nigrocapitata*

_____ *S. n. affinis* — Philippines (s Sierra Madre Mountains of s Luzon)
_____ *S. n. nigrocapitata* — N Philippines (Leyte and Samar)
_____ *S. n. boholensis* — Central Philippines (Bohol)

☐ **Rusty-crowned Babbler** *Stachyris capitalis*

_____ *S. c. capitalis* — S Philippines (Dinagat)
_____ *S. c. euroaustralis* — S Philippines (Mindanao, excluding Zamboanga Peninsula)
_____ *S. c. isabelae* — S Philippines (Basilan and Zamboanga Peninsula of Mindanao)

☐ **Flame-templed Babbler** *Stachyris speciosa*

_____ *S. s. speciosa* — Central Philippines (Negros)
_____ *S. s. ssp.* — Central Philippines (Panay). Undescribed subspecies

☐ **Chestnut-faced Babbler** *Stachyris whiteheadi*

_____ *S. w. whiteheadi* — N Philippines (n Luzon)
_____ *S. w. sorsogonensis* — N Philippines (s Luzon)

☐ **Luzon Striped-Babbler** *Stachyris striata* — N Philippines (n Luzon)

☐ **Panay Striped-Babbler** *Stachyris latistriata* — Central Philippines (montane forests of Panay)

☐ **Negros Striped-Babbler** *Stachyris nigrorum* — Philippines (montane forests of Negros)

☐ **Palawan Striped-Babbler** *Stachyris hypogrammica* — SW Philippines (montane forests of Palawan)

☐ **White-breasted Babbler** *Stachyris grammiceps* — Locally in forests of w Java

☐ **Sooty Babbler** *Stachyris herberti*

Rediscovered in 1995 in central Laos after 74-year absence

☐ **Gray-throated Babbler** *Stachyris nigriceps*

____ S. n. nigriceps	Himalayas (central Nepal to Sikkim, Bhutan and Assam)
____ S. n. coei	E Assam (Mishmi Hills)
____ S. n. coltarti	E Assam (Naga Hills) to n Myanmar and s China (w Yunnan)
____ S. n. spadix	S Assam (s of the Brahmaputra) to s Myanmar and nw Thailand
____ S. n. yunnanensis	E Myanmar to n Thailand, sw China and n Indochina
____ S. n. rileyi	S Vietnam
____ S. n. dipora	Malay Peninsula (Mergui District and Isthmus of Kra to Trang)
____ S. n. davisoni	Malay Peninsula (Pattani Province to Negri Sembilan)
____ S. n. larvata	Sumatra and Lingga Archipelago
____ S. n. natunensis	N Natuna Islands
____ S. n. tionis	Tioman I. (South China Sea)
____ S. n. hartleyi	Highlands of n Borneo (w Sarawak)
____ S. n. borneensis	Highlands of Borneo

☐ **Gray-headed Babbler** *Stachyris poliocephala*

Peninsular Thailand, Malaya, Sumatra, Lingga Arch. and Borneo

☐ **Snowy-throated Babbler** *Stachyris oglei*

Mountains of ne India (ne Assam and se Arunachal Pradesh)

☐ **Spot-necked Babbler** *Stachyris striolata*

____ S. s. tonkinensis	S China (Guangxi and s Yunnan) to n Indochina
____ S. s. swinhoei	Hainan (s China)
____ S. s. helenae	N plateau of Thailand (Nan Province) to n Laos
____ S. s. guttata	S Myanmar and adjacent w Thailand (Tak Province)
____ S. s. nigrescentior	Peninsular Thailand (Isthmus of Kra to Trang Province)
____ S. s. umbrosa	NE Sumatra
____ S. s. striolata	Highlands of w Sumatra

☐ **White-necked Babbler** *Stachyris leucotis*

____ S. l. leucotis	Peninsular Thailand and Malaya
____ S. l. sumatrensis	NE Sumatra (Aceh Province)
____ S. l. obscurata	N Borneo (Mt. Mulu)

☐ **Black-throated Babbler** *Stachyris nigricollis*

Forests of peninsular Thailand, Malaya, e Sumatra and Borneo

☐ **White-bibbed Babbler** *Stachyris thoracica*

____ S. t. thoracica	Foothill forests of s Sumatra, w and central Java
____ S. t. orientalis	E Java

☐ **Chestnut-rumped Babbler** *Stachyris maculata*

____ S. m. pectoralis	Lowlands of peninsular Thailand and Malaya
____ S. m. maculata	Sumatra, Borneo and Riau Archipelago
____ S. m. banjakensis	Banyak I. (off Sumatra)
____ S. m. hypopyrrha	Batu Islands (off Sumatra)

☐ **Chestnut-winged Babbler** *Stachyris erythroptera*

____ S. e. erythroptera	Malay Pen. (Isthmus of Kra to Singapore) and North Natuna Is.
____ S. e. pyrrhophaea (apega)	Sumatra, Bangka, Belitung and Batu islands
____ S. e. fulviventris	Banyak I. (off Sumatra)
____ S. e. bicolor	N and e Borneo and Banggai Islands
____ S. e. rufa	SW Borneo

☐ **Crescent-chested Babbler** *Stachyris melanothorax*

____ S. m. melanothorax	W Java (Mt. Gedeh and Mt. Pangerango)
____ S. m. albigula	W Java (Mt. Papandayan)
____ S. m. mendeni	W Java (Mt. Ciremay)
____ S. m. intermedia	E Java (Mt. Raung)
____ S. m. baliensis	Lowlands of Bali

☐ **Tawny-bellied Babbler** *Dumetia hyperythra*

____	*D. h. hyperythra*	Lowlands of sw Nepal to n and central India
____	*D. h. albogularis*	S India (Aravelli Mountains to Western and Eastern Ghats)
____	*D. h. navarroi*	W India
____	*D. h. phillipsi*	Sri Lanka

☐ **Dark-fronted Babbler** *Rhopocichla atriceps*

____	*R. a. atriceps*	Central India (Western Ghats from Bombay to Nilgiri Hills)
____	*R. a. bourdilloni*	Hill forests of sw India (Kerala)
____	*R. a. siccata*	Arid north, east and central hills of Sri Lanka
____	*R. a. nigrifrons*	Wet lowlands of sw Sri Lanka

☐ **Striped Tit-Babbler** *Macronous gularis*

____	*M. g. rubricapillus*	Lowlands of e Nepal to ne India and extreme n Myanmar
____	*M. g. ticehursti*	W Myanmar (Upper Chindwin District to Arakan)
____	*M. g. sulphureus*	S China (sw Yunnan) to e Myanmar and n plateau of Thailand
____	*M. g. lutescens*	S China (se Yunnan) to n and e Thailand, Laos and Tonkin
____	*M. g. saraburiensis*	E Thailand and w Cambodia
____	*M. g. kinneari*	Central Vietnam
____	*M. g. versuricola*	E Cambodia and s Vietnam
____	*M. g. connectens*	Coastal Gulf of Siam (Isthmus of Kra to Cambodia)
____	*M. g. inveteratus*	Coastal islets off se Thailand and Cambodia
____	*M. g. condorensis*	Pulau Kundur (South China Sea)
____	*M. g. archipelagicus*	Mergui Archipelago (off sw Myanmar)
____	*M. g. chersonesophilus*	Malay Peninsula (Isthmus of Kra to Perak and Trengganu)
____	*M. g. gularis*	S Malay Pen., Sumatra, Banyak, Batu, Lingga and Riau islands
____	*M. g. zopherus*	Anambas Islands
____	*M. g. zaperissus*	North Natuna Islands
____	*M. g. everetti*	Pulau Bunguran (North Natuna Islands)
____	*M. g. ruficoma*	Bangka and Belitung islands
____	*M. g. montanus*	NE Borneo
____	*M. g. bornensis*	Borneo
____	*M. g. argenteus*	Banggai Islands (off n Borneo)
____	*M. g. cagayanensis*	Cagayan Sulu (Sulu Sea)
____	*M. g. woodi*	SW Philippines (Balabac and Palawan)

☐ **Gray-cheeked Tit-Babbler** *Macronous flavicollis*

____	*M. f. javanicus*	Lowlands of w and central Java
____	*M. f. flavicollis*	Lowlands of e Java
____	*M. f. prillwitzi*	Kangean Islands (Java Sea)

☐ **Gray-faced Tit-Babbler** *Macronous kelleyi*

		Forests of s Laos, central and s Vietnam and Cochinchina

☐ **Brown Tit-Babbler** *Macronous striaticeps*

____	*M. s. mindanensis*	S Philippines (Samar, Leyte, Bohol and Mindanao)
____	*M. s. alcasidi*	S Philippines (Dinagat and Siargao)
____	*M. s. striaticeps*	S Philippines (Basilan and Malamaui)
____	*M. s. kettlewelli*	Sulu Archipelago (Bongao, Jolo and Tawitawi islands)

☐ **Fluffy-backed Tit-Babbler** *Macronous ptilosus*

____	*M. p. ptilosus*	Peninsular Thailand and Malaya
____	*M. p. trichorrhos*	Sumatra and Batu Islands
____	*M. p. sordidus*	Bangka and Belitung islands
____	*M. p. reclusus*	Borneo

☐ **Miniature Tit-Babbler** *Micromacronus leytensis*

____	*M. l. leytensis*	S Philippines (Leyte and Samar)
____	*M. l. sordidus*	S Philippines (Mindanao)

☐ **Chestnut-capped Babbler** *Timalia pileata*
____ *T. p. bengalensis*   Submontane Himalayas (Nepal to Assam and nw Myanmar)
____ *T. p. smithi*   N Myanmar to s China, n Thailand and n Indochina
____ *T. p. intermedia*   Central and s Myanmar to sw Thailand
____ *T. p. patriciae*   W portion of central plains of Thailand
____ *T. p. dictator*   E and se Thailand to s Indochina
____ *T. p. pileata*   Java

☐ **Yellow-eyed Babbler** *Chrysomma sinense*
____ *C. s. hypoleucum*   E Pakistan to peninsular India, Bangladesh and w Myanmar
____ *C. s. nasale*   Sri Lanka
____ *C. s. saturatius*   Himalayas from Sikkim to Assam (north of the Brahmaputra)
____ *C. s. sinense*   S China to Myanmar, Thailand and Indochina

☐ **Jerdon's Babbler** *Chrysomma altirostre*
____ *C. a. scindica*   Grasslands of extreme s Pakistan (Mangrani region)
____ *C. a. griseigularis*   Base of Himalayas (Bhutan to s Assam and ne Myanmar)
____ *C. a. altirostre†*   S-c Myanmar (Irawaddy-Sittang grasslands). Extinct ca 1941

☐ **Rufous-tailed Babbler** *Chrysomma poecilotis*

                                         Mts. of sw China (se Qinghai to nw Sichuan and nw Yunnan)

☐ **Spiny Babbler** *Turdoides nipalensis*

                                         Himalayas of w and central Nepal

☐ **Iraq Babbler** *Turdoides altirostris*

                                         SE Iraq and sw Iran (reed beds of lower Tigris-Euphrates Valley)

☐ **Common Babbler** *Turdoides caudatus*
____ *T. c. salvadorii*   SE Iraq to sw Iran
____ *T. c. huttoni*   E Iran to s Afghanistan and s Pakistan
____ *T. c. eclipes*   N Pakistan (Fort Sandeman to Kashmir border)
____ *T. c. caudatus*   Peninsular India, Laccadive Islands and Pamean I.

☐ **Striated Babbler** *Turdoides earlei*
____ *T. e. sonivius*   Pakistan (Rann of Kutch and Indus River Valley) to nw India
____ *T. e. earlei*   Grasslands of ne India to Assam and Myanmar

☐ **White-throated Babbler** *Turdoides gularis*

                                         Dry grassy plains of central and s Myanmar

☐ **Slender-billed Babbler** *Turdoides longirostris*

                                         Grasslands of Nepal to Assam and nw Myanmar

☐ **Large Gray Babbler** *Turdoides malcolmi*

                                         Arid lowland scrub of peninsular India

☐ **Arabian Babbler** *Turdoides squamiceps*
____ *T. s. squamiceps*   Arabian Peninsula (Dead Sea depression to sw Saudi Arabia)
____ *T. s. yemensis*   Yemen and Aden
____ *T. s. muscatensis*   Arabian coast of Gulf of Oman

☐ **Fulvous Chatterer** *Turdoides fulvus*
____ *T. f. maroccanus*   Desert scrub of sw Morocco (valley of the Oued Sous)
____ *T. f. fulvus (billypayni)*   N Algeria to Tunisia and nw Libya
____ *T. f. buchanani*   Central Sahara (Aïr Massif)
____ *T. f. acaciae*   Valley of the Nile (s Egypt to n Sudan and ne Ethiopia)

☐ **Scaly Chatterer** *Turdoides aylmeri*
____ *T. a. aylmeri*   SE Ethiopia to Somalia
____ *T. a. boranensis*   S-central Ethiopia (Arusi region to Boran)
____ *T. a. kenianus*   Central Kenya
____ *T. a. loveridgei*   SE Kenya (Tsavo) and ne Tanzania (Moshi)
____ *T. a. mentalis*   N-central Tanzania

☐ **Rufous Chatterer** *Turdoides rubiginosus*
_____ *T. r. bowdleri* | SE Ethiopia (Diredawa to Somalia border)
_____ *T. r. rubiginosus* | S Sudan to e Uganda, w Kenya, central and s Ethiopia
_____ *T. r. heuglini* | Coastal East Africa (Somalia to Kenya and n Tanzania)
_____ *T. r. schnitzeri* | NW Tanzania

☐ **Rufous Babbler** *Turdoides subrufus*
_____ *T. s. subrufus* | SW India (Western Ghats to n Kerala, Madras and Nilgiri Hills)
_____ *T. s. hyperythrus* | SW India (sw Madras and Kerala)

☐ **Jungle Babbler** *Turdoides striatus*
_____ *T. s. sindianus* | Pakistan and nw India
_____ *T. s. striatus* | Himalayan foothills (n India to e Assam)
_____ *T. s. orientalis* | Central and s India
_____ *T. s. somervillei* | Coastal w India (Surat Dangs to Goa)
_____ *T. s. malabaricus* | SW India (Goa to Kerala)

☐ **Orange-billed Babbler** *Turdoides rufescens*
Humid forests of Sri Lanka

☐ **Yellow-billed Babbler** *Turdoides affinis*
_____ *T. a. affinis* | Arid lowlands and foothills of s India
_____ *T. a. taprobanus* | Sri Lanka

☐ **Blackcap Babbler** *Turdoides reinwardtii*
_____ *T. r. reinwardtii* | Senegambia to Sierra Leone
_____ *T. r. stictilaemus (houyi)* | Ghana to Nigeria, Cameroon, Central African Rep. and n Zaire

☐ **Dusky Babbler** *Turdoides tenebrosus*
Scrub of ne Zaire to Uganda, s Sudan and sw Ethiopia

☐ **Black-lored Babbler** *Turdoides melanops*
_____ *T. m. vepres* | Central Kenya (Nanyuki region)
_____ *T. m. clamosus* | Central Kenya (Great Rift Valley)
_____ *T. m. sharpei* | S Uganda to Rwanda, w Kenya and nw Tanzania
_____ *T. m. angolensis* | Angola (Huila escarpment)
_____ *T. m. melanops* | SW Angola to n Namibia and Botswana
_____ *T. m. querulus* | S Angola to n Namibia

☐ **Scaly Babbler** *Turdoides squamulatus*
_____ *T. s. jubaensis (carolinae)* | Thornscrub of se Ethiopia and s Somalia
_____ *T. s. squamulatus* | Coastal Kenya (Lamu) to ne Tanzania

☐ **White-rumped Babbler** *Turdoides leucopygius*
_____ *T. l. limbatus* | NW Ethiopia
_____ *T. l. leucopygius* | Coastal e Eritrea
_____ *T. l. omoensis* | SE Sudan (Boma Hills) to sw Ethiopia
_____ *T. l. lacuum* | SW Ethiopia
_____ *T. l. smithii* | SE Ethiopia and w Somalia
_____ *T. l. ater* | SE Zaire to Rwanda, Burundi, ne Zambia and sw Tanzania
_____ *T. l. hartlaubii* | S Angola to n Botswana and w Zambia
_____ *T. l. griseosquamatus* | N Botswana

☐ **Southern Pied-Babbler** *Turdoides bicolor*
NE Namibia to Botswana, w Zimbabwe and nw South Africa

☐ **Northern Pied-Babbler** *Turdoides hypoleucus*
_____ *T. h. hypoleucus* | Central Kenya (Mt. Kenya region and Athi River system)
_____ *T. h. rufuensis* | NE Tanzania

☐ **Hinde's Pied-Babbler** *Turdoides hindei*
Locally in foothill scrub of e-central Kenya

☐ **Cretzschmar's Babbler** *Turdoides leucocephalus*

	Thornscrub of e Sudan to ne Ethiopia and Eritrea

☐ **Brown Babbler** *Turdoides plebejus*

_____ *T. p. platycircus (togoensis)* — Senegal to Sierra Leone, Ivory Coast, Togo and w Nigeria
_____ *T. p. plebejus* — N Nigeria to Cameroon, s Chad and central Sudan (Kardofan)
_____ *T. p. cinereus (gularis)* — E Nigeria to Cameroon, s Sudan, Ethiopia, Uganda and w Kenya
_____ *T. p. uamensis* — Grasslands of Cameroon

☐ **Arrow-marked Babbler** *Turdoides jardineii*

_____ *T. j. emini* — Uganda to Rwanda, Burundi and nw Tanzania
_____ *T. j. kikuyuensis* — SW Kenya and adjacent n Tanzania
_____ *T. j. kirkii* — Coastal Kenya (Lamu) to Malawi, Zimbabwe and Mozambique
_____ *T. j. hypostictus* — N Angola (Cabinda) to s Zaire
_____ *T. j. tanganjicae* — SE Zaire to n Zambia
_____ *T. j. tamalakanei* — S Angola to n Botswana, sw Zambia and w Zimbabwe
_____ *T. j. jardineii* — Botswana to Transvaal and Natal

☐ **Bare-cheeked Babbler** *Turdoides gymnogenys*

_____ *T. g. gymnogenys* — Arid bush of sw Angola (Benguela Province)
_____ *T. g. kaokensis* — N Namibia

☐ **Chinese Babax** *Babax lanceolatus*

_____ *B. l. lanceolatus* — Mountains of se Tibet to se Assam, sw China and ne Myanmar
_____ *B. l. woodi* — SE Assam (Lushai Hills) to w Myanmar (Chin Hills)
_____ *B. l. latouchei* — Montane forests of se China

☐ **Giant Babax** *Babax waddelli*

_____ *B. w. lumsdeni* — NE Tibet (on border with Qinghai)
_____ *B. w. waddelli* — SE Tibet (Lhasa, Loti, Chushul, Dzong and Chaksam)
_____ *B. w. jomo* — S-central Tibet (Gyangtse region)

☐ **Tibetan Babax** *Babax koslowi*

_____ *B. k. yuguensis* — Himalayas of se Tibet
_____ *B. k. koslowi* — Himalayas of s-central China (s Qinghai and nw Sichuan)

☐ **Silver-eared Mesia** *Leiothrix argentauris*

_____ *L. a. argentauris* — Himalayas (Garhwal to Nepal, Sikkim, Bhutan and n Assam)
_____ *L. a. aureigularis* — S Assam (s of the Brahmaputra) and sw Myanmar (Chin Hills)
_____ *L. a. vernayi* — NE Assam to n Myanmar and s China (w Yunnan)
_____ *L. a. galbana* — E Myanmar to n Thailand
_____ *L. a. ricketti* — S China (se Yunnan) to n Indochina
_____ *L. a. rubrogularis* — S China (se Yunnan and Guangxi)
_____ *L. a. cunhaci* — S Laos (Bolavens Plateau) and s Annam
_____ *L. a. tahanensis* — Mountains of Malay Peninsula
_____ *L. a. rookmakeri* — Highlands of nw Sumatra (Aceh District)
_____ *L. a. laurinae* — Highlands of w Sumatra

☐ **Red-billed Leiothrix** *Leiothrix lutea*

_____ *L. l. kumaiensis* — Himalayas (Kashmir to nw Uttar Pradesh)
_____ *L. l. calipyga* — W Nepal to Sikkim, Bhutan, e Assam and se Tibet
_____ *L. l. luteola* — S Assam to sw Myanmar (Chin Hills and Arakan Yoma Mts.)
_____ *L. l. yunnanensis* — NE Myanmar to sw China (se Qinghai and nw Yunnan)
_____ *L. l. kwangtungensis* — S China (se Yunnan, Guangxi and Guangdong) to ne Tonkin
_____ *L. l. lutea* — Central and se China

☐ **Cutia** *Cutia nipalensis*

_____ *C. n. nipalensis* — Nepal to e Assam, w Myanmar, s Sichuan and nw Yunnan
_____ *C. n. melanchima* — E Myanmar to s Yunnan, nw Thailand, n Laos and nw Tonkin
_____ *C. n. cervinicrissa* — Highlands of Malay Peninsula (s Perak to s Selangor)
_____ *C. n. legalleni* — S Vietnam (Langbian Plateau)

☐ **Black-headed Shrike-Babbler** *Pteruthius rufiventer*

_____   *P. r. rufiventer*   Nepal to Bhutan, Assam, n Myanmar, Sichuan and nw Yunnan

_____   *P. r. delacouri*   NW Tonkin (Fan Si Pan Mountains)

☐ **White-browed Shrike-Babbler** *Pteruthius flaviscapis*

_____   *P. f. validirostris*   Himalayas (n Pakistan to s China, Assam and nw Myanmar)

_____   *P. f. ricketti*   NE Myanmar to s China, n Thailand and n Indochina

_____   *P. f. lingshuiensis*   Hainan (s China)

_____   *P. f. annamensis*   S Vietnam (Langbian Plateau)

_____   *P. f. aeralatus*   Mountains of e Myanmar to nw Thailand and (?) w Cambodia

_____   *P. f. schauenseei*   Mountains of s Thailand and s Myanmar to Isthmus of Kra

_____   *P. f. cameranoi*   Highlands of Malaya (s Perak to s Selangor) and w Sumatra

_____   *P. f. flaviscapis*   Highlands of Java

_____   *P. f. robinsoni*   Highlands of n Borneo

☐ **Green Shrike-Babbler** *Pteruthius xanthochlorus*

_____   *P. x. occidentalis*   Himalayas (Kashmir to w Nepal)

_____   *P. x. xanthochlorus*   Cent. Nepal to Sikkim, Bhutan, n Assam, se Tibet and w Sichuan

_____   *P. x. hybridus*   Assam (Lushai and Naga Hills) to w Myanmar (Chin Hills)

_____   *P. x. pallidus*   NE Myanmar to sw Qinghai, w Sichuan, Yunnan and nw Fujian

☐ **Black-eared Shrike-Babbler** *Pteruthius melanotis*

_____   *P. m. melanotis*   Nepal to n Myanmar, s Yunnan, n Thailand and n Indochina

_____   *P. m. tahanensis*   Highlands of Malaya (s Perak to Selangor and n Pahang)

☐ **Chestnut-fronted Shrike-Babbler** *Pteruthius aenobarbus*

_____   *P. a. aenobarbulus*   Assam (Garo Hills)

_____   *P. a. intermedius*   E Myanmar to s Yunnan, nw Thailand, Laos and nw Tonkin

_____   *P. a. yaoshanensis*   SE China (Yao Shan region of Guangxi)

_____   *P. a. indochinensis*   S Vietnam (Langbian Plateau)

_____   *P. a. aenobarbus*   Highlands of w Java

☐ **White-hooded Babbler** *Gampsorhynchus rufulus*

_____   *G. r. rufulus*   Nepal to Sikkim, Bhutan, Assam, sw Myanmar and w Yunnan

_____   *G. r. torquatus*   SE Myanmar to se Yunnan, Thailand and n Indochina

_____   *G. r. saturatior*   Highlands of Malaya (s Perak to s Selangor)

☐ **Rusty-fronted Barwing** *Actinodura egertoni*

_____   *A. e. egertoni*   Nepal to Sikkim, Bhutan, n Assam and se Tibet

_____   *A. e. lewisi*   NE Assam (Mishmi Hills)

_____   *A. e. khasiana*   Hill forests of s Assam (south of the Brahmaputra)

_____   *A. e. ripponi*   S China (w Yunnan and sw Guangxi) to sw Myanmar

☐ **Spectacled Barwing** *Actinodura ramsayi*

_____   *A. r. radcliffei*   NE Myanmar (Ruby Mines district) to sw Yunnan and n Laos

_____   *A. r. yunnanensis*   Mountains of s China (se Yunnan and s Guangxi) to n Vietnam

_____   *A. r. ramsayi*   Mountains of extreme se Myanmar and adjacent nw Thailand

☐ **Black-crowned Barwing** *Actinodura sodangorum*

     Western highlands of Vietnam

☐ **Hoary-throated Barwing** *Actinodura nipalensis*

_____   *A. n. nipalensis*   Oak-rhododendron forests of w and central Nepal

_____   *A. n. vinctura*   E Nepal to se Tibet (Pome District), Sikkim and Bhutan

☐ **Streak-throated Barwing** *Actinodura waldeni*

_____   *A. w. daflaensis*   N Assam (north of the Brahmaputra) and se Tibet

_____   *A. w. waldeni*   SE Assam (Naga Hills and Manipur) to nw Myanmar

_____   *A. w. poliotis*   N Myanmar (Mt. Victoria)

_____   *A. w. saturatior*   NE Myanmar (Kachin State) and s China (nw Yunnan)

□ **Streaked Barwing** *Actinodura souliei*
_____ *A. s. souliei* — Oak-rhododendron forests of s China (s Sichuan to nw Yunnan)
_____ *A. s. griseinucha* — Oak-rhododendron forests of nw Tonkin

□ **Taiwan Barwing** *Actinodura morrisoniana*
Montane evergreen forests of Taiwan

□ **Blue-winged Minla** *Minla cyanouroptera*
_____ *M. c. cyanouroptera* — Himalayas (Uttar Pradesh to Nepal, Sikkim, Bhutan, e Assam)
_____ *M. c. aglae* — Hill forests of se Assam and w Myanmar
_____ *M. c. sordida* — E and s Myanmar to nw Thailand
_____ *M. c. wingatei* — NE Myanmar to n Thailand, s China and n Indochina; Hainan
_____ *M. c. croizati* — SW China (se Sichuan in Ipin region)
_____ *M. c. rufodorsalis* — Mountains of se Thailand and sw Cambodia
_____ *M. c. orientalis* — S Vietnam (Langbian Plateau)
_____ *M. c. sordidior* — Mountains of peninsular Thailand and n Malaya

□ **Chestnut-tailed Minla** *Minla strigula*
_____ *M. s. simlaensis* — Himalayas (Kashmir to w Nepal)
_____ *M. s. strigula* — Himalayas (central Nepal to Bhutan, n Assam and se Tibet)
_____ *M. s. cinereigenae* — E Assam (Mt. Japvo)
_____ *M. s. yunnanensis* — E Assam to w Myanmar, sw China, n Laos and n Tonkin
_____ *M. s. castanicauda* — S Myanmar (Karenni Hills) to nw Thailand
_____ *M. s. malayana* — Highlands of Malaya (n Perak to s Selangor and Pahang)

□ **Red-tailed Minla** *Minla ignotincta*
_____ *M. i. ignotincta* — Nepal to Myanmar, se Tibet, Assam and s China (nw Yunnan)
_____ *M. i. mariae* — S China (se Yunnan) to n Tonkin
_____ *M. i. sini* — S China (Yao Shan region of Guangxi)
_____ *M. i. jerdoni (sini)* — S China (s Sichuan, s Hunan and Yao Shan region of Guangxi)

□ **Golden-breasted Fulvetta** *Alcippe chrysotis*
_____ *A. c. chrysotis* — Himalayas (e Nepal to Sikkim, Bhutan and e Assam)
_____ *A. c. albilineata* — Hill forests of s Assam (south of the Brahmaputra)
_____ *A. c. forresti* — NE Myanmar to s China (nw Yunnan)
_____ *A. c. amoena* — S China (se Yunnan) and nw Tonkin
_____ *A. c. swinhoii* — S China (s Shaanxi, central Sichuan, ne Yunnan and nw Guangxi)

□ **Gold-fronted Fulvetta** *Alcippe variegaticeps*
Montane forests of s China (e Sichuan and Guangxi)

□ **Yellow-throated Fulvetta** *Alcippe cinerea*
Nepal to ne Myanmar, s China (Yunnan) and n Laos

□ **Rufous-winged Fulvetta** *Alcippe castaneceps*
_____ *A. c. castaneceps* — Nepal to Assam, Myanmar, se Tibet and nw Thailand
_____ *A. c. exul* — S China (se Yunnan) to n Thailand plateau, Laos and nw Tonkin
_____ *A. c. soror* — Highlands of Malaya (n Perak to s Selangor and Pahang)
_____ *A. c. klossi* — S Vietnam (Langbian Plateau)

□ **White-browed Fulvetta** *Alcippe vinipectus*
_____ *A. v. kangrae* — Himalayas (Kashmir to nw Uttar Pradesh)
_____ *A. v. vinipectus* — Montane forests of w and central Nepal
_____ *A. v. chumbiensis* — Montane forests of e Nepal to se Tibet, Sikkim and Bhutan
_____ *A. v. austeni* — Hill forests of s Assam (south of the Brahmaputra)
_____ *A. v. ripponi* — W Myanmar (highest regions of the Chin Hills)
_____ *A. v. perstriata* — NE Myanmar (Kachin State) to s China (w Yunnan)
_____ *A. v. valentinae* — N Vietnam (Fan Si Pan Mountains)
_____ *A. v. bieti* — S China (Sichuan to nw Yunnan and se Tibet)

□ **Chinese Fulvetta** *Alcippe striaticollis*
Mts. of s-c China (sw Gansu to se Qinghai, Sichuan, nw Yunnan)

☐ **Spectacled Fulvetta** *Alcippe ruficapilla*
- _____ *A. r. ruficapilla* — Central China (s Gansu to s Shaanxi and Sichuan)
- _____ *A. r. sordidior* — S China (w Sichuan and n Yunnan)
- _____ *A. r. danisi* — S China (sw Guizhou and se Yunnan) to nw Tonkin and n Laos

☐ **Streak-throated Fulvetta** *Alcippe cinereiceps*
- _____ *A. c. manipurensis* — Montane forests of ne India to ne Myanmar and nw Yunnan
- _____ *A. c. tonkinensis* — S China (se Yunnan) to nw Tonkin and ne Laos
- _____ *A. c. guttaticollis* — Highlands of se China (nw Fujian); winters in n Guangdong
- _____ *A. c. fucata (berliozi)* — Central China (Hubei to s Hunan and s Shaanxi)
- _____ *A. c. cinereiceps* — W-central China (w Hubei to w Sichuan)
- _____ *A. c. fessa* — W-central China (s Shaanxi and Gansu)
- _____ *A. c. formosana* — Highlands of Taiwan

☐ **Ludlow's Fulvetta** *Alcippe ludlowi* — Himalayas (se Tibet to sw China, e Bhutan and extreme ne India)

☐ **Rufous-throated Fulvetta** *Alcippe rufogularis*
- _____ *A. r. rufogularis* — Himalayas (Bhutan to n Assam north of the Brahmaputra)
- _____ *A. r. collaris* — Hill forests of e Assam to Bangladesh
- _____ *A. r. major* — NE Myanmar to n and e Thailand and n-central Laos
- _____ *A. r. stevensi* — S China (sw Yunnan) and n Indochina
- _____ *A. r. kelleyi* — Central Vietnam (Quangtri Province)
- _____ *A. r. khmerensis* — SE Thailand and adjacent sw Cambodia

☐ **Dusky Fulvetta** *Alcippe brunnea*
- _____ *A. b. mandellii* — S Assam (s of the Brahmaputra) to w Myanmar (Chin Hills)
- _____ *A. b. genestieri* — SW China (se Qinghai, Yunnan and w Guizhou) to n Indochina
- _____ *A. b. olivacea* — S-central China (Hubei, s Shaanxi and e Sichuan)
- _____ *A. b. superciliaris* — Hills of se China (Anhui to Guangxi, Fujian and Guangdong)
- _____ *A. b. intermedia* — E Myanmar (Kachin and Shan States) to s China (Yunnan)
- _____ *A. b. arguta* — Hainan (s China)
- _____ *A. b. brunnea* — Taiwan

☐ **Rusty-capped Fulvetta** *Alcippe dubia* — Pine forests of s Myanmar (Tenasserim)

☐ **Brown Fulvetta** *Alcippe brunneicauda*
- _____ *A. b. brunneicauda* — S Thailand, Malaya, Sumatra, nw Borneo, N Natuna and Batu is.
- _____ *A. b. eriphaea* — Borneo

☐ **Brown-cheeked Fulvetta** *Alcippe poioicephala*
- _____ *A. p. poioicephala* — W India (W Ghats from s Mysore to Kerala and Palni Hills)
- _____ *A. p. brucei* — Central and s peninsular India
- _____ *A. p. fusca* — Assam (south of the Brahmaputra) to nw Myanmar
- _____ *A. p. phayrei* — SW Myanmar (Chin Hills and Arakan Yoma Mountains)
- _____ *A. p. haringtoniae* — NE Myanmar to s China (w Yunnan) and nw Thailand
- _____ *A. p. alearis* — S China (s Yunnan) to n plateau of Thailand and n Indochina
- _____ *A. p. karenni* — SE Myanmar (Karenni State) to sw Thailand
- _____ *A. p. davisoni* — Malay Pen. (Isthmus of Kra to Trang) and Mergui Archipelago

☐ **Gray-cheeked Fulvetta** *Alcippe morrisonia*
- _____ *A. m. yunnanensis* — S China (s Sichuan and e Yunnan) to ne Myanmar (Kachin)
- _____ *A. m. fraterculus* — S China (sw Yunnan) to se Myanmar and n Indochina
- _____ *A. m. schaefferi* — S China (se Yunnan and Guangxi) to nw Vietnam
- _____ *A. m. davidi* — S-central China (w Hubei to Hunan, Sichuan and ne Yunnan)
- _____ *A. m. hueti* — Hill forests of se China (Guangdong to Anhui)
- _____ *A. m. rufescentior* — Hainan (s China)
- _____ *A. m. morrisonia* — Taiwan

☐ **Javan Fulvetta** *Alcippe pyrrhoptera* — Forests of w and central Java

☐ **Mountain Fulvetta** *Alcippe peracensis*
_____ *A. p. grotei*
_____ *A. p. annamensis*
_____ *A. p. eremita*
_____ *A. p. peracensis*

☐ **Nepal Fulvetta** *Alcippe nipalensis*
_____ *A. n. nipalensis*
_____ *A. n. commoda*
_____ *A. n. stanfordi*

☐ **Bush Blackcap** *Lioptilus nigricapillus*

☐ **White-throated Mountain-Babbler** *Kupeornis gilberti*

☐ **Red-collared Mountain-Babbler** *Kupeornis rufocinctus*

☐ **Chapin's Mountain-Babbler** *Kupeornis chapini*
_____ *K. c. chapini*
_____ *K. c. nyombensis*
_____ *K. c. kalindei*

☐ **Abyssinian Catbird** *Parophasma galinieri*

☐ **Capuchin Babbler** *Phyllanthus atripennis*
_____ *P. a. atripennis*
_____ *P. a. rubiginosus*
_____ *P. a. bohndorffi*

☐ **Gray-crowned Crocias** *Crocias langbianis*

☐ **Spotted Crocias** *Crocias albonotatus*

☐ **Rufous-backed Sibia** *Heterophasia annectens*
_____ *H. a. annectens*
_____ *H. a. saturata*
_____ *H. a. mixta*
_____ *H. a. eximia*

☐ **Rufous Sibia** *Heterophasia capistrata*
_____ *H. c. capistrata*
_____ *H. c. nigriceps*
_____ *H. c. bayleyi*

☐ **Gray Sibia** *Heterophasia gracilis*

☐ **Black-backed Sibia** *Heterophasia melanoleuca*
_____ *H. m. melanoleuca*
_____ *H. m. tonkinensis*
_____ *H. m. engelbachi*
_____ *H. m. robinsoni*
_____ *H. m. castanoptera*

☐ **Black-headed Sibia** *Heterophasia desgodinsi*

☐ **White-eared Sibia** *Heterophasia auricularis*

☐ **Beautiful Sibia** *Heterophasia pulchella*

N and central Annam and adjacent Laos
S Laos (Bolaven Plateau), s Annam and adjacent Cochinchina
SE Thailand
Highlands of Malay Pen. (n Perak to s Selangor and Pahang)

Himalayas (Nepal to Sikkim, Bhutan and e Assam)
Assam (south and east of the Brahmaputra) to n Myanmar
Hill forests of sw Myanmar (Chin Hills and Arakan Yoma Mts.)

South Africa (Transvaal to Natal and e Cape Province)

Montane forests of se Nigeria and sw Cameroon

Montane forests of e Zaire and Rwanda

E Zaire (Lake Albert to Lake Edward)
E Zaire (Kahuzi-Biega National Park area)
E Zaire (Kivu region)

Highland juniper and *Hagenia* forests of Ethiopia

Senegal to Liberia
Ivory Coast to s Nigeria, sw Cameroon and Central African Rep.
NE Zaire and extreme w Uganda

Recorded after 57-year absence in s Vietnam (Langbian Plateau)

Montane forests of w and central Java

Sikkim to Bhutan, Assam, nw Myanmar and w Yunnan
SE Myanmar to nw Thailand
SE Myanmar to sw Yunnan, n Thailand, n Laos and nw Tonkin
S Vietnam (Da Lat Plateau)

E Himalayas (Pakistan to Garhwal)
Central Himalayas (Kumaon to central Nepal)
E Himalayas (e Nepal to Sikkim, Bhutan, s Tibet and n Assam)

Montane forests of ne India, Myanmar and s China (w Yunnan)

E Myanmar to nw Thailand
NW Tonkin
S Laos (Bolavens Plateau)
S Vietnam (Langbian Plateau)
SE Myanmar (Southern Shan State and Karenni State)

NE Myanmar to sw China (se Qinghai, s Sichuan, nw Yunnan)

Montane oak forests of Taiwan

Mountains of ne India to se Tibet, sw China and ne Myanmar

☐ **Long-tailed Sibia** *Heterophasia picaoides*
_____ *H. p. picaoides* — Nepal to Sikkim, Bhutan, Assam, nw Yunnan and ne Myanmar
_____ *H. p. cana* — S China (sw Yunnan) to s Myanmar, n Thailand and n Indochina
_____ *H. p. wrayi* — Highlands of Malay Pen. (n Perak to s Selangor and n Pahang)
_____ *H. p. simillima* — Highlands of w Sumatra

☐ **Striated Yuhina** *Yuhina castaniceps*
_____ *Y. c. rufigenis* — NE India (Darjiling) and Sikkim
_____ *Y. c. plumbeiceps* — N Assam to n Myanmar and s China (w Yunnan)
_____ *Y. c. castaniceps* — S Assam to sw Myanmar (Chin Hills and Arakan Yoma Mts.)
_____ *Y. c. striata* — Mountains of e Myanmar to nw Thailand
_____ *Y. c. torqueola* — N plateau of Thailand to s China and n Indochina

☐ **Chestnut-crested Yuhina** *Yuhina everetti* — Montane forests of n Borneo

☐ **White-naped Yuhina** *Yuhina bakeri* — Mts. of ne India (Assam) to Myanmar and s China (nw Yunnan)

☐ **Whiskered Yuhina** *Yuhina flavicollis*
_____ *Y. f. albicollis* — W Himalayas (Kashmir to w Nepal)
_____ *Y. f. flavicollis* — Central Nepal to Bhutan, e Assam (Abor Hills) and se Tibet
_____ *Y. f. rouxi* — S Assam to n Myanmar, s China (Yunnan) and n Indochina
_____ *Y. f. clarki* — Mountains of e Myanmar (S Shan State and Karenni State)
_____ *Y. f. constantiae* — Mountains of n Laos (Chiang Khwang Province)
_____ *Y. f. rogersi* — Extreme n Thailand (Doi Phu Kha)

☐ **Burmese Yuhina** *Yuhina humilis* — Mountains of se Myanmar and adjacent nw Thailand

☐ **Stripe-throated Yuhina** *Yuhina gularis*
_____ *Y. g. vivax* — W Himalayas (Garhwal to Kumaon)
_____ *Y. g. gularis* — Nepal to se Tibet, nw Yunnan, w Myanmar and nw Vietnam
_____ *Y. g. omiensis* — S China (Omei Shan Mountains of Sichuan to nw Yunnan)

☐ **White-collared Yuhina** *Yuhina diademata* — Mountains of sw China to se Myanmar and nw Tonkin

☐ **Rufous-vented Yuhina** *Yuhina occipitalis*
_____ *Y. o. occipitalis* — E Himalayas (Nepal to se Tibet and n Assam)
_____ *Y. o. obscurior* — NE Myanmar (Kachin State) to s China (nw Yunnan)

☐ **Taiwan Yuhina** *Yuhina brunneiceps* — Montane forests of Taiwan

☐ **Black-chinned Yuhina** *Yuhina nigrimenta*
_____ *Y. n. nigrimenta* — Himalayas (Garhwal to e Assam)
_____ *Y. n. intermedia* — Myanmar to s China (Liaoning, Sichuan, Yunnan) and n Indochina
_____ *Y. n. pallida* — Highlands of se China (nw Fujian, Guangxi and Guangdong)

☐ **White-bellied Yuhina** *Yuhina zantholeuca*
_____ *Y. z. zantholeuca* — E Himalayas to n Myanmar, s China (Yunnan) and w Thailand
_____ *Y. z. tyrannula* — NE Thailand to s China (se Yunnan), n Indochina and Hainan
_____ *Y. z. griseiloris* — SE China (Fujian, Guangdong, w Guangxi, se Yunnan); Taiwan
_____ *Y. z. sordida* — Extreme e plateau of Thailand to s Indochina
_____ *Y. z. canescens* — SE Thailand to w Cambodia
_____ *Y. z. interposita* — Malay Peninsula (Mergui District and Isthmus of Kra to Johore)
_____ *Y. z. saani* — NW Sumatra
_____ *Y. z. brunnescens* — Borneo

☐ **Fire-tailed Myzornis** *Myzornis pyrrhoura* — Nepal to se Tibet, s China (Yunnan) and ne Myanmar

☐ **White-throated Oxylabes** *Oxylabes madagascariensis* — Dense humid forests of nw and e Madagascar

☐ **Yellow-browed Oxylabes** *Crossleyia xanthophrys*

Lowland rainforests of e-central Madagascar

☐ **Crossley's Babbler** *Mystacornis crossleyi*

Dense humid forests of e Madagascar

FAMILY: POMATOSTOMIDAE (Pseudo-babblers—5)

☐ **New Guinea Babbler** *Pomatostomus isidorei*
- ____ *P. i. calidus* — N New Guinea (Geelvink Bay to Astrolabe Bay)
- ____ *P. i. isidorei* — S New Guinea, Misool I. and Waigeo I.

☐ **Gray-crowned Babbler** *Pomatostomus temporalis*
- ____ *P. t. strepitans* — S New Guinea (Orimo River to Digul River)
- ____ *P. t. nigrescens* — Western Australia
- ____ *P. t. browni* — N Australia (Cape Arnhem Peninsula of Northern Territory)
- ____ *P. t. mountfordae* — Groote Eylandt (Northern Territory)
- ____ *P. t. rubeculus* — N Australia (Northern Territory)
- ____ *P. t. bamba* — Melville I. (n Australia)
- ____ *P. t. intermedius* — Arid interior of Australia
- ____ *P. t. cornwalli* — Coastal n Queensland (Cape York to Cairns)
- ____ *P. t. temporalis* — NE Australia (coastal central Queensland)
- ____ *P. t. trivirgatus* — E Australia (coastal s Queensland and e New South Wales)
- ____ *P. t. tregellasi* — SE New South Wales, Victoria and se South Australia

☐ **White-browed Babbler** *Pomatostomus superciliosus*
- ____ *P. s. gilgandra* — W New South Wales, Victoria and South Australia
- ____ *P. s. superciliosus* — SE South Australia and (?) adjacent Victoria
- ____ *P. s. ashbyi* — Arid sw Western Australia (north to Tropic of Capricorn)
- ____ *P. s. gwendolenae* — Western Australia (Gascoyne Valley region)

☐ **Hall's Babbler** *Pomatostomus halli*

Locally in *mulga* of sw Queensland and nw New South Wales

☐ **Chestnut-crowned Babbler** *Pomatostomus ruficeps*

Casuarina saltbush country of e-central Australia

FAMILY: PARADOXORNITHIDAE (Parrotbills—20)

☐ **Bearded Reedling** *Panurus biarmicus*
- ____ *P. b. biarmicus* — W Europe to Sweden, Poland, Italy, Balkans and Transcaucasia
- ____ *P. b. russicus* — C Europe (Austria to n Yugoslavia, Asia Minor, c Asia and China)
- ____ *P. b. kosswigi* — Formerly s Turkey (Amik Gölü). Probably extinct

☐ **Great Parrotbill** *Conostoma oemodium*

Bamboo forests of w Nepal to se Tibet, s China and ne Myanmar

☐ **Brown Parrotbill** *Paradoxornis unicolor*

Bamboo forests of Nepal to se Tibet, sw China and ne Myanmar

☐ **Gray-headed Parrotbill** *Paradoxornis gularis*
- ____ *P. g. gularis* — E Himalayas (Sikkim to Bhutan and n Assam)
- ____ *P. g. transfluvialis* — S Assam (s of the Brahmaputra) to Myanmar and nw Thailand
- ____ *P. g. rasus* — W Myanmar (Chin Hills)
- ____ *P. g. laotianus* — E Myanmar (Kengtung) to n Thailand, n Laos and nw Tonkin
- ____ *P. g. fokiensis* — Hill forests of s China (south of the Yangtze River)
- ____ *P. g. hainanus* — Hainan (s China)
- ____ *P. g. margaritae* — Highlands of s Vietnam (s Annam)

☐ **Three-toed Parrotbill** *Paradoxornis paradoxus*
_____ P. p. taipaiensis   Central China (Tsingling Mountains of s Shaanxi)
_____ P. p. paradoxus   S China (n Sichuan and sw Gansu)

☐ **Black-breasted Parrotbill** *Paradoxornis flavirostris*

     Foothills of Nepal to ne Assam and w Myanmar (Chin Hills)

☐ **Spot-breasted Parrotbill** *Paradoxornis guttaticollis*

     Hill forests of Assam to e Myanmar, s China and n Indochina

☐ **Spectacled Parrotbill** *Paradoxornis conspicillatus*
_____ P. c. conspicillatus   Mts. of c China (e Qinghai to e Sichuan, se Gansu, sw Shaanxi)
_____ P. c. rocki   Montane bamboo forests of ne China (w Liaoning)

☐ **Vinous-throated Parrotbill** *Paradoxornis webbianus*
_____ P. w. suffusus   Mts. of nw China (Shaanxi to w Sichuan, Jiangxi, Guangdong)
_____ P. w. mantschuricus   E Manchuria to ne China (e Liaoning)
_____ P. w. fulvicauda   NE China (s Liaoning) to s Korea
_____ P. w. webbianus   Coastal e China (s Jiangsu and n Zhejiang)
_____ P. w. elisabethae   Montane forests of s China (se Yunnan) and nw Tonkin
_____ P. w. bulomachus   Highlands of Taiwan

☐ **Brown-winged Parrotbill** *Paradoxornis brunneus*
_____ P. b. ricketti   S China (s Sichuan and n Yunnan)
_____ P. b. styani   S China (n Yunnan from Mekong Valley to Tali region)
_____ P. b. brunneus   S China (Yunnan from Tali region south to Tengyueh)

☐ **Ashy-throated Parrotbill** *Paradoxornis alphonsianus*
_____ P. a. alphonsianus   Mts. of w-central China (e Qinghai, e Sichuan and Guizhou)
_____ P. a. yunnanensis   Montane forests of s China (se Yunnan) and nw Tonkin

☐ **Gray-hooded Parrotbill** *Paradoxornis zappeyi*

     Mountains of s China (Washan and Omei Shan in e Sichuan)

☐ **Rusty-throated Parrotbill** *Paradoxornis przewalskii*

     Mts. of s-cent. China (se Qinghai to se Gansu and adj. Sichuan)

☐ **Fulvous Parrotbill** *Paradoxornis fulvifrons*
_____ P. f. fulvifrons   Montane forests of Nepal, Sikkim and Bhutan
_____ P. f. chayulensis   Montane forests of se Tibet and ne Myanmar
_____ P. f. albifacies   Montane forests of sw China (se Qinghai and nw Yunnan)
_____ P. f. cyanophrys   Mountains of sw China (w Sichuan, se Gansu and s Shaanxi)

☐ **Black-throated Parrotbill** *Paradoxornis nipalensis*
_____ P. n. nipalensis   Central Nepal (Kathmandu Valley)
_____ P. n. humii   Himalayas of e Nepal, Sikkim and w Bhutan
_____ P. n. crocotius   Mountains of se Tibet and e Bhutan
_____ P. n. poliotis   E Bhutan to Assam, ne Myanmar, se Tibet, s China (nw Yunnan)
_____ P. n. partriciae   SE Assam (Lushai Hills)
_____ P. n. ripponi   N Myanmar (Mt. Victoria)
_____ P. n. feae   Hill forests of se Myanmar (Karenni State) and nw Thailand

☐ **Golden Parrotbill** *Paradoxornis verreauxi*
_____ P. v. verreauxi   Mountains of sw China (e Qinghai to Sichuan and n Yunnan)
_____ P. v. craddocki   S China (ne Guangxi), ne Tonkin (Fan Si Pan Mts.), w Myanmar
_____ P. v. beaulieu   Mountains of n Laos (Chiang Khwang Province)
_____ P. v. pallidus   Mountains of se China (nw Fujian)
_____ P. v. morrisonianus   Highlands of Taiwan

☐ **Short-tailed Parrotbill** *Paradoxornis davidianus*
_____ P. d. davidianus   Highlands of se China (s Zhejiang to central Fujian)
_____ P. d. tonkinensis   Highlands of n Vietnam (Bac Phan)
_____ P. d. thompsoni   S China (s Yunnan) to e Myanmar, e Thailand, nw Laos, n Tonkin

☐ **Black-browed Parrotbill** *Paradoxornis atrosuperciliaris*
____	*P. a. oatesi*	NE India (Darjiling) to Sikkim
____	*P. a. atrosuperciliaris*	Assam to Myanmar, s China (w Yunnan), nw Thailand, n Laos

☐ **Rufous-headed Parrotbill** *Paradoxornis ruficeps*
____	*P. r. ruficeps*	Nepal to Bhutan, n Assam, s China (nw Yunnan) and se Tibet
____	*P. r. bakeri*	S Assam (south of the Brahmaputra) to n and e Myanmar
____	*P. r. magnirostris*	Highlands of central Tonkin

☐ **Reed Parrotbill** *Paradoxornis heudei*
____	*P. h. polivanovi*	Reedbeds of extreme se Siberia (Lake Khanka) and s Ussuriland
____	*P. h. heudei*	Reedbeds of e China (s Heliongjiang, ne Zhejiang and Jiangsu)

FAMILY: ORTHONYCHIDAE (Logrunners—2)

☐ **Logrunner** *Orthonyx temminckii*
____	*O. t. novaguineae*	W New Guinea (Arfak and Tamrau mountains)
____	*O. t. dorsalis*	W New Guinea (Nassau and Snow mountains)
____	*O. t. victoriana*	SE New Guinea (Herzog and Wharton mountains)
____	*O. t. temminckii*	E Australia (se Queensland and e New South Wales)

☐ **Chowchilla** *Orthonyx spaldingii*
	NE Australia (tropical rainforests of Cape York Peninsula)

FAMILY: CINCLOSOMATIDAE (Whipbirds and Quail-thrushes—15)

☐ **Papuan Whipbird** *Androphobus viridis*
	New Guinea (Snow and Weyland mountains)

☐ **Eastern Whipbird** *Psophodes olivaceus*
____	*P. o. lateralis*	NE Australia (Cairns region of n Queensland)
____	*P. o. magnirostris*	NE Australia (Rockhampton region of central Queensland)
____	*P. o. olivaceus*	E Australia (s Queensland, e New South Wales and se Victoria)

☐ **Western Whipbird** *Psophodes nigrogularis*
____	*P. n. leucogaster*	E Australia (*mallee* of nw Victoria and se South Australia)
____	*P. n. nigrogularis*	*Mallee* of sw Western Australia
____	*P. n. pondalowiensis*	SE South Australia and Kangaroo I.

☐ **Chiming Wedgebill** *Psophodes occidentalis*
	Arid western Australia north of *mulga-eucalypt* zone

☐ **Chirruping Wedgebill** *Psophodes cristatus*
	Arid *mulga* zone of interior Australia

☐ **Spotted Quail-thrush** *Cinclosoma punctatum*
____	*C. p. punctatum*	E Australia (se Queensland to s Victoria and se S Australia)
____	*C. p. dovei*	Tasmania

☐ **Chestnut Quail-thrush** *Cinclosoma castanotus*
____	*C. c. castanotus*	SE South Australia and adjacent New South Wales
____	*C. c. mayri*	E Australia (*mallee* region of New South Wales)
____	*C. c. morgani*	South Australia (Eyre Peninsula and Gawler Ranges)
____	*C. c. clarum*	Central Australia
____	*C. c. dundasi*	SW Western Australia

☐ **Chestnut-breasted Quail-thrush** *Cinclosoma castaneothorax*

____	*C. c. marginatum*	Central W Australia to sw N Territory and nw S Australia
____	*C. c. castaneothorax*	S-central Queensland to n-central New South Wales

☐ **Cinnamon Quail-thrush** *Cinclosoma cinnamomeum*

____	*C. c. cinnamomeum*	N Territory, S Australia, se Queensland, nw New South Wales
____	*C. c. alisteri*	Nullarbor Plain of se Western Australia and sw South Australia

☐ **Painted Quail-thrush** *Cinclosoma ajax*

____	*C. a. ajax*	Lowlands of w New Guinea (Geelvink Bay to Triton Bay)
____	*C. a. muscale*	S-central New Guinea (upper Fly River Valley)
____	*C. a. alare*	S-central New Guinea (Oriomo and lower Fly River valleys)
____	*C. a. goldiei*	Lowlands of se New Guinea (Hall Sound to Milne Bay)

☐ **Spotted Jewel-babbler** *Ptilorrhoa leucosticta*

____	*P. l. leucosticta*	W New Guinea (Arfak and Tamrau mountains)
____	*P. l. mayri*	W New Guinea (Wandammen Mountains)
____	*P. l. centralis*	W New Guinea (Weyland, Nassau and Snow mountains)
____	*P. l. sibilans*	N New Guinea (Cyclops Mountains)
____	*P. l. menawa*	Coastal n New Guinea
____	*P. l. amabilis*	E New Guinea (Saruwaged Mountains)
____	*P. l. loriae*	Mountains of se New Guinea

☐ **Blue Jewel-babbler** *Ptilorrhoa caerulescens*

____	*P. c. caerulescens*	W New Guinea (Vogelkop to Etna Bay); Misool I.
____	*P. c. neumanni*	N New Guinea (Mamberamo River to Astrolabe Bay)
____	*P. c. nigricrissa*	S New Guinea (Etna Bay to Milne Bay)
____	*P. c. geislerorum*	E New Guinea (Huon Gulf to Collingwood Bay)

☐ **Chestnut-backed Jewel-babbler** *Ptilorrhoa castanonota*

____	*P. c. castanonota*	W New Guinea (mountains of Vogelkop Peninsula)
____	*P. c. saturata*	W New Guinea (Nassau Mountains)
____	*P. c. uropygialis*	W New Guinea (n slopes of Snow Mountains)
____	*P. c. buergersi*	Central New Guinea (Sepik Mountains)
____	*P. c. par*	E New Guinea (Saruwaged Mountains)
____	*P. c. pulchra*	Mountains of se New Guinea
____	*P. c. gilliardi*	Batanta I. and Yapen I.

☐ **Malaysian Rail-babbler** *Eupetes macrocerus*

____	*E. m. macrocerus*	Peninsular Thailand, Malaya, Sumatra and North Natuna Is.
____	*E. m. borneensis*	Mountains of n Borneo

☐ **Blue-capped Ifrita** *Ifrita kowaldi*

____	*I. k. brunnea*	Mountains of w-central New Guinea
____	*I. k. kowaldi*	New Guinea (Central Highlands and mountains of Huon Pen.)

FAMILY: AEGITHALIDAE (Long-tailed Tits—8)

☐ **Long-tailed Tit** *Aegithalos caudatus*

____	*A. c. rosaceus*	British Isles
____	*A. c. caudatus*	Scandinavia and ne Europe to Siberia, n China, Korea and Japan
____	*A. c. aremoricus*	W France, Channel Islands and Île d'Yeu
____	*A. c. taiti*	S and sw France to nw Spain and Portugal
____	*A. c. irbii*	S Spain, Portugal and Corsica
____	*A. c. europaeus*	France and Germany to n Italy, w Romania and n Bulgaria
____	*A. c. italiae*	Mainland Italy and Yugoslavia

____	*A. c. siculus*	Sicily
____	*A. c. macedonicus*	Albania, Yugoslavia, Greece and s Bulgaria
____	*A. c. tauricus*	S Crimean Peninsula
____	*A. c. tephronotus*	Asia Minor
____	*A. c. major*	Caucasus to w and central Transcaucasia
____	*A. c. alpinus*	SE Azerbaijan to n Iran and sw Turkmenistan
____	*A. c. passekii*	Zagros Mountains (sw Iran)
____	*A. c. glaucogularis*	Central China (mountains of w Sichuan to Yangtze delta)
____	*A. c. vinaceus*	N and w China (Liaoning to Gansu, Qinghai and n Yunnan)
____	*A. c. magnus*	S Korea and Tsushima Is. (Kamino-shima and Shimono-shima)
____	*A. c. trivirgatus*	Japan (Honshu, Awa-shima, Sado and Oki); Cheju-Do Is. (Korea)
____	*A. c. kiusiuensis*	S Japanese islands (Shikoku, Kyushu and Yakushima)

☐ **White-cheeked Tit** *Aegithalos leucogenys*

Juniper and *ilex* scrub of w Kashmir, Afghanistan and n Pakistan

☐ **Black-throated Tit** *Aegithalos concinnus*

____	*A. c. iredalei*	Himalayas (ne Pakistan to n India and s Tibet)
____	*A. c. manipurensis*	NE India (se Arunachal Pradesh) to w Myanmar (Chin Hills)
____	*A. c. concinnus*	Central and e China and Taiwan
____	*A. c. talifuensis*	NE Myanmar to sw China, nw Vietnam and n Laos
____	*A. c. pulchellus*	E Myanmar (s Shan States and Kayah) to extreme nw Thailand
____	*A. c. annamensis*	S Laos (Bolavens Plateau) and Vietnam (central and s Annam)

☐ **White-throated Tit** *Aegithalos niveogularis*

Birch and pine forests of n Pakistan and nw India

☐ **Black-browed Tit** *Aegithalos iouschistos*

____	*A. i. iouschistos*	Himalayas (Nepal to n India and se Tibet
____	*A. i. bonvaloti*	S China (se Tibet to Sichuan and Yunnan) and ne Myanmar
____	*A. i. obscuratus*	Mountains of w China (Sungpan region of ne Sichuan)
____	*A. i. sharpei*	Montane forests of sw Myanmar (Mt. Victoria)

☐ **Sooty Tit** *Aegithalos fuliginosus*

Mts. of cent. China (Sichuan, s Gansu, s Shaanxi and sw Hubei)

☐ **Bushtit** *Psaltriparus minimus*

____	*P. m. saturatus*	S British Columbia, Puget Sound lowlands and Whidbey I.
____	*P. m. minimus*	Pacific coast west of the Cascades (n Oregon to s California)
____	*P. m. plumbeus*	E Oregon to Idaho, Wyoming, Arizona, New Mexico, w Texas
____	*P. m. melanurus*	Coastal s California (n San Diego County) to n Baja
____	*P. m. californicus*	Interior s Oregon to s California (Kern County)
____	*P. m. sociabilis*	S California (Little San Bernardino and Eagle mountains)
____	*P. m. grindae*	Mountains s Baja California (Sierra de la Laguna)
____	*P. m. dimorphicus*	Mountains of nw Mexico (Sonora to Sinaloa and n Coahuila)
____	*P. m. iulus*	Mts. of w Mexico (Durango to s Jalisco and w Tamaulipas)
____	*P. m. personatus*	Mts. of central Mexico (Michoacán to w Veracruz and Puebla)
____	*P. m. melanotis*	Mts. of s Mexico (Guerrero, Oaxaca and Chiapas) to Guatemala

☐ **Pygmy Tit** *Psaltria exilis*

Mountains of w and central Java

FAMILY: MALURIDAE (Fairywrens—25)

☐ **Orange-crowned Fairywren** *Clytomyias insignis*

____	*C. i. insignis*	NW New Guinea (Tamrau and Wandammen mountains)
____	*C. i. oorti*	New Guinea (Snow Mts. to mountains of Huon Peninsula)

☐ **Wallace's Fairywren** *Sipodotus wallacii*

Lowlands of New Guinea, Aru, Misool and Yapen islands

☐ **Broad-billed Fairywren** *Malurus grayi*

____	*M. g. grayi*	N New Guinea (Vogelkop to Sepik River) and Salawati I.
____	*M. g. campbelli*	SE New Guinea (middle Strickland River and Mt. Bosavi area)

☐ **White-shouldered Fairywren** *Malurus alboscapulatus*

____	*M. a. lorentzi*	S and southwestern New Guinea
____	*M. a. alboscapulatus*	NW New Guinea (Arfak and Tamrau mountains)
____	*M. a. naimii*	N and s lowlands and Central Highlands of New Guinea
____	*M. a. aida*	Northwestern New Guinea
____	*M. a. kutubu*	S highlands of central New Guinea
____	*M. a. moretoni*	N and s coasts of se New Guinea and Fergusson I.

☐ **Red-backed Fairywren** *Malurus melanocephalus*

____	*M. m. cruentatus*	N Australia and Melville I.
____	*M. m. melanocephalus*	E Australia (s Queensland and n New South Wales)

☐ **White-winged Fairywren** *Malurus leucopterus*

____	*M. l. leucopterus*	Dirk Hartog I. (Western Australia)
____	*M. l. edouardi*	Barrow I. (Western Australia)
____	*M. l. leuconotus*	Interior of Australia

☐ **Superb Fairywren** *Malurus cyaneus*

____	*M. c. cyanochlamys*	S Queensland to Victoria, e South Australia and Kangaroo I.
____	*M. c. cyaneus*	Tasmania, Flinders I. and King I.

☐ **Splendid Fairywren** *Malurus splendens*

____	*M. s. splendens*	Interior of sw W Australia (north to Shark Bay and Esperance)
____	*M. s. callainus*	Central Australia
____	*M. s. melanotus*	Central Queensland to nw Victoria and e-central S Australia

☐ **Variegated Fairywren** *Malurus lamberti*

____	*M. l. dulcis*	N Northern Territory (east to Arnhem Land)
____	*M. l. rogersi*	NE Western Australia (Kimberley District)
____	*M. l. assimilis*	Interior of Australia
____	*M. l. lamberti*	SE Queensland (Fitzroy River) to se New South Wales

☐ **Lovely Fairywren** *Malurus amabilis*

NE Australia (Cape York Peninsula of n Queensland)

☐ **Red-winged Fairywren** *Malurus elegans*

Swampy undergrowth of coastal sw Australia (Perth to Albany)

☐ **Blue-breasted Fairywren** *Malurus pulcherrimus*

S-central and sw Australia

☐ **Purple-crowned Fairywren** *Malurus coronatus*

____	*M. c. coronatus*	Coastal Northern Territory and n Western Australia
____	*M. c. macgillivrayi*	Coastal ne Northern Territory and nw Queensland

☐ **Emperor Fairywren** *Malurus cyanocephalus*

____	*M. c. cyanocephalus*	Lowlands of w New Guinea, Salawati and Yapen islands
____	*M. c. mysorensis*	Lowlands of Biak I. (n New Guinea)
____	*M. c. bonapartii*	S New Guinea and Aru Islands

☐ **Southern Emuwren** *Stipiturus malachurus*

____	*S. m. westernensis*	S Western Australia and Dirk Hartog I.
____	*S. m. malachurus*	SE South Australia, e New South Wales and Victoria
____	*S. m. parimeda*	South Australia (southern tip of Eyre Peninsula)
____	*S. m. intermedius*	South Australia (southern Mt. Lofty Range)
____	*S. m. halmaturinus*	Kangaroo I. (South Australia)
____	*S. m. littleri*	Tasmania and adjacent inshore islands

□ **Rufous-crowned Emuwren** *Stipiturus ruficeps*

Arid w and central Australia

□ **Mallee Emuwren** *Stipiturus mallee*

Mallee of Victoria, New South Wales and adjacent S Australia

□ **Thick-billed Grasswren** *Amytornis textilis*

_____ *A. t. textilis* — Saltbush flats of Western Australia and w South Australia

_____ *A. t. myall* — Saltbush flats of s-central South Australia

_____ *A. t. modestus* — Interior S Australia to N Territory and w New South Wales

□ **Dusky Grasswren** *Amytornis purnelli*

_____ *A. p. purnelli* — Spinifex of n-central Australia

_____ *A. p. ballarae* — Spinifex of interior w Queensland

□ **Black Grasswren** *Amytornis housei*

Western Australia (Kimberly Divide area)

□ **Striated Grasswren** *Amytornis striatus*

_____ *A. s. whitei* — Locally in nw Western Australia and s Northern Territory

_____ *A. s. merrotsyi* — South Australia (Flinders and Gammon ranges)

_____ *A. s. striatus* — NW New South Wales to central Victoria and se S Australia

□ **White-throated Grasswren** *Amytornis woodwardi*

Northern Territory (nw Arnhem Land)

□ **Carpentarian Grasswren** *Amytornis dorotheae*

Lower MacArthur River and extreme nw Queensland

□ **Gray Grasswren** *Amytornis barbatus*

SW Queensland, adj. New South Wales and ne South Australia

□ **Eyrean Grasswren** *Amytornis goyderi*

Canegrass of lower Macumba River (ne South Australia)

FAMILY: ACANTHIZIDAE (Thornbills and Allies—65)

□ **Western Bristlebird** *Dasyornis longirostris*

Coastal corner of sw Australia (Albany region)

□ **Eastern Bristlebird** *Dasyornis brachypterus*

E Australia (coastal se Queensland to extreme e Victoria)

□ **Rufous Bristlebird** *Dasyornis broadbenti*

_____ *D. b. litoralis* — Coastal sw W Australia (Cape Naturaliste to Cape Leeuwin)

_____ *D. b. broadbenti* — Coastal w Australia to extreme sw Victoria (Otway Range)

_____ *D. b. whitei* — E Australia (se South Australia to sw Victoria)

□ **Pilotbird** *Pycnoptilus floccosus*

SE Australia (e-central New South Wales to s-central Victoria)

□ **Rock Warbler** *Origma solitaria*

E-central New South Wales (Hawkesbury sandstone area)

□ **Fernwren** *Oreoscopus gutturalis*

NE Queensland (Atherton tableland)

□ **Rusty Mouse-Warbler** *Crateroscelis murina*

_____ *C. m. murina* — Lowland forests of Salawati and Yapen islands (New Guinea)

_____ *C. m. monacha* — Lowland forests of Aru Islands (New Guinea)

_____ *C. m. pallida* — Trans-Fly lowlands of se New Guinea

_____ *C. m. capitalis* — Lowland forests of Waigeo and Batanta islands (New Guinea)

_____ *C. m. fumosa* — Lowland forests of Misool I. (New Guinea)

□ **Bicolored Mouse-Warbler** *Crateroscelis nigrorufa*

_____ *C. n. blissi* — New Guinea (Snow Mountains to Central Highlands)

_____ *C. n. nigrorufa* — SE New Guinea (Owen Stanley Mountains)

☐ **Mountain Mouse-Warbler** *Crateroscelis robusta*

____	*C. r. peninsularis*	NW New Guinea (Arfak Mountains)
____	*C. r. ripleyi*	NW New Guinea (Tamrau Mountains)
____	*C. r. bastille*	Coastal n New Guinea (Bewani and Toricelli mountains)
____	*C. r. deficiens*	N New Guinea (Cyclops Mountains)
____	*C. r. sanfordi*	New Guinea (Weyland and Jayawijaya mountains)
____	*C. r. robusta*	SE New Guinea (Herzog and Owen Stanley mountains)

☐ **Yellow-throated Scrubwren** *Sericornis citreogularis*

____	*S. c. cairnsi*	NE Australia (coastal and montane forests of ne Queensland)
____	*S. c. citreogularis*	E Australia (se Queensland to New South Wales)

☐ **White-browed Scrubwren** *Sericornis frontalis*

____	*S. f. laevigaster*	NE Australia (Atherton Plateau to coastal se Queensland)
____	*S. f. frontalis (rosinae)*	SE Australia west to e South Australia (Mt. Lofty Range)
____	*S. f. maculatus (mellori, balstoni)*	Kangaroo I. and s Australian gulfs to W Australia (Shark Bay)
____	*S. f. humilis*	Tasmania and islands in Bass Strait

☐ **Brown Scrubwren** *Sericornis humilis*

Dense forest undergrowth of Tasmania

☐ **Atherton Scrubwren** *Sericornis keri*

NE Australia (Atherton tableland of ne Queensland)

☐ **Beccari's Scrubwren** *Sericornis beccarii*

____	*S. b. wondiwoi*	NW New Guinea (Wondiwoi Mountains)
____	*S. b. cyclopum*	N New Guinea (Cyclops Mountains)
____	*S. b. weylandi*	New Guinea (Weyland Mountains)
____	*S. b. imitator*	NE New Guinea (Arfak Mountains)
____	*S. b. idenburgi*	New Guinea (Gauttier Mts. and slopes above Idenburg River)
____	*S. b. boreonesioticus*	N New Guinea (Toricelli Mountains)
____	*S. b. pontifex*	N New Guinea (Sepik Mountains)
____	*S. b. randi*	S New Guinea (Trans-Fly lowlands)
____	*S. b. beccarii*	Aru Islands
____	*S. b. minimus*	NE Australia (n tip of Cape York Peninsula)
____	*S. b. dubius*	NE Australia (n Queensland south to Cooktown)

☐ **Perplexing Scrubwren** *Sericornis virgatus*

____	*S. v. virgatus*	Vogelkop Mts. and n slopes of Sepik-Ramu river drainage
____	*S. v. jobiensis*	Yapen I. (New Guinea)

☐ **Large Scrubwren** *Sericornis nouhuysi*

____	*S. n. cantans*	NW New Guinea (Vogelkop Mountains)
____	*S. n. adelberti*	NE New Guinea (Adelbert Mountains)
____	*S. n. nouhuysi*	New Guinea (Weyland, Nassau and Snow mountains)
____	*S. n. stresemanni*	Central Highlands of New Guinea
____	*S. n. oorti*	New Guinea (Herzog Mts. and mountains of Huon Peninsula)
____	*S. n. monticola*	SE New Guinea (high Owen Stanley Mountains)

☐ **Large-billed Scrubwren** *Sericornis magnirostris*

____	*S. m. viridior*	NE Australia (coastal and montane forests of Queensland)
____	*S. m. magnirostris*	E Australia (coastal New South Wales and Victoria)

☐ **Vogelkop Scrubwren** *Sericornis rufescens*

W New Guinea (Arfak and Tamrau mts. and Bomberai Pen.)

☐ **Buff-faced Scrubwren** *Sericornis perspicillatus*

Humid montane forests of central and e New Guinea

☐ **Papuan Scrubwren** *Sericornis papuensis*

____	*S. p. meeki*	W New Guinea (Jayawijaya Mountains)
____	*S. p. burgersi*	New Guinea (Weyland Mts. to Cent. Highlands and Sepik Mts.)
____	*S. p. papuensis*	Mountains of se New Guinea

☐ **Gray-green Scrubwren** *Sericornis arfakianus*

Humid montane forests of New Guinea

☐ **Pale-billed Scrubwren** *Sericornis spilodera*
_____ *S. s. spilodera*
_____ *S. s. granti*
_____ *S. s. wuroi*
_____ *S. s. guttatus*
_____ *S. s. ferrugineus*
_____ *S. s. aruensis*
_____ *S. s. batantae*

NW New Guinea (east to Astrolabe Bay) and Yapen I.
W New Guinea (Snow Mountains)
S New Guinea (Trans-Fly lowlands)
Mountains of se New Guinea
Waigeo I. (New Guinea)
Aru Islands (New Guinea)
Batanta I. (New Guinea)

☐ **Scrubtit** *Acanthornis magnus*

Dense forest undergrowth of Tasmania

☐ **Redthroat** *Pyrrholaemus brunneus*

Arid s Australia

☐ **Speckled Warbler** *Chthonicola sagittatus*

S Queensland to New South Wales and sw Victoria

☐ **Rufous Fieldwren** *Calamanthus campestris*
_____ *C. c. rubiginosus*
_____ *C. c. isabellinus*
_____ *C. c. campestris*
_____ *C. c. winiam*
_____ *C. c. ethelae*
_____ *C. c. montanellus*
_____ *C. c. dorrie*

Coastal nw Western Australia
Interior of Western and South Australia
S South Australia, nw Victoria and n New South Wales
Deserts of e South Australia and adjacent nw Victoria
South Australia (Yorke and Eyre peninsulas)
SW Australia north to lower Murchison River
Dirk Hartog I. and Dorre I. (Western Australia)

☐ **Striated Fieldwren** *Calamanthus fuliginosus*

Victoria, South Australia, Tasmania and islands in Bass Strait

☐ **Chestnut-rumped Hylacola** *Hylacola pyrrhopygia*

Extreme se Queensland to s Victoria and se South Australia

☐ **Shy Hylacola** *Hylacola cauta*

S Western Australia to nw Victoria and sw New South Wales

☐ **Papuan Thornbill** *Acanthiza murina*

New Guinea (Snow Mountains to Owen Stanley range)

☐ **Buff-rumped Thornbill** *Acanthiza reguloides*
_____ *A. r. squamata*
_____ *A. r. reguloides*

Atherton Tableland of ne Queensland (south to Burra Range)
S Queensland to Victoria and se South Australia

☐ **Western Thornbill** *Acanthiza inornata*
_____ *A. i. mastersi*
_____ *A. i. inornata*

Dry forests of sw Western Australia (east to Albany)
Dry forests of s-central Western Australia

☐ **Slender-billed Thornbill** *Acanthiza iredalei*
_____ *A. i. iredalei*
_____ *A. i. hedleyi*
_____ *A. i. rosinae*

Samphire zone of Western Australia to w South Australia
Samphire zone of Victoria and South Australia
Samphire zone of s South Australia

☐ **Mountain Thornbill** *Acanthiza katherina*

NE Australia (Atherton tableland of ne Queensland)

☐ **Brown Thornbill** *Acanthiza pusilla*
_____ *A. p. bunya*
_____ *A. p. pusilla*
_____ *A. p. mcgilli*
_____ *A. p. archibaldi*
_____ *A. p. zietzi*
_____ *A. p. diemenensis*

NE Australia (s Queensland and ne New South Wales)
E New South Wales to Victoria and South Australia
E Queensland (Prosperine to Clarke Range)
King I. (Bass Strait)
Kangaroo I. (South Australia)
Tasmania

☐ **Tasmanian Thornbill** *Acanthiza ewingii*

Tasmania, King and Furneaux islands

☐ **Inland Thornbill** *Acanthiza apicalis*

_____	*A. a. whitlocki*	Western Australia (Nullarbor Plain) to s South Australia
_____	*A. a. apicalis*	*Mulga* and *mallee* of sw Australia
_____	*A. a. leeuwinensis*	Humid coastal sw Australia
_____	*A. a. tanami*	W Northern Territory (Tanami Desert)
_____	*A. a. albiventris*	SW Queensland to n S Australia, nw Victoria and w New S Wales

☐ **Yellow-rumped Thornbill** *Acanthiza chrysorrhoa*

_____	*A. c. multi*	Savanna of sw Australia (east to Perth)
_____	*A. c. pallida*	Arid w Australia (north to Murchison River)
_____	*A. c. ferdinandi*	Central Australia and Great Victoria Desert
_____	*A. c. addenda*	*Mallee* of Victoria and South Australia
_____	*A. c. normantoni*	N Queensland (inland from head of Gulf of Carpentaria)
_____	*A. c. chrysorrhoa*	E Australia (s Queensland and New South Wales)
_____	*A. c. sandlandi*	Humid coastal Victoria, South Australia and Tasmania

☐ **Chestnut-rumped Thornbill** *Acanthiza uropygialis*

_____	*A. u. augusta*	Savanna of w-central Australia and w New South Wales
_____	*A. u. uropygialis*	Inland central and s Australia

☐ **Slaty-backed Thornbill** *Acanthiza robustirostris*

	Mulga of inland Australia

☐ **Yellow Thornbill** *Acanthiza nana*

_____	*A. n. flava*	NE Australia (Atherton Tableland of ne Queensland)
_____	*A. n. modesta*	Interior Queensland to se South Australia (Flinders Range)
_____	*A. n. nana*	S Queensland to e New South Wales and Victoria

☐ **Striated Thornbill** *Acanthiza lineata*

_____	*A. l. alberti*	NE Australia (dry forests and woodlands of se Queensland)
_____	*A. l. lineata*	E Australia (e New South Wales)
_____	*A. l. clelandi*	South Australia (west to Mt. Lofty Range)
_____	*A. l. chandleri*	Victoria, coastal se South Australia and Kangaroo I.

☐ **Weebill** *Smicrornis brevirostris*

_____	*S. b. cairns*	NE Australia (dry forests of ne Queensland)
_____	*S. b. pallescens*	NE Australia (central Queensland)
_____	*S. b. flavescens*	N Australia (Kimberly to head of Gulf of Carpentaria)
_____	*S. b. stirlingi*	Southwestern Australia
_____	*S. b. mathewsi*	Central and midwestern Australia (Carnarvon to Roebourne)
_____	*S. b. brevirostris*	S Queensland to coastal Victoria and South Australia
_____	*S. b. mallee*	*Mallee* of New South Wales, Victoria and adj. South Australia

☐ **Mountain Gerygone** *Gerygone cinerea*

	Arfak Mountains to se ranges of New Guinea

☐ **Green-backed Gerygone** *Gerygone chloronotus*

_____	*G. c. cinereiceps*	New Guinea
_____	*G. c. aruensis*	Aru, Waigeo, Salawati and Batanta islands
_____	*G. c. chloronotus*	Coastal nw Australia, Melville I. and Groote Eylandt

☐ **Fairy Gerygone** *Gerygone palpebrosa*

_____	*G. p. palpebrosa*	NW New Guinea, Aru, Waigeo, Misool and Salawati islands
_____	*G. p. wahnesi*	Yapen I. and n New Guinea
_____	*G. p. inconspicua*	SE New Guinea (west to upper Fly River)
_____	*G. p. tarara*	S New Guinea (Moorhead River to mouth of Fly River)
_____	*G. p. personata*	NE Australia (Cape York Peninsula of n Queensland)
_____	*G. p. flavida*	NE Australia (Atherton tableland south to Rockhampton)

☐ **Biak Gerygone** *Gerygone hypoxantha*

	Biak I. (off nw New Guinea)

□ **White-throated Gerygone** *Gerygone olivacea*

____ G. o. cinerascens	Lowlands of se New Guinea (Hall Sound to Port Moresby)
____ G. o. rogersi	NE Western Australia to Northern Territory and nw Queensland
____ G. o. olivacea	N Queensland to Victoria and se South Australia

□ **Yellow-bellied Gerygone** *Gerygone chrysogaster*

____ G. c. leucothorax	Lowlands of w New Guinea (Geelvink Bay region)
____ G. c. notata	W New Guinea, Misool and Batanta islands
____ G. c. neglecta	Waigeo I. (New Guinea)
____ G. c. dohertyi	SW New Guinea (Onin Peninsula to Triton Bay)
____ G. c. chrysogaster	S and e New Guinea, Yapen I. and Aru Islands

□ **Large-billed Gerygone** *Gerygone magnirostris*

____ G. m. conspicillata	NW New Guinea (Vogelkop region)
____ G. m. affinis	N New Guinea, Karkar, Manam and Yapen islands
____ G. m. mimikae	S New Guinea (Onin Peninsula to Port Moresby area)
____ G. m. brunneipectus	Aru Islands (New Guinea)
____ G. m. cobana	Waigeo, Batanta and Salawati islands (New Guinea)
____ G. m. occasa	Kofiau I. (New Guinea)
____ G. m. proxima	D'Entrecasteaux Arch. (Fergusson and Goodenough)
____ G. m. onerosa	Misima I. (Louisiade Archipelago)
____ G. m. tagulana	Tagula I. (Louisiade Archipelago)
____ G. m. rosseliana	Rossel I. (Louisiade Archipelago)
____ G. m. magnirostris	Coastal e W Australia to N Territory; Groote Eylandt; Melville I.
____ G. m. cairnsensis	N Queensland south to Mackay and islands in Torres Strait

□ **Dusky Gerygone** *Gerygone tenebrosa*

____ G. t. tenebrosa	Western Australia (Kimberly coast)
____ G. t. whitlocki	Coastal nw Australia and islands in Dampier Archipelago
____ G. t. christophori	Western Australia (Shark Bay area)

□ **Brown Gerygone** *Gerygone mouki*

____ G. m. mouki	NE Australia (Atherton tableland of n Queensland)
____ G. m. amalia	E Australia (Clarke Range of se Queensland)
____ G. m. richmondi	S Queensland to New South Wales and extreme e Victoria

□ **Golden-bellied Gerygone** *Gerygone sulphurea*

____ G. s. flaveola	Sulawesi, Salayar and Banggai Islands (Peleng and Banggai)
____ G. s. sulphurea	Malay Peninsula, Greater and Lesser Sundas
____ G. s. simplex	Lubang, Luzon, Mindoro, Verde, Negros, Bohol and Cebu
____ G. s. rhizophorae	S Philippines (Mindanao, Basilan and Sulu Archipelago)

□ **Plain Gerygone** *Gerygone inornata*

	Lesser Sundas (Sawu, Roti, Timor and Wetar)

□ **Rufous-sided Gerygone** *Gerygone dorsalis*

____ G. d. senex	Kalaotoa and Madu islands (Flores Sea)
____ G. d. keyensis	Tayandu and Kai Islands (Kai Kecil, Sawa and Ruin)
____ G. d. fulvescens	Lesser Sundas (Moa, Kisar, Leti, Sermata, Babar and Romang)
____ G. d. kuehni	Damar I. (Lesser Sundas)
____ G. d. dorsalis	Tanimbar Islands (Arafura Sea)

□ **Brown-breasted Gerygone** *Gerygone ruficollis*

____ G. r. ruficollis	W New Guinea (Arfak Mountains)
____ G. r. insperata	New Guinea (C Highlands to Owen Stanley Mts. and Huon Pen.)

□ **Western Gerygone** *Gerygone fusca*

____ G. f. fusca	Coastal nw W Australia to w Queensland and n S Australia
____ G. f. mungi	W Australia to s Queensland, Victoria and New South Wales

□ **Mangrove Gerygone** *Gerygone levigaster*
____	*G. l. pallida*	Coastal s New Guinea (Geelvink Bay to Port Moresby)
____	*G. l. levigaster*	Coastal n Australia (n Western Australia to w Queensland)
____	*G. l. cantator*	E Australia (coastal n Queensland to New South Wales)

□ **Norfolk Gerygone** *Gerygone modesta*

Norfolk I.

□ **Gray Gerygone** *Gerygone igata*

Forests of North I., South I. and adjacent islands (New Zealand)

□ **Chatham Gerygone** *Gerygone albofrontata*

Chatham Islands (off New Zealand)

□ **Fan-tailed Gerygone** *Gerygone flavolateralis*
____	*G. f. flavolateralis*	New Caledonia and Maré
____	*G. f. lifuensis*	Lifou (Loyalty Islands)
____	*G. f. correiae*	N Vanuatu and Banks Group
____	*G. f. rouxi*	Uvéa (Vanuatu)
____	*G. f. citrina*	Rennell (se Solomon Islands)

□ **Southern Whiteface** *Aphelocephala leucopsis*
____	*A. l. castaneiventris*	Arid scrub of Western Australia
____	*A. l. whitei*	Arid scrub of central Australia
____	*A. l. leucopsis*	New South Wales, Victoria and South Australia

□ **Chestnut-breasted Whiteface** *Aphelocephala pectoralis*

Arid deserts of South Australia (north to Oodnadatta)

□ **Banded Whiteface** *Aphelocephala nigricincta*

Arid interior of central Australia

FAMILY: EPTHIANURIDAE (Australian Chats—5)

□ **Crimson Chat** *Epthianura tricolor*

Grassy plains and savanna of interior and coastal w Australia

□ **Orange Chat** *Epthianura aurifrons*

Samphire and saltbush areas of interior Australia

□ **Yellow Chat** *Epthianura crocea*
____	*E. c. boweri*	NW Australia (King Sound and Fitzroy River)
____	*E. c. tunneyi*	N Australia (Alligator River region of Northern Territory)
____	*E. c. crocea*	NE Australia (lower Norman River region of w Queensland)
____	*E. c. macgregori*	NE Australia (Rockhampton district of Queensland)

□ **White-fronted Chat** *Epthianura albifrons*
____	*E. a. albifrons*	E Australia (New South Wales to Victoria, Western Australia)
____	*E. a. tasmanica*	Tasmania and islands in Bass Strait

□ **Desert Chat** *Ashbyia lovensis*

Arid stony plains of s-central Australia

FAMILY: NEOSITTIDAE (Sittellas—2)

□ **Black Sittella** *Neositta miranda*
____	*N. m. frontalis*	Mountains of nw New Guinea
____	*N. m. kuboriensis*	Central Highlands of ne New Guinea
____	*N. m. miranda*	Mountains of se New Guinea

☐ **Varied Sittella** *Neositta chrysoptera*

_____ *N. c. papuensis*	W New Guinea (Arfak Mountains)
_____ *N. c. wahgiensis*	New Guinea (Mt. Hagen region)
_____ *N. c. toxopeusi*	NW New Guinea (Snow Mountains)
_____ *N. c. intermedia*	New Guinea (Nassau Mountains)
_____ *N. c. alba*	Central mountains of New Guinea
_____ *N. c. albifrons*	Montane forests of se New Guinea
_____ *N. c. leucoptera*	Northern Territory (Kimberley Division) to central Queensland
_____ *N. c. striata*	N Queensland (Cape York Peninsula to Townsville)
_____ *N. c. pileata*	W New South Wales to w Victoria and e Western Australia
_____ *N. c. lathami*	E Australia (e Victoria)
_____ *N. c. lumholzi*	E Australia (Rockhampton region of e Queensland)
_____ *N. c. magnirostris*	E Australia (Inkerman region of ne Queensland)
_____ *N. c. rothschildi*	NE Australia (Cairns region of n Queensland)
_____ *N. c. leucocephala*	SE Queensland to ne New South Wales (s to Clarence River)
_____ *N. c. chrysoptera*	Extreme s-c interior Queensland, e New S Wales and e Victoria

FAMILY: CLIMACTERIDAE (Australasian Treecreepers—7)

☐ **Papuan Treecreeper** *Cormobates placens*

_____ *C. p. placens*	NW New Guinea (Arfak and Tamrau mountains)
_____ *C. p. steini*	W New Guinea (Weyland Mountains)
_____ *C. p. inexpectata*	N New Guinea (n slope Jayawijaya Mountains)
_____ *C. p. meridionalis*	Mountains of se New Guinea

☐ **White-throated Treecreeper** *Cormobates leucophaeus*

_____ *C. l. minor*	NE Queensland (Cooktown south to the Eungella Range)
_____ *C. l. leucophaeus*	E Australia (e Queensland to extreme se South Australia)

☐ **White-browed Treecreeper** *Climacteris affinis*

_____ *C. a. affinis*	S Australia (east of Spencer Gulf and Simpson Desert)
_____ *C. a. superciliosus*	Dry woodlands of w Australia

☐ **Red-browed Treecreeper** *Climacteris erythrops*

	E Australia (extreme se Queensland to Victoria)

☐ **Brown Treecreeper** *Climacteris picumnus*

_____ *C. p. melanota*	NW Queensland (w Cape York Peninsula south to Normanton)
_____ *C. p. picumnus*	E Australia (Townsville to Victoria and se South Australia)

☐ **Black-tailed Treecreeper** *Climacteris melanura*

_____ *C. m. melanura*	N Western Australia to N Territory and central Queensland
_____ *C. m. wellsi*	Western Australia (between Gascoyne and De Grey rivers)

☐ **Rufous Treecreeper** *Climacteris rufa*

	SW Western Australia to s South Australia

FAMILY: PARIDAE (Chickadees and Tits—55)

☐ **Sombre Tit** *Poecile lugubris*

_____ P. l. lugubris (splendens, lugens)	SE Europe south to n Greece; Crete
_____ P. l. anatoliae	S Greece to Turkey, w Georgia, Armenia, n Iraq and nw Iran
_____ P. l. dubius	W Iran (Zagros Mountains); winters to ne Iraq

☐ **Marsh Tit** *Poecile palustris*

_____ P. p. palustris (dresseri)	Br. Isles, s Scandinavia and c Europe to Pyrénées and Balkans
_____ P. p. stagnatilis	W Russia to n Turkey, e Yugoslavia and Bulgaria
_____ P. p. kabardensis (brandtii)	Caucasus Mountains
_____ P. p. italicus	French Alps and Italy
_____ P. p. brevirostris	Siberia to Mongolia, ne China and Korea
_____ P. p. ernsti	Sakhalin
_____ P. p. hensoni	N Japan (s Kuril Islands and Hokkaido)
_____ P. p. hellmayri	S and e China (Sichuan to Liaoning) and s Korea

☐ **Black-bibbed Tit** *Poecile hypermelaena*

	Central and e China to se Tibet and w Myanmar

☐ **Caspian Tit** *Poecile hyrcanus*

_____ P. h. hyrcanus	N Iran (Elburz Mountains) and adjacent Azerbaijan
_____ P. h. kirmanensis	S Iran (mountains of Kerman region)

☐ **Willow Tit** *Poecile montanus*

_____ P. m. kleinschmidti	Britain
_____ P. m. rhenanus	W Europe to w Germany and n Switzerland
_____ P. m. salicarius	Central Europe to w Poland, sw Germany and nw Austria
_____ P. m. montanus	Central Europe
_____ P. m. borealis (colletti, loennbergi)	Scandinavia to Baltic States, Carpathian Mts. and se Russia
_____ P. m. uralensis	SE Russia to s Urals, sw Siberia and n Kazakstan
_____ P. m. baicalensis	E Siberia to Sea of Okhotsk, Mongolia, Ussuriland and ne China
_____ P. m. anadyrensis	NE Siberia to n coast of Sea of Okhotsk
_____ P. m. kamtschatkensis	Kamchatka Peninsula
_____ P. m. sachalinensis	Sakhalin; vagrant to Hokkaido
_____ P. m. restrictus	Japan

☐ **Songar Tit** *Poecile songarus*

_____ P. s. songarus	Kazakstan (Tien Shan Mountains)
_____ P. s. weigoldicus	SW China (Sichuan to e Tibet, se Qinghai and nw Yunnan)
_____ P. s. affinis	N-central China (Ningxia to s Gansu and ne Qinghai)
_____ P. s. stotzneri	NE China (se Mongolia to Liaoning, Shaanxi and Henan)

☐ **Carolina Chickadee** *Poecile carolinensis*

_____ P. c. atricapilloides	S-central US (Kansas to Oklahoma and Texas)
_____ P. c. agilis	S US (sw Arkansas to w Louisiana and e Texas)
_____ P. c. extimus	E US (e Missouri to n New Jersey, Kentucky and Virginia)
_____ P. c. carolinensis	SE US (e Arkansas to s Virginia, Mississippi and Florida)

☐ **Black-capped Chickadee** *Poecile atricapillus*

_____ P. a. turneri	Alaska and adjacent nw Canada
_____ P. a. occidentalis	Extreme sw Br. Columbia to nw California (west of Cascades)
_____ P. a. fortuitus	S interior British Columbia to nw Montanea and nw Idaho
_____ P. a. garrinus	Rocky Mts. (se Idaho to Wyoming, e Utah and New Mexico)
_____ P. a. nevadensis	Great Basin of sw US (e Oregon to Idaho, Nevada and w Utah)
_____ P. a. bartletti	Newfoundland and Miquelon
_____ P. a. atricapillus	E Canada and ne US
_____ P. a. practicus	NE US (Appalachian Mountains region)
_____ P. a. septentrionalis	W Canada and central US

□ **Mountain Chickadee** *Poecile gambeli*
____ *P. g. abbrebviatus* — SW Canada and coastal ranges of n California
____ *P. g. gambeli* — Rocky Mts. (Montana to Wyoming, New Mexico and sw Texas)
____ *P. g. wasatchensis* — Coniferous forests of s Idaho and Utah
____ *P. g. inyoensis* — Great Basin (se Oregon, sw Idaho to w Utah and e-c California)
____ *P. g. baileyae* — Sierra Nevada of s California
____ *P. g. atratus* — Mountains of n Baja California

□ **Mexican Chickadee** *Poecile sclateri*
____ *P. s. eidos* — Oak-pine forests of se Arizona and New Mexico to nw Mexico
____ *P. s. garzai* — N Mexico (se Coahuila/Nuevo León border)
____ *P. s. sclateri* — Mountains of w Mexico (se Sinaloa to Puebla and w Veracruz)
____ *P. s. rayi* — Mountains of w Mexico (s Jalisco to Guerrero and Oaxaca)

□ **White-browed Tit** *Poecile superciliosus*
Mountains of w China (Qinghai to se Tibet, Gansu and Sichuan)

□ **Père David's Tit** *Poecile davidi*
Mountains of w China (Hubei to Shaanxi, Gansu and Sichuan)

□ **Chestnut-backed Chickadee** *Poecile rufescens*
____ *P. r. rufescens* — Alaska to coastal central California and Sierra Nevada of n Calif.
____ *P. r. neglectus* — Coastal California (sw Marin County)
____ *P. r. barlowi* — Coastal s California (San Francisco Bay to Santa Barbara Co.)

□ **Boreal Chickadee** *Poecile hudsonicus*
____ *P. h. stoneyi* — N Alaska to n Yukon and nw Mackenzie
____ *P. h. hudsonicus* — C Alaska and Yukon to Minnesota, Labrador and Newfoundland
____ *P. h. columbianus* — S Alaska to s Yukon, Br. Columbia, Montana and Washington
____ *P. h. farleyi* — NE British Columbia and Alberta to Saskatchewan and Manitoba
____ *P. h. littoralis* — SE Canada (s Quebec) to Nova Scotia and ne US

□ **Gray-headed Chickadee** *Poecile cinctus*
____ *P. c. lapponicus* — Fenno-Scandia, s Kola Peninsula and n European Russia
____ *P. c. cinctus* — N Ural Mountains to Bering Sea and ne Mongolia
____ *P. c. sayanus* — Altai, Sayan and Tannu-Ola mountains to nw Mongolia
____ *P. c. lathami* — Coniferous forests of Alaska and nw Canada

□ **Coal Tit** *Periparus ater*
____ *P. a. hibernicus* — Ireland (except extreme ne in County Down)
____ *P. a. britannicus* — Britain and ne Ireland
____ *P. a. ater* — Continental Europe to Siberia, Mongolia, Sakhalin and ne China
____ *P. a. vieirae* — Iberian Peninsula
____ *P. a. sardus* — Corsica and Sardinia
____ *P. a. atlas* — N Morocco
____ *P. a. ledouci* — North Africa (n Tunisia and n Algeria)
____ *P. a. cypriotes* — Cyprus
____ *P. a. moltchanovi* — Crimean Peninsula
____ *P. a. derjugini* — Mts. of ne Turkey, w Georgia and Black Sea coast of Russia
____ *P. a. michalowskii* — Caucasus and Transcaucasia
____ *P. a. gaddi* — SE Azerbaijan and Caspian region of n Iran (east to Gorgan)
____ *P. a. chorassanicus* — NE Iran and sw Turkmenistan
____ *P. a. phaeonotus* — Zagros Mountains (sw Iran)
____ *P. a. rufipectus* — Kazakstan (Tien Shan Mountains) to nw China (Xinjiang)
____ *P. a. aemodius* — E Himalayas to ne Myanmar, Tibet and sw China
____ *P. a. pekinensis* — NE China (s Liaoning to Shaanxi and Shantung Peninsula)
____ *P. a. kuatunensis* — Montane forests of se China (Anhui, Fujian and Zhejiang)
____ *P. a. ptilosus* — Montane forests of Taiwan
____ *P. a. insularis* — S Kuril Islands, Japan and Cheju-Do Islands (Korea)

□ **Black-breasted Tit** *Periparus rufonuchalis*
Oak-rhododendron forests of Turkestan to w China and Nepal

☐ **Rufous-vented Tit** *Periparus rubidiventris*
____ P. r. rubidiventris — Rhododendron forests of nw India to central Nepal
____ P. r. beavani — Central Nepal to ne Myanmar, nw India, s Tibet and sw China
____ P. r. saramatii — NW Myanmar (Mount Sarameti in Naga Hills)

☐ **Black-crested Tit** *Periparus melanolophus*

Coniferous forests of e Afghanistan to w Nepal

☐ **Yellow-bellied Tit** *Pardaliparus venustulus*

Mixed woodlands of east, central and s China

☐ **Elegant Tit** *Pardaliparus elegans*
____ P. e. edithae — N Philippines (Calayan and Camiguin Norte)
____ P. e. montigenus — N Philippines (nw Luzon)
____ P. e. gilliardi — N Philippines (Bataan Peninsula of central Luzon)
____ P. e. elegans — Philippines (c and s Luzon, Panay, Mindoro and Catanduanes)
____ P. e. albescens — Philippines (Guimaras, Masbate, Negros and Ticao)
____ P. e. visayanus — Philippines (Cebu)
____ P. e. mindanensis — Philippines (Samar, Leyte, Biliran and Mindanao)
____ P. e. suluensis — Sulu Archipelago (Jolo, Tawitawi and Sanga Sanga)
____ P. e. bongaoensis — Bongao I. (Sulu Archipelago)

☐ **Palawan Tit** *Pardaliparus amabilis*

SW Philippines (Balabac, Calauit and Palawan)

☐ **Crested Tit** *Lophophanes cristatus*
____ L. c. scoticus — Scotland
____ L. c. abadiei — NW France (Bretagne)
____ L. c. cristatus — Fenno-Scandia to European Russia, n Urals and Ukraine
____ L. c. mitratus — Central and w Europe
____ L. c. weigoldi — Portugal and s Spain
____ L. c. baschkirikus — S Urals

☐ **Gray-crested Tit** *Lophophanes dichrous*
____ L. d. kangrae — Coniferous forests of Kashmir to n India (Uttar Pradesh)
____ L. d. dichrous — Coniferous forests of w Nepal to Arunachal Pradesh and s Tibet
____ L. d. dichroides — NE Tibet to sw China (n Sichuan, Qinghai, Gansu and Shaanxi)
____ L. d. wellsi — NE Myanmar and s China (w Sichuan and nw Yunnan)

☐ **White-winged Black-Tit** *Melaniparus leucomelas*
____ M. l. guineensis — Senegambia to s Sudan, sw Ethiopia, Eritrea and n Uganda
____ M. l. leucomelas — Ethiopia
____ M. l. insignis — Gabon to Zaire, Kenya, Zambia, Malawi and n Mozambique

☐ **Southern Black-Tit** *Melaniparus niger*
____ M. n. xanthostomus — Angola to Namibia, Botswana, Zambia, s Tanzania, Mozambique
____ M. n. ravidus — Central Mozambique to plateau of Zimbabwe and n Transvaal
____ M. n. niger — S Mozambique to Natal, Zululand, Swaziland, e Cape Province

☐ **Carp's Tit** *Melaniparus carpi*

SW Angola to n and central Namibia

☐ **White-bellied Tit** *Melaniparus albiventris*

Locally in mountains of Nigeria to Sudan and Tanzania

☐ **White-backed Black-Tit** *Melaniparus leuconotus*

Wooded mountain gorges of Ethiopia

☐ **Rufous-bellied Tit** *Melaniparus rufiventris*
____ M. r. rufiventris — N Angola to w Zaire and central Zambia
____ M. r. diligens — S Angola to ne Namibia, nw Botswana and sw Zambia
____ M. r. masukuensis — Extreme se Zaire to Zambia, Malawi and Mozambique
____ M. r. pallidiventris — C Tanzania to e Zambia, Malawi, Mozambique and e Zimbabwe
____ M. r. stentopicus — Zimbabwe and w-central Mozambique (Manica district)

☐ **Dusky Tit** *Melaniparus funereus*
_____ *M. f. funereus* — Liberia to Cameroon, Zaire, Uganda and Kenya
_____ *M. f. gabela* — W-central Angola (Gabela escarpment)

☐ **Red-throated Tit** *Melaniparus fringillinus*
— Acacia savanna of s Kenya and n Tanzania

☐ **Stripe-breasted Tit** *Melaniparus fasciiventer*
_____ *M. f. fasciiventer* — Montane forests of e Zaire, sw Uganda and Rwanda
_____ *M. f. tanganjicae* — Montane forests of e Zaire (se Kivu Province)
_____ *M. f. kaboboensis* — Montane forests of se Zaire (Mt. Kabobo)

☐ **Somali Tit** *Melaniparus thruppi*
_____ *M. t. thruppi* — Dry acacia of Ethiopia and Somalia
_____ *M. t. barakae* — Dry acacia of sw Somalia to Kenya, Uganda and ne Tanzania

☐ **Miombo Tit** *Melaniparus griseiventris*
— *Miombo* woodlands of Zambia, Tanzania and Zimbabwe

☐ **Ashy Tit** *Melaniparus cinerascens*
_____ *M. c. benguelae* — SW Angola to nw Namibia
_____ *M. c. cinerascens (orphnus)* — Namibia to Botswana, Zimbabwe and South Africa

☐ **Gray Tit** *Melaniparus afer*
_____ *M. a. afer* — Namibia and w Cape Province
_____ *M. a. arens* — Lesotho to sw Orange Free State and e Cape Province

☐ **Great Tit** *Parus major*
_____ *P. m. newtoni* — British Isles
_____ *P. m. major* — Europe to nw Iran, Siberia, Lake Baikal, Altai and Sayan mts.
_____ *P. m. kapustini* — NW China (nw Xinjiang) to Mongolia and e Siberia
_____ *P. m. corsus* — Iberian Peninsula and Corsica
_____ *P. m. mallorcae* — Balearic Islands
_____ *P. m. ecki* — Sardinia
_____ *P. m. excelsus* — NW Africa
_____ *P. m. aphrodite* — S Italy, Sicily, s Greece, Mediterranean islands and Cyprus
_____ *P. m. niethammeri* — Crete
_____ *P. m. terraesanctae* — NW Syria, Lebanon, Israel and Jordan
_____ *P. m. blanfordi (karelini)* — N Iraq and Iran
_____ *P. m. intermedius* — NE Iran and adjacent sw Turkmenistan
_____ *P. m. cashmirensis* — NE Afghanistan to n Pakistan and nw India
_____ *P. m. ziaratensis* — S Afghanistan to n Baluchistan and Pakistan
_____ *P. m. decolorans* — SE Afghanistan (east of Kabul and south of the Hindu Kush)
_____ *P. m. nipalensis* — N India to Nepal, Bhutan, Bangladesh and w Myanmar
_____ *P. m. vauriei* — E Assam (Lakhimpur district) and e Arunachal Pradesh
_____ *P. m. stupae* — Central and peninsular India
_____ *P. m. mahrattarum* — SW India (Kerala) and Sri Lanka
_____ *P. m. templorum* — NE Thailand to s Laos and s Vietnam
_____ *P. m. hainanus* — Hainan (s China)
_____ *P. m. ambiguus* — SE Myanmar, peninsular Thailand, Malaya and Sumatra
_____ *P. m. cinereus* — Java and w Lesser Sundas
_____ *P. m. sarawacensis* — Borneo (w Sarawak)
_____ *P. m. minor* — SE Russia to Japan, Korea, sw China and e Tibet
_____ *P. m. tibetanus* — SW China to se Tibet; single record from Sikkim
_____ *P. m. subtibetanus* — S China to se Tibet and nw Myanmar
_____ *P. m. nubicolus* — SE Myanmar to n Thailand, n Laos and extreme w Tonkin
_____ *P. m. dageletensis* — Ullung I. (South Korea)
_____ *P. m. amamiensis* — N Ryukyu Islands (Amami-O-Shima and Tokuno-Shima)
_____ *P. m. okinawae* — Central Ryukyu Islands (Okinawa and Yagachi)
_____ *P. m. nigriloris* — S Ryukyu Islands (Ishigaki and Iriomote)
_____ *P. m. commixtus* — S China (south of the Yangtze) to Hong Kong and e Tonkin

☐ **Turkestan Tit** *Parus bokharensis*

_____ *P. b. bokharensis* — Russia to Tien Shan and Karatau mts. and nw Afghanistan

_____ *P. b. ferghanensis* — S Kirgiz and w Tien Shan mts. to w Pamirs and Turkestan

_____ *P. b. turkestanicus* — Lake Balkhash to w China (Xinjiang) and sw Mongolia

☐ **Green-backed Tit** *Parus monticolus*

_____ *P. m. monticolus* — W Himalayas to w Nepal and se Tibet

_____ *P. m. yunnanensis* — E Himalayas to ne India, Myanmar, w China and nw Vietnam

_____ *P. m. legendrei* — S Vietnam (Da Lat Plateau)

_____ *P. m. insperatus* — Montane forests of Taiwan

☐ **White-winged Tit** *Parus nuchalis*

Patchily distributed semiarid thorn forests of w and s India

☐ **Black-lored Tit** *Parus xanthogenys*

_____ *P. x. xanthogenys* — Foothills of w Himalayas

_____ *P. x. aplonotus* — N and e peninsular India

_____ *P. x. tranvancoreensis* — S peninsular India

☐ **Yellow-cheeked Tit** *Parus spilonotus*

_____ *P. s. spilonotus* — E Himalayas and adjacent ne Myanmar to s Tibet and sw China

_____ *P. s. subviridis* — NE Indian hill states to Myanmar, n Thailand and nw Laos

_____ *P. s. rex* — S China to nw Vietnam and ne Laos

_____ *P. s. basileus* — S Laos (Bolavens Plateau) and s Vietnam (s Annam)

☐ **Yellow Tit** *Macholophus holsti*

Montane forests of Taiwan

☐ **Blue Tit** *Cyanistes caeruleus*

_____ *C. c. obscurus* — Ireland, Britain and Channel Islands

_____ *C c. caeruleus* — Continental Europe to n Spain, Sicily, n Turkey and n Urals

_____ *C. c. ogilastrae* — Portugal, s Spain, Corsica and Sardinia

_____ *C. c. balearicus* — Majorca I. (Balearic Islands)

_____ *C. c. calamensis* — S Greece, Pelopónnisos, Cyclades, Crete and Rhodes

_____ *C. c. orientalis* — S European Russia (Volga River to central and s Ural Mts.)

_____ *C. c. satunini* — Crimean Pen., Caucasus, Transcaucasia and nw Iran to e Turkey

_____ *C. c. raddei* — N Iran

_____ *C. c. persicus* — SW Iran (Zagros Mountains)

_____ *C. c. ultramarinus* — NW Africa and Pantelleria I. (s Italy)

_____ *C. c. cyrenaicae* — Libya

_____ *C. c. palmensis* — La Palma (w Canary Islands)

_____ *C. c. teneriffae* — Canary Islands (Gomera, Tenerife and Gran Canaria)

_____ *C. c. ombriosus* — Hierro (sw Canary Islands)

_____ *C. c. degener* — E Canary Islands (Fuerteventura and Lanzarote)

☐ **Azure Tit** *Cyanistes cyanus*

_____ *C. c. cyanus* — European Russia to basin of middle Volga River

_____ *C. c. hyperrhiphaeus* — E European Russia to w Siberia and n Kazakstan

_____ *C. c. kotkalensis* — Lowlands of se Kazakstan (south of Lake Balkhash)

_____ *C. c. tianschanicus* — SE Kazakstan to nw China, Manchuria and Pakistan

_____ *C. c. yenisseensis* — SE Siberia to Sea of Japan and lower Amur River

☐ **Yellow-breasted Tit** *Cyanistes flavipectus*

_____ *C. f. carruthersi* — W Pamir Mountains to Fergana basin and e Alayskiy Mountains

_____ *C. f. flavipectus* — W Tien Shan Mountains to n Afghanistan and n Pakistan

_____ *C. f. berezowskii* — N-central China (e Qinghai s of Kokonor on Upper Hwang Ho)

☐ **White-fronted Tit** *Sittiparus semilarvatus*

_____ *S. s. snowi* — N Philippines (n Luzon)

_____ *S. s. semilarvatus* — N Philippines (central and s Luzon)

_____ *S. s. nehrkorni* — S Philippines (Mindanao)

☐ **Varied Tit** *Sittiparus varius*

_____ *S. v. varius*	Kuril Islands, ne China, Korea and main Japanese islands
_____ *S. v. sunsunpi*	Tanegashima (Ryukyu Islands)
_____ *S. v. yakushimensis*	Yakushima (Ryukyu Islands)
_____ *S. v. amamii*	Amami-O-Shima, Tokuno-Shima and Okinawa
_____ *S. v. orii*	Daito Is. (Kita-Daito-jima, Minami-Daito-jima and Daito-jima)
_____ *S. v. olivaceus*	Iriomote (s Ryukyu Islands)
_____ *S. v. castaneoventris*	Taiwan
_____ *S. v. namiyei*	N Izu Islands (To-shima, Nii-jima and Kozu-shima)
_____ *S. v. owstoni*	S Izu Islands (Miyake-jima, Mikura-jima and Hachijo-jima)

☐ **Bridled Titmouse** *Baeolophus wollweberi*

_____ *B. w. vandevenderi*	Oak-juniper forests of Arizona and New Mexico
_____ *B. w. phillipsi*	SE Arizona (south of Gila River) to nw Mexico (Durango)
_____ *B. w. wollweberi*	Central and s highlands of Mexico (Durango to Nuevo León)
_____ *B. w. caliginosus*	W Mexico (Sierra Madre del Sur of Guerrero and Oaxaca)

☐ **Oak Titmouse** *Baeolophus inornatus*

_____ *B. i. sequestriatus*	Interior coast ranges of sw Oregon and nw California
_____ *B. i. inornatus (transpositus, kernensis, restrictus)*	W California (Mendocino to Santa Barbara e to Sierra Nevada)
_____ *B. i. affabilis*	SW California (Ventura County) to n Baja California
_____ *B. i. mohavensis*	Little San Bernardino Mountains of s California
_____ *B. i. ridgwayi*	California (Modoc Plateau south to Providence Mountains)
_____ *B. i. cineraceus*	Cape district of s Baja California

☐ **Juniper Titmouse** *Baeolophus griseus*

_____ *B. g. griseus*	Interior w N Am. (Idaho to Nevada, se Calif., Arizona, ne Sonora)
_____ *B. g. zaleptus*	S Oregon (e of Cascades) to Nevada and e Calif. (Inyo County)

☐ **Tufted Titmouse** *Baeolophus bicolor*

_____ *B. b. bicolor*	S-central Canada (Ontario) to e, central and se US
_____ *B. b. sennetti*	Central and s Texas (s to Brooks County, west to Terrell County)
_____ *B. b. paloduro (dysleptus)*	Texas panhandle and sw Oklahoma; sw Texas and nw Coahuila
_____ *B. b. atricristatus*	S Texas (lower Rio Grande Valley) to se Mexico (Veracruz)

☐ **Yellow-browed Tit** *Sylviparus modestus*

_____ *S. m. simlaensis*	W Himalayas (Kashmir to Uttar Pradesh)
_____ *S. m. modestus*	Nepal to ne India, n Myanmar, sw China, Thailand and n Laos
_____ *S. m. klossi*	S Vietnam (Da Lat Plateau)

☐ **Sultan Tit** *Melanochlora sultanea*

_____ *M. s. sultanea*	Nepal to Assam, Myanmar, n Thailand, n Laos and Vietnam
_____ *M. s. flavocristata*	S Myanmar to s Thailand, Malay Pen., Sumatra and Hainan
_____ *M. s. seorsa*	S China (central Fujian to s Guangxi) to Laos and ne Tonkin
_____ *M. s. gayeti*	Central Annam (Col des Nuages) to s Laos (Bolavens Plateau)

FAMILY: SITTIDAE (Nuthatches—24)

☐ **Chestnut-bellied Nuthatch** *Sitta castanea*

_____ *S. c. castanea*	Foothills of n and central India (Western Ghats)
_____ *S. c. almorae*	Foothills of w Himalayas (Pakistan to e Nepal)
_____ *S. c. cinnamoventris*	E Himalayas (e Nepal to nw Yunnan and Arunachal Pradesh)
_____ *S. c. koelzi*	SE Arunachal Pradesh to Assam and adjacent nw Myanmar
_____ *S. c. tonkinensis*	S Yunnan to n Thailand, n Vietnam, n and central Laos
_____ *S. c. neglecta*	Myanmar to se Yunnan, Thailand, Laos, Cambodia, s Vietnam

☐ **Eurasian Nuthatch** *Sitta europaea*

____	*S. e. caesia*	Britain to Denmark, Carpathian Mts., Pyrénées and Balkan Pen.
____	*S. e. europaea*	Scandinavia and Russia to Volga and Vyatka basins and Ukraine
____	*S. e. asiatica*	E European Russia to Sea of Okhotsk, s Kuril Is. and n Japan
____	*S. e. arctica*	N-central Siberia to Anadyr River (e Russia)
____	*S. e. hispaniensis*	Iberian Peninsula and Morocco
____	*S. e. cisalpina*	S Switzerland, Italy, Sicily and coastal Yugoslavia
____	*S. e. levantina*	W Asia Minor, Levant and s Turkey (e to Euphrates River)
____	*S. e. caucasica*	N and ne Turkey, Caucasus region and Transcaucasia
____	*S. e. rubiginosa*	SE Transcaucasia (Talyshshkiye and Gory mountains) to n Iran
____	*S. e. persica*	Zagros Mountains (sw Iran)
____	*S. e. seorsa*	NW China (e Tien Shan Mountains of n Xinjiang)
____	*S. e. sakhalinensis*	Sakhalin (Russia)
____	*S. e. albifrons*	Kamchatka Peninsula, Paramushir I. and n Kuril Islands
____	*S. e. amurensis*	SE Russia to ne China, Korea and Honshu (n Japan)
____	*S. e. roseillia*	S Japan (se Honshu, Shikoku and Kyushu)
____	*S. e. bedfordi*	Cheju-Do Islands (Korea)
____	*S. e. sinensis*	Central and e China and Taiwan
____	*S. e. nebulosa*	S China (lowlands of s Yunnan)

☐ **Chestnut-vented Nuthatch** *Sitta nagaensis*

____	*S. n. nagaensis (montium)*	N India to central and s China, Myanmar and Thailand
____	*S. n. grisiventris*	S Vietnam and sw Myanmar (Mt. Victoria)

☐ **Kashmir Nuthatch** *Sitta cashmirensis*

Mts. of ne Afghanistan to n Pakistan, nw India and nw Nepal

☐ **White-tailed Nuthatch** *Sitta himalayensis*

Himalayas from n India to se Tibet, sw China and Indochina

☐ **White-browed Nuthatch** *Sitta victoriae*

Alpine forests of sw Myanmar (Mt. Victoria)

☐ **Pygmy Nuthatch** *Sitta pygmaea*

____	*S. p. melanotis*	British Columbia to nw Mexico (Sonora and nw Coahuila)
____	*S. p. pygmaea*	W California (Mendocino County to San Luis Obispo County)
____	*S. p. leuconucha*	S California (San Jacinto and Laguna mts.) to n Baja California
____	*S. p. chihuahuae*	W Mexico (Sierra Madre Occidental of ne Sonora to n Jalisco)
____	*S. p. brunnescens*	SW Mexico (s Jalisco and Michoacán)
____	*S. p. flavinucha*	W Veracruz (Mt. Orizaba) to w Puebla, Morelos and México
____	*S. p. elii*	E Mexico (sw Nuevo León and se Coahuila)

☐ **Brown-headed Nuthatch** *Sitta pusilla*

____	*S. p. pusilla*	Pine forests of se US
____	*S. p. insularis*	Grand Bahama I.

☐ **Corsican Nuthatch** *Sitta whiteheadi*

Montane pine forests of Corsica

☐ **Algerian Nuthatch** *Sitta ledanti*

Montane oak-cedar forests of ne Algeria

☐ **Krueper's Nuthatch** *Sitta krueperi*

Pine, cedar and juniper forests of Turkey to Caucasus Mountains

☐ **Snowy-browed Nuthatch** *Sitta villosa*

____	*S. v. villosa*	Russia to ne China and Korea
____	*S. v. bangsi*	Central China (Qinghai to e Gansu)

☐ **Yunnan Nuthatch** *Sitta yunnanensis*

Mountains of w Sichuan to w Yunnan, se Tibet and nw Guizhou

☐ **Red-breasted Nuthatch** *Sitta canadensis*

Coniferous forests of North America

☐ **White-cheeked Nuthatch** *Sitta leucopsis*

____	*S. l. leucopsis*	Himalayas (ne Afghanistan to nw India and nw Nepal)
____	*S. l. przewalskii*	W China (Qinghai to s Sichuan, sw Gansu, ne Tibet and Yunnan)

☐ **White-breasted Nuthatch** *Sitta carolinensis*

_____	*S. c. tenuissima*	British Columbia and Cascades to Sierra Nevada of n California
_____	*S. c. aculeata*	W Washington to Oregon, California and n Baja (Sierra Juárez)
_____	*S. c. nelsoni*	Rocky Mts. of w US to n Mexico (Sonora and n Chihuahua)
_____	*S. c. carolinensis*	NE North America to Dakotas, Kansas, Oklahoma and e Texas
_____	*S. c. alexandrae*	Mountains of n Baja California (San Pedro Mártir)
_____	*S. c. lagunae*	Mountains of s Baja California (Sierra de la Laguna)
_____	*S. c. oberholseri*	SW Texas (Chisos Mts.) to e Mexico (n Sierra Madre Oriental)
_____	*S. c. mexicana*	Mountains of w Mexico (Sierra Madre Occidental)
_____	*S. c. kinneari*	Mountains of w Mexico (Guerrero and Oaxaca)

☐ **Rock Nuthatch** *Sitta neumayer*

_____	*S. n. neumayer*	Balkan Peninsula
_____	*S. n. syriaca*	W and central Turkey to Syria, Lebanon and Israel
_____	*S. n. rupicola*	Extreme e Turkey to n Iraq and n Iran
_____	*S. n. tschitscherini*	Zagros Mountains (sw Iran)
_____	*S. n. plumbea*	S-central Iran (mountains of s Kerman Province)

☐ **Persian Nuthatch** *Sitta tephronota*

_____	*S. t. dresseri*	Extreme se Turkey to w Iran and Iraq
_____	*S. t. obscura*	S Transcaucasia to n Iran and ne Turkey
_____	*S. t. tephronota*	Extreme e Turkmenistan to Pamirs, Afghanistan and Pakistan
_____	*S. t. iranica*	S Turkmenistan to Uzbekistan (Kyzylkum Desert)

☐ **Velvet-fronted Nuthatch** *Sitta frontalis*

_____	*S. f. frontalis*	Peninsular Thailand to Sumatra, Lingga Arch. and Bangka I.
_____	*S. f. saturatior*	S peninsular Thailand to Malaysia and n Sumatra; Simeulue I.
_____	*S. f. corralipes*	Borneo and Maratua Islands
_____	*S. f. palawana*	S Philippines (Palawan and Balabac)
_____	*S. f. velata*	Java

☐ **Yellow-billed Nuthatch** *Sitta solangiae*

_____	*S. s. solangiae*	N Vietnam (Fan Si Pan Mountains)
_____	*S. s. fortior*	S-central Laos (Langbian Plateau)
_____	*S. s. chienfengensis*	Hainan (s China)

☐ **Sulphur-billed Nuthatch** *Sitta oenochlamys*

_____	*S. o. mesoleuca*	N Philippines (Cordillera Mountains of nw Luzon)
_____	*S. o. isarog*	N Philippines (s and central Luzon)
_____	*S. o. oenochlamys*	Philippines (Cebu, Guimaras, Panay and Negros)
_____	*S. o. lilacea*	Philippines (Samar, Leyte and Biliran)
_____	*S. o. apo*	S Philippines (e Mindanao)
_____	*S. o. zamboanga*	S Philippines (w Mindanao, Basilan and East Blood)

☐ **Blue Nuthatch** *Sitta azurea*

_____	*S. a. expectata*	Malay Peninsula and Sumatra
_____	*S. a. nigriventer*	W Java
_____	*S. a. azurea*	E Java

☐ **Giant Nuthatch** *Sitta magna*

_____	*S. m. ligea*	SW China (extreme s Sichuan, nw Yunnan and sw Guizhou)
_____	*S. m. magna*	S China (w Yunnan) to se Myanmar and nw Thailand

☐ **Beautiful Nuthatch** *Sitta formosa*

Sikkim and Bhutan to Yunnan, Myanmar and nw Tonkin

FAMILY: TICHIDROMIDAE (Wallcreeper—1)

☐ **Wallcreeper** *Tichodroma muraria*
_____	*T. m. muraria*	Europe and sw Asia to n and w Iran
_____	*T. m. nepalensis*	S-central Asia (Turkmenistan) and e Iran to China

FAMILY: CERTHIIDAE (Creepers—7)

☐ **Eurasian Treecreeper** *Certhia familiaris*
_____	*C. f. britannica*	Great Britain and Ireland
_____	*C. f. macrodactyla*	Western Europe to Oder River, Hungary and Yugoslavia
_____	*C. f. corsa*	Corsica
_____	*C. f. familiaris*	Scandinavia and e Europe to w Siberia
_____	*C. f. daurica*	Siberia to Sea of Okhotsk, n Mongolia and ne China
_____	*C. f. orientalis*	Amurland to ne China, Kuril Is., Sakhalin, Hokkaido and Korea
_____	*C. f. japonica*	Japan (Honshu, Shikoku and Kyushu)
_____	*C. f. persica*	Crimean Peninsula, Turkey, Caucasus, Transcaucasus and n Iran
_____	*C. f. tianschanica*	Tien Shan Mts. (Kazakstan) to nw China
_____	*C. f. bianchii*	W-central China (e Qinghai, Gansu, Shaanxi and Shanxi)
_____	*C. f. khamensis*	S China (s Gansu) to s Tibet, Yunnan, ne Myanmar and Bhutan
_____	*C. f. hodgsoni*	W Himalayas (east to Himachal Pradesh)
_____	*C. f. mandellii*	Himalayas (Himachal Pradesh to extreme w Arunachal Pradesh)

☐ **Brown Creeper** *Certhia americana*
_____	*C. a. alascensis*	S-central Alaska; winters to Arizona and New Mexico
_____	*C. a. occidentalis*	Coastal se Alaska to central California
_____	*C. a. stewarti*	Queen Charlotte Islands (British Columbia)
_____	*C. a. montana*	British Columbia to Cascades, Dakotas, s Arizona and w Texas
_____	*C. a. zelotes (phillipsi)*	S Oregon through Cascades and Coast ranges to s California
_____	*C. a. americana*	N Saskatchewan to Newfoundland and ne US; winters to Mexico
_____	*C. a. idahoensis*	N Idaho and nw Montana to central Alberta; winters to Arizona
_____	*C. a. nigrescens*	Great Smoky Mountains of Tennessee and North Carolina
_____	*C. a. albescens*	Mountains of se Arizona, sw New Mexico and nw Mexico
_____	*C. a. alticola*	Mountains of s Mexico
_____	*C. a. pernigra*	Mountains of extreme s Mexico (Chiapas) and n Guatemala
_____	*C. a. extima*	Mountains of e Guatemala, Honduras and nw Nicaragua

☐ **Short-toed Treecreeper** *Certhia brachydactyla*
_____	*C. b. megarhyncha*	W Europe (east to w Germany)
_____	*C. b. brachydactyla*	Continental Europe (east of *megarhyncha*)
_____	*C. b. mauritanica*	Morocco, Algeria and nw Tunisia
_____	*C. b. dorothea*	Cyprus
_____	*C. b. harterti*	Asia Minor and the Caucasus Mountains

☐ **Bar-tailed Treecreeper** *Certhia himalayana*
_____	*C. h. taeniura*	Central Asia and Afghanistan (north of the Hindu Kush)
_____	*C. h. himalayana*	E Afghanistan, n Pakistan and Himalayas (east to central Nepal)
_____	*C. h. yunnanensis*	SW China and adjacent Myanmar
_____	*C. h. ripponi*	W Myanmar (Mt. Victoria)

☐ **Rusty-flanked Treecreeper** *Certhia nipalensis*
	Mountains of w Nepal to ne Myanmar, se Tibet and sw China

☐ **Brown-throated Treecreeper** *Certhia discolor*
_____	*C. d. discolor*	Himalayas of Nepal to s Tibet and nw India
_____	*C. d. manipurensis*	NE India (south of the Brahmaputra) and adjacent sw Myanmar
_____	*C. d. shanensis*	NE Myanmar to sw China (Yunnan), Thailand and nw Vietnam
_____	*C. d. meridionalis*	S Vietnam (Da Lat Plateau)
_____	*C. d. laotiana*	Laos (Tranninh Plateau)

☐ **Spotted Creeper** *Salpornis spilonotus*

____ *S. s. emini*	Senegal to Angola, ne Zaire and nw Uganda
____ *S. s. erlangeri*	Ethiopia
____ *S. s. salvadori*	Extreme e Uganda to w Kenya, Tanzania, Zambia and Malawi
____ *S. s. xylodromus*	Zimbabwe and adjacent Mozambique
____ *S. s. spilonotus*	Central and western India
____ *S. s. rajputanae*	NW India (cent. and se Rajasthan from Sambhar to Mount Abu)

FAMILY: RHABDORNITHIDAE (Philippine Creepers—3)

☐ **Stripe-sided Rhabdornis** *Rhabdornis mysticalis*

____ *R. m. mysticalis*	Philippines (Luzon, Masbate, Negros, Catanduanes and Panay)
____ *R. m. minor*	Philippines (Basilan, Samar, Leyte, Bohol, Dinagat, Mindanao)

☐ **Long-billed Rhabdornis** *Rhabdornis grandis*

N Philippines (Sierra Madre Mountains of n Luzon)

☐ **Stripe-breasted Rhabdornis** *Rhabdornis inornatus*

____ *R. i. inornatus*	Philippines (montane forests of Samar)
____ *R. i. leytensis*	Philippines (Leyte and Biliran)
____ *R. i. rabori*	Philippines (Negros)
____ *R. i. alaris (zamboanga)*	S Philippineas (Mindanao)

FAMILY: REMIZIDAE (Penduline Tits—13)

☐ **Verdin** *Auriparus flaviceps*

____ *A. f. acaciarum*	Deserts of sw US to n Baja California and nw Mexico
____ *A. f. ornatus*	SE Arizona to Oklahoma, Texas, s Coahuila and Tamaulipas
____ *A. f. flaviceps (fraterculus)*	Central Baja California; ne Sonora to n Sinaloa and Tiburón I.
____ *A. f. lamprocephalus*	S Baja California, San José and San Francisco islands
____ *A. f. sinaloae*	NW Mexico (nw Sinaloa from Culiacán to Guamuchil)
____ *A. f. hidalgensis*	W Mexico (ne Jalisco to s San Luis Potosí and e Hidalgo)

☐ **Eurasian Penduline-Tit** *Remiz pendulinus*

____ *R. p. pendulinus*	Europe to Ural Mountains, Caucasus Mountains and w Turkey
____ *R. p. menzbieri*	S and e Turkey to Armenia and nw Iran
____ *R. p. caspius*	NW Kazakstan (Volga and Ural plains) to Caspian Sea
____ *R. p. jaxarticus*	E Urals to w Siberia and n Kazakstan

☐ **Black-headed Penduline-Tit** *Remiz macronyx*

____ *R. m. macronyx*	SW Kazakstan to Uzbekistan, Tajikistan and se Turkmenistan
____ *R. m. neglectus*	SW Turkmenistan and n Iran (Atrak and Gorgan valleys)
____ *R. m. nigricans*	SE Iran
____ *R. m. ssaposhnikowi*	SE Kazakstan (region of lakes Balkhash, Sasykkol and Alakol)

☐ **White-crowned Penduline-Tit** *Remiz coronatus*

Deciduous woodlands of s-central Eurasia; winters to nw India

☐ **Chinese Penduline-Tit** *Remiz consobrinus*

Reedbeds and marshes of n China; winters to s China

☐ **Sennar Penduline-Tit** *Anthoscopus punctifrons*

Savanna and acacia of sub-Saharan Africa

☐ **Mouse-colored Penduline-Tit** *Anthoscopus musculus*

	Thornscrub of Ethiopia and Somalia to ne Tanzania

☐ **Yellow Penduline-Tit** *Anthoscopus parvulus*

____ *A. p. senegalensis*	Senegal to Nigeria and Lake Chad
____ *A. p. aureus*	N Ghana
____ *A. p. citrinus*	N Cameroon to Central African Republic
____ *A. p. parvulus*	Lake Chad to s Sudan and ne Zaire

☐ **Forest Penduline-Tit** *Anthoscopus flavifrons*

____ *A. f. waldroni*	Humid forests of Ghana to Ivory Coast and Liberia
____ *A. f. flavifrons*	E Nigeria to Cameroon, Gabon and n Zaire
____ *A. f. ruthae*	SE Zaire (se Kivu Province)

☐ **African Penduline-Tit** *Anthoscopus caroli*

____ *A. c. ansorgei*	Angola to sw Zaire
____ *A. c. caroli*	SW Angola to Namibia, Botswana, Zimbabwe, s Mozambique
____ *A. c. roccatii*	S Uganda to Rwanda, ne Zaire and extreme nw Tanzania
____ *A. c. rhodesiae*	SE Zaire to ne Zambia and sw Tanzania (Ufipa Plateau)
____ *A. c. sylviella (rothschildi)*	S-central Kenya (e of Rift Valley) to central Tanzania
____ *A. c. sharpei*	SW Kenya to extreme nw Tanzania
____ *A. c. robertsi (taruensis)*	SE Kenya to se Zambia, e Tanzania, Malawi and Mozambique
____ *A. c. pallescens*	W-central Tanzania (Kigoma Province)
____ *A. c. winterbottomi*	NW Zambia and adjacent s Zaire (s Shaba)
____ *A. c. hellmayri*	S Mozambique to e Zimbabwe and South Africa
____ *A. c. rankinei*	Zambesi River between ne Zimbabwe and nw Mozambique

☐ **Southern Penduline-Tit** *Anthoscopus minutus*

____ *A. m. damarensis*	Angola to n Namibia, Botswana, Zimbabwe and w Transvaal
____ *A. m. minutus*	S Namibia to w Cape Province and w Orange Free State
____ *A. m. gigi*	SE Cape Province (Little Karoo and s Great Karoo)

☐ **Fire-capped Tit** *Cephalopyrus flammiceps*

____ *C. f. flammiceps*	W Himalayas (Pakistan to Garhwal and w Nepal)
____ *C. f. olivaceus*	E Himalayas (e Nepal to se Tibet and central China)

☐ **Tit-hylia** *Pholidornis rushiae*

____ *P. r. ussheri*	Sierra Leone to Ghana
____ *P. r. rushiae*	S Nigeria to central Cameroon and Gabon
____ *P. r. bedfordi*	Bioko (Gulf of Guinea)
____ *P. r. denti*	SE Cameroon to nw Angola, C African Rep., e Zaire and Uganda

FAMILY: NECTARINIIDAE (Sunbirds and Spiderhunters—130)

☐ **Ruby-cheeked Sunbird** *Chalcoparia singalensis*

____ *C. s. assamensis*	E Nepal to Bangladesh, Assam, sw China, n Myanmar, n Thailand
____ *C. s. internota*	S Myanmar to s Thailand (Isthmus of Kra)
____ *C. s. koratensis*	Plateau of e Thailand to Laos and Vietnam
____ *C. s. interposita*	S peninsular Thailand (south of Isthmus of Kra)
____ *C. s. singalensis*	Malay Peninsula
____ *C. s. panopsia*	Islands off w Sumatra (Banyak, Nias and Tanahmasa)
____ *C. s. sumatrana*	Sumatra and Belitung I.
____ *C. s. pallida*	North Natuna Islands
____ *C. s. borneana*	Borneo and Banggi I.
____ *C. s. bantenensis*	Extreme w Java (Banten region)
____ *C. s. phoenicotis*	W-central and e Java

☐ **Scarlet-tufted Sunbird** *Deleornis fraseri*
_____ *D. f. idius*	Guinea to Sierra Leone, Mali, Ivory Coast, Ghana and Togo
_____ *D. f. cameroonensis*	S Nigeria to s Cameroon, Central African Rep. and nw Angola
_____ *D. f. fraseri*	Bioko (Gulf of Guinea)

☐ **Gray-headed Sunbird** *Deleornis axillaris*

NE Zaire to Uganda and Tanzania

☐ **Plain-backed Sunbird** *Anthreptes reichenowi*
_____ *A. r. yokanae*	Lowland coastal forests of se Kenya and ne Tanzania
_____ *A. r. reichenowi*	Local in e Zimbabwe, s Mozambique and ne South Africa

☐ **Anchieta's Sunbird** *Anthreptes anchietae*

Angola to se Zaire, Zambia, sw Tanzania, Malawi, n Mozambique

☐ **Plain Sunbird** *Anthreptes simplex*

S Myanmar to Malaya, Sumatra, Borneo, Nias I. and N Natuna Is.

☐ **Plain-throated Sunbird** *Anthreptes malacensis*
_____ *A. m. malacensis*	Myanmar to pen. Thailand, Indochina, Sumatra and s Borneo
_____ *A. m. mjobergi*	Maratua Islands (off Borneo)
_____ *A. m. borneensis*	N Borneo
_____ *A. m. birgitae*	N Philippines (Luzon, Mindoro and Catanduanes)
_____ *A. m. chlorigaster*	Cebu, Masbate, Negros, Panay, Sibuyan, Tablas, Romblon, Ticao
_____ *A. m. griseigularis*	Philippines (Samar, Leyte, Sakuyok, Camiguin Sur, ne Mindanao)
_____ *A. m. heliolusius (basilanicus)*	S Philippines (Basilan, w and central Mindanao and Talicud)
_____ *A. m. cagayensis*	Cagayan Sulu I. (Sulu Sea)
_____ *A. m. paraguae*	S Philippines (Balabac, Culion, Palawan and Calauit)
_____ *A. m. wiglesworthi*	Sulu Archipelago (Bongao, Jolo, Tawitawi and Basbas)
_____ *A. m. iris*	S Philippines (Sibutu and Sitanki)
_____ *A. m. heliocalus*	Sangihe and Siau islands (off Sulawesi)
_____ *A. m. celebensis*	Sulawesi and adjacent islands
_____ *A. m. extremus*	Banggai Islands (Peleng and Banggai) and Sula Islands
_____ *A. m. convergens*	W Lesser Sundas (Lombok to Pantar and Alor)
_____ *A. m. rubrigena*	Sumba (Lesser Sundas)
_____ *A. m. anambae*	Anambas Islands (South China Sea)

☐ **Red-throated Sunbird** *Anthreptes rhodolaema*

Lowlands of s Myanmar, pen. Thailand, Malaya, Sumatra, Borneo

☐ **Mouse-brown Sunbird** *Anthreptes gabonicus*

Senegambia to Cameroon, Gabon and nw Zaire

☐ **Western Violet-backed Sunbird** *Anthreptes longuemarei*
_____ *A. l. longuemarei*	Senegambia to Guinea
_____ *A. l. haussarum*	Liberia to Cameroon, n Zaire, s Sudan, Uganda and w Kenya
_____ *A. l. angolensis*	S Zaire to Angola, Zambia, Malawi and w Tanzania
_____ *A. l. nyassae*	SE Tanzania to se Malawi, n Mozambique and e Zimbabwe

☐ **Kenya Violet-backed Sunbird** *Anthreptes orientalis*
_____ *A. o. orientalis*	SE Sudan to Ethiopia, n Uganda, Kenya and ne Tanzania
_____ *A. o. neumanni*	Somalia to ne Kenya

☐ **Uluguru Violet-backed Sunbird** *Anthreptes neglectus*

Lowland coastal forests of se Kenya, Tanzania and n Mozambique

☐ **Violet-tailed Sunbird** *Anthreptes aurantium*

Cameroon to Gabon, ne Angola, Cent. African Rep. and ne Zaire

☐ **Little Green Sunbird** *Anthreptes seimundi*
_____ *A. s. kruensis*	Sierra Leone to Togo
_____ *A. s. seimundi*	Bioko (Gulf of Guinea)
_____ *A. s. traylori*	Nigeria to Cameroon, n Angola, Zaire, s Sudan, Rwanda, Uganda

☐ **Green Sunbird** *Anthreptes rectirostris*
_____ *A. r. rectirostris*	Sierra Leone to Ghana
_____ *A. r. tephrolaema*	S Nigeria to Angola, s Sudan, Uganda and w Kenya; Bioko

☐ **Banded Sunbird** *Anthreptes rubritorques*

NE Tanzania (Usambara, Nguru and Uluguru mountains)

☐ **Collared Sunbird** *Hedydipna collaris*
_____ *H. c. subcollaris*   Guinea-Bissau to Nigeria
_____ *H. c. hypodilus*   Bioko (Gulf of Guinea)
_____ *H. c. somereni*   Extreme se Nigeria to n Zaire, nw Angola and sw Sudan
_____ *H. c. djamdjamensis*   S Ethiopia
_____ *H. c. garguensis*   E Angola to se Sudan, Uganda, Kenya, nw Tanzania and Zambia
_____ *H. c. elachior*   E Kenya to ne Tanzania, Manda, Zanzibar and Mafia islands
_____ *H. c. zambesiana*   N Namibia to s Tanzania, Zambia, s Mozambique, e Cape Prov.
_____ *H. c. zuluensis*   Highlands of e Zimbabwe and adjacent w Mozambique
_____ *H. c. chobiensis*   Zimbabwe (Limpopo R. drainage) to Mozambique and n Transvaal
_____ *H. c. collaris*   S Natal to w Swaziland, s Zululand and e Cape Province

☐ **Pygmy Sunbird** *Hedydipna platura*

SW Mauritania to n Nigeria, ne Zaire, s Sudan and n Uganda

☐ **Nile Valley Sunbird** *Hedydipna metallica*

N Egypt to Sudan, n Ethiopia, Somalia and sw Arabia

☐ **Amani Sunbird** *Hedydipna pallidigaster*

Coastal se Kenya (Sokoke Forest) and ne Tanzania (rare)

☐ **Purple-naped Sunbird** *Hypogramma hypogrammicum*
_____ *H. h. lisettae*   S China (w Yunnan) to n Myanmar, n Thailand and c Indochina
_____ *H. h. mariae*   Cambodia and s Indochina
_____ *H. h. nuchale*   S Myanmar to s Thailand and Malay Peninsula
_____ *H. h. hypogrammicum*   Sumatra and Borneo
_____ *H. h. natunense*   North Natuna Islands (South China Sea)

☐ **Reichenbach's Sunbird** *Anabathmis reichenbachii*

Liberia to Ivory Coast, Nigeria, Cameroon, n Zaire and ne Angola

☐ **Principe Sunbird** *Anabathmis hartlaubii*

Lowlands of Príncipe (Gulf of Guinea)

☐ **Newton's Sunbird** *Anabathmis newtonii*

Forests of São Tomé (Gulf of Guinea)

☐ **Sao Tome Sunbird** *Dreptes thomensis*

Montane forests of São Tomé (Gulf of Guinea)

☐ **Orange-breasted Sunbird** *Anthobaphes violacea*

Heathlands and *protea* shrubs of Cape Province (South Africa)

☐ **Green-headed Sunbird** *Cyanomitra verticalis*
_____ *C. v. verticalis*   Senegambia to Nigeria
_____ *C. v. cyanocephala*   Cameroon to Gabon, n Angola and e Zaire
_____ *C. v. viridisplendens*   E Zaire to s Sudan, w Kenya, Tanzania, Malawi and ne Zambia
_____ *C. v. bohndorffi*   Coastal Equatorial Guinea to Gabon and Zaire

☐ **Blue-throated Brown Sunbird** *Cyanomitra cyanolaema*
_____ *C. c. magnirostrata*   Sierra Leone to Ghana
_____ *C. c. octaviae*   Togo to Cameroon, n Angola, Zaire, Uganda and nw Tanzania
_____ *C. c. cyanolaema*   Bioko (Gulf of Guinea)

☐ **Blue-headed Sunbird** *Cyanomitra alinae*
_____ *C. a. marungensis*   E Zaire (Marungu highlands)
_____ *C. a. alinae*   Montane forests of e Zaire and w Uganda
_____ *C. a. tanganijicae*   Montane forests of se Zaire, Rwanda and Burundi
_____ *C. a. derooi*   Highlands west of Lake Albert and Lake Edward
_____ *C. a. kaboboensis*   E Zaire (montane forests of Mt. Kabobo)

☐ **Cameroon Sunbird** *Cyanomitra oritis*
_____ *C. o. poensis*   Montane forests of Bioko (Gulf of Guinea)
_____ *C. o. bansoensis*   Highlands of Cameroon
_____ *C. o. oritis*   Montane forests of se Nigeria and s Cameroon

☐ **Bannerman's Sunbird** *Cyanomitra bannermani*

N Angola to se Zaire and extreme nw Zambia

☐ **Eastern Olive-Sunbird** *Cyanomitra olivacea*
_____ *C. o. neglecta*
_____ *C. o. changamwensis*
_____ *C. o. alfredi*
_____ *C. o. olivacina*
_____ *C. o. olivacea*

Highlands of central Kenya (Aberdare Mts.) to n-central Tanzania
Coastal e Kenya, Tanzania and Mafia I.
S Tanzania to Malawi, Mozambique (n of the Zambezi) and Zambia
Coastal plains of e Mozambique and n Natal
Lowlands of central Natal

☐ **Western Olive-Sunbird** *Cyanomitra obscura*
_____ *C. o. guineensis*
_____ *C. o. cephaelis*
_____ *C. o. obscura*
_____ *C. o. ragazzii (vincenti, lowei)*
_____ *C. o. granti*
_____ *C. o. sclateri*

Guinea to w Ghana
E Ghana to s Nigeria, Cameroon, e Zaire and n Angola
Príncipe and Bioko (Gulf of Guinea)
Sudan and c Ethiopia to Kenya, Tanzania, n Zambia and n Malawi
Zanzibar and Pemba I.
E Zimbabwe and immediately adjacent Mozambique

☐ **Mouse-colored Sunbird** *Cyanomitra veroxii*
_____ *C. v. fischeri*
_____ *C. v. zanzibarica*
_____ *C. v. veroxii*

S Somalia to e Kenya, Tanzania, Mozambique and n Natal
Zanzibar
E Natal to e Cape Province

☐ **Buff-throated Sunbird** *Chalcomitra adelberti*
_____ *C. a. adelberti*
_____ *C. a. eboensis*

Sierra Leone to Ghana
Togo to se Nigeria

☐ **Carmelite Sunbird** *Chalcomitra fuliginosa*
_____ *C. f. aurea*
_____ *C. f. fuliginosa*

Sierra Leone to Liberia, Nigeria, Cameroon and Gabon
S Zaire to nw Angola

☐ **Green-throated Sunbird** *Chalcomitra rubescens*
_____ *C. r. stangerii*
_____ *C. r. rubescens (crossensis)*

Bioko (Gulf of Guinea)
Cameroon to n Angola, se Sudan, Kenya, Tanzania and Zambia

☐ **Amethyst Sunbird** *Chalcomitra amethystina*
_____ *C. a. kirkii*
_____ *C. a. deminuta*
_____ *C. a. amethystina (adjuncta)*

SE Zaire to central Tanzania, e Zambia and Zimbabwe
Gabon to Angola, sw Zaire, w Zambia, and nw Botswana
S Mozambique to Transvaal, s Natal, and Cape Province

☐ **Scarlet-chested Sunbird** *Chalcomitra senegalensis*
_____ *C. s. senegalensis*
_____ *C. s. acik (adamauae)*
_____ *C. s. cruentata*
_____ *C. s. lamperti*
_____ *C. s. gutturalis (inaestimata, saturatior)*

Senegambia to n Ghana and n Nigeria
Cameroon to ne Zaire, Cent. African Rep., sw Sudan, nw Uganda
SE Sudan, Eritrea and Ethiopia
E Zaire to Uganda, Kenya and Tanzania
Angola to n Namibia, Zambia, Botswana, Zimbabwe, ne S Africa

☐ **Hunter's Sunbird** *Chalcomitra hunteri*

Extreme se Sudan to s Ethiopia, Somalia, Kenya and ne Tanzania

☐ **Socotra Sunbird** *Chalcomitra balfouri*

Socotra (off ne Somalia)

☐ **Purple-rumped Sunbird** *Leptocoma zeylonica*
_____ *L. z. flaviventris (sola)*
_____ *L. z. zeylonica*

Peninsular India (n to Bombay and e to Bangladesh); w Myanmar
Sri Lanka

☐ **Crimson-backed Sunbird** *Leptocoma minima*

Foothills of coastal w peninsular India

☐ **Copper-throated Sunbird** *Leptocoma calcostetha*

Mangroves and scrub of SE Asia, Palawan and Greater Sundas

547

☐ **Purple-throated Sunbird** *Leptocoma sperata*

____ L. s. brasiliana (phayrei)	S Thailand to Myanmar, Malay Pen., Sumatra, Borneo and Java
____ L. s. emmae	Cambodia to s Laos and s Vietnam
____ L. s. mecynorhyncha	Simeulue I. (off Sumatra)
____ L. s. eumecis	Anambas Islands (South China Sea)
____ L. s. axantha	North Natuna Islands (South China Sea)
____ L. s. henkei	Philippines (Luzon, Babuyan Claro, Calayan, Camiguin Norte)
____ L. s. sperata	N Philippines (Luzon, Polillo and Catanduanes)
____ L. s. marinduquensis	Philippines (Marinduque)
____ L. s. juliae (davaoensis, theresae)	S Philippines (w Mindanao, Basilan and Sulu Archipelago)
____ L. s. oenopa	Sumatra and Nias I.

☐ **Black Sunbird** *Leptocoma sericea*

____ L. s. talautensis	Talaud Islands (Karakelong, Salebabu, Kabruang and Sara)
____ L. s. sangirensis	Sangihe, Siau and Ruang islands
____ L. s. grayi	N Sulawesi, Bangka, Lembeh and Manadotua islands
____ L. s. porphyrolaema	E and s Sulawesi, Muna, Labuan, Blanda, Butung and Togian is.
____ L. s. auriceps	Banggai Islands, Sula Islands and Moluccas
____ L. s. auricapilla	Kayoa (n Moluccas)
____ L. s. proserpina	Buru (s Moluccas)
____ L. s. aspasioides (chlorocephala)	S Moluccas (Seram, Ambon and adj. islands) and Aru Islands
____ L. s. chlorolaema	Kai Islands (Kai Kecil and Kai Besar)
____ L. s. sericea	Mainland New Guinea (except for southeast)
____ L. s. vicina	SE New Guinea
____ L. s. mariae	Kofiau I. (w New Guinea)
____ L. s. cochrani	Misol and Waigeo islands (w New Guinea)
____ L. s. maforensis	Numfor I. (Geelvink Bay off n New Guinea)
____ L. s. salvadorii	Yapen I. (Geelvink Bay off n New Guinea)
____ L. s. mysorensis	Biak I. (n New Guinea)
____ L. s. nigriscapularis	Meos Num and Rani islands (south of Biak I.)
____ L. s. veronica	Liki I. (off n coast of w New Guinea)
____ L. s. cornelia	Tarawai I. (n New Guinea off mouth of Sepik River)
____ L. s. christianae	D'Entrecasteaux and Louisiade archipelagos
____ L. s. caeruleogula	Bismarck Archipelago (New Britain and Umboi)
____ L. s. corinna	Bismarck Arch. (New Ireland, New Hanover, Tabar and Lihir)
____ L. s. eichhorni	Feni I. (Bismarck Archipelago)

☐ **Bocage's Sunbird** *Nectarinia bocagii*

Highlands of central Angola to s Zaire

☐ **Purple-breasted Sunbird** *Nectarinia purpureiventris*

Montane forests of e Zaire, w Uganda, Rwanda and Burundi

☐ **Tacazze Sunbird** *Nectarinia tacazze*

____ N. t. tacazze	Highlands of Eritrea and Ethiopia
____ N. t. jacksoni	Mountains of se Sudan to e Uganda, w Kenya and ne Tanzania

☐ **Bronze Sunbird** *Nectarinia kilimensis*

____ N. k. gadowi	Highlands of central Angola
____ N. k. kilimensis	Highlands of e Zaire to Uganda, w Kenya and Tanzania
____ N. k. arturi	Highlands of s Tanzania to Malawi, ne Zambia and e Zimbabwe

☐ **Golden-winged Sunbird** *Nectarinia reichenowi*

____ N. r. shellyae	Montane forests of e Zaire
____ N. r. lathburyi	Montane forests of extreme n Kenya
____ N. r. reichenowi	Highlands of Kenya to se Uganda and ne Tanzania

☐ **Red-tufted Sunbird** *Nectarinia johnstoni*

____ N. j. johnstoni	Highlands of w Kenya and n Tanzania
____ N. j. dartmouthi	Montane forests of e Zaire and w Uganda
____ N. j. itombwensis	Itombwe Mountains (e Zaire)
____ N. j. nyikensis (salvadorii)	Montane forests of s Tanzania to Zambia and w Malawi

548

☐ **Malachite Sunbird** *Nectarinia famosa*
_____ *N. f. cupreonitens (aeneigularis)*   E Zaire to se Sudan, Ethiopia, Uganda, Kenya, Tanzania, Malawi
_____ *N. f. famosa (major)*   Mountains of e Zimbabwe, Transvaal, Natal, Lesotho and S Africa

☐ **Olive-bellied Sunbird** *Cinnyris chloropygius*
_____ *C. c. kempi*   Senegambia to Ivory Coast
_____ *C. c. chloropygius (lühderi, insularis)*   Ghana to s Nigeria, Cameroon, nw Angola, cent. Zaire; Bioko
_____ *C. c. orphogaster*   NE Angola to e Zaire, s Sudan, Uganda, Kenya and w Tanzania
_____ *C. c. bineschensis*   SW Ethiopia (Binescho region)

☐ **Tiny Sunbird** *Cinnyris minullus*
   Sierra Leone to Cameroon, Gabon, e Zaire and w Uganda; Bioko

☐ **Miombo Sunbird** *Cinnyris manoensis*
_____ *C. m. pintoi*   Central Angola to se Zaire and w Zambia
_____ *C. m. manoensis*   S Tanzania to se Zambia, Zimbabwe and n Mozambique

☐ **Southern Double-collared Sunbird** *Cinnyris chalybeus*
_____ *C. c. subalaris (capricornensis)*   N Transvaal to Swaziland, Natal and e Cape Province
_____ *C. c. chalybeus*   S Cape Province

☐ **Neergaard's Sunbird** *Cinnyris neergaardi*
   Coastal scrub of se Mozambique to extreme n Natal

☐ **Stuhlmann's Sunbird** *Cinnyris stuhlmanni*
_____ *C. s. stuhlmanni*   Ruwenzori Mountains (e Zaire and w Uganda)
_____ *C. s. chapini*   E Zaire and s Burundi (mts. west of Lake Edward to Mt. Kabobo)
_____ *C. s. graueri*   Kivu Volcanos, Rwanda and sw Uganda (Mt. Muhavura)

☐ **Prigogine's Sunbird** *Cinnyris prigoginei*
   Montane forests of se Zaire and w Uganda

☐ **Montane Double-collared Sunbird** *Cinnyris ludovicensis*
_____ *C. l. ludovicensis*   Montane forests of w Angola
_____ *C. l. whytei*   Montane forests of ne Zambia and w Malawi (Nyika Plateau)

☐ **Northern Double-collared Sunbird** *Cinnyris preussi*
_____ *C. p. preussi*   Highlands of se Nigeria to Cameroon
_____ *C. p. kikuyensis*   Highlands of Uganda to se Sudan and w Kenya

☐ **Greater Double-collared Sunbird** *Cinnyris afer*
   W Cape Province (east to Great Fish River)

☐ **Regal Sunbird** *Cinnyris regius*
_____ *C. r. regius*   Ruwenzori Mountains (e Zaire and w Uganda)
_____ *C. r. kivuensis*   Montane forests of se Zaire, sw Uganda, Rwanda and Burundi
_____ *C. r. anderseni*   Kungwe-Mahare Mountains (extreme w Tanzania)

☐ **Rockefeller's Sunbird** *Cinnyris rockefelleri*
   Alpine moorlands of e Zaire

☐ **Eastern Double-collared Sunbird** *Cinnyris mediocris*
_____ *C. m. mediocris*   Highlands of Kenya and n Tanzania
_____ *C. m. usambarica*   Highlands of se Kenya (Taita Hills) and ne Tanzania
_____ *C. m. fuelleborni*   Highlands of Tanzania to Malawi and Zambia
_____ *C. m. bensoni*   Highlands of Malawi and n Mozambique

☐ **Moreau's Sunbird** *Cinnyris moreaui*
   Nguru, Ukaguru and Uvidunda mountains (e Tanzania)

☐ **Beautiful Sunbird** *Cinnyris pulchellus*
_____ *C. p. pulchellus (algra, lucidipectus)*   Senegal to Mali, s Niger (Aïr Massif) and e Sudan
_____ *C. p. melanogastra*   Eritrea to Ethiopia, ne Zaire, Uganda, Kenya and sw Tanzania

☐ **Loveridge's Sunbird** *Cinnyris loveridgei*
   Uluguru Mountains (e Tanzania)

☐ **Mariqua Sunbird** *Cinnyris mariquensis*
_____ *C. m. osiris* — Extreme se Sudan to Eritrea, Ethiopia, n Kenya and n Uganda
_____ *C. m. suahelicus* — E Zaire to central Uganda, Rwanda, Tanzania and ne Zambia
_____ *C. m. mariquensis* — S Angola to n Namibia, sw Zambia, Zimbabwe and ne S Africa

☐ **Shelley's Sunbird** *Cinnyris shelleyi*
_____ *C. s. shelleyi* — Extreme se Zaire to se Tanzania, e Zambia and n Mozambique
_____ *C. s. hofmani* — NE Tanzania (Pangani River to Morogoro region)

☐ **Congo Sunbird** *Cinnyris congensis* — Zaire and Congo (banks of upper Congo and Ubangi rivers)

☐ **Red-chested Sunbird** *Cinnyris erythrocerca* — S Sudan to e Zaire, Uganda, w Kenya and nw Tanzania

☐ **Black-bellied Sunbird** *Cinnyris nectarinioides*
_____ *C. n. erlangeri* — Savanna of se Ethiopia and s Somalia
_____ *C. n. nectarinioides* — Lowlands of e Kenya to extreme ne Tanzania

☐ **Purple-banded Sunbird** *Cinnyris bifasciatus*
_____ *C. b. bifasciatus* — Gabon to central Angola
_____ *C. b. microrhynchus* — NE Angola to Uganda, n Malawi, n Mozambique and Zanzibar
_____ *C. b. strophium* — SE Zambia to Zimbabwe, s Malawi, s Mozambique and n Natal

☐ **Tsavo Sunbird** *Cinnyris tsavoensis* — S Somalia to e Kenya and ne Tanzania

☐ **Violet-breasted Sunbird** *Cinnyris chalcomelas* — Savanna of s Somalia and e Kenya

☐ **Pemba Sunbird** *Cinnyris pembae* — Pemba I. (off se Tanzania)

☐ **Orange-tufted Sunbird** *Cinnyris bouvieri* — Extreme se Nigeria to Cameroon, Gabon, n Angola and w Kenya

☐ **Palestine Sunbird** *Cinnyris oseus*
_____ *C. o. decorsei* — Lake Chad to s Sudan, extreme ne Zaire and nw Uganda
_____ *C. o. oseus* — Syria, Israel and Arabia (east to s Oman)

☐ **Shining Sunbird** *Cinnyris habessinicus*
_____ *C. h. habessinicus* — NE Sudan to Eritrea and w Ethiopia
_____ *C. h. turkanae* — SE Sudan to s Ethiopia, s Somalia, n Kenya and ne Uganda
_____ *C. h. alter* — NW Somalia and adjacent Ethiopia
_____ *C. h. kinneari* — W Saudi Arabia
_____ *C. h. hellmayri* — S Arabia

☐ **Splendid Sunbird** *Cinnyris coccinigaster* — Senegambia to sw Mali, Gabon, ne Zaire, sw Sudan and Uganda

☐ **Johanna's Sunbird** *Cinnyris johannae*
_____ *C. j. fasciatus* — Sierra Leone to Benin
_____ *C. j. johannae* — Nigeria and Cameroon to e Zaire

☐ **Superb Sunbird** *Cinnyris superbus*
_____ *C. s. ashantiensis* — Sierra Leone to Togo
_____ *C. s. nigeriae* — S Nigeria
_____ *C. s. superbus (buvuma)* — S Cameroon to Angola, Zaire, extreme w Kenya and w Tanzania
_____ *C. s. buvuma* — Zaire to Uganda and Kenya

☐ **Rufous-winged Sunbird** *Cinnyris rufipennis* — Known from 2 specimens from e Tanzania (Udzungwa Mts.)

☐ **Oustalet's Sunbird** *Cinnyris oustaleti*
_____ *C. o. oustaleti* — Central and s Angola (Huila to Cuanza Sul and n Bie)
_____ *C. o. rhodesiae* — N Zambia to Malawi and extreme sw Tanzania

☐ **White-breasted Sunbird** *Cinnyris talatala*

Angola to se Zaire, s Tanzania, Mozambique and e South Africa

☐ **Variable Sunbird** *Cinnyris venustus*

_____ *C. v. venustus* — Senegal to Liberia, Nigeria and n Cameroon
_____ *C. v. falkensteini (niassae, kuanzae)* — Gabon to n Angola, e Zaire, Kenya, Tanzania, Zambia, Zimbabwe
_____ *C. v. igneiventris* — Highlands of extreme e Zaire and w Uganda
_____ *C. v. fazolensis (blicki)* — E-central Sudan to Eritrea, Ethiopia and nw Kenya
_____ *C. v. albiventris* — E Ethiopia to Somalia and n Kenya

☐ **Dusky Sunbird** *Cinnyris fuscus*

Coastal s Angola to Namibia, sw Botswana and w Cape Province

☐ **Ursula's Sunbird** *Cinnyris ursulae*

Montane forests of Mt. Cameroon and Bioko (Gulf of Guinea)

☐ **Bates' Sunbird** *Cinnyris batesi*

Ivory Coast to Nigeria, Gabon, s Zaire and nw Zambia; Bioko

☐ **Copper Sunbird** *Cinnyris cupreus*

_____ *C. c. cupreus* — Senegal to e Zaire, Uganda, Ethiopia, w Kenya and w Tanzania
_____ *C. c. chalceus* — Angola to se Zaire, w Zambia, Malawi and Zimbabwe

☐ **Purple Sunbird** *Cinnyris asiaticus*

_____ *C. a. brevirostris* — NE Arabia and se Iran to Afghanistan, Pakistan and n India
_____ *C. a. asiaticus* — S peninsular India and Sri Lanka
_____ *C. a. intermedius* — Bangladesh to Assam, Myanmar, Thailand and Indochina

☐ **Olive-backed Sunbird** *Cinnyris jugularis*

_____ *C. j. andamanicus* — Andaman Islands (Bay of Bengal)
_____ *C. j. klossi* — N Nicobar Islands (Bay of Bengal)
_____ *C. j. proselius* — Car Nicobar I. (Bay of Bengal)
_____ *C. j. flammaxillaris* — Myanmar to Thailand, Cambodia and n Malay Pen. (s to Penang)
_____ *C. j. ornatus* — S Malay Pen. to Sumatra, Borneo, Java, Lesser Sundas and adj. is.
_____ *C. j. rhizophorae* — S China (s Yunnan, Guangxi, Guangdong, Hainan) and n Vietnam
_____ *C. j. polyclystus* — Enggano I. (off w Sumatra)
_____ *C. j. obscurior* — N Philippines (montane forests of n Luzon)
_____ *C. j. jugularis* — S Luzon, central and s Philippine Islands
_____ *C. j. aurorus* — Agutaya, Balabac, Busuanga, Cagayancillo, Culion, Cuyo, Palawan
_____ *C. j. woodi* — Sulu Archipelago
_____ *C. j. plateni* — Sulawesi, Talaud, Salayar and adjacent smaller islands
_____ *C. j. infrenatus* — Tukangbesi Islands (off Sulawesi)
_____ *C. j. robustirostris* — Banggai Islands and Sula Islands
_____ *C. j. frenatus* — N Moluccas, Aru and w Papuan is., New Guinea and n Queensland
_____ *C. j. teysmanni* — Tanahjampea, Kalao, Bonerate, Kalaotoa and Madu islands
_____ *C. j. buruensis* — Buru (s Moluccas)
_____ *C. j. clementiae* — S Moluccas (Seram, Ambon and adjacent islands)
_____ *C. j. keiensis* — Kai Islands (Kai Kecil, Kai Besar, Ohimas and Add)
_____ *C. j. idenburgi* — N New Guinea (lowlands of upper Mamberamo River)
_____ *C. j. flavigaster* — Bismarck Archipelago and Solomon Islands

☐ **Apricot-breasted Sunbird** *Cinnyris buettikoferi*

Lowlands of Sumba (w Lesser Sundas)

☐ **Flame-breasted Sunbird** *Cinnyris solaris*

_____ *C. s. solaris (degener)* — Sumbawa, Flores, Besar, Lomblen, Alor, Semau, Roti and Timor
_____ *C. s. exquisita* — Wetar (e Lesser Sundas)

☐ **Souimanga Sunbird** *Cinnyris sovimanga*

_____ *C. s. aldabrensis* — Aldabra
_____ *C. s. abbotti* — Assumption I. (Aldabra)
_____ *C. s. buchenorum* — Cosmoledo Atoll (Aldabra)
_____ *C. s. sovimanga* — Îles Glorieuses and n Madagascar
_____ *C. s. apolis* — Subdesert of sw Madagascar

☐ **Seychelles Sunbird** *Cinnyris dussumieri*

Seychelles

☐ **Madagascar Sunbird** *Cinnyris notatus*
_____ *C. n. moebii* — Grand Comoro I. (Comoro Islands)
_____ *C. n. voeltzkowi* — Mohéli (Comoro Islands)
_____ *C. n. notatus* — Madagascar

☐ **Humblot's Sunbird** *Cinnyris humbloti*
_____ *C. h. humbloti* — Grand Comoro I. (Comoro Islands)
_____ *C. h. mohelica* — Mohéli (Comoro Islands)

☐ **Anjouan Sunbird** *Cinnyris comorensis*

Anjouan (Comoro Islands)

☐ **Mayotte Sunbird** *Cinnyris coquerellii*

Mayotte (Comoro Islands)

☐ **Long-billed Sunbird** *Cinnyris lotenius*
_____ *C. l. hindustanicus* — S peninsular India (north to Bombay and Andhra Pradesh)
_____ *C. l. lotenius* — Sri Lanka

☐ **Gray-hooded Sunbird** *Aethopyga primigenius*
_____ *A. p. primigenius* — S Philippines (montane forests of central and e Mindanao)
_____ *A. p. diuatae* — S Philippines (Mt. Hilong Hilong on Mindanao)

☐ **Mount Apo Sunbird** *Aethopyga boltoni*
_____ *A. b. boltoni* — S Philippines (montane forests of e Mindanao)
_____ *A. b. malindangensis* — S Philippines (montane forests of Mt. Malindang on w Mindanao)
_____ *A. b. tibolii* — S Philippines (mountains of s Mindanao)

☐ **Lina's Sunbird** *Aethopyga linaraborae*

S Philippines (montane forests of e Mindanao)

☐ **Flaming Sunbird** *Aethopyga flagrans*
_____ *A. f. decolor* — N Philippines (ne Luzon)
_____ *A. f. flagrans* — N Philippines (s Luzon and Catanduanes)
_____ *A. f. guimarasensis* — Philippines (Panay and Guimaras)
_____ *A. f. daphoenonota* — Philippines (Negros)

☐ **Metallic-winged Sunbird** *Aethopyga pulcherrima*
_____ *A. p. jefferyi* — N Philippines (Luzon)
_____ *A. p. pulcherrima* — Basilan, Dinagat, Siargo, Biliran, Samar, Leyte and Mindanao
_____ *A. p. decorosa* — Philippines (Bohol)

☐ **Elegant Sunbird** *Aethopyga duyvenbodei*

Sangihe and Siau islands (off n Sulawesi)

☐ **Lovely Sunbird** *Aethopyga shelleyi*
_____ *A. s. flavipectus* — N Philippines (n Luzon)
_____ *A. s. minuta* — N Philippines (central Luzon, Mindoro and Marinduque)
_____ *A. s. rubrinota* — N Philippines (Lubang)
_____ *A. s. bella* — S Philippines (Samar, Leyte, Dinagat, Siargao and Mindanao)
_____ *A. s. bonita* — Philippines (Ticao, Masbate, Panay, Negros and Cebu)
_____ *A. s. arolasi* — Sulu Archipelago (Jolo and Tawitawi)
_____ *A. s. shelleyi* — S Philippines (Balabac, Busuanga, Culion and Palawan)

☐ **Gould's Sunbird** *Aethopyga gouldiae*
_____ *A. g. gouldiae* — Himalayas (Himachal Pradesh to sw China and se Tibet)
_____ *A. g. isolata* — S Assam to Bangladesh and Myanmar (Chin Hills)
_____ *A. g. dabryii* — W China (Xinjiang to Sichuan and Yunnan) to Myanmar, n Laos
_____ *A. g. annamensis* — S Laos (Bolavens Plateau) and s Vietnam (Langbian Plateau)

☐ **White-flanked Sunbird** *Aethopyga eximia*

Montane forests and scrub of Java

☐ **Green-tailed Sunbird** *Aethopyga nipalensis*

____	*A. n. horsfieldii*	W Himalayas (Garhwal to w Nepal)
____	*A. n. nipalensis*	Central Nepal to ne India (Darjiling) and Sikkim
____	*A. n. koelzi*	Himalayas (Bhutan to ne Myanmar, sw China and nw Tonkin)
____	*A. n. victoriae*	W Myanmar (Chin Hills)
____	*A. n. karenensis*	SE Myanmar (Karen Hills)
____	*A. n. angkanensis*	High mountains of n Thailand (Doi Ang Ka)
____	*A. n. australis*	High mountains of s peninsular Thailand south of Isthmus of Kra
____	*A. n. blanci*	High mountains of Laos
____	*A. n. ezrai*	High mountains of s Vietnam

☐ **Fork-tailed Sunbird** *Aethopyga christinae*

____	*A. c. latouchii*	SE China (e Sichuan, s Hunan, Guandong, Fujian) to n Vietnam
____	*A. c. christinae*	Hainan (s China)
____	*A. c. sokolovi*	S Vietnam

☐ **Black-throated Sunbird** *Aethopyga saturata*

____	*A. s. saturata*	Himalayas (Garhwal to Bhutan and se Tibet)
____	*A. s. assamensis*	Bangladesh to Assam, n Myanmar and sw China (w Yunnan)
____	*A. s. galenae*	Mountains of nw Thailand
____	*A. s. petersi*	E Myanmar to n Thailand, Laos, n Vietnam and se Yunnan
____	*A. s. sanguinipectus*	Hills of se Myanmar (Karenni and n Tenasserim)
____	*A. s. anomala*	Hills of s peninsular Thailand (Phatthalung and Trang)
____	*A. s. wrayi*	Mts. of Malay Peninsula (n Perak to s Selangor and Pahang)
____	*A. s. ochra*	S Laos (Bolavens Plateau) and central Vietnam (Dakto)
____	*A. s. cambodiana*	Mountains of sw Cambodia
____	*A. s. johnsi*	Langbian Plateau (s Vietnam)

☐ **Western Crimson Sunbird** *Aethopyga vigorsii*

Foothills of w India (Gujarat to Bombay)

☐ **Crimson Sunbird** *Aethopyga siparaja*

____	*A. s. seheriae*	Nepal to Assam, Bangladesh, Myanmar, sw China and nw Thailand
____	*A. s. labecula*	E Himalayas (Bhutan to Arundal Pradesh, Assam and Bangladesh)
____	*A. s. owstoni*	S China (Naochow I. off Luichow Peninsula)
____	*A. s. tonkinensis*	S China (se Yunnan) and ne Vietnam
____	*A. s. mangini*	SE Thailand to central and s Indochina
____	*A. s. insularis*	Phu Quoc I. (off extreme s Cambodia)
____	*A. s. cara*	S Myanmar, Thailand and Mergui Archipelago
____	*A. s. trangensis*	Peninsular Thailand and adjacent Myanmar
____	*A. s. siparaja*	Malaya, Sumatra, Borneo and adjacent offshore islands
____	*A. s. nicobarica*	Nicobar Islands
____	*A. s. heliogona*	Java
____	*A. s. natunae*	North Natuna Islands
____	*A. s. magnifica*	Philippines (Cebu, Negros, Panay, Sibuyan and Tablas)
____	*A. s. flavostriata*	N Sulawesi
____	*A. s. beccarii*	Central, se and s Sulawesi and Butung I.

☐ **Scarlet Sunbird** *Aethopyga mystacalis*

Java

☐ **Temminck's Sunbird** *Aethopyga temminckii*

Extreme sw Thailand to Malaya, Sumatra and Borneo

☐ **Fire-tailed Sunbird** *Aethopyga ignicauda*

____	*A. i. ignicauda*	Himalayas (Garhwal to sw China and n Myanmar)
____	*A. i. flavescens*	N Myanmar (Chin Hills)

☐ **Thick-billed Spiderhunter** *Arachnothera crassirostris*

Forests of peninsular Thailand, Malaya, Sumatra and Borneo

☐ **Spectacled Spiderhunter** *Arachnothera flavigaster*

Woodlands of peninsular Thailand, Malaya, Sumatra and Borneo

☐ **Long-billed Spiderhunter** *Arachnothera robusta*

____	*A. r. robusta*	Forests of s peninsular Thailand, Malaya, Sumatra and Borneo
____	*A. r. armata*	Java

☐ **Little Spiderhunter** *Arachnothera longirostra*

____	*A. l. longirostra*	SW India; Nepal to Assam, w Yunnan, Myanmar and w Thailand
____	*A. l. sordida*	SW China (se Yunnan) to ne Thailand and n Indochina
____	*A. l. pallida*	SE Thailand and central Indochina
____	*A. l. cinireicollis*	Pen. Thailand (s of Isthmus of Kra), Malay Pen. and Sumatra
____	*A. l. niasensis*	Nias I. (off w Sumatra)
____	*A. l. prillwitzi*	Java
____	*A. l. buettikoferi*	Borneo
____	*A. l. atita*	South Natuna Islands (South China Sea)
____	*A. l. rothschildi*	North Natuna Islands (South China Sea)
____	*A. l. flammifera*	Philippines (Samar, Leyte, Bohol, Mindanao, Dinagat and Biliran)
____	*A. l. randi*	S Philippines (Basilan)
____	*A. l. dilutior*	SW Philippines (Palawan)

☐ **Yellow-eared Spiderhunter** *Arachnothera chrysogenys*

____	*A. c. chrysogenys*	S Myanmar to s Thailand, Malaya, Sumatra, Java and w Borneo
____	*A. c. harrissoni*	E Borneo

☐ **Naked-faced Spiderhunter** *Arachnothera clarae*

____	*A. c. luzonensis*	N Philippines (Sierra Madre Mountains of e-central Luzon)
____	*A. c. philippensis*	Philippines (Samar, Leyte and Biliran)
____	*A. c. clarae*	S Philippines (e Mindanao in Davao area)
____	*A. c. malindangensis*	S Philippines (central and w Mindanao)

☐ **Gray-breasted Spiderhunter** *Arachnothera modesta*

____	*A. m. caena*	S Myanmar and n peninsular Thailand
____	*A. m. modesta*	S Thailand (s of Isthmus of Kra), Malay Peninsula and w Borneo

☐ **Streaky-breasted Spiderhunter** *Arachnothera affinis*

____	*A. a. everetti*	Mountains of n and central Borneo
____	*A. a. pars*	E Borneo
____	*A. a. affinis*	Java and Bali
____	*A. a. concolor*	Sumatra

☐ **Streaked Spiderhunter** *Arachnothera magna*

____	*A. m. magna*	Himalayas (Garhwal to n Myanmar and sw China)
____	*A. m. aurata*	E-central Myanmar
____	*A. m. musarum*	SE Myanmar (s Shan States) to n Thailand and n Laos
____	*A. m. pagodarum*	S Myanmar and sw Thailand (s Tak and Kanchanaburi provinces)
____	*A. m. remota*	S Vietnam

☐ **Whitehead's Spiderhunter** *Arachnothera juliae*

	Montane forests of n Borneo

FAMILY: MELANOCHARITIDAE (Berrypeckers and Longbills—10)

☐ **Obscure Berrypecker** *Melanocharis arfakiana*

	Known from 2 specimens ca 1900 from mts. of se New Guinea

☐ **Black Berrypecker** *Melanocharis nigra*

____	*M. n. pallida*	Waigeu I. (off w New Guinea)
____	*M. n. nigra*	Misool I., Salawati I. and w New Guinea
____	*M. n. unicolor*	Yapen I., Meos Num I., n and e New Guinea
____	*M. n. chloroptera*	Aru Islands and s New Guinea (Mimika River to Fly River)

☐ **Lemon-breasted Berrypecker** *Melanocharis longicauda*

_____	*M. l. longicauda*	Mountains of nw New Guinea (Vogelkop and Wandammen mts.)
_____	*M. l. umbrosa*	NW New Guinea (slopes above Idenberg River)
_____	*M. l. chloris*	W New Guinea (Weyland Mts. and s slopes of Jayawijaya Mts.)
_____	*M. l. captata*	Mts. of cent. New Guinea (Huon Pen. and Central Highlands)
_____	*M. l. orientalis*	Mountains of se New Guinea

☐ **Fan-tailed Berrypecker** *Melanocharis versteri*

_____	*M. v. versteri*	NW New Guinea (Arfak Mountains)
_____	*M. v. meeki*	W New Guinea (Weyland, Nassau, Orange and Hindenberg mts.)
_____	*M. v. virago*	Mts. of n New Guinea, Central Highlands and Huon Peninsula
_____	*M. v. maculiceps*	Herzog Mountains and mountains of se New Guinea

☐ **Streaked Berrypecker** *Melanocharis striativentris*

_____	*M. s. axillaris*	W New Guinea (Weyland Mts. and south slopes of Snow Mts.)
_____	*M. s. striativentris*	Central Highlands and s slopes of mountains of se New Guinea
_____	*M. s. chrysocome*	E New Guinea (mountains of Huon Peninsula)
_____	*M. s. prasina*	N slopes of mountains of se New Guinea

☐ **Spotted Berrypecker** *Melanocharis crassirostris*

_____	*M. c. crassirostris*	New Guinea (Mts. of Vogelkop Peninsula and Central Highlands)
_____	*M. c. piperata*	Mountains of se New Guinea
_____	*M. c. viridescens*	SE New Guinea (Herzog Mountains)

☐ **Yellow-bellied Longbill** *Toxorhamphus novaeguineae*

_____	*T. n. novaeguineae*	W Papuan islands, w New Guinea and islands in Geelvink Bay
_____	*T. n. flaviventris*	Aru Is. and s New Guinea (Utakwa River to middle Fly River)

☐ **Slaty-chinned Longbill** *Toxorhamphus poliopterus*

_____	*T. p. maximus*	N slopes of c mts. of New Guinea (Weyland to Jayawijaya mts.)
_____	*T. p. poliopterus*	Mountains of se New Guinea

☐ **Dwarf Honeyeater** *Toxorhamphus iliolophus*

_____	*T. i. cinerascens*	Waigeu I. (off w New Guinea)
_____	*T. i. affine*	W New Guinea (mountains of Vogelkop Peninsula)
_____	*T. i. iliolophus*	Yapen and Meos Num islands and n New Guinea
_____	*T. i. flavus*	S and se New Guinea
_____	*T. i. fergussonis*	D'Entrecasteaux Arch. (Fergusson, Goodenough and Normanby)

☐ **Pygmy Honeyeater** *Toxorhamphus pygmaeum*

_____	*T. p. waigeuense*	Waigeu I. (off w New Guinea)
_____	*T. p. pygmaeum*	Misool I. and w New Guinea
_____	*T. p. flavipectus*	S New Guinea (Etna Bay to Milne Bay)
_____	*T. p. olivascens*	N coast of se New Guinea (Milne Bay to Huon Peninsula)
_____	*T. p. meeki*	D'Entrecasteaux Archipelago (Fergusson and Goodenough)

FAMILY: PARAMYTHIIDAE (Tit Berrypecker and Crested Berrypecker—2)

☐ **Tit Berrypecker** *Oreocharis arfaki*

Montane forests of New Guinea

☐ **Crested Berrypecker** *Paramythia montium*

_____	*P. m. montium*	Central Highlands and mountains of se New Guinea
_____	*P. m. olivaceum*	Weyland, Nassau and Jayawijaya mountains (cent. New Guinea)
_____	*P. m. alpinum*	Upper slopes of Jayawijaya Mts. and n slopes of Nassau Mts.
_____	*P. m. brevicauda*	SE New Guinea (mountains of Huon Peninsula)

FAMILY: DICAEIDAE (Flowerpeckers—44)

☐ **Olive-backed Flowerpecker** *Prionochilus olivaceus*

____	*P. o. parsoni*	N Philippines (Sierra Madre Mountains of n Luzon)
____	*P. o. samarensis*	Central Philippines (Samar and Leyte)
____	*P. o. olivaceus*	S Philippines (Basilan, Dinagat, Mindanao and Bohol)

☐ **Yellow-breasted Flowerpecker** *Prionochilus maculatus*

____	*P. m. septentrionalis*	S Myanmar and s peninsular Thailand
____	*P. m. oblitus*	Malay Peninsula
____	*P. m. maculatus*	Sumatra, Belitung I., Nias I. and Borneo
____	*P. m. natunensis*	North Natuna Islands

☐ **Crimson-breasted Flowerpecker** *Prionochilus percussus*

____	*P. p. ignicapillus*	Malaya, s Thailand, Sumatra, Borneo, Riau Arch., N Natuna Is.
____	*P. p. regulus*	Batu Islands (off w Sumatra)
____	*P. p. percussus*	Java

☐ **Palawan Flowerpecker** *Prionochilus plateni*

____	*P. p. plateni*	SW Philippines (Balabac and Palawan)
____	*P. p. culionensis*	SW Philippines (Culion)

☐ **Yellow-rumped Flowerpecker** *Prionochilus xanthopygius*

Lowlands of Borneo and North Natuna Islands

☐ **Scarlet-breasted Flowerpecker** *Prionochilus thoracicus*

S peninsular Thailand, Malaya, Sumatra, Borneo and Belitung I.

☐ **Golden-rumped Flowerpecker** *Dicaeum annae*

____	*D. a. annae*	Flores (w Lesser Sundas)
____	*D. a. sumbawense*	Sumbawa (w Lesser Sundas)

☐ **Thick-billed Flowerpecker** *Dicaeum agile*

____	*D. a. agile*	NE Pakistan and n India
____	*D. a. zeylonicum*	Sri Lanka
____	*D. a. pallescens (modestum)*	Bangladesh to Myanmar, Thailand, Malay Pen. and n Vietnam
____	*D. a. atjehense*	N Sumatra (Aceh Province)
____	*D. a. finschi*	W Java (Sukabumi District)
____	*D. a. tinctum*	Lesser Sundas (Sumbawa, Flores, Besar, Lomblen, Alor, Sumba)
____	*D. a. obsoletum*	Timor (e Lesser Sundas)
____	*D. a. striatissimum*	N Philippines (Lubang, Luzon, Romblon, Sibuyan, Catanduanes)
____	*D. a. aeruginosum*	Cent. and s Philippines (Cebu, Negros, Mindoro and Mindanao)
____	*D. a. affine*	SW Philippines (Palawan)

☐ **Brown-backed Flowerpecker** *Dicaeum everetti*

____	*D. e. everetti (sordidum)*	S Malaya, Riau Archipelago, n Borneo and Labuan I.
____	*D. e. bungurense*	North Natuna Islands

☐ **Whiskered Flowerpecker** *Dicaeum proprium*

S Philippines (montane forests of Mindanao)

☐ **Yellow-vented Flowerpecker** *Dicaeum chrysorrheum*

____	*D. c. chrysochlore*	E Himalayas (Sikkim to sw China, Myanmar and n Indochina)
____	*D. c. chrysorrheum*	S peninsular Thailand to Malaya, Sumatra, Borneo and Java

☐ **Yellow-bellied Flowerpecker** *Dicaeum melanoxanthum*

E Himalayas (Nepal to ne India, sw China and Myanmar)

☐ **White-throated Flowerpecker** *Dicaeum vincens*

Forests of Sri Lanka

☐ **Yellow-sided Flowerpecker** *Dicaeum aureolimbatum*

____	*D. a. aureolimbatum*	Sulawesi, Bangka, Lembeh, Muna and Butung islands
____	*D. a. laterale*	Sangihe I. (off n Sulawesi)

☐ **Olive-capped Flowerpecker** *Dicaeum nigrilore*
_____ *D. n. diuatae* — S Philippines (Diuata Mountains of ne Mindanao)
_____ *D. n. nigrilore* — S Philippines (mountains of Mindanao)

☐ **Flame-crowned Flowerpecker** *Dicaeum anthonyi*
_____ *D. a. anthonyi* — N Philippines (montane forests of Luzon)
_____ *D. a. kampalili* — S Philippines (montane forests of Mindanao)
_____ *D. a. masawan* — S Philippines (Mt. Malindang on nw Mindanao)

☐ **Bicolored Flowerpecker** *Dicaeum bicolor*
_____ *D. b. inexpectatum* — N Philippines (Luzon, Mindoro and Catanduanes)
_____ *D. b. viridissimum* — Central Philippines (Negros and Guimaras)
_____ *D. b. bicolor* — S Philippines (Bohol, Leyte, Dinagat, Mindanao and Samar)

☐ **Cebu Flowerpecker** *Dicaeum quadricolor*
Philippines (rediscovered 1992 after 85-year absence on Cebu)

☐ **Red-striped Flowerpecker** *Dicaeum australe*
Philippines

☐ **Red-keeled Flowerpecker** *Dicaeum haematostictum*
Philippines (Panay and Negros). Extirpated on Guimaras

☐ **Scarlet-collared Flowerpecker** *Dicaeum retrocinctum*
N Philippines (Mindoro)

☐ **Orange-bellied Flowerpecker** *Dicaeum trigonostigma*
_____ *D. t. rubropygium* — NE India (Assam) to s Myanmar and peninsular Thailand
_____ *D. t. trigonostigma* — Extreme s peninsular Thailand (north to Trang)
_____ *D. t. melanostigma* — Malaya, Sumatra, Bangka and Belitung islands
_____ *D. t. antioproctum* — Simeulue I. (off Sumatra)
_____ *D. t. megastoma* — Great Natuna I. (North Natuna Islands)
_____ *D. t. flaviclunis* — Krakatoa I., Java and Bali
_____ *D. t. dayakanum* — Borneo and adjacent offshore northern islands
_____ *D. t. xanthopygium* — N Philippines (Luzon, Marinduque, Mindoro and Polillo)
_____ *D. t. intermedium* — N Philippines (Romblon)
_____ *D. t. cnecolaemum* — N Philippines (Tablas)
_____ *D. t. sibuyanicum* — N Philippines (Sibuyan)
_____ *D. t. dorsale* — Central Philippines (Masbate, Panay and Negros)
_____ *D. t. besti* — S Philippines (Siquijor)
_____ *D. t. cinereigulare* — Philippines (Mindanao, Samar, Leyte, Calicoan, Biliran and Bohol)
_____ *D. t. pallidius* — Central Philippines (Cebu)
_____ *D. t. isidroi* — S Philippines (Camiguin Sur)
_____ *D. t. assimile* — Sulu Archipelago (Tawitawi, Jolo and Siasi)
_____ *D. t. sibutuense* — Sulu Archipelago (Sibutu, Omapoy and Sipangkot)

☐ **Pale-billed Flowerpecker** *Dicaeum erythrorhynchos*
_____ *D. e. erythrorhynchos* — India to s Nepal, Bhutan, Bangladesh and w Myanmar
_____ *D. e. ceylonense* — Sri Lanka

☐ **Plain Flowerpecker** *Dicaeum concolor*
_____ *D. c. olivaceum* — Himalayas (Nepal to s China, Myanmar, Thailand, n Indochina)
_____ *D. c. concolor* — Western Ghats and coastal sw India
_____ *D. c. virescens* — Andaman Islands
_____ *D. c. minullum* — Hainan (s China)
_____ *D. c. uchidai* — Montane forests of Taiwan
_____ *D. c. borneanum* — Malaya, Sumatra, Borneo and North Natuna Islands
_____ *D. c. sollicitans* — Java and Bali

☐ **Flame-breasted Flowerpecker** *Dicaeum erythrothorax*
_____ *D. e. schistaceiceps* — Moluccas (Morotai, Halmahera, Kasiruta, Bacan, Obi and Bisa)
_____ *D. e. erythrothorax* — Buru (s Moluccas)

☐ **White-bellied Flowerpecker** *Dicaeum hypoleucum*

____ *D. h. cagayanensis*	N Philippines (Sierra Madre Mountains of ne Luzon)
____ *D. h. obscurum (lagunae)*	N Philippines (central and s Luzon and Catanduanes)
____ *D. h. pontifex*	Philippines (Bohol, Samar, Leyte, Dinagat, Panaon, Mindanao)
____ *D. h. mindanense*	S Philippines (Zamboanga Peninsula of Mindanao)
____ *D. h. hypoleucum*	S Philippines (Basilan, Bongao, Jolo, Tawitawi and Siasi)

☐ **Pygmy Flowerpecker** *Dicaeum pygmaeum*

____ *D. p. fugaensis*	Fuga (n Philippines off n Luzon)
____ *D. p. salomonseni*	N Philippines (Ilocos Norte Province of extreme n Luzon)
____ *D. p. pygmaeum*	Central and s Luzon and central Philippine Islands
____ *D. p. davao*	S Philippines (Mindanao and Camiguin Sur)
____ *D. p. palawanorum*	S Philippines (Balabac, Culion, Calauit and Palawan)

☐ **Crimson-crowned Flowerpecker** *Dicaeum nehrkorni*

Montane forests of Sulawesi

☐ **Ashy Flowerpecker** *Dicaeum vulneratum*

Moluccas (Boano, Seram, Ambon, Saparua, Gorong, Seram Laut)

☐ **Olive-crowned Flowerpecker** *Dicaeum pectorale*

____ *D. p. ignotum*	Gebe I. (Halmahera Sea off nw New Guinea)
____ *D. p. pectorale*	W Papuan islands and lowlands of w New Guinea

☐ **Red-capped Flowerpecker** *Dicaeum geelvinkianum*

____ *D. g. maforense*	Numfor I. (Geelvink Bay off n New Guinea)
____ *D. g. misoriense*	Biak I. (Geelvink Bay off n New Guinea)
____ *D. g. geelvinkianum*	Yapen and Kurudu islands (Geelvink Bay off n New Guinea)
____ *D. g. obscurifrons*	W New Guinea (Wissel Lakes region)
____ *D. g. setekwa*	SW New Guinea (s slopes of Snow Mts. to Lorentz River)
____ *D. g. diversum*	N New Guinea (Mamberamo River to Humboldt Bay)
____ *D. g. centrale*	Central New Guinea (Nassau and Jayawijaya mountains)
____ *D. g. albopunctatum*	Lowlands of s-central New Guinea
____ *D. g. rubrigulare*	S New Guinea (Palmer Junction to mouth of Fly River)
____ *D. g. rubrocoronatum*	SE New Guinea
____ *D. g. violaceum*	D'Entrecasteaux Arch. (Fergusson, Goodenough and Dobu)

☐ **Louisiade Flowerpecker** *Dicaeum nitidum*

____ *D. n. nitidum*	Louisiade Archipelago (Tagula and Misima)
____ *D. n. rosseli*	Rossel I. (Louisiade Archipelago)

☐ **Red-banded Flowerpecker** *Dicaeum eximium*

____ *D. e. layardorum*	New Britain (Bismarck Archipelago)
____ *D. e. eximium*	Bismarck Archipelago (New Ireland and New Hanover)
____ *D. e. phaeopygium*	Dyaul I. (Bismarck Archipelago)

☐ **Midget Flowerpecker** *Dicaeum aeneum*

____ *D. a. aeneum*	Bougainville, Choiseul, Buka, Florida and adj. n Solomon Islands
____ *D. a. becki*	Guadalcanal (Solomon Islands)
____ *D. a. malaitae*	Malaita (Solomon Islands)

☐ **Mottled Flowerpecker** *Dicaeum tristrami*

San Cristóbal (se Solomon Islands)

☐ **Black-fronted Flowerpecker** *Dicaeum igniferum*

____ *D. i. igniferum*	Lesser Sundas (Sumbawa, Komodo, Flores, Lomblen and Besar)
____ *D. i. aetum*	Lesser Sundas (Pantar and Alor)

☐ **Red-chested Flowerpecker** *Dicaeum maugei*

____ *D. m. splendidum*	Salayar and Tanahjampea islands (Flores Sea)
____ *D. m. neglectum*	W Lesser Sundas (Lombok and Penida)
____ *D. m. maugei*	E Lesser Sundas (Roti, Sawu, Semau, Timor, Romang and Damar)
D. m. salvadorii	E Lesser Sundas (Moa and Babar)

☐ **Fire-breasted Flowerpecker** *Dicaeum ignipectus*

____	*D. i. ignipectus*	E Himalayas (Kashmir) to s-cent. China, Myanmar and Indochina
____	*D. i. dolichorhynchum*	Mountains of s peninsular Thailand and Malay Peninsula
____	*D. i. cambodianum*	Mountains of se Thailand and Cambodia
____	*D. i. formosum*	Montane forests of Taiwan
____	*D. i. luzoniense*	N Philippines (montane forests of n Luzon)
____	*D. i. bonga*	Central Philippines (Samar)
____	*D. i. apo*	Mountains of s Philippines (Negros and Mindanao)
____	*D. i. beccarii*	Montane forests of n Sumatra

☐ **Black-sided Flowerpecker** *Dicaeum monticolum*

Mountains of n Borneo

☐ **Gray-sided Flowerpecker** *Dicaeum celebicum*

____	*D. c. talautense*	Talaud Islands (n Moluccas)
____	*D. c. sanghirense*	Sangihe and Siau islands (off n Sulawesi)
____	*D. c. celebicum*	Manadotua, Bangka, Sulawesi, Lembeh, Togian, Muna and Butung is.
____	*D. c. kuehni*	Tukangbesi Islands (off Sulawesi)
____	*D. c. sulaense*	Banggai Islands and Sula Islands (Taliabu, Mangole and Sanana)

☐ **Blood-breasted Flowerpecker** *Dicaeum sanguinolentum*

____	*D. s. sanguinolentum*	Java and Bali
____	*D. s. rhodopygiale*	Flores (w Lesser Sundas)
____	*D. s. wilhelminae*	Sumba (w Lesser Sundas)
____	*D. s. hanieli*	Timor (e Lesser Sundas)

☐ **Mistletoebird** *Dicaeum hirundinaceum*

____	*D. h. kiense*	S Wallacea (Watubela, Tayandu and Kai islands)
____	*D. h. fulgidum*	Tanimbar Islands (Yamdena, Larat and Lutu)
____	*D. h. ignicolle*	Aru Islands
____	*D. h. hirundinaceum*	Widespread continental Australia and islands in Torres Strait

☐ **Scarlet-backed Flowerpecker** *Dicaeum cruentatum*

____	*D. c. cruentatum (siamensis)*	E Nepal to ne India, s China, Myanmar, Thailand and Indochina
____	*D. c. ignitum*	Malay Peninsula
____	*D. c. sumatranum*	Sumatra
____	*D. c. batuense*	Mentawi Archipelago (off Sumatra)
____	*D. c. simalurense*	Simeulue I. (off w Sumatra)
____	*D. c. niasense*	Nias I. (off w Sumatra)
____	*D. c. nigrimentum*	Borneo and Karimata Islands

☐ **Scarlet-headed Flowerpecker** *Dicaeum trochileum*

____	*D. t. trochileum*	Java, Bali, Madura, se Borneo, Bawean and Kangean islands
____	*D. t. stresemanni*	Lombok (w Lesser Sundas)

FAMILY: PARDALOTIDAE (Pardalotes—4)

☐ **Spotted Pardalote** *Pardalotus punctatus*

____	*P. p. punctatus*	W Australia to Queensland, Victoria, se S Australia; Tasmania
____	*P. p. xanthopygus*	S Western Australia to nw Victoria and Kangaroo I.

☐ **Forty-spotted Pardalote** *Pardalotus quadragintus*

Coastal se Tasmania; formerly King and Furneaux islands

☐ **Red-browed Pardalote** *Pardalotus rubricatus*

____	*P. r. parryi*	Dry eucalyptus forests of n Australia
____	*P. r. rubricatus*	Arid interior of Australia
____	*P. r. carpentariae*	NE Australia (n Queensland along Gulf of Carpentaria)
____	*P. r. yorki*	NE Australia (humid nw Cape York Peninsula)

□ **Striated Pardalote** *Pardalotus striatus*

_____ *P. s. uropygialis*	N Northern Territory to n Queensland (south to Cooktown)
_____ *P. s. melanocephalus*	S Queensland (south of *uropygialis*) to ne New South Wales
_____ *P. s. substriatus*	W Australia to sw Queensland, c New South Wales and Victoria
_____ *P. s. ornatus*	SE Queensland to Victoria and se South Australia
_____ *P. s. striatus*	Tasmania and islands in Bass Strait; winters to Queensland

FAMILY: ZOSTEROPIDAE (White-eyes—94)

□ **Black-capped Speirops** *Speirops lugubris*

São Tomé (Gulf of Guinea)

□ **Cameroon Speirops** *Speirops melanocephalus*

Montane forests of s Cameroon

□ **Fernando Po Speirops** *Speirops brunneus*

Montane forests of Bioko (Gulf of Guinea)

□ **Principe Speirops** *Speirops leucophoeus*

Lowlands of Príncipe (Gulf of Guinea)

□ **African Yellow White-eye** *Zosterops senegalensis*

_____ *Z. s. senegalensis*	Senegal to Uganda, n Congo and w Ethiopia
_____ *Z. s. demeryi*	Sierra Leone to Liberia and Ivory Coast
_____ *Z. s. stenocricota*	SE Nigeria to Cameroon and Gabon; Bioko (Gulf of Guinea)
_____ *Z. s. stuhlmanni*	E Zaire and Uganda
_____ *Z. s. reichenowi*	E Zaire (mountains northwest of Lake Tanganyika)
_____ *Z. s. toroensis*	Lowlands of ne Zaire
_____ *Z. s. kasaica*	SW Congo and ne Angola
_____ *Z. s .heinrichi*	N Angola (Cuanza Norte and Cuanza Sul)
_____ *Z. s. quanzae*	Central Angola (Malange to n Huila)
_____ *Z. s. anderssoni*	S Angola to Zambia, s Tanzania, Malawi, Mozambique and Natal
_____ *Z. s. stierlingi*	Mountains of s Tanzania to Zambia, Malawi and Mozambique
_____ *Z. s. kaffensis*	Highlands of Ethiopia (south of Lake Tana)
_____ *Z. s. kulaensis*	N Kenya (Mt. Kulal)
_____ *Z. s. silvana*	S Kenya (Taita and Kasigau mountains)
_____ *Z. s. mbuluensis*	S Kenya (Chyulu Mountains) and n Tanzania (North Pare Mts.)
_____ *Z. s. winifredae*	NE Tanzania (South Pare Mountains)
_____ *Z. s. tongensis*	S Zimbabwe to n Natal and s Mozambique

□ **Broad-ringed White-eye** *Zosterops poliogaster*

_____ *Z. p. poliogaster (jacksoni)*	Mts. of Eritrea and Ethiopia to Sudan, Kenya and n Tanzania
_____ *Z. p. kikuyensis*	Central Kenya (Aberdare Mountains and Mt. Kenya)
_____ *Z. p. eurycricotus*	NE Tanzania (Mt. Kilimanjaro and Arusha regions)

□ **White-breasted White-eye** *Zosterops abyssinicus*

_____ *Z. a. arabs*	S Arabian Peninsula (Yemen and extreme n Aden)
_____ *Z. a. abyssinicus*	Lowlands of Eritrea and e Ethiopia to se Sudan
_____ *Z. a. socotranus*	N Somalia and Socotra
_____ *Z. a. omoensis*	SW Ethiopia
_____ *Z. a. jubaensis*	SE Ethiopia to Somalia and extreme n Kenya
_____ *Z. a. flavilateralis*	Extreme sw Ethiopia to e Kenya and e-central Tanzania

□ **Cape White-eye** *Zosterops pallidus*

_____ *Z. p. pallidus*	Namibia to Transvaal and nw Cape Province
_____ *Z. p. sundevalli*	N Cape Province
_____ *Z. p. caniviridis*	E Botswana to w Transvaal
_____ *Z. p. virens*	S Mozambique to e Cape Province

☐ **Pemba White-eye** *Zosterops vaughani*

Pemba I. (off Tanzania)

☐ **Mayotte White-eye** *Zosterops mayottensis*

Mayotte (se Comoro Is.); extirpated on Maria Anne I. ca 1940

☐ **Madagascar White-eye** *Zosterops maderaspatanus*

____ *Z. m. menaiensis*	Cosmoledo Atoll (Seychelles Islands)
____ *Z. m. aldabrensis*	Aldabra and Astove islands (Indian Ocean)
____ *Z. m. kirki*	Grand Comoro Island
____ *Z. m. anjouanensis*	Anjouan (Comoro Islands)
____ *Z. m. comorensis*	Mohéli (Comoro Islands)
____ *Z. m. maderaspatanus*	Madagascar and Isles Glorieuses
____ *Z. m. voeltzkowi*	Europa I. (s Mozambique Channel)

☐ **Comoro White-eye** *Zosterops mouroniensis*

Grand Comoro I. (montane heath of Mt. Karthala)

☐ **Sao Tome White-eye** *Zosterops ficedulinus*

____ *Z. f. ficedulinus*	Príncipe (Gulf of Guinea)
____ *Z. f. feae*	São Tomé (Gulf of Guinea)

☐ **Annobon White-eye** *Zosterops griseovirescens*

Pagalu (Gulf of Guinea)

☐ **Mascarene White-eye** *Zosterops borbonicus*

____ *Z. b. borbonicus (alopekion, xerophilus)*	Réunion (w Mascarene Islands)
____ *Z. b. mauritianus*	Mauritius (w Mascarene Islands)

☐ **Reunion White-eye** *Zosterops olivaceus*

Forests of Réunion (w Mascarene Islands)

☐ **Mauritius White-eye** *Zosterops chloronothos*

Highlands of Mauritius (w Mascarene Islands)

☐ **Seychelles White-eye** *Zosterops modestus*

Forests of Mahé (Seychelles Islands). On verge of extinction

☐ **Ceylon White-eye** *Zosterops ceylonensis*

Montane forests of Sri Lanka

☐ **Chestnut-flanked White-eye** *Zosterops erythropleurus*

SE Siberia to sw China and ne Manchuria; winters to SE Asia

☐ **Oriental White-eye** *Zosterops palpebrosus*

____ *Z. p. egregia (occidentis)*	Afghanistan to Pakistan, India, Sri Lanka and Laccadive Islands
____ *Z. p. palpebrosus (siamensis)*	Nepal to se Tibet, sw China, Myanmar, n Thailand and Indochina
____ *Z. p. nilgiriensis*	S India (Nilgiri and Palani hills)
____ *Z. p. salimalii*	SE India (se Hyderabad)
____ *Z. p. nicobaricus*	Andaman and Nicobar islands
____ *Z. p. joannae*	SW China
____ *Z. p. williamsoni*	S Thailand and Malay Peninsula
____ *Z. p. auriventer*	S Myanmar to Malaysia, w Borneo, s Natuna and Bangka islands
____ *Z. p. sumatranus*	W Sumatra
____ *Z. p. buxtoni*	Mountains of e Sumatra and w Java
____ *Z. p. melanurus*	Mountains of central and e Java and Bali
____ *Z. p. unicus*	W Lesser Sundas (Sumbawa and Flores)

☐ **Japanese White-eye** *Zosterops japonicus*

____ *Z. j. yesoensis*	Hokkaido (n Japan)
____ *Z. j. japonicus*	Main Japanese islands (Honshu to Kyushu)
____ *Z. j. stejnegeri*	Izu Islands (s Japan); introduced to Bonin Islands
____ *Z. j. insularis*	Ryukyu Islands (Tanegashima and Yakushima)
____ *Z. j. loochooensis*	Iriomote (Ryukyu Islands)
____ *Z. j. alani*	Volcano Islands (Iwo Jima and Minami-iwo-Jima)
____ *Z. j. daitoensis*	Daito Islands (Philippine Sea)
____ *Z. j. simplex*	W China to Myanmar, n Vietnam and Taiwan; winters to Hainan
____ *Z. j. hainana*	Hainan (s China)

☐ **Lowland White-eye** *Zosterops meyeni*

____	*Z. m. meyeni*	Philippines (Luzon, Banton, Calayan, Lubang, Verde, Caluya)
____	*Z. m. batanis*	Philippines (Batan, Sabtang, Ivojos, Itbayat and Y'Ami)

☐ **Enggano White-eye** *Zosterops salvadorii*

Enggano and Mega islands (off w Sumatra)

☐ **Bridled White-eye** *Zosterops conspicillatus*

____	*Z. c. rotensis*	Sabena Plateau on Rota (n Mariana Islands)
____	*Z. c. conspicillatus*	Guam (s Mariana Islands)
____	*Z. c. saypani*	SE Mariana Islands (Tinian, Agiguan and Saipan)

☐ **Caroline Islands White-eye** *Zosterops semperi*

____	*Z. s. semperi*	Palau Islands (Babelthuap, Koror, Garakayo and Palau)
____	*Z. s. owstoni*	Truk (Caroline Islands)
____	*Z. s. takasukasai*	Pohnpei (Caroline Islands)

☐ **Plain White-eye** *Zosterops hypolais*

Forest and scrub of Yap (nw Caroline Islands)

☐ **Black-capped White-eye** *Zosterops atricapillus*

____	*Z. a. viridicata*	Mountains of n Sumatra
____	*Z. a. atricapillus*	Mountains of central and s Sumatra and n Borneo (Mt. Kinabalu)

☐ **Everett's White-eye** *Zosterops everetti*

____	*Z. e. tahanensis*	Peninsular Thailand to Malaysia and n Borneo
____	*Z. e. wetmorei*	S Thailand
____	*Z. e. everetti*	Philippines (Cebu)
____	*Z. e. basilanicus*	Philippines (Basilan, Dinagat, Mindanao, Siargao, Camiguin Sur)
____	*Z. e. boholensis*	Philippines (Bohol, Leyte, Samar, Calicoan and Biliran)
____	*Z. e. siquijorensis*	Philippines (Siquijor)
____	*Z. e. mandibularis*	Sulu Archipelago (Sulu, Tawitawi, Jolo, Bongao, Sanga Sanga)
____	*Z. e. babelo*	Talaud Islands (Karakelong and Salebabu) and n Sulawesi

☐ **Yellowish White-eye** *Zosterops nigrorum*

____	*Z. n. meyleri*	N Philippines (Camiguin Norte)
____	*Z. n. aureiloris*	N Philippines (mountains of n Luzon)
____	*Z. n. sierramadrensis*	N Philippines (Cagayan Province on s Luzon)
____	*Z. n. luzonicus*	N Philippines (se Luzon and Catanduanes)
____	*Z. n. nigrorum*	Philippines (Masbate, Negros, Ticao, Panay and Caluya)
____	*Z. n. mindorensis*	Philippines (Mindoro)
____	*Z. n. catamarensis*	S Philippines (Camiguin Sur)
____	*Z. n. richmondi*	Cagayancillo I. (Sulu Archipelago)

☐ **Mountain White-eye** *Zosterops montanus*

____	*Z. m. whiteheadi*	N Philippines (n Luzon)
____	*Z. m. halconensis*	Philippines (Mindoro)
____	*Z. m. gilli*	Philippines (Marinduque)
____	*Z. m. pectoralis*	Philippines (n Negros)
____	*Z. m. diuatae*	S Philippines (n Mindanao)
____	*Z. m. vulcani*	S Philippines (Mt. Apo and Mt. Katanglad on Mindanao)
____	*Z. m. parkesi*	SW Philippines (Palawan)
____	*Z. m. obstinatus*	Moluccas (Ternate, Bacan and Seram)
____	*Z. m. montanus*	Sulawesi, Sula Islands, Buru, Lombok, Sumbawa, Flores, Timor
____	*Z. m. difficilis*	S Sumatra

☐ **Christmas Island White-eye** *Zosterops natalis*

Christmas I. (e Indian Ocean)

☐ **Javan White-eye** *Zosterops flavus*

Mangroves and bamboo belt of coastal nw Java and se Borneo

☐ **Yellow-bellied White-eye** *Zosterops chloris*

_____	*Z. c. mentoris*	N-central Sulawesi
_____	*Z. c. intermedius*	S Sulawesi to Muna, Butung, Flores and Sumbawa
_____	*Z. c. flavissimus*	Tukangbesi Islands (Binongka, Kalidupa, Tomea and Wantjee)
_____	*Z. c. maxi*	Lombok, Nusa Penida and adjacent smaller w Lesser Sundas
_____	*Z. c. chloris*	Tayandu Islands and Kai Islands (Banda Sea)
_____	*Z. c. solombensis*	Solombo Besar I. (Java Sea)
_____	*Z. c. zachlorus*	Kalambau I. (Java Sea)

☐ **Ashy-bellied White-eye** *Zosterops citrinellus*

_____	*Z. c. citrinellus*	Lesser Sundas (Timor, Roti, Sawu and Sumba)
_____	*Z. c. albiventris*	Tanimbar Islands and islands in Torres Straits
_____	*Z. c. harterti*	Alor (e Lesser Sundas)

☐ **Great Kai White-eye** *Zosterops grayi*

Kai Besar (Kai Islands)

☐ **Little Kai White-eye** *Zosterops uropygialis*

Kai Kecil (Kai Islands)

☐ **Sulawesi White-eye** *Zosterops consobrinorum*

SE peninsula of Sulawesi

☐ **Black-ringed White-eye** *Zosterops anomalus*

Hills of sw Sulawesi

☐ **Yellow-spectacled White-eye** *Zosterops wallacei*

Lesser Sundas (Sumbawa, Flores, Komodo, Sumba and Lomblen)

☐ **Black-crowned White-eye** *Zosterops atrifrons*

_____	*Z. a. nehrkorni*	Sangihe I. (n of Sulawesi)
_____	*Z. a. atrifrons*	N, n-central and se Sulawesi and Peleng I. (Banggai Is.)
_____	*Z. a. sulaensis*	Sula Islands (Taliabu, Seho, Mangole and Sanana)
_____	*Z. a. stalkeri*	Seram (s Moluccas)

☐ **Cream-throated White-eye** *Zosterops atriceps*

_____	*Z. a. dehaani*	Morotai (n Moluccas)
_____	*Z. a. fuscifrons*	Halmahera (n Moluccas)
_____	*Z. a. atriceps*	N Moluccas (Bacan and Obi)

☐ **Black-fronted White-eye** *Zosterops minor*

_____	*Z. m. chrysolaemus (tenuifrons)*	Mountains of nw New Guinea (Arfak Mts. and Onin Peninsula)
_____	*Z. m. minor*	Mts. of n New Guinea (Cyclops, Sepik and Snow Mts.); Yapen I.
_____	*Z. m. rothschildi*	Mountains of central New Guinea (Weyland Mountains)
_____	*Z. m. gregarius*	Mountains of se New Guinea (Huon Peninsula)
_____	*Z. m. delicatulus*	SE New Guinea (Herzog to Hydrographer mts. and se peninsula)
_____	*Z. m. pallidogularis*	D'Entrecasteaux Archipelago (Fergusson and Goodenough)

☐ **White-throated White-eye** *Zosterops meeki*

Uplands of Tagula I. (Louisiade Archipelago). Status unknown

☐ **Black-headed White-eye** *Zosterops hypoxanthus*

_____	*Z. h. hypoxanthus*	Bismarck Archipelago (New Britain, Uatom and Mioko)
_____	*Z. h. ultimus*	Bismarck Archipelago (New Hanover and New Ireland)
_____	*Z. h. admiralitatis*	Manus I. (Admiralty Islands)

☐ **Biak White-eye** *Zosterops mysorensis*

Mountains of Biak and Supiori islands (off nw New Guinea)

☐ **Capped White-eye** *Zosterops fuscicapillus*

_____	*Z. f. fuscicapillus*	Mountains of coastal n New Guinea
_____	*Z. f. crookshanki*	Mountains of Goodenough I. (D'Entrecasteaux Archipelago)

☐ **Buru White-eye** *Zosterops buruensis*

Mainly montane forests of Buru (s Moluccas)

☐ **Ambon White-eye** *Zosterops kuehni*

S Moluccas (Seram and Ambon)

☐ **New Guinea White-eye** *Zosterops novaeguineae*
___ *Z. n. novaeguineae*
___ *Z. n. aruensis*
___ *Z. n. magnirostris*
___ *Z. n. wahgiensis*
___ *Z. n. wuroi*
___ *Z. n. crissalis*
___ *Z. n. oreophilus*

NW New Guinea (Vogelkop Mountains)
Aru Islands
Coastal ne New Guinea (opposite Manam I.)
C New Guinea (Wahgi Valley, Mt. Kubor and Bismarck Mts.)
Coastal s New Guinea (west of Fly River mouth)
Mountains of se New Guinea (Astrolabe Mountains)
Mountains of e New Guinea (Huon Peninsula)

☐ **Australian Yellow White-eye** *Zosterops luteus*
___ *Z. l. balstoni*
___ *Z. l. luteus*

Mangroves of coastal nw Western Australia
Mangroves of coastal Northern Territory and n Queensland

☐ **Louisiade White-eye** *Zosterops griseotinctus*
___ *Z. g. pallidipes*
___ *Z. g. griseotinctus (aignani)*
___ *Z. g. longirostris*
___ *Z. g. eichhorni*

Rossel I. (Louisiade Archipelago)
Louisiade Arch. (Misima, Deboyne, Duchateau and Conflict)
Bonvouloir, Heath and Alcester islands (Solomon Sea)
Bismarck Archipelago (Nauna, Nissan and Long islands)

☐ **Rennell White-eye** *Zosterops rennellianus*

Rennell (se Solomon Islands)

☐ **Banded White-eye** *Zosterops vellalavella*

Solomon Islands (Vella Lavella and Bagga)

☐ **Ganongga White-eye** *Zosterops splendidus*

Forests of Ranongga (w-central Solomon Islands)

☐ **Splendid White-eye** *Zosterops luteirostris*

Central Solomon Islands (Gizo and Ranongga)

☐ **Solomon Islands White-eye** *Zosterops kulambangrae*

Solomon Is. (Kulambangra and New Georgia group to Rendova)

☐ **Kulambangra White-eye** *Zosterops murphyi*

Kulambangra (central Solomon Islands)

☐ **Yellow-throated White-eye** *Zosterops metcalfii*
___ *Z. m. exigua*
___ *Z. m. metcalfii*
___ *Z. m. floridana*

Solomon Islands (Buka, Bougainville, Shortland and Choiseul)
Solomon Islands (Santa Isabel and San Jorge)
Florida I. (Solomon Islands)

☐ **Gray-throated White-eye** *Zosterops rendovae*
___ *Z. r. rendovae*
___ *Z. r. tetiparia*

Solomon Islands (Bougainville, San Cristóbal and Guadalcanal)
Tetipari (Solomon Islands)

☐ **Malaita White-eye** *Zosterops stresemanni*

Malaita (se Solomon Islands)

☐ **Santa Cruz White-eye** *Zosterops santaecrucis*

Nendo (Santa Cruz Islands se of Solomon Islands)

☐ **Large Lifou White-eye** *Zosterops inornatus*

Forests of Lifou (Loyalty Islands)

☐ **Green-backed White-eye** *Zosterops xanthochrous*

Mountains of New Caledonia, Ile des Pins and Maré

☐ **Small Lifou White-eye** *Zosterops minutus*

Forest and scrub of Lifou (Loyalty Islands)

☐ **Lord Howe White-eye** *Zosterops tephropleurus*

Lord Howe I. (off New Zealand)

☐ **Slender-billed White-eye** *Zosterops tenuirostris*

Norfolk I. (off New Zealand)

☐ **White-chested White-eye** *Zosterops albogularis*

NW Norfolk I. (off New Zealand). Possibly extinct

☐ **Layard's White-eye** *Zosterops explorator*

Fiji (Viti Levu, Ovalau, Gau, Vanua Levu, Taveuni and Kandavu)

☐ **Silver-eye** *Zosterops lateralis*
_____ *Z. l. ramsayi* — E Queensland
_____ *Z. l. lateralis* — SE Queensland to e New South Wales, Victoria and New Zealand
_____ *Z. l. familiaris* — E New South Wales
_____ *Z. l. halmaturinus* — W Victoria to se South Australia, Tasmania and Kangaroo I.
_____ *Z. l. gouldi* — S Western Australia and Récherche Archipelago
_____ *Z. l. chlorocephalus* — Capricorn Islands (Coral Sea off e Queensland)
_____ *Z. l. griseonotus* — New Caledonia
_____ *Z. l. nigrescens* — Loyalty Islands (Maré and Uvea)
_____ *Z. l. melanops* — Lifou (Loyalty Islands)
_____ *Z. l. macmillani* — Vanuatu (Tanna and Aniwa islands)
_____ *Z. l. tropicus* — Espíritu Santo I. (Vanuatu)
_____ *Z. l. vatensis* — N Vanuatu, Banks Group and Torres Islands
_____ *Z. l. valuensis* — Vanua Lava I. (Vanuatu)
_____ *Z. l. flaviceps* — Fiji Archipelago

☐ **Yellow-fronted White-eye** *Zosterops flavifrons*
_____ *Z. f. gauensis* — Gau I. (n Vanuatu)
_____ *Z. f. perplexa* — Vanua Lava I. (n Vanuatu)
_____ *Z. f. brevicauda* — N Vanuatu (Malo and Espíritu Santo)
_____ *Z. f. macgillivrayi* — Malekula I. (Vanuatu)
_____ *Z. f. efatensis* — Vanuatu (Nguna, Efate and Erromanga)
_____ *Z. f. flavifrons* — Tanna I. (Vanuatu)
_____ *Z. f. majuscula* — Aneityum I. (Vanuatu)

☐ **Samoan White-eye** *Zosterops samoensis*
Mountains of Savai'i (Western Samoa)

☐ **Dusky White-eye** *Zosterops finschii*
Woodlands of Palau Archipelago (w Caroline Islands)

☐ **Gray White-eye** *Zosterops cinereus*
_____ *Z. c. ponapensis* — Pohnpei (e Caroline Islands)
_____ *Z. c. cinereus* — Kosrae (e Caroline Islands)

☐ **Yap White-eye** *Zosterops oleagineus*
Forests of Yap (nw Caroline Islands)

☐ **Truk White-eye** *Rukia ruki*
Forests and scrub of Truk (e Caroline Islands)

☐ **Long-billed White-eye** *Rukia longirostra*
Mountains of Pohnpei (e Caroline Islands)

☐ **Golden White-eye** *Cleptornis marchei*
S Mariana Islands (Saipan and Aguijan)

☐ **Rufescent White-eye** *Tephrozosterops stalkeri*
Montane epiphyte forests of Seram (s Moluccas)

☐ **Rufous-throated White-eye** *Madanga ruficollis*
Rediscovered after 75-year absence on Buru (s Moluccas)

☐ **Javan Gray-throated White-eye** *Lophozosterops javanicus*
_____ *L. j. frontalis* — Mountains of w Java (Mt. Karang and Mt. Pangrango-Gedeh)
_____ *L. j. javanicus* — Mountains of central and e Java
_____ *L. j. elongatus* — Mountains of extreme e Java (Idjen Plateau) and Bali

☐ **Streak-headed White-eye** *Lophozosterops squamiceps*
_____ *L. s. heinrichi* — NW Sulawesi (Tentolo-Matinan Mountains)
_____ *L. s. stresemanni* — Mountains of ne Sulawesi
_____ *L. s. striaticeps* — Mountains of n central Sulawesi
_____ *L. s. stachyrinus* — S central Sulawesi (Latimojong Mountains)
_____ *L. s. analogus* — SE Sulawesi (Mengkoka Mountains)
_____ *L. s. squamiceps* — S Sulawesi (Lompobattang Massif)

☐ **Gray-hooded White-eye** *Lophozosterops pinaiae*
Tree-fern forests of Seram (s Moluccas)

☐ **Mindanao White-eye** *Lophozosterops goodfellowi*
____ *L. g. goodfellowi* — S Philippines (Mts. Apo, Matutum, Mayo, Katanglad on Mindanao)
____ *L. g. malindangensis* — S Philippines (Mt. Malindang on Mindanao)
____ *L. g. gracilis* — S Philippines (Mt. Hilong Hilong on ne Mindanao)

☐ **White-browed White-eye** *Lophozosterops superciliaris*
____ *L. s. hartertianus* — Sumbawa (w Lesser Sundas)
____ *L. s. superciliaris* — Flores (w Lesser Sundas)

☐ **Dark-crowned White-eye** *Lophozosterops dohertyi*
____ *L. d. dohertyi* — W Lesser Sundas (mountains of Sumbawa and Satonda)
____ *L. d. subcristatus* — W Lesser Sundas (mountains of Flores)

☐ **Pygmy White-eye** *Oculocincta squamifrons* — Montane moss forests of n Borneo (Sabah)

☐ **Flores White-eye** *Heleia crassirostris* — W Lesser Sundas (Flores and Sumbawa)

☐ **Timor White-eye** *Heleia muelleri* — Lowlands of w Timor (e Lesser Sundas)

☐ **Mountain Black-eye** *Chlorocharis emiliae*
____ *C. e. emiliae* — North Borneo (Mt. Kinabalu)
____ *C. e. trinitae* — North Borneo (Mt. Trus Madi)
____ *C. e. fusciceps* — Mountains of nw Borneo (ne Sarawak)
____ *C. e. moultoni* — Mountains of nw Borneo (w Sarawak)

☐ **Bare-eyed White-eye** *Woodfordia superciliosa* — Open woodlands of Rennell (se Solomon Islands)

☐ **Sanford's White-eye** *Woodfordia lacertosa* — Woodlands and scrub of Nendo (Santa Cruz Islands)

☐ **Giant White-eye** *Megazosterops palauensis* — Palau Archipelago (Babelthuap, Urukthapel and Peleliu)

☐ **Cinnamon White-eye** *Hypocryptadius cinnamomeus* — S Philippines (mountains of Mindanao)

FAMILY: PROMEROPIDAE (Sugarbirds—2)

☐ **Gurney's Sugarbird** *Promerops gurneyi*
____ *P. g. gurneyi* — E Transvaal to Natal and e Cape Province
____ *P. g. ardens* — E Zimbabwe to w-central Mozambique

☐ **Cape Sugarbird** *Promerops cafer* — South Africa (mountains of Cape Province)

FAMILY: MELIPHAGIDAE (Honeyeaters—174)

☐ **Olive Straightbill** *Timeliopsis fulvigula*
____ *T. f. fulvigula* — NW New Guinea (Arfak Mountains)
____ *T. f. montana* — Mts. of c New Guinea (Weyland Mts. to Wharton Range)
____ *T. f. meyeri* — Mountains of se New Guinea
____ *T. f. fuscicapilla* — E New Guinea (mountains of Huon Peninsula)

☐ **Tawny Straightbill** *Timeliopsis griseigula*
____ *T. g. griseigula* — W New Guinea (Vogelkop Peninsula to Weyland Mountains)
____ *T. g. fulviventris* — Mountains of se New Guinea

☐ **Long-billed Honeyeater** *Melilestes megarhynchus*

____	*M. m. vagans*	Batanta and Waigeo islands (New Guinea)
____	*M. m. brunneus*	Mountains of nw New Guinea; Misool and Salawati islands
____	*M. m. megarhynchus*	S New Guinea and Aru Islands
____	*M. m. stresemanni*	N New Guinea (Astrolabe Bay to Geelvink Bay); Yapen I.

☐ **Bougainville Honeyeater** *Stresemannia bougainvillei*

Mountains of Bougainville (nw Solomon Islands)

☐ **Green-backed Honeyeater** *Glycichaera fallax*

____	*G. f. pallida*	Batanta and Waigeo islands (New Guinea)
____	*G. f. poliocephala*	Aru Islands, Misool I. and nw New Guinea
____	*G. f. fallax*	New Guinea (west to Geelvink Bay and Onin Pen.); Yapen I.
____	*G. f. claudi*	NE Australia (Cape York Peninsula of n Queensland)

☐ **Sunda Honeyeater** *Lichmera lombokia*

W Lesser Sundas (Lombok, Sumbawa and Flores)

☐ **Olive Honeyeater** *Lichmera argentauris*

Moluccas and w Papuan islands

☐ **Brown Honeyeater** *Lichmera indistincta*

____	*L. i. ocularis*	SE New Guinea and ne Australia (Cape York Peninsula)
____	*L. i. nupta*	Aru Islands
____	*L. i. indistincta*	Western Australia and Northern Territory
____	*L. i. melvillensis*	Melville I. (n Australia)

☐ **Indonesian Honeyeater** *Lichmera limbata*

Bali and Lesser Sundas to Flores and Timor

☐ **Dark-brown Honeyeater** *Lichmera incana*

____	*L. i. incana*	New Caledonia
____	*L. i. poliotis*	Loyalty Islands (Beautemps, Beaupré, Uvéa and Lifou)
____	*L. i. mareensis*	Maré (Loyalty Islands)
____	*L. i. griseoviridis*	Central Vanuatu islands
____	*L. i. flavotincta*	Erromango I. (Vanuatu)

☐ **White-tufted Honeyeater** *Lichmera squamata*

Lesser Sundas (Wetar to Tanimbar and Kai islands)

☐ **Silver-eared Honeyeater** *Lichmera alboauricularis*

____	*L. a. olivacea*	Lowlands of n New Guinea (Lake Sentani to Ramu River)
____	*L. a. alboauricularis*	South coast of se New Guinea, Doini and Rogeia islands

☐ **Buru Honeyeater** *Lichmera deningeri*

Mountains of Buru (s Moluccas)

☐ **Seram Honeyeater** *Lichmera monticola*

Mountains of Seram (s Moluccas)

☐ **Yellow-eared Honeyeater** *Lichmera flavicans*

Timor (e Lesser Sundas)

☐ **Black-chested Honeyeater** *Lichmera notabilis*

Wetar (Lesser Sundas). Status unknown

☐ **White-streaked Honeyeater** *Trichodere cockerelli*

Tea-tree swamps of ne Queensland

☐ **Seram Myzomela** *Myzomela blasii*

S Moluccas (Seram, Ambon and Boano)

☐ **White-chinned Myzomela** *Myzomela albigula*

____	*M. a. albigula*	Rossell (Louisiade Archipelago)
____	*M. a. pallidior*	Louisiade Arch. (Misima, Bonvouloir, Deboyne and Conflict)

☐ **Red-throated Myzomela** *Myzomela eques*

____	*M. e. eques*	NW New Guinea, Waigeo, Salawati and Misool islands
____	*M. e. primitiva*	N New Guinea (Geelvink Bay to Astrolabe Bay)
____	*M. e. nymani*	S and e New Guinea
____	*M. e. karimuiensis*	E New Guinea

☐ **Ashy Myzomela** *Myzomela cineracea*

New Britain and Umboi islands (w Bismarck Archipelago)

☐ **Dusky Myzomela** *Myzomela obscura*
_____ *M. o. aruensis* — Aru Islands (New Guinea)
_____ *M. o. rubrobrunnea* — Biak I. (New Guinea)
_____ *M. o. fumata* — S New Guinea (Vogelkop to Port Moresby)
_____ *M. o. simplex* — N Moluccas (Halmahera, Damar, Ternate, Tidore and Bacan)
_____ *M. o. rubrotincta* — N Moluccas (Obi and Bisa)
_____ *M. o. mortyana* — Morotai (n Moluccas)
_____ *M. o. harterti* — Coastal e Queensland (Cooktown to Noosa region)
_____ *M. o. munna* — Islands in Torres Strait and Cape York Peninsula
_____ *M. o. obscura* — Coastal Northern Territory and Melville I.

☐ **Red Myzomela** *Myzomela cruentata*
_____ *M. c. cruentata* — New Guinea and Yapen I.
_____ *M. c. coccinea* — Bismarck Archipelago (New Britain and Duke of York)
_____ *M. c. erythrina* — New Ireland (Bismarck Archipelago)
_____ *M. c. lavongai* — New Hanover (Bismarck Archipelago)
_____ *M. c. cantans* — Tabar I. (Bismarck Archipelago)
_____ *M. c. vinacea* — Dyaul I. (Bismarck Archipelago)

☐ **Black Myzomela** *Myzomela nigrita*
_____ *M. n. steini* — Waigeo I. (New Guinea)
_____ *M. n. nigrita* — New Guinea and Aru Islands
_____ *M. n. meyeri* — N New Guinea and Yapen I.
_____ *M. n. nigerrima* — Long Island (ne New Guinea)
_____ *M. n. pluto* — Meos Num I. (New Guinea)
_____ *M. n. forbesi* — D'Entrecasteaux Archipelago
_____ *M. n. louisiadensis* — Louisiade Archipelago
_____ *M. n. hades* — St. Matthias Group (Bismarck Archipelago)
_____ *M. n. ramsayi* — Tingwon Islands (Bismarck Archipelago)
_____ *M. n. ernstmayri* — Manus I. (Admiralty Islands)

☐ **New Ireland Myzomela** *Myzomela pulchella*

New Ireland (Bismarck Archipelago)

☐ **Crimson-hooded Myzomela** *Myzomela kuehni*

Wetar (Lesser Sundas)

☐ **Red-headed Myzomela** *Myzomela erythrocephala*
_____ *M. e. infuscata* — S New Guinea, Aru Islands and coastal ne Australia
_____ *M. e. erythrocephala* — Mangroves of coastal n Western Australia

☐ **Sumba Myzomela** *Myzomela dammermani*

Mangroves of Sumba (w Lesser Sundas)

☐ **Mountain Myzomela** *Myzomela adolphinae*

Patchily distributed mountains of New Guinea

☐ **Sulawesi Myzomela** *Myzomela chloroptera*
_____ *M. c. chloroptera* — N Sulawesi (mountains of Minahassa Peninsula)
_____ *M. c. charlotta* — Mountains of central and se Sulawesi
_____ *M. c. juga* — Mt. Lompobattang (sw Sulawesi)
_____ *M. c. eva* — Salayar, Tanahjampea and Sula Islands (Taliabu)
_____ *M. c. batjanensis* — Bacan (n Moluccas)

☐ **Wakolo Myzomela** *Myzomela wakoloensis*
_____ *M. w. elisabethae* — Mountains of Seram (s Moluccas)
_____ *M. w. wakoloensis* — Mountains of Buru (s Moluccas)

☐ **Banda Myzomela** *Myzomela boiei*
_____ *M. b. boiei* — Banda (e Lesser Sundas)
_____ *M. b. annabellae* — E Lesser Sundas (Babar, Yamdena and Selaru)

☐ **New Caledonian Myzomela** *Myzomela caledonica*

Mangroves and forests of New Caledonia

☐ **Scarlet Myzomela** *Myzomela sanguinolenta*

Coastal e Australia (ne Queensland to extreme e Victoria)

☐ **Micronesian Myzomela** *Myzomela rubratra*
____ *M. r. rubratra*
____ *M. r. dichromata*
____ *M. r. major*
____ *M. r. kurodai*
____ *M. r. kobayashii*
____ *M. r. asuncionis*
____ *M. r. saffordi*

Kosrae (Caroline Islands)
Pohnpei (Caroline Islands)
Truk (Caroline Islands)
Yap (Caroline Islands)
Palau Islands (Babelthuap to Angaur)
N Mariana Islands
S Mariana Islands

☐ **Cardinal Myzomela** *Myzomela cardinalis*
____ *M. c. lifuensis*
____ *M. c. cardinalis*
____ *M. c. tenuis*
____ *M. c. tucopiae*
____ *M. c. nigriventris*
____ *M. c. santaecrucis*
____ *M. c. sanfordi*
____ *M. c. pulcherrima*

Loyalty Islands
Southern Vanuatu
Northern Vanuatu and Banks Group
Tikopia I. (ne of Banks Group)
Samoa (Upolu, Savai'i and Tutuila)
Solomon Islands (Santa Cruz and Torres)
Rennell (se Solomon Islands)
Solomon Islands (San Cristóbal and Ugi)

☐ **Rotuma Myzomela** *Myzomela chermesina*

Rotuma I. (nw of Fiji)

☐ **Scarlet-bibbed Myzomela** *Myzomela sclateri*

Karkar and small islands off ne New Guinea and New Britain

☐ **Ebony Myzomela** *Myzomela pammelaena*

Smaller islands in Bismarck Archipelago

☐ **Scarlet-naped Myzomela** *Myzomela lafargei*

Buka, Bougainville, Shortland, Fauro, Choiseul and Santa Isabel

☐ **Yellow-vented Myzomela** *Myzomela eichhorni*
____ *M. e. eichhorni*
____ *M. e. ganongae*
____ *M. e. atrata*

New Georgia, Rendova, Vangunu and Kulambangra islands
Ranongga (Solomon Islands)
Solomon Islands (Vellalavella and Baga)

☐ **Red-bellied Myzomela** *Myzomela malaitae*

Malaita (se Solomon Islands)

☐ **Black-headed Myzomela** *Myzomela melanocephala*

Solomon Islands (Florida, Savo and Guadalcanal)

☐ **Sooty Myzomela** *Myzomela tristrami*

Solomon Islands (San Cristóbal and Santa Anna)

☐ **Orange-breasted Myzomela** *Myzomela jugularis*

Fiji Islands, Yasawa Group and Lau Archipelago

☐ **Black-bellied Myzomela** *Myzomela erythromelas*

New Britain (Bismarck Archipelago)

☐ **Black-breasted Myzomela** *Myzomela vulnerata*

Timor (Lesser Sundas)

☐ **Red-collared Myzomela** *Myzomela rosenbergii*
____ *M. r. rosenbergii*
____ *M. r. wahgiensis*
____ *M. r. longirostris*

Mountains of nw New Guinea
Mountains of w and central New Guinea
Goodenough I. (D'Entrecasteaux Archipelago)

☐ **Banded Honeyeater** *Certhionyx pectoralis*

N Australia (Kimberleys to n Queensland)

☐ **Black Honeyeater** *Certhionyx niger*

Highly nomadic throughout arid interior of Australia

☐ **Pied Honeyeater** *Certhionyx variegatus*

Highly nomadic throughout arid interior of Australia

☐ **Forest Honeyeater** *Meliphaga montana*

_____ *M. m. montana*	Mountains of nw New Guinea
_____ *M. m. sepik*	N slope of mountains of central New Guinea
_____ *M. m. germanorum*	N New Guinea (Cyclops Mountains)
_____ *M. m. huonensis*	NE New Guinea (mountains of Huon Peninsula)
_____ *M. m. aicora*	N slope of mountains of se New Guinea
_____ *M. m. steini*	Yapen I. (New Guinea)

☐ **Spot-breasted Meliphaga** *Meliphaga mimikae*

_____ *M. m. rara*	N New Guinea (lowlands of upper Mamberamo River)
_____ *M. m. mimikae*	Central mountains of New Guinea
_____ *M. m. bastille*	NE New Guinea (Hydrographic Range)
_____ *M. m. granti*	Mountains of se New Guinea

☐ **Mountain Meliphaga** *Meliphaga orientalis*

_____ *M. o. facialis*	Mountains of central New Guinea and Waigeo I.
_____ *M. o. becki*	Mountains of ne New Guinea
_____ *M. o. orientalis*	Mountains of se New Guinea
_____ *M. o. citreola*	N New Guinea (n slope of Snow Mountains)

☐ **Scrub Honeyeater** *Meliphaga albonotata*

_____ *M. a. setekwa*	Foothills of south-central New Guinea
_____ *M. a. albonotata*	Foothills of s New Guinea

☐ **Puff-backed Honeyeater** *Meliphaga aruensis*

_____ *M. a. sharpei*	New Guinea, w Papuan islands and D'Entrecasteaux Arch.
_____ *M. a. aruensis*	S New Guinea and Aru Islands

☐ **Mimic Honeyeater** *Meliphaga analoga*

_____ *M. a. papuae*	S New Guinea (Fly River to Hall Sound)
_____ *M. a. analoga*	S New Guinea and w Papuan islands
_____ *M. a. longirostris*	Aru Islands
_____ *M. a. flavida*	Lowlands of n New Guinea, Yapen I. and Meos Num I.
_____ *M. a. connectens*	Lowlands of n New Guinea (Wewak to Huon Gulf)

☐ **Tagula Honeyeater** *Meliphaga vicina*

Lowlands of Tagula I. (Louisiade Arch.). Status unknown

☐ **Graceful Honeyeater** *Meliphaga gracilis*

_____ *M. g. stevensi*	N slope of mountains of se New Guinea
_____ *M. g. cinereifrons*	Lowlands of se New Guinea (west to Hall Sound); Sariba I.
_____ *M. g. gracilis*	S New Guinea, Aru Islands and n Queensland
_____ *M. g. imitatrix*	Lowland forests of ne Queensland

☐ **Yellow-spotted Honeyeater** *Meliphaga notata*

_____ *M. n. notata*	Islands in sw Torres Strait
_____ *M. n. mixta*	Lowlands of ne Queensland (Cooktown to Cardwell)

☐ **Yellow-gaped Honeyeater** *Meliphaga flavirictus*

_____ *M. f. crockettorum*	New Guinea (except for range of *flavirictus*)
_____ *M. f. flavirictus*	SE New Guinea (west to lower Fly River)

☐ **Lewin's Honeyeater** *Meliphaga lewinii*

_____ *M. l. lewinii*	NE Australia (e Queensland and e New South Wales)
_____ *M. l. amphochlora*	NE Australia (McIlwraith Range of Cape York Peninsula)
_____ *M. l. nea*	E Australia (rainforests of e Victoria)

☐ **White-lined Honeyeater** *Meliphaga albilineata*

NE Western Australia (w Kimberleys) and ne N Territory

☐ **Streak-breasted Honeyeater** *Meliphaga reticulata*

E Lesser Sundas (Timor and Semau)

☐ **Guadalcanal Honeyeater** *Guadalcanaria inexpectata*

Mountains of Guadacanal (se Solomon Islands)

☐ **Wattled Honeyeater** *Foulehaio carunculata*
____ *F. c. carunculata*
____ *F. c. taviuensis*
____ *F. c. procerior*

Samoa, e Fiji islands, Lau Archipelago and Tonga
Fiji (Taveuni and Vanua Levu)
Fiji (Viti Levu, Ovalau and islands in Yasawa Archipelago)

☐ **Black-throated Honeyeater** *Lichenostomus subfrenatus*
____ *L. s. subfrenatus*
____ *L. s. melanolaemus*
____ *L. s. utakwensis*
____ *L. s. salvadorii*

NW New Guinea (Arfak Mountains)
Central mountains of New Guinea
New Guinea (Weyland and Snow mountains)
Mountains of se New Guinea

☐ **Obscure Honeyeater** *Lichenostomus obscurus*
____ *L. o. viridifrons*
____ *L. o. obscurus*

NE New Guinea (mountains of Vogelkop Peninsula)
New Guinea (Weyland, Snow and Sepik mountains)

☐ **Bridled Honeyeater** *Lichenostomus frenatus*

Rainforests of ne Queensland (Cooktown to Townsville)

☐ **Eungella Honeyeater** *Lichenostomus hindwoodi*

Rainforests of Clarke Range (e-central Queensland)

☐ **Yellow-faced Honeyeater** *Lichenostomus chrysops*
____ *L. c. chrysops*
____ *L. c. samueli*

E Australia (ne Queensland to Victoria)
SE South Australia (west to Mt. Lofty Range and Adelaide)

☐ **Varied Honeyeater** *Lichenostomus versicolor*
____ *L. v. sonoroides*
____ *L. v. vulgaris*
____ *L. v. intermedia*
____ *L. v. versicolor*

NW New Guinea (Vogelkop Peninsula) and w Papuan islands
Coastal n New Guinea, Yapen I. and Fergusson I.
Samarai, Doini and Killerton islands (off e New Guinea)
Coastal s New Guinea, Torres Strait islands and ne Queensland

☐ **Mangrove Honeyeater** *Lichenostomus fasciogularis*

E Australia (e Queensland to n New South Wales)

☐ **Singing Honeyeater** *Lichenostomus virescens*
____ *L. v. virescens*
____ *L. v. insularis*
____ *L. v. westwoodia*
____ *L. v. forresti*
____ *L. v. cooperi*

W Australia and adjacent islands
Rottnest I. (off s Western Australia)
E Australia (s Queensland north to Rockingham)
NW and central Australia and Dampier Archipelago
Melville I. and adjacent coastal Northern Territory

☐ **Yellow Honeyeater** *Lichenostomus flavus*

Cape York Peninsula (s to Flinders River and Broad Sound)

☐ **White-gaped Honeyeater** *Lichenostomus unicolor*

Mangroves and riverine forests of n Australia

☐ **White-eared Honeyeater** *Lichenostomus leucotis*
____ *L. l. novaenorciae*
____ *L. l. leucotis*

S Western Australia
SE Queensland to Victoria, se South Australia and Kangaroo I.

☐ **Yellow-throated Honeyeater** *Lichenostomus flavicollis*

Tasmania, King and Furneaux islands

☐ **Yellow-tufted Honeyeater** *Lichenostomus melanops*
____ *L. m. melanops*
____ *L. m. cassidix*

SE Queensland to e New South Wales, e and central Victoria
S Victoria and extreme se South Australia

☐ **Purple-gaped Honeyeater** *Lichenostomus cratitius*
____ *L. c. cratitius*
____ *L. c. halmaturinus*

W Victoria, se South Australia and sw Western Australia
Kangaroo I. (South Australia)

☐ **Gray-headed Honeyeater** *Lichenostomus keartlandi*

Arid savanna of w and central Australia

☐ **Yellow-tinted Honeyeater** *Lichenostomus flavescens*

Coastal n Australia and savanna of se New Guinea

☐ **Fuscous Honeyeater** *Lichenostomus fuscus*

____ *L. f. deserticolus*	Interior of arid n Western Australia
____ *L. f. melvillensis*	Melville I. (Northern Territory)
____ *L. f. zanda*	N Australia (nw Queensland and adjacent e Northern Territory)
____ *L. f. subgermanus*	E Australia (e Queensland from Cairns to Mackay)
____ *L. f. dawsoni*	E Australia (se Queensland north to Mackay))
____ *L. f. fuscus*	E New South Wales to Victoria and se South Australia

☐ **Gray-fronted Honeyeater** *Lichenostomus plumulus*

____ *L. p. planasi*	N Western Australia (Kimberly Division)
____ *L. p. plumulus*	Arid interior of Australia
____ *L. p. ethelae*	W New South Wales, nw Victoria and e South Australia

☐ **Yellow-plumed Honeyeater** *Lichenostomus ornatus*

Mallee woodlands of s Australia

☐ **White-plumed Honeyeater** *Lichenostomus penicillatus*

____ *L. p. geraldtonensis*	Coastal Western Australia (Geraldton to Point Cloates)
____ *L. p. carteri*	Coastal Western Australia (Point Cloates to De Grey River)
____ *L. p. ladasi*	Central Western Australia
____ *L. p. centralia*	Arid central Australia
____ *L. p. leilavalensis*	Interior and w Queensland and ne South Australia
____ *L. p. interioris*	SW Queensland and nw New South Wales
____ *L. p. penicillatus*	Interior se Queensland to n Victoria and *mallee* of e S Australia
____ *L. p. mellori*	SW Victoria and se South Australia (west to Mt. Lofty Range)

☐ **Tawny-breasted Honeyeater** *Xanthotis flaviventer*

____ *X. f. fusciventris*	Waigeo and Batanta islands (New Guinea)
____ *X. f. flaviventer*	NW New Guinea, Misool and Salawati islands
____ *X. f. rubiensis*	West-central New Guinea
____ *X. f. saturatior*	Aru Is. and s New Guinea (Mimika River to upper Fly River)
____ *X. f. tararae*	Coastal s New Guinea (lower Digul River to Fly River)
____ *X. f. giulianettii*	SE New Guinea (Hall Sound to Port Moresby)
____ *X. f. visi*	SE New Guinea (Cloudy Bay to Milne Bay)
____ *X. f. kumusii*	N coast of se New Guinea (Collingwood Bay to Aicora River)
____ *X. f. madaraszi*	NE New Guinea (Huon Peninsula)
____ *X. f. philemon*	N New Guinea (Astrolabe Bay to Mamberamo River)
____ *X. f. meyeri*	Yapen I. (New Guinea)
____ *X. f. spilogaster*	Trobriand Islands and D'Entrecasteaux Archipelago
____ *X. f. filigera*	NE Australia (n Cape York Peninsula)

☐ **Spotted Honeyeater** *Xanthotis polygramma*

____ *X. p. polygramma*	Waigeo I. (New Guinea)
____ *X. p. keuhni*	Misool I. (New Guinea)
____ *X. p. poikilosternos*	Lower mountain slopes of w New Guinea and Salawati I.
____ *X. p. septentrionalis*	N New Guinea (Mamberamo River to upper Sepik River)
____ *X. p. lophotis*	Mountains of se New Guinea
____ *X. p. candidior*	S New Guinea (Trans-Fly lowlands)

☐ **Macleay's Honeyeater** *Xanthotis macleayana*

Rainforests of ne Queensland (Cooktown to Townsville)

☐ **Kandavu Honeyeater** *Xanthotis provocator*

Forests and scrub of Kandavu (sw Fiji)

☐ **Orange-cheeked Honeyeater** *Oreornis chrysogenys*

W-central New Guinea (timberline zone of Snow Mountains)

☐ **Bonin Honeyeater** *Apalopteron familiare*

____ *A. f. familiare*	Muko-Shima (n Bonin Islands)
____ *A. f. hahasima*	Haha-Shima Group (s Bonin Islands)

☐ White-naped Honeyeater *Melithreptus lunatus*
_____ *M. l. lunatus*   E Queensland to se New South Wales and se South Australia
_____ *M. l. chloropsis*   Locally in sw Western Australia (Moora to Esperance Bay)

☐ Black-headed Honeyeater *Melithreptus affinis*
_____ *M. a. alisteri*   King I. and Furneaux Group (Bass Strait)
_____ *M. a. affinis*   Tasmania

☐ White-throated Honeyeater *Melithreptus albogularis*
_____ *M. a. albogularis*   N Territory, n Queensland, nw New S Wales and s New Guinea
_____ *M. a. subalbogularis*   Tropical n Western Australia

☐ Black-chinned Honeyeater *Melithreptus gularis*
_____ *M. g. parus*   Western Australia (Exmouth Gulf region)
_____ *M. g. laetior*   N Western Australia, s N Territory and n South Australia
_____ *M. g. normantoniensis*   NE Australia (nw Queensland south of Gulf of Carpentaria)
_____ *M. g. carpentarianus*   E Australia (interior of central Queensland)
_____ *M. g. gularis*   NE Australia (Queensland to Victoria and se South Australia)

☐ Strong-billed Honeyeater *Melithreptus validirostris*
_____ *M. v. kingi*   King I. and Furneaux Group (Bass Strait)
_____ *M. v. validirostris*   Tasmania

☐ Brown-headed Honeyeater *Melithreptus brevirostris*
_____ *M. b. augustus*   S Western Australia, s South Australia and nw Victoria
_____ *M. b. brevirostris*   SE Queensland to Victoria and King I.
_____ *M. b. magnirostris*   Kangaroo I. (South Australia)

☐ Stitchbird *Notiomystis cincta*
_____ *N. c. hautura*   Little Barrier I. (New Zealand)
_____ *N. c. cincta†*   Formerly Great Barrier, North and Kapiti is. Extinct ca 1885

☐ Plain Honeyeater *Pycnopygius ixoides*
_____ *P. i. ixoides*   NW New Guinea (east to Geelvink Bay)
_____ *P. i. simplex*   N New Guinea (Mamberamo River to middle Sepik River)
_____ *P. i. proximus*   N New Guinea (middle Sepik River to Astrolabe Bay)
_____ *P. i. unicus*   NE New Guinea
_____ *P. i. cinereifrons*   S New Guinea (Mimika River to upper Fly River)
_____ *P. i. finschi*   N coast of se New Guinea (Kumusi River to Milne Bay)

☐ Marbled Honeyeater *Pycnopygius cinereus*
_____ *P. c. cinereus*   NW New Guinea (mountains of Vogelkop Peninsula)
_____ *P. c. dorsalis*   W New Guinea (Weyland and Nassau mountains)
_____ *P. c. marmoratus*   E New Guinea (Adelbert Mts. and Huon Peninsula mountains)

☐ Streak-headed Honeyeater *Pycnopygius stictocephalus*
Lowlands of New Guinea, Salawati I. and Aru Islands

☐ White-streaked Friarbird *Melitograis gilolensis*
N Moluccas (Morotai, Halmahera, Kasiruta and Bacan)

☐ Meyer's Friarbird *Philemon meyeri*
Lowlands of New Guinea (except for Vogelkop region)

☐ Timor Friarbird *Philemon inornatus*
Timor (e Lesser Sundas)

☐ Gray Friarbird *Philemon kisserensis*
E Lesser Sundas (Kisar, Leti and Moa)

☐ Brass' Friarbird *Philemon brassi*
Unreported since 1940 discovery in nw New Guinea

☐ Dusky Friarbird *Philemon fuscicapillus*
N Moluccas (Halmahera, Bacan and Morotai)

☐ **Little Friarbird** *Philemon citreogularis*

____ *P. c. papuensis*	Trans-Fly savanna of s New Guinea
____ *P. c. occidentalis*	N Western Australia
____ *P. c. breda*	Melville I. (Northern Territory)
____ *P. c .sordidus*	N Northern Territory (Borroloola to Daly River)
____ *P. c. carpenteriae*	NW Queensland (along south coast of Gulf of Carpentaria)
____ *P. c. johnstoni*	NE Queensland (south to Cairns region)
____ *P. c. citreogularis*	E and central Queensland to Victoria and se South Australia

☐ **Black-faced Friarbird** *Philemon moluccensis*

____ *P. m. moluccensis*	Buru (n Moluccas)
____ *P. m. plumigenis*	Tanimbar Is. (Larat, Yamdena); Kai Is. (Kai Kecil, Kai Besar)

☐ **Seram Friarbird** *Philemon subcorniculatus*

Lowlands of Seram (s Moluccas)

☐ **Helmeted Friarbird** *Philemon buceroides*

____ *P. b. novaeguineae*	New Guinea, ne Australia and Melville I.
____ *P. b. buceroides*	E Lesser Sundas (Sawu, Roti, Timor, Semau and Wetar)
____ *P. b. neglectus*	W Lesser Sundas (Lombok and Sumba and Flores)

☐ **White-naped Friarbird** *Philemon albitorques*

Manus I. (nw Bismarck Archipelago)

☐ **New Britain Friarbird** *Philemon cockerelli*

____ *P. c. umboi*	Umboi I. (sw Bismarck Archipelago)
____ *P. c. cockerelli*	Bismarck Archipelago (New Britain and Duke of York)

☐ **New Ireland Friarbird** *Philemon eichhorni*

New Ireland (e Bismarck Archipelago)

☐ **Silver-crowned Friarbird** *Philemon argenticeps*

____ *P. a. argenticeps*	Western Australia (Kimberly Division south to Fitzroy River)
____ *P. a. melvillensis*	Melville I. and Groote Eylandt (Northern Territory)
____ *P. a. alexis*	N Australia (tropical n Northern Territory)
____ *P. a. kempi*	NE Australia (n Queensland south to Townsville region)

☐ **Noisy Friarbird** *Philemon corniculatus*

____ *P. c. ellioti*	Trans-Fly lowlands of se New Guinea and ne Queensland
____ *P. c. clamans*	NE Australia (se Queensland north to Mackay)
____ *P. c. corniculatus*	E New South Wales, ne victoria and se South Australia

☐ **New Caledonian Friarbird** *Philemon diemenensis*

Forests of New Caledonia, Maré and Lifou

☐ **Leaden Honeyeater** *Ptiloprora plumbea*

____ *P. p. granti*	Central Highlands of New Guinea
____ *P. p. plumbea*	Mountains of se New Guinea and Herzog Mountains

☐ **Olive-streaked Honeyeater** *Ptiloprora meekiana*

____ *P. m. occidentalis*	Central New Guinea (Nassau and Snow mountains)
____ *P. m. meekiana*	Herzog Mountains and mountains of se New Guinea

☐ **Rufous-sided Honeyeater** *Ptiloprora erythropleura*

____ *P. e. erythropleura*	NW New Guinea (mountains of Vogelkop Peninsula)
____ *P. e. dammermani*	Central mountain ranges of New Guinea

☐ **Mayr's Honeyeater** *Ptiloprora mayri*

N New Guinea (Foya, Cyclops and Bewani mountains)

☐ **Rufous-backed Honeyeater** *Ptiloprora guisei*

____ *P. g. acrophila*	Coastal n New Guinea
____ *P. g. umbrosa*	N New Guinea (Sepik Mountains)
____ *P. g. guisei*	Herzog Mountains and mountains of se New Guinea

☐ **Black-backed Honeyeater** *Ptiloprora perstriata*

____	*P. p. praedicta*	NW New Guinea (Wandammen Mountains)
____	*P. p. incerta*	Mountains of w-central New Guinea
____	*P. p. perstriata*	Mountains of central and e New Guinea

☐ **Sooty Melidectes** *Melidectes fuscus*

____	*M. f. occidentalis*	Subalpine forests of central mountain ranges of New Guinea
____	*M. f. gilliardi*	E New Guinea (Bismarck Mountains)
____	*M. f. fuscus*	SE New Guinea (Scratchley and Wharton mountains)

☐ **Bismarck Melidectes** *Melidectes whitemanensis*

Mountains of central New Britain (Bismarck Archipelago)

☐ **Short-bearded Melidectes** *Melidectes nouhuysi*

W New Guinea (Mt. Wilhelmina in Snow Mountains)

☐ **Long-bearded Melidectes** *Melidectes princeps*

Alpine grasslands of e-central New Guinea

☐ **Cinnamon-browed Melidectes** *Melidectes ochromelas*

____	*M. o. ochromelas*	W New Guinea (Tamrau, Arfak and Wandammen mountains)
____	*M. o. batesi*	SE New Guinea (Weyland and Nassau mountains)
____	*M. o. lucifer*	NE New Guinea (mountains of Huon Peninsula)

☐ **Vogelkop Melidectes** *Melidectes leucostephes*

W New Guinea (Tamrau, Arfak, Fak Fak and Kumawa mts.)

☐ **Belford's Melidectes** *Melidectes belfordi*

____	*M. b. brassi*	Mountains of nw New Guinea
____	*M. b. joiceyi*	W New Guinea (Weyland Mountains)
____	*M. b. kinneari*	S New Guinea (Nassau and Snow mountains)
____	*M. b. belfordi*	Central Highlands and mountains of se New Guinea
____	*M. b. schraderensis*	NE New Guinea (Schrader Mountains)

☐ **Yellow-browed Melidectes** *Melidectes rufocrissalis*

____	*M. r. rufocrissalis*	Sepik Mts. and central mountain ranges of New Guinea
____	*M. r. thomasi*	Mountains of e New Guinea
____	*M. r. gilliardi*	Mountains of e-central New Guinea

☐ **Huon Melidectes** *Melidectes foersteri*

NE New Guinea (montane forests of Huon Peninsula)

☐ **Ornate Melidectes** *Melidectes torquatus*

____	*M. t. torquatus*	NW New Guinea (mountains of Vogelkop Peninsula)
____	*M. t. nuchalis*	Central New Guinea (Weyland, Nassau and Snow mountains)
____	*M. t. mixtus*	Central New Guinea (Snow Mts. to Victor Emanuel Mountains)
____	*M. t. cahni*	NE New Guinea (mountains of Huon Peninsula)
____	*M. t. polyphonus*	NE New Guinea (Bismarck range to Herzog Mountains)
____	*M. t. emilii*	Mountains of se New Guinea

☐ **San Cristobal Melidectes** *Melidectes sclateri*

Mountains of San Cristóbal (Solomon Islands)

☐ **Arfak Honeyeater** *Melipotes gymnops*

NW New Guinea (Arfak, Tamrau and Wandammen mountains)

☐ **Smoky Honeyeater** *Melipotes fumigatus*

____	*M. f. goliathi*	Mountains of central New Guinea
____	*M. f. fumigatus*	Mountains of se New Guinea
____	*M. f. kumawa*	Extreme nw New Guinea (Kumawa Mountains)

☐ **Spangled Honeyeater** *Melipotes ater*

NE New Guinea (montane forests of Huon Peninsula)

☐ **Dark-eared Honeyeater** *Myza celebensis*

____	*M. c. celebensis*	Mountains of n, central and se Sulawesi
____	*M. c. meriodionalis*	Mountains of s Sulawesi

☐ **Greater Streaked Honeyeater** *Myza sarasinorum*

_____ *M. s. sarasinorum*	Mountains of n Sulawesi
_____ *M. s. chionogenys*	Mountains of n-central and s-central Sulawesi
_____ *M. s. pholidota*	Mountains of se Sulawesi

☐ **Giant Honeyeater** *Gymnomyza viridis*

_____ *G. v. viridis*	Fiji (Taveuni and Vanua Levu)
_____ *G. v. brunneirostris*	Fiji (Viti Levu)

☐ **Mao** *Gymnomyza samoensis*

Samoa (mountains of Savai'i, Upolu and Tutuila)

☐ **Crow Honeyeater** *Gymnomyza aubryana*

New Caledonia

☐ **Kauai Oo** *Moho braccatus*

Alakai Swamp of Kauai (Hawaiian Is.). On verge of extinction

☐ **Bishop's Oo** *Moho bishopi*

Maui (Hawaiian Islands). On verge of extinction

☐ **Crescent Honeyeater** *Phylidonyris pyrrhoptera*

_____ *P. p. pyrrhoptera*	E Australia (e New South Wales and s Victoria)
_____ *P. p. indistincta*	Locally in coastal se South Australia and Mt. Lofty region
_____ *P. p. halmaturina*	Kangaroo I. (Bass Strait)
_____ *P. p. rex*	King I. and Furneaux Group (Bass Strait)
_____ *P. p. inornata*	Tasmania

☐ **New Holland Honeyeater** *Phylidonyris novaehollandiae*

_____ *P. n. longirostris*	SW Western Australia
_____ *P. n. novaehollandiae*	Coastal s Queensland to se South Australia
_____ *P. n. campbelli*	Kangaroo I. (Bass Strait)
_____ *P. n. caudata*	King I. and Furneaux Group (Bass Strait)
_____ *P. n. canescens*	Tasmania

☐ **White-cheeked Honeyeater** *Phylidonyris nigra*

_____ *P. n. nigra*	E Australia (coastal e Queensland and e New South Wales)
_____ *P. n. gouldii*	Coastal sw Western Australia

☐ **White-fronted Honeyeater** *Phylidonyris albifrons*

Arid woodlands of Australia

☐ **Barred Honeyeater** *Phylidonyris undulata*

Montane forests of New Caledonia

☐ **New Hebrides Honeyeater** *Phylidonyris notabilis*

_____ *P. n. notabilis*	Banks Group and nw Vanuatu
_____ *P. n. superciliaris*	N Vanuatu (Espiritu Santo to Epi)

☐ **Tawny-crowned Honeyeater** *Phylidonyris melanops*

_____ *P. m. melanops*	New South Wales, Victoria, S Australia and sw W Australia
_____ *P. m. braba*	Kangaroo I. (Bass Strait)
_____ *P. m. crassirostris*	Tasmania, King I. and Furneaux Group (Bass Strait)

☐ **Brown-backed Honeyeater** *Ramsayornis modestus*

Mangroves of s New Guinea, ne Australia and adjacent islands

☐ **Bar-breasted Honeyeater** *Ramsayornis fasciatus*

_____ *R. f. fasciatus*	N Australia (coastal n Northern Territory and n Queensland)
_____ *R. f. apsleyi*	Melville I. (Northern Territory)
_____ *R. f. broomei*	Coastal n Western Australia (Kimberly Division)

☐ **Striped Honeyeater** *Plectorhyncha lanceolata*

NE Queensland to New South Wales and adj. se S Australia

☐ **Rufous-banded Honeyeater** *Conopophila albogularis*

_____ *C. a. mimikae*	N and s New Guinea and Aru Islands
_____ *C. a. albogularis*	N Territory, Melville I., Cape York Peninsula and n Queensland

☐ **Rufous-throated Honeyeater** *Conopophila rufogularis*
_____ *C. r. rufogularis* — N Western Australia (Kimberly Div.) and n Northern Territory
_____ *C. r. queenslandica* — NE Australia (n Queensland)

☐ **Gray Honeyeater** *Conopophila whitei*
— Arid scrub of w Australia

☐ **Painted Honeyeater** *Grantiella picta*
— Northern Territory to Queensland, New S Wales and Victoria

☐ **Regent Honeyeater** *Xanthomyza phrygia*
— SE Queensland to s Victoria and adjacent se South Australia

☐ **Eastern Spinebill** *Acanthorhynchus tenuirostris*
_____ *A. t. cairnsensis* — NE Queensland (Cooktown south to Bundaberg)
_____ *A. t. trochiloides* — SE Queensland (Bunya Mountains) to n New South Wales
_____ *A. t. tenuirostris* — E New South Wales, e and s Victoria and se South Australia
_____ *A. t. loftyi* — S Australia (Adelaide Plains, Mt. Lofty and Flinders ranges)
_____ *A. t. halmaturinus* — Kangaroo I. (Bass Strait)
_____ *A. t. regius* — King I. and Furneaux Group (Bass Strait)
_____ *A. t. dubius* — Tasmania

☐ **Western Spinebill** *Acanthorhynchus superciliosus*
— Extreme coastal sw Western Australia

☐ **Blue-faced Honeyeater** *Entomyzon cyanotis*
_____ *E. c. harterti* — S New Guinea (Trans-Fly lowlands) and n Queensland
_____ *E. c. albipennis* — N Western Australia and Northern Territory
_____ *E. c. apsleyi* — Melville I. (Northern Territory)
_____ *E. c. cyanotis* — E and central Queensland to Victoria and se South Australia

☐ **Bell Miner** *Manorina melanophrys*
— Coastal e Australia (se Queensland to s Victoria)

☐ **Noisy Miner** *Manorina melanocephala*
_____ *M. m. crassirostris* — E Australia (locally in e Queensland north to Cooktown)
_____ *M. m. melanocephala* — New South Wales, Victoria, se South Australia and Tasmania

☐ **Yellow-throated Miner** *Manorina flavigula*
_____ *M. f. casuarina* — Western Australia (Kimberly Division)
_____ *M. f. lutea* — Arid w Western Australia
_____ *M. f. obscura* — Arid sw Western Australia
_____ *M. f. alligator* — Northern Territory
_____ *M. f. melvillensis* — Melville I. (Northern Territory)
_____ *M. f. pallida* — Central Australia (Musgrave and Macdonnell ranges)
_____ *M. f. flavigula* — Queensland to Victoria, South Australia and se W Australia

☐ **Black-eared Miner** *Manorina melanotis*
— Restricted to *mallee* of south-central Australia

☐ **New Zealand Bellbird** *Anthornis melanura*
_____ *A. m. obscura* — Three Kings Islands (New Zealand)
_____ *A. m. dumerilii* — North I. and adjacent offshore islands (New Zealand)
_____ *A. m. oneho* — Central New Zealand
_____ *A. m. melanocephala†* — Formerly Chatham Islands. Extinct ca 1906
_____ *A. m. melanura* — South I. and Stewart I. (New Zealand)
_____ *A. m. incoronata* — Auckland Islands

☐ **Spiny-cheeked Honeyeater** *Acanthagenys rufogularis*
_____ *A. r. rufogularis* — Arid interior of Australia
_____ *A. r. parker* — Friday I. (Torres Strait)

☐ **Red Wattlebird** *Anthochaera carunculata*
_____ *A. c. carunculata* — SE Queensland to Victoria, Western Australia and Kangaroo I.
_____ *A. c. woodwardi* — SW Western Australia

☐ **Brush Wattlebird** *Anthochaera chrysoptera*

_____ *A. c. chrysoptera*	Coastal se Queensland to Victoria and se South Australia
_____ *A. c. halmaturina*	Kangaroo I. (Bass Strait)
_____ *A. c. tasmanica*	Tasmania

☐ **Little Wattlebird** *Anthochaera lunulata*

Forests and coastal heath of sw Western Australia

☐ **Yellow Wattlebird** *Anthochaera paradoxa*

Tasmania, Furneaux Group and King I. (Bass Strait)

☐ **Tui** *Prosthemadera novaeseelandiae*

_____ *P. n. novaeseelandiae*	New Zealand, Stewart I. and Auckland Islands
_____ *P. n. kermadecensis*	Kermadec Islands
_____ *P. n. chathamensis*	Chatham Islands

FAMILY: ORIOLIDAE (Old World Orioles—29)

☐ **Timor Oriole** *Oriolus melanotis*

_____ *O. m. melanotis*	E Lesser Sundas (Roti, Timor and Semau)
_____ *O. m. finschi*	Wetar (e Lesser Sundas)

☐ **Buru Oriole** *Oriolus bouroensis*

_____ *O. b. bouroensis*	Buru (s Moluccas)
_____ *O. b. decipiens*	Tanimbar Islands (Arafura Sea)

☐ **Seram Oriole** *Oriolus forsteni*

Seram (s Moluccas)

☐ **Halmahera Oriole** *Oriolus phaeochromus*

Halmahera (n Moluccas)

☐ **Brown Oriole** *Oriolus szalayi*

New Guinea and w Papuan islands

☐ **Olive-backed Oriole** *Oriolus sagittatus*

_____ *O. s. magnirostris*	Lowlands of s New Guinea and n Queensland
_____ *O. s. affinis*	Coastal ne W Australia and Northern Territory to Queensland
_____ *O. s. sagittatus*	Queensland to Victoria and coastal se South Australia

☐ **Green Oriole** *Oriolus flavocinctus*

Aru Islands, s New Guinea, e Lesser Sundas and n Australia

☐ **Dark-throated Oriole** *Oriolus xanthonotus*

_____ *O. x. xanthonotus*	S Myanmar, Thailand, Malaysia, Sumatra, sw Borneo and Java
_____ *O. x. consobrinus*	Borneo and adjacent islands
_____ *O. x. mentawi*	Mentawi Archipelago and adjacent islands off Sumatra
_____ *O. x. persuasus*	SW Philippines (Palawan and Culion)

☐ **White-lored Oriole** *Oriolus albiloris*

N Philippines (montane forests of Luzon)

☐ **Philippine Oriole** *Oriolus steerii*

_____ *O. s. samarensis*	Philippines (Leyte, e Mindanao and Samar)
_____ *O. s. steerii*	S Philippines (Basilan and w Mindanao)
_____ *O. s. nigrostriatus*	Philippines (Masbate and Negros)
_____ *O. s. assimilis†*	Philippines. Formerly Cebu (last recorded 1906)
_____ *O. s. cinereogenys*	Sulu Archipelago

☐ **Isabela Oriole** *Oriolus isabellae*

N Philippines (mountains of n Luzon)

☐ **Eurasian Golden Oriole** *Oriolus oriolus*

_____ *O. o. oriolus*	W Palearctic to e Siberia; winters to Africa and nw India
_____ *O. o. kundoo*	W Siberia to Indian subcontinent

☐ African Golden Oriole *Oriolus auratus*
___ *O. a. auratus* — Senegambia to Sudan, Uganda, s Ethiopia and s Somalia
___ *O. a. notatus* — Angola to Tanzania, Mozambique and ne South Africa

☐ Black-naped Oriole *Oriolus chinensis*
___ *O. c. invisus* — S Vietnam
___ *O. c. diffusus* — E Asia; winters to India, Malaysia and Indochina
___ *O. c. andamanensis* — Andaman Islands
___ *O. c. macrourus* — Nicobar Islands
___ *O. c. chinensis* — Philippine Islands
___ *O. c. suluensis* — Sulu Archipelago
___ *O. c. melanisticus* — Talaud Islands (Karakelong and Salebabu)
___ *O. c. sanghirensis* — Sangihe and Tabuken islands (off n Sulawesi)
___ *O. c. formosus* — Siau, Tahulandang, Ruang, Biaro and Mayu is. (off Sulawesi)
___ *O. c. celebensis* — Sulawesi, Bangka, Talisei, Lembeh, Togian Is., Muna, Butung
___ *O. c. frontalis* — Banggai and Sula islands (off Sulawesi)
___ *O. c. oscillans* — Tukangbesi Islands (off Sulawesi)
___ *O. c. boneratensis* — Tanahjampea, Bonerate, Lalaotoa, Madu and Kayuadi islands
___ *O. c. mundus* — Simeulue I. (off Sumatra)
___ *O. c. sipora* — Sipura I. (off Sumatra)
___ *O. c. richmondi* — Siberut and Pagi islands (off Sumatra)
___ *O. c. insularis* — Kangean Islands (Java Sea)
___ *O. c. broderipii* — Lesser Sundas (Lombok, Sumba, Sumbawa, Flores, Bisar, Alor)
___ *O. c. maculatus* — Sumatra, Java, Borneo, Bali, Belitung and Nias islands

☐ Slender-billed Oriole *Oriolus tenuirostris*
E Himalayas to sw China and n SE Asia

☐ Green-headed Oriole *Oriolus chlorocephalus*
___ *O. c. amani* — Montane forests of extreme se Kenya to Tanzania
___ *O. c. chlorocephalus* — Malawi and Mozambique
___ *O. c. speculifer* — S Mozambique

☐ Sao Tome Oriole *Oriolus crassirostris*
Forests of São Tomé (Gulf of Guinea)

☐ Western Black-headed Oriole *Oriolus brachyrhynchus*
___ *O. b. brachyrhynchus* — Sierra Leone and Guinea to Ivory Coast
___ *O. b. laetior* — S Nigeria and Cameroon to s Uganda and extreme w Kenya

☐ Dark-headed Oriole *Oriolus monacha*
___ *O. m. monacha* — Montane juniper forests of n Ethiopia and Eritrea
___ *O. m. meneliki* — Montane juniper forests of s Ethiopia

☐ African Black-headed Oriole *Oriolus larvatus*
___ *O. l. angolensis* — Angola to Namibia, Kenya and Tanzania
___ *O. l. additus* — SE Tanzania and Mozambique
___ *O. l. larvatus* — South Africa

☐ Black-tailed Oriole *Oriolus percivali*
Humid montane forests of e Africa

☐ Black-winged Oriole *Oriolus nigripennis*
___ *O. n. alleni* — West Africa (Sierra Leone to Nigeria)
___ *O. n. nigripennis* — Cameroon to se Sudan, w Uganda and nw Angola; Bioko

☐ Black-hooded Oriole *Oriolus xanthornus*
___ *O. x. xanthornus* — N India, Myanmar, Thailand, Malaysia, Indochina and Sumatra
___ *O. x. maderaspatanus* — S peninsular India
___ *O. x. andamanensis* — Andaman Islands
___ *O. x. ceylonensis* — Sri Lanka
___ *O. x. tanakae* — Coastal ne Borneo and adjacent offshore islands

☐ **Black Oriole** *Oriolus hosii*

Montane forests of n Sarawak (n Borneo)

☐ **Black-and-crimson Oriole** *Oriolus cruentus*
_____ *O. c. malayanus*   Malay Peninsula
_____ *O. c. consanguineus*   Sumatra
_____ *O. c. vulneratus*   Mountains of n Borneo
_____ *O. c. cruentus*   Java

☐ **Maroon Oriole** *Oriolus traillii*
_____ *O. t. traillii*   Himalayan foothills to Myanmar, n Thailand and n Indochina
_____ *O. t. robinsoni*   S Laos and s Vietnam
_____ *O. t. nigellicauda*   N Vietnam and Hainan (s China)
_____ *O. t. ardens*   Taiwan

☐ **Silver Oriole** *Oriolus mellianus*

Mountains of s China; winters to s Thailand and Cambodia

☐ **Wetar Figbird** *Sphecotheres hypoleucus*

Lowlands of Wetar (e Lesser Sundas)

☐ **Green Figbird** *Sphecotheres viridis*
_____ *S. v. vieilloti*   Coastal se New Guinea and ne Australia (s to New South Wales)
_____ *S. v. viridis*   E Lesser Sundas (Roti, Semau and Timor)
_____ *S. v. flaviventris*   Kai Islands; W Australia, Northern Territory and Queensland

FAMILY: IRENIDAE (Fairy-bluebirds—2)

☐ **Asian Fairy-bluebird** *Irena puella*
_____ *I. p. puella*   India to Myanmar, Thailand and Indochina
_____ *I. p. malayensis*   Malaysia
_____ *I. p. criniger*   Sumatra, Borneo and adjacent islands
_____ *I. p. turcosa*   Java
_____ *I. p. tweeddalei*   Philippines (Palawan, Busuanga, Balabac, Culion and Calamian)

☐ **Philippine Fairy-bluebird** *Irena cyanogaster*
_____ *I. c. cyanogaster*   N Philippines (Luzon and Polillo)
_____ *I. c. ellae*   Philippines (Bohol, Samar and Leyte)
_____ *I. c. melanochlamys*   S Philippines (Basilan)
_____ *I. c. hoogstraali*   S Philippines (Mindanao and Dinagat)

☐ FAMILY: LANIIDAE (Shrikes—30)

☐ **Tiger Shrike** *Lanius tigrinus*

NE Asia; winters to SE Asia, Greater Sundas and Philippines

☐ **Bull-headed Shrike** *Lanius bucephalus*
_____ *L. b. bucephalus*   E Asia, Japan, Korea and ne China
_____ *L. b. sicarius*   W-central China (Tao Valley of sw Gansu)

☐ **Red-backed Shrike** *Lanius collurio*
_____ *L. c. juxtus*   Great Britain; winters to s Africa
_____ *L. c. collurio*   Europe and Asia Minor; winters to s Africa
_____ *L. c. pallidifrons*   W Siberia; winters to s Africa
_____ *L. c. kobylini*   Crimean Peninsula to Iran; winters to s Africa

☐ **Rufous-tailed Shrike** *Lanius isabellinus*
_____ *L. i. phoenicuroides* — Iran to Pakistan, s Kazakstan and extreme w China (w Xinjiang)
_____ *L. i. speculigerus* — SE Altai and n-central China; winters to India and e Africa
_____ *L. i. isabellinus* — NW China (Xinjiang); winters to India and e Africa
_____ *L. i. tsaidamensis* — N-central China (Qinghai); winters to India

☐ **Brown Shrike** *Lanius cristatus*
_____ *L. c. cristatus* — E Siberia to nw Mongolia; winters to India and Malay Pen.
_____ *L. c. confusus* — Manchuria and Amurland; winters to Malay Pen. and Sumatra
_____ *L. c. superciliosus* — S Sakhalin and Japan; winters to Sumatra and Lesser Sundas
_____ *L. c. lucionensis* — Korea and e China; winters to Philippines, Borneo, Sulawesi

☐ **Burmese Shrike** *Lanius collurioides*
_____ *L. c. collurioides* — Mountains of Assam to s China, Myanmar and Indochina
_____ *L. c. nigricapillus* — S Vietnam

☐ **Emin's Shrike** *Lanius gubernator*
— Savanna of Ivory Coast to s Sudan, n Uganda and ne Zaire

☐ **Souza's Shrike** *Lanius souzae*
_____ *L. s. souzae* — S Congo to s Zaire and Angola
_____ *L. s. burigi* — NW Tanzania to Rwanda and Burundi
_____ *L. s. tacitus* — SE Angola to n Namibia, Zambia and Mozambique

☐ **Bay-backed Shrike** *Lanius vittatus*
_____ *L. v. vittatus* — W Pakistan (Indus plains)
_____ *L. v. nargianus* — SE Iran, s Turkmenistan, Afghanistan, Baluchistan and Pakistan

☐ **Long-tailed Shrike** *Lanius schach*
_____ *L. s. erythronotus* — NE Iran to Pakistan and n India
_____ *L. s. caniceps* — W and s India and Sri Lanka
_____ *L. s. schach* — E and s China, Taiwan and Hainan
_____ *L. s. tricolor* — Nepal to n Myanmar, Yunnan, n Laos and n Thailand
_____ *L. s. bentet* — Malay Peninsula, Sumatra, Java, Borneo and Lesser Sundas
_____ *L. s. longicaudatus* — Central and se Thailand
_____ *L. s. nasutus* — Philippine Islands
_____ *L. s. suluensis* — Sulu Archipelago
_____ *L. s. stresemanni* — E New Guinea

☐ **Gray-backed Shrike** *Lanius tephronotus*
_____ *L. t. tephronotus* — Nepal to Sikkim, Bhutan, n India and w-central China
_____ *L. t. lahulensis* — N Kashmir to Ladakh and adjacent w Tibet

☐ **Gray-capped Shrike** *Lanius validirostris*
_____ *L. v. validirostris* — N Philippines (n Luzon)
_____ *L. v. tertius* — N Philippines (Mindoro)
_____ *L. v. hachisuka* — S Philippines (Mindanao)

☐ **Loggerhead Shrike** *Lanius ludovicianus*
_____ *L. l. gambeli* — W N America (sw Canada to sw US); winters to w Mexico
_____ *L. l. excubitorides* — Great Plains region of North America; winters to s Mexico
_____ *L. l. migrans* — E North America (se Canada to e Texas); winters to ne Mexico
_____ *L. l. sonoriensis* — Arid sw US to nw Mexico (n Durango and s Sinaloa)
_____ *L. l. anthonyi* — N Channel Islands (off s California)
_____ *L. l. mearnsi* — San Clemente I. (off s California). ±13 birds in wild 1999
_____ *L. l. grinnelli* — S California (San Diego County) and n Baja California
_____ *L. l. nelsoni* — S Baja California
_____ *L. l. ludovicianus* — Coastal se US (Virginia to Florida)
_____ *L. l. miamensis* — S Florida
_____ *L. l. mexicanus* — Central Mexico (s Tamaulipas and Nayarit to Oaxaca)

☐ **Northern Shrike** *Lanius excubitor*

_____ *L. e. excubitor*	W and n Europe to w Siberia
_____ *L. e. homeyeri*	Balkan Peninsula to s Ural Mountains and w Siberia
_____ *L. e. leucopterus*	W Siberia to Yenisey River
_____ *L. e. sibiricus*	E Siberia to n Mongolia and Kamchatka Peninsula
_____ *L. e. bianchii*	Sakhalin and s Kuril Islands (n Japan)
_____ *L. e. mollis*	Russian Altai and nw Mongolia
_____ *L. e. funereus*	W China (Tien Shan Mountains)
_____ *L. e. invictus*	N Alaska to extreme n British Columbia and Alberta
_____ *L. e. borealis*	E Canada (Quebec and n Ontario); winters to ne US

☐ **Southern Gray Shrike** *Lanius meridionalis*

_____ *L. m. meridionalis*	Iberian Peninsula and s France
_____ *L. m. koenigi*	Canary Islands
_____ *L. m. algeriensis*	Morocco (n of Atlas Mountains), coastal n Algeria and Tunisia
_____ *L. m. elegans*	N Sahara (Mauritania to Sinai Peninsula and Red Sea)
_____ *L. m. leucopygos*	S Sahara (Mali to Nile River valley of the Sudan)
_____ *L. m. aucheri*	W coast of Red Sea to s Iran and Arabian Peninsula
_____ *L. m. theresae*	Galilee hills of n Israel and s Lebanon
_____ *L. m. buryi*	Yemen
_____ *L. m. uncinatus*	Socotra
_____ *L. m. lahtora*	E Pakistan and n India
_____ *L. m. pallidirostris*	Iran to arid steppes of w China (Xinjiang, Gansu and Ningsia)

☐ **Lesser Gray Shrike** *Lanius minor*

_____ *L. m. minor*	Iberian Pen. to Balkan Pen. and Turkey; winters to s Africa
_____ *L. m. turanicus*	Iran to Siberia and central Asia (e of Urals); winters to s Africa

☐ **Chinese Gray Shrike** *Lanius sphenocercus*

_____ *L. s. sphenocercus*	Mountains of e Russia (Amur region) to ne and central China
_____ *L. s. giganteus*	Mountains of e Tibet; winters to se China

☐ **Gray-backed Fiscal** *Lanius excubitoroides*

_____ *L. e. excubitoroides*	SE Mauritania to w Sudan
_____ *L. e. intercedens*	Central Ethiopia to nw Uganda and w Kenya
_____ *L. e. bohmi*	W Tanzania to Rwanda and sw Uganda

☐ **Long-tailed Fiscal** *Lanius cabanisi*

	Dry thornscrub of se Somalia to Kenya and ne Tanzania

☐ **Taita Fiscal** *Lanius dorsalis*

	Arid thornscrub of s Sudan and Ethiopia to ne Tanzania

☐ **Somali Fiscal** *Lanius somalicus*

	Arid thornscrub of the Horn of Africa

☐ **Mackinnon's Shrike** *Lanius mackinnoni*

	Equatorial rainforests of central Africa

☐ **Common Fiscal** *Lanius collaris*

_____ *L. c. smithii*	Sierra Leone to Cameroon and s Sudan
_____ *L. c. humeralis*	Eritrea and Ethiopia to Tanzania and n Mozambique
_____ *L. c. marwitzi*	E and s Tanzania
_____ *L. c. capelli*	W Uganda to e Zaire, Angola, Zambia and Malawi
_____ *L. c. predator*	S Mozambique to Natal, Zululand and Transvaal
_____ *L. c. collaris*	Cape Province to Orange River and Transvaal
_____ *L. c. subcoronatus*	Namibia to Botswana and sw Angola

☐ **Newton's Fiscal** *Lanius newtoni*

	São Tomé. Rediscovered 1990 after 50-year absence

☐ **Masked Shrike** *Lanius nubicus*

	Greece to sw Iran; winters to central Africa and sw Arabia

☐ **Woodchat Shrike** *Lanius senator*

____	*L. s. senator*	Europe (Spain to w Turkey) and N Africa; winters to c Africa
____	*L. s. badius*	W Mediterranean islands; winters to central Africa
____	*L. s. niloticus*	E Turkey and Levant to Iran; winters to central Africa

☐ **Yellow-billed Shrike** *Corvinella corvina*

____	*C. c. corvina*	Senegal and Gambia to Niger
____	*C. c. togoensis*	Guinea and Sierra Leone to s Chad and central Sudan
____	*C. c. affinis*	SE Sudan to extreme ne Zaire, n Uganda and w Kenya

☐ **Magpie Shrike** *Corvinella melanoleuca*

____	*C. m. aequatorialis*	E Africa (north of the Zambezi River) north to Kenya
____	*C. m. melanoleuca*	Africa (s of the Zambezi River) to e Angola and South Africa

☐ **White-rumped Shrike** *Eurocephalus rueppelli*

S Sudan to Kenya and Tanzania

☐ **White-crowned Shrike** *Eurocephalus anguitimens*

____	*E. a. anguitimens*	SW Angola to Botswana, Namibia and Zimbabwe
____	*E. a. niveus*	E Zambia to Mozambique and Transvaal

FAMILY: MALACONOTIDAE (Bushshrikes and Allies—43)

☐ **Brubru** *Nilaus afer*

____	*N. a. afer*	Senegal to the Sudan and Ethiopia
____	*N. a. camerunensis*	S Cameroon and Central African Republic to e Zaire
____	*N. a. hilgerti*	Highlands of central Ethiopia
____	*N. a. minor*	S Eritrea to extreme se Sudan and n Kenya
____	*N. a. massaicus*	SW Kenya to n Tanzania, Rwanda and e Zaire
____	*N. a. nigritemporalis*	SE Zaire to Tanzania, Zambia, Malawi and n Mozambique
____	*N. a. brubru*	S Angola to n Cape Province
____	*N. a. solivagus*	Locally in Natal, Swaziland and extreme s Mozambique
____	*N. a. affinis*	Central highlands of w Angola and adjacent Zaire
____	*N. a. miombensis*	Mozambique (Sol do Save region)

☐ **Northern Puffback** *Dryoscopus gambensis*

____	*D. g. gambensis*	Senegal to Cameroon, Chad and n Gabon
____	*D. g. congicus*	Lower Congo River area
____	*D. g. malzacii*	Central African Republic to Sudan and w Kenya
____	*D. g. erythreae*	Extreme e Sudan to Eritrea and Ethiopia
____	*D. g. erwini*	E Zaire to s Uganda and nw Tanzania

☐ **Pringle's Puffback** *Dryoscopus pringlii*

Ethiopia and Somalia to Kenya and ne Tanzania

☐ **Black-backed Puffback** *Dryoscopus cubla*

____	*D. c. affinis*	Coastal e Kenya to n Tanzania, Zanzibar and Mafia I.
____	*D. c. nairobiensis*	Central Kenya to central Tanzania
____	*D. c. hamatus*	S Kenya to Mozambique and Angola
____	*D. c. chapini*	S Mozambique to n Transvaal
____	*D. c. okavangensis*	N Botswana to s Angola and Namibia
____	*D. c. cubla*	Natal to Cape Province

☐ **Red-eyed Puffback** *Dryoscopus senegalensis*

Lowlands of Senegambia to se Zaire, n Angola and Uganda

☐ **Pink-footed Puffback** *Dryoscopus angolensis*

____	*D. a. boydi*	Dense montane forests of Cameroon
____	*D. a. angolensis*	Lower Congo River of sw Zaire and n Angola
____	*D. a. nandensis*	E Zaire to s Sudan and w Kenya
____	*D. a. kungwensis*	W Tanzania (Kungwe-Mahare region)

☐ **Large-billed Puffback** *Dryoscopus sabini*

_____	*D. s. sabini*	Sierra Leone to s Nigeria
_____	*D. s. melanoleucus*	Cameroon and Gabon to central Zaire (Ituri Forest)

☐ **Marsh Tchagra** *Tchagra minuta*

_____	*T. m. minuta*	Sierra Leone to s Sudan, Ethiopia, Kenya and Tanzania
_____	*T. m. reichenowi*	Coastal e Kenya (Lamu) to ne Tanzania
_____	*T. m. anchietae*	S Zaire to Angola, Tanzania and Malawi
_____	*T. m. remota*	SE Zimbabwe and adjacent Mozambique

☐ **Black-crowned Tchagra** *Tchagra senegala*

_____	*T. s. cucullata*	Coastal Morocco to Algeria and Tunisia
_____	*T. s. percivali*	S Arabian Peninsula
_____	*T. s. remigialis*	Central Sudan to Red Sea Province
_____	*T. s. notha*	Mali to Chad
_____	*T. s. senegala*	Senegal to Sierra Leone
_____	*T. s. pallida*	Burkina Faso and Ivory Coast to n Central African Republic
_____	*T. s. camerunensis*	Cameroon to extreme s Sudan and n Uganda
_____	*T. s. habessinica*	E Sudan (upper Nile Province) to Eritrea, Ethiopia and Somalia
_____	*T. s. armena*	S Uganda to se Zaire, central Kenya, Tanzania and Zambia
_____	*T. s. orientalis*	Coastal s Somalia to n Mozambique
_____	*T. s. confusa*	E Transvaal to Natal and e Cape Province
_____	*T. s. kalahari*	Zimbabwe to s Angola and Namibia
_____	*T. s. rufofusca*	SW Zaire to central Angola

☐ **Brown-crowned Tchagra** *Tchagra australis*

_____	*T. a. ussheri*	Sierra Leone to sw Nigeria
_____	*T. a. emini*	S Nigeria to Zaire, s Sudan, w Kenya and w Tanzania
_____	*T. a. minor*	Kenya and nw Tanzania
_____	*T. a. littoralis*	Coastal e Kenya to Zimbabwe and Natal
_____	*T. a. congener*	Coastal s Tanzania to Malawi and Zambia
_____	*T. a. ansorgei*	W Angola (Luanda to Moçamedes)
_____	*T. a. bocagei*	Angola (Cuando region)
_____	*T. a. souzae*	SE Zaire to Angola and extreme n Zambia
_____	*T. a. australis*	E Botswana to Transvaal and s Zimbabwe
_____	*T. a. damarensis*	Namibia to central Botswana

☐ **Three-streaked Tchagra** *Tchagra jamesi*

_____	*T. j. jamesi*	Somalia to Uganda and n Kenya
_____	*T. j. mandana*	Coastal e Kenya, ne Tanzania and adj. is. (Manda and Lamu)

☐ **Southern Tchagra** *Tchagra tchagra*

_____	*T. t. tchagra*	Southern Cape Province
_____	*T. t. natalensis*	Natal to Swaziland, e Transvaal and e Cape Province

☐ **Red-naped Bushshrike** *Laniarius ruficeps*

_____	*L. r. rufinuchalis*	Eritrea to Ethiopia, Djibouti and se Kenya
_____	*L. r. ruficeps*	Extreme nw Somalia
_____	*L. r. kismayensis*	Coastal s Somalia

☐ **Luehder's Bushshrike** *Laniarius luehderi*

_____	*L. l. leuhderi*	E Nigeria to s Cameroon, s Sudan, w Kenya and sw Tanzania
_____	*L. l. brauni*	NW Angola (Cuanza Norte escarpment)
_____	*L. l. amboimensis*	W-central Angola (Gabela escarpment)

☐ **Bulo Burti Boubou** *Laniarius liberatus*

Known from a bird captured 1991 in central Somalia (hybrid?)

☐ **Turati's Boubou** *Laniarius turatii*

Rainforests of Guinea-Bissau, Guinea and Sierra Leone

□ **Tropical Boubou** *Laniarius aethiopicus*

____	*L. a. major*	Sierra Leone to s Sudan, Kenya, Tanzania and Malawi
____	*L. a. aethiopicus*	Extreme e Sudan to Ethiopia, Somalia and n Kenya
____	*L. a. erlangeri*	S Somalia
____	*L. a. ambiguus*	Kenya to n Tanzania
____	*L. a. sublacteus*	Coastal e Kenya (Lamu) to n Tanzania (Dar-es-Salaam); Zanzibar
____	*L. a. limpopoensis*	S Zimbabwe (Limpopo River Valley) to n Transvaal
____	*L. a. mossambicus*	NE Botswana to s Zambia, Malawi and extreme n South Africa

□ **Gabon Boubou** *Laniarius bicolor*

____	*L. b. bicolor*	Mangroves of Cameroon and Gabon
____	*L. b. guttatus*	Lower Congo River (w Zaire and Angola)
____	*L. b. sticturus*	S Angola to n Botswana and sw Zambia

□ **Southern Boubou** *Laniarius ferrugineus*

____	*L. f. savensis*	SE Botswana to se Zimbabwe and s Mozambique
____	*L. f. tongensis*	Coastal s Mozambique and n Natal
____	*L. f. natalensis*	Interior of Natal
____	*L. f. pondoensis*	Coastal Natal to e Cape Province
____	*L. f. transvaalensis*	S and e Transvaal
____	*L. f. ferrugineus*	Southern Cape Province

□ **Common Gonolek** *Laniarius barbarus*

____	*L. b. helenae*	Mangroves of coastal Sierra Leone
____	*L. b. barbarus*	Senegal to Nigeria, extreme n Cameroon and s Chad

□ **Black-headed Gonolek** *Laniarius erythrogaster*

Acacia of Nigeria to Sudan, Ethiopia, Kenya and nw Tanzania

□ **Crimson-breasted Gonolek** *Laniarius atrococcineus*

SW Angola and Namibia to Botswana and nw South Africa

□ **Papyrus Gonolek** *Laniarius mufumbiri*

Papyrus swamps of Zaire to Uganda, Kenya and Tanzania

□ **Yellow-breasted Boubou** *Laniarius atroflavus*

____	*L. a. craterum*	Highlands of se Nigeria
____	*L. a. atroflavus*	Montane forests of Cameroon

□ **Slate-colored Boubou** *Laniarius funebris*

____	*L. f. funebris*	Acacia savanna of s Sudan and Somalia to Tanzania
____	*L. f. degener*	S Ethiopia to s Somalia, e Kenya and n Tanzania

□ **Sooty Boubou** *Laniarius leucorhynchus*

Sierra Leone to Sudan, Uganda, Zaire and ne Angola

□ **Fuelleborn's Boubou** *Laniarius fuelleborni*

____	*L. f. poensis*	Montane forests of e Nigeria; Bioko
____	*L. f. camerunensis*	Highlands of w Cameroon
____	*L. f. holomelas*	Montane forests of e Zaire and Uganda
____	*L. f. usambaricus*	Usambara Mountains (w Tanzania)
____	*L. f. ulugurensis*	Uluguru Mountains (Tanzania)
____	*L. f. fuelleborni*	SW Tanzania (Iringa Mts.), n Malawi and extreme e Zambia

□ **Rosy-patched Bushshrike** *Rhodophoneus cruentus*

____	*R. c. cruentus*	Extreme se Egypt to Eritrea, Ethiopia and extreme se Sudan
____	*R. c. hilgerti*	S Ethiopia to n Kenya
____	*R. c. cathemagmenus*	Kenya (Tsavo and Lake Victoria) to ne Tanzania

□ **Bokmakierie** *Telophorus zeylonus*

____	*T. z. phanus*	S Angola and Namibia
____	*T. z. thermophilus*	Namibia and w Cape Province
____	*T. z. restrictus*	Zimbabwe
____	*T. z. zeylonus*	Transvaal and e Cape Province

☐ **Gray-green Bushshrike** *Telophorus bocagei*
_____ *T. b. bocagei*	S Cameroon to n Angola
_____ *T. b. jacksoni*	Central Zaire to Uganda and w Kenya

☐ **Sulphur-breasted Bushshrike** *Telophorus sulfureopectus*
_____ *T. s. sulfureopectus*	Senegal to ne Zaire
_____ *T. s. terminus*	SE Tanzania to ne South Africa
_____ *T. s. similis*	Ethiopia to Angola and n Cape Province

☐ **Olive Bushshrike** *Telophorus olivaceus*
_____ *T. o. makawa*	Central and s Malawi (west of Shire Valley) and e Zimbabwe
_____ *T. o. bertrandi*	S Malawi (east of Shire Valley)
_____ *T. o. vitorum*	Mozambique (Sol do Save region)
_____ *T. o. interfluvius*	Mozambique
_____ *T. o. olivaceus*	S Mozambique to e Transvaal and e Cape Province

☐ **Many-colored Bushshrike** *Telophorus multicolor*
_____ *T. m. multicolor*	SW Mali and Sierra Leone to Cameroon
_____ *T. m. batesi*	S Cameroon and Gabon to Rwanda, w Uganda and n Angola
_____ *T. m. graueri*	Highlands of e Zaire

☐ **Black-fronted Bushshrike** *Telophorus nigrifrons*
_____ *T. n. nigrifrons*	Central Kenya to Tanzania and n Malawi
_____ *T. n. manningi*	SE Zaire to n Zambia and n Namibia
_____ *T. n. sandgroundi*	S Malawi to Zimbabwe, Mozambique and ne Transvaal

☐ **Mt. Kupe Bushshrike** *Telophorus kupeensis*
	Rainforests of Mt. Kupé (sw Cameroon)

☐ **Four-colored Bushshrike** *Telophorus viridis*
_____ *T. v. viridis*	N Angola to s Zaire and nw Zambia
_____ *T. v. nigricauda*	Coastal se Kenya and e Tanzania
_____ *T. v. quartus*	S Malawi and Mozambique
_____ *T. v. quadricolor*	Zimbabwe to ne South Africa

☐ **Doherty's Bushshrike** *Telophorus dohertyi*
	Mts. of Rwanda, Burundi, w Uganda, e Zaire and w Kenya

☐ **Fiery-breasted Bushshrike** *Malaconotus cruentus*
_____ *M. c. cruentus*	Guinea and Sierra Leone to w Cameroon
_____ *M. c. gabonensis*	E Cameroon and Gabon
_____ *M. c. adolfi-friederici*	E Zaire and extreme w Uganda

☐ **Lagden's Bushshrike** *Malaconotus lagdeni*
_____ *M. l. lagdeni*	Montane forests of Sierra Leone, Liberia and Ivory Coast
_____ *M. l. centralis*	Montane forests of e-central Zaire, Rwanda and w Uganda

☐ **Green-breasted Bushshrike** *Malaconotus gladiator*
	Montane forests of s Cameroon and adjacent e Nigeria

☐ **Gray-headed Bushshrike** *Malaconotus blanchoti*
_____ *M. b. blanchoti*	Senegal to n Nigeria and n Cameroon
_____ *M. b. catharoxanthus*	N Zaire to Eritrea, n Ethiopia, Uganda and w Kenya
_____ *M. b. interpositus*	SE Zaire and w Zambia
_____ *M. b. citrinipectus*	SW Angola
_____ *M. b. approximans*	S Ethiopia to Somalia, Kenya and n Tanzania
_____ *M. b. hypopyrrhus*	Rwanda to Tanzania, Malawi, Mozambique and ne S Africa
_____ *M. b. extremus*	E Cape Province

☐ **Monteiro's Bushshrike** *Malaconotus monteiri*
_____ *M. m. perspicillatus*	SW Cameroon (rediscovered 1992 on Mount Kupé)
_____ *M. m. monteiri*	NW Angola (last recorded 1954)

☐ **Uluguru Bushshrike** *Malaconotus alius*

Uluguru Mountains (central Tanzania)

FAMILY: PRIONOPIDAE (Helmetshrikes and Allies—11)

☐ **White Helmetshrike** *Prionops plumatus*
_____ *P. p. plumatus* — Senegal to Nigeria
_____ *P. p. adamauae* — N Cameroon (Adamawa Plateau)
_____ *P. p. concinnatus* — NE Cameroon to Zaire, extreme se Sudan and n Uganda
_____ *P. p. cristatus* — Eritrea and w Ethiopia to extreme se Sudan
_____ *P. p. melanopterus* — E Ethiopia and Somalia
_____ *P. p. vinaceigularis* — Central Ethiopia to n Kenya
_____ *P. p. angolica* — S-central Kenya to s Uganda, Zaire and Namibia
_____ *P. p. poliocephalus* — E and central Tanzania to Mozambique and ne South Africa

☐ **Gray-crested Helmetshrike** *Prionops poliolophus*

Dry thornscrub of sw Kenya and w Tanzania

☐ **Yellow-crested Helmetshrike** *Prionops alberti*

Montane forests of e-central Zaire and (?) adjacent sw Uganda

☐ **Chestnut-bellied Helmetshrike** *Prionops caniceps*
_____ *P. c. caniceps* — Guinea to Mali, Sierra Leone and s Nigeria
_____ *P. c. rufiventris* — S Cameroon to Gabon, Cent. African Rep., Zaire and w Uganda

☐ **Retz's Helmetshrike** *Prionops retzii*
_____ *P. r. neumanni* — S Somalia
_____ *P. r. graculina* — E Kenya and ne Tanzania
_____ *P. r. tricolor* — Tanzania to Malawi, Zambia and Mozambique
_____ *P. r. intermedia* — NW Tanzania (south of Lake Victoria)
_____ *P. r. nigricans* — W Tanzania to s Zaire, n Zambia and Angola
_____ *P. r. retzii* — Namibia to sw Zimbabwe and ne Transvaal

☐ **Angola Helmetshrike** *Prionops gabela*

W Angola (Gabela escarpment)

☐ **Chestnut-fronted Helmetshrike** *Prionops scopifrons*
_____ *P. s. keniensis* — Extreme s Somalia to central Kenya
_____ *P. s. kirki* — Coastal e Kenya (Lamu) to ne Tanzania
_____ *P. s. scopifrons* — SE Tanzania to extreme e South Africa (n Kwazalu-Natal)

☐ **Large Woodshrike** *Tephrodornis gularis*
_____ *T. g. sylvicola* — SW India (Western Ghats from Narbada River to Kerala)
_____ *T. g. pelvicus* — E Himalayas (Nepal to Assam) to n Myanmar
_____ *T. g. jugans* — S Myanmar and n Thailand
_____ *T. g. vernayi* — SW Thailand
_____ *T. g. annectens* — N peninsular Thailand and n Malaysia
_____ *T. g. fretensis* — S peninsular Thailand, Malaysia and n Sumatra
_____ *T. g. gularis* — Coastal sw and extreme s Sumatra and Java
_____ *T. g. mekongensis* — E and s Thailand, Cambodia and s Indochina
_____ *T. g. hainanus* — N Indochina and Hainan (s China)
_____ *T. g. latouchei* — SE China (Fujian)
_____ *T. g. frenatus* — Borneo

☐ **Common Woodshrike** *Tephrodornis pondicerianus*
_____ *T. p. pallidus* — Pakistan and nw India
_____ *T. p. pondicerianus* — E India to Myanmar, n Thailand and s Laos
_____ *T. p. orientis* — Cambodia and s Vietnam
_____ *T. p. affinis* — Sri Lanka

☐ **Rufous-winged Philentoma** *Philentoma pyrhopterum*
_____ *P. p. pyrhopterum*   S Myanmar, Malaya, Sumatra, Borneo and offshore islands
_____ *P. p. dubium*   Natuna Islands (China Sea)

☐ **Maroon-breasted Philentoma** *Philentoma velatum*
_____ *P. v. caesium*   S Myanmar, pen. Thailand, Malaya, Sumatra, Borneo and Java
_____ *P. v. velatum*   Lowland forests of Java

FAMILY: VANGIDAE (Vangas—14)

☐ **Red-tailed Vanga** *Calicalicus madagascariensis*
    Forested regions of Madagascar

☐ **Rufous Vanga** *Schetba rufa*
_____ *S. r. rufa*   Primary forests of e Madagascar
_____ *S. r. occidentalis*   Primary forests of sw Madagascar

☐ **Hook-billed Vanga** *Vanga curvirostris*
_____ *V. c. curvirostris*   Forests of n and e Madagascar
_____ *V. c. cetera*   Forests of sw Madagascar

☐ **Lafresnaye's Vanga** *Xenopirostris xenopirostris*
    Locally in arid subdeserts of sw Madagascar

☐ **Van Dam's Vanga** *Xenopirostris damii*
    Dry woodlands of nw Madagascar

☐ **Pollen's Vanga** *Xenopirostris polleni*
    Rainforests of nw coastal and e Madagascar

☐ **Sickle-billed Vanga** *Falculea palliata*
    Savanna and mangroves of w and n Madagascar

☐ **White-headed Vanga** *Artamella viridis*
_____ *A. v. viridis*   Forests of e Madagascar
_____ *A. v. annae*   Forests of w Madagascar

☐ **Chabert Vanga** *Leptopterus chabert*
_____ *L. c. chabert*   Forests and savanna of n and e Madagascar
_____ *L. c. schistocercus*   Forests of sw Madagascar

☐ **Blue Vanga** *Cyanolanius madagascarinus*
_____ *C. m. madagascarinus*   Forests of n and central Madagascar
_____ *C. m. comorensis*   Grand Comoro I.
_____ *C. m. bensoni*   Mohéli (Comoro Islands)

☐ **Bernier's Vanga** *Oriolia bernieri*
    Humid forests of e Madagascar

☐ **Helmet Vanga** *Euryceros prevostii*
    Dense forests of ne Madagascar

☐ **Tylas Vanga** *Tylas eduardi*
_____ *T. e. eduardi*   Dense forests of e Madagascar
_____ *T. e. albigularis*   Dense forests of w central Madagascar

☐ **Coral-billed Nuthatch** *Hypositta corallirostris*
    Forests and plateaus of humid e Madagascar

FAMILY: DICRURIDAE (Drongos—23)

☐ **Papuan Drongo** *Chaetorhynchus papuensis*

Montane forests of New Guinea and Yule I.

☐ **Square-tailed Drongo** *Dicrurus ludwigii*
____ *D. l. sharpei* — Senegal to n Angola, Zaire, s Sudan and w Kenya
____ *D. l. saturnus* — Angola
____ *D. l. ludwigii* — S Somalia to e Cape Province
____ *D. l. tephrogaster* — S Malawi to Mozambique and e Zimbabwe

☐ **Shining Drongo** *Dicrurus atripennis*

Forests of Guinea and Sierra Leone to Gabon and e Zaire

☐ **Fork-tailed Drongo** *Dicrurus adsimilis*
____ *D. a. adsimilis* — Africa south of the equatorial rain forests
____ *D. a. fugax* — E Africa to n Natal and Zimbabwe
____ *D. a. divaricatus* — Senegal to Chad, Sudan and Ethiopia
____ *D. a. coracinus* — S Nigeria to Zaire, Uganda and w Kenya
____ *D. a. atactus* — Sierra Leone to s Nigeria and Cameroon; Bioko
____ *D. a. modestus* — Príncipe (Gulf of Guinea)
____ *D. a. apivorus* — Namibia

☐ **Aldabra Drongo** *Dicrurus aldabranus*

Aldabra (w Indian Ocean)

☐ **Comoro Drongo** *Dicrurus fuscipennis*

Grand Comoro I. (w Indian Ocean)

☐ **Crested Drongo** *Dicrurus forficatus*
____ *D. f. forficatus* — Madagascar and Nosy Bé
____ *D. f. potior* — Anjouan (Comoro Islands)

☐ **Mayotte Drongo** *Dicrurus waldenii*

Woodlands of Mayotte (Comoro Islands)

☐ **Black Drongo** *Dicrurus macrocercus*
____ *D. m. albirictus* — SE Iran to Afghanistan and n India
____ *D. m. macrocercus* — Peninsular India
____ *D. m. minor* — Sri Lanka
____ *D. m. cathoecus* — China, n Myanmar, n Thailand, Laos, n Vietnam and Malaysia
____ *D. m. thai* — S Myanmar, s Thailand and s Vietnam
____ *D. m. harterti* — Taiwan
____ *D. m. javanus* — Java and Bali

☐ **Ashy Drongo** *Dicrurus leucophaeus*
____ *D. l. longicaudatus* — E Afghanistan to Sikkim; winters to s India and Sri Lanka
____ *D. l. hopwoodi* — E Himalayas to Myanmar and s China; winters to Indochina
____ *D. l. mouhoti* — S Myanmar and n Thailand; winters to Indochina
____ *D. l. bondi* — S Thailand and Cambodia
____ *D. l. nigrescens* — Extreme s Myanmar, s Thailand and Malaysia
____ *D. l. leucogenis* — Manchuria and e China; winters to Indochina
____ *D. l. salangensis* — SE China and s Thailand; winters to Hainan
____ *D. l. innexus* — Hainan (s China)
____ *D. l. stigmatops* — Mountains of n Borneo
____ *D. l. batakensis* — N Sumatra
____ *D. l. phaedrus* — S Sumatra
____ *D. l. periophthalmicus* — Simeulue I. and adjacent Mentawi Islands (off Sumatra)
____ *D. l. siberu* — Siberut I. (off Sumatra)
____ *D. l. leucophaeus* — Java, Bali, Lombok, Palawan, Calamian and Balabac islands

☐ **White-bellied Drongo** *Dicrurus caerulescens*
____ *D. c. caerulescens* — Foothills of s Nepal and peninsular India
____ *D. c. insularis* — N Sri Lanka
____ *D. c. leucopygialis* — S Sri Lanka

☐ **Crow-billed Drongo** *Dicrurus annectans*

E Himalayas to s China; winters to SE Asia and Greater Sundas

☐ **Bronzed Drongo** *Dicrurus aeneus*

_____ *D. a. aeneus* — India to Myanmar, s China, Thailand, Malaysia and Indochina
_____ *D. a. malayensis* — S Malay Peninsula, Sumatra and Borneo
_____ *D. a. braunianus* — Taiwan

☐ **Lesser Racket-tailed Drongo** *Dicrurus remifer*

_____ *D. r. tectirostris* — Himalayas to s China, Myanmar, Thailand and Indochina
_____ *D. r. peracensis* — S Thailand to w Laos and Malay Peninsula
_____ *D. r. lefoli* — S Cambodia (Chaine d'Éléphant and Cardamomes Mountains)
_____ *D. r. remifer* — Sumatra and Java

☐ **Hair-crested Drongo** *Dicrurus hottentottus*

_____ *D. h. hottentottus* — India to Myanmar, n Thailand and s Indochina
_____ *D. h. brevirostris* — S China to n Myanmar, n Laos and n Vietnam
_____ *D. h. viridinitens* — Mentawi Islands (off Sumatra)
_____ *D. h. borneensis* — N Borneo, Maratua and Matasiri islands
_____ *D. h. jentincki* — Bali and Kangean Islands
_____ *D. h. leucops* — Sulawesi, adjacent islands and n Moluccas
_____ *D. h. guillemardi* — Central Moluccas (Bisa and Obi)
_____ *D. h. pectoralis* — Sula Islands (Taliabu, Mangola and Sanana)

☐ **Balicassiao** *Dicrurus balicassius*

_____ *D. b. abraensis* — N Philippines (n Luzon)
_____ *D. b. balicassius* — C and s Luzon, Lubang, Marinduque, Mindoro and Polillo
_____ *D. b. mirabilis* — Philippines (Panay, Cebu, Negros, Guimaras, Ticao, Masbate)

☐ **Sulawesi Drongo** *Dicrurus montanus*

Hill and montane forests of Sulawesi

☐ **Sumatran Drongo** *Dicrurus sumatranus*

Humid lowlands of Sumatra

☐ **Wallacean Drongo** *Dicrurus densus*

_____ *D. d. bimaensis* — Lesser Sundas (Lombok to Alor)
_____ *D. d. renschi* — Sumbawa (Lesser Sundas)
_____ *D. d. sumbae* — Sumba (Lesser Sundas)
_____ *D. d. densus* — E Lesser Sundas (Roti, Semau, Timor, Wetar, Sermata, Luang)
_____ *D. d. kuehni* — Tanimbar Islands (Arafura Sea)
_____ *D. d. megalornis* — Seram Laut (Gorong, Manawoka), Watubela and Kai Islands

☐ **Ribbon-tailed Drongo** *Dicrurus megarhynchus*

New Ireland (e Bismarck Archipelago)

☐ **Spangled Drongo** *Dicrurus bracteatus*

_____ *D. b. samarensis* — Philippines (Bohol, Leyte, Panaon, Samar and Calicoan)
_____ *D. b. palawanensis* — Philippines (Palawan, Busuanga, Cagayan Sulu, Culion, Balabac)
_____ *D. b. cuyensis* — Philippines (Cuyo and Semirara)
_____ *D. b. menagei* — Philippines (Tablas)
_____ *D. b. striatus* — S Philippines (Basilan, Mindanao and Nipa)
_____ *D. b. suluensis* — Sulu Archipelago
_____ *D. b. morotensis* — Morotai (Moluccas)
_____ *D. b. atrocaeruleus* — N Moluccas (Bacan, Kasiruta and Halmahera)
_____ *D. b. buruensis* — Buru (s Moluccas)
_____ *D. b. amboinensis* — S Moluccas (Seram, Ambon, Haruku and Saparua)
_____ *D. b. carbonarius* — Aru Is., New Guinea, Louisiade Arch., D'Entrecasteaux Arch.
_____ *D. b. laemostictus* — New Britain (Bismarck Archipelago)
_____ *D. b. meeki* — Guadalcanal (Solomon Islands)
_____ *D. b. longirostris* — San Cristóbal (Solomon Islands)
_____ *D. b. bracteatus* — N and e Australia; winters to New Guinea

☐ **Andaman Drongo** *Dicrurus andamanensis*

_____ D. a. andamanensis	Andaman Islands
_____ D. a. dicruriformis	S Myanmar and Cocos Islands (Bay of Bengal)

☐ **Greater Racket-tailed Drongo** *Dicrurus paradiseus*

_____ D. p. grandis	N India to n Myanmar and n Vietnam
_____ D. p. rangoonensis	Central India to s Myanmar, w Thailand and Indochina
_____ D. p. paradiseus	S India to s Thailand and Indochina
_____ D. p. johni	Hainan (s China)
_____ D. p. malayensis	N Malaysia
_____ D. p. platurus	S Malaysia, Sumatra and adjacent nw islands
_____ D. p. ceylonicus	Sri Lanka
_____ D. p. lophorinus	W Sri Lanka
_____ D. p. otiosus	Andaman Islands
_____ D. p. nicobariensis	Nicobar Islands
_____ D. p. banguey	Islands off north Borneo
_____ D. p. brachyphorus	Borneo
_____ D. p. microlophus	North Natuna Islands
_____ D. p. formosus	Java

FAMILY: CALLAEIDAE (Wattlebirds—2)

☐ **Kokako** *Callaeas cinerea*

_____ C. c. wilsoni	North I. and Great Barrier I. (New Zealand)
_____ C. c. cinerea	Formerly South I. and (?) Stewart I. (New Zealand)

☐ **Saddleback** *Creadion carunculatus*

	Hen and South Cape islands (New Zealand)

FAMILY: GRALLINIDAE (Mudnest Builders—2)

☐ **Magpie-lark** *Grallina cyanoleuca*

	Australia and se New Guinea; ranges to Tasmania and Timor

☐ **Torrent-lark** *Grallina bruijni*

	Swift-flowing mountain streams of New Guinea

FAMILY: CORCORACIDAE (White-winged Chough and Apostlebird—2)

☐ **White-winged Chough** *Corcorax melanorhamphos*

	Forests and woodlands of e and se Australia

☐ **Apostlebird** *Struthidea cinerea*

_____ S. c. dalyi	N-central Northern Territory
_____ S. c. cinerea	N Queensland to n Victoria and se South Australia

FAMILY: ARTAMIDAE (Woodswallows—11)

☐ **Ashy Woodswallow** *Artamus fuscus*

	India and Sri Lanka to Myanmar, s China and SE Asia

☐ **Fiji Woodswallow** *Artamus mentalis*

	N Fiji (Yasawa and Viti Levu to Taveuni and Qamea)

☐ **White-backed Woodswallow** *Artamus monachus*

	Sulawesi, Lembeh I., Banggai Islands and Sula Islands

☐ **Great Woodswallow** *Artamus maximus*

	Mountains of New Guinea

☐ **White-breasted Woodswallow** *Artamus leucorynchus*

_____ A. l. pelewensis	Babelthuap I. (Palau Islands)
_____ A. l. leucorhynchus	Philippines, Palawan, Borneo and Natuna Islands
_____ A. l. amydrus	Sumatra, Bangka, Belitung, Kangean islands, Java and Bali
_____ A. l. humei	Andaman and Cocos islands (Bay of Bengal)
_____ A. l. albiventer	Sulawesi and Lesser Sundas
_____ A. l. musschenbroeki	Babar I. and Tanimbar Islands (Larat, Yamdena and Kirimoen)
_____ A. l. leucopygialis	Moluccas, Kai Is., Aru Is., New Guinea and Australia
_____ A. l. melaleucus	New Caledonia, Maré and Lifou (Loyalty Islands)
_____ A. l. tenuis	Vanuatu and Banks Islands

☐ **Bismarck Woodswallow** *Artamus insignis*

Bismarck Archipelago (New Britain and New Ireland)

☐ **Masked Woodswallow** *Artamus personatus*

Savanna of Australia and King I. (Bass Strait)

☐ **White-browed Woodswallow** *Artamus superciliosus*

Savanna of interior Australia (casually to Tasmania and King I.)

☐ **Black-faced Woodswallow** *Artamus cinereus*

_____ A. c. cinereus	E Lesser Sundas (Semau, Timor, Jaco, Leti, Sermata); Australia
_____ A. c. albiventris	N Queensland (south to Normanton and Rockhampton)

☐ **Dusky Woodswallow** *Artamus cyanopterus*

_____ A. c. cyanopterus	SE and e Australia (north to Cairns); Tasmania
_____ A. c. perthi	SW Australia

☐ **Little Woodswallow** *Artamus minor*

Forests and savanna of n and central Australia

FAMILY: PITYRIASEIDAE (Bristlehead—1)

☐ **Bornean Bristlehead** *Pityriasis gymnocephala*

Lowland forests of Borneo

FAMILY: CRACTICIDAE (Bellmagpies and Allies—12)

☐ **Mountain Peltops** *Peltops montanus*

Mountains of New Guinea

☐ **Lowland Peltops** *Peltops blainvillii*

Lowlands of New Guinea, Waigeo, Misool and Salawati islands

☐ **Black-backed Butcherbird** *Cracticus mentalis*

_____ C. m. mentalis	Savanna of se New Guinea (Merauke to Port Moresby)
_____ C. m. kempi	N Queensland (Cape York to Cooktown and Mitchell River)

☐ **Gray Butcherbird** *Cracticus torquatus*

_____ C. t. argenteus	Western Australia (Port Hedland) to Northern Territory
_____ C. t. leucopterus	Interior of Australia
_____ C. t. torquatus	E Australia (s Queensland to Victoria and South Australia)
_____ C. t. cinereus	Tasmania

☐ **Hooded Butcherbird** *Cracticus cassicus*

_____ C. c. cassicus	Lowlands of New Guinea, w Papuan, Aru, Yapen and Biak is.
_____ C. c. hercules	Trobriand Islands and D'Entrecasteaux Archipelago

☐ **Tagula Butcherbird** *Cracticus louisiadensis*

Tagula I. (Louisiade Archipelago)

☐ **Pied Butcherbird** *Cracticus nigrogularis*

____ C. n. picatus	E Kimberly region of Western Australia and Northern Territory
____ C. n. kalgoorli	Western Australia and interior of Australia
____ C. n. nigrogularis	Queensland to Victoria, se Australia and Tasmania

☐ **Black Butcherbird** *Cracticus quoyi*

____ C. q. quoyi	New Guinea, Yapen I. and w Papuan islands
____ C. q. spaldingi	Aru Islands; coastal Northern Territory and n Queensland
____ C. q. rufescens	N central Queensland (south of Cape York Peninsula)

☐ **Australasian Magpie** *Gymnorhina tibicen*

____ G. t. papuana	SE New Guinea (Trans-Fly lowlands)
____ G. t. eylandtensis	Groote Eylandt (Northern Territory)
____ G. t. longirostris	Western Australia (De Grey River to Ashburton River)
____ G. t. finki	Central Australia
____ G. t. terraereginae	Coastal Northern Territory and Queensland
____ G. t. tibicen	New South Wales, Victoria and South Australia
____ G. t. leuconota	SE New South Wales to se South Australia and Kangaroo I.
____ G. t. dorsalis	SW Australia (north to Murchison River and east to Esperance)
____ G. t. hypoleuca	Tasmania and islands in Bass Strait

☐ **Pied Currawong** *Strepera graculina*

____ S. g. robinsoni	NE Australia (Queensland)
____ S. g. graculina	E Australia (New South Wales)
____ S. g. ashbyi	E Australia (Victoria to extreme se South Australia)
____ S. g. crissalis	Lord Howe I.

☐ **Black Currawong** *Strepera fuliginosa*

	Tasmania and islands in Bass Strait

☐ **Gray Currawong** *Strepera versicolor*

____ S. v. versicolor	E Australia (New South Wales and e Victoria)
____ S. v. centralia	N South Australia
____ S. v. plumbea	S Western Australia
____ S. v. melanoptera	SE S Australia, Kangaroo I., sw New S Wales and nw Victoria
____ S. v. intermedia	SE South Australia (Eyre and Yorke peninsulas)
____ S. v. arguta	Tasmania and islands in Bass Strait; winters to nw Victoria

FAMILY: PARADISAEIDAE (Birds-of-paradise—44)

☐ **Loria's Bird-of-paradise** *Cnemophilus loriae*

____ C. l. amethystina	Western, Southern and Eastern Highlands of New Guinea
____ C. l. inexpectata	Weyland, Nassau, Jayawijaya, Hindenberg, Victor Emanuel Mts.
____ C. l. loriae	Mts. of se New Guinea (Herzog Mts. to Owen Stanley Range)

☐ **Crested Bird-of-paradise** *Cnemophilus macgregorii*

____ C. m. sanguineus	Central and Eastern Highlands of Papua New Guinea
____ C. m. macgregorii	Mountains of se Papua New Guinea

☐ **Yellow-breasted Bird-of-paradise** *Loboparadisea sericea*

____ L. s. sericea	Central New Guinea (Weyland Mts. to Victor Emanuel Mts.)
____ L. s. aurora	W New Guinea (Hertzog Mountains)

☐ **Macgregor's Bird-of-paradise** *Macgregoria pulchra*

____ M. p. pulchra	SE New Guinea (high summits of Owen Stanley Mountains)
____ M. p. carolinae	W New Guinea (Snow, Jayawijaya and Star mountains)

☐ **Paradise-crow** *Lycocorax pyrrhopterus*

____ *L. p. morotensis*	N Moluccas (Morotai and Rau)
____ *L. p. pyrrhopterus*	N Moluccas (Bacan, Kasiruta and Halmahera)
____ *L. p. obiensis*	N Moluccas (Obi and Bisa)

☐ **Glossy-mantled Manucode** *Manucodia atra*

____ *M. a. atra*	Western two-thirds of New Guinea
____ *M. a. subalter*	Aru, w Papuan islands and se peninsular Papua New Guinea
____ *M. a. alter*	Tagula I. (Louisiade Archipelago)

☐ **Jobi Manucode** *Manucodia jobiensis*

Lowlands of n New Guinea and Yapen I.

☐ **Crinkle-collared Manucode** *Manucodia chalybata*

Hills and lower montane forests of New Guinea and Misool I.

☐ **Curl-crested Manucode** *Manucodia comrii*

____ *M. c. comrii*	D'Entrecasteaux Archipelago
____ *M. c. trobriandi*	Trobriand Islands (Kiriwina and Kaileuna)

☐ **Trumpet Manucode** *Manucodia keraudrenii*

____ *M. k. keraudrenii*	Vogelkop, Onin Peninsula and Weyland Mts. (w New Guinea)
____ *M. k. aruensis*	Aru Islands (w New Guinea)
____ *M. k. jamesii*	Lowlands of s New Guinea (Mimika River to Port Moresby)
____ *M. k. neumanni*	N escarpment of central range of New Guinea
____ *M. k. adelberti*	Adelbert Mountains (n Papua New Guinea)
____ *M. k. diamondi*	Southern watershed of Eastern Highlands of New Guinea
____ *M. k. purpureoviolacea*	Highlands of se Papua New Guinea
____ *M. k. hunsteini*	D'Entrecasteaux Archipelago
____ *M. k. gouldii*	NE Australia (n Cape York Peninsula)

☐ **Long-tailed Paradigalla** *Paradigalla carunculata*

W New Guinea (Arfak and Farfak mountains)

☐ **Short-tailed Paradigalla** *Paradigalla brevicauda*

Patchily distributed mountains of w and central New Guinea

☐ **Arfak Astrapia** *Astrapia nigra*

W New Guinea (Arfak Mts.). Sight record from Tamrau Mts.

☐ **Splendid Astrapia** *Astrapia splendidissima*

____ *A. s. helios*	W New Guinea (C Range of Irian Jaya to Victor Emanuel Mts.)
____ *A. s. splendidissima*	W segment of central cordillera of New Guinea

☐ **Ribbon-tailed Astrapia** *Astrapia mayeri*

Central cordillera of e New Guinea

☐ **Princess Stephanie's Astrapia** *Astrapia stephaniae*

____ *A. s. feminina*	Schrader and Bismarck ranges and Sepik-Wahgi divide
____ *A. s. stephaniae*	E New Guinea (Central Highlands to Owen Stanley Range)

☐ **Huon Astrapia** *Astrapia rothschildi*

NE New Guinea (mountains of Huon Peninsula)

☐ **Western Parotia** *Parotia sefilata*

W New Guinea (Arfak, Tamrau and Wondiwoi mountains)

☐ **Carola's Parotia** *Parotia carolae*

____ *P. c. carolae*	W New Guinea (Weyland Mountains east to Wissel Lakes)
____ *P. c. meeki*	New Guinea (Snow Mountains to Victor Emanuel Mountains)
____ *P. c. chalcothorax*	W New Guinea (Doorman Mountains)
____ *P. c. berlepschi*	W New Guinea (Van Rees and [?] Foya mountains)
____ *P. c. clelandiae*	Papua New Guinea border to s watershed of Eastern Highlands
____ *P. c. chrysenia*	E New Guinea (n escarpment of Central Highlands)

□ **Lawes' Parotia** *Parotia lawesii*
_____ *P. l. lawesii* — W and s highlands of Papua New Guinea
_____ *P. l. helenae* — N watershed of Papua New Guinea (Waria to Milne Bay)

□ **Wahnes' Parotia** *Parotia wahnesi* — NE New Guinea (n coastal ranges of Huon Peninsula)

□ **King-of-Saxony Bird-of-paradise** *Pteridophora alberti* — Central cordillera of Papua New Guinea

□ **Magnificent Riflebird** *Ptiloris magnificus*
_____ *P. m. magnificus* — Lowlands of w and w-central New Guinea
_____ *P. m. intercedens* — Lowlands of central and se Papua New Guinea
_____ *P. m. alberti* — NE Australia (Cape York Peninsula)

□ **Paradise Riflebird** *Ptiloris paradiseus* — Rainforests of se Queensland and ne New South Wales

□ **Victoria's Riflebird** *Ptiloris victoriae* — Rainforests of n Queensland (Cooktown to Townsville)

□ **Superb Bird-of-paradise** *Lophorina superba*
_____ *L. s. superba* — W New Guinea (Arfak and Tamrau mountains)
_____ *L. s. niedda* — W New Guinea (Mt. Wondiwoi in Wandammen Peninsula)
_____ *L. s. feminina* — W New Guinea (Weyland Mts. to Hindenberg Mts.)
_____ *L. s. latipennis* — E New Guinea (Central and E Highlands to mts. of Huon Pen.)
_____ *L. s. minor* — Mountains of se Papua New Guinea
_____ *L. s. sphinx* — Mountains of extreme se New Guinea

□ **Black Sicklebill** *Epimachus fastuosus*
_____ *E. f. fastuosus* — W New Guinea (Tamrau and Arfak mountains)
_____ *E. f. atratus* — New Guinea (Mts. of Wandammen Peninsula to Kratka Range)
_____ *E. f. ultimus* — Coastal n Papua New Guinea (Mt. Menawa and Mt. Somoro)

□ **Brown Sicklebill** *Epimachus meyeri*
_____ *E. m. meyeri* — Mountains of extreme se New Guinea
_____ *E. m. bloodi* — Central Highlands of New Guinea
_____ *E. m. albicans* — Weyland Mountains to Hindenburg and Victor Emanuel Mts.

□ **Black-billed Sicklebill** *Epimachus albertisi*
_____ *E. a. albertisi* — New Guinea (mountains of Vogelkop and Huon Peninsula)
_____ *E. a. cervinicauda* — Central cordillera of New Guinea

□ **Pale-billed Sicklebill** *Epimachus bruijnii* — Lowlands of n Irian Jaya and nw Papua New Guinea

□ **Magnificent Bird-of-paradise** *Cicinnurus magnificus*
_____ *C. m. magnificus* — Extreme w Irian Jaya and Salawati I.
_____ *C. m. chrysopterus* — W and central New Guinea and Yapen I.
_____ *C. m. hunsteini* — E Papua New Guinea

□ **Wilson's Bird-of-paradise** *Cicinnurus respublica* — W Papuan islands (Waigeo and Batanta)

□ **King Bird-of-paradise** *Cicinnurus regius*
_____ *C. r. regius* — S New Guinea, Aru and w Papuan islands
_____ *C. r. coccineifrons* — N watershed of main body of New Guinea and Yapen I.

□ **Wallace's Standardwing** *Semioptera wallacii*
_____ *S. w. halmaherae* — Hill and montane forests of Halmahera (n Moluccas)
_____ *S. w. wallacii* — Hill and montane forests of Bacan (n Moluccas)

☐ **Twelve-wired Bird-of-paradise** *Seleucidis melanoleuca*

_____ *S. m. melanoleuca* — Lowlands of s New Guinea and Salawati I.

_____ *S. m. auripennis* — N New Guinea (Mamberamo River to Ramu River)

☐ **Lesser Bird-of-paradise** *Paradisaea minor*

_____ *P. m. minor* — Misool I. and w New Guinea (e to Papua New Guinea border)

_____ *P. m. jobiensis* — Yapen I.

_____ *P. m. finschi* — N Papua New Guinea border to Gogol and upper Ramu River

☐ **Greater Bird-of-paradise** *Paradisaea apoda*

_____ *P. a. apoda* — Aru Islands

_____ *P. a. novaeguineae* — S New Guinea (Timika to Fly/Strickland watershed)

☐ **Raggiana Bird-of-paradise** *Paradisaea raggiana*

_____ *P. r. raggiana* — S watershed of se Papua New Guinea

_____ *P. r. salvadorii* — Lowlands of s Papua New Guinea

_____ *P. r. intermedia* — N coast of se Papua New Guinea

_____ *P. r. augustaevictoriae* — New Guinea (Huon Pen. to Waria and lower Mambare rivers)

☐ **Goldie's Bird-of-paradise** *Paradisaea decora*

D'Entrecasteaux Archipelago (Fergusson and Normanby)

☐ **Red Bird-of-paradise** *Paradisaea rubra*

W Papuan islands (Waigeo, Batanta, Gemien and Saonek)

☐ **Emperor Bird-of-paradise** *Paradisaea guilielmi*

NE New Guinea (lower mountains of Huon Peninsula)

☐ **Blue Bird-of-paradise** *Paradisaea rudolphi*

_____ *P. r. rudolphi* — Mountains of se Papua New Guinea

_____ *P. r. margaritae* — Mountains of central Papua New Guinea

☐ **Lesser Melampitta** *Melampitta lugubris*

_____ *M. l. lugubris* — W New Guinea (Arfak Mountains)

_____ *M. l. rostrata* — W New Guinea (Weyland and Nassau mountains)

_____ *M. l. longicauda* — New Guinea (Jayawijaya to Owen Stanley Mts. and Huon Pen.)

☐ **Greater Melampitta** *Melampitta gigantea*

Patchily distributed lower montane slopes of New Guinea

FAMILY: PTILONORHYNCHIDAE (Bowerbirds—20)

☐ **White-eared Catbird** *Ailuroedus buccoides*

_____ *A. b. geislerorum* — Yapen I. and n New Guinea

_____ *A. b. oorti* — W Papuan islands and w New Guinea

_____ *A. b. buccoides* — S New Guinea (Triton Bay to upper Fly River)

_____ *A. b. cinnamomeus* — S New Guinea (Mimika River to upper Fly River)

_____ *A. b. stonii* — S coastal New Guinea (Hall Sound to Port Moresby)

☐ **Spotted Catbird** *Ailuroedus melanotis*

_____ *A. m. melanotis* — Aru Islands and s New Guinea

_____ *A. m. misoliensis* — Misool I. (w Papuan islands)

_____ *A. m. melanocephalus* — Mountains of se New Guinea

_____ *A. m. facialis* — W New Guinea (Nassau and Jayawijaya mountains)

_____ *A. m. guttaticollis* — New Guinea (Sepik River area and Mt. Hagen region)

_____ *A. m. astigmaticus* — NE New Guinea (mountains of Huon Peninsula)

_____ *A. m. jobiensis* — New Guinea (Weyland and Adelbert mountains)

_____ *A. m. arfakianus* — W New Guinea (Arfak Mountains of Vogelkop Peninsula)

_____ *A. m. maculosus* — NE Australia (ne Queensland from Claudie River to Townsville)

☐ **Green Catbird** *Ailuroedus crassirostris*

☐ **Tooth-billed Catbird** *Ailuroedus dentirostris*

☐ **Archbold's Bowerbird** *Archboldia papuensis*

☐ **Sanford's Bowerbird** *Archboldia sanfordi*

☐ **Vogelkop Bowerbird** *Amblyornis inornatus*

☐ **Macgregor's Bowerbird** *Amblyornis macgregoriae*
_____ *A. m. mayri*
_____ *A. m. macgregoriae*
_____ *A. m. germanus*
_____ *A. m. kombok*
_____ *A. m. lecroyae*
_____ *A.. m. nubicola*

☐ **Streaked Bowerbird** *Amblyornis subalaris*

☐ **Golden-fronted Bowerbird** *Amblyornis flavifrons*

☐ **Golden Bowerbird** *Prionodura newtoniana*

☐ **Flame Bowerbird** *Sericulus aureus*
_____ *S. a. aureus*
_____ *S. a. ardens*

☐ **Fire-maned Bowerbird** *Sericulus bakeri*

☐ **Regent Bowerbird** *Sericulus chrysocephalus*
_____ *S. c. rothschildi*
_____ *S. c. chrysocephalus*

☐ **Satin Bowerbird** *Ptilonorhynchus violaceus*
_____ *P. v. minor*
_____ *P. v. violaceus*

☐ **Western Bowerbird** *Chlamydera guttata*

☐ **Spotted Bowerbird** *Chlamydera maculata*

☐ **Great Bowerbird** *Chlamydera nuchalis*
_____ *C. n. nuchalis*
_____ *C. n. yorki*

☐ **Yellow-breasted Bowerbird** *Chlamydera lauterbachi*
_____ *C. l. lauterbachi*
_____ *C. l. uniformis*

☐ **Fawn-breasted Bowerbird** *Chlamydera cerviniventris*

E Australia (se Queensland and e New South Wales)

NE Australia (ne Queensland from Cooktown to Townsville)

W New Guinea (locally in Nassau Mountains)

Humid Central Highlands of New Guinea

NW New Guinea (Arfak, Tamrau and Wandammen mountains)

New Guinea (Weyland, Nassau and Jayawijaya mountains)
New Guinea (Central, Huon and Adelbert mountains)
NE New Guinea (mountains of Huon Peninsula)
Papua New Guinea (Mt. Hagen area)
NE Papua New Guinea (Mt. Bosavi area)
SE Papua New Guinea (Owen Stanley Mountains)

SE Papua New Guinea (Owen Stanley Mountains)

N-central New Guinea (Foya Mountains)

Highland rain forests of ne Australia (ne Queensland)

Lowlands and foothill forests of w New Guinea
S New Guinea (Toricelli and Prince Alexander mountains)

NE New Guinea (humid montane forests of Adelbert Mts.)

E Australia (coastal rainforests of central and s Queensland)
Coastal rainforests of se Queensland to New South Wales

NE Australia (highland rainforests of ne Queensland)
E Australia (se Queensland to Victoria)

Arid interior of Australia

Inland se Australia (central Queensland to n-central Victoria)

W Australia and Northern Territory (e to Gulf of Carpenteria)
Cape York Peninsula and n Queensland; Mornington I.

N-central New Guinea (upper Mamberamo River to Digul River)
S-central New Guinea (Geelvink Bay to Digul River)

New Guinea, ne Queensland and islands in Torres Strait

FAMILY: CORVIDAE (Crows, Jays and Magpies—117)

☐ **Crested Jay** *Platylophus galericulatus*

____	*P. g. ardesiacus*	S Myanmar, peninsular Thailand and Malay Peninsula
____	*P. g. coronatus*	Borneo and Sumatra
____	*P. g. galericulatus*	Java

☐ **Black Magpie** *Platysmurus leucopterus*

____	*P. l. leucopterus*	S Myanmar, peninsular Thailand, Malay Peninsula and Sumatra
____	*P. l. aterrimus*	Borneo

☐ **Siberian Jay** *Perisoreus infaustus*

____	*P. i. infaustus*	Lapland to n Norway, Sweden, Finland and Kola Peninsula
____	*P. i. ostjakorum*	Ural Mountains and nw Siberia
____	*P. i. yakutensis*	NE Asia
____	*P. i. ruthenus*	Central Scandinavia to central Russia and w Siberia
____	*P. i. opicus*	Altai and Sayan mountains
____	*P. i. rogosowi (sibericus)*	Central Siberia to Irkutsk, middle Yenisey River and Outer Siberia
____	*P. i. varnak*	Upper Amur River (north to Stanovoi Mountains)
____	*P. i. sakhalinensis*	N Sakhalin and Shantar islands
____	*P. i. maritimus*	Lower Amur River (Bureya River to ne Manchuria)

☐ **Sichuan Jay** *Perisoreus internigrans*

		Mountains of w China (se Qinghai, sw Gansu and n Sichuan)

☐ **Gray Jay** *Perisoreus canadensis*

____	*P. c. pacificus*	N-central Alaska, n Yukon and nw Mackenzie
____	*P. c. canadensis*	Canada (central Yukon) to n US
____	*P. c. nigricapillus*	E Canada (n Quebec to Newfoundland and Nova Scotia)
____	*P. c. arcus*	SW Canada (coastal mountains of British Columbia)
____	*P. c. albescens*	NE British Columbia to w South Dakota and nw Nebraska
____	*P. c. bicolor*	SE British Columbia to e Washington, ne Oregon and w Montana
____	*P. c. capitalis*	Rocky Mountains (Idaho and Montana to New Mexico)
____	*P. c. griseus*	SW British Columbia and Vancouver I. to ne California
____	*P. c. obscurus*	Coastal nw US (Washington to nw California)

☐ **Steller's Jay** *Cyanocitta stelleri*

____	*C. s. stelleri*	S Alaska and coastal British Columbia to nw Oregon
____	*C. s. carlottae*	Queen Charlotte Islands (British Columbia)
____	*C. s. annectens*	Interior British Columbia to ne Oregon and nw Wyoming
____	*C. s. frontalis*	Central Oregon to s California; winters to extreme n Baja
____	*C. s. carbonacea*	Coastal California (Marin and Contra Costa to Monterey counties)
____	*C. s. macrolopha*	Rocky Mountains (Nevada and Utah to n Sonora)
____	*C. s. diademata*	Sierra Madre Occidental (se Sonora to Chihuahua and Jalisco)
____	*C. s. philippsi*	Central Mexico (San Luis Potosí, Guanajuato and Hidalgo)
____	*C. s. coronata*	Highlands of central Mexico (San Luis Potosí to n Puebla)
____	*C. s. purpurea*	SW Mexico (highlands of w and central Michoacán)
____	*C. s. azteca*	Mts. of c Mexico (México, Morelos, Puebla and w-c Veracruz)
____	*C. s. teotepecencis*	Mountains of s Mexico (central and s Guerrero)
____	*C. s. restricta*	S Mexico (highlands of Oaxaca)
____	*C. s. ridgwayi*	Highlands of s Mexico (Chiapas) to Guatemala and El Salvador
____	*C. s. lazula*	Highlands of El Salvador
____	*C. s. suavis*	Highlands of w Honduras to central Nicaragua

☐ **Blue Jay** *Cyanocitta cristata*

____	*C. c. bromia*	S Canada (Alberta to Quebec) to central US; winters to se US
____	*C. c. cristata*	E-central and se US
____	*C. c. semplei*	S Florida
____	*C. c. cyanoptera*	SE Wyoming and Nebraska to w Kansas, Oklahoma and n Texas

☐ **Black-throated Magpie-Jay** *Calocitta colliei*

Pacific slope of nw Mexico (se Sonora to Jalisco and Colima)

☐ **White-throated Magpie-Jay** *Calocitta formosa*
____ *C. f. formosa*   Coastal s Mexico (Colima, Michoacán and Puebla to Oaxaca)
____ *C. f. azurea*   Pacific slope of se Mexico (Chiapas) and Guatemala
____ *C. f. pompata*   Arid interior of s Mexico (Oaxaca) to nw Costa Rica

☐ **Tufted Jay** *Cyanocorax dickeyi*

Montane forests of nw Mexico (Sinaloa, Durango and Nayarit)

☐ **Black-chested Jay** *Cyanocorax affinis*
____ *C. a. zeledoni*   Humid forests of se Costa Rica and Panama
____ *C. a. affinis*   N Colombia and nw Venezuela

☐ **Green Jay** *Cyanocorax yncas*
____ *C. y. speciosus*   Pacific slope of w Mexico (Nayarit and Jalisco)
____ *C. y. vividus*   Pacific slope of s Mexico (Colima) to w Guatemala
____ *C. y. luxuosus*   S Texas (Rio Grande Valley) to e Mexico (Puebla and Veracruz)
____ *C. y. centralis*   SE Mexico (Tabasco) to Belize, e Guatemala and Honduras
____ *C. y. maya*   SE Mexico (Yucatán Peninsula) and extreme s Quintana Roo
____ *C. y. cozumelae*   Cozumel I.
____ *C. y. galeatus*   Subtropical central Colombia (west of Eastern Andes)
____ *C. y. cyanodorsalis*   E Andes of Colombia and nw Venezuela
____ *C. y. andicolus*   Mountains of n Venezuela
____ *C. y. guatimalensis*   Coastal cordillera of n Venezuela
____ *C. y. yncas*   Subtropical sw Colombia to Ecuador, Peru and central Bolivia
____ *C. y. longirostris*   N Peru (arid upper Marañón Valley)

☐ **Brown Jay** *Cyanocorax morio*
____ *C. m. palliatus*   Gulf-Caribbean slope of se Texas to se Mexico (Veracruz)
____ *C. m. morio*   SE Mexico (coastal c Veracruz to e Tabasco and n Chiapas)
____ *C. m. cyanogenys*   SE Mexico (extreme e Tabasco and Campeche) to nw Panama
____ *C. m. vociferus*   N Yucatán Peninsula (Campeche, Yucatán and Quintana Roo)

☐ **Bushy-crested Jay** *Cyanocorax melanocyaneus*
____ *C. m. melanocyaneus*   Highlands of central Guatemala to Honduras
____ *C. m. chavezi*   Highlands of s Honduras and n Nicaragua

☐ **San Blas Jay** *Cyanocorax sanblasianus*
____ *C. s. nelsoni*   Coastal w Mexico (Nayarit, Jalisco, Colima, Michoacán, Guerrero)
____ *C. s. sanblasianus*   Coastal sw Mexico (central Guerrero)

☐ **Yucatan Jay** *Cyanocorax yucatanicus*
____ *C. y. yucatanicus*   SE Mexico (Yucatán Peninsula) to Belize and Petén of Guatemala
____ *C. y. rivularis*   SE Mexico (Tabasco and sw Campeche)

☐ **Purplish-backed Jay** *Cyanocorax beecheii*

Lowlands of w Mexico (se Sonora and Chihuahua to Nayarit)

☐ **Purplish Jay** *Cyanocorax cyanomelas*

SE Peru to ne Argentina, Paraguay and sw Brazil

☐ **Azure Jay** *Cyanocorax caeruleus*

SE Brazil (São Paulo to Rio Grande do Sul)

☐ **Violaceous Jay** *Cyanocorax violaceus*
____ *C. v. pallidus*   Caribbean littoral of n Venezuela (Anzoátegui)
____ *C. v. violaceus*   E Colombia to Venezuela, Guianas, Brazil, Peru and n Bolivia

☐ **Curl-crested Jay** *Cyanocorax cristatellus*

Woodlands of s-central Brazil and extreme ne Paraguay

☐ **Azure-naped Jay** *Cyanocorax heilprini*

☐ **Cayenne Jay** *Cyanocorax cayanus*
                    SE Colombia to sw Venezuela (Amazonas) and extreme nw Brazil

☐ **Plush-crested Jay** *Cyanocorax chrysops*
                    SE Venezuela (Bolívar) to the Guianas and ne Brazil
      ____ *C. c. diesingii* — N Brazil south of the Amazon
      ____ *C. c. chrysops* — SE Brazil to Paraguay, Uruguay, n Bolivia and ne Argentina
      ____ *C. c. tucumanus* — NW Argentina

☐ **White-naped Jay** *Cyanocorax cyanopogon*
                    Tableland of e Brazil (Pará to Minas Gerais and e Mato Grosso)

☐ **White-tailed Jay** *Cyanocorax mystacalis*
                    Arid sw Ecuador and nw Peru (south to La Libertad)

☐ **Black-collared Jay** *Cyanolyca armillata*
      ____ *C. a. armillata* — Andes of e Colombia and w Venezuela
      ____ *C. a. quindiuna* — Andes of s Colombia and n Ecuador (e Carchi and nw Napo)
      ____ *C. a. meridana* — Andes of nw Venezuela (north to Trujillo)

☐ **Turquoise Jay** *Cyanolyca turcosa*
                    Andes of se Colombia to n Peru (n Piura and nw Cajamarca)

☐ **White-collared Jay** *Cyanolyca viridicyana*
      ____ *C. v. jolyaea* — Andes of n Peru (Amazonas to Junín)
      ____ *C. v. cyanolaema* — Andes of se Peru (Cuzco and Puno)
      ____ *C. v. viridicyana* — Andes of w Bolivia (La Paz and Cochabamba)

☐ **Azure-hooded Jay** *Cyanolyca cucullata*
      ____ *C. c. mitrata* — E Mexico (San Luis Potosí to n-central Oaxaca)
      ____ *C. c. guatemalae* — S Mexico (Chiapas) to central Guatemala
      ____ *C. c. hondurensis* — W Honduras
      ____ *C. c. cucullata* — Costa Rica and w Panama

☐ **Beautiful Jay** *Cyanolyca pulchra*
                    W Andes of sw Colombia and nw Ecuador (south to Pichincha)

☐ **Black-throated Jay** *Cyanolyca pumilo*
                    Montane forests of extreme s Mexico to nw Honduras

☐ **Dwarf Jay** *Cyanolyca nana*
                    Oak-pine forests of sw Mexico (Vera Cruz, Puebla and Oaxaca)

☐ **Silvery-throated Jay** *Cyanolyca argentigula*
      ____ *C. a. albior* — Montane forests of Costa Rica
      ____ *C. a. argentigula* — Montane forests of s Costa Rica and w Panama

☐ **White-throated Jay** *Cyanolyca mirabilis*
                    Oak-pine forests of sw Mexico (s Guerrero and s-central Oaxaca)

☐ **Florida Scrub-Jay** *Aphelocoma coerulescens*
                    Locally in central peninsular and Atlantic coastal Florida

☐ **Island Scrub-Jay** *Aphelocoma insularis*
                    Santa Cruz I. (Channel Islands off s California)

☐ **Western Scrub-Jay** *Aphelocoma californica*
      ____ *A. c. inmanis* — Extreme sw Washington to w Oregon (Willamette Valley)
      ____ *A. c. caurina* — Coastal sw Oregon to c Calif. (Trinity, Lake and Napa counties)
      ____ *A. c. oocleptica* — S-central Oregon to San Francisco Bay and w Nevada
      ____ *A. c. californica* — Coastal ranges of c Calif. (s San Mateo to sw Ventura County)
      ____ *A. c. cana* — Arid s California (Eagle Mountain area of Riverside County)
      ____ *A. c. obscura* — SW California and n Baja California (south to Todos Santos Bay)
      ____ *A. c. cactophila* — Central Baja California (latitude 29°30' to Bahía Magdalena)
      ____ *A. c. hypoleuca* — Cape District of Baja California
      ____ *A. c. nevadae* — SE Oregon s through Great Basin to ne Sonora and nw Chihuahua
      ____ *A. c. woodhouseii* — Rocky Mountains to w Oklahoma, w Texas and n Chihuahua
      ____ *A. c. texana* — W-central Texas

_____ *A. c. grisea*	NW Mexico (e slopes of Sierra Madre Occidental)
_____ *A. c. cyanotis*	Mts. of e central Mexico (s Coahuila and Nuevo León to Hidalgo)
_____ *A. c. sumichrasti*	Highlands of s Mexican plateau (Veracruz to Puebla and Oaxaca)
_____ *A. c. remota*	SW Mexico (Sierra Madre del Sur of Guerrero)

☐ **Mexican Jay** *Aphelocoma ultramarina*

_____ *A. u. arizonae*	Mts. of Arizona and New Mexico to n Sonora and nw Chihuahua
_____ *A. u. wollweberi*	Mts. of w Mexico (se Sonora to Durango, Zacatecas and n Jalisco)
_____ *A. u. gracilis*	Mts. of w-central Mexico (e Nayarit and n Jalisco)
_____ *A. u. couchii*	Mts. of extreme sw Texas to s Nuevo León and c Tamaulipas
_____ *A. u. potosina*	Mts. of e-c Mexico (San Luis Potosí to Querétaro and c Hidalgo)
_____ *A. u. ultramarina*	S Mexican Plateau (Jalisco to Michoacán, Puebla and w Veracruz)
_____ *A. u. colimae*	Mountains w Mexico (nw Jalisco to ne Colima)

☐ **Unicolored Jay** *Aphelocoma unicolor*

_____ *A. u. concolor*	Mountains of se Mexico (w-c Veracruz, e México and Puebla)
_____ *A. u. guerrerensis*	Mountains of w Mexico (s-central Guerrero)
_____ *A. u. oaxacae*	S Mexico (central highlands of Oaxaca)
_____ *A. u. unicolor*	Mountains of se Mexico (Chiapas) and Guatemala
_____ *A. u. griscomi*	Mountains of n El Salvador and w Honduras

☐ **Pinyon Jay** *Gymnorhinus cyanocephalus*

	Pinyon-juniper woodlands of s Oregon to sw US and n Baja

☐ **Eurasian Jay** *Garrulus glandarius*

_____ *G. g. rufitergum*	S Scotland, England, Wales and n France
_____ *G. g. hibernicus*	Ireland
_____ *G. g. glandarius*	N and central Europe
_____ *G. g. severtzowi*	Scandinavia and w Russia
_____ *G. g. lusitanicus*	N Portugal and n Spain
_____ *G. g. fasciatus*	Southern, central and eastern Spain
_____ *G. g. corsicanus*	Corsica
_____ *G. g. albipectus*	Italy, Dalmatian coast of Yugoslavia, Albania and Ionian Islands
_____ *G. g. jordansi*	Sicily
_____ *G. g. ichnusae*	Sardinia
_____ *G. g. graecus*	S Yugoslavia, s Bulgaria and Greece
_____ *G. g. cretorum*	Crete
_____ *G. g. glaszneri*	Cyprus
_____ *G. g. fernandi*	SE Bulgaria to n Turkey (Istranca Mountains)
_____ *G. g. atricapillus*	Lebanon to s Syria, Israel and w Jordan
_____ *G. g. anatolia*	W Turkey and e Aegean Sea to w Asia Minor, n Iraq and sw Iran
_____ *G. g. samios*	Samos and Ikaria region of e Aegean Sea
_____ *G. r. iphigenia*	Crimean Peninsula
_____ *G. g. minor*	Atlas Mountains of Morocco and Algeria
_____ *G. g. cervicalis*	NE Algeria and Tunisia
_____ *G. g. whitakeri*	N Morocco and nw Algeria
_____ *G. g. krynicki*	Caucasus, Transcaucasia and n Asia Minor
_____ *G. r. hyrcanus*	N Iran (Elzburg Mountains and south shore of Caspian Sea)
_____ *G. g. brandtii*	Ural Mountains to Siberia, Lake Baikal and Altai and Sayan mts.
_____ *G. g. bambergi*	Mongolia to Sakhalin, s Kuril Islands, Hokkaido and Korea
_____ *G. g. kansuensis*	Kazakstan (e Tien Shan) and w China (Gansu)
_____ *G. g. pekingensis*	N China (Liaoning) and sw Manchuria
_____ *G. g. sinensis*	W China to n Yunnan and ne Myanmar
_____ *G. g. leucotis*	E Myanmar to s Yunnan, Thailand to central Vietnam
_____ *G. g. oatesi*	Central Myanmar (upper Chindwin and Chin Hills)
_____ *G. g. barringtoni*	Myanmar (Mt. Victoria in s Chin Hills)
_____ *G. g. interstinctus*	E Himalayas and se Tibet
_____ *G. g. persaturatus*	N India (Khasi Hills of Assam)
_____ *G. g. bispecularis*	Himalayas (Kashmir to Nepal)

____	*Garrulus glandarius japonicus*	Japan (Hondo, Shikoku and Kyushu)
____	*G. g. tokugawae*	Sado I. (Japan)
____	*G. g. hiugaensis*	Japan (Isu Peninsula of e Hondo, s Kyushu and Kagoshima)
____	*G. g. orii*	Yakushima I. (Ryukyu Islands)
____	*G. g. namiyei*	Tsushima Islands (sw Japan)
____	*G. g. taivanus*	Taiwan

□ **Black-headed Jay** *Garrulus lanceolatus*

Himalayas (Afghanistan to n India and central Nepal)

□ **Lidth's Jay** *Garrulus lidthi*

Ryukyu Islands (Amami-O-Shima and Tokuno-Shima)

□ **Azure-winged Magpie** *Cyanopica cyana*

____	*C. c. cooki*	Iberian Peninsula
____	*C. c. cyana*	E-central Asia
____	*C. c. pallescens*	Middle and lower Amur River region
____	*C. c. koreensis*	Korea
____	*C. c. stegmanni*	Manchuria
____	*C. c. swinhoei*	E China (Liaoning to Fujian and Sichuan)
____	*C. c. interposita*	N China (Shaanxi)
____	*C. c. kansuensis*	W China (Gansu, Qinghai and nw Sichuan)
____	*C. c. japonica*	Japan (Hondo and Kyushu)

□ **Ceylon Magpie** *Urocissa ornata*

Dense evergreen hill forests of Sri Lanka

□ **Formosan Magpie** *Urocissa caerulea*

Montane forests of Taiwan

□ **Gold-billed Magpie** *Urocissa flavirostris*

____	*U. f. cucullata*	W Himalayas (Hazara to e Nepal)
____	*U. f. flavirostris*	E Himalayas to Assam, s Tibet and n Myanmar
____	*U. f. schaferi*	W Myanmar (Chin Hills)
____	*U. f. robini*	N Vietnam (nw Tonkin)

□ **Blue Magpie** *Urocissa erythrorhyncha*

____	*U. e. brevivexilla*	SW Manchuria and n China
____	*U. e. erythrorhyncha*	Central China to s Yunnan, n Laos and n Vietnam
____	*U. e. alticola*	SW China (n Yunnan) and ne Myanmar
____	*U. e. occipitalis*	Himalayas (Punjab to Sikkim)
____	*U. e. magnirostris*	Hills of Assam to Indochina

□ **White-winged Magpie** *Urocissa whiteheadi*

____	*U. w. xanthomelana*	Mountains of s China to central Laos and n Vietnam
____	*U. w. whiteheadi*	Mountains of Hainan (s China)

□ **Green Magpie** *Cissa chinensis*

____	*C. c. chinensis*	E Himalayas to se Tibet, Myanmar, n Laos and n Vietnam
____	*C. c. robinsoni*	Malaysia
____	*C. c. klossi*	Central Indochina
____	*C. c. margaritae*	S Vietnam (Langbian Mountains)
____	*C. c. minor*	Sumatra and nw Borneo

□ **Yellow-breasted Magpie** *Cissa hypoleuca*

____	*C. h. jini*	SE China (Yaoshan Massif of Guangxi)
____	*C. h. concolor*	N Vietnam
____	*C. h. chauleti*	Central Vietnam
____	*C. h. hypoleuca*	E Thailand and s Indochina
____	*C. h. katsumatae*	Hainan (s China)

□ **Short-tailed Magpie** *Cissa thalassina*
____	*C. t. thalassina*	Java
____	*C. t. jeffreyi*	Mountains of n Borneo

□ **Rufous Treepie** *Dendrocitta vagabunda*
____	*D. v. pallida*	W Himalayas and nw India
____	*D. v. vagabunda*	Lower Himalayas and ne India (south to Hyderabad)
____	*D. v. parvula*	SW India (s Kanara to Cape Comorin)
____	*D. v. vernayi*	SE India
____	*D. v. sclateri*	E Myanmar (upper Chindwin to Chin Hills and Arakan Yoma)
____	*D. v. kinneari*	S Myanmar and nw Thailand
____	*D. v. saturatior*	Tenasserim and s Thailand
____	*D. v. sakeratensis*	E Thailand and Indochina

□ **Gray Treepie** *Dendrocitta formosae*
____	*D. f. occidentalis*	W Himalayas (n Pakistan to Garhwal)
____	*D. f. himalayensis*	E Himalayas to Myanmar and n Laos
____	*D. f. sarkari*	E India (s Jaipur and n Madras)
____	*D. f. assimilis*	S Myanmar to Thailand and Andaman Islands
____	*D. f. sinica*	E and se China to n Vietnam
____	*D. f. sapiens*	S China on Mt. Omei (w Sichuan)
____	*D. f. formosae*	Taiwan
____	*D. f. insulae*	Hainan (s China)

□ **Sumatran Treepie** *Dendrocitta occipitalis*

Mountains of Sumatra

□ **Bornean Treepie** *Dendrocitta cinerascens*

Mountains of Borneo

□ **White-bellied Treepie** *Dendrocitta leucogastra*

Lowlands of sw India (Western Ghats)

□ **Collared Treepie** *Dendrocitta frontalis*

Himalayas of n India, n Myanmar and nw Vietnam

□ **Andaman Treepie** *Dendrocitta bayleyi*

Dense forests of Andaman Islands

□ **Racket-tailed Treepie** *Crypsirina temia*

S Myanmar to n Malaya, Indochina, Java and Bali

□ **Hooded Treepie** *Crypsirina cucullata*

Arid lowlands of Myanmar

□ **Ratchet-tailed Treepie** *Temnurus temnurus*

Forests of central Laos, n Vietnam and Hainan

□ **Black-billed Magpie** *Pica pica*
____	*P. p. hudsonia*	Alaska and Yukon to w Canada and w US
____	*P. p. pica*	British Isles, s Scandinavia, central and e Europe to Asia Minor
____	*P. p. fennorum*	N Scandinavia and w Russia
____	*P. p. galliae*	W Europe to Balkans
____	*P. p. melanotos*	Iberian Peninsula
____	*P. p. mauretanica*	NE Mauritania to Morocco, Algeria and Tunisia
____	*P. p. asirensis*	Assir Mountains (sw Arabia)
____	*P. p. bactriana*	Central Russia to n India and w Tibet
____	*P. p. hemileucoptera*	W and s Siberia to Outer Mongolia
____	*P. p. leucoptera*	S Transbaicalia to e Mongolia and Altai Mountains
____	*P. p. camtschatica*	N shores of Sea of Okhotsk to Kamchatka Peninsula
____	*P. p. bottanensis*	E Himalayas to se Tibet and w China (Qinghai and Xinjiang)
____	*P. p. sericea*	S China to Myanmar, Indochina, Hainan and Taiwan

□ **Yellow-billed Magpie** *Pica nuttalli*

Interior, coastal valleys and foothills of central California

□ **Stresemann's Bush-Crow** *Zavattariornis stresemanni*

S Ethiopia (Sidamo Province)

☐ **Mongolian Ground-Jay** *Podoces hendersoni*

Deserts of central Asia (Kazakstan to Outer and Inner Mongolia)

☐ **Xinjiang Ground-Jay** *Podoces biddulphi*

Deserts of nw China (w Xinjiang)

☐ **Turkestan Ground-Jay** *Podoces panderi*

Deserts of s-central Asia (Russian Turkestan)

☐ **Iranian Ground-Jay** *Podoces pleskei*

Desert steppes of central and e Iran

☐ **Tibetan Ground-Jay** *Pseudopodoces humilis*

Semiarid steppes of Tibetan plateau

☐ **Clark's Nutcracker** *Nucifraga columbiana*

Rocky Mountains (sw Canada to n Baja); casual to nw Mexico

☐ **Eurasian Nutcracker** *Nucifraga caryocatactes*

____	*N. c. caryocatactes*	Scandinavia to n and e Europe; winters to s Russia
____	*N. c. macrorhynchos*	N and ne Asia; irruptions to n Iran, Korea and n China
____	*N. c. rothschildi*	Tien Shan Mountains (Kazakstan)
____	*N. c. japonica*	Central and s Kuril Islands, Hokkaido and Hondo
____	*N. c. owstoni*	Taiwan
____	*N. c. interdicta*	Mountains of n China (Liaoning)
____	*N. c. multipunctata*	Pakistan and nw India
____	*N. c. hemispila*	Himalayas (w Nepal to s Kashmir)
____	*N. c. macella*	E Himalayas to s Tibet, w Nepal, n Myanmar and sw China
____	*N. c. yunnanensis*	SW China (Yunnan)

☐ **Red-billed Chough** *Pyrrhocorax pyrrhocorax*

____	*P. p. pyrrhocorax*	Locally in England, Wales, Isle of Man, Inner Hebrides and Ireland
____	*P. p. erythrorhamphus*	Alps, Pyrénées, Iberian Peninsula and Mediterranean islands
____	*P. p. barbarus*	La Palma (Canary Islands) and nw Africa (Morocco to Algeria)
____	*P. p. baileyi*	Highlands of Ethiopia
____	*P. p. docilis*	Crete and se Europe to n Arabia, n Iraq, Iran and Afghanistan
____	*P. p. centralis*	Central Asia (Tien Shan, Pamir and Altai mountains)
____	*P. p. himalayanus*	Himalayas and n India to w China
____	*P. p. brachypus*	Central and n China to Manchuria and Mongolia

☐ **Yellow-billed Chough** *Pyrrhocorax graculus*

____	*P. g. graculus*	Mountains of Europe, North Africa, Caucasus and s Caspian area
____	*P. g. digitatus*	Lebanon and Iran to s Tibet and Himalayas

☐ **Piapiac** *Ptilostomus afer*

Palm savanna of sub-Saharan Africa

☐ **Eurasian Jackdaw** *Corvus monedula*

____	*C. m. monedula*	Scandinavia; occasionally winters to England and France
____	*C. m. spermologus*	W and central Europe; winters to Canary Islands and Corsica
____	*C. m. soemmerringii*	E Europe, n and c Asia; winters to Iran and nw India (Kashmir)
____	*C. m. cirtensis*	N Africa (Morocco and Algeria)

☐ **Daurian Jackdaw** *Corvus dauuricus*

S Siberia to Mongolia, n China and se Tibet; winters to s China

☐ **House Crow** *Corvus splendens*

____	*C. s. zugmayeri*	Coastal s Iran to s Kashmir and nw India
____	*C. s. splendens*	India south of the Himalayas
____	*C. s. protegatus*	Sri Lanka
____	*C. s. maldevicius*	Laccadive and Maldive islands
____	*C. s. insolens*	S Myanmar to sw Thailand and sw China (w Yunnan)

☐ **New Caledonian Crow** *Corvus moneduloides*

Forests of New Caledonia

☐ **Slender-billed Crow** *Corvus enca*

____	*C. e. sierramadrensis*	N Philippines (Sierra Madre Mountains of Luzon)
____	*C. e. samarensis*	S Philippines (Samar and Mindanao)
____	*C. e. pusillus*	S Philippines (Balabac, Culion, Mindoro and Palawan)
____	*C. e. compilator*	Malaysia, Sumatra, Borneo, Riau Arch. and w Sumatran islands
____	*C. e. enca*	Java, Bali and Mentawi Archipelago
____	*C. e. celebensis*	Sulawesi, Talaud, Is., Togian Is. and Tukangbesi Is.
____	*C. e. mangoli*	Sula Islands (Taliabu, Seho, Mangole and Sanana)
____	*C. e. violaceus*	S Moluccas (Seram, Buru and Ambon)

☐ **Piping Crow** *Corvus typicus*

Central and s Sulawesi, Muna and Butung islands

☐ **Flores Crow** *Corvus florensis*

Lowlands of Flores (w Lesser Sundas)

☐ **Mariana Crow** *Corvus kubaryi*

Mariana Islands (Rota and Guam). On verge of extinction

☐ **Long-billed Crow** *Corvus validus*

N Moluccas (Morotai, Halmahera, Kayoa, Bacan, Obi, Kasiruta)

☐ **Guadalcanal Crow** *Corvus woodfordi*

____	*C. w. woodfordi*	Guadalcanal (Solomon Islands)
____	*C. w. vegetus*	Solomon Islands (Choiseul and Santa Isabel)

☐ **Bougainville Crow** *Corvus meeki*

Solomon Islands (Bougainville and Shortland)

☐ **Brown-headed Crow** *Corvus fuscicapillus*

____	*C. f. megarhynchus*	Waigeo and Gemien islands (w New Guinea)
____	*C. f. fuscicapillus*	Aru Islands and lower Mamberamo River (New Guinea)

☐ **Gray Crow** *Corvus tristis*

New Guinea, Yapen, w Papuan islands and D'Entrecasteaux Arch.

☐ **Cape Crow** *Corvus capensis*

Discontinuously distributed in ne and southern Africa

☐ **Rook** *Corvus frugilegus*

____	*C. f. frugilegus*	W Eurasia; winters to North Africa and nw India
____	*C. f. pastinator*	E Asia; winters to Korea, Japan and se China

☐ **American Crow** *Corvus brachyrhynchos*

____	*C. b. hesperis*	N British Columbia to sw US and n Baja California
____	*C. b. brachyrhynchos*	Central and e Canada to e-central US; winters to se US
____	*C. b. paulus*	E and se US
____	*C. b. pascuus*	Peninsular Florida

☐ **Northwestern Crow** *Corvus caurinus*

Kodiak I. and coastal s Alaska to sw Washington

☐ **Cuban Palm Crow** *Corvus minutus*

W Cuba

☐ **Hispaniolan Palm Crow** *Corvus palmarum*

Hispaniola

☐ **Cuban Crow** *Corvus nasicus*

Cuba, Isle of Pines and s Bahamas (Caicos Islands)

☐ **White-necked Crow** *Corvus leucognaphalus*

Hispaniola; casual on Gonâve and Saona

☐ **Jamaican Crow** *Corvus jamaicensis*

Locally in Jamaica (mainly in uplands)

☐ **Tamaulipas Crow** *Corvus imparatus*

S Texas (lower Rio Grande Valley) to se Mexico (n Veracruz)

☐ **Sinaloa Crow** *Corvus sinaloae*

Coastal lowlands of w Mexico (s Sonora to w Nayarit)

☐ **Fish Crow** *Corvus ossifragus*

Eastern US (New England to s Texas)

☐ **Hawaiian Crow** *Corvus hawaiiensis*

Montane forests of Hawaii (on verge of extinction)

☐ **Chihuahuan Raven** *Corvus cryptoleucus*

Arid sw US to central Mexico

☐ **Carrion Crow** *Corvus corone*
- ____ *C. c. corone* — W Europe
- ____ *C. c. orientalis* — Iran to n China, Korea and Japan
- ____ *C. c. cornix* — N Europe to Yenisey Valley, Ukraine, Corsica and s Italy
- ____ *C. c. sharpii* — Mainland Italy to Yugoslavia, Asia Minor, n Iran and Kazakstan
- ____ *C. c. pallescens* — Coastal s Turkey to Levant, n Iraq and Egypt
- ____ *C. c. capellanus* — S Iraq and adjacent sw Iran

☐ **Large-billed Crow** *Corvus macrorhynchos*
- ____ *C. m. japonensis* — Sakhalin, Kuril Islands and n Japanese Archipelago
- ____ *C. m. connectens* — S Ryukyu Islands (Amami-O-Shima, Okinawa and Miyako-Jima)
- ____ *C. m. osai* — S Ryukyu Is. (Ishigaki, Iriomote, Kobama, Kuru and Aragusuku)
- ____ *C. m. mandschuricus* — NE Asia
- ____ *C. m. colonorum* — N China to n Indochina and Taiwan
- ____ *C. m. hainanus* — Hainan (s China)
- ____ *C. m. mengtszensis* — SW China (s Yunnan)
- ____ *C. m. tibetosinensis* — E Himalayas to se Tibet, n Myanmar and w China
- ____ *C. m. intermedius* — Extreme e Iran to nw India and w Himalayas
- ____ *C. m. culminatus* — S India and Sri Lanka
- ____ *C. m. levaillantii* — Indus River drainage of ne India, Sri Lanka and Andaman Islands
- ____ *C. m. macrorhynchos* — Malaysia, s Indochina, Borneo, Sumatra, Java and Lesser Sundas
- ____ *C. m. philippinus* — Philippine Islands

☐ **Torresian Crow** *Corvus orru*
- ____ *C. o. orru* — N Moluccas, w Papuan is., New Guinea and D'Entrecasteaux Arch.
- ____ *C. o. insularis* — Bismarck Archipelago
- ____ *C. o. latirostris* — Tanimbar Islands and Babar Islands (Arafura Sea)
- ____ *C. o. ceciliae* — Australia and Melville I.

☐ **Little Crow** *Corvus bennetti*

Arid woodlands of interior and w Australia

☐ **Australian Raven** *Corvus coronoides*

Australia

☐ **Little Raven** *Corvus mellori*

New South Wales to Victoria, se South Australia and King I.

☐ **Forest Raven** *Corvus tasmanicus*
- ____ *C. t. boreus* — New South Wales and Victoria
- ____ *C. t. tasmanicus* — Tasmania, King I. and Furneaux Group

☐ **Collared Crow** *Corvus torquatus*

Central and e China to n Vietnam; Hainan and Taiwan

☐ **Pied Crow** *Corvus albus*

Africa s of the Sahara, Madagascar, Aldabra and Comoro Islands

☐ **Brown-necked Raven** *Corvus ruficollis*
- ____ *C. r. ruficollis* — Cape Verde Islands; North Africa to w Pakistan
- ____ *C. r. edithae* — Somalia

☐ **Fan-tailed Raven** *Corvus rhipidurus*

Sub-Saharan Africa and Near East

☐ **White-necked Raven** *Corvus albicollis*	
	Rocks, cliffs and hills of e and s Africa
☐ **Thick-billed Raven** *Corvus crassirostris*	
	Mts. of Ethiopia and Eritrea; vagrant to nw Somalia and se Sudan
☐ **Common Raven** *Corvus corax*	
_____ *C. c. principalis*	Islands in Bering Sea, Alaska, Canada and n US
_____ *C. c. sinuatus*	W-central US to s Baja, Revillagigedo Islands and nw Nicaragua
_____ *C. c. varius*	Iceland and Faeroe Islands
_____ *C. c. corax*	Europe and Mediterranean islands to w Asia
_____ *C. c. subcorax*	SE Europe and Asia Minor to Pakistan
_____ *C. c. tingitanus*	Canary Islands; coastal Morocco to Egypt
_____ *C. c. tibetanus*	Mountains of central Asia and the Himalayas
_____ *C. c. kamtschaticus*	Siberia to Sea of Okhotsk, Sakhalin, Kuril Islands and n Japan

FAMILY: STURNIDAE (Starlings—114)

☐ **Metallic Starling** *Aplonis metallica*	
_____ *A. m. circumscripta*	Tanimbar Islands (Larat and Kirimoen) and Damar I.
_____ *A. m. metallica*	Moluccas, Sula Is. and Aru Is. to New Guinea and ne Queensland
_____ *A. m. inornata*	Biak I. and Numfor I. (n New Guinea)
_____ *A. m. nitida*	Bismarck Archipelago
_____ *A. m. purpureiceps*	Admiralty Islands
☐ **Yellow-eyed Starling** *Aplonis mystacea*	
	Lowland rainforests of s New Guinea
☐ **Singing Starling** *Aplonis cantoroides*	
	Aru Islands and New Guinea to Bismarck Arch. and Solomon Is.
☐ **Tanimbar Starling** *Aplonis crassa*	
	Tanimbar Islands (Larat and Yamdena)
☐ **Atoll Starling** *Aplonis feadensis*	
_____ *A. f. feadensis*	Ontong Java I. (Solomons); Nissan and Nuguria is. (New Guinea)
_____ *A. f. heureka*	Bismarck Archipelago (Ninigo and Hermit Islands)
☐ **Rennell Starling** *Aplonis insularis*	
	Solomon Islands (Rennell and Bellona)
☐ **Long-tailed Starling** *Aplonis magna*	
_____ *A. m. magna*	Biak I. (off n New Guinea)
_____ *A. m. brevicaudus*	Numfor I. (off nw New Guinea)
☐ **White-eyed Starling** *Aplonis brunneicapilla*	
	Solomon Is. (Bougainville, Guadalcanal, Choiseul and Rendova)
☐ **Brown-winged Starling** *Aplonis grandis*	
_____ *A. g. grandis*	Solomon Islands (Bougainville, Choiseul and Santa Isabel)
_____ *A. g. macrura*	Guadalcanal (Solomon Islands)
_____ *A. g. malaita*	Malaita (Solomon Islands)
☐ **San Cristobal Starling** *Aplonis dichroa*	
	Lowland forests of San Cristóbal (s Solomon Islands)
☐ **Rusty-winged Starling** *Aplonis zelandica*	
_____ *A. z. rufipennis*	Central and n Vanuatu and Banks Group
_____ *A. z. maxwelli*	Santa Cruz I. (Vanuatu)
_____ *A. z. zelandica*	Vanikoro I. (Vanuatu)
☐ **Striated Starling** *Aplonis striata*	
_____ *A. s. striata*	Forests of New Caledonia
_____ *A. s. atronitens*	Loyalty Islands

☐ **Mountain Starling** *Aplonis santovestris*

Espíritu Santo (Vanuatu)

☐ **Asian Glossy Starling** *Aplonis panayensis*

_____ *A. p. affinis*	Assam to Bangladesh and Myanmar (Arakan Yoma Mts.)
_____ *A. p. strigata*	S Thailand to Malaysia, Sumatra, Java and w Borneo
_____ *A. p. tytleri*	Andaman Islands and Car Nicobar I.
_____ *A. p. albiris*	Great and Central Nicobar islands
_____ *A. p. heterochlora*	Anambas and Natuna islands (off Borneo)
_____ *A. p. eustathis*	E Borneo
_____ *A. p. alipodis*	Panjang, Maratau and Derawan islands (off e Borneo)
_____ *A. p. panayensis*	N Sulawesi and Philippine Islands
_____ *A. p. sanghirensis*	Talaud, Sangihe, Siau, Tahjlandang, Ruang, and Biaro islands
_____ *A. p. enganensis*	Enggano I. (off s Sumatra)
_____ *A. p. altirostris*	Simuelue, Banyan and Nias islands (off w Sumatra)
_____ *A. p. leptorrhyncha*	Batu I. (off w Sumatra)
_____ *A. p. pachistorhina*	Mentawi Islands (off w Sumatra)
_____ *A. p. gusti*	Bali

☐ **Moluccan Starling** *Aplonis mysolensis*

_____ *A. m. sulaensis*	E Sulawesi, Banggai Islands and Sula Islands
_____ *A. m. mysolensis*	Moluccas and w Papuan islands

☐ **Short-tailed Starling** *Aplonis minor*

Sulawesi, Java, Bali, Lesser Sundas and s Philippines (Mindanao)

☐ **Micronesian Starling** *Aplonis opaca*

_____ *A. o. opaca*	Kosrai (Caroline Islands)
_____ *A. o. angus*	Truk, Ulithi, Fais, Wolea, Ifalik and adjacent Caroline Islands
_____ *A. o. kurodae*	Yap (Caroline Islands)
_____ *A. o. ponapensis*	Pohnpei (Caroline Islands)
_____ *A. o. aeneus*	Mariana Islands (Alamagan, Pagan, Agrihan and Asuncion)
_____ *A. o. guami*	Mariana Islands (Guam, Rota, Tinian and Saipan)
_____ *A. o. orii*	Palau Islands

☐ **Pohnpei Starling** *Aplonis pelzelni*

Rediscovered 1995 in mountains of Pohnpei after 50-year absence

☐ **Polynesian Starling** *Aplonis tabuensis*

_____ *A. t. tabuensis*	S Tonga and Lau Archipelago
_____ *A. t. tenebrosus*	Keppel and Boscawen islands (central Polynesia)
_____ *A. t. nesiotes*	Niuafou I. (central Polynesia)
_____ *A. t. brunnescens*	Niue I. (Cook Isands)
_____ *A. t. vitiensis*	Fiji Islands
_____ *A. t. fortunae*	Futuna, Alofa, Uea and Horne islands (central Polynesia)
_____ *A. t. rotumae*	Rotuma (Fiji)
_____ *A. t. tucopiae*	Tukopia (Solomon Islands east of Santa Cruz Group)
_____ *A. t. pachyramphus*	Reef, Swallow and Tinakula islands (Santa Cruz Group)
_____ *A. t. brevirostris*	Western Samoa
_____ *A. t. tutuilae*	Tutuila (American Samoa)
_____ *A. t. manuae*	Manua Islands (American Samoa)

☐ **Samoan Starling** *Aplonis atrifusca*

Western and American Samoa

☐ **Rarotonga Starling** *Aplonis cinerascens*

Rarotonga (sw Cook Islands). On verge of extinction

☐ **Yellow-faced Myna** *Mino dumontii*

New Guinea, Aru, w Papuan, Solomon Is. and Bismarck Arch.

☐ **Golden Myna** *Mino anais*

_____ *M. a. anais*	Lowlands of nw New Guinea and Salawati I.
_____ *M. a. orientalis*	N New Guinea (east to Huon Peninsula) and Yapen I.
_____ *M. a. robertsoni*	S New Guinea (east to Milne Bay)

☐ **Long-tailed Myna** *Mino kreffti*

Bismarck Archipelago, n and central Solomon Islands

☐ **Sulawesi Myna** *Basilornis celebensis*

Sulawesi, Lembeh, Muna and Butung islands

☐ **Helmeted Myna** *Basilornis galeatus*

Banggai Is. (Peleng and Banggai); Sula Is. (Taliabu and Mangole)

☐ **Long-crested Myna** *Basilornis corythaix*

Forests of Seram (s Moluccas)

☐ **Apo Myna** *Basilornis miranda*

Montane forests of Mindanao (s Philippines)

☐ **Coleto** *Sarcops calvus*
- _____ *S. c. calvus* — N Philippine Islands
- _____ *S. c. melanonotus* — Mindanao, Cebu, Panay, Negros, Bohol, Samar and Ticao
- _____ *S. c. lowii* — Sulu Archipelago

☐ **White-necked Myna** *Streptocitta albicollis*
- _____ *S. a. torquata* — N Sulawesi, Lembeh I. and Togian Islands
- _____ *S. a. albicollis* — S Sulawesi, Muna and Butung islands

☐ **Bare-eyed Myna** *Streptocitta albertinae*

Sula Islands (Taliabu and Mangole)

☐ **Fiery-browed Myna** *Enodes erythrophris*

Mountains of Sulawesi

☐ **Finch-billed Myna** *Scissirostrum dubium*

Sulawesi, Bangka, Lembeh, Butung, Togian, and Banggai islands

☐ **Spot-winged Starling** *Saroglossa spiloptera*

Foothills of n India and Nepal; winters to Myanmar and Thailand

☐ **Madagascar Starling** *Saroglossa aurata*

Forests of Madagascar

☐ **Golden-crested Myna** *Ampeliceps coronatus*

NE India to Myanmar, n Malaya, Thailand and Indochina

☐ **Common Hill Myna** *Gracula religiosa*
- _____ *G. r. religiosa* — Malaysia, Sumatra, Java, Bali, Borneo and Bangka I.
- _____ *G. r. batuensis* — Batu and Mentawi islands (off nw Sumatra)
- _____ *G. r. palawanensis* — Palawan (sw Philippines)
- _____ *G. r. venerata* — W Lesser Sundas (Sumbawa, Flores, Pantar, Lomblen and Alor)
- _____ *G. r. intermedia* — N India to Myanmar, Thailand, Indochina and s China
- _____ *G. r. peninsularis* — NE peninsular India
- _____ *G. r. andamanensis* — Andaman and Nicobar islands

☐ **Southern Hill Myna** *Gracula indica*

SW India (Western Ghats) and s Sri Lanka

☐ **Enggano Myna** *Gracula enganensis*

Enggano I. (off s Sumatra)

☐ **Nias Myna** *Gracula robusta*

Nias, Pulan, Babi, Tuangku and Bangkaru islands (off Sumatra)

☐ **Ceylon Myna** *Gracula ptilogenys*

Humid forests of Sri Lanka

☐ **White-vented Myna** *Acridotheres grandis*

NE India to sw China, Myanmar, Thailand and Indochina

☐ **Crested Myna** *Acridotheres cristatellus*
- _____ *A. c. cristatellus* — E Myanmar to n Indochina, se and central China
- _____ *A. c. brevipennis* — Hainan (s China)
- _____ *A. c. formosanus* — Taiwan

☐ **Javan Myna** *Acridotheres javanicus*

Java and Bali

☐ **Pale-bellied Myna** *Acridotheres cinereus*

S peninsular Sulawesi (north to Rantepao)

☐ **Jungle Myna** *Acridotheres fuscus*
_____ *A. f. fuscus* — Himalayas (Pakistan to Assam, Rajasthan and n Orissa)
_____ *A. f. mahrattensis* — W peninsular India
_____ *A. f. fumidus* — NE Assam
_____ *A. f. torquatus* — Myanmar to n and central Malaysia

☐ **Collared Myna** *Acridotheres albocinctus* — NE India (Manipur) to n Myanmar and sw China (nw Yunnan)

☐ **Bank Myna** *Acridotheres ginginianus* — Foothills of e Pakistan to n Nepal and n-central India

☐ **Common Myna** *Acridotheres tristis*
_____ *A. t. tristis* — SE Iran to India and SE Asia; introduced widely worldwide
_____ *A. t. melanosternus* — Sri Lanka

☐ **Vinous-breasted Starling** *Acridotheres burmannicus*
_____ *A. m .burmannicus* — Myanmar to central Thailand and extreme sw China (Yunnan)
_____ *A. m. leucocephalus* — S Thailand to Cambodia and s Indochina

☐ **Black-winged Starling** *Acridotheres melanopterus* — Lowlands of Java, Bali and Lombok

☐ **Bali Myna** *Leucopsar rothschildi* — Coastal nw Bali (Bali Barat National Park). ±55 birds in 1993

☐ **Black-collared Starling** *Gracupica nigricollis* — Open country and scrub of s China and SE Asia

☐ **Asian Pied Starling** *Gracupica contra*
_____ *G. c. contra* — N and central India
_____ *G. c. sordidus* — N Assam
_____ *G. c. superciliaris* — Manipur and Myanmar south to Tenasserim
_____ *G. c. floweri* — S Myanmar to Thailand and Laos
_____ *G. c. jalla* — Sumatra, Java and Bali

☐ **Daurian Starling** *Sturnia sturnina* — SE Siberia to n Mongolia and n Korea; winters to SE Asia

☐ **Chestnut-cheeked Starling** *Sturnia philippensis* — S Sakhalin, Kuril Is. and n Japan; winters to Philippines, e Indies

☐ **White-shouldered Starling** *Sturnia sinensis* — S China to Indochina; winters to SE Asia and n Philippines

☐ **Chestnut-tailed Starling** *Sturnia malabarica* — Peninsular India to Myanmar, sw China and n SE Asia

☐ **White-headed Starling** *Sturnia erythropygia*
_____ *S. e. erythropygia* — Andaman Islands
_____ *S. e. andamanensis* — Car Nicobar I.
_____ *S. e. katchalensis* — Katchall I. (Nicobar Islands)

☐ **White-faced Starling** *Sturnia albofrontata* — Forests of wet zone of sw Sri Lanka

☐ **Brahminy Starling** *Temenuchus pagodarum* — E Afghanistan to Bangladesh, s Nepal, India and Sri Lanka

☐ **Rosy Starling** *Pastor roseus* — S-central Europe; winters primarily India and se Arabian Pen.

☐ **Red-billed Starling** *Sturnus sericeus* — Lowlands of s-central China; winters to SE Asia and Philippines

☐ **White-cheeked Starling** *Sturnus cineraceus* — NE Asia; winters in s China and Philippines

☐ **European Starling** *Sturnus vulgaris*
_____ *S. v. granti* — Azores
_____ *S. v. vulgaris* — Canary Is. and Iceland to Ural Mts., n Ukraine and se Europe
_____ *S. v. faroensis* — Faeroes
_____ *S. v. zetlandicus* — Shetland Islands
_____ *S. v. tauricus* — E and s Ukraine, Crimea and Asia Minor

_____	*S. v. purpurascens*	W Transcaucasia to Georgia and Armenia
_____	*S. v. caucasicus*	Volga Delta and n Caucasus to Caspian Sea and s Iran
_____	*S. v. nobilior*	Afghanistan, Transcaspia and Khorasan
_____	*S. v. poltaratskyi*	E Ural Mountains to Lake Baikal, Kazakstan and w Mongolia
_____	*S. v. porphyronotus*	S Dzungaria and Tien Shan Mts. to Pamir Mts. and Samarkand
_____	*S. v. humii*	W Himalayas (Kashmir to Garhwal)
_____	*S. v. minor*	Locally in w Pakistan (Sind)

☐ **Spotless Starling** *Sturnus unicolor*

Iberian Peninsula to Corsica, Sardinia, Sicily and nw Africa

☐ **Wattled Starling** *Creatophora cinerea*

Savanna of e and s Africa and Arabian Peninsula

☐ **Cape Glossy-Starling** *Lamprotornis nitens*

_____	*L. n. nitens*	Acacia of w Gabon and Angola
_____	*L. n. phoenicopterus*	Botswana to Zimbabwe, s Mozambique and n South Africa
_____	*L. n. culminator*	South Africa (except for s Cape Province)

☐ **Greater Blue-eared Glossy-Starling** *Lamprotornis chalybaeus*

_____	*L. c. chalybaeus*	Senegambia to Somalia and Kenya
_____	*L. c. cyaniventris*	Ethiopia to w Kenya, Uganda and e Zaire
_____	*L. c. scyobius*	Tanzania to Zambia, Malawi and Mozambique
_____	*L. c. nordmanni*	S Angola to Zambia, Botswana and Transvaal

☐ **Lesser Blue-eared Glossy-Starling** *Lamprotornis chloropterus*

_____	*L. c. chloropterus*	Senegambia to s Sudan, Ethiopia, n Uganda and w Kenya
_____	*L. c. elisabeth*	S Sudan to Uganda, s Kenya, Tanzania, Zambia and Mozambique

☐ **Bronze-tailed Glossy-Starling** *Lamprotornis chalcurus*

Savanna of Senegambia to Cameroon, s Sudan and nw Kenya

☐ **Splendid Glossy-Starling** *Lamprotornis splendidus*

_____	*L. s. chrysonotis*	Senegambia to Ghana
_____	*L. s. splendidus*	Nigeria to Angola, s Sudan, sw Ethiopia and w Tanzania
_____	*L. s. lessoni*	Bioko (Gulf of Guinea)
_____	*L. s. bailundensis*	S Angola to s Zaire, Zambia and s Tanzania

☐ **Principe Glossy-Starling** *Lamprotornis ornatus*

Príncipe (Gulf of Guinea)

☐ **Emerald Starling** *Lamprotornis iris*

Wooded savanna of Guinea, Sierra Leone and Ivory Coast

☐ **Purple Glossy-Starling** *Lamprotornis purpureus*

Senegambia to s Sudan, ne Zaire, Uganda and w Kenya

☐ **Rueppell's Glossy-Starling** *Lamprotornis purpuropterus*

_____	*L. p. aenocephalus*	Eritrea and n Ethiopia
_____	*L. p. purpuropterus*	S Ethiopia to Somalia, s Sudan, Uganda, w Kenya and Tanzania

☐ **Long-tailed Glossy-Starling** *Lamprotornis caudatus*

Savanna of Senegambia to s Sudan (Nile River region)

☐ **Golden-breasted Starling** *Lamprotornis regius*

Arid savanna of s Ethiopia to Somalia, e Kenya and ne Tanzania

☐ **Meves' Glossy-Starling** *Lamprotornis mevesii*

_____	*L. m. mevesii*	Angola and n Namibia to Botswana, s Malawi and ne S Africa
_____	*L. m. benguelensis*	*Mopane* woodlands of sw Angola

☐ **Burchell's Glossy-Starling** *Lamprotornis australis*

S Angola to w Zambia, Namibia, Mozambique and n South Africa

☐ **Sharp-tailed Glossy-Starling** *Lamprotornis acuticaudus*

S Angola to n Namibia, s Zaire, nw Zambia and sw Tanzania

☐ **Black-bellied Glossy-Starling** *Lamprotornis corruscus*

_____	*L. c. corruscus*	Coastal bush of s Somalia to e Swaziland and Cape Province
_____	*L. c. vaughani*	Pemba I. (off Tanzania)

☐ **Superb Starling** *Lamprotornis superbus*

S Sudan and Ethiopia to Somalia, Uganda, Kenya and Tanzania

☐ **Hildebrandt's Starling** *Lamprotornis hildebrandti*

Acacia savanna of s Kenya and n Tanzania

☐ **Shelley's Starling** *Lamprotornis shelleyi*

Acacia of Somalia and s Ethiopia to se Sudan and se Kenya

☐ **Chestnut-bellied Starling** *Lamprotornis pulcher*

Savanna of sub-Saharan Africa (Senegal to n Ethiopia)

☐ **Purple-headed Glossy-Starling** *Lamprotornis purpureiceps*

Guinea to Cameroon, Gabon, n Zaire, Uganda and nw Kenya

☐ **Copper-tailed Glossy-Starling** *Lamprotornis cupreocauda*

Guinea to Sierra Leone, Liberia, Ivory Coast and Ghana

☐ **Violet-backed Starling** *Cinnyricinclus leucogaster*

Woodlands of Africa south of the Sahara and sw Arabia

☐ **African Pied Starling** *Spreo bicolor*

Extreme se Namibia to s Mozambique and South Africa

☐ **Fischer's Starling** *Spreo fischeri*

S Ethiopia and Somalia to e Kenya and ne Tanzania

☐ **Ashy Starling** *Spreo unicolor*

Acacia woodlands of interior Tanzania

☐ **White-crowned Starling** *Spreo albicapillus*
____ *S. a. albicapillus*
____ *S. a. horrensis*

Ethiopia and Somalia to Djibouti and extreme ne Kenya
N edge of Dida Galgulu Desert north to Ethiopian border

☐ **Red-winged Starling** *Onychognathus morio*
____ *O. m. morio*
____ *O. m. rueppellii*

Savanna of Africa south of the Sahara
Eritrea to Ethiopia and extreme n Kenya

☐ **Slender-billed Starling** *Onychognathus tenuirostris*

Mountains of Kenya to Uganda, e Zaire, Tanzania and Malawi

☐ **Chestnut-winged Starling** *Onychognathus fulgidus*

Guinea to Uganda and n Angola; Bioko and São Tomé

☐ **Waller's Starling** *Onychognathus walleri*
____ *O. w. preussi*
____ *O. w. elgonensis*
____ *O. w. walleri*

Highlands of se Nigeria and Cameroon; Bioko
Kenya (west of Rift Valley) to Uganda, se Sudan and e Zaire
E Kenya to Tanzania and Malawi

☐ **Somali Starling** *Onychognathus blythii*

Eritrea and Ethiopia to n Somalia, Abd el Kuri I. and Socotra

☐ **Socotra Starling** *Onychognathus frater*

Rocky hills of Socotra (off ne Somalia)

☐ **Tristram's Starling** *Onychognathus tristramii*

Dead Sea Valley and w Arabia to Yemen and s Oman

☐ **Pale-winged Starling** *Onychognathus nabouroup*

Deserts of sw Angola to Namibia and arid interior South Africa

☐ **Bristle-crowned Starling** *Onychognathus salvadorii*

Extreme se Sudan to ne Uganda, s Ethiopia, Somalia and n Kenya

☐ **White-billed Starling** *Onychognathus albirostris*

Mountains of Eritrea and Ethiopia

☐ **Neumann's Starling** *Onychognathus neumanni*
____ *O. n. neumanni*
____ *O. n. modicus*

N Nigeria to Cameroon, Central African Republic and w Sudan
Senegal to Mali and w Niger

☐ **Narrow-tailed Starling** *Poeoptera lugubris*

Sierra Leone to n Angola, Zaire, w Uganda and Bioko

☐ **Stuhlmann's Starling** *Poeoptera stuhlmanni*

Mts. of s Ethiopia to s Sudan, Uganda, Tanzania and e Zaire

☐ **Kenrick's Starling** *Poeoptera kenricki*

Montane forests of central Kenya and ne Tanzania

☐ **Sharpe's Starling** *Pholia sharpii*

S Sudan to Ethiopia, n Tanzania, w Uganda, Rwanda and e Zaire

☐ **Abbott's Starling** *Pholia femoralis*

Mt. Kenya south to Mt. Meru and Mt. Kilimanjaro

☐ **White-collared Starling** *Grafisia torquata*

Cameroon to Gabon, Central African Republic and n Zaire

☐ **Magpie Starling** *Speculipastor bicolor*

Sudan to s Ethiopia, Somalia, ne Uganda, Kenya and Tanzania

☐ **Babbling Starling** *Neocichla gutturalis*
_____ *N. g. gutturalis* — *Brachystegia* of interior sw Angola and w Zambia
_____ *N. g. angusta* — E Zambia to Tanzania and n Malawi

☐ **Red-billed Oxpecker** *Buphagus erythrorhynchus*

Savanna of e and s Africa

☐ **Yellow-billed Oxpecker** *Buphagus africanus*
_____ *B. a. africanus* — Savanna of Africa south of the Sahara
_____ *B. a. langi* — S Congo basin

FAMILY: PASSERIDAE (Old World Sparrows—35)

☐ **Saxaul Sparrow** *Passer ammodendri*
_____ *P. a. ammodendri* — Aral Sea to Kazakstan, Uzbekistan and Iran border
_____ *P. a. nigricans* — NW China (n Xinjiang to Manas River valley)
_____ *P. a. stoliczkae* — W China (w Xinjiang to n Gansu) and s Mongolia

☐ **House Sparrow** *Passer domesticus*
_____ *P. d. domesticus* — Europe to Mongolia, Amurland and n Manchuria
_____ *P. d. balearoibericus* — Mediterranean Spain, Balearic Is., France, Balkans to Asia Minor
_____ *P. d. tingitanus* — NW Africa (Morocco to Tunisia, Algeria and ne Libya)
_____ *P. d. rufidorsalis* — Nile Valley of the Sudan
_____ *P. d. niloticus* — NE Africa (Suez Canal region to n Sudan)
_____ *P. d. biblicus* — Cyprus and Levant to Turkey, n Saudi Arabia, Iraq and w Iran
_____ *P. d. indicus* — S Israel to n Saudi Arabia, s Iran, India, Sri Lanka and Myanmar
_____ *P. d. hufufae* — NE Arabia (south to n Oman)
_____ *P. d. bactrianus* — Transcaspia to Kazakstan, Afghanistan and nw Pakistan
_____ *P. d. hyrcanus* — N Iran (south to Elburz Mountains) and adjacent Turkmenistan
_____ *P. d. persicus* — Central Iran to sw Afghanistan and extreme w Pakistan
_____ *P. d. parkini* — Himalayas (Pakistan to sw Tibet, Nepal and Sikkim)

☐ **Spanish Sparrow** *Passer hispaniolensis*
_____ *P. h. hispaniolensis (maltae, italiae)* — Cape Verde Is., Canary Is.., Madeira, s Europe and North Africa
_____ *P. h. transcaspicus* — Iran and Transcaspia to e Kazakstan and Afghanistan

☐ **Sind Sparrow** *Passer pyrrhonotus*

Extreme se Iran to Pakistan and nw India

☐ **Somali Sparrow** *Passer castanopterus*
_____ *P. c. castanopterus* — E Ethiopia and Somalia
_____ *P. c. fulgens* — Extreme sw Ethiopia to n-central Kenya

☐ **Russet Sparrow** *Passer rutilans*
_____ *P. r. rutilans* — Sakhalin to Japan, South Korea, e Manchuria, s China and Taiwan
_____ *P. r. intensior* — SW China to n Myanmar, Laos and nw Tonkin
_____ *P. r. cinnamomeus* — Himalayas of ne Afghanistan to ne India and se Tibet

☐ **Plain-backed Sparrow** *Passer flaveolus*

N Myanmar to Thailand, Malay Peninsula and s Vietnam

☐ Dead Sea Sparrow *Passer moabiticus*

____ *P. m. moabiticus* — Israel and Jordan

____ *P. m. mespotamicus* — Cyprus and s Turkey to n Syria, Iraq and sw Iran

____ *P. m. yatii* — E Iran and adjacent sw Afghanistan

☐ Cape Verde Sparrow *Passer iagoensis* — Locally in Cape Verde Islands (except Fogo I.)

☐ Socotra Sparrow *Passer insularis* — Socotra and Abd-al-Küri I. (off Somalia)

☐ Rufous Sparrow *Passer motitensis*

____ *P. m. cordofanicus* — E Chad to w-central Sudan

____ *P. m. shelleyi* — SE Sudan to ne Uganda, e Ethiopia and nw Somalia

____ *P. m. rufocinctus* — Kenya (Rift Valley highlands) to n Tanzania

____ *P. m. benguellensis* — S Angola to Namibia

____ *P. m. motitensis* — Botswana to Transvaal and n Cape Province

____ *P. m. subsolanus* — S Zimbabwe to n Orange Free State and nw Swaziland

☐ Mossie *Passer melanurus*

____ *P. m. damarensis* — SW Angola to Namibia, Zimbabwe and n Cape Province

____ *P. m. melanurus (vicinus)* — S Transvaal to Natal, w Swaziland and Cape Province

☐ Gray-headed Sparrow *Passer griseus*

____ *P. g. griseus* — Senegal to s Chad, n Cameroon, n Gabon and s Sudan

____ *P. g. laeneni* — Mali to extreme n Cameroon and w-central Sudan

____ *P. g. ugandae* — Angola to s Sudan, n Ethiopia, Kenya and ne Tanzania

☐ Swainson's Sparrow *Passer swainsonii* — Extreme ne Sudan to Ethiopia, n Somalia and n-central Kenya

☐ Parrot-billed Sparrow *Passer gongonensis* — Extreme se Sudan to s Ethiopia, s Somalia, Kenya and ne Tanzania

☐ Swaheli Sparrow *Passer suahelicus* — S Kenya to w Tanzania, Malawi and nw Mozambique

☐ Cape Sparrow *Passer diffusus*

____ *P. d. diffusus* — Angola to n Namibia, Mozambique and Cape Province

____ *P. d. luangwae* — E Zambia (upper Luangwa Valley)

____ *P. d. mozambicus* — E Tanzania to n Mozambique, Pemba I. and Zanzibar

☐ Desert Sparrow *Passer simplex*

____ *P. s. saharae* — Sahara of se Morocco to Algeria, s Tunisia and central Libya

____ *P. s. simplex* — S Sahara from Mali to n Niger (Aïr Massif), n Chad and c Sudan

____ *P. s. zarudnyi* — Deserts of s-central Asia (Uzbekistan and Turkmenistan)

☐ Eurasian Tree Sparrow *Passer montanus*

____ *P. m. montanus* — Europe to n Mongolia, Manchuria and Sea of Okhotsk

____ *P. m. transcaucasicus* — S Caucasus (Black Sea coast of Georgia to n Iran)

____ *P. m. dilutus* — Transcaspia to w Pakistan, Gobi Desert and w China (Xinjiang)

____ *P. m. dybowskii* — E Asia (lower Amur River to Manchuria and n Korea)

____ *P. m. kansuensis* — W China (Zaidam basin and n Gansu)

____ *P. m. iubilaeus* — E China (Liaoning to lower Yangtze River and Shaanxi)

____ *P. m. obscuratus* — Nepal to ne India, Myanmar and w-c China (Sichuan to Hubei)

____ *P. m. saturatus* — S Kuril Is., Japan, South Korea, Ryukyu Is., Taiwan and se China

____ *P. m. malaccensis* — Central Myanmar, Malaya, Hainan, Vietnam and w Indonesia

☐ Sudan Golden Sparrow *Passer luteus* — Mauritania to Senegal, Burkina Faso, Sudan and n Ethiopia

☐ Arabian Golden Sparrow *Passer euchlorus* — SW Saudi Arabia to South Yemen, adj. Ethiopia and n Somalia

☐ Chestnut Sparrow *Passer eminibey* — S Sudan and sw Ethiopia to Uganda, Somalia and n Tanzania

☐ **Yellow-spotted Petronia** *Petronia pyrgita*
_____ *P. p. pallida* — S Mauritania and Senegal to Mali, Niger, Chad and c Sudan
_____ *P. p. pyrgita* — SE Sudan to s Ethiopia, Somalia, ne Uganda and ne Tanzania

☐ **Chestnut-shouldered Petronia** *Petronia xanthocollis*
_____ *P. x. transfuga* — SE Turkey to Iraq, s Iran, s Pakistan and nw India
_____ *P. x. xanthocollis* — E Afghanistan to n Pakistan

☐ **Yellow-throated Petronia** *Petronia superciliaris*
— Angola to s Zaire, Mozambique and South Africa

☐ **Bush Petronia** *Petronia dentata*
_____ *P. d. dentata* — Senegambia to Ethiopia and s Arabian Peninsula
_____ *P. d. buchanani* — S Niger (Zinder Province) to Lake Chad

☐ **Rock Petronia** *Petronia petronia*
_____ *P. p. petronia (madeirensis)* — Canary Is., Madeira and Europe to Bulgaria and w Asia Minor
_____ *P. p. barbara* — N Africa (Morocco to Algeria, Tunisia and w Libya)
_____ *P. p. puteicola* — S Turkey to s Syria, n Israel and Jordan
_____ *P. p. exigua* — Central Turkey to n Caucasus, n Iraq and n Iran
_____ *P. p. kirhizica* — Lower Volga River Valley to Turgay depression and Aral Sea
_____ *P. p. intermedia* — Transcaspia to e Iran, n Afghanistan, Pamirs and w Kunlun Shan Mts.
_____ *P. p. brevirostris* — E Siberia to Mongolia, nw Manchuria and sw China (n Sichuan)

☐ **Pale Rockfinch** *Carpospiza brachydactyla*
— Arid Asia Minor; winters to sw Arabia and ne Africa

☐ **White-winged Snowfinch** *Montifringilla nivalis*
_____ *M. n. nivalis* — Pyrénées and Alps to Italy, s Yugoslavia and n Greece
_____ *M. n. leucura* — S and e Asia Minor
_____ *M. n. alpicola* — Caucasus to n Iran, Afghanistan (Hindu Kush) and w Pamirs
_____ *M. n. gaddi* — Zagros Mountains (sw Iran)
_____ *M. n. tianshanica* — Alayskiy and Chatkal'skiy mountains to w Tien Shan Mts.
_____ *M. n. groum-grzimaili* — E Tien Shan Mts. to w China (n Xinjiang) and w Mongolia
_____ *M. n. kwenlunensis* — W China (w Kunlun Shan Mts. to s Tibet and e Qinghai)

☐ **Black-winged Snowfinch** *Montifringilla adamsi*
_____ *M. a. adamsi* — Kashmir to Nepal, Sikkim, s Tibet and sw China
_____ *M. a. xerophila* — W China (nw Nan Shan Mts. to Astin Tagh Mts.)

☐ **White-rumped Snowfinch** *Montifringilla taczanowskii*
— Tibet to w China (Kokonor and Nan Shan Mts. to Sichuan)

☐ **Père David's Snowfinch** *Montifringilla davidiana*
_____ *M. d. davidiana* — Inner Mongolia to w China (Gansu and Qinghai)
_____ *M. d. potanini* — SE Altai Mountains to Outer Mongolia and ne China

☐ **Rufous-necked Snowfinch** *Montifringilla ruficollis*
_____ *M. r. ruficollis* — W Tibet to Sikkim, Kokonor and s Nan Shan Mountains
_____ *M. r. isabellina* — W China (s Xinjiang to nw Qinghai); winters to India

☐ **Blanford's Snowfinch** *Montifringilla blanfordi*
_____ *M. b. ventorum* — Mountains of w-central China (se Xinjiang to w Qinghai)
_____ *M. b. barbata* — Mountains of w China (ne Qinghai to Nan Shan Mts.)
_____ *M. b. blanfordi* — Mountains of Tibet to Sikkim and w China; winters to India

☐ **Afghan Snowfinch** *Montifringilla theresae*
— Hindu Kush Mountains (Afghanistan)

FAMILY: PLOCEIDAE (Weavers and Allies—114)

☐ **White-billed Buffalo-Weaver** *Bubalornis albirostris*
_____ *B. a. albirostris*   Senegambia to s Sudan, Ethiopia, n Uganda and nw Kenya
_____ *B. a. intermedius*   S Ethiopia to Somalia and w-central Kenya

☐ **Red-billed Buffalo-Weaver** *Bubalornis niger*
_____ *B. n. niger*   S Angola to Zambia, Mozambique and Transvaal
_____ *B. n. militaris*   S Zambia to Zimbabwe, s Mozambique, e Transvaal and n Natal

☐ **White-headed Buffalo-Weaver** *Dinemellia dinemelli*
_____ *D. d. dinemelli*   SE Sudan to s Ethiopia, Somalia, e Kenya and ne Tanzania
_____ *D. d. boehmi*   SE Zaire; Tanzania (Kenya border to Lake Malawi)

☐ **Speckle-fronted Weaver** *Sporopipes frontalis*
_____ *S. f. frontalis (pallidior)*   Senegambia to nw Ethiopia and Eritrea
_____ *S. f. emini*   S Sudan to ne Uganda, Kenya and n Tanzania

☐ **Scaly Weaver** *Sporopipes squamifrons*
_____ *S. s. squamifrons (fuligescens)*   SW Angola to Botswana, Zimbabwe, Transvaal and n Cape Prov.
_____ *S. s. pallidus*   Angola (Moçamedes region)

☐ **White-browed Sparrow-Weaver** *Plocepasser mahali*
_____ *P. m. melanorhynchus*   S Sudan to s Ethiopia, Uganda and w Kenya
_____ *P. m. propinquatus*   S Somalia
_____ *P. m. ansorgei*   S Angola to extreme n Namibia
_____ *P. m. stentor (terricolor)*   N Namibia to w Cape Province, s Botswana and Transvaal
_____ *P. m. pectoralis*   Zambia to n Botswana, Zimbabwe, s Tanzania and Mozambique
_____ *P. m. mahali*   South Africa (w Orange Free State to n Cape Province)

☐ **Chestnut-crowned Sparrow-Weaver** *Plocepasser superciliosus*
_____ *P. s. superciliosus*   Senegal to central Sudan
_____ *P. s. brunnescens*   Central African Republic to sw Sudan, n Uganda and nw Kenya

☐ **Chestnut-backed Sparrow-Weaver** *Plocepasser rufoscapulatus*
                                             S Angola to se Zaire, Zambia and w Malawi

☐ **Donaldson-Smith's Sparrow-Weaver** *Plocepasser donaldsoni*
                                             Savanna of sw Ethiopia, extreme s Somalia and n Kenya

☐ **Rufous-tailed Weaver** *Histurgops ruficauda*
                                             Acacia savanna of n Tanzania se of Lake Victoria

☐ **Gray-headed Social-Weaver** *Pseudonigrita arnaudi*
_____ *P. a. arnaudi*   SW Sudan to Kenya, Uganda and extreme n Tanzania
_____ *P. a. australoabyssinicus*   Extreme s Ethiopia
_____ *P. a. dorsalis*   Central Tanzania

☐ **Black-capped Social-Weaver** *Pseudonigrita cabanisi*
                                             Thornscrub of Ethiopia to sw Somalia, Kenya and ne Tanzania

☐ **Social Weaver** *Philetairus socius*
_____ *P. s. geminus*   N and central Namibia
_____ *P. s. xericus*   W Namibia
_____ *P. s. socius (eremus)*   S Namibia to n Cape Province (s Asbestos Mountains)
_____ *P. s. lepidus*   S Botswana to w Transvaal, Orange Free State and n Cape Prov.

☐ **Bannerman's Weaver** *Ploceus bannermani*
                                             Montane forests of se Nigeria and Cameroon

☐ **Bates' Weaver** *Ploceus batesi*
                                             Lowland forests of se Cameroon

☐ **Black-chinned Weaver** *Ploceus nigrimentum*
                                             SE Gabon (Lekoni) to central Angola and adj. Congo Republic

☐ **Baglafecht Weaver** *Ploceus baglafecht*

____	*P. b. neumanni*	Cameroon (Bamenda highlands)
____	*P. b. baglafecht*	Mountains of s Sudan, Eritrea, Ethiopia and n Kenya
____	*P. b. eremobius*	SE Sudan to ne Zaire
____	*P. b. emini*	S Sudan/n Uganda border; se Ethiopia (Harar-Arussi)
____	*P. b. reichenowi*	Extreme s Ethiopia to highlands of Kenya and n Tanzania
____	*P. b. stuhlmanni*	Extreme e Zaire to s Uganda, Rwanda, Burundi and w Tanzania
____	*P. b. sharpii*	Montane forests of sw Tanzania (Ufipa and Iringa)
____	*P. b. nyikae*	Nyika Plateau of Zambia and Malawi

☐ **Bertrand's Weaver** *Ploceus bertrandi*

Highlands of Tanzania, Zambia, Malawi and n Mozambique

☐ **Slender-billed Weaver** *Ploceus pelzelni*

____	*P. p. monachus*	Papyrus swamps of Ghana to Gabon and n Angola
____	*P. p. pelzelni (tuta)*	E Zaire to Uganda, Rwanda, Kenya and extreme nw Tanzania

☐ **Loango Weaver** *Ploceus subpersonatus*

Coastal s Gabon to mouth of Congo River

☐ **Little Weaver** *Ploceus luteolus*

____	*P. l. luteolus*	Savanna of Senegal to ne Zaire, s Sudan, Ethiopia and Eritrea
____	*P. l. kavirondensis*	Uganda to w Kenya and nw Tanzania

☐ **Lesser Masked-Weaver** *Ploceus intermedius*

____	*P. i. intermedius*	SE Sudan to s Ethiopia, Somalia, e Zaire, Kenya and Tanzania
____	*P. i. beattyi*	Arid coastal w Angola (Luanda to Benguela)
____	*P. i. lübberti*	Extreme s Angola to n Namibia
____	*P. i. cabanisii*	SE Zaire to Zambia, Zimbabwe, Botswana and Transvaal

☐ **Spectacled Weaver** *Ploceus ocularis*

____	*P. o. crocatus*	Cameroon to s Sudan and s Ethiopia; winters to Angola
____	*P. o. suahelicus*	E Kenya to e Tanzania, e Zambia, Malawi and Mozambique
____	*P. o. tenuirostris*	N Namibia to n Botswana
____	*P. o. brevior*	South Africa (e Transvaal to n Transkei)
____	*P. o. ocularis*	South Africa (se Transvaal to Natal and Cape Province)

☐ **Black-necked Weaver** *Ploceus nigricollis*

____	*P. n. brachypterus*	Senegal to w Cameroon
____	*P. n. nigricollis*	E Cameroon to n Angola, s Sudan, s Zaire, w Kenya, nw Tanzania
____	*P. n. po*	Bioko (Gulf of Guinea)
____	*P. n. melanoxanthus*	S Ethiopia to Somalia, e Kenya and ne Tanzania

☐ **Black-billed Weaver** *Ploceus melanogaster*

____	*P. m. melanogaster*	Mountains of extreme se Nigeria and w Cameroon; Bioko
____	*P. m. stephanopkhorus*	S Sudan to Uganda, Rwanda, Burundi, w Kenya and w Tanzania

☐ **Strange Weaver** *Ploceus alienus*

Montane forests of e Zaire, w Uganda, Rwanda and Burundi

☐ **Bocage's Weaver** *Ploceus temporalis*

Riparian grasslands of Angola to se Zaire and nw Zambia

☐ **Cape Weaver** *Ploceus capensis*

____	*P. c. olivaceus (rubricomus)*	South Africa (Transvaal to Natal and e Cape Province)
____	*P. c. capensis*	South Africa (w Cape Province)

☐ **African Golden-Weaver** *Ploceus subaureus*

____	*P. s. aureoflavus*	Somalia to e Kenya, e Tanzania, Malawi and n Mozambique
____	*P. s. subaureus (tongensis)*	S Mozambique to Natal, Zululand and e Cape Province

☐ **Holub's Golden-Weaver** *Ploceus xanthops*

Gabon to Angola, Uganda, Kenya, Botswana and Mozambique

☐ **Principe Golden-Weaver** *Ploceus princeps*

Woodlands of Príncipe (Gulf of Guinea)

☐ **Orange Weaver** *Ploceus aurantius*
_____ *P. a. aurantius*
_____ *P. a. rex*

Sierra Leone to Cameroon, Gabon, ne Angola and Zaire
S Uganda (Lake Victoria region) to w Kenya and nw Tanzania

☐ **Golden Palm Weaver** *Ploceus bojeri*

Savanna of Ethiopia to s Somalia, e Kenya and ne Tanzania

☐ **Taveta Golden-Weaver** *Ploceus castaneiceps*

Riverine scrub of extreme se Kenya and ne Tanzania

☐ **Southern Brown-throated Weaver** *Ploceus xanthopterus*
_____ *P. x. castaneigula*
_____ *P. x. xanthopterus*
_____ *P. x. marleyi*

Extreme ne Namibia to sw Zambia, Caprivi Strip and n Botswana
Malawi and Mozambique
Extreme s coastal Mozambique to Natal and Zululand

☐ **Northern Brown-throated Weaver** *Ploceus castanops*

E Zaire to Uganda, Rwanda, w Kenya and nw Tanzania

☐ **Kilombero Weaver** *Ploceus burnieri*

Central Tanzania (floodplain of Kilombero River in Ifakara area)

☐ **Rueppell's Weaver** *Ploceus galbula*

E Sudan to Eritrea, n Ethiopia, Somalia and sw Arabia

☐ **Heuglin's Masked-Weaver** *Ploceus heuglini*

Savanna of Senegambia to sw Sudan, s Uganda and nw Kenya

☐ **Northern Masked-Weaver** *Ploceus taeniopterus*
_____ *P. t. furensis*
_____ *P. t. taeniopterus*

Papyrus swamps of w Sudan (Darfur)
Extreme se Sudan to ne Zaire, n Uganda and s Ethiopia

☐ **African Masked-Weaver** *Ploceus velatus*
_____ *P. v. vitellinus*
_____ *P. v. peixotoi*
_____ *P. v. uluensis*
_____ *P. v. katangae*
_____ *P. v. upembae*
_____ *P. v. velatus (caurinus, shelleyi, finschi)*
_____ *P. v. nigrifrons (tahatali)*

SW Mauritania and Senegal to Chad and w Sudan
São Tomé (Gulf of Guinea)
SE Sudan to e Ethiopia, Somalia, Uganda, Kenya, Tanzania
Extreme se Zaire and adjacent nw Zambia
SE Zaire (Lake Upemba region)
S Angola to n Namibia, Malawi, Mozambique and n Cape Prov.
E Transvaal to Natal and e Cape Province

☐ **Lufira Masked-Weaver** *Ploceus reichardi*
_____ *P. r. reichardi*
_____ *P. r. ruweti*

Swamps of sw Tanzania (Karema to Rukwa) and se Zaire
SE Zaire (known from one specimen from Lufira River)

☐ **Village Weaver** *Ploceus cucullatus*
_____ *P. c. cucullatus*
_____ *P. c. collaris*
_____ *P. c. bohndorffi*
_____ *P. c. frobenii*
_____ *P. c. graueri*
_____ *P. c. abyssinicus*
_____ *P. c. nigriceps (paroptus)*
_____ *P. c. spilonotus (dilutescens)*

Senegal to Cameroon and Chad; Bioko
Gabon to Zaire and n Angola
N Zaire to Uganda, s Sudan and extreme nw Tanzania
S Zaire
E Zaire to Rwanda, Burundi and adjacent w Tanzania
Ethiopia
S Somalia to Kenya, Tanzania, Malawi and n Mozambique
SE Botswana to s Mozambique, Transvaal and e Cape Province

☐ **Giant Weaver** *Ploceus grandis*

São Tomé (Gulf of Guinea)

☐ **Speke's Weaver** *Ploceus spekei*

S Ethiopia to Somalia, Kenya and n Tanzania

☐ **Fox's Weaver** *Ploceus spekeoides*

Swamps of e-central Uganda

☐ **Vieillot's Weaver** *Ploceus nigerrimus*
_____ *P. n. castaneofuscus*
_____ *P. n. nigerrimus*

Sierra Leone to e Nigeria
E Nigeria to Cameroon, s Sudan, Kenya and w Tanzania

☐ **Weyns' Weaver** *Ploceus weynsi*

Lowland forests of n Zaire, Uganda and extreme nw Tanzania

☐ **Clarke's Weaver** *Ploceus golandi*

Coastal e Kenya (Sokoke Forest)

☐ **Black-headed Weaver** *Ploceus melanocephalus*

_____ *P. m. melanocephalus*	Senegal to s Mauritania, Benin, Niger and Lake Chad
_____ *P. m. capitalis*	Niger to s Chad and Central African Republic
_____ *P. m. duboisi*	N and e Zaire to extreme n Zambia
_____ *P. m. dimidiatus (fischeri)*	E Sudan to nw Ethiopia, Uganda, Kenya and nw Tanzania

☐ **Salvadori's Weaver** *Ploceus dichrocephalus*

Riparian vegetation of se Ethiopia, s Somalia and ne Kenya

☐ **Golden-backed Weaver** *Ploceus jacksoni*

Extreme se Sudan to Uganda, Burundi, Kenya and n Tanzania

☐ **Cinnamon Weaver** *Ploceus badius*

_____ *P. b. badius*	Dry savanna of e Sudan (upper Nile River drainage)
_____ *P. b. axillaris*	S Sudan

☐ **Chestnut Weaver** *Ploceus rubiginosus*

_____ *P. r. trothae*	Acacia savanna of sw Angola and n Namibia
_____ *P. r. rubiginosus*	Extreme se Sudan to Ethiopia, Somalia, Kenya and n Tanzania

☐ **Golden-naped Weaver** *Ploceus aureonucha*

NE Zaire (Ituri Forest north of Beni)

☐ **Yellow-mantled Weaver** *Ploceus tricolor*

_____ *P. t. tricolor*	Sierra Leone to se Guinea, Cameroon, Gabon and n Angola
_____ *P. t. interscapularis*	N Zaire to w Uganda and extreme sw Sudan

☐ **Maxwell's Black Weaver** *Ploceus albinucha*

_____ *P. a. albinucha*	Sierra Leone to Liberia, Ivory Coast and Ghana
_____ *P. a. maxwelli*	Bioko (Gulf of Guinea)
_____ *P. a. holomelas*	S Nigeria to Gabon, Cent. African Rep., n Zaire and w Uganda

☐ **Nelicourvi Weaver** *Ploceus nelicourvi*

Evergreen mossy forests of n, w and s Madagascar

☐ **Sakalava Weaver** *Ploceus sakalava*

_____ *P. s. sakalava*	Dry lowland forests of n and ne Madagascar
_____ *P. s. minor*	Subdeserts of w and sw Madagascar

☐ **Streaked Weaver** *Ploceus manyar*

_____ *P. m. flaviceps*	Lowlands of e Pakistan to w India and Sri Lanka
_____ *P. m. peguensis*	NE India (Assam) to Bangladesh and n Myanmar
_____ *P. m. williamsoni*	SW China (Yunnan) to Thailand and Vietnam
_____ *P. m. manyar*	Java, Bali and Bawean I.

☐ **Baya Weaver** *Ploceus philippinus*

_____ *P. p. philippinus*	Lowlands of se Pakistan to w India and Sri Lanka
_____ *P. p. travencoreensis*	SW India (Goa to Travancore and Kerala)
_____ *P. p. Myanmarnicus*	NE India (Bengal) to Bangladesh, Assam and Myanmar
_____ *P. p. infortunatus*	Malay Peninsula to s Vietnam, Sumatra and Nias I.
_____ *P. p. angelorum*	Plains of central Thailand

☐ **Asian Golden Weaver** *Ploceus hypoxanthus*

_____ *P. h. hymenaicus*	S Myanmar to central Thailand, Cambodia and s Vietnam
_____ *P. h. hypoxanthus*	Sumatra and Java

☐ **Yellow Weaver** *Ploceus megarhynchus*

_____ *P. m. megarhynchus*	Foothills of s Himalayas
_____ *P. m. salimalii*	Foothills of ne India

☐ **Bengal Weaver** *Ploceus benghalensis*

Lowlands of Pakistan to peninsular India, Nepal and Bangladesh

☐ **Forest Weaver** *Ploceus bicolor*

____	*P. b. tephronotus (analogus)*	Extreme se Nigeria and Cameroon; Bioko
____	*P. b. amaurocephalus*	N Angola
____	*P. b. mentalis*	S Sudan (Imatong Hills) to ne Zaire, Uganda and w Kenya
____	*P. b. kigomaensis*	S Zaire to Zambia and extreme w Tanzania
____	*P. b. kersteni*	Extreme s Somalia to coastal e Kenya and e Tanzania
____	*P. b. stictifrons*	SE Tanzania to e Zimbabwe, Malawi and Mozambique
____	*P. b. sylvanus*	NE Zimbabwe and adjacent w Mozambique
____	*P. b. bicolor (sclateri, lebomboensis)*	S Mozambique to e Transvaal, Natal and e Cape Province

☐ **Preuss' Weaver** *Ploceus preussi*

Guinea and Sierra Leone to s Cameroon, Gabon and ne Zaire

☐ **Yellow-capped Weaver** *Ploceus dorsomaculatus*

S Cameroon to Gabon, Central African Republic and ne Zaire

☐ **Usambara Weaver** *Ploceus nicolli*

NE Tanzania (Usambara, Uluguru and Udzungwa mountains)

☐ **Olive-headed Weaver** *Ploceus olivaceiceps*

____	*P. o. olivaceiceps*	Mountains of s Tanzania, Zambia, Malawi and n Mozambique
____	*P. o. vicarious*	Mountains of s Mozambique

☐ **Brown-capped Weaver** *Ploceus insignis*

____	*P. i. insignis*	SE Nigeria to n Angola, s Sudan, e Zaire, Kenya and w Tanzania
____	*P. i. unicus*	Bioko (Gulf of Guinea)

☐ **Bar-winged Weaver** *Ploceus angolensis*

Angola to n Zambia and extreme se Zaire

☐ **Sao Tome Weaver** *Ploceus sanctithomae*

Highlands of São Tomé (Gulf of Guinea)

☐ **Compact Weaver** *Pachyphantes superciliosus*

Sierra Leone to Angola, s Sudan, Ethiopia, Uganda and w Kenya

☐ **Yellow-legged Malimbe** *Malimbus flavipes*

NE Zaire (Ituri Forest)

☐ **Red-crowned Malimbe** *Malimbus coronatus*

S Cameroon to Gabon, sw Central African Republic and e Zaire

☐ **Black-throated Malimbe** *Malimbus cassini*

Lowlands of s Ghana and s Cameroon to Gabon and e Zaire

☐ **Ballman's Malimbe** *Malimbus ballmanni*

Humid forests of Sierra Leone, Liberia and sw Ivory Coast

☐ **Rachel's Malimbe** *Malimbus racheliae*

Lowland forests of se Nigeria to s Cameroon and Gabon

☐ **Red-vented Malimbe** *Malimbus scutatus*

____	*M. s. scutatus*	Sierra Leone to Ghana and Benin
____	*M. s. scutopartitus*	S Nigeria to sw Cameroon

☐ **Ibadan Malimbe** *Malimbus ibadanensis*

Savanna of sw Nigeria

☐ **Red-bellied Malimbe** *Malimbus erythrogaster*

S-central Nigeria to e Zaire, extreme sw Sudan and w Uganda

☐ **Gray's Malimbe** *Malimbus nitens*

____	*M. n. nitens*	Lowlands of Senegambia to s Nigeria
____	*M. n. moreaui*	S Cameroon to Gabon, nw Angola and nw Zaire
____	*M. n. microrhynchus*	NE Zaire to w Uganda

☐ **Crested Malimbe** *Malimbus malimbicus*

____	*M. m. nigrifrons*	Sierra Leone to Nigeria
____	*M. m. malimbicus*	Cameroon to nw Angola, s Zaire and w Uganda

☐ **Red-headed Malimbe** *Malimbus rubricollis*
_____ *M. r. bartletti* — Sierra Leone to Ghana
_____ *M. r. nigeriae* — Benin to w Nigeria
_____ *M. r. rubricollis* — E Nigeria to Chad, s Sudan, s Uganda and extreme w Kenya
_____ *M. r. rufovelatus* — Bioko (Gulf of Guinea)
_____ *M. r. praedi* — N Angola

☐ **Red-headed Weaver** *Anaplectes rubriceps*
_____ *A. r. leuconotus* — Senegambia to s Sudan, Ethiopia, Kenya, Tanzania and Malawi
_____ *A. r. jubaensis* — S Somalia and ne coastal Kenya
_____ *A. r. rubriceps* — S Angola to ne Namibia, s Zambia, Mozambique and ne S Africa

☐ **Bob-tailed Weaver** *Brachycope anomala* — SE Cameroon and banks of Congo River system in Zaire

☐ **Cardinal Quelea** *Quelea cardinalis*
_____ *Q. c. cardinalis* — S Sudan to Ethiopia, Uganda, nw Kenya, e Zaire and nw Tanzania
_____ *Q. c. rhodesiae* — Extreme se Kenya to Tanzania and e Zambia

☐ **Red-headed Quelea** *Quelea erythrops* — Grasslands of Africa south of the Sahara

☐ **Red-billed Quelea** *Quelea quelea*
_____ *Q. q. quelea* — Senegal to Chad and Central African Republic
_____ *Q. q. aethiopica* — NW Sudan to Somalia, e Zaire, Uganda, Kenya and n Tanzania
_____ *Q. q. lathami (spoliator)* — Angola to se Zaire, Zambia, Malawi and e Cape Province

☐ **Red Fody** *Foudia madagascariensis* — Forests of Madagascar and Nosy Mitsio

☐ **Red-headed Fody** *Foudia eminentissima*
_____ *F. e. aldabrana* — Aldabra (w Indian Ocean)
_____ *F. e. consobrina* — Grand Comoro I. (Comoro Islands)
_____ *F. e. anjuanensis* — Anjouan (Comoro Islands)
_____ *F. e. eminentissima* — Mohéli (Comoro Islands)
_____ *F. e. algondae* — Mayotte (Comoro Islands)

☐ **Forest Fody** *Foudia omissa* — Forests of e Madagascar

☐ **Mauritius Fody** *Foudia rubra* — Uplands of sw Mauritius (w Mascarene Islands)

☐ **Seychelles Fody** *Foudia sechellarum* — Seychelles Islands (Cousin, Cousine and Frégate)

☐ **Rodrigues Fody** *Foudia flavicans* — Rodrigues (e Mascarene Islands). On verge of extinction

☐ **Yellow-crowned Bishop** *Euplectes afer*
_____ *E. a. afer* — S Mauritania to Chad, Central African Republic and w Sudan
_____ *E. a. ladoensis* — S Sudan to Uganda, n Kenya and n Tanzania
_____ *E. a. strictus* — Highlands of Ethiopia
_____ *E. a. taha* — S Angola to Namibia, Zambia, Mozambique and e Cape Province

☐ **Fire-fronted Bishop** *Euplectes diadematus* — SW Somalia to e Kenya and extreme ne Tanzania

☐ **Black Bishop** *Euplectes gierowii*
_____ *E. g. ansorgei* — Extreme s Sudan to sw Ethiopia, extreme e Zaire and Uganda
_____ *E. g. friederichseni* — SW Kenya to n-central Tanzania
_____ *E. g. gierowii* — N Angola to sw Zaire

☐ **Black-winged Bishop** *Euplectes hordeaceus*
_____ *E. h. hordeaceus* — Senegambia to Angola, s Sudan and south to Zimbabwe
_____ *E. h. craspedopterus* — S Sudan to sw Ethiopia, Uganda and nw Kenya

☐ **Orange Bishop** *Euplectes franciscanus*
_____ *E. f. franciscanus*   Senegal to Sudan, e Zaire, Ethiopia, n Uganda and nw Kenya
_____ *E. f. pusillus*   Eritrea and e Ethiopia to Somalia

☐ **Red Bishop** *Euplectes orix*
_____ *E. o. nigrifrons*   E Zaire to Uganda, Kenya, Tanzania, Malawi and Mozambique
_____ *E. o. orix (turgida)*   S Angola to Namibia, Botswana, Mozambique and n Cape Province
_____ *E. o. sundevalli*   Zimbabwe to s Mozambique and Transvaal

☐ **Zanzibar Bishop** *Euplectes nigroventris*
      SE Kenya to e Tanzania, Zanzibar and n Mozambique

☐ **Golden-backed Bishop** *Euplectes aureus*
      Scrub of coastal Angola; São Tomé (probably introduced)

☐ **Yellow Bishop** *Euplectes capensis*
_____ *E. c. phoenicomerus*   Highlands of se Nigeria and Cameroon; Bioko
_____ *E. c. xanthomelas (crassirostris)*   Mts. of se Sudan to Ethiopia, e Zaire and Kenya s to Transvaal
_____ *E. c. angolensis*   N and central highlands of Angola
_____ *E. c. approximans*   South Africa (e Transvaal to Natal and e Cape Province)
_____ *E. c. macrorhynchus*   South Africa (nw Cape Province)
_____ *E. c. capensis*   South Africa (s Cape Province)

☐ **Fan-tailed Widowbird** *Euplectes axillaris*
_____ *E. a. bocagei (mechowi)*   S Mali to Niger, Cameroon, Angola, s Zaire and n Zambia
_____ *E. a. batesi*   Burkina Faso to upper Niger River
_____ *E. a. quanzae*   Central Angola (lower Cuanza escarpment)
_____ *E. a. traversii*   N and central Ethiopia
_____ *E. a. phoeniceus*   E Sudan to s Ethiopia, Uganda, extreme w Kenya and w Tanzania
_____ *E. a. zanzibaricus*   S Somalia, coastal e Kenya and e Tanzania; Mafia I.
_____ *E. a. axillaris*   Zambia to Zimbabwe, Mozambique and se South Africa

☐ **Yellow-shouldered Widowbird** *Euplectes macrourus*
_____ *E. m. macrourus*   Senegal to s Sudan, Zaire, Angola, Zambia and Malawi
_____ *E. m. macrocercus*   Eritrea and n Ethiopia
_____ *E. m. conradsi*   NW Tanzania (Ukerewe Island in Lake Victoria)
_____ *E. m. intermedius*   W Tanzania and sw shore of Lake Tanganyika

☐ **White-winged Widowbird** *Euplectes albonotatus*
_____ *E. a. eques*   Sudan to s Ethiopia, Uganda, Kenya and Tanzania
_____ *E. a. sassii*   Extreme ne Zaire, Rwanda and Burundi
_____ *E. a. asymmetrurus*   Gabon to Angola and extreme ne Namibia
_____ *E. a. albonotatus*   SE Zaire to Zambia, Botswana, Zimbabwe and ne Cape Province

☐ **Red-collared Widowbird** *Euplectes ardens*
_____ *E. a. concolor*   Guinea to Chad, Cameroon, sw Sudan, Uganda and n Angola
_____ *E. a. laticauda*   Highlands of se Sudan, Eritrea and Ethiopia
_____ *E. a. suahelicus*   Highlands of Kenya and ne Tanzania
_____ *E. a. ardens*   Angola to Uganda, e Zaire, se Kenya, Tanzania and e Cape Prov.

☐ **Marsh Widowbird** *Euplectes hartlaubi*
_____ *E. h. humeralis*   Highlands of Nigeria to Cameroon, Zaire, Uganda and w Kenya
_____ *E. h. hartlaubi*   Angola to s Zaire and Zambia

☐ **Buff-shouldered Widowbird** *Euplectes psammocromius*
      Highlands of sw Tanzania to extreme ne Zambia and n Malawi

☐ **Long-tailed Widowbird** *Euplectes progne*
_____ *E. p. delamerei*   Locally in highlands of Kenya
_____ *E. p. ansorgei*   E-central Angola to se Zaire and w-central Zambia
_____ *E. p. progne (definite)*   Botswana to Zimbabwe, Mozambique and e Cape Province

☐ **Jackson's Widowbird** *Euplectes jacksoni*

Grassy highlands of Kenya and n Tanzania

☐ **Parasitic Weaver** *Anomalospiza imberbis*

Moist grasslands of Afrotropical region

☐ **Grosbeak Weaver** *Amblyospiza albifrons*

____ A. a. capitalba	Sierra Leone to w Nigeria
____ A. a. saturata	E Nigeria to Cameroon, Central African Rep. and n Zaire
____ A. a. melanota	Extreme s Sudan to ne Zaire, Ethiopia, Uganda and nw Kenya
____ A. a. unicolor	Coastal e Kenya, e Tanzania and adjacent offshore islands
____ A. a. montana	Interior s Kenya and Tanzania to Malawi, Zambia and Zimbabwe
____ A. a. tandae	N Angola
____ A. a. kasaica	S Zaire
____ A. a. maxima	Caprivi Strip and extreme n Botswana
____ A. a. albifrons (woltersi)	S Mozambique and e Cape Province

FAMILY: ESTRILDIDAE (Waxbills and Allies—140)

☐ **Jameson's Antpecker** *Parmoptila rubrifrons*

____ P. r. rubrifrons	Liberia (Mt. Nimba) to s Mali and s-central Ghana
____ P. r. jamesoni	E Congo and n Zaire to w Uganda

☐ **Woodhouse's Antpecker** *Parmoptila woodhousei*

____ P. w. woodhousei	SE Nigeria to Cameroon, s Central African Rep. and cent. Zaire
____ P. w. ansorgei	N Angola to sw Zaire

☐ **White-breasted Negrofinch** *Nigrita fusconota*

____ N. f. fusconota	SE Nigeria to Cameroon, Gabon, Angola and w Kenya; Bioko
____ N. f. uropygialis	SE Guinea and Liberia (Mt. Nimba) to s Ghana and sw Nigeria

☐ **Chestnut-breasted Negrofinch** *Nigrita bicolor*

____ N. b. bicolor	SW Senegal to w Gambia, Sierra Leone, Liberia and Ghana
____ N. b. brunnescens	S Nigeria to Angola, w Uganda and w Kenya; Príncipe

☐ **Pale-fronted Negrofinch** *Nigrita luteifrons*

____ N. l. luteifrons	S Nigeria to Central African Republic, n Angola and w Uganda
____ N. l. alexanderi	Bioko (Gulf of Guinea)

☐ **Gray-headed Negrofinch** *Nigrita canicapilla*

____ N. c. emiliae	Guinea and Sierra Leone to Ghana and Togo
____ N. c. canicapilla	S Benin and s Nigeria to Cent. African Rep., w Zaire and Uganda
____ N. c. angolensis	SW Zaire to nw Angola
____ N. c. schistacea	SE Sudan to n Zaire, sw Uganda, w Kenya and n Tanzania
____ N. c. diabolica	Mt. Kenya to Crater Highlands and Mt. Kilimanjaro
____ N. c. candida	W Tanzania (Kungwe-Mahari Mountains)

☐ **White-collared Oliveback** *Nesocharis ansorgei*

Mts. of e Zaire, w Uganda, n Rwanda, Burundi and nw Tanzania

☐ **Fernando Po Oliveback** *Nesocharis shelleyi*

____ N. s. shelleyi	S Cameroon (Mt. Cameroon); Bioko (Moka Highlands)
____ N. s. bansoensis	Highlands of Cameroon and (?) se Nigeria (Obudu Plateau)

☐ **Gray-headed Oliveback** *Nesocharis capistrata*

Guinea to s Mali, Cameroon, n Zaire, sw Sudan and w Uganda

☐ **Orange-winged Pytilia** *Pytilia afra*

Extreme s Sudan and Ethiopia to Angola and n Transvaal

□ **Red-winged Pytilia** *Pytilia phoenicoptera*

____	*P. p. phoenicoptera*	Senegambia to Burkina Faso, n Nigeria and Cameroon
____	*P. p. emini*	Cameroon to n Zaire, n Uganda and extreme s Sudan
____	*P. p. lineata*	Highlands of w and central Ethiopia

□ **Green-winged Pytilia** *Pytilia melba*

____	*P. m. citerior*	Senegal to Burkina Faso, s Chad, n Cameroon and w Sudan
____	*P. m. soudanensis*	E Sudan to Ethiopia, Somalia, Kenya and nw Tanzania
____	*P. m. belli (grotei)*	SE Sudan to w Uganda, e Zaire and sw Kenya to n Mozambique
____	*P. m. percivali*	SW Kenya and n Tanzania
____	*P. m. melba*	W Angola to Namibia, Malawi, sw Tanzania and Transvaal
____	*P. m. thamnophila*	Zimbabwe and s Mozambique to Natal

□ **Red-faced Pytilia** *Pytilia hypogrammica*

NE Guinea and Sierra Leone to Cameroon and nw Zaire

□ **Green-backed Twinspot** *Mandingoa nitidula*

____	*M. n. schlegeli*	Sierra Leone to Cameroon, Angola, Uganda and nw Tanzania
____	*M. n. virginiae*	Bioko (Gulf of Guinea)
____	*M. n. chubbi*	SE Sudan to s Ethiopia, n Tanzania, Zanzibar and Pemba I.
____	*M. n. nitidula*	N Tanzania to s Zaire, n Zambia, Natal and ne Cape Province

□ **Red-faced Crimson-wing** *Cryptospiza reichenovii*

____	*C. r. reichenovii*	SE Nigeria (Obudu Plateau) to w Cameroon; Bioko
____	*C. r. australis*	E Zaire to s Uganda, Zambia, Zimbabwe and n Mozambique
____	*C. r. homogenes*	E Zimbabwe and adjacent Mozambique

□ **Abyssinian Crimson-wing** *Cryptospiza salvadorii*

____	*C. s. kilimensis*	SE Sudan to ne Uganda, Kenya and ne Tanzania
____	*C. s. salvadorii*	S Ethiopia (Shoa Province) to n Kenya
____	*C. s. ruwenzori*	E Zaire (Ruwenzori Mountains) to sw Uganda

□ **Dusky Crimson-wing** *Cryptospiza jacksoni*

Mountains of e Zaire to sw Uganda, Rwanda and Burundi

□ **Shelley's Crimson-wing** *Cryptospiza shelleyi*

Mountains of e Zaire to sw Uganda, Rwanda and Burundi

□ **Crimson Seedcracker** *Pyrenestes sanguineus*

____	*P. s. sanguineus*	Senegambia to s Mali, Sierra Leone and Ivory Coast
____	*P. s. coccineus*	Sierra Leone and Liberia to Ivory Coast

□ **Black-bellied Seedcracker** *Pyrenestes ostrinus*

____	*P. o. ostrinus*	Ivory Coast to Gabon, ne Zaire, Uganda and nw Zambia
____	*P. o. frommi (maximus)*	Togo to Cameroon, sw Sudan, sw Tanzania and ne Zambia
____	*P. o. rothschildi (gabonensis)*	Ghana to s Cameroon, Gabon, n Angola, e Zaire and nw Zambia

□ **Lesser Seedcracker** *Pyrenestes minor*

E Tanzania to s Malawi, e Zimbabwe and n Mozambique

□ **Grant's Bluebill** *Spermophaga poliogenys*

Primary forests of e Zaire and sw Uganda

□ **Western Bluebill** *Spermophaga haematina*

____	*S. h. haematina*	Senegambia to s Mali, Sierra Leone, Liberia and Ghana
____	*S. h. togoensis*	Togo to sw Nigeria
____	*S. h. pustulata*	SE Nigeria to Central African Rep., central Zaire and nw Angola

□ **Red-headed Bluebill** *Spermophaga ruficapilla*

____	*S. r. ruficapilla*	S Sudan to Uganda, w Kenya, w Tanzania and nw Angola
____	*S. r. cana*	NE Tanzania (Usambara Mountains)

□ **Brown Twinspot** *Clytospiza monteiri*

SE Nigeria to s Chad, s Sudan, w Uganda, w Kenya and n Angola

624

☐ **Peters' Twinspot** *Hypargos niveoguttatus*
_____ *H. n. macrospilotus*
_____ *H. n. niveoguttatus*
_____ *H. n. interior*

Angola to e Zaire, Kenya, Somalia, Tanzania and Malawi
Malawi to Zimbabwe, Mozambique and extreme n South Africa
Zimbabwe

☐ **Pink-throated Twinspot** *Hypargos margaritatus*

S Mozambique to e Transvaal, e Swaziland and n Natal

☐ **Dybowski's Twinspot** *Euschistospiza dybowskii*

Senegambia and Guinea to n Zaire and extreme s Sudan

☐ **Dusky Twinspot** *Euschistospiza cinereovinacea*
_____ *E. c. cinereovinacea*
_____ *E. c. graueri (rudolfi)*

Highlands of w and central Angola
Central Zaire to sw Uganda, Rwanda and Burundi

☐ **Bar-breasted Firefinch** *Lagonosticta rufopicta*
_____ *L. r. rufopicta*
_____ *L. r. lateritia*

Senegal and Gambia to Central African Republic and n Zaire
S Sudan to sw Ethiopia, ne Zaire, w Uganda and Kenya

☐ **Brown Firefinch** *Lagonosticta nitidula*
_____ *L. n. nitidula*
_____ *L. n. plumbaria*

Central and e Angola to s Zaire and ne Zambia
S Zambia to nw Zimbabwe, Caprivi strip and n Botswana

☐ **Red-billed Firefinch** *Lagonosticta senegala*
_____ *L. s. senegala*
_____ *L. s. rhodopsis*
_____ *L. s. guineensis*
_____ *L. s. rubrerrima*
_____ *L. s. brunneiceps*
_____ *L. s. somaliensis*
_____ *L. s. pallidicrissa*
_____ *L. s. rendalli*

Cape Verde Islands; Senegal to Cameroon
SW Mauritania and Senegal to Chad, s Sudan and w Ethiopia
Coastal Guinea and Sierra Leone
S Sudan to Uganda, Angola, Zambia, Malawi and Zimbabwe
Highlands of Ethiopia
SE Ethiopia to Somalia, e Kenya and e Tanzania
S Angola to Zimbabwe and n Namibia
S Angola to s Tanzania, Natal, and n-central Cape Province

☐ **Black-bellied Firefinch** *Lagonosticta rara*
_____ *L. r. forbesi*
_____ *L. r. rara*

S Guinea to e Sierra Leone, Liberia and Ghana
N Cameroon to n Zaire, s Sudan, n Uganda and w Kenya

☐ **African Firefinch** *Lagonosticta rubricata*
_____ *L. r. polionota*
_____ *L. r. ugandae (syn. hildebrandti)*
_____ *L. r. congica*
_____ *L. r. haematocephala*
_____ *L. r. rubricata*

Guinea-Bissau to s Mali, Ghana and Nigeria
Cameroon to se Sudan, Uganda, Ethiopia, Kenya and Tanzania
Gabon to central Zaire, ne Angola and nw Zambia
S Tanzania to Malawi, Zambia, Zimbabwe and Mozambique
S Mozambique to e Transvaal and central Cape Province

☐ **Pale-billed Firefinch** *Lagonosticta landanae*

Cabinda and lower Congo River to nw Angola and s Zaire

☐ **Jameson's Firefinch** *Lagonosticta rhodopareia*
_____ *L. r. bruneli*
_____ *L. r. rhodopareia*
_____ *L. r. jamesoni*
_____ *L. r. ansorgei*

S Chad (possibly adjacent ne Nigeria)
Highlands of s Sudan and Ethiopia to Uganda and n Kenya
S Kenya to Mozambique, n Botswana, Transvaal and n Natal
Cabinda to Congo, sw Zaire and w Angola

☐ **Mali Firefinch** *Lagonosticta virata*

S Mali (upper Niger River to Guinea border)

☐ **Rock Firefinch** *Lagonosticta sanguinodorsalis*

N Nigeria (Jos Plateau)

☐ **Black-faced Firefinch** *Lagonosticta larvata*
_____ *L. l. vinacea*
_____ *L. l. togoensis*
_____ *L. l. nigricollis*
_____ *L. l. larvata*

Senegal to Gambia, Guinea-Bissau, Guinea and s Mali
Ghana and Togo to Nigeria, n Cameroon and w Sudan
E Cameroon to Cent. African Rep., n Zaire, n Uganda and s Sudan
SE Sudan to Eritrea and Ethiopia

☐ **Reichenow's Firefinch** *Lagonosticta umbrinodorsalis*

Dry grasslands of s Chad and adjacent Cameroon

☐ **Blue-breasted Cordonbleu** *Uraeginthus angolensis*
_____ *U. a. angolensis*
_____ *U. a. niassensis*
_____ *U. a. damarensis*
_____ *U. a. cyanopleurus*

São Tomé; n Angola to s Zaire, nw Zambia and n Zimbabwe
SE Kenya to Malawi, Mozambique, Transvaal and Natal
N Namibia to n Botswana
N Botswana to Zimbabwe and w Transvaal

☐ **Red-cheeked Cordonbleu** *Uraeginthus bengalus*
_____ *U. b. bengalus*
_____ *U. b. brunneigularis*
_____ *U. b. littoralis*
_____ *U. b. ugogoensis*
_____ *U. b. katangae (semotus)*

Widespread west, n-central and East Africa
Highlands of Kenya (east of Rift Valley)
Extreme s Somalia to se Kenya and ne Tanzania
Mt. Kilimanjaro area to central Tanzania
Extreme e Angola to s Zaire and Zambia

☐ **Blue-capped Cordonbleu** *Uraeginthus cyanocephalus*

Extreme se Sudan to se Ethiopia, s Somalia, Kenya and n Tanzania

☐ **Purple Grenadier** *Uraeginthus ianthinogaster*
_____ *U. i. ugandae*
_____ *U. i. roosevelti*
_____ *U. i. ianthinogaster*

Extreme se Sudan to s Ethiopia, n Kenya and n Uganda
Highlands of central Kenya
Central Kenya to s-central Tanzania

☐ **Violet-eared Waxbill** *Uraeginthus granatina*
_____ *U. g. granatina (siccata)*
_____ *U. g. retusa*

Angola to Namibia, Zambia, s Zimbabwe, Natal and e Cape Prov.
S Mozambique (Inhambane region)

☐ **Lavender Waxbill** *Estrilda caerulescens*

Senegambia to sw Chad, n Cameroon and Central African Republic

☐ **Black-tailed Waxbill** *Estrilda perreini*
_____ *E. p. perreini*
_____ *E. p. poliogastra*
_____ *E. p. incana*

Gabon and lower Congo River to n Zambia and w Tanzania
S Tanzania to Mozambique, e Zimbabwe and n Zululand
S Zimbabwe to s Zululand and Natal

☐ **Cinderella Waxbill** *Estrilda thomensis*

W Angola to extreme n Namibia (Cunene River)

☐ **Yellow-bellied Waxbill** *Estrilda quartinia*
_____ *E. q. bocagei*
_____ *E. q. quartinia*
_____ *E. q. kilimensis*
_____ *E. q. stuartirwini*

Central plateau of w Angola
Highlands of Eritrea, Ethiopia and se Sudan
E Zaire to Rwanda, Uganda, Kenya and Tanzania
S Malawi and e Zimbabwe to n Mozambique

☐ **Swee Waxbill** *Estrilda melanotis*

SW Zimbabwe to extreme s Mozambique and n South Africa

☐ **Fawn-breasted Waxbill** *Estrilda paludicola*
_____ *E. p. ochrogaster*
_____ *E. p. roseicrissa*
_____ *E. p. marwitzi*
_____ *E. p. paludicola*
_____ *E. p. ruthae*
_____ *E. p. benguellensis*

Highlands of extreme se Sudan and Ethiopia
S Uganda to Rwanda, Burundi and extreme nw Tanzania
W Tanzania (Iringa highlands to Shinyanga)
E Congo to s Sudan, ne Zaire, n Uganda and w Kenya
Central Zaire (along middle Congo River)
Central Angola to s Zaire, n Zambia and adjacent Tanzania

☐ **Anambra Waxbill** *Estrilda poliopareia*

S Nigeria (Niger River delta to Benin border)

☐ **Orange-cheeked Waxbill** *Estrilda melpoda*
_____ *E. m. melpoda*
_____ *E. m. tschadensis*

Senegambia to Zaire, n Angola and n Zambia
Lake Chad to n Cameroon (Adamawa Plateau)

☐ **Arabian Waxbill** *Estrilda rufibarba*

SW Arabian Peninsula

☐ **Crimson-rumped Waxbill** *Estrilda rhodopyga*
_____ *E. r. rhodopyga* — Lowlands of s Sudan to Eritrea, Ethiopia and s Somalia
_____ *E. r. centralis* — S Ethiopia and se Sudan to Kenya, nw Tanzania and n Malawi

☐ **Black-rumped Waxbill** *Estrilda troglodytes*

Senegambia to s Sudan, nw Ethiopia, Eritrea and w Kenya

☐ **Common Waxbill** *Estrilda astrild*
_____ *E. a. kempi* — Sierra Leone to s Guinea and Liberia
_____ *E. a. occidentalis* — S Mali to Ivory Coast, Central African Rep. and n-c Zaire; Bioko
_____ *E. a. rubriventris* — Coastal Gabon and lower sw Congo to nw Angola
_____ *E. a. jagoensis* — Coastal w Angola (Benguela and Moçamedes)
_____ *E. a. angolensis* — Plateau of w Angola
_____ *E. a. niediecki (ngamiensis)* — E Angola to n Zambia, Zimbabwe and n Botswana
_____ *E. a. damarensis* — Namibia
_____ *E. a. peasei* — Sudan to e Zaire, Ethiopia, Kenya and nw Tanzania
_____ *E. a. minor* — S Somalia to e Kenya, e Tanzania, Zanzibar and Mafia I.
_____ *E. a. massaica* — Kenya to n Tanzania
_____ *E. a. cavendishi* — S Zaire to Tanzania, Malawi, Zimbabwe and Mozambique
_____ *E. a. schoutedeni* — S Zaire
_____ *E. a. astrild (tenebridorsa)* — S Botswana to s Transvaal, Natal, s Zululand and e Cape Province

☐ **Black-faced Waxbill** *Estrilda nigriloris*

Swamps of se Zaire (no published records since 1950)

☐ **Black-crowned Waxbill** *Estrilda nonnula*
_____ *E. n. nonnula* — Burkina Faso to se Nigeria, Uganda, w Kenya and nw Tanzania
_____ *E. n. elizae* — Bioko (Gulf of Guinea)
_____ *E. n. eisentrauti* — S Cameroon (Mt. Cameroon)

☐ **Black-headed Waxbill** *Estrilda atricapilla*
_____ *E. a. atricapilla* — Extreme se Nigeria to Cameroon, Gabon and nw Zaire
_____ *E. a. avakubi* — Central Zaire to extreme ne Angola
_____ *E. a. graueri (kandti)* — E Zaire to sw Uganda, Rwanda, Burundi and central Kenya

☐ **Black-cheeked Waxbill** *Estrilda erythronotos*
_____ *E. e. soligena* — SW Angola and Namibia to Zimbabwe and n Cape Province
_____ *E. e. delamerei* — Uganda and s Kenya to e Tanzania
_____ *E. e. erythronotos* — S Zimbabwe to Transvaal, w Orange Free State and n Cape Prov.

☐ **Red-rumped Waxbill** *Estrilda charmosyna*
_____ *E. c. charmosyna* — Extreme s Sudan to Ethiopia, Somalia, ne Uganda and ne Kenya
_____ *E. c. kiwanukae* — S Kenya to extreme n Tanzania

☐ **Red Avadavat** *Amandava amandava*
_____ *A. a. amandava* — Lowlands of Pakistan to India, s Nepal and Bangladesh
_____ *A. a. flavidiventris* — SW China (Yunnan) to Myanmar, Malay Pen. and Lesser Sundas
_____ *A. a. punicea* — SE China to se Thailand, Cambodia, Vietnam, Java and Bali

☐ **Green Avadavat** *Amandava formosa*

Locally in grassland and scrub of peninsular India

☐ **Zebra Waxbill** *Amandava subflava*
_____ *A. s. subflava* — Senegal to s Sudan, Ethiopia and w Kenya; South Yemen
_____ *A. s. clarkei* — Gabon and w Angola to Kenya, Tanzania and South Africa

☐ **Red-billed Quailfinch** *Ortygospiza gabonensis*
_____ *O. g. gabonensis* — Rio Muni to Gabon and central Zaire (Congo River)
_____ *O. g. fuscata* — N Angola to s Zaire and Zambia
_____ *O. g. dorsostriata* — Extreme e Zaire to Uganda, Rwanda and nw Tanzania

☐ **African Quailfinch** *Ortygospiza atricollis*
_____ *O. a. atricollis* — Senegambia to Burkina Faso, Lake Chad and n Cameroon
_____ *O. a. ansorgei* — Guinea-Bissau to Liberia, Ivory Coast and coastal Ghana
_____ *O. a. ugandae* — S Sudan and Uganda to n Kenya
_____ *O. a. fuscocrissa* — Highlands of Ethiopia
_____ *O. a. muelleri* — Kenya to Zambia, Angola, Namibia and s Cape Province
_____ *O. a. smithersi* — NE Zambia to n Zimbabwe
_____ *O. a. pallida* — N Botswana to w Zimbabwe

☐ **Locustfinch** *Ortygospiza locustella*
_____ *O. l. locustella* — Angola to s Tanzania, n Mozambique and e Zimbabwe
_____ *O. l. uelensis* — NE Congo to n Zaire (Lake Albert region)

☐ **Painted Firetail** *Emblema pictum* — Porcupine grass of arid interior Australia

☐ **Beautiful Firetail** *Stagonopleura bella* — SE Australia, Tasmania, Kangaroo, Flinders and adjacent islands

☐ **Red-eared Firetail** *Stagonopleura oculata* — Coastal sw Western Australia (Darling Mountains)

☐ **Diamond Firetail** *Stagonopleura guttata* — NE Queensland to Victoria, e South Australia and Kangaroo I.

☐ **Mountain Firetail** *Oreostruthus fuliginosus*
_____ *O. f. pallidus* — W New Guinea (Snow Mountains)
_____ *O. f. hagenensis* — Central highlands of New Guinea
_____ *O. f. fuliginosus* — SE New Guinea (Owen Stanley Mountains)

☐ **Red-browed Firetail** *Neochmia temporalis*
_____ *N. t. minor* — NE Australia (Cape York Peninsula south to Mitchell River)
_____ *N. t. temporalis* — E Queensland to coastal New South Wales and e South Australia
_____ *N. t. loftyi* — S Australia (Mt. Lofty Range and Kangaroo I.)

☐ **Crimson Finch** *Neochmia phaeton*
_____ *N. p. evangelinae* — S New Guinea
_____ *N. p. phaeton* — Northern Territory to Gulf of Carpenteria and e Queensland
_____ *N. p. albiventer* — NE Australia (n Cape York Peninsula)
_____ *N. p. iredalei* — E Australia (Atherton Plateau and e Queensland)

☐ **Star Finch** *Neochmia ruficauda*
_____ *N. r. clarescens* — N Western Australia to n Cape York Peninsula
_____ *N. r. ruficauda* — E Australia (central Queensland to central New South Wales)

☐ **Plum-headed Finch** *Neochmia modesta* — E Australia (ne Queensland to e New South Wales)

☐ **Zebra Finch** *Taeniopygia guttata* — Lesser Sundas (Lombok and Sumba to Timor and Sermata)

☐ **Chestnut-eared Finch** *Taeniopygia castanotis* — Widespread interior of mainland Australia

☐ **Double-barred Finch** *Taeniopygia bichenovii*
_____ *T. b. annulosa* — N Western Australia and Northern Territory
_____ *T. b. bichenovii* — E Northern Territory and Queensland to n Victoria

☐ **Masked Finch** *Poephila personata*
_____ *P. p. personata* — Tropical n Australia (Kimberley Range to Gulf of Carpenteria)
_____ *P. p. leucotis* — Gulf of Carpenteria and Cape York Pen. (south to about 19°S)

☐ **Long-tailed Finch** *Poephila acuticauda*
_____ *P. a. hecki* — NW Australia (Roebuck Bay to Wyndham)
_____ *P. a. acuticauda* — Northern Territory to Gulf of Carpenteria and nw Queensland

☐ **Black-throated Finch** *Poephila cincta*
_____ *P. c. atropygialis*   NE Australia (Cape York Pen. south to Normanton and Cairns)
_____ *P. c. cincta*   E Australia (cent. Queensland to extreme ne New South Wales)

☐ **Tawny-breasted Parrotfinch** *Erythrura hyperythra*
_____ *E. h. malayana*   Mountains of Malay Peninsula
_____ *E. h. brunneiventris*   Philippines (montane forests of Luzon and Mindoro)
_____ *E. h. borneensis*   Borneo (Sarawak and Sabah)
_____ *E. h. microrhyncha*   Montane forests of Sulawesi
_____ *E. h. hyperythra*   Montane forests of Java
_____ *E. h. intermedia*   W Lesser Sundas (Lombok, Sumbawa and Flores)

☐ **Pin-tailed Parrotfinch** *Erythrura prasina*
_____ *E. p. prasina*   S Myanmar to Thailand, Laos, Malay Peninsula, Sumatra and Java
_____ *E. p. coelica*   Borneo

☐ **Green-faced Parrotfinch** *Erythrura viridifacies*
    N Philippines (Luzon and Negros)

☐ **Tricolored Parrotfinch** *Erythrura tricolor*
    Lesser Sundas (Timor, Wetar, Babar, Damar, Romang, Tanimbar)

☐ **Blue-faced Parrotfinch** *Erythrura trichroa*
_____ *E. t. sanfordi*   Sulawesi (Latimojong Mountains and Lore Lindu Nat. Park)
_____ *E. t. modesta*   N Moluccas (Ternate, Tidore, Halmahera and Bacan)
_____ *E. t. pinaiae*   S Moluccas (Seram and Buru)
_____ *E. t. sigillifera*   New Guinea, Bismarck Archipelago and n Queensland
_____ *E. t. eichhorni*   St. Matthias Islands (Bismarck Archipelago)
_____ *E. t. pelewensis*   Palau Islands (e Caroline Islands)
_____ *E. t. clara*   Caroline Islands (Truk, Pohnpei and Kosrae)
_____ *E. t. trichroa*   Kosrae (Caroline Islands)
_____ *E. t. woodfordi*   Guadalcanal and Solomon Islands
_____ *E. t. cyanofrons*   Vanuatu and Loyalty Islands (Lifu and Maré)

☐ **Red-eared Parrotfinch** *Erythrura coloria*
    S Philippines (Mt. Katanglad and Mt. Apo on Mindanao)

☐ **Papuan Parrotfinch** *Erythrura papuana*
    Mountains of New Guinea (Vogelkop Pen. to southeast ranges)

☐ **Red-throated Parrotfinch** *Erythrura psittacea*
    New Caledonia

☐ **Fiji Parrotfinch** *Erythrura pealii*
    Fiji (Kandavu, Viti Levu, Vanua Levu and Taveuni)

☐ **Red-headed Parrotfinch** *Erythrura cyaneovirens*
_____ *E. c. cyaneovirens*   Western Samoa (Savai'i and Upolu)
_____ *E. c. gaughrani*   Savai'i (Western Samoa)
_____ *E. c. efatensis*   Efate (Vanuatu)
_____ *E. c. serena*   Aneityum (Vanuatu)

☐ **Royal Parrotfinch** *Erythrura regia*
    N Vanuatu and Banks Group

☐ **Pink-billed Parrotfinch** *Erythrura kleinschmidti*
    Montane forests of Viti Levu (Fiji)

☐ **Gouldian Finch** *Chloebia gouldiae*
    N Australia (King Sound to n Queensland)

☐ **Madagascar Munia** *Lonchura nana*
    Madagascar

☐ **African Silverbill** *Lonchura cantans*
_____ *L. c. cantans*   Mauritania and Senegal to Chad, n Cameroon and s Sudan
_____ *L. c. orientalis*   SE Egypt to e Sudan, Ethiopia, Kenya, ne Tanzania and s Arabia

☐ **White-throated Munia** *Lonchura malabarica*

Arabian Peninsula to se Iran, India, Sri Lanka, Nepal and Sikkim

☐ **Gray-headed Silverbill** *Lonchura griseicapilla*

S Ethiopia to Kenya and central Tanzania

☐ **Bronze Mannikin** *Lonchura cucullata*

_____ *L. c. cucullata*   Senegal to w Kenya and nw Angola; São Tomé and Príncipe
_____ *L. c. scutata*   Ethiopia and Sudan to Natal and e Cape Province; Comoro Is.

☐ **Black-and-white Mannikin** *Lonchura bicolor*

_____ *L. b. bicolor*   Guinea-Bissau to Guinea, Nigeria and Cameroon
_____ *L. b. poensis*   Cameroon to Ethiopia, Kenya, Tanzania and n Angola; Bioko
_____ *L. b. minor*   S Somalia
_____ *L. b. woltersi*   SE Zaire and nw Zambia

☐ **Brown-backed Mannikin** *Lonchura nigriceps*

S Somalia to ne Zambia, Natal, Zanzibar, Pemba I. and Mafia I.

☐ **Magpie Mannikin** *Lonchura fringilloides*

Senegal to Kenya, south to Tanzania, Zanzibar, Zambia and Natal

☐ **White-rumped Munia** *Lonchura striata*

_____ *L. s. acuticauda*   SE Kashmir and n India to Nepal, Myanmar and n Thailand
_____ *L. s. striata*   S India and Sri Lanka
_____ *L. s. fumigata*   Andaman Islands
_____ *L. s. semistriata*   Nicobar Islands
_____ *L. s. swinhoei*   S China and Taiwan
_____ *L. s. subsquamicollis*   S peninsular Thailand and Malay Peninsula to Indochina
_____ *L. s. sumatrensis*   Sporadic but locally common on Sumatra and Bangka I.

☐ **Javan Munia** *Lonchura leucogastroides*

Lowlands of s Sumatra, Java, Bali and Lombok

☐ **Dusky Munia** *Lonchura fuscans*

Borneo, Natuna, Banggi, Cagayan and Sulu islands

☐ **Black-faced Munia** *Lonchura molucca*

Lowlands of Wallacea (except for Lesser Sundas)

☐ **Black-throated Munia** *Lonchura kelaarti*

_____ *L. k. jerdoni*   SW India (Kerala to w Tamil Nadu) and Eastern Ghats
_____ *L. k. kelaarti*   Highlands of Sri Lanka

☐ **Nutmeg Mannikin** *Lonchura punctulata*

_____ *L. p. punctulata*   Nepal to Sikkim, India and Sri Lanka
_____ *L. p. subundulata*   NE India (Assam) to Bhutan and w Myanmar
_____ *L. p. yunnanensis*   NE Myanmar and sw China
_____ *L. p. topela*   S China to n Thailand, Indochina, Hainan and Taiwan
_____ *L. p. cabanisi*   Philippines (Luzon, Mindoro, Panay, Cebu, Calauit and Palawan)
_____ *L. p. fretensis*   S Thailand and Malay Peninsula to Sumatra and adjacent islands
_____ *L. p. nisoria*   Java, Bali, Lombok and Sumbawa
_____ *L. p. sumbae*   Sumba (Lesser Sundas)
_____ *L. p. blasii*   Flores, Timor, Tanimbar Islands and adj. Lesser Sundas
_____ *L. p. particeps*   Sulawesi
_____ *L. p. baweana*   Bawean I. (Java Sea)
_____ *L. p. holmesi*   Southeast Borneo (Kalimantan)

☐ **White-bellied Munia** *Lonchura leucogastra*

_____ *L. l. leucogastra*   SE Myanmar, peninsular Thailand and Malay Pen. to Sumatra
_____ *L. l. everetti*   Luzon, Mindoro, Camiguin Norte, Catanduanes and Polillo
_____ *L. l. manueli*   Widespread throughout Philippine Islands
_____ *L. l. palawana*   Palawan, islands in Sulu Archipelago and Borneo
_____ *L. l. smythiesi*   N Borneo (Kucing region of sw Sarawak)
_____ *L. l. castanonota*   S Borneo

☐ **Streak-headed Munia** *Lonchura tristissima*

____ *L. t. tristissima*	NW New Guinea (Vogelkop Mountains)
____ *L. t. hypomelaena*	W New Guinea (Weyland Mountains)
____ *L. t. calaminoros*	Jayawijaya and Nassau mountains to Lorentz River and Karkar I.
____ *L. t. bigilae*	SE Papua New Guinea

☐ **White-spotted Munia** *Lonchura leucosticta*

____ *L. l. leucosticta*	Lowlands of s New Guinea (Lorentz River to Turama River)
____ *L. l. moresbyae*	SE Papua New Guinea (Port Moresby)

☐ **Black-headed Munia** *Lonchura malacca*

____ *L. m. rubroniger*	N India (Haryana to n Bihar) and lowlands of Nepal
____ *L. m. malacca*	Lowlands of s India (Tapi River to Raipur) and Sri Lanka

☐ **Chestnut Munia** *Lonchura atricapilla*

____ *L. a. atricapilla*	SE Nepal and ne India to Myanmar and nw Yunnan
____ *L. a. deignani*	SW China (sw Yunnan) to Thailand, Laos and Vietnam
____ *L. a. sinensis*	Pen. Thailand, Malaya, Sumatra, Riau Arch. and Lingga Arch.
____ *L. a. batakana*	Mountains of n Sumatra
____ *L. a. formosana*	Taiwan and n Philippines
____ *L. a. jagori*	Philippines, Sulu Islands, Palawan, Borneo, Sulawesi, Muna and Butung
____ *L. a. obscura*	Borneo (Sampit region of Kalimantan)
____ *L. a. selimbaue*	Borneo (Pontianak region of w Kalimantan)
____ *L. a. brunneiceps*	S Sulawesi (Makassar district)

☐ **White-capped Munia** *Lonchura ferruginosa*

	Lowlands of Java and Bali

☐ **Cream-bellied Munia** *Lonchura pallidiventer*

	SE Borneo (se Kalimantan)

☐ **Five-colored Munia** *Lonchura quinticolor*

____ *L. q. wallacii*	W Lesser Sundas (Lombok and Sumbawa)
____ *L. q. sumbae*	Lesser Sundas (Flores, Alor, Sumba, Roti and w Timor)
____ *L. q. quinticolor*	E Timor, Sermata I., Babar I. and Tanimbar Is. (Yamdena)

☐ **White-headed Munia** *Lonchura maja*

____ *L. m. maja*	Peninsular Thailand, Malaya, Sumatra, Java and Bali
____ *L. m. vietnamensis*	Vietnam

☐ **Pale-headed Munia** *Lonchura pallida*

____ *L. p. pallida*	Sulawesi and Lesser Sundas
____ *L. p. subcastanea*	N-central Sulawesi (lower Palu Valley)

☐ **Grand Munia** *Lonchura grandis*

____ *L. g. ernesti*	N New Guinea (Ramu and Sepik Valley to Astrolabe Bay)
____ *L. g. destructa*	N New Guinea (Hollandia district)
____ *L. g. heurni*	N New Guinea (Idenberg and Hollandia regions)
____ *L. g. grandis*	SE New Guinea (Hall Sound to upper Watut River)

☐ **Gray-banded Munia** *Lonchura vana*

	NW New Guinea (Arfak Mountains)

☐ **Gray-crowned Munia** *Lonchura nevermanni*

	New Guinea (Kurik and Mapa areas to lower Fly River)

☐ **Hooded Munia** *Lonchura spectabilis*

____ *L. s. wahgiensis*	Central and s highlands of New Guinea
____ *L. s. gajduseki*	New Guinea (Karimui basin and e highlands)
____ *L. s. mayri*	New Guinea (Cyclops Mountains and lowlands of Hollandia)
____ *L. s. sepikensis*	NE New Guinea (East Sepik Province)
____ *L. s. spectabilis*	Bismarck Archipelago (New Britain, Long and Umboi)

☐ **Gray-headed Munia** *Lonchura caniceps*
____ *L. c. caniceps* — SE New Guinea (Yule I. and Hall Sound to Port Moresby)
____ *L. c. scratchleyana* — SE New Guinea (Malalaua and Kupriano Mountains)
____ *L. c. kumusii* — SE New Guinea (Kumusi River to upper Musa River)

☐ **Mottled Munia** *Lonchura hunsteini*

____ New Ireland (Bismarck Archipelago)

☐ **New Ireland Munia** *Lonchura forbesi*

____ New Ireland (Bismarck Archipelago)

☐ **New Hanover Munia** *Lonchura nigerrima*

____ New Hanover (Bismarck Archipelago)

☐ **Yellow-rumped Munia** *Lonchura flaviprymna*

____ N Australia (Derby and Kimberlys to Arnhem Land)

☐ **Chestnut-breasted Munia** *Lonchura castaneothorax*
____ *L. c. uropygialis* — NW New Guinea (Geelvink Bay environs)
____ *L. c. sharpii* — New Guinea (Astrolabe Bay to Humboldt Bay and upper Watut R.)
____ *L. c. boschmai* — W New Guinea (Wissel Lakes region)
____ *L. c. ramsayi* — SE New Guinea and D'Entrecasteaux Archipelago
____ *L. c. assimilis* — N Australia (Northern Territory to Groote Eylandt and Melville I.)
____ *L. c. castaneothorax* — E Queensland to e New South Wales and islands in Torres Strait

☐ **Black Munia** *Lonchura stygia*

____ S New Guinea (Trans-Fly lowlands)

☐ **Black-breasted Munia** *Lonchura teerinki*
____ *L. t. mariae* — W New Guinea (Snow Mountains)
____ *L. t. teerinki* — Mountains of w-central New Guinea

☐ **Snow Mountain Munia** *Lonchura montana*

____ W New Guinea (Snow Mts.) and Mt. Capella (Papua NG)

☐ **Alpine Munia** *Lonchura monticola*
____ *L. m. monticola* — SW New Guinea (alpine grasslands of Wharton Mountains)
____ *L. m. myolae* — SW New Guinea (alpine grasslands of Owen Stanley Mountains)

☐ **Bismarck Munia** *Lonchura melaena*
____ *L. m. melaena* — New Britain (se Bismarck Archipelago)
____ *L. m. bukaensis* — Buka (Solomon Islands)

☐ **Pictorella Munia** *Heteromunia pectoralis*

____ N Australia (King Sound to Gulf of Carpenteria)

☐ **Java Sparrow** *Padda oryzivora*

____ Java, Bali, Lombok, Sumbawa and Kangean Islands

☐ **Timor Sparrow** *Padda fuscata*

____ E Lesser Sundas (Timor, Roti and Semau)

☐ **Cut-throat** *Amadina fasciata*
____ *A. f. fasciata* — Senegal to Chad, n Cameroon, Sudan, n Uganda and nw Kenya
____ *A. f. alexanderi* — SE Sudan to Ethiopia, Somalia, Kenya and s Tanzania
____ *A. f. meridionalis* — Malawi to Mozambique, Angola, ne Namibia and n South Africa

☐ **Red-headed Finch** *Amadina erythrocephala*
____ *A. e. erythrocephala* — NW Angola to sw Zimbabwe, Transvaal and Cape Province
____ *A. e. dissita* — E Cape Province (Drakensberg escarpment) to s Natal

FAMILY: VIDUIDAE (Indigobirds—19)

☐ **Village Indigobird** *Vidua chalybeata*
____ *V. c. chalybeata* — Semiarid Senegambia to Sierra Leone and sw Mali
____ *V. c. neumanni* — Mali to Niger, Chad and Sudan
____ *V. c. ultramarina* — Ethiopia
____ *V. c. centralis* — E Zaire to Uganda, Rwanda, Kenya and w Tanzania
____ *V. c. okavangoensis* — Angola to Botswana and w Zambia
____ *V. c. amauropteryx* — S Tanzania to Zambia, Mozambique and Transvaal

☐ **Jambandu Indigobird** *Vidua raricola* — Sierra Leone to n Nigeria, n Cameroon, n Zaire and s Sudan

☐ **Baka Indigobird** *Vidua larvaticola* — Senegambia to Cameroon, n Zaire, Sudan and w Ethiopia

☐ **Jos Plateau Indigobird** *Vidua maryae* — N Nigeria (Jos Plateau)

☐ **Quailfinch Indigobird** *Vidua nigeriae* — N Cameroon (flood plain of Benue River) to s Sudan

☐ **Variable Indigobird** *Vidua funerea*
____ *V. f. nigerrima* — SW Mali to Angola, Zambia and Tanzania
____ *V. f. lusituensis* — NE Namibia (Caprivi Strip) to e Zimbabwe and Mozambique
____ *V. f. funerea* — Natal

☐ **Green Indigobird** *Vidua codringtoni* — Locally in Zambia, sw Tanzania, Malawi and Zimbabwe

☐ **Purple Indigobird** *Vidua purpurascens* — SW Angola to e Namibia, Kenya, Tanzania and Transvaal

☐ **Pale-winged Indigobird** *Vidua wilsoni* — Senegambia to n Zaire, s Sudan and nw Ethiopia

☐ **Cameroon Indigobird** *Vidua camerunensis* — Sierra Leone to e Cameroon, ne Zaire and s Sudan

☐ **Steel-blue Whydah** *Vidua hypocherina* — S Sudan to Ethiopia, Somalia, Uganda, Kenya and Tanzania

☐ **Straw-tailed Whydah** *Vidua fischeri* — Extreme se Sudan to Ethiopia, Somalia, Uganda and Tanzania

☐ **Shaft-tailed Whydah** *Vidua regia* — S Angola to Namibia, Zambia, Botswana, s Mozambique, Natal

☐ **Pin-tailed Whydah** *Vidua macroura* — Senegambia to s Chad, s Sudan, s Somalia and South Africa

☐ **Togo Paradise-Whydah** *Vidua togoensis* — Sierra Leone to Ivory Coast, Ghana and Togo

☐ **Long-tailed Paradise-Whydah** *Vidua interjecta* — Mali to s Nigeria, Cameroon, Central African Rep. and ne Zaire

☐ **Eastern Paradise-Whydah** *Vidua paradisaea* — Angola to se Sudan, Ethiopia and Kenya south to ne S Africa

☐ **Northern Paradise-Whydah** *Vidua orientalis* — Senegal to Mali, s Chad, s Sudan, nw Ethiopia and Eritrea

☐ **Broad-tailed Paradise-Whydah** *Vidua obtusa* — N Angola to Zaire, sw Uganda, Kenya and ne South Africa

FAMILY: VIREONIDAE (Vireos and Allies—52)

☐ **Slaty Vireo** *Vireo brevipennis* — Oak-pine highlands of s-central Mexico

☐ **White-eyed Vireo** *Vireo griseus*

_____ *V. g. noveboracensis*	Central and e US; winters to Bahamas, n Nicaragua and Cuba
_____ *V. g. griseus*	SE US; winters to e Mexico, n Honduras and w Cuba
_____ *V. g. maynardi*	Coastal and insular Florida
_____ *V. g. bermudianus*	Bermuda
_____ *V. g. micrus*	S Texas to e Mexico (south to Puebla and extreme n Veracruz)
_____ *V. g. perquisitor*	E Mexico (ne Puebla and n-central Veracruz)

☐ **Thick-billed Vireo** *Vireo crassirostris*

_____ *V. c. crassirostris*	Bahamas and Cayman Islands
_____ *V. c. stalagmium*	Turks and Caicos Islands
_____ *V. c. tortugae*	Tortue I. (off nw Haiti)
_____ *V. c. approximans*	Isla Providéncia and Isla Santa Catalina (Caribbean Sea)

☐ **Mangrove Vireo** *Vireo pallens*

_____ *V. p. paluster*	Mangroves of nw Mexico (extreme sw Sonora to Nayarit)
_____ *V. p. ochraceus*	Mangroves of Pacific coast of Guatemala and El Salvador
_____ *V. p. pallens*	Mangroves of w Honduras to w Nicaragua and w Costa Rica
_____ *V. p. semiflavus*	SE Mexico (Yucatán Peninsula) to Belize and Nicaragua

☐ **Cozumel Vireo** *Vireo bairdi*

SE Mexico (Cozumel I. off Quintana Roo)

☐ **St. Andrew Vireo** *Vireo caribaeus*

Mangroves of Isla San Andrés (w Caribbean Sea)

☐ **Jamaican Vireo** *Vireo modestus*

Lowlands and mountains of Jamaica

☐ **Cuban Vireo** *Vireo gundlachii*

Wooodlands of Cuba, Isle of Pines and adjacent islands

☐ **Puerto Rican Vireo** *Vireo latimeri*

Confined mainly to limestone hills of w and central Puerto Rico

☐ **Flat-billed Vireo** *Vireo nanus*

Semiarid lowland scrub of Hispaniola and Gonâve I.

☐ **Bell's Vireo** *Vireo bellii*

_____ *V. b. pusillus*	Arid s California; winters to s Baja
_____ *V. b. arizonae*	SW US; winters from Baja and central Sonora to Colima
_____ *V. b. medius*	SW Texas to s Durango and s Coahuila; winters to Oaxaca
_____ *V. b. bellii*	Central and s US; winters from s Mexico to n Nicaragua

☐ **Black-capped Vireo** *Vireo atricapillus*

Breeds Kansas to n Mexico (Coahuila); winters to Guerrero

☐ **Dwarf Vireo** *Vireo nelsoni*

Arid highlands of sw Mexico (se Jalisco to Oaxaca)

☐ **Gray Vireo** *Vireo vicinior*

SW US to n Baja; winters to n Mexico (Sonora)

☐ **Blue Mountain Vireo** *Vireo osburni*

Humid montane forests of nw Jamaica

☐ **Yellow-throated Vireo** *Vireo flavifrons*

E Canada to Gulf States; winters to Venezuela and West Indies

☐ **Plumbeous Vireo** *Vireo plumbeus*

_____ *V. p. plumbeus*	Rocky Mountains of n US to nw Mexico; winters to nw Mexico
_____ *V. p. pinicolus*	Mountains of nw Mexico (Sonora to Durango and Zacatecas)
_____ *V. p. repetens*	Oak-pinyon-juniper belt of central Mexico
_____ *V. p. montanus*	Mountains of s Mexico (Chiapas) to nw Honduras
_____ *V. p. notius*	Pine savanna of Belize

☐ **Cassin's Vireo** *Vireo cassinii*

_____ *V. c. cassinii*	S British Columbia to n Baja; winters to Guatemala
_____ *V. c. lucasanas*	Mountains of s Baja California (Sierra de la Laguna)

☐ **Blue-headed Vireo** *Vireo solitarius*

    ____ *V. s. solitarius*   NE British Columbia to e US; winters to Cuba and Costa Rica

    ____ *V. s. alticola*   S Appalachian Mountains to se US; winters to s Florida

☐ **Yellow-winged Vireo** *Vireo carmioli*

    Montane forests of Costa Rica and w Panama (w Chiriquí)

☐ **Hutton's Vireo** *Vireo huttoni*

    ____ *V. h. insularis*   Vancouver I. (British Columbia)

    ____ *V. h. huttoni (mailliardorum)*   SW British Columbia (west of Cascades and Sierras) to n Baja

    ____ *V. h. obscurus*   Inner coast ranges of California (south to Lake County)

    ____ *V. h. parkesi*   Coastal California (Humboldt County to Marin County)

    ____ *V. h. sierrae*   Sierra Nevada of California

    ____ *V. h. unitti*   Santa Catalina I. (off s California)

    ____ *V. h. oberholseri*   Inner Coast Ranges of California (Monterey Co. to s California)

    ____ *V. h. cognatus*   Mountains of s Baja California (Sierra de la Laguna)

    ____ *V. h. stephensi*   Mts. of se Arizona and New Mexico to nw Mexico (Sinaloa)

    ____ *V. h. carolinae*   Chisos Mountains (Texas) to ne Mexico (sw Tamaulipas)

    ____ *V. h. pacificus*   Coastal mountains of w Mexico (Nayarit to sw Oaxaca)

    ____ *V. h. mexicanus*   Oak-pine forests of Mexican plateau

    ____ *V. h. vulcani*   Mountains of s Mexico (Chiapas) and w Guatemala

☐ **Warbling Vireo** *Vireo gilvus*

    ____ *V. g. swainsonii*   SE Alaska to nw Baja; winters to El Salvador

    ____ *V. g. victoriae*   Mountains of s Baja California (Sierra de la Laguna)

    ____ *V. g. leucopolius*   Great Basin of e Washington to se California and sw Utah

    ____ *V. g. gilvus*   SW Canada to e-central US; winters to ne Costa Rica

    ____ *V. g. brewsteri*   Sierra Madre Occidental of nw Mexico (s Sonora to Nayarit)

    ____ *V. g. eleanorae*   Sierra Madre Oriental of ne Mexico (s Tamaulipas to Hidalgo)

    ____ *V. g. bulli*   Mountains of se Mexico (Oaxaca)

    ____ *V. g. amauronotus*   Mountains of e central Mexico (Puebla and Veracruz)

    ____ *V. g. connectens*   Mountains of s-central Mexico (Michoacán to Oaxaca)

    ____ *V. g. strenuus*   Subtropical s Mexico (Chiapas) to Guatemala and Honduras

☐ **Brown-capped Vireo** *Vireo leucophrys*

    ____ *V. l. leucophrys*   Highlands of e Mexico (San Luis Potosí) to Nicaragua

    ____ *V. l. chiriquensis*   Subtropical Costa Rica and extreme w Panama

    ____ *V. l. disjunctus*   Subtropical Central and (?) Western Andes of Colombia

    ____ *V. l. mirandae*   Santa Marta Mts. (ne Colombia) and mts. of nw Venezuela

    ____ *V. l. dissors*   Western and Central Andes of Colombia

    ____ *V. l. josephae*   Central Andes of sw Colombia (Nariño) and w Ecuador

    ____ *V. l. maranonicus*   Western Andes of n Peru

    ____ *V. l. laetissimus*   Subtropical se Peru and n Bolivia (La Paz and Cochabamba)

☐ **Philadelphia Vireo** *Vireo philadelphicus*

    Breeds e North America; winters to n Colombia

☐ **Red-eyed Vireo** *Vireo olivaceus*

    ____ *V. o. olivaceus*   Canada, w-central and e US; winters to Cuba and c S America

    ____ *V. o. forreri*   W Mexico (Sonora to Jalisco) and Tres Marías Islands

    ____ *V. o. insulanus*   Pearl Islands (Gulf of Panama); winters to upper Amazonia

    ____ *V. o. caucae*   Tropical w Colombia

    ____ *V. o. griseobarbatus*   Tropical w Ecuador and nw Peru

    ____ *V. o. pectoralis*   N Peru (middle Marañón Valley)

    ____ *V. o. solimoensis*   W Amazonian Brazil to e Ecuador and ne Peru

    ____ *V. o. vividior*   Colombia to Venezuela, the Guianas and n Brazil; Trinidad

    ____ *V. o. tobagensis*   Tobago

    ____ *V. o. agilis*   Coastal ne Brazil (Pará to Rio de Janeiro)

    ____ *V. o. diversus*   SE Brazil (São Paulo) to Uruguay, Paraguay and ne Argentina

    ____ *V. o. chivi*   W Amazonian basin; winters north to Colombia and Venezuela

☐ **Choco Vireo** *Vireo masteri*

Rainforests of Pacific slope of Western Andes of Colombia

☐ **Golden Vireo** *Vireo hypochryseus*
_____ *V. h. nitidus* — Lowlands of w Mexico (extreme s Sonora)
_____ *V. h. hypochryseus* — Tropical w Mexico (Sinaloa and w Durango to w Oaxaca)
_____ *V. h. sordidus* — Tres Marías Islands (off w Mexico)

☐ **Yellow-green Vireo** *Vireo flavoviridis*

S Texas to Panama; winters to w Brazil and n Bolivia

☐ **Noronha Vireo** *Vireo gracilirostris*

Ilha Fernando de Noronha (off coastal ne Brazil)

☐ **Black-whiskered Vireo** *Vireo altiloquus*
_____ *V. a. barbatulus* — Coastal s Florida, Cuba and Haiti; winters to Peru and Brazil
_____ *V. a. altiloquus* — Greater Antilles; winters to n South America
_____ *V. a. barbadensis* — St. Croix and Barbados
_____ *V. a. bonairensis* — Netherlands Antilles (Aruba, Curaçao and Bonaire); Margarita I.
_____ *V. a. grandior* — Isla Providéncia and Isla Santa Catalina (w Caribbean Sea)
_____ *V. a. canescens* — Isla San Andrés (w Caribbean Sea)

☐ **Yucatan Vireo** *Vireo magister*
_____ *V. m. magister* — Yucatán Pen., Belize, Cozumel, Isla Mujeres and adj. islands
_____ *V. m. caymanensis* — Grand Cayman I.

☐ **Rufous-crowned Greenlet** *Hylophilus poicilotis*

N Bolivia to e Paraguay, ne Argentina and s Brazil

☐ **Gray-eyed Greenlet** *Hylophilus amaurocephalus*

Lowlands of e Brazil (Piauí and Ceará to extreme n São Paulo)

☐ **Lemon-chested Greenlet** *Hylophilus thoracicus*
_____ *H. t. aemulus* — E slope of Andes of Colombia to se Peru and n Bolivia
_____ *H. t. griseiventris* — E Venezuela (Bolívar) to the Guianas and n Brazil
_____ *H. t. thoracicus* — SE Brazil (Minas Gerais and Espírito Santo to Rio de Janeiro)

☐ **Gray-chested Greenlet** *Hylophilus semicinereus*
_____ *H. s. viridiceps* — S Venezuela (Amazonas and Bolívar), the Guianas and n Brazil
_____ *H. s. semicinereus* — N Brazil south of lower Amazon (Maranhão to n Mato Grosso)
_____ *H. s. juruanus* — NW Brazil (south of Rio Solimões)

☐ **Ashy-headed Greenlet** *Hylophilus pectoralis*

Guianas and e Venezuela to n Bolivia and Amazonian Brazil

☐ **Tepui Greenlet** *Hylophilus sclateri*

Tepuis of s Venezuela, w Guyana and extreme n Brazil

☐ **Buff-cheeked Greenlet** *Hylophilus muscicapinus*
_____ *H. m. muscicapinus* — S Venezuela to the Guianas and Brazil north of the Amazon
_____ *H. m. griseifrons* — N Brazil south of the Amazon (Rio Madeira to Rio Tapajós)

☐ **Brown-headed Greenlet** *Hylophilus brunneiceps*
_____ *H. b. brunneiceps* — E Colombia to s Venezuela and nw Brazil
_____ *H. b. inornatus* — N Brazil south of the Amazon (Rio Tapajós to Rio Tocantins)

☐ **Dusky-capped Greenlet** *Hylophilus hypoxanthus*
_____ *H. h. hypoxanthus* — SE Colombia to extreme sw Venezuela and extreme nw Brazil
_____ *H. h. fuscicapillus* — E Ecuador and n Peru (south to Río Marañón)
_____ *H. h. flaviventris* — Tropical central Peru (San Martín to Ayacucho)
_____ *H. h. ictericus* — W Brazil, extreme se Peru (Puno) and n Bolivia
_____ *H. h. albigula* — N Brazil south of the Amazon (Rio Purús to Rio Xingú)

☐ **Rufous-naped Greenlet** *Hylophilus semibrunneus*

Andes of Colombia to extreme nw Venezuela and e Ecuador

☐ **Olivaceous Greenlet** *Hylophilus olivaceus*

Subtropical Andes of e Ecuador to central Peru (Junín)

☐ **Scrub Greenlet** *Hylophilus flavipes*

____	*H. f. viridiflavus*	Tropical sw Costa Rica and w Panama
____	*H. f. xuthus*	Isla Coiba (Panama)
____	*H. f. flavipes*	Caribbean coast of n Colombia and Magdalena Valley
____	*H. f. melleus*	N Colombia (e tip of Guajira Peninsula)
____	*H. f. galbanus*	Tropical ne Colombia and nw Venezuela
____	*H. f. acuticauda*	Tropical n Venezuela and Isla Margarita
____	*H. f. insularis*	Tobago

☐ **Tawny-crowned Greenlet** *Hylophilus ochraceiceps*

____	*H. o. ochraceiceps*	Gulf lowlands of s Mexico to Guatemala
____	*H. o. pallidipectus*	Tropical Honduras to w Panama
____	*H. o. nelsoni*	E Panama (Veraguas to Darién)
____	*H. o. bulunensis*	Extreme e Panama to Pacific coast of Colombia and w Ecuador
____	*H. o. ferrugineifrons*	SE Colombia to the Guianas, e Peru and nw Amazonian Brazil
____	*H. o. viridior*	Tropical s Peru (Ayacucho and Cuzco) to n Bolivia
____	*H. o. luteifrons*	Extreme e Venezuela, the Guianas and n Amazonian Brazil
____	*H. o. lutescens*	N Brazil south of the Amazon (Rio Madeira to Rio Xingú)
____	*H. o. rubrifrons*	NE Brazil (Rio Tocantins to Pará)

☐ **Golden-fronted Greenlet** *Hylophilus aurantiifrons*

____	*H. a. aurantiifrons*	E Panama and Caribbean coast of n Colombia
____	*H. a. helvinus*	Tropical nw Venezuela (Zulia to n Mérida and s Táchira)
____	*H. a. saturatus*	Tropical e Colombia to n Venezuela; Trinidad

☐ **Lesser Greenlet** *Hylophilus decurtatus*

____	*H. d. decurtatus*	E Mexico (San Luis Potosí) to Panama (Canal Zone)
____	*H. d. dariensis*	Tropical e Panama and n Colombia
____	*H. d. minor*	Trop. sw Colombia (Nariño) to w Ecuador and extreme n Peru

☐ **Chestnut-sided Shrike-Vireo** *Vireolanius melitophrys*

____	*V. m. goldmani*	Oak forests of s central Mexico
____	*V. m. melitophrys*	S Mexico (se Chiapas) to s Guatemala

☐ **Green Shrike-Vireo** *Vireolanius pulchellus*

____	*V. p. pulchellus*	Gulf-Caribbean lowlands of se Mexico to Honduras
____	*V. p. verticalis*	Caribbean slope of Nicaragua and Costa Rica
____	*V. p. viridiceps*	Pacific slope of Costa Rica and w Panama

☐ **Yellow-browed Shrike-Vireo** *Vireolanius eximius*

____	*V. e. mutabilis*	Extreme e Panama (Darién) and nw Colombia
____	*V. e. eximius*	Tropical n Colombia and nw Venezuela (Zulia and Táchira)

☐ **Slaty-capped Shrike-Vireo** *Vireolanius leucotis*

____	*V. l. mikettae*	W slope of Western Andes of Colombia and nw Ecuador
____	*V. l. leucotis*	SE Colombia to e Ecuador, n Peru, the Guianas and nw Brazil
____	*V. l. simplex*	Brazil (south of the Amazon) to s Peru (Huánuco to n Cuzco)
____	*V. l. bolivianus*	SE Peru (Cuzco) to n Bolivia

☐ **Rufous-browed Peppershrike** *Cyclarhis gujanensis*

____	*C. g. flaviventris*	E Mexico (San Luis Potosí) to e Guatemala and n Honduras
____	*C. g. yucatanensis*	SE Mexico (Yucatán Peninsula) and Petén of n Guatemala
____	*C. g. insularis*	Cozumel I. (se Mexico off Quintana Roo)
____	*C. g. nicaraguae*	S Mexico (Chiapas) and Guatemala to Nicaragua
____	*C. g. subflavescens*	Pacific slope of Costa Rica and w Panama
____	*C. g. perrygoi*	W central Panama (Coclé to extreme e Veraguas)
____	*C. g. flavens*	Coastal e Panama
____	*C. g. coibae*	Isla Coiba (Panama)
____	*C. g. canticus*	Tropical Caribbean coast of n Colombia and Magdalena Valley

_____	Cyclarhis gujanensis flavipectus	NE Venezuela (Paría Peninsula) and Trinidad
_____	C. g. parvus	E slope of Eastern Andes of Colombia and n Venezuela
_____	C. g. gujanensis	E Colombia to the Guianas, Amaz. Brazil, e Peru and ne Bolivia
_____	C. g. cearensis	Tableland of e Brazil
_____	C. g. ochrocephala	SE Brazil to Uruguay, e Paraguay and ne Argentina
_____	C. g. viridis	_Chaco_ of Paraguay and n Argentina
_____	C. g. virenticeps	Pacific slope of Ecuador and nw Peru
_____	C. g. contrerasi	Mountains of n Peru (south to La Libertad and San Martín)
_____	C. g. saturatus	N Peru (upper Río Marañón Valley east of Western Andes)
_____	C. g. pax	_Yungas_ of Bolivia (La Paz)
_____	C. g. dorsalis	Highlands of central Bolivia
_____	C. g. tarijae	Extreme se Bolivia (Tarija) and nw Argentina (Jujuy)

☐ **Black-billed Peppershrike** _Cyclarhis nigrirostris_

_____	C. n. nigrirostris	Andes of central Colombia and e Ecuador
_____	C. n. atrirostris	Andes of sw Colombia (Nariño) and w Ecuador

---

FAMILY: FRINGILLIDAE (Siskins, Crossbills and Allies—134)

☐ **Chaffinch** _Fringilla coelebs_

_____	F. c. morelitti	Azores
_____	F. c. maderensis	Madeira
_____	F. c. canariensis	Canary Islands (Gran Canaria, Gomera and Tenerife)
_____	F. c. ombriosa	Hierro (Canary Islands)
_____	F. c. palmae	La Palma (Canary Islands)
_____	F. c. africana	NW Africa (Morocco to w Tunisia)
_____	F. c. spodiogenys	E Tunisia
_____	F. c. coelebs	Continental Europe to Siberia and Asia Minor; winters to Africa
_____	F. c. gengleri	British Isles, Orkneys and Outer Hebrides
_____	F. c. sarda	Sardinia
_____	F. c. schiebeli	Crete
_____	F. c. solomkoi	Crimean Peninsula and Caucasus
_____	F. c. alexandrovi	N Iran
_____	F. c. transcaspica	NE Iran (s Transcaspia in Kopet Dagh and Khorasan)

☐ **Blue Chaffinch** _Fringilla teydea_

_____	F. t. teydea	Tenerife (Canary Islands)
_____	F. t. polatzeki	Gran Canaria (Canary Islands)

☐ **Brambling** _Fringilla montifringilla_

N Eurasia; winters Mediterranean region and s Asia

☐ **Sao Tome Grosbeak** _Neospiza concolor_

São Tomé (rediscovered in 1996 after 101-year absence)

☐ **Oriole Finch** _Linurgus olivaceus_

_____	L. o. olivaceus	Mountains of se Nigeria and Cameroon; Bioko
_____	L. o. prigoginei	Montane forests of e Zaire
_____	L. o. elgonensis	SE Sudan (Imatog Mountains) to Kenya highlands
_____	L. o. kilimensis	Highlands of Tanzania to n Malawi

☐ **Golden-winged Grosbeak** _Rhynchostruthus socotranus_

_____	R. s. louisae	N Somalia
_____	R. s. percivali	Mountains of sw Arabia
_____	R. s. socotranus	Socotra (off Somalia)

☐ **Plain Mountain-Finch** _Leucosticte nemoricola_

_____	L. n. altaica	Mts. of ne Afghanistan to sw China (w Xinjiang) and Altai Mts.
_____	L. n. nemoricola	Himalayas (Nepal to w China); winters to n Myanmar

☐ **Black-headed Mountain-Finch** *Leucosticte brandti*
_____ *L. b. margaritacea* — High barren plains of w Mongolia and se Altai
_____ *L. b. brandti* — W Tien Shan Mts. to Kyrgystan and w China (w Xinjiang)
_____ *L. b. pamirensis* — S Kyrgystan to Pamir Mountains and ne Afghanistan
_____ *L. b. haematopygia (audreyana, walteri, intermedia)* — N Pakistan to Kashmir, Ladakhh, n Punjab, Tibet and w China
_____ *L. b. pallidior* — Mountains of w China (sw Xinjiang to ne Qinghai)

☐ **Tawny-headed Mountain-Finch** *Leucosticte sillemi*

Mountains of western Tibet

☐ **Asian Rosy-Finch** *Leucosticte arctoa*
_____ *L. a. arctoa* — Russian Altai
_____ *L. a. cognata* — Sayan Mts. and adjacent mountains on Russia/Mongolia border
_____ *L. a. sushkini* — N Mongolia (Khangai region)
_____ *L. a. gigliolii* — Mountains north of Lake Baikal (east to Yablonovy Mts.)
_____ *L. a. brunneonucha* — Mts. of e Siberia (Lena River to Kamchatka and Kuril Islands)
_____ *L. a. griseonucha* — Komandorskiye, Aleutian and Kodiak islands to Alaska
_____ *L. a. umbrina* — St. Matthew I. and Pribilof Islands (Bering Sea)
_____ *L. a. irvingi* — Brooks Range (n Alaska)
_____ *L. a. littoralis* — Central Alaska to sw Yukon, w Canada and nw US

☐ **Gray-crowned Rosy-Finch** *Leucosticte tephrocotis*
_____ *L. t. tephrocotis* — Mts. of Yukon and w Alberta to se Br. Columbia and nw Montana
_____ *L. t. wallowa* — Wallowa Mountains (ne Oregon); winters to w-central Nevada
_____ *L. t. dawsoni* — E California (Sierra Nevada, White and Inyo mountains)

☐ **Black Rosy-Finch** *Leucosticte atrata*

Mts. of Idaho and Montana to Nevada and Utah; winters to Arizona

☐ **Brown-capped Rosy-Finch** *Leucosticte australis*

Mountains of se Wyoming, Colorado and n-central New Mexico

☐ **Pine Grosbeak** *Pinicola enucleator*
_____ *P. e. enucleator* — N Scandinavia to Russia and w Siberia (Yenisey River)
_____ *P. e. pacatus* — Siberia (e of Yenisey R.) to Altai Mts., Mongolia and Manchuria
_____ *P. e. kamschatkensis* — W Siberia (Anadyr River) to Kamchatka Peninsula
_____ *P. e. sakhalinensis* — Sakhalin, Kuril Islands and high mountains of Hokkaido
_____ *P. e. alascensis* — NW Alaska to nw Mackenzie and ne Br. Col.; winters to nw US
_____ *P. e. flammulus* — S Alaska to nw British Columbia; winters to nw US
_____ *P. e. carlottae* — Islands and coasts from Queen Charlotte Islands to Vancouver I.
_____ *P. e. montanus* — Interior central British Columbia to Rocky Mountains of sw US
_____ *P. e. californicus* — Sierra Nevada Mountains (e California)
_____ *P. e. leucurus* — Central and e Canada; winters to ne US
_____ *P. e. eschatosus* — Central Quebec and Newfoundland to New England states

☐ **Crimson-browed Finch** *Pinicola subhimachalus*

Mountains of Nepal to se Tibet, sw China and ne Myanmar

☐ **Blanford's Rosefinch** *Carpodacus rubescens*

Coniferous forests of Nepal to se Tibet and sw China

☐ **Dark-breasted Rosefinch** *Carpodacus nipalensis*
_____ *C. n. kangrae* — W Himalayas (Kashmir to Garhwal)
_____ *C. n. nipalensis* — Himalayas (Kumaon to Nepal, Sikkim, Bhutan and se Tibet)
_____ *C. n. intensicolor* — Mts. of sw China to s Tibet and n Vietnam; winters to s Myanmar

☐ **Common Rosefinch** *Carpodacus erythrinus*
_____ *C. e. erythrinus* — E Europe to w Asia; winters to India and Indochina
_____ *C. e. grebnitskii* — E Siberia to Bering Sea and Sea of Okhotsk; winters to se China
_____ *C. e. kubanensis* — Caucasus to nw Iran; winters to sw Iran
_____ *C. e. ferghanensis* — Mts. of ne Iran to n Afghanistan, Pakistan, and w Himalayas
_____ *C. e. roseatus* — E Himalayas to Tibet and China; winters to s India and Indochina

☐ **Cassin's Finch** *Carpodacus cassinii*

Mountains of sw Canada to central Mexico and s Baja California

☐ **Purple Finch** *Carpodacus purpureus*

____	*C. p. purpureus*	E-central Canada to ne US; winters to Florida and Texas
____	*C. p. californicus*	SW British Columbia to sw US and n Baja California

☐ **House Finch** *Carpodacus mexicanus*

____	*C. m. frontalis*	SW Canada to w US, Baja California and nw Mexico
____	*C. m. clementis*	Channel Is. (off s California) and Los Coronados Is. (off n Baja)
____	*C. m. mcgregori†*	Formerly San Benito and Cedros is. (off Baja California). Extinct
____	*C. m. amplus*	Guadalupe I. (off Baja California)
____	*C. m. ruberrimus*	S Baja Calif. and nw Mexico (Sonora, s Sinaloa and sw Chihuahua)
____	*C. m. rhodopnus*	Arid tropical central Sinaloa
____	*C. m. coccineus*	Mts. of sw Mexico (s Nayarit and w Zacatecas to w Michoacán)
____	*C. m. potosinus*	S Texas (Rio Grande Valley) to Chihuahua and sw Tamaulipas
____	*C. m. centralis*	Central Mexican plateau (Guanajuato, Querétaro and adj. states)
____	*C. m. mexicanus*	S central Mexican plateau (e Michoacán to Hidalgo and Oaxaca)
____	*C. m. griscomi*	SW Mexico (Sierra Madre del Sur of Guerrero)

☐ **Beautiful Rosefinch** *Carpodacus pulcherrimus*

____	*C. p. pulcherrimus*	Himalayas (Himachal Pradesh to Nepal, Bhutan and se Tibet)
____	*C. p. waltoni*	SE Tibet to sw China (sw Xinjiang)
____	*C. p. argyrophrys*	W China (Xinjiang, Qinghai, Gansu and w Sichuan)
____	*C. p. davidianus*	Central Mongolia (south to sw Inner Mongolia)

☐ **Pink-rumped Rosefinch** *Carpodacus eos*

Alpine scrub and forests of central China and Tibet

☐ **Pink-browed Rosefinch** *Carpodacus rhodochrous*

Himalayan fir and birch forests from Kashmir to s Tibet

☐ **Vinaceous Rosefinch** *Carpodacus vinaceus*

____	*C. v. vinaceus*	W China (s Gansu and n Shaanxi to Sichuan); winters to Myanmar
____	*C. v. formosanus*	Mountains of Taiwan

☐ **Dark-rumped Rosefinch** *Carpodacus edwardsii*

____	*C. e. edwardsii*	W China (se Tibet to w Sichuan and s Gansu)
____	*C. e. rubicunda*	Himalayas (Nepal to se Tibet and sw China); winters to Myanmar

☐ **Pale Rosefinch** *Carpodacus synoicus*

____	*C. s. synoicus*	Sinai Peninsula
____	*C. s. salimalii*	NE Afghanistan
____	*C. s. stoliczkae*	SW China (sw Xinjiang)
____	*C. s. beicki*	W China (Sining Ho region of ne Qinghai to nw Gansu)

☐ **Pallas' Rosefinch** *Carpodacus roseus*

____	*C. r. roseus*	Siberia and n Mongolia; winters to n China and Japan
____	*C. r. portenko*	Sakhalin; winters to s Korea and n Japan

☐ **Three-banded Rosefinch** *Carpodacus trifasciatus*

Coniferous forests of w China; winters to se Tibet

☐ **Spot-winged Rosefinch** *Carpodacus rhodopeplus*

____	*C. r. rhodopeplus*	Himalayas (Garhwal to Nepal and Sikkim)
____	*C. r. verreauxii*	SW China (extreme se Tibet to n Yunnan); winters to n Myanmar

☐ **White-browed Rosefinch** *Carpodacus thura*

____	*C. t. blythi*	NE Afghanistan and Pakistan through w Himalayas to Kumaon
____	*C. t. thura*	Central Himalayas (Nepal to Bhutan)
____	*C. t. femininus*	SE Tibet to sw China (w Sichuan and n Yunnan)
____	*C. t. dubius*	W China (se Qinghai to se Gansu, s Ningxia and n Sichuan)
____	*C. t. deserticolor*	W China (ne Qinghai)

☐ **Tibetan Rosefinch** *Carpodacus roborowskii*

Mountains of w-central China (central Qinghai)

□ **Red-mantled Rosefinch** *Carpodacus rhodochlamys*

_____ C. r. rhodochlamys — Mts. of extreme e Uzbekistan to sw China, Altai and n Mongolia
_____ C. r. kotschubeii — Alai Mountains (Kyrgyzstan) to Pamirs and Tajikistan
_____ C. r. grandis — Mountains of nw Afghanistan, Pakistan, Ladakh and Kumaon

□ **Streaked Rosefinch** *Carpodacus rubicilloides*

_____ C. r. lucifer — Mts. of Ladakh and se Kashmir to Nepal, Sikkim and sw Tibet
_____ C. r. rubicilloides — W China (Qinghai and Gansu) to se Tibet

□ **Great Rosefinch** *Carpodacus rubicilla*

_____ C. r. rubicilla — Caucasus; winters to Transcaucasus
_____ C. r. diabolica — NE Afghanistan (Sanglech region)
_____ C. r. kobdensis — Alai Mountains of w Mongolia to e and central Altai Mountains
_____ C. r. severtzowi — Kashmir to Nepal, Tibet and sw China

□ **Red-fronted Rosefinch** *Carpodacus puniceus*

_____ C. p. kilianensis — Mts. of Kyrgystan and Tajikistan to sw Xinjiang and ne Ladakh
_____ C. p. humii — W Himalayas (Pakistan to Kumaon)
_____ C. p. puniceus — Central Himalayas (Nepal to se Tibet)
_____ C. p. sikangensis — SW China (Minya Konka to Mula region of extreme w Sichuan)
_____ C. p. longirostris — W China (e Qinghai to Gansu and nw Sichuan)

□ **Parrot Crossbill** *Loxia pytyopsittacus*

Coniferous forests of ne Europe to w Siberia

□ **Scottish Crossbill** *Loxia scotica*

Pine forests of n Scotland

□ **Red Crossbill** *Loxia curvirostra*

_____ L. c. curvirostra — Coniferous forests of n Europe to e Siberia and n Mongolia
_____ L. c. corsicana — Coniferous forests of Corsica
_____ L. c. balearica — Balearic Islands
_____ L. c. poliogyna — Algeria and Tunisia
_____ L. c. guillemardi — Troödos Mountains (Cyprus)
_____ L. c. mariae — SW Crimean Peninsula
_____ L. c. altaiensis — Altai Mountains
_____ L. c. tianschanica — Tien Shan Mountains (Kazakstan)
_____ L. c. himalayensis — Himalayas (Kashmir to Nepal, Sikkim, sw China and sw Tibet)
_____ L. c. meridionalis — Mountains of s Vietnam (Da Lat Plateau)
_____ L. c. japonica — Extreme ne Asia; winters to e-cent. China and s Japanese islands
_____ L. c. luzoniensis — N Philippines (mountains of n Luzon)
_____ L. c. bendirei (neogaea) — S Yukon and n Br. Col. to w US e of Cascades; winters to Baja
_____ L. c. sitkensis — Coastal s Alaska to nw California; winters to ne US
_____ L. c. benti — Mts. of se Montana and ne Wyoming to sw US; winters to s Texas
_____ L. c. minor — S-central Canada and n-central US; winters to se US
_____ L. c. grinnelli — Mountains of sw US
_____ L. c. stricklandi — Mts. of n Baja California, s Arizona and s New Mexico to Chiapas
_____ L. c. mesamericana — Montane pine forests from Guatemala to n Nicaragua
_____ L. c. pusilla — Newfoundland; winters to ne US

□ **White-winged Crossbill** *Loxia leucoptera*

_____ L. l. bifasciata — Coniferous forests of n Eurasia
_____ L. l. leucoptera — N-central Alaska to Newfoundland, Canada and n US
_____ L. l. megaplaga — Cordillera Central of Dominican Republic and adjacent Haiti

□ **Yellow-breasted Greenfinch** *Carduelis spinoides*

_____ C. s. spinoides — Pakistan to se Tibet, sw China, n India, Nepal, Sikkim and Bhutan
_____ C. s. heinrichi — NE India (se Assam and Manipur) to w Myanmar (Mt. Victoria)
_____ C. s. monguilloti — S Vietnam (Langbian Plateau)

□ **Vietnamese Greenfinch** *Carduelis monguilloti*

S Vietnam (Langbian Plateau)

☐ **European Greenfinch** *Carduelis chloris*
- ____ C. c. chloris — British Isles, n Europe, Corsica and Sardinia; winters to s Europe
- ____ C. c. aurantiiventris — S Europe and North Africa
- ____ C. c. chlorotica — Syria, Lebanon, Israel and Jordan; winters to Sinai Pen. and Egypt
- ____ C. c. turkestanica — Crimea to Caucasus, n Iran and Turkmenistan; winters to s Iran

☐ **Black-headed Greenfinch** *Carduelis ambigua*
- ____ C. a. taylori — Mountains of se Tibet and extreme w Sichuan
- ____ C. a. ambigua — Mts. of se Tibet to sw China, n Myanmar, n Laos and nw Tonkin

☐ **Common Redpoll** *Carduelis flammea*
- ____ C. f. flammea — N Eurasia and n North America
- ____ C. f. rostrata — N Labrador, Baffin I. and s Greenland; winters to ne US, Br. Isles
- ____ C. f. islandica — Iceland
- ____ C. f. cabaret — British Isles, Alps and mountains of Czechoslovakia

☐ **Hoary Redpoll** *Carduelis hornemanni*
- ____ C. h. exilipes — Tundra of n Eurasia and n North America
- ____ C. h. hornemanni — Ellesmere I., Baffin I. and n Greenland; winters to n US, Br. Isles

☐ **Eurasian Siskin** *Carduelis spinus*

N Palearctic; winters Mediterranean region, China and Ryukyu Is.

☐ **Pine Siskin** *Carduelis pinus*
- ____ C. p. pinus — Coniferous forests of s Alaska to US; winters to central Mexico
- ____ C. p. macroptera — Coniferous forests of n Baja California, nw and central Mexico
- ____ C. p. perplexa — Mountains of s Mexico (Chiapas) to sw Guatemala

☐ **Black-capped Siskin** *Carduelis atriceps*

Coniferous forests of s Mexico (Chiapas) and w Guatemala

☐ **Black-headed Siskin** *Carduelis notata*
- ____ C. n. notata — Oak-pine forests of e Mexico (San Luis Potosí) to n Guatemala
- ____ C. n. forreri — Oak-pine belt of w Mexico (s Sonora and Chihuahua to Guerrero)
- ____ C. n. oleacea — Coniferous forests of Belize to Honduras and n Nicaragua

☐ **Andean Siskin** *Carduelis spinescens*
- ____ C. s. spinescens (capitanea) — Andes of Colombia to Venezuela and extreme nw Ecuador
- ____ C. s. nigricauda — Temperate Central and Western Andes of n Colombia

☐ **Yellow-faced Siskin** *Carduelis yarrellii*

N Venezuela; interior ne Brazil (Ceará to Bahia)

☐ **Thick-billed Siskin** *Carduelis crassirostris*
- ____ C. c. amadoni — Andes of se Peru (Tacna and Puno)
- ____ C. c. crassirostris — Andes of s Bolivia to central Chile and nw Argentina

☐ **Hooded Siskin** *Carduelis magellanica*
- ____ C. m. capitalis — Mountains of extreme s Colombia to Ecuador and nw Peru
- ____ C. m. longirostris — SE Venezuela to Guyana and n Brazil
- ____ C. m. paula — Tropical and subtrop. s Ecuador and w Peru (south to Arequipa)
- ____ C. m. peruana — Trop. and subtrop. central Peru (Huánuco to Ayacucho and Cuzco)
- ____ C. m. urubambensis — Temperate s Peru (Cuzco) to n Chile (Tarapacá)
- ____ C. m. boliviana — Temperate central and s Bolivia
- ____ C. m. tucumana — NW Argentina (Jujuy, Santiago and Santa Fe to Mendoza)
- ____ C. m. santaecrucis — E foothills of Andes of Bolivia (Santa Cruz)
- ____ C. m. alleni — SE Bolivia to Paraguay, ne Argentina and s Brazil
- ____ C. m. icterica — SE Brazil (Minas Gerais) to Paraguay and extreme ne Argentina
- ____ C. m. magellanica — Uruguay and e Argentina (s Corrientes to Río Negro)

☐ **Yellow-bellied Siskin** *Carduelis xanthogastra*
- ____ C. x. xanthogastra — Local in mts. of Costa Rica to Colombia, Ecuador and Venezuela
- ____ C. x. stejnegeri — SE Peru (Puno) and nw Bolivia (La Paz and Santa Cruz)

☐ **Saffron Siskin** *Carduelis siemiradzkii*

Scrub and woodlands of sw Ecuador and Isla Puná

☐ **Olivaceous Siskin** *Carduelis olivacea*

E slope of Andes of se Ecuador to Peru and w Bolivia

☐ **Red Siskin** *Carduelis cucullata*

Locally in ne Colombia and n Venezuela (on verge of extinction)

☐ **Antillean Siskin** *Carduelis dominicensis*

Montane pine forests of Hispaniola

☐ **Lesser Goldfinch** *Carduelis psaltria*

____	*C. p. hesperophilus*	W US to s Baja California and nw Mexico
____	*C. p. witti*	Tres Marías Islands (off w Mexico)
____	*C. p. psaltria*	S-central US to s Mexico (Guerrero, Veracruz and Oaxaca)
____	*C. p. jouyi*	SE Mexico (Yucatán Peninsula and n Quintana Roo)
____	*C. p. columbianus*	S Mexico (Chiapas) to Colombia, Ecuador, Venezuela and n Peru

☐ **Lawrence's Goldfinch** *Carduelis lawrencei*

S California and nw Baja; winters to Texas and n Sonora

☐ **Black-chinned Siskin** *Carduelis barbata*

Central Chile and s Argentina to Tierra del Fuego and Falkland Is.

☐ **Black Siskin** *Carduelis atrata*

Andes of central Peru to n Chile and Argentina

☐ **Yellow-rumped Siskin** *Carduelis uropygialis*

Andes of central Peru to nw Argentina and n Chile

☐ **American Goldfinch** *Carduelis tristis*

____	*C. t. jewetti*	SW British Columbia to sw Oregon (west of the Cascades)
____	*C. t. pallida*	S-cent. Br. Col. to w-cent. US; winters to Puebla and Veracruz
____	*C. t. salicamans*	California (west of Sierra Nevada) to nw Baja California
____	*C. t. tristis*	E Canada to e-central US; winters to se US and e Mexico

☐ **European Goldfinch** *Carduelis carduelis*

____	*C. c. britannica*	British Isles, Channel Islands and w Netherlands
____	*C. c. carduelis*	W and c Europe; winters to Mediterranean and Black Sea
____	*C. c. parva*	Azores, Madeira, Canary Islands and w Mediterranean region
____	*C. c. tschusii*	Corsica, Sardinia and Sicily
____	*C. c. balcanica*	S Yugoslavia to Bulgaria, Greece and Crete
____	*C. c. niediecki*	Rhodes, Karpathos, Cyprus; Egypt to Asia Minor, n Iraq, sw Iran
____	*C. c. brevirostris*	Crimean Peninsula to Caucasus and ne Turkey
____	*C. c. loudoni*	N Iran (Talysh Mountains to Elburz Mountains)
____	*C. c. paropanisi*	Iran to n Afghanistan and w China (Xinjiang)
____	*C. c. major*	SW Siberia (Ural Mountains to Yenisey River)
____	*C. c. subulata*	S-central Siberia to Lake Baikal and nw Mongolia
____	*C. c. caniceps*	W Himalayas (Kashmir to Nepal and w Tibet)

☐ **Oriental Greenfinch** *Carduelis sinica*

____	*C. s. sinica*	W China (Gansu) to s Manchuria
____	*C. s. chabarowi*	Inner Mongolia to n Manchuria
____	*C. s. ussuriensis*	E Manchuria to s Ussuriland and Korea
____	*C. s. kawarahiba*	Kamchatka, Kuril Is., Sakhalin and Hokkaido; winters to Japan
____	*C. s. minor*	S Japan (Honshu, Shikoku and Kyushu) and Korea (Cheju-Do Is.)
____	*C. s. kittlitzi*	S Japan (Bonin Islands and Volcano Islands)

☐ **Twite** *Carduelis flavirostris*

____	*C. f. flavirostris*	Norway, n Sweden, n Finland and Kola Pen.; winters to s Europe
____	*C. f. pipilans*	Shetland Is., Hebrides, Orkneys, Scotland, n England and Ireland
____	*C. f. brevirostris*	E Turkey and Caucasus to nw Iran
____	*C. f. korejevi*	S Ural Mts. to Caspian Sea, Kirghiz steppes and Tien Shan Mts.
____	*C. f. atlaica*	Altai Mountains of central Russia to nw Outer Mongolia
____	*C. f. montanella (korejevi)*	Kyrgyzstan (Alai Mts.) to Pamirs and w China (w Xinjiang)
____	*C. f. miniakensis*	W China (e Xinjiang, Qinghai and Gansu) to se Tibet
____	*C. f. rufostrigata*	Himalayas (n Kashmir to n Nepal and sw Tibet)

☐ **Eurasian Linnet** *Carduelis cannabina*
_____ *C. c. autochthona* — Scotland
_____ *C. c. nana* — Madeira
_____ *C. c. meadewaldoi* — Tenerife (w Canary Islands)
_____ *C. c. harterti* — Lanzarote (e Canary Islands)
_____ *C. c. cannabina* — Europe to w Siberia, Crimean Peninsula and North Africa
_____ *C. c. bella* — Asia Minor to Caucasus, Afghanistan, sw China; winters to India

☐ **Yemen Linnet** *Carduelis yemenensis*
Mountains of sw Arabia

☐ **Warsangli Linnet** *Carduelis johannis*
Montane juniper forests of n Somalia

☐ **Fire-fronted Serin** *Serinus pusillus*
Mountains of Asia Minor to w China; winters to Israel

☐ **European Serin** *Serinus serinus*
Open woodlands of s Palearctic region

☐ **Syrian Serin** *Serinus syriacus*
Mountains of Lebanon and Syria; winters to Turkey and nw Iraq

☐ **Island Canary** *Serinus canaria*
Madeira, Azores and w Canary Islands

☐ **Citril Finch** *Serinus citrinella*
_____ *S. c. citrinella* — Montane coniferous forests of s Europe
_____ *S. c. corsicana* — Corsica and Sardinia

☐ **Tibetan Serin** *Serinus thibetanus*
Coniferous forests of n India to Nepal, e Tibet and sw China

☐ **Cape Canary** *Serinus canicollis*
_____ *S. c. flavivertex* — Highlands of Eritrea, Ethiopia, Kenya and n Tanzania
_____ *S. c. sassii* — SW Uganda; se Zaire to sw Tanzania, ne Zambia and n Malawi
_____ *S. c. huillensis* — Highlands of central Angola (n Huambo, Huila and Bie)
_____ *S. c. griseitergum* — Highlands of e Zimbabwe and adjacent Mozambique
_____ *S. c. thompsonae* — SE Botswana to n Transvaal and e Cape Province
_____ *S. c. canicollis* — South Africa (w Cape Province to Orange Free State)

☐ **Abyssinian Siskin** *Serinus nigriceps*
Alpine moorlands of n and central Ethiopia

☐ **African Citril** *Serinus citrinelloides*
_____ *S. c. cintrinelloides* — Highlands of se Sudan to Eritrea and Ethiopia
_____ *S. c. kikuyensis* — Highlands of w Kenya
_____ *S. c. frontalis* — E Zaire to w Uganda and nw Tanzania
_____ *S. c. hypostictus* — SE Kenya and Tanzania to e Zambia and n Mozambique
_____ *S. c. martinsi* — Angola (Moxico region)

☐ **Black-faced Canary** *Serinus capistratus*
_____ *S. c. capistratus* — Gabon to central Angola, s Zaire and n Zambia
_____ *S. c. hildegardae* — Central Angola

☐ **Papyrus Canary** *Serinus koliensis*
Papyrus swamps of e Zaire, Uganda, Rwanda and w Kenya

☐ **Forest Canary** *Serinus scotops*
_____ *S. s. transvaalensis* — Highland evergreen forests of n and e Transvaal
_____ *S. s. umbrosus* — SE Transvaal to w Zululand, Natal and coastal s Cape Province
_____ *S. s. scotops* — S Natal and e Cape Province

☐ **White-rumped Seedeater** *Serinus leucopygius*
_____ *S. l. riggenbachi* — Senegal to n Nigeria, Chad, Central African Rep. and w Sudan
_____ *S. l. pallens* — S Niger (Aïr Massif)
_____ *S. l. leucopygius* — Nile basin of e Sudan to Eritrea and n Ethiopia

☐ **Olive-rumped Serin** *Serinus rothschildi*

Mountains of sw Arabia

☐ **Yellow-throated Serin** *Serinus flavigula*

Savanna of Ethiopia

☐ **Salvadori's Serin** *Serinus xantholaemus*

Savanna of Ethiopia

☐ **Black-throated Canary** *Serinus atrogularis*

____	*S. a. reichenowi*	SE Sudan to s Ethiopia, Somalia, ne Uganda, Kenya, ne Tanzania
____	*S. a. somereni*	E Zaire to Uganda and w Kenya
____	*S. a. lwenarum (kasaicus)*	Central Angola to se Zaire, s Tanzania and Zambia
____	*S. a. deserti*	S Angola (Benguela and Huila) to nw Namibia
____	*S. a. semideserti*	S Angola to n Namibia, Botswana, s Zambia and nw Transvaal
____	*S. a. atrogularis*	Zimbabwe to w Transvaal and adjacent n Orange Free State
____	*S. a. impiger*	South Africa (se Transvaal to w Natal and ne Cape Province)

☐ **Yellow-rumped Serin** *Serinus xanthopygius*

Savanna of Eritrea and n Ethiopia

☐ **Lemon-breasted Seedeater** *Serinus citrinipectus*

Savanna of s Malawi and e Zimbabwe to ne South Africa

☐ **Yellow-fronted Canary** *Serinus mozambicus*

____	*S. m. caniceps*	Senegal to Ivory Coast, Nigeria and n Cameroon
____	*S. m. punctigula*	Grasslands of Cameroon
____	*S. m. santhome*	São Tomé (Gulf of Guinea)
____	*S. m. tando*	Gabon to n Angola and sw Zaire
____	*S. m. vansoni*	Extreme se Angola and adj. Namibia to n Botswana, sw Zambia
____	*S. m. barbatus*	NE Zaire to w Sudan, Uganda, w Kenya and nw Tanzania
____	*S. m. samaliyae*	SE Zaire to sw Tanzania and adjacent Zambia
____	*S. m. grotei*	S Sudan (east of the Nile) to Eritrea and w Ethiopia
____	*S. m. gommaensis*	W Ethiopia (Lake Tana to Gomma)
____	*S. m. mozambicus*	Coastal Kenya and Mafia I. to Zambia, Mozambique, n Transvaal
____	*S. m. granti*	S Mozambique (s of Limpopo R.) to e Transvaal and e Cape Prov.

☐ **Northern Grosbeak-Canary** *Serinus donaldsoni*

S Ethiopia to n Kenya; isolated population in Taita Hills

☐ **Southern Grosbeak-Canary** *Serinus buchanani*

Savanna of central Kenya to n Tanzania

☐ **White-bellied Canary** *Serinus dorsostriatus*

____	*S. d. maculicollis*	SE Sudan to ne Uganda, Ethiopia, Somalia and n Kenya
____	*S. d. dorsostriatus*	E-cent. Uganda (Busoga) to sw Kenya (Kisumu) and nw Tanzania

☐ **Yellow Canary** *Serinus flaviventris*

____	*S. f. damarensis*	S Angola to Namibia, Botswana, sw Zambia and sw Zimbabwe
____	*S. f. hesperus*	Coastal sw Namibia and w Cape Province
____	*S. f. flaviventris*	Coastal sw Cape Province (Oliphants River to Bredasdorp)
____	*S. f. aurescens*	N Cape Province
____	*S. f. quintoni*	SW Cape Province east to Great Fish River (e Cape Province)
____	*S. f. marshalli*	Interior nw Cape Province to Orange Free State and w Transvaal
____	*S. f. guillarmodi*	Highlands of Lesotho

☐ **Brimstone Canary** *Serinus sulphuratus*

____	*S. s. frommi*	Angola to Zaire, Zambia, sw Tanzania and n Malawi
____	*S. s. shelleyi (loveridgei)*	E Zaire to Uganda, nw Tanzania, se Zambia and n Mozambique
____	*S. s. sharpii*	Highlands of Kenya to n Tanzania
____	*S. s. languens*	Zimbabwe to s Mozambique and e Natal
____	*S. s. wilsoni*	S Mozambique to Transvaal, Natal and adj. e Cape Province
____	*S. s. sulphuratus*	S Cape Province

☐ **Reichard's Seedeater** *Serinus reichardi*

____	*S. r. striatipectus*	Mts. of s Sudan to s Ethiopia and central highlands of Kenya
____	*S. r. reichardi*	SE Zaire to Zambia, Tanzania, Malawi and n Mozambique

☐ **White-throated Canary** *Serinus albogularis*

_____	S. a. crocopygius	SW Angola to n Namibia and adjacent nw Botswana
_____	S. a. sordahlae	S Namibia and nw Cape Province
_____	S. a. albogularis	Extreme w Cape Province (Cape Town to Orange River)
_____	S. a. hewitti	South Africa (central w Cape Province)
_____	S. a. orangensis	South Africa (Orange Free State)

☐ **Streaky-headed Seedeater** *Serinus gularis*

_____	S. g. canicapillus	Guinea to Sierra Leone, sw Mali, s Niger, Nigeria and n Cameroon
_____	S. g. montanorum	Highlands of e Nigeria and n Cameroon
_____	S. g. uamensis	W Central African Republic
_____	S. g. elgonensis	S Sudan to ne Zaire and w Kenya
_____	S. g. benguellensis	Highlands of central Angola to w Zambia
_____	S. g. mendosus	NE Botswana to w Zimbabwe and nw Transvaal
_____	S. g. gularis	E Zimbabwe to Transvaal and n Cape Province
_____	S. g. endemion	S Mozambique to se Transvaal, Natal and e Cape Province
_____	S. g. humilis	SW Cape Province (east to Great Fish River)

☐ **Black-eared Seedeater** *Serinus mennelli*

Brachystegia woodlands of e Angola to Mozambique

☐ **Brown-rumped Seedeater** *Serinus tristriatus*

Juniper woodlands of n Ethiopia and nw Somalia

☐ **Yemen Serin** *Serinus menachensis*

High altitude bushy hills of sw Saudi Arabia

☐ **Ankober Serin** *Serinus ankoberensis*

Montane scrub of central Ethiopia

☐ **Streaky Seedeater** *Serinus striolatus*

_____	S. s. striolatus	Montane forests of s Eritrea to Ethiopia and n Kenya
_____	S. s. affinis	Highlands of s Ethiopia to Kenya and n Tanzania
_____	S. s. graueri	Ruwenzori Mountains and Lendu Plateau to Mt. Kabobo
_____	S. s. whytii	Highlands of s Tanzania to n Malawi (Vipya)

☐ **Thick-billed Seedeater** *Serinus burtoni*

_____	S. b. burtoni	Cameroon (Mt. Cameroon to Bamenda Highlands)
_____	S. b. tanganjicae	Highlands of w-central Angola; e Zaire and adjacent w Uganda
_____	S. b. kilimensis	Montane forests of e Uganda to n Kenya and n Tanzania
_____	S. b. albifrons	Montane forests of e Kenya (east of the Rift Valley)
_____	S. b. melanochrous	Montane forests of s Tanzania

☐ **Principe Seedeater** *Serinus rufobrunneus*

_____	S. r. rufobruneus	Príncipe (Gulf of Guinea)
_____	S. r. thomensis	São Tomé (Gulf of Guinea)

☐ **Protea Canary** *Serinus leucopterus*

Montane *protea* and heath of sw Cape Province (South Africa)

☐ **Cape Siskin** *Serinus totta*

Montane scrub of South Africa (s Cape Province)

☐ **Drakensberg Siskin** *Serinus symonsi*

Montane scrub of w Natal and Lesotho (Drakensberg Mountains)

☐ **Black-headed Canary** *Serinus alario*

_____	S. a. leucolaema	Arid scrub of Namibia to Botswana and w Cape Province
_____	S. a. alario	South Africa (n and central Cape Province and Lesotho)

☐ **Mountain Serin** *Serinus estherae*

_____	S. e. vanderbilti	Mountains of n Sumatra
_____	S. e. estherae	Mountains of w Java
_____	S. e. orientalis	Tengger Mountains (s-central Java)
_____	S. e. renatae	Mountains of Sulawesi
_____	S. e. mindanensis	S Philippines (Mt. Katanglad and Mt. Apo on Mindanao)

☐ **Brown Bullfinch** *Pyrrhula nipalensis*

____	*P. n. nipalensis*	Himalayas (n Pakistan to n India, Nepal and Bhutan)
____	*P. n. ricketti*	SE Tibet to s China, ne India and n Vietnam
____	*P. n. victoriae*	Myanmar (s Chin Hills)
____	*P. n. waterstradti*	Mountains of Malay Peninsula (Perak, Pahang and Selangor)
____	*P. n. uchidae*	Mountains of s Taiwan

☐ **White-cheeked Bullfinch** *Pyrrhula leucogenis*

____	*P. l. leucogenis*	N Philippines (mountains of nw Luzon)
____	*P. l. steerei (coriaria, apo)*	S Philippines (mountains of Mindanao)

☐ **Orange Bullfinch** *Pyrrhula aurantiaca*

Montane forests of n Pakistan to nw India (Himachal Pradesh)

☐ **Red-headed Bullfinch** *Pyrrhula erythrocephala*

Montane forests of n Pakistan, n India and se Tibet

☐ **Gray-headed Bullfinch** *Pyrrhula erythaca*

____	*P. e. erythaca*	Himalayas (Sikkim to Bhutan, se Tibet, w China and n Myanmar)
____	*P. e. wilderi*	NE China (Liaoning)
____	*P. e. owstoni*	Taiwan (Mt. Ari Shan and Mt. Morrison)

☐ **Eurasian Bullfinch** *Pyrrhula pyrrhula*

____	*P. p. pileata*	British Isles
____	*P. p. europoea*	Denmark, w Germany, Netherlands, Belgium and w France
____	*P. p. pyrrhula*	N Europe to w Mongolia; winters to s Europe and Iran
____	*P. p. iberiae*	Mountains of n Portugal to nw Spain (Pyrénées)
____	*P. p. murina*	San Miguel (Azores)
____	*P. p. rossikowi*	W Turkey to Caucasus and extreme ne Iran
____	*P. p. caspica*	NE and n Iran
____	*P. p. cineracea*	Sayan and n Altai Mts.; winters to Amur region and Manchuria
____	*P. p. cassinii*	Kamchatka Pen., Paramushir I. (n Kurils) and Sea of Okhotsk coast
____	*P. p. griseiventris*	E Manchuria to Sakhalin, Kuril Is. and Honshu; winters to Japan

☐ **Hawfinch** *Coccothraustes coccothraustes*

____	*C. c. coccothraustes*	England and n continental Europe to w Asia; winters to N Africa
____	*C. c. burryi*	Mountains of Morocco, Algeria and Tunisia
____	*C. c. nigricans*	Ukraine to Crimean Peninsula, Caspian Sea and n Iran
____	*C. c. humii*	E Kazakstan to Kyrgystan, Tajikistan and w Afghanistan
____	*C. c. japonicus*	Sakhalin, Hokkaido and n Honshu; winters to e China and Bonin Is.

☐ **Evening Grosbeak** *Coccothraustes vespertinus*

____	*C. v. brooksi*	W-central Canada to mountains of w US; winters to Texas
____	*C. v. vespertinus*	E-cent. Canada (Alberta to New England); winters to se US
____	*C. v. montanus*	Mountains of se Arizona to s Mexico (Sierra Madre Occidental)

☐ **Hooded Grosbeak** *Coccothraustes abeillei*

____	*C. a. pallidus*	Sierra Madre Occidental of Mexico (Chihuahua, Sinaloa, Durango)
____	*C. a. saturatus*	Mountains of e Mexico (San Luis Potosí and sw Tamaulipas)
____	*C. a. abeillei*	Mountains of central and s Mexico
____	*C. a. cobanensis*	Highlands of s Mexico (Chiapas) to central Guatemala

☐ **Yellow-billed Grosbeak** *Eophona migratoria*

____	*E. m. migratoria*	E Manchuria to North Korea; winters to e China
____	*E. m. sowerbyi*	E China

☐ **Japanese Grosbeak** *Eophona personata*

____	*E. p. personata*	Japan (Hokkaido to Honshu); winters to s Japan, e China, Taiwan
____	*E. p. magnirostris*	E Manchuria to ne China (Shandong)

☐ **Black-and-yellow Grosbeak** *Mycerobas icterioides*

Montane forests of ne Afghanistan to central Nepal

☐ **Collared Grosbeak** *Mycerobas affinis*

Mountains of n Pakistan to se Tibet, ne Myanmar and c China

☐ **Spot-winged Grosbeak** *Mycerobas melanozanthos*

Mts. of n Pakistan to s Tibet, sw China, Myanmar and Thailand

☐ **White-winged Grosbeak** *Mycerobas carnipes*
____ *M. c. speculigerus* — Mts. of ne Iran and Transcaspia to n Afghanistan and Pakistan
____ *M. c. carnipes* — Montane forests of Turkestan to Pakistan and w China

☐ **Gold-naped Finch** *Pyrrhoplectes epauletta*

Montane forests of n India to sw China, se Tibet and n Myanmar

☐ **Spectacled Finch** *Callacanthis burtoni*

Himalayas (Kashmir to Nepal and Sikkim)

☐ **Crimson-winged Finch** *Rhodopechys sanguinea*
____ *R. s. aliena* — Atlas Mountains of Morocco
____ *R. s. sanguinea* — Mts. of Turkey to Caucasus, Iran, n Afghanistan and nw India

☐ **Trumpeter Finch** *Rhodopechys githaginea*
____ *R. g. amantum* — Canary Islands
____ *R. g. zedlitzi* — Mauritania to Morocco, Tunisia and Algeria
____ *R. g. githaginea* — S Egypt to n Sudan
____ *R. g. crassirostris* — Israel to Arabia, Iraq, Iran, Afghanistan and Pakistan

☐ **Mongolian Finch** *Rhodopechys mongolica*

Sparse montane vegetation of sw and central Asia

☐ **Desert Finch** *Rhodopechys obsoleta*

Locally in mountains of se Turkey to n China and n Pakistan

☐ **Long-tailed Rosefinch** *Uragus sibiricus*
____ *U. s. sibiricus* — S Siberia to n Mongolia and n Manchuria; winters to Turkestan
____ *U. s. ussuriensis* — Central Manchuria to N Korea; winters to ne China and S Korea
____ *U. s. sanguinolentus* — Sakhalin, s Kuril Is. and Hokkaido; winters to s Japanese islands
____ *U. s. lepidus* — W China (se Gansu and s Shaanxi)
____ *U. s. henrici* — Mountains of w China (se Tibet to w Sichuan and n Yunnan)

☐ **Scarlet Finch** *Haematospiza sipahi*

Himalayas (Nepal to sw China, Myanmar, n Laos and n Vietnam)

FAMILY: DREPANIDIDAE (Hawaiian Honeycreepers—23)

☐ **Laysan Finch** *Telespiza cantans*

Laysan I. (w Hawaiian Islands)

☐ **Nihoa Finch** *Telespiza ultima*

Nihoa I. (nw Hawaiian Islands)

☐ **Ou** *Psittirostra psittacea*

Humid montane forests of Hawaiian Islands (Hawaii and Kauai)

☐ **Palila** *Loxioides bailleui*

Montane *mamame-naio* forests of Hawaii

☐ **Maui Parrotbill** *Pseudonestor xanthophrys*

Maui (*Ohia* montane forests on e slopes of Haleakala Crater)

☐ **Hawaii Amakihi** *Hemignathus virens*
____ *H. v. wilsoni* — *Ohia* and *mamani* forests of Maui; formerly Molokai and Lanai
____ *H. v. virens* — *Ohia* and *mamani* forests of Hawaii

☐ **Oahu Amakihi** *Hemignathus flavus*

Humid montane forests of Oahu

☐ **Kauai Amakihi** *Hemignathus kauaiensis*

Humid montane *ohia/koa* forests of Kauai

☐ **Anianiau** *Hemignathus parvus*

Humid montane forests of Kauai

☐ **Greater Akialo** *Hemignathus ellisianus*

Formerly Lanai, Oahu and Kauai. Last recorded ca 1969

☐ **Nukupuu** *Hemignathus lucidus*
____ *H. l. lucidus* — Wet *ohia* forests of Hawaii
____ *H. l. affinis* — Wet *ohia* forests of Maui
____ *H. l. hanapepe* — Wet *ohia* forests of Kauai

☐ **Akiapolaau** *Hemignathus munroi*

Montane *koa* forests of Hawaii

☐ **Akikiki** *Oreomystis bairdi*

Montane *ohia* forests of Kauai

☐ **Hawaii Creeper** *Oreomystis mana*

Mixed *koa/ohia* forests of Hawaii

☐ **Oahu Alauahio** *Paroreomyza maculata*

Humid montane forests of Oahu

☐ **Kakawahie** *Paroreomyza flammea*

Last reported 1963 in montane forests of Molokai

☐ **Maui Alauahio** *Paroreomyza montana*

Humid montane forests of e Maui

☐ **Akekee** *Loxops caeruleirostris*

Kauai (Kokee and Alakai Swamp environs)

☐ **Akepa** *Loxops coccineus*
____ *L. c. coccineus* — Montane *ohia* and *koa* forests of Hawaii
____ *L. c. wolstenholmei†* — Formerly montane *ohia* and *koa* forests on Oahu. Extinct ca 1900
____ *L. c. ochraceus* — Montane *ohia* and *koa* forests of Maui. Probably extinct

☐ **Iiwi** *Vestiaria coccinea*

Ohia and *mamame* forests of main Hawaiian Islands

☐ **Akohekohe** *Palmeria dolei*

Ohia forests of e Maui. Formerly on Molokai

☐ **Apapane** *Himatione sanguinea*

Wet *ohia* forests from Kauai to Hawaii (e Hawaiian Islands)

☐ **Poo-uli** *Melamprosops phaeosoma*

Maui (*Ohia* forests of Haleakala Crater). On verge of extinction

FAMILY: PEUCEDRAMIDAE (Olive Warbler—1)

☐ **Olive Warbler** *Peucedramus taeniatus*
____ *P. t. arizonae* — Mts. of sw US to n Mexico (n Chihuahua and n Coahuila)
____ *P. t. jaliscensis* — Mts. of nw Mexico (s Chihuahua to sw Jalisco and Colima)
____ *P. t. giraudi* — Mts. of central Mexico (Jalisco to n Puebla and w-c Veracruz)
____ *P. t. taeniatus (aurantiacus)* — Mts. of s Mexico (Guerrero, Oaxaca, Chiapas) to w Guatemala
____ *P. t. micrus* — Mts. of El Salvador, Honduras and n Nicaragua

FAMILY: PARULIDAE (New World Warblers—116)

☐ **Bachman's Warbler** *Vermivora bachmanii*

Formerly se US; winters to Cuba and Bahamas (probably extinct)

☐ **Blue-winged Warbler** *Vermivora pinus*

E US; winters se Mexico to Panama

☐ **Golden-winged Warbler** *Vermivora chrysoptera*

E N America; winters Guatemala to nw S Am. and Greater Antilles

☐ **Tennessee Warbler** *Vermivora peregrina*

SE Alaska and s Yukon to n US; winters s Mexico to nw S Am.

☐ **Orange-crowned Warbler** *Vermivora celata*

_____ *V. c. lutescens*	SE Alaska to Br. Columbia and s Calif.; winters to Guatemala
_____ *V. c. celata*	Central Alaska to s Canada; winters to Guatemala and Bahamas
_____ *V. c. orestera*	Rocky Mountains to sw US and w Texas; winters to s Mexico
_____ *V. c. sordida*	Coastal s California and islands off sw California and Baja

☐ **Nashville Warbler** *Vermivora ruficapilla*

_____ *V. r. ridgwayi*	S Br. Col. to California, Nevada and n Utah; winters to Mexico
_____ *V. r. ruficapilla*	S-cent. Canada to e-central US; winters Mexico to central Honduras

☐ **Virginia's Warbler** *Vermivora virginiae*

Mountains of sw US; winters to sw Mexico

☐ **Colima Warbler** *Vermivora crissalis*

W Texas (Chisos Mountains) to central Mexico

☐ **Lucy's Warbler** *Vermivora luciae*

Arid sw US to ne Baja and ne Sonora; winters to sw Mexico

☐ **Flame-throated Warbler** *Parula gutturalis*

Humid montane forests of Costa Rica and w Panama

☐ **Crescent-chested Warbler** *Parula superciliosa*

_____ *P. s. sodalis*	Sierra Madre Occidental of w Mexico
_____ *P. s. mexicana*	Sierra Madre Oriental of e Mexico
_____ *P. s. palliata*	SW Mexico (s Jalisco to w Michoacán and Guerrero)
_____ *P. s. superciliosa*	Highlands of s Mexico (Chiapas) to Guatemala and w Honduras
_____ *P. s. parva*	Highlands of central and e Honduras and Nicaragua

☐ **Northern Parula** *Parula americana*

E N Am. (s Canada to s US); winters to Nicaragua and West Indies

☐ **Tropical Parula** *Parula pitiayumi*

_____ *P. p. graysoni*	Socorro I. (Revillagigedo Islands off s Baja California)
_____ *P. p. insularis*	Tres Marías Islands (off w Mexico) and adjacent Nayarit
_____ *P. p. pulchra*	Sierra Madre Occidental of nw Mexico (Sonora to Jalisco)
_____ *P. p. nigrilora*	S Texas (lower Rio Grande Valley) to e Coahuila and n Veracruz
_____ *P. p. inornata*	S Mexico (s Veracruz) to e Guatemala and n Honduras
_____ *P.p. speciosa*	Tropical s Honduras to Nicaragua, Costa Rica and w Panama
_____ *P. p. cirrha*	Coiba I. (Panama)
_____ *P. p. nana*	E Panama (Darién) to nw Colombia (Córdoba)
_____ *P. p. elegans*	Trop. n Colombia, n Venezuela and n Brazil; Trinidad and Tobago
_____ *P. p. pacifica*	Tropical sw Colombia (Nariño) to w Ecuador and nw Peru
_____ *P. p. roraimae*	*Tepuis* of s Venezuela and adjacent n Brazil
_____ *P. p. alarum*	Subtrop. e Ecuador and n Peru e of the Andes (s to Huánuco)
_____ *P. p. melanogenys*	S Peru (Junín) to w Bolivia (La Paz and Cochabamba)
_____ *P. p. pitiayumi*	E Bolivia to Paraguay, Brazil, Uruguay and n Argentina

☐ **Yellow Warbler** *Dendroica petechia*

_____ *D. p. amnicola*	Alaska, Canada and Newfoundland; winters to n South America
_____ *D. p. rubiginosa*	S Alaska to w British Columbia; winters to s Baja and Panama
_____ *D. p. aestiva*	S-central Canada and central US; winters to South America
_____ *D. p. morcomi (brewsteri, ineditus)*	SE Br. Columbia, w US and n Baja; winters to n South America
_____ *D. p. sonorana*	SW US to nw Mexico; winters to w Panama, Colombia and Ecuador
_____ *D. p. castaneiceps (hueyi)*	Mangroves of coastal s Baja California (south of latitude 27°N)
_____ *D. p. rhizophorae*	Mangroves of nw Mexico (Sonora to Nayarit); winters to Oaxaca
_____ *D. p. dugesi*	Central plateau of Mexico
_____ *D. p. oraria*	Mangroves of e Mexico (s Tamaulipas to w Tabasco)
_____ *D. p. bryanti*	Mangroves of Yucatán Peninsula to Belize and Costa Rica
_____ *D. p. rufivertex*	Cozumel I. (off Quintana Roo)
_____ *D. p. xanthotera*	Pacific coast of w Guatemala to Costa Rica
_____ *D. p. flavida*	Isla San Andrés (w Caribbean Sea)
_____ *D. p. armouri*	Isla Providéncia (w Caribbean Sea)

_____ D. p. eoa	Jamaica and Cayman Islands
_____ D. p. gundlachi	Lower Florida Keys, Cuba, Isle of Pines and Bahamas
_____ D. p. albicollis	Hispaniola, Gonâve and adjacent islands
_____ D. p. cruciana	Puerto Rico and Virgin Islands
_____ D. p. bartholemica	Montserrat and n Lesser Antilles
_____ D. p. melanoptera	Guadeloupe, Dominica and central Lesser Antilles
_____ D. p. ruficapilla	Martinique (Lesser Antilles)
_____ D. p. babad	St. Lucia (Lesser Antilles)
_____ D. p. petechia	Barbados (Lesser Antilles)
_____ D. p. alsiosa	Grenadines (Lesser Antilles)
_____ D. p. rufopileata	Netherlands Antilles (Aruba, Curaçao, Bonaire and adj. islands)
_____ D. p. obscura	Islas Los Roques (off n Venezuela)
_____ D. p. chrysendeta	NE Colombia (Guajira Peninsula) and nw Venezuela (Zulia)
_____ D. p. paraguanae	NW Venezuela (Paraguaná Peninsula of Falcón)
_____ D. p. cienagae	N Venezuela (coastal Carabobo and Aragua) and offshore islands
_____ D. p. aurifrons	Coastal n-c Venezuela, Islas La Tortuga, Tortuguillas and Piritu
_____ D. p. aureola	Cocos I. (off Costa Rica) and Galapagos Islands
_____ D. p. aequatorialis	Pearl Islands and adjacent mainland Panama
_____ D. p. erithachorides	Atlantic coast of Panama and Caribbean coast of n Colombia
_____ D. p. peruviana	Extreme sw Colombia (Nariño) to w Ecuador and n Peru (Lima)

☐ **Chestnut-sided Warbler** _Dendroica pensylvanica_

E N America; winters Guatemala to Panama (casual n S America)

☐ **Magnolia Warbler** _Dendroica magnolia_

E North America; winters to Panama and West Indies

☐ **Cape May Warbler** _Dendroica tigrina_

Canada and ne US; winters mainly West Indies

☐ **Black-throated Blue Warbler** _Dendroica caerulescens_

_____ D. c. caerulescens	SE Canada to ne US; winters to Bahamas and Greater Antilles
_____ D. c. cairnsi	E-central US; winters to Bahamas and Greater Antilles

☐ **Yellow-rumped Warbler** _Dendroica coronata_

_____ D. c. coronata (hooveri)	N Alaska, Canada and n US; winters to Panama and West Indies
_____ D. c. auduboni (memorabilis)	SW Canada and w US; winters to w Honduras
_____ D. c. nigrifrons	Sierra Madre Occidental of w Mexico (Chihuahua to Durango)
_____ D. c. goldmani	High mountains of s Chiapas (Volcán Tacaná) and w Guatemala

☐ **Black-throated Gray Warbler** _Dendroica nigrescens_

_____ D. n. nigrescens	SW Br. Columbia and w US; winters s California to n Guatemala
_____ D. n. halseii	N Baja California, s Arizona, s New Mexico and n Sonora

☐ **Golden-cheeked Warbler** _Dendroica chrysoparia_

Texas (Edwards Plateau); winters to Nicaragua

☐ **Black-throated Green Warbler** _Dendroica virens_

E N America; winters Mexico to n South America and West Indies

☐ **Townsend's Warbler** _Dendroica townsendi_

Coniferous forests of w North America; winters to Costa Rica

☐ **Hermit Warbler** _Dendroica occidentalis_

Mountains of w US; winters to Nicaragua

☐ **Blackburnian Warbler** _Dendroica fusca_

E North America; winters Costa Rica to Bolivia

☐ **Yellow-throated Warbler** _Dendroica dominica_

_____ D. d. albilora	E-central and se US; winters to Costa Rica, Cuba and Jamaica
_____ D. d. dominica	New Jersey to cent. Florida; winters to Bahamas and Gr. Antilles
_____ D. d. stoddardi	Extreme s Alabama and nw Florida
_____ D. d. flavescens	Grand Bahama, Little Abaco and Great Abaco

☐ **Olive-capped Warbler** _Dendroica pityophila_

Pine barrens of e Cuba, Grand Bahama and Abaco

☐ **Grace's Warbler** *Dendroica graciae*

____	*D. g. graciae*	Mts. of sw US to n Mexico (n Sinaloa); winters to Michoacán
____	*D. g. yaegeri*	Mts. of w Mexico (s Sinaloa to Nayarit, w Zacatecas and w Jalisco)
____	*D. g. remota*	Mts. of s Mexico (Michoacán and Guerrero) to n Nicaragua
____	*D. g. decora*	Pine ridges of coastal Belize, e Honduras and ne Nicaragua

☐ **Adelaide's Warbler** *Dendroica adelaidae*

____	*D. a. adelaidae*	Puerto Rico and Vieques I.
____	*D. a. subita*	Barbuda (Lesser Antilles)
____	*D. a. delicata*	St. Lucia (Lesser Antilles)

☐ **Pine Warbler** *Dendroica pinus*

____	*D. p. pinus*	SE Canada to se Texas and n Florida
____	*D. p. florida*	Peninsular Florida (Gainesville to Everglades National Park)
____	*D. p. achrustera*	Grand Bahama, Little and Great Abaco, Andros and New Providence
____	*D. p. chrysoleuca*	Hispaniola

☐ **Kirtland's Warbler** *Dendroica kirtlandii*

Jack-pine area of Michigan; winters in Bahamas

☐ **Prairie Warbler** *Dendroica discolor*

____	*D. d. discolor*	Central and e-central US; winters Bahamas and West Indies
____	*D. d. paludicola*	SE S Carolina to s Florida; winters to Gr. Antilles and El Salvador

☐ **Vitelline Warbler** *Dendroica vitellina*

____	*D. v. crawfordi*	Little Cayman I. and Cayman Brac
____	*D. v. vitellina*	Grand Cayman I.
____	*D. v. nelsoni*	Swan Islands (w Caribbean Sea)

☐ **Palm Warbler** *Dendroica palmarum*

____	*D. p. palmarum*	Cent. and e Canada to n US; winters to W Indies and Nicaragua
____	*D. p. hypochrysea*	SE Canada and ne US; winters to cent. Florida and n Gulf Coast

☐ **Bay-breasted Warbler** *Dendroica castanea*

Canada and ne US; winters Panama and nw South America

☐ **Blackpoll Warbler** *Dendroica striata*

Alaska and Canada; winters Colombia to Peru and w Amaz. Brazil

☐ **Cerulean Warbler** *Dendroica cerulea*

E N America; winters mts. of Colombia to Venezuela and Bolivia

☐ **Plumbeous Warbler** *Dendroica plumbea*

Dominica, Marie Galante, Guadeloupe and Terre-de-Haut I.

☐ **Arrow-headed Warbler** *Dendroica pharetra*

Montane forests and wooded hills of Jamaica

☐ **Elfin-woods Warbler** *Dendroica angelae*

Montane elfin forests of e Puerto Rico

☐ **Whistling Warbler** *Catharopeza bishopi*

Montane forests of St. Vincent (Lesser Antilles)

☐ **Black-and-white Warbler** *Mniotilta varia*

Canada to Gulf states; winters Mexico to Peru and West Indies

☐ **American Redstart** *Setophaga ruticilla*

Alaska to s US; winters s US to n South America and West Indies

☐ **Prothonotary Warbler** *Protonotaria citrea*

E US; winters se Mexico to w Ecuador and Lesser Antilles

☐ **Worm-eating Warbler** *Helmitheros vermivorus*

E US; winters se Mexico to Panama and Greater Antilles

☐ **Swainson's Warbler** *Limnothlypis swainsonii*

SE US; winters se Mexico and Belize to Guatemala and W Indies

☐ **Ovenbird** *Seiurus aurocapillus*

____	*S. a. aurocapillus*	Central and se Canada to e US; winters to n South America
____	*S. a. cinereus*	Rocky Mts. of s Alberta to w-central US; winters to Costa Rica
____	*S. a. furvior*	Newfoundland; winters to Bahamas, Cuba and Panama

☐ **Northern Waterthrush** *Seiurus noveboracensis*

N North America; winters to West Indies and n South America

☐ **Louisiana Waterthrush** *Seiurus motacilla*

E US; winters s Florida to nw South America and West Indies

☐ **Kentucky Warbler** *Opororis formosus*

E US; winters Mexico to nw South America

☐ **Connecticut Warbler** *Opororis agilis*

N North America; winters S America e of Andes to Peru and Brazil

☐ **Mourning Warbler** *Opororis philadelphia*

SE Canada and ne US; winters Nicaragua to nw South America

☐ **MacGillivray's Warbler** *Opororis tolmiei*

W North America; winters highlands of Mexico to Panama

☐ **Common Yellowthroat** *Geothlypis trichas*

____ *G. t. campicola*	Yukon, w Canada and se Alaska to nw US; winters to n Mexico
____ *G. t. arizela*	Extreme se Alaska to s-c California; winters to s Baja, n Sonora
____ *G. t. occidentalis*	N Oregon to New Mexico and nw Texas; winters to Honduras
____ *G. t. sinuosa*	Saltwater marshes from San Francisco to San Diego
____ *G. t. scirpicola*	S California to Nevada, sw Utah, n Baja and extreme nw Sonora
____ *G. t. trichas (brachidactylus)*	SE Canada and e-cent. US; winters to West Indies, n S America
____ *G. t. typhicola*	SE US; winters to se Mexico (Veracruz)
____ *G. t. ignota*	Coastal se S Carolina to s Florida, s Mississippi and se Louisiana
____ *G. t. insperata*	S Texas (Rio Grande Valley below Brownsville)
____ *G. t. chryseola (riparia)*	SE Arizona to s New Mexico, w Texas and nw Mexico
____ *G. t. modesta*	W Mexico (w-central Sonora south to Colima)
____ *G. t. chapalensis*	NW Mexico (Lake Chapala region of Jalisco)
____ *G. t. melanops*	Cent. Mexico (Zacatecas and n Jalisco to Oaxaca and Veracruz)

☐ **Belding's Yellowthroat** *Geothlypis beldingi*

____ *G. b. goldmani*	Marshes of central Baja California (latitude 28°N to 26°N)
____ *G. b. beldingi*	Marshes of Cape district of s Baja California

☐ **Altamira Yellowthroat** *Geothlypis flavovelata*

Coastal ne Mexico (s Tamaulipas, e San Luis Potosí, n Veracruz)

☐ **Bahama Yellowthroat** *Geothlypis rostrata*

____ *G. r. coryi*	N Bahamas (Eleuthera and Cat I.)
____ *G. r. tanneri*	Grand Bahama, Moranie Cay, Little and Great Abaco, Elbow Cay
____ *G. r. rostrata*	W Bahamas (New Providence and Andros)

☐ **Olive-crowned Yellowthroat** *Geothlypis semiflava*

____ *G. s. bairdi*	Tropical ne Honduras to Nicaragua, Costa Rica and nw Panama
____ *G. s. semiflava*	Pacific lowlands of w Colombia to w Ecuador (El Oro)

☐ **Black-polled Yellowthroat** *Geothlypis speciosa*

Highlands of s-c Mexico (e Michoacán, s Guanajuato and México)

☐ **Masked Yellowthroat** *Geothlypis aequinoctialis*

____ *G. a. chiriquensis*	Lowlands of sw Costa Rica and w Panama (w Chiriquí)
____ *G. a. aequinoctialis*	NE Colombia to Venezuela, Guianas, Suriname, n Brazil; Trinidad
____ *G. a. auricularis*	Pacific slope of w Ecuador to w Peru (south to Ica)
____ *G. a. peruviana*	N Peru (upper Marañon Valley of Cajamarca and La Libertad)
____ *G. a. velata*	SE Peru to Bolivia, Brazil, Paraguay, Uruguay and ne Argentina

☐ **Gray-crowned Yellowthroat** *Geothlypis poliocephala*

____ *G. p. poliocephala (pontilis)*	Pacific slope of nw Mexico (n Sinaloa to extreme w Oaxaca)
____ *G. p. ralphi*	Extreme s Texas to ne Mexico (Tamaulipas and San Luis Potosí)
____ *G. p. palpebralis*	Caribbean slope of s Mexico (Veracruz) to Belize and Costa Rica
____ *G. p. caninucha*	S Mexico (Oaxaca) to w Guatemala, El Salvador and se Honduras
____ *G. p. icterotis*	Pacific slope of w Nicaragua and w Costa Rica
____ *G. p. ridgwayi*	SW Costa Rica (Térraba Valley) to w Panama (Chiriquí)

□ **Hooded Yellowthroat** *Geothlypis nelsoni*
_____ *G. n. nelsoni*   Sierra Madre Oriental of e Mexico (Coahuila to Veracruz, n Puebla)
_____ *G. n. karlenae*   Highlands of s Mexico (Distrito Fed. to Puebla and n-c Oaxaca)

□ **Green-tailed Warbler** *Microligea palustris*
_____ *M. p. palustris*   Higher elevations of Hispaniola
_____ *M. p. vasta*   Xeric lowlands of sw Dominican Republic and Beata I.

□ **Yellow-headed Warbler** *Teretistris fernandinae*

Forest undergrowth of w Cuba, Isle of Pines and Cayo Cantiles

□ **Oriente Warbler** *Teretistris fornsi*

Humid mts. and semiarid coast of e Cuba and Camagüey Arch.

□ **Semper's Warbler** *Leucopeza semperi*

Montane forests of St. Lucia (Lesser Antilles). Possibly extinct

□ **Hooded Warbler** *Wilsonia citrina*

E US; winters Mexico to Panama

□ **Wilson's Warbler** *Wilsonia pusilla*
_____ *W. p. pileolata*   N Alaska and n Yukon to sw US; winters to w Panama
_____ *W. p. chryseola*   SW British Columbia to s California; winters to Panama
_____ *W. p. pusilla*   S and e Canada to ne US; winters to Costa Rica

□ **Canada Warbler** *Wilsonia canadensis*

E North America; winters Panama and mts. of nw South America

□ **Red-faced Warbler** *Cardellina rubrifrons*

Mts. of Ariz. and New Mexico to nw Mexico; winters to Honduras

□ **Red Warbler** *Ergaticus ruber*
_____ *E. r. melanauris*   Sierra Madre Occidental of w Mexico (Chihuahua and Durango)
_____ *E. r. ruber*   Mts. of w Mexico (Jalisco and Michoacán to Veracruz and Oaxaca)
_____ *E. r. rowleyi*   S Mexico (mountains of Oaxaca in Lachao Nuevo region)

□ **Pink-headed Warbler** *Ergaticus versicolor*

Mountains of extreme s Mexico (Chiapas) to Guatemala

□ **Painted Redstart** *Myioborus pictus*
_____ *M. p. pictus*   Mountains of sw US to s Mexico (Guerrero, Oaxaca and Veracruz)
_____ *M. p. guatemalae*   Mountains of s Mexico (Chiapas) to n Nicaragua

□ **Slate-throated Redstart** *Myioborus miniatus*
_____ *M. m. miniatus*   Mts. of w Mexico (s Sonora to Guerrero, Oaxaca and w Chiapas)
_____ *M. m. molochinus*   Mountains of e Mexico (Sierra de Tuxtla in se Veracruz)
_____ *M. m. intermedius*   S Mexico (extreme e Oaxaca and Chiapas) to e Guatemala
_____ *M. m. hellmayri*   Subtropical Pacific cordillera from Guatemala to sw El Salvador
_____ *M. m. connectens*   Subtropical mountains of El Salvador and Honduras
_____ *M. m. comptus*   Subtrop. mts. of Costa Rica (Cordillera Central and Guanacaste)
_____ *M. m. aurantiacus*   Mts. of e Costa Rica (Cordillera de Talamanca) and w Panama
_____ *M. m. ballux*   E Panama (Darién) to Colombia, w Venezuela and nw Ecuador
_____ *M. m. sanctaemartae*   Santa Marta Mountains (ne Colombia)
_____ *M. m. pallidiventris*   Coastal mountains of n Venezuela (e Falcón to Monagas)
_____ *M. m. subsimilis*   W Andes of Ecuador (El Oro) to extreme nw Peru (Piura)
_____ *M. m. verticalis*   SE Ecuador to Peru, Bolivia, se Venezuela, Guyana and nw Brazil

□ **Tepui Redstart** *Myioborus castaneocapillus*
_____ *M. c. duidae*   *Tepuis* of se Venezuela (Mt. Duida, Mt. Parú, Mt. Huachamacari)
_____ *M. c. castaneocapillus*   *Tepuis* of e Venezuela (e Bolívar), w Guyana and extreme n Brazil
_____ *M. c. maguirei*   *Tepuis* of se Venezuela (Cerro de la Neblina)

□ **Brown-capped Redstart** *Myioborus brunniceps*

Andes of Bolivia (La Paz and Cochabamba) to nw Argentina

□ **Yellow-faced Redstart** *Myioborus pariae*

NE Venezuela (humid cloud forests of Paría Peninsula)

☐ **White-faced Redstart** *Myioborus albifacies*

Tepuis of s Venezuela (Cerros Guany, Yaví and Paraque)

☐ **Saffron-breasted Redstart** *Myioborus cardonai*

Tepuis of s Venezuela (Cerro Guaiquinima in w-central Bolívar)

☐ **Collared Redstart** *Myioborus torquatus*

Humid montane forests of Costa Rica and w Panama

☐ **Spectacled Redstart** *Myioborus melanocephalus*

____ *M. m. ruficoronatus*	Andes of sw Colombia (Nariño) to s Ecuador (Loja)
____ *M. m. griseonuchus*	Western Andes of nw Peru (Piura and Cajamarca)
____ *M. m. malaris*	Central Andes of n Peru (north of Chachapoyas in Amazonas)
____ *M. m. melanocephalus*	Eastern Andes of Peru (Amazonas to Ayacucho)
____ *M. m. bolivianus*	Andes of s Peru (Cuzco) to w Bolivia (La Paz and Cochabamba)

☐ **Golden-fronted Redstart** *Myioborus ornatus*

____ *M. o. chrysops*	W and Cent. Andes of Colombia (Antioquia to Cauca and Huila)
____ *M. o. ornatus*	E Andes of Colombia and adjacent sw Venezuela (Táchira)

☐ **White-fronted Redstart** *Myioborus albifrons*

Andes of w Venezuela (Trujillo, Táchira and Mérida)

☐ **Yellow-crowned Redstart** *Myioborus flavivertex*

Santa Marta Mountains (ne Colombia)

☐ **Fan-tailed Warbler** *Euthlypis lachrymosa*

Tropical w Mexico (se Sonora) to n-central Nicaragua

☐ **Gray-and-gold Warbler** *Basileuterus fraseri*

____ *B. f. ochraceicrista*	Arid tropical w Ecuador (Manabí to El Oro) and Isla Puná
____ *B. f. fraseri*	Central Ecuador (Chimborazo) to nw Peru (Lambayeque)

☐ **Two-banded Warbler** *Basileuterus bivittatus*

____ *B. b. roraimae*	*Tepuis* of se Venezuela to Guyana and extreme n Brazil
____ *B. b. bivittatus*	E Andes of se Peru (Cuzco) to w Bolivia
____ *B. b. argentinae*	SE Bolivia (sw Santa Cruz) to nw Argentina (Jujuy and Salta)

☐ **Golden-bellied Warbler** *Basileuterus chrysogaster*

E slope of Andes of Peru (Huánuco and Junín to Puno)

☐ **Choco Warbler** *Basileuterus chlorophrys*

Tropical sw Colombia (Cauca and Nariño) to nw Ecuador

☐ **Pale-legged Warbler** *Basileuterus signatus*

____ *B. s. signatus*	Andes of central Peru (Junín to Cuzco)
____ *B. s. flavovirens*	Andes of se Peru (s Cuzco and Puno) to w Bolivia and nw Argentina

☐ **Citrine Warbler** *Basileuterus luteoviridis*

____ *B. l. luteoviridis*	E Andes of Colombia to sw Venezuela and e Ecuador
____ *B. l. quindianus*	Central Andes of Colombia (Caldas and Tolima)
____ *B. l. richardsoni*	Western Andes of Colombia (Cauca)
____ *B. l. striaticeps*	Andes of n Peru (Amazonas to Cuzco)
____ *B. l. euophrys*	Andes of sw Peru (Puno) to w Bolivia (La Paz and Cochabamba)

☐ **Black-crested Warbler** *Basileuterus nigrocristatus*

Andes of Colombia to n Venezuela, Ecuador and n Peru

☐ **Gray-headed Warbler** *Basileuterus griseiceps*

Cloud forests of coastal mountains of ne Venezuela

☐ **Santa Marta Warbler** *Basileuterus basilicus*

Santa Marta Mountains (ne Colombia)

☐ **Gray-throated Warbler** *Basileuterus cinereicollis*

____ *B. c. pallidulus*	Andes of ne Colombia and w Venezuela
____ *B. c. zuliensis*	Sierra de Perijá (Colombia/Venezuela border)
____ *B. c. cinereicollis*	Eastern Andes of Colombia (Santander del Norte to w Meta)

☐ **White-lored Warbler** *Basileuterus conspicillatus*

Santa Marta Mountains (ne Colombia)

☐ Russet-crowned Warbler *Basileuterus coronatus*

____	*B. c. regulus*	Andes of Colombia and w Venezuela
____	*B. c. elatus*	Andes of sw Colombia (Nariño) and w Ecuador
____	*B. c. orientalis*	E slope of Andes of Ecuador (Pichincha to Chimborazo)
____	*B. c. castaneiceps*	Andes of sw Ecuador to nw Peru (Tumbes and Piura)
____	*B. c. chapmani*	E slope of Western Andes of nw Peru (Cajamarca)
____	*B. c. inaequalis*	Central Andes of n Peru (Amazonas and San Martín)
____	*B. c. coronatus*	E Andes of se Peru (Junín) to w Bolivia
____	*B. c. notius*	E slope of Andes of Bolivia (La Paz and Cochabamba)

☐ Golden-crowned Warbler *Basileuterus culicivorus*

____	*B. c. flavescens*	W Mexico (Nayarit and w Jalisco)
____	*B. c. brasherii*	E Mexico (Nuevo León and Tamaulipas to Hidalgo and n Veracruz)
____	*B. c. culicivorus*	Tropical s Mexico (Puebla) to nw Costa Rica
____	*B. c. godmani*	S Costa Rica and w Panama (e to Veraguas)
____	*B. c. occultus*	Tropical and lower subtropical Andes of Colombia
____	*B. c. olivascens*	E slope of E Andes of Colombia, n Venezuela and Trinidad
____	*B. c. austerus*	E slope of E Andes of Colombia (Boyacá, Cundinamarca and Meta)
____	*B. c. indignus*	Santa Marta Mountains (ne Colombia)
____	*B. c. cabanisi*	Extreme ne Colombia (Santander del Norte) and nw Venezuela
____	*B. c. segrex*	SE Venezuela to w Guyana and adjacent nw Brazil
____	*B. c. auricapillus*	Tropical central Brazil
____	*B. c. azarae*	Paraguay to s Brazil, Uruguay and ne Argentina
____	*B. c. viridescens*	Tropical e Bolivia (Santa Cruz)

☐ Three-banded Warbler *Basileuterus trifasciatus*

____	*B. t. nitidior*	Andes of sw Ecuador (El Oro and Loja) to nw Peru (Tumbes)
____	*B. t. trifasciatus*	Andes of nw Peru (Piura, Cajamarca, Lambayeque, La Libertad)

☐ White-bellied Warbler *Basileuterus hypoleucus*

Lowlands of e Bolivia to ne Paraguay and s-central Brazil

☐ Rufous-capped Warbler *Basileuterus rufifrons*

____	*B. r. caudatus*	Sierra Madre Occidental of w Mexico (Sonora to Durango)
____	*B. r. dugesi*	Mts. of w and central Mexico (s Sinaloa to Guerrero and Oaxaca)
____	*B. r. jouyi*	Sierra Madre Oriental of e Mexico (Nuevo León to Veracruz)
____	*B. r. rufifrons*	Mts. of s Mexico (Puebla to Oaxaca and Chiapas) to n Guatemala
____	*B. r. salvini*	S Mexico (s Veracruz, Tabasco, Chiapas) to Belize and n Guatemala
____	*B. r. delattrii*	S Mexico (se Chiapas) to highlands of n Costa Rica
____	*B. r. mesochrysus*	SW Costa Rica to Panama, n Colombia and w Venezuela
____	*B. r. actuosus*	Coiba I. (off Pacific coast of Panama)

☐ Golden-browed Warbler *Basileuterus belli*

____	*B. b. bateli*	Highlands of w Mexico (se Sinaloa to Jalisco and Michoacán)
____	*B. b. belli*	Highlands of e Mexico (sw Tamaulipas to n Oaxaca)
____	*B. b. clarus*	Highlands of sw Mexico (s Morelos, Guerrero and w Oaxaca)
____	*B. b. scitulus*	Highlands of se Mexico (e Oaxaca and Chiapas) to nw El Salvador
____	*B. b. suboscurus*	High mountains of nw Honduras

☐ Black-cheeked Warbler *Basileuterus melanogenys*

____	*B. m. melanogenys*	Subtropical highlands of Costa Rica
____	*B. m. eximus*	Highlands of w Panama (Chiriquí)
____	*B. m. bensoni*	Highlands of w Panama (Veraguas)

☐ Pirre Warbler *Basileuterus ignotus*

Humid montane forests of e Panama and extreme nw Colombia

☐ **Three-striped Warbler** *Basileuterus tristriatus*

____	*B. t. chitrensis*	Mountains of Costa Rica and w Panama
____	*B. t. tacarcunae*	Highlands of e Panama (Darién) and nw Colombia (Chocó)
____	*B. t. daedalus*	Subtrop. Western and Central Andes of Colombia and w Ecuador
____	*B. t. auricularis*	Subtrop. E and Central Andes of Colombia and sw Venezuela
____	*B. t. meridanus*	Subtropical Andes of w Venezuela (Lara to Táchira)
____	*B. t. bessereri*	Subtropical mountains of n Venezuela (Yaracuy to Miranda)
____	*B. t. pariae*	NE Venezuela (subtropical mountains of Pariá Peninsula)
____	*B. t. baezae*	Andes of e Ecuador (Pichincha to Chimborazo)
____	*B. t. tristriatus*	Andes of se Ecuador (Loja) to central Peru (Cuzco)
____	*B. t. inconspicuus*	Andes of se Peru (Puno) to nw Bolivia (La Paz)
____	*B. t. punctipectus*	Andes of central Bolivia (Cochabamba)
____	*B. t. canens*	E Bolivia (Santa Cruz)

☐ **White-rimmed Warbler** *Basileuterus leucoblepharus*

E Paraguay to se Brazil, Uruguay and ne Argentina

☐ **White-striped Warbler** *Basileuterus leucophrys*

Gallery forests of s-central Brazil

☐ **Flavescent Warbler** *Basileuterus flaveolus*

____	*B. f. pallidirostris*	Tropical ne Colombia to n Venezuela and s Guyana
____	*B. f. flaveolus*	E Bolivia to n Paraguay, interior s Brazil and n Argentina

☐ **Buff-rumped Warbler** *Basileuterus fulvicauda*

____	*B. f. leucopygia*	Tropical n-central Honduras to w Panama (Veraguas)
____	*B. f. veraguensis*	Tropical sw Costa Rica to central Panama (Canal Zone)
____	*B. f. semicervina*	Tropical e Panama (Darién) to nw Peru (Tumbes and Piura)
____	*B. f. motacilla*	N Colombia (upper Magdalena Valley in Tolima and Huila)
____	*B. f. fulvicauda*	Trop. e Colombia to Ecuador, Peru (Junín) and extreme w Brazil
____	*B. f. significans*	Trop. se Peru (Inambari and Tambopata drainages) to nw Bolivia

☐ **Neotropical River Warbler** *Basileuterus rivularis*

____	*B. r. mesoleuca*	E Venezuela to the Guianas and n Brazil
____	*B. r. rivularis*	E Paraguay to se Brazil and ne Argentina
____	*B. r. bolivianus*	Foothills of Bolivia (La Paz, Cochabamba, Santa Cruz and Tarija)

☐ **Wrenthrush** *Zeledonia coronata*

Humid montane forests of Costa Rica and w Panama

☐ **Yellow-breasted Chat** *Icteria virens*

____	*I. v. auricollis (tropicalis)*	S British Columbia to Baja and n Mexico; winters to Guatemala
____	*I. v. virens*	N-central and e US to Florida; winters to Panama

☐ **Red-breasted Chat** *Granatellus venustus*

____	*G. v. venustus (melanotis)*	Coastal w Mexico (n Sinaloa to Chiapas)
____	*G. v. francescae*	Isla María Madre (Tres Marías Islands off w Mexico)

☐ **Gray-throated Chat** *Granatellus sallaei*

____	*G. s. sallaei*	Coastal se Mexico (Veracruz, Tabasco, e Oaxaca and n Chiapas)
____	*G. s. boucardi*	SE Mexico (Yucatán Peninsula) to Belize and e Guatemala

☐ **Rose-breasted Chat** *Granatellus pelzelni*

____	*G. p. pelzelni*	Trop. se Venezuela to Guyana, Suriname, nw Brazil and n Bolivia
____	*G. p. paraensis*	Tropical n Brazil (e Pará)

☐ **White-winged Warbler** *Xenoligea montana*

Montane forests of Hispaniola

FAMILY: COEREBIDAE (Bananaquit—1)

☐ **Bananaquit** *Coereba flaveola*

____	*C. f. mexicana*	SE Mexico (Veracruz) to w Panama (Veraguas) and Coiba I.
____	*C. f. caboti*	E Mexico (Cozumel I., Holbox I., Cancún and Cayo Culebra)
____	*C. f. tricolor*	Isla Providéncia (w Caribbean Sea)
____	*C. f. oblita*	Isla San Andrés (w Caribbean Sea)
____	*C. f. sharpei*	Grand Cayman, Little Cayman and Cayman Brac
____	*C. f. bahamensis*	Bahamas (Great Bahama and Little Abaco to Grand Turk)
____	*C. f. flaveola*	Jamaica
____	*C. f. bananivora*	Hispaniola, Gonâve, Petite Cayemite and Île-à-Vache
____	*C. f. nectarea*	Tortue I. (off n Haiti)
____	*C. f. portoricensis*	Puerto Rico
____	*C. f. sanctithomae*	Virgin Islands (including Vieques and Culebra)
____	*C. f. newtoni*	St. Croix (Virgin Islands)
____	*C. f. bartholemica*	N Lesser Antilles
____	*C. f. martinicana*	Martinique and St. Lucia (Lesser Antilles)
____	*C. f. barbadensis*	Barbados (Lesser Antilles)
____	*C. f. atrata*	St. Vincent (Lesser Antilles)
____	*C. f. aterrima*	Grenada and the Grenadines (Lesser Antilles)
____	*C. f. cerinoclunis*	Pearl Islands (Bay of Panama)
____	*C. f. columbiana*	Trop. e Panama to sw Colombia and s Venezuela (Amazonas)
____	*C. f. uropygialis*	Netherlands Antilles (Aruba and Curaçao)
____	*C. f. bonariensis*	Bonaire I. (Netherlands Antilles)
____	*C. f. melanornis*	N Venezuela (Cayo Sal off Chiririviche)
____	*C. f. lowii*	Islas Los Roques (off n Venezuela)
____	*C. f. ferryi*	Isla La Tortuga (off n Venezuela)
____	*C. f. frailensis*	Isla de Puerto Real and Morro El Fondeadero (off Venezuela)
____	*C. f. laurae*	Isla Testigo Grande and Isla Conejo (off n Venezuela)
____	*C. f. luteola*	Tropical n Colombia to n Venezuela; Trinidad and Tobago
____	*C. f. obscura*	Tropical ne Colombia and w Venezuela
____	*C. f. minima*	Trop. e Colombia to s Venezuela, the Guianas and n Brazil
____	*C. f. montana*	Highlands of w Venezuela (Mérida and Táchira)
____	*C. f. caucae*	W Colombia (upper Cauca Valley)
____	*C. f. gorgonae*	Gorgona I. (off w Colombia)
____	*C. f. intermedia*	SW Colombia to n Peru, sw Venezuela and w Brazil
____	*C. f. bolivari*	E Venezuela (lower Orinoco River Valley)
____	*C. f. guianensis*	Tropical e Venezuela (Bolívar) and adjacent Guyana
____	*C. f. roraimae*	*Tepuis* of se Venezuela, nw Brazil and adjacent sw Guyana
____	*C. f. pacifica*	Arid nw Peru (Lambayeque, w La Libertad and Ancash)
____	*C. f. magnirostris*	N Peru (upper Marañón Valley)
____	*C. f. dispar*	Central Peru (San Martín) to nw Bolivia (La Paz)
____	*C. f. chloropyga*	Trop. s Peru to Bolivia, Paraguay, w Brazil and ne Argentina
____	*C. f. alleni*	Plateau of central Brazil (Mato Grosso) and e Bolivia

FAMILY: THRAUPIDAE (Tanagers and Allies—256)

☐ **Chestnut-vented Conebill** *Conirostrum speciosum*

____	*C. s. amazonum*	E Colombia to sw Venezuela, the Guianas, n Brazil and e Peru
____	*C. s. guaricola*	Tropical cent. Venezuela (e Guárico and w Anzoátegui)
____	*C. s. speciosum*	SE Peru (Puno) to e Brazil, Bolivia, Paraguay and n Argentina

☐ **White-eared Conebill** *Conirostrum leucogenys*

____	*C. l. panamense*	Tropical e Panama to nw Colombia
____	*C. l. leucogenys*	Tropical n Colombia and ne Venezuela
____	*C. l. cyanochrous*	Andes of w Venezuela (Mérida) and Sierra de Perijá

□ **Bicolored Conebill** *Conirostrum bicolor*
_____ *C. b. bicolor* Coastal n Colombia to the Guianas and n Brazil; Trinidad
_____ *C. b. minor* Trop. e Ecuador to extreme ne Peru (Loreto) and w Brazil

□ **Pearly-breasted Conebill** *Conirostrum margaritae*

Tropical ne Peru (Loreto) and w Amazonian Brazil

□ **Cinereous Conebill** *Conirostrum cinereum*
_____ *C. c. fraseri* Central and E Andes of sw Colombia and Andes of Ecuador
_____ *C. c. littorale* West slope of Western Andes of Peru to n Chile
_____ *C. c. cinereum* Andes of se Peru and w Bolivia

□ **Tamarugo Conebill** *Conirostrum tamarugense*

SW Peru (Arequipa and Tacna) to n Chile (Tarapacá)

□ **White-browed Conebill** *Conirostrum ferrugineiventre*

Andes of e Peru (San Martín) and w Bolivia

□ **Rufous-browed Conebill** *Conirostrum rufum*

Mts. of ne Colombia and extreme sw Venezuela (Táchira)

□ **Blue-backed Conebill** *Conirostrum sitticolor*
_____ *C. s. intermedium* Andes of w Venezuela (Mérida and Táchira)
_____ *C. s. sitticolor* Andes of s Colombia, Ecuador and nw Peru
_____ *C. s. cyaneum* Andes of Peru to w Bolivia (La Paz and Cochabamba)

□ **Capped Conebill** *Conirostrum albifrons*
_____ *C. a. albifrons* Central and E Andes of Colombia and w Venezuela (Táchira)
_____ *C. a. centralandium* Central Andes of Colombia (Antioquia to Cauca)
_____ *C. a. cyanonotum* Coastal mts. of n Venezuela (Aragua and Distrito Federal)
_____ *C. a. atrocyaneum* Andes of sw Colombia, Ecuador and n Peru
_____ *C. a. sordidum* Andes of s Peru (Junín) to w Bolivia (La Paz)
_____ *C. a. lugens* *Yungas* of e Bolivia (Cochabamba and Santa Cruz)

□ **Giant Conebill** *Oreomanes fraseri*

Polylepis woodlands of s Colombia to w Bolivia

□ **Brown Tanager** *Orchesticus abeillei*

Foothills of se Brazil (s Bahia and Minas Gerais to Paraná)

□ **Cinnamon Tanager** *Schistochlamys ruficapillus*
_____ *S. r. capistrata* *Caatinga* of ne Brazil (s Pará to Maranhão and Bahia)
_____ *S. r. sicki* SW Brazil (Rio das Mortes region of e Mato Grosso)
_____ *S. r. ruficapillus* SE Brazil (s Minas Gerais to Paraná) and ne Argentina

□ **Black-faced Tanager** *Schistochlamys melanopis*
_____ *S. m. aterrima* NE Colombia to Venezuela, w Guyana and extreme n Brazil
_____ *S. m. melanopis* E Guyana to Suriname, French Guiana and ne Brazil
_____ *S. m. grisea* Subtropical Central Andes of Peru
_____ *S. m. olivina* E Bolivia to Paraguay and s-central Brazil (Mato Grosso)
_____ *S. m. amazonica* Amazonian and se Brazil

□ **White-banded Tanager** *Neothraupis fasciata*

E Bolivia to ne Paraguay and campos of e and s Brazil

□ **White-rumped Tanager** *Cypsnagra hirundinacea*
_____ *C. h. pallidigula* Campos of Suriname and central Brazil to ne Bolivia
_____ *C. h. hirundinacea* E Bolivia to ne Paraguay and campos of s Brazil

□ **Black-and-white Tanager** *Conothraupis speculigera*

Locally from w Ecuador to nw Peru; e Peru to nw Bolivia

□ **Cone-billed Tanager** *Conothraupis mesoleuca*

SW Brazil (known from a 1939 specimen from w Mato Grosso)

□ **Magpie Tanager** *Cissopis leveriana*
_____ *C. l. leveriana* E Colombia to se Venezuela, Guianas, n Bolivia, Amaz. Brazil
_____ *C. l. major* Paraguay to se Brazil and adjacent ne Argentina (Misiones)

☐ **Red-billed Pied Tanager** *Lamprospiza melanoleuca*

Amazonian Brazil, adjacent n Bolivia, e Peru and Guianas

☐ **Grass-green Tanager** *Chlorornis riefferii*

____ *C. r. riefferii* Andes of Colombia and Ecuador
____ *C. r. diluta* Central Andes of n Peru
____ *C. r. elegans* Andes of central Peru (Junín)
____ *C. r. celata* Andes of extreme se Peru (Puno)
____ *C. r. boliviana* Andes of w Bolivia (La Paz and Cochabamba)

☐ **Scarlet-throated Tanager** *Compsothraupis loricata*

Arid interior of ne Brazil

☐ **White-capped Tanager** *Sericossypha albocristata*

Locally in Andes of Colombia and w Venezuela to se Peru

☐ **Puerto Rican Tanager** *Nesospingus speculiferus*

Highlands of Puerto Rico

☐ **Common Bush-Tanager** *Chlorospingus ophthalmicus*

____ *C. o. albifrons* Sierra Madre del Sur of sw Mexico (Guerrero and Oaxaca)
____ *C. o. wetmorei* SE Mexico (Sierra de Tuxtla in Veracruz)
____ *C. o. persimilis* S Mexico (s Oaxaca)
____ *C. o. ophthalmicus* SE Mexico (n Vera Cruz and s San Luis Potosí to w Chiapas)
____ *C. o. dwighti* Caribbean slope of s Mexico (Chiapas) and e Guatemala
____ *C. o. postocularis* Pacific slope of s Mexico (Chiapas) and w Guatemala
____ *C. o. honduratius* Subtropical El Salvador and Honduras
____ *C. o. regionalis* Subtropical Nicaragua and e Costa Rica
____ *C. o. novicius* Subtropical sw Costa Rica and w Panama (Chiriquí)
____ *C. o. punctulatus* Highlands of w Panama (Veraguas and Coclé)
____ *C. o. jaqueti* W slope of Easterm Andes of ne Colombia and n Venezuela
____ *C. o. eminens* E Andes of ne Colombia (Norte de Santander and Boyacá)
____ *C. o. trudis* Colombia (w slope of Andes of Santander at La Pica)
____ *C. o. exitelus* Colombia (e slope of W Andes and C Andes in Antioquia)
____ *C. o. flavopectus* E Andes of Colombia (s Santander and w Cundinamarca)
____ *C. o. macarenae* E Colombia (Macarena Mountains)
____ *C. o. nigriceps* Subtropical and lower temperate Andes of Colombia
____ *C. o. falconensis* NW Venezuela (San Luis Mountains and Sierra de Aroa)
____ *C. o. venezuelanus* Andes of sw Venezuela (Lara, Mérida and Táchira)
____ *C. o. ponsi* Sierra de Perijá (Colombia/Venezuela border)
____ *C. o. phaeocephalus* Subtropical mountains of e and w Ecuador
____ *C. o. cinereocephalus* Subtropical central Peru (Junín)
____ *C. o. hiaticolus* Central Peru
____ *C. o. peruvianus* Subtropical s Peru (Puno)
____ *C. o. bolivianus* W-central Bolivia (Cochabamba and La Paz)
____ *C. o. fulvigularis* Central Bolivia (s Cordillera de Cochabamba)
____ *C. o. argentinus* Cent. Bolivia (upper Río Mizque) to n Argentina (Tucumán)

☐ **Tacarcuna Bush-Tanager** *Chlorospingus tacarcunae*

Montane forests of e Panama and extreme nw Colombia

☐ **Pirre Bush-Tanager** *Chlorospingus inornatus*

Humid montane forests of e Panama

☐ **Dusky Bush-Tanager** *Chlorospingus semifuscus*

____ *C. s. livingstoni* Pacific slope of Western Andes of Colombia
____ *C. s. semifuscus* Pacific slope of sw Colombia (Nariño) and w Ecuador

☐ **Sooty-capped Bush-Tanager** *Chlorospingus pileatus*

____ *C. p. pileatus* Mountains of Costa Rica and w Panama (Volcán de Chiriquí)
____ *C. p. diversus* Mountains of w Panama (e Chiriquí)

☐ **Short-billed Bush-Tanager** *Chlorospingus parvirostris*

____ *C. p. huallagae* E Andes of s Colombia and n Peru
____ *C. p. medianus* Andes of e-central Peru (Junín and Cuzco)
____ *C. p. parvirostris* Andes of extreme se Peru (Puno) and nw Bolivia (La Paz)

☐ **Yellow-throated Bush-Tanager** *Chlorospingus flavigularis*
_____ *C. f. hypophaeus* — Montane forests of w Panama (Volcán Chiriquí to Veraguas)
_____ *C. f. marginatus* — W slope of Western Andes of sw Colombia and w Ecuador
_____ *C. f. flavigularis* — Andes of central Colombia to e Ecuador and e Peru (Cuzco)

☐ **Yellow-green Bush-Tanager** *Chlorospingus flavovirens*

Locally in humid Western Andes of Colombia and nw Ecuador

☐ **Ashy-throated Bush-Tanager** *Chlorospingus canigularis*
_____ *C. c. olivaceiceps* — Subtropical Caribbean slope of w Costa Rica
_____ *C. c. canigularis* — E Andes of Colombia (Cundinamarca) and sw Venezuela
_____ *C. c. conspicillatus* — Western and Central Andes of Colombia
_____ *C. c. paulus* — Subtropical Andes of sw Ecuador
_____ *C. c. signatus* — Subtropical Andes of e Ecuador and Peru (south to Cuzco)

☐ **Gray-hooded Bush-Tanager** *Cnemoscopus rubrirostris*
_____ *C. r. rubrirostris* — Andes of Colombia to sw Venezuela (Táchira) and e Ecuador
_____ *C. r. chrysogaster* — Andes of Peru (Amazonas to Cordillera Vilcabamba in Cuzco)

☐ **Black-capped Hemispingus** *Hemispingus atropileus*
_____ *H. a. atropileus* — Andes of Colombia to sw Venezuela (Táchira) and Ecuador
_____ *H. a. auricularis* — Andes of e Peru (Amazonas to Cuzco)

☐ **Orange-browed Hemispingus** *Hemispingus calophrys*

Andes of se Peru (Puno) and w Bolivia (La Paz, Cochabamba)

☐ **Parodi's Hemispingus** *Hemispingus parodii*

Andes of se Peru (Cuzco)

☐ **Superciliaried Hemispingus** *Hemispingus superciliaris*
_____ *H. s. superciliaris* — E Andes of central Colombia (Cundinamarca)
_____ *H. s. nigrifrons* — Central Andes of Colombia and Ecuador
_____ *H. s. chrysophrys* — Andes of sw Venezuela (Trujillo, Mérida and Táchira)
_____ *H. s. maculifrons* — Andes of extreme sw Ecuador and nw Peru
_____ *H. s. insignis* — Highlands of n Peru (Utcubamba Valley east of Río Marañón)
_____ *H. s. leucogaster* — Temperate Andes of central Peru (Junín)
_____ *H. s. urubambae* — Temperate Andes of s Peru (Cuzco) to w Bolivia (La Paz)

☐ **Gray-capped Hemispingus** *Hemispingus reyi*

Andes of sw Venezuela (Trujillo, Mérida and Táchira)

☐ **Oleaginous Hemispingus** *Hemispingus frontalis*
_____ *H. f. frontalis* — Subtropical Andes of e Colombia, e Ecuador and e Peru
_____ *H. f. ignobilis* — Andes of w Venezuela (s Lara, Trujillo, Mérida and Táchira)
_____ *H. f. flavidorsalis* — Sierra de Perijá (Colombia/Venezuela border)
_____ *H. f. hanieli* — Coastal mountains of n Venezuela (Aragua to Miranda)
_____ *H. f. iteratus* — Coastal mountains of ne Venezuela (Monagas to Sucre)

☐ **Black-eared Hemispingus** *Hemispingus melanotis*
_____ *H. m. melanotis* — Andes of Colombia to sw Venezuela and e Ecuador
_____ *H. m. ochraceus* — W slope of Andes of sw Colombia (Nariño) and w Ecuador
_____ *H. m. piurae* — W Andes of nw Peru (Piura)
_____ *H. m. macrophrys* — Pacific slope of Andes of w Peru (La Libertad)
_____ *H. m. berlepschi* — Subtropical Andes of central Peru (Junín)
_____ *H. m. castaneicollis* — Andes of se Peru (Puno) and *yungas* of w Bolivia

☐ **Slaty-backed Hemispingus** *Hemispingus goeringi*

Andes of w Venezuela (Mérida and n Táchira)

☐ **Rufous-browed Hemispingus** *Hemispingus rufosuperciliaris*

Andes of e Peru (Amazonas to La Libertad and Huánuco)

☐ **Black-headed Hemispingus** *Hemispingus verticalis*

Andes of Colombia to sw Venezuela and extreme n Peru

☐ **Drab Hemispingus** *Hemispingus xanthophthalmus*

Humid Andes of central Peru to nw Bolivia (Puno and La Paz)

☐ **Three-striped Hemispingus** *Hemispingus trifasciatus*

Andes of se Peru to n Bolivia (La Paz and Cochabamba)

☐ **Chestnut-headed Tanager** *Pyrrhocoma ruficeps*

E Paraguay to se Brazil and ne Argentina (Misiones)

☐ **Fulvous-headed Tanager** *Thlypopsis fulviceps*
_____ *T. f. fulviceps* — E slope of Andes of ne Colombia and mountains of n Venezuela
_____ *T. f. intensa* — E Andes of ne Colombia (s Magdalena)
_____ *T. f. obscuriceps* — Sierra de Perijá (Colombia/Venezuela border)
_____ *T. f. meridensis* — Andes of w Venezuela (Mérida)

☐ **Rufous-chested Tanager** *Thlypopsis ornata*
_____ *T. o. ornata* — Andes of sw Colombia (Puracé) and w Ecuador
_____ *T. o. media* — Andes of s Ecuador (Loja) to central Peru (Lima)
_____ *T. o. macropteryx* — E slope of Andes of central and s Peru (Junín and Cuzco)

☐ **Brown-flanked Tanager** *Thlypopsis pectoralis*

Andes of central Peru (Huánuco, Pasco and Junín)

☐ **Orange-headed Tanager** *Thlypopsis sordida*
_____ *T. s. chrysopis* — Extreme s Colombia to e Ecuador, e Peru and w Brazil
_____ *T. s. orinocensis* — Tropical e-central Venezuela (s Anzoátegui and n Bolívar)
_____ *T. s. sordida* — E and s Brazil to e Bolivia, Paraguay and n Argentina

☐ **Buff-bellied Tanager** *Thlypopsis inornata*

Andes of nw Peru; recently recorded in adjacent s Ecuador

☐ **Rust-and-yellow Tanager** *Thlypopsis ruficeps*

Andes of se Peru (Huánuco) to nw Argentina

☐ **Guira Tanager** *Hemithraupis guira*
_____ *H. g. guirina* — W and central Colombia to e Ecuador and extreme nw Peru
_____ *H. g. nigrigula* — N-central Colombia to n Venezuela, the Guianas and ne Brazil
_____ *H. g. huambina* — Tropical se Colombia to e Ecuador, ne Peru and w Brazil
_____ *H. g. roraimae* — *Tepuis* of se Venezuela and Guyana
_____ *H. g. boliviana* — NE Bolivia to nw Argentina and adjacent w Brazil
_____ *H. g. amazonica* — Brazil south of the Amazon (Rio Madeira to Rio Tapajós)
_____ *H. g. guira* — E Brazil (Rio Tocantins to Ceará, Goiás and nw Bahia)
_____ *H. g. forsteri* — E Paraguay to ne Argentina and interior se Brazil

☐ **Rufous-headed Tanager** *Hemithraupis ruficapilla*
_____ *H. r. ruficapilla* — SE Brazil (s Minas Gerais and Espírito Santo to Santa Catarina)
_____ *H. r. bahiae* — E Brazil (se Bahia)

☐ **Yellow-backed Tanager** *Hemithraupis flavicollis*
_____ *H. f. ornata* — Tropical e Panama (Darién) and extreme nw Colombia
_____ *H. f. albigularis* — Colombia (upper Sinú, lower Cauca, middle Magdalena valleys)
_____ *H. f. peruana* — S-cent. Colombia to e Ecuador and ne Peru (n of Río Marañón)
_____ *H. f. aurigularis* — Extreme se Colombia to s Venezuela and n Brazil
_____ *H. f. hellmayri* — SE Venezuela (e Bolívar) to w Guyana (Merumé Mts.)
_____ *H. f. flavicollis* — Suriname, French Guiana and adjacent Brazil n of the Amazon
_____ *H. f. sororia* — N Peru (south of Río Marañón)
_____ *H. f. centralis* — SE Peru to n Bolivia and central Brazil
_____ *H. f. obidensis* — N Brazil (along north bank of the lower Amazon in Pará)
_____ *H. f. melanoxantha* — E Brazil (Pernambuco and Bahia)
_____ *H. f. insignis* — SE Brazil (Espírito Santo and Rio de Janeiro)

☐ **Black-and-yellow Tanager** *Chrysothlypis chrysomelaena*
_____ *C. c. chrysomelaena* — Caribbean slope of e Costa Rica and w Panama
_____ *C. c. ocularis* — Tropical e Panama (Darién)

☐ **Scarlet-and-white Tanager** *Chrysothlypis salmoni*

Pacific slope of Andes of Colombia and nw Ecuador

☐ **Hooded Tanager** *Nemosia pileata*
_____ *N. p. hypoleuca* — Caribbean coast of n Colombia and n Venezuela
_____ *N. p. surinamensis* — Guyana and Suriname
_____ *N. p. pileata* — French Guiana, ne and Amazonian Brazil, extreme n Bolivia
_____ *N. p. interna* — N Brazil (upper Rio Branco and lower Rio Negro)
_____ *N. p. nana* — Tropical Amazon basin of ne Peru and adjacent w Brazil
_____ *N. p. caerulea* — E Bolivia to Paraguay, e and s Brazil and n Argentina

☐ **Cherry-throated Tanager** *Nemosia rourei*
SE Brazil (rediscovered after 47-year absence in Espírito Santo)

☐ **Black-crowned Palm-Tanager** *Phaenicophilus palmarum*
Lowlands of Hispaniola (except s pen. Haiti) and Saona I.

☐ **Gray-crowned Palm-Tanager** *Phaenicophilus poliocephalus*
_____ *P. p. poliocephalus* — S peninsular Haiti, Île-à-Vache and Grande Cayemite I.
_____ *P. p. coryi* — Gonâve I. (e of Haiti)

☐ **Western Chat-Tanager** *Calyptophilus tertius*
Massifs of s Haiti and extreme sw Dominican Republic

☐ **Eastern Chat-Tanager** *Calyptophilus frugivorus*
_____ *C. f. frugivorus* — W Dominican Republic (Benefactor to Sananá)
_____ *C. f. neibei* — Central Dominican Republic
_____ *C. f. abbotti* — Gonâve I. (e of Haiti)

☐ **Rosy Thrush-Tanager** *Rhodinocichla rosea*
_____ *R. r. schistacea* — Tropical Pacific coast of Mexico (Sinaloa to Michoacán)
_____ *R. r. eximia* — SW Costa Rica (Térraba Valley) to w Panama
_____ *R. r. harterti* — W slope of E Andes of central Colombia (Bogotá to e Tolima)
_____ *R. r. beebei* — Sierra de Perijá (Colombia/Venezuela border)
_____ *R. r. rosea* — NW Venezuela (Falcón to Distrito Federal and Miranda)

☐ **Dusky-faced Tanager** *Mitrospingus cassinii*
_____ *M. c. costaricensis* — Caribbean lowlands of e Costa Rica and extreme w Panama
_____ *M. c. cassinii* — Tropical e Panama to w Colombia and w Ecuador

☐ **Olive-backed Tanager** *Mitrospingus oleagineus*
_____ *M. o. obscuripectus* — SE Venezuela (Gran Sabana) and extreme n Brazil (Uei-tepui)
_____ *M. o. oleagineus* — *Tepuis* of se Venezuela (Mt. Roraima) and adjacent Guyana

☐ **Olive Tanager** *Chlorothraupis carmioli*
_____ *C. c. carmioli* — Tropical e Nicaragua to nw Panama (Almirante Bay)
_____ *C. c. magnirostris* — Tropical w Panama (Veraguas)
_____ *C. c. lutescens* — Tropical e Panama (San Blas and Darién) to nw Colombia
_____ *C. c. frenata* — Tropical s Colombia to nw Bolivia (La Paz and Cochabamba)

☐ **Lemon-spectacled Tanager** *Chlorothraupis olivacea*
Tropical e Panama (Darién) to w Colombia and nw Ecuador

☐ **Ochre-breasted Tanager** *Chlorothraupis stolzmanni*
_____ *C. s. dugandi* — W slope of Western Andes of sw Colombia
_____ *C. s. stolzmanni* — Tropical w Ecuador (south to El Oro)

☐ **Olive-green Tanager** *Orthogonys chloricterus*
Montane forests of se Brazil (Espírito Santo to Santa Catarina)

☐ **Gray-headed Tanager** *Eucometis penicillata*
_____ *E. p. pallida* — Tropical se Mexico (Veracruz and Yucatán) to e Guatemala
_____ *E. p. spodocephala* — Tropical Nicaragua and Pacific slope of Costa Rica
_____ *E. p. stictothorax* — Tropical sw Costa Rica and w Panama (east to Veraguas)
_____ *E. p. cristata* — E Panama to n Colombia and extreme w Venezuela
_____ *E. p. penicillata* — SE Colombia east of Andes to the Guianas, e Peru and n Brazil
_____ *E. p. affinis* — Tropical n Venezuela (Falcón to Miranda)
_____ *E. p. albicollis* — E Bolivia to n Paraguay, ne Argentina and s-central Brazil

☐ **Fulvous Shrike-Tanager** *Lanio fulvus*
____ *L. f. peruvianus* — S Colombia (east of the Andes) to e Ecuador and ne Peru
____ *L. f. fulvus* — S Venezuela to the Guianas and n Amazonian Brazil

☐ **White-winged Shrike-Tanager** *Lanio versicolor*
____ *L. v. versicolor* — E Peru (s of Río Marañón) to n Bolivia and w Brazil
____ *L. v. parvus* — S Amazonian Brazil and n Mato Grosso

☐ **Black-throated Shrike-Tanager** *Lanio aurantius*
— Gulf-Caribbean lowlands of se Mexico to nw Honduras

☐ **White-throated Shrike-Tanager** *Lanio leucothorax*
____ *L. l. leucothorax* — Extreme e Honduras to e Nicaragua and e Costa Rica
____ *L. l. reversus* — NW Costa Rica (Nicoya Pen., Puntarenas and Las Agujas)
____ *L. l. melanopygius* — SW Costa Rica and Pacific slope of w Panama
____ *L. l. ictus* — Extreme nw Panama (Almirante Bay environs)

☐ **Rufous-crested Tanager** *Creurgops verticalis*
— Andes of Colombia to sw Venezuela and e Peru (Ayacucho)

☐ **Slaty Tanager** *Creurgops dentata*
— Andes of se Peru to w Bolivia (La Paz and Cochabamba)

☐ **Sulphur-rumped Tanager** *Heterospingus rubrifrons*
— Humid lowlands of e Costa Rica and Panama

☐ **Scarlet-browed Tanager** *Heterospingus xanthopygius*
____ *H. x. xanthopygius* — Extreme e Panama and n Colombia
____ *H. x. berliozi* — Pacific slope of w Colombia and nw Ecuador

☐ **Flame-crested Tanager** *Tachyphonus cristatus*
____ *T. c. fallax* — S Colombia (se Nariño) to e Ecuador and ne Peru
____ *T. c. cristatellus* — Tropical se Colombia to ne Peru, s Venezuela and nw Brazil
____ *T. c. huarandosae* — N Peru (Chinchipe Valley in Río Marañón Valley)
____ *T. c. intercedens* — E Venezuela (e Bolívar), Guyana and Suriname
____ *T. c. cristatus* — French Guiana and ne Brazil (north of the Amazon)
____ *T. c. pallidigula* — NE Brazil (e Pará and lower Rio Tocantins)
____ *T. c. madeirae* — Brazil s of the Amazon (Teffe to Rio Xingú and Mato Grosso)
____ *T. c. nattereri* — SW Brazil (Mato Grosso)
____ *T. c. brunneus* — E Brazil (Pernambuco to São Paulo)

☐ **Yellow-crested Tanager** *Tachyphonus rufiventer*
— E Peru to nw Bolivia and adjacent w Amazonian Brazil

☐ **Fulvous-crested Tanager** *Tachyphonus surinamus*
____ *T. s. surinamus* — E and s Venezuela, the Guianas and Brazil n of the Amazon
____ *T. s. brevipes* — E Colombia to s Venezuela, nw Brazil, e Ecuador and ne Peru
____ *T. s. napensis* — Tropical e Peru (south of the Amazon) and nw Brazil
____ *T. s. insignis* — N Brazil south of the Amazon (lower Rio Madeira to Pará)

☐ **White-shouldered Tanager** *Tachyphonus luctuosus*
____ *T. l. axillaris* — Caribbean slope of e Honduras to w Panama
____ *T. l. nitidissimus* — Pacific slope of sw Costa Rica and extreme w Panama
____ *T. l. panamensis* — E Panama to w Colombia, w Ecuador and w Venezuela
____ *T. l. luctuosus* — SE Colombia e of Andes to Bolivia, the Guianas and n Brazil
____ *T. l. flaviventris* — Extreme ne Venezuela (Sucre) and Trinidad

☐ **Tawny-crested Tanager** *Tachyphonus delatrii*
— Tropical e Honduras to w Ecuador; Isla Gorgona (off Colombia)

☐ **Ruby-crowned Tanager** *Tachyphonus coronatus*
— E Paraguay to se Brazil and ne Argentina

☐ **White-lined Tanager** *Tachyphonus rufus*
— Lowlands of Costa Rica to n Argentina and Amazonian Brazil

☐ **Red-shouldered Tanager** *Tachyphonus phoenicius*
— Guianas and s Venezuela to ne Peru and Amazonian Brazil

☐ **Black-goggled Tanager** *Trichothraupis melanops*

Andes of Peru and w Bolivia; e Brazil, ne Argentina, e Paraguay

☐ **Red-crowned Ant-Tanager** *Habia rubica*

_____ *H. r. holobrunnea*	Subtrop. e Mexico (s Tamaulipas to Veracruz and n Oaxaca)
_____ *H. r. rosea*	Pacific slope of sw Mexico (Nayarit and Jalisco to Guerrero)
_____ *H. r. affinis*	Pacific slope of s Mexico (Oaxaca)
_____ *H. r. nelsoni*	SE Mexico (Yucatán Peninsula north of s Campeche)
_____ *H. r. rubicoides*	S Mexico (Puebla and e Veracruz) to n Nicaragua
_____ *H. r. alfaroana*	NW Costa Rica (Guanacaste Peninsula)
_____ *H. r. vinacea*	Pacific slope of sw Costa Rica (Nicoya Peninsula) to e Panama
_____ *H. r. rubra*	Trinidad
_____ *H. r. crissalis*	Coastal mountains of ne Venezuela (Anzoátegui to Sucre)
_____ *H. r. mesoptamia*	Venezuela (Río Yuruán region of e Bolívar)
_____ *H. r. perijana*	Sierra de Perijá (Colombia/Venezuela border)
_____ *H. r. coccinea*	E base of E Andes of n-central Colombia and w Venezuela
_____ *H. r. rhodinolaema*	SE Colombia e of the Andes to ne Peru and extreme nw Brazil
_____ *H. r. peruviana*	Tropical e Peru to central Bolivia and adjacent w Brazil
_____ *H. r. hesterna*	Central Brazil south of the Amazon to n Mato Grosso
_____ *H. r. bahiae*	Tropical e Brazil (Bahia)
_____ *H. r. rubica*	SE Brazil (s Minas Gerais) to e Paraguay and ne Argentina

☐ **Red-throated Ant-Tanager** *Habia fuscicauda*

_____ *H. f. salvini*	SE Mexico (San Luis Potosí and Veracruz) to El Salvador
_____ *H. f. insularis*	Yucatán Peninsula, Meco I., Isla Mujeres and n Guatemala
_____ *H. f. discolor*	Tropical Nicaragua
_____ *H. f. fuscicauda*	Extreme s Nicaragua to extreme w Panama
_____ *H. f. willisi*	Central Panama (ne Coclé and Colón to w San Blas)
_____ *H. f. erythrolaema*	Caribbean coast of n Colombia

☐ **Sooty Ant-Tanager** *Habia gutturalis*

Foothills of Western Andes of n Colombia

☐ **Black-cheeked Ant-Tanager** *Habia atrimaxillaris*

Pacific lowlands of sw Costa Rica (Golfo Dulce)

☐ **Crested Ant-Tanager** *Habia cristata*

W Andes of Colombia (Antioquia to Cauca)

☐ **Rose-throated Tanager** *Piranga roseogularis*

_____ *P. r. roseogularis*	SE Mexico (arid n Yucatán Peninsula)
_____ *P. r. tincta*	Central and s Yucatán Peninsula, n Belize and n Guatemala
_____ *P. r. cozumelae*	SE Mexico (Cozumel I. and Isla Mujeres)

☐ **Hepatic Tanager** *Piranga flava*

_____ *P. f. hepatica*	SW US and w Mexico (south to Guerrero and Oaxaca)
_____ *P. f. dextra*	SW US (e of Rockies) and e Mexico; winters to w Guatemala
_____ *P. f. figlina*	Lowland pine savanna of e Guatemala and Belize
_____ *P. f. savannarum*	Lowland pine savanna of e Honduras and ne Nicaragua
_____ *P. f. albifacies*	Montane oak-pine belt of w Guatemala to n Nicaragua
_____ *P. f. testacea*	Subtropical Costa Rica and Panama (east to Cape Gararchiné)
_____ *P. f. desidiosa*	Upper tropical and subtropical sw Colombia
_____ *P. f. lutea*	Extreme sw Colombia to w Ecuador, Peru and nw Bolivia
_____ *P. f. haemalea*	Mountains of s Venezuela, w Guyana and extreme n Brazil
_____ *P. f. faceta*	Mountains of n Colombia and n Venezuela; Trinidad
_____ *P. f. toddi*	W slope of Eastern Andes of Colombia (Magdalena)
_____ *P. f. macconnelli*	S Guyana and adjacent extreme n Brazil
_____ *P. f. saira*	E Brazil (Amazon to Mato Grosso and Rio Grande do Sul)
_____ *P. f. rosacea*	E Bolivia (Santa Cruz to Chiquitos)
_____ *P. f. flava*	S Bolivia (Cochabamba) to Uruguay and n Argentina

☐ **Scarlet Tanager** *Piranga olivacea*

E Canada and US; winters mainly upper Amazon basin

☐ **Summer Tanager** *Piranga rubra*
_____ *P. r. cooperi (ochracea)*   SW US and n Mexico; winters to s Baja and s Mexico
_____ *P. r. rubra*   SE US; winters to Amazonian Brazil and n Bolivia

☐ **Western Tanager** *Piranga ludoviciana*

W North America; winters to w Panama

☐ **Flame-colored Tanager** *Piranga bidentata*
_____ *P. b. bidentata*   W Mexico (Sonora and Chihuahua to Guerrero and Morelos)
_____ *P. b. flammea*   Tres Marías Islands (off w Mexico)
_____ *P. b. sanguinolenta*   E Mexico (Nuevo León and Tamaulipas) to El Salvador
_____ *P. b. citrea*   Highlands of Costa Rica and w Panama

☐ **White-winged Tanager** *Piranga leucoptera*
_____ *P. l. leucoptera*   Sierra Madre Oriental of e Mexico (Tamaulipas) to Nicaragua
_____ *P. l. latifasciata*   Costa Rica and w Panama (east to Veraguas)
_____ *P. l. venezuelae*   Andes of Colombia to Venezuela and n Brazil
_____ *P. l. ardens*   Andes of extreme sw Colombia (Nariño) to nw Bolivia

☐ **Red-headed Tanager** *Piranga erythrocephala*
_____ *P. e. candida*   Sierra Madre Occidental of w Mexico (se Sonora to nw Jalisco)
_____ *P. e. erythrocephala*   Mountains of s Mexico (Jalisco and Guanajuato to Oaxaca)

☐ **Red-hooded Tanager** *Piranga rubriceps*

Andes of Colombia to ne Peru (Huánuco)

☐ **Vermilion Tanager** *Calochaetes coccineus*

Andes of se Colombia to Ecuador and e Peru (Cuzco)

☐ **Crimson-collared Tanager** *Ramphocelus sanguinolentus*
_____ *R. s. sanguinolentus*   Tropical se Mexico (Veracruz) to Guatemala and Honduras
_____ *R. s. apricus*   Caribbean slope of e Honduras to nw Panama (Almirante Bay)

☐ **Masked Crimson Tanager** *Ramphocelus nigrogularis*

Humid se Colombia to n Bolivia and w Amazonian Brazil

☐ **Crimson-backed Tanager** *Ramphocelus dimidiatus*
_____ *R. d. isthmicus*   Tropical w and central Panama (east to Río Chepo)
_____ *R. d. arestus*   Coiba I. (Panama)
_____ *R. d. limatus*   Pearl Islands (Bay of Panama)
_____ *R. d. dimidiatus*   Extreme e Panama (Darién) to n Colombia and w Venezuela
_____ *R. d. molochinus*   N Colombia (upper Magdalena Valley)

☐ **Huallaga Tanager** *Ramphocelus melanogaster*
_____ *R. m. melanogaster*   Highlands of n Peru (San Martín)
_____ *R. m. transitus*   E-c Peru (upper Huallaga Valley in Huánuco and San Martín)

☐ **Silver-beaked Tanager** *Ramphocelus carbo*
_____ *R. c. unicolor*   E base of E Andes of Colombia (Cundinamarca and Meta)
_____ *R. c. magnirostris*   Trinidad; single specimen from ne Venezuela (Sucre)
_____ *R. c. carbo*   SE Colombia to the Guianas, e Peru and n Brazil
_____ *R. c. venezuelensis*   E Colombia and w Venezuela
_____ *R. c. capitalis*   NE Venezuela (ne Anzoátegui to se Monagas, Delta Amacuro)
_____ *R. c. connectens*   SE Peru (Cuzco) to nw Bolivia (Río Beni)
_____ *R. c. atrosericeus*   N and e Bolivia
_____ *R. c. centralis*   E-central Brazil and adjacent e Paraguay

☐ **Brazilian Tanager** *Ramphocelus bresilius*
_____ *R. b. bresilius*   NE Brazil (Paraíba to Bahia)
_____ *R. b. dorsalis*   SE Brazil (Minas Gerais and Espírito Santo to Santa Catarina)

☐ **Passerini's Tanager** *Ramphocelus passerinii*

S Mexico (se Veracruz and ne Oaxaca) to w Panama

□ **Cherrie's Tanager** *Ramphocelus costaricensis*

Pacific slope of s Costa Rica (Puntarenas) and w Panama

□ **Flame-rumped Tanager** *Ramphocelus flammigerus*
_____ *R. f. icteronotus* Humid lowlands of Panama to w Colombia and w Ecuador
_____ *R. f. flammigerus* W Colombia (middle Cauca Valley south to Nariño)

□ **Northern Stripe-headed Tanager** *Spindalis zena*
_____ *S. z. townsendi* Grand Bahama I., the Abacos and Green Turtle Cay
_____ *S. z. zena* Central Bahamas
_____ *S. z. pretrei* Cuba, Isle of Pines and adjacent offshore cays
_____ *S. z. salvini* Grand Cayman I.
_____ *S. z. benedicti* Cozumel I. (off Yucatán coast of se Mexico)

□ **Puerto Rican Stripe-headed Tanager** *Spindalis portoricensis*

Puerto Rico

□ **Hispaniolan Stripe-headed Tanager** *Spindalis dominicensis*

Hispaniola and Gonâve I.

□ **Jamaican Stripe-headed Tanager** *Spindalis nigricephala*

Jamaica

□ **Blue-gray Tanager** *Thraupis episcopus*
_____ *T. e. cana* SE Mexico (San Luis Potosí) to n Venezuela; Pearl Islands
_____ *T. e. caesita* Caribbean coast of w Panama (Escudo de Veraguas)
_____ *T. e. cumatilis* Coiba I. (off Pacific coast of Panama)
_____ *T. e. nesophilus* Extreme e Colombia to e Venezuela; Trinidad
_____ *T. e. leucoptera* E slope of Eastern Andes of central Colombia
_____ *T. e. quaesita* Pacific slope of sw Colombia, w Ecuador and nw Peru
_____ *T. e. mediana* SE Colombia to extreme n Bolivia and n Brazil
_____ *T. e. coelestis* Tropical se Colombia to central Peru and w Amaz. Brazil
_____ *T. e. berlepschi* Tobago
_____ *T. e. episcopus* The Guianas and n Brazil
_____ *T. e. caerulea* SE Ecuador and n Peru (south to Huánuco)
_____ *T. e. major* Central Peru (Chanchamayo Valley of Ica)
_____ *T. e. urubambae* SE Peru (Urubamba Valley and Amazonian drainage)

□ **Glaucous Tanager** *Thraupis glaucocolpa*

Arid ne Colombia and n Venezuela; Isla Margarita

□ **Sayaca Tanager** *Thraupis sayaca*
_____ *T. s. boliviana* Tropical nw Bolivia (Río Beni to Río Mapiri)
_____ *T. s. obscura* Central and s Bolivia to w Argentina
_____ *T. s. sayaca* Paraguay to e and s Brazil, Uruguay and ne Argentina

□ **Azure-shouldered Tanager** *Thraupis cyanoptera*

Coastal se Brazil (Minas Gerais to Rio Grande do Sul)

□ **Golden-chevroned Tanager** *Thraupis ornata*

SE Brazil (s Bahia to e Minas Gerais and Santa Catarina)

□ **Blue-capped Tanager** *Thraupis cyanocephala*
_____ *T. c. cyanocephala* Andes of w Ecuador to e Peru and n Bolivia
_____ *T. c. annectens* W and Central Andes of central Colombia
_____ *T. c. auricrissa* E Andes of n-central Colombia and w Venezuela
_____ *T. c. margaritae* Santa Marta Mountains (ne Colombia)
_____ *T. c. hypophaea* Subtropical nw Venezuela (Páramo de las Rosas in Lara)
_____ *T. c. olivicyanea* Coastal mountains of n Venezuela (Aragua to Miranda)
_____ *T. c. subcinerea* Coastal mountains of ne Venezuela (Sucre and Monagas)
_____ *T. c. buesingi* Mountains of ne Venezuela (Pará Peninsula);Trinidad

□ **Blue-and-yellow Tanager** *Thraupis bonariensis*
_____ *T. b. darwinii* Andes of Ecuador to n Chile
_____ *T. b. composita* Andes of e and central Bolivia
_____ *T. b. schulzei* Paraguay and nw Argentina (south to Mendoza and Lavalle)
_____ *T. b. bonariensis* S Brazil (Rio Grande do Sul) to Uruguay and n Argentina

☐ **Yellow-winged Tanager** *Thraupis abbas*

E Mexico to e Nicaragua

☐ **Palm Tanager** *Thraupis palmarum*
____ *T. p. atripennis*
____ *T. p. violilavata*
____ *T. p. melanoptera*
____ *T. p. palmarum*

E Nicaragua to n Colombia and extreme nw Venezuela
Pacific slope of sw Colombia and w Ecuador
E Colombia to n Bolivia, the Guianas and Amazonian Brazil
E and s Brazil to e Bolivia and Paraguay

☐ **Blue-backed Tanager** *Cyanicterus cyanicterus*

E Venezuela to the Guianas and adjacent ne Brazil

☐ **Blue-and-gold Tanager** *Bangsia arcaei*
____ *B. a. caeruleigularis*
____ *B. a. arcaei*

Caribbean slope of Costa Rica
Humid lowlands of w Panama

☐ **Black-and-gold Tanager** *Bangsia melanochlamys*

Central and Western Andes of Colombia

☐ **Golden-chested Tanager** *Bangsia rothschildi*

Andes of w Colombia to nw Ecuador (Esmeraldas)

☐ **Moss-backed Tanager** *Bangsia edwardsi*

Andean foothills of sw Colombia and nw Ecuador

☐ **Gold-ringed Tanager** *Bangsia aureocincta*

Pacific slope of Western Andes of Colombia

☐ **Hooded Mountain-Tanager** *Buthraupis montana*
____ *B. m. gigas*
____ *B. m. cucullata*
____ *B. m. cyanonota*
____ *B. m. saturata*
____ *B. m. montana*

Eastern Andes of Colombia and w Venezuela
Western and Central Andes of Colombia and Ecuador
Andes of Peru (Amazonas to Junín)
Andes of se Peru (Cuzco and Puno)
Andes of w Bolivia (La Paz and Cochabamba)

☐ **Black-chested Mountain-Tanager** *Buthraupis eximia*
____ *B. e. eximia*
____ *B. e. zimmeri*
____ *B. e. chloronota*
____ *B. e. cyanocalyptra*

Eastern Andes of Colombia and sw Venezuela
Western and Central Andes of Colombia
E slope of Andes of se Colombia (Nariño) and nw Ecuador
E slope of Andes of se Ecuador to n Peru

☐ **Golden-backed Mountain-Tanager** *Buthraupis aureodorsalis*

Andes of c Peru (e La Libertad to San Martín and Huánuco)

☐ **Masked Mountain-Tanager** *Buthraupis wetmorei*

Andes of sw Colombia to nw Peru

☐ **Orange-throated Tanager** *Wetmorethraupis sterrhopteron*

N Peru (Marañón Valley) and adjacent s Ecuador

☐ **Santa Marta Mountain-Tanager** *Anisognathus melanogenys*

Santa Marta Mountains (ne Colombia)

☐ **Lacrimose Mountain-Tanager** *Anisognathus lacrymosus*
____ *A. l. pallididorsalis*
____ *A. l. melanops*
____ *A. l. tamae*
____ *A. l. intensus*
____ *A. l. olivaceiceps*
____ *A. l. palpebrosus*
____ *A. l. caerulescens*
____ *A. l. lacrymosus*

Sierra de Perijá (Colombia/Venezuela border)
Andes of w Venezuela (Trujillo, Mérida and Táchira)
Mountains of n-central Colombia and sw Venezuela
E slope of W Andes of sw Colombia (Valle and Cauca)
N part of W and Central Andes of Colombia (s to Quindío)
Andes of sw Colombia (Nariño) and e Ecuador
Mts. of s Ecuador (Loja) to n Peru (Cajamarca, Amazonas)
Andes of central Peru (La Libertad to Junín and n Cuzco)

☐ **Scarlet-bellied Mountain-Tanager** *Anisognathus igniventris*
____ *A. i. lunulatus*
____ *A. i. erythronotus*
____ *A. i. ignicrissus*
____ *A. i. igniventris*

Andes of n-central Colombia and w Venezuela (Táchira)
Central Andes of s Colombia and Ecuador
Andes of Peru (Cajamarca and Amazonas to Junín)
Andes of se Peru (Cuzco) to nw Bolivia

☐ **Blue-winged Mountain-Tanager** *Anisognathus somptuosus*

____	*A. s. antioquiae*	Northern part of Western and Central Andes of Colombia
____	*A. s. victorini*	Andes of central Colombia to sw Venezuela (Táchira)
____	*A. s. cyanopterus*	W slope of Central Andes of sw Colombia and w Ecuador
____	*A. s. baezae*	E slope of Eastern Andes of s Colombia and e Ecuador
____	*A. s. venezuelanus*	Coastal mountains of n Venezuela (Yaracuy to Miranda)
____	*A. s. virididorsalis*	Subtropical n Venezuela (Golfo de Triste area)
____	*A. s. alamoris*	Subtropical sw Ecuador (Cuenca to Loja)
____	*A. s. somptuosus*	Extreme se Ecuador (Zamora) to e Peru (Junín)
____	*A. s. flavinuchus*	Subtropical se Peru (Cuzco) to nw Bolivia

☐ **Black-chinned Mountain-Tanager** *Anisognathus notabilis*

Humid Andes of w Colombia and w Ecuador

☐ **Diademed Tanager** *Stephanophorus diadematus*

Paraguay to se Brazil, Uruguay and ne Argentina

☐ **Purplish-mantled Tanager** *Iridosornis porphyrocephala*

Humid Western Andes of Colombia and nw Ecuador

☐ **Yellow-throated Tanager** *Iridosornis analis*

Andes of se Colombia to Ecuador and se Peru (Puno)

☐ **Golden-collared Tanager** *Iridosornis jelskii*

____	*I. j. jelskii*	Temperate Andes of Peru (La Libertad to Junín)
____	*I. j. bolivianus*	Andes of se Peru (Cuzco) to w Bolivia (La Paz)

☐ **Golden-crowned Tanager** *Iridosornis rufivertex*

____	*I. r. caeruleoventris*	Western and Central Andes of nw Colombia
____	*I. r. ignicapillus*	Western and Central Andes of sw Colombia
____	*I. r. rufivertex*	E Andes of Colombia to sw Venezuela, e Ecuador, e Peru
____	*I. r. subsimilis*	W slope of Western Andes of Ecuador

☐ **Yellow-scarfed Tanager** *Iridosornis reinhardti*

E slope of Andes of Peru (s Amazonas to Cuzco)

☐ **Buff-breasted Mountain-Tanager** *Dubusia taeniata*

____	*D. t. carrikeri*	Santa Marta Mountains (ne Colombia)
____	*D. t. taeniata*	Andes of Colombia to w Venezuela and Ecuador
____	*D. t. stictocephala*	Andes of se Peru (Junín to Cuzco)

☐ **Chestnut-bellied Mountain-Tanager** *Delothraupis castaneoventris*

____	*D. c. peruviana*	Andes of e Peru (north to La Libertad)
____	*D. c. castaneoventris*	Andes of w Bolivia (La Paz, Cochabamba, w Santa Cruz)

☐ **Fawn-breasted Tanager** *Pipraeidea melanonota*

____	*P. m. venezuelensis*	Andes of Colombia to Venezuela and nw Argentina
____	*P. m. melanonota*	E Paraguay to se Brazil, Uruguay and ne Argentina

☐ **Jamaican Euphonia** *Euphonia jamaica*

Woodlands and scrub of Jamaica

☐ **Plumbeous Euphonia** *Euphonia plumbea*

S Venezuela to Guianas, Suriname and n Amazonian Brazil

☐ **Scrub Euphonia** *Euphonia affinis*

____	*E. a. godmani*	Arid tropical w Mexico (se Sonora to Guerrero)
____	*E. a. olmecorum*	S Mexico (Oaxaca and Chiapas)
____	*E. a. affinis*	Tropical e Mexico (Tamaulipas) to nw Costa Rica

☐ **Purple-throated Euphonia** *Euphonia chlorotica*

____	*E. c. cynophora*	Tropical ne Colombia to s Venezuela and extreme n Brazil
____	*E. c. chlorotica*	Tropical Guianas to ne Brazil
____	*E. c. serrirostris*	SE Bolivia to e Paraguay, Uruguay, se Brazil, n Argentina
____	*E. c. taczanowskii*	E Peru and n Bolivia
____	*E. c. amazonica*	Amazonian Brazil

☐ **Yellow-crowned Euphonia** *Euphonia luteicapilla*

☐ **Trinidad Euphonia** *Euphonia trinitatis*

Tropical e Nicaragua to Costa Rica and Panama

☐ **Velvet-fronted Euphonia** *Euphonia concinna*

Trop. n Caribbean Colombia to n Venezuela; Trinidad

☐ **Orange-crowned Euphonia** *Euphonia saturata*

W Colombia (upper Magdalena Valley)

☐ **Finsch's Euphonia** *Euphonia finschi*

Andes of sw Colombia to extreme nw Peru (Tumbes)

☐ **Violaceous Euphonia** *Euphonia violacea*

SE Venezuela to the Guianas and n Brazil (n Roraima)

_____ *E. v. rodwayi*	Tropical e Venezuela (Sucre to n Amazonas); Trinidad
_____ *E. v. violacea*	Tropical Guianas and n Brazil
_____ *E. v. auranticollis*	E Paraguay to se Brazil and ne Argentina (Misiones)

☐ **Thick-billed Euphonia** *Euphonia laniirostris*

_____ *E. l. crassirostris*	Costa Rica to n Colombia and n Venezuela
_____ *E. l. melanura*	E Colombia to e Ecuador, n Peru and w Amazonian Brazil
_____ *E. l. hypoxantha*	W Ecuador and nw Peru
_____ *E. l. zopholega*	Tropical e-central Peru (Junín and Cuzco)
_____ *E. l. laniirostris*	E Bolivia and adjacent sw Brazil

☐ **Yellow-throated Euphonia** *Euphonia hirundinacea*

_____ *E. h. hirundinacea (suttoni, russelli, caribbaea)*	Gulf-Caribbean lowlands of e Mexico to e Nicaragua
_____ *E. h. gnatho*	NW Nicaragua to Costa Rica and extreme w Panama

☐ **Green-chinned Euphonia** *Euphonia chalybea*

Lowlands of e Paraguay to se Brazil and ne Argentina

☐ **Elegant Euphonia** *Euphonia elegantissima*

_____ *E. e. rileyi*	Montane forests of nw Mexico (se Sonora and ne Sinaloa)
_____ *E. e. elegantissima*	N Mexico (s Sinaloa and sw Tamaulipas) to nw Guatemala
_____ *E. e. vincens*	SE Guatemala to w Panama

☐ **Antillean Euphonia** *Euphonia musica*

_____ *E. m. musica*	Hispaniola and Gonâve I.
_____ *E. m. sclateri*	Puerto Rico
_____ *E. m. flavifrons*	Lesser Antilles

☐ **Golden-rumped Euphonia** *Euphonia cyanocephala*

_____ *E. c. pelzelni*	Andes of Colombia to nw Argentina, n Venezuela; Trinidad
_____ *E. c. cyanocephala*	*Tepuis* of se Venezuela to Guyana and Suriname
_____ *E. c. ssp.*	E Paraguay to se Brazil and ne Argentina

☐ **Spot-crowned Euphonia** *Euphonia imitans*

Humid sw Costa Rica and extreme w Panama

☐ **Fulvous-vented Euphonia** *Euphonia fulvicrissa*

_____ *E. f. fulvicrissa*	Humid lowlands of central Panama to nw Colombia
_____ *E. f. omissa*	Tropical central Colombia
_____ *E. f. purpurascens*	Tropical sw Colombia (Nariño) to nw Ecuador (Esmeraldas)

☐ **Olive-backed Euphonia** *Euphonia gouldi*

_____ *E. g. gouldi (loetscheri)*	Caribbean slope of e Mexico (Veracruz) to Honduras
_____ *E. g. praetermissa*	Extreme e Honduras to w Panama (Bocas del Toro)

☐ **Bronze-green Euphonia** *Euphonia mesochrysa*

_____ *E. m. mesochrysa*	Central Colombia (Magdalena Valley) to e Ecuador
_____ *E. m. media*	Subtropical Andes of n and central Peru
_____ *E. m. tavarae*	Andes of se Peru to nw Bolivia

☐ **White-lored Euphonia** *Euphonia chrysopasta*
_____ *E. c. chrysopasta* .... Tropical se Colombia to Bolivia and adjacent w Brazil
_____ *E. c. nitida* .... E Colombia to s Venezuela, the Guianas and n Brazil

☐ **White-vented Euphonia** *Euphonia minuta*
_____ *E. m. humilis* .... Gulf slope of se Mexico (se Chiapas) to w Ecuador
_____ *E. m. minuta* .... Colombia e of Andes to the Guianas, n Bolivia and w Brazil

☐ **Tawny-capped Euphonia** *Euphonia anneae*
_____ *E. a. anneae* .... Caribbean slope of Costa Rica and extreme w Panama
_____ *E. a. rufivertex* .... Tropical w Panama (Veraguas) to nw Colombia (Chocó)

☐ **Orange-bellied Euphonia** *Euphonia xanthogaster*
_____ *E. x. chocoensis* .... Humid e Panama (Darién) to nw Colombia and nw Ecuador
_____ *E. x. exsul (badissima)* .... Mountains of ne Colombia and n Venezuela
_____ *E. x. dilutior* .... Tropical se Colombia to ne Peru (Ucayali Valley)
_____ *E. x. lecroyana* .... W Venezuela (Táchira, Mérida, Lara, Barinas and Zulia)
_____ *E. x. brevirostris* .... E Colombia to Venezuela, Guianas, nw Brazil and e Peru
_____ *E. x. quitensis* .... Tropical and subtropical w Ecuador
_____ *E. x. brunneifrons* .... SE Peru (Cuzco and Puno)
_____ *E. x. ruficeps* .... W Bolivia (La Paz and Cochabamba)
_____ *E. x. cyanonota* .... W Brazil (Rio Juruá and Rio Purús regions)
_____ *E. x. xanthogaster* .... E Brazil (south to Rio de Janeiro)

☐ **Rufous-bellied Euphonia** *Euphonia rufiventris*

SE Colombia to s Venezuela, n Bolivia and w Amaz. Brazil

☐ **Golden-sided Euphonia** *Euphonia cayennensis*

Tropical se Venezuela, the Guianas and e Amazonian Brazil

☐ **Chestnut-bellied Euphonia** *Euphonia pectoralis*

E Brazil (e Alagoas) to e Paraguay and ne Argentina

☐ **Yellow-collared Chlorophonia** *Chlorophonia flavirostris*

Humid forests of sw Colombia and nw Ecuador

☐ **Blue-naped Chlorophonia** *Chlorophonia cyanea*
_____ *C. c. psittacina* .... Santa Marta Mountains (ne Colombia)
_____ *C. c. intensa* .... W slope of Western Andes of Colombia (Caldas and Valle)
_____ *C. c. longipennis* .... Andes of e Colombia to w Venezuela, e Peru and w Bolivia
_____ *C. c. frontalis* .... Mountains of n Venezuela (Falcón and Lara to Miranda)
_____ *C. c. minuscula* .... Coastal mountains of ne Venezuela
_____ *C. c. roraimae* .... S Venezuela to Guyana and extreme nw Brazil
_____ *C. c. cyanea* .... Paraguay to se Brazil (s Bahia) and ne Argentina (Misiones)

☐ **Chestnut-breasted Chlorophonia** *Chlorophonia pyrrhophrys*

Andes of Colombia to w Venezuela and e Peru (Huánuco)

☐ **Blue-crowned Chlorophonia** *Chlorophonia occipitalis*

Montane forests of se Mexico (Veracruz) to Nicaragua

☐ **Golden-browed Chlorophonia** *Chlorophonia callophrys*

Montane forests of Costa Rica and w Panama

☐ **Glistening-green Tanager** *Chlorochrysa phoenicotis*

Andes of w Colombia and w Ecuador

☐ **Orange-eared Tanager** *Chlorochrysa calliparaea*
_____ *C. c. bourcieri* .... W slope of Eastern Andes of Colombia to ne Peru
_____ *C. c. calliparaea* .... Subtropical Andes of e-central Peru
_____ *C. c. fulgentissima* .... Andes of se Peru (Puno) to w Bolivia

☐ **Multicolored Tanager** *Chlorochrysa nitidissima*

Locally in Andes of w Colombia

☐ **Plain-colored Tanager** *Tangara inornata*
_____ *T. i. rava* .... Caribbean lowlands of se Costa Rica and w Panama
_____ *T. i. languens* .... Tropical e Panama to extreme nw Colombia
_____ *T. i. inornata* .... N Colombia (Sinú, lower Cauca, middle Magdalena valleys)

☐ **Turquoise Tanager** *Tangara mexicana*
_____ *T. m. media* — Extreme e Colombia to e Venezuela and nw Brazil
_____ *T. m. vieilloti* — Trinidad
_____ *T. m. boliviana* — E Colombia to n Bolivia and w Amazonian Brazil
_____ *T. m. mexicana* — Tropical zone of the Guianas
_____ *T. m. brasiliensis* — Coastal se Brazil (s Bahia to Rio de Janeiro)

☐ **Azure-rumped Tanager** *Tangara cabanisi*

Cloud forests of s Mexico (Chiapas) and adj. Guatemala

☐ **Gray-and-gold Tanager** *Tangara palmeri*

Humid foothills of e Panama to nw Ecuador (Pichincha)

☐ **Paradise Tanager** *Tangara chilensis*
_____ *T. c. coelicolor* — Colombia east of the Andes to s Venezuela and nw Brazil
_____ *T. c. chilensis* — SE Colombia to n Bolivia and w Amazonian Brazil
_____ *T. c. paradisea* — E Venezuela to the Guianas and n Brazil
_____ *T. c. chlorocorys* — N-central Peru (upper Huallaga Valley)

☐ **Seven-colored Tanager** *Tangara fastuosa*

Coastal ne Brazil (s Paraíba, e Pernambuco and Alagoas)

☐ **Green-headed Tanager** *Tangara seledon*

SE Paraguay to se Brazil and ne Argentina (Misiones)

☐ **Red-necked Tanager** *Tangara cyanocephala*
_____ *T. c. cearensis* — Forests of ne Brazil (Ceará)
_____ *T. c. corallina* — E Brazil (Pernambuco to Bahia)
_____ *T. c. cyanocephala* — SE Brazil (s Bahia) to e Paraguay and ne Argentina

☐ **Brassy-breasted Tanager** *Tangara desmaresti*

Coastal mountains of se Brazil (Espírito Santo to e Paraná)

☐ **Gilt-edged Tanager** *Tangara cyanoventris*

SE Brazil (s Bahia and se Minas Gerais to e São Paulo)

☐ **Blue-whiskered Tanager** *Tangara johannae*

Pacific lowlands of w Colombia and nw Ecuador

☐ **Green-and-gold Tanager** *Tangara schrankii*
_____ *T. s. anchicayae* — W slope of Western Andes of Colombia (Río Anchicayá)
_____ *T. s. schrankii* — SE Colombia to n Bolivia and w Amazonian Brazil
_____ *T. s. venezuelana* — Tropical s Venezuela (s Bolívar and e Amazonas)

☐ **Emerald Tanager** *Tangara florida*
_____ *T. f. florida* — Caribbean slope of Costa Rica and w Panama
_____ *T. f. auriceps* — Extreme e Panama (Darién) to Colombia and nw Ecuador

☐ **Golden Tanager** *Tangara arthus*
_____ *T. a. occidentalis* — W and Central Andes of Colombia (Antioquia to Nariño)
_____ *T. a. palmitae* — W slope of Eastern Andes of Colombia (s Magdalena)
_____ *T. a. sclateri* — Both slopes of Eastern Andes of Colombia
_____ *T. a. aurulenta* — Cent. Colombia (upper Magdalena Valley) to nw Venezuela
_____ *T. a. arthus* — Mts. of n Venezuela (Táchira to Lara, Falcón and Miranda)
_____ *T. a. goodsoni* — Subtropical w Ecuador
_____ *T. a. aequatorialis* — Subtropical e Ecuador and n Peru
_____ *T. a. pulchra* — Central Peru (Chachapoyas to Chanchamayo)
_____ *T. a. sophiae* — Tropical se Peru (Cuzco and Puno) to nw Bolivia

☐ **Silver-throated Tanager** *Tangara icterocephala*
_____ *T. i. frantzii* — Humid highlands of Costa Rica and w Panama
_____ *T. i. oresbia* — Mountains of w-central Panama
_____ *T. i. icterocephala* — E Panama (Darién) to w Colombia and w Ecuador

☐ **Golden-eared Tanager** *Tangara chrysotis*

Andes of sw Colombia to nw Bolivia

☐ **Saffron-crowned Tanager** *Tangara xanthocephala*

____	*T. x. venusta*	Andes of Colombia to w Venezuela and central Peru
____	*T. x. xanthocephala*	Subtropical Andes of central Peru (Chanchamayo region)
____	*T. x. lamprotis*	Andes of se Peru (Cuzco and Puno) to nw Bolivia

☐ **Flame-faced Tanager** *Tangara parzudakii*

____	*T. p. parzudakii*	Andes of Colombia to sw Venezuela, e Ecuador and e Peru
____	*T. p. lunigera*	Pacific slope of Colombia and w Ecuador
____	*T. p. urubambae*	SE Peru (Cordillera Urubamba in Cuzco)

☐ **Yellow-bellied Tanager** *Tangara xanthogastra*

____	*T. x. xanthogastra*	SE Colombia to s Venezuela and n Bolivia
____	*T. x. phelpsi*	S Venezuela and w Amazonian Brazil

☐ **Spotted Tanager** *Tangara punctata*

____	*T. p. punctata*	Tropical s Venezuela, the Guianas and n Amazonian Brazil
____	*T. p. zamorae*	Tropical e Ecuador and n Peru
____	*T. p. perenensis*	Tropical and subtropical e Peru (Chanchamayo region)
____	*T. p. annectens*	Subtropical se Peru (Río Inambari region)
____	*T. p. punctulata*	*Yungas* of n Bolivia (La Paz and Cochabamba)

☐ **Speckled Tanager** *Tangara guttata*

____	*T. g. eusticta*	Caribbean slope of Costa Rica and w Panama
____	*T. g. tolimae*	E slope of Central Andes of Colombia (Tolima)
____	*T. g. bogotensis*	Colombia (east of the Andes) and adjacent w Venezuela
____	*T. g. chrysophrys*	Venezuela and extreme nw Brazil (Sierra de Curupira)
____	*T. g. guttata*	SE Venezuela (s Bolívar) and extreme n Brazil (Roraima)
____	*T. g. trinitatis*	Mountains of n Trinidad

☐ **Dotted Tanager** *Tangara varia*

S Venezuela to the Guianas and n Amazonian Brazil

☐ **Rufous-throated Tanager** *Tangara rufigula*

Andes of w Colombia and w Ecuador (south to El Oro)

☐ **Bay-headed Tanager** *Tangara gyrola*

____	*T. g. bangsi*	Humid tropical and subtropical Costa Rica and w Panama
____	*T. g. deleticia*	E Panama (Darién) and w Colombia
____	*T. g. nupera*	Extreme sw Colombia (Nariño) and w Ecuador
____	*T. g. toddi*	Mountains of n Colombia and nw Venezuela
____	*T. g. viridissima*	Coastal ne Venezuela; Trinidad
____	*T. g. catharinae*	E base of Eastern Andes of Colombia to central Bolivia
____	*T. g. parva*	SE Colombia to s Venezuela, ne Peru and nw Brazil
____	*T. g. gyrola*	S Venezuela to the Guianas and extreme n Brazil
____	*T. g. albertinae*	Brazil s of the Amazon (Rio Purús to Pará, n Mato Grosso)

☐ **Rufous-winged Tanager** *Tangara lavinia*

____	*T. l. cara*	Honduras to Nicaragua and Costa Rica
____	*T. l. dalmasi*	Tropical w Panama (Chiriquí and Veraguas)
____	*T. l. lavinia*	E Panama to w Colombia and nw Ecuador; Isla Gorgona

☐ **Burnished-buff Tanager** *Tangara cayana*

____	*T. c. fulvescens*	Eastern Andes of Colombia
____	*T. c. cayana*	Colombia (e of the Andes) to Guianas, n Brazil and e Peru
____	*T. c. huberi*	NE Brazil (Ilha Marajó region of Pará)
____	*T. c. flava*	NE Brazil (Maranhão and n Goiás to extreme s Bahia)
____	*T. c. sincipitalis*	Central Brazil (Goiás)
____	*T. c. margaritae*	Central Brazil (Mato Grosso)
____	*T. c. chloroptera*	Paraguay to se Brazil (Minas Gerais) and ne Argentina

☐ **Black-backed Tanager** *Tangara peruviana*

Lowlands of se Brazil (Rio de Janeiro to Santa Catarina)

☐ **Lesser Antillean Tanager** *Tangara cucullata*
_____ *T. c. versicolor*   St. Vincent (Lesser Antilles)
_____ *T. c. cucullata*   Grenada (Lesser Antilles)

☐ **Chestnut-backed Tanager** *Tangara preciosa*

E Paraguay to se Brazil, Uruguay and ne Argentina

☐ **Scrub Tanager** *Tangara vitriolina*

Arid scrub of w Colombia and nw Ecuador

☐ **Green-capped Tanager** *Tangara meyerdeschauenseei*

E slope of Andes of extreme se Peru (Puno)

☐ **Rufous-cheeked Tanager** *Tangara rufigenis*

Coastal mts. of n Venezuela (s Lara to Distrito Federal)

☐ **Golden-naped Tanager** *Tangara ruficervix*
_____ *T. r. ruficervix*   Andes of Colombia and Santa Marta Mountains
_____ *T. r. taylori*   SE Colombia (east of the Andes) and e Ecuador
_____ *T. r. leucotis*   Subtropical w Ecuador
_____ *T. r. amabilis*   Subtropical n Peru (south to Huánuco)
_____ *T. r. inca*   Subtropical s Peru (north to Junín)
_____ *T. r. fulvicervix*   *Yungas* of nw Bolivia (La Paz and Cochabamba)

☐ **Metallic-green Tanager** *Tangara labradorides*
_____ *T. l. labradorides*   Andes of w Colombia and w Ecuador
_____ *T. l. chaupensis*   Andes of ne Peru (south to San Martín)

☐ **Blue-browed Tanager** *Tangara cyanotis*
_____ *T. c. lutleyi*   Andes of s Colombia to e Ecuador and e Peru
_____ *T. c. cyanotis*   *Yungas* of nw Bolivia (La Paz and Cochabamba)

☐ **Blue-necked Tanager** *Tangara cyanicollis*
_____ *T. c. granadensis*   Andes of Colombia
_____ *T. c. caeruleocephala*   E Andes of central Colombia to e Ecuador and n Peru
_____ *T. c. hannahiae*   Colombia (east of Eastern Andes) and w Venezuela
_____ *T. c. cyanopygia*   Western Ecuador
_____ *T. c. cyanicollis*   E Peru (north to Huánuco) and e Bolivia
_____ *T. c. melanogaster*   W Amazonian Brazil (Amazon drainage of w Mato Grosso)
_____ *T. c. albotibialis*   E Brazil (s Pará and s Goiás)

☐ **Golden-hooded Tanager** *Tangara larvata*
_____ *T. l. larvata*   Tropical s Mexico (n Oaxaca and Tabasco) to n Costa Rica
_____ *T. l. centralis*   Caribbean slope of Costa Rica and w Panama
_____ *T. l. franciscae*   Pacific slope of Costa Rica and w Panama
_____ *T. l. fanny*   Pacific slope of Panama to Colombia and nw Ecuador

☐ **Masked Tanager** *Tangara nigrocincta*

SE Colombia to s Venezuela, Guianas, n Bolivia and w Brazil

☐ **Spangle-cheeked Tanager** *Tangara dowii*

Humid montane forests of Costa Rica and w Panama

☐ **Green-naped Tanager** *Tangara fucosa*

Highlands of extreme e Panama (Darién) and adj. Colombia

☐ **Beryl-spangled Tanager** *Tangara nigroviridis*
_____ *T. n. cyanescens (consobrina)*   Andes of Colombia to n Venezuela and w Ecuador
_____ *T. n. nigroviridis*   E slope of Eastern Andes of Colombia and e Ecuador
_____ *T. n. lozanoana*   Mts. of Venezuela (Táchira, Mérida, Zulia and Lara)
_____ *T. n. berlepschi*   Andes of e Peru to nw Bolivia (La Paz and Cochabamba)

☐ **Blue-and-black Tanager** *Tangara vassorii*
_____ *T. v. vassorii*   Andes of Colombia to nw Venezuela, Ecuador and nw Peru
_____ *T. v. branickii*   Andes of n and central Peru
_____ *T. v. atrocoerulea*   Andes of s Peru (Huánuco) to w Bolivia

☐ **Black-capped Tanager** *Tangara heinei*

Mountains of n Colombia to n Venezuela and n Ecuador

☐ **Sira Tanager** *Tangara phillipsi*

Andes of e Peru (Cerros del Sira in e Huánuco)

☐ **Silver-backed Tanager** *Tangara viridicollis*

_____ *T. v. fulvigula* Andes of s Ecuador and n Peru
_____ *T. v. viridicollis* Andes of central and s Peru

☐ **Straw-backed Tanager** *Tangara argyrofenges*

_____ *T. a. caeruleigularis* Andes of extreme s Ecuador and n Peru (south to Junín)
_____ *T. a. argyrofenges* *Yungas* of w Bolivia (La Paz, Cochabamba and w Santa Cruz)

☐ **Black-headed Tanager** *Tangara cyanoptera*

_____ *T. c. cyanoptera* Mountains of n Colombia to n Venezuela
_____ *T. c. whitelyi* *Tepuis* of s Venezuela to Guyana and extreme n Brazil

☐ **Opal-rumped Tanager** *Tangara velia*

_____ *T. v. iridina* Colombia (east of the Andes) to n Bolivia and nw Brazil
_____ *T. v. velia* The Guianas and n Amazonian Brazil
_____ *T. v. signata* Tropical ne Brazil (south of the Amazon in Pará)
_____ *T. v. cyanomelaena* Coastal se Brazil (Pernambuco to Rio de Janeiro)

☐ **Opal-crowned Tanager** *Tangara callophrys*

SE Colombia to n Bolivia and w Amazonian Brazil

☐ **Golden-collared Honeycreeper** *Iridophanes pulcherrima*

_____ *I. p. pulcherrima* E slope of Andes of Colombia to e Ecuador and e Peru
_____ *I. p. aureinucha* Subtropical w Ecuador

☐ **Turquoise Dacnis-Tanager** *Pseudodacnis hartlaubi*

Locally in Andes of Colombia

☐ **White-bellied Dacnis** *Dacnis albiventris*

SE Colombia to s Venezuela, ne Peru and c Amaz. Brazil

☐ **Black-faced Dacnis** *Dacnis lineata*

_____ *D. l. egregia* Tropical central Colombia (Magdalena and Cauca valleys)
_____ *D. l. lineata* Colombia (e of the Andes) to n Bolivia and Amaz. Brazil
_____ *D. l. aequatorialis* Tropical w Ecuador (Esmeraldas to Chimbo)

☐ **Yellow-bellied Dacnis** *Dacnis flaviventer*

SE Colombia to s Venezuela, n Bolivia and w Amaz. Brazil

☐ **Black-legged Dacnis** *Dacnis nigripes*

SE Brazil (Minas Gerais to Santa Catarina)

☐ **Scarlet-thighed Dacnis** *Dacnis venusta*

_____ *D. v. venusta* Tropical Costa Rica and w Panama (Chiriquí)
_____ *D. v. fuliginata* E Panama (Caribbean slope of Darién) to nw Ecuador

☐ **Blue Dacnis** *Dacnis cayana*

_____ *D. c. ultramarina* Caribbean slope of ne Honduras to nw Colombia
_____ *D. c. callaina* W Costa Rica and w Panama (Chiriquí)
_____ *D. c. napaea* Tropical n Colombia
_____ *D. c. baudoana* Tropical sw Colombia (Baudó Mts.) to w Ecuador
_____ *D. c. coerbicolor* Central Colombia (Cauca and Magdalena valleys)
_____ *D. c. cayana* E Colombia to Venezuela, Guianas, n and c Brazil; Trinidad
_____ *D. c. glaucogularis* S Colombia to e Ecuador, e Peru and w Bolivia
_____ *D. c. paraguayensis* E Paraguay to e and s Brazil and ne Argentina

☐ **Viridian Dacnis** *Dacnis viguieri*

Lowlands of extreme e Panama and adjacent nw Colombia

☐ **Scarlet-breasted Dacnis** *Dacnis berlepschi*

Lowlands of extreme sw Colombia and nw Ecuador

☐ **Green Honeycreeper** *Chlorophanes spiza*

_____ *C. s. guatemalensis* — S Mexico (Oaxaca) to Guatemala, Belize and Honduras
_____ *C. s. arguta* — Extreme e Honduras to nw Colombia
_____ *C. s. exsul* — Tropical sw Colombia to w Ecuador and extreme nw Peru
_____ *C. s. subtropicalis* — Andes of Colombia and w Venezuela
_____ *C. s. caerulescens* — SE Colombia to e Ecuador, e Peru and w Bolivia
_____ *C. s. spiza* — E Colombia to Venezuela, the Guianas and n Brazil; Trinidad
_____ *C. s. axillaris* — Coastal e Brazil (Pernambuco to Santa Catarina)

☐ **Short-billed Honeycreeper** *Cyanerpes nitidus*

SE Colombia to Venezuela, e Peru and w Amaz. Brazil

☐ **Shining Honeycreeper** *Cyanerpes lucidus*

_____ *C. l. lucidus* — S Mexico (Chiapas) to Belize, Guatemala and n Nicaragua
_____ *C. l. isthmicus* — Costa Rica to Panama and extreme nw Colombia

☐ **Purple Honeycreeper** *Cyanerpes caeruleus*

_____ *C. c. caeruleus* — Extreme e Panama to Venezuela, the Guianas and ne Brazil
_____ *C. c. chocoanus* — Tropical w Colombia and w Ecuador
_____ *C. c. microrhynchus* — E Colombia to s Venezuela, n Bolivia and w Amaz. Brazil
_____ *C. c. longirostris* — Trinidad
_____ *C. c. hellmayri* — Highlands of Guyana

☐ **Red-legged Honeycreeper** *Cyanerpes cyaneus*

_____ *C. c. carneipes* — Gulf slope of s Mexico to n Colombia; Coiba I. and Pearl Is.
_____ *C. c. gemmeus* — N Colombia (Serranía de Macuire on Guajira Peninsula)
_____ *C. c. pacificus* — Pacific coast of w Colombia and w Ecuador
_____ *C. c. gigas* — Gorgona Islands (off Pacific coast of Colombia)
_____ *C. c. eximius* — Tropical n Colombia to n Venezuela; Isla Margarita
_____ *C. c. dispar* — E Colombia to s Venezuela, w Brazil and ne Peru
_____ *C. c. tobagensis* — Tobago
_____ *C. c. cyaneus* — Trop. se Venezuela to the Guianas and ne Brazil; Trinidad
_____ *C. c. brevipes* — Central Amazonian Brazil
_____ *C. c. holti* — E Brazil
_____ *C. c. violaceus* — Central Bolivia and w Brazil

☐ **Tit-like Dacnis** *Xenodacnis parina*

_____ *X. p. bella* — Locally in *polylepis* woodlands of sw Ecuador and n Peru
_____ *X. p. petersi* — Cordillera Blanca (central Peru)
_____ *X. p. parina* — Andes of s-central Peru (Junín, Ayacucho and Cuzco)

☐ **Swallow-Tanager** *Tersina viridis*

_____ *T. v. occidentalis* — E Panama to Venezuela, the Guianas, n Bolivia and n Brazil
_____ *T. v. grisescens* — Santa Marta Mountains (ne Colombia)
_____ *T. v. viridis* — E Bolivia to Paraguay, e Brazil and ne Argentina

☐ **Plush-capped Finch** *Catamblyrhynchus diadema*

_____ *C. d. diadema* — Andes of Colombia to nw Venezuela and s Ecuador
_____ *C. d. federalis* — Coastal mts. of n Venezuela (Aragua and Distrito Federal)
_____ *C. d. citrinifrons* — Andes of Peru to Bolivia and nw Argentina (Jujuy)

☐ **Tanager Finch** *Oreothraupis arremonops*

Pacific slope of w Andes of Colombia and nw Ecuador

☐ **Black-backed Bush-Tanager** *Urothraupis stolzmanni*

Andes of se Colombia and e Ecuador

☐ **Pardusco** *Nephelornis oneilli*

Andes of c Peru (San Martín, La Libertad and Huánuco)

FAMILY: EMBERIZIDAE (Buntings, Sparrows, Seedeaters and Allies—321)

☐ **Przevalski's Rosefinch** *Urocynchramus pylzowi*

Mountains of w China and e Tibet

☐ **Crested Bunting** *Melophus lathami*

N Pakistan to se Tibet, s China, Laos and n Vietnam (Tonkin)

☐ **Slaty Bunting** *Latoucheornis siemsseni*

Mountains of central China (s Shaanxi, se Gansu and ne Sichuan)

☐ **Yellowhammer** *Emberiza citrinella*
____ *E. c. caliginosa* — Ireland, Scotland, Wales and n and w England
____ *E. c. citrinella* — SE England, n and w Europe to c Russia; winters to North Africa
____ *E. c. erythrogenys* — E Europe to central Siberia; winters to n Mongolia and Iraq

☐ **Pine Bunting** *Emberiza leucocephalos*
____ *E. l. leucocephalos* — Siberia to Sakhalin and Tibet; winters to Iraq, India and China
____ *E. l. fronto* — NW China (Kokonor region of ne Qinghai to nw Gansu)

☐ **Cirl Bunting** *Emberiza cirlus*
____ *E. c. cirlus* — Wales and e England to Mediterranean and North Africa
____ *E. c. nigrostriata* — Corsica and Sardinia

☐ **Tibetan Bunting** *Emberiza koslowi*

W China (borders of arid Tibet, sw Qinghai and Sichuan)

☐ **Rock Bunting** *Emberiza cia*
____ *E. c. cia* — Iberian Peninsula and s Europe to w Asia Minor
____ *E. c. africana* — Coastal mountains of s Spain and North Africa
____ *E. c. prageri* — Crimea, Caucasus, ne Turkey and nw Iran
____ *E. c. par* — N and central Iran to Pakistan, nw India and s Altai Mountains

☐ **Godlewski's Bunting** *Emberiza godlewskii*
____ *E. g. stracheyi* — W Himalayas (Chitral to Ladakh)
____ *E. g. decolorata* — W China (foothills of w Tarim Basin in Xinjiang)
____ *E. g. godlewskii* — Mongolia to nw China
____ *E. g. khamensis* — Tibet to w Sichuan and s Qinghai
____ *E. g. yunnanensis* — SE Tibet to n Myanmar, n Yunnan, ne Sichuan and w Hubei
____ *E. g. omissa* — S Mongolia to Hubei, Shaanxi and nw Sichuan
____ *E. g. flemingorum* — Nepal

☐ **Meadow Bunting** *Emberiza cioides*
____ *E. c. tarbagataica* — Mountains of central Asia; winters in n Mongolia
____ *E. c. cioides* — NW Altai Mts. to Transbaikalia and mts. of Mongolia
____ *E. c. weigoldi* — E Transbaikalia to Manchuria, n Liaoning and n Korea
____ *E. c. castaneiceps* — S and central Korea and e China
____ *E. c. ciopsis* — S Kuril and Japanese islands; winters from Honshu southward

☐ **Rufous-backed Bunting** *Emberiza jankowskii*

NE China and extreme ne Korea; winters e-central China

☐ **Gray-hooded Bunting** *Emberiza buchanani*
____ *E. b. cerrutii* — E Turkey, Russia s of the Caucasus to Iran; Mugodzhary Mts.
____ *E. b. buchanani* — Afghanistan to w Pakistan; winters to se India
____ *E. b. neobscura* — Tajikistan to w Xinjiang, e Kazakstan and w Mongolia

☐ **Cinereous Bunting** *Emberiza cineracea*
____ *E. c. cineracea* — Arid rocky slopes of w and s Turkey
____ *E. c. semenowi* — Zagros Mountains (sw Iran); winters to Yemen, Sudan and Eritrea

☐ **Ortolan Bunting** *Emberiza hortulana*

W Palearctic; winters Mediterranean environs and Arabia

☐ **Chestnut-breasted Bunting** *Emberiza stewarti*

S Turkmenistan to n Afghanistan, n Pakistan and nw India

☐ **Cretzschmar's Bunting** *Emberiza caesia*

S Europe to Asia Minor; winters to ne Africa and Arabia

☐ **House Bunting** *Emberiza striolata*

____ *E. s. sahari*	Mountains of Morocco, Algeria and Tunisia to Mali and se Niger
____ *E. s. striolata*	NE Africa to Arabia, Iran, Pakistan and central India
____ *E. s. sanghae*	S Mali (Mopi region)
____ *E. s. saturatior*	Highlands of s Ethiopia and nw Kenya
____ *E. s. jebelmarrae*	Highlands of w-central Sudan (Darfur and Kordofan)

☐ **Lark-like Bunting** *Emberiza impetuani*

____ *E. i. eremica*	S Angola to n Namibia and nw Cape Province
____ *E. i. impetuani*	Arid scrub of w Cape Province to Botswana and sw Zimbabwe
____ *E. i. sloggetti*	Central Cape Province

☐ **Cinnamon-breasted Bunting** *Emberiza tahapisi*

____ *E. t. goslingi*	Sierra Leone to Mali, Nigeria, n Zaire and Sudan (w of the Nile)
____ *E. t. tahapisi (nivenorum)*	Gabon to Uganda, s Sudan, Ethiopia, Somalia and South Africa
____ *E. t. septemstriata*	E Sudan to w and n Ethiopia
____ *E. t. arabica*	S Arabia (Asir to Hadhramaut)
____ *E. t. insularis*	Socotra I. (off ne Somalia)

☐ **Socotra Bunting** *Emberiza socotrana*

Highlands of Socotra I. (off ne Somalia)

☐ **Cape Bunting** *Emberiza capensis*

____ *E. c. nebularum*	SW Angola (Moçamedes and w Huila)
____ *E. c. bradfieldi*	N Namibia (Kaokoveld and highlands of Damaraland)
____ *E. c. capensis*	Namibia to sw Cape Province
____ *E. c. vinacea*	South Africa (Kaap Plateau of n Cape Province)
____ *E. c. cinnamomea (media)*	Central Cape Province to s Transvaal and w Orange Free State
____ *E. c. limpopoensis*	SE Botswana to central and sw Transvaal
____ *E. c. vincenti*	Central Malawi to adjacent n Mozambique and e Zambia
____ *E. c. smithersii*	Mountains on e Zimbabwe/Mozambique border
____ *E c. plowesi*	Plateau of Zimbabwe and adjacent ne Botswana
____ *E. c. reidi*	SE Transvaal to Natal, Orange Free State and n Lesotho
____ *E. c. basutoensis*	Mountains of Lesotho and w Natal

☐ **Ochre-rumped Bunting** *Emberiza yessoensis*

____ *E. y. continentalis*	SE Siberia and e Manchuria; winters to s Korea and e China
____ *E. y. yessoensis*	Japan (Hokkaido, Honshu and s Kuril Islands)

☐ **Tristram's Bunting** *Emberiza tristrami*

Siberia to ne China; winters to s China and n Thailand

☐ **Chestnut-eared Bunting** *Emberiza fucata*

____ *E. f. arcuata*	Himalayas (Pakistan to Bangladesh; n Yunnan); winters to Myanmar
____ *E. f. fucata*	Mountains of Mongolia and Manchuria to Korea and Japan
____ *E. f. kuatunensis*	S China (Jiangsu to Guangdong and s Yunnan)

☐ **Little Bunting** *Emberiza pusilla*

Taiga of n Eurasia; winters to India, SE Asia and Philippines

☐ **Yellow-browed Bunting** *Emberiza chrysophrys*

Taiga of central Siberia; winters in central and se China

☐ **Rustic Bunting** *Emberiza rustica*

____ *E. r. rustica*	*Taiga* of n Eurasia; winters to e China and Japan
____ *E. r. latifascia*	*Taiga* of ne Siberia (Yakutsk to Kamchatka)

☐ **Yellow-throated Bunting** *Emberiza elegans*

____ *E. e. elegans*	Manchuria and n Korea; winters to s Korea, s Japan and e China
____ *E. e. ticehursti*	E Amurland; winters s Manchuria to Shandong Province
____ *E. e. elegantula*	Mountains of sw China; winters to ne Myanmar

☐ **Yellow-breasted Bunting** *Emberiza aureola*
_____ *E. a. aureola* — Boreal forests of Finland to Bering Sea; winters to Indochina
_____ *E. a. ornata* — Amur River to Manchuria, N Korea, Kamchatka and Kuril Is.

☐ **Golden-breasted Bunting** *Emberiza flaviventris*
_____ *E. f. flavigaster* — Mali and n Nigeria to Sudan, Eritrea and n Ethiopia
_____ *E. f. kalaharica (carychroa, princeps)* — S Angola to se Sudan, Kenya, Transvaal and Mozambique
_____ *E. f. flaviventris* — Natal to s Cape Province

☐ **Somali Bunting** *Emberiza poliopleura* — Sudan to Ethiopia, Somalia, Uganda, Kenya and ne Tanzania

☐ **Brown-rumped Bunting** *Emberiza affinis*
_____ *E. a. nigeriae* — Mauritania to n Nigeria, sw Chad and w Cameroon
_____ *E. a. vulpecula* — Cameroon and adjacent Central African Republic
_____ *E. a. affinis* — S Sudan to sw Ethiopia, ne Zaire and n Uganda

☐ **Cabanis' Bunting** *Emberiza cabanisi*
_____ *E. c. cabanisi* — Savanna of Liberia to s Sudan and w Uganda
_____ *E. c. cognominata* — NE Angola to sw Zaire
_____ *E. c. orientalis* — SE Zaire to Tanzania, Zambia, Zimbabwe and s Mozambique

☐ **Chestnut Bunting** *Emberiza rutila* — Siberia to n Mongolia and ne China; winters to India and SE Asia

☐ **Black-headed Bunting** *Emberiza melanocephala* — S-central Eurasia; winters to India

☐ **Red-headed Bunting** *Emberiza bruniceps* — S-central Eurasia; winters in Indian subcontinent

☐ **Yellow Bunting** *Emberiza sulphurata* — Honshu (Japan); winters e China, n Philippines and Taiwan

☐ **Black-faced Bunting** *Emberiza spodocephala*
_____ *E. s. spodocephala* — Central and e Asia; winters to e China and Taiwan
_____ *E. s. personata* — Sakhalin and s Kuril Is. to Honshu; winters to Ryukyu Is.
_____ *E. s. sordida* — W China; winters to e India, n Myanmar and n Indochina

☐ **Gray Bunting** *Emberiza variabilis* — S Kamchatka, Sakhalin, Kuril Is. and n Japan; winters to Ryukyu Is.

☐ **Pallas' Bunting** *Emberiza pallasi*
_____ *E. p. polaris* — Siberia to Sea of Okhotsk; winters Manchuria to e China
_____ *E. p. pallasi* — Mts. of central and e Asia; winters to w China and Mongolia
_____ *E. p. lydiae* — Mountains of central Mongolia

☐ **Reed Bunting** *Emberiza schoeniclus*
_____ *E. s. schoeniclus* — British Isles and nw Europe to c Russia; winters to North Africa
_____ *E. s. witherbyi* — S Portugal, coastal w Spain, France, Balearic Is. and Sardinia
_____ *E. s. canetti (intermedia)* — Italy and Sicily to s Ukraine, Crimea and ne Turkey
_____ *E. s. reiseri* — S Yugoslavia to sw Albania and n Greece
_____ *E. s. caspia* — E Caucasus to w and s Iran, Syria, adj. se Turkey and ne Iraq
_____ *E. s. korejewi* — E Iran
_____ *E. s. pyrrhuloides* — Caspian Sea to Kazakstan, w Xinjiang and w Mongolia
_____ *E. s. passerina* — NW Siberia; winters to n Xinjiang, Mongolia and n Iran
_____ *E. s. parvirostris* — Central Siberia and n Mongolia; winters to n China
_____ *E. s. pyrrhulina* — Transbaikalia to Kamchatka, Kuril Is., Sakhalin, Hokkaido
_____ *E. s. pallidior* — SW Siberia; winters Caucasus to nw India and Mongolia
_____ *E. s. minor* — SE Siberia and adjacent Manchuria
_____ *E. s. ukrainae* — S Russia to n Ukraine and Volga River; winters to Caucasus
_____ *E. s. incognita* — Russia e of Volga to s Urals, n Kazakstan; winters to nw China
_____ *E. s. zaidamensis* — W China (Tsaidam basin in n Qinghai)

☐ **Corn Bunting** *Emberiza calandra* — Grasslands and scrub of Palearctic region

☐ **Coal-crested Finch** *Charitospiza eucosma*

Campos of ne Bolivia to ne and central Brazil and ne Argentina

☐ **Black-masked Finch** *Coryphaspiza melanotis*
_____ *C. m. marajoara*
_____ *C. m. melanotis*

Ilha de Marajó (e Brazil in Pará)
SE Peru to n Bolivia, se Paraguay, se Brazil and ne Argentina

☐ **Many-colored Chaco-Finch** *Saltatricula multicolor*

SE Bolivia to w Paraguay, nw Uruguay and n Argentina

☐ **Pileated Finch** *Coryphospingus pileatus*
_____ *C. p. rostratus*
_____ *C. p. brevicaudus*
_____ *C. p. pileatus*

Colombia (arid upper Magdalena Valley)
N Colombia to n Venezuela; Isla Margarita
E-cent. Brazil (Ceará and Piauí to Minas Gerais and Rio de Janeiro)

☐ **Red-crested Finch** *Coryphospingus cucullatus*
_____ *C. c. cucullatus*
_____ *C. c. rubescens*
_____ *C. c. fargoi*

The Guianas and ne Brazil (east to Pará)
E Paraguay to cent. and s Brazil, Uruguay and ne Argentina
N Peru to Bolivia, w Paraguay and n Argentina

☐ **Crimson-breasted Finch** *Rhodospingus cruentus*

Arid scrub of w Ecuador and extreme nw Peru

☐ **Black-hooded Sierra-Finch** *Phrygilus atriceps*

Andes of sw Peru (Arequipa) to w Bolivia, n Chile, nw Argentina

☐ **Peruvian Sierra-Finch** *Phrygilus punensis*
_____ *P. p. chloronotus*
_____ *P. p. punensis*

Andes of s Peru (Cajamarca to Ayacucho and n Cuzco)
Andes of s Peru (Puno) to nw Bolivia (La Paz)

☐ **Gray-hooded Sierra-Finch** *Phrygilus gayi*
_____ *P. g. gayi*
_____ *P. g. minor*
_____ *P. g. caniceps*

Andes of n Chile (Coquimbo to Colchagua)
Coastal Chile (Atacama to Santiago)
S Chile and Argentina to Tierra del Fuego

☐ **Patagonian Sierra-Finch** *Phrygilus patagonicus*

Central Argentina and Chile to Tierra del Fuego

☐ **Mourning Sierra-Finch** *Phrygilus fruticeti*
_____ *P. f. peruvianus*
_____ *P. f. coracinus*
_____ *P. f. fruticeti*

Andes of n Peru to Bolivia (La Paz and Cochabamba)
Andes of Bolivia (w Oruro and Potosí)
Andes of sw Bolivia to s Chile and s Argentina

☐ **Plumbeous Sierra-Finch** *Phrygilus unicolor*
_____ *P. u. nivarius*
_____ *P. u. geospizopsis*
_____ *P. u. inca*
_____ *P. u. unicolor*
_____ *P. u. tucumanus*
_____ *P. u. ultimus*

NE Colombia (Santa Marta Mts.) and Andes of nw Venezuela
E and Central Andes of Colombia and Ecuador
Andes of Peru to w Bolivia (La Paz)
Andes of sw Peru (Tacna) to s Chile and w Argentina
Andes of Bolivia and nw Argentina
Mountains of s Argentina (Tierra del Fuego)

☐ **Red-backed Sierra-Finch** *Phrygilus dorsalis*

Andes of sw Bolivia to n Chile and nw Argentina

☐ **White-throated Sierra-Finch** *Phrygilus erythronotus*

High Andes of sw Peru, sw Bolivia and n Chile

☐ **Carbonated Sierra-Finch** *Phrygilus carbonarius*

Pampas of central Argentina; winters north to Tucumán

☐ **Band-tailed Sierra-Finch** *Phrygilus alaudinus*
_____ *P. a. bipartitus*
_____ *P. a. humboldti*
_____ *P. a. bracki*
_____ *P. a. excelsus*
_____ *P. a. alaudinus*
_____ *P. a. venturii*

Andes of w Ecuador and Peru (south to Arequipa)
Coastal s Ecuador and n Peru (south to Piura)
Central Peru (arid inter-Andean of upper Río Huallaga)
Andes of s Peru (Puno) and Bolivia
Andes of Chile (Atacama to Valdivia)
Andes of Argentina (Jujuy and Salta to Tucumán and w Córdoba)

☐ **Ash-breasted Sierra-Finch** *Phrygilus plebejus*
_____ *P. p. ocularis*   Andes of Ecuador and extreme n Peru (Tumbes and Piura)
_____ *P. p. plebejus*   Andes of Peru to Bolivia, n Chile and nw Argentina

☐ **Canary-winged Finch** *Melanodera melanodera*
_____ *M. m. princetoniana*   *Llanos* of s Chile and s Argentina to Tierra del Fuego
_____ *M. m. melanodera*   Falkland Islands

☐ **Yellow-bridled Finch** *Melanodera xanthogramma*
_____ *M. x. barrosi*   Mountains of Chile and w Argentina
_____ *M. x. xanthogramma*   S Argentina (Tierra del Fuego and Cape Horn Archipelago)

☐ **Black-crested Finch** *Lophospingus pusillus*
     Chaco of se Bolivia to w Paraguay and n Argentina

☐ **Gray-crested Finch** *Lophospingus griseocristatus*
     Arid Andes of se Bolivia and nw Argentina (Jujuy and Salta)

☐ **Long-tailed Reed-Finch** *Donacospiza albifrons*
     N Bolivia to se Paraguay, se Brazil, Uruguay and ne Argentina

☐ **Gough Island Finch** *Rowettia goughensis*
     Gough I. (s Atlantic Ocean)

☐ **Nightingale Finch** *Nesospiza acunhae*
_____ *N. a. acunhae*   Inaccessible I. (s Atlantic Ocean)
_____ *N. a. questi*   Nightingale I. (s Atlantic Ocean)

☐ **Wilkins' Finch** *Nesospiza wilkinsi*
_____ *N. w. dunnei*   Inaccessible I. (s Atlantic Ocean)
_____ *N. w. wilkinsi*   Nightingale I. (s Atlantic Ocean)

☐ **White-winged Diuca-Finch** *Diuca speculifera*
_____ *D. s. magnirostris*   Andes of central Peru (Ancash and Junín)
_____ *D. s. speculifera*   Andes of s Peru to n Chile, nw Bolivia and nw Argentina

☐ **Common Diuca-Finch** *Diuca diuca*
_____ *D. d. crassirostris*   Andes of n Chile and n Argentina
_____ *D. d. diuca*   Andes of central Chile and central Argentina
_____ *D. d. chiloensis*   Chiloé I. (off w Chile)
_____ *D. d. minor*   Argentina (Córdoba to Santa Cruz); winters to se Brazil

☐ **Short-tailed Finch** *Idiopsar brachyurus*
     Andes of extreme s Peru (Puno) to n Bolivia and nw Argentina

☐ **Cinereous Finch** *Piezorhina cinerea*
     Arid coastal nw Peru (Tumbes to La Libertad)

☐ **Slender-billed Finch** *Xenospingus concolor*
     Coastal w Peru (Lima) to Andes of n Chile

☐ **Great Inca-Finch** *Incaspiza pulchra*
     Arid Andes of Peru (Ancash to s Lima)

☐ **Rufous-backed Inca-Finch** *Incaspiza personata*
     Arid Andes of w Peru (upper Marañón Valley drainage)

☐ **Gray-winged Inca-Finch** *Incaspiza ortizi*
     Arid Andes of w Peru (upper Marañón Valley drainage)

☐ **Buff-bridled Inca-Finch** *Incaspiza laeta*
     Arid Andes of w Peru (upper Marañón Valley drainage)

☐ **Little Inca-Finch** *Incaspiza watkinsi*
     Foothills of arid w Peru (middle Marañón River drainage)

☐ **Bay-chested Warbling-Finch** *Poospiza thoracica*
     Scrub of se Brazil (Minas Gerais to n Rio Grande do Sul)

☐ **Bolivian Warbling-Finch** *Poospiza boliviana*
     Andes of Bolivia and adjacent nw Argentina (Jujuy)

☐ **Plain-tailed Warbling-Finch** *Poospiza alticola*
     Andes of w Peru (s Cajamarca to La Libertad and e Ancash)

681

☐ **Rufous-sided Warbling-Finch** *Poospiza hypochondria*
_____ *P. h. hypochondria*   Andes of w Bolivia (La Paz and Cochabamba)
_____ *P. h. affinis*   Andes of nw Argentina (Jujuy to Mendoza)

☐ **Cinnamon Warbling-Finch** *Poospiza ornata*
     Breeds c Argentina; winters n to Salta, Tucumán and Córdoba

☐ **Rusty-browed Warbling-Finch** *Poospiza erythrophrys*
_____ *P. e. cochabambae*   Andes of w Bolivia (Cochabamba and Chuquisaca)
_____ *P. e. erythrophrys*   Andes of Bolivia (Tarija) and nw Argentina

☐ **Black-and-rufous Warbling-Finch** *Poospiza nigrorufa*
     SE Paraguay to se Brazil, Uruguay and central Argentina

☐ **Black-and-chestnut Warbling-Finch** *Poospiza whitii*
_____ *P. w. whitii*   Andes of w Bolivia (La Paz and Cochabamba) to nw Argentina
_____ *P. w. wagneri*   Andes of Bolivia on Mt. Chulumaní (La Paz)

☐ **Red-rumped Warbling-Finch** *Poospiza lateralis*
_____ *P. l. lateralis*   SE Brazil (sw Minas Gerais and Espírito Santo to n São Paulo)
_____ *P. l. cabanisi*   SE Brazil (s São Paulo) to Uruguay, Paraguay and ne Argentina

☐ **Rufous-breasted Warbling-Finch** *Poospiza rubecula*
     W slope of Andes of Peru (La Libertad to Ica)

☐ **Cochabamba Mountain-Finch** *Poospiza garleppi*
     Andes of w Bolivia (s Cochabamba)

☐ **Tucuman Mountain-Finch** *Poospiza baeri*
     Andes of nw Argentina (Jujuy to Tucumán, Salta and La Rioja)

☐ **Chestnut-breasted Mountain-Finch** *Poospiza caesar*
     Andes of se Peru (Apurímac, Cuzco and Puno)

☐ **Collared Warbling-Finch** *Poospiza hispaniolensis*
     Arid scrub of sw Ecuador and w Peru

☐ **Ringed Warbling-Finch** *Poospiza torquata*
_____ *P. t. torquata*   Arid intermontane valleys of nw Bolivia
_____ *P. t. pectoralis*   Lowlands of se Bolivia to w Paraguay and central Argentina

☐ **Black-capped Warbling-Finch** *Poospiza melanoleuca*
     W Bolivia to n Argentina, Paraguay, Uruguay and sw Brazil

☐ **Cinereous Warbling-Finch** *Poospiza cinerea*
     Locally in *campos* of s-central Brazil

☐ **Blue-black Grassquit** *Volatinia jacarina*
_____ *V. j. splendens*   N Mexico to n South America, Grenada, Trinidad and Tobago
_____ *V. j. peruviensis*   Arid Pacific slope of Ecuador, Peru and extreme n Chile
_____ *V. j. jacarina*   SE Peru to e Bolivia, Paraguay, cent. and e Brazil and n Argentina

☐ **Buffy-fronted Seedeater** *Sporophila frontalis*
     E Paraguay to se Brazil and ne Argentina

☐ **Temminck's Seedeater** *Sporophila falcirostris*
     Lowlands of se Brazil to ne Argentina (Misiones)

☐ **Slate-colored Seedeater** *Sporophila schistacea*
_____ *S. s. subconcolor*   Belize and Guatemala to Nicaragua
_____ *S. s. schistacea*   SW Costa Rica to Panama and n Colombia
_____ *S. s. incerta*   Pacific slope of Andes of Colombia to Ecuador (Pichincha)
_____ *S. s. longipennis*   Trop. e Colombia to Venezuela, Guianas, n Brazil and nw Bolivia

☐ **Plumbeous Seedeater** *Sporophila plumbea*
_____ *S. p. colombiana*   N Colombia (Santa Marta Mts. and lower Magdalena Valley)
_____ *S. p. whiteleyana*   *Llanos* of e Colombia to s Venezuela, the Guianas and n Brazil
_____ *S. p. plumbea*   SE Peru to n Bolivia, e Paraguay, s Brazil and ne Argentina

☐ **Caqueta Seedeater** *Sporophila murallae*
     SE Colombia to e Brazil, e Ecuador and ne Peru

☐ **Gray Seedeater** *Sporophila intermedia*
____ *S. i. bogotensis (agustini)*   Colombia (Western Andes, Magdalena and Cauca valleys)
____ *S. i. anchicayae*   Colombia (valley of the Río Anchicayá in Valle)
____ *S. i. intermedia*   E Colombia to n Venezuela, w Guyana and ne Brazil; Trinidad

☐ **Wing-barred Seedeater** *Sporophila americana*
____ *S. a. americana*   NE Venezuela to Guianas, ne Brazil; Tobago and Chacachacare I.
____ *S. a. dispar*   W Amazonian Brazil

☐ **Variable Seedeater** *Sporophila corvina*
____ *S. c. corvina (badiiventris)*   Caribbean slope of e Mexico (Veracruz) to Nicaragua
____ *S. c. hoffmannii (collaris)*   S Costa Rica and w Panama
____ *S. c. hicksii (chocoana)*   Pacific slope of e Panama (Darién) and w Colombia
____ *S. c. ophthalmica*   SW Colombia w of Andes to Ecuador and n Peru (La Libertad)

☐ **White-collared Seedeater** *Sporophila torqueola*
____ *S. t. sharpei*   S Texas (lower Rio Grande Valley) to e Mexico (Veracruz)
____ *S. t. torqueola*   SW Mexico (Jalisco to Guanajuato, w Puebla and s Oaxaca)
____ *S. t. morelleti*   Caribbean slope of s Mexico (Veracruz) to extreme w Panama
____ *S. t. mutanda*   Pacific slope of s Mexico (Chiapas) to Guatemala and El Salvador

☐ **Rusty-collared Seedeater** *Sporophila collaris*
____ *S. c. ochrascens*   E Bolivia (Beni) to w Brazil (n Mato Grosso and w São Paulo)
____ *S. c. melanocephala*   Paraguay to w Brazil (sw Mato Grosso), Uruguay and n Argentina
____ *S. c. collaris*   E Brazil (s Goiás, Minas Gerais, Espírito Santo and Rio de Janeiro)

☐ **Lesson's Seedeater** *Sporophila bouvronides*
____ *S. b. bouvronides*   E Colombia to Guianas, Trinidad and Tobago; winters to ne Peru
____ *S. b. restricta*   Colombia (lower Magdalena Valley)

☐ **Lined Seedeater** *Sporophila lineola*
____ *S. l. lineola*   Bolivia to Paraguay, se Brazil and n Argentina; winters Amazonia
____ *S. l. ssp.*   *Caatinga* of ne Brazil; winters to Venezuela and the Guianas

☐ **Black-and-white Seedeater** *Sporophila luctuosa*
     Andes of Colombia to w Venezuela, n Bolivia and sw Brazil

☐ **Yellow-bellied Seedeater** *Sporophila nigricollis*
____ *S. n. nigricollis*   S Costa Rica to ne Argentina, Brazil, Trinidad, Tobago and Grenada
____ *S. n. vivida*   SW Colombia (Nariño) and w Ecuador
____ *S. n. inconspicua*   Andes of Peru (south to Cuzco)

☐ **Dubois' Seedeater** *Sporophila ardesiaca*
     E Brazil (s Minas Gerais, Espírito Santo and Rio de Janeiro)

☐ **Hooded Seedeater** *Sporophila melanops*
     Known from an 1870 specimen from se Brazil (possible hybrid)

☐ **Double-collared Seedeater** *Sporophila caerulescens*
____ *S. c. caerulescens*   Bolivia to Paraguay, e Brazil (Pará), Uruguay and Argentina
____ *S. c. yungae*   N Bolivia (La Paz, Cochabamba and Beni)
____ *S. c. hellmayri*   E Brazil (Bahia)

☐ **White-throated Seedeater** *Sporophila albogularis*
     NE Brazil (Piauí and Pernambuco to n Bahia)

☐ **Drab Seedeater** *Sporophila simplex*
     Arid s Ecuador; upper Marañon Valley of n Peru south to Ica

☐ **White-bellied Seedeater** *Sporophila leucoptera*
____ *S. l. mexianae*   S Suriname and Mexiana I. (off ne Brazil in Pará)
____ *S. l. bicolor*   SE Peru (Madre de Dios) to nw Bolivia (Beni and Santa Cruz)
____ *S. l. leucoptera*   E Paraguay to central and sw Brazil and n Argentina
____ *S. l. cinereola*   E Brazil (s Maranhão to Rio de Janeiro)

☐ **Parrot-billed Seedeater** *Sporophila peruviana*
_____ *S. p. devronis* — Arid coastal sw Ecuador (Manabí) to n Peru (Tumbes)
_____ *S. p. peruviana* — Arid coast of Peru (La Libertad to Ica)

☐ **Black-and-tawny Seedeater** *Sporophila nigrorufa*
Extreme e Bolivia and sw Brazil (Mato Grosso)

☐ **Capped Seedeater** *Sporophila bouvreuil*
_____ *S. b. pileata* — E Paraguay to s Brazil (s Mato Grosso) and ne Argentina
_____ *S. b. bouvreuil* — Suriname; e Brazil (Amazon delta to ne São Paulo)
_____ *S. b. crypta* — SE Brazil (Farinha Sêca area near Rio de Janeiro)
_____ *S. b. saturata* — SE Brazil (São Paulo)

☐ **Ruddy-breasted Seedeater** *Sporophila minuta*
_____ *S. m. parva* — Arid Pacific lowlands of sw Mexico (Nayarit) to Nicaragua
_____ *S. m. centralis* — SW Costa Rica and Pacific slope of Panama
_____ *S. m. minuta* — Colombia to Venezuela, Guianas, Amaz. Brazil, Trinidad, Tobago

☐ **Tawny-bellied Seedeater** *Sporophila hypoxantha*
Bolivia to Paraguay, s Brazil and n Argentina

☐ **Dark-throated Seedeater** *Sporophila ruficollis*
N Bolivia to Paraguay, s Brazil, n Uruguay and n Argentina

☐ **Marsh Seedeater** *Sporophila palustris*
Locally in Paraguay, s Brazil, Uruguay and ne Argentina

☐ **Chestnut-bellied Seedeater** *Sporophila castaneiventris*
Guianas and s Venezuela to n Bolivia and Amazonian Brazil

☐ **Gray-and-chestnut Seedeater** *Sporophila hypochroma*
Locally in e Bolivia, Paraguay, sw Brazil and ne Argentina

☐ **Chestnut Seedeater** *Sporophila cinnamomea*
Paraguay to s-central Brazil, Uruguay and ne Argentina

☐ **Narosky's Seedeater** *Sporophila zelichi*
Lowlands of ne Argentina (Entre Ríos)

☐ **Black-bellied Seedeater** *Sporophila melanogaster*
SE Brazil (s Goiás and Minas Gerais to Rio Grande do Sul)

☐ **Chestnut-throated Seedeater** *Sporophila telasco*
Coastal lowlands of sw Colombia to extreme n Chile (Tarapacá)

☐ **Tumaco Seedeater** *Sporophila insulata*
SW Colombia (rediscovered after 82-year absence on Tumaco I.)

☐ **Nicaraguan Seed-Finch** *Oryzoborus nuttingi*
Caribbean lowlands of Nicaragua, Costa Rica and w Panama

☐ **Large-billed Seed-Finch** *Oryzoborus crassirostris*
_____ *O. c. crassirostris* — Colombia east of Andes to Venezuela, the Guianas and n Brazil
_____ *O. c. occidentalis* — Tropical se Colombia to e Ecuador, e Peru and n Bolivia
_____ *O. c. magnirostris* — E Venezuela (Delta Amacuro and n Bolívar) and Trinidad
_____ *O. c. ssp.* — Pacific slope of w Colombia to sw Ecuador

☐ **Black-billed Seed-Finch** *Oryzoborus atrirostris*
_____ *O. a. atrirostris* — E slope of Andes of n Peru (Loreto and San Martín)
_____ *O. a. gigantirostris* — N Bolivia (Beni)

☐ **Great-billed Seed-Finch** *Oryzoborus maximiliani*
SE Colombia to n Bolivia, the Guianas, Amazonian and se Brazil

☐ **Chestnut-bellied Seed-Finch** *Oryzoborus angolensis*
_____ *O. a. torridus* — S Colombia to Peru, Venezuela, the Guianas and Brazil; Trinidad
_____ *O. a. angolensis* — E Brazil to w Bolivia, Paraguay and extreme ne Argentina

☐ **Thick-billed Seed-Finch** *Oryzoborus funereus*
S Mexico (Veracruz) to w Colombia, w Ecuador; Coiba I.; Pearl Is.

☐ **Blackish-blue Seedeater** *Amaurospiza moesta`*
Locally from se Paraguay to e Brazil and ne Argentina (Misiones)

□ **Blue Seedeater** *Amaurospiza concolor*
_____ *A. c. relicta* — Mts. of s Mexico (s Jalisco to Guerrero, Morelos and Oaxaca)
_____ *A. c. concolor* — Mts. of s Mexico (Chiapas) to Nicaragua, Costa Rica and Panama
_____ *A. c. aequatorialis* — Mountains of sw Colombia (Nariño) to s Ecuador (Loja)

□ **Cuban Bullfinch** *Melopyrrha nigra*
_____ *M. n. nigra* — Cuba and Isle of Pines
_____ *M. n. taylori* — Grand Cayman I.

□ **White-naped Seedeater** *Dolospingus fringilloides*
Savanna of e Colombia to s Venezuela and nw Amazonian Brazil

□ **Band-tailed Seedeater** *Catamenia analis*
_____ *C. a. alpica* — Santa Marta Mountains (ne Colombia)
_____ *C. a. schistaceifrons* — Eastern Andes of central Colombia
_____ *C. a. soederstromi* — Andes of n Ecuador (Imbabura to Chimborazo)
_____ *C. a. insignis* — E slope of Andes of Peru (Cajamarca to Ancash)
_____ *C. a. analoides* — W slope of Andes of Peru (Piura to Ayacucho)
_____ *C. a. griseiventris* — Andes of se Peru (Cuzco)
_____ *C. a. analis (subinsignis)* — Andes of n Chile to central Bolivia and nw Argentina

□ **Plain-colored Seedeater** *Catamenia inornata*
_____ *C. i. minor* — Andes of Colombia to w Venezuela, Ecuador and Peru (Junín)
_____ *C. i. mucuchiesi* — Andes of w Venezuela (Mérida)
_____ *C. i. inornata* — Andes of se Peru (Cuzco) to Bolivia, Chile and nw Argentina

□ **Paramo Seedeater** *Catamenia homochroa*
_____ *C. h. homochroa* — Andes of Colombia to w Venezuela, Ecuador, Peru and n Bolivia
_____ *C. h. duncani* — *Tepuis* of s Venezuela (Bolívar and Amazonas) and ne Brazil

□ **Dull-colored Grassquit** *Tiaris obscura*
_____ *T. o. haplochroma* — NE Colombia (Santa Marta Mountains) to nw Venezuela
_____ *T. o. pauper* — Extreme s Colombia (Nariño) to Ecuador and nw Peru
_____ *T. o. obscura* — E slope of Andes of central Peru to w Bolivia and nw Argentina
_____ *T. o. pacific* — *Lomas* of coastal w Peru (n Lima to n Arequipa)

□ **Cuban Grassquit** *Tiaris canora*
Cuba and Isle of Pines; introduced Isla Providéncia

□ **Yellow-faced Grassquit** *Tiaris olivacea*
_____ *T. o. pusilla* — Gulf lowlands of e Mexico to Colombia and w Venezuela
_____ *T. o. intermedia* — Cozumel I. and Holbox I. (off Yucatán Peninsula)
_____ *T. o. ravida* — Isla Coiba (Panama)
_____ *T. o. olivacea* — Cuba, Isle of Pines, Jamaica and Cayman Islands
_____ *T. o. bryanti* — Puerto Rico

□ **Black-faced Grassquit** *Tiaris bicolor*
_____ *T. b. bicolor* — Bahamas and cays off Las Villas Province (Cuba)
_____ *T. b. marchii* — Jamaica, Hispaniola and adjacent islands
_____ *T. b. omissa* — Puerto Rico, Tobago, Isla Margarita, n Colombia and n Venezuela
_____ *T. b. huilae* — S-central Colombia (upper Magdalena Valley)
_____ *T. b. grandior* — Islas Providéncia, Santa Catalina and San Andrés (w Caribbean Sea)
_____ *T. b. johnstonei* — Isla La Blanquilla and Islas Los Hermanos (off Venezuela)
_____ *T. b. sharpei* — Netherlands Antilles (Aruba, Curaçao and Bonaire)
_____ *T. b. tortugensis* — Isla La Tortuga (off Venezuela)

□ **Sooty Grassquit** *Tiaris fuliginosa*
Colombia to Venezuela, Guyana, e and sw Brazil

□ **Yellow-shouldered Grassquit** *Loxipasser anoxanthus*
Hills and mountains of Jamaica

□ **Orangequit** *Euneornis campestris*
Wooded highlands of Jamaica

☐ **St. Lucia Black Finch** *Melanospiza richardsoni*

St. Lucia (Lesser Antilles)

☐ **Puerto Rican Bullfinch** *Loxigilla portoricensis*

Puerto Rico; formerly n Lesser Antilles

☐ **Greater Antillean Bullfinch** *Loxigilla violacea*

____ *L. v. violacea*	Bahamas and Caicos Islands
____ *L. v. maurella*	Tortue, Gonâve and Saona islands (off Puerto Rico)
____ *L. v. affinis*	Hispaniola and Isla Catalina
____ *L. v. parishi*	Île-á-Vache and Beata I. (off Hispaniola)
____ *L. v. ruficollis*	Jamaica

☐ **Lesser Antillean Bullfinch** *Loxigilla noctis*

____ *L. n. coryi*	Lesser Antilles (St. Kitts and Montserrat)
____ *L. n. ridgwayi*	Lesser Antilles (Anguilla, St. Martin, Barbuda and Antigua)
____ *L. n. desiradensis*	Désirade I. (Lesser Antilles)
____ *L. n. dominicana*	Guadeloupe, Marie Galante, Dominica and Iles des Saintes
____ *L. n. noctis*	Martinique (Lesser Antilles)
____ *L. n. sclateri*	St. Lucia (Lesser Antilles)
____ *L. n. crissalis*	St. Vincent (Lesser Antilles)
____ *L. n. grenadensis*	Grenada (Lesser Antilles)
____ *L. n. barbadensis*	Barbados (Lesser Antilles)

☐ **Cocos Island Finch** *Pinaroloxias inornata*

Forests of Cocos I. (off w Costa Rica)

☐ **Slaty Finch** *Haplospiza rustica*

____ *H. r. uniformis*	Highlands of s Mexico (Veracruz and Chiapas)
____ *H. r. barrilesensis*	Highlands of Honduras, Costa Rica and w Panama (Chiriquí)
____ *H. r. rustica*	N Colombia to n Venezuela, Ecuador, Peru and Bolivia
____ *H. r. arcana*	*Tepuis* of s Venezuela (Cerro Chimantá-tepui in Bolívar)

☐ **Uniform Finch** *Haplospiza unicolor*

E Paraguay to se Brazil and ne Argentina

☐ **Peg-billed Finch** *Acanthidops bairdii*

High volcanic peaks of Costa Rica and w Panama

☐ **Cinnamon-bellied Flowerpiercer** *Diglossa baritula*

____ *D. b. baritula*	Highlands of cent. Mexico (se Jalisco to Isthmus of Tehuántepec)
____ *D. b. montana*	Highlands of s Mexico (Chiapas) to Guatemala and El Salvador
____ *D. b. parva*	Highlands of e Guatemala to Honduras and n-central Nicaragua

☐ **Slaty Flowerpiercer** *Diglossa plumbea*

____ *D. p. plumbea*	Highlands of Costa Rica and extreme w Panama (Chiriquí)
____ *D. p. veraguensis*	Pacific slope of w Panama (Veraguas)

☐ **Rusty Flowerpiercer** *Diglossa sittoides*

____ *D. s. hyperythra*	N Colombia (Santa Marta Mts.) and coastal mts. of n Venezuela
____ *D. s. dorbignyi*	Andes of Colombia and w Venezuela (Lara, Mérida and Táchira)
____ *D. s. coelestis*	Sierra de Perijá (Colombia/Venezuela border)
____ *D. s. mandeli*	Subtropical mts. of ne Venezuela (Mt. Turumiquire in Sucre)
____ *D. s. decorata*	Subtropical Andes of Ecuador and Peru
____ *D. s. sittoides*	Subtropical Andes of w Bolivia and nw Argentina

☐ **Venezuelan Flowerpiercer** *Diglossa venezuelensis*

Mountains of ne Venezuela (nw Monagas and s Sucre)

☐ **Chestnut-bellied Flowerpiercer** *Diglossa gloriosissima*

Andes of w Colombia (Antioquia to Cauca)

☐ **White-sided Flowerpiercer** *Diglossa albilatera*

____ *D. a. federalis*	Coastal cordillera of n Venezuela (Aragua to Miranda)
____ *D. a. albilatera*	Santa Marta Mts. and Andes of Colombia to w Venezuela, Ecuador
____ *D. a. schistacea*	Andes of extreme sw Ecuador to nw Peru (Cajamarca)
____ *D. a. affinis*	Highlands of n-central Peru (above Río Utcubamba) to Cuzco

☐ **Glossy Flowerpiercer** *Diglossa lafresnayii*
_____ *D. l. lafresnayii* — Andes of Colombia to w Venezuela, Ecuador and extreme n Peru
_____ *D. l. unicincta* — Andes of n Peru (Cajamarca)

☐ **Moustached Flowerpiercer** *Diglossa mystacalis*
_____ *D. m. pectoralis* — Andes of central Peru (Huánuco and Junín)
_____ *D. m. albilinea* — Andes of se Peru (Cuzco and Puno)
_____ *D. m. mystacalis* — Andes of nw Bolivia (La Paz, Cochabamba and w Santa Cruz)

☐ **Merida Flowerpiercer** *Diglossa gloriosa*
Andes of w Venezuela (Trujillo, Mérida and n Táchira)

☐ **Black Flowerpiercer** *Diglossa humeralis*
_____ *D. h. nocticolor* — Santa Marta Mts. of n Colombia and Sierra de Perijá (w Venezuela)
_____ *D. h. humeralis* — E Andes of Colombia and sw Venezuela (Páramo de Tamá)
_____ *D. h. aterrima* — W and Central Andes of Colombia to Ecuador and nw Peru

☐ **Black-throated Flowerpiercer** *Diglossa brunneiventris*
Andes of n Colombia; Andes of Peru, nw Bolivia and n Chile

☐ **Gray-bellied Flowerpiercer** *Diglossa carbonaria*
Andes of w Bolivia (La Paz to Chuquisaca) and adj. nw Argentina

☐ **Scaled Flowerpiercer** *Diglossa duidae*
_____ *D. d. hitchcocki* — *Tepuis* of s Venezuela (s Amazonas)
_____ *D. d. duidae* — *Tepuis* of s Venezuela (c Amazonas) and adj. n Brazil (Roraima)
_____ *D. d. georgebarrowcloughi* — *Tepuis* of s Venezuela (Cerro Jime)

☐ **Greater Flowerpiercer** *Diglossa major*
_____ *D. m. gilliardi* — *Tepuis* of s Venezuela (Auyan-tepui in se Bolívar)
_____ *D. m. disjuncta* — *Tepuis* of se Venezuela (Gran Sabana in Bolívar)
_____ *D. m. chimantae* — *Tepuis* of se Venezuela (Chimantáa-tepui in Bolívar)
_____ *D. m. major* — Mts. of se Venezuela and adj. n Brazil (Uei-tepui in Roraima)

☐ **Indigo Flowerpiercer** *Diglossopis indigotica*
Andes of w Colombia and nw Ecuador (south to Pichincha)

☐ **Deep-blue Flowerpiercer** *Diglossopis glauca*
_____ *D. g. tyrianthina* — E slope of Andes of sw Colombia (Nariño) and e Ecuador
_____ *D. g. glauca* — SE Peru (Junín) to *yungas* of w Bolivia (La Paz and Cochabamba)

☐ **Bluish Flowerpiercer** *Diglossopis caerulescens*
_____ *D. c. saturata* — Andes of Colombia and sw Venezuela
_____ *D. c. ginesi* — Sierra de Perijá (Colombia/Venezuela border)
_____ *D. c. caerulescens* — Coastal mts. of n Venezuela (Carabobo to Distrito Federal)
_____ *D. c. media* — Andes of s Ecuador (Loja) to nw Peru (Cajamarca and Amazonas)
_____ *D. c. pallida* — Andes of central Peru (La Libertad to Lima and Junín)
_____ *D. c. mentalis* — Andes of se Peru and nw Bolivia (La Paz)

☐ **Masked Flowerpiercer** *Diglossopis cyanea*
_____ *D. c. cyanea* — Andes of Colombia to Ecuador and w Venezuela
_____ *D. c. tovarensis* — Coastal mountains of n Venezuela (Aragua and Distrito Federal)
_____ *D. c. obscura* — Sierra de Perijá (Colombia/Venezuela border)
_____ *D. c. dispar* — Andes of sw Ecuador and nw Peru
_____ *D. c. melanopis* — Andes of Peru and nw Bolivia

☐ **Puna Yellow-Finch** *Sicalis lutea*
Andes of s Peru (Cuzco) to w Bolivia and nw Argentina

☐ **Saffron Finch** *Sicalis flaveola*
_____ *S. f. flaveola* — Tropical e Colombia to Venezuela and the Guianas; Trinidad
_____ *S. f. valida* — Pacific lowlands of Ecuador to nw Peru (Ancash)
_____ *S. f. brasiliensis* — Tropical ne Brazil (Maranhão, Minas Gerais and São Paulo)
_____ *S. f. pelzelni* — E Bolivia to Paraguay, se Brazil, Uruguay and n Argentina

☐ **Grassland Yellow-Finch** *Sicalis luteola*

_____ *S. l. chrysops* — S Mexico (Veracruz and Chiapas) to Guatemala and ne Honduras

_____ *S. l. mexicana* — Pacific slope of s Mexico (sw Puebla and Morelos)

_____ *S. l. eisenmanni* — Pacific slope of nw Costa Rica (Guanacaste) and Panama (Coclé)

_____ *S. l. bogotensis* — E Andes of Colombia to Venezuela, Ecuador and s Peru

_____ *S. l. luteola* — W Andes of Colombia to Venezuela, the Guianas and n Brazil

_____ *S. l. flavissima* — Islands at mouth of Amazon River and adjacent Pará

_____ *S. l. luteiventris* — Lowlands of s South America

☐ **Stripe-tailed Yellow-Finch** *Sicalis citrina*

_____ *S. c. browni* — Highlands of Colombia to Venezuela, the Guianas and ne Brazil

_____ *S. c. citrina* — E Brazil (s Pará to Goiás, Piauí, e Mato Grosso and Paraná)

_____ *S. c. occidentalis* — Andes of extreme s Peru (Puno) and n Argentina (Tucumán)

☐ **Bright-rumped Yellow-Finch** *Sicalis uropygialis*

_____ *S. u. sharpei* — Andes of n Peru (Cajamarca to Junín)

_____ *S. u. connectens* — Andes of s Peru (above upper Urubamba Valley in Cuzco)

_____ *S. u. uropygialis* — Andes of s Peru (Puno) to Bolivia, n Chile and nw Argentina

☐ **Citron-headed Yellow-Finch** *Sicalis luteocephala*

Highlands of w Bolivia and nw Argentina (Jujuy)

☐ **Greater Yellow-Finch** *Sicalis auriventris*

Andes of n and central Chile and adjacent Argentina

☐ **Greenish Yellow-Finch** *Sicalis olivascens*

_____ *S. o. salvini* — Andes of n Peru (La Libertad to Huánuco, Junín and Ayacucho)

_____ *S. o. chloris* — W slope of Andes of Peru (Ancash) to n Chile (Coquimbo)

_____ *S. o. olivascens* — Andes of se Peru (Cuzco) to w Bolivia and nw Argentina

_____ *S. o. mendozae* — Andes of w Argentina (Río Negro to Mendoza and San Luis)

☐ **Patagonian Yellow-Finch** *Sicalis lebruni*

Open plains of s Chile and s Argentina

☐ **Orange-fronted Yellow-Finch** *Sicalis columbiana*

_____ *S. c. columbiana* — Extreme e Colombia to e Venezuela (Orinoco basin); Trinidad

_____ *S. c. leopoldinae* — E Brazil (Piauí to w Bahia and Goiás)

_____ *S. c. goeldii* — E Peru and Amazonian Brazil (to w Pará)

☐ **Raimondi's Yellow-Finch** *Sicalis raimondii*

W Andes of Peru (Cajamarca to Arequipa and Moquegua)

☐ **Sulphur-throated Finch** *Sicalis taczanowskii*

Arid littoral of sw Ecuador and nw Peru

☐ **Wedge-tailed Grass-Finch** *Emberizoides herbicola*

_____ *E. h. lucaris* — SW Costa Rica (Térraba area)

_____ *E. h. hypochondriacus* — Foothills of w Panama (Volcán de Chiriquí) to Panama City

_____ *E. h. floresae* — Mountains of w Panama (Cerro Flores in e Chiriquí)

_____ *E. h. apurensis* — Tropical Colombia (east of Andes) and w Venezuela

_____ *E. h. sphenurus* — N Colombia to Venezuela, the Guianas and n Brazil

_____ *E. h. herbicola* — SE Peru to e Bolivia, Paraguay, ne Argentina, e and se Brazil

☐ **Duida Grass-Finch** *Emberizoides duidae*

Tepuis of s Venezuela (Cerro Duida in Amazonas)

☐ **Lesser Grass-Finch** *Emberizoides ypiranganus*

Marshes of e Paraguay to se Brazil and ne Argentina

☐ **Pale-throated Serra-Finch** *Embernagra longicauda*

Locally on *serras* of e Brazil (interior c Bahia and Minas Gerais)

☐ **Great Pampa-Finch** *Embernagra platensis*

_____ *E. p. olivascens* — Lowlands of se Bolivia to sw Paraguay and nw Argentina

_____ *E. p. platensis* — E Paraguay to se Brazil, Uruguay and central Argentina

☐ **Yellow Cardinal** *Gubernatrix cristata*

Extreme se Brazil and Uruguay to n Argentina

☐ **Red-crested Cardinal** *Paroaria coronata*

Bolivia to central Argentina, Uruguay and extreme se Brazil

☐ **Red-cowled Cardinal** *Paroaria dominicana*

Forests of ne Brazil (Maranhão to Minas Gerais)

☐ **Red-capped Cardinal** *Paroaria gularis*

_____ *P. g. nigrogenis* — E Colombia and Venezuela; Trinidad
_____ *P. g. gularis* — E Colombia to Venezuela, the Guianas, Peru and Amaz. Brazil
_____ *P. g. cervicalis* — N Bolivia and adjacent Brazil (Mato Grosso)

☐ **Crimson-fronted Cardinal** *Paroaria baeri*

_____ *P. b. baeri* — Central Brazil (w Goiás and adjacent ne Mato Grosso)
_____ *P. b. xinguensis* — Central Brazil (upper Rio Xingú in n Mato Grosso)

☐ **Yellow-billed Cardinal** *Paroaria capitata*

_____ *P. c. capitata* — SW Brazil (Mato Grosso) to Paraguay and n Argentina
_____ *P. c. fuscipes* — SE Bolivia (Fortín Campero region in Tarija)

☐ **Sooty-faced Finch** *Lysurus crassirostris*

Humid montane forests of Costa Rica and w Panama

☐ **Olive Finch** *Lysurus castaneiceps*

Locally in Andes of Colombia to Ecuador and se Peru

☐ **Yellow-thighed Finch** *Pselliophorus tibialis*

Humid montane forests of Costa Rica and w Panama

☐ **Yellow-green Finch** *Pselliophorus luteoviridis*

Humid montane forests of w Panama

☐ **Large-footed Finch** *Pezopetes capitalis*

Humid montane forests of Costa Rica and w Panama

☐ **White-naped Brush-Finch** *Atlapetes albinucha*

_____ *A. a. albinucha* — Highlands of s Mexico (Puebla and Veracruz to n Chiapas)
_____ *A. a. griseipectus* — Pacific slope of s Mexico (Chiapas) to w Guatemala and El Salvador
_____ *A. a. fuscipygius* — Highlands of Honduras to nw El Salvador and nw Nicaragua
_____ *A. a. parvirostris* — Subtropical Costa Rica
_____ *A. a. brunnescens* — Subtropical w Panama (w Chiriquí)
_____ *A. a. coloratus* — Subtropical w Panama (e Chiriquí and Veraguas)
_____ *A. a. azuerensis* — W Panama (Azuero Peninsula)
_____ *A. a. gutturalis* — Upper tropical and subtropical n Colombia

☐ **Pale-naped Brush-Finch** *Atlapetes pallidinucha*

_____ *A. p. pallidinucha* — E Andes of Colombia and sw Venezuela (Mérida and Táchira)
_____ *A. p. papallactae* — Central Andes of Colombia to Ecuador and extreme nw Peru

☐ **Rufous-naped Brush-Finch** *Atlapetes rufinucha*

_____ *A. r. phelpsi* — Andes of Colombia to sw Venezuela (Sierra de Perijá)
_____ *A. r. elaeoprorus* — Subtropical n Central Andes of Colombia (Antioquia)
_____ *A. r. simplex* — E Andes of Colombia (Bogotá)
_____ *A. r. caucae* — Western and Central Andes of Colombia (Valle and Cauca)
_____ *A. r. spodionotus* — Andes of s Colombia (Nariño) and n Ecuador
_____ *A. r. comptus* — Andes of sw Ecuador (Cañar to w Loja) and n Peru (Piura)
_____ *A. r. latinuchus* — Andes of se Ecuador (e Azuay and e Loja) to ne Peru (Amazonas)
_____ *A. r. chugurensis* — Pacific slope of nw Peru (Cajamarca)
_____ *A. r. baroni* — N Peru (upper Marañón Valley in Cajamarca and La Libertad)
_____ *A. r. melanolaemus* — Subtropical Andes of se Peru (Cuzco and Puno)
_____ *A. r. rufinucha* — Subtropical Andes of w Bolivia (La Paz and Cochabamba)
_____ *A. r. carrikeri* — Andes of e Bolivia (Santa Cruz)

☐ **White-rimmed Brush-Finch** *Atlapetes leucopis*

Locally in Andes of s Colombia and e Ecuador

☐ **Rufous-capped Brush-Finch** *Atlapetes pileatus*

_____ *A. p. dilutus* — Oak-pine forests of n Mexican plateau
_____ *A. p. pileatus* — Oak-pine forests of s Mexican plateau

☐ **Santa Marta Brush-Finch** *Atlapetes melanocephalus*

Santa Marta Mountains (ne Colombia)

☐ **Olive-headed Brush-Finch** *Atlapetes flaviceps*

Known from two specimens from n Colombia (last recorded 1967)

☐ **Dusky-headed Brush-Finch** *Atlapetes fuscoolivaceus*

Andes of Colombia (upper Magdalena Valley)

☐ **Tricolored Brush-Finch** *Atlapetes tricolor*

_____ *A. t. crassus*	Andes of w Colombia and Ecuador (Pichincha and El Oro)
_____ *A. t. tricolor*	Andes of central Peru (La Libertad and Junín)

☐ **Moustached Brush-Finch** *Atlapetes albofrenatus*

_____ *A. a. albofrenatus*	E Andes of Colombia (Norte de Santander to Cundinamarca)
_____ *A. a. meridae*	Andes of w Venezuela (Táchira and Mérida)

☐ **Slaty Brush-Finch** *Atlapetes schistaceus*

_____ *A. s. schistaceus*	W and Central Andes of Colombia and Ecuador
_____ *A. s. tamae*	Andes of e Colombia and sw Venezuela (Táchira)
_____ *A. s. fumidus*	Sierra de Perijá (Colombia/Venezuela border)
_____ *A. s. castaneifrons*	Andes of w Venezuela (Trujillo, Mérida and e Táchira)
_____ *A. s. taczanowskii*	Andes of central Peru (Huánuco and Junín)
_____ *A. s. canigenis*	Andes of se Peru (Cuzco)

☐ **Bay-crowned Brush-Finch** *Atlapetes seebohmi*

_____ *A. s. celicae*	Andes of extreme s Ecuador (w Loja)
_____ *A. s. simonsi*	Andes of extreme s Ecuador (eastern and central Loja)
_____ *A. s. seebohmi*	Pacific slope of Andes of nw Peru (La Libertad to Ancash)

☐ **Rusty-bellied Brush-Finch** *Atlapetes nationi*

_____ *A. n. nationi*	Western Andes of Peru (Ancash to Arequipa)
_____ *A. n. brunneiceps*	Andes of sw Peru (Ica and Ayacucho)

☐ **White-winged Brush-Finch** *Atlapetes leucopterus*

_____ *A. l. leucopterus*	Andes of w Ecuador (south to Chimbo Valley)
_____ *A. l. dresseri*	Andes of sw Ecuador (El Oro and Loja) to nw Peru (Cajamarca)

☐ **White-headed Brush-Finch** *Atlapetes albiceps*

Arid scrub of se Ecuador and nw Peru

☐ **Pale-headed Brush-Finch** *Atlapetes pallidiceps*

Arid Andes of sw Ecuador (Azuay)

☐ **Rufous-eared Brush-Finch** *Atlapetes rufigenis*

_____ *A. r. rufigenis*	Andes of nw Peru (Cajamarca, La Libertad, Ancash and Huánuco)
_____ *A. r. forbesi*	Andes of s-central Peru (Apurímac, Cuzco and Puno)

☐ **Ochre-breasted Brush-Finch** *Atlapetes semirufus*

_____ *A. s. zimmeri*	E slope of E Andes of ne Colombia and w Venezuela (Táchira)
_____ *A. s. majusculus*	E slope of Eastern Andes of Colombia (n Boyacá)
_____ *A. s. semirufus*	E slope of Eastern Andes of Colombia (Cundinamarca)
_____ *A. s. denisei*	Mts. of n Venezuela (Sucre and Monagas to Aragua and Carabobo)
_____ *A. s. benedettii*	Mountains of n Venezuela (Falcón, Lara and Trujillo)
_____ *A. s. albigula*	Andes of w Venezuela (ne Táchira)

☐ **Fulvous-headed Brush-Finch** *Atlapetes fulviceps*

Andes of Bolivia to nw Argentina

☐ **Tepui Brush-Finch** *Atlapetes personatus*

_____ *A. p. personatus*	*Tepuis* of s Venezuela (Mt. Roraima and adjacent *tepuis*)
_____ *A. p. collaris*	*Tepuis* of s Venezuela (Auyan-tepui in se Bolívar)
_____ *A. p. duidae*	*Tepuis* of s Venezuela (Mt. Duida in Amazonas)
_____ *A. p. parui*	*Tepuis* of s Venezuela (n Amazonas)
_____ *A. p. paraquensis*	*Tepuis* of s Venezuela (Cerro Paraque and Cerro Yaví)
_____ *A. p. jugularis*	Cerro de la Neblina (Venezuela/Brazil border in se Amazonas)

☐ **Yellow-striped Brush-Finch** *Atlapetes citrinellus*

Andes of nw Argentina

☐ **Chestnut-capped Brush-Finch** *Buarremon brunneinucha*

_____ *B. b. suttoni*	Mountains of sw Mexico (Guerrero to central Oaxaca)
_____ *B. b. nigrilatera*	Mountains of s Mexico (Oaxaca)
_____ *B. b. brunneinucha*	Subtrop. e Mexico (San Luis Potosí and Veracruz to ne Oaxaca)
_____ *B. b. apertus*	S Mexico (Sierra de Tuxtla of s Veracruz)
_____ *B. b. macrourus*	Mountains of s Mexico (Chiapas) and sw Guatemala
_____ *B. b. alleni*	Mountains of n El Salvador, Honduras and w Nicaragua
_____ *B. b. elsae*	Mountains of Costa Rica to w and central Panama
_____ *B. b. frontalis*	Mts. of extreme e Panama to Colombia, w Venezuela and s Peru
_____ *B. b. allinornatus*	Mountains of nw Venezuela (Falcón and Yaracuy)
_____ *B. b. inornatus*	Mts. of w-central Ecuador (Río Chimbo and Río Chanchan area)

☐ **Green-striped Brush-Finch** *Buarremon virenticeps*

_____ *B. v. verecundus*	Mountains of w Mexico (s Sinaloa, n Nayarit and s Durango)
_____ *B. v. virenticeps*	Mts. of w Mexico (Jalisco and Colima to Morelos and w Puebla)

☐ **Stripe-headed Brush-Finch** *Buarremon torquatus*

_____ *B. t. costaricensis*	Highlands of sw Costa Rica and w Panama (Chiriquí)
_____ *B. t. tacarcunae*	Mountains of e Panama
_____ *B. t. atricapillus*	Central and Eastern Andes of n Colombia
_____ *B. t. basilicus*	Santa Marta Mountains (ne Colombia)
_____ *B. t. perijanus*	E slope of Andes of e Colombia and w Venezuela (Zulia)
_____ *B. t. larensis*	Andes of w Venezuela (w Lara and w Táchira)
_____ *B. t. phaeopleurus*	Coastal mts. of n Venezuela (Aragua, Miranda, Distrito Federal)
_____ *B. t. phygas*	Mts. of ne Venezuela (Anzoátegui, Monagas and Sucre)
_____ *B. t. assimilis*	Andes of Colombia to w Venezuela, Ecuador and nw Peru
_____ *B. t. nigrifrons*	Andes of sw Ecuador (El Oro and Loja) and nw Peru
_____ *B. t. poliophrys*	Andes of central and se Peru (Huánuco, Junín and Cuzco)
_____ *B. t. torquatus*	Andes of w Bolivia (La Paz and w Cochabamba)
_____ *B. t. fimbriatus*	Andes of Bolivia (e Cochabamba, w Santa Cruz and Chuquisaca)
_____ *B. t. borelli*	Andes of s Bolivia (Tarija) and nw Argentina (Jujuy and Salta)

☐ **Black-masked Brush-Finch** *Buarremon melanops*

Andes of s Peru (Ayacucho and Huancavelica)

☐ **Orange-billed Sparrow** *Arremon aurantiirostris*

_____ *A. a. saturatus*	Caribbean slope of se Mexico (Veracruz) to Guatemala and Belize
_____ *A. a. rufidorsalis*	Caribbean slope of Honduras to Nicaragua and Costa Rica
_____ *A. a. aurantiirostris*	Pacific slope of Costa Rica and Panama
_____ *A. a. strictocollaris*	Extreme e Panama and adjacent nw Colombia (Chocó)
_____ *A. a. occidentalis*	Pacific slope of w Colombia and nw Ecuador
_____ *A. a. erythrorhynchus*	N Colombia (middle Magdalena, lower Cauca, upper Sinú valleys)
_____ *A. a. spectabilis*	SE Colombia (Putumayo) to e Ecuador and ne Peru (San Martín)
_____ *A. a. santarosae*	SW Ecuador

☐ **Pectoral Sparrow** *Arremon taciturnus*

_____ *A. t. axillaris*	Colombia (east of the Andes) and adjacent w Venezuela
_____ *A. t. taciturnus*	E Colombia to s Venezuela, the Guianas and Amazonian Brazil
_____ *A. t. nigrirostris*	Tropical se Peru to n Bolivia and nw Argentina

☐ **Half-collared Sparrow** *Arremon semitorqutus*

SE Brazil (Rio de Janeiro to Rio Grande do Sul)

☐ **Golden-winged Sparrow** *Arremon schlegeli*

_____ *A. s. fratruelis*	N Colombia (Guajira Peninsula)
_____ *A. s. canidorsum*	W slope of Eastern Andes of Colombia (Santander)
_____ *A. s. schlegeli*	Caribbean coast of e Colombia and n Venezuela

☐ **Black-capped Sparrow** *Arremon abeillei*
_____ *A. a. abeillei* | Arid scrub of sw Ecuador (Manabí) to nw Peru (Cajamarca)
_____ *A. a. nigriceps* | NW Peru (upper Marañón Valley)

☐ **Saffron-billed Sparrow** *Arremon flavirostris*
_____ *A. f. flavirostris* | E Brazil (Bahia to s Goiás, w Minas Gerais and se Mato Grosso)
_____ *A. f. dorbignii* | Lowlands of e Bolivia and nw Argentina
_____ *A. f. devillii* | E Bolivia (Santa Cruz) to se Brazil (s São Paulo and adj. Goiás)
_____ *A. f. polionotus* | Paraguay, n Argentina and sw Brazil (w Paraná and Mato Grosso)

☐ **Olive Sparrow** *Arremonops rufivirgatus*
_____ *A. r. sinaloae* | Coastal w Mexico (Sinaloa to Nayarit)
_____ *A. r. sumichrasti* | Coastal sw Mexico (Jalisco to Colima, Michoacán and Oaxaca)
_____ *A. r. rufivirgatus* | S Texas to ne Mexico (Coahuila and Nuevo León to Tamaulipas)
_____ *A. r. ridgwayi* | E Mexico (s Tamaulipas to San Luis Potosí and n Veracruz)
_____ *A. r. crassirostris* | Coastal se Mexico (Veracruz to e Puebla and n Oaxaca)
_____ *A. r. verticalis* | SE Mexico (Yucatán Pen.) to Petén of n Guatemala and n Belize
_____ *A. r. rhypthothorax* | SE Mexico (Yucatán Peninsula)
_____ *A. r. chiapensis* | S Mexico (central valley of Chiapas)
_____ *A. r. superciliosus* | Pacific coast of nw Costa Rica

☐ **Tocuyo Sparrow** *Arremonops tocuyensis*
| Arid scrub of ne Colombia and nw Venezuela

☐ **Green-backed Sparrow** *Arremonops chloronotus*
_____ *A. c. chloronotus* | Gulf slope of se Mexico (Tabasco) to Belize and nw Honduras
_____ *A. c. twomeyi* | Tropical n-central Honduras (Yoro and Olancho)

☐ **Black-striped Sparrow** *Arremonops conirostris*
_____ *A. c. richmondi* | Tropical e Honduras to Nicaragua, Costa Rica and w Panama
_____ *A. c. striaticeps* | Central and e Panama to Pacific slope of Colombia and w Ecuador
_____ *A. c. inexpectatus* | Colombia (arid upper Magdalena Valley)
_____ *A. c. conirostris* | Caribbean coast of Colombia to n Venezuela and extreme n Brazil
_____ *A. c. umbrinus* | E Colombia (Norte de Santander) to w Venezuela

☐ **Rusty-crowned Ground-Sparrow** *Melozone kieneri*
_____ *M. k. grisior* | Arid Pacific slope of nw Mexico (se Sonora and ne Sinaloa)
_____ *M. k. kieneri* | Arid w Mexico (Sinaloa, w Durango, Nayarit, w Jalisco, Colima)
_____ *M. k. rubricatum (obscurior)* | Arid sw Mexico (Michoacán, Puebla, Morelos, Guerrero, Oaxaca)

☐ **Prevost's Ground-Sparrow** *Melozone biarcuatum*
_____ *M. b. hartwegi* | Highlands of s Mexico (Chiapas)
_____ *M. b. biarcuatum* | Highlands of Guatemala, El Salvador and w Honduras
_____ *M. b. cabanisi* | Highlands of central Costa Rica

☐ **White-eared Ground-Sparrow** *Melozone leucotis*
_____ *M. l. occipitalis* | Highlands of s Mexico (Chiapas) to Guatemala and El Salvador
_____ *M. l. nigrior* | Highlands of n-central Nicaragua
_____ *M. l. leucotis* | Highlands of central Costa Rica

☐ **Green-tailed Towhee** *Pipilo chlorurus*
| Highlands of w US; winters to central Mexico

☐ **Collared Towhee** *Pipilo ocai*
_____ *P. o. alticola* | Mountains of w Mexico (w Jalisco and extreme ne Colima)
_____ *P. o. nigrescens* | Mountains of w Mexico (n-central Michoacán)
_____ *P. o. guerrerensis* | Mountains of sw Mexico (Sierra Madre del Sur of Guerrero)
_____ *P. o. brunnescens* | Mountains of s Mexico (central Oaxaca)
_____ *P. o. ocai* | Mountains of se Mexico (e Puebla and w-central Veracruz)

☐ **Socorro Towhee** *Pipilo socorroensis*
| Socorro I. (Revillagigedo Islands off w Mexico)

☐ **Eastern Towhee** *Pipilo erythrophthalmus*
_____ *P. e. erythrophthalmus*   E North America (s Canada to Gulf Coast)
_____ *P. e. rileyi*   Virginia to Georgia, n Florida and se Alabama
_____ *P. e. alleni*   Central peninsular Florida to tip of peninsula
_____ *P. e. canaster*   Tennessee to Louisiana, Alabama and nw Florida
_____ *P. e. arcticus*   Great Plains of North America to sw US; winters to ne Mexico

☐ **Spotted Towhee** *Pipilo maculatus*
_____ *P. m. curtatus*   SE Br. Col. to ne Calif., Nevada and Idaho; winters to se Calif.
_____ *P. m. oregonus*   Coastal sw Br. Col. to sw Oregon; winters to s California
_____ *P. m. falcinellus*   Interior sw Oregon to Sierra Nevada and San Joaquin Valley
_____ *P. m. montanus*   SW US to nw Mexico; winters to n Mexico
_____ *P. m. falcifer*   Coastal n Calif. (Del Norte to Santa Cruz and San Benito counties)
_____ *P. m. megalonyx*   Coastal s Calif. (Monterey) to nw Baja Calif. and Santa Cruz I.
_____ *P. m. clementae*   Santa Rosa, Santa Catalina and San Clemente is. (off s California)
_____ *P. m. umbraticola*   NW Baja California (latitude 32°N to 30°N)
_____ *P. m. consobrinus†*   Formerly Isla Guadalupe (off w Baja California). Extinct
_____ *P. m. magnirostris*   Mountains of s Baja California (Sierra de la Laguna)
_____ *P. m. gaigei*   Mountains of New Mexico, w Texas and n Mexico (n Coahuila)
_____ *P. m. griseipygius*   Mountains of w Mexico (Sierra Madre Occidental)
_____ *P. m. orientalis*   Mountains of e Mexico (Sierra Madre Oriental)
_____ *P. m. maculatus*   Highlands of e Mexico (Hidalgo to Veracruz and e Puebla)
_____ *P. m. sympatricus*   Mountains of e Mexico (Sierra de Tuxtla of Veracruz)
_____ *P. m. macronyx*   Mts. of c Mexico (e Michoacán, México, Morelos, Dist. Federal)
_____ *P. m. vulcanorum*   Mts. of c Mexico (México, ne Morelos, sw Tlaxcala and w Puebla)
_____ *P. m. oaxacae*   Highlands of s Mexico (n and central Oaxaca)
_____ *P. m. chiapensis*   Mountains of s Mexico (central Chiapas)
_____ *P. m. repetens*   Mountains of s Mexico (se Chiapas) and w Guatemala

☐ **California Towhee** *Pipilo crissalis*
_____ *P. c. bullatus*   Semiarid sw Oregon and extreme n-central California
_____ *P. c. carolae*   Interior California (Humboldt County to Kern County)
_____ *P. c. petulans*   Coastal n California (Humboldt County to Santa Cruz County)
_____ *P. c. crissalis*   Coastal cent. Calif. (n Monterey to Kern and Ventura counties)
_____ *P. c. eremophilus*   E-central California (Argus Mts. and nw San Bernardino County)
_____ *P. c. senicula*   Coastal s California (Los Angeles County) and nw Baja California
_____ *P. c. aripolius*   Central Baja California (latitude 29°N to 26°30'N)
_____ *P. c. albigula*   Cape district of s Baja California

☐ **Canyon Towhee** *Pipilo fuscus*
_____ *P. f. mesoleucus*   Arizona and New Mexico to w Texas, Sonora and nw Chihuahua
_____ *P. f. intermedius*   Semiarid nw Mexico (s Sonora to n Sinaloa)
_____ *P. f. jamesi*   Isla Tiburón (n Sea of Cortés off Sonora)
_____ *P. f. mesatus*   SE Colorado to ne New Mexico and extreme nw Oklahoma
_____ *P. f. texanus*   Highlands of w and central Texas to n Mexico (nw Coahuila)
_____ *P. f. perpallidus*   Mountains of w Mexico (Sierra Madre Occidental)
_____ *P. f. fuscus*   Mts. of w Mexico (Nayarit, Jalisco and Colima to Distrito Federal)
_____ *P. f. potosinus*   Highlands of n Mexico (Coahuila to ne Jalisco and sw Tamaulipas)
_____ *P. f. campoi*   Highlands of e-cent. Mexico (Hidalgo, adj. Puebla and Veracruz)
_____ *P. f. toroi*   S-cent. Mexico (Tlaxcala to Veracruz, Puebla and n Oaxaca)

☐ **Abert's Towhee** *Pipilo aberti*
_____ *P. a. aberti*   Deserts of s Utah to sw Nevada and se California
_____ *P. a. dumeticolus*   Colorado Desert of ne Baja and nw Mexico (Sonora)
_____ *P. a. vorhiesi*   S Arizona (Tucson region) to extreme sw New Mexico

☐ **White-throated Towhee** *Pipilo albicollis*
_____ *P. a. marshalli*   Arid oak-pine zone of se Mexico (Puebla)
_____ *P. a. albicollis*   Oak-pine zone of s Mexico (s Puebla and e Guerrero to c Oaxaca)

693

☐ **Bridled Sparrow** *Aimophila mystacalis*

Arid central plateau of Mexico (Puebla to Oaxaca)

☐ **Black-chested Sparrow** *Aimophila humeralis*

Arid highlands of sw Mexico (Jalisco to w Oaxaca)

☐ **Stripe-headed Sparrow** *Aimophila ruficauda*

_____ *A. r. acuminata*   Arid nw Mexico (s Durango to se Guerrero and s Puebla)
_____ *A. r. lawrencii*   Mexico south of Isthmus of Tehuántepec (Oaxaca and w Chiapas)
_____ *A. r. connectens*   E Guatemala (arid valley of Río Motagua)
_____ *A. r. ibarrorum*   Guatemala
_____ *A. r. ruficauda*   SE Guatemala to nw Costa Rica

☐ **Cinnamon-tailed Sparrow** *Aimophila sumichrasti*

Arid Pacific slope of s Mexico (Oaxaca)

☐ **Stripe-capped Sparrow** *Aimophila strigiceps*

_____ *A. s. dabbenei*   NW Argentina (Jujuy, Salta and Tucumán)
_____ *A. s. strigiceps*   NE Argentina to sw Paraguay (Presidente Hayes)

☐ **Tumbes Sparrow** *Aimophila stolzmanni*

Arid littoral of sw Ecuador and nw Peru

☐ **Bachman's Sparrow** *Aimophila aestivalis*

_____ *A. a. illinoensis* Indiana and Illinois to Texas and s Louisiana; winters to Gulf coast
_____ *A. a. bachmani*   Oak-pine woods of Mid-Atlantic states to n Gulf states
_____ *A. a. aestivalis*   Oak-pine woods of e South Carolina and e Georgia to s Florida

☐ **Botteri's Sparrow** *Aimophila botterii*

_____ *A. b. arizonae*   SE Arizona to n Mexico (s Sonora and n Durango)
_____ *A. b. texana*   Extreme s Texas and ne Mexico (e Tamaulipas)
_____ *A. b. mexicana*   Central highlands of Mexico
_____ *A. b. goldmani*   Coastal w Mexico (Sinaloa to Nayarit)
_____ *A. b. botterii*   S highlands of Mexico (s Puebla to Oaxaca and w Chiapas)
_____ *A. b. petencia (tabascensis)* Coastal se Mexico (Veracruz) to Belize, Guatemala and Honduras
_____ *A. b. vantynei*   Highlands of central Guatemala
_____ *A. b. spadiconigrescens*   Lowland pine savanna of n Honduras and ne Nicaragua
_____ *A. b. vulcanica*   Highlands of Nicaragua and n Costa Rica

☐ **Cassin's Sparrow** *Aimophila cassinii*

Arid sw US and adjacent n Mexico; winters to central Mexico

☐ **Rufous-crowned Sparrow** *Aimophila ruficeps*

_____ *A. r. ruficeps*   Coastal ranges of central California and w slopes of Sierra Nevada
_____ *A. r. canescens (lambi)*   SW California and ne Baja (east to base of San Pedro Mártir)
_____ *A. r. obscura*   Channel Islands (Santa Cruz, Anacapa and Catalina)
_____ *A. r. sanctorum*   Todos Santos Islands (off nw Baja California)
_____ *A. r. sororia*   Mountains of s Baja California (Sierra de la Laguna)
_____ *A. r. scottii*   N Arizona to New Mexico, ne Sonora and nw Coahuila
_____ *A. r. rupicola*   Mountains of sw Arizona
_____ *A. r. simulans*   NW Mexico (se Sonora and sw Chihuahua to Nayarit and n Jalisco)
_____ *A. r. eremoeca (pallidissima)* SE Colorado to New Mexico, Texas, n Chihuahua and c Coahuila
_____ *A. r. fusca*   W Mexico (s Nayarit to sw Jalisco, n Colima and Michoacán)
_____ *A. r. boucardi (extima)*   E Mexico (s Coahuila to San Luis Potosí, n Puebla and s Oaxaca)
_____ *A. r. australis*   S Mexico (Guerrero to s Puebla and Oaxaca)

☐ **Rufous-winged Sparrow** *Aimophila carpalis*

_____ *A. c. carpalis*   Arid s Arizona to nw Mexico (central Sonora)
_____ *A. c. bangsi (distinguenda)* NW Mexico (se Sonora to n Sinaloa)
_____ *A. c. cohaerens*   NW Mexico (central Sinaloa)

☐ **Five-striped Sparrow** *Aimophila quinquestriata*

_____ *A. q. septentrionalis*   S Arizona to nw Mexico (Sonora and w Chihuahua to c Sinaloa)
_____ *A. q. quinquestriata*   Arid w Mexico (n Jalisco)

☐ **Oaxaca Sparrow** *Aimophila notosticta*

Arid highlands of s Mexico (central Oaxaca)

☐ **Rusty Sparrow** *Aimophila rufescens*
- _____ *A. r. antonensis*
- _____ *A. r. mcleodii*
- _____ *A. r. rufescens (disjuncta, brodkorbi)*
- _____ *A. r. pyrgitoides (newmani)*
- _____ *A. r. pectoralis (gigas)*
- _____ *A. r. discolor*
- _____ *A. r. hypaethrus*

Arid nw Mexico (Sierra de San Antonio of n-central Sonora)
NW Mexico (e Sonora and w Chihuahua to n Sinaloa, w Durango)
W Mexico (s Sinaloa to Colima, Oaxaca, s Puebla and sw Chiapas)
E Mexico (s Tamaulipas) to Guatemala, Honduras and El Salvador
S Mexico (Chiapas) to cordillera of w Guatemala and El Salvador
S Belize to ne Guatemala, n Honduras and ne Nicaragua
Pacific slope of nw Costa Rica (Cordillera de Guanacaste)

☐ **Striped Sparrow** *Oriturus superciliosus*
- _____ *O. s. palliatus*
- _____ *O. s. superciliosus*

W Mexico (Sierra Madre Occidental from Sonora to Nayarit)
Humid oak-pine forests of southern Central Plateau of Mexico

☐ **Zapata Sparrow** *Torreornis inexpectata*
- _____ *T. i. inexpectata*
- _____ *T. i. sigmani*
- _____ *T. i. varonai*

SW Cuba (arid Zapata Peninsula)
Arid coastal se Cuba
Cayo Coco (off n Cuba)

☐ **American Tree Sparrow** *Spizella arborea*
- _____ *S. a. arborea*
- _____ *S. a. ochracae*

NE Canada and Labrador; winters to e-central US
N Alaska and n Yukon to n British Columbia; winters to sw US

☐ **Chipping Sparrow** *Spizella passerina*
- _____ *S. p. arizonae (boreophila)*
- _____ *S. p. passerina*
- _____ *S. p. atremaeus (comparanda)*
- _____ *S. p. mexicana (repetens)*
- _____ *S. p. pinetorum*

SE Alaska and w Yukon to n Baja, nw Mexico; winters to Oaxaca
SE Canada to s Texas and South Carolina; winters to ne Mexico
Mexico (Sierra Madre Occidental to pine belt of Nuevo León)
Highlands of w Mexico (Nayarit) to nw Guatemala
Pine forests of n Guatemala (Petén) to ne Nicaragua

☐ **Clay-colored Sparrow** *Spizella pallida*

Breeds w Canada and US; winters to Guatemala

☐ **Brewer's Sparrow** *Spizella breweri*
- _____ *S. b. taverneri*
- _____ *S. b. breweri*

SW Yukon and nw Br. Col. to se Br. Col. and sw Alberta
Br. Col. and Alberta to sw US; winters to Baja and cent. Mexico

☐ **Field Sparrow** *Spizella pusilla*
- _____ *S. p. pusilla*
- _____ *S. p. arenacea*

SE Canada to se US; winters to Gulf Coast and s Florida
Great Plains of central US; winters to Gulf Coast and ne Mexico

☐ **Worthen's Sparrow** *Spizella wortheni*
- _____ *S. w. wortheni*
- _____ *S. w. browni*

NE Mexico (Coahuila to Nuevo León, sw Tamaulipas and Veracruz)
Arid montane scrub of n Mexico (w Zacatecas)

☐ **Black-chinned Sparrow** *Spizella atrogularis*
- _____ *S. a. evura*
- _____ *S. a. caurina*
- _____ *S. a. cana*
- _____ *S. a. atrogularis*

SE Calif. to n Nevada, sw Utah, Arizona, w Texas and n Sonora
Coastal central California (Contra Costa to San Benito counties)
Interior coastal mountains of California (Monterey) to n Baja
Cent. plateau of Mexico (Durango to w Nuevo Leon and s Oaxaca)

☐ **Vesper Sparrow** *Pooecetes gramineus*
- _____ *P. g. gramineus*
- _____ *P. g. confinis*
- _____ *P. g. affinis*

SE Canada and e-central US; winters to Texas and Gulf Coast
SW Canada to sw US; winters to s Mexico (Chiapas)
W Washington and w Oregon; winters to nw Baja

☐ **Lark Sparrow** *Chondestes grammacus*
- _____ *C. g. grammacus*
- _____ *C. g. strigatus*

S-cent. Canada (Ontario) to New York, n Texas and w N Carolina
SW Canada and w US to n Mexico; winters to s Mexico

☐ **Black-throated Sparrow** *Amphispiza bilineata*

____	*A. b. bilineata*	N-c Texas to ne Mexico (e Coahuila, Nuevo León and Tamaulipas)
____	*A. b. opuntia*	SE Colorado to e New Mexico, w Texas and nw Coahuila
____	*A. b. deserticola*	Arid w-c US to n Baja, islands in Sea of Cortés and nw Chihuahua
____	*A. b. bangsi*	Cape District of s Baja California and adjacent islands
____	*A. b. tortugae*	Isla La Tortuga (Gulf of California)
____	*A. b. carmenae*	Isla Carmen (Gulf of California)
____	*A. b. belvederei*	Isla Cerralvo (Gulf of California)
____	*A. b. cana*	Isla San Estéban (Gulf of California)
____	*A. b. pacifica*	Arid nw Mexico (s Sonora, n Sinaloa and Isla Tiburón)
____	*A. b. grisea*	W-c Mexico (Chihuahua to s Coahuila, n Jalisco, sw Tamaulipas)

☐ **Sage Sparrow** *Amphispiza belli*

____	*A. b. nevadensis*	Great Basin of w US; winters to n Baja and nw Mexico
____	*A. b. canescens*	Arid interior s-central California to w Nevada and ne Baja
____	*A. b. belli*	S Calif. (w slopes of Sierra Nevada, coastal ranges and nw Baja)
____	*A. b. clementeae*	San Clemente I. (off s California)
____	*A. b. cinerea*	Central Baja California (latitude 29°N to 26°N)

☐ **Lark Bunting** *Calamospiza melanocorys*

Breeds w Canada and w US; winters to n Mexico

☐ **Savannah Sparrow** *Passerculus sandwichensis*

____	*P. s. athinus*	Aleutians and n Alaska to sw Canada; winters to Baja, s Mexico
____	*P. s. sandwichensis*	Amutka I., e Aleutians and w Alaskan Pen.; winters to s California
____	*P. s. crassus*	SE Alaska (Alexander Arch.) and adjacent mainland Alaska
____	*P. s. brooksi*	Vancouver I. and coastal sw Br. Col. to nw Calif.; winters to Baja
____	*P. s. alaudinus*	Coastal n California (Humboldt to San Luis Obispo County)
____	*P. s. beldingi*	Coastal s California (Santa Barbara County) to n Baja California
____	*P. s. anulus*	Bahía Vizcaino area of Baja California
____	*P. s. sanctorum*	San Benito Islands (off w Baja California)
____	*P. s. guttatus*	Coastal w Baja California (Laguna San Ignacio region)
____	*P. s. magdalenae*	Coastal w Baja California (Bahia Magdalena region)
____	*P. s. rostratus*	NE Baja California (mouth of Colorado River and adjacent Sonora)
____	*P. s. rufofuscus*	Central Arizona and n New Mexico to n Mexico (Chihuahua)
____	*P. s. atratus*	Coastal nw Mexico (central Sonora to central Sinaloa)
____	*P. s. brunnescens*	Mexico (Durango to Jalisco, Puebla, Guerrero and Oaxaca)
____	*P. s. wetmorei*	Mountains of extreme sw Guatemala
____	*P. s. nevadensis*	Great Basin and Great Plains of N America; winters to s Mexico
____	*P. s. oblitus*	Central Canada and n-central US; winters to ne Mexico
____	*P. s. mediogriseus*	SE Canada (Ontario to Gaspé Pen.) and ne US; winters se US
____	*P. s. labradorius*	E Quebec, Labrador and Newfoundland; winters to se Texas
____	*P. s. savanna*	Nova Scotia, Prince Edward I. and Magdalen I.; winters to Bahamas
____	*P. s. princeps*	Sable I. (Nova Scotia); winters coastal Massachusetts to Georgia

☐ **Seaside Sparrow** *Ammodramus maritimus*

____	*A. m. maritimus*	Salt marshes from Mass. to n North Carolina; winters to ne Florida
____	*A. m. macgillivraii*	Salt marshes from n North Carolina to s Georgia
____	*A. m. pelonota*	Salt marshes of ne Florida (Georgia border to New Smyrna)
____	*A. m. mirabilis*	Marshes of sw Florida (Everglades to Cape Sable)
____	*A. m. peninsulae*	Salt marshes of w Florida (Dixie County to Old Tampa Bay)
____	*A. m. junicola*	Gulf Coast of n Florida (Escambie County to Taylor County)
____	*A. m. nigrescens*	Salt marshes of e coastal and e Florida
____	*A. m. fisheri*	Marshes of Gulf Coast (San Antonio Bay to Alabama)
____	*A. m. sennetti*	Marshes of Gulf Coast of s Texas (Aransas County to Nueces Bay)

☐ **Nelson's Sharp-tailed Sparrow** *Ammodramus nelsoni*

W North America (s Canada to n US; winters to nw Mexico)

☐ **Saltmarsh Sharp-tailed Sparrow** *Ammodramus caudacutus*

____	*A. c. alterus*	E Canada (s James Bay and w Quebec); winters to n Florida
____	*A. c. subvirgatus*	S Quebec to Nova Scotia and e Maine; winters S Car. to n Florida
____	*A. c. caudacutus*	Marshes of s Maine to s New Jersey; winters to s Florida
____	*A. c. diversus*	Coastal s New Jersey to N Carolina; winters to Florida Gulf Coast

☐ **Le Conte's Sparrow** *Ammodramus leconteii*

Prairies of central North America; winters to Gulf States

☐ **Henslow's Sparrow** *Ammodramus henslowii*

____	*A. h. susurrans*	NY to s N Hamp., e W Virginia and e N Car.; winters to c Florida
____	*A. h. henslowi*	N-central US; winters to Texas, Louisiana and n Florida

☐ **Baird's Sparrow** *Ammodramus bairdii*

Great Plains of North America; winters sw US and n Mexico

☐ **Grasshopper Sparrow** *Ammodramus savannarum*

____	*A. s. perpallidus*	SE Br. Columbia to w Ontario and sw US; winters to El Salvador
____	*A. s. ammolegus*	S Arizona and nw Mexico (n Sonora); winters to Guatemala
____	*A. s. pratensis*	SE Canada and e US; winters to Guatemala and Cuba
____	*A. s. floridanus*	Central peninsular Florida
____	*A. s. bimaculatus*	S Mexico (Veracruz) to Nicaragua, nw Costa Rica and w Panama
____	*A. s. cracens*	Petén and e Guatemala to Belize, e Honduras and ne Nicaragua
____	*A. s. caucae*	Colombia (upper Cauca Valley) and adjacent n Ecuador
____	*A. s. savannarum*	Jamaica
____	*A. s. intricatus*	Hispaniola
____	*A. s. borinquensis*	Puerto Rico
____	*A. s. caribaeus*	Netherlands Antilles (Bonaire and Curaçao)

☐ **Grassland Sparrow** *Ammodramus humeralis*

____	*A. h. humeralis*	Lowlands of e Colombia to Venezuela, the Guianas and Brazil
____	*A. h. pallidulus*	NE Colombia (Guajira Peninsula)
____	*A. h. xanthornus*	E Bolivia (Beni) to Paraguay, Uruguay, s Brazil and n Argentina
____	*A. h. tarijensis*	E Bolivia (Santa Cruz and Tarija)

☐ **Yellow-browed Sparrow** *Ammodramus aurifrons*

____	*A. a. apurensis*	NE Colombia and w Venezuela
____	*A. a. cherriei*	*Llanos* of e Colombia (Meta)
____	*A. a. tenebrosus*	Tropical e Colombia (Vaupés) and Venezuela (sw Amazonas)
____	*A. a. aurifrons*	Trop. se Colombia to e Ecuador, Peru, Bolivia and w Amaz. Brazil

☐ **Fox Sparrow** *Passerella iliaca*

____	*P. i. chilcatensis*	Alaska
____	*P. i. zaboria*	NW Alaska to sw Canada; winters e of Great Plains to c and s US
____	*P. i. altivagans*	Mts. of British Columbia and sw Alberta; winters to nw Baja
____	*P. i. unalaschensis (insularis)*	E Aleutian Islands to Alaska Peninsula; winters to s California
____	*P. i. ridgwayi*	Alaska (Kodiak Island group); winters to s California
____	*P. i. sinuosa*	Kenai Peninsula and Prince William Sound; winters to nw Baja
____	*P. i. annectens*	Alaska (Yakutat Bay region); winters to s California
____	*P. i. townsendi*	SE Alaska (Glacier Bay to Queen Charlotte Is.); winters to c Calif.
____	*P. i. fuliginosa*	Coastal se Alaska to nw Washington; winters to s California
____	*P. i. olivacea*	Mts. of sw Br. Col. to central and e Washington; winters to n Baja
____	*P. i. schistacea*	SW Br. Col. and sw Alberta to n Nevada; winters to w Texas
____	*P. i. swarthi*	Mountains of nw Utah and se Idaho
____	*P. i. fulva*	Oregon e of Cascades to ne California (Modoc); winters to n Baja
____	*P. i. megarhyncha*	Mts. of sw Oregon to c Calif. and w-c Nevada; winters to nw Baja
____	*P. i. brevicauda*	N and inner coast ranges of California; winters to s California
____	*P. i. monoensis*	Mono Lake area of e-c Calif. and adj. Nevada; winters to nw Baja
____	*P. i. canescens*	Mts. of Inyo County (Calif.) and adj. Nevada; winters to n Baja
____	*P. i. stephensi*	Sierra Nevada and high mts. of s Calif.; winters lower elevations
____	*P. i. iliaca*	Labrador and Newfoundland to se Quebec, Ontario; winters e US

☐ **Sierra Madre Sparrow** *Xenospiza baileyi*

Locally in montane pine forests of central Mexico

☐ **Song Sparrow** *Melospiza melodia*

_____ *M. m. maxima*	Aleutian Islands (Attu to Atka)
_____ *M. m. sanaka*	Aleutian Islands (Seguam to Unimak and Sanak to Semidi)
_____ *M. m. amaka*	Amak I. (Aleutian Islands)
_____ *M. m. insignis*	Kodiak Group (Sitkalidak I. to Barren Is.) and adj. Alaskan Pen.
_____ *M. m. kenaiensis*	Coastal s Alaska (Cook Inlet to Copper River)
_____ *M. m. caurina*	Coastal se Alaska (Yakutat Bay to Cross Sound); winters to n Calif.
_____ *M. m. inexspectata*	SE Alaska (Glacier Bay) to interior Br. Col; winters to n Oregon
_____ *M. m. rufina*	Outer islands of se Alaska to c Br. Col.; winters to w Washington
_____ *M. m. merrilli*	S Br. Col. to sw Alberta and nw Montana; winters to n Mexico
_____ *M. m. morphna*	SW British Columbia to sw Oregon; winters to n California
_____ *M. m. fisherella*	Oregon east of Cascades to e-c Calif., w Nevada and sw Idaho
_____ *M. m. cleonensis*	Extreme sw coastal Oregon to n Calif. (w Mendocino County)
_____ *M. m. gouldii*	Coastal central California (Mendocino Co. to n San Benito Co.)
_____ *M. m. mailliardi*	Central Valley of California (Glenn Co. to Stanislaus Co.)
_____ *M. m. samuelis*	Salt marshes of c California (San Pablo and San Francisco bays)
_____ *M. m. maxillaris*	Brackish marshes of central California (Suisan Bay)
_____ *M. m. pusillula*	Salt marshes of c California (south side of San Francisco Bay)
_____ *M. m. heermani*	S California (Merced Co. to Kern County and Kings Canyon)
_____ *M. m. cooperi*	Coastal s Calif. (Santa Cruz) to n Baja, Mojave, Colorado deserts
_____ *M. m. micronyx*	San Miguel I. (off coastal s California)
_____ *M. m. clementae*	Santa Rosa, Santa Cruz and San Clemente is. (off s California)
_____ *M. m. graminea*	Santa Barbara I. (off coastal s California)
_____ *M. m. coronatorum*	Los Coronados Islands (off nw Baja California)
_____ *M. m. rivularis*	S-central Baja California
_____ *M. m. saltonis*	Colorado R. Valley (extreme s Nevada, se California and nw Baja)
_____ *M. m. juddi*	NE Br. Columbia to w-central US; winters to Texas and se US
_____ *M. m. montana*	NE Oregon to w Idaho, e Ariz., and n N. Mex.; winters to Sonora
_____ *M. m. fallax*	SE Nevada to sw Utah, Arizona and nw Mexico (ne Sonora)
_____ *M. m. goldmani*	Sierra Madre Occidental of w Mexico (El Salto area of Durango)
_____ *M. m. niceae*	Wetlands of e-central Mexico (Hidalgo)
_____ *M. m. mexicana*	Wetlands of s central Mexico (Tlaxcala and Puebla)
_____ *M. m. azteca*	Wetlands of valleys of s-c Mexico (Distrito Federal and México)
_____ *M. m. villai*	C Mexico (upper Río Lerma), se Guanajuato and nw Michoacán
_____ *M. m. yuriria*	C Mexico (Río Lerma Valley from Lago Yuriria to s Guanajuato)
_____ *M. m. adusta*	SW Mexico (Lago Pátzcuaro in Michoacán)
_____ *M. m. zacapu*	SW Mexico (Zacapu region of n Michoacán and Laguna Chapala)
_____ *M. m. melodia*	SE Canada and ne US; winters to e Texas and s Florida
_____ *M. m. atlantica*	Coastal New York (Long I.) to N Carolina; winters to n Georgia
_____ *M. m. euphonia*	N-central US; winters to Texas, Alabama, S Carolina and Georgia

☐ **Lincoln's Sparrow** *Melospiza lincolnii*

_____ *M. l. lincolnii*	NW Alaska to Canada and n US; winters to Baja and Guatemala
_____ *M. l. gracilis*	Coastal s Alaska and c Br. Columbia; winters to central California
_____ *M. l. alticola*	Mts. of Oregon to Ariz. and New Mexico; winters to Guatemala

☐ **Swamp Sparrow** *Melospiza georgiana*

_____ *M. g. ericrypta*	E and central Canada; winters to s US and ne Mexico
_____ *M. g. georgiana*	N Dak. to Nova Scotia and ne US; winters to s Texas and Florida

☐ **White-crowned Sparrow** *Zonotrichia leucophrys*

_____ *Z. l. gambelii*	N Alaska and n Yukon to s-central Canada; winters to n Mexico
_____ *Z. l. leucophrys*	C and e Canada to Newfoundland; winters to se US, Cuba, Jamaica
_____ *Z. l. oriantha*	Mts. of sw Canada to sw US; winters to s Baja and cent. Mexico
_____ *Z. l. pugetensis*	Coastal sw Br. Columbia to nw Calif.; winters to sw California
_____ *Z. l. nuttalli*	Coastal central California (Mendocino Co. to Santa Barbara Co.)

☐ **White-throated Sparrow** *Zonotrichia albicollis*

Breeds n North America; winters to s US and n Mexico

☐ **Golden-crowned Sparrow** *Zonotrichia atricapilla*

Breeds Alaska and w Canada; winters to Sonora and Baja Calif.

☐ **Rufous-collared Sparrow** *Zonotrichia capensis*

_____ *Z. c. septentrionalis*	Highlands of s Mexico (Chiapas) to Guatemala and Honduras
_____ *Z. c. antillarum*	Cordillera Central of Dominican Republic
_____ *Z. c. costaricensis*	Mts. of Costa Rica to w Panama; Andes of Colombia, w Venezuela
_____ *Z. c. orestera*	Mountains of w Panama (Cerro Campana)
_____ *Z. c. insularis*	Netherlands Antilles (Curaçao and Aruba)
_____ *Z. c. venezuelae*	Coastal cordillera of n Venezuela
_____ *Z. c. roraimae*	S Colombia (Meta) to e Venezuela, w Guyana and adj. n Brazil
_____ *Z. c. inaccessibilis*	*Tepuis* of s Venezuela (Cerro de la Neblina)
_____ *Z. c. perezchinchillae*	*Tepuis* of s Venezuela (Amazonas)
_____ *Z. c. macconelli*	*Tepuis* of s Venezuela (Mt. Roraima)
_____ *Z. c. capensis*	French Guiana (lower Oyapock River) and adj. Brazil (Amapá)
_____ *Z. c. tocantinsi*	E Brazil (lower Amazonia along Rio Tocantins)
_____ *Z. c. novaesi*	E Brazil (Pará)
_____ *Z. c. matutina*	NE Brazil (Maranhão to Bahia and Mato Grosso) and adj. e Bolivia
_____ *Z. c. huancabambae*	Arid n Peru (Piura, Cajamarca, Amazonas, San Martín and Junín)
_____ *Z. c. illescasensis*	N Peru (Cerro Illescas in Piura)
_____ *Z. c. peruviensis*	Arid coastal Peru and w slope of Andes (La Libertad to Tacna)
_____ *Z. c. carabayae*	E slope of Eastern Andes of Peru (Junín) to w Bolivia
_____ *Z. c. pulacayensis*	Andes of Peru (Junín) to w Bolivia and n Argentina
_____ *Z. c. subtorquata*	E Brazil (Espírito Santo) to Paraguay, Uruguay and ne Argentina
_____ *Z. c. mellea*	Central Paraguay and adjacent n-central Argentina (Formosa)
_____ *Z. c. hypoleuca*	E and s Bolivia to ne Argentina
_____ *Z. c. antofagastae*	N Chile (Tarapacá and Antofagasta)
_____ *Z. c. chilensis*	Chile (Atacama to Islas Guaitecas) and Andes of s Argentina
_____ *Z. c. sanborni*	Andes of Chile (Coquimbo, Aconcagua) and Argentina (San Juan)
_____ *Z. c. arenalensis*	Andes of n Argentina
_____ *Z. c. choraules*	W Argentina (Mendoza, e Neuquén and Río Negro)
_____ *Z. c. australis*	S Chile and s Argentina to Cape Horn; winters n to Bolivia

☐ **Harris' Sparrow** *Zonotrichia querula*

Breeds n-central Canada; winters to s US

☐ **Dark-eyed Junco** *Junco hyemalis*

_____ *J. h. hyemalis*	N Alaska and Yukon to n-central US; winters to n Mexico
_____ *J. h. oreganus*	Coastal se Alaska to cent. Br. Col.; winters to cent. California
_____ *J. h. cismontanus*	S-c Yukon to w-c Alberta; winters to n Baja and central Texas
_____ *J. h. montanus*	Interior Br. Col. and sw Alberta to e Oregon, w Montana, c Idaho
_____ *J. h. mearnsi*	SE Alberta, sw Saskatchewan to e Idaho, Montana, ne Wyoming
_____ *J. h. shufeldti*	W slopes of coastal mts. from sw British Columbia to w Oregon
_____ *J. h. thurberi*	S Oregon to mts. of San Diego Co.; winters to n Baja, sw N Mex.
_____ *J. h. aikeni*	SE Montana to w South Dakota, ne Wyoming and nw Nebraska
_____ *J. h. pinosus*	Coastal ranges of California (San Francisco to s Monterey Co.)
_____ *J. h. pontilus*	Mountains of n Baja California (Sierra Juárez)
_____ *J. h. townsendi*	Mountains of n Baja California (San Pedro Mártir)
_____ *J. h. carolinensis*	Appalachian Mountains to n Georgia

☐ **Yellow-eyed Junco** *Junco phaeonotus*

_____ *J. p. caniceps*	Mts. of s Idaho to Utah and n New Mexico; winters to nw Mexico
_____ *J. p. dorsalis*	Mts. of New Mexico, n Arizona and extreme w Texas
_____ *J. p. mutabilis*	Mts. of s Nevada and adjacent se California
_____ *J. p. palliatus*	Mts. of s Arizona, sw New Mexico and n Mexico
_____ *J. p. phaeonotus*	Mts. of c and s Mexico (Jalisco to Hidalgo, Veracruz and Oaxaca)
_____ *J. p. bairdi*	Mountains of s Baja California (Sierra de la Laguna)
_____ *J. p. fulvescens*	Mts. of s Mexico (interior of Chiapas)
_____ *J. p. alticola*	Mts. of s Mexico (se Chiapas) and w Guatemala

☐ **Guadalupe Junco** *Junco insularis*

Oak-pine forests of Guadalupe I. (off w Baja California)

☐ **Volcano Junco** *Junco vulcani*

Volcanic summits of Costa Rica and w Panama (Chiriquí)

☐ **McCown's Longspur** *Calcarius mccownii*

Breeds w Canada to nw US; winters to nw Mexico

☐ **Lapland Longspur** *Calcarius lapponicus*
_____ *C. l. alascensis*
_____ *C. l. lapponicus*
_____ *C. l. coloratus*

Aleutian and Pribilof is., Alaska and w Canada; winters to n Texas
N Canada across n Siberia to Bering Strait; winters n Europe, c US
E Siberia, Kamchatka Pen. and Komandorskiye Is.; winters to Japan

☐ **Smith's Longspur** *Calcarius pictus*

Breeds Alaska and w Canada; winters in s-central US

☐ **Chestnut-collared Longspur** *Calcarius ornatus*

Prairies of central North America; winters sw US to n Mexico

☐ **Snow Bunting** *Plectrophenax nivalis*
_____ *P. n. townsendi*
_____ *P. n. nivalis*
_____ *P. n. insulae*
_____ *P. n. vlasowae*

Komandorskiye, Pribilof and w Aleutian islands
N North America and n Europe; winters to s US and s Europe
Iceland; winters to Faeroes, Shetland Islands and n Scotland
Tundra of ne Asia; winters to c Asia, Manchuria and Japan

☐ **McKay's Bunting** *Plectrophenax hyperboreus*

Islands in Bering Sea; winters coastal Alaska and Aleutian Islands

☐ **Large Ground-Finch** *Geospiza magnirostris*

Arid scrub of main Galapagos Islands

☐ **Medium Ground-Finch** *Geospiza fortis*

Arid scrub of main Galapagos Islands

☐ **Small Ground-Finch** *Geospiza fuliginosa*

Arid scrub of main Galapagos Islands

☐ **Sharp-beaked Ground-Finch** *Geospiza difficilis*
_____ *G. d. septentrionalis*
_____ *G. d. difficilis*
_____ *G. d. debilirostris*

Galapagos Islands (Culpepper and Wenman)
Galapagos Islands (Tower and Abingdon)
Galapagos Islands (James, Isabela and Fernandina)

☐ **Common Cactus-Finch** *Geospiza scandens*
_____ *G. s. scandens*
_____ *G. s. intermedia*
_____ *G. s. abingdoni*
_____ *G. s. rothschildi*

Galapagos Islands (James and Jervis)
Galapagos Is. (Barrington, Floreana, Duncan, Santa Cruz, Isabela)
Abingdon I. (Galapagos Islands)
Marchena I. (Galapagos Islands)

☐ **Large Cactus-Finch** *Geospiza conirostris*
_____ *G. c. darwinii*
_____ *G. c. conirostris*
_____ *G. c. propinqua*

Galapagos Islands (Culpepper and Wenman)
Hood I. (Galapagos Islands)
Tower I. (Galapagos Islands)

☐ **Vegetarian Finch** *Camarhynchus crassirostris*

Main islands of Galapagos (except for extremely arid islands)

☐ **Mangrove Finch** *Camarhynchus heliobates*

Mangrove swamps of Galapagos Islands (Fernandina and Isabela)

☐ **Large Tree-Finch** *Camarhynchus psittacula*
_____ *C. p. habeli*
_____ *C. p. affinis*
_____ *C. p. psittacula*

Galapagos Islands (Abingdon and Marchena)
Galapagos Islands (Isabela and Fernandina)
Seymour, Barrington, Santa Cruz, Floreana, Duncan, Jervis, James

☐ **Small Tree-Finch** *Camarhynchus parvulus*
_____ *C. p. parvulus*
_____ *C. p. salvini*

Humid scrub of main Galapagos Islands (except Chatham I.)
Chatham I. (Galapagos Islands)

☐ **Medium Tree-Finch** *Camarhynchus pauper*

Humid scrub of Floreana I. (Galapagos Islands)

☐ **Woodpecker Finch** *Camarhynchus pallidus*

_____ *C. p. pallidus*	Galapagos (James, Jervis, Seymour, Duncan, Santa Cruz, Floreana)
_____ *C. p. productus*	Galapagos Islands (Isabela and Fernandina)
_____ *C. p. striatipectus*	San Cristóbal I. (Galapagos Islands)

☐ **Warbler Finch** *Certhidea olivacea*

_____ *C. o. becki*	Galapagos Islands (Culpepper and Wenman)
_____ *C. o. mentalis*	Tower I. (Galapagos Islands)
_____ *C. o. fusca*	Galapagos Islands (Abingdon and Marchena)
_____ *C. o. olivacea*	Galapagos (James, Jervis, Seymour, Duncan, Isabela, Fernandina)
_____ *C. o. bifasciata*	Barrington I. (Galapagos Islands)
_____ *C. o. cinerascens*	Hood I. (Galapagos Islands)
_____ *C. o. ridgwayi*	Floreana I. (Galapagos Islands)

FAMILY: CARDINALIDAE (Saltators, Cardinals and Allies—43)

☐ **Red-and-black Grosbeak** *Periporphyrus erythromelas*

S Venezuela to the Guianas and e Amazonian Brazil

☐ **Lesser Antillean Saltator** *Saltator albicollis*

_____ *S. a. guadelupensis*	Lesser Antilles (Guadeloupe and Dominica)
_____ *S. a. albicollis*	Lesser Antilles (Martinique and St. Lucia)

☐ **Streaked Saltator** *Saltator striatipectus*

_____ *S. s. furax*	Lowlands of sw Costa Rica and w Panama
_____ *S. s. isthmicus*	Panama (except w Chiriquí and Darién)
_____ *S. s. scotinus*	Isla Coiba and Isla Ranchería (off w Panama)
_____ *S. s. melicus*	Isla Taboga (Bay of Panama)
_____ *S. s. speratus*	Pearl Islands (San Miguel, Saboga and Viveros)
_____ *S. s. striatipectus*	E Panama (Darién) and Colombia w of the Andes (south to Cauca)
_____ *S. s. perstriatus*	NE Colombia to mountains of n Venezuela; Trinidad
_____ *S. s. flavidicollis*	SW Colombia (Nariño) to arid w Ecuador and nw Peru (Piura)
_____ *S. s. immaculatus*	Arid coastal Peru (Lambayeque to Ica)
_____ *S. s. peruvianus*	N Peru (upper Marañón Valley in Cajamarca and La Libertad)

☐ **Grayish Saltator** *Saltator coerulescens*

_____ *S. c. vigorsii*	NW Mexico (Sinaloa, w Durango, Nayarit and coastal n Jalisco)
_____ *S. c. richardsoni*	W Mexico (Jalisco to Colima, Guerrero and adj. w Oaxaca)
_____ *S. c. grandis*	E Mexico (Tamaulipas) to Guatemala and central Costa Rica
_____ *S. c. yucatanensis*	SE Mexico (Yucatán Pen., adjacent Tabasco and ne Chiapas)
_____ *S. c. hesperis*	Pacific slope of s Mexico (Chiapas) to Nicaragua
_____ *S. c. brevicaudus*	Pacific slope of w Costa Rica (Gulf of Nicoya region)
_____ *S. c. plumbeus*	Caribbean coast of n Colombia (Río Sinú to Magdalena Valley)
_____ *S. c. brewsteri*	Tropical ne Colombia to Venezuela; Trinidad
_____ *S. c. olivascens*	*Tepuis* of s Venezuela to the Guianas and adjacent n Brazil
_____ *S. c. azarae*	Trop. e Colombia to Ecuador, Peru, Bolivia and w Amaz. Brazil
_____ *S. c. mutus*	N Brazil (lower Solimões to Mexiana I., Amapá and n Maranhão)
_____ *S. c. superciliaris*	NE Brazil (s Piauí to n and e Bahia)
_____ *S. c. coerulescens*	E Bolivia to Paraguay, sw Brazil, Uruguay and n Argentina

☐ **Buff-throated Saltator** *Saltator maximus*

_____ *S. m. gigantodes*	Caribbean slope of e Mexico (Veracruz to n Oaxaca and Tabasco)
_____ *S. m. magnoides*	S Mexico (Chiapas and Quintana Roo) to nw Panama
_____ *S. m. intermedius*	SW Costa Rica to w Panama (Canal Zone)
_____ *S. m. iungens*	E Panama and lowlands of nw Colombia
_____ *S. m. maximus*	E Colombia to Venezuela, Guianas, Brazil, e Bolivia and Paraguay

☐ **Black-headed Saltator** *Saltator atriceps*
_____ S. a. atriceps | Caribbean slope of Mexico to Guatemala and e Costa Rica
_____ S. a. suffuscus | SE Mexico (Sierra de Tuxtla of se Veracruz)
_____ S. a. flavicrissus | W Mexico (central Guerrero)
_____ S. a. peeti | Pacific slope of s Mexico (Chiapas and adjacent Oaxaca)
_____ S. a. raptor | SE Mexico (Yucatán, Quintana Roo and Campeche)
_____ S. a. lacertosus | W Costa Rica and Panama (east to Canal Zone)

☐ **Slate-colored Grosbeak** *Saltator grossus*
_____ S. g. saturatus | Caribbean slope of Nicaragua to w Ecuador
_____ S. g. grossus | E Colombia to Venezuela, the Guianas, Amaz. Brazil and n Bolivia

☐ **Black-throated Grosbeak** *Saltator fuliginosus*

Humid forests and scrub of e Brazil to Paraguay and ne Argentina

☐ **Black-winged Saltator** *Saltator atripennis*
_____ S. a. atripennis | W and Central Andes of Colombia to extreme nw Ecuador
_____ S. a. caniceps | W slope of Eastern Andes of Colombia and w Ecuador

☐ **Green-winged Saltator** *Saltator similis*
_____ S. s. similis | E Bolivia to se Brazil, Paraguay, Uruguay and ne Argentina
_____ S. s. ochraceiventris | SE Brazil (s São Paulo to Paraná and Rio Grande do Sul)

☐ **Orinocan Saltator** *Saltator orenocensis*
_____ S. o. rufescens | NE Colombia (Guajira Peninsula) and arid nw Venezuela
_____ S. o. orenocensis | *Llanos* of Venezuela (north of the Orinoco River)

☐ **Black-cowled Saltator** *Saltator nigriceps*

Humid montane forests of s Ecuador and nw Peru

☐ **Golden-billed Saltator** *Saltator aurantiirostris*
_____ S. a. iteratus | Andes of n Peru (Cajamarca, Amazonas, La Libertad and Ancash)
_____ S. a. albociliaris | Andes of Peru (Ancash and Huánuco) to n Chile (Arica)
_____ S. a. hellmayri | Andes of Bolivia (La Paz and Cochabamba to Potosí and n Tarija)
_____ S. a. aurantiirostris | S Bolivia to Paraguay, Uruguay, s Brazil and n Argentina
_____ S. a. parkesi | S Brazil to Uruguay and ne Argentina
_____ S. a. nasica | W-central Argentina (La Rioja, Mendoza and w La Pampa)

☐ **Thick-billed Saltator** *Saltator maxillosus*

Humid forests of e Paraguay to se Brazil and ne Argentina

☐ **Masked Saltator** *Saltator cinctus*

Andes of extreme se Colombia to ne Peru

☐ **Black-throated Saltator** *Saltator atricollis*

Campos of e Bolivia to ne Paraguay and interior ne and c Brazil

☐ **Rufous-bellied Saltator** *Saltator rufiventris*

Andes of w Bolivia and extreme nw Argentina (Jujuy)

☐ **Black-faced Grosbeak** *Caryothraustes poliogaster*
_____ C. p. poliogaster | Lowlands of se Mexico (Veracruz) to Guatemala and n Honduras
_____ C. p. scapularis | Caribbean lowlands of Nicaragua to Costa Rica and w Panama

☐ **Yellow-green Grosbeak** *Caryothraustes canadensis*
_____ C. c. simulans | Extreme e Panama (Darién)
_____ C. c. canadensis | SE Colombia (Vaupés) to Venezuela, the Guianas and n Brazil
_____ C. c. frontalis | NE Brazil (Ceará, Pernambuco and Alagoas)
_____ C. c. brasiliensis | E-central Brazil (Bahia and e Minas Gerais to Rio de Janeiro)

☐ **Yellow-shouldered Grosbeak** *Parkerthraustes humeralis*

E Colombia to n Bolivia and sw Amazonian Brazil

☐ **Crimson-collared Grosbeak** *Rhodothraupis celaeno*

E Mexico (Nuevo León to n Veracruz and ne Puebla)

□ **Vermilion Cardinal** *Cardinalis phoeniceus*

Caribbean littoral of ne Colombia and n Venezuela; Isla Margarita

□ **Northern Cardinal** *Cardinalis cardinalis*

____	*C. c. superbus*	Extreme se California to Arizona, sw New Mexico and n Sonora
____	*C. c. seftoni*	Central Baja California (south to latitude 27°N)
____	*C. c. igneus*	S Baja California (north to latitude 27°N)
____	*C. c. clintoni*	Isla Cerralvo (Gulf of California)
____	*C. c. townsendi*	Isla Tiburón (Sea of Cortés) and adjacent coastal Sonora
____	*C. c. affinis*	W Mexico (se Sonora to sw Chihuahua and w Durango)
____	*C. c. sinaloensis*	Coastal w Mexico (Sinaloa and Jalisco)
____	*C. c. mariae*	Tres Marías Islands (off w Mexico)
____	*C. c. carneus*	Coastal w Mexico (Colima to Isthmus of Tehuántepec)
____	*C. c. cardinalis*	E US
____	*C. c. floridanus*	SE Georgia and peninsular Florida
____	*C. c. magnirostris*	SE Texas and s Louisiana
____	*C. c. canicaudus*	W Oklahoma and w Texas to e-central Mexico
____	*C. c. coccineus*	E Mexico (e San Luis Potosí, Veracruz, ne Puebla and n Oaxaca)
____	*C. c. littoralis*	Lowlands of e Mexico (s Veracruz and Tabasco)
____	*C. c. yucatanicus*	SE Mexico (Yucatán Peninsula)
____	*C. c. flammigerus*	SE Mexico (s Quintana Roo), Belize and Petén of n Guatemala
____	*C. c. saturatus*	Cozumel I. (off Quintana Roo)

□ **Pyrrhuloxia** *Cardinalis sinuatus*

____	*C. s. fulvescens*	Arid s Arizona and nw Mexico (Sonora to n Nayarit)
____	*C. s. sinuatus*	Arid s New Mexico to se Texas and ne Mexico
____	*C. s. peninsulae*	Baja California (south of latitude 27°N)

□ **Yellow Grosbeak** *Pheucticus chrysopeplus*

____	*P. c. dilutus*	Highlands of nw Mexico (s Sonora, sw Chihuahua and n Sinaloa)
____	*P. c. chrysopeplus (rarissimus)*	Highlands of w Mexico (Sinaloa to Guerrero and sw Puebla)
____	*P. c. aurantiacus*	Highlands of s Mexico (Chiapas) to central Guatemala

□ **Golden-bellied Grosbeak** *Pheucticus chrysogaster*

____	*P. c. laubmanni*	Mountains of n Colombia to coastal cordillera of n Venezuela
____	*P. c. chrysogaster*	Andes of sw Colombia (Nariño) to Ecuador and s Peru

□ **Black-thighed Grosbeak** *Pheucticus tibialis*

Humid montane forests of Costa Rica and w Panama

□ **Black-backed Grosbeak** *Pheucticus aureoventris*

____	*P. a. uropygialis*	E and Central Andes of Colombia
____	*P. a. crissalis*	Andes of sw Colombia (Nariño) and Ecuador
____	*P. a. meridensis*	Andes of w Venezuela (Mérida)
____	*P. a. terminalis*	Andes of e Peru (Amazonas and Cuzco)
____	*P. a. aureoventris*	S Peru (Puno) to e Bolivia, n Paraguay, w Brazil and nw Argentina

□ **Rose-breasted Grosbeak** *Pheucticus ludovicianus*

E Canada and US; winters from Mexico to Peru and w Cuba

□ **Black-headed Grosbeak** *Pheucticus melanocephalus*

____	*P. m. maculatus*	Mountains of sw British Columbia to n Baja California
____	*P. m. melanocephalus*	SE Br. Col. to Rocky Mts., Great Plains and s Mexican Plateau

□ **Ultramarine Grosbeak** *Cyanocompsa brissonii*

____	*C. b. caucae*	W Colombia (valleys of upper Río Patía, upper Cauca and Dagua)
____	*C. b. minor*	Mountains of n Venezuela (Falcón to Lara, Sucre and Monagas)
____	*C. b. brissonii*	NE Brazil (Piauí and Ceará to Bahia)
____	*C. b. sterea*	E Paraguay to e and s Brazil and ne Argentina
____	*C. b. argentina*	E Bolivia to *chaco* of Paraguay, w Brazil and n Argentina

☐ **Blue Bunting** *Cyanocompsa parellina*

_____	*C. p. indigotica*	Pacific slope of Mexico (Sinaloa to Isthmus of Tehuántepec)
_____	*C. p. beneplacita (lucida)*	NE Mexico (s Tamaulipas, e San Luis Potosí and s Nuevo León)
_____	*C. p. parellina*	E Mexico (Veracruz and e Puebla) to Nicaragua

☐ **Blue-black Grosbeak** *Cyanocompsa cyanoides*

_____	*C. c. concreta*	Lowlands of se Mexico (Veracruz) to Guatemala and Honduras
_____	*C. c. toddi*	Nicaragua to Costa Rica and w Panama
_____	*C. c. cyanoides*	Cent. and e Panama to Colombia, nw Venezuela and w Ecuador
_____	*C. c. rothschildii*	E Colombia to Venezuela, the Guianas, Amaz. Brazil and Bolivia

☐ **Glaucous-blue Grosbeak** *Cyanoloxia glaucocaerulea*

E Paraguay to s Brazil, Uruguay and ne Argentina

☐ **Blue Grosbeak** *Guiraca caerulea*

_____	*G. c. salicaria*	N-cent. Calif. and w Nevada to nw Baja; winters to Guerrero
_____	*G. c. interfusa*	SW US to ne Baja and nw Mexico; winters to Honduras
_____	*G. c. deltarhyncha*	Coastal w Mexico (s Sinaloa and Durango to Oaxaca)
_____	*G. c. caerulea*	SE US; winters to Panama and Cuba
_____	*G. c. eurhyncha*	E Mexico (Coahuila to Nuevo León, s Tamaulipas and Oaxaca)
_____	*G. c. chiapensis*	S Mexico (Chiapas and adjacent Oaxaca) to Guatemala
_____	*G. c. lazula*	Honduras to Nicaragua and Costa Rica

☐ **Lazuli Bunting** *Passerina amoena*

S British Columbia to nw Baja and w Texas; winters in Mexico

☐ **Indigo Bunting** *Passerina cyanea*

Canada and US; winters to Gr. Antilles, Colombia and Venezuela

☐ **Varied Bunting** *Passerina versicolor*

_____	*P. v. dickeyae*	S Ariz. to w Mexico (Sonora to w Durango, Jalisco and Colima)
_____	*P. v. versicolor*	S Texas to s Mexico (Oaxaca and Guerrero)
_____	*P. v. pulchra*	S Baja California
_____	*P. v. purpurascens*	S Mexico (Chiapas) to central Guatemala

☐ **Painted Bunting** *Passerina ciris*

_____	*P. c. pallidior*	SW US and n Mexico; winters to w Panama
_____	*P. c. ciris*	Coastal se US; winters to Bahamas, Cuba, Jamaica and Yucatán

☐ **Rose-bellied Bunting** *Passerina rositae*

Pacific slope of sw Mexico (Oaxaca and extreme sw Chiapas)

☐ **Orange-breasted Bunting** *Passerina leclancherii*

_____	*P. l. grandior*	SW Mexico (Jalisco to Michoacán, Guerrero, s Puebla and Chiapas)
_____	*P. l. leclancherii*	Coastal s Mexico (central Guerrero)

☐ **Yellow-billed Blue Finch** *Porphyrospiza caerulescens*

Cerrado of interior of ne and c Brazil

☐ **Dickcissel** *Spiza americana*

Breeds e North America; winters s Mexico to n South America

FAMILY: ICTERIDAE (Troupials and Allies—97)

☐ **Bobolink** *Dolichonyx oryzivorus*

Grasslands and meadows of N America; winters s South America

☐ **Saffron-cowled Blackbird** *Agelaius flavus*

Paraguay to se Brazil, Uruguay and ne Argentina

☐ **Yellow-winged Blackbird** *Agelaius thilius*

_____	*A. t. alticola*	Andes of se Peru (Cuzco) to nw Bolivia
_____	*A. t. thilius*	Andes of Chile (Atacama to Valdivia) and sw Argentina
_____	*A. t. petersii*	Paraguay to extreme se Brazil, Uruguay and n Argentina

☐ **Pale-eyed Blackbird** *Agelaius xanthophthalmus*

Locally in marshes of e Ecuador and e Peru

☐ **Unicolored Blackbird** *Agelaius cyanopus*

_____ *A. c. xenicus* — NE Brazil (Amapá to Pará and nw Maranhão)
_____ *A. c. atroolivaceus* — Coastal se Brazil (Rio de Janeiro)
_____ *A. c. beniensis* — N Bolivia (Beni)
_____ *A. c. cyanopus* — E Bolivia (Santa Cruz) to Paraguay and n Argentina

☐ **Red-winged Blackbird** *Agelaius phoeniceus*

_____ *A. p. arctolegus* — SE Alaska and Yukon to n-central US; winters to s-central US
_____ *A. p. fortis* — Montana to se New Mexico (east of Rocky Mts.); winters to Texas
_____ *A. p. nevadensis* — SE Br. Col. to Idaho, se Calif. and s Nevada; winters to s Arizona
_____ *A. p. caurinus* — Coastal sw Br. Col. to nw California; winters to central California
_____ *A. p. mailliardorum* — Coastal central California
_____ *A. p. californicus* — Central Valley of California
_____ *A. p. aciculatus* — Mountains of s-central California (e-central Kern County)
_____ *A. p. neutralis* — Coastal s California (San Luis Obispo County) to nw Baja
_____ *A. p. sonoriensis* — SE California to ne Baja, s Nevada, cent. Arizona and nw Mexico
_____ *A. p. nyaritensis* — Coastal plains of sw Mexico (Nayarit)
_____ *A. p. gubernator* — Mexican Plateau (Durango to Zacatecas, México and Tlaxcala)
_____ *A. p. pallidulus* — SE Mexico (n Yucatán Peninsula)
_____ *A. p. nelsoni* — S-c Mexico (Morelos and adj. Guerrero to w Puebla and Chiapas)
_____ *A. p. arthuralleni* — N Guatemala
_____ *A. p. grinnelli* — Pacific slope of w Guatemala to nw Costa Rica (Guanacaste)
_____ *A. p. phoeniceus* — SE Canada to Texas and se US
_____ *A. p. littoralis* — Gulf Coast of se Texas to nw Florida
_____ *A. p. mearnsi* — Extreme se Georgia and n Florida
_____ *A. p. floridanus* — S Florida (Everglades to Key West)
_____ *A. p. megapotamus* — C Texas and lower Rio Grande Valley to e Mexico (n Veracruz)
_____ *A. p. richmondi* — Caribbean slope of Mexico (s Veracruz) to Belize and n Guatemala
_____ *A. p. matudae* — Tropical se Mexico
_____ *A. p. brevirostris* — Caribbean slope of Honduras and se Nicaragua
_____ *A. p. bryanti* — NW Bahamas

☐ **Red-shouldered Blackbird** *Agelaius assimilis*

_____ *A. a. assimilis* — W Cuba
_____ *A. a. subniger* — Isle of Pines

☐ **Tricolored Blackbird** *Agelaius tricolor*

Marshes and farmlands of sw Oregon to nw Baja California

☐ **Yellow-hooded Blackbird** *Agelaius icterocephalus*

_____ *A. i. bogotensis* — E Colombia (Bogotá Plateau)
_____ *A. i. icterocephalus* — N Colombia to Venezuela, the Guianas, n Brazil and ne Peru

☐ **Tawny-shouldered Blackbird** *Agelaius humeralis*

_____ *A. h. scopulus* — Cuba, Cayo Cantiles and Jardines de la Reina
_____ *A. h. humeralis* — W Hispaniola (w-central Haiti)

☐ **Yellow-shouldered Blackbird** *Agelaius xanthomus*

_____ *A. x. monensis* — Mona I. (off w Puerto Rico)
_____ *A. x. xanthomus* — Lowlands of sw and ne Puerto Rico

☐ **Chestnut-capped Blackbird** *Agelaius ruficapillus*

_____ *A. r. frontalis* — French Guiana and e Brazil
_____ *A. r. ruficapillus* — SE Bolivia to Paraguay, s Brazil, Uruguay and n Argentina

☐ **Jamaican Blackbird** *Nesopsar nigerrimus*

Humid forests of Jamaica

☐ **Red-breasted Blackbird** *Sturnella militaris*

SW Costa Rica to n Bolivia, Guianas and Amaz. Brazil; Trinidad

☐ **White-browed Blackbird** *Sturnella superciliaris*

Extreme se Peru to Paraguay, Uruguay, n Argentina and Brazil

☐ **Peruvian Meadowlark** *Sturnella bellicosa*
_____ *S. b. bellicosa* — Pacific slope of Ecuador to n Peru
_____ *S. b. albipes* — Arid littoral of sw Peru (Ica) to extreme n Chile
_____ *S. b. catamarcanus* — NW Argentina (Jujuy and Catamarca)

☐ **Pampas Meadowlark** *Sturnella defillippi*

Pampas of e Argentina (rarely Uruguay and se Brazil)

☐ **Long-tailed Meadowlark** *Sturnella loyca*
_____ *S. l. loyca* — S Chile and s Argentina to Tierra del Fuego
_____ *S. l. falklandicus* — Falkland Islands

☐ **Eastern Meadowlark** *Sturnella magna*
_____ *S. m. magna* — S Ontario east to Quebec and south to n Texas and ne Georgia
_____ *S. m. argutula* — SE Kansas and Oklahoma to e US (Carolinas to Florida)
_____ *S. m. hoopesi* — S Texas (Eagle Pass) to n Coahuila, Nuevo León and n Tamaulipas
_____ *S. m. lilianae* — N Ariz. to e New Mexico, sw Texas, s Sonora and nw Chihuahua
_____ *S. m. auropectoralis* — Mexico (Durango and Sinaloa to Michoacán, México and n Puebla)
_____ *S. m. saundersi* — S Mexico (Oaxaca)
_____ *S. m. alticola* — Highlands of s Mexico (Guerrero, s Puebla, Veracruz) to Costa Rica
_____ *S. m. mexicana* — Caribbean slope of se Mexico (Veracruz and Tabasco to Chiapas)
_____ *S. m. griscomi* — SE Mexico (arid coastal n Yucatán Peninsula)
_____ *S. m. hippocrepis* — Cuba and Isle of Pines
_____ *S. m. inexpectata* — Pine savanna of Belize, Petén of Guatemala, Honduras, Nicaragua
_____ *S. m. subulata* — Pacific slope of Panama
_____ *S. m. meridionalis* — E Andes of Colombia to Andes of nw Venezuela
_____ *S. m. paralios* — N Colombia and savannas of w Venezuela
_____ *S. m. monticola* — *Tepuis* of s Venezuela (Mt. Roraima)
_____ *S. m. praticola* — *Llanos* of e Colombia to s Venezuela and n Guyana
_____ *S. m. quinta* — Suriname and ne Amazonian Brazil

☐ **Western Meadowlark** *Sturnella neglecta*
_____ *S. n. confluenta* — SW and central British Columbia to w Idaho and s California
_____ *S. n. neglecta* — SE British Columbia to n Baja, Texas and Gulf States

☐ **Yellow-headed Blackbird** *Xanthocephalus xanthocephalus*

S Canada to n Baja and s US; winters to central Mexico

☐ **Cuban Blackbird** *Dives atroviolacea*

Cuba and Isle of Pines

☐ **Melodious Blackbird** *Dives dives*

Gulf slope of e Mexico to Nicaragua and (rarely) nw Costa Rica

☐ **Scrub Blackbird** *Dives warszewiczi*
_____ *D. d. warszewiczi* — Coastal scrub of sw Ecuador and nw Peru (Tumbes and Piura)
_____ *D. d. kalinowskii* — Coastal scrub of w Peru (La Libertad to Ica)

☐ **Rusty Blackbird** *Euphagus carolinus*
_____ *E. c. carolinus* — N Alaska and n Yukon to ne US; winters to Gulf States
_____ *E. c. nigrans* — Newfoundland, Magdalen I., and Nova Scotia; winters to Georgia

☐ **Brewer's Blackbird** *Euphagus cyanocephalus*

W Canada and w US; winters to s Mexico

☐ **Boat-tailed Grackle** *Quiscalus major*
_____ *Q. m. torreyi* — E US (Atlantic coast from s New Jersey to extreme ne Florida)
_____ *Q. m. major* — E US (Gulf States from se Texas to Florida Keys)

☐ **Common Grackle** *Quiscalus quiscula*
_____ *Q. q. versicolor* — S and se Canada e of Rocky Mts. to c and ne US; winters to s US
_____ *Q. q. stonei* — E US (sw Conn. to Alabama and n Georgia); winters to Florida
_____ *Q. q. quiscula* — SE US (s Louisiana to e South Carolina and Florida Keys)

☐ **Great-tailed Grackle** *Quiscalus mexicanus*

____ *Q. m. nelsoni*	SE California to s Arizona and w Mexico (ne Baja and s Sonora)
____ *Q. m. monsoni*	SE Ariz. to w Texas and Mexican Plateau to Jalisco and Guanajuato
____ *Q. m. prosopidicola*	SE N Mex. to s Texas, Coahuila, San Luis Potosí and s Tamaulipas
____ *Q. m. graysoni*	Coastal nw Mexico (Sinaloa)
____ *Q. m. obscurus*	Coastal sw Mexico (Nayarit to Guerrero)
____ *Q. m. mexicanus*	S Mexico (e Jalisco and San Luis Potosí) to n Nicaragua
____ *Q. m. loweryi*	Coastal Yucatán Peninsula, Belize and adjacent offshore islands
____ *Q. m. peruvianus*	Pacific coast of Costa Rica to nw Peru and nw Venezuela

☐ **Nicaraguan Grackle** *Quiscalus nicaraguensis*

Lake Nicaragua, Lake Managua and n Costa Rica

☐ **Greater Antillean Grackle** *Quiscalus niger*

____ *Q. n. caribaeus*	W Cuba, Isle of Pines and cays east to Cayos de las Doce Leguas
____ *Q. n. gundlachii*	Central and e Cuba and inner cays of Jardines de la Reina
____ *Q. n. caymanensis*	Grand Cayman I.
____ *Q. n. bangsi*	Little Cayman I. and Cayman Brac
____ *Q. n. crassirostris*	Jamaica
____ *Q. n. niger*	Hispaniola, Gonâve, Tortue, Île-a-Vache and Beata islands
____ *Q. n. brachypterus*	Puerto Rico and Vieques I.

☐ **Carib Grackle** *Quiscalus lugubris*

____ *Q. l. guadeloupensis*	Montserrat, Guadeloupe, Marie Galante, Dominica and Martinique
____ *Q. l. inflexirostris*	St. Lucia (Lesser Antilles)
____ *Q. l. contrusus*	St. Vincent (Lesser Antilles)
____ *Q. l. luminosus*	Lesser Antilles (Grenada, the Grenadines and Islas Los Testigos)
____ *Q. l. fortirostris*	Barbados; introduced Barbuda and Antigua
____ *Q. l. orquillensis*	Islas Los Hermanos (off Venezuela)
____ *Q. l. insularis*	Isla Margarita and Islas Los Frailes (off Venezuela)
____ *Q. l. lugubris*	NE Colombia to n Venezuela, the Guianas and ne Brazil; Trinidad

☐ **Bay-winged Cowbird** *Molothrus badius*

____ *M. b. fringillarius*	Campos of ne Brazil (Piauí to Pernambuco, Bahia, Minas Gerais)
____ *M. b. badius*	E Bolivia (Beni and Tarija) to Paraguay, Uruguay and n Argentina
____ *M. b. bolivianus*	Highlands of central and s Bolivia

☐ **Screaming Cowbird** *Molothrus rufoaxillaris*

E Bolivia to Paraguay, s Brazil, Uruguay and n Argentina

☐ **Shiny Cowbird** *Molothrus bonariensis*

____ *M. b. minimus*	L Antilles (n to Martinique), Trinidad, Tobago, Guianas, n Brazil
____ *M. b. cabanisii*	E Panama (Darién) to Colombia
____ *M. b. venezuelensis*	Tropical e Colombia and n Venezuela
____ *M. b. aequatorialis*	Tropical sw Colombia to w Ecuador and Isla Puná
____ *M. b. occidentalis*	Extreme sw Ecuador (Loja) and w Peru (south to Lima)
____ *M. b. riparius*	Tropical e Peru (Río Ucayali) to lower Amazon Valley (Pará)
____ *M. b. bonariensis*	E Bolivia to Paraguay, Brazil, Uruguay and c Argentina

☐ **Bronzed Cowbird** *Molothrus aeneus*

____ *M. a. loyei*	SW US to nw Mexico (Sonora, Chihuahua, Durango and Nayarit)
____ *M. a. assimilis*	SW Mexico (Jalisco to Colima, Guerrero, Puebla, Oaxaca, Chiapas)
____ *M. a. aeneus*	S Texas to s Mexico, Yucatán Peninsula and central Panama
____ *M. a. armenti*	Caribbean coast of n Colombia

☐ **Brown-headed Cowbird** *Molothrus ater*

____ *M. a. artemisiae*	S coastal Alaska to sw US; winters to Baja and s Mexico
____ *M. a. obscurus*	SW US to Guerrero and n Tamaulipas; winters to s Baja and Oaxaca
____ *M. a. ater*	C and e-central US; winters to Gulf Coast, Florida and s Mexico
____ *M. a. californicus*	S California to n Baja and Los Coronados Islands (off nw Baja)

☐ **Giant Cowbird** *Scaphidura oryzivora*
_____ *S. o. impacifa* — Caribbean slope of s Mexico (s Veracruz) to w Panama
_____ *S. o. oryzivora* — E Panama to Bolivia, Paraguay, se Brazil and ne Argentina

☐ **Moriche Oriole** *Icterus chrysocephalus*

E Colombia to Venezuela, Guianas, n Brazil and ne Peru; Trinidad

☐ **Epaulet Oriole** *Icterus cayanensis*
_____ *I. c. cayanensis* — Suriname to French Guiana, Amaz. Brazil, e Peru and e Bolivia
_____ *I. c. tibialis* — E Brazil (Maranhão to Piauí, Pernambuco, Bahia, Rio de Janeiro)
_____ *I. c. valenciobuenoi* — SE Brazil (s Goiás to Minas Gerais, São Paulo and se Mato Grosso)
_____ *I. c. periporphyrus* — NE Bolivia and adjacent w Brazil (w-central Mato Grosso)
_____ *I. c. pyrrhopterus* — SE Bolivia to Paraguay, se Brazil, Uruguay and n Argentina

☐ **Yellow-backed Oriole** *Icterus chrysater*
_____ *I. c. chrysater* — S Mexico (s Veracruz) to Belize, Guatemala and n Nicaragua
_____ *I. c. mayensis* — SE Mexico (n Yucatán Peninsula)
_____ *I. c. hondae* — Panama (west to Veraguas) to n Colombia
_____ *I. c. giraudii* — Central Colombia to n Venezuela

☐ **Yellow Oriole** *Icterus nigrogularis*
_____ *I. n. nigrogularis* — Coastal n Colombia to Venezuela, the Guianas and n Brazil
_____ *I. n. curasoensis* — Netherlands Antilles (Aruba, Curaçao and Bonaire)
_____ *I. n. helioeides* — Isla Margarita (off n Venezuela)
_____ *I. n. trinitatis* — NE Venezuela (e Paria Peninsula); Trinidad and Monos I.

☐ **Jamaican Oriole** *Icterus leucopteryx*
_____ *I. l. bairdi†* — Grand Cayman I. (extinct ca 1967)
_____ *I. l. leucopteryx* — Jamaica
_____ *I. l. lawrencii* — Isla San Andrés (w Caribbean Sea)

☐ **Orange Oriole** *Icterus auratus*

SE Mexico (arid Yucatán Peninsula)

☐ **Yellow-tailed Oriole** *Icterus mesomelas*
_____ *I. m. mesomelas* — Trop. se Mexico (Veracruz and Oaxaca) to Belize and Honduras
_____ *I. m. salvinii* — Caribbean lowlands of Nicaragua to e Panama
_____ *I. m. carrikeri* — Tropical n and w Colombia to nw Venezuela
_____ *I. m. taczanowskii* — Tropical w Ecuador and nw Peru
_____ *I. m. xantholemus* — Ecuador (probable immature *taczanowskii* or unknown hybrid)

☐ **Orange-crowned Oriole** *Icterus auricapillus*

Lowlands of e Panama to n Colombia and n Venezuela

☐ **White-edged Oriole** *Icterus graceannae*

Arid scrub of w Ecuador and nw Peru (south to La Libertad)

☐ **Spot-breasted Oriole** *Icterus pectoralis*
_____ *I. p. pectoralis* — Pacific slope of s Mexico (Colima) to n Nicaragua
_____ *I. p. espinachi* — Pacific coast of s Nicaragua to nw Costa Rica

☐ **Altamira Oriole** *Icterus gularis*
_____ *I. g. tamaulipensis* — S Texas (lower Rio Grande Valley) to se Mexico (Campeche)
_____ *I. g. flavescens* — Coastal sw Mexico (Guerrero)
_____ *I. g. yucatanensis* — SE Mexico (Yucatán Peninsula), Cozumel I. and extreme n Belize
_____ *I. g. gularis* — Arid tropical s Mexico (Oaxaca) to Guatemala and El Salvador
_____ *I. g. troglodytes* — S Mexico (extreme s Chiapas) and Pacific slope of Guatemala
_____ *I. g. gigas* — Interior s Guatemala to Honduras and w-central Nicaragua

☐ **Streak-backed Oriole** *Icterus pustulatus*
_____ *I. p. microstictus* — Tropical w Mexico (n Sonora and Chihuahua)
_____ *I. p. yaegeri* — Coastal lowlands of w Mexico (s Sinaloa to s Nayarit)
_____ *I. p. graysonii* — Tres Marías Islands (off w Mexico)
_____ *I. p. dickermani* — W Mexico (lowlands of sw Jalisco and Colima to s Guerrero)

_____ *I. p. pustulatus*	Tropical sw Mexico (Colima to n Oaxaca, Puebla and Veracruz)
_____ *I. p. formosus*	Arid tropical s Mexico (Oaxaca and Chiapas) to nw Guatemala
_____ *I. p. alticola*	Arid tropical Guatemala and Atlantic slope of Honduras
_____ *I. p. sclateri*	Pacific slope of El Salvador to sw Costa Rica (Nicoya Peninsula)

☐ **Hooded Oriole** *Icterus cucullatus*

_____ *I. c. nelsoni*	Central California to ne Baja and nw Mexico (s Sonora)
_____ *I. c. sennetti*	S Texas (lower Rio Grande Valley) to e Mexico (Tamaulipas)
_____ *I. c. cucullatus*	SW Texas (Del Rio) to se Mexico (Veracruz and Oaxaca)
_____ *I. c. californicus*	N Baja California
_____ *I. c. trochiloides*	S Baja California (latitude 27°N to Cabo San Lucas)
_____ *I. c. restrictus*	NW Mexico (s Sonora)
_____ *I. c. igneus (cozumelae, duplexus, masoni)*	Yucatán Pen., Cozumel, Contoy, Holbox and Mujeres is. to Belize

☐ **Troupial** *Icterus icterus*

_____ *I. i. ridgwayi*	Coastal n Colombia to nw Venezuela; Aruba, Curaçao, Margarita I.
_____ *I. i. icterus*	*Llanos* of e Colombia to n Venezuela
_____ *I. i. metae*	W Venezuela (extreme sw Apure to Colombian border)
_____ *I. i. croconotus*	SW Guyana to n Brazil, e Ecuador and e Peru (Madre de Dios)
_____ *I. i. jamaicaii*	E Brazil
_____ *I. i. strictifrons*	E Bolivia to sw Brazil (Mato Grosso) and *chaco* of Paraguay

☐ **Baltimore Oriole** *Icterus galbula*

	E N America (s Canada to s US); winters to n South America

☐ **Bullock's Oriole** *Icterus bullockii*

_____ *I. b. bullockii*	SW Canada to sw US and n Mexico; winters to nw Costa Rica
_____ *I. b. parvus*	Extreme sw US to n Baja and nw Sonora; winters to Guerrero

☐ **Black-backed Oriole** *Icterus abeillei*

	Riparian woodlands of central plateau and eastern Mexico

☐ **Orchard Oriole** *Icterus spurius*

_____ *I. s. spurius*	SE Canada to ne Mexico; winters to Cuba and Colombia
_____ *I. s. phillipsi*	Central plateau of Mexico
_____ *I. s. fuertesi*	Caribbean coast of Mexico (s Tamaulipas to s Veracruz)

☐ **Black-cowled Oriole** *Icterus dominicensis*

_____ *I. d. prosthemelas*	Caribbean slope of se Mexico (Veracruz) to Nicaragua
_____ *I. d. praecox*	Caribbean slope of Costa Rica and adjacent w Panama
_____ *I. d. northropi*	Bahamas (Andros, Great Abaco and Little Abaco)
_____ *I. d. melanopsis*	Cuba and Isle of Pines
_____ *I. d. dominicensis*	Hispaniola, Gonâve I., Tortue I. and Île-a-Vache
_____ *I. d. portoricensis*	Puerto Rico

☐ **Black-vented Oriole** *Icterus wagleri*

_____ *I. w. castaneopectus*	Arid scrub of nw Mexico (s Sonora to n Sinaloa and Chihuahua)
_____ *I. w. wagleri*	Highlands of w Mexico (Sinaloa and Coahuila) to n Nicaragua

☐ **St. Lucia Oriole** *Icterus laudabilis*

	St. Lucia (Lesser Antilles)

☐ **Martinique Oriole** *Icterus bonana*

	Semiarid hills of Martinique (Lesser Antilles)

☐ **Montserrat Oriole** *Icterus oberi*

	Montane forests of Montserrat (Lesser Antilles)

☐ **Audubon's Oriole** *Icterus graduacauda*

_____ *I. g. audubonii*	S Texas (lower Rio Grande Valley) and e Mexico (Tamaulipas)
_____ *I. g. nayaritensis*	W-c Mexico (s Nayarit to w Jalisco, n Colima and s Michoacán)
_____ *I. g. dickeyae*	Mountains of sw Mexico (Sierra Madre del Sur of Guerrero)
_____ *I. g. graduacauda (richardsoni)*	Southern portion of Mexican Plateau

☐ **Bar-winged Oriole** *Icterus maculialatus*

Oak-pine scrub of s Mexico (se Oaxaca) to El Salvador

☐ **Scott's Oriole** *Icterus parisorum*

Arid sw US to s Mexico

☐ **Yellow-billed Cacique** *Amblycercus holosericeus*
_____ *A. h. holosericeus*
_____ *A. h. flavirostris*
_____ *A. h. australis*

SE Mexico (San Luis Potosí and s Tamaulipas) to n Colombia
W Colombia to w Ecuador and extreme nw Peru (Tumbes)
Colombia to nw Venezuela, e Peru and nw Bolivia

☐ **Yellow-rumped Cacique** *Cacicus cela*
_____ *C. c. vitellinus*
_____ *C. c. flavicrissus*
_____ *C. c. cela*

Tropical e Panama (Canal Zone) to n Colombia
Tropical w Ecuador to extreme nw Peru (Tumbes)
Colombia to Venezuela, the Guianas, Amaz. Brazil and e Bolivia

☐ **Red-rumped Cacique** *Cacicus haemorrhous*
_____ *C. h. haemorrhous*
_____ *C. h. affinis*

SE Colombia to e Ecuador, Peru, Bolivia and n Amazonian Brazil
Paraguay to e and s Brazil and ne Argentina

☐ **Scarlet-rumped Cacique** *Cacicus uropygialis*
_____ *C. u. microrhynchus*
_____ *C. u. pacificus*
_____ *C. u. uropygialis*

Extreme ne Honduras to e Panama (except Darién)
E Panama (Darién) to w Colombia and w Ecuador (El Oro)
Andes of Colombia to nw Venezuela, e Ecuador and se Peru

☐ **Selva Cacique** *Cacicus koepckeae*

SE Peru (known from 2 specimens ca 1965 from se Ucayali)

☐ **Golden-winged Cacique** *Cacicus chrysopterus*

E Bolivia to Paraguay, s Brazil, Uruguay and ne Argentina

☐ **Mountain Cacique** *Cacicus chrysonotus*
_____ *C. c. leucoramphus (peruvianus)*
_____ *C. c. peruvianus*
_____ *C. c. chrysonotus*

Andes of Colombia to sw Venezuela (Táchira) and e Ecuador
Andes of n Peru (south to Junín)
Andes of se Peru and nw Bolivia (La Paz and Cochabamba)

☐ **Ecuadorian Cacique** *Cacicus sclateri*

Tropical forests of e Ecuador and extreme n Peru

☐ **Solitary Cacique** *Cacicus solitarius*

Tropical n Venezuela to central Argentina and Amazonian Brazil

☐ **Yellow-winged Cacique** *Cacicus melanicterus*

Pacific lowlands of w Mexico (se Sonora) to se Guatemala

☐ **Casqued Oropendola** *Psarocolius oseryi*

Tropical e Ecuador, e Peru and extreme sw Brazil (Amazonas)

☐ **Crested Oropendola** *Psarocolius decumanus*
_____ *P. d. melanterus*
_____ *P. d. insularis*
_____ *P. d. decumanus*
_____ *P. d. maculosus*

Tropical Panama and n Colombia
Trinidad and Tobago
E Colombia to Venezuela, Guianas, n Brazil, Ecuador and n Peru
E Peru to Bolivia, Paraguay and n Argentina

☐ **Green Oropendola** *Psarocolius viridis*

Guianas and s Venezuela to ne Peru and Amazonian Brazil

☐ **Dusky-green Oropendola** *Psarocolius atrovirens*

Andes of se Peru and nw Bolivia

☐ **Russet-backed Oropendola** *Psarocolius angustifrons*
_____ *P. a. salmoni*
_____ *P. a. atrocastaneus*
_____ *P. a. sincipitalis*
_____ *P. a. neglectus*
_____ *P. a. oleagineus*
_____ *P. a. angustifrons*
_____ *P. a. alfredi*

W and Central Andes of Colombia
Subtropical w Ecuador
W slope of E Andes of Colombia and upper Magdalena Valley
E slope of Eastern Andes of Colombia and nw Venezuela
Coastal cordillera of n Venezuela and interior mountains (Aragua)
Trop. se Colombia to ne Peru and adjacent w Amazonian Brazil
SE Ecuador to e Peru and nw Bolivia (w Santa Cruz)

☐ **Chestnut-headed Oropendola** *Psarocolius wagleri*
    ____ *P. w. wagleri*
    ____ *P. w. ridgwayi*

Caribbean slope of se Mexico (s Veracruz) to ne Nicaragua
SE Honduras to Panama, w Colombia and nw Ecuador

☐ **Black Oropendola** *Psarocolius guatimozinus*

Humid lowlands of e Panama and n Colombia

☐ **Band-tailed Oropendola** *Ocyalus latirostris*

Tropical se Colombia to ne Peru and extreme w Brazil

☐ **Montezuma Oropendola** *Gymnostinops montezuma*

Gulf-Caribbean lowlands of se Mexico to central Panama

☐ **Baudo Oropendola** *Gymnostinops cassini*

N Colombia (known from 3 specimens ca 1900 from nw Chocó)

☐ **Amazonian Oropendola** *Gymnostinops bifasciatus*
    ____ *G. b. yuracares*
    ____ *G. b. bifasciatus*
    ____ *G. b. neivae*

Trop. se Colombia to s Venezuela, e Bolivia and w Amaz. Brazil
N Brazil s of Amazon (Rio Tocantins to Belém and n Mato Grosso)
N Brazil south of the Amazon (Rio Tapajós to Rio Xingú)

☐ **Oriole Blackbird** *Gymnomystax mexicanus*

E Colombia to Venezuela, the Guianas, Amaz. Brazil and ne Peru

☐ **Yellow-rumped Marshbird** *Pseudoleistes guirahuro*

E Paraguay to s Brazil, Uruguay and n Argentina

☐ **Brown-and-yellow Marshbird** *Pseudoleistes virescens*

Wet pastures of extreme s Brazil, Uruguay and n Argentina

☐ **Scarlet-headed Blackbird** *Amblyramphus holosericeus*

Marshes of n Bolivia, Paraguay, s Brazil and n Argentina

☐ **Red-bellied Grackle** *Hypopyrrhus pyrohypogaster*

Andes of Colombia

☐ **Austral Blackbird** *Curaeus curaeus*
    ____ *C. c. curaeus*
    ____ *C. c. recurvirostris*
    ____ *C. c. reynoldsi*

S Argentina and s Chile to Straits of Magellan
S Chile (Magellanes)
Tierra del Fuego, Navarino and Hoste islands

☐ **Forbes' Blackbird** *Curaeus forbesi*

Known from three localities in extreme e Brazil

☐ **Chopi Blackbird** *Gnorimopsar chopi*
    ____ *G. c. sulcirostris*
    ____ *G. c. chopi*

E Bolivia to ne Brazil and nw Argentina (n Salta)
SE Bolivia to Paraguay, se Brazil, Uruguay and n Argentina

☐ **Bolivian Blackbird** *Oreopsar bolivianus*

Andes of sw Bolivia (Cochabamba, Chuquisaca and Potosí)

☐ **Velvet-fronted Grackle** *Lampropsar tanagrinus*
    ____ *L. t. tanagrinus*
    ____ *L. t. guianensis*
    ____ *L. t. boliviensis*
    ____ *L. t. violaceus*
    ____ *L. t. macropterus*

SE Colombia to e Ecuador, n Peru and w Amazonian Brazil
Tropical n Venezuela to nw Guyana and n Brazil (Roraima)
N Bolivia (along upper Río Beni)
W Brazil (nw Mato Grosso)
W Brazil (upper Rio Juruá)

☐ **Golden-tufted Grackle** *Macroagelaius imthurni*

Tepuis of s Venezuela to w Guyana and n Brazil (Roraima)

☐ **Mountain Grackle** *Macroagelaius subalaris*

Locally in Eastern Andes of ne Colombia

These 85 species have appeared in previous editions of *Birds of the World: A Checklist* and are considered to have become extinct since 1600.

By CITES criteria species not recorded for 50 years or more are considered to be extinct.

Atitlan Grebe *Podilymbus gigas*	Formerly Lake Atitlán (Guatemala). Extinct ca 1980
Colombian Grebe *Podiceps andinus*	Formerly Andes of Colombia. Extinct ca 1980
Alaotra Grebe *Tachybaptus rufolavatus*	Formerly Lake Alaotra (Madagascar)
Guadalupe Storm-Petrel *Oceanodroma macrodactyla*	Formerly Guadalupe I. (off w Mexico). Last recorded 1912
Pallas' Cormorant *Phalacrocorax perspicillatus*	Formerly islands in Bering Sea. Extinct ca 1852
Amchitka Cormorant *Phalacrocorax kenyoni*	Known from skeletal remains from Amchitka I. (Alaska)
Crested Shelduck *Tadorna cristata*	Known from 3 specimens from Siberia and Korea. Extinct ca 1916
Amsterdam Island Wigeon *Anas marecula*	Formerly Amsterdam I. Extinct ca 1780
Pink-headed Duck *Rhodonessa caryophyllacea*	Formerly India and Myanmar. Extinct ca 1935
Labrador Duck *Camptorhynchus labradorius*	Formerly Labrador to ne US. Extinct ca 1878
Auckland Islands Merganser *Mergus australis*	Formerly Auckland Islands (off New Zealand). Extinct ca 1905
Guadalupe Caracara *Polyborus lutosus*	Formerly Guadalupe I. off Baja California. Extinct ca 1900
New Zealand Quail *Coturnix novaezelandiae*	Formerly New Zealand. Extinct ca 1870
Himalayan Quail *Ophrysia superciliosa*	Formerly w-central Himalayas. Extinct ca 1876
Wake Island Rail *Gallirallus wakensis*	Formerly Wake I. (ne Micronesia). Extinct ca 1944
Tahiti Rail *Gallirallus pacificus*	Formerly Tahiti and adj. e Society Islands. Extinct ca 1800
Dieffenbach's Rail *Gallirallus dieffenbachii*	Formerly Chatham Islands off New Zealand. Extinct ca 1900
Chatham Islands Rail *Gallirallus modestus*	Formerly Chatham Islands off New Zealand. Extinct ca 1900
Sharpe's Rail *Gallirallus sharpei*	Known from an 1895 specimen, possibly from Indonesia
Laysan Rail *Porzana palmeri*	Formerly Laysan I. (w Hawaiian Islands). Extinct ca 1944
Hawaiian Rail *Porzana sandwichensis*	Formerly island of Hawaii. Extinct ca 1844
Kosrae Crake *Porzana monasa*	Formerly Kosrae I. (e Caroline Islands). Extinct ca 1828
Lord Howe Swamphen *Porphyrio albus*	Formerly Lord Howe I. (off New Zealand). Extinct ca 1834
Samoan Moorhen *Gallinula pacifica*	Formerly Savai'i I. (Western Samoa). Extinct ca 1908
Canarian Oystercatcher *Haematopus meadewaldoi*	Formerly e Canary Islands. Extinct ca 1913
White-winged Sandpiper *Prosobonia leucoptera*	Formerly Tahiti and Moorea. Extinct ca 1790
Great Auk *Pinguinus impennis*	Formerly Arctic North America. Extinct ca 1844
Dodo *Raphus cucullatus*	Formerly Mauritius I. (w Mascarene Islands). Extinct ca 1662
Reunion Solitaire *Raphus solitarius*	Formerly Réunion I. (w Mascarene Islands). Extinct ca 1715
Rodrigues Solitaire *Pezophaps solitaria*	Formerly Rodrigues I. (e Mascarene Islands). Extinct ca 1760
Bonin Pigeon *Columba versicolor*	Formerly Bonin Islands Extinct ca 1889
Ryukyu Pigeon *Columba jouyi*	Formerly Okinawa, Ryukyu and Daito islands. Extinct ca 1936
Passenger Pigeon *Ectopistes migratorius*	Formerly Canada and US. Extinct ca 1914.
Choiseul Pigeon *Microgoura meeki*	Formerly Choiseul I. (nw Solomon Islands). Extinct ca 1904
Tanna Ground-Dove *Gallicolumba ferruginea*	Formerly Tanna I. (s Vanuatu). Known from a 1774 specimen
Mauritius Blue-Pigeon *Alectroenas nitidissima*	Formerly Mauritius (w Mascarene Is.). Extinct ca 1826
New Caledonian Lorikeet *Charmosyna diadema*	Formerly New Caledonia. Extinct ca 1860
Norfolk Island Kaka *Nestor productus*	Formerly Norfolk I. and Phillip I. Extinct ca 1851
Carolina Parakeet *Conuropsis carolinensis*	Formerly e US. Extinct ca 1918
Black-fronted Parakeet *Cyanoramphus zealandicus*	Formerly Tahiti (e Society Islands). Extinct ca 1844
Raiatea Parakeet *Cyanoramphus ulietanus*	Formerly Raiatea I. (e Society Islands). Extinct ca 1773
Paradise Parrot *Psephotus pulcherrimus*	Formerly e Australia. Presumed extinct ca 1927
Seychelles Parakeet *Psittacula wardi*	Formerly Seychelles Islands (Mahé and Silhouette). Extinct
Newton's Parakeet *Psittacula exsul*	Formerly Rodrigues I. (e Mascarene Islands). Extinct ca 1875
Mascarene Parrot *Mascarinus mascarinus*	Formerly Réunion I. (w Mascarene Islands). Extinct ca 1834
Glaucous Macaw *Anodorhynchus glaucus*	Formerly se Brazil and adjacent Uruguay. Extinct ca 1915
Cuban Macaw *Ara cubensis*	Formerly Cuba and Isle of Pines. Extinct ca 1864
Hispaniolan Macaw *Ara tricolor*	Formerly Hispaniola. Extinct ca 1820
Snail-eating Coua *Coua delalandei*	Formerly Île Sainte-Marie (off Madagascar). Extinct ca 1834
Laughing Owl *Sceloglaux albifacies*	Formerly New Zealand. Extinct ca 1914
Jamaican Poorwill *Siphonorhis americanus*	Formerly Jamaica. Extinct ca 1859
Brace's Emerald *Chlorostilbon bracei*	Known from an 1877 specimen from n Bahamas
Bogota Sunangel *Heliangelus zusii*	Known from a 1909 specimen from Bogotá, Colombia
Stephens Island Wren *Xenicus lyalli*	Formerly Stephens I. (New Zealand). Extinct ca 1894
Banggai Crow *Corvus unicolor*	Formerly Banggai I. Extinct ca 1900
Kittlitz's Thrush *Zoothera terrestris*	Formerly Peel I. (Bonin Group off China). Extinct ca 1860
Amaui *Myadestes woahensis*	Formerly Oahu (Hawaiian Islands). Extinct ca 1825

Grand Cayman Thrush *Turdus ravidus* — Formerly Grand Cayman I. (West Indies). Extinct ca 1938

Chatham Islands Fernbird *Megalurus rufescens* — Formerly Chatham Islands. Extinct ca 1900

Piopio *Turnagra capensis* — Formerly New Zealand. Extinct ca 1908

Damar Flycatcher *Ficedula henrici* — Formerly Damar I. (e Lesser Sundas). Extinct ca 1899

Black-browed Babbler *Malacocincla perspicillata* — Known from an 1850 specimen from s Borneo

Vanderbilt's Babbler *Malacocincla vanderbilti* — Known from a 1940 specimen from n Sumatra

Lord Howe Gerygone *Gerygone insularis* — Formerly Lord Howe I. off New Zealand. Extinct ca 1879

Robust White-eye *Zosterops strenuus* — Formerly Lord Howe I. (off New Zealand). Extinct ca 1920

Oahu Oo *Moho apicalis* — Formerly Oahu (Hawaiian Islands). Extinct ca 1837

Hawaii Oo *Moho nobilis* — Formerly Hawaii. Extinct ca 1898

Kioea *Chaetoptila angustipluma* — Formerly Hawaii. Extinct ca 1859

Huia *Heteralocha acutirostris* — Formerly North I. (New Zealand). Extinct ca 1907

Kosrae Starling *Aplonis corvina* — Formerly Kosrae I. (e Caroline Islands). Extinct ca 1828

Mysterious Starling *Aplonis mavornata* — Formerly Raiatea I. (Society Islands). Extinct ca 1700

Norfolk Starling *Aplonis fusca* — Formerly Lord Howe and Norfolk islands. Extinct ca 1928

Rodrigues Starling *Necropsar rodericanus* — Formerly Met I. s of Rodrigues (Indian Ocean). Extinct ca 1750

Reunion Starling *Fregilupus varius* — Formerly Réunion I. (Mascarene Islands). Extinct ca 1850

Bonin Grosbeak *Chaunoproctus ferreorostris* — Formerly Peel I. (Bonin Islands). Extinct ca 1832

Lanai Hookbill *Dysmorodrepanis munroi* — Known from a 1913 specimen from Lanai (Hawaiian Islands)

Lesser Koa-Finch *Rhodacanthis flaviceps* — Formerly *koa* habitat of Hawaii. Extinct ca 1891

Greater Koa-Finch *Rhodacanthis palmeri* — Formerly *koa* habitat of Hawaii. Extinct ca 1896

Kona Grosbeak *Chloridops kona* — Formerly *koa* habitat of Hawaii. Extinct ca 1896

Greater Amakihi *Hemignathus sagittirostris* — Formerly montane forests of Hawaii. Extinct ca 1910

Lesser Akialoa *Hemignathus obscurus* — Formerly Hawaii. Extinct ca 1967

Ula-ai-hawane *Ciridops anna* — Formerly montane forests of Hawaii. Extinct ca 1890

Hawaii Mamo *Drepanis pacifica* — Formerly montane forests of Hawaii. Extinct ca 1898

Black Mamo *Drepanis funerea* — Formerly montane forests of Molokai. Extinct ca 1907

Slender-billed Grackle *Quiscalus palustris* — Formerly headwaters of Río Lerma (central Mexico)

Complete references to publisher and subtitles are listed in the bibliography

Struthionidae	del Hoyo, J., A. Elliot and J. Sargatal, eds. 1992. *Handbook of Birds of the World*. Vol. 1
Rheidae	del Hoyo, J., A. Elliot and J. Sargatal, eds. 1992. *Handbook of Birds of the World*. Vol. 1
Casuariidae	del Hoyo, J., A. Elliot and J. Sargatal, eds. 1992. *Handbook of Birds of the World*. Vol. 1
Dromaiidae	del Hoyo, J., A. Elliot and J. Sargatal, eds. 1992. *Handbook of Birds of the World*. Vol. 1
Apterygidae	del Hoyo, J., A. Elliot and J. Sargatal, eds. 1992. *Handbook of Birds of the World*. Vol. 1
Tinamidae	del Hoyo, J., A. Elliot and J. Sargatal, eds. 1992. *Handbook of Birds of the World*. Vol. 1
Spheniscidae	del Hoyo, J., A. Elliot and J. Sargatal, eds. 1992. *Handbook of Birds of the World*. Vol. 1
Gaviidae	del Hoyo, J., A. Elliot and J. Sargatal, eds. 1992. *Handbook of Birds of the World*. Vol. 1
Podicipedidae	del Hoyo, J., A. Elliot and J. Sargatal, eds. 1992. *Handbook of Birds of the World*. Vol. 1
Diomedeidae	del Hoyo, J., A. Elliot and J. Sargatal, eds. 1992. *Handbook of Birds of the World*. Vol. 1
Procellariidae	del Hoyo, J., A. Elliot and J. Sargatal, eds. 1992. *Handbook of Birds of the World*. Vol. 1
Hydrobatidae	del Hoyo, J., A. Elliot and J. Sargatal, eds. 1992. *Handbook of Birds of the World*. Vol. 1
Pelecanoididae	del Hoyo, J., A. Elliot and J. Sargatal, eds. 1992. *Handbook of Birds of the World*. Vol. 1
Phaethontidae	del Hoyo, J., A. Elliot and J. Sargatal, eds. 1992. *Handbook of Birds of the World*. Vol. 1
Pelecanidae	del Hoyo, J., A. Elliot and J. Sargatal, eds. 1992. *Handbook of Birds of the World*. Vol. 1
Sulidae	del Hoyo, J., A. Elliot and J. Sargatal, eds. 1992. *Handbook of Birds of the World*. Vol. 1
Phalacrocoracidae	del Hoyo, J., A. Elliot and J. Sargatal, eds. 1992. *Handbook of Birds of the World*. Vol. 1
Anhingidae	del Hoyo, J., A. Elliot and J. Sargatal, eds. 1992. *Handbook of Birds of the World*. Vol. 1
Fregatidae	del Hoyo, J., A. Elliot and J. Sargatal, eds. 1992. *Handbook of Birds of the World*. Vol. 1
Ardeidae	del Hoyo, J., A. Elliot and J. Sargatal, eds. 1992. *Handbook of Birds of the World*. Vol. 1
Scopidae	del Hoyo, J., A. Elliot and J. Sargatal, eds. 1992. *Handbook of Birds of the World*. Vol. 1
Ciconiidae	del Hoyo, J., A. Elliot and J. Sargatal, eds. 1992. *Handbook of Birds of the World*. Vol. 1
Balaenicipitidae	del Hoyo, J., A. Elliot and J. Sargatal, eds. 1992. *Handbook of Birds of the World*. Vol. 1
Threskiornithidae	del Hoyo, J., A. Elliot and J. Sargatal, eds. 1992. *Handbook of Birds of the World*. Vol. 1
Phoenicopteridae	del Hoyo, J., A. Elliot and J. Sargatal, eds. 1992. *Handbook of Birds of the World*. Vol. 1
Anhimidae	del Hoyo, J., A. Elliot and J. Sargatal, eds. 1992. *Handbook of Birds of the World*. Vol. 1
Anatidae	del Hoyo, J., A. Elliot and J. Sargatal, eds. 1992. *Handbook of Birds of the World*. Vol. 1
	Todd, Frank. 1996. *Natural History of the Waterfowl*
Cathartidae	del Hoyo, J., A. Elliot and J. Sargatal, eds. 1992. *Handbook of Birds of the World*. Vol. 2
Pandionidae	del Hoyo, J., A. Elliot and J. Sargatal, eds. 1994. *Handbook of Birds of the World*. Vol. 2
Accipitridae	del Hoyo, J., A. Elliot and J. Sargatal, eds. 1994. *Handbook of Birds of the World*. Vol. 2
Sagittariidae	del Hoyo, J., A. Elliot and J. Sargatal, eds. 1994. *Handbook of Birds of the World*. Vol. 2
Falconidae	del Hoyo, J., A. Elliot and J. Sargatal, eds. 1994. *Handbook of Birds of the World*. Vol. 2
Megapodiidae	Jones, Darryl N., René Dekker and Cees Roselaar. 1995. *The Megapodes*
	del Hoyo, J., A. Elliot and J. Sargatal, eds. 1994. *Handbook of Birds of the World*. Vol. 2
Cracidae	del Hoyo, J., A. Elliot and J. Sargatal, eds. 1994. *Handbook of Birds of the World*. Vol. 2
Meleagridae	del Hoyo, J., A. Elliot and J. Sargatal, eds. 1994. *Handbook of Birds of the World*. Vol. 2
	Delacour, Jean and Dean Amadon. 1973. *Curassows and Related Birds*
Tetraonidae	del Hoyo, J., A. Elliot and J. Sargatal, eds. 1994. *Handbook of Birds of the World*. Vol. 2
Odontophoridae	del Hoyo, J., A. Elliot and J. Sargatal, eds. 1994. *Handbook of Birds of the World*. Vol. 2
Phasianidae	del Hoyo, J., A. Elliot and J. Sargatal, eds. 1994. *Handbook of Birds of the World*. Vol. 2
	Delacour, Jean. 1977. *The Pheasants of the World*
Numididae	del Hoyo, J., A. Elliot and J. Sargatal, eds. 1994. *Handbook of Birds of the World*. Vol. 2
Opisthocomidae	del Hoyo, J., A. Elliot and J. Sargatal, eds. 1996. *Handbook of Birds of the World*. Vol. 3
Mesitornithidae	del Hoyo, J., A. Elliot and J. Sargatal, eds. 1996. *Handbook of Birds of the World*. Vol. 3
Turnicidae	del Hoyo, J., A. Elliot and J. Sargatal, eds. 1996. *Handbook of Birds of the World*. Vol. 3
Gruidae	del Hoyo, J., A. Elliot and J. Sargatal, eds. 1996. *Handbook of Birds of the World*. Vol. 3
Aramidae	del Hoyo, J., A. Elliot and J. Sargatal, eds. 1996. *Handbook of Birds of the World*. Vol. 3
Psophiidae	del Hoyo, J., A. Elliot and J. Sargatal, eds. 1996. *Handbook of Birds of the World*. Vol. 3
Rallidae	del Hoyo, J., A. Elliot and J. Sargatal, eds. 1996. *Handbook of Birds of the World*. Vol. 3
	Taylor, Barry. 1998. *A Guide to the Rails, Crakes, Gallinules and Coots of the World*
Heliornithidae	del Hoyo, J., A. Elliot and J. Sargatal, eds. 1996. *Handbook of Birds of the World*. Vol. 3
Rhynochetidae	del Hoyo, J., A. Elliot and J. Sargatal, eds. 1996. *Handbook of Birds of the World*. Vol. 3
Eurypygidae	del Hoyo, J., A. Elliot and J. Sargatal, eds. 1996. *Handbook of Birds of the World*. Vol. 3
Cariamidae	del Hoyo, J., A. Elliot and J. Sargatal, eds. 1996. *Handbook of Birds of the World*. Vol. 3
Otididae	del Hoyo, J., A. Elliot and J. Sargatal, eds. 1996. *Handbook of Birds of the World*. Vol. 3
Jacanidae	del Hoyo, J., A. Elliot and J. Sargatal, eds. 1996. *Handbook of Birds of the World*. Vol. 3
Rostratulidae	del Hoyo, J., A. Elliot and J. Sargatal, eds. 1996. *Handbook of Birds of the World*. Vol. 3
Dromadidae	del Hoyo, J., A. Elliot and J. Sargatal, eds. 1996. *Handbook of Birds of the World*. Vol. 3
Haematopodidae	del Hoyo, J., A. Elliot and J. Sargatal, eds. 1996. *Handbook of Birds of the World*. Vol. 3

Ibidorhynchidae	del Hoyo, J., A. Elliot and J. Sargatal, eds. 1996. *Handbook of Birds of the World*. Vol. 3
Recurvirostridae	del Hoyo, J., A. Elliot and J. Sargatal, eds. 1996. *Handbook of Birds of the World*. Vol. 3
Burhinidae	del Hoyo, J., A. Elliot and J. Sargatal, eds. 1996. *Handbook of Birds of the World*. Vol. 3
Glareolidae	del Hoyo, J., A. Elliot and J. Sargatal, eds. 1996. *Handbook of Birds of the World*. Vol. 3
Charadriidae	del Hoyo, J., A. Elliot and J. Sargatal, eds. 1996. *Handbook of Birds of the World*. Vol. 3
Pluvianellidae	del Hoyo, J., A. Elliot and J. Sargatal, eds. 1996. *Handbook of Birds of the World*. Vol. 3
Scolopacidae	del Hoyo, J., A. Elliot and J. Sargatal, eds. 1996. *Handbook of Birds of the World*. Vol. 3
Pedionomidae	del Hoyo, J., A. Elliot and J. Sargatal, eds. 1996. *Handbook of Birds of the World*. Vol. 3
Thinocoridae	del Hoyo, J., A. Elliot and J. Sargatal, eds. 1996. *Handbook of Birds of the World*. Vol. 3
Chionidae	del Hoyo, J., A. Elliot and J. Sargatal, eds. 1996. *Handbook of Birds of the World*. Vol. 3
Stercoraiidae	del Hoyo, J., A. Elliot and J. Sargatal, eds. 1996. *Handbook of Birds of the World*. Vol. 3
Laridae	del Hoyo, J., A. Elliot and J. Sargatal, eds. 1996. *Handbook of Birds of the World*. Vol. 3
Sternidae	del Hoyo, J., A. Elliot and J. Sargatal, eds. 1996. *Handbook of Birds of the World*. Vol. 3
Rynchopidae	del Hoyo, J., A. Elliot and J. Sargatal, eds. 1996. *Handbook of Birds of the World*. Vol. 3
Alcidae	del Hoyo, J., A. Elliot and J. Sargatal, eds. 1996. *Handbook of Birds of the World*. Vol. 3
Pteroclidae	del Hoyo, J., A. Elliot and J. Sargatal, eds. 1997. *Handbook of Birds of the World*. Vol. 4
Columbidae	del Hoyo, J., A. Elliot and J. Sargatal, eds. 1997. *Handbook of Birds of the World*. Vol. 4
Cacatuidae	del Hoyo, J., A. Elliot and J. Sargatal, eds. 1997. *Handbook of Birds of the World*. Vol. 4
Psittacidae	del Hoyo, J., A. Elliot and J. Sargatal, eds. 1997. *Handbook of Birds of the World*. Vol. 4
Musophagidae	del Hoyo, J., A. Elliot and J. Sargatal, eds. 1997. *Handbook of Birds of the World*. Vol. 4
Cuculidae	del Hoyo, J., A. Elliot and J. Sargatal, eds. 1997. *Handbook of Birds of the World*. Vol. 4
Tytonidae	del Hoyo, J., A. Elliot and J. Sargatal, eds. 1999. *Handbook of Birds of the World*. Vol. 5
Strigidae	del Hoyo, J., A. Elliot and J. Sargatal, eds. 1999. *Handbook of Birds of the World*. Vol. 5
	Rasmussen, Pamela. 1999. A New Species of Hawk-Owl *Ninox* from North Sulawesi, Indonesia. Wilson Bulletin 111 (4): 457-464
Steatornithidae	del Hoyo, J., A. Elliot and J. Sargatal, eds. 1999. *Handbook of Birds of the World*. Vol. 5
Aegothelidae	Cleere, Nigel. 1998. *Nightjars: A Guide to the Nightjars, Nighthawks, and Their Relatives*
	del Hoyo, J., A. Elliot and J. Sargatal, eds. 1999. *Handbook of Birds of the World*. Vol. 5
Podargidae	Cleere, Nigel. 1998. *Nightjars: A Guide to the Nightjars, Nighthawks, and Their Relatives*
	del Hoyo, J., A. Elliot and J. Sargatal, eds. 1999. *Handbook of Birds of the World*. Vol. 5
Nyctibiidae	Cleere, Nigel. 1998. *Nightjars: A Guide to the Nightjars, Nighthawks, and Their Relatives*
	del Hoyo, J., A. Elliot and J. Sargatal, eds. 1999. *Handbook of Birds of the World*. Vol. 5
Caprimulgidae	Cleere, Nigel. 1998. *Nightjars: A Guide to the Nightjars, Nighthawks, and Their Relatives*
	del Hoyo, J., A. Elliot and J. Sargatal, eds. 1999. *Handbook of Birds of the World*. Vol. 5
Apodidae	Chantler, Phil and Gerald Driessens. 1995. *Swifts: A Guide to the Swifts and Treeswifts of the World*
	del Hoyo, J., A. Elliot and J. Sargatal, eds. 1999. *Handbook of Birds of the World*. Vol. 5
Hemiprocnidae	del Hoyo, J., A. Elliot and J. Sargatal, eds. 1999. *Handbook of Birds of the World*. Vol. 5
Trochilidae	del Hoyo, J., A. Elliot and J. Sargatal, eds. 1999. *Handbook of Birds of the World*. Vol. 5
Coliidae	Fry, C. Hillary, Stuart Keith and Emil Urban, eds. 1988. *The Birds of Africa*. Volume III
Trogonidae	Peters, James Lee. 1945. *Check-list of Birds of the World*. Volume V
Alcedinidae	Fry, C.H., K. Fry and A Harris. 1992. *Kingfishers, Bee-eaters and Rollers*
	Peters, James Lee. 1945. *Check-list of Birds of the World*. Volume V
Todidae	Peters, James Lee. 1945. *Check-list of Birds of the World*. Volume V
Momotidae	Peters, James Lee. 1945. *Check-list of Birds of the World*. Volume V
Meropidae	Fry, C.H., K. Fry and A Harris. 1992. *Kingfishers, Bee-eaters and Rollers*
	Peters, James Lee. 1945. *Check-list of Birds of the World*. Volume V
Coraciidae	Fry, C.H., K. Fry and A Harris. 1992. *Kingfishers, Bee-eaters and Rollers*
	Peters, James Lee. 1945. *Check-list of Birds of the World*. Volume V
Brachypteraciidae	Fry, C.H., K. Fry and A Harris. 1992. *Kingfishers, Bee-eaters and Rollers*
	Peters, James Lee. 1945. *Check-list of Birds of the World*. Volume V
Leptosomidae	Fry, C.H., K. Fry and A Harris. 1992. *Kingfishers, Bee-eaters and Rollers*
	Peters, James Lee. 1945. *Check-list of Birds of the World*. Volume V
Upupidae	Peters, James Lee. 1945. *Check-list of Birds of the World*. Volume V
Phoeniculidae	Peters, James Lee. 1945. *Check-list of Birds of the World*. Volume V
Bucerotidae	Kemp, Alan. 1995. *The Hornbills*. New York: Oxford University Press
Galbulidae	Peters, James Lee. 1948. *Check-list of Birds of the World*. Volume VI
Bucconidae	Peters, James Lee. 1948. *Check-list of Birds of the World*. Volume VI
Capitonidae	Peters, James Lee. 1948. *Check-list of Birds of the World*. Volume VI
Ramphastidae	Peters, James Lee. 1948. *Check-list of Birds of the World*. Volume VI
Indicatoridae	Peters, James Lee. 1948. *Check-list of Birds of the World*. Volume VI

Picidae	Short, Lester. 1982. *Woodpeckers of the World*
	Winkler, Hans, D. A. Christie and D. Nurney. 1995. *Woodpeckers: An Identification Guide to Woodpeckers of the World*
Eurylaimidae	Lambert, Frank and Martin Woodcock. 1996. *Pittas, Broadbills and Asities*
Philepittidea	Lambert, Frank and Martin Woodcock. 1996. *Pittas, Broadbills and Asities*
Furnariidae	Peters, James Lee. 1957. *Check-list of Birds of the World*. Volume VII
	Vaurie, Charles. 1980. *Taxonomy and Geographical Distribution of the Furnariidae.*
Dendrocolaptidae	Peters, James Lee. 1957. *Check-list of Birds of the World*. Volume VII
	Ridgely, Robert and Guy Tudor. 1994. *The Birds of South America*: Vol. II. The suboscine passerines
Thamnophilidae	Peters, James Lee. 1957. *Check-list of Birds of the World*. Volume VII
	Ridgely, Robert and Guy Tudor. 1994. *The Birds of South America*: Vol. II. The suboscine passerines
Formicariidae	Peters, James Lee. 1957. *Check-list of Birds of the World*. Volume VII
	Ridgely, Robert and Guy Tudor. 1994. *The Birds of South America*: Vol. II. The suboscine passerines
Conopophagidae	Peters, James Lee. 1957. *Check-list of Birds of the World*. Volume VII
	Ridgely, Robert and Guy Tudor. 1994. *The Birds of South America*: Vol. II. The suboscine passerines
Rhinocryptidae	Peters, James Lee. 1957. *Check-list of Birds of the World*. Volume VII
	Ridgely, Robert and Guy Tudor. 1994. *The Birds of South America*: Vol. II. The suboscine passerines
Phytotomidae	Peters, James Lee. 1957. *Check-list of Birds of the World*. Volume VII
	Ridgely, Robert and Guy Tudor. 1994. *The Birds of South America*: Vol. II. The suboscine passerines
Cotingidae	Melvin A. Traylor, Jr., ed. 1979. *Check-list of Birds of the World*. Volume VIII. A Continuation of the Work of James L. Peters
	Ridgely, Robert and Guy Tudor. 1994. *The Birds of South America*: Vol. II. The suboscine passerines.
	Snow, David. 1982. *The Cotingas*
Pipridae	Melvin A. Traylor, Jr., ed. 1979. *Check-list of Birds of the World*. Volume VIII. A Continuation of the Work of James L. Peters
	Ridgely, Robert and Guy Tudor. 1994. *The Birds of South America*: Vol. II. The suboscine passerines
Tyrannidae	Melvin A. Traylor, Jr., ed. 1979. *Check-list of Birds of the World*. Volume VIII. A Continuation of the Work of James L. Peters
	Ridgely, Robert and Guy Tudor. 1994. *The Birds of South America*: Vol. II. The suboscine passerines
Oxyruncidae	Melvin A. Traylor, Jr., ed. 1979. *Check-list of Birds of the World*. Volume VIII. A Continuation of the Work of James L. Peters
Pittidae	Lambert, Frank and Martin Woodcock. 1996. *Pittas, Broadbills and Asities*
Atrichornithidae	Melvin A. Traylor, Jr., ed. 1979. *Check-list of Birds of the World*. Volume VIII. A Continuation of the Work of James L. Peters
Menuridae	Melvin A. Traylor, Jr., ed. 1979. *Check-list of Birds of the World*. Volume VIII. A Continuation of the Work of James L. Peters
Acanthisittidae	Melvin A. Traylor, Jr., ed. 1979. *Check-list of Birds of the World*. Volume VIII. A Continuation of the Work of James L. Peters
Alaudidae	Mayr, Ernst and James C. Greenway, Jr., eds. 1960. *Check-list of Birds of the World*. Volume IX. A Continuation of the Work of James L. Peters
Hirundinidae	Turner, Angela and Chris Rose. 1989. *Swallows and Martins*: *An Identification Guide and Handbook*
Motacillidae	Mayr, Ernst and James C. Greenway, Jr., eds. 1960. *Check-list of Birds of the World*. Volume IX. A Continuation of the Work of James L. Peters
Campephagidae	Mayr, Ernst and James C. Greenway, Jr., eds. 1960. *Check-list of Birds of the World*. Volume IX. A Continuation of the Work of James L. Peters
Pycnonotidae	Mayr, Ernst and James C. Greenway, Jr., eds. 1960. *Check-list of Birds of the World*. Volume IX. A Continuation of the Work of James L. Peters
Regulidae	Mayr, Ernst and G. William Cottrell, eds. 1986. *Check-list of Birds of the World*. Volume XI. A Continuation of the Work of James L. Peters. .
Chloropseidae	Mayr, Ernst and James C. Greenway, Jr., eds. 1960. *Check-list of Birds of the World*. Volume IX. A Continuation of the Work of James L. Peters
Aegithinidae	Mayr, Ernst and James C. Greenway, Jr., eds. 1960. *Check-list of Birds of the World*. Volume IX. A Continuation of the Work of James L. Peters
Ptilogonatidae	Mayr, Ernst and James C. Greenway, Jr., eds. 1960. *Check-list of Birds of the World*. Volume IX. A Continuation of the Work of James L. Peters
Bombycillidae	Mayr, Ernst and James C. Greenway, Jr., eds. 1960. *Check-list of Birds of the World*. Volume IX. A Continuation of the Work of James L. Peters
Hypocoliidae	Mayr, Ernst and James C. Greenway, Jr., eds. 1960. *Check-list of Birds of the World*. Volume IX. A Continuation of the Work of James L. Peters
Dulidae	Mayr, Ernst and James C. Greenway, Jr., eds. 1960. *Check-list of Birds of the World*. Volume IX. A Continuation of the Work of James L. Peters

717

Cinclidae	Mayr, Ernst and James C. Greenway, Jr., eds. 1960. *Check-list of Birds of the World.* Volume IX. A Continuation of the Work of James L. Peters
Troglodytidae	Mayr, Ernst and James C. Greenway, Jr., eds. 1960. *Check-list of Birds of the World.* Volume IX. A Continuation of the Work of James L. Peters
Mimidae	Mayr, Ernst and James C. Greenway, Jr., eds. 1960. *Check-list of Birds of the World.* Volume IX. A Continuation of the Work of James L. Peters
Prunellidae	Mayr, Ernst and Raymond A. Paynter, Jr., eds. 1964. *Check-list of Birds of the World.* Volume X. A Continuation of the Work of James L. Peters
Turdidae	Mayr, Ernst and Raymond A. Paynter, Jr., eds. 1964. *Check-list of Birds of the World.* Volume X. A Continuation of the Work of James L. Peters
Cisticolidae	Mayr, Ernst and G. William Cottrell, eds. 1986. *Check-list of Birds of the World.* Volume XI. A Continuation of the Work of James L. Peters
Sylviidae	Mayr, Ernst and G. William Cottrell, eds. 1986. *Check-list of Birds of the World.* Volume XI. A Continuation of the Work of James L. Peters
Polioptilidae	Mayr, Ernst and Raymond A. Paynter, Jr., eds. 1964. *Check-list of Birds of the World.* Volume X. A Continuation of the Work of James L. Peters
Muscicapidae	Mayr, Ernst and G. William Cottrell, eds. 1986. *Check-list of Birds of the World.* Volume XI. A Continuation of the Work of James L. Peters
Platysteiridae	Mayr, Ernst and G. William Cottrell, eds. 1986. *Check-list of Birds of the World.* Volume XI. A Continuation of the Work of James L. Peters
Rhipiduridae	Mayr, Ernst and G. William Cottrell, eds. 1986. *Check-list of Birds of the World.* Volume XI. A Continuation of the Work of James L. Peters
Monarchidae	Mayr, Ernst and G. William Cottrell, eds. 1986. *Check-list of Birds of the World.* Volume XI. A Continuation of the Work of James L. Peters
Petroicidae	Peters, James Lee. 1948. *Check-list of Birds of the World.* Volume VI
Pachycephalidae	Paynter, Raymond A., Jr., ed., in consultation with Ernst Mayr. 1967. *Check-list of Birds of the World.* Volume XII. A Continuation of the Work of James L. Peters
Picathartidae	Mayr, Ernst and Raymond A. Paynter, Jr., eds. 1964. *Check-list of Birds of the World.* Volume X. A Continuation of the Work of James L. Peters
Timaliidae	Mayr, Ernst and Raymond A. Paynter, Jr., eds. 1964. *Check-list of Birds of the World.* Volume X. A Continuation of the Work of James L. Peters
Pomatostomidae	Mayr, Ernst and Raymond A. Paynter, Jr., eds. 1964. *Check-list of Birds of the World.* Volume X. A Continuation of the Work of James L. Peters
Paradoxornithidae	Mayr, Ernst and Raymond A. Paynter, Jr., eds. 1964. *Check-list of Birds of the World.* Volume X. A Continuation of the Work of James L. Peters
Orthonychidae	Mayr, Ernst and Raymond A. Paynter, Jr., eds. 1964. *Check-list of Birds of the World.* Volume X. A Continuation of the Work of James L. Peters
Cinclosomatidae	Mayr, Ernst and Raymond A. Paynter, Jr., eds. 1964. *Check-list of Birds of the World.* Volume X. A Continuation of the Work of James L. Peters
Aegithalidae	Paynter, Raymond A., Jr., ed., in consultation with Ernst Mayr. 1967. *Check-list of Birds of the World.* Volume XII. A Continuation of the Work of James L. Peters
Maluridae	Rowley, Ian and Eleanor Russell. 1997. *Fairy-Wrens and Grasswrens*
	Schodde, Richard. 1982. *The Fairy Wrens*
Acanthizidae	Mayr, Ernst and G. William Cottrell, eds. 1986. *Check-list of Birds of the World.* Volume XI. A Continuation of the Work of James L. Peters
Epthianuridae	Mayr, Ernst and G. William Cottrell, eds. 1986. *Check-list of Birds of the World.* Volume XI. A Continuation of the Work of James L. Peters
Neosittidae	Paynter, Raymond A., Jr., ed., in consultation with Ernst Mayr. 1967. *Check-list of Birds of the World.* Volume XII. A Continuation of the Work of James L. Peters
Climacteridae	Paynter, Raymond A., Jr., ed., in consultation with Ernst Mayr. 1967. *Check-list of Birds of the World.* Volume XII. A Continuation of the Work of James L. Peters
Paridae	Harrap, Simon and David Quinn. 1995. *Chickadees, Tits, Nuthatches and Treecreepers*
Sittidae	Harrap, Simon and David Quinn. 1995. *Chickadees, Tits, Nuthatches and Treecreepers*
Tichidromidae	Harrap, Simon and David Quinn. 1995. *Chickadees, Tits, Nuthatches and Treecreepers*
Certhiidae	Harrap, Simon and David Quinn. 1995. *Chickadees, Tits, Nuthatches and Treecreepers*
Rhabdornithidae	Paynter, Raymond A., Jr., ed., in consultation with Ernst Mayr. 1967. *Check-list of Birds of the World.* Volume XII. A Continuation of the Work of James L. Peters
Remizidae	Paynter, Raymond A., Jr., ed., in consultation with Ernst Mayr. 1967. *Check-list of Birds of the World.* Volume XII. A Continuation of the Work of James L. Peters

Nectarinidae	Chekek, R. A. and Mann, C. F. 2000. *Sunbirds: A Guide to the Sunbirds, Spiderhunters, Sugarbirds and Flowerpeckers of the World*. Sussex, UK: Pica Press
Melanocharitidae	Paynter, Raymond A., Jr., ed., in consultation with Ernst Mayr. 1967. *Check-list of Birds of the World.* Volume XII. A Continuation of the Work of James L. Peters
Paramythiidae	Paynter, Raymond A., Jr., ed., in consultation with Ernst Mayr. 1967. *Check-list of Birds of the World.* Volume XII. A Continuation of the Work of James L. Peters
Dicaeidae	Chekek, R. A. and Mann, C. F. 2000. *Sunbirds: A Guide to the Sunbirds, Spiderhunters, Sugarbirds and Flowerpeckers of the World*
Pardalotidae	Paynter, Raymond A., Jr., ed., in consultation with Ernst Mayr. 1967. *Check-list of Birds of the World.* Volume XII. A Continuation of the Work of James L. Peters
Zosteropidae	Paynter, Raymond A., Jr., ed., in consultation with Ernst Mayr. 1967. *Check-list of Birds of the World.* Volume XII. A Continuation of the Work of James L. Peters
Promeropidae	Chekek, R. A. and Mann, C. F. 2000. *Sunbirds: A Guide to the Sunbirds, Spiderhunters, Sugarbirds and Flowerpeckers of the World*. Sussex, UK: Pica Press
Meliphagidae	Paynter, Raymond A., Jr., ed., in consultation with Ernst Mayr. 1967. *Check-list of Birds of the World.* Volume XII. A Continuation of the Work of James L. Peters
Oriolidae	Mayr, Ernst and James C. Greenway, Jr., eds. 1962. *Check-list of Birds of the World.* Volume XV. A Continuation of the Work of James L. Peters
Irenidae	Mayr, Ernst and James C. Greenway, Jr., eds. 1960. *Check-list of Birds of the World.* Volume IX. A Continuation of the Work of James L. Peters
Laniidae	Lefranc, Norbert. 1997. *Shrikes: A Guide to the Shrikes of the World*
Malaconotidae	Mayr, Ernst and James C. Greenway, Jr., eds. 1960. *Check-list of Birds of the World.* Volume IX. A Continuation of the Work of James L. Peters
Prionopidea	Mayr, Ernst and James C. Greenway, Jr., eds. 1960. *Check-list of Birds of the World.* Volume IX. A Continuation of the Work of James L. Peters
Vangidae	Mayr, Ernst and James C. Greenway, Jr., eds. 1960. *Check-list of Birds of the World.* Volume IX. A Continuation of the Work of James L. Peters
Dicruridae	Mayr, Ernst and James C. Greenway, Jr., eds. 1962. *Check-list of Birds of the World.* Volume XV. A Continuation of the Work of James L. Peters
Callaeidae	Mayr, Ernst and James C. Greenway, Jr., eds. 1962. *Check-list of Birds of the World.* Volume XV. A Continuation of the Work of James L. Peters
Grallinidae	Mayr, Ernst and James C. Greenway, Jr., eds. 1962. *Check-list of Birds of the World.* Volume XV. A Continuation of the Work of James L. Peters
Corcoracidae	Mayr, Ernst and James C. Greenway, Jr., eds. 1962. *Check-list of Birds of the World.* Volume XV. A Continuation of the Work of James L. Peters
Artamidae	Mayr, Ernst and James C. Greenway, Jr., eds. 1962. *Check-list of Birds of the World.* Volume XV. A Continuation of the Work of James L. Peters
Pityriaseidae	Mayr, Ernst and James C. Greenway, Jr., eds. 1960. *Check-list of Birds of the World.* Volume IX. A Continuation of the Work of James L. Peters
Cracticidae	Mayr, Ernst and James C. Greenway, Jr., eds. 1962. *Check-list of Birds of the World.* Volume XV. A Continuation of the Work of James L. Peters
Paradisaeidae	Frith, Clifford and Bruce Beehler. 1998. *The Birds of Paradise*
Ptilonorhynchidae	Mayr, Ernst and James C. Greenway, Jr., eds. 1962. *Check-list of Birds of the World.* Volume XV. A Continuation of the Work of James L. Peters
Corvidae	Goodwin, Derek. 1976. *The Crows of the World*
	Mayr, Ernst and James C. Greenway, Jr., eds. 1962. *Check-list of Birds of the World.* Volume XV. A Continuation of the Work of James L. Peters
Sturnidae	Feare, Chris and Adrian Craig. 1999. *Starlings and Mynas*
Passeridae	Mayr, Ernst and James C. Greenway, Jr., eds. 1962. *Check-list of Birds of the World.* Volume XV. A Continuation of the Work of James L. Peters
Ploceidae	Paynter, Raymond A, Jr., ed., in consultation with Ernst Mayr. 1968. *Check-list of Birds of the World.* Volume XIV. A Continuation of the Work of James L. Peters
Estrildidae	Goodwin, Derek. 1982. *Estrildid Finches of the World*
	Restall, Robin. 1997. *Munias and Mannikins*
	Baptista, Luis F., Robin Lawson, Eleanor Visser and Douglas Bell. 1999. Relationships of some mannikins and waxbills in the estrildidae. *Journal of Ornithology* 140 (179-192)
Viduidae	Paynter, Raymond A, Jr., ed., in consultation with Ernst Mayr. 1968. *Check-list of Birds of the World.* Volume XIV. A Continuation of the Work of James L. Peters
Vireonidae	Paynter, Raymond A, Jr., ed., in consultation with Ernst Mayr. 1968. *Check-list of Birds of the World.* Volume XIV. A Continuation of the Work of James L. Peters

Fringillidae	Clement, Paul, Alan Harris and John Davis. 1993. *Finches and Sparrows.*
	Paynter, Raymond A, Jr., ed., in consultation with Ernst Mayr. 1968. *Check-list of Birds of the World.* Volume XIV. A Continuation of the Work of James L. Peters
Drepanididae	Paynter, Raymond A, Jr., ed., in consultation with Ernst Mayr. 1968. *Check-list of Birds of the World.* Volume XIV. A Continuation of the Work of James L. Peters
Peucedramidae	Paynter, Raymond A, Jr., ed., in consultation with Ernst Mayr. 1968. *Check-list of Birds of the World.* Volume XIV. A Continuation of the Work of James L. Peters
Parulidae	Paynter, Raymond A, Jr., ed., in consultation with Ernst Mayr. 1968. *Check-list of Birds of the World.* Volume XIV. A Continuation of the Work of James L. Peters
Coerebidae	Paynter, Raymond A, Jr., ed., in consultation with Ernst Mayr. 1968. *Check-list of Birds of the World.* Volume XIV. A Continuation of the Work of James L. Peters
Thraupidae	Paynter, Raymond A, Jr., ed., in consultation with Ernst Mayr. 1970. *Check-list of Birds of the World.* Volume XIII. A Continuation of the Work of James L. Peters
Emberizidae	Byers, Clive, Jon Curson and Urban Olsson. 1995. *Sparrows and Buntings*
	Paynter, Raymond A, Jr., ed., in consultation with Ernst Mayr. 1970. *Check-list of Birds of the World.* Volume XIII. A Continuation of the Work of James L. Peters
Cardinalidae	Paynter, Raymond A, Jr., ed., in consultation with Ernst Mayr. 1970. *Check-list of Birds of the World.* Volume XIII. A Continuation of the Work of James L. Peters
Icteridae	Paynter, Raymond A, Jr., ed., in consultation with Ernst Mayr. 1968. *Check-list of Birds of the World.* Volume XIV. A Continuation of the Work of James L. Peters

Ali, Salim. 1962. *The Birds of Sikkim*. London: Oxford University Press

—1969. *Birds of Kerala*. London: Oxford University Press

—1972. *Indian Hill Birds*. Bombay Natural History Society

—1977. *Birds of the Eastern Himalayas*. London: Oxford University Press

Ali, Salim and S. D. Ripley. 1968-1974. *Handbook of the Birds of India and Pakistan* (ten volumes). Bombay: Oxford University Press

—1983. *A Pictorial Guide to the Birds of the Indian Subcontinent*. Delhi: Oxford University Press

—1983. *Handbook of the Birds of India and Pakistan*. Delhi: Oxford University Press

American Ornithologists Union. 1957. *Check-list of North American Birds*. Fifth Edition

—1983. *Check-list of North American Birds*. Sixth Edition

—1998. *Check-list of North American Birds*. Seventh Edition

Baker, R. 1951. *Avifauna of Micronesia*. Lawrence: University of Kansas Press

Bannerman, D. A. 1971. *The Birds of West and Equatorial Africa*. Edinburgh: Oliver and Boyd

Baptista, Luis F., Robin Lawson, Eleanor Visser and Douglas Bell. 1999. Relationships of some mannikins and waxbills in the estrildidae. *Journal of Ornithology* 140 (179-192)

Beehler, Bruce, Thane Pratt and Dale Zimmerman. 1986. *Birds of New Guinea*. Princeton University Press

Benson, S. V. 1970. *Birds of Lebanon and the Jordan Area*. Cambridge: International Council for Bird Preservation

Berger, Andrew. 1981. *Hawaiian Birdlife*. Honolulu: University of Honolulu Press

Binford, L. C. 1989. *A Distributional Survey of the Birds of the Mexican State of Oaxaca*. Ornithological Monographs No. 43. Washington: American Ornithologists' Union

Blake, E. R. 1977. *Manual of Neotropical Birds* (Volume I). Chicago: University of Chicago Press

Bond, James. 1974. *Birds of the West Indies*. London: Collins

Brown, Leslie, E. K. Urban and K. Newman. 1982. *The Birds of Africa* (Volume 1). New York: Academic Press

Brudnell-Bruce, P. G. C. 1975. *Birds of the Bahamas*. New York: Taplinger

Bruner, Phillip. 1972. *Birds of French Polynesia*. Honolulu: Pacific Scientific Information Center

Burton, John. 1973. *Owls of the World*. New York: Dutton

Byers, Clive, Jon Curson and Urban Olsson. 1995. *Sparrows and Buntings*. Boston: Houghton Mifflin

Chantler, Phil and Gerald Driessens. 1995. *Swifts: A Guide to the Swifts and Treeswifts of the World*. South Africa: Russel Friedman Books

Chekek, R. A. and Mann, C. F. 2000. *Sunbirds: A Guide to the Sunbirds, Spiderhunters, Sugarbirds and Flowerpeckers of the World*. Sussex, UK: Pica Press

Christidis, Leslie and Walter E. Boles. 1994. *The Taxonomy and Species of Birds of Australia and its Territories*. Royal Australian Ornithologists Union Monograph 2

Clancy, P.A. 1985. *The Rare Birds of Southern Africa*. Johannesburg: Winchester Press

Cleere, Nigel. 1998. *Nightjars: A Guide to the Nightjars, Nighthawks, and Their Relatives*. Sussex: Pica Press

Clement, Paul, Alan Harris and John Davis. 1993. *Finches and Sparrows*. Princeton University Press

Clements, James F. 1991. *Birds of the World: A Checklist*. Fourth Edition. Vista, CA: Ibis Publishing Company

—1998. Supplement to Birds of the World 1992-1998. *Winging It,* Volume 11, No. 8

Clements, James F. and William Principe, Jr. 1992. *English-Name Index and Supplement to Birds of the World: A Check List*. Vista, CA.: Ibis Publishing Company

Coates, Brian J. and K. David Bishop. 1997. *A Guide to the Birds of Wallacea*. Alderley, Queensland, Australia: Dove Publications

Collar, Nigel and S. N. Stuart. 1985. *Threatened Birds of Africa and Related Islands*. Cambridge: ICBP

Collar, N. J., L. P. Gonzaga, N. Krabbe, A. M. Nieto, L. G. Naranjo, T. A. Parker III and D. C. Wege. 1992. *Threatened Birds of the Americas*. Cambridge: International Council for Bird Preservation

Cramp, Stanley, et al. *Birds of Europe, the Middle East and North Africa*. 1977. Volume 1. London: Oxford Univ. Press

—1980. *Birds of Europe, the Middle East and North Africa*. Volume II. London: Oxford University Press

—1983. *Birds of Europe, the Middle East and North Africa*. Volume III. London: Oxford University Press

—1985. *Birds of Europe, the Middle East and North Africa*. Volume IV. London: Oxford University Press

—1988. *Birds of Europe, the Middle East and North Africa*. Volume V. London: Oxford University Press

—1992. *Birds of Europe, the Middle East and North Africa*. Volume VI. London: Oxford University Press

—1993. *Birds of Europe, the Middle East and North Africa*. Volume VII. London: Oxford University Press

—1994. *Birds of Europe, the Middle East and North Africa*. Volume VIII. London: Oxford University Press

—1994. *Birds of Europe, the Middle East and North Africa*. Volume IX. London: Oxford University Press

Croxall, J. P., P. Evans and R. W. Schreiber. 1982. *Status and Conservation of the World's Seabirds*. Cambridge: International Council for Bird Preservation

Dee, T. J. 1986. *The Endemic Birds of Madagascar*. Cambridge: International Council for Bird Preservation

del Hoyo, Josep, A. Elliot and J. Sargatal, eds. 1992. *Handbook of the Birds of the World*. Volume 1. Ostrich to Ducks.
Barcelona: Lynx Editions
—1994. *Handbook of the Birds of the World*. Volume 2. New World Vultures to Guineafowl. Barcelona: Lynx Editions
—1996. *Handbook of the Birds of the World*. Volume 3. Hoatzin to Auks. Barcelona: Lynx Editions
—1997. *Handbook of the Birds of the World*. Volume 4. Sandgrouse to Cuckoos. Barcelona: Lynx Editions
—1999. *Handbook of the Birds of the World*. Volume 5. Barn Owls to Hummingbirds. Barcelona: Lynx Editions
Delacour, Jean. 1977. *The Pheasants of the World*. Surrey, UK: Spur Publications
Delacour, Jean and Dean Amadon. 1973. *Curassows and Related Birds*. New York: American Museum of Natural History
Diamond, A. W. 1987. *Studies of Mascarene Island Birds*. Cambridge: Cambridge University Press
Diamond, Jared M. 1966. *Avifauna of the Eastern Highlands of New Guinea*. Cambridge: Nuttall Club Publication #12
Dickenson, E. C., Robert S. Kennnedy and Kenneth C. Parkes. 1991. *The Birds of the Philippines*.
British Ornithologists' Union Checklist No. 12
Dowsett, R. J. and F. Dowsett-Lemaire. 1993. *A Contribution to the Distribution and Taxonomy of Afrotropical and
Malagasy Birds*. Liege, Belgium: Tauraco Press
Dowsett, R. J. and Alec Forbes-Watson. 1993. *Checklist of Birds of the Afrotropical and Malagasy Regions*.
Liege, Belgium: Tauraco Press
Etchécopar, R. and F. Hüe. 1967. *The Birds of North Africa*. Edinburgh: Oliver & Boyd
—1978. *Les Oiseaux de Chine (Non Passerines)*. Papeete: Centre National de la Recherche Scientifique
—1983. *Les Oiseaux de Chine (Passerines)*. Paris: Centre National de la Recherche Scientifique
Feare, Chris and Adrian Craig. 1999. *Starlings and Mynas*. Princeton University Press
Fjeldså, Jon and Niels Krabbe. 1990. *Birds of the High Andes*. Zoological Museum: University of Copenhagen
Forshaw, Joseph and W. T. Cooper. 1973. *Parrots of the World*. New York: Doubleday
—1983. *Kingfishers and Related Birds* (Volume I). Melbourne: Lansdowne
—1985. *Kingfishers and Related Birds* (Volume II). Melbourne: Lansdowne
Frith, Clifford and Bruce Beehler. 1998. *The Birds of Paradise*. Oxford: Oxford University Press
Fry, C. H. 1984. *The Bee-eaters*. Vermillion, SD: Buteo Books
Fry, C. H., K. Fry and A Harris. 1992. *Kingfishers, Bee-eaters and Rollers*. London: Christopher Helm
Fuller, E. 1987. *Extinct Birds*. New York: Facts on File
Gill, Frank B. 1995. *Ornithology*. Second edition. New York: W. H. Freeman
Goodwin, Derek. 1982. *Estrildid Finches of the World*. Ithaca: Cornell University Press
—1976. *The Crows of the World*: Ithaca: Cornell University Press
—1983. *Pigeons and Doves of the World*. Ithaca: Cornell University Press
Greenway, J. C. 1967. *Extinct and Vanishing Birds of the World*. New York: Dover Publications
Hadden, D. 1981. *Birds of the North Solomons*. Wau, Papua New Guinea: Wau Ecology Institute
Hall, B. P. and R. E. Moreau. 1970. *An Atlas of Speciation in African Passerine Birds*. London: Trustees of the
British Museum
Halliday, T. 1978. *Vanishing Birds: Their Natural History and Conservation*. New York: Holt, Rinehart and Winston
Hancock, James and Hugh Elliot. 1978. *The Herons of the World*. New York: Harper and Row
Hancock, J., J. Kushlan and M. Kahl. 1992. *Storks, Ibises and Spoonbills of the World*. New York: Academic Press
Hannecart, F. and Y. Letocart. 1983. *Oiseaux de Nouvelle Caledonia et des Loyautes*. Nouméa: Les Editions Cardinalis
Harrap, Simon and David Quinn. 1995. *Chickadees, Tits, Nuthatches and Treecreepers*. Princeton University Press
Harris, M. 1974. *Birds of the Galapagos*. New York: Taplinger
Harrison, C. J. O. 1978. *Bird Families of the World*. New York: Harry Abrams
Harrison, Peter. 1983. *Seabirds: An Identification Guide*. Boston: Houghton Mifflin
Haverschmidt, F. 1971. *The Birds of Surinam*. Edinburgh: Oliver & Boyd
Henry, G. M. 1971. *A Guide to the Birds of Ceylon*. London: Oxford University Press
Hilty, Steven L. and William L. Brown. 1986. *A Guide to the Birds of Colombia*. Princeton University Press
Howard, Richard and Alick Moore. 1994. *A Complete Checklist of the Birds of the World*. Second Edition.
London: Academic Press
Howell, Steve N. G. and Sophie Webb. 1995. *A Guide to the Birds of Mexico and northern Central America*.
Oxford: Oxford University Press
Hume, Rob. 1997. *Owls of the World*. London: Parkgate Books
Inskipp, C. and T. Inskipp. 1985. *A Guide to the Birds of Nepal*. Dover, New Hampshire: Tanager Books
Irwin, M. P. S. 1999. The genus *Nectarinia* and the evolution and diversification of sunbirds: an Afrotropical perspective.
Honeyguide 45: 45-58
Isler, Morton L. and Phyllis R. Isler. 1987. *The Tanagers*. Washington: Smithsonian Institution Press
Johnsgard, Paul. 1981. *The Plovers, Sandpipers and Snipes of the World*. Lincoln: University of Nebraska Press
—1983. *Cranes of the World*. Indiana University Press
—1983. *Grouse of the World*. Lincoln: University of Nebraska Press

—1986. *Pheasants of the World.* Oxford University Press

—1988. *The Quails, Partridges and Francolins of the World.* Oxford: Oxford University Press

—1991. *Bustards, Hemipodes, and Sandgrouse.* Oxford University Press

—1993. *Cormorants, Darters and Pelicans of the World.* Washington: Smithsonian

Jones, Darryl N., René Dekker and Cees Roselaar. 1995. *The Megapodes.* Oxford University Press

Juniper, Tony and Mike Parr. 1998. *Parrots: A Guide to the Parrots of the World.* Yale University Press

Keith, Stuart, Emil Urban, C.H. Fry. 1992. *The Birds of Africa* (Volume IV). New York: Academic Press

Kemp, Alan. 1995. *The Hornbills.* New York: Oxford University Press

King, Ben F. 1997. *Checklist of the Birds of Eurasia.* Vista, CA: Ibis Publishing Company

King, Ben and E. C. Dickenson. 1975. *A Field Guide to the Birds of Southeast Asia.* Boston: Houghton Mifflin

King, Warren. 1981. *Endangered Birds of the World: The ICBP Red Data Book.* Washington: Smithsonian Institution Press

Lambert, Frank and Martin Woodcock. 1996. *Pittas, Broadbills and Asities.* Sussex, UK: Pica Press

Langrand, Olivier. 1990. *Guide to the Birds of Madagascar.* New Haven: Yale University Press

Lefranc, Norbert. 1997. *Shrikes: A Guide to the Shrikes of the World.* New Haven: Yale University Press

Lippens, L. and H. Wille. 1976. *Les Oiseaux de Zaïre.* Brussels: Editions Lannoo Tielt

Mackworth-Praed, C. W. and C. H. B. Grant. 1957. *Birds of Eastern and North Eastern Africa* (Series 1, Volume 1). London: Longmans

—1960. *Birds of Eastern and North Eastern Africa* (Series 1, Volume 2). London: Longmans

—1962. *Birds of the Southern Third of Africa* (Series 2, Volume 1). London: Longmans

—1963. *Birds of the Southern Third of Africa* (Series 2, Volume 2). London: Longmans

—1970. *Birds of the West Central and Western Africa* (Series 3, Volume 1). London: Longmans

—1973. *Birds of the West Central and Western Africa* (Series 3, Volume 2). London: Longmans

Madge, Steve and Hilary Burn. 1988. *Waterfowl: An identification guide to the ducks, geese and swans of the world.* Boston: Houghton Mifflin

Meyer de Schauensee, Rodolphe. 1982. *A Guide to the Birds of South America.* Pan American Section International Council for Bird Preservation

—1984. *The Birds of China.* Smithsonian Institute Press

Monroe, Burt L. and Charles G. Sibley. 1993. *A World Checklist of Birds.* New Haven: Yale University Press

Peters, James L. 1979. *Check-list of Birds of the World.* Volume I, Second Edition. Revision of the Work of James L. Peters. Ernst Mayr and G. William Cottrell, editors. Cambridge, Mass: Museum of Comparative Zoology

—1934. *Check-list of Birds of the World.* Volume II. Cambridge, Mass: Harvard University Press

—1937. *Check-list of Birds of the World.* Volume III. Cambridge, Mass: Harvard University Press

—1940. *Check-list of Birds of the World.* Volume IV. Cambridge, Mass: Harvard University Press

—1945. *Check-list of Birds of the World.* Volume V. Cambridge, Mass: Harvard University Press

—1948. *Check-list of Birds of the World.* Volume VI. Cambridge, Mass: Harvard University Press

—1951. *Check-list of Birds of the World.* Volume VII. Cambridge, Mass: Museum of Comparative Zoology

—1979. *Check-list of Birds of the World.* Volume VIII. A Continuation of the Work of James L. Peters. Melvin A. Traylor, Jr., editor. Cambridge, Mass: Museum of Comparative Zoology

—1960. *Check-list of Birds of the World.* Volume IX. A Continuation of the Work of James L. Peters. Ernst Mayr and James C. Greenway, Jr., editors. Cambridge, Mass: Museum of Comparative Zoology

—1964. *Check-list of Birds of the World.* Volume X. A Continuation of the Work of James L. Peters. Ernst Mayr and Raymond A. Paynter, Jr., editors. Cambridge, Mass: Museum of Comparative Zoology

—1986. *Check-list of Birds of the World.* Volume XI. A Continuation of the Work of James L. Peters. Ernst Mayr and G. William Cottrell, editors. Cambridge, Mass: Museum of Comparative Zoology

—1967. *Check-list of Birds of the World.* Volume XII. A Continuation of the Work of James L. Peters. Raymond A. Paynter, Jr., editor, in consultation with Ernst Mayr. Cambridge, Mass: Museum of Comparative Zoology

—1970. *Check-list of Birds of the World.* Volume XIII. A Continuation of the Work of James L. Peters. Raymond A. Paynter, Jr., editor, in consultation with Ernst Mayr. Cambridge, Mass: Museum of Comparative Zoology

—1968. *Check-list of Birds of the World.* Volume XIV. A Continuation of the Work of James L. Peters. Raymond A. Paynter, Jr., editor, in consultation with Ernst Mayr. Cambridge, Mass: Museum of Comparative Zoology

—1962. *Check-list of Birds of the World.* Volume XV. A Continuation of the Work of James L. Peters. Ernst Mayr and James C. Greenway, Jr., editors. Cambridge, Mass: Museum of Comparative Zoology

Pratt, H. Douglas, P. Bruner and D. Berrett. 1987. *Birds of Hawaii and the Tropical Pacific.* Princeton University Press

Rand McNally. 1999. *New Millennium World Atlas Deluxe.* Skokie, Illinois: Rand McNally Company

Reichel, James D. and Philip O. Glass. 1991. Checklist of the Birds of the Marianas Islands. *Elepaio* 51 (1)

Remsen, J. V., Jr. Editor. 1997. *Studies in Neotropical Ornithology Honoring Ted Parker.* Ornithological Monographs No. 48. Washington, DC: American Ornithologists' Union

Restall, Robin. 1997. *Munias and Mannikins.* New Haven: Yale University Press

Ridgely, Robert S. and John Gwynne. 1989. *A Guide to the Birds of Panama with Costa Rica, Nicaragua and Honduras*. Princeton University Press

Ridgely, Robert S. and Guy Tudor. 1989. *The Birds of South America*: Volume 1. Austin: University of Texas Press

—1994. *The Birds of South America*: Volume 2. Austin: University of Texas Press

Ripley, S. Dillon. 1977. *Rails of the World*. Boston: David Godine

Rowley, Ian and Eleanor Russell. 1997. *Fairy-Wrens and Grasswrens*. Oxford University Press

Schodde, Richard. 1982. *The Fairy Wrens*. Melbourne: Lansdowne Editions

Serle, W., G. J. Morel and W. Hartwig. 1977. *A Field Guide to the Birds of West Africa*. London: Collins

Short, Lester. 1982. *Woodpeckers of the World*. Wilmington: Delaware Museum of Natural History

Sibley, Charles G. and J. E. Ahlquist. 1990. *Phylogeny and Classification of Birds*. New Haven: Yale University Press

Sibley, Charles G. and B. L. Monroe. 1990. *Distribution and Taxonomy of Birds of the World*. Yale University Press

—1992. *A Supplement to Distribution and Taxonomy of Birds of the World*. New Haven: Yale University Press

Sibley, Charles G. and Thayer Birding Software, Ltd. 1994-1996

Sinclair, Ian and Olivier Langrand. 1998. *Birds of the Indian Ocean Islands*. Cape Town: Struik

Slud, P. 1964. *The Birds of Costa Rica*. New York: Bulletin of the American Museum of Natural History, Volume 128

Smythies, B. E. 1960. *The Birds of Borneo*. London: Oliver & Boyd

—1986. *The Birds of Burma*. Pickering, Canada: Silvio Mattacchione & Co.

Snow, David. 1982. *The Cotingas*. Ithaca: Cornell University Press

Stiles, F. Gary and Alexander F. Skutch. 1989. *A Guide to the Birds of Costa Rica*. Ithaca, NY: Cornell University Press

Taylor, Barry. 1998. *A Guide to the Rails, Crakes, Gallinules and Coots of the World*. Yale University Press

Tikader, B. K. 1984. *Birds of the Andaman and Nicobar Islands*. Calcutta: Zoological Survey of India

Todd, Frank. 1996. *Natural History of the Waterfowl*. Vista, CA: Ibis Publishing Company

Turner, Angela and Chris Rose. 1989. *Swallows and Martins*. Boston: Houghton Mifflin Company

Urban, E, K., C. Fry and S. Keith. 1986. *The Birds of Africa. Volume II*. London: Academic Press

Van Marle, J. G. and K. Voous. 1988. *The Birds of Sumatra*. Tring, UK: British Ornithologist's Union

Vaurie, Charles. 1959. *Birds of the Palearctic Fauna (Passeriformes)*. London: Witherby

—1965. *Birds of the Palearctic Fauna (Non-Passeriformes)*. London: Witherby

—1972. *Tibet and its Birds*. London: Witherby

—1980. *Taxonomy and Geographical Distribution of the Furnariidae*. New York: American Museum of Natural History Volume 166: Article 1

Winkler, Hans, D. A. Christie and D. Nurney. 1995. *Woodpeckers: An Identification Guide to Woodpeckers of the World*. Boston: Houghton Mifflin Co

White, C. M. N. 1965. *A Revised Checklist of African Non-Passerine Birds*. Lusaka: Government Printing Office

White, C. M. N. and M. D. Bruce. 1986. *The Birds of Wallacea*. London: British Ornithologists' Union Check-list No. 7

Williams, J. G. and N. Arlott. 1980. *Field Guide to the Birds of East Africa*. London: Collins

Zimmerman, Dale, Donald Turner and David J. Pearson. 1996. *Birds of Kenya and Northern Tanzania*. Princeton: Princeton University Press

Abaco I., *Bahamas*	26	30 N	77	15 W	American Samoa	14	20 S	170	40 W
Abd-al-Küri I., *Somalia*	12	19 N	52	23 E	Amirante Islands, *Seychelles*	6	0 S	53	0 E
Aberdare Mountains, *Kenya*	0	39 S	36	70 E	Amsterdam I., *Indian Ocean*	38	30 S	77	30 E
Abingdon I., *Galapagos Islands*	0	58 N	90	75 W	Amudar'ya, *Uzbekistan*	43	58 N	59	34 E
Abrolhos Bank, *Brazil*	18	0 S	38	0 W	Amur River, *Russia*	53	30 N	122	30 E
Abu, Mt., *India*	24	41 N	72	50 E	Amurland, *Russia*	52	56 N	141	10 E
Acarai, Serra, *Brazil*	1	50 N	57	50 W	Anaa I., *Tuamotu Archipelago*	17	41 S	145	46 W
Acari Mountains, *Guyana*	1	50 N	58	0 W	Anacapa I.. *California*	34	0 N	119	24 W
Aceh Province, *Sumatra*	4	15 N	97	30 E	Anadyr River, *Russia*	64	73 N	177	49 E
Acklins I., *Bahamas*	22	30 N	74	0 W	Anambas Islands, *South China Sea*	3	20 N	106	30 E
Aconcagua, *Chile*	32	39 S	70	0 W	Ancash, *Peru*	9	30 S	77	45 W
Adak I., *Aleutian Islands*	51	40 N	176	30 W	Anchorite Islands, *Admiralty Islands*	2	0 S	145	50 E
Adamawa Highlands, *Cameroon*	6	2 N	10	29 E	Andaman Islands, *Bay of Bengal*	12	30 N	92	30 E
Adana, *Turkey*	37	45 N	35	75 E	Andes, *South America*	20	0 S	68	0 W
Aden	12	45 N	45	0 E	Andra Pradesh, *India*	15	0 N	80	0 E
Admiralty Islands, *Papua New Guinea*	2	0 S	147	0 E	Andros I., *Bahamas*	24	30 N	78	0 W
Adonara I., *Indonesia*	8	15 S	123	5 E	Aneityum I., *Vanuatu*	20	12 S	169	45 E
Adriatic Sea	43	0 N	16	0 E	Angola	12	0 S	30	0 E
Afghanistan	33	0 N	65	0 E	Anguar I., *Palau Islands*	6	45 N	134	5 E
Agrihan I., *n Mariana Islands*	18	76 N	145	66 E	Anhui Province, *China*	37	0 N	117	0 E
Aguijan I., *n Mariana Islands*	14	85 N	145	55 E	Anjouan I., *Comoro Islands*	12	0 S	44	0 E
Ahaggar Mountains, *Algeria*	22	62 N	5	29 E	Ankarata Mountains, *Madagascar*	19	41 S	47	22 E
Aïr Massif, *Niger*	18	30 N	8	0 E	Annam, *n Vietnam*	16	30 N	107	30 E
Aitape district, *Papua New Guinea*	3	11 S	142	22 E	Annamatic Mountains, *Vietnam*	17	0 N	106	0 E
Alabama, *US*	31	8 N	87	57 W	Annobon I. *see* Pagalu	1	43 S	5	62 E
Alabat I., *Philippines*	14	0 N	122	0 E	Anson Bay, *Australia*	13	20 S	130	6 E
Alagoas, *Brazil*	9	0 S	36	0 E	Antalya, *Turkey*	36	97 N	30	68 E
Alai Mountains, *Kyrgyzstan*	39	90 N	72	0 E	Antarctic Peninsula	67	0 S	60	0 W
Alaotra, Lake, *Madagascar*	17	30 S	48	30 E	Antigua I., *West Indies*	17	0 N	61	50 W
Alaschan Mountains, *China*	39	0 N	106	0 E	Anti-Lebanon Mts., *Syria/Lebanon*	33	40 N	36	10 E
Alaska	64	0 N	154	0 W	Antioquia, *Colombia*	7	0 N	75	30 W
Albania	41	50 N	20	0 E	Antipodes Islands, *Pacific Ocean*	49	45 S	178	40 E
Albany, *Australia*	35	1 S	117	58 E	Antofagasta, *Chile*	23	63 S	70	40 W
Albatross I., *Tasmania*	40	24 S	144	40 E	Anzoátegui, *Venezuela*	9	0 N	64	30 W
Albert, Lake, *Zaire/Uganda*	1	30 N	31	0 E	Aoba I., *Vanuatu*	15	30 S	167	70 E
Alberta, *Canada*	54	40 N	115	0 W	Appennine Mountains, *Italy*	44	0 N	10	0 E
Alcester I., *Solomon Sea*	9	56 S	152	42 E	Apo, Mt., *Philippines*	6	98 N	125	25 E
Aldabra I., *Indian Ocean*	9	22 S	46	28 E	Apolima I., *Western Samoa*	13	70 S	172	10 W
Alejandro Selkirk I., *Chile*	33	50 S	80	46 W	Apure, Río, *Venezuela*	7	37 N	66	25 W
Alert Stack I., *Snares Islands*	48	0 S	166	40 E	Apurímac, *Peru*	14	0 S	73	0 W
Aleutian Islands	50	0 N	175	0 W	Aqaba, Gulf of	28	15 N	33	20 E
Alexander Archipelago, *Alaska*	56	28 N	133	25 W	Arabian Peninsula	20	0 N	46	0 E
Algeria	28	30 N	2	0 E	Arabian Sea	16	0 N	65	0 E
Almagan I., *Mariana Islands*	17	80 N	145	45 E	Aragua, *Venezuela*	10	0 N	67	10 W
Alor I., *Lesser Sundas*	8	15 S	124	30 E	Araguaia, Rio, *Brazil*	5	21 S	48	41 W
Altai Mountains, *Mongolia*	46	40 N	92	45 E	Arakan Yoma Mountains, *Myanmar*	20	23 N	94	2 E
Amacuro, Delta, *Venezuela*	8	50 N	61	5 W	Aral Sea	44	30 N	60	0 E
Amak I., *Aleutian Islands*	55	41 N	163	13 W	Arauca, *Colombia*	6	40 N	71	0 W
Amami-O-Shima I., *Japan*	28	0 N	129	0 E	Arequipa, *Peru*	16	0 S	72	50 W
Amapá, *Brazil*	2	5 N	50	50 W	Arfak Mountains, *New Guinea*	2	0 S	133	30 E
Amazon Bay, *New Guinea*	10	20 S	150	0 E	Argentina	35	0 S	66	0 W
Amazon River, *Brazil*	0	5 S	50	0 W	Arica, *Chile*	18	32 S	70	20 W
Amazonas, *Brazil*	4	0 S	64	0 W	Arimã, *Brazil*	5	48 S	63	38 W
Amazonas, *Peru*	5	0 S	78	0 W	Arizona, *USA*	34	0 N	112	0 W
Amazonas, *Venezuela*	3	30 N	66	0 W	Arkansas, *USA*	35	0 N	92	30 W
Ambelau I., *Moluccas*	3	50 S	127	0 W	Armenia	40	20 N	45	0 E
Amberpon I., *New Guinea*	1	50 S	134	10 E	Arnhem Land, *Australia*	13	10 S	134	30 E
Ambon I., *Moluccas*	3	43 S	128	12 E	Arno Atoll., *Marshall Islands.*	7	45 N	172	30 E
Amchitka I., *Alaska*	51	32 N	179	0 W	Aroa River, *New Guinea*	7	30 S	145	0 E

Aru Islands, *New Guinea*	6	0 S	134	30 E	Bangka I., *Sumatra*	2	0 S	105	50 E
Aruba, *Netherlands Antilles*	12	30 N	70	0 W	Bangkaru I., *Sumatra*	2	2 N	97	5 E
Arunachal Pradesh, *India*	28	0 N	95	0 E	Bangladesh	24	0 N	90	0 E
Arvali Hills, *Rajasthan, India*	26	0 N	74	0 E	Banguey I. *see* Banggi I.	7	17 N	117	12 E
Ascension I., *Atlantic Ocean*	8	0 S	14	15 W	Banjak I. *see* Banyak I.	2	10 N	97	10 E
Assam, *India*	26	0 N	93	0 E	Banks Group, *Vanuatu*	13	50 S	167	30 E
Assumption I., *Aldabra*	9	52 S	46	0 E	Banks I., *Canada*	53	20 N	130	0 W
Astin Tagh Mountains, *China*	37	0 N	95	0 E	Banthat Mountains, *Cambodia*	12	0 N	103	30 E
Astrolabe Bay, *New Guinea*	6	0 S	146	0 E	Banton I., *Philippines*	12	56 N	122	4 E
Asuncion I., *Mariana Islands*	19	80 N	145	10 E	Banyak I., *Sumatra*	2	10 N	97	10 E
Aswan, *Egypt*	24	4 N	32	57 E	Barba, Volcán, *Costa Rica*	10	10 N	83	55 W
Atacama, *Chile*	27	30 S	70	0 W	Barbados, *West Indies*	13	10 N	59	30 W
Atherton Tableland, *Australia*	18	0 S	144	30 E	Barbareta Islands, *Honduras*	16	25 N	86	0 W
Atitlán, Lake, *Guatemala*	14	10 N	91	40 W	Barberton, *South Africa*	25	42 S	31	2 E
Atiu, *Cook Islands*	20	0 S	158	0 W	Barbuda, *West Indies*	17	30 N	61	40 W
Atka I., *Aleutian Islands*	60	50 N	151	48 E	Barranquilla, *Colombia*	11	0 N	74	50 W
Atlas Mountains, *North Africa*	32	30 N	5	0 W	Barrington I., *Galapagos Islands*	0	80 S	90	4 W
Atrato Valley, *Colombia*	6	30 N	77	0 W	Barrow I., *Australia*	20	45 S	115	20 E
Attu I., *Aleutian Islands*	53	0 N	173	10 E	Barú, Volcán, *Panama*	8	55 N	83	40 W
Auckland Islands	50	40 S	166	5 E	Basilan I., *Philippines*	6	33 N	122	4 E
Austral Islands *see* Tubai	28	0 S	150	0 W	Basol I., *Philippines*	9	50 N	125	30 E
Australia	23	50 S	133	50E	Bass Strait, *Australia*	39	15 S	146	30 E
Austria	47	50 N	14	0 E	Batan I., *Philippines.*	20	30 N	121	50 E
Auyan-tepui, *Venezuela*	5	48 N	62	41 W	Batanas Islands, *Philippines*	20	30 N	121	50 E
Ayacucho, *Peru*	13	0 S	74	0 W	Batanta I., *w Papuan islands*	0	55 S	130	40 E
Azerbaijan	40	20 N	42	0 E	Batjan I. *see* Bacan	0	35 S	127	30 E
Azores	38	44 N	29	0 W	Batu Islands, *Sumatra*	0	30 S	98	25 E
Azuay, *Ecuador*	2	55 S	79	0 W	Baudó Mountains, *Colombia*	5	30 N	77	0 W
Azuero Peninsula, *Panama*	7	50 N	80	40 W	Bawean I., *Java Sea*	5	49 S	112	39 E
Babar I., *Lesser Sundas*	8	0 S	129	30 E	Bay Islands, *Nicaragua*	12	0 N	83	30 W
Babelthuap I., *Caroline Islands*	7	50 N	134	57 E	Beata I., *Dominican Republic*	17	34 N	71	31 W
Babi I., *Sumatra*	2	9 N	96	64 E	Belém, *Brazil*	1	20 S	48	30 W
Bacan I., *Moluccas*	0	35 S	127	30 E	Belitung I., *Borneo*	3	10 S	107	50 E
Bac Phan, *n Vietnam*	21	54 N	104	3 E	Belize	17	0 N	88	30 W
Baffin Bay, *Canada*	72	0 N	64	0 W	Bellenden Ker Range, *Australia*	18	0 S	145	0 E
Baffin I., *Canada*	68	0 N	75	0 W	Bellona I., *Solomon Islands*	11	17 S	159	47 E
Bagabag I., *New Guinea*	4	79 S	146	23 E	Bengal, *India*	20	0 N	86	0 E
Bahamas, *West Indies*	24	0 N	75	0 W	Benguela, *Angola*	13	0 S	13	30 E
Bahia, *Brazil*	12	0 S	42	0 W	Beni, *Bolivia*	10	23 S	65	24 W
Bahia, Islas de la, *Honduras*	16	18 N	86	35 W	Beni, Río, *Bolivia*	11	0 S	66	0 W
Bahrain, *Persian Gulf*	26	0 N	56	0 E	Benin	10	0 N	2	0 E
Baikal, Lake, *Russia*	53	0 N	108	0 E	Bensbach River, *New Guinea*	8	0 S	141	50 E
Baja California, *Mexico*	30	0 N	115	0 W	Bequia I., *Lesser Antilles*	12	50 N	61	20 W
Balabac I., *Palawan*	8	0 N	117	0 E	Bering Sea	58	0 N	171	0 E
Bale Province, *Ethiopia*	6	20 N	41	30 E	Berlenga Islands, *Portugal*	39	29 N	9	30 W
Balearic Islands *Spain*	39	30 N	3	0 E	Bermuda	32	45 N	65	0 W
Bali, *Indonesia*	8	20 S	115	0 E	Bernier I., *Australia*	24	50 S	113	12 E
Balkan Peninsula	43	15 N	23	0 E	Bhamo District, *Myanmar*	24	28 N	97	25 E
Balkhash, Lake, *Kazakstan*	46	50 N	74	50 E	Bhutan	27	0 N	90	0 E
Balleny I., *Antarctica*	66	30 S	163	0 E	Biak I., *New Guinea*	1	10 S	136	30 E
Baltic Peninsula	56	0 N	26	0 E	Bié, *Angola*	13	0 S	17	0 E
Baluchistan, *Pakistan*	27	30 N	65	0 E	Bihar, *India*	25	0 N	86	0 E
Bamenda Highlands, *Cameroon*	5	57 N	10	11 E	Biliran I., *Philippines*	12	0 N	124	50 E
Banc d'Arguin, *Mauritania*	21	0 N	16	0 W	Billiton I. *see* Belitung I.	3	10 S	107	50 E
Banda I., *Banda Sea*	4	37 S	129	50 E	Binaia, Mt., *Seram*	3	18 S	129	43 E
Banda Sea, *Indonesia*	6	5 S	130	0 E	Bioko, *Gulf of Guinea*	3	30 N	8	40 E
Banggai Islands, *Banda Sea*	1	43 S	123	22 E	Bisa I., *Moluccas*	1	15 S	127	32 E
Banggi I., *Borneo*	7	17 N	117	12 E	Bismarck Archipelago	2	30 S	150	0 E
Bangka I., *Sulawesi*	1	30 N	125	50 E	Black Sea	43	30 N	35	0 E

Blue Nile	15	38 N	32	31 E	Calayan I., *Philippines*	19	20 N	121	27 E
Boang I., *see* Tanga I.	3	0 S	153	10 E	Calicoan I., *Philippines*	11	0 N	125	50 E
Boano I., *s Moluccas*	2	97 S	127	91 E	Camagüey Archipelago, *Cuba*	22	20 N	77	95 W
Bocas del Toro, *Panama*	9	30 N	82	30 W	Cambodia	12	15 N	105	0 E
Bogotá, *Colombia*	4	34 N	74	0 W	Cameron Highlands, *Malaysia*	4	30 N	101	34 E
Bohol I., *Philippines*	9	50 N	124	10 E	Cameroon	4	0 N	12	0 E
Bolívar, *Colombia*	9	0 N	74	40 W	Cameroon, Mt., *Cameroon*	4	13 N	9	10 E
Bolívar, *Venezuela*	6	20 N	63	30 W	Camiguin Norte, *Philippines*	18	56 N	121	55 E
Bolivia	17	6 S	64	0 W	Camiguin Sur, *s Philippines*	9	16 N	124	73 E
Bolavens Plateau, *Laos*	15	10 N	106	30 E	Camorta I., *Nicobar Islands*	8	5 N	93	50 E
Boma Hills, *Sudan*	6	20 N	34	30 E	Campbell I., *New Zealand*	52	30 S	169	0 E
Bonaire, *Netherlands Antilles*	12	10 N	68	15 W	Campeche, *Mexico*	19	50 N	90	32 W
Bongao I., *Sulu Arch*ipelago	5	0 N	119	60 E	Canada	56	0 N	99	0 W
Bonin Islands, *Japan*	27	10 N	142	20 E	Canal Zone, *Panama*	9	0 N	80	0 W
Borabora, *French Polynesia*	16	30 S	151	45 W	Canary Islands, *Atlantic Ocean*	28	30N	16	0 W
Borneo	1	0 N	115	0 E	Cantabrian Mountains, *Spain*	43	0 N	5	85 W
Borodino Islands *see* Daito Islands	25	92 N	131	31 E	Cantiles Keys, *Cuba*	21	40 N	81	30 W
Bosavi, Mt., *Papua New Guinea*	6	30 S	142	49 E	Cape Barren I., *Australia*	40	25 S	148	15 E
Botswana	22	0 S	24	0 E	Cape Cod, *Massachusetts*	42	0 N	70	0 W
Bougainville, *Solomon Islands*	6	0 S	155	0 E	Cape Comorin, *India*	8	3 N	77	40 E
Bounty Islands	48	0 S	178	30 E	Cape Horn, *Argentina*	56	0 S	67	0 W
Boyacá, *Colombia*	5	30 N	72	0 W	Cape Mala Peninsula *see* Azuero Pen.	7	50 N	80	40 W
Brahmaputra River, *India*	23	58 N	89	50 E	Cape Province, *South Africa*	33	50 S	18	22 E
Branco, Rio, *Brazil*	1	20 S	61	50 W	Cape Sable, *Florida*	25	6 N	81	7 W
Brava I., *Cape Verde Islands*	14	85 N	24	72 W	Cape Town, South Africa	33	90 S	18	49 E
Brazil	12	0 S	50	0 W	Cape Verde Islands, *Atlantic Ocean*	17	10 N	25	20 W
Brisbane, *Australia*	27	24 S	153	9 E	Cape York Peninsula, *Australia*	12	0 S	142	30 E
Bristol Bay, *Alaska*	58	0 N	160	0 W	Capella, Mt., *Papua New Guinea*	5	4 S	141	8 E
British Columbia, *Canada*	55	0 N	125	15 W	Capricorn Islands, *Coral Sea*	23	44 S	151	91 E
Broughton I., *New Zealand*	48	2 S	166	37 E	Caprivi Strip, *Zambia*	18	0 S	23	0 E
Brunei, *Borneo*	4	75 N	114	55 E	Caquetá, *Colombia*	1	0 N	74	0 W
Buad I., *Philippines.*	11	40 N	124	50 E	Car Nicobar Island, *Nicobar Islands*	9	10 N	93	0 E
Bucaramanga, *Colombia*	7	0 N	73	0 W	Carabobo, *Venezuela*	10	10 N	68	5 W
Buenaventura, *Colombia*	3	54 N	77	2 W	Caracas, *Venezuela*	10	30 N	66	55 W
Buenos Aires Province, *Argentina*	36	30 S	60	0 W	Caribbean Sea	15	0 N	75	0 W
Buka, *Solomon Islands*	5	10 S	154	50 E	Caripe, *Venezuela*	10	30 N	63	25 W
Buldir I., *Aleutians*	52	30 N	175	50 E	Carnamah District, *Australia*	29	0 S	115	0 E
Bulgaria	42	35 N	25	30 E	Caroline Islands, *Pacific Ocean*	8	0 N	150	0 E
Bulubuk, *Sulu Archipelago*	5	0 N	120	0 E	Carpathian Mountains, *Europe*	49	30 N	21	0 E
Burdekin-Lynd Divide, *Australia*	19	38 S	147	25 E	Carpentaria, Gulf of, *Australia*	14	0 S	139	0 E
Burkina Faso	12	0 N	1	0 W	Cartagena, *Colombia*	10	25 N	75	33 W
Burma *see* Myanmar	21	0 N	96	30 E	Casablanca, *Morocco*	33	36 N	7	36 W
Buru I., *Moluccas*	3	0 S	126	50 E	Cascade Mountains, *US*	45	0 N	121	45 W
Burundi	3	15 S	30	0 E	Caspian Sea	43	0 N	50	0 E
Busuanga I., *Philippines*	12	5 N	120	5 E	Catamarca, *Argentina*	27	0 S	65	50 W
Buto Song Mountains, *Borneo*	2	23 N	113	84 E	Catanduanes, *Philippines*	13	50 N	124	20 E
Buton I. *see* Butung I., *Sulawesi*	5	0 S	122	45 E	Cauca Valley, *Colombia*	8	54 N	74	28 W
Butung I., *Sulawesi*	5	0 S	122	45 E	Caucasus Mountains	42	50 N	44	0 E
Bwamba Forest, *Uganda*	0	87 N	30	10 E	Caura, Río, *Venezuela*	6	0 N	64	25 W
Cabinda, *Angola*	5	34 S	12	12 E	Cavilli I., *New Zealand*	35	0 S	173	58 E
Cacahuatique Mountains, *El Salvador*	13	45 N	91	30 W	Cayman Brac, *West Indies*	19	43 N	79	49 W
Cagayan Sulu, *Philippines*	7	0 N	118	47 E	Cayman Islands, *West Indies*	19	40 N	80	30 W
Cagayancillo I., *Palawan*	9	59 N	121	21 E	Cayo Cantilles, *Cuba*	21	62 N	81	99 W
Caicara, *Venezuela*	7	38 N	66	10 W	Cayo Coco, *Cuba*	22	48 N	78	47 W
Caicos Islands, *West Indies*	21	40 N	71	40 W	Cayo Largo, *Cuba*	21	40 N	80	30 W
Cairns, *Australia*	16	57 S	145	45 E	Cayo Real, *Cuba*	21	40 N	80	10 W
Cajamarca, *Peru*	6	15 S	78	50 W	Ceará, *Brazil*	5	0 S	40	0 W
Calamian Group, *Philippines*	11	50 N	119	55 E	Cébaco I., *Panama*	7	33 N	81	9 W
Calauit I., *Philippines*	12	30 N	119	60 E	Cebu I., *Philippines*	10	18 N	123	54 E

Cedros, Isla, *Baja California*	28	14 N	115	22 W	Congo	0	1 S	15	15 E
Celebes *see* Sulawesi	2	0 S	120	0 E	Connecticut, *US*	41	30 N	72	45 W
Central African Republic	7	0 N	20	0 E	Cook Islands, *Pacific Ocean*	17	0 S	160	0 W
Ceram I. *see* Seram	3	10 S	129	0 E	Cook Strait. *New Zealand*	41	15 S	174	29 E
Cerralvo, Isla, *Gulf of California*	24	23 N	109	87 W	Cooktown, *Australia*	15	30 N	145	16 E
Ceylon see Sri Lanka	7	30 N	80	50 E	Copper River Delta, *Canada*	61	0 N	145	0 W
Chad	15	0 N	17	15 E	Coquimbo, *Chile*	30	0 S	71	20 W
Chad, Lake	13	0 N	14	40 E	Córdoba, *Argentina*	31	22 S	64	15 W
Chagos Archipelago, *Indian Ocean*	6	0 S	72	0 E	Coroico, Río, *Bolivia*	16	0 S	68	18 W
Chalatenango, *El Salvador*	13	30 N	89	0 W	Coronados Islands, *Mexico*	32	25 N	117	15 W
Chanchamayo, *Peru*	12	30 S	72	30 W	Corrientes Province, *Argentina*	30	42 S	59	38 W
Channel Islands, *California*	33	40 N	119	15 W	Corsica	42	0 N	9	0 E
Chaparé, Río, *Bolivia*	15	58 S	64	43 W	Cosmoledo Atoll, *Aldabra*	9	7 S	47	58 E
Chari River, *Chad*	12	0 N	15	0 E	Costa Rica	10	0 N	84	0 W
Chatham I. *see* San Cristóbal	0	52 S	89	27 W	Cousin I., *Seychelles*	4	20S	55	40E
Chatham Islands, *New Zealand*	44	0 S	176	40 W	Cozumel I., *Mexico*	20	30 N	86	40 W
Cheju-Do Islands, *South Korea*	33	29 N	126	34 E	Crater Highlands, *Tanzania*	3	8 S	35	40 E
Chekiang *see* Zhejiang	29	0 N	120	0 E	Crete	36	0 N	25	0 E
Chepo, Río, *Panama*	9	10 N	79	6 W	Crimean Peninsula	45	0 N	34	0 E
Chiapas, *Mexico*	17	0 N	92	45 W	Cross River, *Nigeria*	5	30 N	8	0 E
Chihuahua, *Mexico*	28	40 N	106	3 W	Crozet Islands, *Indian Ocean*	46	27 S	52	0 E
Chile	35	0 S	72	0 W	Cuanza River, *Angola*	9	2 S	13	30 E
Chiloé I., *Chile*	42	30 S	73	50 W	Cuanza Sul, *Angola*	12	0 S	15	0 E
Chilpancingo, *Mexico*	17	30 N	99	30 W	Cuba, *West Indies*	22	0 N	79	0 W
Chimborazo, Mt., *Ecuador*	1	5 S	78	40 W	Cuenca, *Ecuador*	2	50 S	79	9 W
Chin Hills, *Myanmar*	22	30 N	93	30 E	Culebra I., *Puerto Rico*	18	20 N	65	20 W
China	30	0 N	110	0 E	Culiacán, Rio, *Mexico*	24	30 N	107	42 W
Chinchorro Bank, *Mexico*	18	35 N	87	20 W	Culion I., *Philippines*	11	54 N	120	1 E
Chiribiquete, Sierra de, *Colombia*	1	0 N	73	0 W	Culpepper I., *Galapagos Islands*	1	10 N	92	0 W
Chiriquí, *Panama*	8	50 N	82	50 W	Cumaná, *Venezuela*	10	30 N	64	5 W
Chisos Mountains, *Texas*	29	5 N	103	15 W	Cundinamarca, *Colombia*	5	0 N	74	0 W
Chocó, *Colombia*	6	0 N	77	0 W	Cunene River, *Angola*	17	20 S	11	50 E
Choiseul I., *Solomon Islands*	7	0 S	157	0 E	Curaçao, *Netherlands Antilles*	12	10 N	69	0 W
Christmas I., *Indian Ocean*	10	30 S	105	40 E	Curupira, Serra de, *Brazil*	0	5 N	63	61 W
Christmas I. *see* Kiritimati	1	58 N	157	27 W	Cururu, Rio, *Brazil*	7	10 S	58	3 W
Chubut, *Argentina*	43	30 S	69	0 W	Cuyo Islands, *Philippines*	10	50 N	121	5 E
Chucantí, Cerro, *Panama*	8	50 N	78	40 W	Cuzco, *Peru*	13	31 S	72	0 W
Chukotsk Peninsula, *Russia*	68	0 N	175	0 E	Cyclops Mountains, *New Guinea*	4	5 S	139	0 E
Chuquisaca, *Bolivia*	20	30 S	63	30 W	Cyprus	35	0 N	33	0 E
Ciremay, Mt., *Java*	6	91 S	108	37 E	D'Entrecasteaux Archipelago	9	0 S	151	0 E
Clarión Isla, *Mexico*	18	25 N	114	40 W	Dagelet I. *see* Ullung I.	37	50 N	130	87 E
Clipperton I., *Pacific Ocean*	10	18 N	109	13 W	Daito Islands, *Japan*	25	92 N	131	31 E
Coahuila, *Mexico*	27	0 N	103	0 W	Dakhla Oasis, *Egypt*	25	30 N	28	50 E
Cochabamba, *Bolivia*	17	26 S	66	10 W	Da Lat Plateau, *Vietnam*	15	4 N	107	59 E
Cocos Islands, *Bay of Bengal*	12	10 S	96	55 E	Dalupiri, *Philippines*	19	5 N	121	12 E
Cocos, Isla del, *Costa Rica*	5	0 N	87	0 W	Damar I., *Banda Sea*	7	7 S	128	40 E
Codfish I., *New Zealand*	46	76 S	167	64 E	Damaraland, *Namibia*	22	40 S	17	0 E
Coiba, Isla, *Panama*	7	48 N	81	78 W	Dampier Islands, *New Guinea*	0	40 S	131	0 E
Col de Nuages, *Vietnam*	16	11 N	108	8 E	Dao I., *Philippines.*	10	28 N	121	57 E
Colchagua, *Chile*	34	30 S	71	0 W	Dar es Salaam, *Tanzania*	6	51 S	39	18 E
Colima, *Mexico*	19	10 N	103	40 W	Darfur Province, *Sudan*	13	40 N	24	0 E
Colombia	3	45 N	73	0 W	Darién, *Panama*	8	50 N	78	0 E
Colorado River basin	32	0 N	115	0 W	Darjiling, *ne India*	27	4 N	88	26 E
Colorado, *US*	39	30 N	105	30 W	Darling Mountains, *Australia*	34	4 S	141	54 E
Commander Is. *see* Komandorskiye Is.	55	0 N	167	0 E	Darnley I., *New Guinea*	9	39 S	143	46 E
Comodoro Rivadavia, *Argentina*	45	50 S	67	40 W	De Grey River, *Australia*	20	12 S	119	13 E
Comoro Islands, *Indian Ocean*	12	10 S	44	15 E	Denmark	55	30 N	9	0 E
Cóndor, Cordillera de, *Peru*	5	0 S	78	51 W	Derby District, *Australia*	17	18 S	128	38 E
Conflict Islands, *Louisiade Arch.*	10	77 S	151	81 E	Desertas Islands, *Madeira*	32	30 N	16	30 W

Place	°	′	°	′
Dicabaito I., *Philippines*	10	50 N	121	5 E
Diego Garcia I., *Indian Ocean*	7	50 S	72	50 E
Digul River, *New Guinea*	7	7 S	138	42 E
Dinagat I., *Philippines*	10	0 S	126	0 E
Dirk Hartog I., *Australia*	25	50 S	113	5 E
Distrito Federal, *Mexico*	19	20 N	99	10 W
Djampea I. *see* Tanahjampea	7	10 S	120	35 E
Djibouti	12	0 N	43	0 E
Doi I., *Moluccas*	2	14 N	127	49 E
Doi Luang Chiang, *Thailand*	19	25 N	98	55 E
Dominica, *West Indies*	15	20 N	61	20 W
Dominican Republic	19	0 N	70	30 W
Douala, *Cameroon*	4	4 N	9	43 E
Drakensberg Mountains, *South Africa*	31	0 S	28	0 E
Duff Group, *Santa Cruz Islands*	9	0 S	167	10 E
Duida, Mt., *Venezuela*	3	45 N	65	0 W
Duke of York I., *Bismarck Archipelago*	4	0 S	152	50 E
Duncan I., *Galapagos Islands*	0	60 S	90	63 W
Dunk I., *Australia*	17	59 S	146	29 E
Dyaul I., *Bismarck Archipelago*	2	95 S	150	88 E
Durango, *Mexico*	25	0 N	105	0 W
Easter I., *Pacific Ocean*	27	0 S	109	0 W
Eastern Ghats, *India*	18	0 N	83	0 E
Ecuador	2	0 S	78	0 W
Efate I., *Vanuatu*	17	60 S	168	30 E
Egum Atoll, *Trobriand Group*	9	20 S	151	56 E
Egypt	28	0 N	31	0 E
Eiao I., *Marquesas Islands*	7	98 S	140	69 W
Eirú, Rio, *Brazil*	7	0 S	71	0 W
El Oro, *Ecuador*	3	30 S	79	50 W
El Salvador	13	50 N	89	0 W
Elba I., *Italy*	42	46 N	10	17 E
Elburz Mountains, *Iran*	36	0 N	52	0 E
Eleuthera I., *Bahamas*	25	0 N	76	20 W
Elgon, Mt., *Kenya*	1	13 N	34	54 E
Ellesmere I., *Canada*	79	30 N	80	0 W
Ellice I., *Pacific Ocean*	8	0 S	178	0 E
Enggano I., *Sumatra*	5	20 S	102	40 E
England, *United Kingdom*	53	0 N	2	0 W
Epi I., *Vanuatu*	16	43 S	168	15 E
Eritrea	14	0 N	38	30 E
Erromango I., *Vanuatu*	18	45 S	169	5 E
Escazú, Cerros de, *Costa Rica*	9	55 N	84	7 W
Escudo de Veraguas I., *Panama*	9	3 N	81	30 W
Esmeraldas, *Ecuador*	0	56 N	79	40 W
Espinhaço, Serra, *Brazil*	16	90 S	43	25 W
Espírito Santo I., *Mexico*	24	30 N	110	23 W
Espírito Santo, *Brazil*	20	0 S	40	45 W
Espíritu Santo I., *Vanuatu*	15	15 S	166	50 E
Essaouira, *Morocco*	31	32 N	9	42 W
Ethiopia	8	0 N	40	0 E
Etna Bay, *New Guinea*	4	1 S	134	20 E
Etosha, *Namibia*	18	40 S	16	30 E
Europa I., *s Mozambique Channel*	22	20 S	40	21 E
Exmouth Gulf, *Australia*	22	20 S	114	9 E
Eyre, Lake, *Australia*	29	30 S	137	26 E
Faeroes, *Atlantic Ocean*	62	0 N	7	0 W
Faial I., *Azores*	38	40 N	29	19 W
Falcón, *Venezuela*	11	0 N	69	50 W
Falkland Islands, *Atlantic Ocean*	51	30 S	59	0 W
Fanning I. *see* Tabuaeran I.	3	87 N	159	32 W
Fan Si Pan Mountains, *n Vietnam*	22	25 N	103	76 E
Farallon Islands, *California*	37	45 N	123	0 W
Fatuhiva I., *Marquesas Islands*	10	47 S	138	63 W
Fatuhuku I., *Marquesas Islands*	9	26 S	136	55 W
Fauro I., *Solomon Islands*	6	55 S	156	50 E
Fayal I. *see* Faial, *Azores*	38	40 N	29	19 W
Feni I., *Bismarck Archipelago*	4	0 S	153	62 E
Fenualoa I., *Bismarck Archipelago*	10	20 S	166	40 E
Fergana basin, *Uzbekistan*	40	39 N	71	78 E
Fergusson I., *D'Entrecasteaux Arch.*	9	30S	150	45 E
Fernandina I., *Galapagos Islands*	0	36 S	91	54 W
Fernando de Noronha, Ilha, *Brazil*	4	0 S	33	10 W
Fernando Po *see* Bioko	3	30 N	8	40 E
Fiji Islands, *Pacific Ocean*	17	20 S	179	0 E
Finland	63	0 N	26	0 E
Fitzroy River, *Australia*	17	31 S	123	35 E
Flinders I., *Australia*	40	0 S	148	0 E
Flinders Range, *Australia*	31	30 S	138	30 E
Floreana I., *Galapagos Islands*	1	28 S	90	45 W
Flores, *Lesser Sundas*	8	35 S	121	0 E
Florida, *US*	28	0 N	82	0 W
Florida Group, *Solomon Islands*	9	55 S	160	15 E
Fly River, *New Guinea*	8	25 S	143	0 E
Fogo I., *Cape Verde Islands*	17	0 N	24	10 W
Fôret du Day, *Djibouti*	12	0 N	43	0 E
Formosa *see* Taiwan	23	70 N	121	0 E
Formosa, *Argentina*	26	15 S	58	10 W
France	7	0 N	3	0 E
Franz Josef Land, *Russia*	82	0 N	55	0 E
Frégate I., *Seychelles*	4	20S	55	50E
French Guiana	4	0 N	53	0 W
French Polynesia	18	0 S	145	0 W
Fresco, Rio, *Brazil*	7	15 S	51	30 W
Frontier Province, *Pakistan*	35	0 N	73	0 E
Fuerte, Río, *Mexico*	25	50 N	109	25 W
Fuerteventura, *Canary Islands*	28	30 N	14	0 W
Fuga I., *Luzon*	18	52 N	121	20 E
Fujian Province, *China*	25	85 N	118	30 E
Fukien *see* Fujian	26	0 N	118	0 E
Furneaux Group, *Australia*	40	10 S	147	50 E
Futuna, *Wallis and Futuna*	14	25 S	178	20 E
Gabon	0	10 S	10	0 E
Galapagos Islands, *Ecuador*	0	0 S	91	0 W
Gambia	13	28 N	16	34 W
Ganges River, *India*	23	20 N	90	30 E
Ganongga I. *see* Ranongga	8	5 S	156	35 E
Gansu Province, *China*	36	0 N	104	0 E
Garhwal, *India*	30	30 N	78	30 E
Gascoyne River, *Australia*	25	0 S	115	0 E
Gaspé Peninsula, *Quebec*	48	63 N	65	71 W
Gau I., *Fiji*	18	0 S	179	30 E
Gebe I., *Halmahera*	0	9 N	129	43 E
Gedeh, Mt., *Java*	6	47 S	106	59 E
Geelvink Bay, *New Guinea*	3	0 S	135	0 E
Gemien I., *New Guinea*	0	20 S	130	30 E
Georgia, *Eurasia*	42	0 N	43	0 E
Georgia, *US*	32	50 N	83	15 W

Germany	51	0 N	10	0 E	Gunong Tahan, *Malaysia*	4	63 N	102	22 E
Ghana	8	0 N	1	0 W	Gunungapi I., *Banda Sea*	6	55 S	126	80 E
Giannutri I., *Tyrrhenian Sea*	42	25 N	11	9 E	Guyana	5	0 N	59	0 W
Gizo I., *Solomon Islands*	8	7 S	156	50 E	Hachijo-jima, *Japan*	33	10 N	139	80 E
Glacier Bay, *Alaska*	58	40 N	136	0 W	Hadramaut, *Saudi Arabia*	14	19 N	46	72 E
Glorieuses, Îles, *Indian Ocean*	11	30 S	47	20 E	Haifa, *Israel*	32	46 N	35	0 E
Gobi Desert	44	0 N	111	0 E	Hainan, *China*	19	0 N	109	30 E
Godavari River, *India*	20	0 N	75	0 E	Haiti, *Hispaniola*	19	0 N	72	30 W
Goiás, *Brazil*	12	10 S	48	0 W	Hall I., *Bering Sea*	60	39 N	173	0 W
Goliath, Mt., *Irian Jaya*	4	41 S	139	48 E	Hall Sound, *New Guinea*	9	0 S	147	0 E
Gonâve I., *Haiti*	18	45 N	73	0 W	Halmahera, *Moluccas*	0	4 N	128	0 E
Gongga Shan, Mt., *China*	29	58 N	101	85 E	Hamersley region, *Australia*	21	50 S	117	30 E
Goodenough I., *D'Entrecasteaux Arch.*	9	20 S	150	15 E	Harar, *Ethiopia*	9	31 N	42	12 E
Gorgona I., *Colombia*	2	97 N	78	18 W	Haruku I., *Moluccas*	3	34 N	128	28 E
Gorong I., *s Moluccas*	4	0 S	131	40 E	Hatutu I., *Marquesas Islands*	7	93 S	140	58 W
Gorongoza, Mt., *Mozambique*	18	39 N	34	4 E	Hawaii, *Hawaiian Islands*	20	0 N	155	0 W
Gough I., *Atlantic Ocean*	40	10 S	9	45 W	Heard I., *Indian Ocean*	53	0 S	74	0 E
Gran Canaria I., *Canary Islands*	27	55 N	15	35 W	Hebei Province *see* Liaoning	40	75 N	122	20 E
Grand Bahama I., *Bahama Islands*	26	40 N	78	30 W	Hejaz, *Saudi Arabia*	26	57 N	37	58 E
Grand Cayman I., *Cayman Islands*	19	40 N	80	30 W	Helgoland, *Germany*	54	10 N	7	53 E
Grand Comoro I., *Indian Ocean*	12	0 S	44	1 E	Heliongjiant, *ne China*	47	20 N	127	70 E
Great Coco I., *Andaman Islands*	14	5 N	93	25 E	Henan Province, *China*	33	87 N	113	53 E
Great Inagua I., *Bahamas*	21	0 N	73	20 W	Henderson I., *French Polynesia*	24	20 S	128	20 W
Great Kei River, *South Africa*	32	0 S	28	0 E	Herald I., *Australia*	16	58 S	149	9 E
Great Nicobar I., *Nicobar Islands*	7	0 N	94	0 E	Hermit Islands, *Bismarck Archipelago*	1	50 S	145	10 E
Great Slave Lake, *Canada*	61	23 N	115	38 W	Hertzog Mountains, *New Guinea*	8	0 S	147	20 E
Greater Antilles, *West Indies*	17	40 N	74	0 W	Hidalgo, *Mexico*	20	30 N	99	10 W
Greece	40	0 N	23	0 E	Hierro I., *Canary Islands*	27	44 N	18	0 W
Green I., *Bismarck Archipelago*	4	35 S	154	10 E	Himachal Pradesh, *India*	31	30 N	77	0 E
Greenland	66	0 N	45	0 W	Himalayas	29	0 N	84	0 E
Grenada, *West Indies*	12	10 N	61	40 W	Hinchinbrook I., *Australia*	18	20 S	146	15 E
Griqualand, *South Africa*	28	49 S	23	15 E	Hindenberg Mountains, *New Guinea*	5	20 S	140	45 E
Groote Eylandt, *Australia*	14	0 S	136	40 E	Hindu Kush Mountains, *Afghanistan*	37	0 N	70	0 E
Grootfontein, *Namibia*	19	31 S	18	6 E	Hispaniola, *West Indies*	10	0 N	71	0 W
Guadalcanal, *Solomon Islands*	9	32 S	160	12 E	Hiu I., *Vanuatu*	13	50 S	166	50 E
Guadalupe I., *Mexico*	29	0 N	118	50 W	Hivaoa, *Marquesas Islands*	9	77 S	139	2 W
Guadeloupe, *West Indies*	16	20 N	61	40 W	Hokkaido, *Japan*	42	0 N	157	0 E
Guaiquinima, Cerro, *Venezuela*	5	82 N	63	69 W	Holbox I., *Mexico*	21	30 N	87	20 W
Guaitecas Islands, *Chile*	44	0 S	74	30 W	Holland *see* Netherlands	52	0 N	5	30 E
Guajira Peninsula, *Colombia*	12	0 N	71	30 W	Honduras	14	40 N	86	30 W
Guam, *Mariana Islands*	13	50 N	144	70 E	Hong Kong	22	11 N	114	14 E
Guanaja I., *Honduras*	16	0 N	87	0 W	Honshu, *Japan*	36	0 N	138	0 E
Guanajuato, *Mexico*	20	40 N	101	20 W	Hood I., *Galapagos Islands*	1	30 S	89	30 W
Guangdong, *China*	23	0 N	113	0 E	Hoste, Isla, *Chile*	55	31 S	68	94 W
Guangxi Province, *China*	24	0 N	109	0 E	Houtman Abrolhos Islands, *Australia*	28	43 S	113	48 E
Guatemala	15	40 N	90	30 W	Hpimaw Hills, *Myanmar*	21	10 N	97	9 E
Guayaquil, Gulf of, *Ecuador*	3	10 S	81	0 W	Hsikang *see* Qinghai, *China*	36	0N	98	0E
Guayas, *Ecuador*	2	30 S	80	35 W	Huahine I., *Society Islands*	16	50 S	150	70 W
Guerrero, *Mexico*	17	30 N	100	0 W	Huallaga, Río, *Peru*	5	15 S	75	30 W
Guimaras I., *Philippines*	10	35 N	122	37 E	Huambo, *Angola*	13	30 S	15	30 E
Guinea	10	20 N	11	30 W	Huambo, *Peru*	6	30 S	79	59 W
Guinea-Bissau	12	0 N	15	0 E	Huancavelica, *Peru*	12	50 S	75	5 W
Guizhou Province, *China*	27	0 N	107	0 E	Huánuco, *Peru*	9	55 S	76	14 W
Gujrat, *Pakistan*	32	40 N	74	2 E	Huapu I. *see* Uapou	9	40 S	140	0 W
Gulf Coast, *US*	30	0 N	88	0 W	Hubei Province, *China*	31	0 N	112	0 E
Gulf of California, *Mexico*	30	0 N	113	0 W	Hudson Bay, *Canada*	60	0 N	86	0 W
Gulf of Guinea	3	0 N	2	30 E	Huila, *Angola*	14	80 S	14	90 E
Gulf of Honduras	16	50 N	87	0 W	Humboldt Bay, *California*	40	45 N	124	25 W
Gulf of St. Lawrence, *Canada*	48	25 N	62	0 W	Humboldt Bay, *New Guinea*	2	40 S	140	0 E

Place					Place				
Hunan Province, *China*	27	30 N	112	0 E	Jordan Valley	31	48 N	34	32 E
Hungary	47	45 N	10	0 E	Jos Plateau, *n Nigeria*	9	53N	8	59 E
Huon Peninsula, *New Guinea*	6	20 S	147	30 E	Juan Fernández Archipelago	33	50 S	80	0 W
Hupeh *see* Hubei	31	0 N	113	0 E	Juárez, Sierra de, *Baja California*	32	0 N	116	0 W
Iberian Peninsula	40	0 N	5	0 W	Jujuy, *Argentina*	23	20 S	65	40 W
Ibuhos I., *Philippines*	20	19 N	121	49 E	Junín, Lake, *Peru*	11	0 S	76	10 W
Ica, *Peru*	14	20 S	75	30 W	Junín, *Peru*	11	30 S	73	0 W
Iceland	64	45 N	19	0 W	Jupiter, *Florida*	27	0 N	80	5 W
Idenburg River, *New Guinea*	13	0 S	138	20 E	Juruá, Rio, *Brazil*	37	0 S	65	44 W
Île-á-Vache, *Haiti*	18	7 N	73	63 W	Kabobo, Mt., *Zaire*	5	2 S	29	5 E
Illinois, *US*	40	15 N	89	30 W	Kadavu I. *see* Kandavu	19	0 S	178	15 E
Inaccessible I., *s Atlantic Ocean*	37	30 S	12	68 W	Kai Islands, *Ceram Sea*	5	55 S	132	45 E
Imbabura, *Ecuador*	0	35 N	78	57 W	Kakemega Forest, *Kenya*	0	20 N	34	46 E
India	20	0 N	78	0 E	Kalahari Desert	24	0 S	21	30 E
Indochina	15	0 N	108	0 E	Kalao I., *Flores Sea*	7	20 S	120	94 E
Inhambane District, *Mozambique*	23	54 S	35	30 E	Kalaotoa I., *Flores Sea*	7	18 S	121	30 E
Innamincka, *Australia*	27	44 S	140	46 E	Kaledupa I., *Banda Sea*	5	51 S	123	73 E
Inner Hebrides, *UK*	57	0 N	6	30 W	Kamchatka Peninsula	55	0 N	160	0 E
Inyo Mountains, *California*	36	40 N	118	0 W	Kampong Baru, *Yapen I.*	1	48 S	136	18 E
Iran	33	0 N	53	0 E	Kampuchea *see* Cambodia	12	15 N	105	0 E
Iraq	33	0 N	44	0 E	Kanaga I., *Aleutians*	51	55 N	177	20 W
Irazú, Volcán, *Costa Rica*	10	0 N	83	55 W	Kandavu I., *Fiji*	19	0 S	178	15 E
Ireland	53	50 N	7	52 W	Kangaroo I., *Australia*	35	45 S	137	0 E
Irian Jaya, *Indonesia*	4	0 S	137	0 E	Kangean Islands, *Java Sea*	6	91 S	115	35 E
Iringa region, *Tanzania*	7	50 S	35	40 E	Kangra, *India*	32	10 N	76	23 E
Iriomote, *Ryukyu Islands*	24	20 N	123	55 E	Kansas, *US*	38	30 N	99	0 W
Irrawaddy River, *Myanmar*	20	0 N	95	0 E	Kansu *see* Gansu	36	0 N	104	0 E
Isabela I., *Galapagos Islands*	0	5 S	91	0 W	Kapiti I., *New Zealand*	40	50 S	174	56 E
Ishigaki, *Ryukyu Islands*	24	30 N	124	7 E	Kara Kum Mountains, *Turkmenistan*	39	30 N	60	0 E
Isiolo, *Kenya*	0	24 N	37	33 E	Karakelong I., *Talaud Islands*	4	29 N	126	79 E
Israel	32	0 N	34	50 E	Karelia, *Russia*	63	70 N	33	60 E
Italy	42	0 N	13	0 E	Karimata Islands, *sw Borneo*	1	0 S	107	10 E
Itbayat I., *Philippines*	20	47 N	121	51 E	Karimunjawa Islands *Java Sea*	5	81 S	110	46 E
Itombwe Mountains, *Zaire/Uganda*	0	33 S	29	16 E	Karkar I., *Papua New Guinea*	4	40 S	146	0 E
Ituri Forest, *Zaire*	1	40 N	27	1 E	Kashmir, *India*	34	0 N	76	0 E
Ivojos I., *Philippines*	20	19 N	121	49 E	Katanglad, Mt., *Philippines*	8	6 N	124	54 E
Ivory Coast	7	30 N	5	0 W	Katchall I., *Nicobar Islands*	8	0 N	93	30 E
Iwo Jima, *Volcano Islands*	24	78 N	141	32 E	Kathiawar Peninsula, *nw India*	21	81 N	70	66 E
Izu Islands, *Japan*	34	30 N	140	0 W	Kauai, *Hawaiian Islands*	22	3 N	159	30 W
Jalisco, *Mexico*	20	0 N	104	0 W	Kayoa I., *Moluccas*	0	4 N	127	42 E
Jaluit I., *Marshall Islands*	6	0 N	169	30 E	Kazakstan	48	0 N	55	0 E
Jamaica, *West Indies*	18	10 N	77	30 W	Kazan-Retto *see* Volcano Islands	25	10 N	143	50 E
James Bay, *Canada*	51	30 N	80	0 W	Keeling Islands *see* Cocos Islands	12	10 S	96	55 E
James I., *Galapagos Islands*	0	23 S	90	75 W	Kemp Welch River, *New Guinea*	9	20 S	147	40 E
Jan Mayen I., *Arctic*	71	0 N	9	0 W	Kenai Peninsula, *Alaska*	60	0 N	150	0 W
Japan	36	0 N	139	0 E	Kenya	1	0 N	38	0 E
Japen I. *see* Yapen	1	50 S	136	0 E	Kenya, Mt., *Kenya*	0	14 S	37	30 E
Java Sea, *Indonesia*	4	35 S	107	15 E	Kerala, *India*	11	0 N	76	15 E
Java, *Indonesia*	7	0 S	110	0 E	Kerguelen Islands, *Indian Ocean*	49	15 S	69	10 E
Javarí, Rio, *Brazil/Peru*	5	0 S	72	0 W	Kericho, *Kenya*	0	36 S	35	26 E
Jayawijaya Mountains	4	30 S	139	30 E	Kermadec I., *Pacific Ocean*	30	0 S	178	15 W
Jebel Marra Massif, *Sudan*	13	6 N	24	22 E	Key West, *Florida*	24	40 N	81	30 W
Jervis I., *Galapagos Islands*	0	40 S	90	72 W	Khao Kuap, *Thailand*	12	25 N	102	50 E
Jiangsu Province, *e China*	33	0 N	119	0 E	Kharga Oasis, *Egypt*	25	10 N	30	35 E
Jiangxi Province, *se China*	27	26 N	116	1 E	Khartoum, *Egypt*	15	31 N	32	35 E
Jimi River, *New Guinea*	5	0 S	145	25 E	Khasi Hills, *India*	25	30 N	91	30 E
Johnston Atoll, *Pacific Ocean*	16	70 N	169	51 W	Khingan Mountains, *n Manchuria*	48	12 N	130	78 E
Jolo Group, *Sulu Archipelago*	6	0 N	121	9 E	Kiangsi *see* Jiangxi	27	26 N	116	1 E
Jordan	31	0 N	36	0 E	Kilimanjaro, Mt., *Tanzania*	3	7 S	38	0 E

Kimberley Division, *Australia*	17	30 S	127	30 E	Labrador, *Canada*	53	20 N	61	0 W
Kinabalu, Mt., *Borneo*	6	3 N	116	14 E	Labuan I., *nw Borneo*	5	31 N	115	21 E
King I., *Australia*	39	50 S	144	0 E	Laccadive Islands, *Indian Ocean*	10	0 N	72	30 E
King Sound, *Australia*	16	50 S	123	20 E	Ladakh, *India*	34	0 N	78	0 E
Kioa I., *Fiji*	16	40 S	179	58 E	Lahul, *India*	31	40 N	78	0 E
Kirgiz Mountains, *Kyrgystan*	41	64 N	74	94 E	Lakhimpur, *ne India*	27	95 N	80	77 E
Kiribati, *Micronesia*	11	64 N	166	43 E	Lali Hills, *Kenya*	2	55 S	39	20 E
Kiritimati I., *Kiribati*	1	89 N	157	38 W	Lambayeque, *Peru*	6	45 S	80	0 W
Kisar I., *Lesser Sundas*	8	5 S	127	0 E	Lamu, *Kenya*	2	17 S	40	54 E
Kiska I., *Aleutians*	51	59 N	177	30 E	Lanai, *Hawaiian Islands*	20	83 N	156	92 W
Kita-Daito-jima I., *Japan*	25	94 N	131	31 E	Langbian Plateau, *Laos*	20	0 N	102	20 E
Kivu Mountains, *Zaire*	3	10 S	27	0 E	Lan-yü I., *Taiwan*	22	4 N	121	55 E
Kobrar I. *see* Kobroor	6	10 S	134	30 E	Lanzarote I., *Canary Islands*	29	0 N	13	40 W
Kobroor I., *New Guinea*	6	10 S	134	30 E	Laos	17	45 N	105	0 E
Kodiak I., *Alaska*	57	30 N	152	45 W	Lapland, *Europe*	68	7 N	24	0 E
Kofiau I., *New Guinea*	1	11 S	129	50 E	Lara, *Venezuela*	10	10 N	69	50 W
Kokonor, *China*	37	0 N	100	3 E	Larat I., *Sulawesi*	7	13 S	131	85 E
Ko Kut I., *Thailand*	11	66 N	102	56 E	Lasia I., *Sumatra*	2	17 N	96	63 E
Kola Peninsula, *Russia*	67	30 N	38	0 E	Lau Archipelago, *Fiji*	17	0 S	178	30 W
Kolombangara I. *see* Kulambangra I.	7	98 S	157	6 E	Laysan I., *Pacific Ocean*	25	30 N	167	0 W
Kolyma River, *Russia*	69	30 N	161	0 E	Lebanon	34	0 N	36	0 E
Komandorskiye Islands, *Russia*	55	0 N	167	0 E	Leeward Islands, *Atlantic Ocean*	17	85 N	42	60 W
Kongelia, *Kenya*	2	5 N	35	0 E	Leizhou Bandao Peninsula, *China*	20	84 N	110	0 E
Kordofan Province, *Sudan*	12	0 N	30	0 E	Lelet Plateau, *New Ireland*	3	4 S	151	50 E
Korea	38	0 N	127	50 E	Lembeh I., *Sulawesi*	1	50 N	125	25 E
Koro I., *Fiji*	17	20 S	179	50 E	Lena River, *Russia*	72	52 N	126	40 E
Kosrae, *Caroline Islands*	5	20 N	163	0 E	Lenkoran, *Azerbaijan*	38	45 N	48	50 E
Kra, Isthmus of, *Malaysia*	10	15 N	99	30 E	Lerma, Río, *Mexico*	19	20 N	99	10 W
Krakatau I., *Java*	6	14 S	105	44 E	Lesotho	29	50 S	28	50 E
Kuching District, *Sarawak*	1	33 N	110	25 E	Lesser Antilles	15	0 N	61	0 W
Kulal, Mt., *Kenya*	2	77 N	36	92 E	Lesser Sundas, *Indonesia*	9	0 S	120	0 E
Kulambangra I., *Solomon Islands*	7	98 S	157	6 E	Leti I., *Timor*	8	10 S	128	0 E
Kumaon, *Himalayas*	30	5 N	79	92 E	Leyte, *Philippines*	11	0 N	125	0 E
Kumawa Mountains, *Irian Jaya*	3	85 S	133	0 E	Liaoning Province, *China*	40	75 N	122	20 E
Kumbo Highlands, *Cameroon*	6	15 N	10	36 E	Liberia	6	30 N	9	30 W
Kumusi River, *Papua New Guinea*	8	16 S	148	13 E	Libya	27	0 N	17	0 E
Kungwe-Mahali Mountains, *Tanzania*	6	20 S	30	0 E	Lifou I., *New Caledonia*	21	0 S	167	20 E
Kunlun Shan Mountains, *China*	36	0 N	86	30 E	Lihir Group, *Bismarck Archipelago*	3	0 S	152	35 E
Kur I., *Banda Sea*	5	33 S	131	92 E	Likiang Mountains, *China*	24	0 N	102	40 E
Kuril Islands, *Russia*	45	0 N	150	0 E	Lima, *Peru*	12	0 S	77	0 W
Kusaie *see* Kosrae	5	20 N	163	0 E	Limpopo River, *Africa*	25	5 S	33	30 E
Kutch, *India*	24	0 N	70	0 E	Linapacan I., *Palawan*	11	48 N	120	3 E
Kwangsi *see* Guangxi	24	0 N	109	0 E	Linchow Pen. *see* Leizhou Bandao	20	84 N	110	0 E
Kwangtung *see* Guangdong	23	0 N	113	0 E	Line Islands	0	0 S	160	0 W
Kwazulu-Natal, *South Africa*	27	30 S	31	0 E	Lingga Archipelago, *Malaysia*	0	10 S	104	30 E
Kweichow *see* Guizhou	27	0 N	107	0 E	Little Barrier I., *New Zealand*	36	12 S	175	8 E
Kyrgyzstan	41	64 N	74	94 E	Little Cayman I., *West Indies*	19	41 N	80	3 W
Kyushu I., *Japan*	33	0 N	131	0 E	Little Coco I., *Andaman Islands*	12	30 N	92	30 E
Kyzl Kum Mountains, *Uzbekistan*	42	30 N	65	0 E	Little Kiska I., *Aleutians*	51	59 N	178	0 E
La Blanquilla, Isla, *Venezuela*	11	50 N	64	40 W	Llanquihue, *Chile*	41	30 S	73	0 W
La Digue I., *Seychelles*	4	22 S	55	50 E	Lofoten I., *Norway*	68	30 N	14	0 E
La Gomera I., *Canary Islands*	28	3 N	17	15 W	Lofty Range, *Australia*	24	0 S	119	0 E
La Libertad, *Peru*	8	0 S	78	30 W	Loh I., *Vanuatu*	13	55 S	166	55 E
La Palma I., *Canary Islands*	28	40 N	17	50 W	Loja, *Ecuador*	3	59 S	79	16 W
La Pampa, *Argentina*	36	50 S	60	0 W	Loliondo, *Tanzania*	2	3 S	35	40 E
La Paz, *Bolivia*	15	30 S	68	0 W	Lolobau I., *New Britain*	4	92 S	151	16 E
La Plata, Isla, *Ecuador*	1	18 S	81	5 W	Lomblen I., *Lesser Sundas*	8	30 S	123	32 E
La Rioja, *Argentina*	29	2 S	67	0 W	Lombok, *Lesser Sundas*	8	45 S	116	30 E
La Tortuga, Isla, *Venezuela*	11	0 N	65	30 W	Lomlon I., *Solomon Islands*	10	30 S	166	50 E

Place	Lat °	Lat ′	Long °	Long ′
Lompobattang, Mt., *Sulawesi*	5	22 S	119	58 E
Long I, *Papua New Guinea*	5	20 S	147	5 E
Long I., *US*	40	45 N	73	30 W
Lop Nur, *China*	40	31 N	90	28 E
Lord Howe I., *New Zealand*	31	33 S	159	6 E
Lore Lindu National Park, *Sulawesi*	1	35 S	120	20 E
Lorentz River, *New Guinea*	5	52 S	138	42 E
Los Frailes, Islas, *Venezuela*	11	15 N	64	45 W
Los Hermanos, Islas, *Venezuela*	11	45 N	64	25 W
Los Roques, Islas, *Venezuela*	11	82 N	66	74 W
Los Testigos, Islas, *Venezuela*	11	37 N	63	13 W
Louisiade Arch., *Papua New Guinea*	11	10 S	153	0 E
Louisiana, *US*	30	50 N	92	0 W
Loyalty Islands, *New Caledonia*	20	50 S	166	30 E
Luang I., *Lesser Sundas*	8	11 S	128	43 E
Luangwa Valley, *Zambia*	13	30 S	31	30 E
Lubang I., *Philippines*	13	52 N	120	7 E
Luzon, *Philippines*	16	0 N	121	0 E
Mackay, *Australia*	21	8 S	149	11 E
Mackenzie Basin, *New Zealand*	44	10 S	170	25 E
Mackenzie River, *Canada*	69	10 N	134	20 W
Macquarie I., *Australia*	54	36 S	158	55 E
Madagascar	20	0 S	47	0 E
Madeira, *Atlantic Ocean*	32	50 N	17	0 W
Madeira, Rio, *Brazil*	3	22 S	58	45 W
Madhya Pradesh, *India*	22	50 N	78	0 E
Madras, *India*	13	8 N	80	19 E
Madre de Dios, *Peru*	12	0 S	71	0 W
Madu I., *Flores Sea*	7	31 S	121	47 E
Madura I., *Lesser Sundas*	7	30 S	113	0 E
Maewo I., *Vanuatu*	15	10 S	168	10 E
Mafia I., *Tanzania*	7	45 S	39	50 E
Magdalena Bay, *Baja California*	24	30 N	112	10 W
Magdalena Valley, *Colombia*	11	06 N	74	57 W
Magellan, Straits of	52	30 S	75	0 W
Magellanes, *Chile*	54	5 S	72	39 W
Mahé, *Seychelles*	5	0 S	55	30 E
Mahenge, *Tanzania*	8	41 S	36	41 E
Maine, *USA*	45	20 N	69	0 W
Makatea, *Tuamotu Archipelago*	15	83 S	148	25 W
Makgadikgadi, *Botswana*	20	40 S	25	45 E
Makira I. *see San Cristóbal I.*	10	30 S	161	0 E
Malabar coast, *India*	11	0 N	75	0 E
Malaita I., *Solomon Islands*	9	0 S	161	0 E
Malakulu I., *Vanuatu*	16	23 S	167	46 E
Malamaui I., *Philippines*	6	73 N	121	95 E
Malanje, *Angola*	9	32 S	16	20 E
Malawi	11	55 S	34	0 E
Malay Peninsula	7	27 N	100	0 E
Maldive Islands, *Indian Ocean*	5	0 N	73	0 E
Mali	17	0 N	3	0 W
Malindang, Mt., *Philippines*	8	21 N	123	62 E
Malleco, *Chile*	38	10 S	72	20 W
Malo I., *Vanuatu*	15	67 S	167	16 E
Malta, *Mediterranean Sea*	35	90 N	14	40 E
Maltahöhe, *Namibia*	24	55 S	17	0 E
Mamberamo River, *New Guinea*	2	0 S	137	50 E
Mamberiok Peninsula *see* Vogelkop	1	25 S	133	0 E
Mamoré, Río, *Bolivia*	10	23 S	65	53 W
Manabi, *Ecuador*	0	30 S	80	0 W
Manacapurú, *Brazil*	3	16 S	60	37 W
Manam I., *Papua New Guinea.*	4	5 S	145	0 E
Manchuria, *China*	42	0 N	125	0 E
Manda I., *Kenya*	2	25 S	40	94 E
Mangaia I., *Cook Islands*	21	80 S	158	0 W
Mangareva I., *Tuamotu Archipelago*	23	30 S	134	50 W
Mangere I., *Chatham Islands*	18	55 S	159	45 W
Mango I., *Tonga*	20	15 S	174	30 W
Mangole I., *Sula Islands*	1	50 S	125	55 E
Manipa I., *Moluccas*	3	18 S	127	33 E
Manipur Hills, *India*	25	0 N	94	0 E
Manitoba, *Canada*	55	30 N	97	0 W
Mantanani I., *Borneo*	6	50 N	116	30 E
Manua Islands, *American Samoa*	14	13 S	169	35 W
Manipa I., *Moluccas*	3	30 S	127	54 E
Manus I., *Admiralty Islands*	2	0 S	147	0 E
Maracaibo, Lake, *Venezuela*	9	40 N	71	30 W
Maranhão, *Brazil*	5	0 S	46	0 W
Marajó, Ilha de, *Brazil*	1	1 S	49	74 W
Marañón, Río, *Peru*	6	0 S	76	0 W
Maratua Archipelago, *Borneo*	21	0 N	118	35 E
Marcapata Valley, *Peru*	13	31 S	70	52 W
Marchena I, *Galapagos Islands*	0	35 N	90	47 W
Marcus I., *Japan*	24	28 N	153	97 E
Maré, *Loyalty Islands*	21	30 S	168	0 E
Margarita I., *Venezuela*	11	0 N	64	0 W
María Madre I., *Mexico*	21	40 N	106	45 W
Mariana Islands, *Pacific Ocean*	13	0 N	145	0 E
Marinduque, *Philippines*	13	25 N	122	0 E
Marion I., *Indian Ocean*	47	0 S	38	0 E
Marquesas Islands, *French Polynesia*	9	30 S	140	0 W
Marshall Islands, *Pacific Ocean*	9	0 N	171	0 E
Martín Vaz I., *Atlantic Ocean*	20	20 S	28	50 W
Martinique, *West Indies*	14	40 N	61	0 W
Marungu, *Zaire*	7	71 S	29	86 E
Masafuera I. *see* Alejandro Selkirk I.	33	50 S	79	0 W
Masalembu Besar, *Java Sea*	5	55 S	114	43 E
Masatierra I. *see* Robinson Crusoe I.	33	50 S	80	46 W
Masbate I., *Philippines*	12	21 N	123	36 E
Mascarene Islands, *Indian Ocean*	22	0 S	55	0 E
Matasiri I., *Java Sea*	4	48 S	115	45 E
Mato Grosso, *Brazil*	14	0 S	55	0 W
Maui, *Hawaiian Islands*	20	48 N	156	20 W
Mauke I., *Cook Islands*	20	5 S	156	0 W
Maule, *Chile*	36	05 S	72	30 W
Maupiti I., *Society Islands*	16	30 S	152	50 W
Mauritania	20	50 N	10	0 W
Mauritius, *Indian Ocean*	20	0 S	57	0 E
Mayotte, *Indian Ocean*	12	50 S	45	10 E
Mayu I., *Moluccas*	1	33 N	126	39 E
Mbua I., *Fiji*	16	41 S	179	7 E
McArthur River, *Australia*	16	27 S	136	7 E
McDonald I., *Indian Ocean*	53	0 S	73	0 E
McKinley, Mt., *Philippine Islands*	6	59 N	125	16 E
Mediterranean Sea	35	0 N	15	0 E
Mednyi I., *Russia*	78	50 N	95	0 E
Mega, *Ethiopia*	3	57 N	38	19 E
Mekong Delta, *Indochina*	9	30 N	106	15 E

Mekonga, Mt., *Sulawesi*	3	63 S	121	24 E	Moorea, *French Polynesia*	17	30 S	149	60 E
Melville I., *Australia*	11	30 S	131	0 E	Mopti, *Ghana*	6	82 N	0	13 W
Menawa, Mt., *New Guinea*	3	18 S	141	33 E	Morelos, *Mexico*	18	40 N	99	10 W
Mendoza, *Argentina*	33	0 S	69	0 W	Mores I., *Bahamas*	26	20 N	77	35 W
Mentawi Archipelago, *Sumatra*	2	0 S	99	0 E	Morocco	32	0 N	5	50 W
Meos Num I, *New Guinea*	1	25 S	136	21 E	Morogoro, *Tanzania*	6	81 S	37	66 E
Merauke, *New Guinea*	8	29 S	140	24 E	Morotai, *Moluccas*	2	10 N	128	30 E
Mergui Archipelago, *Myanmar*	11	30 N	97	30 E	Motagua River, *Guatemala*	15	44 N	88	14 W
Mérida, *Venezuela*	9	0 N	71	0 W	Motagua Valley, *Guatemala*	15	0 N	90	0 W
Merumé Mountains, *Guyana*	5	40 N	60	0 W	Motane, *Marquesas Islands*	9	98 S	138	82 W
Meta, *Colombia*	3	30 N	73	0 W	Mozambique	19	0 S	35	0 E
Mexiana, Ilha, *Brazil*	0	2 S	49	56 W	Mugodzhary Mountains, *Kazakstan*	48	83 N	58	55 E
Mexico	25	0 N	105	0 W	Mujeres, Isla de, *Mexico*	21	30 N	86	0 W
Miahuatlán, Sierra de, *Mexico*	16	21 N	96	36 W	Mulanje, Mt., *Malawi*	16	0 S	35	30 E
Miangas I., *Sulawesi*	5	55 N	126	58 E	Müller Mountains, *Borneo*	0	35 N	113	50 E
Michigan, *US*	44	0 N	85	0 W	Mulu, Mt., *Sarawak*	4	6 N	114	92 E
Michoacán, *Mexico*	19	0 N	102	0 W	Muna I., *Sulawesi*	5	0 S	122	30 E
Micronesia, *Oceania*	11	0 N	155	0 E	Murchison River, *Australia*	27	45 S	114	0 E
Mikura-jima, *Japan*	33	87 N	139	60 E	Murmansk, *Russia*	68	57 N	33	10 E
Milne Bay, *New Guinea*	10	30 S	150	40 E	Murua I. *see* Woodlark I.	9	10 S	152	50 E
Mimika River, *New Guinea*	4	30 S	137	30 E	Mussau I., *Bismarck Archipelago*	1	30 S	149	40 E
Minami-Daito-jima, *Japan*	25	84 N	131	24 E	Mwali I. *see* Mohéli I.	12	20 S	43	30 E
Minami-Io-jima, *Volcano Islands*	24	24 N	141	46 E	Myanmar	21	0 N	96	30 E
Minami-Torishima *see* Marcus I.	24	28 N	153	97 E	Mysore, *India*	12	17 N	76	41 E
Minas Gerais, *Brazil*	18	50 S	46	0 W	Naga Hills, *Myanmar*	26	0 N	95	0 E
Mindanao, *Philippines*	8	40 N	125	0 E	Namaqualand, *South Africa*	30	0 S	17	25 E
Mindoro, *Philippines*	13	0 N	121	0 E	Namibia	22	0 S	18	9 E
Minnesota, *US*	46	0 N	94	15 W	Namuli, Mt., *Mozambique*	15	25 S	37	0 E
Miquelon, *Newfoundland*	47	4 N	56	33 W	Nan Shan Mountains, *China*	39	0 N	97	0 E
Miranda, *Venezuela*	10	15 N	66	25 W	Nandi Hills, *Kenya*	0	11 N	35	18 E
Mirituba, *Brazil*	4	25 S	55	88 W	Nanyuki, *Kenya*	0	2 N	37	7 E
Mishmi Hills, *ne India*	29	0 N	90	0 E	Naochow I., *China*	20	90 N	110	60 E
Misima I., *Louisiade Archipelago*	10	38 S	152	45 E	Napo, Río, *Ecuador*	3	20 S	72	40 W
Misiones Province, *Argentina*	27	0 S	56	0 W	Narcondam I., *Andaman Islands*	13	24 N	94	15 E
Misool I., *New Guinea*	1	52 S	130	10 E	Nariño, *Colombia*	1	30 N	78	0 W
Mississippi River, *US*	38	37 N	90	12 W	Nassau Range, *New Guinea*	4	0 S	139	30 E
Missouri, *USA*	38	25 N	92	30 W	Nasser, Lake, *Egypt*	23	0 N	33	0 E
Misuku Hills, *Malawi*	10	30 S	33	30 E	Natal, *South Africa*	28	5 S	32	0 E
Mitchell River, *Australia*	15	12 S	141	35 E	Natuna Islands, *China Sea*	4	0 N	108	15 E
Mitiaro I., *Cook Islands*	19	80 S	157	71 W	Nauru I., *Melanesia*	2	49 S	164	83 E
Miyake-Jima, *Ryukyu Islands*	24	45 N	125	20 E	Navarino I., *Chile*	55	0 S	67	40 W
Moa I., *Timor*	8	0 S	128	0 E	Navassa I., *Hispaniola*	18	41 N	75	0 W
Moçamedes, *Angola*	15	22 S	12	38 E	Nayarit, *Mexico*	22	0 N	105	0 W
Mocha I., *Chile*	38	22 S	73	56 W	Neblina, Cerro de la, *Venezuela*	0	83 N	65	99 W
Mogador *see* Essaouira	31	32 N	9	42 W	Nebraska, *US*	41	30 N	99	30 W
Mohéli, *Comoro Islands*	12	20 S	43	30 E	Negro, Río, *Argentina*	39	74 S	65	31 W
Moka Highlands, *Bioko*	3	30 N	8	40 E	Negro, Rio, *Brazil*	3	0 S	60	0 W
Molokai, *Hawaiian Islands*	21	14 N	157	1 W	Negro, Río, *Guatemala*	15	9 N	90	0 W
Moluccas, *Indonesia*	1	60 S	128	0 E	Negros I., *Philippines*	9	30 N	122	40 E
Mona I., *Puerto Rico*	18	30 N	67	45 W	Nenusa Islands, *Moluccas*	4	74 N	127	11 E
Mona I. *see* Muna I., *Sulawesi*	5	0 S	122	30 E	Nepal	28	0 N	84	0 E
Monagas, *Venezuela*	9	20 N	63	0 W	Netherlands	52	0 N	5	30 E
Mongolia	47	0 N	103	0 E	Netherlands Antilles	12	15 N	69	0 W
Mono I., *Solomon Islands*	7	20 S	155	35 E	Neuquén, *Argentina*	38	55 S	68	5 W
Montana, *US*	47	0 N	110	0 W	Nevis I., *West Indies*	17	0 N	62	30 W
Montecristo I., *Tyrrhenian Sea*	42	34 N	10	30 E	New Britain, *Bismarck Archipelago*	5	50 S	150	20 E
Monterey Bay, *California*	36	50 N	122	0 W	New Caledonia	21	0 S	165	0 E
Montserrat, *West Indies*	16	40 N	62	10 W	New Georgia Group, *Solomon Islands*	8	15 S	157	30 E
Moore River, *Australia*	31	22 S	115	30 E	New Guinea	4	0 S	136	0 E

Place	Lat °		Lon °	
New Hanover, *Bismarck Archipelago*	2	30 S	150	10 E
New Hebrides *see* Vanuatu	15	0 S	168	0 E
New Ireland, *Bismarck Archipelago*	3	20 S	151	50 E
New Mexico, *US*	34	30 N	106	0 W
New Providence I., *Bahamas*	25	25 N	78	35 W
New Siberian Islands, *Russia*	75	0 N	142	0 E
New South Wales, *Australia*	33	0 S	146	0 E
New York, *US*	41	0 N	74	0 W
New Zealand	41	40 S	174	0 E
Newfoundland, *Canada*	53	0 N	58	0 W
Ngau I., *Fiji*	18	0 S	179	30 E
Ngoc Linh, Mount, *Vietnam*	15	4 N	107	59 E
Ngorongoro Crater, *Tanzania*	3	8 S	35	40 E
Nias I., *Sumatra*	1	0 N	97	30 E
Niau I., *Tuamotu Archipelago*	16	0 S	147	0 W
Nibo, *Papua New Guinea*	3	28 S	142	12 E
Nicaragua	11	40 N	85	30 W
Nicobar Islands, *Bay of Bengal*	9	0 N	93	0 E
Niue I., *Cook Islands*	19	0 S	178	0 W
Niger	17	30 N	10	0 E
Niger River, *Africa*	6	0 N	6	47 E
Nigeria	8	30 N	8	0 E
Nightingale I., *s Atlantic Ocean*	37	41 S	12	48 W
Nihoa, *w Hawaiian Islands*	23	6 N	161	92 W
Nila I., *Lesser Sundas*	7	0 S	129	30 E
Nile Valley, *Egypt*	25	0 N	31	0 E
Nilgiri Hills, *India*	12	0 N	78	0 E
Nimba, Mt., *Liberia*	7	30 N	8	35 W
Ningxia Province, *China*	37	26 N	105	94 E
Ninigo Group, *Admiralty Islands*	1	10 S	144	30 E
Nipa I., *Papua New Guinea*	6	11 S	143	27 E
Nissan I., *Bismarck Archipelago*	5	0 S	154	20 E
Niuafou I., *central Polynesia*	15	30 S	175	58 W
Niue I., *Cook Islands*	19	2 S	169	54 W
Noir I., *Chile*	54	48 S	73	1 W
Nonsuch I., *Bermuda*	32	45 N	65	0 W
Noord River *see* Lorentz River	4	52 S	138	42 E
Norfolk I., *New Zealand*	28	58 S	168	3 E
Normanton, *Australia*	17	40 S	141	5 E
Norte de Santander, *Colombia*	8	0 N	73	0 W
North Carolina, *US*	35	30 N	80	0 W
North Dakota, *US*	47	30 N	100	15 W
North I., *New Zealand*	38	0 S	175	0 E
North Korea	40	0 N	127	0 E
North Yemen	16	0 N	44	0 E
Northeast I., *Snares Islands*	48	1 S	166	34 E
Northern Territory, *Australia*	20	0 S	133	0 E
Norway	63	0 N	11	0 E
Nosy Bé, *Madagascar*	13	30 S	48	10 E
Nosy Mitsio, *Madagascar*	12	88 S	48	61 E
Nova Scotia	45	10 N	63	0 W
Novaya Zemlya, *Russia*	75	0 N	56	0 E
Ñuble, *Chile*	37	0 S	72	0 W
Nuevo León, *Mexico*	25	0 N	100	0 W
Nuguria Islands, *Bismarck Archipelago*	3	28 S	150	49 E
Nukuhiva, *Marquesas*	8	87 S	140	14 W
Nullarbor Plain	31	0 S	128	0 E
Num I. *see* Meos Num	1	30 S	135	10 E
Numfor I., *New Guinea*	1	4 S	134	89 E
Nusa Penida, *Lesser Sundas*	8	25 S	115	27 E
Nzwani I. *see* Anjouan I.	12	0 S	44	0 E
Oahu, *Hawaiian Islands*	21	28 N	157	58 W
Oaxaca, *Mexico*	17	0 N	97	0 W
Ob River, *Russia*	66	45 N	69	30 E
Obi I., *n Moluccas*	1	23 S	127	45 E
Obidos, *Brazil*	1	50 S	55	30 W
Obilatu I., *Moluccas*	1	25 S	127	20 E
Obudu Plateau, *Nigeria*	6	38 N	9	5 E
Ocaña, Sierra de, *Colombia*	8	15 N	73	20 W
Ofu I., *American Samoa*	14	11 S	169	41 W
Ogaden Depression, *Ethiopia*	7	30 N	45	30 E
Ogasawara Islands *see* Bonin Islands	27	0 N	144	0 E
Ogea Levu I., *Fiji Islands*	19	15 S	178	39 W
Okhotsk, Sea of, *Russia*	55	0 N	145	0 E
Okinawa, *Japan*	26	40 N	128	0 E
Oklahoma, *US*	35	20 N	97	30 W
Oku, Mt., *Cameroon*	6	20 N	10	45 E
Olancho Department, *Honduras*	15	30 N	86	30 W
Olosega I., *American Samoa*	14	11 S	169	40 W
Olympic Peninsula, *Washington*	47	80 N	123	60 W
Oman	23	0 N	58	0 E
Ométepe, Isla de, *Nicaragua*	11	32 N	85	35 W
Onin Peninsula, *Irian Jaya*	2	50 S	132	0 E
Ono I., *Fiji*	18	55 S	178	29 E
Ontario, *Canada*	48	0 N	83	0 W
Orange Free State, *South Africa*	28	30 S	27	0 E
Orange River, *South Africa*	30	50 S	27	15 E
Orangerie Bay, *New Guinea*	10	16 S	148	48 E
Oranje Mountains *see* Jayawijaya Mts.	4	30 S	139	30 E
Oregon, *US*	44	0 N	121	0 W
Orinoco River, *Venezuela*	9	15 N	61	30 W
Orissa, *ne India*	20	20 N	84	26 E
Orizaba, Mt, *Mexico*	18	51 N	97	6 W
Orkney Islands, *UK*	59	0 N	3	0 W
Otago I., *New Zealand*	45	15 S	170	0 E
Ouarzazarte, *Morocco*	30	94 N	6	89 W
Ouvéa I. *see* Uvéa I.	20	30 S	166	35 E
Ovalau, *Fiji*	17	40 S	178	48 E
Owen Stanley Mountains, *New Guinea*	8	30 S	147	0 E
Owens Valley, *California*	36	32 N	117	59 W
Oyapock River, *French Guiana*	2	86 N	52	43 W
Pacasmayo, *Peru*	7	20 S	79	35 W
Pagai Islands, *Sumatra*	3	0 S	100	15 E
Pagalu, *Gulf of Guinea*	1	25 S	5	36 E
Pagan I., *n Mariana Islands*	18	12 N	145	77 E
Pahang, *Malaysia*	3	62 N	102	85 E
Paita, *Peru*	5	11 S	81	9 W
Pakistan	30	0 N	70	0 E
Palau Islands, *Caroline Islands*	7	30 N	134	30 E
Palawan, *Philippines*	9	30 N	118	30 E
Paloe I., *Flores*	8	33 S	121	71 E
Palu, Gulf of, *Sulawesi*	1	0 S	119	52 E
Pamean I., *India*	9	28 N	79	30 E
Pamir Mountains, *Tajikistan*	37	40 N	73	0 E
Pan de Azucar, *Philippines*	11	17 N	123	10 E
Panama	8	48 N	79	55 W
Panaitan I. *w Java*	6	58 S	105	19 E
Panaon I., *Philippines*	10	3 N	125	13 E

Location	Lat °	Lat ′	Lon °	Lon ′
Panay I., *Philippines*	11	10 N	122	30 E
Pantar I., *Lesser Sundas*	8	28 S	124	10 E
Pantelleria I., *Mediterranean Sea*	36	78 N	12	0 E
Papandayan, Mt., *Java*	7	20 S	107	44 E
Pará, *Brazil*	3	20 S	52	0 W
Paracas Peninsula, *Peru*	13	53 S	76	20 W
Paracel Islands, *South China Sea*	17	0 N	112	30 E
Paraguai-Paraná system	25	36 S	57	0 W
Paraguay	23	0 S	57	0 W
Paraíba, *Brazil*	7	03 S	36	0 W
Paramushir I., *Sea of Okhotsk*	50	36 N	155	78 E
Paraná, *Brazil*	12	30 S	47	48 W
Paraná, Río, *Argentina*	33	43 S	59	15 W
Paría Peninsula, *Venezuela*	11	0 N	62	0 W
Pasco, *Peru*	10	40 S	75	0 W
Patagonia, *Argentina*	45	0 S	69	0 W
Patía Valley, *Colombia*	1	56 N	78	0 W
Pavuvu, *Solomon Islands*	9	4 S	159	8 E
Pearl Islands, *Panama*	8	41 N	79	7 W
Pebas, *Peru*	3	10 S	71	46 W
Pegu Yoma Mountains, *Myanmar*	19	30 N	95	82 E
Peleng I., *Sulawesi*	1	20 S	123	30 E
Pemba I., *Tanzania*	5	0 S	39	45 E
Peña Blanca, *Nicaragua*	14	0 N	85	0 W
Penang I., *Malaysia*	5	25 E	100	15 E
Pegunungan Barisan Mts., *Sumatra*	3	5 S	102	30 E
Penner Valley, *India*	14	35 N	80	10 E
Pennsylvania, *US*	40	45 N	77	30 W
Pensacola, *Florida*	30	25 N	87	13 W
Pequeni Río, *Panama*	9	20 N	79	30 W
Perijá, Sierra de, *Colombia/Venezuela*	9	30 N	73	3 W
Pernambuco, *Brazil*	8	0 S	35	0 W
Persian Gulf	27	0 N	50	0 E
Perth, *Australia*	31	57 S	115	52 E
Peru	4	0 S	75	0 W
Pescadores Islands, *China*	23	57 N	119	60 E
Petén, *Guatemala*	16	58 N	89	50 W
Philippines	12	0 N	123	0 E
Phillip I., *Australia*	38	30 S	145	12 E
Phoenix Islands, *Kiribati*	3	30 S	172	0 W
Phu Quoc I., *Vietnam*	10	31 N	103	93 e
Piauí, *Brazil*	7	0 S	43	0 W
Pichincha, *Ecuador*	0	10 S	78	40 W
Pinang I. *see* Penang	5	25 N	100	15 E
Pines, Isle of, *Cuba*	21	40 N	82	40 W
Pines, Isle of, *New Caledonia*	22	30 S	167	30 E
Pirre, Mt., *Panama*	7	57 N	77	52 W
Pitcairn I., *Pacific Ocean*	25	5 S	130	5 W
Pitt I., *New Zealand*	44	17 S	176	10 W
Piura, *Peru*	5	15 S	80	38 W
Poás, Volcán, *Costa Rica*	10	20 N	83	55 W
Pohnpei, *Caroline Islands*	6	55 N	158	10 E
Poland	52	0 N	20	0 E
Polillo I., *Philippines*	14	56 N	121	56 E
Poopo, Lake, *Bolivia*	18	30 S	67	35 W
Port Elizabeth, *South Africa*	33	58 S	25	40 E
Port Moresby, *New Guinea*	9	24 S	147	8 E
Portland Parish, *Jamaica*	18	10 N	76	20 W
Porto Santo I., *Madeira*	33	5 N	16	20 W
Portugal	40	0 N	8	0 W
Praslin, *Seychelles*	4	20 S	55	45 E
Pribilof Islands, *Bering Sea*	56	0 N	170	0 W
Prince Edward I., *Gulf of St. Lawrence*	46	31 N	63	23 W
Prince Edward Islands, *s Indian Ocean*	46	35 S	38	0 E
Prince William Sound, *Alaska*	61	0 N	147	0 W
Princess Marianne Str., *New Guinea*	7	99 S	139	30 E
Príncipe I., *Gulf of Guinea*	1	37 N	7	27 E
Prinsen I., *Sunda Strait*	5	94 S	105	85 E
Providéncia, Isla, *Caribbean*	13	25 N	81	26 W
Prussia	50	43 N	8	35 E
Puebla, *Mexico*	18	30 N	98	0 W
Puerto Rico, *West Indies*	18	15 N	66	45 W
Pulau Bunguran., *N Natuna Islands*	4	0 N	105	0 E
Pulau Kundur I., *South China Sea*	0	74 N	103	42 E
Puná, Isla, *Ecuador*	2	52 S	80	7 W
Puno, *Peru*	15	55 S	70	3 W
Purús, Río, *Brazil*	3	42 S	61	28 W
Pyrénées Mountains, *Europe*	43	10 N	0	50 W
Qinghai, *China*	36	0 N	98	0 E
Quebec, *Canada*	48	0 N	74	0 W
Queen Charlotte Islands, *Canada*	53	20 N	132	10 W
Queensland, *Australia*	22	0 S	142	0 E
Quelpart Islands *see* Cheju-Do Islands	33	29 N	126	34 E
Quilotoa, Mt., *Ecuador*	0	50 S	78	52 W
Qinghai, *China*	36	0N	98	0E
Quintana Roo, *Mexico*	19	0 N	88	0 W
Rabat, *Morocco*	34	2 N	6	48 W
Raiatea I., *Society Islands*	17	0 S	151	0 W
Rajasthan, *India*	26	45 N	73	30 E
Rambi I., *Fiji*	16	30 S	179	59 W
Ramu River, *New Guinea*	4	0 S	144	41 E
Rani I., *New Guinea*	1	25 S	136	21 E
Rann of Kutch, *India*	24	0 N	70	0 E
Ranongga I., *Solomon Islands*	8	5 S	156	35 E
Rapa I., *Austral Archipelago*	27	35 S	144	20 W
Rarotonga, *Cook Islands*	21	30 S	160	0 W
Rasa I., *Borneo*	6	50 N	116	30 E
Rat I., *Aleutian Islands*	52	0 N	178	0 E
Ratnagiri district, *India*	10	0 N	73	20 E
Rau I., *Moluccas*	2	10 N	128	0 E
Raung, Mt., *Java*	8	12 S	114	23 E
Récherche Archipelago, *Australia*	34	15 S	122	50 E
Red Sea	20	0 N	40	0 E
Redonda I., *Galapagos*	1	0 N	91	47 W
Reef Islands, *Vanuatu*	14	0 S	168	0 E
Rendova, *Solomon Islands*	8	33 S	157	17 E
Rennell, *Solomon Islands*	11	40 S	160	10 E
Réunion, *Indian Ocean*	21	0 S	56	0 E
Revillagigedo Islands, *Mexico*	18	40 N	112	0 W
Rhio Arch. *see* Riau Archipelago	0	30 N	104	20 E
Rhodes, *Greece*	36	15 N	28	10 E
Rhodope Mountains, *Bulgaria*	41	62 N	24	85 E
Riau Archipelago, *Indonesia*	0	30 N	104	20 E
Rif Mountains, *North Africa*	35	0 N	5	0 W
Rift Valley, *Kenya*	0	20 N	36	0 E
Rio de Janeiro, *Brazil*	23	0 S	43	12 W
Rio Grande do Sul, *Brazil*	32	0 S	52	20 W
Rio Grande Valley, *Texas*	29	20 N	101	0 W

Place	Lat°	Lat′	Lon°	Lon′
Rio Muni	1	34 N	9	38 E
Rishiri-To I., *n Japan*	45	11 N	141	15 E
Roatán I., *Honduras*	16	18 N	86	35 W
Robinson Crusoe I., *Chile*	33	50 S	80	46 W
Rocky Mountains, *US*	42	0 N	110	0 W
Rodrigues I., *Indian Ocean*	19	45 S	63	20 E
Roebuck Bay, *Australia*	18	5 S	122	20 E
Rokupr, *Sierra Leone*	9	1 N	12	95 W
Rôlas, Ilha das, *São Tomé*	0	1 S	6	31 E
Roma I. *see* Romang I.	7	30 S	127	20 E
Romang I., *Timor*	7	30 S	127	20 E
Romania	46	0 N	25	0 E
Romblon I., *Philippines*	12	30 N	122	15 E
Rondo Plateau, *Tanzania*	10	18 S	39	25 E
Rondônia, *Brazil*	11	05 S	63	0 W
Rook I. *see* Umboi I.	5	50 S	147	70 E
Roraima, *Brazil*	2	0 N	61	30 W
Roraima, Mt., *Venezuela/Guyana*	5	14 N	60	44 W
Rossel I., *Louisiade Archipelago*	11	0 S	154	30 E
Rota I., *Mariana Islands*	14	10 N	145	10 E
Roti I., *Timor*	10	50 S	123	0 E
Rottnest I., *Australia*	32	0 S	115	27 E
Rotuma I., *Fiji*	12	25 S	177	5 E
Russam I., *Sumatra*	2	11 N	96	42 E
Russell Group, *Solomon Islands*	9	10 S	159	10 E
Russia	62	0 N	105	0 E
Rutshuru, *Zaire*	1	35 S	29	25 E
Ruwenzori Mountains, *Zaire/Uganda*	0	3 N	29	55 E
Rwanda	2	0 S	30	0 E
Ryukyu Islands, *Japan*	28	0 N	127	0 E
Sabah, *Borneo*	6	0 N	117	0 E
Sable I., *Nova Scotia*	43	94 N	59	94 W
Sabtang I., *Philippines*	20	15 N	121	46 E
Sacramento Valley, *California*	36	3 N	121	56 W
Sado I., *Japan*	38	0 N	138	25 E
Sahel, *Africa*	14	20 N	6	0 W
Sainte-Marie, Ile de, *Madagascar*	16	50 S	45	55 E
Saipan I., *Mariana Islands*	15	12 N	145	45 E
Sakalava, *Madagascar*	22	54 S	44	31 E
Sakaraha, *Madagascar*	23	0 N	44	0 E
Sakhalin, *Russia*	51	0 N	143	0 E
Salawati I., *w Papuan islands*	1	07 S	130	52 E
Sala y Gómez I., *Chile*	26	42 S	105	45 W
Salayar I., *Flores Sea*	6	7 S	120	30 E
Salebabu I., *Talaud Islands*	3	92 N	126	68 E
Salta, *Argentina*	24	48 S	65	30 W
Salton Sea, *California*	33	15 N	115	45 W
Salvage Islands, *Canary Islands*	30	0 N	16	0 W
Salween River, *Myanmar*	19	95 N	97	80 E
Samar I., *Philippines*	11	50 N	125	0 E
Samarai I., *Papua New Guinea*	10	39 S	150	41 E
Samoa, *Pacific Ocean*	14	0 S	171	0 W
San Ambrosio I., *Chile*	26	28 S	79	53 W
San Andrés, Isla, *Caribbean*	12	42 N	81	46 W
San Benedicto I., *Mexico*	19	0 N	110	0 W
San Benito Islands, *Mexico*	28	15 N	115	30 W
San Bernardino Mountains, *California*	34	10 N	116	45 W
San Blas, *Mexico*	26	4 N	108	46 W
San Cristóbal, *Galapagos Islands*	0	83 S	89	35 W
San Cristóbal, *Solomon Islands*	10	30 S	161	0 E
San Diego County, *California*	33	0 N	116	30 W
San Esteban, Isla, *Gulf of California*	28	70 N	112	57 W
San Félix I., *Chile*	26	23 S	80	0 W
San Ignacio, Laguna, *Baja California*	27	0 N	113	19 W
San Jeronomo, Serrania de, *Colombia*	8	0 N	76	0 W
San Jorge I., *Solomon Islands*	8	40 S	159	45 E
San José I., *Panama*	8	0 N	79	10 W
San Juan, *Argentina*	31	09 S	60	0 W
San Juancito Mountains, *Honduras*	14	10 N	87	5 W
San Luis Obispo, *California*	35	17 N	120	40 W
San Luis Potosí, *Mexico*	22	10 N	101	0 W
San Luís, *Argentina*	34	0 S	66	0 W
San Martín, *Peru*	12	3 S	76	45 W
San Miguel del Rey I., *Panama*	8	27 N	78	55 W
San Miguel, Volcán, *El Salvador*	13	30 N	88	12 W
San Pedro Mártir, *Baja California*	31	0 N	115	30 W
San Salvador I., *Bahamas*	24	0 N	74	40 W
Sanana I., *Sula Islands*	2	04 S	125	58 E
Sanga Sanga, *Sulu Archipelago*	5	4 N	119	46 E
Sangihe I., *Sulawesi*	3	53 N	125	52 E
Santa Anna I., *Solomon Islands*	10	70 S	162	40 E
Santa Barbara, *California*	34	25 N	119	42 W
Santa Catalina I., *California*	33	29 N	119	2 W
Santa Catarina, *Brazil*	27	25 S	48	30 W
Santa Cruz County, *California*	36	58 N	122	1 W
Santa Cruz Group, *Solomon Islands*	10	30 S	166	0 E
Santa Cruz I., *California*	34	1 N	119	43 W
Santa Cruz I., *Galapagos Islands*	0	62 S	90	34 W
Santa Cruz, *Argentina*	49	0 S	70	0 W
Santa Cruz, *Bolivia*	17	43 S	63	10 W
Santa Isabel, *Solomon Islands*	8	0 S	159	0 E
Santa Marta Mountains, *Colombia*	10	55 N	73	50 W
Santa Rosa I., *California*	33	58 N	120	6 W
Santarém, *Brazil*	2	25 S	54	42 W
Santiago, *Cape Verde Islands*	15	0 N	23	64 W
São Nicolau, *Cape Verde Islands*	16	60 N	24	24 W
São Paulo de Olivença, *Brazil*	3	34 S	68	55 W
São Paulo, *Brazil*	22	0 S	49	0 W
São Salvador, *Brazil*	7	0 S	73	0 W
São Tomé, *Gulf of Guinea*	0	10 N	6	39 E
Saona I., *Dominican Republic*	18	10 N	68	40 W
Saparua I., *Moluccas*	3	33 S	128	40 E
Sarawak, *Malaysia*	2	0 N	113	0 E
Sardinia, *Italy*	40	0 N	90	0 E
Saribas District, *Sarawak*	2	0 N	113	0 E
Saskatchewan, *Canada*	54	40 N	106	0 W
Saudi Arabia	23	0 N	46	0 E
Savai'i, *Western Samoa*	13	28 S	172	24 W
Savo I., *Solomon Islands*	9	8 S	159	48 E
Sawu I., *Lesser Sundas*	10	52 S	121	87 E
Sayan Mountains, *s Russia*	53	49 N	97	97 E
Scammon's Lagoon, *Baja California*	27	30 N	114	0 E
Scandinavia	64	0 N	12	0 E
Schrader Range, *New Guinea*	5	8 S	144	35 E
Schwaner Mountains, *Borneo*	0	73 S	112	9 E
Scotia Arc, *Antarctica*	56	5 S	56	0 W
Scotland	57	0 N	4	0 W
Scott Islands, *Antarctica*	67	0 S	179	0 E

Place				
Selangor, *Malaysia*	3	39 N	102	24 E
Semau I., *Timor*	10	13 S	123	22 E
Semipalatinsk, *Kazakstan*	50	26 N	80	16 E
Semirara I., *Philippines*	12	4 N	124	23 E
Semliki Valley, *Zaire*	0	1 S	29	30 E
Senegal	15	48 N	16	32 W
Senegambia	12	45 N	12	0 W
Sennar District, *Sudan*	13	0 N	33	10 E
Sepik River, *New Guinea*	3	49 S	144	30 E
Seram I., *Moluccas*	3	10 S	129	0 E
Serengeti National Park, *Tanzania*	3	0 S	35	0 E
Seridó, *Brazil*	6	82 S	36	40 W
Sermata I., *Lesser Sundas*	8	15 S	128	50 E
Seven Finger Mountains, *Hainan*	9	0 N	109	70 E
Seven Islands of Izu *see* Izu Islands	34	30 N	139	30 E
Seychelles Islands, *Indian Ocean*	5	0 S	56	0 E
Shaanxi Province, *China*	37	0 N	108	70 E
Shan States, *Myanmar*	21	30 N	98	30 E
Shandong Province, *China*	36	0 N	118	0 E
Shantar Islands, *Sea of Okhotsk*	54	90 N	137	72 E
Shanxi Province, *China*	37	79 N	111	78 E
Shensi *see* Shaanxi	37	0 N	108	70 E
Shetland Islands, *UK*	60	30 N	1	30 W
Shewa Province, *Ethiopia*	9	0 N	38	45 E
Shikoku I., *Japan*	33	0 N	133	30 E
Shire River, *Malawi*	15	0 S	35	30 E
Shoa Province *see* Shewa	9	0 N	38	45 E
Shortland Islands, *Solomon Islands*	6	55 S	155	53 E
Shweli-Salween divide, *Myanmar*	24	0 N	98	0 E
Siargao I., *Philippines*	9	52 N	126	3 E
Siasi I., *Sulu Archipelago*	5	33 N	120	52 E
Siau I., *Sulawesi*	2	5 N	125	25 E
Siberia, *Russia*	60	0 N	100	0 E
Siberut I. *Sumatra*	1	30 S	99	0 E
Sibutu I., *Sulu Archipelago*	4	45 N	119	30 E
Sibuyan I., *Philippines*	12	25 N	122	40 E
Sichuan Province, *China*	31	0 N	104	0 E
Sicily, *Italy*	37	30 N	14	30 E
Sicogon I., *Philippines*	11	26 N	123	16 E
Sidamo Province, *Ethiopia*	5	0 N	37	50 E
Sierra Leone	9	0 N	12	0 W
Sierra Madre del Sur, *Mexico*	17	30 N	97	40 W
Sierra Madre Occidental, *Mexico*	25	0 N	103	0 W
Sierra Madre Oriental, *Mexico*	23	0 N	97	0 W
Sierra Nevada Mountains, *California*	36	35 N	118	18 W
Sikkim	27	50 N	88	20 E
Silhouette, *Seychelles*	4	30 S	55	15 E
Simeulue I., *Sumatra*	2	45 N	99	45 E
Sinai Peninsula, *Egypt*	29	30 N	34	0 E
Sinaloa, *Mexico*	25	0 N	107	30 W
Singapore	1	30 N	104	0 E
Singida, *Tanzania*	4	45 S	34	48 E
Sinkiang *see* Xinjiang	42	0 N	86	0 E
Sinú Valley, *Colombia*	3	30 N	76	20 W
Sipoura I., *Sumatra*	2	18 S	99	40 E
Siquijor I., *Philippines*	9	12 N	123	35 E
Sira, Cerros del, *Peru*	9	21 S	74	43 W
Slamet, Mt., *Java*	7	23 S	109	19 E
Snares I., *New Zealand*	48	0 S	166	40 E
Snow Mountains, New Guinea	4	0 S	139	30 E
Society Islands, *Pacific Ocean*	17	0 S	151	0 W
Socorro I., *Mexico*	18	45 N	110	58 W
Socotra I., *Indian Ocean*	12	30 N	54	0 E
Sokoke-Arabuku Forest, *Kenya*	2	40 S	40	15 E
Solander I., *New Zealand*	46	34 S	166	54 E
Solimões, Rio, *Brazil*	0	5 S	50	0 W
Solomon Islands	8	70 S	159	0 E
Solor I., *Lesser Sundas*	8	27 S	123	0 E
Somalia	7	0 N	47	0 E
Sonora, *Mexico*	28	50 N	111	33 W
South Africa	32	0 S	23	0 E
South Australia	32	0 S	139	0 E
South Carolina, *US*	34	0 N	81	0 W
South Dakota, *US*	44	15 N	100	0 W
South Georgia I., *Antarctica*	54	30 S	37	0 W
South I., *New Zealand*	44	0 S	170	0 E
South Korea	36	0 N	128	0 E
South Orkney Islands, *Antarctica*	63	0 S	45	0 W
South Shetland Islands, *Antarctica*	62	0 S	59	0 W
South Yemen	15	0 N	47	0 E
Spain	39	0 N	4	0 W
Spitzbergen, *Arctic*	78	0 N	17	0 E
Sri Lanka	7	30 N	80	50 E
St. Croix, *Virgin Islands*	17	45 N	64	45 W
St. Helena I., *Atlantic Ocean*	15	55 S	5	44 W
St. John I., *Virgin Islands*	18	21 N	64	48 W
St. Lawrence I., *Bering Sea*	63	30 N	170	30 W
St. Lucia, *West Indies*	14	0 N	60	50 W
St. Matthew I., *Alaska*	60	20 N	172	30 W
St. Matthias Is., *Bismarck Archipelago*	1	30 S	150	0 E
St. Paul I., *Indian Ocean*	38	55 S	77	34 E
St. Pierre I., *Newfoundland*	46	78 N	56	20 W
St. Thomas, *Virgin Islands*	18	20 N	64	55 W
St. Vincent, *West Indies*	13	0 N	61	10 W
Star Keys I., *Chatham Islands*	44	12 S	175	58 W
Staten I., *Argentina*	54	40 S	64	30 W
Stewart I., *New Zealand*	46	58 S	167	54 W
Sucre, *Venezuela*	10	25 N	63	30 W
Sudan	15	0 N	30	0 E
Sudest I. *see* Tagula I.	11	30 S	153	30 E
Suez Canal, *Egypt*	31	0 N	32	20 E
Sula Islands, *Sulawesi*	1	45 S	125	0 E
Sulawesi, *Indonesia*	2	0 S	120	0 E
Sulu Archipelago, *Philippines*	6	0 N	121	0 E
Sumatra, *Indonesia*	0	40 N	100	20 E
Sumba, *Lesser Sundas*	9	45 S	119	35 E
Sumbawa, *Lesser Sundas*	8	30 S	117	30 E
Suriname	4	0 N	56	0 W
Svalbard, *Arctic*	78	0 N	17	0 E
Swallow I., *Solomon Islands*	10	21 S	166	17 E
Swan Islands, *w Caribbean Sea*	17	42 N	83	93 W
Swaziland	26	30 S	31	30 E
Sweden	57	0 N	15	0 E
Syrdarya River, *Kazakstan*	46	3 N	61	0 E
Syria	35	0 N	38	0 E
Szechwan *see* Sichuan	31	0 N	104	0 E
Tabar Group, *Bismarck Archipelago*	2	50 S	152	0 E
Tabasco, *Mexico*	17	45 N	93	30 W

Place	Lat°	Lat′	Lon°	Lon′
Tablas I., *Philippines*	12	25 N	122	2 E
Taboga I., *Bay of Panama*	8	79 N	79	55 W
Tabora, *Tanzania*	5	4 S	32	49 E
Tabuaeran I., *Kiribati*	3	87 N	159	32 W
Táchira, *Venezuela*	8	7 N	72	15 W
Tacna, *Peru*	17	40 S	70	20 W
Tadzhikistan *see* Tajikistan	38	30 N	70	0 E
Tagula I., *Louisiade Archipelago*	11	30 S	153	30 E
Tahaa I., *Society Islands*	16	50 S	151	10 W
Tahiti, *French Polynesia*	17	37 S	149	27 W
Tahuata, *Marquesas Islands*	9	94 S	139	7 W
Taita Hills, *Kenya*	4	7 S	38	62 E
Taiwan	23	30 N	121	0 E
Tajikistan	38	30 N	70	0 E
Talamanca, Cordillera de, *Panama*	9	20 N	83	20 W
Talaud Islands, *n Moluccas*	4	30 N	127	10 E
Taliabu I., *Sula Islands*	2	30 S	125	0 E
Talisei I., *Sulawesi*	1	84 N	125	7 E
Tamaulipas, *Mexico*	24	0 N	99	0 W
Tamil Nadu, *India*	11	0 N	77	0 E
Tamrau Mountains, *New Guinea*	2	30 S	137	40 E
Tana, Lake, *Ethiopia*	12	0 N	37	30 E
Tana River, *Kenya*	2	32 S	40	31 E
Tanaga I., *Aleutians*	51	55 N	178	0 W
Tanahjampea I., *Flores Sea*	7	10 S	120	35 E
Tanahmasa I., *Sumatra*	0	12 S	98	39 E
Tanakeke I., *Sulawesi*	5	51 S	119	28 E
Tanegashima, *Japan*	30	30 N	131	0 E
Tanga I., *Bismarck Archipelago*	3	20 S	153	15 E
Tanganyika, Lake	6	40 S	30	0 E
Tanimbar Islands, *Arafura Sea*	7	30 S	131	30 E
Tanna I., *Vanuatu*	19	30 S	169	20 E
Tannu-Ola Mountains, *Mongolia*	50	82 N	92	36 E
Tanzania	6	0 S	34	0 E
Tapajós, Rio, *Brazil*	2	24 S	54	41 W
Tarapacá, *Chile*	20	45 S	69	30 W
Tarbagatay Mountains, *Russia*	51	30 N	107	20 E
Tarija, *Bolivia*	21	30 S	63	30 W
Tarim Basin, *China*	41	15 N	84	4 E
Tasman Sea	36	0 S	160	0 E
Tasmania	42	0 S	146	30 E
Tatau I., *Bismarck Archipelago*	3	0 S	152	0 E
Tau I., *American Samoa*	14	55 S	169	30 W
Taurus Mountains, *w Turkey*	37	19 N	31	64 E
Taveuni I., *Fiji*	16	51 S	179	58 W
Tawitawi I., *Sulu Archipelago*	5	10 N	120	0 E
Tayandu Islands, *Banda Sea*	5	60 S	132	29 E
Taymyr Peninsula, *Russia*	75	0 N	100	0 E
Tegucigalpa, *Honduras*	14	5 N	87	14 W
Tehuántepec, Isthmus of, *Mexico*	17	0 N	94	30 W
Tenasserim, *s Myanmar*	14	0 N	99	0 E
Tengger Mountains, *Java*	7	89 S	110	75 E
Teraina I., *Line Islands*	4	71 N	160	75 W
Tenerife, *Canary Islands*	28	15 N	16	35 W
Tentolo-Matinan Mountains, *Sulawesi*	0	92 N	121	73 E
Terciera I., *Azores*	38	30 N	27	10 W
Ternate I., *Moluccas*	0	45 N	127	25 E
Teun I., *Lesser Sundas*	6	59 S	129	8 E
Texas, *US*	31	40 N	98	30 W
Thailand	16	0 N	102	0 E
Tiandu I. *see* Tyandu I.	5	50 S	132	40 E
Tibet	32	0 N	86	0 E
Tiburón, Isla, *Mexico*	29	0 N	112	30 W
Ticao I., *Philippine Islands*	12	31 N	123	42 E
Tidore I., *Moluccas*	0	40 N	127	25 E
Tien Shan Mountains, *Kazakstan*	42	0 N	76	0 E
Tierra del Fuego	54	0 S	69	0 W
Timor, *Lesser Sundas*	9	0 S	125	0 E
Tinakula I., *Santa Cruz Islands*	10	40 S	165	60 E
Tinian I., *Mariana Islands*	15	0 N	145	40 E
Tioman I., *South China Sea*	2	77 N	104	17 E
Titicaca, Lake, *Bolivia/Peru*	15	30 S	69	30 W
Tobago, *West Indies*	11	10 N	60	30 W
Tocantins, Rio, *Brazil*	10	0 S	48	0 W
Todos Santos Bay, *Baja California*	31	80 N	116	78 W
Toga I., *Vanuatu*	13	26 S	166	42 E
Togian Islands, *Sulawesi*	0	37 S	122	5 E
Togo	8	30 N	1	35 E
Tokashiki-Shima I., *Japan*	26	11 N	127	21 E
Tokelau Islands, *Oceania*	9	0 S	171	0 E
Tokuno-Shima I., *Japan*	27	56 N	128	55 E
Tolima, *Colombia*	4	40 N	75	19 W
Tonga, *Pacific Ocean*	19	50 S	174	30 W
Tongatapu I., *Tonga*	21	10 S	170	0 W
Tonkin, *n Vietnam*	22	0 N	105	0 E
Torishima I., *Japan*	34	30 N	139	15 E
Torres I., *Vanuatu*	13	15 S	166	37 E
Torres Straits, *Australia*	9	50 S	142	20 E
Tortola I., *Virgin Islands*	18	19 W	64	45 W
Tortue I., *Haiti*	20	5 N	72	80 W
Tortuga, Isla, *Gulf of California*	27	44 N	111	97 W
Tower I., *Galapagos Islands*	0	32 N	89	96 W
Townsend, *Australia*	22	10 S	150	30 E
Townsville, *Australia*	19	15 S	146	45 E
Trang, *Thailand*	7	55 N	98	59 E
Trangan I., *New Guinea*	6	40 S	134	20 E
Transbaikal	53	0 N	108	0 E
Transcaucasia	40	0 N	45	0 E
Trans-Fly region, *New Guinea*	8	0 S	142	0 E
Transkei, *South Africa*	30	0 S	28	15
Transvaal, *South Africa*	25	0 S	30	0 E
Tres Marías Islands, *Mexico*	21	25 N	106	28 W
Trindade I., *Atlantic Ocean*	20	20 S	29	50 W
Trinidad, *West Indies*	10	30 N	61	20 W
Tristan da Cunha I., *Atlantic Ocean*	37	6 S	12	20 W
Triton Bay, *South China Sea*	16	0 N	111	30 E
Trobriand Islands, *Solomon Sea*	8	30 S	151	0 E
Trondheim Fjord, *Norway*	63	35 N	10	30 E
Trujillo, *Peru*	8	6 S	79	0 W
Trujillo, *Venezuela*	9	22 N	70	30 W
Truk. *Caroline Islands*	7	34 N	151	74 E
Tsaidam Basin, *w China*	38	0 N	92	0 E
Tsinghai *see* Qinghai	36	0 N	98	0 E
Tsinling Mountains, *China*	35	0 N	110	0 E
Tsushima Islands, *Japan*	34	20 N	129	20 E
Tuamotu Arch., *French Polynesia*	17	0 S	144	0 W
Tuangku I., *Sumatra*	2	4 N	97	18 E
Tubai Islands, *French Polynesia*	28	0 S	150	0 W

Place				
Tubbataha Reefs, *Sulu Sea*	8	30 N	120	0 E
Tucumán, *Argentina*	26	48 S	66	2 W
Tukangbesi Islands, *Banda Sea*	5	54 S	123	71 E
Tumaco I., *Colombia*	2	0 N	79	0 W
Tumbatu Islands, *Tanzania*	5	50 S	39	13 E
Tumbes, *Peru*	3	50 S	80	30 W
Tumindao I., *Sulu Archipelago*	4	42 N	119	10 E
Tunisia	33	30 N	9	10 E
Turama River, *New Guinea*	7	48 S	143	50 E
Turkana, Lake, *Kenya*	3	30 N	36	5 E
Turkestan	43	30 N	68	25 E
Turkey	39	0 N	36	0 E
Turkmenistan	39	0 N	60	0 E
Turneffe Islands, *Belize*	17	20 N	87	50 W
Turner River, *Australia*	17	46 S	128	13 E
Turrialba, Volcán, *Costa Rica*	10	5 N	83	30 W
Tutuila I., *American Samoa*	14	19 S	170	50 W
Tuvalu, *Melanesia*	9	0 S	175	0 E
Twek-quay, Mt., *Guyana*	5	35 N	60	83 W
Uahuka I., *Marquesas Islands*	8	91 S	139	55 W
Uapou I, *Marquesas*	9	43 S	138	92 W
Uaupés, Rio, *Brazil*	0	2 N	68	0 E
Ucayalí, Río, *Peru*	4	30 S	73	30 W
Udzungwa Mountains, *Tanzania*	8	30 S	35	45 E
Uganda	2	0 N	32	0 E
Ugi I., *Solomon Islands*	10	30 S	161	10 E
Uki Ni Masi, *Solomon Islands*	10	20 S	161	50 E
Ukraine, *Russia*	49	0 N	32	0 E
Ullung I., *South Korea*	37	50 N	130	87 E
Uluguru Mts., *Tanzania*	7	0 S	37	30 E
Umboi I., *Bismarck Archipelago*	5	50 S	147	70 E
Union I., *Grenadines*	12	36 N	61	26 W
Upemba, Lake, *Zaire*	8	63 S	26	38 E
Upolu I., *Western Samoa*	14	0 S	171	60 W
Upper Volta *see* Burkina Faso	12	0 N	1	0 W
Ural Mountains	60	0 N	59	0 E
Ural River, *Kazakstan*	49	0 N	52	0 E
Ursula I., *Borneo*	6	50 N	116	30 E
Urubamba Valley, *Peru*	10	43 S	73	48 W
Uruguay	32	30 S	56	30 W
Usambara Mountains, *Tanzania*	4	0 S	39	0 E
Ussuriland, *Russia*	48	27 N	135	0 E
Utah, *US*	39	20 N	111	30 W
Utila I., *Honduras*	16	0 N	87	0 W
Uttar Pradesh, *India*	27	0 N	80	0 E
Utupua I., *Solomon Islands*	11	20 S	166	55 E
Uvéa I., *Loyalty Islands*	20	30 S	166	35 E
Uzbekistan	41	30 N	65	0 E
Valdivia, *Chile*	39	50 S	73	14 W
Vancouver I., *Canada*	49	50 N	126	0 W
Vangunu I., *Solomon Islands*	8	40 S	158	5 E
Vanikoro I., *Santa Cruz Islands*	11	50 S	166	70 E
Vanua Kula I., *Fiji*	17	0 S	179	0 W
Vanua Lava, *Vanuatu*	13	79 S	167	47 E
Vanua Levu, *Fiji*	16	33 S	179	15 E
Vanuatu	15	0 S	168	0 E
Vava'u Group, *Tonga*	18	36 S	174	0 W
Vellalavella I., *Solomon Islands*	7	45 S	156	40 E
Venezuela	8	0 N	65	0 W

Place				
Ventuari, Río, *Venezuela*	3	58 N	67	2 W
Veracruz, *Mexico*	19	0 N	96	15 W
Veraguas, *Panama*	8	50 N	81	0 W
Victor Emanuel Mts., *New Guinea*	5	20 S	142	15 E
Victoria Falls, *Africa*	17	58 S	25	52 E
Victoria, *Australia*	37	0 S	144	0 E
Victoria, Lake, *Africa*	1	30 S	33	0 E
Victoria, Mt., *Myanmar*	21	23 N	93	90 E
Vieques I., *Puerto Rico*	18	10 N	65	30 W
Vietnam	19	0 N	106	0 E
Vilcabamba Mountains, *Peru*	13	05 S	73	0 W
Villavicencio, *Colombia*	4	9 N	73	37 W
Virgin Islands, *West Indies*	18	20 N	65	0 W
Virginia, *USA*	37	30 N	78	45 W
Viti Levu, *Fiji*	17	30 S	178	0 E
Vizcaino, Bahia, *Baja California*	27	79 N	114	20 W
Vogelkop Peninsula, *New Guinea*	1	25 S	133	0 E
Volcano Islands, *Japan*	25	10 N	143	50 E
Volga River, *Russia*	46	0 N	48	30 E
Vulcan I. *see* Manam I.	4	5 S	145	0 E
Wadi Natrun, *Libyan Desert*	30	35 N	30	24 E
Waigeo I., *New Guinea*	0	20 S	130	77 E
Wake I., *Pacific Ocean*	18	18 N	166	36 E
Wales, *UK*	52	30 N	4	0 W
Wallis Islands, *Pacific Ocean*	13	18 S	176	10 W
Wandammen Mountains, *New Guinea*	2	35 S	134	30 E
Waria River, *New Guinea*	8	0 S	147	30 E
Warner Valley, *Oregon*	41	40 N	120	15 W
Washington, *US*	47	30 N	120	30 W
Watling I. *see* San Salvador I.	24	0 N	74	40 W
Watubela Islands, *Moluccas*	4	47 S	131	64 E
Watut River, *New Guinea*	6	48 S	146	24 E
Weda I., *Moluccas*	0	21 N	127	50 E
Wenman I., *Galapagos Islands*	1	0 N	91	45 W
Western Australia	25	0 S	118	0 E
Western Ghats, *India*	14	0 N	75	0 E
Western Samoa, *Pacific Ocean*	14	0 S	172	0 W
Wetar I., *Lesser Sundas*	7	30 S	126	30 E
Weyland Mountains, *New Guinea*	3	40 S	137	20 E
Wharton Mountains, *New Guinea*	8	30 S	147	10 E
Whidbey I., *Washington*	48	12 N	122	17 W
White Nile region, *Sudan*	13	0 N	32	40 E
White Pass, *Alaska*	59	40 N	135	3 W
White Sea, *Russia*	66	30 N	38	0 E
Whitney I. *see* Shortland I.	6	55 S	155	53 E
Wilhelm, Mt., *New Guinea*	5	46 S	144	59 E
Wilhelmina, Mt., *New Guinea*	4	16 S	138	69 E
Windhoek, *Namibia*	22	35 S	17	4 E
Wisconsin, *US*	44	45 N	89	30 W

Wissel Lakes, *Irian Jaya*	3	55 S	136	18 E
Witu I., *Bismarck Archipelago*	4	30 S	149	10 E
Wokam I., *New Guinea*	5	45 S	134	28 E
Woodlark I. *see* Misima I.	9	10 S	152	50 E
Wotje Atoll, *Marshall Islands*	10	0 N	171	3 E
Wrangel I., *Russia*	71	23 N	179	42 W
Wrangell I., *Alaska*	56	16 N	132	12 W
Wyndham, *Australia*	15	33 S	128	3 E
Wyoming, *USA*	43	0 N	107	30 W
Xingú, Rio, *Brazil*	1	30 S	51	53 W
Xinjiang, *China*	42	0 N	86	0 E
Yabelo, *Ethiopia*	4	9 N	38	7 E
Yablonovy Mountains, *Transbaicalia*	52	50 N	115	0 E
Yakushima I., *Ryukyu Islands*	32	20 N	130	30 E
Yakutat Peninsula, *Alaska*	59	30 N	139	30 W
Yambaru Mountains, *Okinawa*	26	50 N	128	30 E
Yamdena I., *Arafura Sea*	7	56 S	131	41 E
Yangtze River, *China*	30	0 N	116	0 E
Yap, *Caroline Islands*	9	30 N	138	10 E
Yapen I., *New Guinea*	1	50 S	136	0 E
Ycacos Lagoon, *Belize*	16	30 N	89	0 W
Yemen	15	0 N	44	0 E
Yenisey River, *Russia*	71	50 N	82	40 E
Yeppoon, *Australia*	23	5 S	150	47 E
Yibin, *China*	28	78 N	104	61 E
Yonaguni I., *Ryukyu Islands*	24	27 N	123	0 E
Yucatán Peninsula, *Mexico*	19	30 N	89	0 W
Yugoslavia	44	0 N	20	0 E
Yukon Territory	63	0 N	135	0 W
Yule I., *Papua New Guinea*	8	81 S	146	53 E
Yunaska I., *Aleutians*	52	40 N	170	45 W
Yunnan Province, *China*	25	0 N	102	0 E
Yurimaguas, *Peru*	5	55 S	76	7 W
Zacapa Plains, *Guatemala*	15	0 N	89	30 W
Zacatecas, *Mexico*	23	30 N	103	0 W
Zagros Mountains, *Iran*	33	45 N	48	5 E
Zaire	3	0 S	23	0 E
Zaire River	6	4 S	12	24 E
Zambezi River	18	35 S	36	20 E
Zambia	15	0 S	28	0 E
Zamboanga Peninsula, *Mindanao*	7	30 N	122	10 E
Zanzibar I., *Tanzania*	6	12 S	39	12 E
Zembra I., *Tunisia*	37	13 N	10	80 E
Zhejiang Province, *China*	29	0 N	120	0 E
Zimbabwe	19	0 S	30	0 E
Zinder Province, *Niger*	13	48 N	9	0 E
Zulia, *Venezuela*	10	0 N	72	30 W
Zululand *see* Kwazulu-Natal	27	30 S	31	0 E

Distribution of endemic bird species of the world. Adapted with permission from *BirdArea for Windows*. © 1996 Santa Barbara Software Products, Inc. Research courtesy Shawneen Finnegan

Country	Species	Endemics	Country	Species	Endemics
New Guinea	736	330	Samoa	63	10
Australia	754	238	US contiguous 48 states	908	9
Philippines	572	185	Chile	437	9
Brazil	1656	181	Guam and Marianas	114	9
Peru	1716	114	Cocos (Keeling Islands)	30	9
Madagascar	255	98	Ecuador	1481	8
Sulawesi (Celebes)	388	96	Timor	210	8
Mexico	1049	88	Mauritius	82	7
Solomon Islands	245	68	Cook Islands	55	7
Moluccas	359	67	Kenya	1105	6
Colombia	1725	62	Costa Rica	838	6
New Zealand	295	56	Socotra	99	6
China	1204	50	Gough/Tristan da Cunha	76	6
Lesser Sundas	382	46	Canary Islands	256	5
Venezuela	1337	41	Admiralty Islands	89	5
Bismarck Archipelago	246	38	Réunion	58	5
India	1167	36	Burma (Myanmar)	985	4
Hawaii	275	36	Saint Lucia	128	4
Borneo	599	31	Pitcairn Island	30	4
Java and Bali	500	28	Cape Verde	130	3
Jamaica	265	27	Norfolk Island	57	3
São Tomé and Príncipe	86	27	Uganda	1015	2
Galapagos Islands	138	25	Sudan	961	2
Fiji	119	25	Thailand	918	2
French Polynesia	92	24	Nigeria	868	2
Sri Lanka	359	23	Nepal	853	2
Zaire	1135	19	Malaysia (Peninsular)	663	2
Tanzania	1050	19	St. Vincent	113	2
Ethiopia	828	18	Aldabra Island	110	2
Sumatra	611	18	Dominica	107	2
Cuba	346	17	Kiribati (Micronesia)	63	2
Andaman and Nicobar Is.	213	17	Tonga	59	2
Comoro Islands	84	16	Kiritimati I. (Christmas I.)	48	2
Argentina	976	15	St. Helena/Ascension Is.	44	2
New Caledonia	122	15	Rodrigues Island	29	2
Taiwan (Formosa)	474	14	Zambia	753	1
Angola	914	13	Honduras	690	1
Tasmania	272	13	Pakistan	672	1
Micronesia	102	13	French Guiana	624	1
South Africa	812	12	Namibia	618	1
Puerto Rico	258	12	Mali	616	1
Palau and Caroline Is.	136	12	Liberia	574	1
Vanuatu	75	12	United Kingdom	542	1
Cameroon	874	11	Eritrea	516	1
Japan	549	11	Iran	497	1
Seychelles Islands	178	11	France	483	1
Panama	907	10	Trinidad and Tobago	427	1
Vietnam	761	10	Algeria	374	1
Somalia	662	10	Djibouti	320	1

Country	Species	Endemics	Country	Species	Endemics
Bahamas	319	1	Benin	434	0
Haiti	243	1	Oman	433	0
Madeira Island	208	1	Morocco	429	0
Guadeloupe	193	1	Kampuchea (Cambodia)	426	0
Martinique	187	1	Turkey	425	0
Cayman Islands	180	1	Denmark	420	0
Leeward Islands	167	1	Finland	420	0
Falkland Islands	160	1	Poland	418	0
Grenada	120	1	Ireland	416	0
Antarctica	49	1	Kazakstan	414	0
Nauru Island	24	1	Belgium	411	0
Guyana	728	0	Ukraine	406	0
Ghana	723	0	Austria	403	0
Russia	697	0	Albania	396	0
Ivory Coast	696	0	Greece	389	0
Guatemala	691	0	Czech Republic	382	0
Mozambique	690	0	United Arab Emirates	382	0
Bangladesh	679	0	Portugal	379	0
Suriname	664	0	Iraq	378	0
Central African Republic	656	0	Switzerland	377	0
Nicaragua	656	0	Afghanistan	375	0
Paraguay	655	0	Uruguay	375	0
Zimbabwe	653	0	Turkmenistan	374	0
Malawi	651	0	Yugoslavia	370	0
Rwanda	646	0	Malta	366	0
Gabon	643	0	Yemen	365	0
Canada	625	0	Mongolia	364	0
Laos	618	0	Hungary	362	0
Senegal	609	0	Slovenia	362	0
Sierra Leone	600	0	Bulgaria	356	0
Burundi	599	0	Croatia	356	0
Bhutan	585	0	Romania	353	0
Congo	562	0	Bermuda	352	0
Botswana	559	0	Tunisia	351	0
Togo	554	0	Jordan	344	0
Guinea	543	0	Slovakia	343	0
Mauritania	529	0	Cyprus	338	0
Chad	528	0	North Korea	336	0
Gambia	511	0	Uzbekistan	334	0
Israel	494	0	South Korea	333	0
Niger	473	0	Estonia	332	0
Spain	470	0	Iceland	331	0
Germany	469	0	Guinea-Bissau	328	0
Swaziland	469	0	Brunei	327	0
El Salvador	467	0	Singapore	326	0
Sweden	451	0	Lebanon	323	0
Norway	448	0	Azerbaijan	322	0
Egypt	446	0	Latvia	317	0
Italy	444	0	Lithuania	313	0
Saudi Arabia	442	0	Syrian Arab Republic	313	0
Hong Kong	440	0	Libyan Arab Jamahiriya	312	0
Netherlands	439	0	Armenia	310	0

Country	Species	Endemics	Country	Species	Endemics
Bahrain	309	0	US Virgin Islands	181	0
Georgia	308	0	Greenland	153	0
Macedonia	295	0	Barbados Island	150	0
St. Pierre and Miquelon Is.	294	0	Andorra	148	0
Belarus	292	0	Maldive Islands	147	0
Tadzhikistan	287	0	British Virgin Islands	142	0
Kirghizia	286	0	Svalbard and Jan Mayen	121	0
Moldova	285	0	Monaco	105	0
Kuwait	281	0	San Marino	103	0
Lesotho	281	0	Burkina-Faso	89	0
Equatorial Guinea	280	0	Marshall Islands	77	0
Luxembourg	276	0	Canton and Phoenix Is.	55	0
Faeroe Islands	259	0	American Samoa	54	0
Gibraltar	258	0	Macau	40	0
Bosnia and Herzegovina	246	0	Wake Island	30	0
Dominican Republic	246	0	Midway Islands	28	0
Qatar	240	0	Niue	28	0
Liechtenstein	239	0	Tuvalu	27	0
Netherlands Antilles	239	0	Wallis and Futuna Islands	23	0
Azores Islands	207	0	Tokelau	15	0
Western Sahara	194	0	Johnston Island	13	0
Turks and Caicos Islands	192	0	Easter Island	9	0

Distribution of avifauna of the world. Adapted with permission from *BirdArea for Windows*. © 1996 Santa Barbara Software Products, Inc. Research courtesy of Shawneen Finnegan

Country	Code	Species	Endemics	Country	Code	Species	Endemics
Colombia	CO	1725	62	French Guiana	GF	624	1
Peru	PE	1711	104	Lao People's Republic	LA	618	0
Brazil	BR	1656	181	Namibia	NA	618	1
Ecuador	EC	1481	8	Mali	ML	616	1
Venezuela	VE	1337	41	Sumatra	TA	611	18
China	CN	1204	50	Senegal	SN	609	0
India	IN	1167	36	Sierra Leone	SL	600	0
Zaire	ZR	1135	19	Borneo	IB	599	31
Kenya	KE	1105	6	Burundi	BI	599	0
Tanzania	TZ	1050	19	Bhutan	BT	585	0
Mexico	MX	1049	88	Liberia	LR	574	1
Uganda	UG	1015	2	Philippines	PH	572	185
Burma (Myanmar)	BU	985	4	Congo	CG	562	0
Argentina	AR	976	15	Botswana	BW	559	0
Sudan	SD	961	2	Togo	TG	554	0
Thailand	TH	918	2	Japan	JP	549	11
Angola	AO	914	13	Guinea	GN	543	0
US contiguous 48 states	US	908	9	United Kingdom	GB	542	1
Panama	PA	907	10	Mauritania	MR	529	0
Cameroon	CM	874	11	Chad	TD	528	0
Nigeria	NG	868	2	Eritrea	ER	516	1
Nepal	NP	853	2	Gambia	GM	511	0
Costa Rica	CR	838	6	Java and Bali	ID	500	28
Ethiopia	ET	828	18	Iran	IR	497	1
South Africa	ZA	812	12	Israel	IL	494	0
Vietnam	VN	761	10	France	FR	483	1
Australia	AU	754	238	Taiwan (Formosa)	TW	474	14
Zambia	ZM	753	1	Niger	NE	473	0
New Guinea	PG	736	330	Spain	ES	470	0
Guyana	GY	728	0	Germany	DE	469	0
Ghana	GH	723	0	Swaziland	SZ	469	0
Russia	RS	697	0	El Salvador	SV	467	0
Ivory Coast	CI	696	0	Sweden	SE	451	0
Guatemala	GT	691	0	Norway	NO	448	0
Honduras	HN	690	1	Egypt	EG	446	0
Mozambique	MZ	690	0	Italy	IT	444	0
Bangladesh	BD	679	0	Saudi Arabia	SA	442	0
Pakistan	PK	672	1	Hong Kong	HK	440	0
Suriname	SR	664	0	Netherlands	NL	439	0
Malaysia (Peninsular)	MY	663	2	Chile	CL	437	9
Somalia	SO	662	10	Benin	BJ	434	0
Central African Republic	CF	656	0	Oman	OM	433	0
Nicaragua	NI	656	0	Morocco	MA	429	0
Paraguay	PY	655	0	Trinidad and Tobago	TT	427	1
Zimbabwe	ZW	653	0	Kampuchea	KH	426	0
Malawi	MW	651	0	Turkey	TR	425	0
Rwanda	RW	646	0	Denmark	DK	420	0
Gabon	GA	643	0	Finland	FI	420	0
Canada	CA	625	0	Poland	PL	418	0

Country	Code	Species	Endemics	Country	Code	Species	Endemics
Ireland	IE	416	0	Bahrain	BH	309	0
Kazakstan	KZ	414	0	Georgia	GG	308	0
Belgium	BE	411	0	Macedonia	ME	295	0
Ukraine	UR	406	0	New Zealand	NZ	295	56
Austria	AT	403	0	St. Pierre and Miquelon	PM	294	0
Albania	AL	396	0	Belarus	BL	292	0
Greece	GR	389	0	Tadzhikistan	ZS	287	0
Sulawesi (Celebes)	SW	388	96	Kirghizia	GZ	286	0
Czech Republic	CZ	382	0	Moldova	DV	285	0
Lesser Sundas	SS	382	46	Kuwait	KW	281	0
United Arab Emirates	AE	382	0	Lesotho	LS	281	0
Portugal	PT	379	0	Equatorial Guinea	GQ	280	0
Iraq	IQ	378	0	Luxembourg	LU	276	0
Switzerland	CH	377	0	Hawaii	hi	275	36
Afghanistan	AF	375	0	Tasmania	TS	272	13
Uruguay	UY	375	0	Jamaica	JM	265	27
Algeria	DZ	374	1	Faeroe Islands	FO	259	0
Turkmenia	TM	374	0	Gibraltar	GI	258	0
Yugoslavia	YU	370	0	Puerto Rico	PR	258	12
Malta	MT	366	0	Canary Islands	IC	256	5
Yemen	YE	365	0	Madagascar	MG	255	98
Mongolia	MN	364	0	Bismarck Archipelago	MK	246	38
Hungary	HU	362	0	Bosnia and Herzegovina	BA	246	0
Slovenia	SI	362	0	Dominican Republic	DO	246	0
Moluccas	CS	359	67	Solomon Islands	SB	245	68
Sri Lanka	LK	359	23	Haiti	HT	243	1
Bulgaria	BG	356	0	Qatar	QA	240	0
Croatia	RT	356	0	Liechtenstein	LI	239	0
Romania	RO	353	0	Netherlands Antilles	AN	239	0
Bermuda	BM	352	0	Andamans and Nicobars	AI	213	17
Tunisia	TN	351	0	Timor	TP	210	8
Cuba	CU	346	17	Madeira Islands	MD	208	1
Jordan	JO	344	0	Azores	AZ	207	0
Slovakia	SK	343	0	Western Sahara	EH	194	0
Cyprus	CY	338	0	Guadeloupe	GP	193	1
North Korea	KP	336	0	Turks and Caicos Islands	TC	192	0
Uzbekistan	BK	334	0	Martinique	MQ	187	1
South Korea	KR	333	0	U. S. Virgin Islands	VI	181	0
Estonia	EN	332	0	Cayman Islands	KY	180	1
Iceland	IS	331	0	Seychelles	SC	178	11
Guinea-Bissau	GW	328	0	Leeward Islands	MS	167	1
Brunei	BN	327	0	Falkland Islands	FK	160	1
Singapore	SG	326	0	Greenland	GL	153	0
Lebanon	LB	323	0	Barbados	BB	150	0
Azerbaijan	ZB	322	0	Andorra	AD	148	0
Djibouti	DJ	320	1	Maldives	MV	147	0
Bahamas	BS	319	1	British Virgin Islands	VG	142	0
Latvia	LV	317	0	Galapagos Islands	GS	138	25
Lithuania	LN	313	0	Palau and Caroline Is.	PU	136	12
Syrian Arab Republic	SY	313	0	Cape Verde	CV	130	3
Libyan Arab Jamahiriya	LY	312	0	Saint Lucia	LC	128	4
Armenia	AM	310	0	New Caledonia	NC	122	15

Country	Code	Species	Endemics	Country	Code	Species	Endemics
Svalbard and Jan Mayen	SJ	121	0	Tonga	TO	59	2
Grenada	GD	120	1	Réunion	RE	58	5
Fiji	FJ	119	25	Norfolk Island	NF	57	3
Guam and Marianas	GU	114	9	Canton and Phoenix Is.	CT	55	0
St. Vincent	VC	113	2	Cook Islands	CK	55	7
Aldabra	DB	110	2	American Samoa	AS	54	0
Dominica	DM	107	2	Antarctica	AA	49	1
Monaco	MC	105	0	Christmas Island	CX	48	2
San Marino	SM	103	0	St. Helena/Ascension Is.	ZH	44	2
Micronesia	FM	102	13	Macau	MO	40	0
Socotra	RA	99	6	Cocos (Keeling Islands)	CC	30	9
French Polynesia	PF	92	24	Pitcairn Island	PN	30	4
Admiralty Islands	RL	89	5	Wake Island	WK	30	0
Burkina-Faso	HV	89	0	Rodrigues	RZ	29	2
São Tomé and Príncipe	ST	86	27	Midway Islands	MI	28	0
Comoro Islands	KM	84	16	Niue	NU	28	0
Mauritius	MU	82	7	Tuvalu	TV	27	0
Marshall Islands	RM	77	0	Nauru	NR	24	1
Gough/Tristan da Cunha	ZC	76	6	Wallis and Futuna Is.	WF	23	0
Vanuatu	VU	75	12	Tokelau	TK	15	0
Kiribati	KI	63	2	Johnston Island	JT	13	0
Samoa	WS	63	10	Easter Island	IP	9	0

autumnalis, Amazona 151
  Dendrocygna 26
averano, Procnias 318
Aviceda 34
Avocettula 198
avosetta, Recurvirostra 90
awokera, Picus 264
axillaris, Aramides 82
  Deleornis 545
  Elanus 35
  Euplectes 622
  Herpsilochmus 300
  Monarcha 485
  Myrmotherula 299
  Pterodroma 10
  Saxicola 472
aylmeri, Turdoides 513
aymara, Psilopsiagon 148
  Metriopelia 119
ayresi, Sarothrura 78
ayresii, Cisticola 428
  Hieraaetus 48
Aythya 31-32
azara, Pteroglossus 245
azarae, Synallaxis 274
azurea, Alcedo 218
  Cochoa 472
  Coracina 379
  Hypothymis 482
  Sitta 541
azureocapilla, Myiagra 488
azureus, Eurystomus 230

Babax 515
baboecala, Bradypterus 436
bacchus, Ardeola 20
bachmani, Haematopus 89
bachmanii, Vermivora 649
badeigularis, Spelaeornis 509
badia, Ducula 130
  Halcyon 221
badiceps, Eremomela 444
badius, Accipiter 40
  Caprimulgus 182
  Molothrus 707
  Phodilus 163
  Ploceus 619
Baeolophus 539
Baeopogon 388
baeri, Asthenes 278
  Aythya 31
  Leucippus 202
  Paroaria 689
  Poospiza 682
baeticatus, Acrocephalus 439
bafirawari, Bradornis 456
baglafecht, Ploceus 617
bahamensis, Anas 30
  Coereba 658
baileyi, Xenospiza 698
bailleui, Loxioides 648
bailloni, Baillonius 246
Baillonius 246
bairdi, Oreomystis 649
  Vireo 634
bairdii, Acanthidops 686
  Ammodramus 697
  Calidris 99
  Campephilus 263
  Myiodynastes 349
  Prinia 431
  Trogon 215

bakeri, Ducula 129
  Sericulus 597
  Yuhina 520
bakkamoena, Otus 164
balaenarum, Sterna 105
Balaeniceps 23
balasiensis, Cypsiurus 191
Balearica 76
balfouri, Cyanomitra 547
balicassius, Dicrurus 590
balli, Otus 163
balliviani, Odontophorus 63
ballmanni, Malimbus 620
balstoni, Apus 193
bambla, Microcerculus 406
Bambusicola 70
bamendae Apalis 433
bangsi, Grallaria 309
Bangsia 668
bangwaensis, Bradypterus 437
banksiana, Neolalage 484
banksii, Calyptorhynchus 131
bannermani, Cyanomitra 547
  Ploceus 616
  Puffinus 12
  Tauraco 153
banyumas, Cyornis 463
baraui, Pterodroma 10
barbadensis, Amazona 151
barbara, Alectoris 64
barbarus, Laniarius 585
  Otus 167
barbata, Carduelis 643
  Cercotrichas 468
  Penelope 55
barbatus, Amytornis 527
  Apus 192
  Criniger 391
  Dendrortyx 60
  Gypaetus 37
  Monarcha 487
  Myiobius 337
  Pycnonotus 385
barbirostris, Myiarchus 346
baritula, Diglossa 686
barlowi, Certhilauda 359
barklyi, Coracopsis 143
barnardi, Barnardius 137
Barnardius 137
baroni, Cranioleuca 276
  Metallura 211
barrabandi, Pionopsitta 149
barratti, Bradypterus 437
barroti, Heliothryx 212
bartelsi, Spizaetus 48
bartletti, Crypturellus 4
Bartramia 98
bartschi, Aerodramus 189
Baryphthengus 227
basalis, Chrysococcyx 155
basilanica, Ficedula 461
Basileuterus 655-657
basilica, Ducula 129
basilicus, Basileuterus 655
Basilornis 609
bassanus, Morus 15
Batara 293
batavica, Touit 149
batesi, Apus 193
  Caprimulgus 185
  Cinnyris 551
  Ploceus 616

  Terpsiphone 483
Bathmocercus 438
Batis 476-477
Batrachostomus 179
battyi, Leptotila 119
baudii, Pitta 353
baudinii, Calyptorhynchus 131
baumanni, Phyllastrephus 389
bayleyi, Dendrocitta 603
beaudouini, Circaetus 37
beauharnaesii, Pteroglossus 246
Bebrornis see Acrocephalus
beccarii, Cochoa 472
  Gallicolumba 122
  Otus 166
  Sericornis 528
beckeri, Phylloscartes 327
becki, Pterodroma 9
bedfordi, Terpsiphone 483
beecheii, Cyanocorax 599
behni, Myrmotherula 299
belcheri, Larus 101
  Pachyptila 11
beldingi, Geothlypis 653
  Passerculus 696
belfordi, Melidectes 575
bella, Goethalsia 200
  Stagonopleura 628
belli, Amphispiza 696
  Basileuterus 656
bellicosa, Hirundinea 338
  Sturnella 706
bellicosus, Polemaetus 48
bellii, Vireo 634
bellulus, Margarornis 281
bendirei, Toxostoma 408
bengalensis, Bubo 169
  Centropus 160
  Houbaropsis 88
  Graminicola 452
  Gyps 37
  Sterna 104
bengalus, Uraeginthus 626
benghalense, Dinopium 264
benghalensis, Coracias 230
  Ploceus 620
  Rostratula 89
benguelensis, Certhilauda 359
benjamini, Urosticte 210
bennetti, Casuarius 1
  Corvus 606
bennettii, Aegotheles 178
  Campethera 252
benschi, Monias 75
bensoni, Pseudocossyphus 410
berard, Pelecanoides 14
bergii, Sterna 104
berigora, Falco 52
berlepschi, Chaetocercus 213
  Aglaiocercus 211
  Asthenes 278
  Crypturellus 2
  Dacnis 675
  Hylopezus 311
  Phacellodomus 280
  Rhegmatorhina 306
berlepschi, Myrmeciza 305
Berlepschia 283
berliozi, Apus 192
bernardi, Sakesphorus 293
bernicla, Branta 27

semicincta, Malacoptila 237
semicinerea, Cranioleuca 277
semicinereus, Hylophilus 636
semicollaris, Rostratula 89
　Streptoprocne 186
semifasciata, Tityra 352
semiflava, Geothlypis 653
semiflavum, Ornithion 322
semifuscus, Chlorospingus 660
semilarvata, Eos 132
semilarvatus, Sittiparus 538
Semioptera 595
semipalmata, Anseranas 25
semipalmatus, Catoptrophorus 98
　Charadrius 94
　Limnodromus 97
semipartitus, Empidornis 456
semiplumbea, Leucopternis 44
semiplumbeus, Rallus 81
semirubra, Rhipidura 481
semirufa, Cossypha 467
　Hirundo 369
　Thamnolaea 476
semirufus, Atlapetes 690
　Myiarchus 346
semitorquata, Alcedo 218
　Certhilauda 359
　Ficedula 460
　Streptopelia 114
semitorquatus, Arremon 691
　Lurocalis 180
　Micrastur 49
　Polihierax 50
semitorques, Spizixos 384
　Otus 164
Semnornis 244-245
semperi, Leucopeza 654
　Zosterops 562
senator, Lanius 583
senegala, Lagonosticta 625
　Tchagra 584
senegalensis, Batis 477
　Burhinus 91
　Centropus 160
　Cyanomitra 547
　Dryoscopus 583
　Ephippiorhynchus 23
　Eupodotis 88
　Halcyon 222
　Hirundo 370
　Otus 165
　Podica 86
　Streptopelia 114
　Zosterops 560
senegallus, Pterocles 109
　Vanellus 93
senegaloides, Halcyon 222
senegalus, Poicephalus 143
senex, Cypseloides 186
　Todirostrum 333
senilis, Myornis 313
　Pionus 150
sephaena, Francolinus 65
sephaniodes, Sephanoides 208
Sephanoides 208
sepiarium, Malacocincla 503
sepium, Orthotomus 443
septimus, Batrachostomus 179
sepulcralis, Cacomantis 155
serena, Lepidothrix 321
sericea, Leptocoma 548
　Loboparadisea 593

sericeus, Orthotomus 443
　Sturnus 610
sericocaudatus, Caprimulgus 182
Sericornis 528-529
Sericossypha 660
Sericulus 597
Serilophus 270
serina, Calyptocichla 388
Serinus 644-646
serinus, Serinus 644
serpentarius, Sagittarius 49
Serpophaga 325
serrana, Formicivora 301
　Upucerthia 271
serranus, Larus 103
　Turdus 420
serrator, Mergus 32
　Morus 15
serriana, Coua 158
serripennis, Stelgidopteryx 367
serrirostris, Colibri 197
serva, Cercomacra 303
setaria, Leptasthenura 273
sethsmithi, Muscicapa 459
setifrons, Xenornis 297
Setophaga 652
Setornis 392
severa, Ara 144
　Mackenziaena 293
severus, Falco 52
sewerzowi, Bonasa 59
sganzini, Alectroenas 128
sharpei, Gallirallus 713
　Lalage 381
　Macronyx 373
　Pseudocossyphus 410
　Sheppardia 465
　Smithornis 269
　Terenura 302
　Turdoides 514
sharpii, Apalis 433
　Pholia 613
shelleyi, Aethopyga 552
　Bubo 169
　Cinnyris 550
　Cryptospiza 624
　Francolinus 66
　Lamprotornis 612
　Nesocharis 623
Sheppardia 465
shorii, Dinopium 264
Sialia 414
sialis, Sialia 414
sibilans, Luscinia 466
sibilator, Sirystes 346
sibilatrix, Anas 29
　Phacellodomus 280
　Phylloscopus 447
　Syrigma 18
sibirica, Muscicapa 458
　Zoothera 412
sibiricus, Uragus 648
Sicalis 687-688
sichuanensis, Phylloscopus 447
sicki, Terenura 302
sidamoensis, Heteromirafra 358
sieboldii, Treron 124
siemiradzkii, Carduelis 643
siemsseni, Latoucheornis 677
Sigelus 457
sigillatus, Peneothello 491
signata, Cercotrichas 468

　Eremopterix 360
signatus, Basileuterus 655
　Knipolegus 344
siju, Glaucidium 173
silens, Sigelus 457
sillemi, Leucosticte 639
silvestris, Gallinula 85
silvicola, Otus 164
Silvicultrix 341
similis, Anthus 374
　Chloropeta 442
　Myiozetetes 348
　Saltator 702
simonsi, Scytalopus 314
Simoxenops 283
simplex, Anthreptes 545
　Calamonastes 434
　Chlorocichla 388
　Columba 113
　Geoffroyus 139
　Myrmothera 311
　Pachycephala 494
　Passer 614
　Phaetusa 106
　Piculus 259
　Pogoniulus 241
　Pseudotriccus 326
　Pycnonotus 387
　Rhytipterna 346
　Sporophila 683
sinaloa, Thryothorus 401
sinaloae, Corvus 606
　Progne 365
sindianus, Phylloscopus 447
sinense, Chrysomma 513
sinensis, Centropus 159
　Ixobrychus 21
　Pycnonotus 385
　Sturnia 610
singalensis, Chalcoparia 544
singularis, Xenerpestes 281
sinica, Carduelis 643
sintillata, Chalcopsitta 132
sinuata, Cercomela 474
sinuatus, Cardinalis 703
sipahi, Haematospiza 648
siparaja, Aethopyga 553
Siphonorhis 181; 713
Sipodotus 525
Siptornis 281
Siptornopsis 276
siquijorensis, Ixos 392
sirintarae, Pseudochelidon 365
Sirystes 346
sissonii, Thryomanes 402
Sitta 539-541
Sittasomus 287
sitticolor, Conirostrum 659
Sittiparus 538-539
sittoides, Diglossa 686
Siva see Minla
sjostedti, Columba 111
　Glaucidium 173
skua, Catharacta 101
Skutchia 307
sladeni, Gymnobucco 240
sloetii, Campochaera 381
Smicrornis 530
smithii, Anas 31
　Geophaps 117
　Hirundo 369
Smithornis 269

tatei, Aegotheles 178
　Premnoplex 281
Tauraco 152-153
Tchagra 584
tchagra, Tchagra 584
tectes, Saxicola 472
tectus, Notharchus 236
　Vanellus 93
teerinki, Lonchura 632
teesa, Butastur 43
tegimae, Pericrocotus 383
telasco, Sporophila 684
Telacanthura 190
Teledromas 313
telescophthalmus, Arses 487
Telespiza 648
Telophorus 585-586
Temenuchus 610
temia, Crypsirina 603
temminckii, Aethopyga 553
Calidris 99
　Coracias 230
　Coracina 378
　Cursorius 91
　Dendrocopos 254
　Eurostopodus 181
　Orthonyx 523
　Picumnus 250
　Tragopan 71
Temnurus 603
temnurus, Priotelus 215
　Temnurus 603
temporalis, Neochmia 628
　Ploceus 617
　Pomatostomus 521
tenebricosa, Tyto 162
tenebrosa, Chelidoptera 238
　Colluricincla 497
　Gallinula 85
　Gerygone 531
　Pachycephala 497
　Rhipidura 480
tenebrosus, Phyllastrephus 390
　Turdoides 514
tenella, Neomixis 509
tenellipes, Phylloscopus 448
tenellus, Tmetothylacus 372
tener, Loriculus 142
teneriffae, Regulus 394
tenimberensis, Megapodius 54
tenuepunctatus, Thamnophilus 294
tenuirostris, Acanthorhynchus 577
　Anous 106
　Cacatua 131
　Calidris 99
　Coracina 379
　Geositta 271
　Gyps 37
　Inezia 329
　Macropygia 115
　Numenius 98
　Onychognathus 612
　Oriolus 579
　Puffinus 11
　Rallus 81
　Xenops 281
　Zosterops 564
tephrocotis, Leucosticte 639
Tephrodornis 587
tephrolaemus, Andropadus 388
tephronota, Sitta 541
tephronotum, Glaucidium 173

tephronotus, Lanius 581
　Turdus 418
tephropleurus, Zosterops 564
Tephrozosterops 565
Terathopius 37
Terenotriccus 337
Terenura 302
Teretistris 654
terminalis, Pheucticus 703
Terpsiphone 483-484
terraereginae, Aerodramus 188
terrestris, Phyllastrephus 389
　Trugon 122
　Zoothera 714
terrisi, Rhynchopsitta 144
Tersina 676
tertius, Calyptophilus 663
Tesia 435
tessmanni, Muscicapa 459
tethys, Oceanodroma 13
Tetrao 58-59
Tetraogallus 63-64
Tetraophasis 63
Tetrax 88
tetrax, Tetrax 88
tetrix, Tetrao 59
textilis, Amytornis 527
textrix, Cisticola 428
teydea, Fringilla 638
teysmanni, Rhipidura 480
teysmannii, Treron 123
thagus, Pelecanus 14
Thalassarche 8-9
thalassina, Cissa 603
　Eumyias 462
　Tachycineta 366
thalassinus, Colibri 197
Thalassoica 9
Thalassornis 26
Thalurania 200-201
Thamnistes 297
Thamnolaea 475-476
Thamnomanes 297-298
Thamnophilus 294-296
Thamnornis 438
Thaumastura 212
thayeri, Larus 102
theklae, Galerida 363
thenca, Mimus 407
theomacha, Ninox 176
theresae, Montifringilla 615
theresiae, Metallura 211
　Polytmus 202
Theristicus 24
Thescelocichla 389
thibetanus, Serinus 644
thilius, Agelaius 704
Thinocorus 100
Thinornis 95
Thlypopsis 662
tholloni, Myrmecocichla 475
thomensis, Alcedo 219
　Columba 111
　Dreptes 546
　Estrilda 626
　Zoonavena 190
thompsoni, Hypsipetes 394
thoracica, Apalis 432
　Bambusicola 70
　Poospiza 681
　Stachyris 511
thoracicus, Bradypterus 437

Charadrius 94
Cyphorhinus 406
Dactylortyx 63
Hylophilus 636
Liosceles 313
Prionochilus 556
Thryothorus 401
Thraupis 667-668
Threnetes 194
threnothorax, Rhipidura 479
Threskiornis 23
Thripadectes 283
Thripophaga 280
thruppi, Melaniparus 537
Thryomanes 402
Thryorchilus 405
Thryothorus 399-402
thula, Egretta 19
thura, Carpodacus 640
thyroideus, Sphyrapicus 252
Tiaris 685
tibetanus, Syrrhaptes 109
　Tetraogallus 64
tibialis, Neochelidon 366
　Pheucticus 703
　Pselliophorus 689
tibicen, Gymnorhina 593
ticehursti, Sylvia 454
Tichodroma 542
tickelli, Anorrhinus 233
　Pellorneum 504
Tickellia 451
tickelliae, Cyornis 464
tigrina, Dendroica 651
tigrinus, Lanius 580
Tigriornis 21
Tigrisoma 21
Tijuca 315
Tilmatura 212
Timalia 513
Timeliopsis 566
timorensis, Ficedula 462
timoriensis, Megalurus 451
Tinamotis 5
Tinamus 2
tinniens, Cisticola 426
tinnunculus, Falco 50
tiphia, Aegithina 395
tirica, Brotogeris 148
tithys, Synallaxis 276
Tityra 352
Tmetothylacus 372
tobaci, Saucerottia 204
Tockus 232-233
toco, Ramphastos 247
tocuyensis, Arremonops 692
Todirhamphus 222-224
Todirostrum 333-334
Todus 226-227
todus, Todus 227
togoensis, Vidua 633
tolmiei, Oporornis 653
Tolmomyias 335
tombacea, Galbula 236
tomentosa, Mitu 56
tonsa, Platysteira 476
Topaza 198
torda, Alca 108
Torgos 37
torotoro, Syma 225
torquata, Ceryle 226
torquata, Chauna 25

DISTRIBUTION OF ENDEMIC BIRDS

50

36

185

18

19

19

27

31

96

330

74

98

238

200-300   100-200   50-100